D1558610

Contemporary
Literary Criticism

Guide to Gale Literary Criticism Series

For criticism on	Consult these Gale series
Authors now living or who died after December 31, 1999	*CONTEMPORARY LITERARY CRITICISM (CLC)*
Authors who died between 1900 and 1999	*TWENTIETH-CENTURY LITERARY CRITICISM (TCLC)*
Authors who died between 1800 and 1899	*NINETEENTH-CENTURY LITERATURE CRITICISM (NCLC)*
Authors who died between 1400 and 1799	*LITERATURE CRITICISM FROM 1400 TO 1800 (LC)* *SHAKESPEAREAN CRITICISM (SC)*
Authors who died before 1400	*CLASSICAL AND MEDIEVAL LITERATURE CRITICISM (CMLC)*
Authors of books for children and young adults	*CHILDREN'S LITERATURE REVIEW (CLR)*
Dramatists	*DRAMA CRITICISM (DC)*
Poets	*POETRY CRITICISM (PC)*
Short story writers	*SHORT STORY CRITICISM (SSC)*
Literary topics and movements	*HARLEM RENAISSANCE: A GALE CRITICAL COMPANION (HR)* *THE BEAT GENERATION: A GALE CRITICAL COMPANION (BG)* *FEMINISM IN LITERATURE: A GALE CRITICAL COMPANION (FL)* *GOTHIC LITERATURE: A GALE CRITICAL COMPANION (GL)*
Asian American writers of the last two hundred years	*ASIAN AMERICAN LITERATURE (AAL)*
Black writers of the past two hundred years	*BLACK LITERATURE CRITICISM (BLC-1)* *BLACK LITERATURE CRITICISM SUPPLEMENT (BLCS)* *BLACK LITERATURE CRITICISM: CLASSIC AND EMERGING AUTHORS SINCE 1950 (BLC-2)*
Hispanic writers of the late nineteenth and twentieth centuries	*HISPANIC LITERATURE CRITICISM (HLC)* *HISPANIC LITERATURE CRITICISM SUPPLEMENT (HLCS)*
Native North American writers and orators of the eighteenth, nineteenth, and twentieth centuries	*NATIVE NORTH AMERICAN LITERATURE (NNAL)*
Major authors from the Renaissance to the present	*WORLD LITERATURE CRITICISM, 1500 TO THE PRESENT (WLC)* *WORLD LITERATURE CRITICISM SUPPLEMENT (WLCS)*

ISSN 0091-3421

Volume 293

Contemporary Literary Criticism

Criticism of the Works
of Today's Novelists, Poets, Playwrights,
Short Story Writers, Scriptwriters, and
Other Creative Writers

Jeffrey W. Hunter
PROJECT EDITOR

 GALE
CENGAGE Learning

Detroit • New York • San Francisco • New Haven, Conn • Waterville, Maine • London

Contemporary Literary Criticism, Vol. 293

Project Editor: Jeffrey W. Hunter

Editorial: Dana Ramel Barnes, Maria Carter-Ewald, Sara Constantakis, Kathy D. Darrow, Kristen Dorsch, Dana Ferguson, Michelle Kazensky, Jelena O. Krstović, Michelle Lee, Marie Toft, Lawrence J. Trudeau

Content Conversion: Katrina Coach, Gwen Tucker

Indexing Services: Laurie Andriot

Rights and Acquisitions: Sari Gordon, Tracie Richardson, Jhanay Williams

Composition and Electronic Capture: Gary Oudersluys

Manufacturing: Cynde Lentz

Associate Product Manager: Marc Cormier

For product information and technology assistance, contact us at
Gale Customer Support, 1-800-877-4253.
For permission to use material from this text or product,
submit all requests online at **www.cengage.com/permissions.**
Further permissions questions can be emailed to
permissionrequest@cengage.com

While every effort has been made to ensure the reliability of the information presented in this publication, Gale, a part of Cengage Learning, does not guarantee the accuracy of the data contained herein. Gale accepts no payment for listing; and inclusion in the publication of any organization, agency, institution, publication, service, or individual does not imply endorsement of the editors or publisher. Errors brought to the attention of the publisher and verified to the satisfaction of the publisher will be corrected in future editions.

Gale
27500 Drake Rd.
Farmington Hills, MI, 48331-3535

LIBRARY OF CONGRESS CATALOG CARD NUMBER 76-46132

ISBN-13: 978-1-4144-4607-3
ISBN-10: 1-4144-4607-1

ISSN 0091-3421

Printed in the United States of America
1 2 3 4 5 6 7 14 13 12 11 10

Contents

Preface

Named "one of the twenty-five most distinguished reference titles published during the past twenty-five years" by *Reference Quarterly,* the *Contemporary Literary Criticism* (*CLC*) series provides readers with critical commentary and general information on more than 2,000 authors now living or who died after December 31, 1999. Volumes published from 1973 through 1999 include authors who died after December 31, 1959. Previous to the publication of the first volume of *CLC* in 1973, there was no ongoing digest monitoring scholarly and popular sources of critical opinion and explication of modern literature. *CLC,* therefore, has fulfilled an essential need, particularly since the complexity and variety of contemporary literature makes the function of criticism especially important to today's reader.

Scope of the Series

CLC provides significant passages from published criticism of works by creative writers. Since many of the authors covered in *CLC* inspire continual critical commentary, writers are often represented in more than one volume. There is, of course, no duplication of reprinted criticism.

Authors are selected for inclusion for a variety of reasons, among them the publication or dramatic production of a critically acclaimed new work, the reception of a major literary award, revival of interest in past writings, or the adaptation of a literary work to film or television.

Attention is also given to several other groups of writers—authors of considerable public interest—about whose work criticism is often difficult to locate. These include mystery and science fiction writers, literary and social critics, foreign authors, and authors who represent particular ethnic groups.

Each *CLC* volume contains individual essays and reviews taken from hundreds of book review periodicals, general magazines, scholarly journals, monographs, and books. Entries include critical evaluations spanning from the beginning of an author's career to the most current commentary. Interviews, feature articles, and other published writings that offer insight into the author's works are also presented. Students, teachers, librarians, and researchers will find that the general critical and biographical material in *CLC* provides them with vital information required to write a term paper, analyze a poem, or lead a book discussion group. In addition, complete bibliographical citations note the original source and all of the information necessary for a term paper footnote or bibliography.

Organization of the Book

A *CLC* entry consists of the following elements:

- The **Author Heading** cites the name under which the author most commonly wrote, followed by birth and death dates. Also located here are any name variations under which an author wrote, including transliterated forms for authors whose native languages use nonroman alphabets. If the author wrote consistently under a pseudonym, the pseudonym will be listed in the author heading and the author's actual name given in parenthesis on the first line of the biographical and critical information. Uncertain birth or death dates are indicated by question marks. Single-work entries are preceded by a heading that consists of the most common form of the title in English translation (if applicable) and the original date of composition.

- The **Introduction** contains background information that introduces the reader to the author, work, or topic that is the subject of the entry.

- The list of **Principal Works** is ordered chronologically by date of first publication and lists the most important works by the author. The genre and publication date of each work is given. In the case of foreign authors whose works have been translated into English, the English-language version of the title follows in brackets. Unless otherwise indicated, dramas are dated by first performance, not first publication.

- Reprinted **Criticism** is arranged chronologically in each entry to provide a useful perspective on changes in critical evaluation over time. The critic's name and the date of composition or publication of the critical work are given at the beginning of each piece of criticism. Unsigned criticism is preceded by the title of the source in which it appeared. All titles by the author featured in the text are printed in boldface type. Footnotes are reprinted at the end of each essay or excerpt. In the case of excerpted criticism, only those footnotes that pertain to the excerpted texts are included.

- A complete **Bibliographical Citation** of the original essay or book precedes each piece of criticism. Source citations in the Literary Criticism Series follow University of Chicago Press style, as outlined in *The Chicago Manual of Style,* 15th ed. (Chicago: The University of Chicago Press, 2003).

- Critical essays are prefaced by brief **Annotations** explicating each piece.

- Whenever possible, a recent **Author Interview** accompanies each entry.

- An annotated bibliography of **Further Reading** appears at the end of each entry and suggests resources for additional study. In some cases, significant essays for which the editors could not obtain reprint rights are included here. Boxed material following the further reading list provides references to other biographical and critical sources on the author in series published by Gale.

Indexes

A **Cumulative Author Index** lists all of the authors that appear in a wide variety of reference sources published by Gale, including *CLC*. A complete list of these sources is found facing the first page of the Author Index. The index also includes birth and death dates and cross references between pseudonyms and actual names.

A **Cumulative Nationality Index** lists all authors featured in *CLC* by nationality, followed by the number of the *CLC* volume in which their entry appears.

A **Cumulative Topic Index** lists the literary themes and topics treated in the series as well as in other Literature Criticism series.

An alphabetical **Title Index** accompanies each volume of *CLC*. Listings of titles by authors covered in the given volume are followed by the author's name and the corresponding page numbers where the titles are discussed. English translations of foreign titles and variations of titles are cross-referenced to the title under which a work was originally published. Titles of novels, dramas, films, nonfiction books, and poetry, short story, or essay collections are printed in italics, while individual poems, short stories, and essays are printed in roman type within quotation marks.

In response to numerous suggestions from librarians, Gale also produces an annual cumulative title index that alphabetically lists all titles reviewed in *CLC* and is available to all customers. Additional copies of this index are available upon request. Librarians and patrons will welcome this separate index; it saves shelf space, is easy to use, and is recyclable upon receipt of the next edition.

Citing *Contemporary Literary Criticism*

When citing criticism reprinted in the Literary Criticism Series, students should provide complete bibliographic information so that the cited essay can be located in the original print or electronic source. Students who quote directly from reprinted criticism may use any accepted bibliographic format, such as University of Chicago Press style or Modern Language Association (MLA) style. Both the MLA and the University of Chicago formats are acceptable and recognized as being the current standards for citations. It is important, however, to choose one format for all citations; do not mix the two formats within a list of citations.

The examples below follow recommendations for preparing a bibliography set forth in *The Chicago Manual of Style,* 15th ed. (Chicago: The University of Chicago Press, 2003); the first example pertains to material drawn from periodicals, the second to material reprinted from books:

James, Harold. "Narrative Engagement with *Atonement* and *The Blind Assassin.*" *Philosophy and Literature* 29, no. 1 (April 2005): 130-45. Reprinted in *Contemporary Literary Criticism.* Vol. 246, edited by Jeffrey W. Hunter, 188-95. Detroit: Gale, 2008.

Wesley, Marilyn C. "Anne Hèbert: The Tragic Melodramas." In *Canadian Women Writing Fiction,* edited by Mickey Pearlman, 41-52. Jackson: University Press of Mississippi, 1993. Reprinted in *Contemporary Literary Criticism.* Vol. 246, edited by Jeffrey W. Hunter, 276-82. Detroit: Gale, 2008.

The examples below follow recommendations for preparing a works cited list set forth in the *MLA Handbook for Writers of Research Papers,* 7th ed. (New York: The Modern Language Association of America, 2009); the first example pertains to material drawn from periodicals, the second to material reprinted from books:

James, Harold. "Narrative Engagement with *Atonement* and *The Blind Assassin.*" *Philosophy and Literature* 29.1 (April 2005): 130-45. Rpt. in *Contemporary Literary Criticism.* Ed. Jeffrey W. Hunter. Vol. 246. Detroit: Gale, 2008. 188-95. Print.

Wesley, Marilyn C. "Anne Hèbert: The Tragic Melodramas." *Canadian Women Writing Fiction.* Ed. Mickey Pearlman. Jackson: University Press of Mississippi, 1993. 41-52. Rpt. in *Contemporary Literary Criticism.* Ed. Jeffrey W. Hunter. Vol. 246. Detroit: Gale, 2008. 276-82. Print.

Suggestions are Welcome

Readers who wish to suggest new features, topics, or authors to appear in future volumes, or who have other suggestions or comments are cordially invited to call, write, or fax the Associate Product Manager:

Associate Product Manager, Literary Criticism Series
Gale
27500 Drake Road
Farmington Hills, MI 48331-3535
1-800-347-4253 (GALE)
Fax: 248-699-8983

Acknowledgments

The editors wish to thank the copyright holders of the criticism included in this volume and the permissions managers of many book and magazine publishing companies for assisting us in securing reproduction rights. Following is a list of the copyright holders who have granted us permission to reproduce material in this volume of *CLC*. Every effort has been made to trace copyright, but if omissions have been made, please let us know.

COPYRIGHTED MATERIAL IN *CLC*, VOLUME 293, WAS REPRODUCED FROM THE FOLLOWING PERIODICALS:

America, v. 200, January 19, 2009. Copyright © 2009 www.americamagazine.org. All rights reserved. Reproduced by permission of America Press. For subscription information, visit www.americamagazine.org.—*American Poetry Review,* v. 35, May-June, 2006 for "A Curious Gladness: A Garden Conversation with Stanley Kunitz and Genine Lentine" by Genine Lentine. Copyright © 2006 by World Poetry, Inc. Reproduced by permission of the author.—*Booklist,* v. 100, May 1, 2004. Copyright © 2004 by the American Library Association. Reproduced by permission.—*The Bookseller,* February 10, 2006; July 21, 2006. Copyright © 2006 VNU Business Media, Inc. All rights reserved. Both reproduced by permission.— *Christianity and Literature,* v. 57, spring, 2008. Copyright 2008 Conference on Christianity and Literature. Reproduced by permission.—*Editor & Publisher,* June 3, 2009. Copyright © 2009 VNU Business Media, Inc. All rights reserved. Reproduced by permission.—*The Hemingway Review,* v. 22, fall, 2002. Copyright © 2002 The Ernest Hemingway Foundation. Reproduced by permission.—*Kirkus Reviews,* v. 74, June 1, 2006; August 15, 2008. Copyright © 2006, 2008 VNU Business Media, Inc. All rights reserved. Both reproduced by permission.—*Mosaic,* v. 36, September, 2003; v. 41, March, 2008. Copyright © *Mosaic* 2003, 2008. Acknowledgment of previous publication is herewith made.—*The Nation,* v. 279, November 1, 2004. Copyright © 2004 by *The Nation Magazine*/The Nation Company, Inc. Reproduced by permission.—*New Statesman,* v. 131, December 16, 2002; 133, September 6, 2004; v. 137, June 2, 2008. Copyright © 2002, 2004, 2008 New Statesman, Ltd. All reproduced by permission.—*Publishers Weekly,* v. 245, July 6, 1998; v. 250, March 17, 2003; v. 251, April 12, 2004; v. 252, April 4, 2005. Copyright © 1998, 2003, 2004, 2005 by Reed Publishing USA. All reproduced from *Publishers Weekly,* published by the Bowker Magazine Group of Cahners Publishing Co., a division of Reed Publishing USA, by permission.—*Research in African Literatures,* v. 40, summer, 2009. Copyright © 2009 Indiana University Press. Reproduced by permission.—*The Romanic Review,* v. 86, November, 1995. Copyright © 1995 by the Trustees of Columbia University in the City of New York. Reproduced by permission.—*South Florida Sun Sentinel,* May 31, 2006. Reproduced by permission.—*The Spectator,* v. 296, September 11, 2004; v. 307, May 3, 2008. Copyright © 2004, 2008 by *The Spectator.* Both reproduced by permission of *The Spectator.*—*Style,* v. 37, summer, 2003. Copyright © *Style,* 2003. All rights reserved. Reproduced by permission of the publisher.—*Victoria,* v. 16, February, 2002, for "Romancing the Word" by Michele Slung. Reproduced by permission of the author.

COPYRIGHTED MATERIAL IN *CLC*, VOLUME 293, WAS REPRODUCED FROM THE FOLLOWING BOOKS:

Ashton, Dore. From *A Celebration for Stanley Kunitz on His Eightieth Birthday.* The Sheep Meadow Press, 1986. © 1986 by The Sheep Meadow Press. All rights reserved. Reproduced by permission.—Bergonzi, Bernard. From *David Lodge.* Northcote House, 1995. Copyright © 1995 by Bernard Bergonzi. All rights reserved. Reproduced by permission.— Crowe, Marian E. From *Aiming at Heaven, Getting the Earth: The English Catholic Novel Today.* Lexington Books, 2007. Copyright © 2007 by Lexington Books. All rights reserved. Reproduced by permission.—Daly, Brenda O. From "Ann Beattie's *Picturing Will*: Changing Our Images of 'Good' Mothers and Fathers," in *The Critical Response to Ann Beattie.* Edited by Jaye Berman Montresor. Greenwood Press, 1993. Copyright © 1993 by Jaye Berman Montresor. All rights reserved. Reproduced with permission of ABC-CLIO, LLC, Santa Barbara, CA.—Dillard, R. H. W. From "Letters from a Distant Lover: The Novels of Fred Chappell," in *More Lights than One: On the Fiction of Fred Chappell.* Edited by Patrick Bizzaro. Louisiana State University Press, 2004. Copyright © 2004 by Louisiana State University Press. All rights reserved. Reproduced by permission.—Gallagher, Tess. From *A Celebration for Stanley Kunitz on His Eightieth Birthday.* The Sheep Meadow Press, 1986. © 1986 by The Sheep Meadow Press. All rights reserved. Reproduced by permission.—Harriott, Esther. From "I'm Not Sleepy," in *Interviews and Encounters with Stanley Kunitz.* Edited by Stanley Moss. The Sheep Meadow Press, 1993. Copyright © 1986 by Stanley Kunitz. All rights reserved. Reproduced by

Gale Literature Product Advisory Board

Ann Beattie
1947-

American novelist and short story writer.

The following entry presents an overview of Beattie's career through 2007. For further information on her life and works, see *CLC*, Volumes 8, 13, 18, 40, 63, and 146.

INTRODUCTION

Beattie's work is widely recognized for its psychologically nuanced characters and insight into the human condition as it existed in the 1970s. Influenced by modernist poetics and reacting to the decline of postmodernism, Beattie's writing reflects the sense of aimlessness and lack of purpose that characterizes modern life while employing a distant, sometimes cold, deadpan style. Her themes are reminiscent of those of F. Scott Fitzgerald, Ernest Hemingway, and J. D. Salinger, and she has been compared stylistically to Hemingway and Raymond Carver.

BIOGRAPHICAL INFORMATION

Beattie was born September 8, 1947, in Washington, D.C., to Charlotte Crosby and James A. Beattie, a grants-management specialist for the federal government. She grew up in a middle-class suburban neighborhood and performed poorly in elementary school but earned a bachelor's degree from American University in 1969 and a master's degree from the University of Connecticut in 1972. She published both her first novel and her first book of short stories in 1976. Beattie has a son with her first husband, David Gates, whom she married in 1973. After their divorce, she married artist Lincoln Perry, with whom she has collaborated on various projects. Beattie has received a Guggenheim Fellowship (1977) and an American Academy Award (1980) among other accolades and has been a member of the American Academy and Institute of Arts and Letters since 1983. She currently occupies the Edgar Allan Poe Chair of the Department of English and Creative Writing at the University of Virginia.

MAJOR WORKS

Beattie's first novel, *Chilly Scenes of Winter* (1976), received a warm response from readers and critics. A love story that expertly depicts the "Me Decade" mentality of the 1970s, *Chilly Scenes of Winter* presents Charles and his love interest, Laura, who is married to Jim. Laura represents Charles's ideal domestic fantasy: Through her, he can lose himself entirely and escape into what he sees as a perfect life which demands nothing from him. Charles's relationship with his own family, however, is less idyllic. His mother, Clara, claims she is dying, but Charles believes she is using illness to manipulate him and to live as an existentially free person; the similarity to his own escapist aspirations is lost on him. Clara's husband, Pete, is disliked by his stepchildren—Charles and his sister Susan—and Charles harbors increasingly hostile feelings toward Pete as Clara's health deteriorates. The relationships in this novel present a negative portrayal of marriage congruent with themes of self-absorption that have typified this era for many.

The short story collection *Distortions* (1976) echoes some of the themes and subject matter of *Chilly Scenes of Winter*. The pursuit of happiness is a central motif in the collection, and it proves almost always unattainable. The first story in the collection, "Dwarf House," contrasts the miserable existences of several characters with the relatively contented lives of a group of dwarfs who live together. Due to their marginalization, Beattie implies, the dwarfs are not obligated to observe societal standards of happiness and are therefore free to create their own. Among them is James, the son of a self-pitying mother who bemoans her son's disability and insists that his choice to live in the dwarf house is unhealthy escapism. James's non-dwarf brother, meanwhile, wallows in ennui despite his life of relative ease. The story ends with the wedding of James and another dwarf, whose obviously genuine joy challenges James's mother and brother to reflect on their conceptualizations of happiness. The theme of discontent in *Distortions* continues with the story "The Parking Lot," in which Jim and his wife have agreed to alternate the years in which they work. In the year the story takes place, Jim's wife, who is never named, has taken an office job, which allows her to escape the banal, mundane existence of her married life. The office represents for her a vast, blank void, unchanging, where she can avoid the life she has resigned herself to. She begins an affair with a man from her office, meeting him in the parking lot after work before their trysts. While aware that she will eventually be caught, she is, like many Beattie characters, irresistibly attracted to the freedom the relationship affords her. Beattie's fourth novel, *Picturing Will* (1989), revisits the author's themes of marriage and intimate relationships but reveals a shift in narrative voice from cold distance to a closer but more disdainful view of her characters. Will, the title character, is a five-year-old boy whose father abandoned the family shortly after he was born and whose mother, Jody, became a wedding photographer to support them. Jody remarries and Mel, Will's stepfather, gives up his vocation to care for Will while Jody pursues her new career. The novel questions the factors by which parenting is defined and assessed.

The novel *The Doctor's House* (2002) depicts the wife, son, and daughter of a tyrannical, unfaithful man whose harshness and unpredictability have shaped each family member differently. Daughter Nina, a young widow, attempts to live in solitude but remains attached to her brother, Andrew, who embarks on an effort to reconnect with old flames; meanwhile their alcoholic mother wonders why Nina and Andrew are so close to each other and so aloof with her. The father, as often happens in Beattie's fiction, is present in the story only through the reflections of the characters upon whom he is such a significant influence. Strained family relationships are also a theme of Beattie's collection *Follies* (2005), which contains nine short stories and a novella.

CRITICAL RECEPTION

Beattie's early fiction has been lauded as heralding a break from the postmodernist poetics that dominated literature for decades. The world of literary fiction at the time was widely viewed as weary of the academic strictures of postmodernism and ready for a return to realism, and Beattie's writings are described as having provided it. Her early publications were well received by critics who were impressed with her unique voice and sharp insight into human motivations. However, some critics have expressed frustration at what they perceive as a repetitive inertia in Beattie's characters across several novels and short story collections. Reflecting on the impact of *Distortions* a decade after its publication, Christina Murphy argued against the complaint that Beattie's characters are all cut from the same cloth, observing that in some stories Beattie is "less a writer depicting a certain character type of the 'lost, counterculture wastrel' than she is a writer revealing deep insights into the nature of the human psyche and the human will."

A motif running through much of Beattie's work is that of miscommunication and the inability of couples and families to express themselves to each other.

Frequently, it has been noted, Beattie's characters become cut off from real experience and withdraw entirely in her books. This leaves room for endings that offer no resolution, and critics have been divided over whether Beattie, or any author, should be held responsible for supplying answers rather than merely describing problems and situations. However, Beattie has also been criticized by some for the conclusion of *Chilly Scenes of Winter,* which was perceived not as ambiguous but as overly upbeat when viewed in the context of the rest of the novel. In response Beattie observed that the end of any narrative is never the end of the story, and she leaves it to readers to imagine what happened next. *Picturing Will* fared somewhat poorly with critics, many of whom complained that too much attention was devoted to peripheral characters of little influence within the story, but the novel generated much discussion about the requisite qualities of a good parent.

Some reviewers of Beattie's recent works have expressed impatience for the author to move away from the tone and subjects that defined her early career. As Donna Rifkind opined in a review of *Follies,* Beattie's typically unsettled and melancholy characters, "once the pioneers of a directionless generation, are now at best supporting players in a drama whose mood has changed. The trademark passivity of Beattie's characters has given way to a new generation's urgency, passion, religious and political conviction, determination and certitude. Serving as a generation's voice has its limits: One day the action moves on."

PRINCIPAL WORKS

Chilly Scenes of Winter (novel) 1976
Distortions (short stories) 1976
Secrets and Surprises (short stories) 1978
Falling in Place (novel) 1980
The Burning House (short stories) 1982
Love Always (novel) 1985
Where You'll Find Me, and Other Stories (short stories) 1986
Picturing Will (novel) 1989
What Was Mine (short stories) 1991
Another You (novel) 1995
My Life, Starring Dara Falcon (novel) 1997
Park City: New and Selected Stories (short stories) 1998
Perfect Recall: New Stories (short stories) 2001
The Doctor's House (novel) 2002
Follies: New Stories (short stories) 2005
Walks with Men (novella) 2010

CRITICISM

Ann Beattie, Larry McCaffery, and Sinda Gregory (interview date 27 January 1982)

SOURCE: Beattie, Ann, Larry McCaffery, and Sinda Gregory. "A Conversation with Ann Beattie." In *Conversations with Ann Beattie*, edited by Dawn Trouard, pp. 41-54. Jackson: University Press of Mississippi, 2007.

[*In the following interview, conducted January 27, 1982, and originally published in the* Literary Review *in 1984, Beattie discusses her themes, her writing process, and critical reaction to her fiction.*]

Since Ann Beattie's short stories first began appearing, in the mid 1970s, mainly in the *New Yorker,* she has quickly emerged as one of the most distinctive voices in contemporary American fiction. Her first two books, **Chilly Scenes of Winter** (a novel, 1976) and **Distortions** (stories, 1976), with their coolly dispassionate prose rhythms and their vivid portrayals of the disaffections, anguish, and boredom of middle America, were widely praised by reviewers. Her second story collection, **Secrets and Surprises** (1978), and her second novel, **Falling in Place** (1980), solidified her reputation and exhibited a growing maturity as a stylist. A third collection, **The Burning House,** was published by Random House in the fall of 1982.

Sinda Gregory and Larry McCaffery interviewed Ann Beattie in Los Angeles on January 27, 1982. Their questions and comments during the interview are identified SG and LM, respectively.

[SG]: *In your interview in the* New York Times Book Review, *you respond to the comment made by Joyce Maynard that you are primarily a chronicler of the sixties counterculture by saying, "It's certainly true that the people I write about are essentially my age, and so they were a certain age in the sixties and had certain common experiences and tend to listen to the same kind of music and get stoned and wear the same kind of clothes, but what I've always hoped for is that somebody will then start talking more about the meat and bones of what I'm writing about." The "meat and bones" that you refer to seems to me to involve the difficulties involved in people understanding each other—the difficulty of saying what we feel, of making ourselves clear, of having the courage or honesty to say what we mean. Would you agree that this issue of the breakdown of communication is one of the meat-and-bones areas you're referring to?*

[Beattie]: Yes, my fiction often has to do with that. A direct result of this breakdown of communication is the breakdown of relationships. I don't think the people in my stories are representative, by the way—that's really off the point of what you just asked me, but it's behind Maynard's comment, and behind what a lot of people have said about my work. I'd say that the people in my fiction reflect some of my own personal problems and concerns, perhaps to an exaggerated degree, but I don't mean them to be taken as representative of the culture. So that's part one of the answer. As to part two, what you're saying sounds perfectly insightful to me—I'd agree that these breakdowns do have a lot to do with my work—but even this, I think, tends to generalize a great deal. I mean if I were to ask you to be specific and cite to me what the common denominator is between two different stories of mine, I wonder what it would be?

[SG]: *I'd probably say that a lot of your stories that differ in many respects still seem to focus on relationships in the process of breaking down.*

Okay, I can see what you mean, but often the people in my stories are unstable in some way even before the relationship—their problems often predate the relationship we see, or there's no reason to think the breakdown is a consequence of the relationship itself.

[LM]: *In quite a few of your stories you seem to imply that one of the reasons that people's relationships break down is because they can't express themselves. You don't always explain why they are unable to talk to each other, but often your stories have scenes with characters who are totally cut off from each other or who misunderstand each other.*

[SG]: *A good example of this is the scene in* **Falling in Place** *where the whole family is sitting around while John has taken them out for a Chinese dinner: at one line each one of them makes a gesture of generosity towards the others that is misconstrued and rejected, so they draw back; in that scene it seems impossible for anyone to express what they want to express.*

Yes, I'll have to agree that these kinds of scenes do appear in my work, in one form or another. But this is not something I'm doing deliberately. Personally, of course, I believe that many people have a lot of trouble communicating, but I'm afraid this sounds so banal that I hate to dwell on it because it's hardly something I originated. When I was working on that scene Sinda just mentioned, for instance, I was mainly thinking of the literary effects—the tension it creates—and not the general issue involved. I guess I feel that if you're mainly interested in showing people not communicating you ought to be at least as interesting as Harold Pinter.

[LM]: *You know, what I really tend to notice in your fiction is not so much the issues you raise but the specific people you place into your stories. What interests you about your characters?*

I'm often interested in my characters because they can't break away from the situation they find themselves in. If they can't communicate to begin with, you'd think more of them would fly off than they do. Part of this interest is a reflection of my own experiences with people. I find it very hard to envy most of the couples I know. I can't imagine exchanging places with those that are together, even those that are happy, because it seems to me they have made so many compromises to be together. So I'm very interested in the fact that there are these personalities who have compromised in so many ways. On the other hand, there are so many people who are together because of all the obvious reasons: they don't want to be lonely or they are in the habit of being together, or this whole Beckettian thing—I can't stay and I can't go. This tug interests me more than the fact that they're not communicating—I want to find out why they're staying and not going.

[LM]: *A lot of your characters are very self-conscious individuals—self-conscious about their roles, about the cliches they use to express themselves, about just about everything. Sinda and I notice this same sense of self-consciousness in ourselves and with the people we associate with—maybe it has to do with education or the kinds of people we have as friends—but we notice that this tends to intrude into relationships. It almost seems as if the more self-aware you become, this self-awareness gets to the way of spontaneity or whatever it is that is "natural" in relationships.*

Yes, I know just what you mean. This kind of intellectualizing or self-consciousness just allows you to hide from yourself forever. People can easily fall into the trap of thinking that to label something is to explain it.

[SG]: *It's the same thing with the irony your characters often seem to have—it's a kind of defense mechanism. . . .*

Yeah, all these artifices assist in helping people delude themselves.

[SG]:—*even though these artifices and intellectualizing are supposedly, on the surface, helping people develop insights about their behavior and that of others.*

These insights aren't very profound, though. If you notice, usually in my stories one person is insightful and the other person isn't. They end up in a tug-of-war when it becomes inconsequential whether they're insightful or not. In a story like **"Colorado"** Robert knows what the score is with Penelope, but so what? And she understands why they've ended up in Vermont and her understanding doesn't matter. Charles Manson

said there was a particular voice telling him to do something, and David Berkowitz said that it was a dog, Sam, up in the sky motivating him. Don't people always say that what motivates them is logical? What matters is that they're getting through life and they're unhappy and there's something missing. If I knew what it was that was missing, I'd write about it, I'd write for Hallmark cards. That would please a lot of my critics.

[LM]: *Yeah, I've noticed that some critics have complained that your stories don't offer "solutions" or resolutions to your characters' problems. How do you respond to this idea—championed recently by John Gardner—that writers need to supply answers and not simply describe problems or situations?*

I don't expect answers of anyone other than a medical doctor, so no, it wouldn't occur to me that writers should have to supply answers. I certainly don't feel that it's the obligation of any artist to supply answers.

[LM]: *What about your trying other fictional approaches? Are you ever tempted to try, say, a detective story, or an historical novel, or something like that?*

Falling in Place was meant to be an "historical novel."

[LM]: *I can see that, but what about writing about historical periods other than our own? One reviewer said, half-jokingly I think, that no tune exists in your work before 1968. . . .*

No, I've never tried that type of work because that would require research and I fear libraries. No kidding, I don't know if I could do it or not, so, in brief, the answer is that I've not been tempted in that direction. I'm very much interested in writers who are tempted and do it. Mary Lee Settle is one of my favorite writers, and the research she undertakes to find out background is amazing: she gets herself in a rowboat and goes down the banks of a river in West Virginia to see the way it curves at a particular point; and then she studies topographical maps, circa 1890, to see if that bend was in the river at that time or not; then she flies to Boston to listen to a speech JFK gave in a particular town in West Virginia to see how this relates to her material. I'm fascinated with this approach, but it seems like Perry Mason stuff to me. Sleuthing and trying to keep all that in one's mind would be impossible for me. I hate writing novels to begin with because I can't remember what the character did five days ago; so I write everything quickly, including novels, which is why complexity fouls me up. If I can't remember in a fifteen-page story what one of my characters did on page five, I can take a few minutes and look it up and make sure that the X who walked in on page five was a shit. But if I can't remember if this character is a shit or not and I have to take the time to go through chapters one through nineteen to find out what his off-the-wall comment was that showed he was a shit, then my train of thought is gone. So for me it would be just agonizing to try to go back and write from research and then imagine something, because at least with my own writing I have a touchstone in that I'm writing out of what happened yesterday. I could never assimilate things the way that Mary Lee Settle does and then get them down into a coherent form.

[SG]: *You just said that you work very quickly. What kinds of work habits do you have—have you always worked in spurts like this?*

No, at first when I found out there was something I could do—I was learning, teaching myself, mostly, how to write—I wrote a lot more than I do today. Those stories were more speculative and funnier than what I write now. I don't think I have as much to say today. Some of the things that interested me when I was starting out don't interest me as much now—or they interest me in a different way. I've always had what people call "writer's block," but it's never scared me because I never thought of it as that. My total output is pretty large and I can't be too frightened about deviating from work habits that have always never been a routine. So my work habits have been erratic.

[SG]: *What about the mundane details, like whether or not you work at a typewriter, or during the day, and things like that?*

I always work at a typewriter. I can make some revisions or do fine editing in longhand, but if I'm revising a whole page I always go back to the typewriter. When I lived in the country I usually worked at night, although this isn't true any longer. I find that I'm very lethargic during the day, and everything seems distracting and it's very hard to concentrate. Of course, now I do different kinds of work—when a revised script for PBS is due in forty-eight hours, what are you going to do? Explain that you don't start writing until after midnight? I get in there and start writing right after breakfast. I'm also very neurotic about my work habits. To this day I have my mother mail to me, from Washington DC, a special kind of typing paper—which isn't even particularly *good* typing paper—from People's Drugstore. It costs about $1.29 a pack. I used to always work in my husband's clothes. He's not my husband any longer, but I still occasionally put on the essential plaid shirt.

[SG]: *Are you a coffee-drinker while you work—or do you go more for the straight gin or dope method?*

Not coffee, but I find writing is surprisingly oral—when you're not talking you need something. But I never take drugs when I write and I never drink either. I have gotten really out of it to remember what something feels like, and then managed to crawl to the typewriter two days later. People will say to me, "Boy, you must have been really stoned to write that stoned scene in **Falling in Place**." They forget that writers have memories. When I wrote that scene I had probably had two aspirin and a glass of water. There's such an energy rush when you do it cold.

[LM]: *What seems to get you to sit down at the typewriter in the first place? Do you have a specific scene or character or sentence in mind?*

My stories always seem to begin with something very small, whether it be one or the other of those things you've just mentioned. If I were to say I usually begin with a character, that wouldn't mean that I would know the character's occupation or whether the character is happy or sad, or what the character's age was. I would know that the character is named "Joe," and, yes, sometimes the idea that the character's name is "Joe" has gotten me to the typewriter. More often it's really a physiological feeling that I should write something—this feeling doesn't always work out. Many times I'm wrong about it.

[LM]: *What do you mean by a "physiological feeling"?*

I don't know how to talk about this without sounding like Yeats saying that the "Voices" were driving him into a room and dictating to him, but it's almost like that, almost that crazy to me. Something in me has built up and this is a compulsion to go and write something at the typewriter. And, yes, it's not totally amorphous, there is something in the back of my mind: it's a name, it's a sentence, it's a sense of remembering what it is like to be in the dead of winter and wanting to go to the beach in the summer, some vague notion like that. It's never more than that. I've never in my life sat down and said to myself, "Now I will write something about somebody to whom such-and-such will happen."

[SG]: *What you're saying is very interesting because I think most people assume that because your characters are so particularized and real-seeming that they must be based on people you've actually known. Does this happen very often?*

I probably shouldn't answer that because, given the nature of most of my characters, it wouldn't be much to my advantage to admit it if I did. It's interesting to me, though, that there have been some instances when I thought I've come very close to capturing the essence of somebody even though I've made some little change in their clothing or in the location of the story. These changes are made subconsciously, it's not something I do deliberately, but these changes are always enough to throw people off. That's what interesting to me—I don't think someone has ever said to me, "Hey, that's me," and been right.

[*LM*]: *That's never happened?*

Not even when I thought it was most obvious. On the other hand in places where a character I've created has nothing to do with anyone I know, people have insisted that a particular line is something they've said. I had a sentence in a story called **"Like Glass"** and I was showing it to a friend; the woman who's narrating the story says of her husband that when he talked about his dreams his dreams were never full of the usual things like symbols but were summaries of things that had happened. And the friend of mine who was reading the story stopped and said to me, "This isn't true of my dreams!" So there you have it.

[*SG*]: *You said somewhere that when you began* **Falling in Place** *that you had no idea of where it was heading, that you only knew you wanted it to be about children.*

That wasn't quite true. I knew the beginnings of the first sentence. "John Joel was high up in a tree . . ." and then it occurred to me that if somebody was up high in a tree, it would probably be a child, and if it were a child it was likely that there would have to be a family surrounding him. So then with that as an idea I proceeded to write the novel. I had seven weeks to go with this deadline at Random House. I understand that in the real world people don't come after you with whips that say "Random House" on the handles; but it still makes me very nervous to have deadlines because I don't like to have deadlines—and I've organized my life so that I don't have deadlines very often. But in this case I had this deadline that was making me very nervous, and I looked out my window and there was this wonderful peach tree out there. That's what started **Falling in Place.**

[*LM*]: *But despite being written in seven weeks under the pressures of these Random House whips,* **Falling in Place** *seems to me to have a much greater sense of structure or "plot" in the traditional sense than, say,* **Chilly Scenes**—*that is, it seems to be working towards that climax, the shooting of Mary by John Joel.*

I was so surprised when that shooting happened.

[*LM*]: *How far in advance had you realized that this is where the book was heading?*

Never. I was totally amazed to find the gun in the kid's hands. But then I remembered there had been that odd box which belonged to Parker's grandfather.

[*SG*]: *So you hadn't planted that box there with the gun in it?*

No, in fact, after the shooting happened I thought, "Oh, my God, we're only three weeks into the book and here Mary is dead on the ground—what am I going to do to resurrect her?" So I resurrected her. Really, I was very upset when that shooting happened.

[*LM*]: *But despite these kinds of surprises, wouldn't you agree that* **Falling in Place** *is a more "writerly novel" than* **Chilly Scenes of Winter**—*that it has a tighter structure and is governed by a more coherent set of images and metaphors?*

Sure. Remember **Falling in Place** was written several years after my first novel. I wrote **Chilly Scenes** in 1975, and it was all dialogue, basically; it was really more like a play than a novel. And that book was written in three weeks. I hope that I did know more about writing in the summer of 1979 than I did four years earlier. And, of course, things happen to you that also help create a focus for your work. I was living in Redding, Connecticut, when I wrote **Falling in Place,** and I had been living there about a year. While I was actually working on **Falling in Place** I didn't really realize how much of Redding had gotten into my head. Actually I guess I had grown very hostile to Redding and was very upset by being there, so in a way it was almost a relief to write something like **Falling in Place** and sort of purge myself of these feelings. We had had more than a year of very bad times and total isolation living in this wealthy commuter community that had nothing to do with us. And I was watching the people at the market and it was like when you're sick and have a fever and everything seems in sharper focus. I went around with that kind of fever for about a year, and then I had this deadline, so I wrote **Falling in Place.** I don't think that it follows that this is the way I always work—if you put me in Alaska for a year I'm not sure I'd write about igloos—but it did happen that way in Redding, Connecticut. There was so much more I had subconsciously stored away that I wanted to get out than there had been about anywhere else I've lived before.

[*SG*]: *I have a question about the structure of* **Falling in Place.**

Yeah, what is the structure of that book? I've been wondering about that myself.

[*SG*]: *Why did you have every other chapter take the form of those brief, italicized sections?*

You want to know the truth about those chapters? I started out that novel by writing chapters—I would write a chapter a day. But after I wrote the first chapter—it was the opening chapter that's there now—I realized that I had forgotten to put any background information in it, so I made notes to myself of what I had to go back and include in the first chapter. The second day I wrote a chapter and then thought, "Here's what I left out of this one." The third day I thought, "I wonder if anyone has ever written a whole book like this. I wonder if this isn't too artsy?" Then I thought, "Who cares?" Eventually I went back and made these lists a little more articulate and they became the italicized chapters. If I were teaching this book, I could imagine myself making any number of pretentious guesses about why the book is structured this way, but in point of fact the book is structured this way because I left in these notes and comments to myself. Another thing I should mention is that I'll do anything to trick myself into thinking that I'm not writing a novel—it's easier if I just think in terms of chapter one, chapter two, chapter three—I can deal with that. So I thought of the italics at the end of Chapter One in *Falling in Place* as being a kind of coda. And of course the chapters in that book don't all function in the same way: some of them repeat what you already know, some of them tell you what you know is an absolute lie, some of them tell you what to anticipate later on. I think Random House was a little baffled and wondered, "What do we call these?"

[LM]: *One of the things I like about your fiction is precisely the thing that some critics seem most troubled with—that is, your work often seems to recreate a sense of modern life's aimlessness, its lack of coherency and resolution. Is this a conscious strategy on your part—a desire to suggest life's formlessness, that life isn't shaped like most well-made stories and novels suggest—or does, this sense emerge mainly as a function of your writing habits? In other words, does this "aimlessness" result from your view of the world or mainly from the fact that you don't know where your works are headed?*

There are at least two honest answers to that question. One is to repeat what I've said before that I've never known beforehand what I'm setting out to write, so that even when I write the ending to a piece it's only at that point that I know how it ends. I do agree how you characterize my endings—the sense of them is "aimless," but the language used to create this sense isn't. I imagine, though, that subconsciously this is aesthetically what I believe in. . . .

[LM]: *You mean that you can't wrap things up neatly with a nice climax and denouement?*

Not the people and situations that I'm writing about. I don't hate books in which this happens; in fact, I rather admire them. One of my favorite books is non-fiction,

Blood and Money by Thomas Thompson. The last page is so apocalyptic and satisfying. If I could do anything like that—see things with such an overview—I would wrap things up neatly. But it's not the way my mind works; it would seem inappropriate to what I've done, and I've never been able to overhaul a story. In fact, stories often get thrown away in the last paragraph, even the last sentence, because I don't know how it can end. It seems to me most honest personally to write something that still implies further complexity. I'm not writing confessionally. If I want to do that I can write my grandmother and say, "The day began here and it ended here." It wouldn't occur to me that this approach would be pleasurable or meaningful in a story.

[SG]: *You've mentioned how* **Falling in Place** *started. Do you recall what the opening image was in* **Chilly Scenes of Winter***?*

No, not really. All I remember about that is that I had an idea in mind about the friendship between two men, Charles and Sam. I wrote quite a bit of background about them, and I showed it to a good friend of mine who handed it back to me and there was only a little shard of paper left—the remains of page 51 with Charles saying, "Permettez-moi de vous presenter Sam McGuire." And everything about how Charles came to meet Sam, what town they lived in, everything else had been scissored away. And I thought, you're right, just jump in. So whatever had been my original intention as I began the book was gone. The book that now stands is what took over. My friend had done the perfect job of editing. When the book came out I was amused when reviewers would talk about "Beattie's amazing, stark beginning," when in fact my friend had actually taken the scissors to it. My friend J. D. O'Hara, to whom *Falling in Place* is dedicated and who teaches at the University of Connecticut, used to take the scissors to the ends of my stories. Maybe I'm just a victim of my friends' Freudian obsessions, but in both cases they were right. It was really O'Hara who, in literally taking the scissors to my pages, suggested that more elliptical endings to my stories might be advantageous.

[LM]: *I've also noticed that you seem to almost be deliberately refusing to provide the kinds of background and psychological information that most writers do— you just put your characters in a situation and show the reader that situation.*

I don't think that my characters are what they are because of interesting psychological complexities. They're not clinical studies to me. That would be a mind that worked in a different way than mine works. It's like: I like *you*, but I don't care about your childhood; if we know each other for the next ten years I would no doubt be interested if you were to tell me about your childhood, but to think that having known you at some point in time would change my impression, help me in any way to uncover what I'm looking for in our personal relationship, isn't true for me. For whatever reasons, I just seem to react to what is right there in front of me. So that's usually the way I write. There is often background information—though I supply it late in the story.

[SG]: Your prose style is one that most reviewers have called "deadpan" or "emotionless." Are you consciously aiming for a certain kind of effect in relying on this kind of style?

I think that's the way people talk. I know I think that way—in short sentences. If I didn't describe things neutrally I would be editorializing, which is not at all what I mean to do. It may be that I have gone too far with my prose style in this direction. It's a very mannered style, really—or the effect of it is very mannered—but that effect is no more conscious on my part when I sit down at the typewriter than these other things we've been talking about. I write so fast that I couldn't possibly think about whether or not I'm putting compound or complex sentences into my prose, or whether I'm writing like a dope, or whatever. I mean, we're talking about writing a whole story in two or three hours.

[LM]: But from what you just said I take it that you are conscious about trying to eliminate an intrusive, editorializing narrator?

Usually, but not always. There's a story of mine called **"Greenwich Time,"** which was in the *New Yorker*; it doesn't exactly have editorializing but it does have what is purple prose for me. So I won't say I never change my prose style or point of view. I don't think you would even recognize that **"Greenwich Time"** is by me, except maybe in terms of the characters—it's full of analogies, it's constructed like a prism, the language is extremely deliberate and insistent; it's ostensibly seen through the main character's eyes, but the author is so completely and obviously there that you couldn't possibly remove her.

[SG]: Is this kind of different approach something you've been doing more of recently in your stories, or is it just an isolated incident?

It's something I realize more that I can do now. But it certainly would be so damn hard for me to do it all the time that I avoid it. And, of course, the most important thing is that this different approach seemed appropriate for that story, whereas it wouldn't be in others.

[SG]: When you say that you write the way you do because it's "too hard" to write in other ways, what do you mean?

I don't think I have an overall view of things to express.

[SG]: So you focus on trying to observe small things. . . .

Not so much small things as small moments. I wish that writing these stories would suddenly lead me to some revelation that could help me as well as existing as art, as well as pleasing others. But don't think I've ever written anything that's allowed me to put pieces together; or maybe I have a psychological problem that makes me resist putting pieces together, that's the flip side of it. But one or the other is true.

[SG]: It's interesting that you relate this to your own psychological makeup because I noticed that your characters often seem to have moments where they seem unable to put the pieces of their lives together, unable to understand their own or others' motivations.

This particular problem may indeed be particular to me. Based on what I've experienced, even with the people I'm closest to, I can't predict or always find consistency to others' behavior—and I don't think I'm especially bad about reading people. What I'm perceiving, though, is probably correct I suspect: people are unpredictable. What I tend to think about someone is not something like, "X will always be cheerful on a given evening; therefore I should call X and we'll go out and get a pizza." Rather, I think, "I'll call X—anything might happen." I think this way even if I've known X for fifteen years. Obviously this attitude works its way into my fiction in all sorts of ways because I can't pretend to project myself into any other position.

[LM]: What other contemporary writers do you especially admire?

This is a hard question for me to answer because it makes me seem like a fool to like so many. I do read a lot these days, whereas years ago I didn't. If you asked me, "Who do you think is always good?" that would be really hard—I'd say "Almost nobody, me included." But for individual moments or books or stories, there's so many. Obviously one writer I like is Mary Lee Settle, whose name seems to have come up several times tonight. Barthelme—I think he's the true genius of our time. Ann Tyler is really good. Joy Williams is one of the best short story writers in America; she has a collection out called *Taking Care* which is great. I just read a Tobias Wolff collection called *In the Garden of the North American Martyrs*, a terrible title but the first story in it is absolutely magnificent and the whole book is really first rate. Raymond Carver. If there's one story I could die happy having written, it's "What Is It?" by Raymond Carver. If there's one novel I could have written, it would have been Steven Millhauser's *Edwin Mullhouse.* Stanley Crawford, whose last book, *Some Instructions for My Wife,* is a bitterly witty book; my favorite book of his is *Log of the S.S. The Mrs. Unquentine.* I also read a lot of poetry. I'm a great admirer of Louise Gluck, Jay Parini, Gregory Orr, Michael Ryan, Sidney Lea.

[*LM*]: *In your story* "*A Reasonable Man*" *one of your characters points to all the books lining his walls and then wonders whether or not any of them were written by happy people. Has writing made you happy, or does it tend to aggravate things, open up wounds, the way it apparently did for Sylvia Plath?*

Writing doesn't open up wounds for me; during the writing of them it has made me happy. There have been a couple of times, only three I can think of, where I have finished a story—and remember that when I start to write something I don't know what it is I'm going to write and have gotten to the end of it and thought, "I really wish I had never had to put these pieces together." These were "**The Burning House,**" a story in *Vogue* called "**Playback,**" and a story that will be out in the *New Yorker* in a few months called "**Desire.**"

[*SG*]: *Why did you regret finishing these?*

Each of these made me realize that I had kept at bay and deliberately misinterpreted painful truths. But it is worth the price of discovering what you don't want to know because you can also have the sheer pleasure of writing something absurd like "**It's Just Another Day at Big Bear City, California,**" and deciding to have spacemen take pornographic pictures. I mean, that's fun and I basically write because I think it's fun. There are a few things I wish I never had written only because I wish I hadn't found out the things I found out.

[*LM*]: *So at least occasionally you feel that the process of writing allows you to discover things about yourself.*

Yes, but always only in retrospect. I don't ever sit down thinking that. I just do it, the way I get my groceries.

Christina Murphy (essay date 1986)

SOURCE: Murphy, Christina. "*Distortions*: The Early Fiction." In *Ann Beattie,* pp. 20-41. Boston: Twayne, 1986.

[*In the following essay, Murphy presents a detailed analysis of the stories collected in Beattie's* Distortions.]

Distortions, Ann Beattie's first volume of short stories, was published in 1976. At the time, the prevailing mode of postmodernism had largely run its course, all its literary experiments had been tried, all the rebellions against the constraints of traditional mimetic fiction undertaken, and all the ways of looking at the "story-shaped world" of postmodernist aesthetics established.[1] In Ann Beattie's opinion, and in the opinion of many critics, the literary world was ripe for a return to realism, even if that realism was mediated through postmodernist influences.[2] It was a time, too, in which the literary and social worlds were both interested in understanding the decade of the 1960s in American culture, a decade of individualism, social rebellion, and romanticism wedged between the halcyon conformity of the Eisenhower era and the frenetic materialism of the 1970s. It was a time in which, as Ann Beattie states, people were and continued to be "tremendously interested in either fancifying or romanticizing the 1960's." A conflux of events served to establish Beattie's reputation as an important literary newcomer: she was a neorealist in an era interested in a return to literary realism; she was, as she describes it, "a writer of a romantic period" that people were interested in learning more about,[3] and she was, by all accounts, a highly talented writer whose first volume of stories revealed a unique style and a keen awareness of human motivations.

"Dwarf House"

"**Dwarf House,**" the first story in *Distortions,* opens with a question: "Are you happy? Because if you're happy I'll leave you alone."[4]

The question is a key one, for all the stories in the volume focus upon happiness and the distortions of perception, need, and self-deceit that make the search for happiness frustrated and incomplete. If one central theme unites the stories, it is that the pursuit of happiness is the most elusive and complex of human quests and yet also the most highly valued.

The question about happiness is posed by MacDonald to his brother James. MacDonald has been sent by his mother to ask James to leave the "dwarf house" he shares with several other dwarfs and return home. When James refuses, MacDonald responds that he needs to reassure their mother that James is happy.

> "Tell her I'm as happy as she is."
>
> "You know she's not happy."
>
> "She knows I'm not, too. Why does she keep sending you?"
>
> "She's concerned about you. She'd like you to live at home. She'd come herself . . ."
>
> "I know. But she gets nervous around freaks."
>
>   (15)

James tells MacDonald that he is in love with a woman who lives in the "dwarf house" and that he intends to marry her. MacDonald is deeply distressed and knows that the news will throw their mother into a paroxysm of self-pity and despair.

Three houses or "families" shape the thematic import of **"Dwarf House,"** each representing different social and personal definitions of happiness. The first is the mother's house, which is described in distinctly unhappy terms as being closed-off, dark, and isolated. The mother is immersed emotionally in her sorrows over James's deformity. She is filled with self-pity that such a terrible tragedy as to be the mother of a dwarf could be imposed upon her by fate. Yet, she wants James to return and live with her because loneliness is a worse state of unhappiness than living daily with James and facing the fact of his handicap, a paradoxical perspective that makes her more histrionically and self-destructively "unhappy."

The second house is the "dwarf house" itself, inhabited by a group of dwarfs and one giant. In the "dwarf house," a true spirit of camaraderie, loyalty, and family exists. The dwarfs and the giant are bound together by an appreciation of their role as outcasts and "freaks," and their knowledge of their state gives them a type of existential freedom. Since they can never fit into society's definition of "happiness," they are free to pursue their own. They are existentially free to choose self-definition, because they have abandoned all illusions that they will ever find "happiness" in the conventional sense of the word.

The middle zone between the self-centered and self-reflexive "happiness" of the mother and the existentially defined freedom of the "dwarf house" is conventional reality, the house occupied by Mac-Donald. MacDonald is essentially a passive observer of the types of "happiness" he sees in his mother's house and in the "dwarf house." He is aware that he really belongs in neither realm, yet he is unable to formulate a definition of his own.

MacDonald often calls his wife from work to tell her that he is going to be tied up in a meeting for several hours and will be late coming home, but the phone call is a practiced and regular deception. At least once a week, MacDonald goes to a run-down bar across town. On one occasion, he asks his secretary Betty to come along with him. As they drive to the bar, Mac-Donald asks Betty her age, and she responds that she is thirty. He asks her how she can be thirty years old and not be a cynic yet. Betty replies, "Actually, if I didn't take two kinds of pills, I couldn't smile every morning and evening for you" (20).

When they arrive at the bar, MacDonald tells Betty,

> "If you don't feel like smiling, don't smile."
>
> "Then all the pills would be for nothing."
>
> "Everything is for nothing," he says.
>
> "If you weren't drinking, you could take one of the pills," Betty says. "Then you wouldn't feel that way."
>
> (20-21)

In the story's denouement, MacDonald, his wife, and his mother "stand amid a cluster of dwarfs and one giant" waiting for James's wedding to begin (22). The couple is married on the lawn outside the church. When the ceremony is over, James kisses the bride and the dwarfs swarm around them. "MacDonald thinks of a piece of Hershey bar he dropped in the woods once on a camping trip, and how the ants were all over it before he finished lacing his boot" (22-23). MacDonald steps forward to congratulate the couple, and he "sees that the bride is smiling beautifully—a smile no pills could produce—and that the sun is shining on her hair so that it sparkles. She looks small, and bright, and so lovely that MacDonald, on his knees to kiss her, doesn't want to get up" (23).

The ending of **"Dwarf House"** is characteristic of the type of "miniaturized epiphanies" that Gilder sees adorning Beattie's fiction. Beattie has described her endings as "elliptical"[5] and has commented that her endings are "very important" to her—much more important than beginnings."[6]

The image of the Hershey candy bar with the ants swarming over it, symbolic of hunger and of human need, is a classic example of a "miniaturized epiphany" in which large insights into human nature are revealed through small, almost trivial, gestures and events. The people at the wedding are so desperate for "happiness" that wherever they encounter it, in whatever form, they descend upon it, trying to devour whatever little piece they can find. This same theme is recapitulated in the image of MacDonald on his knees staring into the bride's face and being mesmerized by her smile of radiant, true happiness. MacDonald is literally hungry for the type of joy that the bride and James possess, and, as he stares into the bride's face in a moment of longing and loneliness, he wishes to possess a bit of the happiness the couple has found.

The ending of the story is not only effective as the symbolic and thematic keel of the story but for embodying what Jay Parini views as the most carefully developed and aesthetically significant aspect of Beattie's writings: "As always in Beattie's fiction, the real story takes place at the edge of what is shown. Her statements are really questions. And she poses hard questions for her readers about human relations, about what will suffice to make us happy."[7] At the edge of **"Dwarf House,"** the reader is left to ponder the silence that surrounds the moment of insight and to wonder what type of "happiness" will be available to MacDonald now that he has glimpsed true happiness in the bride's beatific look of love and total self-acceptance.

"SNAKES' SHOES"

"Snakes' Shoes" is another fictive universe in which "the real story takes place at the edge of what is shown." It focuses upon the emotional permutations involved in the relationships between Sam, his brother Richard, and Richard's ex-wife, Alice.

The story opens with the trio sitting on a rock in the middle of Hall's Pond, an image perhaps suggestive of the distance and isolation the three share—although Ann Beattie has stated that she likes "to bury things too obviously symbolic" in her stories.[8]

Richard, Sam, and Alice have agreed to get together again, at Sam's suggestion. To the meeting, Alice brings her ten-month-old baby from her second marriage and her daughter from her marriage with Richard. The little girl is never identified by name, nor is her age specifically given.

When the little girl notices a snake crawl out from a crack between two rocks on the shore, Sam, her uncle, tells her how snakes tuck their tails into their mouths and turn into hoops so they can roll down hill more easily.

> "Why don't they just walk?" [the child asks].
>
> "They don't have feet. See?" [Sam says].
>
> At Alice's urging to tell the child the truth, Sam responds, "They have feet, but they shed them in the summer. If you ever see tiny shoes in the woods, they belong to the snakes."
>
> "Tell her the truth," [Alice says again].
>
> "Imagination is better than reality," [Sam says to the little girl].
>
> (26)

There is a strong emphasis in the story upon Sam's statement that "imagination is better than reality." In fact, there is the suggestion that imagination is all that enables humans to endure the vagaries of life and especially the vagaries of human relationships.

When Richard and Alice were engaged, Sam had tried to talk Richard out of the marriage; his intense conviction was based upon not wanting to see Richard dominated by a wife in the same fashion that he was controlled by his mother and regimented out of his identity in the Air Force. The wedding takes place, however, and Richard and Alice invite Sam to spend the summer with them. He is so impressed with the love and devotion the two express to each other that he continues to return for part of each summer and for every Thanksgiving thereafter. Just as he is convinced that "everything was perfect" (28), Richard tells him that he and Alice are getting a divorce.

Sam has admired Alice for her patience, for the way in which she appears not to hold a grudge against her husband for burning a hole in an armchair or for tearing the mainsail on their sailboat (done by irresponsibly going out on the lake in a storm). But when he talks to Alice about the breakup, Alice says of Richard, "He burns up all the furniture. He acts like a madman with that boat. He's swamped her three times this year. I've been seeing someone else" (28).

Sam takes Richard to a bar to sympathize with him about Alice's affair with Hans, her German lover. Richard knows about Hans and seems to be more troubled by the fact that Hans is German than by the fact that Alice has taken a lover.

After much urging from Richard, Sam agrees to let Richard move in with him in New York, and Richard proceeds to turn Sam's apartment into a menagerie, filling it with a dog, a cat, a parakeet, and a rabbit. When the rabbit contracts a fever, it costs Sam one hundred sixty dollars to treat the animal's illness because Richard is unemployed and cannot pay for anything.

Sam keeps a record book of the debts that Richard owes him. In it he writes, "Death of rabbit—$160 to vet." When Richard does get a job, he looks over the debt book and goes into a rage at what Sam has done.

"Why couldn't you have just written down the sum?" he asks Sam. "Why did you want to remind me about the rabbit?" The incident so upsets Richard that he misses the second day on his job. "That was inhuman," he says to Sam. "'Death of rabbit—$160'—that was horrible. The poor rabbit. God damn you." Sam's perception is that Richard "couldn't get control of himself" (30-31).

Sam hears from Alice when his mother dies. It is an odd letter of condolence, and it seems to Sam that Alice is not very happy. Sam writes her a long letter saying that they should all get together. He knows of a motel out in the country where they can stay, perhaps for the weekend. Alice agrees to the idea, and the trio meet to stay at the same hotel but in different rooms. One afternoon, out on the rock in the pond, the "family" is again reunited, and the little girl asks Sam to tell her a story. Sam responds that he cannot think of one, noticing that the girl "had bony knees" and "was not going to be as pretty as her mother" (32). Richard asks Alice why she married Hans, and she replies, "I don't know why I married either of you" (33). Perhaps sensing the tension mounting between the couple, Sam offers to take the girl for a walk. He takes her hand, this time observing that "the little girl's knees stuck out. Sam felt sorry for her. He lifted her on his shoulders and cupped his hands over her knees so he wouldn't have to look at them" (33).

That evening, the "family" once more returns to the rock. The little girl, recalling a previous scene in which she had looked through a man's binoculars, says she wishes she could look through them again. "Here," Sam says, making two circles with the thumb and first finger of each hand. "Look through these" (29). The little girl leans over and looks up at the trees through Sam's fingers. "Much clearer, huh?" Sam says. The little girl is enjoying the game. "Let me see," Richard says, and looks through his brother's fingers. "Don't forget me," Alice says as she leans across Richard to "peer through the circles" (34). As Alice leans across him, Richard kisses the back of her neck, and the story closes.

The ending of the story provides not only another of the "miniaturized epiphanies" that characterize and define Beattie's fiction but a simultaneous union of the concept of vision and illusion. Certainly, the ending forces the reader to discover that what goes on at the surface in human action and in human relationships is not the full or even the clear picture. On the surface, Alice and Richard act the politest of ex-spouses; their marriage is in the past, and they are moving on to form and to share a friendship. Richard helps to take care of Alice's son by Hans, and Alice is cooperative in carrying out the suggestions and requests for the weekend that both Richard and Sam present. As the ending of the story indicates, however, Richard's emotions have not fallen so easily into social politeness and group cooperation. His kiss on Alice's neck is one of tenderness, perhaps, perhaps one of sadness or desire. It is both ironic and intriguing that the kiss takes place only within the illusory security of distorted vision—as the couple peers through the imaginary binoculars made by Sam's fingers and pretends to see something not actually seen. Only in this moment of distorted perception, of perception distorted toward the realm of fantasy, can Richard's real feelings surface.

Earlier in the story, Sam has tried to coax the little girl into believing that he wrote *Alice in Wonderland,* and perhaps no finer metaphor exists for the thematic dimensions of **"Snakes' Shoes"** than an allusion to a child's fairy tale about perception and insight—about the looking glass and its magical powers to distort reality and, in those distortions, reveal more truths than otherwise could be found. Through the looking glass, Richard and Alice discover truths about themselves and their feelings, and those truths, one hopes, are ultimately freeing. In **"Snakes' Shoes,"** however, as in **"Dwarf House,"** much of the power of the story takes place in the suggestive silence that surrounds the story's end. The reader can only wonder in **"Dwarf House"** what MacDonald will see or refuse to see once the spell of looking into the bride's face is broken. Similarly, the reader can only wonder or imagine what Richard and Alice, perhaps even Sam, will see once the protective circle of the imaginary looking glass is withdrawn and reality must be seen in a different light, a different focus.

"THE PARKING LOT"

Adulterous affairs and the romantic illusions associated with passionate, sexual love seem to be the predominant mode of escapism in **Distortions.** Characters search for the love they do not possess by involving themselves in temporary liaisons they know will not keep them secure (or even desired) for long. The romances and attractions seem to be only temporary stays against confusion, distractions from the deeper pain of these characters' lives; but the characters find their real lives to be even more emotionally unfulfilled than the fantasies they pursue.

In **"The Parking Lot,"** a couple's marriage is shown to be an empty series of domestic rituals centering upon food and its preparation. The woman, who is never named, works in an office building surrounded by a vast parking lot. Throughout the story, the parking lot itself becomes a metaphor for the work place—vast, empty, demarcated, never-changing—a place in which the woman can lose herself and not have to face the larger and more real loss of her own identity. Each time she walks across the parking lot, she becomes fascinated by "the sameness of the surface: so black and regular" (188), yet, the same regularity and "sameness of the surface" associated with her marriage begin to feel isolating and deadening to her.

The woman has an arrangement with her husband, Jim; they alternate the years in which they work. Last year, he worked as a house painter; this year, she has an office job. They survive, too, by sharing not only the economic responsibilities of the marriage but the domestic responsibilities as well. Jim does all the grocery shopping, and the woman is a superb cook, consistently preparing gourmet meals of exotic combinations.

During the day, Jim searches for spices and herbs and whatever delicacies his wife might need that evening, while the woman immerses herself in her work at the office. "Only work has seemed real to her since she began her job"; "the wide, shining hallway gives her a sense of purpose" (189).

The couple has a friend, Sam, who often comes to visit them. Sam is separated from his wife and seems to come to the couple's home for a vicarious sense of participating in marriage and in a domestic routine. Sam and Jim often go out together and invite the woman to go along with them, but she declines. "When they leave the apartment it seems suddenly as though space is opening up around her" (190).

The woman is aware that "Sam has always been a little in love with her," and she "likes him a little more because she knows about his secret love" (191). But she also feels uncomfortable around Sam because his presence is "a reminder of what can happen to a marriage, the distressing realization that two adults who care about each other as Sam and his wife do, can't reach some agreement, have some arrangement that will make them both happy" (192).

One day, the woman is walking from work toward her car in the parking lot, and a car pulls up along side of her. She recognizes the driver as "a man she has spoken to several times in the elevator" (192). He asks her if she is parked in the back of the lot and offers her a ride. She gets in, and they are at her car in less than a minute—"'too short a time to start a conversation,' he says" (192). She agrees and remains in the car for awhile longer. "She smiles, which is something she hasn't done all weekend" (192). "During the next hour they have a conversation—in a bar. The conversation lasts about an hour, and then they go to a motel and go to bed. She thinks, then, of Jim—as she has most of the afternoon. She cannot decide what to tell him, so she stays in the motel for another hour, thinking. Eventually they leave. He drives her back to her car. They smile again. This time there is no conversation, and she gets out" (192-93).

The next day she does not go to work but loses herself in a shopping spree in a department store, buying expensive perfume, and in making an elaborate meal for Jim. The following day she returns to work and expects that the man "will be in her office waiting for her, but she doesn't see him all that day" (194). At the day's close, she leaves work, crosses the parking lot, and then she sees his car. She approaches the car, and, for a moment, stands with her hand against the window "until he reaches across the seat and opens the door on her side. Then she gets into the car" (194-95).

The woman knows that eventually her husband will find out. One evening she is particularly late and had delayed calling for hours. She uses the phone at the entrance to the parking lot, trying to keep her voice calm and regular. She counts the white lines that divide the lot into parking places until Jim answers. She tells him that her car has broken down and that there is a man there who will help her. Jim listens and asks several questions; then there is silence. He tells her to call him if there is any real trouble.

The man drives her to her car at the back of the lot. She watches in the rearview mirror as his car drives away, and then she gets out of her car and stands in the parking lot. "Standing there, she thinks of her lover, gone in one direction, and of Jim, in another." Then "she gets in the car and drives home to make dinner" (196).

"The Parking Lot" is an interesting study in loneliness. The woman feels confined by her marriage and her life. Her work, which exhausts her by the end of the day, also frees her because it provides her a reason to be away from home and to immerse herself in another perspective, another environment. For love and real communication, she and her husband have substituted cooking and eating rituals, perhaps in an attempt to fill themselves physically in ways they cannot emotionally. The emotional bankruptcy of their marriage makes the woman seek a type of fulfillment through an affair with a coworker.

One might wonder why the woman does not become involved with Sam since he loves her, and she is attracted both to Sam and to his admiration of her. Yet, it is apparent from the story's context that Sam represents the reality of a failed union, of the inability of love and marriage to conquer all and to survive. This is a realization that the woman is not yet ready to face in her own life. She clings to the hope that she can find emotional fulfillment by losing herself in a sexual involvement that does not even attempt or pretend to involve love or commitment. In this distraction, she pulls herself away from her marriage, which has become a phantasm of unexpressed and unfulfilled emotions.

Because reality is too harsh and the awareness that love does not conquer all too difficult to accept at this point in her life, the woman substitutes the temporary self-deception that an affair with a virtual stranger will at least free her from some of the emotional pain and alienation she feels. Her pursuit of emotional wholeness and fulfillment is a quest fostered by resignation and despair and sustained by illusion. The woman is aware that her marriage has not become the type of union she desires; yet, rather than accept this realization and its implications for personal growth and change, she endeavors to let a chance encounter in the parking lot outside her office building alchemize her life. When reality cannot be accepted and vision cannot be joined with action, escapism remains the only option, and, for Beattie's characters, escapism is often only the visible expression of failed attempts at meaningful self-definition.

"IMAGINED SCENES"

Like **"The Parking Lot," "Imagined Scenes"** addresses the themes of loneliness, longing, and frustrated love, but this time measured and assessed against the themes of old age and loss. The life and emotional interaction of a married couple, David and his wife (who remains unnamed throughout the story) are examined in contrast to the life of an elderly widower; the loneliness of the old man serves as a symbolic comment upon the emotional drift and distancing David and his wife undergo.

The story opens with a note of emotional intensity between the couple but also with suggestions of the compromises their relationship has exacted. The woman is dreaming of a trip to Greece and awakens to share her excitement with her husband. David is awake already, and she remembers a time the previous year, the week before Christmas, when they had both come home with their purchases. She was at the front door struggling with her keys when David drove up. He jumped out of the car, excited about his purchases, and reached around to put his key in the lock for her. "Now she expects him to wake up when she does, that they will arrive home simultaneously" (54). But her husband still surprises her. At the end of the summer he had told her that he would not return to work but would be going back to school to finish his Ph.D.

Since that decision, their life had become, in part, a series of unspoken compromises, manifested as rituals. He sits in a chair by the fireplace and reads; she brings coffee to the table by his chair. When she is tired, he turns off the lights and goes upstairs with her to bed. "By unspoken agreement, he has learned to like Roquefort dressing" (54), and he pokes the logs in the fireplace for her because she is afraid of the hot red coals.

The woman works at night. She is a nurse and has been hired by an old man's daughter and son-in-law to stay with him at night for a week while they are out of town. His sister is to stay with him during the days.

One afternoon, the woman returns home early from work and finds that David has gone for a walk with the dog. Company has been in the house. She finds coffee cups, spoons, and forks scattered about the kitchen and an apple pie she does not remember buying. When David comes in, he tells her that he has met the people who moved in down the hill, Katherine and Larry Duane. He has agreed to help them put in a sink, and, as he leaves to go back to the Duanes, he does not take the dog with him.

The next night, late in the evening, she looks at her watch to see if it is time to give the old man his medicine and discovers that her watch is not there. She calls David to find out if she has left her watch at home. She lets the phone ring a long time, but there is no answer.

The following night at work, she calls David at four in the morning. There is no answer. When the old man awakens, he can tell that she is very worried.

> "I tried to get my husband last night but there was no answer."
>
> "Men are heavy sleepers."
>
> "No," she says. "He'd wake up."
>
> (60)

It is snowing heavily. The old man asks her to call his sister and tell her not to come. If anything happens, he can call. She phones the sister and gives her the message, but she is coming anyway. "It's terrible to be old," the old man says. "You have no power" (61).

David comes to get his wife, knowing that her car will never make it up the hill in the snow and sleet. They drive through the blinding snow, and the woman says to David, "I called you last night and there was no answer."

> "You called?"
>
> "Yes. You weren't there."
>
> "I didn't know it was you. I was asleep. Why were you calling?"
>
> "I guess you were walking the dog in the woods."
>
> "I just told you, I was asleep."
>
> (62-63)

As they drive home, she closes her eyes and imagines a series of scenes about David: David sleeping; David playing with the dog, holding a branch high into the air for the dog to jump up to; David asleep again, under the covers; David walking up the hill. She tries to imagine more but is afraid that if she does not open her eyes she will fall asleep.

Back home, she closes her eyes again. The curtains are drawn, and the house is dark. David says he is going downstairs to clean up. The phone rings, and she comes downstairs to answer it. "The table is clear. Everything has been cleared away" (63).

It is the old man's sister on the phone. She is snowed in and cannot reach her husband. The old man's daughter and son-in-law cannot return. Their plane is grounded in Florida. The sister is asking if the woman can possibly come back and stay the night with the old man.

As she listens to the sister, the woman imagines the runway in Florida filling up with snow. No planes will land tonight, and no one is at home in the United States; "they're up in the air, above the snow" (64). She wonders what was on the table when she came in and notices that David has also cleaned up the room. "You're so lucky," the sister says to her. "You can come and go. You don't know what it's like to be caught" (64).

"Imagined Scenes" combines the triad of vision, imagination, and escapism that so largely determines Beattie's philosophical stance and the thematic structuring of her stories. The woman in **"Imagined Scenes"** goes through a variety of emotional stages representative of changes in her vision. As the story begins, she is lost in a dream. When she awakens, she retreats into memories of fond times in her life with David. Interacting with David, she believes that she sees him and their marriage clearly, envisioning David as impulsive and whimsical in his career choice, perhaps, but overall the epitome of devoted love. Her interaction with David indicates that she sees him as the center of her experience. She wants always to be with him—to awaken with him, to share enthusiastic and exciting moments with him, to help him attain his goals in his career. In her daily routine with David, she feels strongly that she knows him well and that the unspoken agreements they have made to give structure to their marriage have been positive and effective. In truth, however, as John Romano points out, "the daily schedules of the couple barely overlap. They do not inhabit the same hours, and there is something chilling and mysterious about the gap between them."[9]

The woman is more obviously attached to David than he is to her. She is only separated from David when he leaves her to take a walk, or to visit the Duanes, or when she goes to stay with the old man. In these moments with the old man, she must imagine David and recreate him in her mind. As the story progresses, she can find less and less refuge in fantasy and memory—in "imagined scenes"—and must face some very difficult and unsettling realities that necessitate a reshaping of her vision of her life with David.

In contrast to **"The Parking Lot,"** the adultery in **"Imagined Scenes"** is only hinted at. As Romano indicates, the "frequent signs of inexplicable activity"

(such as the coffee cups on the table and a favorite plant given away to the Duanes) combined with David's plausible though sketchy explanations "seem slightly sinister in the haze of mutual incomprehension. The glimpses, the physical data, which the woman has of her husband's life in her absence tell her nothing, though they hint at guilty secrets. They cannot be either ignored or interpreted."[10]

The fact that David is not home the two nights the woman calls, that he is reluctant to take his wife down to meet the Duanes, and that he is so obviously uncomfortable in discussing where he has been and what he has been doing in his wife's absence are key indications that he has most likely been involved in an affair. For David, perhaps, the adultery is an escape from the unspoken agreements by which he and his wife have structured their lives. Perhaps it is indicative of a certain loss of direction in his life, exemplified by his desire to complete his doctorate but his inability to get any academic work done during the course of the story.

As in many of Beattie's stories, the adultery is indicative of Beattie's belief that what is most significant in individual human lives and relationships occurs below the visible level of everyday existence. In **"Imagined Scenes,"** the woman's subconscious mind—her memories and fantasies—are far more revealing of her true emotional state than her conscious mind. Similarly, David's adultery, which takes place "off stage" in the story and within the obscurity of night, is far more important and revealing than his daily and daytime interactions with his wife.

The great metaphor in the story for the encroachment of reality is the snow that falls until it finally traps everyone in a kind of nebulous inertia. The story begins with a dream of warmth on the summer beaches of Greece and ends with the snow immobilizing all the characters and freezing the entire city into a virtual standstill. From the warmth of their house, David goes out into the snow and meets the Duanes; his liaison with Katherine will eventually take away the warmth from his home and leave his wife feeling emotionally exhausted and trapped. It is in nights of heavy snow that the woman calls her house and discovers David's absences. In the worst storm of the winter, David and his wife drive home in angered, tense silence after the woman has discovered and admitted to herself David's infidelity, and the most poignant and thematically rich line of the story is presented. The radio in the car is turned on, and "the weather forecast calls for more snow" (63).

The snow that surrounds the town, the couple, their home, their lives, is emblematic of the slow and deep disillusionment that occurs in the story. The dream of

Greece that began the story has become, by its end, a symbol of immobility and of unattainable fantasy. The woman must confront the painful loss of illusions in the same fashion that the old man must envision age as another threatening and immobilizing agent.

"It's terrible to be old. You have no power," the old man says (61). Just as easily, the woman could state, "It's terrible to be disillusioned. You have no power."

John Romano describes **"Imagined Scenes"** as a story that shows the unique way in which Beattie makes her material her own. "We do not realize, or not all at once, that what the young woman has 'imagined' is not her husband's private or guilty activity. She has accepted not the explanations but the sufficiency unto themselves of the physical facts. She 'imagines' only that she is in Greece, or some place warm, by the sea, while the scene of her actual present life is snowy. It is the reader who has been seduced into guessing at the husband's hidden life." Romano sees **"Imagined Scenes"** as representative of Beattie's skill in the short story genre.

> We guess at the "real facts" of the woman's life because we care about her, her sadness has been made significant. It follows that the author has cared about her in the making. But then it is more astonishing to perceive that the woman cares so little, so indistinctly, for herself. She is not suspicious, she has no imagination; the mark of Beattie's respect for this creation is not to have slipped her some healthy suspicion, as it were, under the counter. In this forbearance the writer resembles some impossible ideal of a loving parent who succeeds in not interfering in her children's lives. To love one's characters—Tolstoy is the presiding genius here—is to allow them to be who they are.[11]

Countering those critics who attack Beattie for her dispassionate, restrained, and seemingly aloof style, Romano argues that, in a Beattie story, "only later does the sympathetic center of her work betray itself. We may feel misled by the outward reserve, but, again, her willingness to distort when necessary, her passion for the particular, is ultimately an index of her concern for the integrity of things and people in themselves."[12]

"FANCY FLIGHTS"

If one envisions **"Snakes' Shoes"** and **"Imagined Scenes"** as commentaries upon the theme of illusion versus reality, or, more specifically, the theme of the imagination as a protection against the intrusion of too much painful reality, it is interesting to view the story **"Fancy Flights"** as a comment upon the total rejection of reality in favor of the world of illusion, specifically a drug-induced flight away from the strictures and responsibilities of everyday social and personal interaction.

Much has been made of Beattie's focus upon drugs in her fiction and the illusory worlds that drugs generate for her characters. Joshua Gilder considers this focus "one reason why Beattie People never seem to do much of anything."[13] Gilder is particularly disturbed by the pervasive presence of marijuana, cocaine, and Valium in Beattie's fiction, describing this aspect of her work as fiction operating in "the comatose mode." The presentation of characters so in need of escapism by such vacuous and self-destructive means is one more proof, Gilder contends, of Beattie's inability to deal ethically and realistically with human choice and freedom.[14]

Clearly, Beattie's fiction does include a strong emphasis upon characters who rely on drugs, and **_Distortions_** is no exception. It is a limiting critical notion, however, to regard the depiction of characters dependent upon chemical alterations of their perceptions of reality as indicative of Beattie's inability or refusal to write moral fiction. Rather, one should view Beattie as a neorealist whose faithfully realistic descriptions of life in the 1970s and 1980s must include depictions of drug use and drug dependency.

Like many of Beattie's fictions, **"Fancy Flights"** centers upon alienation and emotionally fractured lives. Michael, the central character, is separated from his wife, Elsa, and from his four-and-a-half-year-old daughter, Mary Anne. His deepest emotional bond, in fact, seems to be with his dog Silas, and his interaction with Silas is the story's opening motif.

Silas is afraid of vacuum cleaners, little children, and music, all of which he growls at, and "his growling always gets him in trouble; nobody thinks he is entitled to growl" (36). Silas gets extremely agitated at Bob Dylan's song "Positively Fourth Street," and Michael believes that "if the dog had his way, he would get Dylan by the leg in a dark alley" (36). He imagines that maybe he and Silas could take a trip to a recording studio or concert hall, "wherever Dylan was playing," and then "Silas could get him" (36). "Thoughts like these ('fancy flights,' his foreman called them) were responsible for Michael's no longer having a job" (36).

Michael had worked in a furniture factory. During his breaks, he smoked hash in the parking lot in the back of the factory. Often, during his shifts, he would break into hysterical laughter at jokes his fellow employees would tell. "Every day he smoked as much hash as he could stand" (36).

Michael depends on his grandmother for support in the form of "words of encouragement, mail-order delicacies, and money" (37). He lives in a house that belongs to his friends Prudence and Richard, who are in Manila. Michael is house-sitting for his friends and does not have to pay rent, only the utility bills. He spends his days and evenings listening to music, smoking hash, playing with Silas, and going through Prudence's and Richard's bureau drawers. "He usually eats two cans of Campbell's Vegetarian Vegetable soup for lunch and four Chunky Pecan candy bars for dinner. If he is awake in time for breakfast, he smokes hash" (38).

One day, Michael calls his wife. He learns that his daughter, Mary Anne, is having trouble in the day-care center. Mary Anne wants to quit, stay home, and watch television. His wife asks if Michael would stay with Mary Anne during the day and let her have her wish, "since her maladjustment is obviously caused by Michael's walking out on them when he *knew* the child adored him" (41).

Michael says he called to say he was lonesome because Silas has run away.

> "I really love that dog," [Michael says].
>
> "What about Mary Anne?" [Elsa asks].
>
> "I don't know. I'd like to care, but what you said didn't make any impression on me."
>
> (42)

Michael has a friend named Carlos who amazes Michael because he can cast curses upon people and objects and "roll a joint in fifteen seconds" (43). Carlos speaks to Michael about the possibility of getting a job in Carlos's father's factory. Michael tells him that he is through with jobs and with all machinery and tells Carlos to put a curse on his father's machines.

> "What if I put a curse on you?" Carlos asks.
>
> "I'm already cursed," Michael says, ". . . I myself am cursed with ill luck."
>
> (44)

The next day, Silas returns home. Michael finds him standing in the front yard. He takes Silas inside, hugs and pets him; then there is a knock at the door. It is Michael's wife, Elsa, who tells him, "I've come to get you and make you come home and share the responsibility for Mary Anne."

> "I don't want to come home," [Michael says].
>
> "I don't care. If you don't come home, we'll move in here."
>
> "Silas will kill you."
>
> "I know the dog doesn't like me, but he certainly won't kill me."
>
> (46)

Elsa tells Michael decisively to come home and help with Mary Anne, who is driving Elsa crazy. Michael gets Silas, his bag of grass and his pipe, and what remains of a bag of pecans his grandmother has sent him, and goes with Elsa.

> "I'm not asking you to work right away," [Elsa says]. I just want you in the house during the day with Mary Anne."
>
> "I don't want to hang around with her."
>
> "Well, you can fake it. She's your daughter."
>
> "I know. That doesn't make any impression on me."
>
> "I realize that," [Elsa says].
>
> (47)

Michael spends his days taking care of Mary Anne and watching soap operas. One afternoon, Mary Anne and a friend are having an imaginary tea party. Carlos calls, and Michael asks him, "Why don't you cast a spell and make things better?" (50).

Michael "looks at his daughter and her friend enjoying their tea party" (50-51) and then goes into the bathroom, closes the door, and lights up his pipe. He sits on the bathroom floor with his legs crossed and gets very stoned. He can hear a woman crying on the soap opera. Mary Anne's pink plastic bunny stares at him from the bathtub. "'What else can I do?' he whispers to the bunny. He envies the bunny—the way it clutches the bar of soap to its chest" (51).

When Elsa returns, Michael goes into the hall and "puts his arms around her, thinking about the bunny and the soap. Mick Jagger sings to him: 'All the dreams we held so close seemed to all go up in smoke . . .'" (51).

> "Elsa," he says, "What are your dreams?"
>
> "That your dealer will die," she says.

He asks her to be serious and tell him "one real dream." "I told you," Elsa says (51).

Michael lets Elsa go and walks into the living room. He sees Carlos pull up and goes out and gets into Carlos's car. Michael is somber and noncommunicative, and his mood is "contagious." Carlos angrily starts the car and drives off, "throwing a curse on a boxwood at the edge of the lawn" (51).

While ostensibly a story about the impact of drug dependency upon Michael's life, **"Fancy Flights"** is, on a much deeper level, a story about loneliness and emotional suffering. Michael's drug use is only symptomatic of deeper emotional hurts and longings—

the cumulative effect of which is to present a picture of a man unable to cope with his life or to function within it in a meaningful fashion.

Clearly, in his interpersonal relationships, Michael is capable of very little closeness or responsibility. He frees himself of anything that might place strictures upon his life or make demands upon his emotional energies—his wife, daughter, job, self-esteem, motivation, and capacity for inner-directed vision. In ridding himself of both his marriage and his job, Michael, in a sense, regresses to a type of adolescence (and a very childlike adolescence at that), staying home and getting stoned all day; refusing to work and letting his grandmother and his wife support him; eating soup and Chunky Pecan candies; playing with Silas as his only true companion or buddy—being, in essence, as free as possible from any of the responsibilities and implications of self-definition.

In his talks with Carlos, Michael blames his dysfunctional and apathetic state upon "ill luck" (44), failing (perhaps even refusing) to realize how many of his own problems and troubles he has brought upon himself. Like many adolescents, Michael blames his misfortunes and problems on others and remains happy as long as he can be self-indulgent and irresponsible. In his world of self-induced self-deception, he does not have to face up to the existential implications of personal freedom; instead, all Michael has to do is live in an imagined, euphoric world of "fancy flights."

Michael's adolescent refuge is violated and altered when his wife, Elsa, comes to take him home. The irony of his wife's coming for him as if he were a child who has misbehaved is surpassed only by the heavy parent-child interaction that Michael and Elsa engage in until the last scene of the story. Perhaps most significantly, the world that Elsa brings Michael into is that of a type of illusory childhood—he is to serve as a kind of playmate and companion for his four-and-a-half-year-old daughter, a role for which Michael seems ideally suited in terms of his own emotional immaturity, but one that he does not want because of the implied adult responsibilities caring for Mary Anne encompasses.

In the last scene of the story, Michael is forced into a painful realization of his emotional state and his lot in life. Watching his daughter having her tea party with her friend, knowing that his wife and even Carlos (with all his magic) are at work, Michael experiences a sense of displacement and alienation that is exceedingly painful, yet illuminating. Admiring with poignant longing the bond that his daughter and her friend share at the tea party, Michael goes into the bathroom to

smoke pot, his usual custom and his usual way of dealing with both loneliness and painful emotions. Even here, in his drug-induced fantasies of a world protected from painful intrusions, he cannot escape the realization that even the plastic bunny, which functions as both a bath toy and a soap holder, has more purpose in life than he.

"What else can I do?" (51) he asks of the bunny, meaning that since Michael does not truly fit into the world of childhood represented by his daughter and her friend, or into the world of adulthood, represented by his wife and Carlos at work, what else can he do but get stoned and try to live in a world of delusions and self-imposed deceptions?

This time, however, the magic of the drugs to transport him away from adulthood and responsibility is not sufficient, and Michael is forced to face a measure of truth about his world and his life. He remembers a line from Mick Jagger's song "Angie," and, as he embraces his wife, he realizes that "all the dreams we held so close seemed to all go up in smoke . . ." (51), a clear indication that Michael is beginning to realize how much of his own state of dysfunction and apathy he has brought upon himself. His life and his dreams are going up in smoke, and he feels powerless to do anything about the dissipation he is experiencing. Rather than fight it, Michael chooses to leave his wife, and the clarity of vision she represents, to go off with Carlos, and to reidentify himself with the world of magic and drug-induced "fancy flights."

Gilder has stated that "perhaps the most telling of Beattie's emotional economies is her characters' inability to muster the energy to pass beyond adolescence. Their limit to growth is about age eighteen, which among other things explains their nostalgia for the Sixties, when the whole culture seemed to have regressed into adolescence."[15] While **"Fancy Flights"** is indeed a story about one character's "inability to muster the energy to pass beyond adolescence," it is also a story representative of failings in human character and relationships. The weaknesses that Michael reveals are emblematic of personal failings that are generated by a preference for refuge and security, however illusory, over the terrifying implications of taking responsibility for one's own life. In this regard, Beattie is less a writer depicting a certain character type of the "lost, counterculture wastrel" than she is a writer revealing deep insights into the nature of the human psyche and the human will.

DARKNESS AND LIGHT

Peter Glassman has commented that, in assembling in *Distortions* a "bizarre collection of the lonely, the disoriented, and the dispossessed," Beattie has achieved a "measure of consummate technical virtuosity." Beattie's "frigid prose, the shocking inexorableness of her humor and narrative designs, the macabre and spare efficiency of her thought, conspire to project her tales as actual—if rather awful—occurrences of modern existence."[16] Glassman is aware that, in contrast to many contemporary writers, Beattie does not assume an ironic distance from her characters, which might make their sufferings and conundrums seem like parodies of contemporary life. Instead, "Beattie constructs her stories from within a soft and subtle sensibility of sympathy, participation, and hopefulness. She understands that, however capricious or queer, her characters' pains have their origin less in the morasses of individual neurosis than in the insipidity of the culture at large, the withering vapidity of the historical processes which envelop one and with which one must manage to coexist in some sort of emotional relation." The collapse of characters' inner lives is but a reflection of the spiritually bankrupt world in which they live, for Beattie comprehends, in Glassman's opinion, "that we are driven into our misery and peculiarity because, appropriately, we cannot accommodate the abstraction and absurdity which surround us."[17]

Larry Husten, in considering both the merit and philosophical implications of *Distortions,* envisions Beattie as "a sharp cultural observer" who "focuses on the interaction between her characters and their culture." In Husten's view, those of Beattie's characters "who abandon their selves to the cultural moment lose the ability to experience genuine emotion."[18] Husten's construct for Beattie's philosophical dichotomy of will and apathy, feeling and emptiness, is the metaphor of darkness and light that he says pervades Beattie's fictive universe in *Distortions.* Characters who are lost in their culture's mazes of emotional and spiritual entropy are often identified with the dark; other characters, who deny the sterility and the penchant for self-annihilation in the modern world, "retain a core of self and the ability to feel."[19] For these characters, who struggle for self-definition, light, in the form of self-insight and the will to self-determination, is their bounty. As Husten states, all Beattie's characters in *Distortions* "face, or will face, the darkness. What makes Beattie so interesting and popular a writer . . . is not *her* response to this darkness (by now a trite concept) but the ways in which she imagines her characters' responses."[20]

For characters like MacDonald, facing the darkness and the silence while staring into the light in the bride's face in **"Dwarf House,"** or the wife in **"Imagined Scenes,"** watching the snow falling and immersing her life in darkness and freezing cold, the light of existential self-definition is still a possibility. That some, like Michael in **"Fancy Flights,"** allow their lives and dreams to go up in smoke, or others, like the wife in **"The Parking Lot,"** wait for circumstances to overwhelm them and force change upon them, does not negate that the light, the other choice that might have been made, waits (like the silence) at the edge of Beattie's fictional world. Were the choices between darkness and light clear-cut and easy for her characters, Beattie would be the type of moral writer with ready ethical and existential answers that Gilder and many other critics admire. As it is, Beattie is concerned with defining a universe of distortions, of fluctuations in darkness and light, that make the choices seem more ambiguous, more obscure. Through these distortions, Beattie depicts not only the essences of her characters' lives but presents powerful insights into the patterns of contemporary life.

Notes

1. Brian Wicker, *The Story-Shaped World: Fiction and Metaphysics* (Notre Dame, Ind.: University of Notre Dame Press, 1975).

2. Maynard, "Visiting Ann Beattie," 39-40.

3. Ibid.

4. *Distortions* (New York: Doubleday, 1976), 14. Subsequent page references will appear within parentheses in the text.

5. McCaffery and Gregory, "Conversation," 174.

6. Maynard, "Visiting Ann Beattie," 41.

7. Parini, "Writer Comes of Age," 24.

8. Ibid., 23.

9. John Romano, "Ann Beattie and the 60's" *Commentary,* February 1977, 63.

10. Ibid.

11. Ibid.

12. Ibid.

13. Gilder, "Down and Out," 51.

14. Ibid., 54-56.

15. Ibid., 56.

16. Peter Glassman, review of *Distortions, Hudson Review* 30, no. 3 (1977): 447.

17. Ibid.

18. Larry Husten, "On Ann Beattie," *Salmagundi* 40 (1978): 164.

19. Ibid., 161.

20. Ibid.

Selected Bibliography

Primary Sources

1. Novels

Chilly Scenes of Winter. New York: Doubleday, 1976. Reprint. New York: Fawcett Popular Library, 1978, (paperback); New York: Warner Books, 1983 (paperback).

Falling in Place. New York: Random House, 1980. Reprint. New York: Fawcett Popular Library, 1980 (paperback); London: Secker & Warburg, 1981; Harmondsworth: Penguin, 1982 (paperback); New York: Warner Books, 1983 (paperback).

Love Always. New York: Random House, 1985. Reprint. London: Joseph, 1985.

2. Short Stories

Distortions. New York: Doubleday, 1976. Reprint. New York: Fawcett Popular Library, 1979 (paperback); New York: Warner Books, 1976 and 1983 (paperback).

Jacklighting. Metacom Limited Editions Series, no. 3. Worcester, Mass.: Metacom Press, 1981.

Secrets and Surprises. New York: Random House, 1978. Reprint. New York: Fawcett Popular Library, 1978 (paperback); London: Hamilton, 1979; New York: Warner Books, 1983 (paperback).

The Burning House. New York: Random House, 1982. Reprint. New York: Ballantine, 1982 (paperback); London: Secker & Warburg, 1983.

Secondary Sources

1. Interviews

Maynard, Joyce. "Visiting Ann Beattie." *New York Times Book Review,* 11 May 1980, 39-41. A discussion of Beattie's views of her literary career and critical reputation; especially interesting for Beattie's perspectives upon the writing of *Falling in Place.*

McCaffery, Larry and Sinda Gregory. "A Conversation with Ann Beattie." *Literary Review* 27 (Winter 1984): 165-77. Significant for Beattie's discussion of her "mannered" prose style and the overall focus of her work upon the breakdown of communications in human relationships.

Miner, Bob. "Ann Beattie: 'I Write Best When I Am Sick.'" *Village Voice,* 9 August 1976, 33-34. Focuses, in large measure, upon Beattie's reputation as a counterculture writer and upon the techniques Beattie employs in structuring her fiction.

Murray, G. E. "A Conversation with Ann Beattie." *Story Quarterly* 7/8 (1978): 62-68. Emphasizes *Distortions* and *Chilly Scenes of Winter*; Murray espouses the view

that "faith and despair" are the major themes in Beattie's fiction. Beattie talks about the concepts of illusions and disillusionment in Charles's quest for Laura in *Chilly Scenes of Winter.*

2. Articles

Bell, Pearl K. "Literary Waifs." *Commentary,* February 1979, 67-71. Considers Beattie's "literary waifs" to be in the tradition of John Cheever; "Miss Beattie tells us what happened to the children of Shady Hill and Proxmire Manor."

————. "Marge Piercy and Ann Beattie." *Commentary,* July 1980, 59-61. Contrasts Beattie's *Falling in Place* with Marge Piercy's *Vida*; finds Piercy's world "is a place of heady conflicts between absolutes," while Beattie, "at the opposite extreme, sees a world devoid of all such schematic fitness and order, political or otherwise."

Brown, Georgia A. "Chilly Views of Beattie." *Canto* 3 (January 1981): 165-73. Praises Beattie's distinctive prose style for capturing the essence of lives enmeshed in vacillation and ennui, but finds that Beattie's emphasis upon lives of "quiet desperation" only deals in "surfaces and images—in fashion, and in the fashionable emotions of nostalgia and sentimentality."

Epstein, Joseph. "Ann Beattie and the Hippoisie." *Commentary,* March 1983, 54-58. Envisions Beattie's primary subject as "the fate of her own generation, the generation that was in college and graduate school in the late 60's and early 70's." Beattie's emphasis upon disillusionment and defeat arises from the fact that hers was "a generation of promise," yet one unable to find purpose, direction and self-definition in the 1970s and 1980s.

Gelfant, Blanche H. "Ann Beattie's Magic Slate, or The End of the Sixties." *New England Review* 1 (1979): 374-84. Analyzes *Chilly Scenes of Winter* and selected stories from *Distortions*; finds that Beattie, like J. D. Salinger, "values childlike innocence, precociousness, and whimsy," and is at her best when "she tells stories that embody these qualities while she shows them imperiled."

Gerlach, John. "Through 'The Octascope': A View of Ann Beattie." *Studies in Short Fiction* 17 (Fall 1980): 489-94. An extended critical analysis of Beattie's short story "The Octascope" in *Secrets and Surprises*; finds the male characters in "The Octascope" and in Beattie's fiction in general to be suffering from a kind of passivity that makes them unable to form strong commitments; Beattie's fiction demonstrates "the need for personal growth while depicting the allure of retreat and security."

Gilder, Joshua. "Down and Out: The Stories of Ann Beattie." *New Criterion* 1 (October 1982): 51-56. Severely criticizes Beattie's fiction for failing to offer viable moral solutions to the philosophical problems raised in her fiction; finds Beattie's prose lifeless and tedious and her themes vapid and ephemeral.

————. "Less Is Less." *New Criterion* 2 (February 1983): 78-82. A general discussion of minimalism and of such minimalist authors as Beattie, Raymond Carver, and Mary Robison. Minimalism, with its emphasis upon a "constriction" of artistic vision, represents "a kind of literary personal bankruptcy."

Griffith, Thomas. "Rejoice If You Can." *Atlantic Monthly,* September 1980, 28-29. Counters the prevailing view of Beattie as a pessimistic and defeatist writer by arguing that her portrayals of the problems of her generation offer insight into the contemporary psyche and therefore hope for personal growth and change.

Hammond, Karla M. "Ann Beattie: Still with the Sixties." *Denver Quarterly* 15, no. 2 (1980): 115-17. Beattie's fiction chronicles the "sense of desperation entailed in choice" and emphasizes "nihilistic environments" and "a feeling of entrapment."

Iyer, Pico. "The World According to Beattie." *Partisan Review* 50, no. 4 (1983): 548-53. Like J. D. Salinger, John Cheever, and John Updike, Beattie coolly chronicles "the sad eccentricities, plaintive longings, and quiet frustrations" of a generation.

Parini, Jay. "A Writer Comes of Age." *Horizon* December 1982, 22-24. Surveys Beattie's accomplishments in fiction from *Distortions* through *The Burning House* and praises Beattie for her sociological realism and psychological insight; provides useful biographical information on Beattie.

Romano, John. "Ann Beattie & the 60's." *Commentary,* February 1977, 62-64. Beattie's subject matter is "a certain shiftlessness and lack of self-apprehension besetting people in their twenties and thirties"; Beattie "conveys the drabness of these lives by her tone and an almost hallucinatory particularity of detail."

Taylor, David M. "Ann Beattie." *Dictionary of Literary Biography Yearbook* 1982. Detroit: Gale Research Co., 1983, 206-12. A biographical and critical discussion; Beattie's fiction focuses upon capturing the essence of lives composed of "indirection, indecision, and angst."

Christina Murphy (essay date 1986)

SOURCE: Murphy, Christina. *"Chilly Scenes of Winter."* In *Ann Beattie,* pp. 42-51. Boston: Twayne, 1986.

[*In the following essay, Murphy describes critical reaction to Beattie's* Chilly Scenes of Winter, *noting that it deftly captures the spirit of the era in which it was written and during which the story is set.*]

"CHILLY SCENES"

Ann Beattie's formal literary debut as an author of books was both unique and impressive, with Doubleday simultaneously publishing her first novel, *Chilly Scenes of Winter,* and her first volume of short stories, *Distortions,* on 13 August 1976. The move was designed by the publisher to draw attention to Beattie as a new talent, and it proved an extremely effective technique.[1] *Chilly Scenes of Winter* was offered as a Book-of-the-Month Club alternate, and reviewers who critiqued Beattie's achievement generally responded to both works in their assessments.

While the critical response to *Distortions* was generally favorable, though somewhat mixed, the response to *Chilly Scenes of Winter* was almost universally laudatory. Beattie was praised as a mesmerizing and unique literary talent, and *Chilly Scenes of Winter* was compared to J. D. Salinger's *Catcher in the Rye* for capturing and distilling the mood of the 1970s as Salinger's novel had etched into literary memory the atmosphere of the 1950s.[2]

In essence, *Chilly Scenes of Winter* is a love story, played out against scenes of the 1970s in America. Benjamin DeMott in *Surviving the 70's* describes the decade as unique, for, following on the heels of the highly idealistic and ideologically defined 1960s, it was the first era to substitute trends and fads for personal and cultural mythologies. DeMott sees the *The Whole Earth Catalogue,* the archetypal icon and the Bible of the seventies, as indicative of the era's values and perspectives—a type of "mod wishbook" in which all trendy fantasies could be satisfied and the earth itself could be contained within faddish categories and hip definitions.[3]

One may think of *Chilly Scenes of Winter* as a type of "mod wishbook" on love in the seventies, for the novel explores and satirizes many of the clichés of romantic love dominant at the time, and most of the characters of *Chilly Scenes of Winter* are known more by their wishes or fantasies than by what they actually do with their lives.

The central character in the novel is Charles, who is in love with Laura, a married woman who lives in an A-frame house, bakes bread, and cares for her husband, Jim, and her stepdaughter Rebecca. Laura is alternately envisioned by Charles as a symbol of settled, domestic bliss or of an exotic romantic life freed from social restraints and petty bourgeois considerations. Laura has come to mean so much to Charles, to have taken on so much significance in his personal life, that he is literally obsessed with her and with his desire to win her away from Jim and to have her love forever.

Charles's quest for Laura's love is by turns comic and pathetic and is enacted amidst the emotional chaos of Charles's relationship to his own family, who represent, metaphorically, another perspective on love and marriage. Charles's mother, Clara, is a self-centered neurotic given to histrionics and hypochondria. She regularly calls Charles and his sister Susan at odd hours to come and minister to her imagined physical woes. Clara is convinced that she is dying and that her children do not care about her because they do not take an interest in her sufferings. Susan tends to view Clara's sufferings as genuine, though somewhat overly dramatized; Charles, however, views his mother's theatrics as both manipulations and existential statements. "If you want to know what I really think," he says to Susan, "I think that one day she just decided to go nuts because that was easier. This way she can say whatever she wants to say, and she can drink and lie around naked and just not do anything."[4]

Clara is married to Pete, her second husband. Her first husband, Charles and Susan's father, died at thirty-nine and is perceived by both Clara and his children as a model of virtue and understanding. Pete, on the other hand, is intensely disliked by Charles and only moderately tolerated by Susan—largely because she feels sorry for him and does not want to add any additional pressures on her mother's delicate emotional condition. Pete openly seeks Charles's and Susan's attention and love and becomes even more obnoxious to them by constantly pressuring them to admit that they dislike him and then endeavoring to manipulate them into loving him out of a sense of guilt and responsibility.

While Susan is generally tolerant and patient with Pete, attributing his demanding nature to insecurities and the pressures of living with Clara, Charles dismisses Pete as an eccentric loser who is incapable of seeing Clara (and therefore his marriage to Clara) clearly. Charles describes Pete as "a grown man with a messed-up wife" (78) who refuses to face the reality of his situation by making up comfortable fantasies about Clara and then trying to foist them off on others. When Clara is confined to a hospital for what she claims is an appendicitis attack, Pete tries to minimize the incident by telling both Charles and Susan that "Mommy" (as Pete calls Clara) is prone to exaggeration. When "Mommy" goes into the bathroom and swallows twelve laxative tablets because no one will believe she is really sick, Pete claims that the doctors do not understand her. Finally, when "Mommy" is placed in a mental hospital because of her increasingly aberrant behavior, Pete's solution is to enroll them both in a Fred Astaire dancing class so that "Mommy" will have something to take her mind off her troubles.

One of the most effective ironies of *Chilly Scenes of Winter* is that Charles is exceedingly hostile toward Pete because he envisions Pete as a fool for being unable to recognize Clara for what she is—in other words, for being unable to see clearly and realistically the woman he loves. Yet, this failure to perceive one's beloved clearly is exactly the malady Charles suffers from in the exaggerated and highly romanticized notions of Laura that he maintains throughout the novel, despite much realistic evidence to the contrary. Thematically, it is an interesting twist in the novel that Charles, who thinks he is insightful because he can see the absurdities of Pete's distorted perceptions of Clara, is guilty of the same misperceptions generated by obsessive love.

Images of marriage in *Chilly Scenes of Winter* are generally negative. Pete and Clara's marriage is portrayed as a maze of twisted emotional needs predicated upon neuroses and a distorted sense of reality. Jim and Laura's marriage is shown to be emotionally vacuous and compromised by Laura's adultery with Charles. One couple, whom Charles knows only vaguely, sends him a Christmas card in which the wife details the husband's adulterous affair with a younger woman and the couple's reconciliation, which is due to the fact that the younger woman kicked the husband out after only a short time. "It's nuts to get married," Sam, Charles's best friend, says. "What would you get married for?" (65), summing up the prevailing motif in the novel that marriage is both a pointless and a perilous venture.

In the thematic design of the novel, Sam serves as an effective contrast to Charles. The two have been friends since childhood, and Charles admits to worshipping Sam because he sees him as everything that Charles is not. Sam "always has great success with women" (2), while Charles is an admitted failure. Sam's self-confidence is matched by Charles's self-doubt, and, while Sam is able to avoid all deep emotional involvements and commitments, Charles falls deeply in love with Laura and cannot free himself from her memory. In many ways, Sam is the contemporary image of youth in the 1970s. He is a college graduate, a member of Phi Beta Kappa, who works as a clothing salesman because he does not have the motivation to go to law school. His romantic involvements are short-term and based solely upon sexual attraction. He has no place in his life for love or marriage, and his predominant concern in the novel is in seeking a way of life that does not encumber him with the traditional obligations of middle-class existence. He is a self-centered free spirit, at once cynical and highly aware. He asks little of himself and expects even less from others. His strongest emotional tie in the novel is to Charles, with whom he shares a bond of strong, affectionate love.

If Sam represents a contemporary type, perfectly in tune with the bland, self-centered values of the 1970s, Charles is the dreamy romantic, slightly out of step with his times but yet very much a product of them. Charles is immersed in the world of rock 'n roll. Everywhere he goes, he is aware of songs on the radio, stereo, or juke box and relates the messages in the songs to his own life. His sense of reality is tied up with Bob Dylan's songs, or Janis Joplin's overdose, or Mick Jagger's search for satisfaction. Charles lives what appears to be an adult life, having his own apartment, working at a government job, searching for someone to love and for a lasting relationship, but his consciousness (and thus his true identity) is wrapped up in a more adolescent sense of life and love. He fixates upon songs because he identifies them with his more carefree youth in which he had fewer worries and in which he never felt sorry for himself. Now that he has fallen in love with Laura, he pities himself all the time, and his sister tells him that he is a juvenile, sometimes even infantile, egomaniac. "You deliberately make yourself suffer all the time," she says, "because then you can be aware of *yourself*" (82). Susan tells Charles that he allows Laura to dominate his consciousness because he has little identity of his own and even less sense of direction for his life. Being wrapped up in thoughts of Laura gives Charles a ready and seemingly noble excuse to avoid examining his own life. Susan believes that, because self-definition (or making something of himself) is too difficult for Charles, he prefers to invest himself in an emotionally dependent relationship with Laura that mimics a home, mother, and family life—all the qualities of security that a child would seek.

There seems to be much merit to Susan's claim that Charles is "infantile" (82) in his desires. Charles himself admits to having a childlike desire to escape reality by spending his days imagining scenes about Laura that never took place. He chides himself for being overly dependent upon food, an oral fixation that in Freudian terms signifies an immature sense of seeking emotional gratification. He keeps a number of Laura's cookbooks on hand as comforting symbols of security, and he dreams throughout the novel of a special dessert Laura used to make for him of cognac and fresh oranges. "He often craves that dessert, and the recipe is probably in one of those books, but he can't bring himself to look. He wants to think of it as magic" (16). Rather than make the dessert himself and end his craving (in essence, meet his own emotional needs), he prefers to hunger and long (both physically and emotionally) for an imaginary ideal that he hopes

will appear one day by magic. Like a child, he prefers magical, wishful thinking to purposeful choice, and the metaphor of his childlike longing for the dessert is an apt symbol of his immature longing for Laura as the "magic" that will set his life right.

As Charles's personal life collapses around him, Laura increasingly becomes the ideal that holds his existence together. Clara's neuroses intensify into periodic disassociations from reality, while Pete becomes more and more emotionally demanding of Charles's time and attention. Sam loses his job and moves in with Charles, becoming an economic (and, at times, an emotional) drain. Pamela Smith, Charles's ex-lover, who has become a compendium of 1970s cultural clichés as a bisexual, feminist vegetarian, returns to plague Charles with her own emotional insecurities and problems that need resolving. Susan has fallen in love with Mark, a somewhat pompous and obtuse medical student who drives a maroon Cadillac, will not pollute his body with toxins, and is, in Charles's opinion, a "dress for success" phony who exemplifies the worst superficialities and shortcomings of youthful ambition.

In the midst of his loneliness and isolation, Charles further exacerbates his emotional dilemmas by asking Betty, a co-worker, out for a date. Charles is drawn to Betty because she is Laura's close friend, and he hopes to feel a certain closeness to Laura through Betty. It is from Betty that Charles learns that Laura has left her husband and is living in an apartment. Charles's immediate reactions are shock, delight, and hurt that Laura would leave her husband and not tell him. He gets Laura's phone number from Betty and anguishes over what to say when he calls her. He is worried that her failure to call him is a sign that she does not love him. He broods about his situation, much to the dismay of Sam, who believes that Charles's affection for Laura is "disproportionate" (242). Finally, he calls Laura.

She says she did not call because she needs time alone to figure out what she wants in life and does not want to be pressured by his emotional demands. Charles protests that he is not demanding, that he loves her and wants her back, and Laura responds, "I don't think you're thinking of me. I think you're thinking about what's best for you" (244). Charles replies that he loves Laura and asks to see her just one more time.

Driving to Laura's, Charles tries to understand "why he seemed so incapable of impressing upon her, why he had always—almost always—been incapable of impressing upon her, that he loved her and had to have her" (245). He enters Laura's apartment intent upon letting her know that he will not be dissuaded from his love for her.

"Stop thinking about yourself and think about me," Laura says. "I need peace. I don't need to be told what to do. I've lost Rebecca and my marriage has fallen apart and I can't find a job, and you're telling me it can be like it was before." "It can!" Charles asserts (256).

Laura wants Charles to leave, but he cannot bring himself to go. He wanders through the apartment instead, lost in reveries of Laura, and only agrees to go when she promises that he can return the next evening and she will make the special dessert of oranges and cognac.

Upon his return, in the novel's final scene and denouement, he brings Laura tulips in a ceramic pot and watches Laura as she peels the oranges and warms the cream. The dessert signifies the fulfillment of his deepest longings, a type of symbolic filling of his emotional hunger for Laura and the romantic ideal that she represents to him.

> "I got my way," he says.
>
> "You did," she says.
>
> "A story with a happy ending," he says.
>
> (299)

A number of critics have commented upon the ending of *Chilly Scenes of Winter* as being too romantically facile and unrealistically happy, given the depth and range of complexities in the novel that have kept Charles and Laura apart. To these objections, Beattie responds that "Charles has pursued this woman all through the book and he does get her. But you should understand by that point that he's a strange enough character and that they're mismatched enough that the rest of their life clearly isn't going to be easy. It's not as though it's just a frieze for all time that you can do with a movie camera and really capture something. The characters presumably still walk and breathe after the last period, and who knows what's going to happen?"[5]

Clearly, attempts to view the ending of *Chilly Scenes of Winter* as a happy union of two young lovers are greatly weakened by the novel's heavy emphasis upon romantic misperceptions of reality and the subsequent distortions in both understanding and feeling that such illusory notions bring to life. Charles himself states that "he has always had problems with reality encroaching on his fantasies" (140), and David M. Taylor sees Charles's idée fixe, his endless longing for Laura, as a romantic refuge, a form of emotional solace Charles seeks from the "psychic intrusions of relatives, friends, and acquaintances—each with his own nebulous yearning."[6]

In seeking to escape his drab and unfulfilling real life by positing a romantic ideal of perfect, blissful love, Charles is no different from one of his literary models and progenitors, Jay Gatsby, who psychologically and emotionally divorces himself from his mundane past to embrace the visionary and romantic ideal of his love for Daisy Buchanan. Certainly, comparisons of *Chilly Scenes of Winter* to *The Great Gatsby* are made more striking by the many references to *The Great Gatsby* in the novel. Charles is always after Sam to ride with him over to Laura's just so Charles can drive by the house and imagine that Laura is there. Sam never wants to go because he considers the whole idea "pointless."

> "She might be outside," [Charles says].
>
> "Just walking around at the end of the drive, soaking up the cold air?" [Sam responds].
>
> "The light might be on."
>
> "Of course the light will be on. She wouldn't be in bed this early."
>
> "Then I want to see the light."
>
> "What's this, *The Great Gatsby* or something?"
>
> (213)

When Charles insists that he is going to Laura's, Sam says, "Take me home. I can't bear to watch you make a fool of yourself" (214). Charles stubbornly persists, however, and proceeds to drive over to Laura's.

> "I mean it," Sam says. "This is pathetic. It's not like you call her and write her and make yourself obnoxious. All you do is slink over there to look at the lights on in her house. If she killed somebody you'd take the rap for her, wouldn't you? The whole Gatsby trip."
>
> "She wouldn't ever kill anybody."
>
> "Yeah, but what if she was driving your roadster along and a woman ran out in front of it?"
>
> "Okay, okay. Enough."
>
> "What can I say that will talk you out of this dreary driving by her house?"
>
> "Nothing."
>
> "There's no point to it. What does driving by her house prove?"
>
> "Nothing."
>
> "You just intend to do it anyway."
>
> "I just intend to do it anyway."
>
> (215)

Critics have seen parallels to *The Great Gatsby* in *Chilly Scenes of Winter,* comparing Charles to Gatsby, Laura to Daisy, and the slightly cynical, emotionally aloof, Sam to Nick Carroway. In response, Beattie states, "The spirit of what Fitzgerald was getting at was something I wanted to restate. I do see some similarities between the 1920's and 1960's—that whole idea of being in a frantic state and still seeing real-life possibilities. That was deliberate. So there are echoes there, but not that strongly. It's not a rehash of *Gatsby* by any means."[7]

The concept of romantic love and the inevitable distortions of perception and of self it engenders is certainly a major theme of *Chilly Scenes of Winter,* but, as Beattie states, it is not the novel's major focus, but, rather, an outgrowth of her concern to depict the milieu and consciousness of a period in American culture. Charles and his circle of friends are products of the 1960s, embodying the idealism and frenetic energy of a highly motivated, highly politicized generation that sought major societal reforms and vast personal growth. Entering into the 1970s, on the verge of turning thirty, and both needing and seeking a way to stabilize their lives, they find themselves isolated and lost, their efforts at self-definition largely purposeless and ineffectual. In typical romantic fashion, they look to their past and find no acceptable answers. "'The goddamn sixties,' Charles says. 'How'd we ever end up like this?'" (210).

After drinking with J. D., a friend and another lost soul, Sam says to Charles,

> "Everybody's so pathetic. . . . What is it? Is it just the end of the sixties?"
>
> "J. D. says it's the end of the world."
>
> "It's not," Sam says. "But everything's such a mess."
>
> (187)

Like all romantics, they look to their past but find no helpful insights. "'I sure am waiting for that Dylan album,' Sam says. 'I really want to know what Bob Dylan's got to say in 1975'" (218).

Devoid of heroes, prophets, meaningful goals, Charles and his friends wander in a type of existential malaise, searching for a new faith, a new purpose—acting very much like their counterparts of "the lost generation" of the 1920s. They search for explanations of why their lives have come to such emotional standstills and wonder if their culture is to blame. In a Kentucky Fried Chicken restaurant, Charles "looks around at all the families eating fried chicken" and thinks, "America is getting so gauche. If there's a McDonald's in Paris, is the Colonel there, too? Kentucky Fried bones thrown around the Eiffel Tower?" (194). What metaphor, what value has their era given them to long for, and what image of American life do they see around them that would give their personal aspirations significance?

Charles's answer, of course, is undying, romantic love, but there is much in *Chilly Scenes of Winter* to indicate that even Charles suspects the illusions and self-deceptions, large and small, at the heart of his quest. He wants to live with Laura in a house that they have picked out together and bought, raise a family, and have a dog. Yet, he admits to himself that "it sounds too Norman Rockwellish to be true" (251). He knows that Clara and Pete's marriage did not last, that no one he can think of has a happy marriage, yet he still believes that he and Laura will be happy together forever. He bases this belief on the fact that they will communicate their problems to one another and work them out, but he also acknowledges that "they never really understood each other. Most people can read signals; they never could" (41). If Charles, by virtue of his romantic and idealistic longings in an age of jaded cynicism, is the moral center of *Chilly Scenes of Winter* just as Gatsby, the dreamer, was the axiological center of *The Great Gatsby,* he is, very definitely, a qualified and somewhat self-doubting romantic, and his quest for Laura's love is both strikingly noble and pathetic. This dual resonance of the dignity and foolishness of Charles's struggle to win Laura's love gives a greater dimension to *Chilly Scenes of Winter* than its surface context of the mores of the 1970s would seem to allow.

CRITICAL RESPONSES

In responding to *Chilly Scenes of Winter,* critics found much to admire in both Beattie's themes and her style. John Updike, in the *New Yorker,* stated that *Chilly Scenes of Winter* "thaws quite beautifully" with its "uncanny fidelity to the low-level heartbreaks behind the banal" and saw Beattie's work as comparable to that of Virginia Woolf and Nathalie Sarraute in achievement.[8] J. D. O'Hara, writing for the *New York Times Book Review,* commented that the novel was a "wide-screen panorama of Life in These United States" through which Beattie "understands and dramatizes our formlessness." Remarking that *Chilly Scenes of Winter* is "the funniest novel of unhappy yearning that one could imagine," O'Hara added that "Beattie renews for us the commonplaces of the lonesome lover and the life of quiet desperation. . . . The novel's major theme . . . is not waiting for an answer or Laura or love, but waiting itself, wistful anticipation, life unfulfilled and yearning. Immersing us in specificity, Beattie makes us feel these generalities on our pulse."[9] David Thorburn, in the *Yale Review,* praised Beattie's "powers of observation and dramatic representation" expressed in "a purified declarative prose not unlike good Hemingway" and judged *Chilly Scenes of Winter* to be a novel rich in "psychological nuance and in documentary power."[10] Thorburn's assessment was ratified by Sheila Weller who said of Beattie that "satirically, sadly, and truthfully, she writes of familiar fights against the damning arbitrariness of our charmed post-industrial lives."[11] John Romano emphasized the novel's sociological realism: "In *Chilly Scenes of Winter* . . . our attention is called to a contemporary pathos whose effects few have yet begun to gauge: the sadness over the passing of the 60's. . . . Beattie's presentation of Charles's nostalgia for the 60's suggests that such longing has the limits of an elegy to lost innocence, and the advantages, too. It distorts, but it also provides . . . the idea that things can be better than they are, because they have been better before now. As usual, the prospects for hope seem to depend upon some degree of mystification."[12]

In all, critics found in Beattie's depictions of hope and despair in the 1970s, through the "chilly scenes of winter" that represent the emotional seasons of the soul, a new voice and a strong, original talent. Praising Beattie's accomplishment in her first novel, critics applauded a significant writer on the contemporary scene and forecast even greater literary achievements from Beattie in the future.

Notes

1. Murray, "Conversation," 63.

2. John Updike, review of *Chilly Scenes of Winter, New Yorker,* 29 November 1976, 164-66.

3. Benjamin DeMott, *Surviving the 70's* (New York: E. P. Dutton, 1971), 67.

4. *Chilly Scenes of Winter* (New York: Doubleday, 1976), 14. Subsequent page references will appear in parentheses in the text.

5. Maynard, "Visiting Ann Beattie," 40.

6. Taylor, "Ann Beattie," 209.

7. Murray, "Conversation," 66.

8. Updike, review, 164.

9. O'Hara, *"Chilly Scenes,"* 14, 18.

10. David Thorburn, "Recent Novels: Realism Redux," *Yale Review* 76 (Summer 1977): 585-86.

11. Sheila Weller, "A Valentine to the Guys who Grew Up in the '60s," *Ms.,* December 1976, 47.

12. Romano, "Ann Beattie," 64.

Selected Bibliography

[Editor's Note: See previous essay for Selected Bibliography.]

Susan Jaret McKinstry (essay date 1993)

SOURCE: McKinstry, Susan Jaret. "The Speaking Silence of Ann Beattie's Voice." In *The Critical Response to Ann Beattie,* edited by Jaye Berman Montresor, pp. 134-40. Westport, Conn.: Greenwood, 1993.

[*In the following essay, McKinstry identifies elements of Beattie's stories which frequently create discomfort in her readers, including ambiguous endings and subtexts that seem imperfectly related to the author's surface messages.*]

"I've just told these stories to my daughter Eliza," says the female narrator in Ann Beattie's story **"Like Glass,"** "She used to like her stories to end with a moral, like a fairy tale, but now she thinks that's kid's stuff. She still wants to know what stories mean, but she wants me to tell her. The point of the two stories—well, I don't know what the point is, I'm always telling her."[1] Beattie's speakers often seem to miss the point of their stories. And so do many readers. For like other *New Yorker* writers, Beattie contravenes our generic expectations. As J. D. O'Hara writes in *The New York Times*: "Traditionally the novel has relied on action spun out and woven into a plot, complete with beginning and end. Little in our own lives corresponds to this orderliness."[2] Noting that "most of Miss Beattie's stories end without a feeling of closure," Anatole Broyard wonders "whether it is unreasonable to expect closure nowadays. . . . Perhaps fiction is being discriminated against when we look to it to satisfy orderly expectations."[3] Thomas Griffith, in the *Atlantic Monthly,* praises the "*New Yorker* fiction . . . in its rejection of moralizing and pat endings. . . . Nothing is ever summed up, or brought to an end; a moment passes and is wryly commented upon. It is a fictional approximation of value-free science."[4]

But narrative cannot be value-free. The act of speaking is an act of choosing speech over silence, deciding where to begin and end. Frank Kermode argues that "stories as we know them begin as interpretations,"[5] while Paul Hernadi sees "self-assertive entertainment and self-transcending commitment as two kinds of ultimate motivation for our countless narratives."[6] Beattie's female speakers are telling stories with value, self-assertion, and closure. But they puzzle readers because they tell two stories at once: the open story of the objective, detailed present is juxtaposed with a closed story of the subjective past, a story the speaker tries hard not to tell. In the space between these two narratives lies the point of the story.

Seymour Chatman makes a useful distinction between the closed and open narrative, which he calls the resolved plot and the revealed plot:

In the traditional narrative of resolution, there is a sense of problem solving . . . of a kind of ratiocinative or emotional teleology . . . "What will happen?" is the basic question. In the modern plot of revelation, however, the emphasis is elsewhere, the function of the discourse not to answer that question or even pose it. . . . It is not that events are resolved (happily or tragically) but rather that a state of affairs is revealed.[7]

Unlike Chatman, Beattie does not distinguish between the two plots, but juxtaposes them. Trying to avoid telling the closed story, Beattie's speakers create unintentional resolution as they tell stories of undesired revelation. This narrative reluctance results in a disembodied, objective voice whose analytical language and photographic descriptions—often using free indirect speech rather than a more traditional first or third-person perspective—emphasize the disparity between the emotional past and the seemingly objective present, between the closed story and the open story. In **"Waiting,"** for example, the narrator talks about her husband's leaving in terms of things, not emotions: "He forgot: his big battery lantern and his can opener. He remembered: his tent, the cooler filled with ice, . . . a camera, a suitcase, a fiddle, and a banjo" (p. 167). The narrator herself is omitted from either list.

"Give me the hand," says the narrator to her unfaithful lover in **"Gravity"** (p. 118). This sentence exemplifies the double narrative I am describing. Here, while the sentence expresses physical desire for him—for his hand—the narrator's use of the indefinite article rather than the possessive reflects her desire for linguistic neutrality. "*Anybody* else would have said 'your hand,'" he responds. "When you said it that way, *it* made it sound as if my hand was disembodied" (p. 122, my emphasis). He in turn converts her to "it," severing her from her verbal action and missing the point. Yet she still tells her stories. She describes the disembodied hand as an object detached from their ended love and thus open to other interpretations: "His right hand is extended, finger on the bone between my breasts. I look down for a second, the way a surgeon must have a moment of doubt, or even a moment of confidence, looking at the translucent, skin-tight rubber glove: his hand and not his hand, about to do something important or not important at all. . . . Disembodied, that hand would be a symbol from Magritte. . . . Alone, I'd know it anywhere" (p. 122).

Carolyn Heilbrun comments that "women, like children, have told stories in which the details are more important than the plot, in which their own action is not possible, not imagined."[8] For Beattie's speakers, action seems impossible because the story has already ended; the details allow the narrator to objectify the present and disguise her emotional response to the past. For example, **"Like Glass"** suspends the narrative present by beginning with a description of an old family photograph of a father, baby and dog that puzzles the narrator because the baby is "gazing into the distance" (p. 201). When her husband explains the picture to her, she says, "I was amazed that I had made a mystery of something that had such a simple answer. It is a picture of a baby looking at its mother" (p. 205). But her original interpretation, based on what is missing in the photograph, reflects the complex juxtaposition of closed and open stories. What is absent may reveal what is present: "The collie is dead. The man with a pompadour . . . was alive, the last time I heard. The baby grew up and became my husband, and now is no longer married to me" (p. 201). Her narrative is motivated by the desire to reopen the past by describing two events—glass broken in celebration and glass broken in anger—and thus link "two things that are similar, although they have nothing in common" (p. 201) in order to create a happy ending. "The point is that broken glass is broken glass" (p. 205) she tells her daughter, but her narrative connects these past events and the present failure of her marriage as resolution and revelation meet. "One mistake and glass shatters," the narrator warns (p. 205). And the story ends with the question, "What do you do with a shard of sorrow?" (p. 206). What the narrator's dual stories have in common is loss: focusing on details rather than on closure—"What's new with me? My divorce is final" (p. 205)—the narrator still tells us, through the resolved tales she tells her daughter and the revealed tale she tells us, that broken glass is more than broken glass.

Margaret Atwood claims that "these stories are not of suspense but of suspension."[9] I think this effect is caused by the double narrative that juxtaposes open and closed story, revealed and resolved plot. Beattie's stories use images of physical suspension, like characters ascending in glass elevators in **"The Cinderella Waltz,"** treading water in **"Afloat"** in "the desire, for one brief minute, simply to get off the earth" (p. 183), and "looking down . . . from space" in **"The Burning House"** (p. 241). In **"Downhill,"** a story from her first collection, Beattie's narrator describes this suspension: "As he leads he tilts me back, and suddenly I can't feel the weight of his arms anymore. My body is very heavy and my neck stretches farther and farther back until my body seems to stretch out of the room, passing painlessly through the floor into blackness."[10] This narrative disembodiment is physical, emotional and verbal, creating a subtle interpretive suspension. In **"Gravity,"** the narrator thinks of astronauts and feels "the lightness of a person who isn't being kept in place by gravity, but my weightlessness has been from sadness and fear" (p. 122). Atwood compares a Beattie narrator to a "climber seizing the next rung on the ladder without having any idea of where he's going or wants to go,"[11] and in one Beattie story a professor ridicules a student's interpretation by asking her if she would "also climb a ladder using the spaces between rungs" (**"Sunshine and Shadow"** p. 126).

In their desire to speak themselves into silence, Beattie's narrators try to erase their individuality by comparisons and doublings. They always fail. "People often mistake us for sisters," brags the narrator in **"Playback"** (p. 65), but her story is really about their differences: "Simple, fortune-cookie fact: someone loved Holly more than anyone had ever loved me" (p. 72) and "that went a long way toward explaining why we looked so much alike, yet she was more beautiful" (p. 73). In **"Afloat,"** the narrator explains to her stepdaughter "that there should be solidarity between women, but that when you look for a common bond you're really looking for a common denominator, and you can't do that with women" (p. 179). Even so, she claims that "our common denominator is that none of us was married in a church and all of us worried about the results of the blood test we had before we could get a marriage license" (p. 179). "Most of these things have to do with love, in some odd way" admits the narrator in **"Running Dreams"** (p. 190), and in these stories love (and its failure) inevitably reinforces individuality rather than commonality.

In Beattie's world of multiple divorce and infidelity, these speakers dream of conventional romance and its happy ending to disguise the failure of love in their individual stories. Repeatedly, Beattie's speakers seek "erotic texts," in Nancy K. Miller's phrase, in which "the heroine" will not just triumph "in some *conventionally* positive way but . . . will transcend the perils of plot with a self-exalting dignity" and marry the man she loves.[12] Repeatedly, Beattie's women fail to find such endings. As Claudine Hermann notes, "If women did not generally experience the love they desire as a repeated impossibility, they would dream about it less. They would dream of other, perhaps more interesting things. . . . Woman's 'daydreaming' is a function of a world in which nothing comes true on her terms."[13] Miller comments that "the daydream, then, is both the stuff of fairy tales ('Someday my prince will come') and their rewriting ('Someday my prince will come, but we will not live happily ever after')."[14] Beattie's narrators dream of the happy ending even as they speak its sad revision in their own lives. They seek fairytales, but "Was my persistence willfulness, or belief in magic?" asks the narrator in **"The Cinderella Waltz"** (p. 50). "Who could really believe that there was some way to find protection in

this world—or someone who could offer it?" asks the bereaved mother in **"In the White Night."** "What happened happened at random, and one horrible thing hardly precluded the possibility of others happening next."[15] And the narrator of **"Learning to Fall"** ends her story with a sort of moral: "What will happen can't be stopped. Aim for grace" (p. 14).

Beattie's story **"In the White Night"** ends with this grace. Although the story employs the narrative doubling I have described, it is unusual in Beattie's works because there is a reconciliation between the open and closed stories. Recalling her dead daughter's camera, the central character Carol thinks, "There were two images when you looked through the finder, and you had to make the adjustment yourself so that one superimposed itself upon the other and the figure suddenly leaped into clarity" (p. 15). This struggle to juxtapose separate images describes the technique of the story itself. Trying not "to bring up a sore subject" (p. 14), the story focuses on mundane details as Carol and Vernon return from a party at Matt and Gaye Brinkley's house, yet the resolved story that is revealed is the death of Carol and Vernon's daughter Sharon. Such closure is unchangeable. Yet endings—as a sort of narrative death—become the focus of the story, which includes three resolved anecdotes: Vernon's illness, the death of their dog, "the time when the Christmas tree caught fire, . . . and Vernon pushed her away just in time," (p. 15) and even "the moment when Sharon died . . . (Carol had backed up against the door for some reason)" (p. 14). Carol's desire to remove herself from Sharon's death fails in both past and present, and the story re-embodies both grieving mother and dead daughter. The narrative juxtaposes that closed story with an open present in a connotative metonymy of desire: "one signified acts as the signifier of another signified not actually named"[16] as the narrative present signifies the unspeakable past.

This linguistic and temporal elision makes absence present. "Don't think about an apple," says Matt to his departing guests, and Carol responds: "Why had Matt conjured up the image of an apple? Now she saw an apple where there was no apple, suspended in midair, transforming the scene in front of her into a silly surrealist painting" (pp. 11-12). The signifier "apple" becomes a disembodied signified, linking word and object, absence and presence. The story follows this pattern throughout, as Carol and Vernon focus on precisely what they are trying to avoid: the past presence that has become present absence, the death of their daughter. The story signifies a transcendence of closure: just as the apple became image, Sharon has become a verbal ghost haunting the text.

Like Beattie's other speakers, Carol tries to refuse the closure of the past through narrative disembodiment.

She has to "blink herself into focus" (p. 15) after crying for her daughter Sharon, and she and her husband Vernon try to superimpose the two families to erase the difference between them, closure of death. "Vernon said, quite sincerely, that Matt and Gaye were their alter egos, who absorbed and enacted crises, saving the two of them from having to experience such chaos" (p. 14); Carol thinks that the husbands "looked like two children," and the daughters "had sat side by side, or kneecap to kneecap, and whispered that way when they were children—a privacy so rushed that it obliterated anything else" (p. 12). Yet the mother, "remembering that scene now, could not think of what passed between Sharon and Becky without thinking of sexual intimacy" (p. 12); her attempted evasion does not distance Carol from the story, but instead reinforces her loss as the sexuality that created Sharon is displaced onto a past scene and thus effectively disembodied.

Carol's narrative desire to regain the past and thus her daughter recognizes the transformative power of language. As Carol and Vernon drive home through the snowstorm, in the light of a streetlamp "there seemed for a second to be some logic to all the swirling snow. If time itself could only freeze, the snowflakes could become the lacy filigree of a valentine" (p. 12). Through metonymic transformations, the physical world evokes the emotional, the dangerous snow becomes beautiful, transparent lace, and emotion and language meet in a *love letter*. The narrative itself becomes a sort of love letter as Carol's perspective illuminates the double narrative by such transformations.

Carol is faced with three alternatives when Vernon falls asleep on the couch: "The sofa was too narrow to curl up with him. She didn't want to wake him. Neither did she want to go to bed alone" (p. 16). Since nothing is just right, the heroine must make her own ending. Lying down on the floor next to the couch, she wonders: "What would anyone think? She knew the answer to that question, of course"—that their physical positions would be interpreted as drunkenness (p. 17). But she understands that even common events tell tales, that the everyday is not protection from painful stories: "Such odd things happened. Very few days were like the ones before" (p. 16). "In time," the grief for Sharon and the love for Vernon have both become part of "the inevitable sadness that set in, always unexpectedly but so real that it was met with the instant acceptance one gave to a snowfall" (p. 17). Thus absence meets presence. Like the superimposed images in Sharon's camera, the story focuses. In accepting the story of death that she is really telling, Carol tells herself exactly the ending that she needs to hear: "In the white night world outside, their daughter might be drifting past like an angel, and she would see this tableau, for the second that she hovered, as a necessary small adjustment" (p. 17). Beattie's narratives surprise us because they demand the sort of double vision I have been describing, and it is no small adjustment. Anatole Broyard claims in *The New York Times* that Beattie causes "the shock of unrecognition": after reading Beattie's stories he admits that "I felt like a psychiatrist at the end of a hard day. I would like to run out and hug the first stodgy person I can find. I am beginning to feel like an alarmed ecologist of personality."[17] But like any good analyst, like any careful reader, we must listen to the tale not being told in order to understand Beattie's narrative acts. Fortunately for readers, Beattie's speakers do not choose silence.

Notes

1. Ann Beattie, *The Burning House* (New York: Ballantine Books, 1983), p. 204. Further references to this collection will be cited in parentheses.

2. J. D. O'Hara, *"Chilly Scenes of Winter, Distortions"* in *The New York Times Book Review,* 15 August 1976, p. 14.

3. Anatole Broyard, "Books of the Times: *Secrets and Surprises*" in *The New York Times,* 3 January 1979, p. C17.

4. Thomas Griffith, "Rejoice If You Can" in *Atlantic Monthly,* 246 (September 1980), 28.

5. Frank Kermode, "Secrets and Narrative Sequence" in *On Narrative,* edited by W. J. T. Mitchell (Chicago: University of Chicago Press, 1981), p. 81.

6. Paul Hernadi, "On the How, What, and Why of Narrative" in *On Narrative,* edited by W. J. T. Mitchell, p. 198.

7. Seymour Chatman, *Story and Discourse: Narrative Structure in Fiction and Film* (New York: Cornell University Press, 1978), p. 48.

8. Carolyn Heilbrun, *Reinventing Womanhood* (New York: W. W. Norton, 1979), p. 124.

9. Margaret Atwood, "Stories from an American Front" in *The New York Times Book Review,* 26 September 1982, p. 34.

10. Ann Beattie, *Distortions* (New York: Popular Library, 1979), p. 95.

11. Margaret Atwood, "Stories from an American Front," p. 1.

12. Nancy K. Miller, "Emphasis Added: Plots and Plausibilities in Women's Fiction" in *PMLA,* 96 (January 1981), 40.

13. Claudine Hermann, quoted in Miller, p. 42.

14. Nancy K. Miller, "Emphasis Added," 43.

15. Ann Beattie, "In the White Night" in *Where You'll Find Me* (New York: Simon and Schuster, 1986), p. 14. Further references to this story will be cited in parentheses.

16. David Lodge, *Working with Structuralism* (Boston: Routledge and Kegan Paul, 1981), p. 22.

17. Anatole Broyard, "The Shock of Unrecognition" in *The New York Times,* 24 August 1976, p. 27.

17. Mere thanks cannot express my gratitude to Peter Jaret for his contributions to every stage of this article—thinking, writing, and editing.

Brenda O. Daly (essay date 1993)

SOURCE: Daly, Brenda O. "Ann Beattie's *Picturing Will*: Changing Our Images of 'Good' Mothers and Fathers." In *The Critical Response to Ann Beattie,* edited by Jaye Berman Montresor, pp. 158-76. Westport, Conn.: Greenwood, 1993.

[*In the following essay, Daly develops the argument that Beattie portrays Mel, the stepfather in* Picturing Will, *as a better parent than Jody, Will's biological mother, and notes how unsettling this concept will likely be to female readers.*]

"Who Is the Truest Parent?" asks the headline of a review of Ann Beattie's latest novel, *Picturing Will.* According to the reviewer, Beattie gives two related answers to this question: first, that the truest parent is the one most capable of "picturing Will," and second, that the truest parent is Mel, the child's step-father. In other words, neither of Will's biological parents, his mother Jody nor his father Wayne, is the truest parent because neither succeeds in fully imagining or meeting the child's needs. What makes a true parent, one might then conclude, is the ability to imagine a child's world. But reviewer T. Boyle Coraghessan gives an even more expansive role to the imagination, arguing that "To picture Will is to capture the world around him, the world of his mother, of his father, of his stepfather-to-be, and of all the characters who crowd his life and the lives of the supporting cast" (1). The truest parent, it would appear, is the novelist herself. Yet the character who most closely approximates the author is not a woman, but a man, a gender reversal that further complicates what is most radical in *Picturing Will*—the proposition that mothering requires thinking.[1] Moreover, because Will's mother Jody is a successful photographer whereas Mel is an unpublished writer, the novel raises the question of whether public success can be achieved only at the cost of sacrificing one's (maternal) competence at "picturing Will."

This possibility may trouble some women readers, especially those who are trying to combine motherhood and careers, and who may have mixed feelings about Beattie's decision to portray Mel, rather than Jody, as most successful at "picturing Will." The fact that photography, not maternity, becomes Jody's top priority, may stimulate a form of mother-guilt which, according to Susan Suleiman in "Writing and Motherhood,"[2] originates in a fantasy of maternal perfection that is impossible for anyone merely human to achieve. Readers who harbor such maternal guilt are likely to judge harshly the professionally ambitious Jody, especially when she exposes Will to potential danger by turning his care over to Mel even before he has become her second husband. By contrast, Mel may have sacrificed potential fame as a writer in order to be a true parent to Will, a possibility that comes as a surprise in the novel's final chapter. This chapter, set twenty years later, pictures Will as an adult who has come home to celebrate his mother's birthday. His step-father chooses this occasion to hand him the key to "papers" he asks Will to read, commenting: "'They're only things I've written—not official documents'" (229). But when Will opens the journal, it begins, *"Of course you do not want the child to be a ventriloquist's dummy,"* words certain to surprise readers who recognize how they echo the first of a number of such italicized meditations, interspersed throughout the novel. Upon discovering that Mel is the author of these meditations, readers are likely to abruptly change their understanding of him, not only as a parent, but as an artist. After all, if Mel is as capable of picturing Will in his words, as Jody is in her photographs, it is possible that Beattie means to declare him both the "truest" parent and the "truest" artist.

Yet *Picturing Will* need not be read as a contest of "true" parenting or true artistry. Beattie's answer may not be a simple either/or, either Jody or Mel, but rather, both/and, both Jody and Mel. In other words, she may imagine the winner of at least the literary contest as neither photographer nor writer, but rather as the marriage of the two who, together, create a narrative of shared images,[3] whether of memories or photographs. Beattie is suggesting, I think, that both artistry and parenting are meaningful only when they are understood as shared acts, communal or familial. Without narrative, images cannot be comprehended, Beattie implies, a point that Susan Sontag also makes about photographs. Photography, Sontag says, creates a world "of unrelated, freestanding particles . . . which denies interconnectedness, [and] continuity," but "this is the opposite of understanding" (23). "Only that which narrates can make us understand" (23) Sontag declares, a proposition also asserted in *Picturing Will.*

Characteristically, Beattie makes her thematic point—in this case, the assertion that understanding occurs through narration—through a dramatic emphasis upon absence or lack. For example, it is Wayne's lack of narrative knowledge of his wife and son, whom he has abandoned, that makes it impossible for him to interpret the random contents of manila envelopes that Jody occasionally sends him—envelopes containing "Will's printed request for another G. I. Joe," or "a computer letter offering Jody two free days in a Key West condo," or "the cartoon that came with a cube of bubble gum" (8). Wayne's lack of understanding upon receipt of Jody's envelopes makes the point that only through a marriage of imaginations, joined together in the shared task of creating a family narrative, is it possible to both "picture Will" and care for him.

Without narrative, Beattie also implies, images may deceive us. For example, while our memories or photographs may give parents the illusion of having stopped time, the movement of narrative—especially the child's narrative—subverts this desire. The novel's exploration of the relationship between images and the flow of time surfaces in one of Mel's meditations on Will's childhood:

> *He will be standing the way he stood in the snapshot, with an expanse of field—maybe the beach—around him. A little thing, but you will remember that distinctly without having a photograph in front of you. That will be the way, in fact, the child will stay: a visual image—one that, even at the time, you squinted to look harder at, whether or not a camera was raised to your eye.*
>
> (53)

Mel's meditation ends, *"As you remember him, the child is always two,"* but this image of Will is undercut at the end of the novel when, along with a now adult Will, we re-read this passage as Mel's journal. The recurrence of this passage foregrounds a temporal disparity, creating an awareness in readers of the novel's double-visioned narrative movement: the time at which a passage is written (or a picture taken) and the time of its being read (or viewed).

In **Picturing Will,** Beattie's strategic placement of such meditative passages, as well as photographs, accentuates a sense of loss or absence. Carolyn Porter has noted Beattie's use of photographs to emphasize loss, but in **Picturing Will** this use of photography is even more complex. By marrying a photographer-mother and a writer-father, she also explores the narrative possibilities of family life in our postmodern period. More specifically, this novel asks how writers and photographers are using images, not just to mourn but to transform the "nuclear" family of the modern age into a postmodern family which still retains its capacity for imagining the needs of children.[4] This concern with the transformation of family life is most obvious in the novel's depiction of changing roles—for example, in the reversal of parenting roles as surrogate father Mel becomes "mother" to Will while Jody pursues her career. At times, however, Beattie's characterization of Jody verges on the negative, as if she mourns the passing of the nuclear family, with its stay-at-home mother, even as she records its demise. It should be noted, however, that among contemporary women writers, Beattie is not alone in her ambivalence about the demise of—or is it the transformation of?—the nuclear family. Authorial ambivalence surfaces in recent novels by Marilyn French and Sue Miller, both of which depict mother-photographers.[5]

Initially, the appearance of mother-photographers in these novels may seem quite unremarkable. After all, these novels are clearly about family life, and "Cameras go with family life," as Sontag remarks in *On Photography* (8). Historically, photography and families appeared at about the same time, according to Sontag, who says that just "as that claustrophobic unit, the nuclear family, was being carved out of a much larger family aggregate, photography came along to memorialize, to restate symbolically, the imperiled continuity and vanishing extendedness of family life" (9). Since that time, with a brief lag between the camera's invention in the 1840s and its use by amateurs, it has been used to record the rites of nuclear family life—weddings, birthdays, and holidays—even as it has also recorded what Sontag describes as the "ghostly traces" of an extended family system already in decline by the early nineteenth century. Now, in the late twentieth century, it is possible that the professional woman photographer is not simply recording the rites of the modern family, but actually helping to hasten its demise.

This, at least, seems to be the possibility—along with the attendant anxieties—being portrayed in these recent novels. Is the movement of women into the public realm an unmitigated "good," these novelists are asking, particularly when we no longer have a community narrative that affirms shared beliefs and rites, and when we see no parallel movement of men into the private realm? To put the question somewhat differently, and in the specific terms of these novels: is it "good" if women photographers unquestioningly accept "masculine" values, such as objectivity or a lack of affect, that govern the profession of photography? If so, how does the practice of "masculine" photography affect their ability to nurture? What happens to children when the "feminine" capacity to nurture disappears from the family? The question, crudely stated, is simply: Who will care for the children—and, more generally, for the family—if women refuse to do it?

Given the absence of community, or extended families, the threat of losing the nuclear family, however oppressive it has been to women, is understandably threatening to many, regardless of gender. At the same time, as feminist critics have clearly demonstrated, for centuries the family has been defined in such as way as to force most women to sacrifice themselves, and their potential as artists, on the altar of motherhood. *Picturing Will* examines this puzzle from an aesthetic point of view, as well as from the perspective of different family members. The novel depicts the impact of Jody's career upon her family, but it also raises questions about how photography, as an art whose conventions have been defined by men, may adversely affect a woman. Like both French and Miller, Beattie raises the possibility that the act of taking pictures—at least in the male-defined professional manner—may have a potentially destructive impact upon a woman's abilities to nurture children. In short, these novels ask not only whether a woman can hold a baby and a camera at the same time—that is, whether she can have both a career and a child—but whether a woman's work as a photographer will change her from an empathic, imaginative nurturer of children, one capable of "picturing Will," into an aggressive, emotionally distant recorder of life.

In fact, Beattie's own lack of emotion in the early fiction might make her, according to some critics, the Diane Arbus of contemporary literature. One critic has, for example, described her early fiction as "'listless writing [that] replicates in prose the affectless inner life of her characters.'"[6] It does seem that some of the early stories, such as those in *Distortions,* could have been recorded by the eye of the camera. Such a lack of affect, or compassionate purpose, is a characteristic that Sontag also sees, and criticizes, in the photographs of Diane Arbus. Sontag could as easily be commenting on some of Beattie's early stories such as **"Wally Whistles Dixie"** or **"Marshall's Dog,"** when she describes Arbus as having "enrolled in one of art photography's most vigorous enterprises—concentrating on victims, on the unfortunate—but without the compassionate purpose that such a project is expected to serve" (33). Beattie concentrates on the victims in these early stories, but no compassionate purpose is served when the characters, often members of the same family, not only remain "other" to each other, but also to readers. Even so, some critics praised Beattie's stories for their lack of affect, just as, according to Sontag, Arbus's photographs were "praised for their candor and for an unsentimental empathy with their subjects" (33). Nevertheless, Sontag argues that Arbus's work "is based on distance, on privilege, on a feeling that what the viewer is asked to look at is really *other*" (33-34).[7] Like Arbus's photographs, Beattie's early stories sometimes invite readers to experience this otherness without encouraging them to move beyond it, without encouraging a sense of community.

By contrast, *Picturing Will* asks whether the absence of affect in Jody's photographs is somehow inherent in the act of taking pictures and, if so, whether this will be detrimental to Jody's capacity to mother. If it is true, as Sontag declares, that "the act of taking pictures is a semblance of appropriation, a semblance of rape" (24), must the professional woman photographer develop an aggressive persona? In other words, if Jody is to succeed as a photographer, must she conform to a profession that has been defined in terms of masculine conventions, and in a rhetoric which defines a camera as a gun and the photographer as one who "hunts" for "prey," "aims" his camera, and "shoots" a picture? This masculine rhetoric prevails in the profession, creating discomfort for women like Jody who strive to establish themselves in the field. In Marilyn French's *Her Mother's Daughter,* a similar problem occurs when the mother/photographer turns over childcare responsibilities to her second husband while she plays the man's part, taking "manly" photos and, at the same time, frequently, ignoring the needs of her husband and children.

Of course, women do have in Dorothea Lange a different model than Diane Arbus. Lange, who is best known for her compassionate pictures of the poor during the Great Depression, is a photographer whose work demonstrates that a lack of affect is not inherent in the act of taking pictures. Nevertheless, the women in these novels assume that if they are to succeed as professional photographers, they must accept the masculine convention of "objectivity." In fact, perhaps like Diane Arbus, they attempt to outdo male competitors in their capacity for objectifying—for making "other"—their photographic subjects. The danger is, Beattie implies (as do French and Miller), that if Jody assumes this stance of detachment toward her photographic subjects, she will also take this stance in her private life. Indeed, the moment Jody begins to make her living as a photographer, this process of emotional-distancing begins. As Jody photographs weddings to support herself and Will after having been abandoned by Wayne, she begins to use her camera to shield herself from the painful memories aroused by such family occasions. This sense of loss is palpable in Jody's first successful photograph, called "After the Wedding." But this is only the first of two photos, both of which are carefully embedded in the narrative, that illustrate how Jody sublimates the painful experience of loss—loss of marriage and community—in her art.

Beattie develops the ethical complexity of Jody's entry into the world of professional photography through the narrative placement, and thematic variation, of three key photographs: the two taken by Jody, "After the Wedding," as mentioned above, and a second photo that might be called, "After the Halloween Party," which launches Jody's career as a professional photographer; and a third, a mother-and-child photo of Jody and Will, taken by a *Vogue* photographer. Perhaps the most significant of these is the Halloween photo which has the effect of "carnivalizing"[8] the family narrative; that is, the effect of altering conventional hierarchies and familial roles, often by reversal. After first shifting the novel's focus from the conventional romance plot—from *before* the wedding to *after*—Beattie then signals, with the Halloween photo, a transformation of the traditional family narrative. In other words, Beattie is "writing beyond the ending" of the romance plot, to use a phrase coined by Rachel Blau Du Plessis, to direct our attention to what happens after the wedding. It is, however, the "after-Halloween" photo that launches Jody's professional career, and, at the same time, sets in motion the carnivalization of her family's narrative. Traditional family roles are reversed as, for example, when Jody's lover acts as more of a father to Will than does the child's biological father, or when Jody takes the part of the traditional "father," spending more time and energy on her career, while Mel acts the part of "mother," attending to Will's needs. The change in roles is also evident in Mel's choice to write privately to his son, rather than seeking public fame, a reversal of spheres—private and public—that have long been defined as "feminine" and "masculine," respectively.

Yet, as I said, Beattie also seems to be examining an aesthetic puzzle in ***Picturing Will,*** exploring the differences between photography and writing, as if to determine how the marriage between these two—as between Jody who photographs and Mel who writes—works to nurture, or picture, a child's life. The division of the novel into three parts, called "Mother," "Father," and "Child" invites such an examination of both Beattie's aesthetic practice and this "nuclear" concept of the family. For example, the last part of the novel, "Child," consists of a single chapter; by contrast, both Part One and Part Two, "Mother" and "Father," consist of ten chapters each. Why such brevity for "Child"? As if in answer to this question, chapter twenty-one, "Child," places emphasis on Will's capacity for independent narrative, a narrative that will occur beyond the "end" of the story of Mel and Jody. Part Three, or chapter twenty-one, opens as Will, who has come home for Jody's birthday, looks at the old *Vogue* photo of his mother holding him. Both the photo and the birthday party accentuate the passage of time and, by placing the photo in this new temporal context, Beattie heightens its emotional impact and interpretive power. The sense of loss is further accented in Mel's journal where Will reads this description of Jody's art: "Her feeling has been that people do things, then abandon the worlds they have created. She is interested in what remains, after the fact. No doubt she also feels abandoned" (219).

Apparently, years after being abandoned by her first husband, Jody's photographs continue to depict the loss—even the damage—that often takes place following such communal celebrations. Jody was earning a living by photographing weddings when, in Part One, she had returned, the day afterward, to photograph the abandoned site of a marriage ceremony. On that day she had first considered photographing a crushed plastic champagne glass in the driveway; later, seeing the remains of an empty bird's nest, she had looked for broken eggshells to photograph. Finding no broken shells, she had waited. And she was rewarded, for, in just a few minutes, two men had driven up to the house in a rusty blue pickup.

She waited until they got to the door, then began photographing in earnest. And luck was with her: the wind got in the photograph. A wind blew up, and in an almost palpable way it reinforced the empty space that surrounded the men. Then she moved quickly to stand behind the tripod and photograph the men as the door opened, the lens compressing distance until their truck was no longer a respectable distance from the house but a huge presence, large and threatening. It existed in stark contrast to the branches blowing in the breeze. The housekeeper was squinting against the rush of air. Jody clicked and knew she had the right picture. (18) With the caption, "After the Wedding," it was a photo that made people "stop dead in their tracks to stare" (18). Apparently, though this photograph mirrors Jody's emotional state, it also happens to mirror the collective consciousness of the era.

But it is Jody's photograph of the Halloween party which most powerfully depicts her own psychic landscape in a way that also mirrors the postmodern world of the late twentieth century. The Halloween photograph speaks to viewers not only because of its ghostly traces of something missing, but because of the carnivalesque quality of the images. In this photo, Cinderella, a woman about to be abandoned by her alcoholic husband, has just left a Halloween party when she accidentally hits and kills a deer with her car. The party, itself the remnant of an ancient community celebration, had taken place in an abandoned church.[9] Afterward, Jody had snapped her best picture as Casper the Ghost and Peter Pan crouch in the headlights, surveying the "crumpled" deer. People had stopped to help, but Jody had deliberately taken her photo at the instant Cinderella stood completely alone, as if abandoned by the Prince, her fairy godmother, everyone. The photo is described in these words: "Mary Vickers's eyes, bright enough to bore a hole through the camera lens, full moon shining to one side, people clotted together on the road, and in the background the large form of a ghost, white body billowing in the wind, looking down at who knew what" (49). The ghost and, once again, the wind, both suggest that something is missing. What is it? What loss do the revelers see in Mary Vickers's eyes?

For some readers, this something missing is as much outside as inside the photo. It is disturbing, for example, that Jody responds first, not as a friend, but as a photographer. Of course, Jody's lack of intervention is the characteristic stance of a photographer, as Sontag points out. But for this same reason, photography suits Jody's psychological needs because, after her wedding and subsequent abandonment, she seeks protection from the pain that is always possible in relationships. After the Halloween party, for example, she puts her camera between herself and her friend's pain just as earlier, at the Halloween party, when she "felt vulnerable and sentimental, as if she wanted to rush into Mel's arms," she had picked up her camera, thinking: "That was the good thing about having a camera between you and the rest of the world: It afforded some protection, a way to stall for time" (45). But this self-protective use of her camera also allows Jody to disavow her sympathy with others, with her friend Mary and her lover Mel. According to Sontag, "A disavowal of empathy, a disdain for message-mongering, a claim to be invisible—these are strategies endorsed by most professional photographers" (77). Such a disavowal of empathy is, of course, precisely what Jody believes is required in order to survive in the post-1960s world.

In her previous fiction, Beattie herself has used photographs to effect this same "disavowal of empathy," but a change is apparent in *Picturing Will,* as it is in Beattie's more recent short fiction, according to Carolyn Porter. Particularly in *The Burning House* (1982), photographs such as "Winter: 1978" or "Lake Champlain: 1978," Porter says, "resemble Beattie's earlier stories in their insistence on simply portraying a scene without comment or interpretation" (24), but now these photographs "serve a larger narrative interest," primarily because of their placement "within a narrative about time and loss" (24). The same can be said of placement of photos in *Picturing Will,* as il-

lustrated above. Whereas it is Jody's purpose to disavow empathy, placing distance between herself and her photographic subject, Beattie now uses photographs not only to comment upon time and loss, but to criticize her former aesthetic practice. With her use of photography in *Picturing Will.* Beattie implies that artists or parents (and perhaps readers) who want to succeed in caring for a child, in "picturing Will," cannot hide behind a camera, cannot disavow empathy.

In terms of her capacity for empathy, her capacity to enter the imaginative world of another, Jody is portrayed as a less successful parent and artist than Mel. To a degree, Jody herself is aware of this characteristic stance in her life and her art. For example, as she considers the way her life is becoming entangled with Mel's—her toothbrush at his house, his shirt in her laundry basket—she reflects upon her use of photography:

> That was the thing about taking photographs. About taking wedding photographs, at least: that the people you were seeing wanted so sincerely to belong. It was a desperation rather than vanity that made them look soulfully into the camera, because the camera had the power to stop time and to verify that they were part of a tradition. That was why brides wore their grandmothers' wedding dress.
>
> (65-66)

Taking photographs such as "After the Wedding" gives Jody the illusion of having mastered this "desperation" to belong. In other words, rather than taking photographs that preserve the "illusion" of belonging to generations of an extended family, Jody takes photographs that freeze time at moments of profound isolation, moments that record, and accentuate, the absence of family, tradition, or community. Both "After the Wedding" and "After the Halloween Party" depict the ghostly traces of a community once defined in terms of kinship.

A different kind of loss is implied by the narrative placement of the picture of Jody and Will which is taken by a *Vogue* photographer. This photo is taken at the very moment Jody chooses to put her career first and her son second. Understood in this context, the picture functions as a parody of the centuries-old mythical image of "Madonna and Child" women have been expected to fulfill. However, Beattie's transformation of this image can only be interpreted in relationship to her use of other kinds of images, particularly metaphor. For example, Jody's shift in priorities from maternity to photography is signalled by a movement away from metaphor, associated with her intimacy with Will during his childhood, and toward metonymy, associated with postmodern discontinuities of a man named Haverford who represents the worst of the commercial New York world. It is Mel who puts Jody in touch with Haverford, but it is also Mel who establishes, in one of his meditations, the link between metaphor and childhood. Childhood, he writes, is a world in which a road "might not be a road but the sea" (92). What does it mean, then, that Jody reads Blake to Will at bedtime, and that, though Will enjoys his mother's attention, he probably cannot understand what she is saying? Jody certainly understands the power of metaphor. In fact, as her career is just beginning, she uses metaphor to assert herself with Haverford, a man who is successful at selling art but incapable of comprehending any of Jody's conversational images, whether similes or metaphors.

During her first meeting with Haveabud (a man Beattie first calls Haverford, but subsequently calls "Haveabud," using Jody's name for a man who, it turns out, prefers sex with budding boys), Jody had used the power of metaphor to resist his personality. Sensing that he did not genuinely understand art—that she and her photographs had only commercial value for him—she had used images, both metaphor and simile, to break "whatever mood he had meant to establish" (84). Asking Haveabud if he would understand an analogy, Jody then "told him that after the pictures were taken they were pieces of a puzzle. That in the darkroom they would float for a while, like a rose petal that had fallen into a glass of champagne. . . . They were images ruffled by currents, she said. Those slips of paper in the developing fluid" (84). Haveabud can only echo Jody's phrase "images ruffled by currents," without understanding, without entering into her world.[10] He sees Jody, as he later sees the boy Spencer, whom he molests, merely as a commodity that he can exploit to meet his needs. However, as Jody moves toward the world of Haveabud and away from the maternal world, her own capacity for metaphor and relationship appears to diminish. At one point in his meditations, Mel even wonders whether Jody has had an affair with Haveabud.

However, Beattie might be engaging in self-parody in this depiction of Jody's shift from metaphor to metonymy, from Will to Haveabud. To be specific, when Jody sends manila envelopes to Wayne containing random items, she is using a technique that, according to Porter, Beattie had once used herself in stories such as **"Marshall's Dog,"** where items are "arranged without apparent regard for chronology, plot sequence, or thematic development" (14). In these stories, Porter explains, whenever a metaphor surfaced, it would be transformed into metonymy which would then generate more narrative. In **"Marshall's Dog,"** for example, the moment spaghetti "snapped in half" becomes a metaphor for "bones cracking," Porter says that Beattie's narrator refuses to build the metaphor but rather talks of sauce or butter, food items associated with actual spaghetti. Porter explains this technique as a refusal of metaphor. "Even when metaphors appear," she says, "they refuse to function normally—that is, to create and develop symbolic meanings. Instead, they act as metonymy does in Roman Jakobson's theory, returning to relationships of contiguity which generate narrative movement" (15). Jody's pursuit of a career is portrayed as a similar movement away from Will's intimate world of metaphor and into Haveabud's random world of metonymy.

Jody's association with Haveabud leads her into the carnivalesque New York scene, a world in which community relationships, as well as authentic intimacy, are lacking. Although the carnivalesque quality of Haveabud's New York might seem a fairy tale to a child—and the narrator asks, "Why read fairy tales to your child when you can take him to a party in New York?" (62-63)—this very lack of instability makes it an unsuitable, or at least very difficult place in which to raise a child. Beattie emphasizes this instability in her description of the kind of New Yorkers who might easily exist in fairy tales or in the topsy-turvy realm of carnivals or Halloween parties. For example, while in New York Jody meets a caterer named Angela in the kitchen of one of Mel's acquaintances. In a short conversation with Angela, Jody learns that the caterer's entourage includes a boyfriend who offers legal advice or "Rolfing," as well as a dishwasher who teaches "the Alexander Technique and with whom she was two-timing her boyfriend, and a fleet of people who served food, among them a dwarf who worked nights when he was between movie-stuntman jobs" (62). In this carnival of characters, no stable identity or relationship seems possible.

Intimacy of a certain kind is immediate—as, for example, when the caterer tells Jody that she "had grown up in a family of four brothers who treated her like one of the horses" (68)—but Jody isn't sure what this means since she lacks any knowledge of Angela's narrative. It may be, however, that Angela herself has no sense of living a life of narrative continuity. Narrative discontinuity is apparent when, just a few nights later, Jody meets Angela again. The woman no longer has a boyfriend, and though she is the caterer for Mel's party, she has come dressed for Halloween:

> in stone-washed jeans, probably about size three, and an enormous sweatshirt with a green-faced, red-lipped Oriental on it and raised red letters spelling SUMO. Her hair was yellow—not any shade of blond but yellow, Crayola-crayon yellow. Pink ballet slippers. No socks. On her wrist a coiled bracelet that ended in the

triangular head of a spitting snake. An earcuff and a diamond stud in one ear, a replica of the Empire State Building dangling from the other.

(68)

As Angela's costume suggests, this world is one in which the individual exists in particles, without a clear relationship to herself, her family, or kin. Jody's choice to become part of this world, rather than resisting it as she had initially resisted Haveabud, affects her relationship with Will.

The change is underscored by Beattie's placement of the *Vogue* photo in the novel's final section, called "Child." As Will looks at the mother-and-child photo, he remembers that it was taken just at the moment his mother was about to become a famous photographer: "It sits on the piano in the living room—the *Vogue* photograph taken twenty years before" (225). The narrative placement of this photo doubles its interpretive power by linking the present and the past. In the present, as Will looks through the window at his own wife, he finds the photo "not as evocative as the photographer had hoped" (225). But readers also know that, twenty years earlier, at the time the photo was taken, Jody had already begun to detach herself from Will by turning over child-care responsibilities to Mel. This shifting of traditional maternal responsibilities to Mel is hardly incriminating; as feminists have argued, though women give birth to children,[11] it should not be automatically assumed that they must also be the caretakers of children. On the other hand, when Mel first began taking care of Will, as we learn retrospectively, his motives had not been completely altruistic; Mel admits in his journal that, initially, Will was "simply a stepping-stone to [Jody's] heart" (221). Love came later. How much later Mel comes to love Will, we aren't told.

However, we do know that before their marriage, Jody had entrusted Mel to drive her son to Florida to visit his biological father, Wayne, the man who had abandoned her and who has, since then, shown little interest in Will. In protest against Wayne's indifference, as stated above, Jody occasionally sends him a manila envelope filled with unrelated items from her present life: a drawing of Will's, a bank overdraft notice, unopened letters, a grocery receipt. However, readers are left to ponder why, if she recognizes Wayne's indifference, she sends Will to visit him in Florida. Of course, the divorce decree may have required such visitations, but Wayne would not have forced Jody's compliance with such a ruling. Even more damaging, however, is the fact that Jody allows Haveabud, whom she obviously doesn't trust but who can further her career, to accompany Mel and Will on the trip to Florida. In fact, the night before Will leaves,

his mother tells him that "Haveabud liked to act wild, and that usually the easiest thing to do was to try to get into the spirit of things" (109). Will does "try to get into the spirit of things" as Haveabud, who has brought along his "nephew" Spencer, molests the boy in his hotel room. The innocent Will watches, disturbed but not quite sure why; meanwhile, Mel lies asleep in a nearby hotel room, recovering from a headache.

Looking at the *Vogue* photo twenty years later, Will recalls that when he tried to tell his mother about this disturbing event, she hadn't cared to listen. She had not wanted to hear anything negative about Haveabud. "Years ago," writes Beattie, "Will had started to tell Jody about Haveabud, and she had shushed him. Nothing negative could be said about her manic mentor" (228). Will's memory of this conversation, which as an adult he can now interpret, places the mother-and-child photo in quite a different frame of reference. He may also recall that his mother interrupted his trip to Florida, breaking a promise she had made to him that, if he spent a short time with his father, he could then visit his friend Wag. At the time, Jody was quite willing to place her career before her child's needs, calling Florida—not out of a desire to protect Will from his irresponsible father—but to ask that he be returned to New York "so he could be photographed with her for the July issue of *Vogue*. She was going to be one of five women photographed with their children—a full page picture. And her show opened in July." (197).

This interpretation of Jody's priorities is verified by Mel's document of their family history where Will reads, "She pursued fame, and left [me] to pursue the baby-sitters" (216). Nevertheless, after reading the document, Will also senses in Mel "a sort of narcissism difficult to separate, at times, from true involvement: an almost militant desire that things go well, or at least have a rationale, after the fact," and this despite the fact that "he always knew the care Mel took raising him" (229). At the same time, in contrast to Wayne, Mel is close to an ideal parent, whether readers think of him as "father" or "mother." Part Two, "Father," raises questions about such roles while, at the same time, it is primarily a narrative of Will's visit to his biological father. For example, although Wayne is the biological father, he lacks the ability—he lacks the imagination—to care for anyone. From the outset, as we learn, Wayne had wanted Jody to have an abortion. He had regarded Will's birth as "a distraction," as an unwanted responsibility which, he pretends later, had prevented him from doing something with his life. So immature is he, we discover, that "many dawns, Wayne had considered stuffing a diaper into [Will's] mouth, plugging the entrance to the cave of the noise, or pinching him, holding him upside down, pushing a pillow into his face" (131). It is possible that Wayne avoided such violent behavior only by leaving his wife and child. Leaving, it seems, is Wayne's only method of solving problems. By contrast, Mel writes, "Imagine this: You love someone whose birth had nothing to do with you" (215), and though Mel's love has its narcissistic aspects, Beattie identifies him as the most nurturing adult in Will's life. She does so, not only by depicting Mel's actions—his willingness to arrange for baby sitters, for example—but also by her use of Mel's writing. Retrospectively, when we recognize these recurring italicized writings as Mel's meditations on the nature of childhood, we see his effort to understand the world that Will inhabits.

The surprise of Mel's writing invites us to examine the contrast between Jody and Mel's art, between the photographer and the writer. Their differences as artists also point to their differences as parents. Jody uses her camera to protect herself from the "other," whereas Mel uses his writing to enter into the world of the "other," in this instance, the world of a child. This contrast is sharpened by Beattie's careful placement of Mel's first meditation on childhood immediately following the Halloween accident that Jody photographs with almost Arbus-like detachment. Mel's meditation, which begins, *"Of course, you do not want the child to be a ventriloquist's dummy"* (50), goes on to reflect upon the fact that a parent can no more ventriloquate a child than s/he can stop the flow of time. However powerful parents may seem to children—like the gods of myths or the ogres of fairy tales—their desires cannot stop a child from growing up. Even if we remember a child as "always two" (54), the child doesn't stay that way. Moreover, though Jody may try to keep a threatening world at bay with her camera, Mel reflects upon the impossibility of doing so. Mel's entry into a child's world, his effort to diminish the distance between self and other, presents a sharp contrast to Jody's photo of Halloween carnage, an attempt to increase the distance between herself and Mary Vickers. When, for example, Jody pictures Mary Vickers standing alone in the midst of unrelated masqueraders, she deliberately emphasizes the trauma that isolates her from others, as if friendship itself is a masquerade.

Such a vision is not *all* of life, but rather a nightmarish moment of life chosen out of many possible others. This same Halloween image surfaces later, this time as part of Mel's dream, a dream in which he sees not only "carnage: the deer on the road again, the Halloween revelers squatting and standing in the glow of the headlights, the bright eye of the deer" (68), but also a woman "photographing fish" (70) in a drowning world. Awakening in the night and observing Mel's REM (rapid eye movement, which indicates that the sleeper is dreaming), Jody has no access to Mel's dreams. Yet, as if intuiting Mel's dream, she thinks of

a line from "The Wasteland," a poem about spiritual drought, recalling the line, *"Those are pearls that were his eyes,"* but not recalling "the line before that line" (70). Jody remembers only that someone drowns, but most readers will recall the warning, "Fear death by water." In "The Wasteland," water may bring death, but it also brings re-birth, ending the community's spiritual drought. If Jody is unconsciously associating the lines, *"Those are pearls that were his eyes"* with Shakespeare's "The Tempest," the reference to water takes on more positive connotations. For in "The Tempest," a play that happens to be about fathering, water symbolizes the potential for a rebirth or a "sea change" (footnote 5, 2173-75).

What point is Beattie making in this scene? The novel's allusion to "The Wasteland" certainly does not solve the riddle of who is the truest parent; indeed, mothers are conspicuously absent in "The Tempest." Nevertheless, the marriage of Mel and Jody may end a spiritual drought, bringing about a sea change for both. Such an interpretation of Beattie's allusion to "The Wasteland" gains credibility when read in relationship to an earlier allusion to the sacred grounds on which Mel and Jody conduct their courtship. Indeed, just a few pages before the reference to Eliot's poem, the narrator tells us that Mel lives "across the street from General Theological Seminary," and that he "had in his possession a key that would open the big iron gate" (62) to the seminary courtyard. During their courtship, Jody and Mel sometimes enjoy this yard "with grass so green it shocked you into remembering the country," and their entry into the seminary "garden" is described as "analogous . . . to finding a way into heaven" (62). But if Mel has the only key to heaven for Jody, Jody might, in turn, hold the only key to Mel's salvation, as intimated by Beattie's allusion to Eliot's poem.

The line of "The Wasteland" that Jody cannot recall—the line preceding "Those are pearls that were his eyes"—comes from this passage in Part I, "The Burial of the Dead," which reads as follows:

> Madame Sosostris, famous clairvoyante,
> Had a bad cold, nevertheless
> Is known to be the wisest woman in Europe,
> With a wicked pack of cards. Here, said she,
> Is your card, the drowned Phoenician Sailor,
> (Those are pearls that were his eyes. Look!)
> Here is Belladonna, the Lady of the Rocks,
> The lady of situations.
>
> (2173-2174)

As Jody watches the dreaming Mel, her continuing presence in his life seems certain, yet she has neither the power of Madame Sosostris, nor is she as treacherously beautiful as that "Belladonna, the Lady of the Rocks." This allusion to the threat of powerful women in "The Wasteland" may indicate some degree of fantasy in Beattie's attitude toward Jody who does have the power to affect the lives of both Mel and Will, either positively or negatively. Yet Beattie depicts Jody in human, rather than in mythical terms so that, finally, our judgments of her must be rendered, not in the realm of fantasy, speaking in psycho-social terms, but on the human plane. And since Jody had the wisdom to find a father who would mother Will, should she be judged "wrong" or "selfish"? There is no simple answer to this question.

However, if it takes imagination to be a good parent, not just the day-to-day expenditure of time and energy, as Beattie suggests in her title, then Jody's choice of Mel for her second husband and Will's father should establish her as at least a "good enough,"[12] if not quite a "good" parent. And what ordinary parent—a description that fits most parents—can lay claim to more? As Mel reminds us in one of his meditations, even the best parents cannot control a child's future:

> *Do everything right and the child will prosper. It's as simple as that, except for fate, luck, heredity, chance, the astrological sign under which the child was born, his order of birth, his first encounter with evil, the girl who jilts him in spite of his excellent qualities, the war that is being fought when he is a young man, the drugs he may try once or too many times, the friends he makes, how he scores on tests, how well he endures kidding about his shortcomings, how ambitious he becomes, how far he falls behind, circumstantial evidence, ironic perspective, danger when it is least expected, difficulty in triumphing over circumstance, people with hidden agendas, and animals with rabies.*
>
> (52)

Though Beattie is certainly not the first nor the only writer who has made children her central concern, it is still rare to find a novel organized around the theme that good parenting, like good writing, requires imagination.

It may be Mel who explores in writing the idea of "picturing Will," but it should be noted that it is Jody who decides to marry Mel, a choice that shows considerable imagination and, following her experience with Wayne, considerable wisdom. Furthermore, though Jody is not the author/narrator of **Picturing Will,** she exerts considerable narrative power by turning over the tasks of mothering to Mel. And since Will appears not to have suffered from this reversal of roles, the novel's outcome may prompt readers to be as generous as Mel, perhaps even more generous, when deciding how good a parent Jody is. For example, if Jody tries to avoid celebrating birthdays or Christmas, she does counter this impulse by allowing Mel to take charge of these family occasions. Her ambivalence

toward holidays may arise from the impulse to avoid painful memories, pain that surfaces in many people during the holidays, if only from reminders of our own mortality. Families remind us of our impending deaths even as, through the generations, they enable us to care for our children. But family narrative can change. As we see in **Picturing Will,** roles may be transformed in the postmodern family, but this does not necessarily spell the end of families. By carefully embedding photographs and passages of writing in a narrative that is divided according to traditional family roles, Beattie enables readers to both mourn the passing of the modern family and, at the same time, to critique anachronistic roles, along with traditional plots and endings.

Notes

1. Sara Ruddick stresses this point in *Maternal Thinking* when she says, "Mothers think" (23), explaining that "daily, mothers think out strategies of protection, nurturance, and training. Frequently conflicts between strategies or between fundamental demands provoke mothers to think about the meaning and relative weight of preservation, growth, and acceptability. In quieter moments, mothers reflect upon their practice as a whole" (23-4).

2. This guilt, as Ruth Perry explains, differs from "the guilt of working women who must earn their bread while entrusting their children to others or leaving them alone;" instead, it is "the free floating mother-guilt felt by nearly all mothers in Anglo-American culture, independent of their individual circumstances—a guilt ready to attach itself to any phenomenon, a nagging feeling that we never do enough for our children or do it quite right, never properly protect them from danger and disappointment in the world, and are never quite sure that we have always acted in their best interest" ("Mary Gordon's Mothers" in *Narrating Mothers,* 210).

3. *People* magazine reports that Ann Beattie's husband, the artist Lincoln Perry, gave the novel its title. Neither Beattie nor Perry has "the slightest desire to reproduce," but Beattie explained that she wrote the novel "'because somehow not having children made it more mysterious, more interesting to look at'" (Hubbard, 91).

4. I am using this term as defined by Judith Stacey. According to Stacey, "The 'modern' family of sociological theory and historical convention designates a form no longer prevalent in the United States—an intact nuclear household unit composed of a male breadwinner, his full-time homemaker wife, and their dependent children" (5).

5. Both Marilyn French's *Her Mother's Daughter* and Sue Miller's *Family Pictures* portray mothers who become professional photographers and, as a result, change their own life narratives along with their fam-

ily narratives. The role of mother-photographer is not always an unambiguous "good" for a mother or her children.

6. See, for example, Joshua Gilder who, according to Christina Murphy, criticizes Beattie because her fiction says, "'there is no redemption from despair and hopelessness, especially not in art'" (18).

7. Edward Steichen may have tried to emphasize unity in the famous "Family of Man," whereas Arbus's work insists, Sontag says, that "humanity is not 'one'" (32). Yet both Steichen and Arbus lack a sense of history, according to Sontag who comments: "The Steichen show was an up and the Arbus show was a down, but either experience serves equally well to rule out a historical understanding of reality" (33).

8. This term comes from Mikhail Bakhtin. See especially "Epic and Novel" (3-40) and "From the Prehistory of Novelistic Discourse" (41-83). In her Halloween photo, Jody alludes to the ghostly traces of carnival, an ancient community celebration. See also Michael Andre Bernstein's "When the Carnival Turns Bitter: Preliminary Reflections Upon the Abject Hero" in which he says, "It is largely from the writings of Mikhail Bakhtin that we have learned to apply terms like 'carnivalization' to the collapse of hierarchic distinctions upon which all such dialogues depend, and it is a major part of Bakhtin's legacy to have taught us how to value the liberating energy of the carnivalesque" (100). At the same time, Bernstein points out that the spirit of carnival may place us in an ironic, if non-mimetic relationship to events so that, as in the case of Rabelais, "we never respond to all the killings, maimings, humiliations, and catastrophes as if they happened to human beings" (117). Jody's Halloween photo has a similar effect, distancing viewers from the catastrophe.

9. Beattie's Halloween party (parody) on holy ground has ancient precedent. Bakhtin tells us in "From the Prehistory of Novelistic Discourse" that "holy laughter" was permitted during the medieval period. Written parody of the Bible was also permitted, and in a work called *Cyprian Feasts* "the entire Sacred Writ is transformed into carnival, or more correctly into Saturnalia" (70). Of course, Beattie's tone is mournful, conveying a sense of loss, rather than celebration.

10. For a discussion of how the transaction between the maker and the appreciator of metaphor "constitutes the acknowledgement of community" and "the achievement of intimacy," see Ted Cohen's "Metaphor and the Cultivation of Intimacy" (6). According to Cohen, "[The appreciator of metaphor] must penetrate your remark, so to speak, in order to explore you yourself, in order to grasp the import" (7). When Haveabud fails to respond to Jody's invitation, he fails either to acknowledge a community or build one. On the other hand, Jody's use of figurative language might be a power play since, as Cohen says, "A figurative use [of language] can be inaccessible to all but those who share information about one another's knowledge, beliefs, intentions, attitudes" (7). Jody may be demonstrating her superior knowledge of an art form about which Haveabud knows nothing—except what sells.

11. See, for example, Sara Ruddick, Marianne Hirsch, or Brenda O. Daly and Maureen T. Reddy.

12. Winnicott says that "the good-enough 'mother' is one who makes active adaptation to the infant's needs, an active adaptation that gradually lessens, according to the infant's growing ability to account for failure of adaptation and to tolerate the results of frustration" (10). Such gradually lessening maternal adaptation is as apparent in Jody's willingness to share parenting with Mel as it is in Mel's meditations on parenting.

Works Cited

Bakhtin, Mikhail M. *The Dialogic Imagination: Four Essays*. Trans. Caryl Emerson and Michael Holquist. Ed. Michael Holquist. Austin: U of Texas P, 1983.

———. "Epic and Novel." 3-40.

———. "From the Prehistory of Novelistic Discourse." 41-83.

Beattie, Ann. *Chilly Scenes of Winter*. New York: Doubleday & Co., 1976.

———. *Distortions*. New York: Doubleday & Co., 1976.

———. *Picturing Will*. New York: Random House, 1989.

Bernstein, Michael Andre. "When the Carnival Turns Bitter: Preliminary Reflections Upon the Abject Hero." *Bakhtin: Essays and Dialogues on His Work*. Ed. Gary Saul Morson. Chicago: U of Chicago P, 1986. 99-121.

Blau Du Plessis, Rachel. *Writing beyond the Ending*. Bloomington: Indiana UP, 1985.

Cohen, Ted. "Metaphor and the Cultivation of Intimacy." *On Metaphor*. Ed. Sheldon Sacks. Chicago: U of Chicago P, 1979. 1-10.

Coraghessan Boyle, T. "Who Is the Truest Parent?" *The New York Times Book Review,* 7 January 1990: 1+.

Daly, Brenda O., and Maureen T. Reddy. *Narrating Mothers: Theorizing Maternal Subjectivities*. Knoxville: U of Tennessee P, 1991.

Eliot, T. S. "The Wasteland." *The Norton Anthology of English Literature*. Vol. 2. New York: W. W. Norton & Co., 1974. 2172-2188.

French, Marilyn. *Her Mother's Daughter*. New York: Ballantine Books, 1987.

Gilder, Joshua. "Less Is Less." *New Criterion* 2 (February 1983): 78-82.

Greene, Gayle. *Changing the Story: Feminist Fiction and the Tradition.* Bloomington: Indiana UP, 1991.

Hirsch, Marianne. *The Mother/Daughter Plot: Narrative, Psychoanalysis, Feminism.* Bloomington: Indiana UP, 1989.

Hubbard, Kim. "For Writer Ann Beattie, Winter's Anything but Chilly since Her Marriage to Artist Lincoln Perry." *People* (5 Feb. 1991): 89-95.

Miller, Sue. *Family Pictures.* New York: HarperCollins Publishers, 1990.

Murphy, Christina. *Ann Beattie.* New York: Twayne Pubs., 1986.

Perry, Ruth. "Mary Gordon's Mothers." *Narrating Mothers: Theorizing Maternal Subjectivities.* Eds. Brenda O. Daly and Maureen T. Reddy. Knoxville: U of Tennessee P, 1991. 209-221.

Porter, Carolyn. "Ann Beattie: The Art of the Missing." *Contemporary American Women Writers: Narrative Strategies.* Eds. Catherine Rainwater and William J. Scheick. Lexington: The U P of Kentucky, 1985. 9-28.

Ruddick, Sara. *Maternal Thinking: Toward a Politics of Peace.* Boston: Beacon P, 1989.

Sontag, Susan. *On Photography.* New York: Farrar, Straus and Giroux, 1977.

Stacey, Judith. *Brave New Families: Stories of Domestic Upheaval in Late Twentieth Century America.* New York: Basic Books, 1990.

Suleiman, Susan. "Motherhood and Writing." *The (M)Other Tongue: Essays in Feminist Psychoanalytic Interpretation.* Eds. Shirley Nelson Garner, Clare Kahane, and Madelon Sprengnether. Ithaca, NY: Cornell UP, 1989. 352-77.

Winnicott, D. W. *Playing and Reality.* Reading, MA: Addison-Wesley, 1987.

Michele Slung (review date February 2002)

SOURCE: Slung, Michele. "Romancing the Word." *Victoria* 16, no. 2 (February 2002): 38-9.

[*In the following review, Slung praises Beattie's novel* The Doctor's House *as unusually constructed and mesmerizing.*]

When the measure of love's reach is taken no two findings are ever alike. Yet it is the investigation itself that always especially when embarked upon by such writers as Berg, Beattie and Templeton, whose powers of observation are as keen as their empathies are deep.

Following a string of highly praised, best-selling novels, Elizabeth Berg's latest book, *Ordinary Life* (Random House), comes to us as her first short story collection. In a foreword, she comments that she's most often drawn to exploring "the seemingly irreconcilable differences between men and women."

Yet, poignantly, the title story, "Ordinary Life," which takes as its milieu the rocky territory where those differences collide, bears the subtitle 'A Love Story.'

But what an unexpected one it is! Seventy-nine-year-old Mavis Elaine McPherson has never spent a night apart from her husband, Al, in their long life together, yet now she has locked herself in the bathroom, surrounded by pillows and library books, fortified by candy bars and a bowl of apples. Refusing all his entreaties to come out, she's focused instead on the Andrews Sisters, a particular red lipstick and a pair of open-toed shoes she once owned.

This escape to the bathtub is an act of transformation as well as meditation because the woman who finally emerges several days later is almost the same Mavis Elaine McPherson who went in—only not quite.

Many of the passages here—as Berg sketches for us Mavis's random reveries of her lost years as a little girl, a young bride, a new mother—have a lovely reflective quality. "Who knew whom you would be born to, befriend, live out your life with? Those were accidents, too, weren't they? Completely arbitrary things, barely noticed, most often. And yet." It's that phrase that summons up truth in a mere two words: And yet.

Watching Mavis, locked away and lost in her memories as she stubbornly struggles to remember, for example, the names of forgotten pets or the fate of a certain favorite flowered sofa, is to watch her, really, attack the puzzle of her own existence—and to share, also, in her affirmation of it.

Other of the selections in *Ordinary Life* include "The Matchmaker," in which an eleven-year-old would-be Cupid suffers an early sting of betrayal, and "The Thief," in which a busy but neglected suburban wife is jolted out of her boredom by the attentions of an amateur abductor whose longings—for romance? adventure? connection?—mirror her own. Berg's heroines have an Everywoman quality: Each of them could easily be someone we know.

The Doctor's House (Scribner) by Ann Beattie is also a book of stories, though not in the usual sense. It is actually the same tale told from different, overlapping perspectives. And we understand fairly quickly that none of the three narrators—a mother and her grown son and daughter—can we count on as perfectly reliable.

At the book's center is Nina, a young widow living in Cambridge, Massachusetts. She is finding it difficult to remain as remote as she'd like when Andrew, her brother, is continually churning up the dust of old romances, and his former girlfriends keep arriving on her doorstep.

As a little girl, Nina fantasized a magical world in which she and Andrew flew on the night wind, "up very very high where all the noise faded. They couldn't hear mothers and fathers fighting or dogs barking or even a telephone ring, and even the silence was beautiful." To her mother, from whom she is now estranged Nina seems an "Ice Princess" while a friend regards her as a different kind of fairy-tale figure—a "Cinderella who preferred to go barefoot, unescorted."

But what Nina actually is, as she carefully nurtures her own emotional paralysis, is a self-willed Sleeping Beauty, trapped in the brambles of her family's messy past. And it is her various shifting aspects that make this account of love's labors and losses so mesmerizing.

Unlike Ann Beattie and Elizabeth Berg, writers whose works are known to American readers, Prague-born Edith Templeton has remained a forgotten literary presence on this side of the Atlantic for many decades. In *The Darts of Cupid and Other Stories*—some of which originally appeared more than forty years ago in *The New Yorker* and are being collected here for the first time—the author proves herself to be adept at portraying eccentric personalities engaged in or recovering from unexpected affairs of the heart.

Templeton lived in India for much of her life and now at eighty-six makes her home in Italy. There are moments when she reminds me of a more sensual Barbara Pym: For example, the title story, "The Darts of Cupid," shows how an office of women, thrown together in wartime and attached to military staff, is fertile ground for flirtations and the gossip that inevitably follows.

In other stories, Templeton's scenes resemble what might be outtakes from (a less dour) Anita Brookner—as when, in the charming "Equality Cake," a woman returns, after long exile, to visit as a tourist what was once her grandmother's castle in Bohemia. Or when, in a different story of return, the protagonist encounters the maddening mystery of the man who has been to her, actually, more than "A Coffeehouse Acquaintance." We collect people as we go along, she reminds us. But few manage to defy tidy labels until the very end. This particular friend's ultimate elusiveness, though, is what provides the twist to her wry account of him.

Templeton's voice is always sharp and shrewd, and the central character of several of her tales undoubtedly possesses a biography that closely resembles her creator's. Indeed the lives of both seem to have similarly crisscrossed Europe at the same time history was continually redrawing its map. The goings-on in these stories are both drolly sophisticated and deceptively straightforward, as Templeton offers up comic clashes—not just between the sexes but also between the Old World and the New.

Robert Beuka (essay date fall 2002)

SOURCE: Beuka, Robert. "Tales from 'The Big Outside World': Ann Beattie's Hemingway." *Hemingway Review* 22, no. 1 (fall 2002): 109-17.

[*In the following essay, Beuka traces the influence of Ernest Hemingway on Beattie's writing and compares Beattie's short story "The Big Outside World" to its inspiration, the Hemingway story "Cat in the Rain."*]

Assessing Ann Beattie's literary influences can prove a bit difficult, for a number of reasons. For one thing, there is the matter of Beattie's own literary reputation; on the one hand, her style seems to have been pinned down rather specifically by reviewers and critics, as evidenced by the variety of interchangeable appellations affixed to her work: Beattie has been described as a "minimalist, a "K-Mart realist," a writer of *"New Yorker* fiction," and—in a phrase that is one of my personal favorites—a practitioner of the "Frank went to stand by the window" school of fiction writing (Birkerts 317). Still, Beattie has nonetheless amassed a body of work varied enough to resist such simplistic categorization, as is evidenced by the marked stylistic and tonal differences between her earliest work in *Distortions* (1976) and *Chilly Scenes of Winter* (1976) and her more emotionally complex recent fiction. Complicating the assessment of Beattie's literary influences is the author's own hesitance to discuss her relationship to literary forebears. But despite this general resistance to discussing influences, Beattie has affirmed the frequent comparisons between her work and Hemingway's, noting the distinct impact Hemingway's writing has had on her own. In an unpublished 1996 interview, Beattie mentioned the specific connection she feels to Hemingway:

> Surely I learned things from Hemingway. . . . [On first reading him] it was unusual to me . . . that someone would put together what looked like a very

oblique story that really made its demands between the lines. . . . I learned that from Hemingway, and it had a really strong impact. I'm sure that my ability to have things transpire off the page, and the innuendo that I have in a story and so forth, really is rooted in Hemingway.[1]

It is worth exploring the relationship between Beattie's and Hemingway's fiction, I will argue, because doing so might offer a window into assessing Hemingway's ongoing influence in contemporary fiction; at the same time, the nature of Beattie's borrowings from Hemingway might also tell us something more about the successful yet often maligned school of minimalist fiction to which Beattie, however unwillingly, has been assigned. Certainly, Beattie's most pointed, specific acknowledgment of Hemingway's influence can be found in the story **"The Big Outside World"** from her 1986 collection, ***Where You'll Find Me.*** Beattie describes this story as a "deliberate variation" on her favorite Hemingway story "Cat in the Rain" (Centola 419). Much like her cohort Raymond Carver whose story "The Train" stands as an homage to John Cheever, Beattie here uses the fictional medium to pay tribute to a primary literary influence. But while Carver fashioned his story as an extension of Cheever's "The Five-Forty-Eight" Beattie instead offers in **"The Big Outside World"** an entirely independent story, yet one with clear connections to Hemingway's "Cat in the Rain." In this essay I will discuss the two stories with an eye toward assaying the larger connections between the fictional approaches of Hemingway and Beattie.

Though it occupies a relatively minor place in the canon of Hemingway's fiction, "Cat in the Rain" nonetheless remains one of the most stylistically intriguing stories from *In Our Time,* its craftsmanship prompting John Hagopian to suggest that it is "probably Hemingway's best-made short story" (230). In a particularly terse and understated narrative, Hemingway tells the story of an American couple whose unsatisfactory afternoon alone in an Italian hotel room bespeaks larger issues of dissatisfaction within the relationship. The lone American visitors in the resort-town hotel, the couple remain cut off from the outside world by an afternoon rainstorm. Gazing upon the dreary scene outside, the wife spots a "poor kitty" crouched under a dripping table, and resolves to rescue it. Though her husband, George, makes an empty offer to go fetch the cat for her, he never moves from his position reading on the bed and never even sees the cat. After the wife's unsuccessful attempt to retrieve the animal—with the assistance of the hotel's maid and the tacit support of the innkeeper, a solicitous older man—we come to learn that the cat represents for the wife certain unfulfilled desires in her relationship with George. Specifically, she tells him, "I want

to eat at a table with my own silver and I want candles. And I want it to be spring and I want to brush my hair out in front of a mirror and I want a kitty and I want some new clothes" (*IOT* 121). Utterly dismissive of all of his wife's desires, George tells her to "shut up and get something to read" (121), whereupon the maid appears at the door carrying a "big tortoise-shell cat," explaining "the padrone asked me to bring this for the Signora" (122).

With this abrupt closing, Hemingway leaves his readers hanging—because we cannot know for sure whether the cat delivered is the cat the wife had imbued with such symbolic resonance, we have simply no way of understanding the significance of this closing action. One assumes from the wife's actions and stated desires that the kitty in the rain represents, for her, a complex of material, emotional, and sexual desires not being met in her relationship; hence, the unresolved status of the cat at the end of the story mirrors the unresolved troubles of the relationship itself. Extant critical work on the story bears out its open-endedness: Carlos Baker, for example, assumes that the two cats are one and the same; in his reading, the delivery of the cat—which for him symbolizes the wife's desire for a "comfortable bourgeois domesticity"—by the hotel manager only emphasizes the split between the wife's dreams and her life with an unresponsive husband (135). Hagopian, on the other hand, argues that the cat in the rain is an "obvious symbol for a child" and that its replacement by a different cat altogether at the end ironically highlights the central theme of the story, which for him turns on "a crisis in the marriage . . . involving the lack of fertility" (232). While both interpretations emphasize the bitter divide between the wife's desires and reality, their very different readings of Hemingway's central symbol underscore both the craftsmanship and the peculiar difficulty of this story.

As David Lodge points out in his structuralist interpretation, divergent opinions such as these result from teleologically oriented readings that attempt to affix closure on a story whose very structure offers no such finality. Lodge notes that "Cat in the Rain" is exemplary in its use of a metonymic, rather than metaphoric, mode of signification, one that reveals meaning gradually through a contiguous chain of thematic and symbolic oppositions (31). Contrasts between the wife's desires and George's reaction, between George and the hotel manager, and between the Italian setting and the couple's own Americanness, for example, build upon one another to create our understanding of the wife's plight.[2] Nevertheless, we as readers are left, at story's end, without closure and with nothing definitive to say about the story. As in a story such as "Hills Like White Elephants," here Hemingway achieves an intense narrative compression; his displacement of an emotional center, onto physical objects such as the claustrophobic hotel room, the cat, and the empty, rain-drenched square works to preclude narrative resolution, even as it allows us a glimpse of the protagonist's own emotional displacement.

It is precisely such a decentered, metonymic mode of signification that Beattie seizes upon in her reworking of the story in **"The Big Outside World."** In Beattie's story, a couple are in the midst of packing the belongings of their small New York City apartment in preparation for a move to suburban Connecticut. Having suffered a miscarriage, Beattie's 35-year-old protagonist, Renee, fears the prospect of a childless future with her emotionally distant husband, Tadd, who no longer seems to care about having children. The couples' dog serves as a child surrogate for Renee; her suggestion to add another dog to the family meets with anger and scorn from Tadd. In a nod to Hemingway, Beattie has Renee planning instead to adopt a cat upon their move to Connecticut. Preparing for the move, Renee takes bags of clothing to a Goodwill store; on the street outside the locked store, she is accosted by a pair of transvestites, who gleefully try on her clothing as Renee can only stand and watch, shocked and dumbfounded. On her return to the apartment, Tadd relates a story from his teenage years, in which he and a former girlfriend had, on several occasions, used clothing from Goodwill bins as bedding for their sexual trysts. Angered and emotionally alienated by Tadd's admission, Renee resolves to exit the apartment and take the dog for a walk, away from the scene at the Goodwill store, as the story closes.

While the action of Beattie's plot seems almost random (which would support the recurring charge among critics of a sense of "aimlessness" in her fiction), in fact the accumulation of detail in this story does work eventually to signify Renee's predicament. As in Hemingway's "Cat in the Rain," the central concerns of the story emerge through the author's use of contrasting, cumulative references; the freedom and adventurousness of the outside world, for example, contrasts to the stifling enclosure of an apartment literally being "boxed up," while sexuality and "Goodwill," metonymically linked, remain inaccessible to Renee. Ultimately, Renee's emotional isolation is revealed most directly through her identification with the pets her husband rejects. Through the accumulation of such related details and images, Beattie in the end presents us with a protagonist similar to Hemingway's—a sexually frustrated woman confined within an increasingly claustrophobic relationship, one that has separated her from a larger sense of belonging in the "big outside world."

Notwithstanding this thematic similarity, it is the structural and technical resemblance between the two stories that is of most importance in assessing Hemingway's larger influence on Beattie. In **"The Big Outside World,"** as in most of her fiction, Beattie resists, in Carolyn Porter's apt phrasing, "the rewards of the symbolic"; that is, following Hemingway's lead, she rejects the power and immediacy of metaphoric signification in favor of the more allusive, associative mode of metonymy (12). Central to this process is the use, well known to Hemingway's readers and fans of the minimalist school he helped to inspire, of the objective correlative, the telling detail from the physical environment which evokes otherwise suppressed or omitted emotions. In Beattie's words, what she gained from Hemingway in this regard was the ability to "have things transpire off the page." For detractors of minimalism such as Sven Birkerts, one of Beattie's harshest critics, her second-generation poetics of omission pales in comparison to the real thing. Arguing that the use of what he calls "the gap," or "the unstated," is the primary link between Hemingway and the minimalists, Birkerts goes on to make a sharp qualitative distinction between Papa and his children:

> We should note, by the way, the difference between the vaporized minimalism of an Ann Beattie and the laconic repressions of a Hemingway. For the latter, the unstated was a solid presence, a specific emotion or complex of emotions to be avoided—he knew, and we knew, what was being left out. For Beattie and her cohort, however, minimalism became a way of not dealing with that which could not be dealt with—the thousand and one grades of anomie that may not have existed fifty or a hundred years ago.
>
> (133)

Birkerts' assessment of minimalist poetics is by no means unique, and it may not be entirely unfair; nonetheless, it ought to be pointed out that he grounds this fairly representative condemnation of minimalism on the notion that this school of writers fails to name what he concedes is unnameable—a broadly generational sense of social disconnection. The circularity of this argument is daunting, but I believe another look at Hemingway's "Cat in the Rain" might suggest a means of better understanding the nature of the minimalists' inheritance from Hemingway.

Central among the many opposing images Hemingway uses in this story to convey the protagonist's dilemma are those that suggest the couples' dislocation from a sense of cultural "place" and belonging. Their physical position on the inside of an abandoned resort hotel looking out on an empty Italian cityscape emphasizes not only their "foreignness" but also their isolation.[3] As Thomas Strychacz succinctly puts it, "George and the 'American wife' seem gripped by a deep-rooted anomie born of their aimlessness . . . the Americans have no apparent purpose for being there" in Italy (76). One would imagine this aspect of the story attracted Beattie, as a similar sense of "aimlessness" or dislocation drives **"The Big Outside World"** and much of Beattie's fiction: from her countless protagonists who seem trapped in their cramped New York City apartments, to drifters like the narrator of the early story **"Vermont"** who search in vain for a place to inhabit, to disaffected suburbanites such as the protagonists of her 1980 novel *Falling in Place*. Beattie seems consistently to draw characters whose inability to connect to physical place parallels their emotional estrangement. Indeed, I would argue, along with Birkerts, that such a dynamic fuels a good deal of minimalist fiction in addition to Beattie's work; one need only think of the desultory landscapes of Raymond Carver or Bobbie Ann Mason, for example, to see how physical displacement tends to connote emotional estrangement in minimalist fiction. Beattie's antagonist from **"The Big Outside World,"** Tadd, utters a line that alludes to such a sense of dislocation from the surrounding environment: Upon Renee's return from the Goodwill store, seeing the frenzied reaction of the dog who wishes to escape the apartment, Tadd jokes, "Tell him that the big outside world wasn't that much fun. . . . Make him feel better" (41). Unwittingly summing up Renee's predicament, Tadd's joke also references the problem faced by her fictional predecessor, Hemingway's "American wife": for both characters, the "big outside world" remains, ultimately, inaccessible.

I concede that it may sound a bit odd to cite Hemingway as a pioneering voice for a school of "placeless," "dislocated" fiction that would emerge a half-century later. After all, as J. Gerald Kennedy has recently pointed out, profound attachments to place fueled so much of Hemingway's fiction.[4] And yet there are moments, and "Cat in the Rain" is by no means the only one, where we see Hemingway's characters either trapped, coerced or forced into a retreat from the "big outside world," alienated from place and community. One thinks as well of Krebs on his parents' porch in "Soldier's Home," the elder waiter of "A Clean, Well-Lighted Place," the narrator of "A Canary for One," Jig in "Hills Like White Elephants," and others—characters whose outward gazes toward landscapes devoid of meaning connote a larger sense of disconnection from not only physical, but also cultural, place. As poet Deborah Tall suggests, through characters such as these Hemingway "epitomizes the twentieth-century archetype of the uneasy, 'lost' individual whose identity is created in isolation rather than communally enacted" (343). And it is in this sense that we might see a larger connection, both stylistic and thematic, to the work of minimalists such as Ann Beattie. Following Hemingway's lead, Beattie consistently creates meticulously rendered visions of physical environments that, paradoxically, serve to emphasize her protagonists' social withdrawal. If her aim is indeed to suggest through this fictional approach a generational sense of anomie, she would not be the first to have done so.

In assessing Hemingway's influence on Beattie's fiction, we can quite readily speak of a shared minimalist poetics, the tendency to evoke emotion obliquely through both clipped dialogue and the use of the telling physical detail. Reading Beattie's homage, **"The Big Outside World,"** alongside the story that inspired it, "Cat in the Rain," reveals as much, but also suggests further avenues for understanding Hemingway's importance to Beattie. Ann Beattie's Ernest Hemingway is the Hemingway of the homeless, those suffering broken connections to the "Big Outside World"—characters whose desire for a sense of place, physically and emotionally, is matched only by their inability to make such a connection. Like Hemingway's characters, many protagonists of minimalist fictions represent the broken connections of their contemporary culture. Members of a generation not so much "lost" as displaced, protagonists of minimalist fiction of the past three decades tend to traverse physical and emotional landscapes devoid of abiding contours and connections. Not coincidentally, their stories are typically told by a process of displacement as well—through an ongoing, associative, metonymic drift. This technique, precisely realized by Hemingway in "Cat in the Rain" and other stories, in one sense highlights the protagonists' subjectivity, while in another sense it brings into focus their utter lack of connection to others around them. Among the generation who share this narrative style of Hemingway's, Beattie is surely at the forefront. Like Hemingway, she employs an allusive, decentered narrative technique that mirrors the physical and emotional displacement, or decenteredness, of her protagonists. And though Beattie resolutely declines the role of spokesperson for her generation, it ought to be noted that her poetics of displacement, like Hemingway's, resonates with lived experience in an age of virtual community. For this reason, to write off her fiction as mere stylization devoid of meaning is to catch, if you will forgive me, merely the tip of the iceberg.

Notes

1. This observation comes from an interview with Beattie conducted by J. Gerald Kennedy at Louisiana State University on 23 September 1996. My thanks to Professor Kennedy for allowing me access to the transcript of this interview.

2. To be sure, Lodge's approach has its limits as well; for example, his insistence on reading the entire narrative in terms of binary oppositions leaves him at a loss to account for Hemingway's fluid gender constructions, which are central to the dynamics of the story. As both Mark Spilka, in Hemingway's *Quarrel with Androgyny* (Lincoln; University of Nebraska Press, 1990) and Warren Bennett, in "The Poor Kitty and the Padrone and the Tortoise-shell Cat in 'Cat in the Rain,'" *The Hemingway Review* 8.1 (Fall 1988), have pointed out, the story's androgynous play marks "Cat in the Rain" as an early exploration of territory Hemingway would revisit in *The Garden of Eden.* Nor does a strictly narratological reading shed much light on the fetishistic elements of the story, recently examined in compelling fashion by Carl Eby in Hemingway's *Fetishism: Psychoanalysis and the Mirror of Manhood* (Albany: SUNY 1999). In a larger sense, some of the most compelling critical work on Hemingway from recent years has resisted binary formulations of gender and instead served to complicate and energize discussions of gender dynamics in Hemingway's fiction. See, for example, *Hemingway's Genders: Rereading the Hemingway Text,* by Nancy Comley and Robert Scholes (New Haven: Yale UP, 1994).

3. Extending Lodge's structuralist argument, Oddvar Holmesland claims that the spatial division of inside/outside is the central opposition that drives the narrative of "Cat in the Rain." See his essay "Structuralism and Interpretation: Ernest Hemingway's "Cat in the Rain," 58-72 in *New Critical Approaches to the Short Stories of Ernest Hemingway,* ed. Jackson Benson (Durham, NC: Duke UP, 1992).

4. See Kennedy's essay "Doing Country: Hemingway's Geographical Imagination" in *The Southern Review* 35 (Spring 1999): 325-329, for this discussion of the dynamics of place in Hemingway's fiction. The essay is one of four related pieces in a special section titled "Hemingway's Attachment to Place: A Symposium."

Works Cited

Baker, Carlos. *Hemingway: The Writer as Artist.* Princeton: Princeton UP, 1972.

Beattie, Ann. "The Big Outside World." In *Where You'll Find Me and Other Stories.* New York: Simon and Schuster, 1986.

Birkerts, Sven. *American Energies: Essays on Fiction.* New York: William Morrow. 1992.

Centola, Steven R. "An Interview with Ann Beattie." *Contemporary Literature* 31 (Winter 1990): 405-22.

Hagopian, John. "Symmetry in 'Cat in the Rain.'" *The Short Stones of Ernest Hemingway: Critical Essays.* Ed. Jackson J. Benson. Durham, NC: Duke UP, 1975. 230-232.

Hemingway, Ernest. "Cat in the Rain." *In Our Time.* New York: Charles Scribner's Sons, 1930.

Kennedy, J. Gerald. "Doing Country: Hemingway's Geographical Imagination." *The Southern Review* 35 (Spring 1999): 325-29.

Lodge, David. *Working with Structuralism: Essays and Reviews on Nineteenth- and Twentieth-Century Literature.* Boston: Routledge and Kegan Paul, 1981.

Porter, Carolyn. "Ann Beattie: The Art of the Missing." *Contemporary American Women Writers: Narrative Strategies.* Ed. Catherine Rainwater and William J. Scheik, Lexington: U of Kentucky P, 1985. 9-25.

Strychacz, Thomas. "In Our Time, Out of Season." *The Cambridge Companion to Ernest Hemingway.* Ed. Scott Donaldson, Cambridge UP, 1996. 55-86.

Tall, Deborah. "The Where of Writing: Hemingway's Sense of Place." *The Southern Review* 35, (Spring 1999): 338-43.

Ann Beattie and Dawn Trouard (interview date 1-2 October 2004)

SOURCE: Beattie, Ann, and Dawn Trouard. "Ann Beattie at Home." In *Conversations with Ann Beattie,* edited by Dawn Trouard, pp. 175-84. Jackson: University Press of Mississippi, 2007.

[*In the following interview, conducted in October 2004, Trouard questions Beattie about her writing process, the challenge of maintaining workspaces in three homes, and how her techniques influence what she teaches writing students.*]

The interview was conducted over two extended sessions on October 1-2 in the Maine summer home of Ann Beattie and her husband, artist Lincoln Perry. Beattie was expecting the page proofs for her eighth short story collection, **Follies** (Scribner). She has published seven novels in addition to her work on painters and photographers. Beattie is the Edgar Allan Poe Professor of Literature and Creative Writing at the University of Virginia.

The house itself is full of light, eclectic décor, and assorted constellations of books, sculpture, photos, paintings, and toys. Life was very much in-progress and Beattie's pleasure in her marriage and the work she does is palpable. The couple was preparing for their annual winter relocation to Florida and the house was in various stages of departure. The interview was punctuated by Perry's occasional appearance in a doorway to corroborate a story, embellish an account, or provide sustenance.

[*Trouard*]: *Of your three homes, the last place I expected to meet with you was the one in Maine. What's it like living amongst Mainers?*

[Beattie]: Like being a ghost. I mean, sometimes I say to my husband when I look at *Preservation* magazine and see those little ads in the back for what look like wonderful Georgian mansions in Tennessee and they're fifty-five thousand dollars, I think that's what we should do. That's what we should do! And he says, "What do you like about that?" and I say, "Nobody would know where we were, and we wouldn't even have to have a telephone." He says, "Well, you could take your telephone out, and that *is* the life you live in Maine." It's quite true. I think if you don't have a history with the place and you don't have any easy way to connect, like having kids in school, or a need to be part of certain groups, you can have a great deal of anonymity.

Can you have too much anonymity?

[smiling slyly] I really have pretty much failed in making friends.

Is there a book store in this town?

No. But a lot of books appear FedEx, delivered right into my hands because publishers send me books. And I order from Amazon and I go into Cambridge once a year. I shop in Harvard Square for books, then I have dinner with Don Lee and he drives me back to the bus. He can't believe that I won't drive in Boston.

Even with your map and phone directions, I had to stop four times to get help from locals just to find this road. I missed it three times. It seems they haven't made it all that easy to even get to you.

No, but it's not about making it easy. In Maine, it's really, really not about making it easy.

Does that carry over to householding? I notice that you have lots of projects around the place—the garage, some work by your porch? Are these your projects or are they couple projects?

They're not all my projects. Sometimes I have a project that isn't Lincoln's, but he's a Gemini, so often he has a project that isn't mine. I was on record as saying that as far as I was concerned the garage could fall into the ground and we could park in the driveway, rather than pay to do all the repairs. It was endless. So finally Lincoln wrote a check to pay for the garage repair. I still have a very bad relationship with the garage. We're still waiting for the patio guy. We've had several appointments. He's supposed to come. But he never actually does.

And is writing a check the same as getting someone to come do the work here?

Very rarely, unless it's over a certain sum, can you get anyone to come do any work under any circumstances. And, if so, not during the time period, they said. We waited three years to have the outside of our house painted.

Was there a waiting list? How selective are the house painters in Maine?

I don't think they liked the colors.

And, do they give preferences to Mainers?

I can only assume [laughing]. I can only assume.

So of the areas not under construction, do you have a favorite space in this home?

The living room is nice, and I love the color of the walls, but it will always be the living room, you know? I can't get over the fact that it's the living room and therefore I almost always avoid it. Except in cold months when it's very nice to be warm in the living room. I like the kitchen in some ways because you can see in many different directions, and also because it's the mail sorting room and there's room on the walls for paintings I really like, instead of spice racks, or whatever we're supposed to have in there. I also don't feel that there are any particular things required of me in the kitchen, though every now and then my husband looks very hopeful that I might cook. There's a kitchen island but there's not a table or chairs or anything like that, and I wouldn't want them. I like to lean on the island like it's a big flat lectern, though there are a few stools for people to sit on if they want. I like to feel like I'm improvising. We've even lugged the TV onto the porch, hooked up lots of extension cords, and simulated our own drive-in movie theater. The changing light through the summer viewed from the porch is one of our favorite things.

[Laughing] Would it help your wait list ranking if you make Maine news? "Couple torched among pigs with faulty electrical hook-ups."

[Laughing] We're very attached to the pig lights on the porch. They're the last things I put away when we close the house, and when they're put up again, it indicates that summer has arrived.

[At this point the door bell rings and the longed for semi-mythical patio man arrives.]

With three residences, do you have different supplies and favorite things in each house? Do you have duplicate libraries?

Well, believe it or not, one triplicate is a grammar book [laughing]. I occasionally need to check something before I send a piece in, so I do have a copy of Harcourt Brace . . .

Standard bible?

Yes, the very standard bible. I have that everywhere. I think I probably have a book of mythology everywhere. I probably have *Grimm's Fairy Tales* everywhere too. I know I have Flannery O'Connor's *Mystery and Manners* at all three places, I know I have a collection of essays with Joan Didion's "Why I Write" in it. I think it's called *The Writer on Her Work*. It has very good essays in it. I can never tell when I'll be called upon to write something and there are certain little touchstone essays that are just so wonderful that even though I remember them pretty well, I think "Oh great, Didion would be the perfect source to look at for that." *The Great Gatsby* is in all three houses. But works of fiction tend to be one place or another in order to thwart me, because they're never where I need them. Of course with Lincoln the essential reference work would be the Atlas.

I noticed that in addition to the strings of pig lights around your porch that you have dragon flies in the first floor bath. Is there a theme?

No, I love toys and I do think they are visually exciting, and they serve the purpose of undercutting any notions I have of seriousness. So does our friends' dog, Sandy, who comes to stay for a month or so every summer. I would feel inhibited, having nothing but nice antiques. I sort of equate formality with things that are expected of me. Artists don't usually want to deal with such things; they really don't like expectations. I'm an odd mixture in that I do like things to be in their place, and I like to have comfortable chairs, but I like rugs to be as wildly patterned as possible and houseplants to be from nowhere in the region. It's my temperament: I try to undercut seriousness as much as possible. And also, I love odd little things, whether it's a series of photographs of someone I don't know, or some lamp that has a story attached to it (my lamps have quite good stories attached to them), or something absurd, like the frog pitcher that reminds me of the way Pavarotti stands when he's going for the high notes that our friends Bob and Jane gave us. There's almost nothing anywhere we live that doesn't have a story. I've always had a cluttered desk, and everything, everything, is meaningful. In fact, if I'm going someplace new, like the time Lincoln and I spent a couple of months in Rome, I take along a panoramic picture of my Maine desk because I know it'll reassure me that I can make a big mess again on a new desk and everything will be okay.

The photograph has to do for a while, because how could I immediately find fifty amusing things in Rome to make an instant landslide? As a joke, once, I went out and bought lots of vegetables and draped my Missoni scarf over a corner of Lincoln's drafting table and had an instant still life set up for him to paint when he came back.

Does the clutter calm you or does it play a role in your writing?

When I'm writing, I find that when I can't see the details of what I'm writing about distinctly any more, it helps if I can actually move my eyes to something real, something I can appropriate. If it's right in front of me, it'll do for the moment. The writing may be revised—the artichoke might disappear—but in the moment, it will keep me going. At some point, if things are distinct but become too disembodied, it's helpful just to be able to look at the simplest thing—a little vase or a framed photograph or something like that; they're "grab things" and they're the little life rafts that keep the story afloat. More often than not, they stay in the final version.

Do you advise your students to keep clutter or just tell them about "grab things"?

I do try to indicate to them the point at which I start to feel either that things are too vague, or that I've become too myopic as a reader. That's usually the result of the writer keeping the external world too much at bay. In other words, there need to be little moments of chaos: those erratic little intrusions you always experience when you least want to in real life. What I try to do is get them to avoid writing things that are hermetically sealed; to find places where they might open up a story with a bit of randomness or an overheard song or a flower pot that falls for no reason. The story can't really go out of control, but there has to be the possibility that it might. It's a sort of wink given by the writer to the reader that the writer knows perfectly well he or she is working within narrow parameters, but that there is a larger world. I question extreme order all the time in the fiction writers' stories. They make fun of me, of course. They'll put in one sentence, almost like they're throwing me a bone, almost as mockery: "At this point comma a bird flew by the window." I'm made much fun of for saying, "No bird ever flies past the window? The character has looked toward the window three times. What has the character seen?" These are small things and they sound funny in paraphrase, but of course I'm also expressing my philosophy of the story. If the unexpected starts to intrude in the lives of the characters, too, the uncontainability of life tends to make the story more convincing.

Did you get such practical advice from your teachers?

I did get very astute marginal notes from J. D. O'Hara, who taught at the University of Connecticut, though he wasn't my teacher. I was scared to take a class with him. I'd be even more scared this many years later. Frank Turaj, who taught me in undergraduate school, persuaded me very subtly to learn to read, and J. D. O'Hara was invaluable in letting me know what I might aspire to as a writer. His notes were absolutely wonderful because I could look at them privately, I could look at them in my own time, I could understand without embarrassment, especially after I began to catch on to what his way of reading was and what he was looking for. I admired it, and he really taught me a lot.

How did he get a hold of your stories? I'm picturing him skulking about saying, "Give me that story. . . ."

Almost true. He stopped me in the hallway one day and said that he understood I was a short story writer. I was a graduate student—B minus all the way—but another student had told him my real love was writing stories. He said he'd be curious to see what I wrote. So I gave him a story and he crossed out lines, asked questions, put the story back in my mailbox, and then I gave him another story and he did the same thing, and finally we had a real editor/writer relationship going. It was incredibly kind of him. I try to remember that, not so much when I'm teaching (though probably my students wish I would remember), but those times I might be able to do a young writer a favor.

I know you were doing doctoral work in literature when you broke through as a writer. Do you believe going to a Writing Program benefits aspiring writers?

Look at the numbers of MFA programs these days. You're talking to somebody who avoids the expectations she feels people have of her in her own living room. There are so many of these programs now, and there's no going back. Of course there are good things about them and there are bad things about them. If I'd known I wanted to spend my life writing, I wonder if it would've occurred to me to go to a Creative Writing Program. I'll never know, because it wasn't at all clear to me (and that's no reflection on my students it is clear to), that I was going to find writing stories so endlessly interesting. I wasn't thinking about specializing in that way; I was thinking about what period of literature I might specialize in. I was also avoiding work. I'm really glad I had all that reading time. Maybe it would have been better if I'd been part of a writing program, but I was lucky enough to do okay being lost. Now, an immoderate number of people are rushing into MFA programs. It's obvious that it's an industry that is sustaining and perpetuating itself. A

few years ago when I met Patricia Hampl in Prague she made an extremely good point. She said something like, "Because the regular curriculum is so theory-driven, students who want to study literature have started going into Creative Writing because you're still reading the book at hand; you're still talking about formal concerns about how that book was put together." I hadn't gone back to teaching at that point and I was surprised by the information.

My biggest frustration with your reviewers has been how often they miss your comedy or balk—or almost disapprove—at the overwhelming ironies you capture. Forget appreciation for how your sentences pop or the stunning emphasis of the finales. What do you do with student writers to help them get irony, humor, emphasis?

Even though they're writers, I work with them almost continually as readers. There are good things and bad things about going to readings, but writers who are good readers of their work do help students understand not only what they're hearing, but by extension, how that keen hearing can lead to good writing. I can remember some audiences, years ago, who were rather hostile to Donald Barthelme's stories. Once they heard his delivery, though, once they got the tone, they felt relief, and they were rolling in the aisles. And believe it or not, even after constant exposure, not everyone understands Raymond Carver's tone. At first, many people had a tin ear for Carver; they had no idea that within these very serious stories there were hilarious, deliberately irreverent moments. And there were. They got it when Carver read, too. So, in some ways you want them to hear their own voices, but you also hope they'll hear echoes of other voices worth admiring. It's fine if they want to sit in their room and read their own stories out loud, but they also have to develop that ability to hear when they've done it right and when they've done it wrong. In general, beginning writers are rather afraid of humor, because it's potentially so unmanageable and also sometimes so unrecognizable, even to them.

I think very often when students read a confusing line they do notice that it's different than other lines, off-kilter, but humor isn't the first thing they think of. They fear the writer has made a faux pas. A student will say, "Wait a minute, this is really weird, why does the character say something so dumb?" It's okay to ask the question, but asking also takes you farther away from the spontaneous, instinctive response the writer means to elicit. Don't overlook the obvious. The writer wrote a deliberately silly sentence so you'd laugh. The writer did it because writing good dialogue gets boring. Or because he knew his girlfriend would like it that she got the joke. It's as simple as that.

So, maybe part of the solution is Jon Stewart needs to start a reading club to teach reading. Forget Oprah.

Oh, that would be great! Jon Stewart has an automatic advantage in that it's visual and he can give you a sidelong look, or he can put his head in his hands, or he can roll his eyes and express emotion without relying on words. He shows a clip of something inherently absurd, he lets just the right amount of time transpire, then he communicates with expression, rather than with words. But that's not analogous to how people read, unless you train them to read that way: "Wait a minute, pause after that paragraph, be Jon Stewart after you've read that paragraph and then you might be on the track of what the writer is trying to do."

So, maybe the handbooks that accompany literature anthologies should provide stage directions instead of fact-based questions about the story. Or The Daily Show *could produce handbooks for literature.*

Yes. I'm sure Jon Stewart's questions to go with a story would only enlarge the story. So often the questions developed for stories are terribly reductive and absolutely unanswerable—even by the author. I actually think it would be a great idea to have philosophers and your mechanic writing the questions.

Sometimes you can get quite far into a discussion about a story before you realize they haven't understood something on a very basic level. Or if something's a satire and based on something else. I'm guilty of it, myself. I just tend to teach things that I do get. One of the funniest teaching stories I have happened when I taught a story by Frederick Barthelme that I really like called "Box Step." I was not communicating with the students very well, I could tell. The problem finally occurred to me. I looked at these young kids and said, "You know what the box step is, right?" They shook their heads no, so I sprang up from my chair and said, "Here's the box step." I finished, and they continued to stare at me—at least, those who weren't looking at the floor. I said, "It's the first step they teach you so you could move around the floor even if you didn't know the tango." I did a very mechanical box step again, bringing my feet together in a sort of militaristic way, and I said, "That's the box step." There was complete silence. Of course they were humiliated for me, that I had done this odd dance twice. Finally somebody raised his hand and asked, "Professor, where would someone do this?"

I guess if nothing else, if I go in there and inadvertently show them I'm just a person in her own little world, it makes for a livelier connection to the work.

I fell into despair years back when I noticed they'd felt the need to gloss maître'd in "Babylon Revisited." I was lamenting this at a conference and in perfect English a French scholar said, "It really is *over for you people, isn't it?"*

Any secrets on teaching complexity and nuance?

One thing that I had my graduate students do that I thought was helpful had to do with noticing the careful level at which an excellent story is crafted. I went through an Alice Munro story myself, and I footnoted and cross-referenced it and pointed out every allusion I got. This was Munro at her best, so of course everything was loaded and about to explode. I wrote longhand, because I was lying on my sofa and so many hours were required. My minimum notes came to about fifty-five pages. Then I had the students read what I'd written, read my footnotes, then later I had them footnote their own work. Not to show the class, but to show me. I wanted them to also account for why every single word was in their story. Their stories got to be a lot more carefully written. The danger, of course, is that when everything's in close-up, a story can come to seem very schematic, too perfect, in a way. But as an exercise, I thought it would be interesting. Then I brought in some footnotes I'd made of a story I hadn't yet distributed that I thought was pretty obscure, and said "Here are my footnotes. Read them, and when you're through, tell me what you think the story is." They considered all the cultural references, all the allusions, everything I managed to mention, and had a fine time spinning their wheels about what they thought the story was. And also, don't think I didn't learn something about that Alice Munro story, even though I'd read it several times before and thought I understood everything about it. I'd realize that a footnote on page twenty was inadequate, because by page thirty it was a much more complicated matter. So I would have to go back to re-footnote page twenty. This was my idea of great fun. It has been suggested that I take up computer solitaire.

I've heard you read your own stories (and they can be bought through Audible.com and Amazon.com). Do you think there will come a time when no one much wants to actually read words on the page, preferring to have the author and others just read to them through ipods? What will be lost?

I think people will always want to open books because it's like the excitement of opening a package. And what you find inside, with a book, is present after present. Also, people like an excuse to hunch their shoulders and slip low in chairs and be elsewhere. Always elsewhere.

A friend of mine suggested that I not ask you the traditional question, what is your biggest regret or to name the thing you'd do differently, but instead, ask you the question, what's the thing you think you did right?

I think my perseverance was one of the biggest factors. I was young, and I didn't realize that I was persevering; I was just doing something I was compelled to do, and fascinated by. I guess writing a lot and also hanging in there was the thing I did right. Other things were out of my control. They're largely out of everyone's control, like whether the *New Yorker* will accept a story or not. They might or might not have ever accepted my work. I kept at it. I figured out a lot of stuff when I was making the transition from reader to writer—not to say that I didn't have very, very good feedback from friends, which helped enormously. But I don't think there's any substitute for teaching yourself something.

What projects are in the works now?

I'm writing an introduction to a book of my husband's paintings: *Lincoln Perry's Charlottesville.* It should be out by Christmas.

[At this point Lincoln Perry returns from the backyard and asks Ann to join him and the patio man.]

Is there anything you had hoped I'd ask before we end? I got a great price on my patio in Orlando. I know you've been waiting for this encounter for some time so I don't want to hold you up.

Come with me and tell him about your bargain price and prompt service. Take a picture of him, too, so we'll recognize him if he ever comes back.

FURTHER READING

Criticism

Gairaud Ruiz, Hilda. "The Fragmentation of Style in Ann Beattie's *Picturing Will.*" *Káñina* 29, no. 2 (July-December 2005): 273-84.

Describes *Picturing Will* as a more complex narrative than Beattie's previous works.

Gordic-Petkovic, Vladislava. "The Single Girl and the City: Gender Issues and Role Models." In *History, Politics, Identity: Reading Literature in a Changing World,* edited by Marija Knezevic and Aleksandra Nikcevic-Batricevic, pp. 135-41. Newcastle upon Tyne, England: Cambridge Scholars, 2008.

Examines Beattie's short stories and her treatments of women living in urban environments, comparing Beattie's characters to those in the television shows *Ally McBeal* and *Sex and the City.*

Rifkind, Donna. "In a Generation's Wake." *Washington Post* (19 June 2005): http://www.washingtonpost.com/wp-dyn/content/article/2005/06/16/AR2005061601192.html.

Mixed review of *Follies.*

Additional coverage of Beattie's life and career is contained in the following sources published by Gale: *American Writers Supplement,* **Vol. 5;** *Beacham's Encyclopedia of Popular Fiction: Biography & Resources,* **Vol. 1;** *Bestsellers,* **Vol. 90:2;** *Concise Major 21st-Century Writers,* **Ed. 1;** *Contemporary Authors,* **Vols. 81-84;** *Contemporary Authors New Revision Series,* **Vols. 53, 73, 128;** *Contemporary Literary Criticism,* **Vols. 8, 13, 18, 40, 63, 146;** *Contemporary Novelists,* **Eds. 4, 5, 6, 7;** *Contemporary Popular Writers; Dictionary of Literary Biography,* **Vols. 218, 278;** *Dictionary of Literary Biography Yearbook,* **1982;** *DISCovering Authors Modules: Novelists* **and** *Popular Fiction and Genre Authors;* *DISCovering Authors 3.0; Encyclopedia of World Literature in the 20th Century,* **Ed. 3;** *Literature Resource Center; Major 20th-Century Writers,* **Eds. 1, 2;** *Major 21st-Century Writers,* **(eBook) 2005;** *Modern American Literature,* **Ed. 5;** *Reference Guide to American Literature,* **Ed. 4;** *Reference Guide to Short Fiction,* **Ed. 2;** *Short Stories for Students,* **Vol. 9;** *Short Story Criticism,* **Vol. 11; and** *Twayne's United States Authors.*

Fred Chappell
1936-

(Full name Fred Davis Chappell) American short story writer, novelist, and poet.

The following entry presents an overview of Chappell's career through 2007. For further information on his life and works, see *CLC*, Volumes 40, 78, and 162.

INTRODUCTION

Known for writing in the Southern Gothic tradition, Chappell draws heavily on influences such as Edgar Allan Poe and has been compared to William Faulkner. Over his career he has experimented with different stylistic techniques, adapting classical elements to modern styles, and is widely recognized for illuminating the nature of simple farm life through complex academic writing.

BIOGRAPHICAL INFORMATION

Chappell was born on May 28, 1936, in Canton, a town along the Pigeon River in the mountains of Western North Carolina. He earned B.A. and M.A. degrees at Duke University and has taught advanced composition, poetry, and fiction at the University of North Carolina, Greensborough, since 1964. He has written three short story collections, eight novels, and more than a dozen books of verse. In December 1997, Chappell was appointed North Carolina's first poet laureate. He has received many awards, including the North Carolina Award for Literature (1980), the Bollingen Prize in Poetry (1985), the T. S. Eliot Prize of the Ingersoll Foundation (1993), and the Aiken Taylor Award for Modern American Poetry (1996). His novel *Dagon* (1968) was awarded the Best Foreign Book Prize from the Academie Française in 1972. Chappell lives with his wife, Susan, in Greensborough, North Carolina; their son, Heath, is a jazz drummer in Chicago.

MAJOR WORKS

Although Chappell maintains that poetry is his first passion, he published three novels before his first poetry collection. His publishing career began the year before he finished his master's degree at Duke, with the novel *It Is Time, Lord* (1963), which drew on his experiences in the rural American South. *It Is Time, Lord,* which takes place in the 1940s, is frequently cited by critics as a modern example of Gothic fiction and remains a source of comparisons between Chappell and Edgar Allan Poe. Like Poe's "Man of the Crowd" and Nathaniel Hawthorne's "Wakefield," Chappell's story features a narrator, James Christopher, who is a liar—to the reader and to himself—and who has a relationship with time and memory that is thorny at best. Christopher, entering his thirties, has quit his job at a college press to write a novel. He struggles with the guilt of having burned down his grandfather's house when he was nine and is burdened by his father, who has resigned himself to and grown weary of his son's shortcomings. Christopher plunges headlong into a midlife crisis, commenting, "My memory of former days is a wound which can in a moment make itself known by uncorking a rotten stink" (95). Christopher adopts a drinking buddy, Preacher, who is mistaken for Christopher and killed by the husband of Christopher's lover, Judy. When Judy blames Christopher for Preacher's death, he feels no guilt but instead a cathartic unburdening which he equates to burning down "a house with all of the bad things in the world in it"—an existential redemption that brings closure to his childhood guilt.

Chappell's third novel, *Dagon,* also features a protagonist who attempts to distance himself from his family and his past, much to his own detriment. While it contains recognizable Gothic settings and themes, *Dagon* also includes elements of mysticism and horror associated with H. P. Lovecraft, Algernon Blackwood, and Poe. While using Lovecraft's fictional mythology as a source, Chappell weaves in actual historical sources along with abundant symbolism, making *Dagon* his most ambitious and difficult novel. The story presents a Methodist preacher, Peter Leland, who inherits his grandparents' house in the mountains of western North Carolina and immerses himself in the study of a form of ancient pagan worship that he is convinced still exists, hidden in the mountain landscape. When he meets Mina, a woman whose family has inhabited the area for generations, he becomes obsessed, gradually falls under her spell, and ultimately murders his wife, Sheila. Leland loses more and more of himself to Mina and finally offers himself as a sacrifice to the pagan god Dagon. Although in this novel Chappell relies on many of the same themes and settings of his previous work, *Dagon* represents a departure in terms of its conceptual nature and disparate source material. While his previous two novels were written in six-week intervals, he reportedly worked on *Dagon* for three years and vacillated over whether he considered the book a success or a failure.

Beginning in 1985 with *I Am One of You Forever,* Chappell embarked on a series of semi-autobiographical works that explore in depth his Appalachian roots and the history of the region from shortly before his birth through the 1940s. Relayed through the perspective and experiences of Jess Kirkman from childhood to his adult life as a writer and professor, the series is considered a masterful depiction of Appalachian life and is generally described as Chappell's best work. In each of the titles, Jess reveals more of his family's history: *I Am One of You Forever* introduces the Kirkman clan through a series of Jess's childhood memories; *Brighten the Corner Where You Are* (1989) recounts Jess's father's conflict with the school board when he teaches evolution to his high-school students; *Farewell, I'm Bound to Leave You* (1996) features folklore passed down to Jess by his mother and grandmother; and *Look Back All the Green Valley* (1999) follows Jess as his mother's illness prompts him to return to the family homestead.

Chappell's long poem *Midquest* (1981), for which he was awarded the Bollingen Prize in Poetry, was originally published as four separate volumes—*River* (1975), *Bloodfire* (1978), *Wind Mountain* (1979), and *Earthsleep* (1980)—though conceived from the start as a single work. The semi-autobiographical poem draws again on the theme of memory as the narrator, Ole Fred, looks back and takes stock of his life on the occasion of his thirty-fifth birthday. Ole Fred was brought up on a farm but abandoned rural life for an intellectual, urban existence. While many critics have read these roles as oppositional or in conflict, the poems in *Midquest* suggest that they work in tandem, one informing the other. Structurally and thematically similar to Dante's *Divine Comedy,* the poem allows itself forays into different styles and strategies without losing its larger structure. Also, with its allusions to Dante and also Virgil, *Midquest* shows that Chappell understands both worlds, allowing him to cover more poetic ground without becoming mired in nostalgia. The poetry collection *Family Gathering* (2000) includes short, rhyming, light verse that considers the idiosyncrasies and closeted skeletons typical of extended families. The poems in this volume are bookended by pieces about eight-year-old Elizabeth. The first, "Elizabeth Retreats," finds her dancing on the porch, avoiding the adult conversation of the family

inside the house and looking out at the darkness beyond the porch. The other poems in the collection examine the difficulties of the family dynamic, often using humor to illustrate the problems that people frequently bring upon themselves. The final poem returns to the setting of the first: "Elizabeth in the Porch Swing" concludes, "at this stage / When all that's good is past or yet to come," and is reminiscent of Phoebe Caulfield in J. D. Salinger's *The Catcher in the Rye* reaching for the carousel's brass ring. Chappell's most recent short story collection, *Ancestors and Others* (2009), brings together several different genres, including Southern Gothic, science fiction, satire, fable, and metanarrative essay, while his latest poetry collection, *Shadow Box* (2009), experiments with structure, presenting poems within poems and a variety of styles to demonstrate his ongoing interest in innovation.

CRITICAL RECEPTION

From his first published work, Chappell has garnered popular and critical attention and praise. He is considered by many scholars of Southern literature to be America's leading talent and is among a small number of authors described as excellent in the writing of both prose and poetry. While his earlier publications do not reveal the penchant for fantasy demonstrated in his later poetry and stories, they do show real concern for and interest in the metaphysical. Over his career, Chappell has enamored critics with his use of allusions, references to classicism, and ongoing experimentation, and scholarly assessments of his work often identify a spiritual vision. One flat note in his oeuvre, *Dagon,* was so far afield from Chappell's other works and those of his contemporaries that it was resoundingly rejected by critics, readers, and even the author himself, who declared it a failure. However, in recent years, scholars have reconsidered *Dagon* and, while still acknowledging its significant flaws, have found its symbolism to be a component worthy of further exploration. In contrast, much attention has been paid to Chappell's Kirkman Family tetralogy, often described as his best work and praised for the author's enigmatic depiction of the region of his birth. Chappell's development of the character of Jess Kirkman is viewed as having provided the author with an opportunity for exploration of some autobiographical elements as well as a challenge worthy of his considerable skills.

PRINCIPAL WORKS

It Is Time, Lord (novel) 1963
The Inkling (novel) 1965

Dagon (novel) 1968
The World between the Eyes (poetry) 1971
The Gaudy Place (novel) 1973
River (poetry) 1975
Bloodfire (poetry) 1978
Wind Mountain (poetry) 1979
Earthsleep (poetry) 1980
Moments of Light (short stories) 1980
*Midquest (poetry) 1981
Castle Tzingal (poetry) 1984
†*I Am One of You Forever* (novel) 1985
Source (poetry) 1985
The Fred Chappell Reader [edited by Dabney Stuart]
    (poetry, novels, and short stories) 1987
†*Brighten the Corner Where You Are* (novel) 1989
First and Last Words: Poems (poetry) 1989
More Shapes Than One (short stories) 1991
C: Poems (poetry) 1993
Plow Naked: Selected Writings on Poetry (essays) 1993
Spring Garden: New and Selected Poems (poetry) 1995
†*Farewell, I'm Bound to Leave You* (short stories) 1996
*Way of Happening: Observations of Contemporary Po-
    etry* (essays) 1998
†*Look Back All the Green Valley* (novel) 1999
Family Gathering (poetry) 2000
Backsass (poetry) 2004
Ancestors and Others: New and Selected Stories (short
    stories) 2009
Shadow Box (poetry) 2009

*This volume contains the previously published collections *River, Blood-
fire, Wind Mountain,* and *Earthsleep.*

†These novels make up the "Kirkman Family" tetralogy.

CRITICISM

R. H. W. Dillard (essay date 1973)

SOURCE: Dillard, R. H. W. "Letters from a Distant Lover: The Novels of Fred Chappell." In *More Lights than One: On the Fiction of Fred Chappell,* edited by Patrick Bizzaro, pp. 6-26. Baton Rouge: Louisiana State University Press, 2004.

[*In the following essay, originally published in the* Hollins Critic *in 1973, Dillard presents an introduction to the first four novels by Chappell, who was a little-known author at that time.*]

This essay was written for and published by the *Hollins Critic* in 1973. It was the first critical essay to consider Fred Chappell's first four novels as a whole,

as a body of work by a new, relatively unknown American writer of substance and promise. It was intended to be an introduction to those novels, for readers who might not know them, rather than a definitive reading of them. Looking over it twenty-seven years later, I realized that any attempt to revise it and its tentative conclusions for this volume would be a disservice to its young, relatively unknown author, a person with whom I feel a close kinship but with whom I identify in only the least substantial ways. Therefore, I offer it here with only a few housekeeping changes—a bit of dust flicked away here, a bibelot moved slightly there.

I have added a postscript, written in 2000, one that looks back upon the essay, makes an additional confession or two, and goes on to make a couple of observations about Chappell's second set of four novels and their poetic mirror image, the four-volume poem *Midquest* (1981), as well.

[I. 1973]

Consider Fred Chappell.

(As he considers the world.)

In the last decade, Fred Chappell has written four novels, a book of poems, and a number of uncollected short stories. In France, like his predecessors Poe and Faulkner, he is a critical and popular success, a best seller. In this country, his novels have been praised by such varied readers as Wright Morris, Granville Hicks, and the Prescotts (Orville and Peter). William Blackburn, when asked who was the best writer among the students he had taught at Duke University (they included Mac Hyman, William Styron, Reynolds Price, and Anne Tyler) answered without qualification, "Fred Chappell. He's the best of them all."

The best of them all, and possibly the one we know the least.

The reasons for his audience in this country's not being larger are not hard to find. In the first place, he is a southerner, and his novels are set in the mountains of North Carolina. The phrase "Southern Gothic" has all too easily been attached to his work, and that phrase has automatically excluded him from much of the audience he deserves—readers who savor the wonders and complexities of Barth, Coover, or Hawkes. Even the dust jacket of his new novel *The Gaudy Place* will only allow that his works "have earned him the reputation of being one of the most gifted of the younger North Carolina writers."

And not only is he southern, but he is Gothic. The landscape of his fiction is often frighteningly ugly, and it is peopled with grotesques—with grotesques and with ordinary people awash in the flesh, drowning in its pains, suffocating in an absence of spirit. It is a world which, at least at first acquaintance, is as barren and deadly as Lovecraft's Arkham or Kafka's castled K-land. Or, if it is not barren, its very fecundity can be deadly. When Peter Leland, in **Dagon,** first visits the Morgans' house tucked away like a hidden sin on the land of his inheritance, he comes face to face with this nightmarishly living world:

> He entered. At first he couldn't breathe. The air was hot and viscous; it seemed to cling to his hair and his skin. The black wood range was fired and three or four kettles and pans sat on it, steaming away industriously. The ceiling was low, spotted with grease, and all the heat lay like a blanket about his head. The floor was bare, laid with cracked boards, and through the spaces between them he could see the ground beneath the house. There was a small uncertain-looking table before the window on his right, and from the oilcloth which covered it large patches of the red-and-white pattern were rubbed away, showing a dull clay color. From the ceiling hung two streamers of brown flypaper which seemed to be perfectly useless; the snot-sized creatures crawled about everywhere; in an instant his hands and arms were covered with them. And through the steamy smell of whatever unimaginable sort of meal was cooking, the real odor of the house came: not sharp but heavy, a heated odor, oily, distinctly bearing in it something fishlike, sweetly bad-smelling; he had the quick impression of dark vegetation of immense luxuriance blooming and momentarily rotting away; it was the smell of rank incredibly rich semen.

No wonder a reader might hesitate before willingly entering such a place.

But, of course, his being southern and Gothic are not the whole answer. Styron, Price, and Dickey—not to mention O'Connor, McCullers, and Capote, have made the southern grotesque quite acceptable and even profitable. The difference between the work of these familiar Southern Gothic writers and that of Fred Chappell is that, despite the clarity and ease of his prose, Chappell is a difficult writer—a consciously, uncompromisingly, and originally difficult writer. He is what used to be known as an "experimental" writer, a writer deeply and intensely involved with the complexity of his vision who writes fiction that demands of its reader an imaginative commitment of an equivalent depth and intensity. Like Alain Robbe-Grillet or John Hawkes or Borges or Nabokov, Chappell demands of his reader that he "read the page, every page, as hard as if it were a letter from a distant, and reticent, lover. Which is, in a way, exactly what a page from a novel is."

The difficulty of Chappell's fiction is further compounded by the nature of his perception. The sources of his understanding are not psychological or social like those of Thomas Wolfe or Styron. They are, rather, philosophical. In the early 1920s, Wolfe complained to his notebook that North Carolina seemed incapable of producing any genuine thought. "Can there be," he asked, "any advanced intellectual life where a condition exists, where people look furtively about before even arguing the existence of truths which have been known and accepted for over half a century?" And so Wolfe, logically enough, set out to devour the whole of the vast world of impenetrable fact that his upbringing seemed to deny him. Fred Chappell's is a new generation, however, one raised on science fiction, to whom the galaxy seems and feels as real and immediate as the stonecutter's lot down the street or the whores at the foot of the hill. His is a generation ready for and at ease with ideas and no longer able to write a fiction which is unaware of the vast curve of space or the lawless variety of subatomic matter, even though it may be focused on the conversation in the room or the mysterious events next door. (How many of Chappell's generation, I wonder, came to Kafka not as adult readers or as students in a classroom but in the pages of Ray Bradbury's *Timeless Stories for Today and Tomorrow?*)

"I've written two novels which are philosophical novels," Chappell told John Graham in a 1970 interview. "They're not easy to read. None of my books are easy to read. But what I try to do . . . is let the philosophical structure stand behind the novel, and the drama that the philosophical notions generate just takes place in it. And if you follow the story perhaps the system would be intimated to you. But if you don't ever get the system, the story may just appear to be nonsense."

Consider, then, Fred Chappell.

(Southern, Gothic, difficult, philosophical.)

Edgar Allan Poe, who was also southern and Gothic and difficult and philosophical, whose work has often seemed "to be nonsense," felt the need to assure his readers in the preface to the 1840 edition of *Tales of the Grotesque and Arabesque* that his work was not of the school of German "pseudo-horror" that was popular at the time. Instead, he wrote, "If in many of my productions terror has been the thesis, I maintain that terror is not of Germany, but of the soul,—that I have deduced this terror only from its legitimate sources, and urged it only to its legitimate results." Like Poe, Fred Chappell has deduced his terrors from their legitimate sources; they are not of the South but of the soul, the mind, and the heart. If his pages are, as he says, letters from a distant and reticent lover, then I should like this essay to be read as a hesitant, uncertain but enthusiastic and excited reply.

1

> Herr: est ist Zeit. Der Sommer war sehr gross.
> —RAINER MARIA RILKE

James Christopher, the narrator of Fred Chappell's first novel *It Is Time, Lord* (1963), is a familiar figure in modern (and romantic) literature. He has just entered his thirtieth year, and he has come to a halt. He has resigned his job with the local university press, and he has settled into a life of surrender. He drinks; he rereads the books of his youth; he examines the universe for signs and portents; he gives in to sin and despair. Like Melville's Bartleby, he has reached a point of preferring not to do anything active or positive. The sole code of behavior that he attempts to live by and to understand is the army Code of Conduct, which does not seem to apply to him, since it states that "I will never surrender of my own free will." He is sporadically writing his story ("I was born May 23, 1931, in the house of my grandmother"), while at the same time recognizing that "There is no story to tell, there is only a story to look for." James Christopher is a prisoner of life, like Bellow's dangling man or Mailer's nameless watcher on the Barbary shore, "obliged to live waiting for the signs which tell me I must move on again."

It Is Time, Lord is not, however, just another existential tale of entropic decline, for James Christopher is a great deal more than he seems to be. For one thing, he is a liar, to himself, to those around him, and to the reader. His life story moves along for three chapters with few surprises, handsomely composed, meditative, intelligent; the third chapter is a sermon concluding, "Do not love your neighbor as yourself; love him as your brother. One loves oneself too dangerously." But, then, in the fourth chapter, James Christopher's sister finds the manuscript of those chapters and asks him, "The story of your life?"

"No," he tells her, "The way that thing turns out, I'm a Methodist preacher."

"It's not your life then?" she says, and he replies, "I don't think so." And what are we to think? We are forced to think, to unravel fact and fancy, and to see with great clarity the inextricable complicity of truth with the lie, and of the lie with truth. "What is paramount here," Christopher the preacher tells us, "is

that I am by nature blind to a greater part of the world about; I am sealed away from the most of my life. This is an invaginate existence: much too dull to think about for its own value." The liar tells the truth; Christopher has become blind to most of his life. But the truth-teller cannot see the truth of his telling; at least not yet.

Christopher's clouded perception sees his thirtieth summer as the beginning of a draining autumn (even as a child in the dead cold of winter, he dreamed not of summer but of the fall). The last stanza of Rilke's "Herbsttag" defines the tone of Christopher's stalled thought and life (the translation is Annie Dillard's):

> Who now has no house, never will build one.
> Who now is alone, alone will remain,
> and will wake, read, write long letters,
> and wander the roadsides, up and down,
> restless, while all the leaves rain.

James Christopher is homeless, having rejected his home even as he lives in it, and he is alone even when he is with his wife and children because of that same act of rejection: waking, reading, writing, wandering, and without rest. "It is time, Lord," he cries out in the foul rag-and-bone shop of his heart.

But James Christopher is more than one man. He was born under the sign of Gemini, the twins (as he carefully does not remind us, even as he discusses the sign), and the preacher James Christopher tells us in his sermon that "I do not trust my friendly Doppelgänger who ranges my dreams and daydreams." Just as the liar and the truth-teller live together in the same phrase, so James Christopher the false preacher and prisoner of life shares the same identity with James Christopher the true Christ-bearer and free man. It is this inner man who as a boy wrote the vast epic poem about the Ironbird, "a long, unrhymed, non-metrical poem about a bird whose wings were door hinges, whose brain was an abacus, whose tail was a poker hand of cards. This bird flew around the world twice daily. It could see into the far past and the far future, prophesying in unintelligible language. It preached against the horrible sin of cannibalism." It is the prisoner who later loses the poem. And it was the prisoner, even in the boy James, who decided to commit suicide at the age of twelve, his blood draining away like that of Petronius while he lay reading great literature, just as it was the living James who did not commit suicide because he became so interested in *The Hunchback of Notre Dame* with which his double chose to die.

If Rilke's poem dominates the world of the prisoner, H. G. Wells's *When the Sleeper Wakes* stands as an emblem of the other James's nature, struggling to awake from the cannibalistic autumn dream of his double. The prisoner, in his guise as preacher, advises James that the past is not unchanging:

> It grows up soon with weeds and underbrush like a dangerous trail. It sours and rots like old meat in the mind. It is a huge sea with titanic currents—like any sea. And he who fishes it must use a golden hook, he must plunge himself as bait into its depths, and if his past does not destroy and devour him wholly, his luck is insuperable. The self is the golden hook which is too valuable to cast into former days; no line is strong enough to hold it to the present and to the hope of futurity once the cast is made.

But James Christopher makes the cast into that mutable past, and instead of losing himself, he awakens the sleeper in his heart. By descending into the sea of sin and betrayal and the darkness of himself, by losing hope and gaining vision, James Christopher learns the lessons of the day and finds the summer of his life. By accepting the blame for burning down his grandfather's house (and we never really know if he did it, or whether the mysterious and devilish red-haired man whom he had previously blamed really did), he learns the lesson of forgiveness, the healing and regenerative lie, the truth beyond all lies. He regains his home and his loving wife by betraying them and redeeming his own betrayal. He learns to love his neighbor only after he is able to forgive (and love) himself. His no-good drinking buddy (who is named Preacher, appropriately and ironically) is killed for James's sins, and he gains from that death and his own betrayals and recoveries a set of three recurring dreams (not nightmares) in which he is able to enact his fall and redemption again and again. In the last of them he finds the sleeping giant of himself, and he struggles to awaken him even as he knows "that when this cold figure wakes I myself, a figure in his dreaming, will be forever obliterated."

"I dream my dream," he says, "and swim slowly awake." And awake, he finds himself to be not a giant but a man, living again in time, not alone, not wandering, rested and waiting for his family to awake and rise. "The roof is dripping with the morning dew, a patient zodiac sprawls the sky." He has ceased to demand of himself and of life the purity of absolute truth, and he is now able, by his refusal to surrender himself or "his men" for good and all, to see the day for what it is and to live in it, summer moving into fall, fall into winter, secure in the present and the hope of futurity.

2

> Mon âme éternelle,
> Observe ton voeu

> Malgré la nuit seule
> Et le jour en feu.

> —ARTHUR RIMBAUD

It Is Time, Lord is a rich and complex novel, difficult and rewarding far beyond the outline I have suggested, but its duplicitous narrative and textual complexity seem nevertheless clear and uninvolved beside the difficulties of Chappell's second novel *The Inkling* (1965).

Like the first novel, *The Inkling* is at first glance simple enough, even familiar—the story of a small and fatherless family, a mother who is fading away in her loneliness; her brother who is the type of ordinary fallen man ("as long as Uncle Hake was around you knew the universe was still identical with the one you had always known: it had not suddenly been cleansed overnight"); her son who is nearing madness in his attempt to master his life and the world around him by the exercise of his will; and her daughter who is a mentally retarded visionary. After the introduction of an outsider—Lora, Uncle Hake's young, sexy wife—into the family, the mother dies, the boy commits adultery with his uncle's wife, the sister finds them, and the boy shoots his uncle in the heart.

Simple and familiar, that is, in the light of countless southern tales of distorted families and mad children which have followed in the strong wake of *The Sound and the Fury*. And *The Inkling* is that story, the story of a group of people who allow themselves to be cut off from the normal flow of life around them. But it is much more, for it is also the story of the awful and essential struggle within the human consciousness between will and desire, between mind's desperate need to subsume the material unto itself and flesh's equally desperate need to assert its own reality by joining that materiality utterly and without cease.

The Inkling begins and ends at one moment in time. In it, the small boy Jan and his sister Timmie are warned by a terrible yellow-haired man, are given an inkling of what is to come. But all the man says is, "Hanh, you goddam kids! . . . What if you was to die? What if you was to die one day?" They cannot see what stands before them, and their lives move into tragedy because neither of them can see the terrible and awesome fact of mortality as something integral to their own needs and desires. When the scene occurs again at the end of the book, the reader discovers what the children did not, that the yellow-haired man is Jan, that he has burst back through time propelled by the fury of his thwarted will like one of Feynman's positrons, unable "to warn them . . . to admonish this Jan, to preach to him," able only to stagger away, laughing at the joke he has discovered at the heart of his own being, the very earth ebbing and swaying beneath "his confused feet . . . as it might ebb and sway beneath the feet of a man who had been hanged."

The events of that day on fire—when the yellow-haired man of sixteen stands in the field, existing "so weightily . . . that he might have created it," the sun reflected in the plain glass of his spectacles "a tiny yellow dot, the size of the pupils of his eyes," and cries out his terrible question to his silver-haired six-year-old self—cannot be explained by the terms of the familiar tale of the southern decaying family. Nor can it really be explained by the terms of science fiction, from which it borrows the time warp that enables the confrontation to occur. A science-fiction reader might explain that the older Jan, moving in negative time, is now composed of contraterrene (or anti-) matter and that, had he touched his younger self, they would have merged in an act of collision and would have vanished completely leaving only a new ray of free energy, a day even more brightly on fire. But that would not explain the nature of the two Jans' meeting nor its terrible significance.

The Inkling is not a rerun of either *The Sound and the Fury* or of Jack Williamson's *Seetee Shock*. It uses the familiar ground of the Southern Gothic just as it uses the metaphorical freedom of science fiction to give imaginative substance and aesthetic value to a philosophical examination of the awful and awesome tension in the human mind and flesh between will and desire and of the terrible consequences for us all if that tension is not resolved in understanding.

Jan Anderson is a boy who looks hard at the world and attempts to master it with the force of his stare. He stares down the family cat Buddha and then kills it with a stone. Having mastered the animate and sentient, he turns to that inanimate and insentient weapon itself:

> The stone he took up and carried back from the field to the house and put down near the back door. It was smeared on one awkward side with blood and there were other, whitish, stains here and there upon it. It was to be a new obstacle for him to vanquish; and in time he came to know every mark, the contour of every stain, each minuscule protuberance, the vague course of every vein, each tiny pit in the texture of the surface. He squatted before it, gazing hotly, and it looked as if he might be worshiping a god in the stone. This time he managed the exercise without gathering rancor and he and the stone in the end became brothers, and Jan was satisfied that he had overcome the will of the stone without having to displace it.

Jan's sister Timmie is a creature of "unwillingly sentient desire," possessed of visions of bleeding hands and feet, the extremities of Christ's sacrifice without

the central significance. Jan attempts to protect her from reality by telling her that all evil is just "joking," not understanding that what she desires is a world of tangible reality, of bleeding good and evil available to the senses. And she, in turn, sees Jan's coming to terms with the stone as an act of worship and his acts of will as a "willing himself out of being" and therefore attempts to protect him by blunting his will, by covering his eyes with the plain glass spectacles to prevent "him from seeing clearly, or even guessing clearly, what he was to bring upon himself." Jan strives to control everything; Timmie yearns "to allow everything, to let it come down."

These two characters are enriched by a subtle web of allusions to the relationship of Rimbaud and Verlaine. Jan has Rimbaud's features, his stare, his powerful will; Timmie has Verlaine's sensuous and sensual imagination, his desperate need for physical love, his commingling of ecstasy and painful despair. As Verlaine shot Rimbaud finally, so Timmie stabs Jan in the hand. She makes him bow to her gods, phallic and obscene, and she sacrifices him to her need for an evil that cannot be explained away. Caught "under the paw of that one big tiger, his will," blinded by that will, by his sister's desire, and by the physical presence of his uncle's wife whose breasts are "sealed but observant eyes" and whose sex is "a coy sticky sidewise wink," Jan misses the admonitory signs around him, does not see (as his sister does) "how the clean path he had laid was curling back upon itself under his feet." He is caught up in the fate of his blind making, kills his uncle, and enters literally the sun-blazing world of Rimbaud's day on fire.

In the field under the sun, he waits for "things to make sense." Instead a baseball lands at his feet, contesting "his supremacy of existence" by its very fact, its simple being apart from Jan's will. He wishes to crush it, but he merely throws it away. It bounces against a tree, and Jan sees at last the joke of his life. The world simply is, like the ball and the tree. He simply is, alive in a world that one need not master but in which one is free to live, filled perhaps with will and desire but above all simply and amazingly alive.

Jan laughs and walks away; he turns "a big invisible corner of the airy light," out of negative time and into time, the world ebbing and swaying beneath his feet as beneath those of a hanged man, confused, lost perhaps in time but also possibly found at last, a burnt-out case moving in the heat of the day. "As soon as he had begun to walk he felt cooler," we were told in the first chapter of the book, and perhaps we can believe that, freed now of will and desire, alert to the cosmic joke, Jan may say, as Rimbaud did before him, "All that is past. Today I know how to greet beauty."

3

What but design of darkness to appall?

—ROBERT FROST

Fred Chappell's third novel, **Dagon** (1968), picks up strands of idea and metaphor from the first two novels and weaves them into an utterly different substance. Peter Leland, its central character, is a preacher as James Christopher dreamed of being, and like Jan he is appalled by the power of materiality, "the invalidity of his desires, how they could be so easily canceled, simply marked out, by the impersonal presence of something, a place, an object, anything vehemently and uncaringly itself." The novel is the story of a man who comes into his inheritance in his thirty-third year, a puritan inheritance of revulsion toward the living world, of surrender to the evil that he finds in the very urgings of his blood. Peter Leland is Young Goodman Brown in the modern world. Aware of sin, of the "fast deep iciness, pure recalcitrant cold" at the center of the earth, of "the fault in mankind to act without reflecting, to *do* without knowing why, to go, without knowing where," he loses his faith (and his wife, whom he kills) as fully as did Hawthorne's young puritan. He becomes increasingly passive, losing everything that he was and had, becoming finally a helpless and happy sacrifice on the idol of the mutilated god **Dagon,** the embodiment to Leland of "naked will uncontrollable."

Dagon is an elaborate texture of allusions to and parodies of the puritanical works of many of our literary forebears—Hawthorne, Melville, and especially H. P. Lovecraft, from whom the book takes its title and its central metaphor. Lovecraft was really the final and fullest expression of the dark vision of American Puritanism in our literature, a Puritanism in which God is finally not only silent but actually nonexistent. Lovecraft saw himself as a materialist, a believer in a mechanistic and meaningless universe, so vast in time and space that it reduces all human significance to nothing. But his Puritan needs asserted themselves in the creation of a "mythos" with ancient gods (among them Dagon) and future ones, dark and horrible gods who once ruled and may again rule an earth on which humans are mere passing shadows, less permanent than mayflies, smaller than motes of dust. He gave himself over in his dreams and his fiction to these dark gods, sure in his surrender that, no matter how man may strive to endure or prevail, endless time and his own unending decay will finally destroy him and leave him forgotten in the "paleogian gulfs of time."

Chappell's Peter Leland, whose name should have warned him that he was of the earth, earthy, stone and soil, a weak man whose wife pins him easily when they wrestle playfully, is a preacher who is more interested in the horror of the world (sex, money, needless productivity) than in the love of God and the promises of life. He inherits his grandfather's house and with it apparently the Morgan family, whose daughter Mina, noseless and rank as a beached fish, priestess of the cult of Dagon in the back hills of North Carolina, is an emblem of Leland's own "self-minatory" nature. Once he has seen her, he cannot "unthink her image," and he sinks into the darkness that she represents for him. He sinks into materiality because he is unable to see that he was of it from the first. He creates out of the stuff of himself a new theology of the snake; unable to bear the weight of Adam's sin, of his own progenitors' worship of Dagon, he abandons his humanity and its strength, choosing the dark source of sinful temptation itself as his totem:

> We live as serpents, sucking in the dust, sucking it up. The stuff we were formed of, and we ought to inhabit it. We ought to struggle to make ourselves secret and detestable, we should cultivate our sickness and bruise our own heads with our own heels. What's the profit in claiming to walk upright? There's no poisonous animal that walks upright, a desecration. It's better to show your true shape, always.

As he debases himself, he preserves himself. He does not reconstruct and free himself like James Christopher, nor does he see through his blindness like Jan; he merely maintains his static identity: "He had faced the incomprehensible manifestation and he still maintained himself, he was still Peter Leland." It is this sort of self-maintenance that Chappell has referred to in another context as "existential desperation." Leland dies at the hands of Mina, still himself, nothing more, nothing less (for to his own eyes, there could be nothing less).

Dagon is not, however, just a reworking of Kafka's *The Trial* in an American Puritan context. It is much closer to that sad novel's cheerful Doppelgänger, Nabokov's *Invitation to a Beheading.* Peter Leland may not find beings akin to him at the end of the novel in the way that Nabokov's Cincinnatus C. does, but he does come through death to a new mode of existence. In the concluding chapter, which alludes to and parodies Chaucer's *Troilus and Criseyde,* Leland looks back at his life and laughs "without rancor and without regret." He swims in a realm of metaphors, contemplating "with joy the unity of himself and what surrounded him," deliberating "what form his self should take now." He does not choose the serpent, but rather the fish, Leviathan: "Peter took the form of the great fish, a glowing shape some scores of light-years in length. He was filled with calm; and joyfully bellowing, he wallowed and sported upon the rich darkness that flows between the stars."

Peter Leland was his own executioner just as Nabokov's Cincinnatus C. almost was in his novel, and *Dagon,* for all its overwhelming physicality, is an interior adventure, again like that of Nabokov's novel. Peter, a self-mutilated man, dives into the depths of his consciousness; the line does not hold for him as it did for James Christopher, and he destroys his life as surely as he murdered his wife *within himself.* He chooses his own evil but finally finds the only unity available to him beyond that evil. The novel may be the account of a descent into madness, but to limit its realities to hallucinations is to deny its metaphysical implications. The human mind believes what it sees, but it also sees what it believes and shapes its world to the needs of its belief. Peter Leland's Puritan consciousness gives him literally the fallen and nightmarish world of Puritan belief. The joke is on him, and he is the unwitting joker as well.

Perhaps Peter Leland's Nabokovian namesake, "the melancholy, extravagant, wise, witty, magical, and altogether delightful Pierre Delalande," states the moral (for what Puritan book would be without a moral) of *Dagon* best in the epigraph to *Invitation to a Beheading*: "Comme un fou se croit Dieu, nous nous croyons mortels."

4

> If design govern in a thing so small.
>
> —ROBERT FROST

Of course, *Dagon* may also be read as a criticism of American society, of the dark puritanical sources of its commitment to blind productivity, but it is in Fred Chappell's new novel *The Gaudy Place* (1973) that we find the fullest rendering of society, of the social and economic levels of a small town from bottom to top, from A(rkie) to Z(ebulon Johns Mackie). The novel is a tracing of the events leading up to an act of violence, an act comic and trivial in itself but which reveals with a startling clarity the terrible patterns of human striving and knowing.

The novel is comic; its tone is far lighter than anything Chappell has written before, the prose lively and witty. Its characters are the familiar victims of vice and folly that we have come to know from centuries of comic art—Arkie, the fourteen-year-old boy who ranges tawdry Gimlet Street and his fourteen-block world looking for a good con; Clemmie, the nineteen-year-old whore tied to her life because the rest of the world seems to her "as flossy and unbelievable as a Technicolor movie"; Oxie her pimp who is rising above Gimlet Street toward politics and respectability; Linn Harper, an idealistic and intelligent seventeen-year-old boy who learns the limits of ideas and ideals by

discovering for himself "whether a code of behavior crudely extrapolated from the printed page can find an arena of action in quotidian reality"; Andrew Harper, Linn's historian father, whose "muddied perceptions and not particularly admirable life" have led him to believe in a "humanity helpless because choice is absent"; and Zebulon Johns Mackie, Andrew's uncle by marriage, a corrupt small-town political boss and businessman, an expert at urban charading, a gangster who looks like our sentimentalized image of Benjamin Franklin. Assorted characters mixed ready to begin the morning right, and their lives do mix and mingle, all of them ready, for one reason or another, to turn their backs "on this feverish gaudy place for good," all of them knowing that Gimlet Street "could take you anywhere in the world, it was joined to all the other streets there were," but none of them able to leave that gaudy place behind.

Chappell's first three novels, dark in texture, filled with physical and spiritual suffering, all have at center a faith in life, in something inexpressibly larger than the bare self in the barren world. But *The Gaudy Place,* the brightest and lightest of them all, has at its heart the deepest darkness of them all, for at the center of this exercise in cause and effect is an absence of meaning, of first cause. It is as if, in these lives, design does not govern at all.

The book takes its epigraph from Yeats: "What's right and wrong? / My grand-dad got the girl and the money." The lines are from *Purgatory,* the play that, as John Rees Moore reminds us, "goes further than any other Yeats play in the direction of unredeemed and apparently unredeemable blackness." The characters in *The Gaudy Place* all feel themselves to be at a turning place, but when the turn comes it is unexpected, and the road leads into a new and strange country quite different from anything they might have dreamed. "I don't know whether a novelist believes finally and philosophically in cause and effect," Fred Chappell admitted to John Graham. "I don't frankly philosophically believe in it. I've studied too much Erwin Schrödinger to go with that. But, in human terms, I think there is a cause and effect. In sub-atomic physics, I'm sure there isn't." In *The Gaudy Place,* this purgatory without apparent exit, the chaos of the subatomic world seems to be the metaphorical figure at the moral center of the novel.

"Anything can happen," Clemmie says when discussing a science-fiction book with a barfly named Teacher, "but I don't believe in it." But anything can and does happen, believe it or not. Arkie gets up his courage and tells his dream to Clemmie. When it begins to come true, partly because he told it, she invents a lie to tell back to Arkie. Arkie, who has come to love

Clemmie, acts upon her lie, leading Clemmie to believe that she is "on the verge of a strange and important revelation. She was going to know things that she had never known before. . . . Something big was going to take place and she was going to have a piece of it." And it does, but with consequences neither of them could imagine. Dreams feed fact; new fact gives rise to new dreams which feed new fact; the whole process careening along, a giddy nightmare of cause and effect, unpredictable and formless, the mad world of "anything can happen."

Even Linn Harper, the boy whose world is the largest in the book, whose imagination (fed by science fiction) can expand to galaxies and even to the farthest reaches of the universe, lands in jail, lured there by the very mental integrity that enables him to see so far. Science fiction has led him to physics and to the writing of Conrad, and from Conrad the path has led dangerously on to Kafka, to Sartre, and to Camus's *The Stranger*. Linn's faith in the course he has followed makes him willing to risk himself for what he believes, which happens to be a dim understanding of Meursault's gratuitous act. So he lands in jail, a place far worse than anything he had ever imagined. He begins there to see for himself a free and exhilarating future life of crime, apart from all morals, but he ends up in the grip of a dream in which his old faith in the right and the good reasserts itself, but now (and forever) mixed with "other images, unrelated, discordant and dismaying."

We consider them all, and we consider ourselves.

But there is more to the gaudy place than this random mix of blind cause and effect. We do live "upon this lonely blue planet Earth, burning like a sunny atom of dust on the farthest rim of its galaxy," and "The universe is, after all, a gaudy place in which to live." Andrew Harper, speaking of the shooting at the end of the novel, does manage to find a way of coming to terms with events:

> What happened next was at first almost incomprehensible to me—and, in fact, I do not yet understand it. That is, I cannot know the causes and mechanics of the event. But it does take a shape in my mind, it does make itself at least credible. Even at the time it occurred it must have appealed to me as a pattern, for by the time it was over I was laughing uncontrollably.

Laughing out of control, but laughing; unaware of causes and mechanics, but taking pleasure in the shape of things. Andrew Harper's laughter rings with Jan's and Peter Leland's. Oh, we learn the hard way, the hardest ways, but we learn. And we forgive. And we love. We care for these poor fools in Gimlet Street, and by that caring, we love life itself a bit more. Like Camus's Meursault, we at least come to appreciate the wonder of the gaudy place.

"The act of literature is a moral act," Fred Chappell told John Carr and John Sopko in a 1969 interview, and certainly the care and caring at the heart of *The Gaudy Place* make it a moral act. "What's right and wrong?" That we cannot ever know, because the right and the wrong are as fluid as the chaotic moment itself. But we can know the good. "I think the human spirit can surmount its materialism," Fred Chappell continued. "After all, materialism is really just an invention of the spirit. Anything we can invent we can get over. I hope." And that hope is at the source of *The Gaudy Place* as well as the earlier novels. The universe is, after all, such a grand and gaudy place in which to live.

5

A confession and one last anecdote:

I have, despite all my efforts, failed to do the novels of Fred Chappell justice, but I hope that I have managed to convey some of their values and something of their value. But perhaps this personal anecdote will at least say simply what I have been struggling to express. One of the best of our graduate students asked me not long ago which novelist of my generation (and by generation, she meant my age) did I really think she ought to read. Really read, grapple with, learn from, experience.

I could have named a great number. I did name a handful to myself; all, writers whose work I value. The list came easily, and it was an honest list. But I knew from the start that the exercise was futile, because I knew the answer all along.

"Fred Chappell," I said. "He's the best of them all."

[II. 2000]

To that concluding confession, I should like to add three others:

> 1. In the section of the essay dealing with *The Gaudy Place*, I called Zebulon John Mackie "an expert at urban charading." Since the phrase makes sense in its context (or at least I think it does), its oddness may have slipped by its readers unnoticed, but I now feel the need to confess that it is actually a reference to an even more odd mistake in one of Fred Chappell's interviews (which I alluded to obliquely a bit further down the page). The transcriber of the taped interview, not entirely familiar with Chappell's western North Carolina accent, made Fred into a student of "urban charading" rather than of the physicist Erwin Schrödinger. I confess that I could not resist the joke. Mea culpa.

> 2. Although I could not have been expected to know how important the number 4 with all of its Pythagorean solidity would become in Chappell's later work, I

confess that I should nevertheless in my discussion of *It Is Time, Lord* have made mention of James Christopher's wife's lying by him in bed at the end of the novel, "her slender legs crossed with her right ankle on her left knee, making the number 4." I remember developing a tentative theory about it, one actually based on post-Pythagorean numerology (in which that most primitive of numbers stands for steadiness and endurance—certainly appropriate to Sylvia in the novel), but I must have lost my nerve. That it may also refer to the four elements (earth, air, fire, and water), I had not a clue. Mea culpa.

3. I will also confess that I was immensely pleased to discover, in a most startling and pleasant way, that Fred Chappell approved of at least one part of my essay. In his poem, **"Burning the Frankenstein Monster: An Elegiac Letter to Richard Dillard,"** he says, "You were right, Richard, / What I mostly ripped off from Rimbaud was the notion of fire / As symbolic of tortured, transcendent-striving will." I was perhaps even more pleased by being in *Bloodfire* (1978, the second volume of *Midquest*) at all and, thus, like James Dickey, attaining immortality the easy way. For being so pleased and even worse for bragging about it here, I can only say, "Mea culpa."

I should also like to make three comments or observations having to do with Chappell's second group of four novels, the Kirkman tetralogy:

1. Once, when writing a notice of the first volume of the tetralogy, I attempted to locate or "place" the novel's unique nature by a process of what might be called literary rectangulation, i.e., a process using three fixed points rather than the usual two used in trigonometric triangulation. Since I now believe that the discovery I made using this process applies equally well to the entire tetralogy, I shall repeat it here. If one wishes to define the special flavor of these books, one would do well to draw a line stretching from Gabriel Garcia Márquez's *One Hundred Years of Solitude* (1967) to Erskine Caldwell's *Georgia Boy* (1943) to Ray Bradbury's *Dandelion Wine* (1957), closing the rectangle with Chappell's tetralogy. By examining closely the literary context formed by these books, each unique and radically different from the others, I predict that one will find at least a clue as to just what gives Chappell's novels their satisfying and unique taste. Of course, there are references and echoes and allusions to the work of many other writers in Chappell's novels, ranging from Robert A. Heinlein (in chapter 9, "Into the Unknown!" of *Look Back All the Green Valley*) to Dante, Virgil, Shakespeare, et al., but I still believe that those particular three novels I've hitched to the Kirkman tetralogy's star will give an interested reader at least a good start toward a richer understanding of Chappell's achievement.

2. I do have one bone to pick with Fred Chappell. In *The Finish Line,* the Leidig lecture that Chappell gave at Emory and Henry College on April 10, 2000, and which was published by the college the following fall, he delivers himself of an unusually tart attack on "postmodernist metafiction":

For my money, metafiction is a nasty adolescent habit one strives to outgrow—like smoking. . . . When I

depart this world and a just Deity hands out my allotted punishment, he shall set me to writing metafiction. That is a sign of his mercy, of course, for he could condemn me to an eternity of reading the stuff.

As a fully accredited (and aggrieved) writer of "postmodern metafiction," I guess that it is up to me to take on the onerous task of pointing out to Fred Chappell that the Kirkman tetralogy is, whether he likes it or not, and whether he admits it or not, a metafiction. How could it not be, with its shifting narrative strategies, cross-genre devices and references, multilayered allusions, and, of course, its playing of the significant game that "Fred Chappell" is the pseudonym used by Jess Kirkman to write his tetralogy of poems (*Midquest*)? Why else would I have put Chappell in the company of "a Barth or a Coover or a Hawkes" in my 1973 essay had it not been that his first four novels struck me as being metafictional, too? I don't know exactly why he is denying the metafictional nature of his fiction so much these days, but I have to admit that, while doing so, he sounds to me an awful lot like an adolescent farm boy caught smoking behind the barn, who protests his innocence loudly while one of his horny heels is busily grinding the still smoldering butt out in the red clay.

3. In *The Finish Line,* Fred Chappell also speaks tellingly of the Kirkman tetralogy and the four volumes of *Midquest* as a "double quartet, or octave, of books: about 1,000 pages of fiction, about 200 pages of poetry." There is no need for me here to explore the connections between the parts of that octave, a task begun so well by Richard Abowitz in Patrick Bizzaro's *Dream Garden: The Poetic Vision of Fred Chappell.* That work is now safely, I am sure, in better hands than mine. I would like, rather, to make the possibly heretical suggestion that the first four novels, the four *Midquest* volumes, and the four Kirkman novels form an even larger, twelve-volume work, a *Divina Commedia Nuova,* if you will. The connections between the first four novels and the octave are, at least to my mind, clear enough—the autobiographical echoes and parallels, for example, or the parallels among Fred Chappell, Jess Kirkman (as Abowitz pointed out, *chapel* and *churchman*), and, say, James Christopher (*Christ bearer*) in *It Is Time, Lord,* or, for that matter, Preacher in that novel and the preacher Peter Leland in *Dagon.* The connection of Chappell's work with Dante's great *Commedia* is quite explicit in both the situation and design of *Midquest* and is brought full circle in *Look Back All the Green Valley,* in which not only is Jess Kirkman translating the *Commedia,* but his quest for his father's secrets comically and significantly replicates Dante's revelatory journey. The first four novels are also to my mind sufficiently hellish to form an *Inferno*; Chappell admits in his autobiographical essay in the *Contemporary Authors Autobiography Series* that his design in the early novels "was as much to harrow the reader as to entertain him." *Midquest,* I think, could also interestingly be read as a *Purgatorio,* and the Kirkman tetralogy as a *Paradiso.* I offer this observation not as a fact, but as a speculation. I doubt that Chappell had this *Commedia Nuova* in mind all along, but then, since he is such a complicated and thoughtful and quite duplicitous artist, I also wouldn't be surprised if he did. It may just be that I see this larger pattern in

Chappell's work because I am concerned that Chappell's first four novels not be overlooked in the midst of all the quite legitimate interest in the last four; for I still believe, as I did in 1973, that they are major novels, certainly worthy of thorough and serious critical examination. To further that cause, I'll even make another and final confession: like many readers of Dante, for all my admiration of the books that make up what I've called Chappell's *Purgatorio* and *Paradiso*, I nevertheless still like his *Inferno* best.

Dabney Stuart (essay date 1997)

SOURCE: Stuart, Dabney. "Spiritual Matter in Fred Chappell's Poetry: A Prologue." In *Dream Garden: The Poetic Vision of Fred Chappell*, edited by Patrick Bizzaro, pp. 48-70. Baton Rouge: Louisiana State University Press, 1997.

[*In the following essay, Stuart examines the combination of scientific and spiritual concepts embodied in Chappell's poetry.*]

> Tanto giú cadde, che tutti argomenti
>   à la salute sua eran giá corti
> fuor che mostrarli le perdute genté.
>
> —Dante, *Purgatorio*, XXX, 136-38

Our faith must be earned from terror.

> —Fred Chappell, *Bloodfire*, IX

FLESH AND SPIRIT

The first two words of the title of this essay are a subdued version of Fred Chappell's more spritely rhymed phrase "attar of matter" (in **"Firewood"**). I intend, however, the same complementary attachment of terms. Chappell's phrase suggests, in sound as well as substance, that there is an essence embedded in matter and releasable from it—a sweet, intangible spirit inexplicably meshed in the molecular arrangement of the elemental stuff of which all things, including human and other creatures, are composed. One direction in which Chappell aims the atomistic possibilities inherent in this perspective is Lucretian. The other primary direction is not, however, subject to the contained reshuffling of atoms. Chappell is more essentially preoccupied with and hopeful of images of release and transformation, which are Christian in their orientation. The two modes of understanding are, needless to say, not always cleanly separable.

Perhaps a finer distinction is in order. The Lucretian perspective doesn't employ the complementary duality of flesh and spirit but rather transposes it into the fluid, imperceptible molecular composition of apparently solid material bodies. This, of course, was Lucretius' understanding of how the transience of individual instances of forms could be reconciled with the equally obvious recurrence, apparently eternal, of the forms themselves. Individual people die, but the human race does not; we eat this carrot today, but another grows for us to eat tomorrow; we may pulverize this stone, but stones are everywhere. Mutation and recurrence are complementary motions, rearranging the atoms out of whose coalescence particular things are made, and because of whose dispersal they disappear. But the atoms are irreducible and everlasting, as is the process of rearrangement—carried out by the forces he called Love and Strife—by which perceptible forms occur, pass away, and recur.

The interpenetration of earth, air, fire, and water is one expression of the Lucretian dispensation in *Midquest* and seems to me in no need of elaborate elucidation. The titles of the frame poems of Volumes II, III, and IV serve as sufficient indicators, as do the abundance of phrases in those same poems in which two or more of the elements cohere: "dewfired," for instance, and "Earthsmoke," "earth / with its mouths of wind," "water in stone," and "blind windcurrent of the soil." It shows more explicitly, however, in passages where Chappell uses Lucretius' terms and images. In **"Bloodfire Garden,"** it is in the fire of love that "we are / whole again, / our atoms driven and / interlocked as heat in air" (91-92). When the "untenable trombone tones" Chappell imagines riding "out upon the blue-bleached air" pops, it lets him "slide the effervescent atoms" alone (**"The Autumn Bleat of the Weathervane Trombone,"** 114-15). In the same poem, he refers to "the hail of impulse Nature keeps tossing over / Her shoulder" (115). The recurrent "coming apart to" constructions (as in "fire coming apart now to wind") extend this explicit evocation across some of the frame poems. In the world beyond the "four-square crucis of elements" in **"Earth Emergent Drifts the Fire River"** (a cold world of nothingness, which I will comment on in more detail later), "the single atoms stray / Lost and touchless" (146-47). This poem is, in fact, dotted with Lucretian infusions, perceptions more accessible because of the atomistic backdrop. As Fred wakes in the first poem of *Bloodfire,* "the seeds, ignis semina, of fire / Put forth in me their rootlets" (56).[1] *Ignis semina* is, in fact, a phrase from Lucretius, which Chappell identifies later in **"Firewood."**

"Susan Bathing" and **"Firewood"** comprise the two most probing, subtle, and thorough embodiments of the Lucretian vision in *Midquest.* They are rather miraculous poems in many ways, not least in their personal and local dimensions and in the careful psychological progression their disguised narrative lines reveal. But my space and context limit me to some brief comments on the process of atomistic transmutations that occur in **"Firewood."**

It is "Flame, flame" that Fred's ax strikes first; he imagines the fire in the hearth that the log he is splitting will eventually afford. The dimensions the language implies become more complex immediately, as he speaks of the "heart / red in the oak where sun / climbed vein by vein" (67). It's not until he tangles with the walnut log some seventy-five lines later that these implications begin to receive their fullest development. This time he sees "the life" of the blazing log, "yellow / red and orange and blue & hasting your dark gasses / starward, on the silverblue night splaying a new tree / shape, tree of spirit spread on the night wind" (69). This new tree lifted from the burning of the old one sifts "upward to the needle pricks of fire" of the constellations. The roots of the tree of fire

> sizzle in our fireplace, the
> ghostly arms of it embrace the moon, the lancet
> glance of the star pierces its leafage, this tree
> in our fireplace is the sun risen at midnight,
> capillaries of heat light lift out the chimney,
> the rose trellis of stars is afire, sun reaches
> homeward again to the *vacant interlunar spaces,*
> chimney is its shrunk trunk & pins our dwelling
> to the earth and to the stars equally, this spirit
> trunk in the chimney is the spine of the world.
>
> (69)

Chappell suggests at least a double cycle here: the sun's energy enters the tree, causes it to grow, and then, in the burning of the logs, is released again into the vastness of space where it originated; the physical form of the tree rooted in the earth is released as a tree of spirit rooted in the hearth fire and foliated among the stars. That the stars themselves are fire spreads further the impress of transformation focused in this passage. The fire, however, remains mysterious, no matter the language invented to image it, because it gives us light in which to "read" everything but itself. It is also mortal. As the fire in the hearth dwindles so does the tree of spirit rising from it: "Lucretius' / seed of fire ignis semina is seed semina mortuis / . . . of death in that same split second" (70).

Three other sorts of transformations parallel this central one. In the brief parenthetical phrase that echoes the burden of **"My Grandmother Washes Her Feet"**—*"dirt we rose from, dirt we'll never forget"* (70)—human beings rise from the ground and are rooted there, no matter the changes that transpire in any individual life. Human will, similarly, may cast "forward / into the flesh of light itself / . . . angry against the stream of time" (70-71). Perhaps the poet, too, "*can* transform all / germens with an incantatory perception of what's / what or what's supposed" (71). These palimpsest possibilities layered against the basic image of the tree of spirit follow one another in the

poem pell-mell, each growing from the other, the form enacting transformation while articulating its stages. The energy of language and prophetic will, twined together, leads Fred to a credo: it can make

> every tree that stands a *Christmas tree,* Christmas
> on Earth, though even as I recall the beautiful
> manifesto my faith flickers & dwindles, we are not
> born for the rarer destinies only for the rarest,
> we are born to enter the tree of smoke, backbone of
> the world of substance, born to smear our life stuff
> against the zodiac, & as I take down in matter
> the spine of the world & will send it up again in
> spirit a feeling that these things are so indelibly
> correct overtakes me.
>
> (71)

Part of the primary drama of this extraordinary poem consists of its entertainment. It is interesting, first of all, various and full of surprising turns, holding together voice and attention (poet's and reader's), as well as holding out alternative ways of speaking about the relationship of matter to spirit. The Lucretian focus, a naturalistic philosophy both ancient and contemporary, balances, as it were, in the middle of a spectrum.

At one end is nothingness, the terrifying possibility that a "roaming / puddle of gravitons, a winter's night the black / hole, comes this way striding & yanks the tree / of light elongate like a sunny licorice down / the drain" (70).

Fred explicitly rejects the terror of nothingness, along with the will-less condition of Nirvana (which he has earlier called "a sterile and joyless blasphemy"), in the opening poem of *Earthsleep,* indicating by their juxtaposition that the latter is a version of the former. "What there is in emptiness," he says,

> . . . let it consume itself,
> Let it mass and flounder yonder from the skin
> Of things, let it not come nigh this hearth, this hold,
> This house, let the cloud of unbeing never touch
> Our garish boxes of fervor.
>
> (146)

In the same series of refusals he seems also to include Lucretius' eternal atomistic dispersal and configuration; he mentions "another" world, "where no water sings with / Its breath of fire, where sunlight the cloud never / Ripens to peach, where the single atoms stray / Lost and touchless" (146-47). Lucretius' vision, I think, slides to the negative end of the spectrum here.[2] The double nadir of **"Susan Bathing,"** which produces abject fear in Fred, is first, that he will not be able to praise her adequately (in *River*'s **"Birthday 35,"** to have his mouth stopped is "despair") and second, that Susan will vaporize and disappear. After confronting such motions toward vacuum, Fred pushes his face "more fiercely" to Susan's breast and begins a series of allusive reprises of earlier poems that have centered on experiences of healing contact with people he loves.

It is not surprising given Fred's heritage that atomistic philosophy is insufficient, since Lucretius includes the soul among material things. A central thrust of his arguments in *De Rerum Natura* is to remove from his auditors their fear of punishment after life by arguing that the soul, like everything else, disperses into autonomous, anonymous atoms. There *was,* therefore, no hereafter to fear. This is not only too neat and reductive for a mind as probing, doubtful, and inventive as Fred Chappell's, it also dismisses too cerebrally what he has absorbed into the veins of his imagination from birth. If Lucretius had grown up with Fred's grandparents and parents, he would have rejected atomism, too. Chappell's profound disinclination also proceeds from his sensuality and, perhaps above all, from his unstaunchable love of life. In his splendid essay on Lucretius in *Three Philosophical Poets,* George Santayana observed that at the bottom of Lucretius' insistent opposition to immortality was a fear of life.[3] Santayana called this an "untenable ideal." He asserted that "What is dreaded is the defeat of a present will directed upon life and its various undertakings. . . . To introduce ascetic discipline, to bring out the irony of experience, to expose the self-contradictions of the will, would be the true means of mitigating the love of life; and if the love of life were extinguished, the fear of death, like smoke rising from that fire, would have vanished also" (53).

Fred clearly is no ascetic. He seeks everywhere to embrace life, to fire the world with his will, in the local and temporal frame of *Midquest* to celebrate his birthday, and to continue his fundamentally hopeful, Dantesque journey toward light.

At the other extreme is the Christmas tree and its extension at the end of **"Firewood"** into images of marriage, procreation, and finally, salvation. The sexual and marital similes salted into the opening page of the poem (*e.g.,* "*marriage / vow* joints," "nice girls back in high school") receive more serious resolution in such phrases as "the wedge goes in like semen" and "the river-clean smell of opened / flesh comes at me as the annunciation to Mary" (73). The latter reference also echoes the more extended annunciation passage in **"Susan Bathing."** Immediately following these focuses is Fred's assertion "I'm washed in the blood / of the sun," a variation of "blood of the Lamb" in a context suggesting, with "Christmas on Earth," a Christian salvation, an implicit answer to the parenthetical question "but where / shall I sit when once this flesh is spirit?" (73) The "flesh! more flesh" at the

heart of the riven log is analogous to the Christian incarnation and helps one understand the source of Fred's love of the earth and life on it that pervades *Midquest.* ("The flesh the earth is suits me fine" is a representative instance.) The poem following **"Firewood"** deals with a real fire, the conflagration that destroyed Fred's grandfather's church. Its concluding passage reinforces the sacramental, transforming vision of **"Firewood."** In form and language imitating Old English alliterative verse, the poem presents Fred and Susan coming to the site of the fire years later to find it altogether revivified, a "victory of spirit":

> Time took it anew
> and changed that church-plot to an enchanted chrisom
> of leaf and flower of lithe light and shade.
>
> *Pilgrim, the past becomes prayer*
> *becomes remembrance rock-real of Resurrection*
> *when the Willer so willeth works his wild wonders.*
>
> (77)

This is stated as unequivocally as "the spine of the world" passage quoted above.

Other less extended instances of the Christian mode of transformation abound. The world was formed as "the purer spirits surged ever upward, / Shucking the gross pig-matter their bodies" (**"Fire Now Wakening on the River,"** 56). Sexual union in **"Bloodfire Garden"** burns the lovers "down again to the ghost of us, . . . Burnt-off, we are being prepared" (94). For the grandmother in **"Second Wind,"** the stirring of a slight breeze becomes "the breath of life. . . . / Renewal of spirit such as I could never / Deny" (106). In a richly evocative scene on Wind Mountain, "the resplendent house of spirit bursts around the body" (**"Earth Emergent Drifts the Fire River,"** 149). The four elements carried by the winds are "suffering of spirit, suffering of elements, / In one mass," in **"Dawn Wind Unlocks the River Sky"** (98). Both the poems celebrating jazz in *Wind Mountain* embody the idea from Schopenhauer that serves as epigraph in Chappell's homage to Louis Armstrong—"*Music is the world over again,*" but in impalpable sound, in another form altogether (99). At the close of that poem, man becomes "half funky animal, half pure music, / Meat and spirit drunk together" (102).

The spiritual choice I am suggesting *Midquest* reticulately and dramatically enacts is more sharply underlined by three poems at the close of *Source,* published in 1985, four years after *Midquest*'s serially printed volumes (1975, 1978, 1979, 1980) were collected into one. In **"Urlied,"** Chappell puts words (some anachronistic) into Lucretius' mouth, having him reject immortality via Rilke and the familiar anthropomorphism of Olympus. Conversely, Lucretius reiterates his "trust" in the forces of dissolution and coalescence (love/strife, Venus/Mars) and draws this comfort from his system: "There's nothing personal in it" (*Source,* 53). The evaluation is heavily ironic, however, being true as a description of the movement of matter but devastatingly false when applied to the emotional effect of losing one's identity. Chappell articulates this dreadful rift in the last section of the poem, where he evaluates Lucretius' endeavor as fundamentally courageous and integral but finally without solace. He leaves Lucretius in the "white fountain of delirium / Burning but not purified" (54), recalling both the close of T. S. Eliot's "The Fire Sermon" and the final stanza of his own **"Feverscape: The Silver Planet"** in *Midquest.* Once again, the Lucretian vision, for all its radically compelling perception into the material nature of things, is bleak and isolate, not transforming in a way Chappell finds desirable.

The other two poems set against **"Urlied"** involve ascent. **"Message"** employs Lucretian terminology, but Chappell's context involves three dimensions basically apostate to the Roman poet's system: the controlling metaphor of ascension; an increased understanding by the grief-stricken sufferer; and a concern with expressing that understanding in language. In choosing among his sorrows, the "he" of the poem becomes the measure of his own grief. In the opening lines' use of an angel as messenger "purely clothed in terror," there is also an implicit acceptance of this aspect of Rilke, contrasted to his dismissal by Lucretius in the preceding poem.

More telling still is **"Forever Mountain,"** the final poem in *Source.* Chappell presents his father ascending, after death, Mt. Pisgah, about fifteen miles southeast of Canton, North Carolina—Chappell's hometown but also the mountain from which God showed Moses the promised land. Words from the hymn "Sweet Hour of Prayer" are relevant to the vision the poem renders: "Til from Mt. Pisgah's lofty height / I view my home and take my flight." J. T. Chappell doesn't fly, but he does leisurely ascend the mountain, "taking the time / He's got a world of" (57). He observes "the quality of light come over him," spends a dreamful night, "rises glad and early and goes his way, / Taking by plateaus the mountain that possesses him." He has come a far piece from the Pilate-like figure he cut when we last saw him in *Midquest.* At the poem's close, Chappell's "vision blurs . . . with distance," Pisgah becomes Forever Mountain, "a cloud / That light turns gold, that wind dislimns." The shift from the figure of his father to Chappell's blurred vision has much the same effect as would an unmitigated focus on the father's assumption

into a new form. We witness an ascension of body to light and transformation, the context and perspective explicitly biblical, implicitly Christian. Between **"Message"** and **"Forever Mountain,"** in fact, Chappell places a terse and rending avatar of another hymn, "O Sacred Head Now Wounded," concerned with the mocking of Jesus' suffering during his trial and crucifixion.

PRAYER; ORTHODOXIES

I called **"Forever Mountain"** a vision, but in an italicized line appended to the poem, Chappell calls it a prayer. It is noteworthy that it's not a vision or a wish or a hope, but specifically *a prayer. Source,* in fact, contains three other poems so labeled, each of them depicting a merging of the one who prays with the particular conditions he prays about ("about" in the sense of concerning, and circling). In the first, **"A Prayer for the Mountains,"** it is a peaceable kingdom he both accepts as existing and desires to exist, wanting to "share the sleep / Of the cool ground's mildest children" (5). In **"A Prayer for Slowness,"** he seeks to be not content but filled with giving, as the cow in the poem has "her rich welcome / . . . taken from her" (6). **"A Prayer for Truthfulness"** concerns the poet's release of his poem from his control into its own illumination, able to say finally "its last abandonment" (7). The three prayers are, in short, not self-focused or escapist or acquisitive; in fact, insofar as they ask for anything, it is a place among the portions of other creatures into which Chappell may meld his being and talent.

Prayer is, of course, as complex an area as the other spiritual matters in Fred Chappell's work. I'm no expert on it by any stretch of the imagination, but a few thoughts may at least serve to disperse its associations beyond mere petition.

The extraordinary act of paying conscious attention may be considered a form of prayer. Prayer may be a tonality, an indication in declarative statements or questions that the speaker is tuned somewhere to spiritual dimensions he may not be addressing directly. "Where've you been?" asked in a certain way, for instance, can be a prayer, as Kathy Mattea's recent song by that name shows. A lived life can be a prayer, though that is difficult to specify, except perhaps in the cases of some saints. Prayer is not necessarily even supplication but may be homage, or gratitude, or acceptance, or lament, or bewilderment spoken or enacted or felt toward the immanent presence of a power greater than oneself. It may be a habit or an attitude. In *Hamlet,* Claudius' prayer, though his thoughts "remain below," is still a prayer. That which impels our attention away from the self or turns the will toward imagination may, speaking as broadly as possible, be considered prayer. Chappell refers to *Midquest* in his Preface as "in its largest design a love poem" (xi); from a number of these perspectives, the book could also be thought of as a prayer.

Individual poems, too, embody this possibility. **"Susan Bathing"** is a prayer of worship, praise, and adoration, **"My Grandmother's Dream of Plowing,"** a prayer for release and forgiveness, **"My Father Allergic to Fire,"** for acknowledgement and continuance. And so on.

The prayers per se dispersed throughout *Midquest,* though not explicitly indicated as the ones in *Source,* are not so much disguised as diverse. Chappell composes and aims them variously.

"Birthday 35: Diary Entry" concludes with a prayer in the more traditional mode of petition: "Please, Lord. I want to go to some forever / Where water is, and live there" (7). Until the final three lines, the poem is a plea for an anthropomorphic afterlife (part of the pattern **"How to Build the Earthly Paradise"** and **"At the Grave of Virgil Campbell"** later extend) where current pleasures pertain, an "Elysium . . . plentifully planted / With trout streams and waterfalls and suburban / Swimming pools, and sufficient chaser for bourbon" (8). Its tone is wise-ass jaunty, its diction hip, its beat and varying line lengths accumulating a pseudo music-hall effect that seeks to minimize the prayerful imploring, much as a sophisticated dude cultivates a cool exterior to cover his sensitivity. But in the last three lines, the more serious underlying concern breaks through: he wants the water of heaven to wash away sin.

The going up in flames of Fred's grandfather's church (*Bloodfire,* VI) and the site's transformation seventeen years later "to the stark beginning where the first stars burned" (77) becomes the ground for the definition of prayer that ends the poem. What has been a catastrophe is subsequently seen as part of a reenactment of the resurrection of Jesus.

> *Pilgrim, the past becomes prayer*
> *becomes remembrance rock-real of Resurrection*
> *when the Willer so willeth works his wild wonders.*
>
> (77)

"The Willer," presumably not a human being, is involved in the process of prayer defined here. The experience itself is prayer, in which the divine will is inextricably woven, suggesting that God's involvement in history is not limited to the incarnation of Jesus.

I'm not sure if the more dire self-immolation of the Buddhist monks in **"Bloodfire"** should be included in

this context, but it seems possible. What miraculous renewal may be hidden in the most awful destruction is part of the dread mystery of God's will.

Chappell uses fire as an agent of transformation again in connection with prayer in **"Bloodfire Garden."** In a remarkable merging of garden and bed, brushfire and loinfire ("the disease / necessary to know God"), Fred remembers praying as he watched the blackberry vines, scythed and "raked up in barbarous heaps," put to the torch (92). It was, he says, a moment in which

> I went stark sane, feeling under my feet
> the hands of blackberry fire
> rummaging
> unfurrowed earth.
>
> (93)

What, if anything, he prays for is unspecified, but his act is imbedded in images that suggest not only fire as incipient plow ("rummaging": the area is being cleared for planting) but also the burning of human bodies ("frying lattice / of dry bones") and the incarnation of spirits ("ghosts began again to take flesh") (93). In the other half of the poem's context of burning—the bedroom—after the lovers' climax "a cool invisible smoke goes up / from our bodies, it is grateful / prayer, sigil / of warm silence between us" (94).

> In this garden our bed we have burned
> down again to the ghost of us . . .
>
> (94)

In both contexts, the burning down has resulted in renewal or the readying for it. "Burnt-off," the lovers "are being prepared"; the burning off of the wild blackberry vines is a preparation as well for new growth. The image of dry bones suggests the vulnerability of the apparently solid human body and has driven young Fred to sanity and prayer; the aftermath of the fire of sexual union is prayer as well, associated with gratitude. In this context, the fresh rain blowing up "out of the green isles / of Eden," with its implication of renewed creative harmony with the Creator, seems entirely appropriate (94).

Fred's first prayer, the one in **"Birthday 35"** to which I've referred above, follows a vision of Time in which he sees "nothing human,"

> No man, no woman,
>
> No animals or plants; only moon
> Upon moon, sterile stone
>
> Climbing the steep hill of void.
>
> (7)

This waste land (part of a longer passage that I think consciously echoes T. S. Eliot's poem) leads to Fred's admission, "I was afraid." This process of a fearful vision of bleakness leading to prayer occurs again in at least two noteworthy places. In *Earthsleep* I, Fred talks to himself or, more accurately, to his "Mind," which he calls "Old Crusoe." In the context of wondering if they are both lost on "this bright and lonely spark" (149), he asks three questions about their eventual fate. The questions are directed at "Earth" but involve the other three elements central to *Midquest*. All of the alternatives are terrifying: "black waters streaming / Deathward," "In wind to suffer shorn of flesh," and "fire . . . the raging ecstasy / . . . of burning foreknowledge" (149). After such imagined vistas, the next utterance is a prayer.

>   Do not us Earth
> Remember.
>   Leave us, mud jumble of mirk
> And humus, tucked in the rock heart
> Of the mountain, in these stones are seeds of fire,
> Dream-seeds which taking root shall renew the world,
> Tree of Spirit lifting from the mountain of earth.
>
>   (149)

I take this prayer to be a refusal to identify the human creature as simply a concatenation of elemental substances. We are no more fully accounted for as such a composite than we are as Lucretian molecular aggregates or energy diminishing toward the cold will-lessness of Nirvana. Human creatures are elemental, yes, but also infused with spirit. Fred's prayer here is childlike in its desire that Earth simply forget him and Susan and tend to some other business. They'll take a spiritual form (the tree of spirit from **"Firewood"**) analogous to the earthly tree—an appeasing gesture?—and grow on transmuted, as spirit mysteriously grows. This eases into two afterprayers, asking **"Earth"** for gentleness and **"Destiny"** for sweet treatment. The tone and focus here is relief after the exhausting effort of imagination that precedes it.

The same process occurs finally in starker, more condensed form in the closing poem of the volume (and the book):

>   Here where I find
> I am I founder.
>   Lord Lord
> Let this lost dark not.
>
>   (186)

Not what? is the inevitable question. Swallow us up, as the sea overwhelms a foundering ship? That seems the most immediate likelihood. The prayer itself is so close to the terror that impels it that it cannot be completely uttered. The pattern of zeroes that occupy the volume (the "darkest vowel" of the well opening, for instance, the drains in the grandmother's and Susan's tub, the black hole in space in **"Firewood"**) has been perhaps the best preparation for what is most feared here from the dark.

These various spiritual radiations are rarely orthodox in any sense. But institutional Christian orthodoxies, too, occupy a substantial place in the spiritual experience of *Midquest.* The most accessibly presented are made part of the lives of Fred's forebears. Concerned for his salvation, his grandfather changes denominations (*River,* VII) and is baptized in the West Fork of the Pigeon River. Later, speaking from the grave (*Earthsleep,* IX), "Here where it's / Still not Absolute" (181-82), he awaits "Judgment Day / When we can see once more in the Judgment Book / All that we've seen already, each nook / And cranny of us forever on display" (182). The tone of the latter poem is nettled and testy, a strong modulation of the comic surface of the former one; in both poems, the man is of two minds about the perspectives the church has saddled him with, but there's no doubt he accepts its terms and forms, and takes them seriously.

These two poems deal with sacraments: baptism and burial. Fred's grandmother confronts another—marriage (*River,* VII), seeing this commitment as analogous to Caesar's Rubicon: *"If I cross this river I won't turn back."* When her husband dies (**Wind Mountain,** III) and she is faced with the public anonymity of everything, as well as the distracting hodge-podge of the funeral gathering, she wants to join him. Immediately, however, she aborts the idea on orthodox grounds: "It's a sin to want yourself to die" (103). She utters this fundamental belief before the poem is well begun, then suffers the family and their best intentions until, unable to take any more, she walks outdoors, away from the house, to a place "where the rose / Vine climbed the cowlot fence and looked away / Toward Chambers Cove" (105). It is also a place in her spiritual life "where everything is hard as flint: breathing, / Walking, crying even. It's a heathen / Sorrow over us" (105). In such a condition, she is unable to help herself, but in the immobilizing heat of the day, she feels a breeze stir, coming cornstalk leaf by cornstalk leaf across the field toward her. She understands this to be "the breath of life . . . / Renewal of spirit such as I could never / Deny and still name myself a believer" (106). This utterly convincing account ends with the freshening wind touching her face "so strong it poured on me the weight of grace" (106).

At the other extreme from this visitation of saving grace, Chappell places Fred's father's guilt over the manner in which he's buried Honey, an old mule dead after generations of labor on the farm (*Earthsleep,* III). Because the clayey ground makes the digging of a grave nearly impossible, J. T. breaks the animal's legs so he won't need so deep a hole. What he does and is witnessed doing is ineradicable, however, from his memory, in his "head for good and all and ever" (155). It's no wonder, given his account of it:

I busted her legs.
I busted her legs with the mattock, her eyes all open
And watching me crack her bones and bulging out
Farther slightly with every blow. These fields
Were in her eyes, and a picture of me against
The sky blood-raw savage with my mattock.

(154)

"Heavy is how / I felt," he says, "empty-heavy and blue as poison" (154). The context of the poem is J. T.'s washing at the pump two weeks later. He scrubs his hands for "maybe seven minutes," dries them, and when he gives Fred the towel back, "there was his handprint, / Earth-colored, indelible, on the linen" (155). The figures of Pontius Pilate and Lady Mac-Beth lurk in the shadowy background here, and for the moment anyhow, no grace pours down on anything.

The mule is already dead when J. T. breaks her legs, and his sense of guilt is mostly a projection of his sensitivity and compassion. The experience revealed in the grandmother's dream of plowing (**Earthsleep**, VIII), however, is a fundamental sin, the bearing of a child either prior to her marriage to Frank or through adultery during it. The skillfully dovetailed phases of her dream show her progressively unsuccessful attempts to disguise her act, its issue, and their consequences. Frank's plowing, itself an unprecedented vision for her, provides an apt contextual metaphor: something hidden is uncovered. Frank both unearths the object and asks the question that pitches the dream toward its identification: *"Is that your baby that was never mine?"* (179). Anne—the grandmother, too, is named for the first time in the book, becoming a person not wholly identified through a role—"expects" at the start of her dream a church bell to be turned up by the plow, an object associated with Frank's past misfortune (the burning of his church) rather than with her own sin. This is the first of the dream's series of displacements. The object turns out to be in its first incarnation a lump of gold, which she cradles "to [her] breast." Following Frank's question, Anne denies (to herself) it's a baby, but then suddenly "I knew it *was* a baby in my arm, / The strangest baby" (179). The displacements continue: the infant is compared to Jesus as he is depicted in the *Upper Room*—a daily devotional publication—and then becomes a "golden child" who will "bring us luck." The creature she holds, however, continues to metamorphose toward the truth the dream is unlayering, finally becoming "'an ugly little man,'" "an evil little goblin / With an evil smile" (179). This truth is, of course, how Anne feels about the child, a slow revelation of her shame and awful self-condemnation projected outward into the form the dream work has presented as separate from her. She wishes it dead, and—"the awfullest part" (180)—it dies. It's only after this that she is able to say, "It was

my fault," but her admission of responsibility is focused only on her desire for the figure's death. Her guilt, insofar as she articulates it to Fred, to whom she's recounting the dream, seems focused on this, too; she also considers the child as separate from herself in its innocence at this point: "Whatever harm had the little goblin done?" (180). There seems no conscious owning up to her responsibility for its birth. Whether we are to take the death in the dream as indicating what happened to the actual baby is inconclusive, but the guilt is real enough: she has never waked from this dream. Incidentally, the revelation of this buried secret from her past casts a sharp light on her preoccupation in previous poems with the "Shadow Cousins," the profound hesitation she experienced before committing herself to marrying Frank, and out seeing her in two situations where she is washing something (her feet, her milk cans).[4]

These poems compose behavior and attitudes derived from sectarian Christian assumptions undergirding central aspects of what one might call primary theology. Suicide, adultery, and the wish to murder are sins; guilt is inevitably consequent upon sin; grace is God-given and mysterious, coming in unpredictable forms and at unpredictable times; the sacraments are inviolable, no matter how one might seek to hedge one's bets through them, their seriousness ingrained in the soul.

One of the assumptions inherent in **Midquest** appears to be that human beings, as Fred's grandmother fears, do grow away from their sources (this occurs both to individuals and to generations), but they appear to do so as a tree grows away from its roots, remaining one organism. Human beings are mobile, of course. I mean this analogy more to suggest temporal than spatial wholeness: as a tree grows in space, so a person grows in time. Human beings can make disorienting and potentially destructive choices, but there is as well a genetic and behavioral determinism woven into their development. **Midquest** embodies Fred Chappell's fulfillment of the grandmother's vision by becoming a professor and author, leaving the farm behind, deserting, as he says, "manual labor for intellectual labor." But the restless, doubt-ridden entertainments of his imaginative mind are largely informed by and directed at the physical, religious, and moral dimensions of the farm environment in which he was raised. I think this is the source, finally, of the spiritual and psychic healing and regeneration that **Midquest** seeks in its widest intention. In my context here, the central orthodox beliefs that define the family members seep into Fred's ways of probing his own diverse options.

This is clearest in the preoccupation with the relationship between matter and spirit—how to view incarnation—that pervades **Midquest** and informs much of

Chappell's poetry subsequent to it. His terror in the face of nothingness and the anonymous dispersal of atoms is bearable because the Christian mode of understanding affords him a richer, more hopeful alternative. He is, of course, predisposed toward it, but too given to the mind's uncertainties to accept it without first testing the abysmal ontological possibilities that contradict it. His use of Dante's *Divine Comedy* as model and guide further underscores the influence orthodox configurations have on his work. (Below I comment on Dante more specifically.)[5]

Other more local instances arise frequently throughout the book. I have mentioned both the transformation Fred witnesses in **Bloodfire** VI and the serious note ("Washing away sin") toward which his prayer at the close of **"Birthday 35"** tends (8), and I will discuss his use of Jonah, Lazarus, and Joseph. Not surprisingly, in the pattern of praise for Susan in **"Susan Bathing,"** phrases from the Christian vocabulary of belief appear: *"plenia gratia"* (from the Catholic "Hail Mary" and Luke 1:28) in the Madonna passage; *"let there be,"* from the creation story in Genesis. As a whole, the poem and the narrator's role in it are informed by the conception of God as Word (John 1:1ff.). In **"Firewood,"** he alludes to man "in his fallen state." In *Earthsleep* VI, he tells the dead Virgil Campbell, "All the world is lit for your delight, / old Buddy, hook it to your hulk both hands, / It's a worship of God, though kinda primitive / I admit."

These last two examples are drops in the larger welter of Fred's ruminations about the afterlife. They range from the pleasant, relaxed, anthropomorphic excursions in such poems as **"The Peaceable Kingdom of Emerald Windows," "At the Grave of Virgil Campbell,"** and *Wind Mountain* V, to the bleak visions of nothingness in **"Firewood"** and *Earthsleep* I. What can be envisioned in familiar terms we can project ourselves into, evaluate and decide about, but a Christian vision of the soul's form after death is more troublesome. A genuine transformation—the Pauline idea of the "body imperishable" of I Corinthians, 35-57, for instance—is, like grace, a mystery and therefore by definition cannot be imaged (though the conditions of its mystery may be). Consequently, the alternative, desirable vision is only vaguely implied in *Midquest,* a spindrift of thought and faith. This quandary is sharply presented in **"Birthday 35"**:

> But, Lord, You stand on one side
>
> Of the infinite black ditch
> And I on the other. *And that's a bitch.*
>
> (7-8)

Fred is as fascinated, however, with how life may have begun as with what may follow it. From the touching desire to uncover with his grandfather "the final source of West Fork Pigeon River," through the brief hints in the opening poem of each volume about "how the world was formed," to the more complexly developed myths of creation in *Wind Mountain* V ("a slightly different Big Bang theory") and *River* IX ("The Novel"), he reveals an inventive, fervent desire to be present at beginnings (which in the myths at least, he is). The title section (**"Two"**) of *Source* elaborates this impulse, being composed of scattered, disparate myths, many dealing with first causes, each apparently seeking to embody an "explanation," but finally explaining nothing.

In this preoccupation with the unknowns that border human life at either verge, he keeps in uneasy balance his inventive, informed intellectual curiosity and his spiritual tendency to accept the unknowable, or at least his place outside it. Here, as at so many other junctures of *Midquest,* a passage from **"Birthday 35,"** the true prelude to the volume, is pertinent:

> I'd sleep in the eiderdown of the True Believer
> And never nightmare about Either/Or
>
> If I had a different person in my head.
> But this gnawing worm shows that I'm not dead.
>
> Therefore: either I live with doubt
> Or get out.
>
> (5)

STRUCTURES

One may enter Chappell's *Midquest* at any point and find, as with all coherent visions emanating from a center, the basic terms and images that shadow the whole. The poems radiate from and revolve around a hub—though within most of them there is a nicely composed narrative linearity sometimes (*e.g.,* **"Susan Bathing," "Second Wind"**) reinforced by a psychological progression—so that one poem or a sequence of poems may enact the volume.

"Cleaning the Well" offers an instance of this, embodying in a single piece the general construction of *Midquest* as a Dantesque descent into hell and a rising toward light and redemption. Fred assists his grandfather in cleaning the well, the literal experience graphically presented from the double perspective of a young (eight- to ten-year-old) boy doing the work and an adult creating a shape for his memory. Chappell gives various indications of the figurative perspective from which he sees the experience and by which he wishes it evaluated. Dante's descent is, of course, the fundamental metaphoric enclosure, the "soundless dreaming / O" (14) of the well's mouth functioning effectively as a fearsome gate to the netherworld, prefiguring *Inferno*'s circles and the further possibility that nothingness may be at the bottom of things. The grandfather lowers Fred on pulley rope and harness, thus supporting him and becoming a "guide" (like Virgil) in a way appropriate to the context. The well itself is a version of the well at the center of the declining valleys of Malebolge through which Dante enters Cocytus, the frozen wasteland of the final circle of *Inferno.* Two of the boy's phrases particularize the broad connection. As he hits the water, he cries, "Whoo! It's *God / Damn* cold!" (14) and later, in response to his grandfather's asking how it's going, thinks, "It goes like Hell" (15). Two italicized phrases express more formally the implications of these colloquial ones: at the terrifying point where the boy has been reduced to the condition of a non-creature (nerveless, sexless, breathless, mindless, and bodiless) occur the words *"I shall arise never"* (15); similarly, at the other extreme of readjustment to the ground above, we read, *"I had not found death good"* (17).

Within the Dantesque frame, Chappell has Fred compare himself to Jonah, Joseph, and Lazarus, adding a biblical lens through which the homey, local experience is considered. A particularly telling merging of psychological insight and literary allusion takes place in this stanza (14). Fred's return to upper earth has disoriented him as much as had the earlier descent into the gelid water. He recalls the foreboding dark as "holy" and tries, in his new disorientation, "to fetch [it] / Back" (16). He then wonders if the three biblical figures had also been "ript untimely / From black wellspring of death" (16). There is the understanding of the human psyche's conservative nature, to want to remain in the condition to which it's become accustomed, so that the usual view of the miracles of the restoring of Jonah, Joseph, and Lazarus to the world is given an unexpected twist. In terms of the other allusive dimension here, Fred's resistance to his return recalls the resistance to waking with which each of the four volumes of **Midquest** begins, itself derived partly from Dante's tendency to sleep or swoon when faced with the pressure of attention and discovery (*e.g., Inferno,* I, ll, III, 136, and V, 142; *Purgatorio,* XVIII, 145). Finally, "wellspring of death" encapsulates the paradoxical understanding the *Divine Comedy* assumes, eventually tracing back to the *felix culpa* of Christianity.

Poems VI, VII, and VIII of **Wind Mountain** accomplish as a series what **"Cleaning the Well"** does as a single poem. A comic inversion of the poem it precedes, **"My Father's Hurricane"** is a tall tale with which J. T. regales eleven-year-old Fred over "the ruins / Of an April supper" (116). The hurricane is immortalized as "Bad Egg," which suggests it is the destructive opposite of "Egg," the source of all life

that Fred refers to hyperbolically in **"Birthday 35."** It is a five-layer conglomeration of all the stuff its power has uprooted and carried who knows where. J. T. travels upward through each layer, fending off young Fred's common-sense questions, until he reaches layer five, composed of "'Lovebirds, honeypies, sweethearts—whatever / You want to call them'" (119). The mother stops the story at the point where it tends toward raunchiness, the lovers "'Rolling and sporting in the wind like face cards / From a stag poker deck'" (120). The simile indicates the more serious substance the poem makes light of—lust and the gamble one takes with one's soul when one gives in to it. Paulo and Francesca are among those J. T. sees in layer five, and the potential cost of lust becomes even more sharply focused by Fred's question, "'But how did you get down without / Getting killed?'" (120). The answer to the question never comes, for the poem ends with J. T.'s voice cut off. Getting out is another story.

These last three details—the reference to Paulo and Francesca, the figurative implication that lust is a high-stakes gamble, and the allusion to death—would be sufficient to key the spiritual implications of this inverted hell. It is humorously presented, of course, and a dazzlingly inventive entertainment, but it is also from the outset suspiciously unsettling, beginning as it does with the comparison of J. T.'s cigarette smoke to a "dust cloud over a bombed-out city" (116).

The corrective to this odd *ascent* into a layer of "honeypies," begins with the title of the next poem. **"In Parte Ove Non E Che Luca"** is most of the final line of Canto IV of Dante's *Inferno,* and the poem it labels is a pretty fair country translation of Canto V. The chaotic uprooting of the previous poem becomes the "storm infernal" (Dante's *"bufera"* could be translated "hurricane") of the second circle of Hell. Here the winds also conflict, unceasingly driving the damned Spirits "onward with brute force":

> Up they go to the very edge of the Course
>   Of Ruin, complaining, lamenting, aghast.
>   For them the Word Divine is sheer remorse.
>
> Into this pain the lovers of flesh are thrust,
>   All those who gave their human reason over
>   To the delicious fever of carnal lust.
>
>   (122)

In short, J. T.'s "lovebirds" are here, hovering "in the torn air," and this time no humor relieves their predicament. Chappell, however, updates the population by adding Casanova, a couple of poets, and from his own book, Virgil Campbell.

Campbell, in response to Fred's request that his Master and guide, the *other* Virgil, stop and bring him over to them, becomes the subject and speaker (à la Francesca) of the third poem in this group, **"Three Sheets in the Wind: Virgil Campbell Confesses."** He tells his own tale, balancing formally J. T.'s hurricane story. It concerns his getting caught by his wife and the preacher *in flagrante delicto* with a willing country "gal you always hear about / And generally never meet" (124). It's another funny experience, well stitched together, but for all Campbell's ingratiating humor, cajolery, and wit, it is finally quite serious because of the context in which Chappell sets it. Ironies proceed from that context, too. The poem, a confession, begins with Campbell calling himself "a solid by God citizen," but his country is the second circle of the Inferno.[6] He understands his youthful penchant for moonshine and women as "a kind of crazy" in his blood that "nothing but / The worst that can happen will ever get . . . out" (124). He then says, "The worst that can happen never happened to me," which is a lie, given his condition of damnation; it is also a sign of the rationalization and evasion of the truth that is traditionally characteristic of the damned. Virgil Campbell could have sold cider to Eve. His story leads him to make the familiar promise of those caught in a terrifying trap—he believes, sewed up in one of his wife's sheets, that he's died and gone to hell, and so he thinks

> how I'd do it all different if
> I could only live my earthly life again:
> I'd be a sweet and silent religious man.
>
> (126)

He gets out of the story's *contretemps,* of course, and the final line of the poem, in which he decides to have a drink, indicates how ineptly he's kept that rash promise. "'Well, where's the harm?'" (127) he asks rhetorically, ready to bend his elbow, repeating the same question he's asked earlier in the poem in justifying with wonderful sophistic logic his adultery. The harm is perdition, no matter the charm of the lothario; Campbell is a convincing embodiment of the giving over of human reason "to the delicious fever of carnal lust." In the larger series of poems centering on Virgil Campbell in *Midquest,* it's clear that Fred is affectionately and generously disposed toward him; Fred feels great kinship with Virgil in the last of these, **"At the Grave of Virgil Campbell."** But a lovable reprobate is still a reprobate, and in a book that takes seriously the fallen nature of humankind and traditional modes of dealing with that condition, the implications of this trio of poems are inescapable.

This group, then, repeats in extended form and with more widely varying tonalities the descent motif of **"Cleaning the Well,"** using Dante's model more pervasively, making explicit the dimension of Hell's eternal enclosure. These four poems focus also *Midquest*'s recurrent entertainment from different perspectives of the possibility of an afterlife and what spiritual alternatives face its central figure, the pilgrim Fred Chappell on his thirty-fifth birthday, pressing toward "the love that moves itself in light to loving."

Notes

1. Because both the author and the narrator of *Midquest* share the same name but are not identical to each other, I have used "Fred Chappell" or "Chappell" to refer to the former and "Fred" for the latter. Chappell comments on this matter in his Preface to *Midquest.*

2. A complementary comic rejection occurs in *Earthsleep,* IV, where "the Ideal World," Platonic in its evocative details, "sounds like a Grand Hotel / Emptied out because of chicken pox."

3. George Santayana, *Three Philosophical Poets* (Cambridge, Mass., 1910), 53.

4. Fred's guilt at turning his back on the voices of the poor (*Wind Mountain,* IX) may be considered part of this pattern.

5. The musical aspect of this part of Chappell's quest may be as crucial as the philosophical. The absence of jazz in Nirvana is another telling argument against its appeal.

6. I have taken Virgil Campbell's placement in the second circle of Dante's Hell so literally because of the sequence of these poems, particularly the segue between the second and third. The presence of J. T. Chappell as listener in the dramatic monologue of the confession complicates this choice, however. Is J. T. damned, too? Perhaps he is a *nonce* extension of Fred, a "listener" of context, no more trapped in hell than Dante was. Or perhaps we are gradually to ease back into the familiar general-store setting of "Firewater."

John Lang (essay date 2000)

SOURCE: Lang, John. "Shaping the Self in Poetry: *The World between the Eyes* and *Midquest*." In *Understanding Fred Chappell,* pp. 58-94. Columbia: University of South Carolina Press, 2000.

[*In the following essay, Lang considers Chappell's early poetry, published first in* The World between the Eyes *and subsequently released in* Midquest, *along with four other collections of poems.*]

By the time Chappell's first book of poems, ***The World between the Eyes,*** appeared in 1971, the author had already published three novels and had completed a draft of his fourth. Yet despite the variety of fictional forms in which he has worked, Chappell's first allegiance has always been to poetry, which he calls a "nobler sort of art" than fiction.[1] "It's enormously more fun writing poetry than fiction and nonfiction," he told an interviewer, "because of the concentration on themes and on language, particularly language. . . . It's also more difficult."[2] That challenge is one he has successfully embraced in ten book-length collections of poems as well as three chapbooks.[3]

Chappell's poetics derives from the organicism first espoused in American literature by Ralph Waldo Emerson, for whom the poem originates in "a thought so passionate and alive that, like the spirit of a plant or an animal, it has an architecture of its own, and adorns nature with a new thing."[4] As Chappell puts it, "Every work of art . . . creates its own separate aesthetic laws, the way in which it's to be understood. I think that really means that it must have created its own special way to be written if it's a genuine work of art."[5] Chappell has repeatedly avowed his commitment to the Horatian aims of literature, to entertain and to instruct, and has said that "the only important considerations" in assessing a poem or a book of poems "[are] that it be beautiful, honest, and interesting—that is, that it intrigue the mind or affect the feelings."[6] These aesthetic principles help to account for the range of forms that readers encounter in Chappell's poetry as well as the varied styles he uses. Chappell has often written in free verse, not just in traditional forms, while the range of such forms, especially in *Midquest,* demonstrates his mastery of poetic craft and technique. As for the absence of a distinctive poetic style in his work, Chappell has commented: "I'm not interested in creating a fixed poetic style for myself, but [in] matching each separate poem to the subject matter. I deliberately try to be as fluid as possible."[7]

Yet another important aesthetic principle governing Chappell's collections of poetry is his assumption that a book of poems should form a whole and not be simply a gathering of discrete individual poems. The four books that compose *Midquest,* each of them organized around one of the four classical elements, exhibit such unity, as does the text as a whole, which is subtitled *A Poem. Castle Tzingal* (1984) certainly has such unity, as do, in varying degrees, each of his subsequent volumes, whether the book's impression of wholeness results from similarity of themes and motifs, as in *Source* (1985); similarity of subject matter and approach, as in *First and Last Words* (1989); or similarity of poetic form, as in the epigrams of *C* (1993). Chappell's most important precursor in this regard is Charles Baudelaire's *Fleurs du mal.* "Baudelaire said," Chappell told an interviewer, "if you have twenty-four poems, the order of the poems makes up

the twenty-fifth poem; that is, the design of the whole book is a poem itself."[8]

THE WORLD BETWEEN THE EYES

It is for the absence of such design, among other flaws, that Chappell has criticized *The World between the Eyes,* calling it "weak in conception and execution."[9] Yet while it is true that the thirty-seven poems collected in this initial volume lack the structural unity and the refinement of Chappell's later poetic compositions, the book contains a number of poems, as Kathryn Stripling Byer has noted, "which are [among] the most intense in contemporary poetry, almost overwhelming in their obsessive imagery and unrelenting rhythms."[10] These qualities are especially notable in the eight longer narrative poems that fill nearly half of the book's pages. In fact those eight poems—**"February," "The World between the Eyes," "The Farm," "The Father," "The Mother," "Tin Roof Blues," "Sunday,"** and **"The Dying"**—though often separated from one another by shorter lyric poems, can usefully be read as a sequence. Taken together, they provide an insightful portrait of the artist as child and young man, and they thus anticipate both the narrative structure of many of *Midquest*'s poems and some of that later volume's major subjects, themes, images, and stances.

The World between the Eyes opens with **"February,"** a poem that vividly describes, in a syntax often disjointed and a free verse that frequently employs an iambic base, a hog killing. This subject matter situates poet and reader squarely in the rural environment so typical of Chappell's work. The poem's events are presented from the perspective of "the boy," a semiautobiographical point of view to which Chappell returns not only in much of *Midquest* but also in *I Am One of You Forever* and the other Kirkman novels. The child's ambivalence toward the hog killing is captured in such phrases as "dismayed / With delight" and "elated-drunk / With the horror."[11] The communal dimension of this activity is one of its most important features, for Chappell seeks to locate the reader not only in proximity to the natural world but also in relationships with others. Nature, through this "most unlikely prodigious pig" (5), affords the family both food and an occasion for affirming friendship and interdependence.

One of Chappell's pervasive poetic concerns has been his resistance to the self-absorption that characterizes so much contemporary poetry, the retreat into the individual psyche that marked the confessional poetry of the late 1950s and 1960s. Despite this concern, the longer narrative poems of *The World between the Eyes* do indeed record the efforts of "the child" to achieve individuation, self-identity. The title poem emphasizes the issue of subjectivity and the child's struggle for selfhood by opening with the boy imagining a scene of troops preparing for battle. Casting himself in the role of "the Swarthy Spy" who "hones a talent for precision" in his reports (12), the child becomes an emblem of the adult poet.

The title of this collection highlights the role that mind and imagination play in shaping the world. But the title also recalls the phrase "a bullet between the eyes," thereby reinforcing the child's sense of being menaced by the world, of being embattled. It is significant that these narrative poems begin with a hog killing and end, in **"The Dying,"** with the death of the boy's sister, while including in **"The Father"** the child's contemplation of suicide. Death haunts many of these poems, as it haunted Chappell's first three novels. The book's title is open to a third interpretation as well. The world between the eyes is also a world shared among various I's—that is, shared among different people (families, communities) and shared among the different selves (or different voices) that contribute to a single individual's identity. The child shares his world with his ancestors, with the past, as he wanders "the house of his fathers," "rooms of his fathers" (12). He shares it with his father and mother, with the inhabitants of Canton (in **"Tin Roof Blues"**), with the religious community in which his parents immerse him (in **"Sunday"**), with his dying sister, and with the natural phenomena portrayed in **"The Farm,"** That poem too, as it moves from the work required by summer haying to the paralysis of winter, is shadowed by death: "Stupor of cold wide stars" (20), "The world, locked bone" (21).

To make a place for himself in such a world, the developing poet must master his memories, must overcome the stasis they often induce, and must come to recognize, like James Christopher of *It Is Time, Lord,* the resources they offer. Even more importantly, he must achieve a vision of the future, grounding that future in an accurate understanding of his past. Over against "things that bloom and burn," the child sets "words [that] bloom / and burn" (13) and embraces "his duty to read aright, / To know" (14). Surrounded by "signs" and filled with a sense of time "charged past endurance with the future" (14), the child of the title poem nevertheless realizes that "he's blest in his skins, an old stone / House, and a sky eaten up with stars" (15). Time and eternity are yoked in the images of house and star, and brooding on both is the figure of the developing poet.

Though Chappell grounds these narrative poems in the rural and in family, he does not idealize either of those subjects. The seasonal progression from summer to winter in **"The Farm"** makes this attitude clear, as

does the difficulty of the work portrayed. The child's relationships with his father and mother, presented in two consecutive poems, the latter at the virtual midpoint of the book, reveal a similar ambivalence. The father's judgmental stance mirrors that of James Christopher's father in the **"January"** episodes of *It Is Time, Lord.* Yet the boy's success in fulfilling the task his father assigns—to discover a new spring to replenish the family's water supply—leads the child to a renewed sense of life's possibilities. Having rejected the temptation to commit suicide, he feels like "someone who's lived through his death, come out grinning, / Mind surcharged with the future" (27). While this easy confidence is treated ironically, the child does acquire a new sense of equanimity.

Although the boy's mother promptly shatters that equanimity, he is able to restore it, and what makes his resilience possible is humor—humor and a hard-won capacity for detachment. Significantly, it is precisely such a discovery of the usefulness of humor that helped effect the transition in Chappell's fiction from the gloom of *Dagon* to the lighter tone of *The Gaudy Place,* not to mention the broad comedy of many of the poems in *Midquest* and of many of the characters and events in the Kirkman tetralogy. What Chappell says of humor in Carolyn Kizer's poetry seems applicable to his own increasing reliance on humor after the publication of *Dagon*: "Kizer seems to look upon humor as one of the most welcome parts of her personal, as well as her human, heritage. It is for her not only necessary for balance and tolerance, it is a necessity for survival."[12]

For the child in **"The Mother,"** it is humor that enables him to triumph over hatred and rage. Storming out of the house, he longs to "squash it from sight with his palm" (29). Rejecting that option, he retreats to the woods to consider others. Yet the very shapes of his fantasies subvert their appeal: "Could live in the woods and eat bugs! / Or, handily build Snug Cabin, chink it with mud / . . . // Could murder his mother, conquer the world! / Or, rob banks and live rich on the loot" (30). By acknowledging the absurdity of his fantasies, the child manages to return home.

In this poem at the midpoint of Chappell's first book of poetry, the child-poet comes to recognize that the function of the imagination is not to evade reality but to confront it and to illuminate it. The world between the eyes emerges from and engages with the world those eyes observe, not a world they invent. Chappell's later short stories and novels and poems reveal his penchant for fantasy, but it is fantasy in the service of a deeper understanding of life, not fantasy as an alternative to lived social experience. The child in **"The Mother"** returns home, "his pace . . . deliberately fashioned." Unlike the figure in this volume's **"Face to Face,"** who, standing at his door, decides that "he'll sleep the ditch tonight" (22), the child-poet "stops to take the measure of the family door. / And then he enters" (31). As Byer says of **"The Father"** and **"The Mother,"** "Each poem concludes with a real, earned breakthrough into a life-sustaining vision."[13] The return home that the latter poem records becomes the pivotal event in the poet's psychological and artistic development.

The eight longer narrative poems in *The World between the Eyes* are linked by repeated images and phrases; by their narrative structure; by the themes of time, mortality, family ties, and the function of the imagination; and, most importantly, by the figure of the boy or young man who appears in each of them. Although the poems are not presented as a sequence, they can profitably be read as one. Yet as the striking contrast between the endings of **"Face to Face"** and **"The Mother"** shows, Chappell has also established connections between several of the shorter poems in this volume and the longer narrative poems as well as connections among some of the shorter poems. Three poems on the poet's son, Heath, for example, serve as a bridge between the title poem and **"The Farm,"** depicting Heath's wrestling with the world of objects and his efforts to acquire a language expressive of his needs and feelings. Five witty poems on baseball are grouped together, illustrating Chappell's skill with figurative language and apt allusions as well as his sense of humor, but those poems fail to contribute to a sense of underlying unity in the book as a whole. Nevertheless, as Byer remarks, "What continues to fascinate any reader of *The World between the Eyes* is the range of voice, tone, and style the book displays."[14]

Such range has become one of the hallmarks of Chappell's achievement, not only in poetry but also in fiction. In other ways too *The World between the Eyes* adumbrates his later poetic forms, themes, and techniques. The ease with which he moves, for instance, from free verse to a variety of rhyme schemes, meters, and stanza structures is amply evident. His extensive use of narratives that focus on childhood memories and experiences provides another example of the continuity between this initial book of poems and his later work. Even the place names in some of these early narrative poems—Smathers Hill, Wind River—either reappear in *Midquest* or anticipate that book's dominant images. The allusiveness of Chappell's poetry, along with its philosophical concerns, is also evident at many points, starting with the volume's second poem, **"A Transcendental Idealist Dreams in Springtime,"** a poem dedicated to James Applewhite. That allusiveness marks even the opening and closing lines of **"Third Base Coach,"**

with its references to the ghost of Hamlet's father and to Aeschylean tragedy. Chappell's willingness to address such seemingly unpoetic material and to dignify the products of popular culture is also apparent in a poem like **"Weird Tales,"** with its celebration of the practitioners of horror stories and science fiction. In form, moreover, **"Weird Tales"** is an epistolary poem, addressed to R. H. W. Dillard, and it thus looks forward to the four letter-poems that play a crucial role in *Midquest.*

Chappell chose to reprint only four poems from *The World between the Eyes* in *The Fred Chappell Reader,* but he selected ten of them (at times greatly revised) for inclusion in *Spring Garden.* While some of the poems—**"Erasures," "Guess Who," "The Survivors,"** and **"Northwest Airlines,"** among others—are indeed slight, a number of the poems remain of interest both for their insights into the poet's later development and for their own artistic merit.

MIDQUEST

In the title poem of *The World between the Eyes,* the narrator remarks of the child-poet, "Of the elements his is water" (14). It was, in fact, to water that Chappell turned in composing his next book of poems, *River* (1975), the first volume of what was to become *Midquest* (1981), his semiautobiographical epic, "something like a verse novel," as he notes in the preface to that book.[15] Chappell has traced the genesis of *Midquest* to **"Familiar Poem,"** first published in *The Archive* while he was a student at Duke.[16] But he didn't begin working on this material consciously, he says, until May 28, 1971, his thirty-fifth birthday, when he was preparing *The World between the Eyes* for publication. Early on Chappell realized the potential scope of this new body of material: "By the time I'd written the second poem [in *River*] . . . I saw the shape of the whole thing. Not the exact structure but the shape of it."[17] Asked by an interviewer, "How old were you when you found the grain [of your poetic sensibility] and kept going with it?" Chappell responded, "I was thirty-five. . . . I started writing *Midquest.* It became important to me. And that became the theme of the book—to take stock and change directions."[18] To another interviewer Chappell remarked, "The whole poem, *Midquest,* is about rebirth."[19]

Now widely recognized as what Patrick Bizzaro calls "the structural and thematic centerpiece of Chappell's poetic achievement thus far,"[20] *Midquest* is an extraordinarily ambitious, complexly structured, deeply humane book. Some five thousand lines in length, it gathers together the four previously published volumes *River, Bloodfire* (1978), *Wind Mountain* (1979), and *Earthsleep* (1980). Each of those volumes consists of eleven poems, with each volume organized around one of the four elements—water, fire, air, and earth—that Pythagoras and other ancient philosophers viewed as fundamental to all life. Chappell allows each of these elements to assume a variety of meanings and also has them interact with and upon one another, as when he describes "the burning river of this morning / That earth and wind overtake" (187) or speaks of "the morning flush of loosed wind-spirit, exhalation / Of fire-seed and gusty waters and of every dirt" (98). In *Bloodfire* alone, the image of fire is linked to dawn, to a Rimbaudian derangement of the senses, to the Ku Klux Klan's cross burnings, to sexual desire, to spiritual longing, to Pentecost and the Christian symbolism associated with the Holy Spirit, to hellfire, to the violence of war, to martyrdom (political as well as religious), to hearth and home, to the fevers of physical illness, to natural disasters, to Lucretius's *ignis semina* as building blocks of the physical world, to illumination or revelation, to alcohol ("firewater"), to "fire / As symbolic of tortured, transcendent-striving will" (85), and to many other objects and significations. A similar multiplicity of meanings attaches to the other elements, allowing the poet enormous latitude for the exercise of his ingenuity while at the same time insuring a comprehensive and comprehensible focus for the book.

In addition to using the four elements as a unifying device within and between volumes, Chappell conjoins the four books that comprise *Midquest* in a number of other ways. Each volume opens, for instance, with the poet-narrator (Ole Fred) in bed with his wife, Susan, on the morning of his thirty-fifth birthday, and each volume closes with the couple back in bed. Susan likewise appears in at least one other poem in each volume. Ole Fred's grandparents and parents speak at length in various narrative poems throughout the four volumes. Yet another unifying character is Virgil Campbell, the country storekeeper first introduced in *It Is Time, Lord.* One poem in each of *Midquest*'s four volumes is devoted to Virgil, "who is supposed to give to the whole," Chappell states in the preface, "its specifically regional, its Appalachian, context" (x). Each volume also contains a lengthy stream-of-consciousness poem that meditates on such philosophical issues as the relationship between body and mind, flesh and spirit, time and eternity; and each volume contains a poem that portrays a natural disaster appropriate to the element around which that book is organized: a flood, a fire, a hurricane, and in *Earthsleep* death itself. Similarly helping to unify all four volumes are Chappell's varied allusions to and echoes of Dante's *Divine Comedy,* with its quest for moral and spiritual rebirth at the midpoint of one's life. The motif of pilgrimage is implicit throughout *Midquest,*

as is Thoreau's idea that "morning is moral reform" (101). Chappell subtitles *Midquest* "A Poem," thus indicating the unity of impression to which the work aspires, and which, I believe, it achieves—a unity amidst astonishing and engaging variety. The careful design of the book infuses in the reader a sense both of order and of the richness of life's possibilities; yet *Midquest* never slights the struggles that are required to attain and sustain such a vision.

Chappell's preface to *Midquest* indicates a great deal about the author's intentions and about the book's design. The preface has generated some controversy, however, because of several inconsistencies between Chappell's statements there and the book's actual structure. Chappell notes, for example, that the sixth poem in each volume is devoted to Virgil Campbell, when in fact Virgil appears in the seventh poem of *Bloodfire* and the eighth poem of *Wind Mountain.* Likewise, Chappell claims that "the fifth poem in each [volume] is given to stream of consciousness" (x), though it seems clear that it is the fourth poem in *Earthsleep,* "**The Peaceable Kingdom of Emerald Windows,**" that parallels the narrator's stream-of-consciousness meditations in *Midquest*'s first three volumes. Chappell also explains in the preface that "each of the volumes (except *Wind Mountain*) is organized as a balancing act. The first poem is mirrored by the last; the second by the next to last, and so on inward" (ix). Although Randolph Paul Runyon has traced many of these parallels, they ultimately seem far less significant than the narrative and thematic momentum of the book as it moves forward through the poems in a given volume and through the entire text. As Runyon himself concedes, "*Midquest* is probably as rich in sequential echoes as it is in symmetrical ones."[21]

Chappell's preface is more useful, it seems to me, in its comments on the poet's general intentions than on the book's details of design. Chappell characterizes *Midquest,* for instance, as "a reactionary work," one that aimed "to restore . . . qualities sometimes lacking in the larger body of contemporary poetry: detachment, social scope, humor, portrayal of character and background, discursiveness, wide range of subject matter" (x). The longer version of the preface that appeared in *The Small Farm,* a year prior to *Midquest*'s publication, helps to clarify to what and to whom the poet was reacting. There he indicates his dissatisfaction both with the autobiographical lyric and with the long poem as represented by Ezra Pound's *Cantos,* William Carlos Williams's *Paterson,* Charles Olson's *Maximus Poems,* Louis Zukovsky's *A,* and Hart Crane's *The Bridge.* These long poems he faults for their "structural failures" as they "limn down to lyric moments stuck together with the bland glue of raw data."[22] It is within the tradition of the long poem that Chappell places *Midquest,* and his achievement within that tradition is truly extraordinary. *Midquest* combines lyric, narrative, and meditative poems to create a larger structure that derives from the epic, most obviously Dante's *Divine Comedy.*

The title of one of Chappell's book reviews, reprinted in *A Way of Happening,* indicates his assessment of the contemporary long poem—**"Piecework: The Longer Poem Returns."** In that review he speaks of the "mosaic structures" rather than "extended wholes" that the majority of American long poems offer.[23] One of the consequences of such structures, as he points out in *Plow Naked,* is that "whatever the subject matter of the modern epic, and whatever the ostensible and announced themes, three secondary themes will inevitably be articulated[:] . . . disintegration, disconnection, and loneliness."[24] According to Chappell, "It is a wild connect-the-dots scheme, this construction of the contemporary epic," and he contrasts the fragmentation of perception and structure in such works with Homer's "faith that in fashioning a plot from all the random matter [of his world], he would find meaning, and a truth that would have value."[25] In *Midquest* the poet has striven for a sense of design, an architecture, in which "each part supports every other and a homogeneity of interest results."[26] While the resulting poem clearly lacks the narrative flow of *The Odyssey* or *The Aeneid,* it tries to recover the "sense of community with the people of the past" so often absent from the contemporary epic.[27] Instead of portraying Ole Fred in terms of disconnection and loneliness, Chappell presents him as rooted in family and place and as representative of both the folk culture of the Appalachian South and the formal literary culture of the university. The social dimension of Chappell's poetic vision cannot be overemphasized. As Robert Morgan has remarked: "There is an assumption of community in all [Chappell's] work, a sense of belonging not just to a family and a place . . . but also to the terrain of history. It is a community in time that is implied and evoked, a world of parents and ancestors both literal and literary."[28]

Chappell's reservations about the contemporary autobiographical lyric, like his reservations about the modern epic, stem from its loss of community, its creation of intensely private, fragmentary modes of consciousness. He also criticizes such lyrics for their "attenuation of subject matter" and their "phony mysticism, the substitution of excited language for hard-won perception."[29] Shaped by "the Symbolist prescription that the poet should be a seer, a prophet," the autobiographical lyric, in Chappell's opinion, has reinforced the Romantic notion of the poet as social outsider, as social outcast. Too often, then, he adds,

"The subject matter to be perceived lay on or beyond the outer borders of common experience."[30]

Chappell's rejection of this last assumption pervades *Midquest.* As Henry Taylor has written, "*Midquest* is a poem celebrating the world most of us live in and the play of mind and language over it."[31] It is to human beings' ordinary yet remarkable relationships and experiences that Ole Fred turns in his portraits of his grandparents, parents, spouse, and friends. The sense of community is fundamental to the book, and that community extends well beyond the mountain setting of Ole Fred's childhood. Similarly, the self the poet portrays is not simply—or even primarily—an autobiographical self. While the figure of Ole Fred borrows heavily from the author's personal experiences, he is meant to be, like Dante the pilgrim or Walt Whitman's persona, "widely representative" (x). Chappell seeks not the novelties of private moments of illumination but the revelations that result from engagement with tradition and with other people. He resists entrapment in the isolated ego and rejects elitist conceptions of art; instead he situates the reader in a vivid social milieu and draws upon the oral tradition and folk materials to underscore his imagination's democratic inclusiveness. As the poet told an interviewer while the book was still in progress, "Although [*Midquest*] is autobiographical, in many ways, the last thing I want it to be about is the self. . . . And a sense of history, a sense of tradition, is one way to get away from the extremely *personal* tone of so much present-day poetry."[32]

While dissociating himself from the intensely subjective autobiographical lyric, Chappell does not—despite his disclaimer in the preface—sacrifice "intensity, urgency, metaphysical trial, emotional revelation" (x). Such qualities are regularly present in *Midquest,* particularly in the opening and closing poems of each volume and in Ole Fred's stream-of-consciousness meditations, but they occur within the larger context of the relationships, the extended sense of community and tradition, that the poem explores. Nor does Chappell abandon the idea of the poet as a seer, though he employs other conceptions of the poet's identity as well in order to recover for poetry the breadth of subject matter it enjoyed in pre-Symbolist eras. Spiritual vision is crucial to *Midquest,* a text in which Chappell affirms what he has called the traditional role of the poet "as celebrator of divinity and of the created objects of the universe."[33] As seer, Ole Fred embraces both body and spirit, sings the physical world without neglecting "the Mountains Outside Time" (169), and wonders whether the "Earthly Paradise" isn't already "among our amidst" (177). The meditative poems in each volume are especially imbued with visionary insights, which manifest themselves at many other points in *Midquest* too.

Part of what distinguishes this book from Chappell's earlier work is its attitude toward the past. For James Christopher of *It Is Time, Lord,* the past was filled with memories of his father's misjudgment of him and memories of burning down his grandparents' house. For Peter Leland of *Dagon,* the weight of the past meant bondage to Mina and ensnarement in a degrading religious cult. Even for "the child" of the narrative poems in *The World between the Eyes,* the past is often tormenting as he struggles to come to terms with his father and mother, with his sense of alienation from community and church in **"Tin Roof Blues"** and **"Sunday,"** and with the death of his sister. For Ole Fred, however, as well as for his author, the past is a valuable resource, a strong foundation upon which to build. As Chappell says of his persona in the preface to *Midquest,* "He is cut off from his disappearing cultural traditions but finds them, in remembering, his real values" (x). Yet Chappell does not idealize or romanticize that past. The "Georgic center" of Chappell's poetry, in Don Johnson's phrase,[34] may be the farm, but like the Roman poet Virgil, Chappell is keenly aware of the hardships of agrarian living, especially on hardscrabble mountain farms, as a poem like **"My Father Washes His Hands"** demonstrates. Chappell is not a neo-Agrarian, but he does find in farming a meaningful—though not financially rewarding—lifestyle, one that heightens recognition of humanity's dependence on nature and that encourages both humility and a sense of stewardship. As he declares in his essay, **"Poet and Plowman,"** "[Farming] is the one life besides poetry and natural philosophy that still touches an essential harmony of things, and when a civilization discards that way of life, it breaks the most fundamental covenant mankind can remember."[35] In *Midquest* farming also becomes a metaphor for the cultivation of the physical world that eventuates in spiritual vision. For Chappell, immersion in the physical world, not flight from it, leads to religious insight.

The agrarian tradition is only one dimension of the past that the poet celebrates in *Midquest.* Memories of his grandparents and parents as well as of Virgil Campbell elicit some of the book's most humorous and affectionate poems. Often those poems are monologues spoken by the characters themselves, though a younger Fred may serve as interlocutor. It is in such narrative poems as **"My Grandmother Washes Her Feet,"** **"My Father Allergic to Fire," "Firewater," "My Mother Shoots the Breeze," "My Father's Hurricane,"** and **"Three Sheets in the Wind: Virgil Campbell Confesses"** that Chappell utilizes most ef-fectively the oral tradition of his native Appalachia. At the same time, these narrative poems, with their vivid characters and incidents and their use of traditional folk materials, were inspired, Chappell says, by his admiration for Chaucer's achievement in *The Canterbury Tales.*[36]

The humor of the oral tradition—especially that distinctively American art form, the tall tale—had a major impact on the development of nineteenth-century literature in the United States, most notably in the writing of George Washington Harris and Mark Twain. Chappell's reading of both authors is apparent on more than one occasion in *Midquest* (and throughout the Kirkman tetralogy). Ole Fred's father's account of the multilayered windstorm in **"My Father's Hurricane,"** for instance, originates in the Washoe Zephyr that Twain describes in chapter 21 of *Roughing It.* And Harris's Sut Lovingood puts words in Virgil Campbell's mouth—*"Feet don't fail me now"*—in **"Three Sheets in the Wind."**[37]

Such borrowings and the frequent literary, musical, philosophical, and religious allusions in *Midquest* attest to the poet's celebration of the past and to the inclusiveness of his sense of community. His use of Dante's pilgrimage motif and other Dantean materials further affirms the continuity between past and present, as do the epigraphs he chooses for each of the book's four volumes, epigraphs taken from Melville, René Char, Dante, and Hawthorne, respectively. Of this group, only Char represents the twentieth century. The challenges faced by Chappell's "widely representative" persona are perennial human concerns.

Even while evoking the immense resources of the past, Chappell also emphasizes the importance of community in the present. This emphasis results not only from his attachment to place and to family but also from the poem's sociopolitical dimension and from the relationships Ole Fred cultivates with fellow writers. Sociopolitical issues are raised in each volume of *Midquest,* and the responsibilities of citizenship are never far from the poet's mind because the text's present, May 1971, finds the United States still fighting a war in Vietnam. **"Bloodfire"** deals most directly with that war, referring to its "fire-martyrs," "the immolated and self-immolated" (88). But the penultimate poem in *River* also speaks of "slow rain twitching wounds and eyelids / of murdered soldiers, / daily snail-white corpses / bloating the Mekong" (48). The opening poem of *Earthsleep* likewise notes how "fire colors the military maps, each village a red coal" (145). In addition to the bloodshed in Vietnam, Chappell protests economic injustice, from the paper mill's role in augmenting the flood's destruction in **"Dead Soldiers"** to the indifference of the rich toward the poor in **"Remembering Wind Mountain at Sunset"** By making such issues, including the racism alluded to in **"My Father Allergic to Fire,"** a significant part of the book, Chappell indicates that, for him, poetry is a means of confronting sociopolitical realities, not retreating from them into aestheticism.

Yet aesthetics, as distinct from aestheticism, is certainly another of the issues that *Midquest* addresses. The nature and function of the literary imagination have become one of the dominant themes in twentieth-century poetry, as is evident in the poetry of Wallace Stevens, for example. Unlike Stevens, however, for whom this theme is ubiquitous, Chappell assigns it a carefully delimited role in *Midquest,* as if to suggest that, for all its importance to the poet, it is only one of several ways of approaching the work of the mind. The poems in which aesthetic issues receive the most extended treatment are the playlet in which Reynolds Price appears and the four epistolary poems Ole Fred writes to friends and fellow writers Guy Lillian, James Applewhite, Richard Dillard, and George Garrett. Through their epistolary format, the latter poems reinforce the theme of community and help to dispel the image of the writer as *isolato*. These poems also reveal several of the major literary influences that shaped Chappell's imagination, influences he had learned to question. In **"Science Fiction Water Letter to Guy Lillian,"** for instance, the poet recalls his youthful fascination with this genre. Despite his continuing use of science fiction in a story like **"The Somewhere Doors"** (*More Shapes Than One*), this poem expresses Chappell's dissatisfaction with the genre, primarily because of its inattention to the physical world, its failure to develop a "feel for pastness," and its disregard for suffering (38-39). After this critique of science fiction, however, the poet proceeds to comment on the plight of contemporary poetry, especially among confessional poets, "still whining, like flawed Dylan records, about their poor / lost innocence" (40). Rejecting such an egocentric stance and its obsession with the personal past, Chappell proclaims, "Fresh wonders clamor for language," and he recommends (as T. S. Eliot's essays do) a return to Andrew Marvell and John Donne and Henry Vaughan, for "they had senses / alive apart from their egos, and took delight in / every new page of Natural Theology" (40).

This poem's emphasis on utilizing the senses to experience creation's abundance is echoed by the critique of the Symbolist sensibility set forth in **"Rimbaud Fire Letter to Jim Applewhite."** There Ole Fred renounces the derangement of the senses he had practiced so assiduously under Rimbaud's tutelage. What altered his poetic vision, he explains, following his suspension

from Duke, was his return to the mountain landscape and then, following his re-enrollment at Duke, his immersion in the writings of Samuel Johnson, Alexander Pope, and other representatives of neoclassical rationalism. Yet Ole Fred signs this letter, only partly ironically, "Yours for terror and symbolism" (61), for symbolism—though not the Symbolist sensibility—informs all of *Midquest.* As for terror, that term, reminiscent perhaps of the emotion prompted by Rimbaud's "Drunken Boat," assumes for Chappell the added meaning of gazing into the abyss of suffering and meaninglessness. As he writes Richard Dillard in another of these epistolary poems, "Our faith must be earned from terror" (87) to be credible.

The aesthetic issues raised in the preceding epistolary poems are recapitulated in **"Hallowind"** and in the letter Chappell addresses to George Garrett titled **"How to Build the Earthly Paradise."** The playlet posits a contrast between Fred as poet and Reynolds Price as fiction writer, the former committed to generalizing symbols or archetypes, to a poetry of paradigms, the latter espousing "local clarities" (136) and declaring, "I regard the 'symbol' as a thief" (137). For Price, as Chappell presents him, "Poems are maimed by their timelessness, / . . . / The *symbol* is at last inhuman" (137; Chappell's italics). In actuality, of course, Chappell and Price write both fiction and poetry, and both authors use symbolism extensively. The conflict this poem articulates is intentionally oversimplified. In *Midquest* Chappell creates a text that reconciles the opposing principles the playlet depicts, combining the "local clarities" of the mountain community in which he was raised with the paradigm of spiritual quest limned in Dante's *Divine Comedy,* itself a poem steeped in symbolism and allegory. Chappell's use of the four elements as unifying images also contributes to the symbolic thrust of the poem, its archetypal and mythic dimensions. But at the same time, the images derived from those four elements anchor the text in the material world, in the realm of time and mortality, even as the pilgrim strives to soar toward eternity, toward a vision of the divine. It is precisely the substantiality of the Earthly Paradise—its composition from stone, sand, earth, water, air, plants and animals, men and women and children—that Ole Fred's epistle to Garrett insists upon. And the last word of that letter, before its valediction, is "yes," a word that voices both persona's and poet's affirmation of "the seething / homebrew of creation creating" (177). For Chappell both spiritual rebirth and authentic poetic insight depend upon this recognition of the wonder and mystery of nature and of human existence itself. As he writes in **"Susan Bathing,"** "Unattending beauty is danger & mortal sin," whereas "speech-praise" is the "instrument of unclosing and rising toward light" (19).

To enter the presence of such light is the ultimate goal of the pilgrim-poet in *Midquest,* as it is of Dante the pilgrim, and Chappell establishes many parallels between the two works. Both pilgrims commence their journeys in their thirty-fifth years; both have guides named Virgil; and both also experience divine love mediated by a woman (Beatrice, Susan). Though Virgil Campbell speaks for far earthier values than the author of the *Aeneid,* both Virgils are storytellers who, in different ways, represent the power of the vernacular. As in Dante's epic, the disappearance of *Midquest*'s Virgil from the text (Ole Fred visits his grave in the sixth poem of *Earthsleep*) is followed by a vision of the Earthly Paradise. Some of Chappell's parallels to Dante's poem occur in humorous contexts, as when Chappell, by adding Casanova, Lord Byron, and James Dickey, updates the Italian poet's Second Circle, where the carnal are punished. Chappell achieves similar humorous effects by using Dante's *terza rima* in Ole Fred's account of his grandfather's decision to hedge "his final bet" by converting from Methodism to "hard-believer / Baptist" (30), a conversion that necessitates baptism by total immersion, in the irreverently titled **"My Grandfather Gets Doused."** Such humorous adaptations of Dantean materials and poetic techniques are clearly meant to counterbalance the visionary flights of *Midquest*'s persona. Ole Fred lacks the certitude of his Dantean counterpart, and Chappell thus makes his pilgrim's affirmations more credible by detailing the "wilderness of doubt" (56) from which Fred's faith ultimately arises. The poet's skillful use of humor and irony, his perfectly timed moments of self-deprecation and self-mockery, strengthen the book.

"Birthday 35: Diary Entry," the second poem in *Midquest,* marks the point of departure for Ole Fred's spiritual quest and provides an effective example of the poet's self-directed humor and irony.

> Multiplying my age by 2 in my head,
> I'm a grandfather. Or dead.
>
> "Midway in this life I came to a darksome wood."
> But Dante, however befuddled, was Good.
>   . . . . .
>
> I'm still in flight, still unsteadily in pursuit,
> Always becoming more sordid, pale, and acute . . .
>
>   (3)

In the book's opening poem Ole Fred is portrayed as "wishing never to wake" (2). His diary entry helps explain this impulse by describing the spiritual

wasteland he wanders. Yet Ole Fred's response to this emptiness is not to despair but to pray. **"Birthday 35"** concludes with a prayer that runs for twenty-two lines. A striking admixture of the humorous, the grotesque, the self-ironic, and the sincere, that prayer distances readers from Ole Fred's longing for rebirth without undercutting the sincerity and significance of his yearning.

That yearning is powerfully conveyed in *Midquest*'s fourth poem too, **"Cleaning the Well,"** with its archetypal descent into the underworld, its confrontation with death. Hauled up into the light, the "most willing fish that was ever caught" (16), young Fred wonders, "Jonah, Joseph, Lazarus, / Were you delivered so?" (16) and remarks, *I had not found death good* (17; Chappell's italics). The prospect of death and the possibility of resurrection preoccupy Fred in many of the book's poems, especially in *Earthsleep,* for as his grandmother tells him as early as *Midquest*'s third poem, "It's dirt you rose from, dirt you'll bury in" (12). For her, this thought is more fact than threat, a fact of nature that does not negate her hope of resurrection. Indeed the natural and the supernatural cohabit throughout *Midquest,* as they frequently do in the Judeo-Christian tradition. Each of the four elements around which Chappell organizes *Midquest* assumes religious significance. Water, often a symbol of materiality, becomes an emblem of the intersection of time and eternity in **"The River Awakening in the Sea,"** as in Anne Bradstreet's "Contemplations." Water is also, in baptism, a means of grace, an instrument of spiritual regeneration. Fire is both instrument of divine wrath and means of purification. It witnesses to God's presence in the burning bush from which God spoke to Moses and in the tongues of flame associated with the Holy Spirit. Wind—bodiless, invisible, yet observable in its effects—is similarly linked to the Holy Spirit, and in **"Second Wind"** it touches Fred's grandmother with "the weight of grace" (106). Chappell regularly associates wind with music as well and has noted that "music probably stands in my poems most of the time for exaltation, exalted spirits, ecstatic visionary knowledge."[38] As for earth, with its gaping graves, it is the foundation of the Earthly Paradise and the soil from which the "Tree of Spirit lift[s] from the mountain of earth" (149) to "the Mountains Outside Time" (169).

Midquest is a poem that evokes the mythos of Eden and "a final shore" (141) beyond the fevered river of time. Implicit in the sleep of *Earthsleep* is the prospect of awakening, and the epigraph from Hawthorne that opens the book's final volume depicts the peaceful transition from waking to the "temporary death" of sleep, comparing that transition to the experience of dying itself. "So calm, perhaps, will be the final change; so undisturbed, as if among familiar things the entrance of the soul to its Eternal home" (143). Hawthorne's "perhaps" in this passage registers the ineluctable mystery of the human encounter with death, and the sketch from which Chappell excerpts this epigraph is titled "The Haunted Mind." Yet while the questions death poses are irresolvable for the mind situated on this side of the grave—as the varied definitions of the term "earthsleep" in *Midquest*'s closing poem indicate—Chappell concludes that poem by invoking Dante's vision of God: "The love that moves the sun and other stars / The love that moves itself in light to loving" (187). The first of these lines translates the final line of the *Paradiso,* while the second is Chappell's attempt to capture the tone and spirit of Dante's poem. In the final line of **"Earthsleep"** Fred and Susan lie side by side "here in the earliest morning of the world" (187), an image suggestive not of death but of new life. Dabney Stuart is thus correct when he argues that Chappell is "preoccupied with and hopeful of images of release and transformation, which are Christian in their orientation."[39] The Fred who resists waking in *Midquest*'s opening poem learns to "invite the mornings" (185).[40]

In addition to tracing this explicitly religious quest, Chappell fills *Midquest* with metaphysical speculations of various sorts. For Chappell, the experience of wonder prompts not only spiritual meditation but also the reflections of poet and philosopher alike. Chappell's repeated probing of philosophical issues, what one critic has called Chappell's "abiding concern with Ultimates,"[41] contributes significantly to both the breadth of *Midquest*'s subject matter and the substantiality of its themes. Yet the book does not simply juxtapose humorous narrative poems with more somber meditative poems. Instead, Chappell's narrative poems address philosophical and religious themes while his meditative poems are leavened by a buoyant humor that prevents reader and poet alike from taking themselves too seriously. The book's more lyric poems—those, for example, that open and close each of the four volumes—are similarly infused with philosophical inquiry. In fact cosmogony is a recurring motif in the initial poems of *River, Bloodfire,* and *Wind Mountain,* introduced in each case by references to "how the world was formed" (2, 56, 98). Myths of origin are also evident in Ole Fred's "slightly different Big Bang theory" in **"The Autumn Bleat of the Weathervane Trombone"** ("In the beginning was the Trombone" [115]) and in the excerpt from his novel-in-progress in **"Science Fiction Water Letter"** (41-43). Obviously, a concern for cosmogony also underpins Chappell's use of the four elements to

structure *Midquest*. Renouncing the abstraction of Plato's realm of Ideal Forms (as he had done in his early poem **"A Transcendental Idealist Dreams in Springtime"**), Chappell recurs to the pre-Socratic naturalistic era in Greek philosophy. What he offers, finally, is a profoundly incarnational view of the relationship between matter and spirit, time and eternity, a view shaped by Christian thought.

This incarnational perspective is most fully developed in *Midquest*'s four long meditative poems: **"Susan Bathing," "Firewood," "The Autumn Bleat of the Weathervane Trombone,"** and **"The Peaceable Kingdom of Emerald Windows."** The first two are single-sentence stream-of-consciousness poems, each seven pages in length, and they thus contrast in structure with the greater formal and syntactical clarity of the latter two poems, differences intended to mirror, Chappell says, his pilgrim's progress "as the speaker begins to order his life" (x). To term these poems "interior monologues," however, as Chappell does in the preface, is somewhat misleading, for each includes features of direct address that again reinforce the network of relationships in which the poet embeds Ole Fred.

"Susan Bathing" incorporates both philosophical and explicitly religious themes while also confirming Chappell's claim that *Midquest* is "in its largest design a love poem" (xi). The epigraph to **"Susan Bathing,"** taken from Pope's "Windsor Forest," asserts that harmonious confusion, not chaos, governs the world, and thus underscores the fundamental outlook of *Midquest* as a whole and the artistic impression of order that the book conveys. The Susan of this poem takes on a variety of identities. On the literal level she is simply Fred's wife, the object of his love, but marriage in *Midquest* assumes a metaphoric significance that extends well beyond its social function. Marriage illustrates the union of apparent opposites: not only women and men but also humankind and nature, as well as in Christian theology, the human and the divine. Susan herself functions allegorically in this poem both as Beatrice and as the Virgin Mary. In **"Susan Bathing"** body and spirit are conjoined, and Chappell's wide-ranging diction reflects this yoking of the earthy and the ethereal. In addition to her roles as Beatrice and Mary, Susan becomes the poet's muse, her "clean / flesh the synonym of love," eliciting his "speech praise" (23), reminding the poet of his "responsibilities to whatever is genuine" (19). In traditional Christian terms, the poet describes his will as "stricken and contort" and declares that "only intercession from / without can restore it" (21). Through Susan and the outpouring of praise she provokes, he gains access to self-transformation, "for

once the mind prepares to praise & garbs / in worshipful robe it enlarges to plenitude" (19), a plenitude, as
in the annunciation to Mary, "plena gratia" (20), full
of grace. Significantly, it is the sight of Susan's body
that prompts this epiphany, just as her physical act of
bathing promises the poet spiritual regeneration.

In contrast to **"Susan Bathing," "Firewood"** is less
explicitly religious and more overtly philosophical in
its exploration of the relationship between flesh and
spirit, matter and mind. It too employs the metaphor
of marriage, however, and discusses the role of art in
bonding humanity and nature. Much more than **"Susan
Bathing," "Firewood"** confronts the fact of death and
attempts to reconcile that fact with the longing for immortality. The wood Ole Fred splits in this poem is
destined for his fireplace, where the sun (imaged as
stored in the wood) will be released as heat and light,
"the sun risen at midnight" to ascend "the rose trellis
of stars . . . afire" (69). Burning, this wood will
become "tree of spirit," with the poet's chimney linking the corporeal and the immaterial and suggesting
humanity's dual identity as flesh and spirit—the world
of spirit symbolized, here as elsewhere in Chappell's
work, by the stars. The chimney "pins our dwelling /
to the earth and to the stars equally" (69), the poet
observes. Yet despite the beauty and the rhetorical effect of an image like "the rose trellis of stars," Ole
Fred remains skeptical, fearful that "the cold dark will
tear our tree of fire / away complete" (69) and
conscious that Lucretius's "seed of fire ignis semina is
seed semina mortuis," that is, seed of death (70). Unable to endorse, as he once did, Rimbaud's conception
of "the vatic will" (71) capable of utterly transforming
reality through the powers of the poetic imagination,
Ole Fred yields to thoughts of death. For a moment he
even longs to jettison human consciousness in
exchange for the apparent contentment of the animal
world. But, finally, he can neither surrender the uniqueness of human selfhood nor evade its often anguished
doubts. As he continues to wonder, "but where / shall
I sit when once this flesh is spirit?" (73), the reader
notices that Ole Fred has undercut the Lucretian view
of a purely physical universe in the very formulation
of that question. **"Firewood"** concludes by comparing
the ultimately successful splitting of the wood to the
annunciation to Mary and by depicting that experience
as a kind of baptism: "I'm washed in the blood / of
the sun, the ghostly holy of the deep deep log" (73).
The punning religious diction here is meant to resolve,
to some extent at least, the tensions between secular
and sacred, flesh and spirit, time and eternity, that this
poem examines. Yet, as Ole Fred states in the poem's
final lines, "It doesn't come easy, I'm / here to tell
you that."

What the other two long meditative poems in *Midquest*
make clear is that, for Chappell, this "ghostly holy" is
not to be sought at the expense of the physical world.
To both **"The Autumn Bleat of the Weathervane
Trombone"** and **The Peaceable Kingdom of Emerald
Windows,"** the poet introduces a new character,
someone whom Ole Fred refers to as Uncle Body.
This figure is intended to subvert the philosophical
idealism espoused by Plato, Plotinus, Descartes, and
Emerson as well as the otherworldliness of a Protestant
Christianity too often misled by Gnostic and Neo-
Platonic thought. For the Emerson of *Nature,* personal
identity was purely a mental or spiritual phenomenon;
even one's body belonged to the category of the "NOT
ME."[42] The playfulness and linguistic exuberance of
both these poems reflect the expansiveness of the
poet's sense of selfhood. In **"The Autumn Bleat"**
[**"The Autumn Bleat of the Weathervane Trombone"**] fall is less a time of decay than of rebirth. Yellow, gold, and blue are the dominant colors, the last
recalling Wallace Stevens's use of blue as the color of
the imagination in "The Man with the Blue Guitar."
That connection is evident here in Fred's music, a
"bluesy A" (115) emerging to drift "the bluebleached
air" (114). As the title's term "bleat" implies, that
music is scarcely elegant, but the poem provides a
cornucopia of sound effects, of levels of diction and
allusion too. "There's something in air in love with
rounded notes, / The goldenrod's a-groan at the globèd
beauty," Chappell writes, in lines of consciously exaggerated alliteration (110). "Bring me my trombone of
burning gold, bring me / My harrowing desire," he
adds, paraphrasing Blake's *Milton*. Obviously, Chappell takes risks in such passages, as he attempts to
communicate Fred's vision of life's fullness; occasionally those fanciful flights collapse under the weight of
their distended diction. In general, however, readers
are likely to be borne along by the sweeping sense of
elation Ole Fred expresses, by the sheer energy and
inventiveness of his words.

Like **"Firewood,"** both **"Autumn Bleat"** and **"The
Peaceable Kingdom of Emerald Windows"** address
the fact of death. In contrast to **"Firewood"** the latter
two poems actually contain portraits of the afterlife
(as does *Earthsleep*'s **"At the Grave of Virgil
Campbell"**). At times, these visions of the afterlife
are wildly comic, verging on the blasphemous, as
when Fred states his certainty that there is "Whiskey-
after-Death" and refers to God as "the Holy Bartender"
(173). But the different versions of the afterlife Ole
Fred offers all have in common their being grounded
upon human relationships and the physical world. In
"Autumn Bleat," for example, he anticipates—with
some apprehension—the prospect of spending eternity
in the company of his fellow poets. In **"Peaceable**

Kingdom" it is naturalists like Gilbert White and William Bartram, a novelist like Colette, and "rare Ben Franklin" whom he envisions joining, all of them people firmly attached in their earthly lives to the physical world. Moreover, since the phrase **"Emerald Windows"** refers to raindrops, nature becomes precious in itself, associated through the color green with seasonal rebirth and providing a source of spiritual vision, a window on eternity. At odds with the philosophical idealism of Emerson, Chappell nevertheless seems to concur with the Transcendentalist precept, "Nature is the symbol of Spirit."

Yet while Ole Fred celebrates nature and renounces Nirvana as "a sterile and joyless blasphemy" (113), he is decidedly unwilling to resign himself to physicality alone. He refuses to surrender to matter his powers of mind and spirit. Thus in **"Autumn Bleat"** he attempts to induce Uncle Body to voyage with him through the realms of philosophical speculation: "To swim from Singapore / To Hermeneutics and through the Dardanelles / To Transcendentalism, back through the Straits / of Hegel" (113). Here, as in many other poems in *Midquest,* Chappell attempts to naturalize metaphysical thought and thus to create for poetry—and for its readers—a commitment to philosophical reflection, to the Socratic ideal of examined lives. Just as the Virgil of the *Georgics* identifies the natural philosopher (along with the farmer and the poet) as one of the three kinds of people most attuned to the harmonies of the universe, so Chappell makes philosophical thought one of *Midquest*'s central activities, along with farming and artistic creation and the religious quest itself.

Perhaps the most persistent philosophical and religious problem Chappell's book addresses, especially in *Earthsleep,* is human mortality, the inescapable reality that Martin Heidegger terms *Sein zum Tod* (being toward death). **"The Peaceable Kingdom,"** the meditative poem in that final volume, includes the statement, "Goodbye I perceive to be a human creature" (156). Yet the tone of that poem is not one of fear or anxiety but serenity. Chappell achieves this effect in part by invoking the utopian vision of the Edward Hicks painting mentioned in the title, in part by making green one of the poem's dominant colors (as that color predominates in several other poems in *Earthsleep*), and in part by organizing the latter portions of the poem around the activity of harvesting hay. That activity, successfully completed despite the threat of rain, lends to the poem an aura of fruition and reaffirms the bonds of family and community which the entire book cultivates. Rejecting again idealism's "sleepy flea market of Forms" (158), Ole Fred emphasizes the goodness of the creation, informing Uncle Body, "All the world is lit for your delight"

(159). Integral to this vision of oneness with nature are those passages in which the poet personifies Maude and Jackson, the horses pulling the hay wagon, endowing them with speech. Through this device Chappell bridges the accustomed gap between humanity and nature and suspends the reader's commitment to the purely factual. His appeal to a wider conception of truth encourages the reader to assent as well to his image of the sun nestling "in the form / In the hay in the world in the green green hand" (157).

Clearly the resolution **"The Peaceable Kingdom"** offers is more emotional than logical. Like the repeated sound of the church bell calling *home, home, home* at key points throughout the last two volumes of *Midquest* (100, 133, 161, 185), it appeals more to the heart than to the head. But Chappell has already conceded as much in **"Firewood"** in his account of the postlapsarian intellect as "all alert and doubtful" (72). What Chappell manages to accomplish in *Midquest*—and it is no small achievement in what is commonly considered a postmodern, post-Christian age—is to awaken readers to the presence of Spirit, both in nature and in themselves. The ***Book of Earth,*** as Ole Fred discovers, is "brimming over with matter, / Matter aye and spirit, too, each / And every page is chock to stupefying" (160). Or, as Fred puts it after visiting the site of a burned church in **"My Grandfather's Church Goes Up"**:

> *Pilgrim, the past becomes prayer*
> *becomes remembrance rock-real of Resurrection*
> *when the Willer so willeth works his wild wonders.*
>
> (77; Chappell's italics)

Among the types of resurrection to which *Midquest* testifies is that of traditional poetic forms. **"My Grandfather's Church"** employs Anglo-Saxon alliterative verse; the epistolary poem to Richard Dillard is in elegiacs; the letter to Guy Lillian in syllabics; **"My Grandmother's Hard Row to Hoe"** uses chant royal. While blank verse and free verse predominate, other traditional forms abound: rhymed couplets in lines of varying lengths, heroic couplets, *terza rima,* Yeatsian tetrameter, even a variation on classical hexameter in **"Susan Bathing."** The rhyme scheme in the playlet **"Hallowind"** consists of three successively rhymed tetrameter lines, with the rhymes carrying over from one speaker to the next. In the grandmother's monologue in **"Second Wind"** the poet uses iambic pentameter octets based on an abba abba rhyme scheme, yet maintains the impression of a vernacular voice. Few poets since Robert Frost have captured the natural speaking voice as effectively as Chappell does in both rhymed forms and blank verse. The book's varied stanza structures—couplets, tercets, quatrains, sestets, octets, verse paragraphs of differing lengths, seven-page single-sentence stream-of-consciousness meditations—help keep the poems continually fresh as the reader accompanies Ole Fred on his quest. As one critic has remarked, "The poems fairly exult in their technical invention. . . . The range is extraordinary."[43] Chappell's skill with such structural matters is especially evident in the epistolary poem to George Garrett titled **"How to Build the Earthly Paradise."** There the poet creates a nine-line stanza, each end stopped, to represent the blocks of material used to construct this utopia. Each stanza opens and closes, moreover, with a single-syllable line, as if to evince the solidity of the workmanship, and the second and eighth lines contain just two syllables per line. The ponderous rhythms these four lines establish at each stanza's beginning and end suggest the thought and care that underlie the poet's making. Chappell's mastery of his craft is readily, though unostentatiously, apparent throughout *Midquest,* reminding readers of the poetic resources many contemporary poets have neglected in their commitment to free verse.

The revival of the narrative impulse in poetry is another of the aesthetic resurrections that this book attains. As one interviewer has noted, there are at least three kinds of narrative in *Midquest*: "the movement of images," "the repetition of narratives within a poem, the story lines themselves, the plots," and "the whole poetic narrative of the self, a biography of sorts."[44] It is in the second of these categories that the poet allows his gifts for storytelling their freest rein, particularly when his grandparents and parents and Virgil Campbell speak; and it is often in these poems (for example, **"My Father's Hurricane"** and **"Three Sheets in the Wind"**) that Chappell's comic vision reaches its greatest heights. Because of the accessibility and humor of these poems, general readers as well as critics have sometimes seen them as the most distinctive or original aspect of the book. Yet for all their vividness and directness of appeal, these poems are subsumed within *Midquest*'s larger narrative and thematic structure, which is centered upon Ole Fred's search for moral and spiritual renewal and for a deeper understanding of his place both in the human community and in the cosmos.

Midquest is ultimately most original in its elaborate interweaving of the regional and the universal and in its intricacy of design, a design in which lyric, narrative, epistolary, and meditative poems echo and enrich one another. Chappell's enormous range of allusions ties his individual Appalachian voices to many of the most significant features of the Western literary, philosophical, and religious traditions. To declare, as one reviewer of *Earthsleep* did, that Chappell's "real subject" is "the hard but satisfyingly essential dirt-farming life as it used to be in the South," a subject

from which the reviewer felt the poems in *Earthsleep* had strayed, is to badly misread both the poet's intentions and his accomplishment.[45] *Midquest* is a book that requires and rewards rereading. It is, to quote Kelly Cherry, "a terrifically . . . powerful poem, full of the pleasures of surfaces and the deep gratification of complex structure."[46] As the book receives the kind of searching critical analysis its achievement merits, it will increasingly be seen for what, in fact, it is—one of the finest long poems in twentieth-century American literature.

Notes

1. Broughton, "Fred Chappell," 118.

2. Palmer, "Fred Chappell," 407.

3. Chappell's three chapbooks—*The Man Twice Married to Fire* (Greensboro: Unicorn, 1977), *Awakening to Music* (Davidson, N.C.: Briarpatch, 1979), and *Driftlake: A Lieder Cycle* (Emory, Va.: Iron Mountain Press, 1981)—have often been erroneously listed among his book-length publications in standard reference works. "How I Lost It"—another title so listed—though planned, never appeared in print.

4. Ralph Waldo Emerson, *Selected Prose and Poetry,* 2d ed., ed. Reginald L. Cook (San Francisco: Rinehart, 1969), 124.

5. Stephenson, "'The Way It Is,'" 8.

6. Chappell, *A Way of Happening: Observations of Contemporary Poetry* (New York: Picador, 1998), 9.

7. Walsh, "Fred Chappell," 71.

8. Ibid., 75.

9. Chappell, "Fred Chappell," 122.

10. Kathryn Stripling Byer, "Turning the Windlass at the Well: Fred Chappell's Early Poetry," in *Dream Garden,* 88.

11. Chappell, *The World between the Eyes* (Baton Rouge: Louisiana State University Press, 1971), 3, 4. Further references noted parenthetically are to this edition.

12. Chappell, *Plow Naked: Selected Writings on Poetry* (Ann Arbor: University of Michigan Press, 1993), 112.

13. Byer, "Turning the Windlass at the Well," 93-94.

14. Ibid., 95.

15. Chappell, *Midquest* (Baton Rouge: Louisiana State University Press, 1981), ix. Further references noted parenthetically are to this edition.

16. Broughton, "Fred Chappell," 108. "Familiar Poem" is reprinted in *Under Twenty-five: Duke Narrative and Verse, 1945-1962,* ed. William Blackburn (Durham, N.C.: Duke University Press, 1963), 198-201.

17. Crane and Kirkland, "First and Last Words," 16.

18. Dannye Romine Powell, "Fred Chappell," in *Parting the Curtains: Interviews with Southern Writers* (Winston-Salem: Blair, 1994), 36.

19. Jackson, "On the Margins of Dreams," 156.

20. Bizzaro, "Introduction: Fred Chappell's Community of Readers," in *Dream Garden*, 4.

21. Randolph Paul Runyon, "Fred Chappell: Midquestions," in *Southern Writers at Century's End*, ed. Jeffrey J. Folks and James A. Perkins (Lexington: University of Kentucky Press, 1997), 197.

22. Chappell, "Midquest," *The Small Farm* 11-12 (Spring-Fall 1980): 13.

23. Chappell, *A Way of Happening*, 215.

24. Chappell, *Plow Naked*, 90.

25. Ibid., 89, 92.

26. Chappell, *A Way of Happening*, 235.

27. Chappell, *Plow Naked*, 91.

28. Morgan, "*Midquest* and the Gift of Narrative," in *Dream Garden*, 139.

29. Chappell, "Midquest," 13.

30. Ibid.

31. Taylor, "Fred Chappell," in *Contemporary Poets*, 6th ed., ed. Thomas Riggs (New York: St. James Press, 1996), 154.

32. Philip Pierson, "Interview with Fred Chappell," *New River Review* 2 (Spring 1977): 13. As Rodney Jones also notes, "We never have the sense that *Midquest* is inventing itself apart from other consciousness." See Jones's essay "The Large Vision: Fred Chappell's *Midquest*," *Appalachian Journal* 9, no. 1 (1981): 63.

33. Chappell, "Towards a Beginning," *The Small Farm* 4-5 (Oct. 1976-Mar. 1977): 98.

34. Don Johnson, "The Cultivated Mind: The Georgic Center of Fred Chappell's Poetry," in *Dream Garden*, 170-79.

35. Chappell, *Plow Naked*, 79.

36. Pierson, "Interview with Fred Chappell," 11. See also Crane and Kirkland, "First and Last Words," 20.

37. For an extensive analysis of the sources of many of Chappell's allusions in *Midquest*, see John Lang, "Points of Kinship: Community and Allusion in Fred Chappell's *Midquest*," in *Dream Garden*, 97-117.

38. Broughton, "Fred Chappell," 109.

39. Dabney Stuart, "Spiritual Matter in Fred Chappell's Poetry," in *Dream Garden*, 48.

40. Alan Nadel mistakenly assumes that Chappell's aim in *Midquest* is to "attempt to freeze the day of his 35th birthday," an attempt that Nadel calls "the governing futility of the whole tetralogy." See his essay "Quest and Midquest: Fred Chappell and the First-Person Personal Epic," *New England Review and Bread Loaf Quarterly* 6 (Winter 1983): 324.

41. Peter Makuck, "Chappell's Continuities: *First and Last Words*," in *Dream Garden*, 180.

42. Emerson, *Selected Prose and Poetry*, 4.

43. Cherry, "The Idea of Odyssey in *Midquest*," in *Dream Garden*, 122.

44. Jackson, "On the Margins of Dreams," 155.

45. Richard Tillinghast, "Scattered Nebulae," *Sewanee Review* 90, no. 2 (1982): 300.

46. Cherry, "The Idea of Odyssey in *Midquest*," 132.

Works by Fred Chappell

Listed in order of publication.

NOVELS

It Is Time, Lord. New York: Atheneum, 1963. London: Dent, 1965.

The Inkling. New York: Harcourt, Brace and World, 1965. London: Chapman and Hall, 1966.

Dagon. New York: Harcourt, Brace and World, 1968.

The Gaudy Place. New York: Harcourt, Brace and World, 1973.

I Am One of You Forever. Baton Rouge: Louisiana State University Press, 1985.

Brighten the Corner Where You Are. New York: St. Martin's, 1989.

Farewell, I'm Bound to Leave You. New York: Picador, 1996.

Look Back All the Green Valley. New York: Picador, 1999.

COLLECTIONS OF POETRY

The World between the Eyes. Baton Rouge: Louisiana State University Press, 1971.

River, Baton Rouge: Louisiana State University Press, 1975.

Bloodfire. Baton Rouge: Louisiana State University Press, 1978.

Wind Mountain. Baton Rouge: Louisiana State University Press, 1979.

Earthsleep. Baton Rouge: Louisiana State University Press, 1980.

Midquest. Baton Rouge: Louisiana State University Press, 1981.

Castle Tzingal. Baton Rouge: Louisiana State University Press, 1984.

Source. Baton Rouge: Louisiana State University Press, 1985.

First and Last Words. Baton Rouge: Louisiana State University Press, 1989.

C. Baton Rouge: Louisiana State University Press, 1993.

Spring Garden: New and Selected Poems. Baton Rouge: Louisiana State University Press, 1995.

COLLECTIONS OF SHORT STORIES

Moments of Light. Los Angeles: New South, 1980.

More Shapes Than One. New York: St. Martin's, 1991.

COLLECTIONS OF ESSAYS

Plow Naked: Selected Writings on Poetry. Ann Arbor: University of Michigan Press, 1993.

A Way of Happening: Observations of Contemporary Poetry. New York: Picador, 1998.

OTHER BOOKS

The Fred Chappell Reader. New York: St. Martin's, 1987.

SELECTED UNCOLLECTED ESSAYS AND OTHER NONFICTION

"Seven Propositions about Poetry and Personality." *Above Ground Review* 1 (Winter 1969): 41-44.

"Six Propositions about Literature and History." *New Literary History* 1, no. 3 (1970): 513-22.

"Unpeaceable Kingdoms: The Novels of Sylvia Wilkinson." *Hollins Critic* 8 (Apr. 1971): 1-10.

"*The Surface of Earth*: A Pavement of Good Intentions." *The Archive* 88 (Fall 1975): 75-82.

"The Image of the South in Film." *Southern Humanities Review* 12 (Fall 1978): 303-11.

"Two Modes: A Plea for Tolerance." *Appalachian Journal* 5, no. 3 (1978): 335-39.

"The Comic Structure of *The Sound and the Fury.*" *Mississippi Quarterly* 31, no. 3 (1978): 381-86.

"Science and the Artist's Vision." *New England Review* 3, no. 1 (1980): 132-40.

"The Vocation of Literature." *Colonnades* 32 (Spring 1981): 78-82.

"The Seamless Vision of James Still." *Appalachian Journal* 8, no. 3 (1981): 196-202.

"Viable Allegiances." *Abatis One* (1983): 52-63.

"A Pact with Faustus." *Mississippi Quarterly* 37 (Winter 1983-84): 9-20. Reprinted in *The Fred Chappell Reader,* 479-90.

"'Menfolks Are Heathens': Cruelty in James Still's Short Stories." *Iron Mountain Review* 2 (Summer 1984): 11-15.

"The Ninety-Ninth Foxfire Book." *Appalachian Journal* 11, no. 3 (1984): 260-67.

"Fred Chappell." Vol. 4 of *Contemporary Authors Autobiography Series,* edited by Adele Sarkissian, 113-26. Detroit: Gale, 1986.

"Visionary Fiction." *Chronicles* 11 (May 1987): 19-21.

"A Detail in a Poem." *Kentucky Poetry Review* 26 (Fall 1990): 66-75.

"Fantasia on the Theme of Theme and Fantasy." *Studies in Short Fiction* 27, no. 2 (1990): 179-89.

"Fictional Characterization as Infinite Regressive Series: George Garrett's Strangers in the Mirror." In *Southern Literature and Literary Theory,* edited by Jefferson Humphries, 66-74. Athens: University of Georgia Press, 1990.

"The Long Mirror: Dabney Stuart's Film Allusion." *Kentucky Poetry Review* 27 (Spring 1991): 85-92.

"Remarks on *Dagon.*" In *The H. P. Lovecraft Centennial Conference Proceedings,* edited by S. T. Joshi, 43-45. West Warwick, R.I.: Necronomicon, 1991.

"'Rich with Disappearances': Betty Adcock's Time Paradoxes." *Shenandoah* 45 (Summer 1995): 58-75.

"The Shape of Appalachian Literature to Come." In *The Future of Southern Letters,* edited by Jefferson Humphries and John Lowe, 54-60. New York: Oxford University Press, 1996.

"Peter Taylor: The Genial Mentor." *North Carolina Literary Review* 6 (1997): 45-54.

"Jim Wayne Miller: The Gentle Partisan." *North Carolina Literary Review* 6 (1997): 7-13.

"'Not as a Leaf': Southern Poetry and the Innovation of Tradition." *Georgia Review* 51, no. 3 (1997): 477-89.

"The Music of 'Each in His Season.'" In *Tuned and Under Tension: The Recent Poetry of W. D. Snodgrass,* edited by Philip Raisor, 72-87. Newark: University of Delaware Press, 1998.

INTERVIEWS

Graham, John. "Fred Chappell." In *Craft So Hard to Learn,* edited by George Garrett. New York: Morrow, 1972.

Sopko, John, and John Carr. "Dealing with the Grotesque: Fred Chappell." In *Kite-Flying and Other Irrational Acts: Conversations with Twelve Southern Writers,* edited by John Carr. Baton Rouge: Louisiana State University Press, 1972.

Graham, John. "Fred Chappell." In *The Writer's Voice,* edited by George Garrett. New York: Morrow, 1973.

Pierson, Philip. "Interview with Fred Chappell." *New River Review* 2 (Spring 1977): 5-16, 61-73.

West, James L. W., III, and August Nigro. "William Blackburn and His Pupils: A Conversation." *Mississippi Quarterly* 31, no. 4 (1978): 605-14.

Jackson, Richard. "On the Margins of Dreams." In *Acts of Mind: Conversations with Contemporary Poets,* edited by Richard Jackson. Tuscaloosa: University of Alabama Press, 1983.

Patterson, Sarah, and Dan Lindsey. "Interview with Fred Chappell." *Davidson Miscellany* 19 (Spring 1984): 62-76.

Stephenson, Shelby. "'The Way It Is': An Interview with Fred Chappell." *Iron Mountain Review* 2 (Spring 1985): 7-11.

Ruffin, Paul. "Interview with Fred Chappell." *Pembroke Magazine* 17 (1985): 131-35.

Redd, Chris. "A Man of Letters in the Modern World: An Interview with Fred Chappell." *Arts Journal* 14 (May 1989): 7-9.

Tarkington, Tim. "An Interview with Fred Chappell." *Chattahoochee Review* 9 (Winter 1989): 44-48.

Stewart, Mary Lass. "Interviews with Clyde Edgerton and Fred Chappell." *Cellar Door* 17 (Spring 1990): 26-28.

Stirnemann, S. A. "Fred Chappell: Poet with 'Ah! Bright Wings.'" *South Florida Poetry Review* 7 (Winter 1990): 41-51.

Broughton, Irv. "Fred Chappell." Vol. 3 of *The Writer's Mind: Interviews with American Authors.* Fayetteville: University of Arkansas Press, 1990.

Walsh, William J. "Fred Chappell." In *Speak So I Shall Know Thee: Interviews with Southern Writers.* Asheboro, N.C.: Down Home Press, 1990.

Palmer, Tersh. "Fred Chappell." *Appalachian Journal* 19, no. 4 (1992): 402-10.

Brannon, Melissa. "On Process: An Interview," In *Plow Naked: Selected Writings on Poetry,* edited by Fred Chappell. Ann Arbor: University of Michigan Press, 1993.

Schweitzer, Darrell. "A Talk with Fred Chappell." *Worlds of Fantasy and Horror* 1 (Summer 1994): 40-43.

Powell, Dannye Romine. "Fred Chappell." In *Parting the Curtains: Interviews with Southern Writers.* Winston-Salem, N.C.: John F. Blair, 1994.

Easa, Leila. "A Conversation with Fred Chappell." *The Archive* 108 (Fall 1995): 49-60.

Corbett, Kevin. "Fred Chappell," *Notre Dame Review* 2 (Summer 1996): 64-67.

Howard, Jennifer. "Fred Chappell: From the Mountains to the Mainstream." *Publishers Weekly,* 30 Sept. 1996, 55-56.

Brown, Fred, and Jeanne McDonald. "Fred Chappell." In *Growing up Southern: How the South Shapes Its Writers.* Greenville, S.C.: Blue Ridge, 1997.

Crane, Resa, and James Kirkland. "First and Last Words: A Conversation with Fred Chappell." In *Dream Garden: Vie Poetic Vision of Fred Chappell,* edited by Patrick Bizzaro. Baton Rouge: Louisiana State University Press, 1997.

Ragan, David Paul. "'Flying by Night': An Early Interview with Fred Chappell." *North Carolina Literary Review* 7 (1998): 105-19.

Sullivan, Sally. "'Citizens Who Observe': A Conversation with Fred Chappell." *North Carolina Literary Review* 7 (1998): 145-55.

SELECTED WORKS ABOUT CHAPPELL

Listed in alphabetical order by author.

BIBLIOGRAPHIES

Kibler, James Everett, Jr. "A Fred Chappell Bibliography, 1963-1983." *Mississippi Quarterly* 37 (Winter 1983-84): 63-88. Detailed record of Chappell's primary works.

BOOKS

Bizzaro, Patrick, ed. *Dream Garden: The Poetic Vision of Fred Chappell.* Baton Rouge: Louisiana State University Press, 1997. Extremely valuable collection of essays on Chappell's poetry through *Spring Garden.*

SELECTED CRITICAL AND BIOGRAPHICAL ESSAYS

Abowitz, Richard. "Chappell's Aesthetic Agenda: The Binding of *Midquest* to *I Am One of You Forever* and *Brighten the Corner Where You Are.*" In *Dream Garden: The Poetic Vision of Fred Chappell,* edited by Patrick Bizzaro, 145-53. Baton Rouge: Louisiana State University Press, 1997. Thorough analysis of the characters, images, and literary techniques that link *Midquest* to the first two Kirkman novels.

Albright, Alex. "Friend of Reason: Surveying the Fred Chappell Papers at Duke University." In *Dream Garden: The Poetic Vision of Fred Chappell,* edited by Patrick

Bizzaro, 222-39. Baton Rouge: Louisiana State University Press, 1997. Useful inventory of the major holdings of Chappell manuscripts and letters at Duke.

Bizzaro, Patrick. "The Singer Dissolved in Song: The Poetic as Modern Alternative in Chappell's *Castle Tzingal.*" In *Dream Garden: The Poetic Vision of Fred Chappell,* edited by Patrick Bizzaro, 154-69. Baton Rouge: Louisiana State University Press, 1997. Views *Castle Tzingal* as an allegory on the survival powers of art in the *modern* age.

Byer, Kathryn Stripling. "Turning the Windlass at the Well: Fred Chappell's Early Poetry." In *Dream Garden: The Poetic Vision of Fred Chappell,* edited by Patrick Bizzaro, 88-96. Baton Rouge: Louisiana State University Press, 1997. Excellent assessment of *The World between the Eyes,* especially its longer narrative poems.

Campbell, Hilbert. "Fred Chappell's Urn of Memory: *I Am One of You Forever.*" *Southern Literary Journal* 25 (Spring 1993): 103-11. Brilliant analysis of Chappell's use of memory and imagination to transform childhood experience into art. Also points out similarities between this novel and *Midquest.*

Cherry, Kelly. "A Writer's Harmonious World." *Parnassus* 9 (Fall-Winter 1981): 115-29. Reprinted as "The Idea of Odyssey in *Midquest*" in *Dream Garden: The Poetic Vision of Fred Chappell,* edited by Patrick Bizzaro, 118-32. Baton Rouge: Louisiana State University Press, 1997. Detailed analysis of the motif of the spiritual journey in *Midquest.*

Coindreau, Maurice-Edgar. Preface to *Le Dieu-Poisson* [*Dagon*]. Paris: Christian Bourgois, 1971.

Cooper, Kate. "Reading between the Lines: Fred Chappell's *Castle Tzingal.*" In *Southern Literature and Literary Theory,* edited by Jefferson Humphries, 88-108. Athens: University of Georgia Press, 1990. Offers a postmodernist reading of this poem, emphasizing the indeterminacy and limitations of linguistic representation.

de Abruna, Laura Niesen. "Fred Chappell." In *Encyclopedia of American Humorists,* edited by Steven H. Gale, 75-81. New York: Garland, 1988. Discusses *Midquest* and Virgil Campbell as the high points of Chappell's contributions to American humor.

Dillard, Annie. Foreword to *Moments of Light,* ix-xvii. Los Angeles: New South, 1980. Insightful, appreciative assessment of the literary achievement of Chappell's first book of stories.

Dillard, R. H. W. "Letters from a Distant Lover: The Novels of Fred Chappell." *Hollins Critic* 10 (Apr. 1973): 1-15. This first scholarly article on Chappell provides a superb analysis of the major themes in the writer's first four novels.

Dziemianowicz, Stefan. "Fred Chappell." In *St. James Guide to Horror, Ghost, and Gothic Writers,* edited by David Pringle, 132-33.

Detroit: St. James, 1998. Brief discussion of *Dagon* and several short stories.

Eubanks, Georgann. "Fred Chappell: The Bard of Canton." *Duke Magazine,* Nov.-Dec. 1993, 6-11. Useful overview of Chappell's career, including his teaching at the University of North Carolina-Greensboro.

Forkner, Ben. "Contemporary Stories of the American South." *Revue française d'etudes americaines* 23 (Feb. 1985): 51-61. Discussion of *Moments of Light* that refers to "Children of Strikers" and "Blue Dive" as "Southern masterpieces."

Garrett, George. "A Few Things about Fred Chappell." *Mississippi Quarterly* 37 (Winter 1983-84): 3-8. Lively assessment of Chappell's personality and achievement.

Gingher, Marianne. "I Wish I'd Written That Story." *Southern Review* 33, no. 4 (1997): 846-52. Illuminating essay on Chappell as a teacher of creative writing in the early 1970s.

Gray, Amy Tipton. "Fred Chappell's *I Am One of You Forever*: The Oneiros of Childhood Transformed." In *The Poetics of Appalachian Space,* edited by Parks Lanier, Jr., 28-39. Knoxville: University of Tennessee Press, 1991. A Bachelardian interpretation of this novel.

————. "R'lyeh in Appalachia: Lovecraft's Influence on Fred Chappell's *Dagon.*" In *Remembrance, Reunion, and Revival: Celebrating a Decade of Appalachian Studies,* edited by Helen Roseberry, 73-79. Boone, N.C.: Appalachian Consortium Press, 1988. Informative analysis of Chappell's debt to Lovecraft and the ways in which he diverges from Lovecraft's premises.

Gresset, Michel. Preface to *L'Hamçon d'or* [*It Is Time, Lord*]. Paris: Gallimard, 1965.

Hobson, Fred. *The Southern Writer in the Postmodern World,* 82-91. Athens: University of Georgia Press, 1991. Superb commentary on *I Am One of You Forever* as an example of Donald Davidson's "autochthonous ideal" of unself-conscious regionalism.

Johnson, Don. "The Cultivated Mind: The Georgic Center of Fred Chappell's Poetry." In *Dream Garden: The Poetic Vision of Fred Chappell,* edited by Patrick Bizzaro, 170-79. Baton Rouge: Louisiana State University Press, 1997. Informative discussion of Chappell's debt to Virgil and the agrarian vision of the *Georgics.*

Jones, Rodney. "The Large Vision: Fred Chappell's *Midquest.*" *Appalachian Journal* 9, no. 1 (1981): 59-65. Enthusiastic assessment of *Midquest* that emphasizes the volume's meditative poems.

Lang, John. "Breathing a New Universe: The Poetry of Fred Chappell." *Kentucky Poetry Review* 26 (Fall 1990): 61-65. Brief overview of Chappell's poetry for this Chappell issue of *Kentucky Poetry Review.*

————. "Fred Chappell." In *American Poets since World War II,* edited by R. S. Gwynn, 25-38. Vol. 105 of *Dictionary of Literary Biography* Detroit: Gale, 1991. Surveys Chappell's poetry through *First and Last Words.*

————. "Illuminating the Stricken World: Fred Chappell's *Moments of Light.*" *South Central Review* 3 (Winter 1986): 95-103. Explores the stories' religious themes.

————. "Intimations of Order: Fred Chappell's *More Shapes Than One.*" *North Carolina Literary Review* 7 (1998): 140-44. Analyzes the stories' unifying themes and character types, especially scientists and artists.

————. "Points of Kinship: Community and Allusion in Fred Chappell's *Midquest.*" In *Dream Garden: The Poetic Vision of Fred Chappell,* edited by Patrick Bizzaro, 97-117. Baton Rouge: Louisiana State University Press, 1997. Includes a useful appendix that lists Chappell's many references and allusions in this poem and that demonstrates the varied sources that have influenced his work.

Lynskey, Edward C. "Fred Chappell's *Castle Tzingal:* Modern Revival of Elizabethan Revenge Tragedy." *Pembroke Magazine* 25 (1993): 73-87. Applies Fredson T. Bowers's "Kydian formula" to this book of poems.

Makuck, Peter. "Chappell's Continuities: *First and Last Words.*" *Virginia Quarterly Review* 68, no. 2 (1992): 315-36. Reprinted in *Dream Garden: The Poetic Vision of Fred Chappell,* edited by Patrick Bizzaro, 180-97. Baton Rouge: Louisiana State University Press, 1997. Perceptive placement of this volume in the context of Chappell's abiding philosophical and religious concerns.

McDonald, Hal. "Fred Chappell as Magic Realist." *North Carolina Literary Review* 7 (1998): 127-39. Uses William Spindler's typology of magic realism to analyze striking features of *The Inkling, Dagon,* and the first three Kirkman novels.

McFee, Michael. "The Epigrammatical Fred Chappell." *Southern Literary Journal* 31 (Spring 1999): 95-108. Thorough analysis of *C* that sets the book in its literary historical contexts and in the context of Chappell's entire career.

Morgan, Robert. *"Midquest." American Poetry Review* 11 (July-Aug. 1982): 45-47. Reprinted as "*Midquest* and the Gift of Narrative" in *Dream Garden: The Poetic Vision of Fred Chappell,* edited by Patrick Bizzaro, 133-44. Baton Rouge: Louisiana State University Press, 1997. Also reprinted in Morgan's *Good Measure* (Baton Rouge: Louisiana State University Press, 1993). Superb analysis of *Midquest* as "lyric narrative."

Morrison, Gail M. "'The Sign of the Arms': Chappell's *It Is Time, Lord.*" *Mississippi Quarterly* 37 (Winter 1983-84): 45-54. A character analysis that focuses on the protagonist's quest for balance amidst the dualities and polarities he confronts.

Mosby, Charmaine Allmon. "*The Gaudy Place:* Six Characters in Search of an Illusion." *Mississippi Quarterly* 37 (Winter 1983-84): 55-62. Exploration of the novel's plot and characters in terms of the contrast between coincidence and causality.

Nadel, Alan. "Quest and Midquest: Fred Chappell and the First-Person Personal Epic." *New England Review and Bread Loaf Quarterly* 6 (Winter 1983): 323-31. Argues that Chappell's quest is doomed because it tries to freeze the day of his thirty-fifth birthday to stop the passage of time.

Quillen, Rita. *Looking for Native Ground,* 21-34. Boone, N.C.: Appalachian Consortium Press, 1989. Discusses the theme of family in *The World between the Eyes* and *Midquest.*

Ragan, David Paul. "At the Grave of Sut Lovingood: Virgil Campbell in the Work of Fred Chappell." *Mississippi Quarterly* 37 (Winter 1983-84): 21-30. Traces Campbell's role as a representative of freedom and independence in both *It Is Time, Lord* and *Midquest.*

————. "Fred Chappell." In *Contemporary Poets, Dramatists, Essayists, and Novelists of the South: A Bio-Bibliographical Sourcebook,* edited by Robert Bain and Joseph M. Flora, 91-103. Westport, Conn.: Greenwood, 1994. Extremely useful overview of Chappell's career and his major themes. Includes a lengthy bibliography.

————. "Fred Chappell." In *American Novelists since World War II, Second Series,* edited by James E. Kibler, Jr., 36-48. Vol. 6 of *Dictionary of Literary Biography.* Detroit: Gale, 1980. Insightful analysis of Chappell's first four novels.

Ragan, Sam et al. "Tributes to Fred Chappell." *Pembroke Magazine* 23 (1991): 77-89. Appreciative assessment of Chappell's career by several fellow writers, including Clyde Edgerton.

Runyon, Randolph Paul. "Fred Chappell: Midquestions." *Southern Writers at Century's Turn.* Ed. Jeffrey J. Folks and James A. Perkins, 185-200. Lexington: University Press of Kentucky, 1997. Detailed analysis of the "symmetrical" structure of *Midquest* and some of the inconsistencies between Chappell's preface and the poem's practice.

Secreast, Donald. "Images of Impure Water in Chappell's *River.*" *Mississippi Quarterly* 37 (Winter 1983-84): 39-44. Surveys the thematic significance of water imagery in the opening volume of *Midquest.*

Slavitt, David. "The Comedian as the Letter *C* Strikes Again." *New England Review* 16 (Spring 1994): 155-58. Reprinted in *Dream Garden: The Poetic Vision of Fred Chappell,* edited by Patrick Bizzaro, 198-202. Baton Rouge: Louisiana State University Press, 1997. Celebrates Chappell's use of the epigram in *C.*

Smith, R. T. "Fred Chappell's Rural Virgil and the Fifth Element in *Midquest.*" *Mississippi Quarterly* 37 (Winter 1983-84): 31-38. Discusses alcohol as a "fifth element" unifying *Midquest,* a sacramental substance often linked to Virgil Campbell as Ole Fred's guide.

——. "Proteus Loose in the Baptismal Font." In *Dream Garden: The Poetic Vision of Fred Chappell,* edited by Patrick Bizzaro, 35-47. Baton Rouge: Louisiana State University Press, 1997. Insightful overview that emphasizes the diversity of Chappell's writing.

Stephenson, Shelby. "*Midquest*: Fred Chappell's Mythical Kingdom." *Iron Mountain Review* 2 (Spring 1985): 22-26. Appreciative overview of Chappell's "metaphysical humanist" stance in this poem, his yoking of world and word.

——. "Vision in Fred Chappell's Poetry and Fiction." *Abatis One* (1983): 33-45. Surveys Chappell's career through *Moments of Light.*

Stuart, Dabney. "'Blue Pee': Fred Chappell's Short Fiction." *Iron Mountain Review* 2 (Summer 1985): 13-21. Perceptive analysis of the moral preoccupations and thematic relationships of the stories in *Moments of Light.*

——. "Spiritual Matter in Fred Chappell's Poetry: A Prologue." *Southern Review* 27, no. 1 (1991): 200-220. Reprinted in *Dream Garden: The Poetic Vision of Fred Chappell,* edited by Patrick Bizzaro, 48-70. Baton Rouge: Louisiana State University Press, 1997. Brilliant discussion of the Lucretian and Christian influences on Chappell's poetry.

——. "'What's Artichokes?': An Introduction to the Work of Fred Chappell." In *The Fred Chappell Reader,* xi-xx. New York: St. Martin's, 1987. Insightful survey of Chappell's career.

Sullivan, Sally. "Irony and Allegory in *I Am One of You Forever*: How Fantasy and the Ideal Become the Real." *North Carolina Literary Review* 7 (1998): 120-26. Detailed analysis of this novel's literary techniques, especially irony, allegory, and fantasy—all three in the service of life's "splendid mystery."

Taylor, Henry. "Fred Chappell: The World Was Plenty." *Compulsory Figures: Essays on Recent American Poets,* 69-86. Baton Rouge: Louisiana State University Press, 1992. Reprinted in *Dream Garden: The Poetic Vision of Fred Chappell,* edited by Patrick Bizzaro, 71-87. Baton Rouge: Louisiana State University Press, 1997. Informative overview of Chappell's poetry through *First and Last Words.*

Tucker, Ellen. "His Life in Mid-Course." *Chicago Review* 33 (Summer 1981): 85-91. Enthusiastic discussion of the narrative, lyric, and epistolary poems in *Midquest,* but Tucker finds the meditative stream-of-consciousness poems unsatisfying.

Underwood, Susan O'Dell. "The Light of Transformation in Fred Chappell's *Spring Garden.*" In *Dream Garden: The Poetic Vision of Fred Chappell,* edited by Patrick Bizzaro, 203-21. Baton Rouge: Louisiana State University Press, 1997. Detailed thematic analysis of the seven sections that compose *Spring Garden.*

Ward, Kurt C. "Fred Chappell: North Carolina Poet Laureate Reflects on Thirty-four Years at UNCG." *UNCG Graduate,* Spring 1998, 2-5. Valuable source of biographical information.

John Lang (essay date 2000)

SOURCE: Lang, John. "The Short Stories: *Moments of Light* and *More Shapes Than One.*" In *Understanding Fred Chappell,* pp. 166-200. Columbia: University of South Carolina Press, 2000.

[*Below, Lang presents a comprehensive overview of the works in Chappell's first two short-story collections.*]

"Of all the forms I have attempted," Chappell has remarked, "the short story is the most difficult. . . . It is the prose form I most admire."[1] Although he has published only two collections in this genre, **Moments of Light** (1980) and **More Shapes Than One** (1991), he has been steadily writing short fiction since at least his high school days. Moreover, as many reviewers and critics have observed, his novels in the Kirkman tetralogy that began with *I Am One of You Forever* often read more like volumes of interrelated short stories than like traditional novels, an assessment that underscores the importance of this genre in Chappell's total writing career.

As early as 1965, just as **The Inkling** was about to appear, Chappell offered Hiram Haydn, his editor at Harcourt, Brace and World, a manuscript of fourteen stories under the title **"The Thousand Ways."** According to Alex Albright, Chappell received a contract for that book of stories, but Haydn later persuaded the author to substitute a contract to publish **Dagon.**[2] Over half of those stories were subsequently printed in magazines and literary journals, but only two, the title story and **"January,"** found their way into **Moments of Light.** By 1980 Chappell had published some three dozen stories from which to draw the selections for that volume.

As in his collections of poetry, in his books of short fiction Chappell strives to create an impression of unity among the individual stories. The ordering of the stories, their temporal and thematic progression, and their recurring motifs are central to each book's meaning. And as in his poems, so in his short stories, Chappell writes in a wide variety of literary forms in these two volumes: mythic fable (**"The Three Boxes"**), tales of horror and fantasy (**"Weird Tales," "The Somewhere Doors"**), tall tales (**"Mankind Journeys through Forests of Symbols"**), fictions involving historical figures, ghost stories (**"Ember"** and **"Miss Prue"**), straightforwardly realistic fiction (**"Duet"**), and texts that blend two or more of these genres. This impressive variety of forms is matched by an equal diversity of voices and tones and styles. As in *Castle Tzingal,* Chappell is wonderfully adept at using a diction and syntax appropriate to the historical period in which a work is set and to the specific characters he depicts. Humor, satire, and parody regularly lighten the tone of these stories, especially in *More Shapes Than One.* Yet the playfulness of Chappell's imagination is almost always in the service of substantive themes, if not in each story individually, then in the collection as a whole. Chappell the moralist is never entirely absent from these fictions no matter how comically exuberant or whimsical they may be, for Chappell numbers himself among those authors and citizens "seriously concerned about the tone of our literature and the tenor of our lives."[3]

One of the major subjects in these two books is the partnership of the sciences and the arts in ordering the world and endowing it with meaning. Chappell's use of historical figures like Benjamin Franklin and William Herschel, like Franz Joseph Haydn and Carl Linnaeus and the composer Jacques Offenbach, both reinforces his characteristic insistence on the value of the past and reflects his desire to bridge the gap between the arts and sciences posited by C. P. Snow in his influential book *The Two Cultures.* Chappell seeks to reconcile these two modes of acquiring knowledge by featuring scientists and artists, not just the historical figures cited but also characters like Stovebolt Johnson of **"Blue Dive,"** Kermit Wilson of **"Duet,"** and Arthur Strakl of **"The Somewhere Doors."** Chappell's interest in promoting greater understanding of science, evident in the Kirkman tetralogy as well, stems from his recognition that much of the general populace "thinks of science as incomprehensible, unapproachable, elitist, and inhumane."[4] For Chappell, in contrast, "Both science and art are humanist endeavors."[5] In a number of his essays he has dealt with the interrelationship of science and the arts, especially in their search for truth, their usefulness in enlarging and refining our senses and our sympathies, and their promotion of curiosity and wonder. His portraits of men like Herschel and Linnaeus are meant to humanize science and scientific research while emphasizing the fundamental human yearning for truth and order and beauty.

The eleven stories that comprise *Moments of Light* dramatize this quest for truth, moral order, and spiritual transcendence. As the title indicates, many of these stories offer epiphanies, instants of illumination, that transform the characters' and/or the readers' outlook. The world Chappell portrays is clearly postlapsarian, a "stricken world," as the narrator of **"The Weather"** puts it.[6] Yet the acceptance of moral responsibility remains both possible and necessary. Chappell insists that human beings have the capacity to act justly despite their fallen condition, and it is that capacity— not the recovery of a specious innocence—on which the stories focus.

Writing six years after the book's publication, Chappell stated that "*Moments of Light* may well be my favorite child among my books of fiction."[7] Reviewers were equally enthusiastic. One said, "Chappell's stories are consistently thought-provoking and well written," while another called the book "a memorable . . . collection." Yet a third praised it for being "as satisfying a moral fiction as we can find in contemporary literature, . . . a remarkable collection."[8] Such comments are well deserved in light of the volume's originality of conception and high level of achievement both in characterization and in theme, qualities warmly acknowledged in Annie Dillard's foreword to the book.

In its chronological structure *Moments of Light* moves from an explanatory fable set in mythic time and a brief first-person account narrated by Judas to three stories set in the eighteenth century and six set in the twentieth. This temporal progression does not trace a simplistic history of either decline or progress; instead Chappell emphasizes the perennial nature of the moral challenges human beings face, the individual's recurring opportunities to enact justice or to reject its claims, to embrace or to betray love. Yet Chappell does seem to sense in the modern world a lack of commitment to active pursuit of the good, a failure of will that Dante's age identified as *acedia,* spiritual sloth. In Chappell's view, moral lassitude rather than outright evil characterizes the modern age, as an increasingly secularized culture obscures the very existence of values beyond material interests. *Moments of Light* thus recalls the reader to the possibilities for self-realization and self-transcendence in art, love, and the quest for justice.

The book's opening story, **"The Three Boxes,"** based on a folktale Chappell found retold in Simone Weil's *Notebooks,*[9] deals directly with the quest for justice and the need to affirm individual and collective moral responsibility. At the same time, **"The Three Boxes"** makes use of the archetypal journey motif, which recurs in various forms in seven of the remaining ten stories, and introduces music as a means of transcendence, thereby anticipating the role music plays not only in the title story but also in the book's final story, **"Blue Dive."** For Chappell's characters, the journey usually leads to heightened moral and spiritual insight, because they are pilgrims rather than merely travelers.

"The Three Boxes" attests to Chappell's religious concerns not only by using this metaphor of pilgrimage but also by numbering God among its characters. Annie Dillard refers to the story as "a hieratic parable" (ix-x), one that addresses racial differences. Each of the three men presented in the opening paragraph assumes a different racial identity as he swims across a river emblematic of time. Once across the river, he is permitted to open one of three boxes. The man who turns black is the last to traverse the river, and he discovers in his box not the treasures afforded the Caucasian and Asian figures who precede him but chains and branding irons and hang nooses, instruments of oppression. Pain and suffering all but fill the box, though patience and endurance and music are also among its contents. While this story seems to originate in a troublingly Eurocentric conception of African culture and history, Chappell is writing primarily in the context of the African American experience, in which slavery was the predominant reality. When God appears to this black man, the man rightfully protests the injustice of the gifts' distribution, and God concedes, "It is not fair."

> "The reason the distribution is not fair," God said, "is that the principle of justice is not yet established in the world. I—even I—cannot act justly until justice itself comes into being."
>
> "When then will justice happen?"
>
> "Justice will not happen," God said. "Justice must be created, and it is you who shall create it."
>
> . . . . .
>
> "But there have fallen to me only the means and emblems of injustice."
>
> "Out of these justice shall be created. For it cannot come into being in the abstract, by fiat. It can inhabit only the human soul and the human body."
>
> (12)

In this dialogue Chappell raises perplexing issues about the principle of justice, issues as complex as those that attend divine command theory in the realm of ethics. Chappell's main point, however, seems to be that just as God cannot compel people's love without violating their freedom, so God cannot create justice by fiat, cannot compel just action. As **"The Three Boxes"** concludes, the black man journeys forth to find his companions and to present them with "the gift of justice, the one thing in the whole world worth knowing that can be learned in the world, and is not divinely revealed" (14). The last five words in this quotation point to the problem of evil that Chappell also confronts in such poems as **"Windows"** and **"An Old Mountain Woman Reading the Book of Job."**

The gift of freedom makes possible the abuse of that gift, and it is to such abuse that Chappell turns in the volume's second story, **"Judas."** Less than three pages long, **"Judas"** recounts its title character's reasons for betraying Christ. It wasn't the money, he declares. It was the "insupportable feeling of responsibility" that Jesus engendered (17). The figure of Judas is meant to contrast with the black man of **"The Three Boxes,"** who accepts the burden of striving for justice despite the world's inequities. These two characters represent, respectively, fidelity and betrayal, the acceptance of moral responsibility and its rejection, and they enable Chappell to measure the characters in many of the subsequent stories against the conduct these two display. Among the characters found wanting are Blackbeard of **"Thatch Retaliates,"** Mark Vance of **"The Thousand Ways,"** the narrator of **"Broken Blossoms,"** and Locklear Hawkins of **"Blue Dive."**

"Thatch Retaliates" is one of the three historical fictions Chappell sets in the eighteenth century, commonly called the Age of Reason or the Age of Enlightenment. It is, indeed, enlightenment on which he focuses in the first and third of these stories, **"Mrs. Franklin Ascends"** and **"Moments of Light."** The former was Chappell's first effort in the genre of historical short fiction, a text he wrote, he explains, to give his students in an American literature survey some understanding of the personality of Benjamin Franklin and some sense of the texture of eighteenth-century life.[10] One of the main pleasures of this story, however, is the portrait it provides of Deborah Franklin, who is far more complex than Dillard suggests when she says, "Sweet Mrs. Franklin is, I'm afraid, as simple and material as a bolt of cloth" (x). The repartee between the Franklins is echoed by the playful tone of the story itself, which culminates in a comic anticlimax when Deborah awakens to what she perceives to be celestial music and mistakenly assumes that she and Ben have died—only to discover that the music originates from the *armonica* her husband has brought back from England and is playing in their attic. In the person of Ben Franklin, Chappell unites the scientist and the artist, suggesting that both are inspired by the quest for order, the quest for harmony, symbolized here by Ben's new musical invention.

Between the comedy of **"Mrs. Franklin Ascends"** and the book's title story falls the shadow of **"Thatch Retaliates."** The title character, Blackbeard, parallels

Judas as a figure of evil and challenges the eighteenth century's assumptions about the innate goodness of human nature and the power of reason to guide human conduct. Chappell effectively contrasts the setting, events, and tone of this and the preceding story. Instead of focusing on domestic life, as does **"Mrs. Franklin Ascends," "Thatch Retaliates"** opens in "the primeval Carolina forest" amid "the discomfort of wilderness travel" (29) before shifting to the primitive colonial town of Bath. The story's main characters, in addition to Blackbeard, are Toby Milliver and Hyde Prescott, the former a bookseller intent on founding a print shop and bookstore in Bath. Toby, the spokesperson for education and reason, believes that "the great flaws of personality both in the state and in the individual [are] historical products rather than inbred propensities" (34). Thus, through Toby, Chappell invokes the mythos of the New World as a second Eden and the American as a new Adam liberated from the errors and evils of the past. In Hyde Prescott, in contrast, Chappell creates an opposing voice, one that undercuts the myth of American innocence, that insists "that the old Adam [is] still heartily at work in every man" (34).

In **"Thatch Retaliates,"** as in *The Inkling* and *Dagon,* Chappell's outlook is closer to Hawthorne's than to Toby Milliver's. Indeed "the heavy American darkness" through which Prescott and Milliver travel resembles "the benighted wilderness" of "Young Goodman Brown." Yet unlike Brown, Toby has his shattering experience in town, not in the wilderness, for within hours of his arrival in Bath, he is shot to death by Blackbeard. Despite this violent rebuttal of Toby's assumptions about human nature, the young optimist retains the reader's sympathy. Lying on his deathbed, Toby continues to identify himself as "a friend to Reason in this place" (48), a statement that Chappell might well make about himself. What is needed, Chappell implies, is not an abandonment of reason but a renewed commitment to cultivating its strengths while acknowledging its limitations. In this story Blackbeard comes to represent what Melville called in *Billy Budd* "the mystery of iniquity." For Chappell as for Melville, the eruption of moral evil is an irreducible fact of human experience, one that appears to lend credence to the theological concept of Original Sin.

As this collection's title story makes clear, however, the quests for truth and goodness and spiritual insight persist despite such eruptions of evil. While **"Thatch Retaliates"** bears witness to the presence of irrational evil even amid the Age of Reason, Chappell's placement of that story between two that highlight the pursuit of science and music demonstrates the fundamental hopefulness of his artistic vision. In **"Moments of Light"** Chappell brings together the astronomer William Herschel and the composer Franz Joseph Haydn, describing their meeting in 1792 during Haydn's first London sojourn. In addition to linking science and art, this story emphasizes the compatibility of science and religious faith.

Chappell's convincing portraits of both Herschel and Haydn, his skillful use of a secondary character like Doctor Burney, his subtle re-creation of the style and temper of the eighteenth century, and his effective blending of historical fact and visionary fancy—these are among the qualities that make **"Moments of Light"** one of the finest stories in this collection. Equally significant are the themes this story develops and its use of the stars, one of the prominent images throughout Chappell's writing, as a symbol of eternity and of spiritual realities. Haydn conceives of astronomy as a matter of "searching out new moments of light" (56), an apt definition of literature's function as well. In this story, science and art join forces in their effort to illuminate the human condition. Herschel, himself both an oboe player and a former organist, praises the scientific insights provided by such poets as Lucretius and Homer and Virgil. And he rejects Doctor Burney's suggestion that modern science makes untenable the ancient notion of the music of the spheres. For Chappell, as for Herschel, "the Harmony of the Universe . . . is surely the conception of greatest grandeur the ancient world could claim" (55), a conception to which Chappell continues to give his allegiance through his repeated references to music in both his poetry and fiction. But Haydn's acts of creation, as Chappell points out, ultimately derive not from his imagination alone but from the divine fiat that, according to the Judeo-Christian tradition, gave rise to the universe: "Let there be light." The artist's and scientist's quests for illumination are thus mutually grounded upon that primordial act. Like Chappell himself, both figures seek to assert harmony and order, a vision of wholeness, without denying the contradictions and complexities, the real chaos, that also attends human experience.

It is chaos rather than order that Chappell emphasizes in **"The Thousand Ways,"** the first of six stories set in the twentieth century. This story, the longest in the book, takes its title from the lyrics of a popular song that serve as the story's epigraph: "Love, O love, O careless love, / You broke my heart a thousand ways" (71). Yet this story and those that follow deal not so much with outright betrayals of love as with *carelessness,* with moral lassitude. To underscore the distance between the world of **"Mrs. Franklin Ascends"** and **"The Thousand Ways,"** Chappell sets the latter in 1962, two hundred years after the 1762 date of Franklin's homecoming. The change in emotional and intellectual climate is apparent in Chappell's shift from the "deep certitude and serenity" of Haydn's temperament (53) to the "indecision and dismay" (71) that characterize Mark Vance, the would-be poet who is the protagonist of **"The Thousand Ways."** The setting in which Mark finds himself, a cheap hotel room where "no light burned," also contrasts with both the domestic comforts of the Franklin household and the emphasis on light throughout the title story. Though Mark eats in the Venus Grill, that name functions ironically, for Mark is shown, over the one-day span of the story, struggling to extricate himself from a loveless affair with Norma Lang, a forty-five-year-old alcoholic divorcée nearly twice his age. The physical disorder in Norma's home mirrors the moral and emotional chaos of both her life and Mark's. In their mutual lack of direction these two characters typify an aimlessness that promotes self-betrayal as well as disregard for others. **"The Thousand Ways"** opens and closes with Mark alone in bed in his hotel room, a circularity of structure that confirms the characters' entrapment in their lives. Yet the story ends, significantly, with Mark's thrice-repeated whisper of the word "Help," the words functioning as a largely unconscious prayer. Like the final gesture of **"Moments of Light,"** Haydn's pointing of his baton toward heaven, Mark's whispered plea orients him toward something beyond the self.

The three stories that follow **"The Thousand Ways"** are first-person retrospective narratives that depict childhood experiences. The first, **"January,"** which was also incorporated in three variations in *It Is Time, Lord,* returns to the theme of injustice raised in **"The Three Boxes"** and **"Thatch Retaliates."** At the same time, **"January"** extends the book's concern with moral responsibility. Like **"Judas,"** this story is just three pages in length, another instance of Chappell's striking economy of storytelling. Yet it is among the most evocative and ambiguous texts in *Moments of Light,* its very ambiguity one measure of the complexity of moral judgment. Is the narrator guilty of neglecting his three-year-old sister's welfare? Are the assumptions his parents make accurate? Has he done all he could to protect his sister from the harsh winter weather? And what is the meaning of the boy's remaining silent before his parents and of his blotting out the moon with his frosty breath upon the window pane? The boy clearly feels the injustice of his parents' attitude, for he has not been trying to hurt his sister but to help her home. Yet his response to the men in the barn, "I told her not to come" (103), sounds too glibly self-exculpatory. The winter weather points to a physical cold that requires the warmth of human compassion to combat it, the capacity to recognize and then to alleviate others' suffering. On this occasion,

then, the boy's blotting out of the moon, a common symbol of the imagination, may reflect his failure of empathy, his lack of moral imagination.

"The Weather" and **"Broken Blossoms"** raise much more directly this issue of moral lassitude, of an innocence that consists of inactivity, of a withdrawal from the world that unintentionally abets injustice. The narrator of **"The Weather"** acknowledges his preference for passivity, while the narrator of **"Broken Blossoms"** exhibits an inattentiveness, a "dreaming reverie" (129), dangerous not only to others but also to himself. In the latter story Chappell vividly recreates the perspective of an imaginative yet self-absorbed child. This story stands out from the others in *Moments of Light* because it deals with an extended time period, nearly a year rather than the twenty-four-to forty-eight-hour time frames of almost all the other stories. **"Broken Blossoms"** is also one of the two stories, along with **"Thatch Retaliates,"** that most clearly evoke the biblical account of the fall. When the narrator, searching for a rare stamp that he imagines will bring him fame and fortune, breaks into a locked trunk belonging to his parents, he unwittingly comes upon a box of blasting caps, which he gently shakes before returning the box to the trunk. The child's father learns what has happened and asks the hired man, Mr. Cody, to show the boy the blasting caps' destructive power. Mr. Cody lodges one of the caps in a disfigured apple tree and, from a safe distance, fires a bullet into the cap. The resulting explosion destroys the tree. "From this instant I can date my awkward tumble into the world," the narrator remarks (133).

Together with the stars and light itself, this tree is one of the book's major symbols, reminiscent of Eden's tree of knowledge but also of the duality of human nature itself. Mr. Cody's lesson forces the child to recognize that inaction and passivity also have consequences, that self-absorption and inattention are among "the thousand ways" to betray love. Chappell's sense of the insidious appeal of irresponsibility can be gauged by his adult narrator's admission that, despite what he learned from Mr. Cody, "If I could get it back, if I could return, I would undo it all. I would wrap myself in dream ever more warmly and would sink to the bottom of the stream of time, a stone uncaring, swaddled in moss" (133). Resistance to moral awakening is fierce, Chappell concedes, but awakening remains possible, even for someone as inclined to sleep as this unnamed narrator, whose very anonymity makes him a representative figure, an everyman.

The need for such wakefulness, for moral alertness, is underscored in **"Children of Strikers,"** the succeeding story. Almost as brief as **"Judas"** and **"January,"** this story provides a third-person account of two children's confrontation with evil. Chappell sets this encounter alongside a mill town's "black chemical river," thus highlighting the paper mill's pollution of the physical environment, but the strike of the story's title also suggests a context of social and economic injustice. The children's discovery of a doll's severed foot introduces yet a third species of evil, individual cruelty of the sort embodied in Blackbeard, for the children realize that only an adult could have used a knife so skillfully. Thus the maimed doll comes to symbolize what Chappell calls the "unguessable violence" of the mill town itself. Once again in this story, Chappell leaves the principal characters nameless, hence widely representative. Minimalist in length, **"Children of Strikers"** resonates powerfully both in its own right and in the framework of the entire collection.

The concluding story, **"Blue Dive,"** is another third-person narrative that focuses on injustice. Its protagonist, Stovebolt Johnson, is an African American blues guitarist recently released from prison who is looking for a job he was promised three years earlier by the owner of the Blue Dive. That owner is gone, however, and the new owner, an African American named Locklear Hawkins, has no interest in the kind of music Johnson plays. Though "Hawk" gives Johnson an opportunity to audition and though Stovebolt wins the patrons' approval, Hawkins's decision is already made: "There is no room in this nightclub for any Rastuses or any Sambos. . . . And there's no room for anybody named *Stovebolt*" (165; Chappell's italics).

Chappell's use of both music and African American characters in this final story links it to **"The Three Boxes,"** while his use of music and of star imagery also connects **"Blue Dive"** to **"Moments of Light."** Ironically, the injustice Stovebolt experiences here comes not from whites but from another African American. The tellingly named Locklear Hawkins fails to grasp the significance of the blues, deriding them as "those old-time nigger whining songs" (158). He ignores their function as a means of transcending suffering and injustice and as a means of ordering and understanding experience through the power of art. For novelist Ralph Ellison, in contrast, "The blues is . . . an assertion of the irrepressibly human over all circumstance whether created by others or by one's own human failings."[11] Of the blues as an expression of freedom and transcendence, Hawk knows nothing, and he thus epitomizes those who abandon the cultural resources of the past without ever understanding what it is they are discarding. *Moments of Light,* like *Midquest* and *C* and *Spring Garden,* is structured to affirm the ongoing value of the past. The lives of Judas and Blackbeard, of the Franklins and Herschel and

Haydn, all speak to contemporary human conduct and values, though in different ways. Among the most important elements in **"Blue Dive,"** then, is its implicit critique of the modern world's willingness to jettison the traditional. Hawkins, while obsessed with the new, seems finally to be the same old Adam of whom Hyde Prescott spoke.

One of the other major strengths of **"Blue Dive"** is its sensitive portrait of Stovebolt himself. As Dabney Stuart has noted, in addition to musical skill, "Stovebolt has more important qualities to recommend him: decency, delicacy, balance, dignity, a sense of proportion and humor and perspective."[12] Despite the insulting treatment Stovebolt receives, he retains something of the serenity Chappell associates with Haydn. Walking away from the Blue Dive late at night, Stovebolt is also linked with Haydn through the stars he observes. "There was one clear yellow star," Chappell writes, "that stood in the sky directly behind the twiggy tip of a wild cherry tree. As the wind moved, the tip kept brushing through the light of it. But, Stovebolt knew, it was never going to brush that light away" (166)

On this note of affirmation *Moments of Light* concludes. Justice has not been established, nor has fallen humanity returned to innocence. The fall is an absolute in Chappell's fiction, a fundamental datum. At book's end humanity, in the person of Stovebolt, remains a pilgrim. But the stars still shine, emblems of the mysterious source of life, with their promise of illumination and revelation. Moreover, the "falling star" of the toppled candle that marks Toby Milliver's death (48) is here replaced by the star whose permanence Stovebolt emphasizes. Like Haydn at the end of the volume's title story, Stovebolt looks heavenward, another of the many sentinels of the stars that fill Chappell's work and testify to its moral and spiritual concerns.

MORE SHAPES THAN ONE

The book that ultimately became *More Shapes Than One* had been conceived as early as 1983, at which time it bore the title **"Waltzes Noble and Sentimental."**[13] Among the Chappell papers at Duke University there is a table of contents page for this projected volume, showing that the author made a number of major changes before the book appeared in 1991, including the deletion of two of the eleven stories in the original manuscript and the addition of four new stories: **"The Adder," "Ember," "Duet,"** and **"Miss Prue."** Chappell also altered the tenor of the collection substantially by choosing to omit **"Bloodshadow"**—a tale of witchcraft, an indelible bloodstain, and cosmic convulsion—which had originally been intended to conclude the book. Several of the stories were also retitled. Chappell's dramatic transformation of **"The Sleeping Orchid"** into **"The Somewhere Doors"** is one measure of the care and skill with which he revises as he moves from periodical to book publication.[14]

The thirteen stories of **More Shapes Than One** are preceded by an epigraph from Milton's *Areopagitica* that provides the volume's title. That epigraph again directs attention to Chappell's moral and religious concerns as well as to his commitment to what might be called literary pluralism, that is, his willingness to embrace the genres of popular culture and folk culture, not just the genres of canonical literature. The passage Chappell draws from Milton reads in part, "For who knows not that Truth is strong, next to the Almighty. She needs no policies, nor stratagems nor licensings to make her victorious. . . . Yet is it not impossible that she may have more shapes than one."[15] The diverse stories that follow confirm the variety noted in the book's title. At the same time, by invoking Truth with a capital *T,* Chappell suggests that the quest for knowledge has a spiritual dimension, that it aims to achieve an ultimately unified and unifying vision. As the mathematician Feuerbach declares in one of these stories, "The mind makes no mistake in intuiting intimations of a high and eternal order" (36-37), although the precise nature of that order may elude the mind's grasp.

In addition to containing two more stories than *Moments of Light, More Shapes Than One* differs from Chappell's first collection of short fiction in several other significant ways. First, it contains a greater range of stories, a variety evident not only in their literary forms but also in their historical settings and casts of characters. Second, **More Shapes Than One** includes more historical fictions and a larger number that deal with scientists (Linnaeus, Maupertuis, Feuerbach), though Chappell continues to examine artist figures as well, composers like Jacques Offenbach and writers like Lovecraft and Hart Crane. A third difference between the two volumes is the latter's more detailed use of the mountains of western North Carolina as a setting. But the most striking difference arises from Chappell's extensive use of fantasy in *More Shapes Than One,* a literary strategy already apparent to readers of *I Am One of You Forever* and *Brighten the Corner Where You Are,* both published before this second collection of stories.

The prominence of fantasy elements in *More Shapes Than One* tends to underscore the playfulness and inventiveness of Chappell's imagination. Yet that appearance of whimsicality should not lead readers to overlook the thematic substance of such tales. For Chappell, fantasy is not escapist. Instead it is a means of seeing reality anew. "Our problem is not that we imagine too much, and therefore become unreal," Chappell told an interviewer, "but that we don't imagine fully enough, and don't understand the reality that's out there. . . . We discover the world by imagining it."[16] The writer who diverges from factual accuracy, Chappell observes, does so "in order to illuminate, and not to deceive."[17] His interest in fantasy and in what he calls visionary fiction has been evident throughout his career, and he has commented on what he sees as critics' arbitrary division of his stories into two types, the realistic and the fantastic: "For me there's no important difference between them in terms of treatment; . . . both ways of writing are ways to try to deal with reality on the plane of literature."[18] The mimetic aim of fantasy in Chappell's hands is implicit in the verbal interplay of his title "Fantasia on the Theme of Theme and Fantasy," an essay in which he identifies as works of fantasy not only science fiction and horror stories but also texts by E. T. A. Hoffmann, Nathaniel Hawthorne, Lewis Carroll, Henry James, Franz Kafka, and Thomas Mann.[19] Such folk traditions as fairy tales and tall tales also involve fantasy, but Chappell traces the *literary* ancestry of contemporary "visionary fiction" to such varied sources as Genesis and Revelation, *The Odyssey, The Faerie Queene, A Midsummer Night's Dream,* the Gothic novel, and narrative poems like "The Rime of the Ancient Mariner" and especially *The Divine Comedy,* which he calls "the single most important influence."[20] "What is most at stake" in such visionary literature, says Chappell, "is a transfiguration of quotidian *secular* life,"[21] a renewed awareness of the immanence of the sacred.

It is precisely such a visionary moment that Chappell celebrates in the opening story of **More Shapes Than One, "Linnaeus Forgets."** By focusing on the eighteenth-century Swedish botanist who established the system of binomial nomenclature, Chappell immediately introduces the theme of the quest for order in nature, a major subject of both science and art. Yet the story turns not on the discoveries of empirical science but on the fantastical vision Linnaeus experiences while studying a plant sent to him from the South Seas. Examining that plant, the scientist observes within its leaves "a little world . . . in which the mundane and the fanciful commingled" (13), a world that revolves around a pageant procession honoring the goddess Flora.[22] This vision of harmony and beauty grows so intense that Linnaeus faints, awakening later to find that the plant has disappeared and that the notes he made during this experience are unreadable. The very effort to decipher them causes the entire scene to vanish from his memory. Yet this visionary interlude does have enduring effects. Linnaeus's "love for metaphor sharpened" (18), Chappell writes, linking scientist and artist as he does Herschel and Haydn in **"Moments of Light."** The vision also instills a new confidence in Linnaeus, whose theories about the sexuality of plants were extremely controversial and sometimes subjected him to accusations of immorality. The story concludes by affirming Linnaeus's newfound confidence: "He was finally certain that the plants of this earth carry on their love affairs in uncaring merry freedom, making whatever sexual arrangements best suit them, and that they go to replenish the globe guiltlessly, in high and winsome delight" (18).

Although the details of Linnaeus's vision recall the Golden Age, this opening story clearly contrasts the paradisal condition of nature with what Linnaeus himself thinks of as "the fallen world of mankind" (7). Plants and animals exist apart from the moral order that originates in humanity's capacity to reflect, to empathize, and to act in accordance with the dictates of conscience. The very fact that Linnaeus *forgets* his extraordinary experience may be meant to indicate the distance between physical nature and human nature, between the kind of innocence that nature possesses and humanity's consciousness of moral evil. Humanity's expulsion from paradise is apparent or implied in many of the book's subsequent stories, most notably in **"Weird Tales," "The Adder," "Ember,"** and **"After Revelation."** *More Shapes Than One* thus continues to investigate "the stricken world" of human conduct that Chappell also explores in such stories as **"Judas," "Thatch Retaliates,"** and **"Broken Blossoms"** in *Moments of Light.*

In other ways too **"Linnaeus Forgets"** introduces major figures and themes that help to unify the book. The figure of the scientist, for instance, reappears not only in some of the volume's additional historical fictions but also in the concluding story, **"After Revelation,"** whose narrator has been imprisoned "for practicing science" (186). The scientist as seeker after truth is associated with various artist figures in stories that analyze the origins of artistic creativity (**"Barcarole," "Duet,"** and **"Mankind Journeys through Forests of Symbols"**). **"Linnaeus Forgets"** also raises at least three themes developed in subsequent stories. First of all, this opening story reminds the reader of humanity's dependence on nature, no matter how much human consciousness transcends the capacities of physical nature. In both **"The Somewhere Doors"** and **"Duet,"** the protagonists' moments of insight stem from contact with nature (96-97; 141-42), from their awareness of what Linnaeus calls the "ordinary amazing errands" of nature's creatures (11). The awakening of a sense of wonder and reverence

and gratitude is among the primary aims of Chappell's writing, here and elsewhere. Secondly, despite the verb in the story's title, **"Linnaeus Forgets"** paradoxically demonstrates the need to *remember.* As in *Moments of Light,* the historical figures in the first five stories of *More Shapes Than One* affirm the temporal continuum of which the present is a part. Just as Linnaeus's scientific studies require the collection and classification of specimens, so Chappell's art involves acts of recollection, of memory as well as invention. To ignore the past Chappell repeatedly implies, is to lose much of the potential of the future.

Yet a third major theme introduced by **"Linnaeus Forgets"** involves love and sexuality. The volume's second story, **"Ladies from Lapland"**—along with **"Ember," "Miss Prue,"** and **"Alma"**—reveals that *human* sexual relationships are far more complicated than those Linnaeus observes in his botanical studies. The transition Chappell creates between these first two stories demonstrates his usual care in structuring a collection of poems or short fiction. The protagonist of **"Ladies from Lapland"** is Pierre de Maupertuis, a French mathematician, biologist, and physicist, the leading Continental proponent of Newton's theories. Maupertuis is linked to Linnaeus not only because both are scientists but also because both conducted research in Lapland during the 1730s. But Chappell's account of Maupertuis focuses not on the latter's scientific pursuits but on his sexual exploits in Lapland, conduct satirized by Voltaire in *Micromégas.* Maupertuis's behavior highlights his egotism and his general disregard for the scientific responsibilities that brought him to Lapland, research that others must complete for him.

As a mathematician, among other things, Maupertuis in turn anticipates the central character in this volume's third story, **"The Snow That Is Nothing in the Triangle,"** which traces the mental disintegration of the nineteenth-century German mathematician Karl Wilhelm Feuerbach, originator of the Feuerbach Theorem on the nine-point circle of a triangle. Yet Chappell's portrait of Feuerbach is obviously meant to contrast with his sketch of Maupertuis. The Frenchman's self-centered conduct is juxtaposed with Feuerbach's conviction, after his arrest on charges of anarchy, that "if one man die, the others shall be freed" (37), a belief that leads him to two attempts at suicide while imprisoned. His willingness to sacrifice himself for others clearly differentiates him from Maupertuis, as does his inability to forget, once he is released from prison, the death of his fellow mathematician and presumed co-conspirator Klaus Hörnli. Chappell uses Feuerbach to re-emphasize the quest for order that is one of the central themes of *More Shapes Than One.* Feuerbach is astounded that a geometer should be accused of anarchy since for him, "the propositions of Euclid follow as inevitably from one another as the roses spring from the vine" (35), an analogy that reminds the reader of Linnaeus's similar confidence in a divine order underlying the natural world. Feuerbach points to the snowflake, another striking example of "more shapes than one," explaining that "in the snowflake nature reaches out to us as if it were reassuringly . . . suggesting that the mind makes no mistake in intuiting intimations of a high and eternal order" (36-37). The image of the snowflake recalls the story's title, which conjoins natural and geometric forms but which may also be meant to affirm nature's own creation of beauty and order. The boundary between the products of nature and the products of human artifice blurs when we consider such a geometric form as the circle, for circles abound in the natural world. Both scientist and artist build upon designs or structures inherent in nature itself, as Feuerbach avows and Chappell intimates.

While Chappell shifts from scientists to artist figures in the book's other two historical fictions, the concern for moral responsibility introduced in **"Ladies from Lapland"** recurs in both. Like Feuerbach, the composer Offenbach of **"Barcarole"** reveals a concern for others that Maupertuis lacks. In fact **"Barcarole,"** set in 1871, opens with an encounter reminiscent of the parable of the Good Samaritan when Offenbach discovers a dying violinist, Rudolf Zimmer, lying on a sidewalk in Vienna. Momentarily mistaking the stranger for his brother Julius, Offenbach also discerns his own features in Zimmer's face. Using the literary motif of the double, Chappell stresses the imagination's role not, in this case, as an instrument of scientific research or artistic creation but as an instrument of moral vision, of compassion in its root sense of "suffering with" others.

"Barcarole" is a superb example of Chappell's skill in selecting and developing the figures who populate his historical fictions, in dramatizing the events that befall them, and in establishing a broad network of thematic implications and allusions that tie a particular story to others in *More Shapes Than One.* Given Chappell's own interest in popular literary forms, Offenbach is an apt choice as protagonist because of his contributions to such musical genres as the operetta, which he helped to popularize internationally. Like much of Chappell's writing, Offenbach's compositions are marked by their gaiety and tunefulness. Moreover, at the time of his death, Offenbach was working on a comic opera based on the tales of E. T. A. Hoffmann, whose fiction shares Chappell's predilection for the fanciful and the supernatural in this book. Hoffmann was himself a musician as well as a writer, and Chappell's work repeatedly exhibits its author's love of music.

Thematically, **"Barcarole"** not only extends Chappell's treatment of moral responsibility but also initiates a new theme, the origins of artistic creativity, a theme pursued in several subsequent stories set in the twentieth century. The dying Zimmer's gift to Offenbach is a copy of the one piece of music the violinist ever composed, a waltz tune that has long haunted Offenbach because his sisters had hummed it to him in his childhood. That tune, which inspires the famous "Barcarolle" in Offenbach's *Les Contes d'Hoffmann,* was prompted by the death of Zimmer's fiancée Rosalie. Grief, intense suffering, Zimmer says, is the origin of his art, perhaps of all great art. "For another song like this one to be written," he declares, "another Rosalie would have to die" (55). Like the Wallace Stevens of **"Sunday Morning,"** for whom "death is the mother of beauty," Zimmer seems to ground artistic creation in the experience of loss. This viewpoint is reinforced in the later story **"Duet,"** whose protagonist traces his success as a country music singer to the death of his best friend. Yet this assumption about the necessary connection between art and suffering is challenged in other stories in *More Shapes Than One,* especially in **"Weird Tales"** and **"Mankind Journeys through Forests of Symbols."**

"Weird Tales," the book's final historical fiction, deals with events that occur in the 1920s and 1930s, but it is narrated, as the final paragraph makes clear, from some point in the future, after the Old Ones of Lovecraft's Cthulhu mythos have seized control of the world from humankind. The story's title is also the name of the pulp magazine that began publishing Lovecraft's fiction in the 1920s, one of the magazines which the adolescent Chappell read avidly and for which he aspired to write. Like *Dagon,* then, **"Weird Tales"** is in part a tribute to Lovecraft and the kind of horror fiction Lovecraft popularized. "The visionary poet Hart Crane and the equally visionary horror-story writer H. P. Lovecraft met four times," the story begins, but its focus soon shifts away from Lovecraft himself to Sterling Croydon, a member of Lovecraft's circle, who suffers a ghastly death as a result of his experiments with "spatial emplacement," a concept derived from one of Lovecraft's own stories, "The Dreams in the Witch House," to which Chappell refers in **"Weird Tales."** Similarly, the Antarctic setting of Croydon's death stems from Lovecraft's use of that region in his novel *At the Mountains of Madness.* Chappell obviously relishes the opportunity to create a horror story to rival one of Lovecraft's own and to fill it with details from Lovecraft's fiction.

"Weird Tales" is more, however, than a *jeu d'esprit* in the horror genre. In fact the story raises questions about the struggle between free will and fate that are fundamental to the very possibility of moral choice. The implied narrator of this third-person tale (which shifts to first-person plural only in its closing paragraph) shares the pessimism bred by Lovecraft's mythos. "Lovecraft," writes the narrator, from whom Chappell distances himself, "described a cosmos that threw dark Lucretian doubt on the proposition 'that such things as . . . good and evil, love and hate, and all such local attributes of a negligible and temporary race called mankind, have any existence at all'" (60). The words quoted by the narrator in this passage are taken from one of Lovecraft's letters to Farnsworth Wright, the editor of *Weird Tales*.[23] In the context of Lovecraft's mythos, the narrator presents Hart Crane's suicide as a surrender to the prehistoric gods, represented by "the immense serpentine manifestation of Dzhaimbú, . . . *this fabulous shadow only the sea keeps*" (70). The last phrase, which serves as the closing line of Crane's poem "At Melville's Tomb," seems intended to remind readers of the Old Testament's Leviathan, God's archetypal enemy, personified for Melville's Ahab in the white whale, while the "serpentine" shape of Dzhaimbú recalls Satan's disguise in Genesis.[24]

But Chappell's mythos is not Lovecraft's. Nor does he share Croydon's theory that "all human speech [is] merely the elaboration of an original shriek of terror" (63). For Chappell, literary creation often seems to originate in delight, in the exuberant playfulness of the artistic imagination. Instead of invoking the cruel prehistoric gods of Lovecraft and Croydon, Chappell's fiction and poetry are informed by the Christian mythos, with its emphasis on the radical distinction between good and evil, its ethic of self-sacrificial love, and its sense of the crucial role choices play in defining moral character.

This issue of choice is also central to **"The Somewhere Doors,"** the first of the book's nonhistorical fictions. Like **"Barcarole"** and **"Weird Tales,"** this story deals with an artist figure, Arthur Strakl, a writer of science fiction. In German the verb *strakln* means "to stretch" or "to stretch one's arms," and one of the effects of Strakl's fiction, like Chappell's itself, is to enlarge the reader's mind and imagination and heart. The plot, as is appropriate to a science fiction tale, involves a visitor from another dimension, a person who calls herself Francesca and who announces that Arthur will soon be receiving two doors. He is to choose between them, entering a new world from which he can never return. One of the doors will open on a pastoral paradise, a second Eden, with Arthur its only inhabitant. The other door will give him access to a utopian civilization of "great cities." Ultimately—and perhaps too predictably—Strakl recognizes a third option: to remain where he is, to embrace earthly existence. Before Francesca's appearance, however, Strakl had tended to disdain the earth. "Arthur did not read invasion stories," Chappell writes; "he could not imagine that Earth . . . would be a desirable prize" (72). Like Virgil Campbell and Uncle Body in **Midquest** though without their bawdiness, Strakl learns to celebrate the physical world. As with Linnaeus, Strakl's moment of insight occurs in the presence of nature, amid sights he has long overlooked, sights "he could remember . . . and yet he would always mostly forget" (97). Such forgetfulness seems to constitute one major category of error, if not of sin, in the moral universe Chappell's fiction postulates. It is thus significant that Strakl rejects both "paradise" and "utopia" because they "could not remember. They were eternal and unaging and had no history to come to nor any to leave behind" (97). Chappell concludes **"The Somewhere Doors"** by inviting his readers to make a choice, an interpretive choice involving the story's final image: Strakl "weeping aloud like a child deceived or undeceived."

This story earned Chappell the 1992 World Fantasy Award, an award he won again two years later for the chapbook publication of **The Lodger**.[25] Despite its award-winning status, however, **"The Somewhere Doors"** is too schematic and didactic to reach the level of artistry Chappell achieves in **"Linnaeus Forgets"** and **"Barcarole"** and **"Weird Tales."** The story is also flawed by a sentimental subplot involving Arthur's relationship with his employer. Yet Chappell endears Strakl himself to the reader, in part by referring to the protagonist by his first name after using surnames for the characters in the five historical fictions. **"The Somewhere Doors"** plays a key thematic role in the book, moreover, by underscoring the primacy of choice, by enlarging Chappell's cast of artist figures, by insisting on the importance of memory, and by again distancing humanity from paradise.

That distance is re-emphasized in the volume's seventh—and thus central—story, **"The Adder,"** which is narrated by a book dealer in Durham. Like **"Weird Tales,"** this story invokes Lovecraft's mythos, for its title refers to *The Necronomicon,* a book of black magic invented by Lovecraft, who attributed it to a fictitious Arabic author, Abdul Alhazred. In contrast to **"Weird Tales,"** however, with its visions of violent destruction, the tone of **"The Adder"** is more comic than minatory. Although *The Necronomicon*'s presumed capacity for evil is immense, Chappell focuses specifically on the book's power to alter other texts and even people's memories of those texts. The narrator discovers this power when he conceals the book beneath a tattered copy of Milton's poems, only to find that the opening lines of *Paradise Lost* and of Milton's sonnet on his blindness have been grotesquely distorted. The variant readings Chappell cites are themselves delightful parodies: *"When I consider how my loot is spent"* (108), *"When I consider to whom my spode is lent"* (109), among several others. But Chappell does more than entertain. **"The Adder"** also makes clear that language and literature are not exempt from moral categories. Nor is the writer, as Chappell's use of Milton, both here and in the collection's epigraph, appears to suggest. Whimsical as this story is, it limns a world well east of Eden. To paraphrase Melville's assessment of the Encantadas, "In no world but a fallen one could such [a book] exist." It is Chappell's conception of literature's moral responsibilities, its role in preserving and promoting humane values, that accounts for his placement of **"The Adder"** at the very center of *More Shapes Than One.*

Like **"The Adder,"** four of the book's final six stories use first-person narrators. These narrators range from a jealous lover who has just killed his sweetheart (**"Ember"**) to a persecuted practitioner of science (**"After Revelation"**), from a country music star still mourning the death of his best friend (**"Duet"**) to a frontiersman in an unspecified era who abhors "the woman trade" as it is practiced by his contemporaries, for whom women are so much livestock (**"Alma"**). Chappell individualizes each of these narrators, endowing them with personalities as varied as those of the volume's earlier historical figures. Although several of these later stories are set in the North Carolina mountains, Chappell usually avoids nonstandard English except in spoken dialogue. When his narrators address the reader or another silent auditor (as Bill Puckett does in **"Ember"** or Kermit Wilson does in **"Duet"**), it is their diction, syntax, and figurative language that reflect the stories' mountain settings. Puckett says, "My face got laid open by a bramble or a twig" and reports how he struggled through a laurel thicket "as puzzledy as a roll of barbwire" (124, 125). He sees "a little old granny woman" transformed into something "all gnarled and rooty like the bottom of a rotted oak stump turned up" (126). Such images and expressions derive from authentic regional dialect and the circumstances of mountain life without reinforcing regional stereotypes.

In a third-person narrative like **"Mankind Journeys"** Chappell both exploits and subverts such stereotypes. Sheriff Balsam and his deputies, "tall tobacco-chewing mountain boys," seem initially the stock-in-trade of Southern fiction. Yet one of the deputies, as it happens, is a closet symbolist poet who can identify the French wine (Château Beychevelle '78) in a soupcon of barbecue sauce. **"Mankind Journeys"** is the most wildly humorous of all the stories in *More Shapes Than One.* Part parody, part satire, part sheer comic extravagance, it draws on both the tall tale tradition and the exotic fabulations of an author like Donald Barthelme. By taking the story's title from Baudelaire's famous poem "Corréspondances" and by parodying Symbolist poetry, Chappell also pokes fun at his own youthful literary influences, as he did in *Midquest*'s **"Rimbaud Fire Letter."** At the same time, this story presents variations on the artist and scientist figures who appear throughout the volume.

The story's opening paragraph illustrates Chappell's seamless blending of fantasy and realism when an immense dream, "about two stories tall and five hundred yards wide," is discovered blocking a highway. To remove this obstruction, the sheriff eventually learns, he must sponsor a poetry contest, for the dream originates in the unconscious or blocked work of deputy Bill's poetic imagination. In **"Mankind Journeys"** Chappell hilariously interweaves a frustrated artist figure, a pseudoscientific expert, and French Symbolist speculations on the origins of literary creativity. Unlike Linnaeus, Dr. Litmouse, the scientist in this story, is caricatured. After ingesting a piece of the dream to determine its composition, Litmouse spouts several lines of Baudelaire's poem, then collapses, the apparent victim of a Rimbaudian derangement of the senses. Moreover, his quart jar of what the sheriff assumes to be secret formula turns out to be barbecue sauce. Part of the pleasure of this story stems from Chappell's outlandish comic similes, as when he echoes one of Apollinaire's definitions of surrealism by stating, "Dusk had come to the mountains like a sewing machine crawling over an operating table" (160). But Chappell also uses this story to puncture the Symbolists' conception of the suffering artist, the poet *maudit.* His hyperbolic account of the deputy's agonizing efforts to complete his poem serves to undercut the views of Rudolf Zimmer in **"Barcarole"** that artistic creation arises *only* amid anguish.

"After Revelation," the final story in *More Shapes Than One,* looks back to **"Linnaeus Forgets"** by focusing on a botanist and looks forward to the extraliterary world to which the reader will return beyond the text's epiphanies. Set in a vaguely European locale at an unspecified time in the future, the story might be labeled an eschatological fable. It opens in medias res with the words, "Then one evening I woke from a nap to find the door of my cell open and I walked out" (186). The narrator, George, owes his liberation to the return of "the Owners" of the human race, whose presence on earth ultimately prompts him to become a pilgrim in search of his Owner. This quest motif, treated comically in **"Mankind Journeys,"** recalls both *Midquest* and *Moments of Light.* Significantly, the arrival of the Owners does not negate the fact of death. Indeed the narrator's beloved, Larilla, dies "of happiness" in the company of her Owner. The initially disconsolate George is placed at a table, given a loaf of bread and a cup of water, and urged to rest, eat, and remember (196), images and commands (though wine is absent) similar to those involved in the sacrament of Communion. Religious revelation does not, Chappell implies, enable believers to evade suffering and death, nor does it free people from the continuing need to make complex moral choices and to search for truth. The same obligations attend those who are the beneficiaries of the epiphanies offered by the arts and sciences.

This concluding story also clarifies the moral implications of Chappell's earlier portraits of Maupertuis, Feuerbach, and Offenbach. "The Owners are, I believe," says George, "those who can pay full attention to someone else" (191). Here is the heart of Chappell's moral vision, and herein, he suggests, lies the principal challenge and achievement of literature. Chappell's fiction and poetry strive to become such acts of attention, enabling their readers to share the experiences of others and thus nurturing understanding and compassion. His work promotes respect for the resources of the past while recognizing the reader's need to act in an extraliterary present. "After revelation, what then?" asks George in the story's—and the book's—final sentence. By juxtaposing this story with "Alma," whose narrator has had a revelation about the injustice of the woman trade and vows to free the brutalized women he encounters, Chappell underscores the ethical implications of both extraliterary experience and the experiences mediated by literary texts. Literature, he insists, illuminates the world, enlarging our conception of reality, but it does not replace that world.

More Shapes Than One was widely and enthusiastically reviewed. Michael Dirda, who called the stories "terrifically enjoyable," remarked that "these entrancing pages deserve all the readers they can get," while Orson Scott Card concluded his review by observing, "You'll be glad to have [this] book on your shelf, and even gladder to have Fred Chappell's sweet and searing stories in your memory."[26] Jacqueline Adams spoke of the collection's "13 marvelous stories" and stated, "Chappell is a talented writer who deserves a wider audience."[27] Yet it seems uncertain that Chappell's volumes of short stories will gain the broad readership both Dirda and Adams recommend, for as Chappell himself has noted, historical fictions, especially those about scientists, have "limited audience appeal,"[28] and both his collections contain such work. Allusive as those stories may be, however, they are among Chappell's finest and most thought-provoking short fiction.

They appear, moreover, in volumes that offer an impressive variety of stories. What Francesca says of Arthur Strakl's fiction in **"The Somewhere Doors"** can be said with even greater justice of Chappell's own stories; they afford "many fine pleasures" (77).

Notes

1. Chappell, "Fred Chappell," 123.

2. Alex Albright, "Friend of Reason: Surveying the Fred Chappell Papers at Duke University," in *Dream Garden,* 229.

3. Chappell, "Introduction," in *Editor's Choice* 3, ed. Morty Sklar (New York: Spirit That Moves Us Press, 1991), 10.

4. Chappell, "Science and the Artist's Vision," *New England Review* 3, no. 1 (1980): 133.

5. Chappell, "A Little Houyhnhnm in Your Life," in *Editor's Choice,* ed. Morty Sklar and Jim Mulac (Iowa City: Spirit That Moves Us Press, 1980), 387.

6. Chappell, *Moments of Light* (Los Angeles: New South Company, 1980), 110. Further references noted parenthetically are to this edition.

7. Chappell, "Fred Chappell," 123.

8. Reviews of *Moments of Light,* by Chappell, *Choice,* Mar. 1981, 946; Robert D. Walsh, *Library Journal,* 15 Jan. 1981, 165; Robert Gingher, "Fred Chappell's Intelligent Heart," *Greensboro Daily News/Record,* 23 Nov. 1980, G5.

9. *The Notebooks of Simone Weil,* vol. 2, trans. Arthur Wills (London: Routledge and Kegan Paul, 1956), 500.

10. Chappell, "Fred Chappell," 124.

11. Quoted by Robert Bone in Ralph Ellison, "Ralph Ellison and the Uses of Imagination," in *Twentieth Century Interpretations of* Invisible Man, ed. John M. Reilly (Englewood Cliffs, N.J.: Prentice-Hall, 1970), 24.

12. Stuart, "'Blue Pee': Fred Chappell's Short Fiction," *Iron Mountain Review* 2 (Spring 1985): 19.

13. See James Everett Kibler, Jr., "A Fred Chappell Bibliography, 1963-1983," *Mississippi Quarterly* 37 (Winter 1983-84): 65. Of "Waltzes Noble and Sentimental," Kibler states, "Chappell describes this as a short-story collection completed and pending approval for publication."

14. See "The Dreaming Orchid," *New Mexico Humanities Review* 5, no. 1 (Spring 1982): 61-76.

15. Chappell, *More Shapes Than One* (New York: St. Martin's, 1991), ix. Further references noted parenthetically are to this edition.

16. Darrell Schweitzer, "A Talk with Fred Chappell," *Worlds of Fantasy and Horror* 1 (Summer 1994): 42.

17. Sullivan, "'Citizens Who Observe,'" 148.

18. Palmer, "Fred Chappell," 405.

19. Chappell, "Fantasia," 179-89.

20. Chappell, "Visionary Fiction," *Chronicles* 11 (May 1987): 19.

21. Ibid., 21; Chappell's italics.

22. Linnaeus's vision of the triumph of Flora, as Chappell describes it, is based on the frontispiece to Linnaeus's *Hortus Cliffortianus* (1737). That frontispiece is reproduced in Wilfrid Blunt's *The Complete Naturalist: A Life of Linnaeus* (New York: Viking, 1971), 128.

23. I am indebted to S. T. Joshi's introduction to *The Annotated H. P. Lovecraft* (New York: Dell, 1997) for my knowledge of the specific letter from which Chappell drew this quotation. Joshi cites that letter in his introduction (p. 15) but does not discuss Chappell's story. Chappell himself says in the interview with Darrell Schweitzer cited above, "All the quotations that are in documents in ["Weird Tales"] are real. Those came from Hart Crane's letters or from H. P. Lovecraft's letters" (42).

24. The name Dzhaimbú, as Chappell noted in a personal letter dated 29 March 1999, is not of Lovecraftian origin but is a variation on Xingu or Shango, a West African voodoo god transported to the Caribbean.

25. Chappell, *The Lodger* (West Warwick, R.I.: Necronomicon Press, 1993). This twenty-eight-page chapbook spoofs Lovecraftian horror tales of demonic possession. The exorcism in this case is accomplished by reading aloud assorted passages of postmodern literary criticism from books with such titles as *Despotic Signifiers and the Babylonian Antireactionary Episteme*.

26. Michael Dirda, *Washington Post Book World,* 6 Oct. 1991, 5; Orson Scott Card, "Books to Look For." *Magazine of Fantasy and Science Fiction* 83 (Aug. 1992): 20.

27. Jacqueline Adams, *Library Journal,* 1 Sept. 1991, 233.

28. Chappell, "Fred Chappell," 124.

Bibliography

[Editor's Note: See previous essay for complete bibliography.]

Casey Clabough (essay date September 2003)

SOURCE: Clabough, Casey. "Appropriations of History, Gothicism, and Cthulhu: Fred Chappell's *Dagon*." *Mosaic* 36, no. 3 (September 2003): 37-53.

[*In the following essay, Clabough examines* Dagon *in depth, deeming it "Chappell's most versatile novel, as well as his most ambitiously experimental."*]

The Nile flows north [. . .] to Wisconsin
Where August Derleth prints the books
Of Lovecraft, dreamer of
The Book of Thoth.
The Necronomicon, lost work of Abdul Alhazred,
Lovecraft who wrote of Nug and Dagon,
Old gods. Nyogtha and Cthulhu,
And east of this train, south of Virginia,
In western North Carolina, Fred Chappell
Has written a novel, Dagon.

—*R. H. W. Dillard,* News of the Nile

At first glance, Fred Chappell's third book, **Dagon** (pronounced *dā'gŏn'*, possesses a number of striking similarities with his first two novels, **It Is Time, Lord** and **The Inkling.** Once again, the reader is confronted with a rural area of the American South, an unhappy inward-looking male protagonist, an element of domestic unrest, and symbolic acts of violence. However, these seemingly significant commonalities ultimately melt away as the reader sinks progressively deeper into **Dagon**'s suffocatingly unique and even bizarre combination of history, horror, and wide-ranging intertextuality. With its myriad sources, multiple levels of meaning, and an aesthetic technique utilizing various conventions of gothicism, horror, and southern grotesque, **Dagon**—a winner of the Best Foreign Novel award from the French Academy—constitutes Chappell's most versatile novel, as well as his most ambitiously experimental.

Dagon is singular in a number of disparately important respects, and this essay begins with an account of its composition—an anguished three-year process that stands out against the succinct development of his first two books, each written in less than two months. Using **Dagon**'s composition as a visceral foundation, the argument moves into a discussion of the book's preliminary sources, those texts that fueled its initial conception. **Dagon**'s models also inform some of the book's specific internal dynamics, and the essay proceeds to consider the relationship between its gender-conscious construction of character and its Gothic qualities, demonstrating how each informs the other. Working both behind and with this dynamic is the book's innovative appropriation of a fictional historical source: the constructed mythology of H. P. Lovecraft. Chappell couples Lovecraft's work with genuine historical sources in delivering serious commentary on debilitating American materialism. The argument concludes with a demonstration of how the book's amalgamating and transcendent resolution reiterates its Gothic and fantastic qualities, while also pressing the boundaries of the genres from which it appropriates material.

* * *

More than thirty years after **Dagon**'s publication, Chappell appeared uneasy and slightly reluctant when asked about his third book, the composition of which he paints in unpleasant terms: "I recall sweating out that novel over here on Spring Garden Street and having great agonies with it" (personal interview). In an autobiographical essay he elaborates: "*Dagon,* my third novel and the shortest of my books of fiction, gave me trouble from which I never quite recovered. Though I was willing to harrow readers with my books, I never expected one of my books to harrow me" (**"Fred"** 21). In addition to its psychologically trying subject matter, *Dagon* harried Chappell in terms of its largely irreconcilable themes and labyrinthine concepts, upon which he spent massive amounts of time and energy trying to resolve. He recalls, "Well, I put a lot into it. I put a lot of horrible feelings—all my fears and doubts and pride—into that novel. And I tried real hard. Of the novels I've written, I had the most ambition for that one. It was a difficult failure . . . but then I was trying for difficult things" (Stirnemann 45). Chappell's struggles with the book are obvious in a number of respects. A fluid and prodigious writer who produces essays, reviews, poems, and stories with little revision and at a consistently rapid rate, he toiled over *Dagon* for three arduous years. By contrast, as a result of economic and publication pressures, Chappell had written both *It Is Time, Lord* and *The Inkling* in remarkable six-week intervals. Yet *Dagon* constantly evaded and exhausted him, driving him to bouts of heavy drinking and numerous fruitless efforts: "When I worked on it, I worked on it furiously. But then I kept throwing away large sections, great patches of it, so that it was a case of writing ten pages and throwing away 40" (Palmer 404). After multiple drafts and months of turmoil, having reached a point where he felt he could go no further or achieve anything better, Chappell settled on a manuscript and arrived at the conclusion, "I'd given it my best shot and failed" (**"Remarks"** 5). His editor at Harcourt, Brace and World, Hiram Hadyn, had reservations about publishing *Dagon* and insisted on extensive changes. Yet, having nothing left to offer the book, Chappell simply placed the rejected manuscript in a drawer for a year and sent it back to Hadyn unchanged. It was accepted (**"Fred"** 23-24).

When Chappell labels *Dagon* a "failure," he points to his professed inability to carry out and reconcile the book's complex themes. He maintains, "I think it's the best of the novels, in that it's the most adventurous and most courageous. I think it's the worst in terms of execution. It simply just does not work" (Ragan 110). Indeed, the book possesses a kind of mesmerizing and suffocating aura that resists organization and is difficult to measure in terms of technical proficiency. As was the case with his second novel, *The Inkling,* Chappell's intricate themes, obscured and buried beneath a dense, dark narrative, confused and frustrated early reviewers. He recounts, "*Dagon* received puzzled, irritated, and even furious reviews and sold, I would guess, 4000 copies" (**"Remarks"** 3). Confronted with another challenging and enigmatic Chappell novel, reviewers—as they had done with *The Inkling*—characterized *Dagon* in terms of its most superficial characteristics, hoping to arrive at convenient and conventional estimations of its literary value. Peter Buitenhuis, for example, makes the oblique comment, "The style of the novel is of a very high order. Its precise, dry elegance contrasts piquantly with its sleazy material" (58). Another early reviewer, Allen Cohen, was nearly as opaque in describing his protagonist Peter Leland's actions during the second half of the novel: "For the rest of the book he indulges in alcohol, and in sexual, physical, and mental degradation with the help of a farm girl" (3,576). Reducing Mina Morgan's dark, perverse, archetypal character to a simple "farm girl" underscores the half-hearted and superficial analysis with which the book initially was greeted. Furthermore, as with Chappell's first two novels, those readers who succeeded in noting *Dagon*'s considerable symbolic depth generally were confused and put off by it. One reviewer, in the Winter 1969 issue of *Virginia Quarterly Review,* complains that "symbolism is scattered throughout with almost too heavy a hand." Confronted with a text that conceded few ready meanings, puzzled early reviewers criticized its baffling depth and most literal qualities, readily dismissing the book without having successfully delved into it.

* * *

The underlying themes of *Dagon* that so evaded and confused early reviewers are revealed initially through the sources that supplied them, which are numerous and wide-ranging, making it Chappell's most thoroughly researched and ambitious novel. He says of his intentions for the book, "I had erected too many ambitions for the story to fulfill: it was to be a thesis about American fecklessness and wastefulness; it was to be an expose of a hidden American religion; it was to tell the biblical story of Samson in modern terms; it was to employ the artificial mythology of the H. P. Lovecraft circle of writers, the Cthulhu mythos, in a sarcastic pop-art fashion" (**"Fantasia"** 181-82). Disparate and even contradictory, Chappell's attempted reconciliations of *Dagon*'s general themes frustrated him, resulting in the book's arduous and prolonged composition process. However, Chappell had very specific literary texts in mind while he laboured on *Dagon,* which he hoped would serve as models for working out his numerous philosophical concerns. He relates, "I had ambitions for it I could not bring off. I had hoped that it might be thought of somewhere along the level of Thomas Mann's *Death in Venice.* [. . .] Now you can find it in stores as a horror novel—which is what it is—with covers that my mother would *not* like. I love them, though" (Stirnemann 45-46). *Death in Venice* anticipates **Dagon** in the way the aesthete Aschenbach becomes a slave to pagan passions through his fascination with the sensual young boy, Tadzio. Aschenbach becomes irrationally attached to the boy, to the point that he does not leave Venice even when a deadly Asiatic cholera strikes the city. Similarly, the bookish Peter Leland remains inextricably bound to young Mina Morgan, even as his perverse dedication threatens to pervert and destroy him.

Chappell notes that his appropriation of *Death in Venice* did not keep the novel off the shelves of bookstores' horror sections. In fact, in addition to his confessed use of Lovecraft, Chappell seems to have drawn on his extensive fantasy reading in assembling various aspects of **Dagon.** For example, Leland's investigation of his grandparents' cryptic letters in the big "dark secretary" (**Dagon** 9) suggests identical episodes from George MacDonald's novels *Lilith* and *Phantastes.* MacDonald is one of Chappell's favourite writers in a fantastic genre he labels "visionary fiction" (**"Visionary"** 19), and he cites *Lilith* and *Phantastes* as two of the best exemplars of this tradition. A former Scottish clergyman, MacDonald often worked interesting theological concepts into his somewhat didactic plots, just as Chappell effectively uses Leland's theological scholarship and sermons to address some of his book's philosophical concerns.

Chappell also drew on his own western North Carolina background in establishing some of the novel's more literal characteristics. For example, he admits, "The house from **Dagon** is a variation on my grandfolks' house. The house I grew up in for the latter part of my adolescence. This is also the house of *I Am One of You Forever*" (qtd. in Palumbo 195). Chappell compares the physical aspects of the farm to various aesthetic and symbolic components in his work, the literal geography of the Leland land projecting psychological and artistic qualities. Early in **Dagon,** the narrator remarks, "The big ugly house sat almost in the center of the wide farm, the four hundred acres shaped vaguely like an open hand" (16). Resembling "an open hand" and surrounded by large hills, the very physical nature of the farm symbolically suggests Leland's diminutive insignificance and imminent confinement. As Leland progressively succumbs to his family's dark past, the farm's fingers slowly close in on him.

In his summary of **Dagon,** John Lang likens the Leland house to that in Hawthorne's *The House of the Seven Gables* (35). Although Chappell does not specifically mention Hawthorne's third novel, he readily admits to its author's influence on **Dagon**: "There is always Hawthorne in my work; after Poe, he's my principle author, almost, of American literature" (qtd. in Palumbo 198). Instead of *The House of the Seven Gables,* Chappell notes that **Dagon**'s initial conception was based on one of Hawthorne's more distinguished short stories: "**Dagon** started first in my mind as a sort of short story that would make a pendant to Hawthorne's story 'My Kinsman, Major Molineaux,' but then when I got to thinking about it a little more it would seem to be more fun as a short novel, because I could retell the story of Samson at the same time. And as a kind of dark joke I could use H. P. Lovecraft's Cthulhu mythology as background" (Palmer 404). Putting aside, for the time being, the influential mythology of Lovecraft and the Bible, it is especially noteworthy and illuminating that Chappell's novel had its genesis in one of Hawthorne's dark *Bildungsroman,* for **Dagon** is a kind of initiation narrative for Peter Leland, a youthful and naïve Methodist preacher, whose half-hearted, postured theological idealism blinds him to the presence of evil, both in others and in himself. Lacking the moral and theological seriousness of Hawthorne's Hooper or Dimmesdale, Leland nonetheless shares with them a dimension of harsh self-analysis that borders on the perverse. Yet, this dynamic is essential to his character, paving the way for his descent into self-abasement. In fact, Chappell maintains that he is drawn to ministerial characters "because they have a little more leisure time than other folks, more time to explore their psyches than other folks" (Easa 53). Although "My Kinsman, Major Molineaux" lacks a ministerial protagonist, its similarities with **Dagon** are difficult to ignore. Both Leland and Hawthorne's young protagonist, Robin, journey eastward, from western rural areas to seaport towns, where dark epiphanies await them that are both violent and perverse in their implications. In addition, both young men are inhibited by their dark, Puritan *Umwelten,* or self-worlds, which inform their myopic misinterpretations and hesitant inabilities to act decisively. At the end of **Dagon**'s first chapter, the narrator reveals that Leland "had never before felt his will to be so ringed about, so much at bay" (12). Moreover, in Hawthorne's story, Robin's cudgel, like Leland's water-pump handle (**Dagon** 119), is brandished but never used—an obvious corresponding symbol of physical and psychological impotence.

* * *

Hawthorne's story gave Chappell the idea for a young naïve male character haunted by a Puritanical legacy and wholly predisposed to impotence. He explains, "My protagonist, a misguided minister named Peter Leland, turned out to be the most gullible and spineless creature who ever haunted book paper" (**"Fantasia"** 187). Although Leland is weak and ineffective, his character is neither pointlessly shallow nor superficial. As Chappell notes, convincing the reader of Leland's flat passivity proved to be an extraordinarily difficult chore: "The hardest character I've ever had to draw was the protagonist of **Dagon,** Peter Leland, because he was so bleeding passive. All he did was sit there, and I stuck pins into him, and it was very difficult to give him any character at all" (qtd. in Broughton 117). Although Chappell views Leland's flatness as a shortcoming in the novel, it is perhaps an unavoidable one. After all, a strong, well-developed character likely would have resisted Mina's influence altogether, or at least held out against it for a much longer period of time. Leland's puny willpower and unsympathetic underdevelopment are necessary for him to function as a kind of symbol for both the deluded Puritan *Umwelt* and the American Gothic tradition, his name calling to mind Brockden Brown's novel *Wieland, or The Transformation* (1798), generally considered the first successful Gothic narrative written in America. Leland's impotence also balances the book's symbolic gendered narrative since Mina, his erotic puerile captor, embodies a potently dominant female authority, channelled through a cruel ancient fertility god with brutal Gothic qualities. At the etymological root of "Gothic" is "Goth," the term Roman writers employed in identifying the various wandering pagan tribes of northern Europe who swept down upon Rome in the early fifth century, raping and looting as they came. As Richard Davenport-Hines recounts, "their love of plunder and revenge ushered in a dark age, and the word 'goth' is still associated with dark powers, the lust for domination and inveterate cruelty" (1).

Channelled through Mina's willful, sexualized character, the novel's Gothic ruthlessness and authority take on a potently feminine hue. Not surprisingly, aspects of the text's dense symbolism are illuminated through a consideration of gender power relationships between the characters. In his extreme psychological sensitivity and inability to act, Leland demonstrates qualities of the traditional weak Gothic female—the beleaguered and objectified damsel in distress. Leland's incapacity for action and unlimited potential for victimization are made obvious from the book's beginning: "Never before had he realized so acutely the invalidity of his desires, how they could be so easily canceled, simply marked out, by the impersonal presence of something, a place, an object, anything vehemently and uncaringly itself" (12). Chappell repeatedly underscores Leland's reluctance for action, paving the way for his abdication to Mina's dark feminine authority. For example, like the irresolute speaker in D. H.

Lawrence's poem "Snake," Leland hesitates to kill the serpent that frightens his wife (76), becoming churlish after Sheila finally taunts him into destroying the hapless reptile. More indicative of his weak incapacity, he is unable to hold his liquor and, by the end of the novel, incapable of having sex, an impotent condition magnified by his traditionally asexual and emasculating vocation. As Cyndy Hendershot notes in *The Animal Within: Masculinity and the Gothic,* "the Gothic disrupts. It takes societal norms and invades them with an unassimilable force" (1). Fatigued, nervous, and alone, Leland is completely enervated of any normative masculine potency, taking on instead the feminine qualities of the traditional Gothic heroine, and becoming victim to a powerfully irresistible and equally non-traditional feminine evil.

What little inkling of manhood Leland possesses at the beginning of the book is defused from him in the first few chapters. His lack of masculinity is also underscored and countered early in the novel by his seemingly traditional feminine wife Sheila, a "pretty little wife" (26) who cooks, cleans, sews (47), and wears "pink cotton slacks" (17). However, for all her stereotypical ultra-feminine qualities, Sheila is both smarter (21) and physically stronger than Peter, mocking his dense theological doctrines (41) and outmuscling him during their wrestling match/foreplay (22). When he accidentally locks himself in the attic, she comes to his rescue and chides him, "Just like a child, can't stay out of trouble" (54). Immediately after this episode, the narrator muses, "How often it had seemed to Peter that she was a man, maybe more male in the way it counted than he" (66). However, Sheila's indefatigable patience and blind wet-nursing of Leland ultimately alienate her to the reader and compromise her safety. Like Ellen Trainer in E. F. Benson's rural thriller "At the Farmhouse," Sheila is made unsympathetic and left underdeveloped to the point that her murder goes unlamented and even unremarked. However, her general physical and mental superiority to Leland made Chappell worry that Leland's murder of her would seem impractical and unconvincing. Years after the book's publication, he confessed, "The difficult thing was in getting the reader to accept a sudden violent event, the murder of the wife, which opened the doorway to the supernatural" (qtd. in Broughton 101). Having made Leland, like the traditional Gothic heroine, a figure of passivity and mental and emotional instability, Chappell all but compromised his protagonist's ability to act. However, through Leland's dreams and irrational behaviour, he drops enough hints along the way to suggest that the backsliding minister's deepening madness might conceivably drive him to murder. At one point, the narrator says of Leland, "Nor was he delighted to see his mind so often turning upon himself" (8). Though stronger and more intelligent than her husband, Sheila, blinded by her ill-advised devotion, becomes a casualty of the degenerate homicidal madness that plagues him.

As Chappell remarks, Sheila's murder opens "the doorway to the supernatural," a dark realm where the nature of evil is potently feminine. In one of their barely literate letters, Leland's grandparents remark that the members of the Morgan family are "the most high adepts" (74) in the Dagon cult and, although her parents possess unusual qualities, Mina appears to be the dominant Morgan in administering the religion. Chappell uses archetypal feminine traits in describing both the Morgan women and the cult in order "to get the powerful female principle in there" (qtd. in Palumbo 198). For example, he based Mina's mother, Mrs. Morgan, with her enormous breasts and belly (29), on the Heidelberg Venus—an ancient depiction of a fertility goddess. Although she is large and potent, Mrs. Morgan never speaks in the novel, functioning instead as a symbol of primitive and powerful, though unthinking and inarticulate, female sexuality. Mina too, despite being "maybe fourteen or fifteen or sixteen" (30), projects a vigorous sexuality, copulating incessantly with Leland, Coke Rymer, and random hillbillies. Leland imagines, "She had no nose, Mina, any more than a fish. She deeped in oceans of semen" (51). Yet, there is much more to Mina than powerful, perverse sexuality. Whereas Mrs. Morgan constitutes a stolid, large, dominant feminine sexuality, the spirit or intellect of the novel's dark femininity resides in her prodigious daughter, whose character suggests the seductive Philistine Dagon-worshiper Delila in the well-known biblical narrative.

As Chappell notes, to an extent, Mina also grew out of the sensual character Lora Bowen in **The Inkling**: "It seemed to me that the kind of personality or force that Mina represents, is present to some degree in Lora" (Ragan 111). Just as Lora unravels Jan Anderson's rationalistic will, wearing it down with maddening lust, so Mina seduces Leland into a state of debilitating psychological agitation that leads to the senseless murder of his wife. As Joseph Andriano remarks in *Our Ladies of Darkness: Feminine Daemonology in Male Gothic Fiction,* "the female demon in Gothic fiction, then, is often an image of the archetypal feminine, with which men must struggle in their attempts to define themselves and their relation to the female Other" (146). Having been weakened and perverted by his brooding, repressive Puritanical *Umwelt,* Leland is unable to resist the dark feminine archetypal urges manifested through Mina's supernatural enchantments, becoming instead a slave to his basest impulses, which is the same as becoming Mina's

slave. In their literal form and function, Mina's demonic supernatural characteristics suggest those of the protagonist in Arthur Machen's tale "The White People," in which a young girl is taught the orgiastic rites of an ancient witch cult. Incidentally, H. P. Lovecraft based aspects of his Cthulhu terminology on passages from "The White People." Mina's role as priestess, or at least prime participant, in a cult ceremony that amounts to little more than a hillbilly gang-bang (107-09), underscores her centrality both as a sexual object and prime authority figure in the worship of **Dagon.** Although, in the course of the ceremony, she has sex with several men, it is evident that she controls—in the same way she commands Leland and Coke Rymer—both the unfolding of the ritual and the men involved.

* * *

Chappell draws on legitimate historical and literary texts in constructing **Dagon**; however, not all of his sources are historically authentic, his dominant basis for the Dagon religion deriving from the fictional work of H. P. Lovecraft, perhaps the most important and influential writer of supernatural fiction in the twentieth century. In *The Weird Tale,* Lovecraft scholar S. T. Joshi explains his system of interpretation in terms of the practice of appropriation and variation among writers of the "weird": "Weird writers utilize the schemas I have outlined (or various permutations of them) precisely in accordance with their philosophical predispositions" (10). Possessing his own particular philosophical agenda, Chappell utilizes Lovecraft's original philosophical and mythological system and plays by its rules in order to achieve a specific supernatural effect in his novel. He comments significantly and at great length on his appropriation of Lovecraft's material:

> I was especially pleased with myself for appropriating and using in a contemporary fashion the fantasy materials of H. P. Lovecraft; my notion was that I could take inferior literary matter from the old pulp horror magazines and by including it in a distinctly modernist story, reinterpret it and rework it into artistic respectability. I had in mind the use of such quotidian "inferior" materials as newspaper pages, matchbooks, bicycle wheels, and so forth by such renowned artists as Picasso, Kurt Schwitters, and Man Ray.
>
> Now I recognize how woefully I deceived myself. In the first place, Lovecraft in his best works is a good writer, and certainly much more expert in the art of the horror story than I was or am likely to become. His work did not need me to give it a literary legitimacy that was not in my power to give—a legitimacy already inherent. In the second place, any inclusion of such highly specific fantasy materials—the Cthulhu Mythos had already acquired a largish literary "cult" following—aroused certain expectations in readers who

recognized the materials, expectations which *Dagon,* a little too self-important, a little too pretentious entirely, could not fulfill.

("Fantasia" 182)

Although few of Chappell's readers, excepting Lovecraft enthusiasts, have recognized *Dagon*'s Lovecraft motif, the dynamic is essential to understanding both the internal nature of the Dagon cult and much of the novel's abstract language and imagery. Lovecraft's mythology is revealed in many of his stories through individuals, cults, and towns that worship the Old Ones, cosmic beings who ages ago journeyed from another part of the universe to rule the earth from the now-submerged city of R'lyeh—a word that appears in one of the few widely translated passages of *The Necronomicon,* which Chappell uses as an epigraph for his book: "Ph'nglui mglw'nafh Cthulhu R'lyeh wgah'nagl fhtagn." (In his house at R'lyeh, dead Cthulhu lies dreaming.) In selecting a constructed fictional mythology as the dominant intertexual source for his book, Chappell made the conscious decision to blur the fiction and reality of the real world in the one he had created.

In his little-known poem **"H. P. Lovecraft,"** Chappell attempts to portray the disquieting atmosphere that Lovecraft achieves in his work:

> The worst of it, everything alive.
> Had you thought to escape without dreaming?
> The walls bulge with what you come to know.
> Squamous. Obscene. Hybrid. Eldritch.

(1)

As the poem's last line demonstrates, a major component of Lovecraft's weird power is based on the compelling alien words he so convincingly adopted and created. This dynamic translates into *Dagon* through the enigmatic Lovecraftian terms that Leland discovers in his grandparents' correspondence. As he seeks to open the secret tongue, one gets the impression that the ugly infectious phrases are fueling Leland's madness, crippling his ability to organize language and rational thought. The narrator remarks, "He felt that the letters were obscurely responsible for the bad dreams that came on him late in the mornings" (47). As Leland degenerates further, he studies the letters more regularly and intently, as if the words and his madness are feeding off each other.

The protagonist of Lovecraft's story "The Thing on the Doorstep" is a Mina-like co-ed student—small and dark, with a touch of the "Innsmouth look"—who seduces a hapless professor. In his review of L. Sprague De Camp's Lovecraft biography, Chappell observes that Lovecraft's work often is made up of "scholars who pursue their psychological lives until they are utterly—and logically—destroyed by them" (1). Besides serving as an important critical comment on Lovecraft's work, Chappell's remark suggests the hapless protagonists in two of his early attempts at composing *Dagon.* In an untitled early hand-written version of *Dagon,* the Leland-figure, Vaughn Newcome, appears as a Renaissance scholar preparing to go on sabbatical. Although Mina does not appear as a tenant girl, she is almost identical to her namesake in the novel, "flat-nosed," with "wet and cold" hands (**"Untitled"** 10). Newcome encounters Mina at a college party and, like the estimable academic in Lovecraft's "The Thing on the Doorstep," proceeds to fall under her debilitating influence. Also suggestive of *Dagon,* in **"The Bad Luck,"** a sixty-page unpublished novella, a young, delinquent outlaw couple kidnap a spineless professor pretentiously, yet aptly, named Percival Norman. Uneducated, apathetic, and amoral, the young couple, resembling Mina and Coke Rymer, contrast dramatically with the pompous, ineffective, and Leland-like Norman. Furthermore, Anna Long's voice hisses like Mina's and the highway abduction sequence mirrors the eastward trek of Mina, Rymer, and Leland in *Dagon.* When asked to comment on these interesting early versions of *Dagon,* Chappell humorously replies, "I don't even remember those [laughter]. Are those actual versions? I have no idea. [. . .] I'm sorry, I don't recall either of those versions. [. . .] I think I must have written other versions too and simply discarded them. I'm surprised to hear that there are any of those versions left. I think what I finally had published probably takes from a number of discarded versions, certainly a lot of discarded chapters and pages" (personal interview). Although Chappell does not recollect them now, these interesting early versions of *Dagon* are significant in the way they may be used to trace the development of specific characters and events, as well as Chappell's various compelling applications of Lovecraft's fictional techniques and extraordinary mythological world.

* * *

Not all of Chappell's historical commentary is fictional, his pairing of the decadent Dagon cult with wasteful corporate America functioning as an indictment of the fanatical Puritan work ethic. Chappell says that "the secret cult is a metaphor for the whole of Detroit, Gleem toothpaste and that whole business" (qtd. in Sopko and Carr 230). The narrator's family history reveals that Leland's Puritanical Methodist ancestors were obsessed with money, their correspondence containing numerous references to property values and bills of sale (*Dagon* 10). *Dagon* explores the relationship between capitalist materialism and depraved inhumanity in a number of ways.

For example, Mina's materialism—her seizure of Leland's cheque book and car, along with the manner in which she uses him up as an object—is inextricably bound with her perverse sexuality. In his unpublished poem **"Detroit Pontiac,"** Chappell connects the midwestern industrial hub with carnal lust, describing it as "Furiously decaying, bubbling / With red erotic dreams" (1). Confronting the perverse sexualized materialism of the Dagon cult with his naïve esoteric intellect. Leland's senses are drowned and he becomes an object of consumption for the cult. In the end, his feeble rationalistic constructs are no match for the pervasive, mindless power of the Dagon cult, using up objects and people for no apparent constructive purpose. At the conclusion of his sermon, Leland traces the shadowy legacy of Dagon in contemporary America at great length:

> Didn't the Dagon notion of fertility dominate? Frenzied, incessant, unreasoning sexual activity was invited on all sides; every entertainment, even the serious entertainment, the arts, seemed to suppose this activity as basis. This blind sexual Bacchanalia was inevitably linked to money—one had only to think of the omnipresent advertisements, with all those girls who alarmed the eye. A mere single example. And wasn't the power of money finally dependent upon the continued proliferation of product after product, dead objects produced without any thought given to their uses? Weren't these mostly objects without any truly justifiable need? Didn't the whole of American culture exhibit this endless irrational productivity, clear analogue to sexual orgy? And yet productivity without regard to eventual need was, Peter maintained, actually unproductivity, it was really a kind of impotence. This was the paradox which the figure of Dagon contained.
>
> (39-40)

Fuelled by the Puritan legacy of blind duty and work, American capitalism simultaneously produces useless products and the constructed and skillfully marketed, propagandic lust for them, resulting in a fruitless masturbatory cycle of waste. Such also is the microcosmic purpose of Dagon and his decadent cult, breeding desire and lustfully using up everything in its path without thought or rationale.

At one point in the novel, Leland says of Mina, "No question about her purposes with his possessions; she would waste them totally and carefully" (129). Leland's sermon turns out to be prophetic when he, himself, becomes the wasted material object of the mutated Puritan *Umwelt*. Just as the repressive Puritanical work ethic had created both the Dagon cult and corporate American waste, so Leland's Puritanical world view eventually transforms him into the pathetic and deranged object he becomes—a being devoid of intellect, a figure of wasteful dissipation. As Leland enters the last stages of alcoholic dementia, he

strangles a chicken to death (151) and performs humiliating acts for Mina and her friends/followers in order to obtain his precious ration of moonshine—the primary object of his materialistic addiction. Chappell drew on a number of interesting sources in portraying his broken-down protagonist as a senseless, used-up material commodity, basing the chicken-strangling aspect of Leland's character on a carnival geek he encountered who ate raw chickens and committed other strange acts in order to earn enough money for the next bottle. He also made use of Erskine Caldwell's dark novella, *Poor Fool,* in which the protagonist, Blondy, a punch-drunk boxer, falls under the influence of Mrs. Boxx, a woman who possesses a hypnotic power similar to Mina's, and who, having already castrated her husband, plans to emasculate Blondy as well. Like Leland, Blondy ultimately is measured in terms of his literal usefulness—an object to be appraised, devoured, and thrown away.

* * *

Although Chappell wanted to make a serious and powerful point about wasteful American materialism, he found Leland's ritualized death to be too hopeless and heartless a way to conclude his novel. Rather than leaving his protagonist drained and broken, literally an article of objectified trash, Chappell follows Leland's consciousness as it dwindles into infinity, a phantom afterlife in which he roams the universe contemplating its mysteries. One of the relatively early studies of contemporary gothicism, Linda Bayer-Berenbaum's *The Gothic Imagination: Expansion in Gothic Literature and Art,* maintains, "The Gothic philosophy deals with the nature of transcendence" (12). This bears upon Chappell's novel in the manner that Leland, through his suffering, becomes more an object than a human being, until finally, with his death, he becomes a part of the universe. Chappell describes Leland's transformation in the following terms:

> It seems to me we define ourselves by suffering. That's what the human being is very good at; much of his existence is suffering in one form or another. In order to live with this suffering, in order to endure, we make myths of it; we make narratives and meaning of it. [. . .] In that chapter. I tried to imagine another kind of existence, an afterlife if you will, in which idea and physicality are co-terminals, co-equals. An existence in which the fact of idea can influence the shape and "punch" of the physical. That seemed to me very close to what I can imagine an ideal world must be like, a world in which sensual objects embody and show forth their mathematical forms and relationships immediately to the senses.
>
> (Redd 9)

Giving Leland's extensive suffering a constructive and redeeming purpose, Chappell imagines an afterlife in which idea and physical form enjoy a symbiotic relationship. Like the figure in Chappell's poem **"Message,"** Leland ascends:

> a finer dimension of event, he feels with senses
> newly evolved the wide horizons unknown till now.
> He is transformed head to foot, taproot to polestar.
> He breathes a new universe, the blinding whirlpool
> galaxies drift round him and begin to converse.
>
> (*Source* 55)

Having become privy to the universal relationships of objects and ideas, Leland "contemplated with joy the unity of himself and what surrounded him" (180), exploring both galactic space and the spaces between things and thoughts.

Leland's preparation for this final transformation is reflected in a parody of *Moby Dick,* in which Mina and the other *Dagon* initiates tattoo religious symbols on his body before sacrificing him to their deity. The final section of the novel, concerning Leland's afterlife, extends the parodic *Moby Dick* motif when Peter assumes the form of a spiritual leviathan, a huge, inscrutable, and omniscient being. Furthermore, the final chapter owes its tone and form to Chaucer's *Troilus and Criseyde,* the conclusion of which constitutes a trivialization of a powerful succession of events. Finally, the meditative finale of *Dagon* is suggestive of William Hope Hodgson's conclusion to *The House on the Borderland,* in which the protagonist finds himself a naked explorer of outer space. *Dagon*'s sudden and dramatic shift from Leland's literal sacrifice to his fantastic afterlife, which troubles some readers, is an obvious convention of Hodgson's work. In the second chapter of *The Nightland,* for example, Hodgson's milieu shifts suddenly from a quaint English countryside to a black nightmarish future.

More important than its intertexual antecedents, Leland's supernatural condition at the end of *Dagon* informs the structure of the text. Just as Leland's essence transcends the natural world, so the book transcends conventional Gothic tropes to create something artistically authentic. Although the result of Chappell's appropriations is an often-fragmented and confusing narrative, *Dagon* is ultimately protected from claims of organizational disintegration by what critics interpret as the Gothic novel's inherent tendency to disrupt form. George Haggerty perhaps makes this point the best in *Gothic Fiction/Gothic Form*: "What really takes place is a process of formal insurgency, a rejection of the conventional demands of novel form, first within the gloomy confines of Gothic novel, causing disruption and inconsistency, and later as a liberated and liberating alternative to the conventional novel" (3). Long before Haggerty's book existed, H.

P. Lovecraft, in his important extended meditation, "Supernatural Horror in Literature," had stated as much: "Naturally we cannot expect all weird tales to conform absolutely to any theoretical model. [. . .] Much of the choicest weird work is unconscious. [. . .] Atmosphere is the all-important thing, for the final criterion of authenticity is not the dove-tailing of a plot but the creation of a given sensation" (144). Just as Matthew Lewis's novel *The Monk* broke the Radcliffian Gothic tradition of creating natural explanations for supernatural events, and opened up a new world of fantastic imagination, so *Dagon* compromises conventional genre paradigms with its remarkable and unorthodox meshing of wide-ranging intertextuality, gender, history, humour, and horror. As Haggerty and Lovecraft likely would contend, its singular fragmented form is simply a continuation of what memorable Gothic narratives and weird tales have always done: breaking and reinventing the rules of the genre and forcing it to evolve as an aesthetic form. *Dagon* participates in this tradition, or anti-tradition, skillfully and artfully, and likely deserves greater recognition in the contemporary cannon of Gothic narratives. In a genre overpopulated by superfluous clichéd texts, Chappell's novel shines as a rich and innovative work, genuinely embracing the tradition and shaping it into something new.

Works Cited

Alhazred, Abdul. *The Necronomicon (Al Azif).* Damascus: 730 A.D.

Andriano, Joseph. *Our Ladies of Darkness: Feminine Daemonology in Male Gothic Fiction.* University Park: Pennsylvania State UP, 1993.

Bayer-Berenbaum, Linda. *The Gothic Imagination: Expansion in Gothic Literature and Art.* Rutherford, NJ: Fairleigh Dickinson UP, 1982.

Benson, E. F. *The Collected Ghost Stories of E. F. Benson.* New York: Carroll and Graf, 1996.

Broughton, Irv. "Fred Chappell." *The Writer's Mind.* Ed. Irv Broughton. Vol. 3. Fayetteville: U of Arkansas P, 1990. 91-122.

Brown, Charles Brockden. *Wieland, or the Transformation.* New York: Swords, 1798.

Buitenhuis, Peter. "Desire under the Magnolias." Rev. of *Dagon,* by Fred Chappell. *New York Times Book Review* (29 September 1968): 58.

Caldwell, Erskine. *Poor Fool.* New York: Rariora, 1930.

Chappell, Fred. "The Bad Luck." Chappell manuscript. Fiction subseries. Duke University Special Collections.

———. *Dagon.* New York: Harcourt, Brace and World, 1968.

————. "Detroit Pontiac." Box WP-2. Writings by Chappell. Poetry subseries. Duke University Special Collections.

————. "Fantasia: On the Theme of Theme and Fantasy." *Studies in Short Fiction* 27.2 (Spring 1990): 179-89.

————. "Fred Chappell." Box WM-1. Writings by Chappell. Miscellaneous subseries. Duke University Special Collections.

————. "H. P. Lovecraft." Box WP-2. Writings by Chappell. Poetry subseries, 1960-1996. Duke University Special Collections.

————. *The Inkling.* New York: Harcourt, Brace, and World, 1965.

————. Personal interview, 6 August 2001.

————. *It Is Time, Lord.* New York: Atheneum, 1963.

————. "Lovecraft: A Biography." Box WR-1. Writings by Chappell. Reviews subseries. Duke University Special Collections.

————. "Remarks on *Dagon* for Lovecraft Conference." Box WF-1. Writings by Chappell. Fiction subseries. Duke University Special Collections.

————. *Source.* Baton Rouge: Louisiana State UP, 1985.

————. "Untitled." Box WF-1. Writings by Chappell. Fiction subseries. Duke University Special Collections.

————. "Visionary Fiction." *Chronicles* 11.5 (May 1987): 19-21.

Cohen, Allen. Rev. of *Dagon. Library Journal* 93.17 (1 October 1968): 3,576.

Davenport-Hines, Richard. *Gothic: 400 Years of Excess, Horror, Evil and Ruin.* London: Fourth Estate, 1998.

De Camp, L. Sprague. *Lovecraft: A Biography.* Garden City: Doubleday, 1975.

Dillard, R. H. W. *News of the Nile.* Chapel Hill: U of North Carolina P, 1971.

Easa, Leila. "A Conversation with Fred Chappell." *The Archive* 108.1 (Fall 1995): 49-60.

Haggerty, George E. *Gothic Fiction/Gothic Form.* University Park: Pennsylvania State UP, 1989.

Hawthorne, Nathaniel. *The Complete Short Stories of Nathaniel Hawthorne,* Garden City, NY: Doubleday, 1959.

————. *The House of the Seven Gables.* Boston: Ticknor, Reed, and Fields, 1851.

Hendershot, Cyndy. *The Animal Within: Masculinity and the Gothic.* Ann Arbor: U of Michigan P, 1998.

Hodgson, William Hope. *The Nightland.* London: Eveleigh Nash, 1912.

Joshi, S. T. *The Weird Tale.* Austin: U of Texas P, 1990.

Lang, John. *Understanding Fred Chappell.* Columbia: U of South Carolina P, 2000.

Lawrence, D. H. *The Complete Poems of D. H. Lawrence.* New York: Penguin, 1977.

Lewis, Matthew. *The Monk.* London: Bell, 1796.

Lovecraft, H. P. "Supernatural Horror in Literature." *Dagon and Other Macabre Tales.* London: Panther, 1969.

————. "The Thing on the Doorstep." *Weird Tales* 29.1 (January 1937): 52-70.

MacDonald, George. *Visionary Novels: Lilith, Phantastes.* New York: Noonday, 1954.

Machen, Arthur. "The White People." *The House of Souls.* New York: Knopf, 1906.

Palmer, Tersh. "Fred Chappell." *Appalachian Journal* 19.4 (Summer 1992): 402-11.

Palumbo, Carmine. "Folklore and Literature: The Poetry and Fiction of Fred Chappell." Diss. U of Southwestern Louisiana, 1997.

Ragan, David Paul. "Flying by Night: An Early Interview with Fred Chappell." *North Carolina Literary Review* 7 (1998): 105-19.

Redd, Chris. "A Man of Letters in the Modern World: An Interview with Fred Chappell." *The Arts Journal* 14.8 (May 1989): 7-9.

Rev. of *Dagon,* by Fred Chappell. *Virginia Quarterly Review* 45.1 (Winter 1969): viii.

Sopko, John, and John Carr. "Dealing with the Grotesque: Fred Chappell." *Kite-Flying and Other Irrational Acts: Conversations with Twelve Southern Writers.* Ed. John Carr. Baton Rouge: Louisiana State UP, 1972. 216-35.

Stirnemann, S. A. "Fred Chappell: Poet with 'Ah! Bright Wings.'" *Poetry Review* (Winter 1990): 41-51.

Rebecca Smith (essay date 2004)

SOURCE: Smith, Rebecca. "The Search for Moral Order in *Moments of Light*." In *More Lights than One: On the Fiction of Fred Chappell,* edited by Patrick Bizzaro, pp. 119-31. Baton Rouge: Louisiana State University Press, 2004.

[*In the following essay, Smith traces themes of morality in the stories of Chappell's* Moments of Light.]

In a 1970 response to a letter disparaging his novel *The Inkling* for its vulgarity, Fred Chappell retorts that astute readers might in fact see *The Inkling* as a religious book and defends himself as "a modern moralist."[1] This label describes well the author of the eleven narratives that make up his first short-story collection *Moments of Light* (1980), which present a chronological history of human moral development, from the beginning to modern times. We find within this collection human beings at their moral best and at their moral worst; in between, we find those struggling to bridge the gap between their dream of moral order and the chaos of the fallen world. Throughout the stories, music recurs as an emblem of characters' search for the music of the spheres, or a universal moral harmony, as they ply their art to impose an order on the disordered world.

The first story, **"Three Boxes,"** presents a parable of humans' introduction to choice, the basic component of moral consciousness. That the three men are naked and of "indeterminate color" suggests they live prior to racial prejudice, a detail rendering the moral failure of the volume's final story all the more poignant. Without the trappings of materialism or competition, these men represent pure intellectual and moral innocence. Having no complicating sense of past or future, they find complete satisfaction in their journey of unknown destination. But the end of their innocent enjoyment of nature's music in the wind, bird song, and rippling water is foreshadowed by a leaf twirling in the clear river, portending the moral complexity that will soon face them and the characters in the following stories.

When the three men discover three boxes on the far side of the river, they enter a world of covetousness and moral detachment suggested by the objective, detached narrative style. The first man to swim the river, seeking the material goods hidden in the boxes, muddies the water, leaving a "yellow stain" representing both the origin of different races and a disrupting of the natural universal harmony that humans struggle to reestablish in the rest of the book. The first swimmer remains white, and as soon as he owns the wealth he finds in the box, he is unable to see his brothers on the far shore and so turns his back on them. His figure becomes grotesquely distorted by the burden of the material world; his eyesight is impaired. Immediately, the two remaining men covet the first man's possessions and risk their own safety to explore the other boxes. The second swimmer takes on the water's yellow stain, to represent the oriental race, and leaves the water behind him (which will stain the skin of the last swimmer) black. The material wealth of each box diminishes; the second swimmer finds not gold but

paper money, implements of work, civil order, diplomacy, and a tranquility of spirit that obscures his face, suggesting that utter serenity blinds us to our fellow human beings' needs. Again, a diminution of the man's stature symbolizes the burden of material gain. And Chappell's allegory of the distribution of wealth becomes even more poignant as the final man receives his color and embraces the material world.

When the first two swimmers are unable to see the third remaining on the shore, the air around him becomes cold, and darkness threatens. The third man's swim in the black water is "a kind of death." His skin becomes black, and he has "no choice" but to open the last box, which emanates "no light" and reveals to him only "misery"—chains, scars, hatred, diseases, pests, but also patience to endure the suffering of slavery and oppression. The now-black man, seeing the disparity among the three boxes, asks God humanity's ultimate theological question: why is there no justice in the world? If God is omnipotent, can't He make the world fair? God's answer opens the way for the actions of all the following stories: humans, He says, must create justice. Justice can be fashioned only out of injustice, and not in the abstract but only from real, physical suffering. Then, lightening the black man's palms and soles, God explains: "It is for you to remember that when you are oppressed and beaten down by men of other color, that it is themselves also they crush into the earth. . . . For I tell you now forever, that until oppression of you shall quit not one step toward victory shall have been taken by a single person."[2] What better statement could Chappell—or any writer—create as a guide to moral responsibility?

Significantly, only the man carrying the box of suffering and injustice away from the river's shore finds music, the gourds and bones of early African music, and only he walks tall and erect under his load. He has a mission, a purpose that will take him outside himself, and he is thrilled to have the gift of justice to take to his comrades. Only he feels a "warm candle-flame," a moment of divinely revealed light that leads him to understand the morally ambiguous truth that injustice must exist to lead the way to justice, that the gift of justice is "the one thing in the whole world worth knowing that can be learned in the world, and is not divinely revealed" (14). In the following stories, the characters who confront some of mankind's most frustrating dilemmas thus become Chappell's experiments in human strength. Can they create justice from the suffering of their fellow man? Will they allow the music of the spheres to play a harmony all people can enjoy?

The hope of moral engagement and harmonious existence falls quickly into despair in the second story,

"Judas." This first-person account of Judas's betrayal of Christ recounts humanity's choosing material gain and a secular moral order over a transcendent order that yet, Christ implies, must be grounded in the physical world because it must guide the physical world. The excitement that the black man of **"The Three Boxes"** feels when challenged to spread the gift of justice is lost to Judas's petty obsession with Christ's difference from his own moral system. By associating with whores, thieves, lepers, and others whom Judas deems "useless refuse" (16), Christ overturns the secular order that Judas values, and Christ's holier-than-thou certainty of a transcendent order incenses Judas because that order is incomprehensible to him. Judas represses his intuitive sense that Christ is right and shies away from Christ because of this main objection: "he engendered an insupportable feeling of responsibility" (17). We leave the betrayer in a state of dissatisfied guilt and darkness, uneasy in his awareness that he has failed in his moral obligation. Judas botches mankind's gift of choice, of responsibility for justice. His secularly formed prejudices preclude his thinking outside their boundaries, and his reasoning with the rules of a secular order leaves him emotionally and morally bankrupt. But without Judas's treachery Christ would not have been crucified and hence not resurrected, so we must recognize that this story, despite its darkness, signifies the oppositions—and their potential reconciliation—that form the core of this book.[3]

The third story jumps to the eighteenth century, the first of three consecutive stories set during the Age of Reason. The first, **"Mrs. Franklin Ascends,"** takes place in the new Eden, the United States, in 1762, upon Benjamin Franklin's return from a trip to London, and so presents the possibility that the New World will give rise to a new Adam and a perfect moral order. Deborah Franklin has deliberately overspent during her husband's absence, creating disorder in their financial accounts so that her husband can set them straight—exemplifying again the book's emphasis on people's search for order. This story presents no weighty moral dilemma such as Judas's betrayal of Christ: the main moral failure here seems to be Benjamin's failure to recognize his wife's exasperation with his scientific investigations. But Ben Franklin is pursuing a transcendent kind of order, the music of the spheres, and this story is the first to focus on man-made music as a path to universal harmony. Benjamin arises during his first night home to play the armonica, his new musical invention, creating tones from the rubbing of glasses. Deborah hears the tones in a kind of half-dream and ascends to the attic to find Ben; she believes that they have died together and gone to heaven. He is, she thinks, "unleashing the music of the spheres" (28). This story leaves us with hope for a harmonious universal moral order.

But the order of the first eighteenth-century tale turns quickly to chaos in the succeeding story, **"Thatch Retaliates,"** when the New World fails to live up to its Edenic potential. Toby Milliver, newly arrived from England, believes most ardently in this New World myth: "He saw the colonies as a fresh beginning, a place where the old mistakes did not have to be repeated . . . *Reason* was . . . to be the guildmark of America, for every man is first guided by self-interest and can only injure his affairs with unreason. Therefore, injustice and prejudicial opinion and baseless cruelty could never importantly take root here, for each man's personal welfare was posed against them." Milliver's faith in humanity's moral development is corrected by his friend Prescott's perception that "the Old Adam [is] still heartily at work in every man and that a new-found landscape [can] hardly be a panacea for all the ills of human character" (34). The reference to Mr. Tidrow's owning slaves in Williamsburg suggests such a flaw, and the remainder of the story quickly verifies that Milliver's idealism is only that. For the title character of this tale is none other than Blackbeard the Pirate (Edward Teach, whom Chappell fictionalizes as Edward Thatch), "one of the arrantest villains that God has ever made to creep upon the earth" (39). The drunken Blackbeard kills Toby Milliver, supposedly mistaking him for another man. Man at his moral worst senselessly destroys man at his moral best.

"Thatch Retaliates" recalls **"Judas"** in that the secular order Judas embraces is shown to be absolutely corrupt in the Bath, North Carolina, society: Governor Eden (note the irony of the name) is in league with Blackbeard, leaving the community no hope of ridding itself of evil. Amazingly, Milliver, the most optimistic character in the entire collection, never loses his faith in the human spirit, nor is he the story's only good character: James MacCollum and William Jameson befriend Milliver and Prescott; bystanders do the right thing by taking the injured Milliver and Prescott into their home for aid; and Prescott, himself in pain from being pistol-whipped by the demonic Blackbeard, pulls himself to the dying Milliver's side, crying, "He is my responsibility in this place. I cannot have it on my conscience that I did not go to him" (47). Thus while Prescott epitomizes the ideal of moral accountability that Chappell's collection of stories explores, he cannot save Milliver or the town from the dark forces of evil. This story ends with "a little more of the relentless American nighttime" (48) entering the room when Milliver's foot topples a candle during his final death jerk, extinguishing the moment of light that seems to have shone in Milliver and the other generous-of-spirit characters.

This darkness comes between two stories offering clear hope for a harmonious world. Chappell seems to have arranged the stories in this collection to create a rhythmic cycle of hope and despair rather than a perfectly chronological series. **"Thatch Retaliates"** takes place in 1718, prior to the previous story's time of 1782. After **"Judas," "Mrs. Franklin Ascends"** offers the hope of a better world; **"Thatch Retaliates"** then shows a descent into moral depravity. True to the movement of the collection, the next story answers with an ascent of enlightenment.

"Moments of Light" moves from America to England, centering on the 1792 convergence of art and science in the meeting of composer Franz Joseph Haydn and astronomer William Herschel, both German immigrants to England. Having discovered the planet Uranus eleven years earlier, Herschel is presently working on his "grand treatise on the construction of the heavens" (51), a scientific metaphor for the music of the spheres that Annie Dillard notes in the foreword as the central notion of Chappell's collection. Since late-eighteenth-century thought no longer considers the artist and the scientist antipodal but rather sees "the advancement of learning and the refinement of the senses" as complements (50), Haydn and Herschel are expected to meet. Haydn, on whom the story focuses through its limited omniscient point of view, dreads and delays the rendezvous, for he finds the new celestial discoveries disturbing. They present a rift in the world order that he knows. The disorder he observes in his earthly surroundings likewise unnerves him: he is bothered by discovering "butchers with more gracious manners than counts . . . and carters who had a broader knowledge of the world than princes" (51). As any artist, Haydn seeks in his music the order he finds missing in his environment, and through this fellow artist Fred Chappell presents his most overt statement on the power of art to soothe humanity's troubled existence in a world that seems at best morally neutral, resistant to our attempts to understand and perfect its flaws.

Haydn is pleasantly surprised to find that the scientist Herschel appreciates and understands the arts' contributions to humanity's knowledge: "We must never forget how much our present state of scientific knowledge is indebted to the writings of the ancient poets," Herschel asserts (54). Amazingly, this world-renowned scientist does not discredit the notion of the music of the spheres, either, and Haydn in turn recognizes the astronomer's admirable pursuit of "new

moments of light" in the heavens (56). The musician soon experiences his own moment of light when he learns from Herschel that astronomy is not the glorious, inspired calling he assumes, but a profession of tedious, hard work and physical discomfort. This new enlightenment prepares Haydn for the truly transcendent experience he enjoys when looking through the scientist's telescope.

What follows represents a veritable marriage of art and science. This story in fact encapsulates the moral dilemma that has characterized the twentieth century in such controversies as evolution versus creationism, and science versus the arts. Haydn is physically transported by the sight of the stars to an alien city where he hears, literally, the music of the spheres emanating from a fountain as well as from a dragonfly music box floating in the void of space. Haydn learns, in his out-of-body experience soaring through the interstellar spaces of the heavens, that "if music and poetry are not mindless, but instead the appreciable workings of personality, then this drama of light [is] intelligently assertive in the same way" (63). His epiphany creates in him a "flight of genius" that soon leads to his oratorio *The Creation,* whose musical description of chaos transfixes his audience, and to his accepting Beethoven as a music pupil. The absolutely positive ending of this title story, with Haydn pointing his baton toward heaven at the end of a performance of his oratorio and giving credit to a greater spirit for his music, "Not from me. . . . From thence comes everything" (70), seems to reinstate an Edenic purity and hope for a universal moral order. From the music of the spheres comes the glorious music of Haydn and Beethoven, a bit of heaven come down to earth. Haydn's epiphany represents the demise of humans' intellectual innocence and the birth of a new hope, hope in a beauty that man admittedly cannot fully discern. Only art can articulate this mystery, as humanity uses and reflects the music of the spheres in its own musical creations.

The next story, which introduces modern-day (mid-twentieth-century) narratives, presents another kind of artist figure, the writer Mark Vance, and introduces the focus on individual fragmented personalities that seems to characterize the second half of *Moments of Light.* This story ends the same way that it begins, with Mark tossing and turning on his bed, trying to write a long, philosophical poem on human suffering, trying to order with words the disorder he observes about him. The story chronicles Mark's two-day journey of encounters with misery and his attempts to soothe humanity's wounds of despair. The suffering he sees when he ventures from his room explains the story's title, **"The Thousand Ways,"** for through its examples, the story suggests that human beings misuse their own and others' lives in a thousand different ways.

Although the story centers on the failing of human moral action, it also presents two of the book's most earnest characters, Mark Vance and George Palinopolous, a Greek immigrant working hard at a grubby local grill. George forfeits his daughter's chance to attend a good college when he makes a moral decision—to help his brother-in-law out of drug-related trouble. George feels an essential debt to humanity for his success in America, a debt that he repays by customarily giving Mark his supper free of charge. George's moral responsibility is paralleled by the actions and sensibility of the main character. When he chances upon a young boy sent out by his mother to wander the streets while she has a sexual encounter, Mark gives the boy, Joe Starret, all the money in his pocket. Mark also wants to save his girlfriend Norma Lang from her self-imposed turmoil. Living in squalor, neglecting her personal hygiene, and drinking excessively, Norma chastises Mark for his moral rectitude, the prudishness that causes his outrage at Joe's mother's negligence and her alcoholism, part of her unhealthy lifestyle that apparently has led to a serious, incurable sickness. Mark's final confrontation of the day solidifies his sense of the world's need. Back at his hotel, he befriends a teenaged girl who shoulders responsibility for her stumbling father, whose drunkenness she denies. He is aghast when this fourteen- or fifteen-year-old, attracted by his kindness, kisses him quite sensuously. Sexual innocence is lost to both this girl, Edwina Tumperling, and Joe Starret, the children whose names he records when he returns to his philosophical poem at the story's end. Mark Vance seeks to order through his art the chaos he has witnessed, but despair overwhelms him. His ending call of "help" portrays him as an artist lost because he discerns too keenly others' suffering and lack of moral accountability. This story's continual juxtaposition of light and dark imagery intensifies its message that the light of moral decency lingers always just beyond the fringes of our failures.

The very short first-person narrative that follows shows us, possibly, a young Mark Vance, a boy just facing the fact that we cannot escape our accountability to other human beings. **"January"** is the genesis for chapter 1 of Chappell's novel *It Is Time, Lord,* which is set in the 1940s, so the 1962 setting of **"The Thousand Ways"** strengthens the argument that the young narrator of **"January"** is indeed a childhood version of Mark Vance. **"January"** is in many ways a cold story, its style providing little narrative reflection to give the reader a sense of the teller's emotions.

Rather, the objective, childlike language (simple words, short paragraphs) creates an innocent narrative voice recalling a simple scene: a boy's inadequately clad young sister follows him to a cold barn, where unnamed men worry that the child will freeze to death; the father appears suddenly and carries the girl back home with the boy following; the waiting mother wonders what the children were doing out in the cold. The boy's denial of responsibility for the three-year-old innocent, "I told her not to come with me," rings hollow when he offers it to the strange men in the barn. He doesn't even bother to repeat his excuse to his reprimanding father. **"January"** presents in little more than two pages a boy's moral coming of age, his learning about the ambiguity at the heart of human relationships. He did tell his sister not to follow him, but he knows he is still responsible, and he realizes that telling his father the truth, ironically, will not absolve his culpability. As the lonely boy looks heavenward, a spot emerges to obscure his view of the moon, a symbol of enlightenment and humanity's spiritual life. This young boy's moment of light has darkened his world, for he has moved, unwillingly, from the innocence of childhood into the adult world of accountability, a world that weighs heavily on the adult Mark Vance in the previous story.

The next story reiterates the loss of innocence presented in **"January,"** this time through a sexual coming of age. **"The Weather,"** unlike the other stories in *Moments of Light,* is published only in this collection, and Chappell explains that he wrote it as a link between stories.[4] **"The Weather"** is the most sensual of all the narratives. Full of color (golden skin, licorice-black hair, streams of sunlight), misting rain, the smell of alfalfa, kisses redolent of bittersweet chocolate, **"The Weather"** recreates both the emotional and the physical intensity of an adolescent boy's first sexual encounter. The child of **"January"** has become an adolescent; in the barn of the previous story, he loses his sexual innocence at the hands of an older but still puerile Rosemary McKay, daughter of a local drunkard. Like **"January,"** this story is told as a memory, but in **"The Weather,"** the adult narrator speaks overtly to an unnamed but specific listener, a current lover. His openly nostalgic, now-experienced voice speaks philosophically at the end of the story to this lover and the reader, creating a bridge between the physical enjoyment he remembers and its spiritual parallels that form the basis of this collection's theme of moral responsibility:

> So that is what I meant when you suggested we make love and I replied, "No, you make love and I'll just lie here." For a moment it seemed to me that by imitating lassitude I might recapture the lassitude of innocence . . .

But it doesn't work that way, does it? Innocence is not recaptured in an awkward dance of the body simple. Let us do then whatever we please; we shall always remember and always forget.

Like the rest of the stricken world.

(110)

This reminder of time's passage recalls the collection's movement through centuries of human moral development and reminds us that moral passivity will not suffice. When we forget our accountability, we become one with the ill-fated world.

"The Weather" leads to the fine story **"Broken Blossoms,"** the last of four narratives that might be seen as a "portrait of the artist as a young man" series, culminating, in reverse order, with the artistic anxiety of Mark Vance in **"The Thousand Ways."** **"Broken Blossoms"** makes clear that the dreaming boy must wake up to the practical world where people are accountable, as Annie Dillard explains in her introduction to the collection, not only for what they do know but also for what they do not. As the first-person speaker describes his boyhood fascination with stamp-collecting as part of his awakening to a world outside himself, we realize that the voice here is a learned, retrospective voice, that of a poet looking back at his coming of age. It is reminiscent of **"Moments of Light,"** for art and science converge when the young boy forsakes chemistry experiments and cryptography in favor of writing romantic nature poetry. He sets his poems on a fantasy planet inhabited by butterfly-like creatures "whose method of communication was a music composed of tones beyond the range of human hearing" (122), similar to the heavenly harmonies Haydn hears when transported through Herschel's telescope in the earlier story. The adolescent's poetry ensues from an imagination that dominates his mind, rendering him practically useless as a farm boy. Finally, he recognizes the danger of living totally in a world of self-centered dreaminess, a state of existence rendered as moral indifference on the part of adults in other stories in this collection.

The boy's first epiphany turns out to be a misleading one, but his final awakening brings him fully into adulthood. Looking for exotic stamps, he explores without permission keepsakes that his parents have stored in an old trunk, which he opens with a claw hammer. Realizing for the first time that his parents were people with interests and dreams of their own before his birth, he vows to become a better son and convinces himself that his destiny lies not in stamp-collecting but in diving even more deeply into his fanciful introspection. His practical father, ever frustrated with the son's inadequacies, ironically orchestrates the young poet's awakening to the world of moral responsibility. He sends him on a walk with the farmhand Harmon Cody, who illustrates symbolically to the boy the entire meaning of existence by blowing to smithereens a box of blasting caps the boy luckily did not disturb as he rambled through the forbidden trunk. "You see, honey, you're going to have to take better care. Happened you hit one of those caps a lick up in your attic, you'd been blowed to pieces. Blowed half the roof off" (132). The boy's poetic sensibility has already led him to recognize the fragile juxtaposition of life and death as he contemplates the apple tree into which Mr. Cody places the caps, a tree stunted by a lightning strike so that its missing half, seared with a firescar, offsets a side yet blooming with pinkish-white, bee-laden flowers. Mr. Cody's shot obliterates another portion of the tree in an eye-opening act of violence reminiscent of the violence it takes to open Flannery O'Connor's characters' eyes to their own shortcomings. Remembering this scene, the adult narrator describes his epiphany as a physical undressing, allowing the world "so long closed away" to rush in upon him and change him forever: "And in this same moment that someone who is myself is born again, someone who is myself also dies. From this instant I can date my awkward tumble into the world." Like most of us, he regrets his fall into the world of knowledge, wishing that he could have spent his life in a warm dream of innocence, never hurting anyone, so that he could say at the Judgment Day, "*'I slept and never woke. . . . I am so innocent I might never have existed'*" (133).

This wish encapsulates the definitive statement on moral accountability that Chappell makes in this collection of stories. To live as human beings, we must act—not only on our own behalf but on others' as well. We cannot remain indifferent to the consequences of our actions, a fact that haunts Mark Vance in **"The Thousand Ways"** because he cannot make everyone see that basic tenet of human existence. The last two stories in *Moments of Light* continue Chappell's critique of the failings of human responsibility.

"Children of Strikers" is a dark story whose sensuous imagery enhances its picture of human suffering in a world gone awry. Two children, a girl and a boy, find by the edge of a stinking, black chemical river—no doubt inspired by the paper mills of Chappell's Canton, North Carolina—a severed baby doll's foot—a perfect symbolic blend of innocence and sordid experience. The boy argues that the smooth edge of the stub indicates that an adult, not a child, must have cut the doll's foot as practice "before he went and kilt a real baby." Such an assumption strikes the reader as amusing, until the omniscient narrator's descriptions of the "strained" faces of unshaven men and crying women, of strangers "saying hard wild sentences" and "banging tabletops" in rooms of "unguessable violence" suggest the real possibility of domestic disorder in the milltown shanties (137). The toy foot, representing a fallen innocent, makes the children who find it face unaware the pain caused by moral irresponsibility.

The final story of Chappell's distinguished collection returns overtly to the motifs of journeys, music, and race introduced in the opening narrative, **"The Three Boxes."** The racial discrimination suggested when the dark-skinned man of the first story is left with chains, scars, cotton sack, mule harness, and endurance has come to ironic fruition in **"Blue Dive."** In the ending selection, a black bluesman just out of prison travels on a Greyhound bus in the 1960s or '70s to find a nightclub, The Blue Dive, where the owner once promised him a job. Stovebolt Johnson is on a journey of moral redemption, trying to make a living after serving time for his moral failings. The story begins on a hopeful note, with Stovebolt gazing frequently at the horizon and in fact being welcomed at his first stop, the house of a kind-hearted couple who enjoy his guitar playing and give him food. B. J. and Darlene represent the best of human moral potential, but their goodness is overshadowed by the selfish materialism of The Blue Dive's new owner, Locklear Hawkins. Mr. Hawkins, who is, like the other characters, African American, will not risk hiring an ex-convict even though his patrons clearly love Stovebolt's live music. "In my plans there is no room for any Rastuses or any Sambos," he explains. "And there's no room for anybody named Stovebolt" (165). The denigrating racial stereotype intensifies Hawkins's rejection of his fellow human being, for he colludes in the stereotyping of his own race. Through Hawkins's complicity, Chappell implicates us all as conspirers in the world's evil.

Annie Dillard suggests in her foreword to *Moments of Light* that Hawkins's rejection of Stovebolt parallels Judas's betrayal of Christ, a reading reinforced by the "one clear yellow star" lighting the sky as Stovebolt leaves The Blue Dive. Like the story **"Judas," "The Blue Dive"** shows us what happens when justice is left in mankind's hands, as God explains in **"The Three Boxes"** that it must be. We see in the end allegiance to self outweighing responsibility to others, as in the opening story when the first two men become literally blind to their fellow travelers upon opening their own box of material goods. But the conclusion of this final story also provides a ray of hope for humanity's continuing moral development: when the tip of a wild cherry tree blowing in the wind brushes through the light of that one yellow star, Stovebolt is confident that it is "never going to brush that light

away" (166). The universal transcendent order will not abandon us despite our moral failings. Stovebolt continues on his way, as we all must, with his music grounding him in the world's often unfathomable beauty.

In an essay titled **"A Pact with Faustus,"** published in a special Chappell issue of *Mississippi Quarterly* cited earlier, Fred Chappell speaks of his early fascination with the magic of music, his passion for the drama of its harmonies. His comments elucidate his choice of music as the art that is successful, in *Moments of Light,* at helping humans to satisfy their longing for order. I want to cite once more Annie Dillard's discerning introduction to Chappell's first story collection, as she offers her interpretation of the role of art in human survival as well as in these stories: "[Man] casts his spiritual longing [for order] into the very teeth of the matter—and comes up with art. . . . art, the heavenly harmonies translated into the soul's own lowdown blues."[5] Fred Chappell's art, with its well-crafted symmetries and delights, forms his action against the disharmony he sees in the world about him. In *Moments of Light,* his moral and artistic imperative is this: our actions and our art make a difference in this imperfect material world.

Notes

1. Alex Albright, "Friend of Reason: Surveying the Fred Chappell Papers at Duke University," in *Dream Garden: The Poetic Vision of Fred Chappell,* ed. Patrick Bizzaro (Baton Rouge: Louisiana State University Press, 1997), 226.

2. Fred Chappell, *Moments of Light* (Los Angeles: New South, 1980), 9-13. References to the text are in parentheses.

3. Dabney Stuart, "'Blue Pee': Fred Chappell's Mythical Kingdom," *Iron Mountain Review* 2 (spring 1985): 13-21, discusses these stories' concern with the harmonizing of polarities.

4. James Everett Kibler Jr., "A Fred Chappell Bibliography, 1963-1983," *Mississippi Quarterly* 37 (winter 1983-84): 79.

5. Annie Dillard, foreword to *Moments of Light,* by Fred Chappell (Los Angeles: New South, 1980), vii.

George Hovis (essay date 2007)

SOURCE: Hovis, George. "Fred Chappell's Prison/ Arcadia: Plain Folk in Appalachia." In *Vale of Humility: Plain Folk in Contemporary North Carolina Fiction,* pp. 97-137. Columbia: University of South Carolina Press, 2007.

[*In the following essay, Hovis explores Chappell's identification with Appalachian culture and the region's influence on his writings.*]

In a 1999 interview, I asked Fred Chappell whether he more considered himself to be a "southern" or an "Appalachian" writer. He quickly responded:

> Appalachian. That's easy. To me "southern" means Deep South, a region that I really don't know very much about. And I haven't had very much experience with it. The problem of race relations was never an important part of my early experience. I really only got involved with it when I was in graduate school at Duke. I was a member of CORE for a little while. But where I was from, there was such little contact, at least on my part, with black people that it just didn't seem that this great topic that ought to exercise the South was much of a force among us. Other things—large land holdings, southern aristocracy, cotton—these things were not a part of my experience. My experience was small land holdings, no aristocracy—we're all white trash together, I guess, in the mountains. Little wealth. And absence of any kind of a historical perspective on family that they seem to have in the Deep South. We didn't talk about our family histories, hardly at all. Well, we talked about members of the family, but not in the terms of "Our family's been here for generations and we did such and such." You hear that in the Deep South. You don't hear it where I'm from.[1]

Chappell's identification of Appalachia as a place apart from the rest of the South resembles the plain-folk bravado of Thomas Wolfe. Chappell's statement provides a clear articulation of yeoman values: egalitarianism, independence, and an identification of the small family farm as the basic social unit. Missing from this overview of his Appalachian experience— what for Chappell is perhaps the "elephant in the living room"—is the pervasiveness of an intrusive lumber and pulpwood industry, which around the turn of the twentieth century led the way to modernization of the region, producing devastating environmental and economic changes that made the yeoman freehold farm increasingly less viable.

In *Miners, Millhands, and Mountaineers,* Ronald D. Eller describes the rapid rise of industrialization throughout southern Appalachia during the years 1880-1930. While coal mining made much less of an impact in western North Carolina than elsewhere in the region, the timber industry irrevocably changed the mountains of North Carolina and the lives of its people. This process began in 1880 with the arrival, after twenty-five years of intermittent construction, of the Western North Carolina Railroad in Asheville. By 1890 the rail line had passed through Haywood County and the future site of Canton, Chappell's hometown. The railroad brought a tourist boom to Asheville, which grew from a population of 2,000 in 1880 to 10,000 by 1890. It also brought to the region speculators and lumbermen who bought up vast tracts of mountain land. By 1900, lumber and timber manufacturing had become the second leading industry in North Carolina,

and most of this manufacturing was located in the western portion of the state. By the industry's peak in 1909, southern Appalachia was providing almost 40 percent of the nation's timber production. By the eve of World War I, however, timber production in southern Appalachia experienced a rapid decline as the industry moved to the Pacific Northwest, leaving behind unemployed mountaineers and a devastated natural environment. The clear-cut mountains suffered extensive erosion, and the bottom lands experienced frequent flooding, which made them largely unfit for agriculture.[2]

One timber company that established a sustainable business in western North Carolina was the Champion Paper and Fiber Company, with its primary regional manufacturing site located in Haywood County. In 1905, the company's owner, Peter G. Thompson, from Hamilton, Ohio, "secured" roughly 300,000 acres of timberland throughout Haywood County and began building a pulp mill and a company town which came to be named Canton, after Canton, Ohio. According to Eller, "No other lumber company had as great or as lasting an impact upon the Blue Ridge and the Smokes."[3] In *Birth of Forestry in America,* Carl Alwin Schenck observes of the Champion operation, "The whole scheme was the most gigantic enterprise which western North Carolina had seen."[4] By the beginning of World War I, the company had expanded further throughout Haywood County and into Swain County and eastern Tennessee, producing 200 tons of wood pulp per day, most of which was being shipped to Ohio for conversion to paper. By 1930, six years before Fred Chappell's birth, the Canton operation had developed the capacity to produce postcard paper and had "grown into the largest paper and pulp mill in the nation."[5]

The impact of industrialization on Appalachian yeoman farmers can be measured by the decline in the size of the average farm and total land under cultivation, as well as the declining number of farmers relative to the region's total population. As extractive industries appropriated larger portions of the region's available land—and then later left former farmland unusable—the size of the average farm decreased from 187 acres in the 1880s to 76 acres in 1930. Even though the total number of farmers increased, the available farmland declined by 20 percent, and, although the region's urban population quadrupled and the rural nonagricultural population doubled, the agricultural population increased only by 5 percent.[6] Furthermore, family farms were increasingly integrated into (and threatened by) an expanding market economy.

The industrialization of Haywood County and of western North Carolina, in general, along with the tenuous position of the yeoman farmer produced by this industrialization, affected Chappell's family directly and, not surprisingly, has exerted a powerful shaping force on his fiction. Born in 1936, at a time when the Champion Company was converting pulp into paper more rapidly than any paper mill in the country and pouring its waste into the Pigeon River, Chappell grew up on his mother's family's small farm two miles outside of Canton. The Champion factory, thinly disguised as the Challenger mill, appears as a target of scorn in much of his work. His father struggled to make a small dairy farm financially viable and discovered, like many small Appalachian farmers,[7] that the family's subsistence depended upon his entering public work. In fact, both of Chappell's parents supplemented the family's income by teaching school, and his father also worked for a time as a lineman with Carolina Power & Light. Eventually, they closed the farm and opened a retail furniture business. Much of Chappell's poetry and his later fiction provides fairly autobiographical treatments of his family's struggle to keep their farm in operation. Moreover, at stake in this struggle is the larger effort to retain the preindustrial values and folkways of the yeoman, which are threatened by encroaching capitalism and industrialization.

Such a privileging of an agrarian past has long manifested itself in southern literature in forms that have been associated with a pastoral tradition extending back to classical pastoralists such as Virgil and Theocritus. As Lucinda MacKethan notes, however, southern pastoralists have traditionally chronicled the experience of the planter rather than that of the yeoman. In *The Dream of Arcady,* MacKethan surveys southern pastoral from the antebellum period to the early twentieth century, including writers such as John Pendleton Kennedy, William Gilmore Simms, Thomas Nelson Page, and William Faulkner. Of the major southern pastoralists she examines, all but one represent the plantation tradition—or the antiplantation tradition. MacKethan identifies only Sidney Lanier as writing about the yeoman experience, stating that his "version of the pastoral reflects, for southern literature, the road not taken."[8] Were she to extend her study into the late twentieth century, MacKethan would find a radically different scenario. Recent novels by Chappell—as well as by Robert Morgan, Charles Frazier, Tony Earley, and other western North Carolina writers—offer very positive treatments of a past culture centered around the yeoman farmer. In each case, the North Carolina mountains appear as an extremely insular space, one that is depicted—with all of its hardships—as being purer and in many ways more healthy than the modern culture that has replaced it.

Because, in the wake of the civil rights movement, the plantation tradition is no longer viable as a pastoral mode, pastoral literature has taken root elsewhere, largely in the rocky soil of Appalachia. In later years even Reynolds Price has found it increasingly difficult to employ the pastoral as a means of exploring race relations in eastern North Carolina. Although rarely is it entirely absent, race plays significantly less of a role in the fiction by contemporary writers from Appalachia, making pastoral, with its idealization of an agrarian social order, more viable. The rapid development of tourism in western North Carolina, along with the crowding of indigenous populations by summer homes owned by absentee landlords, has created in the late twentieth century a further pastoral impetus toward cultural preservation.

In light of the history of his family and region, as well as the ever-present contrast during his boyhood of his family's farm with the polluting Champion paper mill, it comes as no great surprise that Chappell became a pastoralist. It is more surprising, perhaps, that he did not, like Reynolds Price, *begin* his career as one. Very unlike Price's debut novel, which celebrates the childhood farming town he knew as a rural utopia, Chappell began his career by rebelling against his past. (This difference between the early careers of Price and Chappell can be explained, in part, by the fact that Chappell was actually required to work on the farm where he lived, whereas Price observed with fond detachment the lives of farmers who frequently lived nearby.) After twenty years away from the mountains—first as a student at Duke University and then as a professor at the University of North Carolina at Greensboro—Chappell began to reassess his troubled relationship with his own Appalachian past, and the rebellion of his earlier novels became replaced by reconciliation.

It is difficult to imagine a career more bifurcated than Chappell's—the first decade of major publications dominated by a fascination with alienation and degenerating states of the self—including alcoholism, deviant sexuality, prostitution, accounts of paranoid schizophrenia, and nihilism—and the later three decades characterized by the qualities of pastoral—a reverence for nature and family, a preoccupation with social order out of which meaning and value are derived, and an imagining of the past as an innocent golden age. Chappell's first four novels were out of print until they recently reappeared in Louisiana State University Press's invaluable *Voices of the South* series. Most scholarship on Chappell has focused on the later work. Even in recent scholarship, critics seem in a quandary to reconcile these two very different modes of fiction from the same pen. This chapter will briefly investigate the earlier studies in alienation before studying at greater length the later pastorals, examining how both are very different reactions to the same Appalachian yeoman culture, especially with respect to the region's insularity and the resulting tension between the mountaineer's fierce *independence* and his *interdependence* with family and community.

The amazing diversity of Chappell's literary productivity was already apparent during his years at Duke University, where he earned a B.A. and in 1964 a M.A. in English literature. Chappell studied under the legendary William Blackburn, who also taught William Styron, Anne Tyler, and Reynolds Price. In writing workshops Chappell demonstrated a raw genius that much later prompted Blackburn, in conversation with George Garrett, to call him "the most gifted writer and the best of the bunch," even while admitting his doubts whether Chappell would "ever 'succeed' as a writer" the way the others had.[9] Chappell's "success" in the form of widespread recognition was slower in coming than it was for the other writers mentioned, which may be because of his penchant for experimentation. If Price's career began with considerably more fanfare, a critical reevaluation over the last two decades—sparked, in part, by the appearance of *The Fred Chappell Reader* (1987)—has begun to bring Chappell the attention he deserves. Among the many prestigious awards offered in recognition of Chappell's diverse achievements are the Best Foreign Novel Prize from the French Academy (for *Dagon*), the Bollingen Prize in Poetry, the Ingersoll Foundation's T. S. Eliot Award for Poetry, a Rockefeller Grant, the Award in Literature from the National Institute of Arts and Letters, and the World Fantasy Award. In 1997 Chappell became the fourth official poet laureate of North Carolina. George Garrett places Chappell "among the best American poets alive" and, recognizing his vast skills in long and short fiction as well as criticism, calls him "our preeminent man of letters."[10] Lee Smith has famously written that "anybody who knows anything about Southern writing knows that Fred Chappell is our resident genius, our shining light, the one truly great writer we have among us."[11]

His first decade of major publication was devoted to novels: *It Is Time, Lord* (1963), *The Inkling* (1965), *Dagon* (1968), and *The Gaudy Place* (1973). The first three novels are wonderful examples of gothic fiction and, like many of his short stories, demonstrate the important early influence of Poe. *The Gaudy Place* is an abrupt shift toward comic realism, an urban satire showing the influence of Twain and other southwestern humorists. *The Gaudy Place* marks a transition from his earlier studies in alienation, one that anticipates his later pastorals. Throughout the 1970s, Chappell's attention shifted to poetry with the appearance of *The World between the Eyes* (1971), followed by *River* (1975), *Bloodfire* (1978), *Wind Mountain* (1979), and *Earthsleep* (1980). These latter four volumes were

conceived of as equal parts of one long poem and in 1981 were published together as *Midquest,* which won the prestigious Bollingen Prize. In *Midquest,* Chappell continued to employ the elements of southwestern humor that he had used in *The Gaudy Place*; however, the dark satire of the former novel gives way to an elegiac pastoral vision, which he continued to employ in the tetralogy of novels that follow: *I Am One of You Forever* (1985); *Brighten the Corner Where You Are* (1989); *Farewell, I'm Bound to Leave You* (1996); and *Look Back All the Green Valley* (1999). These autobiographical novels, which chronicle the maturation of a poet named Jess Kirkman, serve as a counterpart to the four volumes of *Midquest* thus comprising an octave. The pastoral quality of the Kirkman tetralogy may be observed not only in its celebration of an agrarian culture but by the fact that, with the exception of the last novel, each part is set in the past of the poet's boyhood on the farm, whereas Chappell's first four novels all have contemporary settings. Since 1980 Chappell has also produced numerous other works, including two volumes of short fiction, seven additional volumes of poetry, and two collections of criticism.

The majority of his writing exhibits the basic tension between a longing for unity with his Appalachian past and his recognition of his alienation from that past. He has named Faulkner, Eliot, Pound, and Joyce among the numerous important models especially of his earlier writing, and, like these and other great writers of the high modernist period, Chappell has responded to his loss of a traditional culture by reconstructing the raw materials in forms borrowed from both within and without the culture. Many readers have noted what Michael McFee calls Chappell's "split literary personality." "On the one side," McFee explains, "we have 'Ole Fred,' the kind of persona readers tend to remember, a character of extreme Romantic temperament and habits. Ole Fred is feisty; he cusses, he jokes, he drinks, he misbehaves; he is cheerfully politically incorrect; he overstates and exaggerates. . . . On the other side . . . is Professor Chappell, a neo-classical polymath of the first order, deeply and widely read, profoundly learned: a genuine scholar."[12] This split literary persona arguably indicates an actual "split" within the writer, who understands himself and his world by means of two divided cultures, one belonging to his present life in the Piedmont city of Greensboro, where for four decades he served as a professor of English at that campus of the University of North Carolina, and the other to his childhood on the Appalachian farm of his ancestors.

Just as McFee observes the tension in Chappell between a Romantic and a neoclassical temperament, Chappell's literary influences, while impressively diverse, are dominated by the antithetical traditions of Romanticism and neoclassicism. These two antagonistic aesthetic tendencies manifest themselves in Chappell's work as competing attitudes toward the yeoman culture of Appalachia he knew from boyhood. His later pastorals have been largely indebted to writers who were themselves of or largely indebted to the literature of classical antiquity, figures such as Virgil, Dante, and Pope, poets who were concerned with depicting a vision of an ordered, ideal society and were acutely aware of how their depictions were informed and limited by a long cultural tradition. To the contrary, Chappell's earlier novels were more inspired by the "dark" Romantics, writers such as Poe, Baudelaire, and Rimbaud, who—even when they were impressively cultivated—conceived of themselves as inventing something wholly new, writers who saw themselves as alienated artists working in opposition to the conformist tendencies of their publics.

What cannot be emphasized too strongly is the extent to which this bifurcated literary personality derives from Chappell's Appalachian heritage and its competing values of independence and interdependence, values reflected both in the pattern of farm settlement in the mountains and the resulting social structure. Ronald Eller notes of the settlement of the mountains that "houses were seldom constructed within sight of each other but, instead, were spread out, each in its own separate hollow or cove. Solitude and privacy were such dominant cultural values that they fostered dispersed settlement patterns and the continual penetration of the deeper mountain wilderness long after the passing of the frontier."[13] Several pages later, Eller discusses the "familism" that characterized Appalachian farming culture, observing that in "preindustrial Appalachia, as in most traditional rural societies, the family was the central organizing force of social life. . . . Obligations to the family came first, and this economic condition created intense family loyalties that not only insured the survival of the group, but also provided a strong feeling of security and belonging for individuals."[14] Eller, astonishingly, does not seem to recognize the inherent conflict between the mountaineer's independence and his interdependence with family, but perhaps such a consideration concerns the historian less than the creative writer, who responds to the culture not as an objective observer, viewing the culture through the lens of multiple texts, but as an individual participant, in whom these contradictory impulses are intensely and personally felt. Certainly this tension between independence and interdependence is one of the most pronounced features of Chappell's oeuvre. He seems to have begun writing in oedipal rebellion as a declaration of independence from his family and community, portray-

ing Appalachian families that are extremely dysfunctional and depicting independence taken to the extreme of alienation. Later, having found that position spiritually depleting, he began to chronicle interdependent farming families and communities in a much more positive light, finding the isolated family farm not a prison to be escaped but, rather, an Arcadia to be preserved.

"Darker Vices and Nearly Incomprehensible Sins": Chappell's Early Novels

Although Chappell claims that Jess Kirkman is by far a more autobiographical figure than the protagonists of his earlier novels, he admits that Jess has been "highly romanticized and cleaned up a great deal."[15] Unlike the earlier protagonists, Jess's attitude toward his family and community is characterized by innocent acceptance and an often reverent attentiveness to detail that demonstrates the adult narrator's longing for a vanished past. Two autobiographical essays chronicling Chappell's adolescence—**"First Attempts"** and **"A Pact with Faustus"**—provide a very different picture of his relationship to family and community. As a boy with an intense interest in books and writing, it comes as no surprise that he was less than content with life on the farm. Just as Thomas Wolfe had felt about his native Asheville twenty miles to the east, Chappell grew up seeing the hills around Canton as a prison, holding him back from the cosmopolitan experience—and the career of a writer—of which he dreamed. Remembering his adolescent penchant for melodrama, he writes that it was clear to him that as an artist he was "never going to catch up with the twentieth century," that he was already "starting from too far behind."[16]

By the age of fifteen, he had determined to become a writer and was already publishing stories in various science fiction and fantasy magazines, whose editors gave him what little encouragement and instruction he received. "My experience with [these] editors," he writes, "was that they were sinister spectral entities who occasionally scribbled crabbed notes on little blue rejections slips: 'Your exposition is silly'; 'This is not how Martians talk to each other.'"[17] Despite the thanks he gives to certain high school teachers who at least did not discourage him from writing, Chappell's account of his own adolescence is one that might be expected from an aspiring writer growing up on an isolated mountain farm: the dreamy autodidact, who began teaching himself to write through "an eon of trial . . . followed by an infinitude of error."[18] His parents were, at times, both school teachers, and so they instilled in him a sense of the value of education and made books readily available, including the classics of Western literature. Of his high school years he remembers that he "was reading Shelley and Shakespeare by wholesale acreage and had bought a copy of Yeats's early plays for twenty-five cents from a junk dealer."[19] Although he believes that his parents had themselves once entertained literary aspirations, they strongly discouraged his because they found them impractical.

In **"A Pact with Faustus,"** Chappell recalls his adolescent friendship with Harry ("Fuzz") Fincher, another Canton boy, who aspired to become a composer. Chappell recalls their mutual "conspiracy against the placid town and against [their] perfectly nice parents": "We felt—God forgive us!—superior in some way that we could not articulate, and much put upon, despised for our interests and aspirations."[20] The boys felt cut off from any meaningful discussion of the arts beyond their own company of two, and in typical adolescent fashion they luxuriated in their alienation and eventually joined in a spree of vandalism through the nighttime streets of Canton, "breaking random store windows and wreaking other damage," a night that for Fred resulted in "severe" and "unforgettable" punishments involving "physical ordeals" and an "interminable" ban on reading, an activity his parents associated with his waywardness.[21]

If he was taught that reading was a guilty pleasure, writing seemed to have been doubly so. In a community of farmers and mill workers, a pursuit of the arts was seen as self-indulgent. Parents, teachers, and "everyone else" constantly lectured Fred about the valuelessness of his pursuits.[22] He remembers his family's attitude toward the long evenings he spent secluded upstairs writing. "My bedroom was too small to accommodate a desk and typewriter, but I had found a niche in the upstairs hall. When I set the Royal clattering the sound could be heard all over the house. Visitors who asked about the racket were informed that Oh, that's only Fred working on his typing. Their embarrassment was just that acute; I was not trying to write, I was learning to type. Typing was a useful skill that might come in handy someday. Writing was impractical and impracticality was worse than heresy, thievery, or some kinds of homicide. These were the tag-end years of the Depression; it was imperative to be practical."[23] He had discovered that to be a writer was to be at odds with his culture, and he clung to this newfound identity of the outsider. What a contrast Chappell's situation offers to that of Reynolds Price, who in *Clear Pictures* describes family and teachers only as being thoroughly supportive of his artistic ambitions. Even though there were no literary members of Price's family, the family's genteel history made possible the identity of the artist for young Reynolds in a way that such an identity was completely alien to

Chappell's frontier, yeoman culture. At the same time, Chappell's embracing the role of the alienated artist is a manifestation of the fierce independence so prevalent in Appalachian culture.

Chappell makes comically clear in **"First Attempts"** that, in fact, what attracted him as a young person to the literary profession was the extreme eccentricity—and, thus, the glamour—that his people associated with "being a writer." At the same time, the problem he faced was a lack of models:

> The only other writer [besides Hemingway] of whose personal life one ever heard anything was Poe—and he was regarded as both scandalous and tragic. Whenever my parents, teachers, and ministers tried to dissuade me from a life of writing—as they did regularly and assiduously—it was the fate of Poe they threatened me with. They pictured him as a wild-eyed genius who was an alcoholic and drug addict, and they hinted too at darker vices and nearly incomprehensible sins.
>
> Well, I could see that being Edgar Allan Poe had it all over being Ernest Hemingway. . . . To all of us [writing] seemed such an exotic occupation, such a dangerous ambition, that when we tried to imagine the way of life a writer might trace we could come up with only the most lurid and improbable scenarios, visions that horrified and repulsed my elders while they attracted me with all the force a two-ton electromagnet exerts on a single crumb of iron filing.[24]

Poe would serve as an appropriate icon to represent the alienation he felt, and, along with the French Symbolists, would fix very firmly in his mind the image of the young genius at odds with his world, composing obscure lyrical gems that would some day after his early death bring him the fame he had deserved.

How striking it is that the young Chappell did not find in Thomas Wolfe a model of the alienated artist—considering that Wolfe grew up in and wrote about Asheville, just twenty miles to the east. Like Reynolds Price, however, Chappell missed reading Wolfe, recalling that, as a teenager, he had only read later works, *The Hills Beyond* and "Only the Dead Know Brooklyn."[25] Perhaps like Lin Harper, the teenage founder of a literary club called the Skylark Society in *The Gaudy Place,* the young Chappell felt that Wolfe, a "local" writer "too much lauded by parents and teachers," would have nothing to say to him of the outside world.[26] While Chappell names Poe as his "first and most lasting influence,"[27] the influence of Camus and Faulkner is also evident in his first four novels.[28]

In fact, the protagonists in the first four novels might be seen as Appalachian Quentin Compsons, trapped and determined by their environments and by their personal and familial pasts. James Christopher, the protagonist of his first novel, *It Is Time, Lord,* describes the past as "an eternally current danger, in effect, a suicide. We desire the past, we call to it just as men who have fallen overboard an ocean liner call. . . . it sours and rots like old meat in the mind."[29] In addition to confronting the repressed trauma of sexual molestation he seems to have suffered during childhood, James Christopher is still wrestling at age thirty-one with the guilt of having as a nine-year-old burned down his family's ancestral homeplace. His fixation on the past has produced a midlife crisis, the symptoms of which include alcoholism and the loss of purpose in his professional and family life. James tells his wife of his plan to straighten himself out by visiting his parents in the mountains, whom he has not seen or corresponded with in five years. "Isn't it true," he says, "that if I could get my past settled in the right groove my present life would trundle along the way it's supposed to? It's like getting a nut cross-threaded on a bolt: you have to twist it back and try until it fits correctly" (160).

His attempts to "settle" his past depend largely on making peace with his father, a plan that fails abruptly. When James first enters the front yard, his father begins a withering speech, rehearsing—in a lazy and "preoccupied" voice, a "good voice for reading Tennyson"—all of his son's failures, past and present. In effect, he verbally divests James of his manhood, just as he had done throughout James's boyhood, constantly, criticizing his bookishness and his disinclination for farm labor, making James re-experience the guilt of having burned his family's homeplace. After showing anything but enthusiasm for his son's visit, the father mentions plans for having James's wife and children make an extended visit—without James:

> "In the first place, I don't like to think about your kids inheriting your hatred—or do they call it an allergy now?—whatever—of clean air and sunlight. But if they do come, I want *them.* And every time I see you around I'll just try to drive you off with a shotgun."
>
> "Why?"
>
> "Well, that's hyperbole, of course. I don't like the thought of turning a gun on a mewling baby, especially one over thirty years old. What I can't understand is how you ever thought of coming up here. You could have everything that's on my mind, and I believe I can speak pretty fairly for your mother too, over the telephone in a few minutes."
>
> "I don't know."
>
> "The only thing I could figure was that you've been reading too many novels. Telemachus. Stephen Dedalus. The boy with the golden screw for a navel. The search for a father. All that literary stuff. I've read it myself, one time or another. It's hogwash. Bull shit. I've just about stopped reading, and only just now I've

> started hoping that I've stopped in time. Even our damn barn cat has got enough sense to chase its younguns off when they get old enough."
>
> (157-58)

Like James, his father is a man threatened by any degree of intimacy, and his rejection of his son appears to be a spontaneous response to that threat. Shortly thereafter, James's mother comes to his bedroom and explains that she is supposed to let him know that his father is still his "good buddy." "Your father's got in his head," she says, "that the only way a real masculine man ought to talk is in grunts and profanity. But the trouble is, he likes to talk too much for that to satisfy him. So he runs on. I've lived with him long enough to know he doesn't mean anything he says for an hour at a time." She further remarks that he "almost jumps out of his skin" when he hears the word "love" (161).

In *Look Back All the Green Valley,* Jess Kirkman observes that "to be well spoken is not in the tradition of the Appalachian mountaineer, whose sometimes inscrutable taciturnity is locally regarded as a virtue having something to do with valor and manliness."[30] If to show oneself a "well spoken man" in Appalachia is to invite suspicions of one's masculinity, to show oneself as "bookish" confirms those suspicions. In both cases, not only emotional warmth, but communication through language, is degraded in contrast to "action." James's father has obviously internalized these cultural values and, because, as his wife observes, he is a compulsive talker, he compromises by divorcing any emotional warmth from his speeches to his son. Chappell acknowledges "the taciturn farmer father" as a staple of American realism, finding examples in Hamlin Garland, Sarah Orne Jewett, Mary Wilkins Freeman, and "all the regionalists."[31] Such taciturnity and emotional paralysis appear throughout Chappell's fiction as the downside of yeoman independence. *It Is Time, Lord,* especially, launches a steady critique against Appalachian ideals of manhood, viewing the figure of the yeoman farmer as insensitive, alienated, and completely incapable of nurturing.

Interestingly enough, even in this darkly pessimistic first novel, Chappell shows signs of the pastoralist he would later become. The novel depicts James Christopher's intense preoccupation with his rural past and his desire to reconcile himself to that past—and to his father—even if that desire is thoroughly balked. Moreover, the description of James's boyhood on the farm is in many ways idyllic, though the idyll is corrupted by self-loathing: James recalls himself as "the toad in the garden of what [his] family . . . might call Eden" (95).

The psychological/supernatural thriller *Dagon* also depicts a return to a family homeplace in the mountains that goes awry. Peter Leland returns with his wife to his family's Appalachian farm, which he has just inherited and finds to be literally haunted by a familial past that he, like Poe's Roderick Usher, cannot escape. Upon first exploring the downstairs parlors, Leland remarks that "the pastness which these two rooms . . . enclosed was not simply the impersonal weight of dead personality but a willful belligerence, active hostility. Standing still in the center of the first room, he felt the floor stirring faintly beneath his feet, and he was convinced that the house was gathering its muscles to do him harm."[32] Over the following weeks, the house does in fact do him serious harm, exerting an influence over his moods and his frame of mind, leading him to morbid thoughts and ultimately to the brutal and motiveless murder of his wife. Up until the murder it seems that if Leland could only escape the homeplace of his ancestors he could avoid the malaise that has overtaken him.

Like Poe's stories of dementia that Chappell so admired growing up, the energy driving Chappell's first three novels[33] derives from within the self rather than from the social milieu in which the self finds itself. For all their intensity and frequent lyricism, the first three novels lack the breadth and social scope typically associated with long fiction. Admittedly, the length of each stays under 200 pages, and, considering the economy and intensity of the narratives, these novels have the advantage—which Poe attributes to the short story—of possibly being read in a single sitting.[34] Nevertheless, W. H. Auden's criticism of Poe's stories would equally apply to Chappell's. According to Auden, there is "no place" in any of Poe's fiction "for the human individual as he actually exists in space and time, that is, as simultaneously a natural creature subject in his feelings to the influences and limitations of the natural order, and an historical person, creating novelty and relations by his free choice and modified in unforeseen ways by the choices of others."[35] As with Poe's stories, each of Chappell's first three novels demonstrates an unease with society, and in particular, an unease with the yeoman society of Appalachia. The characters' self-destructive behaviors result not from interactions with others so much as from their withdrawal from society and the internal compulsions they cannot escape.

Even though Chappell has acknowledged this problem, noting a "claustrophobic feeling" that he "could not get out" of his early fiction,[36] in my estimation the "claustrophobia" of Chappell's earlier work is not necessarily a problem; as with Poe's stories, Chappell's early novels are so engaging precisely because of the characters' withdrawal into dementia. Alienation is not only a very real part of the modern experience but also the traditional yeoman experience in Ap-

palachia as well. James Christopher or Peter Leland might be described in the very words Joe Robert Kirkman uses to describe one of his shy rural students who is more comfortable alone in the woods than in a high school classroom: "It was the mountaineer strain in his blood as pure . . . as it might have been a century ago" (*Brighten*, [*Brighten the Corner Where You Are*] 57). Nevertheless, having acknowledged the insight of Poe and of Chappell's early work into the alienated psyche, Auden's critique of Poe is equally applicable to Chappell, prompting us to declare that not all the world looks so dark and determined. Even in the loneliest valleys of Appalachia, people form communities, however small, which they creatively engage and in which they define themselves. Chappell obviously recognized this same dilemma, having remarked of his fourth novel, *The Gaudy Place* (1973), "I set myself very deliberately the challenge . . . of writing a novel about the same length as the others, but having scope in it, and trying to draw a larger social picture . . . [and] more variety of character."[37] *The Gaudy Place* marks Chappell's first attempt in long fiction to escape the prison of the self and to describe a social world.

The Gaudy Place is Chappell's first and only fully urban novel, taking in all of the bustle of the Gimlett Street red-light district of Braceboro, the fictional version of Lexington Avenue and Flint Street in Asheville, where Chappell spent numerous hours doing research.[38] A strikingly different sensibility is at work in this fourth novel; although the earlier fiction is replete with delicious irony, this is Chappell's first fully comic novel, a social satire reminiscent of Twain that pokes brutal fun at the American myth of the self-made man. With its Kafkaesque interest in the dissemination of power, *The Gaudy Place* is easily Chappell's most explicitly sociopolitical novel, one in which not family so much as economics and politics determine social and personal realities. But, then again, as the novel's Andrew Harper discovers upon moving to Appalachia with his mountain-born wife, mountain politics is a *family* business.

As satire, *The Gaudy Place* takes the first step toward the pastoral vision of yeoman society found in *Midquest* and the Kirkman novels. Frank Kermode observes that, like pastoral, satire is an urban genre, designed to contrast the "degeneracy" of the "metropolis" with some "better way of life—that is, some earlier way of life; the farther back you go the better."[39] Such a dichotomy appears, for example, in *Adventures of Huckleberry Finn,* in which the pastoral life of the river is juxtaposed with the social quagmires the boy finds along the river's shores. *The Gaudy Place* offers no such easy geographic demarcations; however, strata of corruption are associated with the extent to which individuals have insinuated themselves into the city's social structures by which power, wealth, and status are acquired.

The lowest stratum represented in the novel is occupied by Arkie, a resourceful fourteen-year-old orphan, an urban Huck Finn who survives day to day by running cons on the slow-witted truck farmers, who have come to the city to sell their produce, and on the unsuspecting "johns" waiting for their "girl friends." Arkie speaks a tough, comic street slang, full of both hyperbolic boasting and self-deprecation and is known all along Gimlett Street for a subservient song-and-dance routine that has all the characteristics of minstrelsy; whenever a tense moment appears, he sings out his namesake couplet: "Fried cornbread and cold coleslaw, I'm traveling down to Arkansas" (26) or some variant thereof. At a slightly more elevated level of society there is Oxie, a Gimlett Street pimp, who also works as a bondsman and reads Dale Carnegie in an effort to ingratiate himself with the "respectable" racket of local politics. The city's highest level of power and corruption is represented by Zebulon Johns Mackie, or Uncle Zeb, a local politician and self-made man described as a "dead ringer" for Benjamin Franklin. A member of both the city council and the board of directors for the local Green Ridge Construction Company, respectable Uncle Zeb has his own con in the works, one that involves someone with Oxie's contacts on Gimlett Street.

This novel's considerable power derives from the vertigo of watching what at first seems to be a random sampling of society drawn into a web of power that robs each of them of agency—demonstrating that in *The Gaudy Place* Chappell feels the same mistrust of society that appears in his earlier novels of alienation. Admittedly, the novel ends somewhat hopefully for Arkie, with him running from the law after singing out that he is "going down to ARKANSAS!" (177) and thereby eluding the city's corrupting influences that have entrapped the other characters. Nevertheless, like Huck Finn, Arkie's final statement that he plans to light out for the territory of the old Southwest suggests that, equally for Twain and Chappell, freedom only exists for the individual removed from society.

"THE GREEN POISON OF MONEY HAS LEACHED INTO THE GROUND AND TURNED IT BLUE"

The Gaudy Place is easily Chappell's most class-conscious novel. It not only provides a complete overview of the social classes of this mountain city but also shows how power flows from the upper classes downward to determine the lives of those below, how market capital in general perverts society's better instincts, including the truck farmers who often spend in a single day along the city's red light district a good portion of the cash they earned from selling their produce.

Although industrialization and urbanization, which developed throughout Appalachia during the late nineteenth and early twentieth centuries, certainly accelerated the threat to the yeoman's economic independence and exacerbated class conflict, Wilma Dunaway dates the introduction of capitalism into the region to the arrival of the first European settlers in the early eighteenth century and finds that class conflict was already present during the antebellum period.[40] Paul Salstrom demonstrates the rapid expansion of a market economy in the region following the Civil War—even before the growth of industrialization. Because of the war's devastation, the rising imbalance between population growth and depleted resources, and the restructuring of the national bank system (which favored capital investment available only from and controlled by sources outside the region), Appalachian farmers increasingly fell prey to market forces. The rise of a market economy devalued labor, kept the landless poor in a state of dependency and struggling for subsistence, and made a "competency" more difficult for yeomen to secure. Ironically, Salstrom explains, even as this struggle for subsistence became more acute, Appalachian farmers "increasingly abandoned their subsistence-barter-and-borrow systems and increasingly adopted the capitalist system," which depended on "increasing quantities of money" for survival.[41]

Chappell investigates the deleterious effects of this dependence on capital in the darkly comic poem **"My Father Burns Washington"** from *Midquest*. The poet recalls his boyhood during the latter years of the Great Depression when, lying in bed, he and his sister would overhear his parents as they frequently talked through their financial troubles and stalked the "phantom dollar and ghostly dime," after which they "went to bed in the grip / Of money and dreamed of money" (81). One night, the boy's father came home in tears and railed, "In outrage: 'Money. Money. Money. It's the death of the world. If it wasn't for goddam money a man might think a thought, might draw a breath of freedom. But all I can think is, Money. Money by God is death.'" (82)

As if to defy the control of capital over the farm and their lives there, and its delimitation of the farmers' "freedom," the father strikes a match and sets fire to a dollar bill. The poem's title, **"My Father Burns Washington,"** suggests the symbolism of the Appalachian farmer's defiance of the national bank and what a world-systems analysis would describe as the exploitation of poor farmers in a capitalist system's periphery for the benefit of the capitalist core in the industrialized Northeast.[42] The poem ends with the repentant father stomping out the fire, before the bill completely burns, and asking his wife, like "a beaten child," *"Mother, will it still spend?"* (84). In **"My Father Washes His Hands,"** also from *Midquest,* the older Fred, now away at college, returns to find his father broken and ready to give up the farm and "sell / Cheap furniture to poor folks" (153). Declaring that a "man's a fool in this age / Of money to turn the soil," the father intends not "to die in the traces like poor Honey" (153), the mule that died two weeks before. He tells Fred of the ordeal of burial, which involved digging through "pipe clay as blue and sticky as Buick paint" (153). "The green poison / Of money," the father explains, "has leached into the ground / And turned it blue" (154).

One of the most unfortunate effects of capitalism in Appalachia, as elsewhere, has been the production of barriers between social classes and resulting class conflict. Ronald Eller locates the appearance of class consciousness in Appalachia during the period of industrialization that began in the late nineteenth century, largely in mining company towns, where the mine owners and supervisors were segregated in nicer homes but always in view of their impoverished work force.[43] Both Salstrom and Dunaway observe a rigid stratification of social classes to have developed much earlier. Throughout most of the region, Salstrom finds that by 1880 the capitalization of agriculture had already stymied a spirit of entrepreneurship, making farm ownership available to fewer mountaineers and producing a nearly insurmountable division between upper and lower classes.[44] Dunaway demonstrates how the prevalence of absentee landlords even in the antebellum period exacerbated the exploitation of labor in the form of tenancy, sharecropping, wage labor, and slavery.

Contrary to the prevailing myth of a nearly slaveless mountain South, Dunaway demonstrates how pervasive slavery was throughout southern Appalachia. Her research shows, however, that, compared to Appalachian Virginia, Alabama, Georgia, and South Carolina, where one-fifth to one-quarter of households owned slaves, coming near the southern average, 1860 census data show that in western North Carolina, as in eastern Kentucky, only about 10 percent of households owned slaves.[45] And even in western North Carolina this figure varies considerably, with the foothills showing a higher incidence of slavery than the more remote mountainous regions.[46] Dunaway observes one of the most significant effects of slavery in western North Carolina to be the production of an inequitable distribution of resources and developing social classes, including the rise of a large population of landless

poor. According to Dunaway, despite their relatively low representation in the population, North Carolina's Appalachian slaveholders "engrossed more than two-fifths of the farm acreage, leaving only one-seventh of the resources available to the poorer bottom half of the farm households."[47] Furthermore, whereas "subsistence producers made up nearly one-fifth of the owner households," they owned "only 4 to 8 percent of the farm land."[48] Even more troubling, while distribution of wealth elsewhere in the United States remained fairly unchanged throughout the antebellum period, in Appalachia, Dunaway demonstrates, the polarization of wealth between slaveholders and nonslaveholders increased dramatically.[49] This disparity in landholdings during the antebellum period produced widespread landlessness, forcing a significant portion of the agricultural population into wage labor, tenancy, and sharecropping, and thereby threatening the yeoman ideal of a classless, egalitarian society.

Chappell's fiction depicts the persistence of these class divisions well into the twentieth century. The legacy of slavery in the form of conflict between Appalachian whites and descendants of slaves is not entirely absent in his work, as exemplified by **"My Father Allergic to Fire"** from *Midquest* or in the acknowledgement of racism by Jubal Henry, Tipton High School's African American janitor in *Brighten the Corner Where You Are.* Nevertheless Chappell's concern with class conflict focuses much more often on the tensions between white tenant farmers and their yeoman landlords, with both groups struggling for subsistence in response to market pressures. Class conflict is most troubling in his early fiction. If *The Gaudy Place* represents Chappell's most conscious engagement of the strata of Appalachian social classes, *Dagon* yields the most unnerving depiction of conflict between yeoman and tenant. Peter Leland, a Methodist minister, and scion of an Appalachian yeoman family, returns to the abandoned Leland homeplace to complete a book that treats, among other subjects, the spiritually deadening influence of capitalism throughout American history. Leland concludes, "And wasn't the power of money finally dependent upon the continued proliferation of product after product, dead objects produced without any thought given to their uses? Weren't these mostly objects without any truly justifiable need? Didn't the whole of American commercial culture exhibit this endless irrational productivity, clear analogue to sexual orgy? And yet productivity without regard to eventual need was, Peter maintained, actual unproductivity, it was really a kind of impotence" (70-71). This preoccupation with capitalism, coupled with his return to his family's farm, produces in Leland psychological instability, which results in his motiveless murder of his wife, followed by his flight from the family homestead to the home of a sharecropping family named Morgan, who for generations has sustained itself on the sale of moonshine. Leland gives himself over to the Morgans' moonshine and spends the rest of the summer drunk in the bed of the daughter Mina, who serves as his dominatrix, subjugating him to her every whim, delighting in his increasing degradation. At the end of the summer, Mina uses Leland's automobile to drive eastward with Leland and another young man to a Piedmont town where they settle into an abandoned house. Mina employs two other women as prostitutes and begins a campaign of ritually desecrating Leland's body through torture and tattooing. The story ends with Leland emaciated and covered in tattoos, reduced to a state of bestiality and total withdrawal, grunting and mooing being his only forms of communication, and a metal bar that he identifies as his "man-thing" being the only object he values. When Mina finally takes his life in ritual sacrifice, Leland welcomes the knife.

A reduction of this novel to a mere diatribe against the unhealthy influence of market capital on Appalachian social classes would represent a serious misreading—or at least an incomplete one. Nevertheless, as the descendant of an established yeoman family, Leland's aberrant behavior toward the Morgans, who have for generations occupied the position of tenant farmers, certainly deserves investigation. His sexual behavior toward Mina obviously bears all the marks of masochism, which, when considered in light of the economic relationship of their respective families, along with Leland's developing thesis on capitalism, suggests a manifestation of his repressed class-based guilt. The same dynamic appears in *It Is Time, Lord*: James Christopher, a successful middle-class editor at a university press, leaves his job, undertakes an extended drunk, goes on the lam with a cast of lower-class characters, and becomes masochistically involved with a "redneck" woman named Judy. This relationship may, in part, be a failed effort at reconciliation with his own past and, in particular, with his family's tenant farmer, "Uncle" George, who served the young James as a surrogate father while nevertheless neglecting and abusing his own son. Other than Uncle George's nurturing of James, no healthy relationship appears between poor whites and yeomen (and their middle-class descendants) in Chappell's early work. The yeoman fathers are cold and distant. Their sons are self-loathing drunks—not unlike the besotted aristocrats in decline who appear in Faulkner or Percy or Styron. And the poor whites are brutish, narrow-minded, and cruel.

Chappell's later work marks a departure from such negative portraits of Appalachian society, a difference particularly evident in the Jess Kirkman tetralogy. In these four novels interactions between social classes appear less frequently or are downplayed, given that three of the novels focus on relations within the Kirkman family or within what appears to be a seemingly classless, agrarian society. When, for example, the Kirkman family hires Johnson Gibbs to work on their farm, paying him primarily with room and board, providing a better life than that to which he had been accustomed growing up in an orphanage, little mention is made of the economic incentives for his presence, so thoroughly is he embraced as a part of the family. The various elderly figures who proliferate the stories that make up *I Am One of You Forever* and *Farewell, I'm Bound to Leave You* are either kinfolk or apparently of the yeoman class.

The Kirkman novel that most directly addresses issues of class is *Brighten the Corner Where You Are*. Here, Jess's father, Joe Robert Kirkman, is a yeoman farmer/educator of modest means, who, with quiet grace and humility, assumes a position of noblesse oblige toward the less fortunate of his community. Contrary to the paternalism typically displayed by planters toward their dependents, however, Joe Robert takes pains to diminish any sense of social hierarchy or difference of status that might appear between himself and other members of his community. When as a high school science teacher he stumbles upon Jubal Henry's hideaway in the school's basement, Joe Robert absorbs without retaliation the African American janitor's repressed aggression toward "white folks." Even though Joe Robert advises Jubal to stand up to the perpetrators of racism rather than taking out his anger on a man who "never did [Jubal] a bad turn," he seems to understand when Jubal explains, "The man that will give me trouble is the one that will just as soon kill me. I rather take it out on you. A little backsass don't do you no hurt and does me a profit of good" (123).

Joe Robert takes a similarly pacifist stance toward the wrathful tenant, Hob Farnum, whom he employs on his dairy farm, as described in the central chapter of *Brighten,* entitled **"Shares."** When counseling his son not to fight back against tenant children, even when attacked, he tells Jess, *"Poor people have got plenty enough problems without you hitting them"* (109). Jess, who is being emotionally abused by Hob Farnum and physically bullied by the tenant's son, Burrell, counters, *"But what if I had to? What if he was to start picking on me, or we had a quarrel?"* Joe Robert responds, *"Oh, you've got a quarrel, all right. You had a quarrel before either of you were born"* (111). Joe Robert's efforts to enlighten his son about the complex of emotions involved between the *"haves and have-nots"* (111), however, are lost on his young son (but not on the adult Jess, who serves as the novel's retrospective narrator). Young Jess is thoroughly invested in the values of manly honor that come to him from Hollywood westerns (values that Bertram Wyatt-Brown finds pervasive throughout the Old South); filled with self-loathing as a result of his own cowardice, Jess thinks to himself, *"Roy Rogers wouldn't [even] spit on me"* (112). After months of cowering before the abuse of the tenants, feelings of dishonor drive Jess nearly to the brink of madness. *"It was all upside down,"* he reflects. *"They were the tenants and lived in the little weathered house with its bare yard pecked over by listless chickens; I lived in the brick house under the trees. Yet I was the one who was getting bossed around, the one who felt petty and subservient"* (110). Finally, after standing up to and defeating Burrell, Jess remarks, *"I wish I was grown up now already and owned me a farm with some poor folks on it. I wish I had me some tenants on a farm. I'd whip their ass three times a day"* (114). The abyss of self-loathing and alienation into which young Jess sinks here in this twelve-page chapter resembles the demented psychological states suffered by the protagonists of Chappell's first three novels. Unlike the earlier novels, however, Jess's suffering in the role reversal recounted in "Shares" is necessary for his maturation and his willingness as an adult to embrace his father's yeoman ideal of an egalitarian society, one in which no one should have to feel "petty" or "subservient."

Despite the conflicts that will arise in any society—and that are necessary for any fiction—the octave composed of the Kirkman novels and the four volumes of *Midquest* emphasize the possibility for social harmony grounded in the basic unit of the yeoman family farm. In "Shares," Jess observes, *"My father and Hob Farnum found one point upon which they enjoyed perfect agreement. They both hated and passionately despised the system of tenant farming"* (103). Both men realize that this system is necessitated by their participation in the market economy, which is equally for the tenant and the yeoman landlord an unavoidable trap. Implicit in this critique of capitalized agriculture, which deprives both men of independence and autonomy, is the ideal of a farm free of market pressures, providing economic competency for all willing to work, and freedom from hierarchies based on wealth. This yeoman ideal fairly characterizes the society that Paul Salstrom finds more prevalent throughout Appalachia in its earlier frontier stages, before capitalism so thoroughly ensnared the vast majority of the region's population.[50] In *Midquest* and the Kirkman novels, just such a golden age informs the vision of the pastoralist Chappell would become by his second decade of publishing. Quite in contrast to his earlier studies of alienation, in which the Appalachian tendency toward independence is taken to its extreme, in his later work there emerges the pos-

sibility of a balance between independence and interdependence, as he explores the lives of individuals whose identities emerge not exclusively in rebellion *against* the social order but nurtured *within* it, as well.

Midquest: "When You Got True Dirt You Got Everything You Need"

In **"The Poet and the Plowman,"** Chappell ponders what he considers to be one of the fundamental issues facing poets ever since the classical age: the fact that it is impractical, if not impossible, to pursue both a life of poetry and a life of farming. As the essay begins, Chappell recalls long Sunday afternoons in the mid-1960s when he and his guest Allen Tate (who was then a guest lecturer at the University of North Carolina at Greensboro) would watch football on television and bemoan the disappearance of their Latin skills, along with the diminishing allure of the "traditional attractions of farm life."[51] Chappell recalls Tate's conclusion that poets should be only "spectator farmers": "Then he would smile and say in his breathy ironic genteel Kentucky accent: 'But we would make dreadful farmers, Fred, you and I.'"[52] In Chappell's portrait of the aging Agrarian, "genteel" Tate comes off unmistakably more comfortable in his resignation than does Chappell himself, who goes on restlessly to ponder the age-old kinship between the poet—or, more generally, the writer—and the plowman. This connection between the writer and the farmer is one that Chappell explores throughout the long poem *Midquest* and the subsequent Kirkman tetralogy of novels.

In the preface to *Midquest,* which Chappell therein calls a "verse novel" (ix), he describes the poem's "protagonist," Ole Fred, as a "demographic sample" of the twentieth century: "He was reared on a farm but has moved to the city; he has deserted manual for intellectual labor, is 'upwardly mobile'; he is cut off from his disappearing cultural traditions but finds them, in remembering, his real values" (x). This contrast between an ideal agrarian childhood and a corrupted urban age is one of the principal hallmarks of pastoral, which, as Frank Kermode notes, is always "an urban product."[53] Kermode observes that the "first condition of pastoral . . . is that there should be a sharp difference between two ways of life, the rustic and the urban. The city is an artificial product, and the pastoral poet invariably lives in it, or is the product of its schools and universities."[54] Kermode's description fits both Chappell and "Ole Fred," the autobiographical protagonist of *Midquest.* Chappell grew up observing the remnants of a traditional culture, as well as the emergence of industry in western North Carolina. The "loud, smoky, noisome" Champion Paper and Fiber Company[55] is a ubiquitous presence in Chappell's pastorals (appearing under the name of *Challenger*), as is the figure of the farmer father tenaciously scratching out a living from the soil, and the dreamy adolescent boy destined to leave the farm for the Piedmont cities of Durham and Greensboro. The world Chappell describes is one very much in flux, which makes his recollections of childhood appear all the more valued. Kermode has noted that pastoral "flourishes at a particular moment in the urban development, the phase in which the relationship of metropolis and country is still evident, and there are no children (as there are now) who have never seen a cow."[56] This precondition for pastoral sounds very like the necessity of the "backward glance" to the Southern Literary Renascence, or, more generally, to the experience of modernism. In each case, the artist has witnessed the disappearance of the old verities, an experience that leaves him dislocated, alienated, full of epistemological uncertainty, and longing for some source of truth by which to reorient himself. *Midquest* is full of folk tales, jokes, and convincing accounts of farm life, and at the same time it abounds in literary allusions. Chappell's style conflates examples of high and low cultures and derives a high lyricism from a rural Appalachian vernacular. In its largest design, *Midquest* attempts to heal the schism between Ole Fred and Professor Chappell, to restore a sense of wholeness by employing the breadth of the poet's learning to recreate the world of his childhood.

Following the model of Dante's *Divine Comedy,* each of *Midquest*'s four volumes begins with Ole Fred awakening on his thirty-fifth birthday in a state of spiritual longing. Of the eleven poems that compose each volume, most take the form of dialogues with family members remembered from the poet's childhood. These recollections serve as a source of inspiration and direction for Ole Fred, who at mid-life finds himself disenchanted with his suburban existence. In **"Birthday 35: Diary Entry,"** the second poem in the first volume, Ole Fred pessimistically considers—from the comfort of his living room—the results of his life's work: "On paper I scribble mottoes and epigrams, / Blessings and epithets, O-Holy's and Damn's— / Not matter sufficient to guard a week by. / The wisdom I hoard you could stuff in your eye" (4). The heroic couplets enhance the comic deflation of his vocational crisis. Throughout the poem Ole Fred employs humor to shield himself from raw feelings of despair and loss, as well as from the fear that the spiritual restoration for which he yearns is no longer available. Ultimately, though, he achieves that restoration through memory.

The past is no longer a "suicide," as it is described by James Christopher in *It Is Time, Lord,* but, rather, an antidote for the aridity of modern existence, a touchstone by which the poet finds meaning to live in the present. Nearing its conclusion, the tone of **"Birthday 35"** shifts from witty erudition to genuine desperation, as wasteland imagery proliferates:

> A wilderness of wind and ash.
> When I went to the river . . .
> 　　　. . . . .
> I saw, darkened, my own face.
> On the bank of Time I saw nothing human,
> 　　　. . . . .
> . . . only moon
> Upon moon, sterile stone
> Climbing the steep hill of void.
> And I was afraid.
>
> 　　　　　　　　　　　　　　　　(7)

This sterile landscape is characterized by dryness and dreary uniformity. In addition to conjuring images of mountains denuded by timber companies, these lines express Ole Fred's anxiety concerning his own tendency toward solipsism and the possibility that, as in the case of James Christopher, the world he observes or remembers is merely a projection of his own subconscious. These lines clearly echo the language from the final section of *The Waste Land:*[57] "Here is no water but only rock / Rock and no water and the sandy road."[58] Chappell's reaction to the dilemma is a parody of Eliot's climactic prayer, with Ole Fred praying for transcendence in the form of "Elysium . . . plentifully planted // With trout streams and waterfalls and suburban / Swimming pools, and sufficient chaser for bourbon" (8). In characteristic fashion, he switches back and forth between adolescent cheekiness and heartfelt sincerity; these lines are immediately followed by a shift in tone from cynicism to reverential pleading. Note also that the suburban references are absent from the concluding lines:

> Lead me then, Lord, to the thundering valleys where
> Cool silver droplets feather the air;
> Where rain like thimbles smacks roofs of tin,
> Washing away sin;
> Where daily a vast and wholesome cloud
> Announces itself aloud.
> Amen.
>
> 　　　　　　　　　　　　　　　　(8)

The wasteland imagery in **"Birthday 35"** evokes Ole Fred's spiritual estrangement and draws a distinction, in typical pastoral fashion, between the emptiness of his present urban/suburban condition and the spiritual sustenance to be found in a long-past rural golden age.

The prayer for cleansing and quenching that ends **"Birthday 35"** is provisionally answered in the following dramatic dialogue set in Ole Fred's boyhood, **"My Grandmother Washes Her Feet."** While washing her feet, the grandmother lectures the boy Fred about the dangers of pretension and the unrecognized history of his family's less respectable plain folk, which she accepts as family, despite what might be seen by mainstream society as undesirable idiosyncrasies. Again, intellectual pursuits occupy an antagonistic position to the farming life, as indicated in the grandmother's warning to the boy:

> You're bookish. I can see you easy a lawyer
> Or a county clerk in a big white suit and tie,
> Feeding the preacher and bribing the sheriff and the
>   judge.
> Second-generation respectable
> Don't come to any better destiny.
> But it's dirt you rose from, dirt you'll bury in.
> Just about the time you'll think your blood
> Is clean, here will come dirt in a natural shape
> You never dreamed. . . .
>   . . . . .
> . . . When you got true dirt, you got
> Everything you need . . .
>
>   (12)

The shift in consciousness that occurs from **"Birthday 35"** to the following **"My Grandmother Washes Her Feet"**—from a jaded scholar, listening to himself pontificate in the prison of his suburban living room, to the mostly passive and humble boy auditor, receptive to the wisdom of another—reveals the strategy Chappell will employ in the following poems, many of which take the form of dramatic dialogues, letters, prayers, and metaphysical love poems, all forms that emphasize the desire to make contact with another rather than only pursuing introspection. He will consistently seek to escape self-absorption and alienation, which he identifies as the problem of his age, and make contact with the concrete and authentic world of his plain-folk relatives, evoked in **"My Grandmother Washes Her Feet"** and elsewhere as "dirt."

Dirt has multiple connotations: the basis of agriculture and the source of all life; a symbol for the cycle of life and death; and a representation of the eternal and substantial versus the ephemeral and superficial. *Dirt* also contains the biblical allusions to the creation of Adam, as well as original sin. As in Betts's fiction, original sin becomes changed by Ole Fred's pious grandmother into a positive attribute of the human condition, reminding us of our common proclivities to error, and thereby requiring the assumption of humility that comes with the acknowledgment of our common humanity. Classical pastoral relies upon a concept of human nature not altogether inconsistent with such a vision of original sin; as Kermode notes, classical pastorals frequently portray the people of a golden age in their natural states as "hedonistic and sinless, though wanton."[59] The grandmother's list of cousins in their

"natural" states includes drunks, womanizers, a "Jack-leg" preacher, and a great aunt named Paregoric Annie who would beg for drug-money by removing her glass eye and asking for assistance in replacing it. Fred idealizes these cousins as still vitally connected to the earth through farming, and thereby exempt from the fallen state and subsequent need for salvation attributed to civilized humanity. Furthermore, their connection with the earth diminishes differences of social status, which contrasts sharply with the urban future the grandmother foresees for Fred.

Fred longs to forge a lost connection to this extended family that the grandmother and her generation took for granted. In an effort to visualize better these shadow cousins he has never met, the boy Fred—like God creating Adam—shapes their earthen effigies from the mud produced by his grandmother's footbath water. The adult Fred concludes the poem dejectedly, contemplating the economic necessity that forced his father to give up farming, then comparing himself unfavorably to his imagined cousins: "I never had the grit to stir those guts. / I never had the guts to stir that earth" (13). The reciprocal substitution of the terms "grit," or its synonym "earth," with "guts" in these lines equates the terms syntactically, thereby conflating their meanings, an effect enhanced by the consonance in "grit" and "guts."

This same tendency to ennoble mountain folk by equating them physically with the land itself is found in ***Brighten the Corner Where You Are*** when Joe Robert Kirkman is visited by Pruitt and Ginny Dorson, an extremely rural couple whom he characterizes as "silent farm folk from the genuine old-time mountain stock. . . . Salt of the earth: That was the common phrase for families like the Dorsons, but my father considered that it was all too common. Soul of the earth, he thought, earth's own earth" (56). The purest expression of Chappell's longing for a complete reunification with his Appalachian heritage is found in his desire to be one with the earth itself, which Jess Kirkman symbolically achieves at the end of ***Look Back All the Green Valley*** (also the culmination of the entire octave), when he finds himself on a rainy night covered in the mud of his father's grave.

The Dorsons, Fred's "shadow cousins," the "dirt poor" as Fred's grandmother calls them (12), and all the other "genuine old-time mountain" folk in Chappell's narratives figure the same way that shepherds do in traditional pastoral poetry, as a liaison between the pure and simple world of nature and the complicated and impure urban world of the pastoral poet. As J. E. Congleton explains, "The shepherd, actually, is half man and half Nature; he has enough in common with man to be his universal representative and has enough in common with Nature to be at one with it. Because the shepherd is so close to Nature, man, through him, can become united with Nature and consequently feel that he is a harmonious part of the whole and that his ideas are reconciled with the fundamental truths."[60]

Kenneth Lynn similarly observes how frontier story-tellers often presented their characters as part man, part beast. Lynn quotes Christian Schultz's 1808 report from Natchez, Mississippi, where Schultz heard two drunken rivermen competing for a Choctaw woman: "One said, 'I am a man; I am a horse; I am a team. I can whip any man *in all Kentucky,* by G-d.' The other replied, I am an alligator, half man, half horse; can whip any man on the *Mississippi,* by G-d. . . . I am a Mississippi snapping turtle: have bear's claws, al-ligator's teeth, and the devil's tail.'"[61] Although the frontier humorist's "shepherds" are considerably more violent and bawdy than the shepherds of pastoral poetry, they perform one of the same essential func-tions—vicariously reconnecting the civilized reader with the wildness and simplicity of the natural world. In *Midquest* and the Jess Kirkman tetralogy, high and low cultures meet as Chappell employs elements of both classical pastoral and frontier humor to get in touch with the simple, the concrete, what he feels to be his own essential nature.

The error of leaving the farm and forgetting one's birthright of "dirt" involves the dominant theme of *Midquest*: the loss of the concrete world through a process of abstraction. Pastoral promises a reunifica-tion with nature by means of considering human culture at its most basic level, and yet, as Kermode observes, the challenge to the pastoral poet is to avoid merely, an inauthentic imitation of established conven-tions. This challenge is one familiar to any reader of southern literature. Just as the earlier pastorals often tended toward derivative accounts of shepherds and nymphs, southern writers have felt the temptation toward predictable representations of pastoral types: the pure and virtuous belle, the noble colonel-father, the faithful Negro retainer, the hillbilly farmer.

In *Midquest* Chappell frequently calls attention to this problem, as in the poem **"Firewater,"** in which the boy Fred listens to his father, J.T., and his father's drinking buddy Virgil Campbell as they lament the passing of the old ways and of the genuine Ap-palachian farmers. What their dialogue makes obvious to the reader is the difficulty of knowing or represent-ing a "genuine" Appalachian farmer—and how the label itself implies a level of self-consciousness in which the organic and traditional have been extracted from their living medium to be displayed for their picturesque value. Virgil begins the poem by describ-ing his recent visit to rural Clay County—where some

of his backwater cousins live—for the purpose of watching their centennial celebration. The festival's main attraction was the "Grand Parade, / Celebrating their most famous products" (78), with moonshine topping the list. In an effort to celebrate their culture, the local officials have traveled up Standing Indian Mountain to invite Big Mama and her family (whom they have been trying to prosecute for ten years) to "build a model still" and "waltz it down Main Street in broad daylight" (79). The plan backfires during the middle of the parade when a mule following behind Big Mama's float staggers and then collapses, "Drunk as an owl, / Just from breathing the smoke that was pouring out / From Big Mama's *model* still" (79). A deputy attempts to make an arrest, but "smiling so the crowd would think / It was part of the act" (80), at which point

> Big Mama's boys stood up—
> Wearing phony beards, barefoot with beat-up hats,
> Just like the hillbillies in the funny papers—
> And threw down on the deputy three shotguns.
> Whether they were loaded I don't know.
> He didn't know. Except Big Mama's bunch
> *Nobody* knew.
>
> (80)

The use of disguises here calls attention to the stereotype and thus forces the reader to guess at the authentic identity hidden from view. These are the pastoral's real shepherds wearing shepherd masks. As Houston Baker notes of the minstrel mask and its adoption by black speakers during the Jim Crow era,[62] Big Mama's boys assume their hillbilly disguises as a means of protecting their genuine identities. That they alone know whether their guns are loaded further sug-gests their control over their own identity and culture, thereby invalidating Virgil Campbell and J.T.'s nostalgic lament of cultural erosion.

By choosing in *Midquest* to differentiate experience into four rubrics associated with the four pre-Socratic elements, Chappell examines experience at its most fundamental level. The effect of the repeated images of water, fire, air, and earth relentlessly locates human experience in a natural, primitive context. The speak-ers in these poems are constantly in contact with the natural elements and interpret their lives by means of metaphors derived from the natural world. In **"Second Wind,"** for example, the grandmother tells the boy Fred the story of his grandfather's funeral and embod-ies the despair she felt in the hot, still August weather. Similarly the freshening of a breeze breaks her emotional stasis and leads to hope. Time in *Midquest* is cyclical, which is reinforced by the book's four-part structure; in each volume, the poet's birthday begins with first light and progresses toward evening. The farming community depicted in *Midquest* measures time in a premodern way, planting crops by the phases of the moon, paying attention to the progress of the seasons, locating memory by references not to calendar dates so much as significant events, often natural disasters, such as the storm described in **"My Father's Hurricane"** the flood in **"Dead Soldiers,"** or the fire in **"My Grandfather's Church Goes Up."**

Midquest's structure reinforces this vision of a society in harmony with the cosmos. Unlike the montage of fragments in *It Is Time, Lord,* which resists not only closure but also the production of any sort of stable meaning, *Midquest* presents an ordered repetition of image and event, which reflects a psychic balance and harmony, rather than discord. And, in contrast to the five isolated perspectives that comprise *The Gaudy Place,* the multiple subjectivities represented in *Midquest*'s dramatic monologues and dialogues create the sense of a community of interdependent speakers. In addition to the numerous parallels between *Midquest* and the Kirkman tetralogy, Chappell alerts the reader in *Midquest*'s preface that the poems in each of the four volumes balance each other and make orderly connections with similarly placed poems in each of the other four volumes. Just as Lucinda MacKethan argues that southern pastorals have always been motivated by the "need of people in a rapidly changing world to have a vision of an understandable order,"[63] Chappell's attention to a carefully ordered structure throughout his octave underscores his desire to preserve in poetry a disappearing social structure: the network of relationships that define the farming family, the basic unit of yeoman society.

Like Thomas Jefferson, Chappell promotes yeomanry as the ideal society, one that makes possible the difficult balance between individual freedom and social integrity. Further still, Chappell's reliance on classical aesthetics suggests metaphysical implications, as he makes clear in his essay on Virgil's *Georgics,* **"The Poet and the Plowman."** Chappell examines Virgil's dictum, *"Nudas ara, sere nudus,* Plow naked, naked sow,"* and declares, "The words are there to remind us of the ceremonial, and ultimately religious nature of farming; they remind us of the selfless rituals we must undergo in order to keep faith."[64] Further on, he continues this theme: "The largest purpose of the *Georgics* is not to dignify, but to sanctify, honest farm labor. A reader who has not looked at it in a long time finds he has forgotten that the poem is full of stars. Even the smallest task must be undertaken in due season under the proper constellations. These prescriptions are not mere meteorology; they connect the order of the earth to the order of the stars. The farmer moves by the motion of the stars, and his labors determine the concerns of the government. The Roman State is not founded upon the soil, it is founded in the universe.

And so were all the other civilizations which managed to endure for any length of time. If poets do not wish to study these matters and treat of them, they shirk their responsibilities and fail their society."[65]

In this passage Chappell makes explicit his belief in the spiritual harmony that exists between yeomen and the cosmos. Chappell's conviction that the artist bears a responsibility to his public—that he should show that public a vision of its better self—is a distinctly premodern notion, and indeed *Midquest* comes as close to the epic as anything likely to be found in contemporary poetry. As with Virgil, for Chappell poetry's greatest value lies in its ability to capture not only a life but a world. One of Chappell's most notable frustrations with contemporary poetry derives from his observation that the vast majority of it, good and bad, takes the shape of the "autobiographical lyric" with little in the way of "social scope" (*Midquest,* x). How ironic it is, of course, that Chappell would himself first come to find the full expression of "social scope" in his poetry, rather than in fiction, the more natural genre—at least in contemporary writing—for such explorations. However, when he returned to writing long fiction, after devoting his greatest energies during the 1970s to *Midquest,* the vision of an ordered life—rooted in the yeoman farming community—remained a guiding principle.

FRONTIER HUMOR IN *I AM ONE OF YOU FOREVER* AND *FAREWELL, I'M BOUND TO LEAVE YOU*

As in the companion quartet of long poems that make up *Midquest,* the Jess Kirkman tetralogy features an autobiographical figure who struggles to access the Appalachian culture of his childhood. The entire octave serves as an extended kunstlerroman, which depicts Jess's maturation as a poet. Like Ole Fred of *Midquest,* Jess Kirkman discovers the unavoidable tension—common to all pastoral—between the necessity of employing the individual imagination and the danger of falsifying or abstracting the concrete experience he seeks to recover. In his effort to recreate Appalachian culture authentically, Chappell reconstructs personal experience and family legend according to models indigenous to his folk culture—principally, the tall tale, the windy, and the fairy tale.[66] As in *Midquest,* the characters spend considerable time telling each other tall tales, which lends the tetralogy its prevalent element of fantasy. Like the episodic collections of frontier humor from the nineteenth century, the term "novel-of-stories" might be applied to the first and third novels, *I Am One of You Forever* (1985) and *Farewell, I'm Bound to Leave You* (1996). The tetralogy's second and fourth novels—*Brighten the Corner Where You Are* (1989) and *Look Back All the*

Green Valley (1999)—also form a pair in that they both dramatize Jess's attempt to connect with his father and, through him, the culture of the yeoman farmer Jess recalls from childhood.

A comparison of *I Am One of You Forever* and *Farewell, I'm Bound to Leave You* is especially fruitful when considering how the model of the frontier storyteller facilitates and limits Chappell's ability to immerse himself in his Appalachian culture. These two novels balance each other in that *One of You* focuses on the many solitary men in the extended family and *Farewell* focuses on a community of women, a difference that helps to illustrate the development of Jess's poetic vision and the tension he feels as a young artist caught between his Romantic impulse to follow the lead of his own individual imagination and his constant longing for unity with an interdependent family and farming community. This tension is dramatized by the playful contestation between Jess's father, who aligns himself with the masculine ideal of frontier independence, and Jess's mother and grandmother, who seek to domesticate the frontier and promote order through the maintenance of family ties.

Four of the chapters in *One of You* dramatize a series of visits by Jess's maternal uncles, solitary men who pay brief visits to the farm. Jess's memories of these visits focus on the uncles' eccentricities and the extent to which they remain separate from the family. Jess begins the tale of Uncle Zeno's visit by observing, "Uncle Zeno came to visit us. Or did he? Not even the bare fact of his visit is incontestable" (97). Zeno is a legendary storyteller, one who fits Twain's description of the frontier tale teller in that he consistently appears oblivious to the reaction of his audience. Furthermore, even though he periodically entrances them with his stories, Zeno never once engages Jess or his family in even the simplest of dialogues. Like Uncle Zeno, each of Jess's other visiting uncles is physically but not mentally or emotionally present. Each uncle is absorbed by his own subjective reality to the extent that communication with the family is severely limited. Each has his own individual obsession. Like Uncle Zeno, bearded Uncle Gurton will not be tempted into dialogue. Gurton will speak only one sentence, and only after mealtime: "I've had an elegant sufficiency; any more would be a superfluity."[67] Uncle Luden is so driven by his dependence on whiskey and women that he finds it difficult to fit in time for his family whom he has traveled all the way from the far west, California, to visit. Luden, too, has his favorite expression: he sums up his renegade individuality in the melancholy war cry "Wahoo!" Uncle Runkin prefers the world beyond the grave to the world of the living; he is obsessed with graveyards and sleeps in the casket he has brought with him for his visit with the Kirk-

mans. Each of these uncles is larger than life, eccentric to the point of inspiring legend—or tall tale, which is essentially the genre that each of the chapters devoted to the visiting uncles best fits. In assuming the role of frontier storyteller, Jess understands his responsibility to let the tale grow larger than life, as for example in the chapter entitled **"The Beard,"** which ends with Uncle Gurton's fabled long beard pouring down the steps of the farmhouse, flowing out the windows and blending with the stars in the night sky. Additional chapters of *One of You* feature a talking horse, storm angels, a shape-shifting telegram, a storyteller who creates the future by speaking his tales, and numerous other fantastic instances.

Because Jess *receives* the stories in *Farewell, I'm Bound to Leave You* from his mother and grandmother, the stories (and the values encoded therein) have been more faithfully rendered this time, less transformed, less tampered with than they were in the earlier novel. In contrast to the string of visiting uncles in *One of You,* who are treated more as grotesques than as fully human characters, the stories in *Farewell* typically present legendary women who, nevertheless, appear to be flesh and blood and capable of interacting with their community. The association of these differences of representation with the gender of the respective narrators is supported by Carol Mitchell's research of gender differences among joke tellers. She observes how men "often seem to enjoy competitive joke-telling sessions," whereas women "very rarely participate" in them,[68] Women prefer to tell jokes in more intimate settings involving one or two close friends or family members, whereas men are "much more likely than women to tell jokes in the presence of casual acquaintances and even strangers."[69] Furthermore, a woman is more likely to "speak amusingly or wittily about herself or others in an informal way rather than using the formal conventions of the joke."[70] In contrast to the intimacy that develops as a result of women's humorous anecdotes, Mitchell finds that the aggressive competitiveness among male joke tellers prevents "friendships from becoming too intimate."[71]

A similar difference distinguishes *Farewell* from *One of You*: much more actual dialogue takes place between the boy and his mother and grandmother than between him and his father. As in the dramatic dialogues of *Midquest,* in Chappell's novels the women are more capable of responding to Jess's questions, and their dialogue is marked by an emotional directness that is lacking between the father and son. Chappell himself observes, "It's noticeable in my work that the father actually *says* very little, except when he is showing off and teasing."[72] The women's stories contain an explicit moral purpose, while the father's are filled with humor and hyperbole; he delights in the tales for their own sake as artistic performance. Furthermore, the competitive aspect of Joe Robert's tale telling becomes quite clear when the renowned storyteller Uncle Zeno visits the family, and Joe Robert feels that his very existence is called into question.

Considering the degree to which in Appalachia an "inscrutable taciturnity is locally regarded as a virtue having something to do with valor and manliness,"[73] such a premium on silence creates serious obstacles for an Appalachian storyteller, and, in its broadest sense, *I Am One of You Forever* involves Jess's struggle to find an appropriate voice to articulate his experience. Reviewers have often acknowledged *One of You* as an initiation story; as such, it describes the paradoxical initiations into the norms of his community and, by doing so, into the independence and emotional isolation of frontier manhood. Although Jess seeks to preserve his family's Appalachian culture by becoming its spokesperson, his very assumption of this role—in which he speaks in the detached voice of the frontier teller of tall tales—perpetuates his isolation from his community.

Like *One of You,* the third Kirkman novel, *Farewell, I'm Bound to Leave You* is very much an initiation story, though initiation not into the isolation of manhood but rather into the adult community defined by his mother, grandmother, and all the other mountain women they visit both literally and in their stories. These stories are told within a domestic space—around the kitchen table, out on the front porch, down in the cellar—and they usually coincide with some shared chore such as peeling apples, stringing beans, or washing dishes. One of the most obvious purposes of these stories is to feminize the young Jess, to expose him to both women's labor and women's stories. Often the subjects of the stories are women who exemplify some quality that the men of their frontier community have exclusively associated with masculinity, such as marksmanship, physical toughness, or shrewdness. In stories with fairy tale titles that clue the listener/reader into the story's moral purpose—such as **"The Figuring Woman," "The Fisherwoman,"** and **"The Feistiest Woman"**—Jess's grandmother and mother seek to deconstruct chauvinistic gender stereotypes and simultaneously promote "feminine" values of nurturing and collectivism versus what they identify as destructive masculine values of the frontier, based upon competition, domination, and exploitation.

"The Child Is Father of the Man": *Brighten the Corner Where You Are* and *Look Back All the Green Valley*

Though Chappell pays tribute to Appalachian women in *Farewell, I'm Bound to Leave You* and in many of the poems in *Midquest,* the figure of the farmer father remains for him the most significant door to his native culture. Whereas that door remains firmly closed in the early novels, in the second and fourth novels of the Kirkman tetralogy Chappell explores the relationship between father and son as a means for Jess Kirkman to reconnect with his homeland. Except for demeanor, Jess's affable father, Joe Robert Kirkman, very closely resembles James Christopher's emotionally abusive father from *It Is Time, Lord.* Each father is a farmer-teacher who abandons a job teaching science at the nearby high school because of his unwillingness to refrain from teaching evolution. Both men are rugged individualists who cultivate a friendship with a local grocery store owner named Virgil Campbell, the hard-drinking epitome of Appalachian independence. In these respects, both fathers closely resemble Chappell's own father. What changes, obviously, is Chappell's attitude toward his father. An oedipal struggle appears in the early work that is absent or at least muted in the Kirkman tetralogy. In these later four novels, the father is a benign, harmless, fun-loving trickster figure, whom the boy idolizes and emulates. For all his adolescent pranks, Joe Robert Kirkman demonstrates an emotional distance from his son, which the adult Jess seeks to close. Whereas James Christopher's father ridicules the son's search for the father found throughout Western literature, from Homer to Joyce, in the Kirkman tetralogy, Jess successfully enacts just such an epic quest.

The first three novels chronicle Jess's maturation from elementary-school age to late adolescence, and in each the adult narrator almost entirely effaces himself. The final novel, *Look Back All the Green Valley,* skips ahead to Jess's middle age, collapsing the distance between Jess the narrator and his dramatic self-characterization. He finds himself returning to the mountains (after living away from them for twenty-one years) to help arrange for his terminally ill mother and his father, who died ten years earlier, to share a final resting place. As he assumes the task of traveling the countryside looking for an appropriate site, Jess ends up tracking down kin and family friends whom he has not seen since childhood. In the process, he retraces his father's old stomping grounds in the still extremely rural Hardison County, searching for the world his father knew. In this attempt to become reconciled to a father from whom he always felt estranged, Jess simultaneously seeks to become reconciled to the mountain culture.

Upon his return home, he meets his sister, Mitzi, who has become successful in the business and politics of Asheville. In contrast to her active life—which he likens to their father's faith in the practical benefits of education—Jess finds that his scholarly work at the university does not lead him into a vital connection with his community. He recalls beginning the composition of a steamy novel based upon departmental gossip, "a tale of intrigue, betrayal, sabotage" that "involved a married chairman of a Romance languages department who was carrying on a weird affair with a junior colleague" (13). After observing that he was not busy "describing telling incidents at all, but paying off ancient grudges and unforgiven slights," he abandons the novel and decides "ruefully but not reluctantly, that Jess Kirkman was not born to write novels. [He] was condemned to poetry. . . . a dreamer: nose in a book, head in the clouds" (13). Jess is presently busy translating Dante's *Divine Comedy* into Appalachian vernacular and finishing, under the pen name Fred Chappell, a book of Appalachian poems called *Earthsleep,* the last in a series of four volumes (that is, *Midquest*). In retreating to poetry and poetry translation, Jess withdraws from his actual community in Greensboro and returns to the purer, more ideal worlds of Dante's medieval Europe and the Appalachian farm of his own boyhood.

Similarly, by imaginatively inhabiting his father in **Brighten the Corner** [**Brighten the Corner Where You Are**], Jess finds an avenue to escape his own tendency to introversion. He manages to live the active life vicariously, to immerse himself—through his father, a teacher in a public high school—in the life of the farming community of Tipton. This strategy of escaping the self is suggested in the text; in his civics class, Joe Robert struggles with the challenge of drawing out some of his shy rural students and happens upon a strategy of role playing that enables his very shyest student, Scotty Vann, miraculously to overcome his stuttering and speak with the authority of Socrates. Joe Robert identifies "the principle of the mask" at work in his student (158), and the reader should recognize the same principle at work in the novel's narrative voice, which involves Jess—as first-person narrator—assuming the consciousness of his father. Except for several instances, Jess effaces himself from the narrative, usually referring to his father neutrally as "Joe Robert" and assuming the detached voice of an omniscient narrator; the reader easily forgets that the novel is actually told in first person. If Jess's role as narrator is kept in mind, however, Jess's personality becomes readily apparent in the character of his father, or at least in his father's voice. Joe Robert's chameleon ability to speak both down-home language around the campfire with a group of old farmers and not only correct but highly cultivated English in the classroom (while operating a dairy farm in the mornings and evenings) is more than heroic; it is not quite believable. Despite Chappell's assertion that his father, J. T. Chappell, actually was multivoiced like his fictional counterpart,[74] the very act of assuming his father's

point of view throughout the novel makes it nearly inconceivable that Jess would not, to a large extent, project his own voice, especially when we consider his powerful desire to connect with his father. This connection is best illustrated by a scene late in the novel when Joe Robert steps into his son's bedroom to find him asleep with a volume of the *Aeneid* by his side, dreaming of his father's heroic deeds, so that the entire narrative can be read as the son's Virgilian dream of his father. The point of view is, in fact, even a little more complicated: the adult Jess imagines his father thinking of his son lying in bed thinking of him (201-2), a point of view that approximates a hall of mirrors, so that ultimately the father's and son's consciousnesses merge into one, which is exactly Jess's purpose in telling the story about his dead father. The entire action of the novel occurs during this one day in which the dreaming boy imaginatively follows his father to work at Tipton High School. Indeed, it is *the* pivotal day of Joe Robert's career as an educator; he has been called upon by the school board to address the concerns of certain parents who have questioned his teaching of evolution in his science class. By imaginatively reconstructing that single day from the past, Jess (the adult classical scholar and poet) not only observes the classical unities but combines elements from Virgil's *Aeneid* and *Eclogues* in order to idealize his father as a hero of classical proportions.

Joe Robert serves Jess as an apt conduit to the Appalachian culture because, like Jess, he, too, is something of an outsider and so acts out the drama of struggling to integrate himself into the culture, a struggle Jess would himself find impossible. Having grown up not in the mountains but in the middle eastern part of the state (like Andrew Harper of **The Gaudy Place**), Joe Robert is capable of observing the mountain folk with some degree of detachment, which allows him more fully to idealize and seek to emulate them, while nevertheless finding it necessary to bring to them an alien perspective and thereby disrupt their homogenous world. As a science teacher and a believer in the Enlightenment philosophy of progress through "the advancement of knowledge" and through "education and biological and cultural evolution," Joe Robert is often opposed by the more conventionally religious members of his community, whom he refers to as "our local medievals" (**Look Back,** 26). Jess is one step further removed from them, finding his father's Victorian optimism "quaint and outdated" (26), though Jess frequently yearns for his father's innocent faith in progress.

Of all of Chappell's novels, **Brighten the Corner** confronts the issue of cultural change most relentlessly and with the most explicitly universal ramifications. Joe Robert may be an optimist, but he is not a blind one. Early in the novel he confronts the question of whether the Promethean gift of knowledge will lead to mankind's enlightenment or its demise. More specifically, he questions the uncertain results of his own mission to bring scientific enlightenment to his corner of the world, which has for generations lived according to traditional folkways and beliefs. When the parents of one of his former students visit the school to tell him that their son has recently committed suicide, Joe Robert is forced to consider the influence of his classroom discussions on the boy's decision. Lewis Dorson had recently returned from World War II decorated but physically and psychologically damaged, alienated from his rural family; after a brief visit, Lewis left for Detroit, where he took his own life. Lewis's father, Pruitt, who claims that for generations his family had read only the Bible, blames Lewis's death on his education. Although the mother explains that Pruitt's reaction is only temporary, Joe Robert is left to ponder the connection between science and the world-shattering technologies derived therefrom. If he'd been "a praying man," reflects Joe Robert, he "would have prayed that Pruitt Dorson was wrong, that it wasn't the lessons and the books and the teachers that had brought this century to nothing but disaster. But how could you be sure? Every time you looked anywhere, there was the schoolhouse smack in the middle of it with its fool ideas and its silly hopes. Maybe it was not the cure but the disease, maybe it would have been better always to let well enough alone" (**Brighten,** 66). The rest of the novel involves a series of dialectics, which, in one form or another, engage this question of enlightenment—thus, informing the novel's title. As in Virgil's eclogues, which feature shepherds who engage each other in a variety of philosophical topics, **Brighten the Corner Where You Are** takes the shape of a series of debates through which Joe Robert, as philosopher in shepherd's disguise, seeks to define his relation to his world—in his case as an apostle of Enlightenment idealism in this rural backwater.

Joe Robert's function as philosopher-shepherd is underscored by the fact that he spends the entire novel literally in the guise of a yeoman farmer. Early in the novel, after saving a drowning girl from Trivett Creek on his way to teach school, Joe Robert stops by his friend Virgil Campbell's Bound for Hell Gro. & Dry Goods and, after getting the girl dry and warm, exchanges his own wet suit for the only clothes Virgil's store carries, a pair of overalls and "a pair of new brogans of the cornball old-fashioned sort" (45). He wears this farmer outfit while teaching school, which helps to provide a comic contrast between his erudition and his good-ol'-boy posturing.

Joe Robert's characterization as an incorrigible paramour further aligns him with the shepherds of classical pastoral, who wile away their days fashioning not only philosophical speculations on the nature of life but also, more frequently, plaintive ballads for the nymphs they are wooing. *I Am One of You Forever* begins with his construction of an elaborate bridge that will lead his wife, Cora, into a pastoral garden, in which he no doubt imagines a variety of amorous possibilities. In **Midquest, Farewell,** and **Look Back,** we hear three different versions of the family legend regarding his unorthodox courtship of Cora: how, while they were both teachers at Tipton High School, he attempted to duplicate for his general science class Ben Franklin's famous electricity experiment by fashioning a kite out of Cora's red silk slip and then flying it outside her classroom window. Throughout **Brighten the Corner,** Joe Robert comically pretends a serious flirtation with one of his female students, Janie Forbes. In **Look Back,** Jess finds a map of Hardison County that he at first suspects to be a record of his father's amorous adventures across the rural countryside, only later realizing the absurdity of such a notion. While Jess frequently depicts his father as playfully amorous, Joe Robert's flirtations take the form of an adolescent boy's mischief rather than genuine erotic passion. Nevertheless, this constant posturing, like that of the shepherds from classical pastoral, aligns Joe Robert with the generative processes of nature and thereby connects Jess with these same processes and draws him out of the spiritual stasis to which he has succumbed while living in the city.

As in Virgil, Joe Robert's amorous adventures concretely locate him within the pastoral milieu, balancing the more serious philosophical and social issues he engages. Whether discussing race relations with Tipton High School's elderly black custodian, arguing for scientific skepticism with his general science class, or defending his right to teach evolution before the inquisition of "Socrates," Joe Robert addresses the possibility of effecting positive changes in society. In **Look Back,** Jess calls his father "your classic folklore trickster" (26), and, like most trickster figures, Joe Robert is an agent of unpredictable change. From the opening chapter of **Brighten the Corner** in which Joe Robert steals the moon from the sky and holds it captive in a milk can, this "wizard" appears as a threat to the natural order. His entrance into the community disrupts the present order but thereby makes the creation of a new order possible. Whether that new order is preferable to the old is in this case, as in most, a matter of debate. The inevitability of change from a simpler to a more complex state has always been central to pastoral. Kermode notes that, during the Renaissance, pastoral flourished in part as a response to the discovery of the New World and its inhabitants, who were "living in a state of nature, unaffected by Art, and outside the scope of Grace" (40). Western society divided into two positions regarding those New World natives: those who recognized the duty of civilizing them and bringing them into "the scope of Grace" extended by the Christian church and those such as Montaigne, who saw them as "virtuous because unspoilt."[75] In bringing modern science into the Appalachian hinterlands, Joe Robert confronts just such a dilemma, one that by the end of **Brighten the Corner** he is unable to resolve completely.

The novel ends with Joe Robert's dream—inspired by the school board's debate about allowing him to teach Darwin in the schools. In his dream Darwin is brought up to a scaffold in a back lot of the high school and Joe Robert is called upon to defend him. He begins eloquently defending the theories of evolution and cultural progress but ends by expressing repressed doubts: "We began as innocent germs and added to our original nature cunning, deceit, self-loathing, treachery, betrayal, murder, and blasphemy. We began lowly and have fallen from even that humble estate" (211). Despite his belief in the doctrine of modern science, Joe Robert is a reluctant missionary. His respect for—and idealization of—the yeoman independence of his community gives him pause, even though his pursuit of science derives from the same instinct for independence that he observes in the most rugged mountaineers. Before teaching school, he worked for Carolina Power and Light stringing electrical lines across the remotest mountains, bringing light into the darkness. Joe Robert views his role as an educator in the same terms: he is a Promethean liberator from the darkness of superstition. While religion subjugates the individual to the authority of the church—an authority outside the self—Joe Robert embraces the Enlightenment values of human perfectibility and promotes the scientific attitude because he believes that it locates authority for truth within the individual. Thus, he believes that by following science rather than religion the essential yeoman spirit of Appalachian independence will best flourish.

If in **The Gaudy Place** the image of Ben Franklin is borrowed for the sake of undercutting the myth of the self-made man, in **Brighten the Corner** Joe Robert is associated with a positive image of Franklin as scientist and Renaissance man. Whereas in his characterization of Uncle Zeb, the corrupt Asheville politician, Chappell shows how the yeoman spirit is degraded by society, politics, and money, in Joe Robert, Chappell offers the pure ideal of the public man, one whose private nature has not been compromised by his public role. Whereas Uncle Zeb seeks to impose a social hierarchy that will subjugate the masses to a position of relative powerlessness, Joe Robert consistently champions the individual liberty and egalitarianism at the heart of the yeoman ideal. By defending his right to teach Darwin's theory, of evolution in his general science class, he promotes independent thought and expression. In his brief role as high school principal, he similarly seeks to dismantle social hierarchy among the faculty; he combats their tendency to be "too concerned with personal status among equal colleagues" by inventing "the Ungodly Terror, a mysterious and utterly rotten kid, a student who was a danger to them all" (51). To convince his faculty that the threat is real, he spends a significant part of his time as principal exploding firecrackers in lockers, painting doorknobs with kerosene, filling teachers' desk drawers with wet oatmeal, and virtually every other "naughty schoolboy fantasy he could remember. / It must have been for him the Earthly Paradise" (52). Joe Robert plays the trickster to bring about a siege mentality and thereby foster an egalitarian community spirit among his faculty.

At home on the farm he embraces the same defiance of authority—in the form of his mother-in-law—by pulling an ongoing string of pranks, or "rusties." Whenever he dons his working clothes to milk the cows, he imagines that he is wearing his "Peasant Costume" and says, "Every time I get into these duds . . . it makes me want to overthrow the Czar" (**Brighten,** 31). This Romantic antagonism to authority finds a very real outlet in Joe Robert's opposition to tenancy, a system that presses landless farmers into a feudal dependency. Joe Robert is fully aware that tenancy is a system that perpetuates itself, for a lack of economic independence often leads to a lack of spiritual independence that keeps the tenant "poor forever" and that "breaks his pride. Turns him mean sometimes" (103-4). Unfortunately, Joe Robert is pressed by financial necessity into hiring the tenant, Hob Farnum, whose Dickensian characterization suggests deprivation and perversion of nature. Hob is "a short man, slightly hunchbacked . . . filled with an angry narrow energy" (104). By creating the loss of economic and social independence, tenancy degrades the sharecropper's connection to nature and even potentially reduces the spiritual act of farming to the materialistic function of production, not unlike the mill jobs so many sharecroppers found preferable to tenancy.

As opposed to the "angry, narrow energy" of his tenant, Joe Robert finds his own life so rewarding because he is capable of channeling his energies into such a broad scope of freely chosen activities. He has worked as a farmer, schoolteacher, school principal, lineman for Carolina Power & Light, and, in his off time, a tinkerer. As a self-proclaimed jack-of-all-trades, Joe Robert approximates the whole man whose disappearance from any specialized society Emerson laments in "The American Scholar." Emerson examines an ancient creation story in which the gods "divided Man into men" so that Man "might be more helpful to himself"—an act that nevertheless left the disassociated men longing for the original wholeness. In an ideal state, Emerson finds that "Man is not a farmer, or a professor, or an engineer, but he is all. Man is priest, and scholar, and statesman, and producer, and soldier."[76] The yeoman farmer, out of necessity a generalist, comes as close to fulfilling Emerson's ideal of the whole man as any profession—except that of the poet, whom Emerson identifies as "representative. He stands among partial men for the complete man."[77] Echoing Emerson, in the preface to *Midquest* Chappell explicitly identifies his task to be one of writing the "widely representative" experience. Throughout *Midquest* and the Jess Kirkman novels, Chappell strives to capture the wholeness of life, for which the farming community serves as an apt model. By making Joe Robert a generalist, someone with a wide range of vocational interests and diverse friendships, Jess (and Chappell) solves the dilemma that faces him as a poet who earns his living in the "ivory tower" of the university. Separated even from his immediate colleagues by his academic specialty, Jess recovers a sense of wholeness through his idealization of the self-reliant yeoman farmer.

In *Look Back All the Green Valley,* Jess similarly makes use of Joe Robert's avocation of tinkerer to gain for himself proper orientation as a poet. As he seeks a final resting place for his parents, Jess stumbles across a secret workshop his father had kept in the basement of an antique clock store. In his readings of the notes and journals he discovers there, Jess reconstructs his father's identity as a self-educated scientist: a botanist, engineer, and natural philosopher. Among the records of his father's intellectual life, Jess finds a hand-drawn, cryptic map of Hardison County, which Jess finally discovers to be a key to his father's horticulture experiments; Joe Robert has planted diverse cultivars of roses all across the rural county, partly in an effort to determine the effect of environment on growth. Jess finds his father's diagram for a mechanism that would enact revenge on an engineer at the Challenger Paper and Fiber Company, whom Joe Robert holds personally responsible for the factory's egregious pollution. Jess also finds a collection of epigrammatic meditations on time entitled "The Thoughts of Fugio"; adolescent fantasies of space travel; and Joe Robert's theories for a "Floriloge," an

ideal timepiece that would be "organic" rather than mechanical, a clock that would be a "living thing, connected with the cosmos" (78).

These various artifacts point Jess toward the discovery of his father's private life of the imagination, and this inner journey coincides with Jess's search for traces of his father upon the landscape of Hardison County. The two ultimately converge, in a Dante-esque vision of paradise, in the pristine region of True-love, where Jess witnesses a flourishing yellow rose that his father had planted years before. His father's interest in horticulture and his pseudo-scientific design of the Floriloge coalesce with Jess's immersion in the task of translating *The Divine Comedy* into Appalachian vernacular, signifying their common idealization of unspoiled Appalachia as a fitting image of the golden age, a place and time where life is unified and "connected with the cosmos." Jess's ability to recognize the spiritual affinity between his own profession as a poet and his father's interest in science and agriculture becomes a final means of reconciliation, a reconciliation he has sorely needed, considering his father's silence on the subject of Jess's profession and Jess's mother's clear denunciation. According to Cora, "*Poetry* explained [his] wayward and drifting existence. . . . It was the vice that had brought [him] low and made [him] crazy" (175). It is not surprising that she had a similar reaction to her husband's excessive absorption in his "projects." In his short fiction, Chappell has explored the lives of a variety of historical scientists, including William Herschel, Carl Linnaeus, and Benjamin Franklin. As in these stories, Joe Robert the tinkerer/scientist is interested in *seeing* the world accurately. *Seeing* accurately requires a right relation to the universe, which Chappell, like Virgil, finds equally necessary for the farmer and the poet.

As Fred Hobson observes in his treatment of *I Am One of You Forever,* Chappell's attempt to become utterly one with his native Appalachian culture forces him ultimately to recognize the impossibility of doing so, to recognize—and celebrate—the importance of the individual imagination in the process of cultural recovery. In fact, the individual imagination is still as distinct and separate from the concrete world it observes in Chappell's pastorals as in his earlier dramas of alienation. Indeed, extravagant products of the imagination proliferate throughout the octave of *Midquest* and the Jess Kirkman novels. Even after adopting a classical aesthetic, Chappell is no less of an "experimental" writer than when he worked from a darkly Romantic sensibility. What has profoundly changed is the orientation of the imagination—from an inward to an outward gaze—as well as an affirmation that the efforts of the imagination can be a collaborative effort, one that balances the *independent* perspective with involvement in an *interdependent* community for the production of meaning. By using the father—who is farmer, teacher, scientist—as a means to access the world of Appalachia, Chappell manages to reimagine that insular world and to transform it from a hill-ringed prison into Arcadia. As the entire octave comes to a conclusion, Jess tells his wife, "You know, I am the son who went searching for his father, just like the characters do in all those important well-received literary novels. But I didn't find a man. I found a boy" (**Look Back,** 271). Jess's words suggest both his father's perpetual adolescence and that, in finding his father, Jess has reclaimed the wholeness of his own Appalachian boyhood.

Notes

1. George Hovis, "An Interview with Fred Chappell," *Carolina Quarterly* 52.1 (Fall/Winter 1999): 72.

2. Ronald Eller, *Miners, Millhands, and Mountaineers: Industrialization of the Appalachian South, 1880-1930* (Knoxville: University of Tennessee Press, 1982), 99-111.

3. Ibid., 108.

4. Carl Alwin Schenck, *The Birth of Forestry in America: Biltmore Forest School, 1898-1913* (Santa Cruz, Calif.: Forest History Society, 1974), 148.

5. Eller, *Miners,* 109.

6. Ibid., xix-xx.

7. See Paul Salstrom, *Appalachia's Path to Dependency: Rethinking a Region's Economic History, 1730-1940* (Lexington: University Press of Kentucky, 1994), xx-xxi.

8. Lucinda Hardwick MacKethan, *The Dream of Arcady: Place and Time in Southern Literature* (Baton Rouge: Louisiana State University Press, 1980), 16.

9. George Garrett, foreword to *Dream Garden: The Poetic Vision of Fred Chappell,* ed. Patrick Baser (Baton Rouge: Louisiana State University Press, 1997), xiii.

10. Ibid., xiv.

11. Lee Smith, critical blurb, dust jacket to Fred Chappell, *I Am One of You Forever* (Baton Rouge: Louisiana State University Press, 1985).

12. Michael McFee, "The Epigrammatical Fred Chappell," *Southern Literary Journal* 31.2 (1999): 96.

13. Eller, *Miners,* 25-26.

14. Ibid., 28-29.

15. Hovis, "Interview," 71.

16. Fred Chappell, "A Pact With Faustus," *Mississippi Quarterly* 37 (1984). Rpt. in *The Fred Chappell Reader,* ed. Dabney Stuart (New York: St. Martin's, 1987), 481.

17. Chappell, *Plow Naked,* 20.

18. Ibid., 14.

19. Ibid., 6.

20. Chappell, "Pact," 480.

21. Chappell, "Pact," 481.

22. Ibid., 481.

23. Chappell, *Plow Naked,* 12.

24. Ibid., 9.

25. Letter to the author, March 22, 2002.

26. Fred Chappell, *The Gaudy Place* (New York: Harcourt Brace, 1973), 65. Further references noted parenthetically are to this edition.

27. Hovis, "Interview," 75.

28. Chappell acknowledges the important influence of Faulkner and Camus on his first novel in "An Interview with Fred Chappell" (Hovis, 71). Also, in "A Pact With Faustus" he lists *The Sound and The Fury* among the five novels he has most often read, the others being *Doctor Faustus, Don Quixote, Adventures of Huckleberry Finn,* and *The Sun Also Rises* (479).

29. Fred Chappell, *It Is Time, Lord* (New York: Atheneum, 1963), 34-35. Further references noted parenthetically are to this edition.

30. Fred Chappell, *Look Back All the Green Valley* (New York: Picador, 1999), 183. Further references noted parenthetically are to this edition.

31. Hovis, "Interview," 71.

32. Fred Chappell, *Dagon,* in *The Fred Chappell Reader,* 53. Further references noted parenthetically are to this edition.

33. While I do not discuss *The Inkling* here, it very much fits the pattern found in both *It Is Time, Lord* and *Dagon.* The boy protagonist, Jan, and his sister, Timmie, both spiral into states of increasing dementia, which their dysfunctional home life only serves to exacerbate. David Paul Ragan notes that the relationship between Jan and Timmie "almost seems an extension of the childhood relationship between James Christopher and his sister" in *It Is Time, Lord,* and that "the relationship between Laura and Jan at the end of *The Inkling* seems to prefigure the relationship between Peter Leland and Mina" in *Dagon.* David Paul Ragan, "Flying by Night: An Early Interview with Fred Chappell," *North Carolina Literary Review* 7 (1998): 111.

34. In an early interview, Chappell actually used Poe's language in describing his own goal to write novels that were capable of being read in "one sitting." See John Sopko and John Carr, "Dealing with the

Grotesque: Fred Chappell," in *Kite Flying and Other Irrational Acts: Conversations with Twelve Southern Writers,* ed. John Carr (Baton Rouge: Louisiana State University Press, 1972), 225.

35. W. H. Auden, introduction to *Edgar Allan Poe: Selected Prose, Poetry, and Eureka,* ed. W. H. Auden (New York: Hold, Rinehart, 1950), vi.

36. Hovis, "Interview," 71.

37. David Paul Ragan, "Fred Chappell (1936-)," in *Contemporary Poets, Dramatists, Essayists, and Novelists of the South: A Bio-Bibliographical Sourcebook,* eds. Robert Bain and Joseph M. Flora (Westport, Conn.: Greenwood, 1994), 93.

38. Fred Chappell, personal interview, September 12, 1999. Chapel Hill, N.C. Note that each of the other citations of this interview refer to the version published in the *Carolina Quarterly* 52.1.

39. Frank Kermode, *English Pastoral Poetry: From the Beginnings to Marvell* (New York: Barnes and Noble, 1952), 15.

40. Wilma Dunaway, *The First American Frontier: Transition to Capitalism in Southern Appalachia, 1700-1860* (Chapel Hill: University of North Carolina Press, 1996).

41. Salstrom, *Appalachia's Path,* xxiii.

42. See, for example, Dunaway's *The First American Frontier.*

43. Eller, *Miners,* 9-12.

44. Salstrom, *Appalachia's Path,* xv.

45. Dunaway, *Slavery,* 25.

46. Ibid., 32.

47. Ibid., 34-35.

48. Ibid., 35.

49. Ibid., 37-38.

50. Salstrom, *Appalachia's Path,* xiii-xxiii.

51. Chappell, *Plow Naked,* 73.

52. Ibid., 73.

53. Kermode, *English Pastoral Poetry,* 15.

54. Ibid., 14.

55. Chappell, "Pact," 489.

56. Kermode, *English Pastoral Poetry,* 15.

57. While a student at Duke, Chappell was heavily influenced by Eliot and labored upon a "longish, heavily Eliotic" poem through as many as forty drafts. See Chappell, *Plow Naked,* 23.

58. T. S. Eliot, *The Waste Land and Other Poems* (New York: Harvest, 1934), 42.

59. Kermode, *English Pastoral Poetry,* 43.

60. J. E. Congleton, *Theories of Pastoral Poetry in England, 1684-1798* (Gainesville: University of Florida Press, 1952), 4.

61. Quoted in Kenneth S. Lynn, *Mark Twain and Southwestern Humor* (Westport, Conn.: Greenwood, 1972), 27.

62. Houston A. Baker, Jr., *Modernism and the Harlem Renaissance* (Chicago: University of Chicago Press, 1987).

63. MacKethan, *Dream of Arcady,* 6.

64. Chappell, *Plow Naked,* 76.

65. Ibid., 77.

66. Hovis, "Interview," 78.

67. Fred Chappell, *I Am One of You Forever* (Baton Rouge: Louisiana State University Press, 1985), 51. Further references noted parenthetically are to this edition.

68. Carol Mitchell, "Some Differences in Male and Female Joke-Telling," in *Women's Folklore, Women's Culture* (Philadelphia: University of Pennsylvania Press, 1985), 167.

69. Ibid., 169-70.

70. Ibid., 170.

71. Ibid., 169.

72. Hovis, "Interview," 71.

73. Fred Chappell, *Look Back All the Green Valley* (New York: Picador, 1999), 183. Further references noted parenthetically are to this edition.

74. Fred Chappell, letter to the author, March 4, 2000.

75. Kermode, *English Pastoral Poetry,* 40.

76. Ralph Waldo Emerson, "The American Scholar," in *Selected Writings of Emerson,* ed. Donald McQuade (New York: Modern Library, 1981), 46.

77. Ralph Waldo Emerson, "The Poet," in *Selected Writings of Emerson,* ed. Donald McQuade (New York: Modern Library, 1981), 304.

Bibliography

Auden, W. H. Introduction. *Edgar Allan Poe: Selected Prose, Poetry, and Eureka.* Ed. W. H. Auden. New York: Hold, Rinehart, 1950.

Baker, Houston A., Jr. *Modernism and the Harlem Renaissance.* 1987. Chicago: University of Chicago Press, 1989.

Chappell, Fred. *Brighten the Corner Where You Are.* New York: St. Martin's, 1989.

————. *Dagon.* 1968. *The Fred Chappell Reader.* Ed. Dabney Stuart. New York: St. Martin's, 1987. 47-163.

————. *Farewell, I'm Bound to Leave You.* New York: Picador, 1996.

————. *The Gaudy Place.* New York: Harcourt Brace, 1973.

————. *I Am One of You Forever.* Baton Rouge: Louisiana State University Press, 1985.

————. *It Is Time, Lord.* New York: Atheneum, 1963.

————. *Look Back All the Green Valley.* New York: Picador, 1999.

————. *Midquest: A Poem.* Baton Rouge: Louisiana State University Press, 1981.

————. *Moments of Light.* Los Angeles: New South, 1980.

————. *More Shapes Than One.* New York: St. Martin's, 1991.

————. "A Pact with Faustus." *Mississippi Quarterly* 37 (1984). Rpt. in *The Fred Chappell Reader.* Ed. Dabney Stuart. New York: St. Martin's, 1987.

————. *Plow Naked: Selected Writings on Poetry.* Ann Arbor: University of Michigan Press, 1993.

————. *"The Surface of Earth."* Review of *The Surface of Earth,* by Reynolds Price. *Duke Alumni Register* 62.1 (October 1975): 6.

Congleton, J. E. *Theories of Pastoral Poetry in England, 1684-1798.* Gainesville: University of Florida Press, 1952.

Dunaway, Wilma A. *The First American Frontier: Transition to Capitalism in Southern Appalachia, 1700-1860.* Chapel Hill: University of North Carolina Press, 1996.

————. *Slavery in the American Mountain South.* Cambridge: Cambridge University Press, 2003.

Eliot, T. S. *The Waste Land and Other Poems.* New York: Harvest, 1934.

Eller, Ronald D. *Miners, Millhands, and Mountaineers: Industrialization of the Appalachian South, 1880-1930.* Knoxville: University of Tennessee Press, 1982.

Emerson, Ralph Waldo. *Selected Writings of Emerson.* Ed. Donald McQuade. New York: Modern Library, 1981.

Garrett, George. Foreword. *Dream Garden.* Ed. Patrick Bizzaro. Baton Rouge: Louisiana State University Press, 1997. xiii-xv.

Hovis, George. "Assuming the Mantle of Storyteller: Fred Chappell and Frontier Humor." *The Enduring Legacy of Old Southwest Humor.* Ed. Ed Piacentino. Baton Rouge: Louisiana State University Press, 2006. 156-73.

————. "Darker Vices and Nearly Incomprehensible Sins: The Fate of Poe in Fred Chappell's Early Novels." *More Lights than One: On The Fiction of Fred Chappell.* Ed. Patrick Bizzaro. Louisiana State University Press, 2004. 28-50.

————. "'I Contain Multitudes': Randall Kenan's *Walking on Water* as Collective Autobiography." *Southern Literary Journal* 36.2 (Spring 2004): 100-125.

————. "Industry Meets Agriculture: The Emergence of the Farmer/Peddler in the Carolina Piedmont." *North Carolina Folklore Journal* 41.1 (1994): 24-34.

————. "An Interview with Fred Chappell." *Carolina Quarterly* 52.1 (Fall/Winter 1999): 67-79.

————. "The Legacy of Thomas Wolfe in Contemporary North Carolina Fiction." *Thomas Wolfe Review* 29.1 and 2 (2005): 76-90.

————. "The *Raney* Controversy: Clyde Edgerton's Battle with Campbell University over Creative Freedom." *Southern Cultures* (Summer 2001): 60-83.

————. "'When You Got True Dirt, You Got Everything You Need': Forging an Appalachian Arcadia in Fred Chappell's *Midquest.*" *Mississippi Quarterly* 53.3 (Summer 2000): 389-414.

Hovis, George, and Timothy Williams. "Old Times on the Haw: An Interview with Dale Ray Phillips." *Carolina Quarterly* 55.3 (Summer 2003): 63-73.

Kermode, Frank. *English Pastoral Poetry: From the Beginnings to Marvell.* New York: Barnes & Noble, 1952.

Lang, John. "Points of Kinship: Community and Allusion in Fred Chappell's *Midquest.*" *Dream Garden.* Ed. Patrick Bizzaro. Baton Rouge: Louisiana State University Press, 1997. 97-117.

————. *Understanding Fred Chappell.* Columbia: University of South Carolina Press, 2000.

————. "Windies and Rusties: Fred Chappell as Humorist." *More Lights than One: The Fiction of Fred Chappell.* Ed., Patrick Bizzaro. Baton Rouge: Louisiana State University Press, 2004.

Lefler, Hugh Talmage. *North Carolina Told by Contemporaries.* Chapel Hill: University of North Carolina Press, 1965.

Lynn, Kenneth S. *Mark Twain and Southwestern Humor.* Westport, Conn.: Greenwood, 1972.

MacKethan, Lucinda Hardwick. *The Dream of Arcady: Place and Time in Southern Literature.* Baton Rouge: Louisiana State University Press, 1980.

McFee, Michael. "The Epigrammatical Fred Chappell." *Southern Literary Journal* 31.2 (1999): 95-108.

———. Introduction. *This Is Where We Live: Short Stories by 25 Contemporary North Carolina Writers.* Ed. Michael McFee. Chapel Hill: University of North Carolina Press, 2000.

Mitchell, Carol. "Some Differences in Male and Female Joke-Telling." In *Women's Folklore, Women's Culture.* Eds. Rosan A. Jordan and Susan J. Kalcik. Philadelphia: University of Pennsylvania Press, 1985. 163-86.

Ragan, David Paul. "Flying by Night: An Early Interview with Fred Chappell" *North Carolina Literary Review* 7 (1998): 111.

———. "Fred Chappell (1936-)." *Contemporary Poets, Dramatists, Essayists, and Novelists of the South: A Bio-Bibliographical Sourcebook,* eds. Robert Bain and Joseph M. Flora (Westport, Conn.: Greenwood, 1994). 91-103.

Salstrom, Paul. *Appalachia's Path to Dependency: Rethinking a Region's Economic History, 1730-1940.* Lexington: University Press of Kentucky, 1994.

Schenck, Carl Alwin. *The Birth of Forestry in America: Biltmore Forest School, 1898-1913.* Santa Cruz, Calif.: Forest History Society, 1974.

Sopko, John, and John Carr. "Dealing with the Grotesque: Fred Chappell." In *Kite Flying and Other Irrational Acts: Conversations with Twelve Southern Writers.* Ed. John Carr. Baton Rouge: Louisiana State University Press, 1972.

Stuart, Dabney. Introduction. *The Fred Chappell Reader.* Ed. Dabney Stuart. New York: St. Martin's, 1987.

FURTHER READING

Criticism

Clabough, Casey Howard. "Will, Appetite, Alchemy, Faulkner, and Two French Poets: *The Inkling.*" In *Experimentation and Versatility: The Early Novels and Short Fiction of Fred Chappell,* pp. 32-48. Macon, Ga.: Mercer University Press, 2005.
    Analysis of Chappell's early novel *The Inkling.*

———. "'Great' Men and 'Weird' Events: Historical and Fantastic Narratives." In *Experimentation and Versatility: The Early Novels and Short Fiction of Fred Chappell,* pp. 122-44. Macon, Ga.: Mercer University Press, 2005.
    Considers the portion of Chappell's short stories that may be classified as fantasy.

Johnson, Don. "The Cultivated Mind: The Georgic Center of Fred Chappell's Poetry." In *Dream Garden: The Poetic Vision of Fred Chappell,* edited by Patrick Bizzaro, pp. 170-79. Baton Rouge: Louisiana State University Press, 1997.
    Close reading of Chappell's poetry which identifies connections to Virgil's "Georgics."

Additional coverage of Chappell's life and career is contained in the following sources published by Gale: *Contemporary Authors,* Vols. 5-8R, 198; *Contemporary Authors Autobiography Series,* Vol. 4; *Contemporary Authors New Revision Series,* Vols. 8, 33, 67, 110; *Contemporary Literary Criticism,* Vols. 40, 78, 162; *Contemporary Novelists,* Ed. 6; *Contemporary Poets,* Eds. 6, 7; *Contemporary Southern Writers; Dictionary of Literary Biography,* Vols. 6, 105; *Literature Resource Center;* **and** *St. James Guide to Horror, Ghost & Gothic Writers.*

Michael Connelly
1956-

American novelist and essayist.

The following entry presents an overview of Connelly's career through 2009.

INTRODUCTION

Connelly is a crime-fiction writer known for detailed procedural descriptions, complex plots, and multifaceted characters. He maintains a prolific output, averaging one novel per year since his debut, *The Black Echo* (1992), and many of his stories feature the popular character Hieronymus (Harry) Bosch, a hardboiled Los Angeles detective. Connelly has received every major award given in his field.

BIOGRAPHICAL INFORMATION

Connelly was born July 21, 1956, in Philadelphia, Pennsylvania. Both of his parents encouraged success in their children, and Connelly's mother introduced him to the crime-fiction genre. When he was eleven, the family moved to Fort Lauderdale, Florida, and at age sixteen, he saw a suspicious-looking man throw away an object which proved to be a murder weapon. Connelly reported the incident to the police, who investigated and interviewed him extensively, and he has remarked that the experience of being immersed in their world for that short time was formative for him. In 1980, he completed a bachelor's degree in journalism at the University of Florida at Gainesville, minoring in creative writing and studying under the tutelage of author Harry Crews. After graduation he worked the crime beat for several South Florida newspapers and later the *Los Angeles Times,* all the while gathering background for his planned career as a crime novelist—a strategy eventually declared successful by both critics and readers. In 1993, he left journalism to concentrate on fiction-writing, a move he later said was not without some reluctance despite his growing success as a novelist. Connelly's books have been lauded from the beginning: *The Black Echo,* his debut title and the first to feature Harry Bosch, earned the Edgar Award for Best First Novel from the Mystery Writers of America, and since then Connelly has been included in the *Los Angeles Times* Best Books of the Year list at least four times and has received numerous awards, including the Anthony Award for best mystery novel (1997, 1999, 2003, and 2009), Audie Award for best mystery audio book (2004 and 2007), Barry Award for best novel from *Deadly Pleasures Mystery Magazine* (1998 and 2003), Carvalho Prize for detective fiction (2009), Dilys Award from the Independent Mystery Booksellers Association (1996 and 1997), and the Grand Prix de Littérature Policière for best international crime novel (1999). In addition, he has won the *Los Angeles Times* Best Mystery/Thriller Award (2006), Macavity Award for best mystery novel from Mystery Readers International (1999 and 2006), Falcon Award from the Maltese Falcon Society for best hardboiled novel published in Japan (1995 and 2006), Nero Award for excellence in the mystery genre (1997), Premio Bancarella Award for literature (2000), and Shamus Award from the Private Eye Writers of America (2006). He served as president of Mystery Writers of America from 2003 to 2004. Connelly lives in Florida with his wife, Linda, and their daughter, Callie.

MAJOR WORKS

The fictional Detective Harry Bosch is the linchpin of Connelly's mystery-writing career. Bosch, named after the painter Hieronymus Bosch who produced gruesome visions of Heaven and Hell, is the protagonist of Connelly's first four novels and most of the rest, sometimes sharing the spotlight with other recurring Connelly characters such as investigator and former FBI agent Terry McCaleb and attorney Mickey Haller, Bosch's half-brother. Over the span of sixteen novels to date, Bosch progresses from Los Angeles Police Department detective to private investigator and back, all the while maintaining both a mistrust of and a love for the justice system that weaves a strand of tension through each story. Bosch's assignment to various divisions of the LAPD plus his independent P.I. work have provided ample fodder for Connelly to create mysteries and settings in which to place them.

Connelly's career received a boost in 1994 when then-President Bill Clinton was photographed carrying a copy of his third novel, *The Concrete Blonde* (1994). This novel places Bosch on trial for having killed a suspected serial killer when the suspect was reaching for a toupee rather than for the presumed pistol. Bosch feels the man he killed was really the serial killer, but the female district attorney goes after him, seeing police brutality in the case. While Bosch is on trial, new murder victims crop up, bearing the *modus operandi* of the psychopath Bosch supposedly put out of action. *Blood Work* (1998), Connelly's first Terry McCaleb novel, took the author's sales to new heights. In this novel, the story centers on retired FBI agent McCaleb, who had specialized in tracking down Los Angeles-area serial killers. Suffering from cardiac problems, McCaleb has endured an agonizing two-year wait before finally receiving a heart transplant. McCaleb is under doctor's orders to avoid stress, particularly the anxiety-laden investigations that precipitated his heart problems. This work was adapted into a film starring Clint Eastwood in 2002; the film's plot differs significantly from that of the novel. The eleventh Harry Bosch novel, *The Closers* (2005), debuted at number one on the *New York Times* best-seller list, setting yet another new precedent for the author's success. This work features Bosch returning to the LAPD, after having resigned from the police force at the conclusion of *City of Bones* (2002). The title of *The Closers* refers to a group within the force consisting of officers who are assigned to investigate cold cases and resolve them. Bosch and his partner begin to search for information that might help them solve a kidnapping and murder that took place seventeen years ago. The victim was a mixed-race teenage girl. Newly uncovered DNA evidence points them toward several leads, including a white supremacist, as the novel examines racial issues as well as crime-solving, with Bosch wondering if racial bias on the part of police interfered with the original investigation. In *Nine Dragons* (2009), Harry is forced to travel to Hong Kong, now the home of his ex-wife, Eleanor, and his daughter, Maddie. While Harry investigates a case in L.A. Maddie is apparently kidnapped by members of a Chinese Triad gang, and Bosch, believing her disappearance is tied to his case, travels overseas to rescue her. Connelly's books continue to sell well, with each publishing to heavy reader anticipation and critical attention and spawning speculation about possible future screenplays.

CRITICAL RECEPTION

Connelly's depiction of Los Angeles has been compared to that of Raymond Chandler, with scholars noting that while Chandler clearly yearned for a less gritty, more innocent L.A. of years past, Connelly has embraced the city as it is, honoring its fine points and acknowledging its negative traits. His development of the character Harry Bosch has been described as well-

nuanced and empathic, and some reviewers have declared incredulously that, at a point when many other series would have declined into banal repetition and cheap marketing tricks to retain readers, Connelly continues to produce stories with actual literary worth. A *Publishers Weekly* reviewer of *The Closers* concluded, "Connelly comes as close as anyone to being today's Dostoyevsky of crime literature."

PRINCIPAL WORKS

The Black Echo (novel) 1992
The Black Ice (novel) 1993
The Concrete Blonde (novel) 1994
The Last Coyote (novel) 1995
The Poet (novel) 1996
Trunk Music (novel) 1997
*Blood Work (novel) 1998
Angels Flight (novel) 1999
Void Moon (novel) 2000
A Darkness More than Night (novel) 2001
Chasing the Dime (novel) 2002
City of Bones (novel) 2002
Lost Light (novel) 2003
The Narrows (novel) 2004
The Closers (novel) 2005
The Lincoln Lawyer (novel) 2005
Crime Beat: A Decade of Covering Cops and Killers (essays) 2006
Echo Park (novel) 2006
The Overlook (novel) 2007
The Brass Verdict (novel) 2008
Nine Dragons (novel) 2009
The Scarecrow (novel) 2009
The Reversal (novel) 2010

*This novel was adapted as a film in 2002, directed by and starring Clint Eastwood.

CRITICISM

Judy Quinn (essay date 6 July 1998)

SOURCE: Quinn, Judy. "A Michael Connelly Movie Soon?" *Publishers Weekly* 245, no. 27 (6 July 1998): 16.

[*In the essay below, Quinn comments on the possibility of the development of film adaptations of one or more of Connelly's novels. The film version of* Blood Work *was released in 2002.*]

It's starting to look that way, with still another film deal for thriller writer Michael Connelly. On the basis of just a 37-page proposal, Renaissance agent Joel Gotler, working on behalf of Connelly's agent, Philip G. Spitzer, made a $1-million deal, plus another $500,000 to come at production, with producer Bill Gerber and Warner Bros. for an outright sale of *Void Moon,* a non-Harry Bosch thriller about a female prowler who steals from the wrong person. Connelly is writing the screenplay first and then the novel, which is expected to be part of his current deal with Little, Brown, an amazing (and rare) five-book, world rights deal that has already led the house to sell five books outright to Orion U.K. and begins with this coming fall's title *Angels Flight,* which will once again feature L.A. police detective Bosch. Interestingly, it is Connelly's non-Bosch thrillers that have achieved some of Connelly's biggest jumps in sales, says his editor, Michael Pietsch. First there was the serial-killer thriller *The Poet,* currently under development at HBO, and then *Blood Work,* Connelly's bestseller breakout that jumped him from a previous hardcover net of about 75,000 to more than 200,000. The latter is under development in a seven-figure deal with Warner Bros. Pictures and Clint Eastwood's Malpaso Productions. "I bet you'll see a Connelly movie within the year," predicts Gotler.

Publishers Weekly (review date 17 March 2003)

SOURCE: Review of *Lost Light,* by Michael Connelly. *Publishers Weekly* 250, no. 11 (17 March 2003): 52.

[*In the following review, the critic praises Connelly's ninth Harry Bosch novel,* Lost Light, *concluding that despite its longevity the series remains engaging.*]

Award-winning former crime reporter Connelly (*The Black Echo*; *City of Bones*) hits all the right notes with this latest [*Lost Light*] in his Edgar-winning mystery series featuring sax-playing L.A. detective Harry Bosch. Even though this marks the ninth outing for Harry, the principled, incorruptible investigator shows little sign of slowing in his unrelenting pursuit of justice for all. Disillusioned by his constant battle with police hypocrisy and bureaucracy, Harry quits the department after 28 years on the job. Like so many ex-cops before him, he finds retirement boring: "I was staying up late, staring at the walls and drinking too much red wine." He decides to take advantage of his newly minted private-eye license and get back to work. The case he chooses—one that he had been briefly involved in four years before—is the puzzling unsolved murder of 24-year-old Angella Benton. Angella's death is linked to the theft of $2 million from a film company foolishly employing real cash as a prop on an action movie set. Harry patiently follows the bloody trail from Angella's violated body through the Hollywood heist to the disappearance of an FBI computer expert and the shooting of two LAPD cops. His investigation eventually leads him to the elite terrorist hunters of the new Department of Homeland Security. Few will follow every twist and turn of the labyrinthine plot, but no matter. The fun comes in watching Harry slowly and brilliantly separate the seemingly impossibly knotted strands and then knit them back into whole cloth. This exciting procedural is as good as any in the series, and Connelly's concluding coda has a kicker about Harry's private life that will draw gasps of astonishment from longtime readers. [. . .]

Forecast: All the usual marketing and promotion jams have been kicked out on this one—television, radio and print advertising; transit ads; multi-city author tour; postcards; etc.—which should push it to the top of the lists. Special bonus: fans at Connelly's readings will receive a compilation CD featuring Bosch's favorite jazz tunes.

Christiana Gregoriou (essay date summer 2003)

SOURCE: Gregoriou, Christiana. "Criminally Minded: The Stylistics of Justification in Contemporary American Crime Fiction." *Style* 37, no. 2 (summer 2003): 144.

[*In the following essay, Gregoriou compares the character development approaches of Michael Connelly, Patricia Cornwell, and James Patterson.*]

1. INTRODUCTION

Much has been written about crime fiction, from a range of approaches. While some writers view the genre as mere entertainment, crime fiction has been elsewhere treated seriously. Critics such as Ball, Winks, Roth, Messent, and others have described both the history of the genre and changing attitudes to it. According to Knight (1), less evaluative approaches have tried to establish why crime fiction is so compelling; psychoanalysts found the basis of the form's patterns in the psychic anxieties of writers and readers, while another type of analysis has seen the social attitudes and pressures of the modern environment as the basic drive in crime fiction. Overall, though the development of the genre has been traced by literary critics, psychoanalysts, and sociologists, little linguistic work has been undertaken in the area.

This article is part of a study that aims to explore the stylistic forms involved in the production of contemporary American crime novels and therefore aims to contribute to both the discipline of literary criticism and that of cognitive stylistics. The study focuses on the portrayal of the criminal mind as figured in contemporary works by James Patterson, Michael Connelly, and Patricia Cornwell, and this paper directly addresses the issue of how this mind comes to be morally situated.

These three have been chosen not only because they are best-selling authors, but also to illustrate three different criminal types. Extracts are taken from Patterson's *Cat and Mouse,* Connelly's **The Poet,** and Cornwell's *Southern Cross.* Whereas Patterson's portrayed criminal is indeed a serial killer, that of Connelly is a pedophile, and that of Cornwell a thief.

In addition, whereas the first two excerpts allow access to the criminal's consciousness correspondingly in the form of third person internal and first person narration, the third excerpt is in the form of a third person external narration, and hence the selection would cover various forms of the criminal portrayal in the field. Though the excerpt from the Cornwell novel is not one from her best-known series (featuring Chief Medical Examiner Kay Scarpetta) and is not an excerpt from the criminal's viewpoint, it does however implicitly deal with the matter at hand: the issue of how the criminal's actions are evaluated and justified. Altogether, the selection will allow me to contrast the different criminals in an attempt to provide answers to the question, "Are contemporary American crime fiction criminals presented as having been born evil or are their actions justified for instance by means of their childhood traumatic experiences?"

The stylistic models I will be using to analyze the extracts, namely those of type of narration, point of view, and mind style, are introduced in section 3. I will apply the frameworks to the three extracts and discuss the extent to which such forms of stylistic analysis would explain the different justifications of the actions of the portrayed criminals. That is, I will claim that it is by manipulating these three stylistic variants that the reader is given the impression that the criminal has been born evil, made evil, or both. In other words, I consider mind style to be one of the vital mediums for one to get from the stylistic analysis of such extracts to the nature of the moral justification of crimes. I will finally draw on the implications that this study has raised as to the notion of mind style in particular.

2. CONTEXTUALISING THE CRIME FICTION EXTRACTS

As Porter puts it, historians of detective literature may be differentiated according to whether they take the long or the short view of their subject:

> Those taking the long view claim that the detective is as old as Oedipus and serendipity of at least eighteenth-century China. Those maintaining the short view assume that detective fiction did not appear before the nineteenth century and the creation of the new police in Paris and London, that its inventor, in the 1840s, was Edgar Allan Poe, and that it reached its golden age in the opening decades of the twentieth century with the nonviolent problem novel.

According to Porter, a case may be made for both views that chiefly depends upon the preliminary definition adopted, while the view preferred will also be conditioned by the way one evaluates the representation of crime in literature. In other words, in order to decide who wrote the first detective novel we need to define the genre, as well as consider briefly its relationship to the much larger and vaguer category of crime literature.

Here, I define crime fiction as a text that combines two forms of suspense: the desire to know whodunit along with that suspense derived by the fear that whoever it was might repeat his/her crime. In other words, it is that short view of historians of detective literature that I adopt when referring to the crime novel.

Rankin (3) argues that the golden age of crime fiction was the 1920s and '30s when the traditional English whodunit was at its height, with practitioners such as Agatha Christie establishing its style and substance. He goes on to argue that, in the United States, Chandler and Hammett reacted against this cosy style. Whereas in Britain detective fiction developed towards a deeper characterization of protagonists—approaching mainstream fiction—in America, the genre has taken a rather different turn. For instance, a whole new sub-genre of detective fiction developed in the U.S. (the feminist hard-boiled novel) while various other ironic varieties have also emerged in the form of parodies and pastiches.

In his study of detective fiction, Symons argues that what detective fiction lacks as literature is character. In effect, and as Roth also points out, since only two characters are central to the plot of the genre, the remedy is rather simple: the detective failed to pay off in literary currency, so writers had to invest in the criminal. "Refocus the form on the criminal, and the potential for growth would be as various as in the novel itself" (4). Roth claims that the groundwork was already there because every work of detective fiction contains, however implicitly, the story of a murderer (and, by extension, criminal) and his or her crime; a story of psychological depth and intensity therefore lies buried in the form already.

One way in which this is accomplished is by giving the criminal a voice of his/her own and allowing the readers access to his/her consciousness. This in effect gives rise to the notion of the glamorous or sympathetic criminal in twentieth-century fiction, a figure that, according to Priestman (39), forcefully emerged as a primary object of reader identification. Novels focusing on the criminal in this manner intend to shock the reader into accepting that there are people for whom cruelty, in both its physical and psychological sense, is a normal way of life.

Finally, this focus on the criminal gives rise to a distinction between those crimes placed in the world of social cause and effect and those consigned to the category of pure evil. It is, however, the latter type of criminal violence that readers seem to find of most interest. They are fascinated by that criminal violence which is monstrous and dependent on the purely personal motivation and disturbed psychological condition of the single criminal figure.

One of the criminals under analysis in this paper is Gary Soneji, a psychopathic serial killer who recurrently figures in a James Patterson series featuring detective/psychologist Alex Cross. Cross makes his fourth appearance in Patterson's *Cat and Mouse,* which also marks the return of the villain Soneji from *Along Came a Spider.* Soneji goes on a murder spree at train stations in Washington and New York, but his ultimate goal is killing Alex Cross. In the extract under analysis, Gary Soneji's evil mind appears to be as twisted as ever, as he somehow gains access to the detective's cellar to go through his family's personal belongings and "fuel his hatred." The killer is back to wreak vengeance on the detective and his family while the latter is on the trail of an equally dangerous madman terrorizing Europe, Mr Smith.

He was inside the Cross house!

He was in the cellar: The cellar was a clue for those who collected them. The cellar was worth a thousand words. A thousand forensic pictures, too.

It was important to everything that would happen in the very near future. The Cross murders.

There were no large windows, but Soneji decided not to take any chances by turning on the lights. He used a Maglite flashlight. Just to look around, to learn a few more things about Cross and his family, to fuel his hatred, if that was possible.

The cellar was cleanly swept, as he had expected it would be. Cross's tools were haphazardly arranged on a pegged Masonite board. A stained Georgetown ballcap was hung on a hook. Soneji put it on his own head. He couldn't resist.

He ran his hands over folded laundry laid out on a long wooden table. He felt close to the doomed family now. He despised them more than ever. He felt around the hammocks of the old woman's bra. He touched the boy's small Jockey underwear. He felt like a total creep, and he loved it.

Soneji picked up a small red reindeer sweater. It would fit Cross's little girl, Jannie. He held it to his face and tried to smell the girl. He anticipated Jannie's murder and only wished that Cross would get to see it, too.

He saw a pair of Everlast gloves and black Pony shoes tied around a hook next to a weathered old punching bag. They belonged to Cross's son, Damon, who must be nine years old now. Gary Soneji thought he would punch out the boy's heart.

Finally, he turned off the flashlight and sat alone in the dark. Once upon a time, he had been a famous kidnapper and murderer. It was going to happen again. He was coming back with a vengeance that would blow everybody's mind.

He folded his hands in his lap and sighed. He had spun his web perfectly.

Alex Cross would soon be dead, and so would everyone he loved.

(Patterson, *Cat and Mouse* 4)

The second criminal under analysis is the Eidolon, featuring in Michael Connelly's ***The Poet,*** the author's first non-series book that broke into the bestseller lists. Though the novel is a pulse-pounding mystery about a serial killer, Gladden, it is the Eidolon and his criminal role as a pedophile that is the focus of the extract's analysis. In ***The Poet,*** an embittered journalist investigating the death of his police officer brother is stalked by a twisted aficionado of internet child porn and betrayed at every turn by the officials he thought would help him. It is the Eidolon's pedophilia that is portrayed in the extract, which is a script Gladden comes across at a website from and for pedophiles.

Gladden looked at the words on the screen. They were beautiful, as if written by the unseen hand of God. So right. So knowledgeable. He read them again.

They know about me now and I am ready. I await them. I am prepared to take my place in the pantheon of faces. I feel as I did as a child when I waited for the closet door to be opened so that I could receive him. The line of light at the bottom. My beacon. I watched the light and the shadows each of his footfalls made. Then I knew he was there and that I would have his love. The apple of his eye.

We are what they make us and yet they turn from us. We are cast off. We become nomads in the world of the moan. My rejection is my pain and motivation. I carry with me the vengeance of all the children. I am the Eidolon. I am called the predator, the one to watch for in your midst. I am the cucoloris, the blur of light and dark. My story is not one of deprivation and abuse. I welcomed the touch. I can admit it. Can you? I wanted, craved, welcomed the touch. It was only the rejection—when my bones grew too large—that cut me so deeply and forced on me the life of a wanderer. I am the cast off. And the children must stay forever young.

(Connelly 299)

The third and final criminal I investigate is Smoke, featured in Patricia Cornwell's *Southern Cross*. This teenager is the head of a gang referred to as The Pikes, who seem to be responsible for a series of robberies taking place in Virginia. The fast-moving adventure follows the work of the police department in its attempts to eradicate the teenage gangs and prevent the robberies from cash dispensers. Multiple points of view add change of pace to the narrative, in the course of which southern personalities make up the fabric of the interwoven story lines. The extract under analysis is the narrative's first reference to Smoke and is the only extract out of the three analyzed that is not taken from the criminal's viewpoint.

> Smoke was a special needs child. This had become apparent in second grade when he had stolen his teacher's wallet, punched a female classmate, carried a revolver to school, set several cats on fire and smashed up the principal's station wagon with a pipe.
>
> Since those early misguided days in his hometown of Durham, North Carolina, Smoke had been written up fifty-two times for assault, cheating, plagiarism, extortion, harassment, gambling, truancy, dishonesty, larceny, disruptive dress, indecent literature and bus misconduct.
>
> He had been arrested six times for crimes ranging from sexual assault to murder, and had been on probation, on supervised probation with special conditions, in an Alternative to Detention Program, in detention, in a wilderness camp therapeutic program, in a community guidance clinic where he received psychological evaluation and in an anger-coping group.
>
> Unlike most juveniles who are delinquent, Smoke had parents who showed up for all of his court appearances. They visited him in detention. They paid for attorneys and dismissed one right after another when Smoke complained and found fault. Smoke's parents enrolled him in four different private schools and blamed each one when it didn't work out.
>
> It was clear to Smoke's father, a hardworking banker, that his son was unusually bright and misunderstood. Smoke's mother was devoted to Smoke and always took his side. She never believed he was guilty. Both parents believed their son had been set up because the police were corrupt, didn't like Smoke and wanted to clear cases. Both parents wrote scathing letters to the district attorney, the mayor, the attorney general, the governor and a U.S. senator when Smoke was finally locked up in C. A. Dillon Training School in Butner.
>
> Of course, Smoke didn't stay there long because when he turned sixteen, he was no longer a minor according to North Carolina law and was released. His juvenile record was expunged. His fingertips and mug shots were destroyed. He had no past. His parents thought it wise to relocate to a city where the police, whose memories were not expunged, would not know Smoke or harass him any more. So it was that Smoke moved to Richmond, Virginia, where this morning he was feeling especially in a good mood to cause trouble.

(Cornwell 17)

It is not until later in the chapter that readers are allowed access to the criminal's consciousness as he cruises the streets of the city looking for other teenagers to recruit into his gang. It is for this reason that this extract is only to be analyzed in terms of the type of narration chosen and the scale of interference that narration allows. Since we do not get access to this character's consciousness, we cannot analyze his individual mind style.

The following section is concerned with analyzing the excerpts in terms of (a) the type and tone of narration employed, and (b) in the case of the first two excerpts, in terms of the nature of the criminal mind style and viewpoint portrayed. I will try to show that such analyses are central in demystifying the criminal mind, as well as in explaining the ways in which it comes to be morally situated.

3. STYLISTIC ANALYSIS OF THE EXTRACTS

3.1 TYPE OF NARRATION

To begin with, the narration portraying Soneji's consciousness seems to be of the "internal" type, meaning that it is mediated through the subjective viewpoint of this particular character's consciousness (Simpson 39). In other words, the narrator is here presented as omniscient, controlling the narration of events and displaying "privileged access to the thoughts and feelings of the characters in a way that an ordinary external observer [would] not" (Fowler, *Linguistic Criticism* 127).

Furthermore, this type of narration is one that produces a personal relationship with the reader as well as sympathy, both of which inevitably bias the reader in favor of the character. Despite this effect, the fact that what is represented is a criminal slipping in and out of fantasies of murdering little children will produce some sort of tension for readers. On one hand, the omniscient narration has readers sympathizing with the character, and yet on the other we might feel that we should not do so, on account of the content of the thoughts and fantasies Soneji is engaging in. In effect, we get a strong impression that this animal-like criminal has no remorse for the crimes he has committed, and since the only justification he gives for his actions is that of getting vengeance over the detective, we are invited to believe that he was born evil.

The type of narration employed in the Eidolon's written message is rather different. Though the narration is still that of the internal type, allowing readers access to the pedophile's consciousness, it nevertheless is homodiegetic, as presented in the first-person. Such a narration is instead expected to be limited (the characters don't know all the facts) as opposed to omniscient (Short 257), as well as flawed and opinionated. Here, the omniscient narrator describes a character's (Gladden's) reading/response to a text written by another character (the Eidolon), in the first person. In effect, the analyzed passage is a quotation. The voice the Eidolon adopts is additionally rather biblical in that it draws on language to be found in religious material ("beacon," "pantheon," "Eidolon") with even Gladden marking it as such: "as if written by the unseen hand of God."

This piece nevertheless can also be argued to produce tension amongst readers, mostly due to the fact that the text is written for other pedophiles to read, and uses the second person: "My story is not one of deprivation and abuse. I welcomed the touch. I can admit it. Can you?" This level of personal involvement with pedophilia is likely to make most readers uncomfortable in that it presupposes not only that the readers are pedophiles themselves, but also that they are unable to admit to the fact that they enjoyed the abuse, here referred to as "love": "Then I knew he was there and that I would have his love." Further tension is created by the use of the inclusive "we" and "us" in "We are what they make us and yet they turn from us. We are cast off. We become nomads in the world of the moan." Here, it also seems to be the case that "we" and "they" are used to refer to the same group of people, the pedophiles. It gives the impression that, not unlike vampires, pedophiles abuse children who grow up to become pedophiles themselves. It is for this reason that readers might get the impression that the Eidolon was made evil when abused as a child and therefore it is his traumatic childhood experience that is to blame for his current pedophilia.

One can however argue that since the reader of the novel is not the intended audience of the character's website (which is written for fellow pedophiles), and the reader is in fact aware of this at the time, the excerpt additionally provides insight into Gladden's consciousness. His reaction to the words on the screen ("They were beautiful, as if written by the unseen hand of God. So right. So knowledgeable") therefore gives the impression that Gladden shares the same positioning as the Eidolon. Both pedophiles are presumed to have been through similar experiences, and hence both are thought of as having been made evil.

In contrast to the narration of these two extracts, that displaying the character of Smoke is of the external type, in that events are described outside the consciousness of any participating character (Simpson 39). Here, the third-person narration adopted relates to events

and describes people from a position outside Smoke's consciousness, while the fact that the narrator declines to report any of the character's psychological processes adds an intuitively objective, neutral, and impersonal impression to the theme.

The type of impersonal third-person narration employed here is additionally interesting in that it draws on the sort of register one would expect from a social worker, a probation officer, or a psychologist as the jargon "special needs child," "misguided days," and "juveniles who are delinquent" reflects. However, this formal, distant, and apparently objective register is often interrupted by casual conversational jargon such as "had been written up," "smashed," and "showed up," which adds a strong sense of irony to the claims made. Additional irony is produced by the fact that while the narrator uses a format suggesting that Smoke shares little if any responsibility for the crimes he committed, the actual content of the extract gives a rather different story. His early crimes and punishments are provided in lists, while some responsibility is indirectly assigned to the youth's parents who appear to have been over-supportive and extremely suspicious of the police. It is this duality of the narrator's voice that makes the extract appear to be so ironic. On one hand, the format and the grammatical and lexical choices (from the field of social work) suggest that the narrator is giving Smoke the benefit of the doubt. On the other hand, the actual content of the piece, the informal register creeping in, and the narrator's assertiveness leave no doubt as to his guilt.

Interesting forms are also in use when we get shifts to the parents' viewpoints, such as in reference to the mother who "never believed he was guilty," where it is the fact that we get a negation of the expectation that he was indeed guilty, which raises the expectation in the first place. A similar impression is achieved when we are given access to the father's viewpoint: "It was clear to Smoke's father, a hardworking banker, that his son was unusually bright and misunderstood." Here, the subordination of the claim for the son's intelligence and individuality adds an additional ironic layer to the claim itself. We are strongly asked to believe ("It was clear") that the teenager was misunderstood even though we are given a rather large list of crimes, one that he is highly unlikely to have been set up for by the police.

Even further, the extract is suffused with words that are linked to criminality and the semantic field of finding fault, and yet these come to be attached to either the boy's attorneys, the schools the boy attended, or the police, but never to the boy himself: "when Smoke complained and found fault," "enrolled him in four different schools and blamed each one when it didn't work out," "Both parents believed their son had been set up because the police were corrupt," "would not know Smoke or harass him any more." In effect, we are given the impression that though Smoke and his parents were indeed in search of someone to blame for the situation the boy constantly found himself in, they never looked to the boy for fault. Overall, the blind trust the parents maintain as to the boy's innocence is reinforced in more ways than one, making it even clearer how likely it is that he was indeed guilty.

Finally, irony is further diffused over the last paragraph, where the readers are told that once the juvenile turned sixteen, his record and therefore his past was expunged. In contrast to the long subordinated sentences of the previous paragraphs, we are given a series of three short sentences: "His juvenile record was expunged. His fingertips and mug shots destroyed. He had no past," which may be argued to suggest that the cause of actions was unfair. The last sentence ("He had no past") especially conveys irony in that it states an impossible state of affairs: everybody has a past, and yet Smoke got away with his because of his age. A loophole in the American legal system is revealed, and, therefore, some responsibility as to the course of criminal action that Smoke is to engage in later on is indirectly assigned to the system itself.

It is not until the final sentence of the extract that we are allowed access to Smoke's actual consciousness: "he was feeling especially in a good mood to cause trouble." Here, the fact that Smoke was the type of teenager who would be in a mood for trouble, something so far only implied, is now confirmed. The overall impression we are given as to Smoke is that of a spoiled child who was both born and made evil; though it was rather early on in life that he displayed criminal behavior, it is also the parents' over-sympathizing that may have led him to become the criminal he is at this point in the narrative. In addition, the system appears to also be at blame, in that by deleting his records it allowed him to make a new start in an even more criminal new life.

3.2 CRIMINAL MIND STYLE AND VIEWPOINT

Roger Fowler (*Linguistics and the Novel*) coined the term *mind style* to describe the phenomenon in which the language of a text projects a characteristic world view, a particular way of perceiving and making sense of the world.

> A mind style may analyse a character's mental life more or less radically; may be concerned with relatively superficial or relatively fundamental aspects of the mind; may seek to dramatize the order and structure of conscious thoughts, or just present the topics on which

a character reflects, or displays preoccupations prejudices, perspectives and values which strongly bias a character's world-view but of which s/he may be unaware.

(Fowler, *Linguistics and the Novel* 103)

Fowler uses the term to refer to any distinctive linguistic presentation of an individual mental self and, according to Semino and Swindlehurst (145), introduced this notion of mind style as an alternative to ideological point of view or point of view on the ideological plane. According to the same source, ideological viewpoint refers specifically to the attitudes, beliefs, values, and judgments shared by people with similar social, cultural, and political backgrounds.

Since then, however, the notions of ideological viewpoint and mind style seem to have taken on separate definitions, and studies have tended to deal exclusively with either one (on ideological viewpoint see, for example, Simpson) or the other (on mind style see Leech and Short; Bockting; Semino and Swindlehurst). The definition I adopt for the term mind style is the following one, which Bockting offers: "Mind style is concerned with the construction and expression in language of the conceptualisation of reality in a particular mind" (159). This definition, Semino and Swindlehurst (144) argue, rests on two central assumptions. The first assumption is that what we call reality is the result of perceptual and cognitive processes that may vary in part from person to person, and the second assumption is that language is a central part of the process by which we make sense of the world around us; thus the texts we produce reflect our particular way of conceptualizing reality. Such a definition of mind style appears to be rather distinct from that of ideological viewpoint; whereas the latter term is now taken to capture the evaluative and socially shared aspects of world views, mind style captures their cognitive and more idiosyncratic aspects.

Since I take this latter sense of the term mind style to refer to the way in which a particular reality is perceived and conceptualized in cognitive terms, it may now relate to the mental abilities and tendencies of an individual, traits that may be completely personal and idiosyncratic, or ones that may be shared, for example by people with similar cognitive habits or disorders. It is for this reason that I borrow this sense of the term in reference to the criminal persona and mind. Even though I would not go to the extent of marking criminality as a mental disorder, it can surely be taken to be an idiosyncratic tendency certain people are prone to, regardless of whether they are born with it or whether they have come to adopt it later on in life. Criminality could be perceived as some rather special mental tendency, one that may be idiosyncratic, or one that is shared among other criminals with similar tendencies.

The range of linguistic phenomena portraying such a distinctive presentation of an individual mental self includes primarily choices of transitivity (Leech and Short 189), where semantic matters like agency and responsibility are indicated, and metaphorical patterns (Semino and Swindlehurst). In addition, choices of register and lexis, the figure of metonymy, as well as certain instances of speech and thought presentation can prove to be important aspects of mind style. Rather distinct linguistic patterns can be seen in my three extracts, leading towards the construction of quite distinct mind styles.

Firstly, with regards to register, the extract portraying Soneji's viewpoint marks the criminal as a persona that is intelligent and careful, in that he takes precautions in his trespassing of the Cross household. Despite this fact, the narration contains elements that portray a rather child-like viewpoint. The anticipation and excitement marking out every single one of Soneji's actions in the cellar seem more appropriate for a child rather than a serial killer: "A stained Georgetown ball-cap was hung on a hook. Soneji put it in his head. He couldn't resist." In addition, the structure of the passage is simple, full of co-ordinated clauses, while constructions such as "Once upon a time, he had been a famous kidnapper and murderer" are there to mark out the fact that, though a criminal, his viewpoint often blends with that of a child at play.

He additionally seems to be in control as much of his actions as he is of his thoughts, in that his free indirect thought processes represent not only clues to the cause of his past criminal actions, but also clues to the nature of those that are to come next. For instance, "The cellar was a clue to those who collected them. The cellar was worth a thousand words. A thousand forensic pictures, too" is marked out as a clue regarding the sort of death he anticipates for the family. The fact that this passage is in italics further signals its prominence from the remaining text.

The word *feel* is used both literally (to mark out physical perceptions)—"He felt around the hammocks of the old woman's bra"—and in a non-tactile sense (to mark out emotions and mental sensations): "He felt close to the doomed family now," "He felt like a total creep, and he loved it." The use of the verb *feel* in its various senses brings out sinister qualities to the criminal persona.

The extract further contains metaphors that are literalized such as "He was coming back with a vengeance that would blow everybody's mind." The narrator plays around with the "blowing someone's mind" metaphor that he uses as a clue, as the criminal indeed intends to set off to a murder spree at a train station and blow people's heads off. More remarkably, this narration includes a few instances of metonymy, such as "Soneji picked up a small reindeer sweater [. . .]. He held it to his face and tried to smell the girl." Even though the criminal appears to smell the sweater, in his mind it is the girl that he smells. It is also worth pointing out that the original referent is phonologically as well as graphologically associated with "sweat," therefore bringing out the impression that the criminal attempts to smell the girl's sweat.

Overall, even though there is nothing in Gary Soneji's actions to cause terror or fear directly, the nature of his thought processes as well as the way he uses metaphors literally and as clues could make readers feel uncomfortable with such an access to the disturbed individual's mental consciousness. Sentences such as "He had spun his web perfectly" are used to mark out the killer as an individual who is so disturbed that he even sees himself as a spider looking out for victims to catch in his web. Even though this metaphor is rather conventional, it is used to such a great extent (note especially the title of a previous novel in the series—*Along Came a Spider*) that it may be said to be a "sustained metaphor" (see Werth), meaning one that provides a sustained frame of reference as well as a means of thematic coherence.

The narrator however distances himself from the criminal's position by repeatedly stating that it is Soneji's thoughts that are represented, and therefore naming him where a personal pronoun would be more normal: "but Soneji decided not to take any chances," "Soneji put it on his head," "Soneji picked up a small reindeer sweater," "Gary Soneji thought he would punch out the boy's heart." The narrator avoids repeatedly using the pronoun "he" to signal that the thoughts are strictly the responsibility of the killer, while the criminal's full name is given in the last instance to distance the narrator even further from the killer's disturbing fantasies.

The Eidolon's mind-style on the other hand portrays rather different linguistic forms. The structure "My story is not one of deprivation and abuse" negates the expectation that he regards his abuse as such, and therefore raises it in the first place. In other words, this structure confirms the fact that he is aware of people in general viewing stories such as his as ones of abuse. Even though the pedophile makes reference to vengeance, he does so in the context of being vengeful towards his abusers not for carrying on the abuse in the first place, but for rejecting him once he became too old for their tastes. That is, though he does admit to feeling motivated and in pain, he claims that it was because the abuse eventually had to come to an end. In his mind, the pedophile appears to be of the belief that he keeps the children young by abusing them and sees it as his duty to carry on abusing them, which in turn helps them maintain their youth: "And the children must stay forever young." In addition, it is worth pointing out that this belief is reinforced by the fact that this last statement is one of the few in this extract that are given in an impersonal and rather generalized tone. Rather than claim that he is the one who is to help children stay forever young, he uses this impersonal tone to take no responsibility for this claim and yet imply that he would be involved in the process of keeping them young.

The extract portraying the Eidolon is extremely personal, though there appears to be a short shift from the "I" of the first paragraph ("I await them. I am prepared to take my place [. . .] I feel as I did as a child [. . .] I could receive him [. . .] I watched the light [. . .] I knew that be was there and that I would have his love") to the "we" of the beginning of the second paragraph ("We are what they make us [. . .] We are cast off. We become nomads [. . .]"), only to switch back to the first person singular later on ("I carry with me the vengeance [. . .] I am called the predator [. . .] I am the cucoloris"). This transition points out the pedophile's belief that his view of pedophilia is one shared among other pedophiles surfing the net. (At this point, it is also worth pointing out that the name the criminal adopts—Eidolon—comes from Greek, and means idol or image. By choosing such a name for himself, the pedophile is portrayed as a mental representation of others who share his state of mind and views on pedophilia.) It also reinforces his belief that these others need feel not only that they are not on their own in their search for young victims, but also that they are right to do so.

There appear also to be verbless clauses such as "The line of light at the bottom," "My beacon," and "The apple of his eye," which have connotations of inactivity and repress the agency function. This choice of structuring has the connotation of reduction in the strength of the will in those human characters to whom this style is applied (Fowler, *Linguistics and the Novel* 111). In other words, it adds to the impressions that those carrying out the abuse had little or no choice in the matter and that they ought not be blamed for it. Moreover in the extract feelings, states, and responses tend to be given in a non-judgmental tone through the process of nominalization: "the moan," "my rejection," "my pain and motivation," "the touch." This pattern allows emotions and qualities to be presented as possessions which can be discarded, passed from

person to person, traded, manipulated—non-inherent, not demanding commitment (112). In other words, these feelings and emotions appear to be taken for granted, are passed on from the abuser to the abused, and simultaneously take responsibility away from those who experience them and act upon them.

The extract is at the same time full of metaphors ("The apple of his eye," "nomads in the world of the moan") as well as some literal, identificational, or predicative constructions ("I am the predator," "my rejection is my pain and motivation"). Cognitive linguists such as Lakoff and Gibbs have stressed that metaphors are part of the fabric of language, even of thought. The author (who, in the analyzed extract, is the Eidolon whose writing is being quoted by Gladden), however, appears to elaborate on and combine conventional and unconventional metaphors with certain literal, identificational, or predicative constructions to project a distinctive mind style. It has also been suggested that personifying metaphors are often used to project a world view that attributes a potentially threatening animacy to nature (Semino and Swindlehurst 148). When discussing a similar occurrence in the mind style of Lambert Strether in *The Ambassadors,* Fowler argues, "It is as if his feelings are disconnected from his own psyche; as if his perceptions assail him from the outside, beyond his control; as if he relates to others and himself only through intermediaries; and it seems that he pictures others as suffering the same divided self' (*Linguistics and the Novel* 112). A similar effect seems to be achieved in the Eidolon's extract. Even though it is not inanimate objects but the feelings and emotions of the pedophile that come to be animated here, the effect achieved is still just as strong. The man who experiences the emotional states becomes merely a potential onlooker of the states themselves that are animated by movement, motive, and awareness. The feelings are the ones that overtake the pedophile, acting on his behalf, and taking responsibility of those actions away from him who performs them.

4. CONCLUSIONS

Overall, there appear to be certain correlations between the stylistic forms chosen and the way in which the criminal mind is morally situated.

In the case of Soneji, the third person narration is of the internal type and correlates with the impression of a criminal who was born as such. No justifications for his actions are provided and no excuses given. The literalizing of the everyday metaphors add to an image of an animal-like criminal who is not only proud of the crimes he has committed in the past, but willing to commit many more in the future. The criminal consciousness portrayed often blends with that of a child at play, while the use of the various senses of feel combined with metaphors and metonymies add sinister qualities to the disturbed persona. These are used as clues not only to the nature of his past crimes, but also to the nature of those to come. Overall, strong tensions are created in the use of stylistic forms that convey sympathy with the consciousness portrayed, with a content of fantasies that draw on anything but sympathy.

The Eidolon's first-person internal narration instead correlates with the impression of a criminal who was made: it is his traumatic childhood experience that is to blame for the abuse he currently carries out. The pedophile holds the belief that, much like the myth of vampires, he was made into the abuser he now is by the abuse(s) he himself suffered when he was a child. Though he admits to feeling vengeful and in pain, he claims that it was only because the abuse ended and not because it took place. The form of the language adopted causes tension in that it comes to presuppose not only that the readers are pedophiles themselves, but also that they are in denial as to having enjoyed the abuse. The extract is further suffused with first person pronouns adding a strong personal impression to the theme, while the occurrence of verbless clauses carries connotations of inactivity and the repression of agency. Moreover, the recurring metaphorical expressions, identificational constructions, and process of nominalization project a mind that views its feelings as disconnected from its own psyche. The feelings and emotions are presented as animate entities, taking the responsibility of the crimes away from the criminal who experiences them and acts upon them.

The overall impression we get of Smoke is that of a spoilt child who was both born and made evil. Though Smoke's consciousness does not get portrayed through the Cornwell extract (with the exception of the last sentence), the third person external narration adopted has strong ironic effects and deals however implicitly with issues of responsibility. The extract draws on a social worker's jargon, which gives the theme a rather objective tone, and yet the everyday expressions encountered, the grammar, as well as the content portray a narrator that is anything but objective. Interesting forms are in use when we get momentary shifts to the parents' viewpoint, where expectations are negated and strong implicatures are drawn upon. Responsibility as to the crimes carried out gets therefore implicitly assigned not only to the juvenile himself, but also to the parents' blind trust, and the system's loopholes.

Overall, though these correlations have been made, I do not mean to argue that each of these three types of narration would correlate with each of these justifications for the crime directly or necessarily. It is not the case that all first person narrations allow access to criminals who were made, or that third person internal narrations would correlate with criminals who were born, or that third person external narrations would bring out the impression of ones who were both born and made. The content of each excerpt would certainly contribute to the effect just as much as the type/tone of narration would. But it does seem to be the case that the positioning of the criminal on the cline of the moral justifications of crime would depend upon the nature of the narration chosen, the extent to which the reader is allowed access to the criminal's consciousness, and the way in which that consciousness is portrayed. And all these are aspects of what I shall refer to as criminal mind style.

This study has several implications as to the notion of mind style in particular. Even though the notion was originally coined as an alternative to that of ideological viewpoint, the definition I adopt for the term in this study is rather different. I instead use the term to refer to the way in which a particular reality is perceived and conceptualized, and it may hence relate to the idiosyncratic tendencies of individuals. Therefore, the term now has an interesting application in reference to the criminal persona and mind. Though primarily the range of linguistic phenomena portraying such a distinctive presentation of an individual mental self includes metaphorical patterns, transitivity, and lexical choices, other linguistic choices have also proved to be relevant. Certain instances of thought presentation, the grammatical process of nominalization, the deletion of agency, the figure of metonymy, as well as the type and tone of narration can all contribute to the construction of the criminal mind. It is the use of patterns involving these aspects of the language of such extracts that need be further explored, as these not only reveal the poetic structure of the criminal mind but also the ways in which it comes to be morally situated.

In the context of the larger study of which this paper is a part, I aim to concentrate on a larger variety of excerpts that portray the criminal consciousness and examine the extent to which the figurative language of such excerpts can specifically mirror the way in which authors realize the notion of criminality. Overall, I aim to prove that since the constraints of how we speak and write are not imposed by the limits of language but by the ways we actually think of our everyday experiences (Gibbs 8), it follows that the way that the criminal mind is linguistically portrayed is closely tied to the way the criminals are believed to conceptualize their lives and actions.

WORKS CITED

Ball, John, ed. *The Mystery Story*. California: U of California P, 1976.

Bockting, Ineke. "Mind Style as an Interdisciplinary Approach to Characterisation in Faulkner." *Language and Literature* 3.3 (1994): 157-74.

Connelly, Michael. *The Poet*. London: Orion, 1996.

Cornwell, Patricia. *Southern Cross*. London: Warner, 1998.

Fowler, Roger. *Linguistic Criticism*. Oxford: Oxford UP, 1986.

———. *Linguistics and the Novel*. London: Methuen, 1977.

Gibbs, Raymond W. *The Poetics of Mind: Figurative Thought, Language, and Understanding*. Cambridge: Cambridge UP, 1994.

Knight, Steven T. *Form and Ideology in Crime Fiction*. London: Macmillan, 1980.

Lakoff, George, and Mark Johnson. *Metaphors We Live By*. Chicago: U Chicago P, 1980.

Leech, Geoffrey N., and Michael H. Short. *Style in Fiction*. London: Longman, 1981.

Messent, Peter, ed. *Criminal Proceedings: The Contemporary American Crime Novel*. London: Pluto, 1997.

Patterson, James. *Along Came a Spider*. London: Harper Collins, 1993.

———. *Cat and Mouse*. London: Headline, 1997.

Porter, Dennis. "The Pursuit of Crime." *Art and Ideology in Detective Fiction*. New Haven: Yale UP, 1981.

Priestman, Martin. *Crime Fiction: From Poe to the Present*. Plymouth: Northcote House, 1998.

Rankin, Ian. *Criminal Minded*. Edinburgh: Canongate, 2000.

Roth, Marty. *Foul and Fair Play: Reading Genre in Classic Detective Fiction*. Athens: U Georgia P, 1995.

Semino, Elena, and Kate Swindlehurst. "Metaphor and Mind Style in Ken Kesey's *One Flew Over the Cuckoo's Nest*." *Style* 30.1 (1996): 143-65.

Short, Michael H. *Exploring the Language of Poems, Plays, and Prose*. London: Longman, 1996.

Simpson, Paul. *Language, Ideology, and Point of View*. London: Routledge, 1993.

Symons, Julian. *Bloody Murder: From the Detective Story to the Crime Novel: A History*. 3rd ed. London: Pan, 1994.

Werth, Paul. *Text Worlds: Representing Conceptual Space in Discourse*. Harlow: Longman, 1999.

Winks, Robin W., ed. *Detective Fiction*. Englewood Cliffs: Prentice-Hall, 1980.

***Publishers Weekly* (review date 12 April 2004)**

SOURCE: Review of *The Narrows*, by Michael Connelly. *Publishers Weekly* 251, no. 15 (12 April 2004): 38.

[*In the following review, the critic praises "some nifty hooks to this new Connelly," titled* The Narrows.]

There's a gravitas to the mystery/thrillers of Michael Connelly, a bedrock commitment to the value of human life and the need for law enforcement pros to defend that value, that sets his work apart and above that of many of his contemporaries. That gravitas is in full force in Connelly's newest [*The Narrows*], and as nearly always in the work of this talented writer, it supports a dynamite plot, fully flowered characters and a meticulous attention to the details of investigative procedure.

There are also some nifty hooks to this new Connelly: it features his most popular series character, retired L.A. homicide cop Harry Bosch, but it's also a sequel to his first stand-alone, *The Poet* (1996), and is only his second novel (along with *The Poet*) to be written in both first and third person. The first-person sections are narrated by Bosch, who agrees as a favor to the widow to investigate the death of Bosch's erstwhile colleague and friend Terry McCaleb (of *Blood Work* and *A Darkness More than Night*). Bosch's digging brings him into contact with Rachel Walling, the FBI agent heroine of *The Poet*, and the third-person narrative concerns mostly her. Though generally presumed dead, the Poet—the serial killer who was a highly placed Fed and Walling's mentor—is alive and killing anew, with, we soon learn, McCaleb among his victims and his sights now set on Walling. The story shuttles between Bosch's California and the Nevada desert, where the Poet has buried his victims to lure Walling.

The suspense is steady throughout but, until a breathtaking climactic chase, arises more from Bosch and Walling's patient and inspired following of clues and dealing with bureaucratic obstacles than from slash-and-dash: an unusually intelligent approach to generating thrills. Connelly is a master and this novel is yet another of his masterpieces. [. . .]

Forecast: Connelly should hit #1 with this even without trying, but he and Little, Brown are going all out to support the novel, with plans including a 15-city author tour, a *Today Show* appearance and the distribution to media and bookstores of a DVD, *Michael Connelly's Los Angeles,* narrated by CSI star William Petersen. Simultaneous Time Warner Audio and large print edition.

Michael Connelly and Jeff Zaleski (interview date 12 April 2004)

SOURCE: Connelly, Michael, and Jeff Zaleski. "Writing Toward Justice." *Publishers Weekly* 251, no. 15 (12 April 2004): 39.

[*In the following interview, Connelly discusses his novel* The Narrows, *a sequel to* The Poet.]

[*PW*]: **The Narrows** [. . .] *is a sequel to your 1996 novel* **The Poet.** *Why a sequel?*

[Connelly]: The real question is, "Why did I write a sequel to **The Poet** when for years I was saying I will not write one?" I think it had something to do with me coming to the world of fiction from journalism. One of my guidelines in fiction is to make it as close to reality as possible. So there's that contradiction: bookshelves are full of mystery novels where the bad guy is caught. And the reality I came from in the newspaper business is that 70% of the time the bad guy is caught, but a lot of bad guys get away. I wrote **The Poet** right after I quit being a journalist, and it was kind of a personal statement that I was going to keep my stories real. So I had the bad guy get away. As years went by, it started to bother me that in this fictional world I had let somebody loose to do what he wanted to do, which was not good stuff. I guess that was also a reflection for me of the times starting to be more uncertain, and I felt that I should set a little bit of my fictional world right. So I started thinking about going after the guy that I'd let go free.

On your Web site, there's offered for sale a special edition of **The Poet** *for which Stephen King wrote an introduction. We just got in the sixth book in his* Dark Tower *series, and King has made himself a character in the book. Do you have any plans along those lines, for Michael Connelly to interact with Harry Bosch [the detective hero of most Connelly novels]?*

I don't have a plan, but I'm curious about the line between fiction and nonfiction. And I cross it in ways in **The Narrows.** Some of the people there are real people. There's a detective who calls Harry [who's a

retired cop] and plants the seed of him coming back to the department—he's a real guy. And then there's the banter about the movie **Blood Work** [based on a Connelly novel]. And one time I wrote, for my Web site, an interview between me and Harry Bosch. That was a lot of fun to do. That exercise alone makes me think that some day the character Michael Connelly could intrude into fiction.

Along with the blurring of lines between reality and fiction, there's been a blurring within your novels of story lines, with characters from one series moving to another series—and that's especially true of **The Narrows.** *Why are you going in that direction?*

It's fun to do. Another reason is that I try to be loyal to people who have been riding with me. And in some ways loyalty means giving stuff back. If you've read 13 Michael Connelly books and there's some vague reference to a character who's in book number four or something, I think it's fun. And then there's a correlation between writing and painting. I look at my work as one big canvas, almost like a Hieronymus Bosch painting. All these stories are moving on the same canvas, so you're bound to have cross currents.

You've spent a lot of time as a journalist working the cop beat, and you've spent a lot of time writing about serial killers. Do you believe in evil? And if so, where does it come from?

Yes, I do believe in evil. My sense is that it's nurtured, and it's nurtured quite early. Some of the reading I've done is in regard to how behavioral patterns are set by the time you're five years old, and if you're messed with in some way by parents or neglected in some way, that's like the pebble going into water and the ripples go through your life. What's interesting, in writing about cops, is that for the most part they have a mentality of, "We'll leave it to the shrinks to figure out where evil comes from. All I know is that I'm taking evil out of this world." And that is more interesting to me as a writer, because it's very hard to do that, and it's very hard to do that without costing yourself something.

When you kill someone, as cops occasionally have to do, nothing puts your own humanity at more risk. It needs to be done, but you're making a choice, aren't you? A life for a life.

That's exactly right. And when I write about this guy [Bosch] and in every story he goes into the abyss, at some point you ask, "What damage have I done to this character?" and "What damage has the character done to himself by doing this?" And that to me is a more fascinating question than where evil comes from.

Bill Ott (review date 1 May 2004)

SOURCE: Ott, Bill. Review of *Michael Connelly's Los Angeles* (*Blue Neon Night* DVD). *Booklist* 100, no. 17 (1 May 2004): 1576.

[*In the review below, Ott describes Connelly's ability to evoke the character of the city of Los Angeles and finds that Connelly's depiction is far more loving than that of his literary predecessor, Raymond Chandler.*]

A sense of place is one of those terms, like noir or character-driven, that reviewers bandy about when they are having trouble getting at the heart of the matter. Hiding behind a phalanx of recognizable critical catch-phrases allows us to move forward without ever really making sense of such questions as why, in the works of certain writers, the landscape of the story seems to acquire a level of meaning far beyond geography. Sure, readers of crime fiction recognize that Raymond Chandler's Los Angeles is a special place, intimately connected to the birth of the hard-boiled novel, and that, more recently, Michael Connelly's Los Angeles is special, too, a kind of redrawn version of Chandler's map, but what is it precisely that makes those places special? To say that Chandler's or Connelly's novels possess a "great sense of place" is hopelessly vague, like directing a Chicagoan to Los Angeles by telling him to go south and then turn right.

What we need to help us understand landscape in fiction is a different kind of map, one that recognizes the intersection of metaphor and meaning the way a topographical map shows varying kinds of terrain. Readers who are quick to buy Connelly's superb new novel, *The Narrows,* will receive something like that metaphorical map in the form of a limited-edition DVD, *Blue Neon Night: Michael Connelly's Los Angeles.* Combining excerpts from Connelly's 14 books (read by William Petersen, star of *To Live and Die in L.A.*) with the author's musings on why he finds the city such a fertile setting for crime fiction, the DVD sets Connelly's words against expertly photographed footage of the places he discusses. (Interestingly, the DVD is directed by filmmaker Terrill Lee Lankford, whose first novel, *Earthquake Weather,* is a moody crime tale set in Los Angeles . . .)

But the DVD is no simple travelogue. Lankford wisely has Connelly do much of his talking while driving the streets of the city, thus capturing the single most significant aspect of landscape in Connelly's novels: motion. Harry Bosch, Connelly's hero, sees the city, usually at night, through the windshield of his car, and he describes it to us from that vantage point. Occasionally, he comments on the vista from the porch of his stilt house in the Hollywood Hills, but even then, mo-

tion is implied, both by the "carpet of lights" he sees on the freeway below him and by the ever-present possibility of an earthquake, which would "send his house down the hill like a sled."

Motion is significant in Connelly's world because it suggests constant change, which in turn creates an all-pervasive sense of randomness: If the victim had taken the Santa Monica Freeway instead of Wilshire Boulevard, he might not have stopped for a drink at that particular bar and met that particular woman. . . . Life can seem random anywhere, of course, even in relatively stationary landscapes, but it is exaggerated when we are so often in motion and when the distance between safety and danger is never a fixed point.

Raymond Chandler knew about motion, too. The "carpet of lights" wasn't quite as long when he was writing, but it was growing steadily. Chandler saw the birth of Connelly's L.A., and he hated it. When his hero, Philip Marlowe, was driving the streets, his eyes never quite left the rear-view mirror, looking back to a different city, a more innocent place, a more static place, a place not quite so prone to random violence. Chandler gave us our first detailed map of Los Angeles as a nightmare landscape, our first glimpse of where the wild things are. Nobody (except Nathanael West) had seen Los Angeles that way before Chandler, but now it's become second nature, the way we see urban life in general, the reason Connelly named his hero, known as Harry to his friends, after the master of surrealistic nightmare, painter Hieronymus Bosch.

The difference between Chandler's landscape and Connelly's is the way Chandler fights it. He wants to be somewhere else—the England of his childhood, perhaps, where the white cliffs of Dover don't move in the night. Marlowe dreams bitterly of a house in the country; Bosch knows he could never live anywhere except L.A.: "He loved the city most at night. . . . It was in the dark slipstream that he believed he moved most freely, behind the cover of shadows, like a rider in a limo. There was a random feel to the dark, the quirkiness of chance played out in the blue neon night. So many ways to live, and to die."

Toward the end of the DVD, Connelly makes a curious remark: "In their own way, I want my books to be love letters to Los Angeles." Chandler never wrote love letters to his city, or if he did, it was only to the city the way it used to be. Connelly finds and treasures emblems of lost innocence, or at least lost beauty, in the past of Los Angeles, too, in the Bradbury Building, for example, which Bosch celebrates in *Angels Flight* (1999). But the difference is that, for Connelly, the nightmare side of Los Angeles today is a source of energy as well as pain, of grace under pressure as well as random bursts of senselessness, and he sees that duality every day through his windshield. You won't find that concept on a map, though, not even a metaphorical one, but it's not so hard to visualize as Bosch steers his way down Sunset Boulevard, "from the barrios to the beaches," or as he gazes at the city from his deck, admiring the sunset even as he remembers that it's the smog that makes the colors so beautiful. Maybe, in fact, if we can start to understand how the blue neon nights of a character named Hieronymus Bosch are the stuff of both nightmares and love letters, we'll begin to know what it means to say that Michael Connelly's novels have a great sense of place.

Publishers Weekly (review date 4 April 2005)

SOURCE: Review of *The Closers,* by Michael Connelly. *Publishers Weekly* 252, no. 14 (4 April 2005): 40.

[*In the following review, the critic offers high praise for* The Closers, *describing it as one of Connelly's best efforts and deems the author "as close as anyone to being today's Dostoyevsky of crime literature."*]

LAPD detective Harry Bosch, hero of last year's **The Narrows** and other Connelly thrillers, is back on the force after a two-year retirement [in **The Closers**]. Assigned to the Open Unsolved (cold cases) unit and teamed with former partner Kiz Rider, Harry's first case back involves the killing of a high school girl 17 years before, reopened because of a DNA match to blood found on the murder gun. That premise could be a formula for a routine outing, but not with Connelly. Nor does the author rely on violent action to propel his story; there's next to none. In Connelly/Bosch's world, character, context and procedure are what count, and once again the author proves a master at all. The blood on the gun belongs to a local lowlife white supremacist, Roland Mackey; the victim had a black father and a white mother. But the blood indicates only that Mackey had possession of the gun, so how to pin him to the crime? Connelly meticulously leads the reader along with Bosch and Rider as they explore the links to Mackey and along the way connect the initial investigation of the crime to a police conspiracy. Most striking of all, in developments that give this novel astonishing moral force, the pair explore the "ripples" of the long ago crime, how it has destroyed the young girl's family—leaving the mother trapped in the past and plunging the father into a nightmare of homelessness and drink—and how it drives Rider, and especially Bosch, into deeper understanding of their own purposes in life. Connelly comes as close as anyone to being today's Dos-

toyevsky of crime literature, and this is one of his finest novels to date, a likely candidate not only for book award nominations but for major bestsellerdom.

Benedicte Page (interview date 10 February 2006)

SOURCE: Page, Benedicte. "Witnessing Hell: Michael Connelly, Creator of Detective Harry Bosch, Tells about His First Encounter with Murder—at the Age of 16." *Bookseller* 5216 (10 February 2006): 21.

[*In the following interview, Connelly reveals the origins of his interest in crime writing and reflects on some differences between American and British crime novels and their readers.*]

With Michael Connelly's most recent novel **The Lincoln Lawyer** selected to be on Richard & Judy's Book Club on the 22nd March, a new title from Connelly in the summer will throw light on the author's early career as a crime reporter.

Connelly's collected journalism from the decade to 1992 (**Crime Beat,** Orion, June) includes accounts of key murder cases he reported on during his time at the *Los Angeles Times*—cases that went on to inform his novels, sometimes in background detail, but sometimes directly. The novel **The Poet** grew out of one case he followed, while **Trunk Music** was inspired by another that remained unsolved.

In fact, Connelly's first exposure to the world of crime had come long before he even graduated in journalism, when at the age of 16 he was working nights as a dishwasher in a Florida hotel. One evening he witnessed a suspicious-looking man dumping a package in a hedge. It turned out to be a gun; someone had been shot dead during a robbery nearby and the bag contained the murder weapon. Connelly, the sole witness, was interviewed at length by the detective bureau that night, but the killer was never found.

"That night of being immersed in the police department and being interviewed repeatedly by these detectives, who seemed to me very hardened individuals, this really impressed something upon me," says Connelly. "That's when I started being fascinated with their lives and how they worked. From that point I was reading crime newspapers every day, true crime, mystery novels."

He took on the crime reporter's role to learn more, always with a view to eventually writing fiction. "I tried to specialise in crime and police and the courts because it was a training ground for what I wanted to do," he says. "Traditionally in my country there's a rotation in newsrooms where you don't spend too much time on a police beat because of the tendency to get cynical about things. I always deflected efforts to rotate me."

In his own novels he has always preferred to focus on the psychology of the policeman, rather than that of the criminal. "There's a great emphasis in crime fiction on what makes the bad guy turn bad. I was more fascinated in the police officer and the difficulty of doing the job correctly and dealing with the darkness of human nature every day."

"There's a price they pay for doing their jobs. That's what I took to Harry Bosch—the moments by himself when he tries to work out what his place is in the world and what it all means are some of the most important in the books."

Harry Bosch's name comes from that of the 15th-century artist Hieronymus Bosch; a Bosch depiction of hell and its sufferings used to hang in Connelly's study. He took it down, though, when his daughter (now eight) grew old enough to take it in. "Having family around, having my daughter come see me after school, it keeps you out of the darkness," he observes.

He is appreciative of his British readers. "In the States, if people like the books, they love the twists and trying to guess the story. But in the UK and other European countries, they see them more as social novels, as a reflection of what is happening in society, which is a more fulfilling response to get."

"I enjoy reading crime novels that aren't set in the United States for escapism—if they're set in America, I find myself analysing them. I find I can escape more if I'm reading Ian Rankin, Peter Robinson, Val McDermid or Mo Hayder."

Oline H. Cogdill (review date 31 May 2006)

SOURCE: Cogdill, Oline H. "The Genesis of a Top Crime Writer: A Review of *Crime Beat: A Decade of Covering Cops and Killers.*" *South Florida Sun-Sentinel* (31 May 2006): http://articles.sun-sentinel.com/2006-05-28/entertainment/0605240944_1_crime-harry-bosch-michael-connelly.

[*In the following review of the essay collection* Crime Beat, *Cogdill traces the origins of Connelly's fiction-writing to his years as a police-beat journalist in southern Florida and Los Angeles.*]

Harry Bosch, the brooding and insightful LAPD detective, doesn't make an appearance in Michael Connelly's latest book, *Crime Beat.* Neither does Terry Mc-

Caleb, the former FBI agent whose adventures literally pulled at the heartstrings in *Blood Work.* Nor are any of the assorted villains, killers and con men (and women) who have supplied plot lines in Connelly's 16 novels.

While none of these fictional characters shows up in *Crime Beat,* their shadows are a vital part of Connelly's first nonfiction book. *Crime Beat* is a collection of 22 newspaper articles that Connelly wrote while covering the police beat at the *South Florida Sun-Sentinel* and the *Los Angeles Times.*

Crime Beat reveals the genesis of one of the top mystery writers in the world, a foundation that began when he was a teenager in Fort Lauderdale and later cemented as a reporter on the crime beat.

In an intriguing introduction, Connelly shows how his work as a journalist was "seeded" into his fiction, as the author pulled details about personality quirks, habits and crimes into his novels. The writing is lean and economical, unburdened by embellishments; yet this no-frills approach captures situations so perfectly. These are the same techniques that Connelly brought to his novels.

Crime Beat also illustrates the art of solid police reporting, which doesn't have to be dull sentences about who did what to whom, ending with the attribution "police said." Instead, the crime beat can be a window into a specific time, capturing a society's worst moments as well as its heroes.

And heroes abound in *Crime Beat,* especially in a series of articles Connelly did after spending a week with the Fort Lauderdale Police Department's homicide squad during 1987. Certainly Connelly, who grew up in Fort Lauderdale and worked at the *Sun-Sentinel* from 1981 to 1987, reports on one of Fort Lauderdale's most murderous years, but he also shows the detectives' compassion, insight, frustration and hard work. It's easy to see the fictional Harry Bosch's embryonic roots. In [his] chapter, "The Call," Connelly says that what he observed during this week set the stage for all his fiction writing.

Connelly's articles give a complete picture of everyone involved in a crime, including the victims, a trait that he continues in his fiction. In a chapter titled "The Gang That Couldn't Shoot Straight," originally published in the *Sun-Sentinel* in 1987, Connelly describes the tragedy in the killing of Anita Spearman, a well-liked assistant city manager in West Palm Beach. The same story pinpoints the ineptness and stupidity of the hit men who had been hired from want ads.

The author's reporting for the *Los Angeles Times,* where he worked from 1987 to 1994, was similarly serendipitous for his future career. The day before his interview with the *Times,* thieves had pulled a bank heist by going through the city's water system tunnels. The real life event became the basis of Connelly's Edgar Award-winning debut, ***The Black Echo.***

Crime Beat ends with an equally intriguing essay about Connelly, written by Michael Carlson, a correspondent for several British publications. Carlson says that Connelly never stopped being a reporter, that each of his novels is an extension of journalism written with "empathy and perception."

And that insight began while on the Crime Beat.

Kirkus Reviews (review date 1 June 2006)

SOURCE: Review of *The Closers,* by Michael Connelly. *Kirkus Reviews* 74, no. 11 (1 June 2006): 533.

[*In the following review, the critic offers a plot summary of* The Closers *and finds it consistent with Connelly's other novels in its ability to surprise readers.*]

Harry Bosch, back with the LAPD in the Open-Unresolved Unit (***The Closers,*** 2005), wrestles with a teasing case from his salad days in Hollywood homicide.

Back in 1993, equestrienne Marie Gesto vanished without a trace. Ten days later, her car turned up in the garage of a landmark apartment building, her clothing neatly folded inside. Then nothing, from that day to this. Harry Bosch, who caught the case, worked it obsessively and even took a copy of the open file into retirement with him. Frustrated that he could never make a case against Anthony Garland, the worthless son of a high-rolling oilman, Bosch reviewed the evidence every chance he had when he was back on the job in Open Unresolved. Now, suddenly, the crime has evidently been solved without his lifting a finger. Raynard Waits, a window-cleaner caught red-handed with the dismembered body parts of two murder victims in his car, is trying to avoid the needle by confessing to nine earlier homicides, including Marie Gesto's. But Harry can't help looking this gift horse in the mouth. He doesn't trust Freddy Olivas, the Northeast homicide detective in charge of the case, or Rick O'Shea, the prosecutor who plans to ride it into the top job at the DA's office. And he doesn't trust Waits, not even when he provides information about the crime only the killer could know and offers to lead the cops to the spot where he buried Marie Gesto.

Readers who feel confident they can see what's coming will be thrown off-stride by the crafty series of surprises Connelly has up his sleeve. But nobody familiar with Bosch's checkered career will be shocked when the malfeasance reaches past Raynard Waits to the highest levels of city government.

Connelly offers a stellar demonstration of why, as Harry says, "taking it straight to the heart is the way of the true detective," whatever the costs to himself and others.

Aislinn McCormick (essay date 21 July 2006)

SOURCE: McCormick, Aislinn. "Branding Michael Connelly: A Selection for Richard and Judy's Book Club Prompted Orion to Research Michael Connelly's Readers." *Bookseller* 5239 (21 July 2006): 26.

[*In the following essay, McCormick describes the marketing push behind Connelly's novel* The Lincoln Lawyer, *noting that the campaign emphasized the author's uncommon ability to keep readers enthralled.*]

The marketing campaign for Michael Connelly's ***The Lincoln Lawyer*** began when the trade paperback was selected in January for the "Richard & Judy" Book Club. This promoted Connelly to a larger, more diverse reader base, and encouraged Orion to redefine his brand name.

Research into what Connelly readers enjoy about his writing helped to shape a core brand message. "What triggers people to read on is the addictive quality from page one, and the fact that he always delivers 100%," Anthony Keates, Orion paperback marketing director, says. For the mass market edition of ***The Lincoln Lawyer,*** [. . .] the new brand logo, "100% Connelly, 100% addictive", is used on all marketing and promotional material. The research will inform the style of the author's new cover look, to be used from March 2007.

"The message came through of the maturity in the storytelling and his ability to use a crime as the catalyst for other revelations," Keates says. "We developed this into a multi-layered design style in the creative."

Lucie Stericker, Orion art director, says: "We used icons hidden within a pattern to show there's always something more. Connelly deserves more than the normal packshot with a tagline that so many authors—particularly crime—seem to get."

A national outdoor campaign began on 3rd July, running for two weeks with four-sheet posters and advertising at mainline London stations. A 20-ft supersign at London Charing Cross and a transvision screen at London Victoria featured ads with quotes from Mickey Haller, *The Lincoln Lawyer*'s main character.

The rest of the outdoor drive took place in central London over five days, consisting of 100,000 teaser postcard drops and ad vans circulating around Oxford Street and Russell Square. Telephone kiosk advertising ran in the same area. "We invested our money in advertising that the publishing trade doesn't usually use," Keates says. "The design of the brand was taken from contemporary advertising. We made the product shot small and used the rest of the canvas to hook you in."

The Lincoln Lawyer features in campaigns in all the major book retail chains throughout the year. Keates says: "Orion is putting Connelly ahead of the pack. You can't pigeonhole him as a crime writer. Richard and Judy saw he was more than that, too."

Kirkus Reviews (review date 15 August 2008)

SOURCE: Review of *The Brass Verdict,* by Michael Connelly. *Kirkus Reviews* (15 August 2008): http://www.kirkusreviews.com.

[*In the following review of* The Lincoln Lawyer, *the critic describes the book as satisfying although the case at its center is "less than baffling."*]

The answer to every Connelly fan's dream [is presented in **The Brass Verdict**]: Hieronymus Bosch meets the Lincoln Lawyer.

Away from the courtroom for two years after he was shot (**The Lincoln Lawyer,** 2005), Mickey Haller plans a gradual return to the legal practice he runs from the back seat of his car. But the plan is abruptly accelerated by the murder of his colleague Jerry Vincent, who designated Mickey as the attorney who'd take over his list of clients if anything happened to him. One client is a high-profile defendant guaranteed to put Mickey back on the map. Hollywood studio head Walter Elliot is accused of killing his much younger wife Mitzi, who evidently took the recent vesting of her prenup as the signal to file for divorce, and her even younger lover, interior decorator Johan Rilz, who wasn't nearly as gay as Mitzi had hinted. Before Mickey can claim victory, however, he'll have to explain away the gunpowder residue on his client's hands; he'll have to figure out what secret the client is hiding from him that makes him so sure he's going to get off; and he'll have to be ready to go to trial in ten days. While he's racing around trying to fit the pieces

together, he'll cross swords repeatedly with Connelly's long-running hero, Det. Harry Bosch, the 33-year veteran of Robbery-Homicide (**The Overlook,** 2007, etc.) who's investigating Vincent's murder. Despite twists aplenty, the trial drags on for so many pages that savvy readers will solve the mystery ahead of Mickey. But his relationship with Bosch, whom he doesn't recognize as his half brother, is satisfyingly resourceful—by turns wary, competitive, complementary, cooperative and mutually predatory.

Even if the case is less than baffling, Connelly brings his two sleuths together in a way that honors them both.

Mark Fitzgerald (review date 3 June 2009)

SOURCE: Fitzgerald, Mark. "In New Thriller, Hero Is an *L. A. Times* Reporter with a Pink Slip." *Editor & Publisher* (3 June 2009): http://www.editorandpublisher.com.

[*In the following review of* The Scarecrow, *Fitzgerald describes the impact of changes in the journalism industry on Connelly and his fiction-writing.*]

Michael Connelly's newest novel **The Scarecrow** has all the elements of a page-turner thriller: Flawed protagonist and rekindled love interest on a collision course with a seemingly omniscient killer whose deviance might give even Hannibal Lecter the creeps.

The Scarecrow could also be described as a story ripped from the headlines . . . of *E&P*.

Scarecrow hero Jack McEvoy isn't just a *Los Angeles Times* reporter—he's just been given his layoff notice as the book begins, and told to acquaint his much-younger, Twitter-friendly, blogaholic colleague with the cop shop beat. Himself a former reporter for the *Times* and the South Florida *Sun-Sentinel,* Connelly has written a thriller that plays out against the background of a declining newspaper industry: Tribune Co. declares bankruptcy, the *Rocky Mountain News* folds, the *Times* tries unsuccessfully to sell its building.

"Like the paper and ink newspaper itself, my time was over," the character McEvoy reflects at one point. He is not interested in the flash and distraction, as he sees it, of the mobile journalist. "I'm not a mojo," he says, "I'm an oldjo."

So many of the newspaper developments in **Scarecrow,** in fact, are so recent that when I got Connelly on the phone from his home in Tampa, one of my first questions had to be about the publishing logistics of getting in details such as the Feb. 27 closing of the *Rocky.*

"With the way they physically print and manufacture books now, you can make changes pretty late into the process," he said.

The *Rocky* closing was a particularly urgent change for Connelly. "The first time I wrote about Jack McEvoy in 1996 (in the thriller ***The Poet***), he wrote for the *Rocky Mountain News*. Now, of course, he's in Los Angeles. When I first turned the manuscript in the Friday after Thanksgiving, when Jack gets laid off at the *Times,* a guy from the *Rocky Mountain News* calls and offers him a job."

Galleys with that passage were being distributed to booksellers when the *Rocky* shut down. "That would have been pretty embarrassing if it went in" the hardcover, Connelly said.

In writing ***Scarecrow,*** Connelly said, he wanted to reflect on "this downward spiral" of the newspaper business.

"I write thrillers so that obviously has to be my priority here," he said. "But in any story there's always an open window to let something in, some reflection of what's been. Sure, I haven't been a reporter for whatever it is, 14 or 15 years. But I act like a reporter when I'm researching, I use those skills, and of course the business means something to me, so I wanted this to be a sort of torch song for newspapers."

Connelly says he always wanted to write crime novels, and majored in journalism at the University of Florida "because I knew it would take me into police stations with the police beat and I would develop my writing." After graduating in 1980, he worked at the Daytona Beach *News-Journal* and then the *Sun-Sentinel* before moving in 1988 to the Los Angeles *Times,* where the great noir novelists Raymond Chandler and Dashiell Hammett plied their trade.

A *Sun-Sentinel* editor told him he was going to the Velvet Coffin, the old nickname for the newspaper under Times-Mirror Co. ownership, when it indulged writers with space and expense accounts.

Connelly found success inside and out of the paper. His first novel, ***The Black Echo,*** in 1992 won an Edgar Award for best first novel. Its plot came from a *Times* newspaper story an editor used as a test when Connelly was interviewing for the job. Soon, he says, he felt he had to pick between journalism and thrillers. He took a leave of absence to write one book and realized, when he returned to the newsroom, how much better he could work concentrating only on fiction.

"It was a very reluctant choice on a number of levels," Connelly said. He liked the job, but also worried that giving up his press pass might mean giving up access to the cops and detectives who inspired story ideas and offered real-life details.

He needn't have worried. The *Times* and the Los Angeles Police Department are mutually suspicious organizations. Connelly could call on the people he knew from his beat—and they no longer worried something they told him would wind up in the paper.

But writing ***Scarecrow,*** he came to realize how much had changed in newspapers since he left the *Times* in 1994. "I gave the manuscript to people I knew, and they told me, 'The thriller part is great, but you haven't been in a newsroom in 10 years, have you?'" In went references to mojos and Twitter—and a certain despondency. Connelly calls himself "naturally pessimistic," and that view extends to the future of newspapers as well.

In ***Scarecrow,*** reporter McEvoy and an FBI agent/love interest traverse motel corridors where death could be waiting around the corner. They trespass on their serial killer's high-tech lair. But there's a striking passage in ***Scarecrow*** in which the Los Angeles *Times* newsroom seems just as spooky:

> The place was completely dead, not a reporter or editor in sight, and I got a stark feeling for what the future held. At one time the newsroom was the best place in the world to work. A bustling place of camaraderie, competition, gossip, cynical wit and humor, it was at the crossroads of ideas and debate . . . Now thousands of pages of editorial content were being cut each year and soon the paper would be like the newsroom, an intellectual ghost town. In many ways I was relieved that I would not be around to see it.

FURTHER READING

Biographies

Ayers, Jeff. "Interview: Michael Connelly." *Library Journal* 130, no. 16 (1 October 2005): 66.
    Connelly discusses Mickey Haller, a new character introduced in *The Lincoln Lawyer.*

Simon, Scott. "Novelist Connelly Revisits His 'Crime Beat' Days." *National Public Radio Weekend Edition* (29 April 2006): http://www.npr.org/templates/story/story.php?storyId=5368001.
    Interview with Connelly in which he discusses his essay collection, *Crime Beat.*

Criticism

Ogle, Connie. "*The Closers*: The Former L.A.P.D. Cop Is Back on the Force, and He's Learned a Thing or Two." *Miami Herald* (18 May 2005): np.

> Review of *The Closers* in which Ogle praises Connelly's ability to keep his Harry Bosch series engaging.

————. "Tour the Darkness with Torture and Suicide Bombers." *Miami Herald* (3 June 2009): np.

> Review of *The Scarecrow*, by Michael Connelly.

Signor, Randy Michael. Review of *A Darkness More than Night*, by Michael Connelly. *Book* (January 2001): 68.

> Review focusing on the interaction between Harry Bosch and Terry McCaleb in Connelly's *A Darkness More than Night*.

Swartley, Ariel. "Michael Connelly Doesn't Live Here Anymore. . . . but L.A.'s Always on His Mind." *Book* (November-December 2002): 48.

> Reviews Connelly's career to date during a visit to Los Angeles.

Additional coverage of Connelly's life and career is contained in the following sources published by Gale: *Contemporary Authors,* **Vol. 158;** *Contemporary Authors New Revision Series,* **Vols. 91, 180;** *Literature Resource Center***; and** *St. James Guide to Crime & Mystery Writers,* **Ed. 4.**

Stanley Kunitz
1905-2006

(Full name Stanley Jasspon Kunitz; also wrote under pseudonym Dilly Tante) American poet, essayist, and nonfiction writer.

The following entry presents an overview of Kunitz's career through 2007. For further information on his life and works, see *CLC,* Volumes 6, 11, 14, and 148.

INTRODUCTION

Considered a "poet's poet" and highly respected by his peers, Kunitz published a great number of poems over a career that spanned almost eighty years. His early work was influenced by John Keats, Alfred Lord Tennyson, and especially Robert Herrick, and was recognized by scholars for its technical excellence and complex themes dealing largely with loss and inner turmoil. Kunitz's later work, marked by simpler language and a more open style, has been deemed more accessible and prompted the critical community to take a serious interest in his work.

BIOGRAPHICAL INFORMATION

Kunitz was born in Worcester, Massachusetts, in 1905 to Solomon and Yetta Kunitz, who owned a dressmaking company. His father committed suicide by drinking carbolic acid a few weeks before Stanley was born. When Kunitz was eight, his mother married Mark Dine, whom Kunitz adored. Mr. Dine, as Kunitz called him, died in 1918, when Kunitz was fourteen. In high school, Kunitz was inspired by Romantic poets such as Keats, Tennyson, William Wordsworth, and William Blake. He won a scholarship to Harvard College, earning a bachelor's degree in 1926 and a master's degree in 1927, and worked briefly for the English department but was told he could not continue due to his Jewish heritage. After leaving Harvard, Kunitz worked as a reporter and editor, editing the Wilson Library Bulletin from abroad. During this time he contributed poetry to several magazines, including *Poetry,* the *Nation,* and the *New Republic.* His first collection, *Intellectual Things* (1930), earned moderate praise, and he spent some time during the 1930s and 1940s co-editing a series of literary reference books for the H. W. Wilson Company. During World War II, Kunitz served

in the army after being denied deferment as a conscientious objector. He was discharged in 1945 and spent a year in Santa Fe on a Guggenheim grant before his friend and fellow poet Theodore Roethke secured a teaching position for him at Bennington College. Kunitz's tenure at Bennington was brief, and he subsequently accepted another teaching position in upstate New York. In 1952, after the birth of his daughter, Gretchen, he and his wife separated, and he spent two years in Europe on a traveling fellowship. Ultimately, Kunitz's teaching career included positions at Columbia, Yale, Princeton, Rutgers, the New School for Social Research, and the University of Washington. During the 1960s and 1970s, Kunitz traveled throughout Europe and Africa on lecture and reading tours. He visited the Soviet Union in 1967 and in time earned recognition for his translations of the works of several Russian poets, most notably Anna Akhmatova. Kunitz has been lauded with numerous awards, including the Pulitzer Prize for poetry in 1959, the National Medal of Arts in 1993, the National Book Award in 1995 for *Passing Through,* (1995) and the Peace Abbey Courage of Conscience award in 1998. In 1974, Kunitz was appointed the 22nd Consultant in Poetry to the Library of Congress where he served two terms, concluding his tenure in 1976. In 2000, he was appointed the tenth Poet Laureate Consultant in Poetry to the Library of Congress, making him the third poet to serve as both consultant in poetry and poet laureate. Kunitz remained active, writing daily and tending his elaborate garden, until his death from pneumonia on May 14, 2006, at age 100.

MAJOR WORKS

Kunitz's first published collection, *Intellectual Things,* established him as an erudite poet. The collection contains fifty poems that are carefully arranged, as in Eisensteinian montage, to create something new through their juxtaposition. The poems in *Intellectual Things* were written when Kunitz was very young and he later commented, "I had developed intellectually more than I had emotionally or experientially." Critics have observed that Kunitz's immaturity as a poet is evident in this collection, especially in the second half, which comprises mostly love poems. Most of these preliminary efforts, acknowledged by Kunitz as technically flawed and awkward, were excluded from his *Selected Poems, 1928-1958* (1958), which received the Pulitzer Prize for poetry. His sophomore collection, *Passport to the War* (1944), contains the poem "Father and Son," establishing a recurring motif in his works. The deaths of his father and stepfather are explored in several other Kunitz poems, including "Three Floors," which contains the passage, "Bolt upright in my bed that night / I saw my father flying; / the wind was walking on my neck, / the windowpanes were crying." *Passport to the War* again focuses on organization and contains twenty-four poems from *Intellectual Things,* some with minor revisions. The reprinted poems are arranged as they were in the earlier collection, but the omission of some pieces allowed for clearer and smoother transitions. New poems, considering the war and equating timeless themes with contemporary events, were also added to Kunitz's second collection.

After *Selected Poems, 1928-1958,* Kunitz published *The Testing-Tree* (1971). The new collection marked a stylistic departure for Kunitz, now writing in a more open, accessible style. The title poem resurrects the father-son motif when the speaker says, "Father wherever you are / I have only three throws / bless my good right arm. / In the haze of afternoon, / while the air flowed saffron, / I played my game for keeps— / for love, for poetry, / and for eternal life." Published when Kunitz was sixty-five years old, these poems are looser and incorporate free verse, a starkly different approach than the rhymed, five-foot, ten-syllable meter of his earliest work. The National Book Award-winning *Passing Through,* published when Kunitz was ninety, includes most of his work since *The Testing-Tree* and marks a more optimistic vision, as is shown in the foreword where he writes, "Poetry . . . is ultimately mythology, the telling of the stories of the soul. This would seem to be an inverted, even solipsistic, enterprise, if it were not that these stories recount the soul's passage through the valley of this life—that is to say, its adventure in time, in history."

CRITICAL RECEPTION

Kunitz's early work was appreciated by critics for its use of language but failed to gain widespread acclaim until *Selected Poems* earned the Pulitzer Prize. Still, while acknowledged as profound and well written, critics largely viewed his work as derivative of the poets from whom he drew inspiration. Always hugely popular among other poets and championed by Roethke and his peers, Kunitz came to represent a kind of elder statesman—a "poet's poet." His later work, dating from the 1970s, was regarded in much higher esteem than his early work, and his technical prowess continued to improve over his career. Appreciation for Kunitz's longevity and devotion to his craft was clear by the time of his publication of *Passing Through* at age ninety and appointment to the U.S. Poet Laureate post at age ninety-five. Concluding an overview of his career published shortly after his death, Jeanne Braham wrote, "On the day Kunitz died I overheard a colleague remark, with a mixture of sorrow and admiration, 'He cast a long shadow.' I prefer to think he cast a long light."

PRINCIPAL WORKS

Intellectual Things (poetry) 1930

Living Authors: A Book of Biographies [editor; as Dilly Tante] (nonfiction) 1931

Authors Today and Yesterday: A Companion Volume to Living Authors [editor, with Howard Haycraft] (nonfiction) 1933

Passport to the War: A Selection of Poems (poetry) 1944

Selected Poems, 1928-1958 (poetry) 1958

The Testing-Tree (poetry) 1971

Poems of Anna Akhmatova [translator, with Max Hayward] (poetry) 1973

The Coat without a Seam: Sixty Poems, 1930-1972 (poetry) 1974

The Terrible Threshold: Selected Poems, 1940-1970 (poetry) 1974

A Kind of Order, a Kind of Folly: Essays and Conversations (essays and interviews) 1975

The Lincoln Relics (poetry) 1978

The Poems of Stanley Kunitz, 1928-1978 (poetry) 1979

The Wellfleet Whale and Companion Poems (poetry) 1983

Next-to-Last Things: New Poems and Essays (poetry and essays) 1985

Passing Through: Later Poems, New and Selected (poetry) 1995

The Collected Poems of Stanley Kunitz (poetry) 2000

The Wild Braid: A Poet Reflects on a Century in the Garden (nonfiction) 2005

CRITICISM

Stanley Kunitz and William Packard (interview date 1970)

SOURCE: Kunitz, Stanley, and William Packard. "Speaking of Craft." In *Interviews and Encounters with Stanley Kunitz,* edited by Stanley Moss, pp. 10-18. Riverdale-on-Hudson, N.Y.: Sheep Meadow Press, 1993.

[*In the following interview, originally conducted in 1970, Kunitz discusses the state of poetry as a literary discipline and his own processes and themes as a poet.*]

[*Packard*]: *A few years ago, many of our poets were also serious critics. Today there doesn't seem to be the same interest in critical theory that there was when Mr. Ransom, Mr. Winters, Mr. Brooks, and Mr. Warren—*

[Kunitz]: Oh well, it's part of the revolt against the establishment, which is also a revolt against conventions and standards, including critical standards.

And it seems also as if some poets are their own aestheticians, such as Mr. Olson. Now, does this take part of a poet's energy, part of what used to be given to him?

Yes, but on the other hand it means that the possibilities are more open; that nobody is required to write in the prevailing style or in the voice of the master. The danger, of course, is in thinking that anything goes in the new dispensation.

Perhaps there will be a swing back; perhaps there will be new criticism after this period is over.

I suspect there will be. These are energetic and confusing times. There will have to be an evaluation of the work of a whole generation. In fact, it is already happening—look at the spate of freshly minted anthologies. I note, by the way, that reputations are being shuffled faster than ever.

This must be one of the freest periods of your whole career, in terms of what can be done.

Freer than ever—but tied to the same old carcass! Incidentally, I can't think of it as a career. To me it's a life.

Mr. Auden has complained about the abuses of this period, that there seems to be a lack of interest in history on the part of some young poets, a lack of interest in meter, in craft, in prosody. He was very concerned, distressed.

Who will be left to admire his great craft? When I first began to teach, in the late forties, it seemed quite obvious that instruction in prosody was part of a workshop discipline. Today the young are mostly indifferent to such matters; not only indifferent but even strongly antipathetic. They praise novelty, spontaneity, and ease, and they resist the very concept of form, which they relate to mechanism and chains. Few understand that, for a poet, even breathing comes under the heading of prosody.

You once said that the originality of any poetry consists to a large degree in the poet's finding his own key images, those that go back to his roots and traumas. Can a poet talk about these images?

Not unless he's very sick, or very foolish. Some poets are both. One oughtn't to try to explain everything away, even if one could. It's enough to reconcile oneself to the existence of an image from which one never gets very far. No matter how one turns or where one travels in the mind, there inescapably it is, sending out vibrations—and you know it's waiting, waiting to be seized again.

Several years ago, you said that certain themes—those of the quest, the night journey, and death and rebirth—preoccupied you.

I must have been reading Jung then. Those are archetypes built into the structure of the mind.

In discussing "Father and Son" in the Ostroff book (The Contemporary Poet as Artist and Critic), *you referred to your sister, and to the big house on the hill, and you said, "They belong to that part of my life which I keep trying to rework into legend." What does that mean?*

What the alchemists meant when they spoke of converting dross into gold.

The voice in the poem you call simply **"Poem"** *is intensely personal, and at the same time the events described have a sense of universal myth behind them.*

When I wrote that poem I was young and ignorant. But even then, as now, I wanted to get below the floor of consciousness, to wipe off the smudge of the day. The poems I like best, I suppose, are the ones that are steeped in "the taste of self"—Hopkins's phrase. Such poems are hard fought for.

What do you feel about improvisations, about randomness as a prime creative principle?

My advice to myself is, Trust in your luck, but don't trust in it absolutely. I recall that after a couple of excruciating experiences as an amateur mycologist, John Cage saw that though the principle of chance operations was good enough for his music, it could not be extended to his mushroom hunting without killing him. Was he aware of the irony implicit in that revelation? Maybe he didn't pursue his insight far enough.

So far, The New York Quarterly *is more or less dependent on the quality of the poems that are submitted to us. What do you feel about the level of the poems that are appearing in the* Quarterly, *and what should we do to improve the quality? We're always looking for that one poem that will be "below the floor of consciousness," as you have said.*

Standards were easier to maintain in an aristocratic society. Emerson said somewhere that democracy descends to meet. All the modern arts are being threatened by the cult of the amateur. And being nourished, too. You have to know the difference between naiveté and simplicity, novelty and originality, rhetoric and passion. The most insidious enemy of the good is not so much the bad as it is the second-best. I mean particularly, in this context, the inferior productions of first-rate reputations. Anyone can see that we have plenty of talent around—what civilization had more? The trouble is that our gifts are not being used well. On the face of it, our literature reflects a mediocre or silly age, sometimes an angry one. When are we going to wake up to the fact that it's tragic?

Have you had any experience with editing, with magazines?

The only magazine I ever edited, after the Classical High School *Argus* (Worcester, Massachusetts), was a library periodical. But last year [1969] I became editor of the Yale Series of Younger Poets, succeeding the late Dudley Fitts. That means reading some five hundred book-length manuscripts a year. Nobody believes me, but I actually make an effort to read every one of them, though not necessarily every page. It's a responsibility I refuse to unload on others, because—who knows?—the most miraculous, most original work of all might get weeded out in the first round, as sometimes happens in competitions of this kind. At least half the submissions can be put aside at once as hopelessly inept or maudlin—usually both. It isn't asking much of a manuscript that it prove reasonably competent and tolerably readable, but I've learned that no more than one hundred out of the five hundred can be expected to pass that test. Eventually it becomes clear that there are only three or four manuscripts, maybe, in the lot from which any sort of fire breaks each time you turn to them. As far as I am concerned, these finalists are all winners, and I wish the rules of the game didn't require me to make an arbitrary choice. I have always hated the business of ranking poets. What was it Blake said? "I cannot think that Real Poets have any competition. None are greatest in the Kingdom of Heaven."

You have said that you used to play technical games, and do craft exercises. Have any of your poems come out of one of those games?

Not that I can recall. But, of course, there is a game element in all poetry. In the very act of writing a poem one is playing with language, playing with the capacities of the mind to hold together its most disparate elements. The object of the game is to fuse as many of one's contradictions and possibilities as one can.

Before we began to record our interview, you said that most of your poems have begun with something that was "given" to you, a very strong opening voice. Doesn't, then, the challenge of realizing the poem require a great understanding of craft in extending the impulse through to the end? So many poems by mediocre poets seem to start beautifully and then are not brought off.

Practically all my poems start with something given to me, that is, a line or a phrase, or a set of lines, that takes me by surprise. When that happens, the challenge is to accept the blessing and go along with it. Only in the process of writing the poem do you discover why the gift was bestowed on you and where it will lead you. Craft is there to sustain and fortify the original impulse, and to preserve the momentum, now by letting go, now by pulling back. Sometimes you find in the end you have to throw out the very lines that gave the poem its start, because they have become embodied in the whole act of the poem and are no longer necessary. Sometimes they require modification, because they may not have come to you perfect. For example, in **"End of Summer,"** the opening lines, as they announced themselves to me, were "*The* agitation of the air, / *The* perturbation of the light." At a certain point in the revision my ear told me that the four definite articles thickened the lines unpleasantly. I changed them to "*An* agitation of the air, / *A* perturbation of the light"—much more open, airy, fluid.

Now surely this process of rewriting and trying to fulfill the intention of the given lines must require a full understanding of verse and prosody. This is the whole reason for craft.

As I indicated earlier, prosody isn't just metrics. It's closer to biology than to mechanics. It involves everything that has to do with the making of a poem, the way it moves, the way it sounds, the way it lives from word to word, the way it breathes.

It is interesting to hear that the beginnings of your poems often consist of "inspired" material, because so much attention has been paid to the way you have ended your poems—particularly those that turn at the end in a line or two in a way that seems both to come out of the poem and to be something new. Do you ever begin the writing of a poem with the ending?

Occasionally I am astonished to find, through all the devious windings of a poem, that my destination is something I've written six months or a year or two years before, and that is what the poem's been seeking out. The mind's stuff is wonderfully patient.

This process of retention, of being able to carry these lines for years and years, requires a tremendous memory. Is there ever any confusion with lines that have been written by other poets? Do you ever find yourself not sure if you wrote a line?

In the beginning, sometimes, I would say to myself, I wonder—is this line really mine? And I discovered quite soon that if I questioned it, the only thing to do was to forget it, because the mind has its own conscience, which has to be trusted. A little doubt is all you need to know.

You keep a notebook of quotations that mean something to you. Has an entry from that notebook ever inspired a poem of yours? Or, do you ever incorporate other people's words into the body of a poem?

The mind is a prolix gut. That's a phrase I suspect I stole from Woodrow Wilson, of all people, though I can't be sure. All poets are thieves—or magpies, if you want me to be euphemistic. The imagination keeps looking for information to digest, and digestion is a process of reconstitution. I don't really care much for paste-and-scissors jobs.

Do you consciously try to control the speed of lines in your poems? In "Benediction," the line "God drive them whistling out" has speed and force, and in the same poem the line "No shy, soft, tigrish fear" is suspended and slow.

The variable pulse of a poem shows that it is alive. Too regular a beat is soporific. I like to hear a poem arguing with itself. Even before it is ready to change into language a poem may begin to assert its buried life in the mind with wordless surges of rhythm and counterrhythm. Gradually the rhythms attach themselves to objects and feelings. At this relatively advanced stage, the movement of a poem is from the known to the unknown, even to the unknowable. Once you have left familiar things behind, you swim through levels of darkness toward some kind of light, uncertain where you will surface.

It's improbable, isn't it, that this kind of experience would ever be given in sum to a poet, without the long struggle, without the long process of—

I wish it were easier. How I envy prolific poets!

To go back to your underwater metaphor for the creative process, what is the sensation at the point of surfacing?

Joy. As though a burden had been removed. One is freer than before.

Then a false ending to a poem would be an attempt to create this result without actually achieving it.

If you fake it, your rhetoric betrays you.

Have you always written in the way you have just described?

I think so. Even the earliest poems. **"For the Word Is Flesh,"** for example.

How young were you when you began to write poetry?

Even in grade school I was rhyming—doggerel, mainly. But I enjoyed that. And I was reading all the bad poets, along with some good ones, and loving them equally. Words always fascinated me, regardless of whether I knew what they meant. In fourth grade, I recall, I began a composition on the Father of Our Country with the sentence: "George Washington was a tall, petite, handsome man."

Which of the poets you read as a young person had the most influence on the development of your own writing? Did reading Tennyson affect the development of your ear?

During my high school years I admired Keats and Tennyson for their music. One day my English teacher read Herrick in class. Later, a neighbor gave me Wordsworth's collected poems. Those were red-letter days. At Harvard I discovered the metaphysicals and Hopkins, and they shook me up. Afterwards, in the thirties, the later Yeats became important to me, and I began my long friendship with Roethke.

Would you say something about your feelings concerning faith and religion? This process you describe of struggling with the given lines of a poem might almost be an Old Testament scene of Jacob wrestling with the Dark Angel in order to find God through intuition rather than through outside revelation.

I suppose I am a religious person without a religion. Maybe because I have no faith, I need it more than others. And the wrestling is damn good exercise.

Do you often change words in poems after they have been printed? There are two versions of "Deciduous Branch" in print—the first says "Passion" where the later one has "Summer."

"Summer" made the metaphor harder and cleaner. I can't usually bear to read my early poems, but once in a while I am tempted to see whether I can make some small improvements in the ones I want to keep. I haven't the slightest interest in rewriting them *in toto*, even if I could, nor do I propose to make major changes.

This brings up the matter of a poet's going back and revising, or even disclaiming, early poems which the public has already come to know. How can he blot them out? Should a poet keep trying to bring his work up to date, or should he let the record stand?

A poet tends to be a perfectionist. I see no reason why he should be disqualified from trying to improve his own work, published or unpublished. As long as he's alive, it's his property. After his death, posterity will have the privilege of determining which versions of his poems, if any, it chooses to remember.

What prompted you to edit those massive collections of literary biographies, Twentieth Century Authors, European Authors, *and the rest?*

Simply that I had to earn a living. After college I went to work for a publisher in New York and soon discovered that I wasn't geared for an office existence. So I fled to a farm in Connecticut, where I produced a crop of herbs, flowers, and reference books. And, perennially, poems.

Now you seem to be spending a good part of your time on Cape Cod, in Provincetown.

I'm truly happier there. I have a great world of friends in New York, but the city depletes me. I need to grow things and to breathe clean air. Then, I have my involvement with the Fine Arts Work Center in Provincetown. A few of us have banded together, with the help of some foundation money, including a grant from the National Endowment for the Arts, to invite a selected group of young writers and artists each year to join a productive winter community up there by the sea. We give what help we can. Alan Dugan and I are the ones most concerned with the poets. And we bring in all sorts of brilliant people from the outside for weekly seminars.

That sounds like an exciting program. How does one find out more about it?

By writing to the Fine Arts Work Center, Box 565, Provincetown, Massachusetts, 02657.

Poetry seems to be the orphan child of the arts—it is always difficult to find public support for projects involving poetry. Do you see any sign of improvement? Will a person who wants to become a poet always have to look forward to a lifetime of struggling, and working at vocations he doesn't really enjoy in order to support his art?

Hasn't that usually been true? I'm not sure that a poet should expect to be rewarded for his voluntary choice of a vocation. If he has any sense at all, he should realize that he's going to have a hard time surviving, particularly in a society whose main drives are exactly opposite to his. If he chooses, against the odds, to be a poet, he ought to be tough enough, cunning enough, to take advantage of the system in order to survive. And if he doesn't, it's sad, but the world is full of the most terrible kinds of sadness.

What do you think of the way in which poetry and literature have been presented to elementary school children through our present educational system?

Almost anybody would have to agree that the American system of education has been a dismal failure. Certainly one of the areas in which it has most significantly failed is in teaching students how to cope with poetry. The failure begins at the grade school level. But there are some promising signs—first of all, a general recognition of the failure. The new young educators, clearly, know the essential truth about the injury done to the imagination of the child, and there are many signs of revolt against the educational system, just as there is a revolt against the political system.

Many high school and college students feel that poetry has no importance for them, in their lives.

So many of the young today doubt that classroom instruction in general and the reading of poetry in particular are what they need most. I can understand their negativism. They fail to see that the work of the imagination is precisely what has to be achieved if we are going to save our civilization from disaster. And that a poem, regardless of its theme, can embody for us a principle of the free mind engaged in a free action.

Wasn't "The Mound Builders" written out of a political situation?

Many of my poems are, but in an oblique way. By its nature poetry is hostile to opinions, and the opinions of a poet on public affairs are, in any case, of no special interest. The poems that attract me most, out of the contemporary dilemma, are the peripheral ones that are yet obviously the product of a mind engaged with history. **"The Mound Builders,"** I can recall, came out of the resumption of nuclear testing by President Kennedy in 1962, when I was traveling through the South, and looking at the archeological traces of a civilization that flourished in this country between 900 and 1100 A.D., the greatest civilization of the Eastern seaboard, and maybe the greatest civilization north of Mexico, of which nothing now remains except a few shards. There in Georgia the inscription reads, "Macon is the seventh layer of civilization on this spot." Macon, one of the seats of racist injustice in this country. So all these elements entered into the making of the poem, including the fact that I was traveling, and reading my work, and talking to college students in the South. But most readers would say, not without justification, "It's a poem about mound builders."

Are you writing dramatic monologues now?

My new book has several poems that are basically dramatic in their structure. They're not quite dramatic monologues—I don't know really what to call them—but in each case there is a dramatic action incorporated in the poem, sometimes appearing and sometimes disappearing. The very last poem I wrote for the book is called **"Around Pastor Bonhoeffer."** Bonhoeffer, you know, was the Lutheran pastor in Germany who, after a great struggle with his conscience, joined the plot to kill Hitler. The plot failed, and he was exterminated. The conflict between his Christian principle of nonviolence and the political necessity for action seems to me a parable for our times. I myself am a nonviolent man with radical feelings about the way things are.

When will that book be published?

Next March.

And it's called **The Testing-Tree***?*

With a hyphen.

Marie Henault (essay date 1980)

SOURCE: Henault, Marie. "The 'Interior Logic' of Kunitz's First Three Books of Poetry." In *Stanley Kunitz,* pp. 65-85. Boston: Twayne, 1980.

[*In the following essay, Henault examines Kunitz's concept of interior logic as a goal in the compilation of his poetry collections.*]

Kunitz tends "to think," he said, "of a book as a composition, a joining of parts into an architectural whole, not just a throwing-together of the poems as written. A book ought to have an interior logic. . . ."[1] What is the "interior logic" of each of Kunitz's first three volumes? Both *Intellectual Things* and *Passport to the War* contained exactly fifty poems each, and each began and ended with significant poems. The first book began with **"Change"** and without internal divisions proceeded on to conclude with **"Vita Nuova."** The second book in turn began with a war

poem congruent with its date of publication, **"Reflection by a Mailbox,"** and finished off with the same poem as the first book, **"Vita Nuova."**

Part I of this second book *Passport to the War* contained twenty-six new poems, all those written since 1930 that Kunitz wished to retain; Part II, twenty-four poems from *Intellectual Things*. All fifty of these poems reappeared in *Selected Poems* with the addition of two poems from *Intellectual Things* which had not been carried over into *Passport to the War*. With that latter book already including poems from *Intellectual Things* and the poems from that book (*Passport*) all reprinted in *Selected Poems,* one gathers that *Selected Poems* is a collection of all the poems written up to that time that Kunitz wanted to keep, a kind of "collected poems" after all: more than half the poems from his first book and the whole of his second book. Yet, since Kunitz never arranged his poems chronologically, their juxtapositions in each book have significance, an "interior logic," as he phrased it; thus, next is an examination of this "interior logic" in each of his first three books along with a brief look at the poems rejected for one inadequacy or another.

I *INTELLECTUAL THINGS* (1930)

First of all, as Kunitz reminds us, the poems in his first book, *Intellectual Things,* "date from 1927, when I was 22." He was, then, he says, "an innocent in so many ways. I had developed intellectually more than I had emotionally or experientially."[2] One can add "technically," too, for the failure of a good many of the poems in this book is due not to the inadequacy of theme or content but to questions of form and control. But first the book itself, its "interior logic": Lacking marked internal divisions and subtitles, the fifty poems rest rather heavily on the Blake epigraph "The tear is an intellectual thing." He "meant to demonstrate," Kunitz said, "if I could, not that the poem was a cerebral exercise, but the contrary, that the intellect and the passions were inseparable. . . ."[3]

This unity is, I think, the main emphasis in the volume, and the arrangement of the poems appears to be from generalities to particulars. Thus the first half of the book has poems which are relatively general visions of man, the poet, and destiny—poems like **"Change," "Geometry of Moods," "Single Vision," "The Words of the Preacher," "Mens Creatrix,"** and **"Ambergris."** The second half has a good number of love poems, many of which were ultimately discarded. Seventeen of the twenty-six poems not reprinted in *Passport to the War* are from the second half of *Intellectual Things*. The earlier poems in this first book, the general ones, have overtones of doom, intimations of vision as, one can suppose, the poet grows. Finally, it seems that the poems attempt to reconcile or bring together "mind" and "heart," which along with "blood," "Time," and "thought," are among the most frequently used words in the book. Out of love and the suffering and pain it causes come poetry and the unity of the mind and the passions.

The book ends with some meditative-philosophical poems, **"Who Tears the Serpent from the Flesh,"** **"Organic Bloom,"** and, last of all, **"Vita Nuova,"** presenting a hard, more terrifying vision of life—or of a "new life": the poet's dedication of himself to a more iron control. He had been "a part-time creature," and what he desires is "The single beam of all my life intense." This final assertion, the last line in *Intellectual Things,* confirms directly some of the incidental wisdom of other poems—in **"The Words of the Preacher,"** for instance, "By piecemeal living a man is doomed . . . ," and in **"Beyond Reason"** he tames the passions "with the sections of my mind" and teaches his "mind to love its thoughtless crack."

II REJECTED POEMS

Of the two dozen or so poems from *Intellectual Things* which did not fit into the "interior logic" of *Passport to the War,* Kunitz has said that his own "main feeling" about them was "that they were immature. Maybe I felt a little embarrassed reading them, so I thought it would be better to drop them. . . ."[4] "Immature," yes, and sometimes embarrassing, too, but mostly they lack technical control, are awkward in imagery, and, at times, are awkward in form also.

The greater number of these rejected poems, more than one-half, can be grouped as "love" poems in which, often, "love is coming or is passing by" (*IT,* 32). **"Thumb-Nail Biography"** (*IT,* 27-28) shares weaknesses with many of the other poems in this grouping. It has an ugly title, for one thing, as do also **"Particular Lullaby"** and **"Regard of Tangents"** and other abandoned poems. Then in six short-lined quatrains with an abab rhyme the subject of a too-soon blossoming love is presented in rather infelicitous imagery ("delicate knobs of blooms," "electric light"):

> Her dim corolla-love,
> Believing there was sun,
> Received too early shivering proof
> Of corruption.
>
> (Stanza 4)

The last stanza wafts off helplessly in two sets of periods of ellipses as though the poem could not be brought to a conclusion.

Another love poem, **"First Love"** (*IT,* 47-48), too, fails in imagery, diction, and resolution. Here the Lady awakes to love so:

> At his incipient sun
> The ice of twenty winters broke,
> Crackling, in her eyes.
>
> (Stanza 1)

In the final, eighth stanza, she is said ineffectively to be,

> . . . a tree in spring
> Trembling with the hope of leaves,
> Of which the leaves are tongues.

"Me and the Rock" (*IT,* 42) also has a disagreeable title, and while its minimal punctuation gives it some interest as an early experimental poem, its untypical diction—"train," "cars," "planes," and "motors"—and unsuccessful images—"coals of remembrance," "blind / Punctures of sleep"—might be why it was not retained.

Two other eliminated poems, **"Thou Unbelieving Heart"** and **"Sad Song"** (*IT,* 43-44 and 45) might, it seems to me, be retitled, slightly revised, and revived. They are not highly significant, but both interestingly experiment with form, few rhymes, and a certain re-frainlike quality. **"Sad Song"** is somewhat in "La Belle Dame sans Merci" tradition: "I married me a fay, / I was a merry gnome . . ." of stanza I becomes "I married me a fay, / I am a withered gnome . . ." of the third and final stanza.

In a four-stanza form (stanzas of 7, 8, 9, and 7 lines) reminiscent of the ballade, **"Thou Unbelieving Heart"** with pseudomedieval matter ("lady," "lord," "hawk," "hound," "beast") tells a mysterious story the sinister implications of which are not clear. "Lady," the second stanza reads,

> . . . the bird still screams,
> The old dog licks his hand,
> Do not study your dreams.

The last stanza repeats the two opening lines of the poem:

> Lady that flutters in the bridal cage
> Waiting love's absent lord,

and then recasts the remaining five lines of stanza 1 using almost identical rhymes:

> The beast he hunts and may not find
> Is hunting you who shall be found.
> Erase the picture from your floor.
> Innocent Lady, you have heard
> The lion thunder at your door.

In contrast to these cast-off poems, the two poems resurrected from *Intellectual Things* for inclusion in *Selected Poems,* **"Postscript"** and **"Benediction"** (*SP,*

16-17 and 11-12), are more specific and more typical of Kunitz in both tone and idiom. The only changes in **"Postscript"** between its publication in 1930 and that in 1958, twenty-eight years later, are the excisings of the two archaic "unto's" in lines 3 and 39. The forty-three unrhymed lines of this single verse paragraph are, it seems, a "postscript" to a love affair. The speaker calls his dream journey of the first five lines "the perilous way without return," making it archetypal. He sums up what has happened in lines 14 and 15: "I lost by winning, and I shall not win / Again except by loss." Meanwhile he remembers and finds "Some little comfort" in thinking that "Yet will its lyric history be saved. . . ."

Yet, as the speaker says in the most memorable lines of the poem, art cannot feed man:

> A man can starve upon the golden-sweet
> Impossible apples of Cezanne; a man
> Can eagerly consult a woman's head
> (Picasso's), but her slow and stupid eyes
> Drink light in vegetative apathy.

With a final "O darling" cry he ends, rather weakly,

> The meaning of a mouth, a breast, is plain,
> But what you mean to me is dipped in blood
> And tangled like the bright threads of a dream.

What "a breast, a mouth" are in themselves "is plain," but what the poet means by their "meaning" is not. And "what you mean to me" in the next line is Valentine phrasing unredeemed by the strong phrase "dipped in blood" or the imprecise "tangled like the bright threads of a dream."

The other revived poem, **"Benediction,"** in fifteen equal open couplets, is what its title says it is, a "benediction," a blessing, in which the speaker asks God first to

> . . . banish from your house
> The fly, the roach, the mouse . . .

and also to "Admonish from your door / The hypocrite and liar. . . ." Fear, doubt, evil are in turn to be excluded, as are surprise and delirium. In the last four couplets the speaker asks God to grant "you" tears, love, and his own "(My sweet) sweet company." It is a slight, uncomplicated occasional poem with no outstanding lines except for the wordplay on "sweet" in the final couplet, but overall a directness and competence that make it worth preserving.

III *PASSPORT TO THE WAR* (1944)

Arranged in two parts, part I new poems and part II poems from *Intellectual Things, Passport to the War,* Kunitz's second book, is in a sense his selected poems

of 1944—and so it is subtitled: "A Selection of Poems." The twenty-four reprinted poems, "some of them revised," according to Kunitz's note, are grouped as they were in the 1930 volume; the excisions make the progress from **"Change"** to **"Vita Nuova"** clearer than it had been previously, though part II reads rather like a separate volume than as a section intrinsically and necessarily following the twenty-six new poems of part I.

These new poems, quite a bit more concrete, less abstract than those in part II, are concerned with contemporary events seen as timeless equivalents of the ills of the world. The time itself is that of World War II, and the poems move from the poet's summons to take part in the conflict (**"Reflection by a Mailbox"**) through further reflections on this and on the meaning of what is happening to him "whirling between two wars," who "Yesterday . . . had a world to lose." Much of the imagery and many of the themes of these poems relate to his enlisting in wrath's "brindled generation" and going "forth to war." About midway in the section the poems seem to locate the source of the world's evil in man himself, his "ancient wrongs," as in **"Between the Acts," "The Guilty Man,"** and **"The Fitting of the Mask."** It is his "wound," he says in the last poem of part I. The title of this poem, in quotation marks, poses a question asked of the poet, **"'What Have You Done?'"** He answers it by asking his questioner, "Pigeon," a loved one, to

> Be patient with my wound:
> Too long I lay
> In the folds of my preparation,
> Sinuous in the sun,
> A golden skin,
> All pride, sores, excretion,
> Blazing with death. O child,
> From my angry side
> Tumbles this agate heart,
> Your prize, veined with the root
> Of guilty life,
> From which flow love and art.

(*SP,* 87)

The title phrase, "'What Have You Done?'", is sufficiently everyday in diction to be a question actually asked of the "I" of the poem; still, the quotation marks make it seem more than that. Possibly it is an allusion to Pliny's "Hodie quid egisti?" so that while the question, first of all, asks about a specific act (such as going off to war) it radiates out to ask about the whole of one's life. Samuel Johnson's Idler 88, with Pliny's words as a title, comments, for instance, "This fatal question ['What have ye done?'] has disturbed the quiet of many other minds. He that in the latter part of his life too strictly enquires what he has done, can very seldom receive from his own heart such an account as will give him satisfaction."[5] The "wound" that the speaker is asking his loved one to be "patient" with here could be one's universal limitations as a human being, the damage of something like Original Sin, those elements of oneself that lead him to act in ways which require explanation or at least patience from those one loves.

The poems in **Intellectual Things** seem to be abstract and concerned with universals while those in **Passport to the War** are concrete and concerned with particulars. Kunitz himself has remarked that one of his "great influences was Plato, and I was very deep in Platonic lore . . . at this period of my first work." **"Very Tree,"** one of the poems not reprinted from **Intellectual Things** in the 1944 volume, has as its theme, in Kunitz's added words, "the idea of tree, treeness as opposed to the shadow of the idea."[6] In the poem the poet rejects bark, leaves, a bird: "let there be / Only tree." Mostly, however, the Platonism in his first book is in the starting from generalities as in **"Change"** and **"Geometry of Moods,"** the first two poems, or in **"Motion of Wish"** and **"So Intricately Is This World Resolved,"** near the end of the book.

Partly no doubt the change between the two sets of poems came about as a result of experience and growth as well as the circumstances of the time. At least since the Romantics, poets have often seen themselves caught up in history, and, like Kunitz, young and not-so-young American men of the 1940s were more than most others snatched from their routines and lives and transported into another "curious life"—that of the drafted or enlisted. M. L. Rosenthal devotes several pages of the first chapter of his *New Poets,* a study of "American and British Poetry Since World War II," to "the deep, and literal, absorption of our age in the terrors of war . . ." and says,

> War is more than a theme or subject for modern writers. It is a condition of consciousness, a destructive fact that explodes within the literature as without it. Just because the fact is so grossly obvious, we are in danger of overlooking its omnipresence.[7]

"The bloodied envelope addressed to you / Is history . . . ," Kunitz writes at the end of **"Night Letter,"** and one has to emphasize the adjective "bloodied." A poet who is, in Kunitz's view, "more like others than anybody else,"[8] a representative man, can also more than others see himself *in* history. As Rosenthal says, so "the private life of the poet himself, especially under stress of psychological crisis, becomes a major theme. Often it is felt at the same time as a symbolic embodiment of national and cultural crisis."[9] In other words, "a gang of personal devils / . . . clank their jigging bones as public evils . . ." (*SP,* 113). Many of

the new poems in **Passport to the War** do "clank their jigging bones as public evils. . . ." The full clarification of what Kunitz had to say, nonetheless, had to wait for the thematic grouping and rethinking that came fourteen years later with **Selected Poems.**

IV *SELECTED POEMS* (1958)

The arrangement of the fifty-two poems from the first two books of poetry is completely discarded in **Selected Poems,** in which the earlier poems at no time maintain the same sequence. Thus it seems that Kunitz reexamined the relationships among his poems before "composing" this third book, which, as he says in his **"Author's Note,"** are "in groups that bear some relevance to the themes, the arguments, that have preoccupied me since I began to write" (*SP,* front matter).

As noted below these groupings are made clear with titles taken from poems central to the sections; the five division titles are "The Serpent's Word," "The Terrible Threshold," "Prince of Counterfeits," "A World to Lose," and "The Coat without a Seam," each of them a highly figurative and suggestive phrase in itself.[10] The second of these section titles, "The Terrible Threshold," Kunitz used again as the title for his 1974 book of selected poems published in England (discussed in the next chapter).

The Serpent's Word. The first section, "The Serpent's Word," contains twenty-seven poems, more than half of them ones new in **Selected Poems**; the twin themes here are love and poetry. The section begins and ends with poems of the 1950s and includes in between a dozen poems from Kunitz's two earlier books. **"The Dark and the Fair,"** from which the title of the section comes, in eight elegiac quatrains interrelates love and art (*SP,* 33-34).

The poem itself is a small archetypal drama: While the speaker is engaged in a heated discussion at a party, the Fair Lady, his present companion, comes to his side and puts in his hand her own "small impulsive" one, "Five-fingered gift." For him "The moment clanged . . . ," and he is reminded, like Marcel Proust tasting the madeleine soaked in tea, of the past: "risen from the past" the Dark Lady "eventually usurps the scene," Kunitz said in commenting on this poem.[11] Like the present Fair Lady, once years before the Dark Lady had similarly come to his side. "What brought her now, in the semblance of the warm," he asks in the sixth stanza, "Out of cold spaces, damned by colder blood?"

The Dark Lady had wronged him in that past time, and for her he had "killed the propitiatory bird . . . ," a sinful, symbolic action, apparently, like that of the

Ancient Mariner. Now, though, "Peace to her bitter bones," he says in the last stanza, "Who taught me the serpent's word, but yet the word." Although the "word," given the association with "serpent," can be read as evil or the knowledge of good and evil, in the context of Kunitz's work as a whole, clearly it is poetry or this particular poem. From such hurtful experiences comes art.

Kunitz chose this poem as "a favorite or crucial poem"[12] from his own work for Engle and Langland's *Poet's Choice* (1962), saying that one of his reasons was that he liked "a poem that rides the beast of an action," and many of his strongest poems, like this one, do just that. **"The Science of the Night,"** which opens this section and *Selected Poems,* so rides "the beast of an action," as does also **"The Thief,"** the long, lively poem which closes "The Serpent's Word."

The Terrible Threshold. Most of the twenty-four poems in "The Terrible Threshold," section 2 of this book, are visionary, "religious" pieces from *Intellectual Things* with only four new poems and four from *Passport to the War.* Some of these are **"Single Vision," "For the Word Is Flesh," "Father and Son,"** and the sonnet **"So Intricately Is This World Resolved,"** all discussed above. **"Open the Gates"** (*SP,* 41), the short Blakean lyric from which the title of the section comes, is typical of the poems in "The Terrible Threshold." The three tetrameter quatrains, the "In Memoriam" stanza, present a strange action in which the naked "I" prowls through "the city of the burning cloud" dragging his life behind him in a sack. He knocks at a door; the door opens, and he stands "on the terrible threshold" where he sees "The end and the beginning in each other's arms."

Ralph J. Mills, Jr., points to the "nightmare effects" in this poem, and I think "nightmare" sums up both this poem and many of the other poems in this section. The "Gates" of the title may refer to Penelope's story in the *Odyssey,* Book XIX, of the two gates of dreams, the one of ivory for deceitful dreams, the other of horn for prophetic dreams. The vision in this poem surely is that of the latter kind; here as in another poem in this section he seems, prophetically, to live all his life "at once" (*SP,* 51). The situation is similar to those in **"I Dreamed That I Was Old"** and in **"Change"** (*SP,* 59 and 65):

> Here, Now, and Always, man would be
> Inviolate eternally:
> This is his spirit's trinity.

(*SP,* 65)

Prince of Counterfeits. The third and middle section of *Selected Poems,* "Prince of Counterfeits," has seventeen poems; only one of them is from Kunitz's first book; nine are from *Passport to the War,* and seven are new to this volume. The theme here is the treachery and grief of the Self as singled out in such statements as "its own self turns Christian-cannibal" and "The thing that eats the heart is mostly heart" of the final poem in the section (*SP,* 71). In **"My Surgeons"** the "I's" "butcher-boys" "cut" him up and squeeze out of his veins "The bright liquor of sympathy. . . ."

> "No hope for persons any more,"
> They cry, "on either side of the grave."

(*SP,* 73)

The situation seems to be that as he matures the "I" sees what "the world's game" (*SP,* 75) is, and he does not like it. A world of disharmony, violence, and betrayal, it constantly imperils the Self. In **"The Guilty Man"** the "I" says that "the darkness of the self goes out / And spreads contagion on the flowing air." And what is it like in the world?

> Heart against mouth is singing out of tune,
> Night's whisperings and blanks betrayed; this is
> The end of lies: my bones are angry with me.

(*SP,* 75)

By his title phrase, "The Guilty Man," Kunitz said, he does not "mean someone who has sinned more than anybody else." Rather, he means "the person who, simply by virtue of being mortal, is in a way condemned; he's mortal and he's fallible, and his life is inevitably a series of errors and consequences."[13]

This particular poem, then, **"The Guilty Man,"** is an important one for Kunitz, perhaps a troublesome one, too, for he continued to revise it. In 1944 the last line was "None may forgive us for the ancient wrongs" (*PW,* 27). Possibly this phrasing seemed to point overmuch to Original Sin—an idea which certainly is in the poem—though, as Kunitz pointed out, it is there "Without the theological furniture."[14] At any rate for *Selected Poems* he altered it to "The souls of numbers kiss the perfect stars," a line of nearly baffling complexity (*SP,* 75). For the selection of his poems published in England in 1974, *The Terrible Threshold,* Kunitz extensively changed the final four lines of the poem moving them toward clarity and simplicity, also, I think, shifting the meaning somewhat, and leaving the poem less resolved—purposefully less resolved, it seems:

> I hate the excellence that spoils the world.
> So leave me now, you honorable men
> Whose treason is to turn the conscience kind,
> And do not turn until you hear a child.

(pp. 16-17)

The poem from which the title of this section of *Selected Poems* comes, **"The Fitting of the Mask,"** most explicitly outlines this implicit fable of the "treason" of the Self. A dialogue poem in eight stanzas, it has seven sestets rhyming abacbc; the seventh stanza, an italicized song, is eight lines, ababcbcb. The setting is a shop in which masks are sold, and the two speakers are a customer, the Self, who must have a mask to wear at the dance (of life, no doubt), and a merchant, a devil-figure. Two images which the customer would like he cannot buy and the one he is offered at the end he would rather not have seen. In the first line the Self says, "Again I come to buy the image fated" (*SP,* 82). The seller tells him that that image, "the youth, the undefeated," is gone. The customer chides the merchant for this and is given excuses.

"Enough!" the Self says in the third stanza; he will buy instead "another face," one described in the catalogue as "Fool of Love," clearly an image of another phase in the Self's life. The other protests that that mask is shopworn, and while rummaging around for yet another face, he sings a song about the various other faces that similarly cannot be sold: *"There's nothing left that's decent in our stock, / And what are we to do, and what to do?"* At last, however, he finds another mask. "But look!" he says,

> "—here's something rare, macabre, a true
> Invention of the time's insomniac wits.
> Perhaps we ought to sell it to the zoo.
> Go to the darkening glass that traps your shames
> And tell me what you see."

"O Prince of Counterfeits," the customer cries in answer, "This is the Self I hunted and knifed in dreams!"

A World to Lose. Section 4 of *Selected Poems,* "A World to Lose," has one new poem, **"The Economist's Song,"** consistent in theme and tone with the eight poems from *Passport to the War* that complete the section. In a sense all nine poems are both political and personal poems, the self horrified by what has happened but certain too that he and everyone else are not without responsibility in the catastrophe by which all are overtaken. "Our failures creep with soldier hearts, / Pointing their guns at what we love," the speaker says in **"The Last Picnic"** (*SP,* 93), the first poem in the section and the one from which the title of the section comes—"Yesterday we had a world to lose."

In the meditative poem **"Reflection by a Mailbox,"** waiting for the postman to bring him his "passport to the war," presumably his draft notice, the speaker reflects on the contemporary political situation—Hitler, the Jewish persecution in Europe. His ancestors "step" from his "American bones," he says, and he sees his immigrant parents, "mother in a woven shawl,"

> . . . father picking up his pack
> For the return voyage through those dreadful years
> Into the winter of the raging eye.

> (*SP,* 94)

His people, the Jews, are "game," he says, "For the hunters of manskins in the warrens of Europe . . . ," and he asks what it means:

> Are these the citizens of the new estate
> To which the continental shelves aspire;
> Or the powerful get of a dying age, corrupt
> And passion-smeared, with fluid on their lips,
> As if a soul had been given to petroleum?
> How shall we uncreate that lawless energy?

In the final stanza he thinks "of Pavlov and his dogs / And the motto carved on the broad lintel of his brain: / 'Sequence, consequence, and again consequence.'" And so these awful things, animalized humans, are not without their beginnings somewhere in our own selves.

The ironically titled poem **"Careless Love"** (*SP,* 95) which follows reflects on man's attraction to war in an extended conceit: soldiers "Are comforted by their guns . . . ," as though these instruments of killing were loved ones. Here war is a "nymphomaniac" and what she "enjoys / Inexhaustibly is boys." Similarly in **"Confidential Instructions"** (*SP,* 98) and **"This Day This World,"** with diction and tone like those in some of Auden's satiric poems, the blame is put on man himself.

Closing the section, **"Night Letter,"** one of Kunitz's best poems, brings all the elements together—"in the torment of our time," all are guilty, "self-accused," and suicidal. The sixty blank-verse lines of this dramatic monologue cannot be quoted in full, though they speak so clearly for themselves that one is tempted to do just that, or at least to quote three-quarters of them, as Ralph J. Mills, Jr., does in his discussion of the poem.[15]

The circumstances of **"Night Letter"** seem to be these: Away at the war "Night after night" the speaker tries to write to his beloved, but is beset instead by the horrors of his time. "Where is your ministry?" he asks, and adds,

> . . . I thought I heard
> A piece of laughter break upon the stair
> Like glass, but when I wheeled around I saw
> Disorder, in a tall magician's hat,

Keeping his rabbit-madness crouched inside,
Sit at my desk and scramble all the news.
The strangest things are happening. Christ! the dead,
Pushing the membrane from their face, salute
The dead and scribble slogans on our walls;
Phantoms and phobias mobilize, thronging
The roads; and in the Bitch's streets the men
Are lying down, great crowds with fractured wills
Dumping the shapeless burden of their lives
Into the rivers where the motors flowed.

                                            (*SP*, 101)

"What have we done to them," he asks, "that what they are / Shrinks from the touch of what they hoped to be?" Out of his personal guilt, "Pardon," he pleads, "clutching the fragile sleeve / Of my poor father's ghost returned to howl / His wrongs."

> I suffer the twentieth century,
> The nerves of commerce wither in my arm;
> Violence shakes my dreams; I am so cold,
> Chilled by the persecuting wind abroad,
> The oratory of the rodent's tooth,
> The slaughter of the blue-eyed open towns,
> And principle disgraced, and art denied.

As Mills says, this "hell of Kunitz's poem is a hell of our own invention, wherein we lock ourselves with greed, exploitation, and hatred of self and others."[16] This terrifying death-in-life that war, particularly, has brought us to, is conveyed through not only the vividness of the Mad Hatter image of Disorder but also that of the rising of the dead as they push "the membrane from their face," in a rebirth image. In addition, the simplicity of "I am so cold" is followed by what he is "Chilled by": "the persecuting wind," "The oratory of the rodent's tooth, / The slaughter of the blue-eyed open towns." The personification here, giving human "blue eyes" to "towns," works, I think, because of the connotations of childlike innocence and defenselessness in "blue-eyed" and "open" and as well the wartime meaning of an "open" city.[17]

After the abstract summation, "principle disgraced, and art denied," the speaker addresses his beloved simply, personally, as "My dear" and asks if it is "too late for us / To say, 'Let us be good unto each other'?" Then, emotion expended, in a peaceful few lines he sees

> The lamps go singly out; the valley sleeps;
> I tend the last light shining on the farms
> And keep for you the thought of love alive. . . .

His conclusion is that though this is a bad time for man, it is not the end of the world:

> Cities shall suffer siege and some shall fall,
> But man's not taken. What the deep heart means,
> Its message of the big, round, childish hand,

> Its wonder, its simple lonely cry,
> The bloodied envelope addressed to you,
> Is history, that wide and mortal pang.

This final "you" is no longer the beloved woman but all of us, man, and, as Kunitz says so often, "the deep heart," compassion, may yet save us if we but accept "The bloodied envelope addressed to" us.

Although **"Night Letter"** is by no means an imitation of Arnold's "Dover Beach," or even necessarily influenced by it, that is the poem it most resembles in tone, subject, and resolution, and the two poems might profitably be read side by side. Both are nocturnal addresses to a beloved; the speakers are both shaken by the miseries and doubts of their time; and both poems find a refuge in love: "Ah, love, let us be true / To one another!" ("Dover Beach"), and "'Let us be good unto each other.' / . . . I tend the last light shining on the farms / And keep for you the thought of love alive . . ." (**"Night Letter"**).

The Coat without a Seam. The fifth and final section of **Selected Poems**, "The Coat without a Seam" is fittingly a strong one with only one poem each from each of Kunitz's previous volumes and six new poems, some of them the best in the collection. Three of these are fairly long poems with short lines—**"The Way Down,"** seventy-two lines; **"Revolving Meditation,"** seventy-four lines; and **"A Spark of Laurel,"** thirty-six lines—a kind of poem new in Kunitz's work and a kind of poem, too, that becomes increasingly characteristic. He commented himself that as time went on his "line has been getting shorter, partly because I'm cutting down on adjectives—I'm usually down to two or three stresses to a line. This permits any number of syllables, within reason, as long as the ground pattern is preserved."[18]

These short-lined poems themselves, like the other poems in this section, are poems about poetry or art. In **"The Way Down"** the action seems to be an archetypal allegory of a journey through time, a descent and a return. "Time swings her burning hands," and the "I" sees an unspecified "him going down . . . / To a cabin underground / Where his hermit father lives. . . ." His hermit father's coat is "The coat without a seam" of the title phrase, the coat

> That the race, in its usury, bought
> For the agonist to redeem,
> By dying in it, one
> Degree a day till the whole
> Circle's run.

                                            (*SP*, 106)

These lines connect "The coat without a seam" to both Adam and Christ as in John's gospel, yet Kunitz appears not to be using the phrase in its strict theological meaning;[19] rather the coat is a magical garment symbolical of unity as such a remarkably woven piece of clothing easily can be. In the second stich the "I" dies at the same time as "the magician," but then revives. "Must I learn again to breathe?" he asks, and everything wakes with him. Finally, in section 3 he asks his "father in the wood, / Mad father of us all" to "Receive your dazzling child / Drunk with the morning-dew / Into your fibrous love. . . ."

Too explicit explaining of the allegory might detract from the poem, though one can say at least that it touches on the poetic process, the necessity of knowing one's depths, and is in the tranced poet tradition of Coleridge's poet in "Kubla Khan":

> His flashing eyes, his floating hair!
> Weave a circle round him thrice,
> And close your eyes with holy dread,
> For he on honeydew hath fed,
> And drunk the milk of Paradise.

Besides, the poem does what Kunitz has said he likes a poem to do; it "rides the beast of an action," a descent in this case. As he explained to inquiring students in a biographical aside, he could not expect them "to know that I began to write the poem after making the steep descent down to the Grotto of Neptune in Tivoli, not far from Rome."[20] Yet the physical details of the poem are specific enough for readers to infer a physical setting, the quite specific "miracle" of sewing a "coat without a seam," with the Apollo, Christ, and father images making up the backbone of the poem. Still, "The actual physical setting," as Kunitz went on to say, "is of no consequence, for 'the way down' of the poem is into a mythic underground, older than self or history. Down there the protagonist confronts the mystery of his roots, endures his fate, and is restored to life."[21]

The dithyrambic force of the poem comes across partly through the form, that of the Cowleyan or irregular ode, suitable to the exalted rapture of the material: here quick six-syllabled lines in the first and third numbered parts, mostly longer lines in part 2, and irregular rhyming. "Hands," at the end of the first line, for example, links with "lands" in line three; but "down" of line 2 is not echoed until line 9 when it is repeated. "Gold" of line 4 has no rhyme, but lines 5-8 are alternately rhymed—"specked," "mind," "crack," "grind"—a pattern of rhyme recurring here and there throughout the poem to give an overall highly musical effect.

Three of the other poems in this final part of *Selected Poems,* like **"The Thief"** in the first section, are uncharacteristically (for Kunitz) relaxed and even exuberant—**"The Class Will Come to Order," "A Choice of Weapons,"** and **"Revolving Meditation."** In the first of these, one of Kunitz's most engaging poems, the speaker walks on a college campus prior to a class. He has received a letter from his beloved, from whom he is temporarily separated, and the thought of love and the feel of this letter in his pocket give him joy; later in the classroom he smiles to himself but does not tell his students why he smiles.

The poem has two epigraphs, an unusual practice for Kunitz, one from Joyce's *Finnegans Wake* and another from Dante's *Vita Nuova.* They set the academic scene and prepare for some of the content of the poem.

> O tell me all about Anna Livia! I want to hear all about Anna Livia. Well, you know Anna Livia? Yes, of course, we all know Anna Livia. Tell me all. Tell me now. You'll die when you hear.
>
> . . . *ed io sorridendo li guardava, e nulla dicea loro.*
>
> (*SP,* 110)

That he has his own tale to tell runs through the poem, as do also allusions to Joyce, who is familiarly dubbed "Our Irish friend," "old father," and "Artificer." The Dante quotation is paraphrased in the last two lines of the poem (Dante: "I, smiling, looked at them and said nothing"[22]).

The speaker begins by describing what is around him in a playful tone.

> Amid that Platonic statuary, of athletes
> Playing their passionate and sexless games,
> The governors-to-be struck careless on the lawns,
> The soldiers' monument, the sparrow-bronzes,
> Through that museum of Corinthian elms
> I walked among them in the
> Soliloquy of summer, a gravel-scholar.

The speaker's own soliloquy runs over Joyce's phrase "silence, exile, and cunning": he will himself be silent—"not . . . the silence of the cowed, / But hold your tongue, sir, rather than betray." Silent, he can then

> . . . hear a music not prescribed, a tendril-tune
> That climbs the porches of the ear,
> Green, cool, like cucumber-vine.
> What if the face starts threatening the man?
> Then exile, cunning.

This last line, neatly sliced in half by the caesura, goes on,

> Yes, old father, yes,
> The newspapers were right,
> Youth is general all over America. . . .

With this turn on Joyce's words at the end of "The Dead," the concluding story of *Dubliners*—"Yes, the newspapers were right: snow was general all over

Ireland."—the "I" of the poem thinks of the snow and the westward journey in that story and quotes his beloved's words in the letter:

> "The almonds bloom," she wrote. But will they hold,
> While I remain to teach the alphabet
> I still must learn, the alphabet on fire,
> Those wizard stones? As always, where the text ends
> Lurks the self, so shamed and magical. Away!

This "Away!" at the end of this last line could echo Stephen's two "Away's" at the end of *A Portrait of the Artist as a Young Man,* as Stephen's in turn possibly echoes Keats's in "Ode to a Nightingale," bringing in some of the "magical" atmosphere of that poem:

> Away! Away! for I will fly to thee,
>   Not charioted by Bacchus and his pards,
> But on the viewless wings of Poesy.

Kunitz's line itself, with a terminal caesura like other lines in the poem, has a colloquial rhythm and force partly because of the high proportion of monosyllables. The line that follows, "Who stays here long enough will stay too long," is monosyllabic except for the middle word, "enough," and it balances speech stress and metrical stress; Harvey Gross has noted that the final lines of the poem similarly do so ("I smiled . . .").[23]

The speaker prefers change and disorder to the order of the academy. "Time snaps her fan, and there's her creature caught. . . ." He introduces the important lines of the poem with a foreshortened trimeter line followed by six pentameters:

> Absurd though it may seem, [trimeter]
> Perhaps there's too much order in this world;
> The poets love to haul disorder in,
> Braiding their wrists with her long mistress hair,
> And when the house is tossed about our ears,
> The governors must set it right again.
> How wise was he who banned them from his state!

Clearly the "I" is thinking about his own roles as teacher and poet, the subverting of the order of the world. As Kunitz comments in an essay, "Plato . . . felt that the right words for the poet might be the wrong words for the state," and when he "banned" poets "from his state" he specified, Kunitz rightly insists, that he had

> nothing against poets . . . content to exercise their craft by writing hymns to the gods and praises of famous men. The poets to guard against are those who nourish the passions and desires. These are the sons of Dionysus, the god of wine and ecstasy, as opposed to the rulers of the state, who are sons of Apollo, a relatively moderate divinity.[24]

The speaker of the poem could toss the house about the ears of his students should he choose to tell his tale, as he feels he is asked to do in the chiming line "O tell me a tale before the lecture-bell!" fashioned on the epigraph from Joyce. In the classroom, he invokes Joyce, as Daedalus, in an alliterative, mostly monosyllabic epizeuxis (doubling words for emphasis: "I swear"), "I swear, Artificer, I swear I saw / Their souls awaiting me, with notebooks primed." He continues with a crucial question:

> The lesson for today, the lesson's what?
> I must have known, but did not care to know.
> There is a single theme, the heart declares,
> That circumnavigates curriculum.
> The letter in my pocket kissed my hand.
> I smiled but I did not tell them,
> I did not tell them why it was I smiled.

Concluding the poem these last four lines individually deserve attention: "The letter in my pocket kissed my hand" for its everyday simplicity metaphorically lifted up by the substitution of "kissed" for the expected "touched" and for the reversal of the actual, which would be "My hand touched the letter. . . ." The final two lines paraphrase the Dante epigraph and, doubling again for emphasis, another epizeuxis ("I did not tell them, / I did not tell them. . . ."), begin and end with the same words ("I smiled").

Then, finally, "circumnavigates curriculum," nine syllables in two words, verb and object, surrounded by less weighty words, has a whole verbal and visual humor that is consistent with the rest of the poem. "But hold your tongue, sir, rather than betray. / Decorum is a face the brave can wear . . . ," for instance, and "The poets love to haul disorder in . . ."—both of these begin with colloquial diction ("hold your tongue," "love to haul") and rhythm and continue with consciously formal, "poetic," elegant phrases. After "to haul disorder in" comes "Braiding their wrists with her long mistress hair," a play on Donne's "celebrated line from *The Reliquc*," as Harvey Gross says: "A bracelet of bright hair about the bone." Kunitz's line here, Gross further notes, has a "sinuous beauty . . . produced by the strategically place short *i*'s as well as by the reversed first foot and the double foot standing in the third and fourth positions."[25]

An accomplished prosodist, Kunitz shows his skill perhaps nowhere so clearly as in this line and generally throughout this lighthearted, felicitous blank-verse poem. Each of the four poems that follow **"The Class Will Come to Order"** in *Selected Poems,* however, is similarly varied in prosody and diction. In the eight lines of **"The Summing-Up"** the high proportion of monosyllables speeds reading as the relaxed diction— "scribbled," "cheap," "my gear," "damn the cost!"— lightens the portentousness of its content and of some of the heavier words ("disburdened," "ransomed," "lintel"):

When young I scribbled, boasting, on my wall,
No Love, No Property, No Wages.
In youth's good time I somehow bought them all,
And cheap, you'd think, for maybe a hundred pages.

Now in my prime, disburdened of my gear,
My trophies ransomed, broken, lost,
I carve again on the lintel of the year
My sign: *Mobility*—and damn the cost!

(*SP,* 112)

In **"A Choice of Weapons"** witty feminine rhymes ("elation-reputation," "devils-evils," "empiric-lyric," "folly-melancholy," "garden-harden") convey a teasing tone; and in **"Revolving Meditation"** the diction, especially, makes its grave material readable: the pleasant colloquialism of "God knows," "a sprig or two," "in a nutshell," or "this perjured quid of mine" (*SP,* 114-15).

Along with **"A Spark of Laurel"** these are the fine new poems with which *Selected Poems* ends. Harvey Gross noted Kunitz's maintenance of "iambic discipline" up to this point; subsequently Kunitz began publishing in journals poems in freer meters. Gross points to **"The Mound-Builders,"** published in 1963, five years later, as a poem "written in a free meter very close to Lowell's."[26] In a long review article published the year after *Selected Poems,* Kunitz noted that his own age happened "*not* to be a time of great innovation in poetic technique; it is rather a period in which the technical gains of past decades, particularly the 'twenties, are being tested and consolidated."[27] Now this testing and consolidating he was doing himself, having, possibly, "exhausted," as he has said, the potentialities of strict forms.

"As one matures and changes, the voice must change too," Kunitz said in an interview in 1968. "It cannot remain the voice of a young man of twenty-five when you are sixty." In his own case, he added, he noticed that he was "moving toward a much more open style. . . . I somehow no longer feel right within a tight structure, and I'm trying to crack it."[28] How he achieved this "cracking" of "a tight structure," his next and fourth book, *The Testing-Tree,* shows.

Notes

1. *Contemporary Literature,* p. 11.

2. *Iowa Review,* p. 76; *Contemporary Literature,* p. 4.

3. *Contemporary Literature,* p. 3.

4. Ibid., pp. 2-3.

5. Pliny the Younger, Epistles I.9.1. See also Pythagoras, *Aurea Carmina* 42.

6. *Contemporary Literature,* p. 4.

7. M. L. Rosenthal, *The New Poets: American and British Poetry Since World War II* (New York, 1967), pp. 6 and 10.

8. *Contemporary Literature,* p. 14.

9. Rosenthal, *New Poets,* p. 15.

10. The phrase "The Serpent's Word" comes from the poem "The Dark and the Fair," SP, 34; "The Terrible Threshold," from "Open the Gates," SP, 41; "Prince of Counterfeits," from "The Fitting of the Mask," SP, 83; "A World to Lose," from "The Last Picnic," SP, 93; and "The Coat Without a Seam," from "The Way Down," SP, 106.

11. Paul Engle and Joseph Langland, eds., *Poet's Choice* (New York, 1962), p. 68.

12. Ibid., p. xiii.

13. *Contemporary Literature,* p. 5.

14. Ibid.

15. *Contemporary American Poetry* (New York, 1966), pp. 44-47.

16. Ibid., p. 46.

17. An "open city" is one which is "a military objective but is completely demilitarized and left open to enemy occupation in order to gain immunity, under international law, from bombardment and attack."

18. *Iowa Review,* p. 77.

19. In John, 19:23-24. The outer coat worn by the High Priest is woven as one piece without a seam. In the Rabbinic tradition God gave Adam an unstitched coat and after him Moses and the High Priest. When the tradition was taken over into Christian theology the Adam-Moses-Redeemer typology applied it also to Christ.

20. Russell, "Poet in the Classroom," p. 584.

21. Ibid.

22. The one-paragraph prose section (IV) of *Vita Nuova,* of which this is the last sentence, concerns Dante's wasting away with love and being questioned about it by his friends: "And I, perceiving their evil questioning, through the will of Love, who commanded me according to the counsel of the reason, replied to them, that it was Love who had brought me to this pass. I spoke of Love, because I bore on my face so many of his signs that this could not be concealed. And when they asked me: 'For whom has Love thus wasted thee?' I, smiling, looked at them and said nothing." Charles Eliot Norton, trans., *The New Life of Dante Alighieri* (Boston, 1898), p. 7.

Part of one line in the last section of the poem, "The lesson for today," is identical to the title of Robert Frost's earlier 1941 Harvard Phi Beta Kappa poem. I do not perceive any important connections between the two poems such as to suggest that Kunitz might have been alluding in any way to the Frost poem. The two poems have some similarities of subject, poetry, the state, and the world; Frost's poem is much longer (161 lines), is rhymed, and "rides no beast of action." Frost's "lesson for today / Is how to be unhappy yet polite." The poem ends with Frost's memorable epitaph, "I had a lover's quarrel with the world." The phrase, "The lesson for today," is sufficiently everyday for the identity to be coincidental. "The Lesson for Today," *The Complete Poems of Robert Frost* (New York, 1964), pp. 471-476.

23. Harvey Gross, *Sound and Form in Modern Poetry: A Study of Prosody from Thomas Hardy to Robert Lowell* (Ann Arbor, Mich., 1968), p. 280.

24. *A Kind of Order,* p. 50.

25. Gross, pp. 279 and 280. Gross's reading is "Braiding | their wrists | with her long mis | tress hair. . . ."

26. Ibid., p. 326.

27. "American Poetry's Silver Age," *Harper's,* 219 (June 1959), 178.

28. *Yale Literary Magazine,* p. 9.

Selected Bibliography

This bibliography begins with a list of Stanley Kunitz's books of poetry and prose and continues with those that he translated and those that he edited. Important articles and reviews by him follow. After these, some of his contributions to other books are listed. The arrangement is chronological, and all except the first three are annotated.

In the Secondary Sources, the pieces of consequence are those by Hagstrum and Mills. Some citations relevant in the Notes and References are omitted here.

PRIMARY SOURCES

1. BOOKS OF POETRY AND PROSE

Intellectual Things. New York: Doubleday, Doran, 1930.

Passport to the War. A Selection of Poems. New York: Henry Holt, 1944.

Selected Poems, 1928-1958. Boston: Atlantic-Little, Brown, 1958.

The Testing-Tree. Poems. Boston: Atlantic-Little, Brown, 1971.

The Terrible Threshold. Selected Poems, 1940-1970. London: Secker & Warburg, 1974.

A Kind of Order, a Kind of Folly: Essays and Conversations. Boston: Atlantic-Little, Brown, 1975.

The Poems of Stanley Kunitz, 1928-1978. Boston: Atlantic-Little, Brown, 1979.

2. BOOKS TRANSLATED

Poems of Akhmatova. Selected, Translated and Introduced by Stanley Kunitz with Max Hayward. Boston: Atlantic-Little, Brown, 1973.

Story under Full Sail by Andrei Voznesensky. Translated from the Russian by Stanley Kunitz with Vera Reck, Maureen Sager, Catherine Leach. Garden City, New York: Doubleday, 1974.

Orchard Lamps by Ivan Drach. Edited and translated by Stanley Kunitz. Sheep Meadow Press, 1978.

3. BOOKS EDITED

Living Authors: A Book of Biographies. Ed. by Dilly Tante [pseud.]. New York: H. W. Wilson, 1933.

Authors Today and Yesterday. A Companion Volume to Living Authors. With Howard Haycraft; Wilbur C. Hadden, ed. asst. New York: H. W. Wilson, 1933.

The Junior Book of Authors. With Howard Haycraft. New York: H. W. Wilson, 1934.

British Authors of the Nineteenth Century. With Howard Haycraft. New York: H. W. Wilson, 1936.

American Authors, 1600-1900. A Biographical Dictionary of American Literature. With Howard Haycraft. New York: H. W. Wilson, 1938.

Twentieth Century Authors. A Biographical Dictionary of Modern Literature. With Howard Haycraft. New York: H. W. Wilson, 1942.

British Authors before 1800. A Biographical Dictionary. With Howard Haycraft. New York: H. W. Wilson, 1952.

Twentieth Century Authors. First Supplement. With Vineta Colby. New York: H. W. Wilson, 1955.

Poems of John Keats. New York: Crowell, 1965.

European Authors, 1000-1900. A Biographical Dictionary of European Literature. With Vineta Colby. New York: H. W. Wilson, c. 1967.

World Authors, 1950-1970. Ed. John Wakeman. Stanley Kunitz, Editorial Consultant.

4. SELECTED ARTICLES AND REVIEWS

"Dilly Tante Observes," column beginning in January 1928 in *Wilson Bulletin for Librarians* (title changed to *Wilson Library Bulletin,* September 1939). Continued as "The Roving Eye" with initials "S. J. K." Final column: *Wilson Library Bulletin,* 17 (March 1943), 562. As titles of column suggest, this monthly piece by Kunitz in the H. W. Wilson Company house organ is informal and anecdotal with interesting incidental and topical comments.

"Creative Writing Workshop," *Education,* 73 (November 1952), 152-56. Both this and the report that follows are valuable for an account by Kunitz of his teaching aims and methods.

"Seminar in the Arts," *Education,* 73 (November 1952), 172-76.

"American Poetry's Silver Age," *Harper's,* 219 (October 1959), 173-79. "An improbable dialogue" between The Poet and The Young Man, this piece is an excellent survey of the poetic scene from Eliot and Frost to Ginsberg.

"Process and Thing: A Year of Poetry," *Harper's,* 221 (September 1960), 96+. The second of Kunitz's yearly surveys; comments on about a dozen of the year's books with acute observations about poetry.

"New Books," *Harper's,* 223 (August 1961), 86-91. The third of Kunitz's yearly surveys; as above.

"Frost, Williams, and Company," *Harper's,* 225 (October 1962), 100-103+. The fourth of Kunitz's yearly surveys; as above.

"Auden on Poetry: A Conversation with Stanley Kunitz," *Atlantic,* 218 (August 1966), 94-102. Like Kunitz's conversations with Robert Lowell and Andrei Voznesensky (both included in *A Kind of Order*), here it is mostly the other poet, W. H. Auden, who is heard, but there are some valuable observations about Kunitz, too.

5. BOOKS CONTRIBUTED TO

"Poetry's Silver Age: An Improbable Dialogue," in *Writing in America,* ed. by John Fischer and Robert B. Silvers. New Brunswick, N.J.: Rutgers University Press, 1960. A reprint of Kunitz's 1959 survey of the contemporary poetic scene for *Harper's,* cited above.

"The Taste of Self (On Theodore Roethke's 'In a Dark Time')," in *The Contemporary Poet as Artist and Critic,* ed. by Anthony Ostroff. Boston: Little, Brown, 1964. Kunitz's close analysis of his friend Roethke's poem for Ostroff's symposia.

"On 'Father and Son,'" in *The Contemporary Poet as Artist and Critic,* ed. by Anthony Ostroff. Boston: Little, Brown, 1964. Kunitz's comments on his own poem for Ostroff's symposia.

"Out of the Cage," in *Randall Jarrell, 1914-1965,* ed. by Robert Lowell, Peter Taylor, and Robert Penn Warren. New York: Farrar, Straus, 1967. Brief, personal, this memoir mostly comments on Jarrell's poem "The Woman at the Washington Zoo" as representative of the pain in Jarrell's poetry.

SECONDARY SOURCES

In preparing this first full-length study of Kunitz, I have consulted only materials in periodicals and books.

1. BIOGRAPHY

Useful biographical accounts are those in *Current Biography,* 1959, and the *Encylopaedia Judaica* (1971). Some additional biographical facts are in Michael True, *Worcester Poets. With Notes Toward a Literary History* (Worcester: The Worcester County Poetry Association, 1972), pp. 27-30. An account of Kunitz's career compiled in 1974 is in *Contemporary Authors,* volumes 41-44. *Twentieth Century Authors. First Supplement (1955),* edited by Kunitz himself with Vineta Colby, contains no Kunitz entry, though it includes entries for his peers, Lowell, Roethke, and Wilbur. Since he was by then the Editorial Consultant, not an editor, Kunitz prepared an autobiographical sketch for *World Authors, 1950-1970* (ed. by John Wakeman), H. W. Wilson's "companion" to *Twentieth Century Authors* and its *First Supplement.* There in two pages he gives a narrative of his life; the subsequent commentary and appended bibliography make this entry the best survey of him and his work in reference volumes. Some few details here and there in my text are from correspondence I had with Kunitz while I was writing this book and from a visit with him the afternoon of August 20, 1975, at his summer home in Provincetown. Generally I have not thought it necessary to document these specifically. Some published accounts with biographical data are listed immediately below. The anonymous "Craft Interview" in the *New York Quarterly* and the Davis, Lupher, and Ryan interviews are referred to in the Notes as, respectively, *New York Quarterly, Contemporary Literature, Yale Literary Magazine,* and *Iowa Review.*

Allen, Henry. "The Poets' Poet: Stanley Kunitz at the Library of Congress," *Potomac* (Washington *Post* Sunday Supplement), January 9, 1975, pp. 10+. A brief account of Kunitz's life and an interview with him; focusses on his work as Consultant in Poetry to the Library of Congress.

Anon. "Craft Interview with Stanley Kunitz," *New York Quarterly,* 1 (Fall 1970), 9-22. As the title suggests, mostly about the craft of poetry. Valuable, with some interesting biographical informaedion, especially about Kunitz's work with the Fine Arts Work Center in Provincetown.

Brantley, Robin. "A Touch of the Poet," *New York Times Magazine,* September 7, 1975, pp. 80-83. An excellent commentary on and description of Kunitz's gardens at his homes in New York City and in Provincetown. "Gardening," Kunitz says, "is a very deep, intimate part of my poetic life."

[Davis, Cynthia]. "An Interview with Stanley Kunitz—*Conducted by Cynthia Davis,*" *Contemporary Literature,* 15 (Winter 1974), 1-14. An excellent, wide-ranging interview.

Gross, Harvey. "Stanley Kunitz, Action and Incantation," *Antaeus,* 30/31 (Spring 1978), 283-295. An interview mostly on prosody.

Loxterman, Alan, Moderator. "Poetry in the Classroom: A Symposium with Marvin Bell, Donald Hall, and Stanley Kunitz," *American Poetry Review,* 6 (No. 1, 1977), 9-13. A symposium on "The Continuing Revolution in American Poetry" held at the University of Virginia in January 1976 shows Kunitz giving some new considerations as well as repeating favorite ideas.

Lupher, David. "Stanley Kunitz on Poetry: A Yale Lit Interview," *Yale Literary Magazine,* 136 (May 1968), 6-13. The earliest of the Kunitz interviews; photographs of Kunitz at home among his flowers and books.

Mills, Ralph J., Jr. "Kunitz, Stanley (Jasspon)," in *Contemporary Poets of the English Language,* ed. by Rosalie Murphy. New York: St. Martin's Press, 1970. As with the other entries in this excellent compilation, this one on Kunitz by Mills is brief but of great value.

Russell, Robert. "The Poet in the Classroom," *College English,* 28 (May 1967), 580-86. An account of Kunitz's visit to a college classroom.

Ryan, Michael. "An Interview with Stanley Kunitz," *Iowa Review* (Spring 1974), 76-85. His "best interview," in Kunitz's opinion.

2. Articles, Sections in Books, and
Selected Reviews

Beloof, Robert. "On Stanley Kunitz's 'Father and Son,'" in *The Contemporary Poet as Artist and Critic,* ed. by Anthony Ostroff. Boston: Little, Brown, 1964. Analysis of "Father and Son."

Brodsky, Joseph. "Translating Akhmatova," *New York Review of Books,* August 9, 1973, pp. 9-10. The most severe of the critics about the quality of Kunitz's translation, but ultimately approving.

Ciardi, John. "[A review of *Selected Poems*]," *Saturday Review of Literature,* 41 (September 27, 1958), 18. Concludes that "Kunitz is certainly the most neglected good poet of the last quarter-century."

Elliott, George P. "[A review of *Selected Poems*]," *Accent,* 18 (Autumn 1958), 267-70. A detailed, perceptive review.

Gross, Harvey. *Sound and Form in Modern Poetry: A Study of Prosody from Thomas Hardy to Robert Lowell.* Ann Arbor: University of Michigan Press, 1968. Three pages of praise for Kunitz as a prosodist: "Kunitz' ear for quantity and monosyllabic harmonies is nearly unmatched among American poets."

Hagstrum,. Jean H. "The Poetry of Stanley Kunitz: An Introductory Essay," in *Poets in Progress,* ed. by Edward Hungerford. Evanston, Ill.: Northwestern University Press, 1967. The most complete and thorough of the articles on Kunitz's poetry.

Huddle, David. "In Fierce Decay a Stripe of Honey: The Poetry of Stanley Kunitz," *Northern New England*

Review, 1 (1975), 20-26. A fine commentary on Kunitz's poetry by a young poet; especially good on the differences between the early verse and that of *The Testing-Tree.*

Kermode, Frank. "[A review of *Selected Poems*]," *Spectator,* July 17, 1959, p. 81. A brief, perceptive review. "A Roman Thief" is "a splendid maledictory poem," and Kunitz is "indeed a big poet."

Lowell, Robert. "On Stanley Kunitz's 'Father and Son,'" in *The Contemporary Poet as Artist and Critic,* ed. by Anthony Ostroff. Boston: Little, Brown, 1964. A relaxed, informal analysis of "Father and Son."

Mercier, Vivian. "[A review of *Selected Poems*]," *Commonweal,* 69 (February 13, 1959), 523. "Like several of the greatest modern poets, Kunitz speaks more directly to us—and more richly, too—as he grows older."

Mesic, Michael. "[A review of *Poems of Akhmatova*]," *Poetry,* 124 (July 1974), 238-40. The Akhmatova translations "are excellent, better than one ever expected them to be, conscientiously respectful of the original and aware of the demands of English."

Miles, Josephine. "On Stanley Kunitz's 'Father and Son,'" in *The Contemporary Poet as Artist and Critic,* ed. by Anthony Ostroff. Boston: Little, Brown, 1964. Another excellent analysis of "Father and Son."

Mills, Ralph J., Jr. *Contemporary American Poetry.* New York: Random House, 1966. Along with Hagstrum's essay, one of the best essays on Kunitz's poetry.

——. "Kunitz, Stanley (Jasspon)," in *Contemporary Poets of the English Language,* ed. by Rosalie Murphy. New York: St. Martin's Press, 1970. The best brief exposition of Kunitz's ideas and biography.

Moss, Stanley. "[A review of *The Testing-Tree*]," *Nation,* 213 (September 20, 1971), 250. A superior review of *The Testing-Tree.* "Kunitz' accomplishment . . . should occasion a national holiday."

Muchnic, Helen. "[A review of *Poems of Akhmatova*]," *New York Times Book Review,* October 21, 1973, p. 6. Though the translations are "on the whole as good as any we have had so far," they "are not great poems."

Nyren, Dorothy, comp. and ed. *A Library of Literary Criticism. Modern American Literature.* New York: Frederick Ungar, 1971. Collects comments from ten reviews, 1930-1959.

Rosenthal, M. L. *The Modern Poets. A Critical Introduction.* New York: Oxford University Press, 1965. Though brief, like most of Rosenthal's discussions, judicious and discriminating.

——. "[A review of *Selected Poems*]," *Nation,* 187 (October 11, 1958), 214. "Stanley Kunitz has a rich lyrical style; sometimes a redundancy of it."

Russell, Robert. "The Poet in the Classroom," *College English*, 28 (May 1967), 580-86. In addition to a portrayal of Kunitz talking with students, this article contains some explication of "The Science of the Night," "The Way Down," and other poems.

Schorer, Mark. "[A review of *Passport to the War*]," *New York Times*, March 26, 1944, p. 21. The "metaphysical" style characteristic of the early Kunitz "Now . . . has become entirely his own, and he writes with terse, fresh imagery at nearly every point."

Vine, Richard. "[A review of *A Kind of Order, a Kind of Folly*]," *Salmagundi*, No. 36 (Winter 1977), 117-123. Not given nearly the consideration that it deserved, the book almost in this review alone has its superb qualities and importance truly estimated.

Wagoner, David. "[A review of *Selected Poems*]," *Poetry*, 93 (December 1958), 174-78. A detailed review with analysis of two of Kunitz's poems; comments that *Selected Poems* should "end . . . Kunitz's quiet Thirty Years War for a place among the very best poets of our time."

Winters, Yvor. "[A review of *Intellectual Things*]," *New Republic*, 63 (June 4, 1930), 77. "The experience in which Mr. Kunitz deals is normal, rich and complex; he is firm on his feet, and, now and again, quick on them."

Wright, James. "[A review of *Selected Poems*]," *Sewanee Review*, 67 (January-March 1959), 330-36. "In the hands of this poet, the subject [of love] flinches and wails. It is not pretty. It has grandeur."

Zabel, Morton Dauwen. "[A review of *Intellectual Things*]," *Poetry*, 36 (July 1930), 218-23. ". . . Kunitz plunges into his elaborate imagery, conceits, and phraseology with none of the hesitation that detains the poet stricter in matters of form and logic."

Marie Henault (essay date 1980)

SOURCE: Henault, Marie. "Seedcorn and Windfall: Kunitz's Prose Book." In *Stanley Kunitz*, pp. 126-39. Boston: Twayne, 1980.

[*In the following essay, Henault presents a detailed analysis of Kunitz's essay collection,* A Kind of Order, a Kind of Folly, *drawing parallels between the author's prose and poetry.*]

Kunitz's one book of prose, *A Kind of Order, a Kind of Folly: Essays and Conversations* (1975), is made up of fifty pieces, some quite long, some brief, some published for the first time, most selected from the published prose of five decades—essays, conversations, reviews, introductions, personal reflections. Mostly these concern poets and poetry; four are about

art and artists; some are autobiographical reminiscences; and some are semiphilosophical, aphoristic journal notes (**"Seedcorn and Windfall"**). The fifty separate items themselves are arranged under eight main headings, each of which points to the main subject of each section, as, for instance, "Four for Roethke," a collection of Kunitz's writings about Theodore Roethke, or "Root Images," about Kunitz's own boyhood.

The book opens with a brief, explanatory **"Foreword,"** admitting the inevitably "random aspect" that such a gathering together as this must have. Yet, too, Kunitz insists on his stubbornness or "the durability of the psyche" through the years. One of his "unshakable convictions," he writes, "has been that poetry is more than a craft, important as the craft may be: it is a vocation, a passionate enterprise, rooted in human sympathies and aspirations."[1] And this is mostly what the book is about—poetry as a high vocation.

A Kind of Order itself contains both reminiscences and theoretical and analytical essays on poetry and art, personal and informative. "Produced over a span of years"—forty-four, by my count—Kunitz's prose in this book has no one describable style. He did no rewriting, he says in his **"Foreword,"** "for the sake of improving or squaring my opinions," but he did try "to eliminate matter that seemed peripheral to the main thrust of this volume, or patently ephemeral, or boring, or redundant" (xii). Having made comparisons, I can testify that this is indeed fully true. Some passages have been altered to excise details that "date" the writing, others to banish a cliché, something already used elsewhere, or the obvious ("The publication of *The Letters of Wallace Stevens* is an event in American literary history.").

No extensive rewriting was undertaken, however—rightly, I think, for how could one, one might ask in a Kunitzian question, reenvision such random writings as these? What I take to be the latest pieces—**"A Kind of Order"** and **"Seedcorn and Windfall"**—have a mature, bright rightness of language, simple elegance of syntax, and aphoristic splendor. The earliest pieces—**"The Vaudeville of the Mind (Conrad Aiken)"** and **"A Lesson from Rilke,"** two from among more than two dozen reviews and essays of Kunitz's early years—date from his middle and late twenties and are abstruse and rather showy in style. Hence Kunitz's prose changed in a way similar to his poetry. As he noted in **"Seedcorn and Windfall,"** his "early writing was dense and involuted—so, I guess, was I." Now what he seeks "is a transparency of language and vision" (301). At least two pieces, the first and the last (just named above), achieve this "transparency of language and vision"; others similarly have an easygoing, colloquial swing—for instance, the autobiographical essays in "Root Images." But Kunitz's medium is verse, not prose, and one reads *A Kind of Order* for *what* it is saying, not *how*. That is not to say that the book is ill-written, for it assuredly is not. Mainly, though, what the reader gets is lucidity of *thought* and, generally, great good sense. "It is no doubt a judgment of our age," one reviewer wrote, "that we find good sense astounding. Mr. Kunitz has it, and to an astonishing degree. He says a great many things which, in this late frantic hour of our art, need desperately once again to be said—which is to say of course that they need desperately once again to be heard."[2] Even more important, "Romantic notions of the poet notwithstanding," this reviewer, Richard Vine, adds, "poetic sensibility manifestly does not preclude precision of thought; one can be a good poet *and* an accurate thinker. Stanley Kunitz is both."[3]

Outstanding items in the book are Kunitz's portraits of his friends Theodore Roethke and Robert Lowell. Part II brings together four pieces on Roethke written between 1949 and 1965, expert analyses and pertinent personal estimates. The "Conversation" with Robert Lowell, in which only Lowell speaks, has important statements on poetry ranging from Lowell's opinions about other poets to remarks about his own poetry.

Another notable characteristic of *A Kind of Order* is the great number of quotations that it contains. As Kunitz acknowledges in his **"Foreword,"** "A writer's obsessions and quotations are the indispensable baggage he carries with him from year to year and from page to page," and so obsessive, favorite quotations occur more than once; to "expunge" them, as Kunitz says, would leave "too big a hole in the text" (xii). Each section and each essay begin with quotations; the first section, for example, with quotations from Osip Mandelstam and Herbert Marcuse; the first essay, Siegfried Giedion. Quoted or alluded to in the first essay are Nietzsche, Kierkegaard, Freud, Pascal, Heisenberg, Niels Bohr, Yeats, Einstein, Carlyle, Stevens, Franz Kline, Valéry, Emerson, Lionel Johnson, Pope, Plato, and Tillich. Some others in other essays are Camus, Rilke, Malraux, Whitman, Goethe, Pound, Ortega y Gasset, Serge Diaghilev, Solzhenitsyn, Voznesensky, Belinsky, Yevtushenko, Akhmatova, Joseph Brodsky, Shakespeare, Pasternak, Keats, William Carlos Williams, Confucius, Christopher Caudwell, Whitehead, Chekhov, Blake, Hopkins, Coleridge, Brecht, Fanon, Wordsworth, Joyce, Thomas Mann, Roethke, Lévi-Strauss, Shelley, Frost, Sartre, Lao-Tzu, St. John of the Cross, Dr. Rollo May, and many others—to a total number of about 100 writers, painters, sculptors, and composers. A mind reveals itself by whom and what it remembers, and in his quotations and allusions Kunitz shows himself to be widely read, liberal,

humanitarian, reflective—and consistent, in the best sense. Richard Vine, for instance, observes "a uniform quality of mind [that] pervades" the book and adds that it is "a quality marked by reasonableness, sensitivity, lucidity, and balance. One thinks inevitably of Aristotle's Magnanimous Man, of Camus' *homme du midi*."[4] So here Stanley Kunitz's highly individual voice is echoed and counterpointed by those of others to create a polyphony of thought, one of the more admirable aspects of *A Kind of Order, a Kind of Folly*.

I THE STYLE OF AN AGE

At the end of his **"Foreword"** Kunitz plays on Yeats's words by saying that "In the medium of prose a poet walks more naked than in his verse" (xii), and so here in the first section one sees Kunitz's ideas plain. The first long essay, **"A Kind of Order,"** is one of six on "The Style of an Age," part I of the book, and like **"Seedcorn and Windfall,"** the essay that makes up part VIII and ends the book, it is a major expression of Kunitz's thoughts on poets and poetry. Though less so than **"Seedcorn,"** **"A Kind of Order"** still tends to be an essay in the Emersonian tradition of bits of journal jottings stitched into a single whole. In other words, it shines with flashes of insight pithily stated. Still, some paragraphs remain under- or undeveloped and its main idea—the necessity of balancing inner and outer realities, as pointed to in the Giedion epigraph[5]—is more outlined than analyzed. Yet, overall, as might be expected, **"A Kind of Order"** is a brilliant discussion of its subject.

To begin with, Kunitz traces the familiar ancestral lines of our present disorder—the destructive fragmentation of our world by Darwin, Marx, Freud, and Einstein in one arena; by Cezanne and Picasso, Rimbaud and Eliot, Whitman and Lawrence, Dostoevsky and Joyce in others (3). Hence, in our age "poetry inevitably tends to become increasingly aware of itself, to turn inward" (8), Kunitz writes, and like Heisenberg's demonstration "that the very act of observation changes the phenomena to be observed" (6), so "the work modifies the author . . . as a woman modifies herself in front of a mirror" (9). He thinks, Kunitz continues,

> . . . of those women in the paintings of de Kooning who sit in front of a window that is also a mirror and also a picture on a wall. How can you tell the inside from the outside, the reality from its reflection? Yeats had asked the question before, "How can we know the dancer from the dance?"
>
> (9)

However, "Since the art of our time is the only art we can get," it must be defended, and it can be, too, if one makes "the effort toward compassionate understanding . . ." (10). And, finally, in all its disorder, the art of our time wrestles through to "a kind of order," an order of the "greatest," one "which holds in suspension the most disorder; holds it in such precarious balance that each instant threatens its overthrow" (13). The material in this essay is heady and theoretical, abstract and knowledgeable. Its apothegms, of which I have quoted a few, and supporting examples and quotations make it an understandable and central statement of Kunitz's aesthetic ideas and also gloss his earlier lines in the poem **"The Class Will Come to Order"**:

Perhaps there's too much order in this world;
The poets love to haul disorder in,
Braiding their wrists with her long mistress hair,
And when the house is tossed about our ears,
The governors must set it right again.
How wise was he who banned them from his state!

(*SP*, 111)

The second essay in this part of the book, **"The Search for a Style,"** is as short and to the point as the first was long and discursive. In eight, mostly long, paragraphs Kunitz tries to clarify the style of an age "so that its outlines become unmistakable" (14). The recent effort to reject "academic verse and . . . to convert poetry into a popular art . . . is doomed to fail" (15, 16), Kunitz asserts, because, in seeming paradox, while a closed society such as that in Soviet Russia favors an open, public poetry, an open society conversely tends to promote a closed, private poetry: "where the poet is free to pursue his deepest and most arcane thoughts and feelings to their source, his art tends to embrace the personal and to prefer an intimate tone" (15).

Still, Kunitz adds, the contemporary work that "interests" him "most . . . are poems that, stemming out of the great closed art of this century, are nevertheless relaxed in the line, fluid in their development, organic in their form, and immediate in feeling. I begin to see the possibility of a poetry that will recapture from the novel much of the territory that has been forfeited to it" (16). So possibly poetry *has* "become over-specialized, too different from prose" (16), and, as Kunitz also said about his effort in teaching, "Why should not all men of imagination feel that poetry is their medium, as long as they have a language of the imagination to offer . . . ?" (16).

Following these two general essays on the conditions of poetry are three others on specific subjects along with another general, theoretical essay. **"A Visit to Russia"** is mostly a narrative, with some analysis, of his visit to the Soviet Union in 1967, making points about the oppressiveness of the Soviet system under

which, nonetheless, poets and poetry flourish. As the Osip Mandelstam opening epigraph to section 1 puts it, "Poetry is respected only in this country [Russia]—people are killed for it" ([xiii]).

"On Translating Akhmatova" and **"The Modernity of Keats"** derive from prefatory remarks to two of Kunitz's previous books, his translations of Akhmatova and his selection from the poems and letters of Keats. In the Keats essay Kunitz attempts to examine the poetry without the encrustations of the years. "We do not clearly focus on the poets of the past," he writes,

for we regard them through the eyeball of an ancestral giant who has already thumbed their pages, underscored their most sentimental passages, memorized their worst lines; and this Cyclopean organ with its superfluity of moisture, can scarcely be termed an ideal instrument of perception.

(60)

He had had to fight himself free from "the idolatry" of his youth, and so has "been impelled to return intermittently to the pages of Keats as to a battlefield in the history of one man's taste, over which have raged certain small but savage wars" (60).

"Poet and State," the fifth essay in this first section, previously unpublished, returns to and expands on some of the themes in **"A Kind of Order."** Longer and more wide-ranging than that first essay, it implicitly continues the Herbert Marcuse epigraph for section 1: "Today the fight for life, the fight for Eros, is the *political* fight." Exploring connections between poet and state, "between good government and right words," Kunitz quotes Confucius's statement that language "matters above everything" (49) and contrasts that with the Platonic banishment of the poet from the state. For Plato, "the right words for the poet might be the wrong words for the state," especially the words of "the sons of Dionysus, the god of wine and ecstasy, as opposed to the rulers of the state, who are sons of Apollo, a relatively moderate divinity" (49-50).

"Among writers," Kunitz thinks, "the poet is freer than his brothers the novelist and playwright . . . more fortunate . . . than the contemporary painter or sculptor" because "nothing he can do will make his labor profitable" (52-53). He believes "that the shape of the future will be determined politically" (56). Thus some of "the causes that have agitated" Kunitz in what he calls "this unquiet century" in his **"Foreword"** ([xi]) covertly figure in this essay—anti-Semitism and Fascism. Overtly, the essay is about other matters: the indifference or even contempt with which poets are treated. "Even so fine a critical intellect as Edmund

Wilson could ask," Kunitz writes, "'Does it really constitute a career for a man to do nothing but write lyric poetry?'" (56). In addition to the "impolite retort" which fortifies him but which he does not record, Kunitz wishes "that [former President] Nixon had been capable of reading Berryman's *Dream Songs*" (56).

The necessary full humanity for the poet would be an absolute awareness of the world and of the dangers around him with special attention to the dictum to "stay healthy in a sick world" (58). The charge Kunitz makes against the great writers who immediately preceded him—Joyce, Proust, Eliot, Frost, Stevens, Pound, and Yeats, too—is that they lacked wide sympathy: They cannot "be said to have cultivated their humanity, to have fulfilled themselves outside their art" (57). So "it was possible," Kunitz says, "a generation ago, . . . though I still find it hardly credible—to be both a reactionary and a poet, even a major poet" (55). Something like his own political position, that of a philosophical anarchist, he implies here, should be that of good and sane poets. Of the truly alive and "radiant" poets, Pasternak and William Carlos Williams, "it can be said that they did more than merely care about their art: they cared about others" (58). Yet, of course, "a poet isn't going to change the world with even the most powerful of his poems. The best he can reasonably hope for is to conquer a piece of himself" (58). But that, surely, he must constantly strive to do.

II FOUR FOR ROETHKE

The four pieces on Theodore Roethke that make up section 2 of **A Kind of Order, a Kind of Folly** were published over a period of sixteen years and are a record of Kunitz's consistent high estimate of his friend's work. The first, the 1963 essay, **"Remembering Roethke (1908-1963),"** is an "in memoriam" piece. The second, **"News of the Root,"** is a 1949 review of Roethke's *Lost Son*. The third, **"The Taste of Self,"** from Ostroff's symposium *The Contemporary Poet as Artist and Critic,* is a 1961 close analysis of Roethke's "In a Dark Time." The fourth essay, **"Poet of Transformations,"** is a magnificent coda, a consideration of Roethke's total achievement and especially a review of *The Far Field,* a posthumously published volume of Roethke's poems.

The first of these, a tender, autobiographical memoir, gauges the importance of Roethke to Kunitz himself— "The poet of my generation who meant most to me, in his person and in his art . . ." ([77])—and details their first meeting:

> My recollection is of a traditionally battered jalopy from which a perfectly tremendous raccoon coat emerged, with my first book of poems tucked under its

> left paw. . . . The image that never left me was of a blond, smooth, shambling giant, irrevocably Teutonic, with a cold pudding of a face, somehow contradicted by the sullen downturn of the mouth and the pale furious eyes: a countenance ready to be touched by time, waiting to be transfigured, with a few subtle lines, into a tragic mask.
>
> (78)

Kunitz and Roethke talked about poetry then and later; Kunitz suggested *Open House* as the title for Roethke's first book of poems (1941), a suggestion that Roethke both took and wrote a poem to go with the title as well (78). Kunitz, too, read Sir John Davies's *Orchestra* to Roethke and so began "Four for Sir John Davies," one of Roethke's important sequences (79). They played tennis together also and, later, croquet and badminton, and Kunitz introduced Roethke at his last reading in New York City at the Poetry Center in 1960 (79, 82).

In 1963 Kunitz continued to think of Roethke's *Lost Son* (1948) "as the great one" (80) of Roethke's books, and the 1949 review **"News of the Root,"** the next essay, gives Kunitz's first reasons for so thinking: Roethke, he wrote then (1949), "stands among the original and powerful contemporary poets" ([83]). His "greenhouse world," Kunitz insisted, is not "rosy, innocent, optimistic. On the contrary, it swarms with malevolent forces" (84). And, he concluded, *The Lost Son,* "by virtue of its indomitable creativeness and audacity, includes much more chaos in its cosmos" than did *Open House*; "it is difficult, heroic, moving, and profoundly disquieting" (86).

In **"The Taste of Self,"** a stanza-by-stanza analysis of Roethke's "In a Dark Time," Kunitz begins by making a connection with Gerard Manley Hopkins through Hopkins's "I taste *self* but at one tankard, that of my own being" (88). The self in Roethke, as Kunitz sees it, "is divided, and the hostile parts are seen as voraciously cannibalistic: 'My meat eats me'" (88). In the poem **"In a Dark Time"** itself, diction, line, and stanzaic units are tightly patterned, "fiercely won controls," which keep the poem from collapsing into "a cry, a tremendous outpouring of wordless agitation" (88).

In "his land of desolation," Kunitz writes, the speaker in the poem "struggles to recover his identity," seeks self-justification; in the motion-filled climax in stanza III, he dies to himself; and in IV, "returns to the prison-house of his senses" (89, 93). The strength and assurance of Kunitz's analysis here rest greatly on his thorough knowledge of Roethke's other poems, from which he quotes frequently, for "Roethke belongs," in Kunitz's estimation, to that superior order of poets who will not let us rest in any one of their poems, who keep driving us back through the whole body of their work to that live cluster of images, ideas, memories, and obsessions that constitutes the individuating source of the creative personality, the nib of art, the very selfhood of the imagination.

(88)

The last of the "Four for Roethke" essays begins with a graceful retelling of the myth of Proteus and goes on to point out in Roethke's work transformations, shape-shiftings, transmutations, and metamorphoses. In Roethke's "most heroic enterprise, the sequence of interior monologues which he initiated with the title poem of *The Lost Son* . . . , continued in *Praise to the End* (1951), and which he persisted up to the last in returning to . . ." (100), he is "Proteus and all the forms of Proteus—flower, fish, reptile, amphibian, bird, dog, etc. . . ." (101). Ranging through Roethke's works and themes, Kunitz concludes with a detailed consideration of Roethke's *Far Field,* fifty new poems arranged by Roethke just before his death. Here Roethke "evokes his own valedictory image, Whitman is with him, and Prospero, and—in the shifting light Proteus, the old man of the sea, fatigued by his changes . . ." (108-109). Kunitz has high praise for these final words from Roethke.

III ROOT IMAGES

The third and most pleasing section of *A Kind of Order, a Kind of Folly* unites three mostly autobiographical pieces and concerns mainly Kunitz's interest in words and comments on two of his own poems. The first of these essays, **"Swimming in Lake Chauggogagogmanchauggagogchabunagungamaugg,"** with a tongue-tangling title that is a compositor's nightmare, presents the time-honored picture of the precocious youngster's infatuation with words. For the Worcester-born Kunitz the magical word was the Indian name for nearby Lake Webster:

Chauggogagogmanchauggagogchabunagungamaugg. To think that this was reputed to be the longest lake-name in the world! To know, moreover, that this fantastic porridge of syllables made sense, and what delicious sense, signifying: "I-fish-on-my-side, you-fish-on-your-side, nobody-fishes-in-the-middle!" I practiced how to say it, priding myself on talking Indian . . . nor to this very day have I forgotten the combination.

([113]-14; Kunitz's ellipsis)

Giving this lake "its secret name," he says, "was somehow to possess it, to assert my power over the spot, as by an act of magic" (114).

Unfortunately, most of our words have lost their magical aspect, and the poet's problem is "how to make words potent and magical again, how to restore their lost vitality. . . . A poet is a man who yearns to swim in Lake Chauggogagogmanchauggagogch-abunagungamaugg, not in Lake Webster" (114). For himself, Kunitz writes, he has "an ideal lyric" in his head "whose words flow together to form a single word-sentence, an unremitting stream of sound, as in the Indian lake-name; I am not reconciled to the knowledge that I shall never be able to write it" (114).

Meanwhile, how does a poet write his poems? Craft, will, solitude. Once asked what he considered to be his "chief asset as a poet," Kunitz answered, "'My ability to stay awake after midnight.' Perhaps," he goes on,

I was more serious than I intended. Certainly the poems of mine that I am most committed to are those that I recall fighting for hardest, through the anxious hours, until I managed to come out on the other side of fatigue, where I could begin to breathe again, as though the air had changed and I had found my second wind.

(115)

In illustration he tells, "not without trepidation," the story of the gestation of his 1953 poem **"End of Summer,"** already retold above in Chapter 3.

"The Worcester Poets," the second of the essays in "Root Images," written as a Foreword to Michael True's brief study (forty-four pages), *Worcester Poets: With Notes toward a Literary History* (1972), gracefully comments on the curious fact that two of his "most admired colleagues"—Elizabeth Bishop and Charles Olson—"had at least a birthplace in common" with himself (118).

Suppose, I speculate, we had stayed home—what would have become of us? In that parochial climate, given our different backgrounds, would we have managed to find one another? All three of us, curiously, developed an inordinate love of place, but not of *that* place.

(118-19)

For Elizabeth Bishop it was Nova Scotia and, later, Brazil; for Olson, Gloucester; for Kunitz, the countryside, Connecticut, Bucks County, Pennsylvania, and Cape Cod. "Elizabeth and Charles were able to forget Worcester," Kunitz adds; "I doubt that I ever shall" (119).

Worcester for Kunitz is memories—Halley's Comet, school days, teachers, the public library, the art museum, the woods beyond his house. Tantalizingly, he notes that he has "much, much more to tell, but this is scarcely the proper occasion for spilling everything" (121). Some day, he promises, he "must set down, if only as a chapter of Americana, the narrative of my horse-and-buggy adventures, when I was lamplighter on the Quinapoxet roads" (121). He ends by quoting the one sentence that makes up the three stanzas of the concluding half of **"Goose Pond,"** a 1956 poem in which the protagonist "meets his child-hood beating back / To find what furies made him man" (121).

The third essay in section 3 is the one on Kunitz's own poem **"Father and Son"** from the symposium on that poem in Anthony Ostroff's *Contemporary Poet as Artist and Critic*. This essay, short to the point of terseness, candidly admits to dream as the starting point for the poem and adds a few illuminating details. He wrote about the poem reluctantly, Kunitz confesses at the end of the essay, because he is "fearful of sur-rendering to the temptation of saying more than I should" (127). Anyway, "Once a poem has been distributed, it is no longer the property of the poet" (123) and "the words of the poem stand forever separate from the words about it . . ." (127). The poet "has already had his chance" (127).

IV SECTIONS 4 THROUGH 7 OF *A KIND OF ORDER*

Since the first three parts of *A Kind of Order, a Kind of Folly* are the most important in my judgment, I have surveyed them in some detail. Now I shall glance briefly at sections 4 through 7, before examining the concluding part 8, "Recapitulations." These thirty-five pieces in the middle of the book are good reading in themselves—I know no better single article on Robert Lowell than the "Conversation" in **"Tête-à-Tête"**—but the variety here is too great and some of the items themselves too brief (but four or five paragraphs) for any organized individual comment.

The first of these sections, 4, "Studio Life," has as its theme the close relationship between poets and artists. In **"The Sister Arts"** Kunitz makes the admission that he prefers "the company of painters and sculptors to that of poets" because poets "tend to be rather surly and withdrawn," while artists "are temperamentally gregarious" ([131]). And while they greatly enjoy each other's company, artists seem to like to have poets around too, as such poet-artist friendships as Keats-Haydon, Baudelaire-Delacroix, Rilke-Rodin, and oth-ers testify (132). Poet-painters and painter-poets, combining in one being both talents, are further "evidence of the natural affinity between poet and painter . . ." (132). The outstanding examples are Michelangelo and Blake and also the Chinese masters Wang Wei and Buson (132).

But, as Kunitz says, getting to the point of his essay, introducing a portfolio of contemporary poems chosen and illustrated by American painters, the "contempo-rary western artist . . . lacks a . . . convention" (133) comparable to that in the Orient of *haiku* and *haiga*, poem and picture inextricably entwined, and what is he to do with a self-sufficient poem? An artist does not illustrate it merely, but "must invent a style of graphic translation that enables him to register his variable sense of the poem" (133). Today, Kunitz concludes, "while the style of an age, or at least of a generation, is evolving, it seems to me imperative that poets and painters should continue their civilized discourse" (134).

Besides his reflections on having his head sculpted by James Rosati, the section on "Studio Life" also contains a long essay on **"The Temptations of the Artist"** and a short, moving tribute to Kunitz's friend the artist Mark Rothko. The one is an informed survey of recent trends in art, with remarks on the overex-panded role of the critic and an inveighing against the "dehumanization of art." Rothko, the artist who took his own life in 1970, was, in Kunitz's view, "a poet among painters"; to describe Rothko's work Kunitz quotes from his own extensively revised poem from 1930, **"Among the Gods"**: "Shapes of things interior to Time, / Hewn out of chaos when the Pure was plain" (149; *SP,* 7).

Following the two "Conversations," one with Robert Lowell and the other with Andrei Voznesensky, of part 5 of *A Kind of Order,* is "Works and Lives," part 6, an anthology of reviews of various works of some twenty or so poets ranging, alphabetically, from Conrad Aiken to William Carlos Williams. Mostly quite short these are confined in subject matter to the particular works reviewed. Part 7 collects five of Kunitz's introductions to the works of the "Younger Poets" that he selected for inclusion in the Yale Series; these are models of essays of this kind, biographical, judiciously analyti-cal, kindly, and accurate. Each isolates each poet's strengths, places him in a tradition, makes judgments about the worth of his accomplishment, and, if faulty, is so in an overgenerosity of praise. Indeed, in a certain sense, though these five essays are quite good in themselves, placed together as they are here, they make this the least interesting part of *A Kind of Order.* For Hugh Seidman, Peter Klappert, Michael Casey, Robert Hass, and Michael Ryan are at the moment little-known poets, a condition time may correct, but now without the support of the poems that follow in the books in the series, these introductions are too brief to be thoroughly convincing.

V RECAPITULATIONS

The eighth and final section of Kunitz's prose book is made up of one item entitled **"Seedcorn and Wind-fall,"** a collection of observations, thoughts, and ruminations taken from "notebooks, articles, and transcripts of interviews" ([297]). The nouns of the title point to the use for and the characteristics of what is here: "Seedcorn" is corn set aside for planting a new crop; so some of these paragraphs might later grow into something else. "Windfall" is something blown down by the wind, as fruit from a tree; so some of these comments are accidental accumulations of a lifetime.

Engrossing reading, **"Seedcorn and Windfall"** does not lend itself to analysis or summary; what I can say is that almost all of it is good. An occasional aphorism may seem glib or even mechanical: "An old poet ought never to be caught with his technique showing" (307). "I have no religion—perhaps that is why I think so much about God" (308). Mainly, though, notations are stringent and memorable: "I have no patience with the Midas-fingered who complain that poetry resists being turned into gold. It is better than gold" (300). "You don't know why you're writing poems, any more than a cat knows why it claws at the bark of a tree" (300). "To remain a poet after forty requires an awareness of your darkest Africa, that part of your self that will never be tamed" (301). "If we did not wear masks, we should be frightened of mirrors" (305). "People don't have to be taught to suffer—they have to be taught how to live" (305).

A "seedcorn" might be such a passage as this one:

> In the beginning Nature threatened Man. Now their roles are reversed. Is there anything on earth more to be feared than the hairless biped *homo sapiens,* the beast that knows so much and loves so little?
>
> (303-304)

Another seedcorn might be the anecdote about the foundered whale on Cape Cod who

> . . . was lying there, in monstrous desolation, making the most terrifying noises—rumbling—groaning. I put my hands on his flanks and I could feel the life inside him. And while I was standing there, suddenly he opened his eye. It was a big, red, cold eye, and it was staring directly at me. A shudder of recognition passed between us. Then the eye closed forever.
>
> (306)

The simplicity and exactness of the language here, this planed, plain prose without tropes, characterizes the writing of many parts of this final piece of *A Kind of Order, a Kind of Folly.*

"Seedcorn and Windfall" is, then, finally, a splendid piece with which to end the book. No organized essay could offer as much—sixteen pages of reflective wisdom, autobiographical information, and a muted

melancholy of tone aptly caught in the epigraph from Sappho: "The moon has set, and the Pleiades; it is the middle of the night and time passes, time passes, and I lie alone" ([297]). Seventy, the aging poet is mellower but not mellowed, not serene, still unreconciled to "the good-enough that spoils the world" (*SP,* 75). He is, he says, "moving toward a more expansive universe," and he proposes "to take more risks" than he ever did before (312). **"Seedcorn and Windfall"** is a risk, a fine risk well worth taking.

Notes

1. *A Kind of Order, a Kind of Folly: Essays and Conversations* (Boston 1975), p. [xi]. Hereafter in this chapter, page references to this book are in parentheses following each citation.

2. Richard Vine, "The Language That Saves," *Salmagundi,* No. 36 (Winter 1977), 122-3.

3. Ibid., p. 118.

4. Ibid.

5. "Our period demands a type of man who can restore the lost equilibrium between inner and outer reality . . . who can control his own existence by the process of balancing forces often regarded as irreconcilable: man in equipoise" ([3]); Kunitz's ellipsis).

Selected Bibliography

[Editor's Note: See previous essay for Selected Bibliography.]

Michael Ryan (essay date September/October 1985)

SOURCE: Ryan, Michael. "Life between Scylla and Charybdis." In *Interviews and Encounters with Stanley Kunitz,* edited by Stanley Moss, pp. 128-36. Riverdale-on-Hudson, N.Y.: Sheep Meadow Press, 1993.

[*In the following essay, originally published in the September/October 1985 issue of* American Poetry Review, *Ryan presents a close reading of Kunitz's poem "My Sisters" and places it within the context of Kunitz's oeuvre.*]

> *The life of a poet is crystallized in his work, that's how you know him.*
>
> —Stanley Kunitz

This is one of the poems by Stanley Kunitz I love the most:

"My Sisters"

Who whispered, souls have shapes?
So has the wind, I say.
But I don't know,
I only feel things blow.

> I had two sisters once
> with long black hair
> who walked apart from me
> and wrote the history of tears.
> Their story's faded with their names,
> but the candlelight they carried,
> like dancers in a dream,
> still flickers on their gowns
> as they bend over me
> to comfort my night-fears.
>
> Let nothing grieve you,
> Sarah and Sophia.
> Shush, shush, my dears,
> now and forever.

The poem is beyond comment, or underneath it, at least in the language of criticism, which is "a kind of translation," Eudora Welty says, "like a headphone we can clamp on at the U.N. when they are speaking the Arabian tongue." **"My Sisters"** resists this translation exceptionally well because its Arabic is silence—the silences of the past, of lost time, death, and eternity. These are different silences, I think, and one of the accomplishments of the poem is that it differentiates them, it makes them distinct and present and felt as such, and then gathers them into that tender, heartbreaking final sentence—"Shush, shush," a comforting gesture, a wish for silence as relief from sadness or grief or a child's night-fears (and so calling back to stanza two), a wish for silence as relief from frailty and mortality. Just as the past becomes present (through the agency of "the candlelight they carried" that "still flickers"), and the comforted finally becomes the comforter (and vice versa), that last gesture transforms the preceding silences into one silence that includes not only the poem's characters but also its readers. At least this reader. It makes me feel the intimate texture of the simple, inexhaustible fact that—as Kunitz put it in an interview—"we are living and dying at the same time."

The way it does this is primarily nondiscursive, through structure, movement, music, and drama. "The best part" of a poem, Frost said, is "the unspoken part." Almost all of **"My Sisters"** is unspoken in this sense, like Hardy's "During Wind and Rain," which so exceeds its commonplace idea, that human beings are mortal, by embodying its emotional truth in structure and rhythm, refrain and variation, in the voice that begins each stanza and begins the poem, "They sing their dearest songs," and the voice that invariably answers and closes the poem, "Down their carved names the rain-drop plows."

"My Sisters" has two voices, too, but their function and relationship are very different from those of Hardy's poem. The voice of the first stanza frames the rest of **"My Sisters"** like one of Vermeer's half-opened windows that filter and admit the light in which everything appears at once palpable and numinous. It strikes me as a voice out of nowhere, from the wilderness of inner space, not the same "I" that speaks the second and third stanzas but given terrestrial life by the second "I." "There is an aspect of one's existence that has nothing to do with personal identity, but that falls away from self, blends into the natural universe," Kunitz wrote in *A Kind of Order, a Kind of Folly.* This, I believe, is the first "I" of **"My Sisters,"** appropriately distinguished by italics from the personal "I" who has memories and affections and a life in time; one of the dramatic undercurrents of the poem is probably *their* blending together "into the natural universe" of silence.

In any case, the first line—*"Who whispered, souls have shapes?"*—sets the tone. It echoes in my ear "Who said, 'Peacock Pie'?"—the beginning of a strange, wonderful poem by a strange, sometimes wonderful poet, Walter de la Mare, who is much loved in England and mostly unread in the United States. De la Mare's is another poem in two voices, one that questions and one that replies, a mechanical arrangement meant to go nowhere, unlike **"My Sisters,"** which moves great distances gracefully "like dancers in a dream." **"My Sisters"** is, in fact, a miracle of movement, traveling from the impersonal undervoice of the opening to the intimate direct address of the ending, invariably immediate and increasingly dramatic. Is it this movement over the fluid three-beat lines marked by irregular rhymes and half-rhymes which makes the form feel like a membrane that can barely contain an overwhelming grief and sweetness? The way the three-beat line is used is a joy to look at closely. The second sentence of the second stanza, besides being a wonder syntactically and lodging in the dramatic image so it won't be forgotten, is cut into lines of extraordinary rhythmical beauty and function. "Like dancers in a dream" is the pivotal line of the six-line sentence. The return to the strict iambic trimeter after the rhythmical variation of the previous three lines physiologically and psychologically brings the line home. The satisfaction of the rhythmical expectation mounting since the last strict iambic trimeter ("who walked apart from me") is bonded to content, and the image of the "dancers in a dream" acquires the authority of that satisfaction. "Like dancers in a dream" also immediately reestablishes the ground beat, the rhythmical context for the lines following it. "Still flickers on their gowns"—another iambic trimeter—reinforces this, but unlike the previous three lines it isn't end-stopped, a subtle variation, but enough with the line's slightly increased duration to echo the ground beat yet still keep the rhythm fluid. Now, in the next line, when the second beat occurs before it "should"—"as they *bend* over me"—that moment takes on terrific emphasis, even if, especially if, this emphasis is registered subconsciously while we are attending to the drama, the meaning of the words. The gesture of bending becomes palpable beneath its description or representation.

Also, the subconscious rhythmical effect is so powerful at that moment, it keeps us locked in the remembered scene to a degree that makes the astonishing move into direct address after the stanza-break feel simple and natural. This kind of pivot or "turn"—what Petrarch called the "volta" between the octave and sestet of the sonnet—seems inherent to poetic form, and there are all sorts of turns in all sorts of poems, but this one, because of its marriage of solidity and wildness, seems to me inspired: "Let nothing grieve you, / Sarah and Sophia." And, by saying the names, the story that had "faded with their names" is restored; the sisters are given life, as in a ritual of the dead, at least for the ritualistic, rhythmic time of the poem. Their silence is shaped and, in the poem's last gesture, accepted and honored.

A great deal could be written about how the last stanza uses the established iambic trimeter to depart from it, but I want to look at only two lines, both examples of foreshortening but of different kinds. The first line— "Let nothing grieve you"—has three beats but a syllable missing in a strategic position. The unexpected silence extends the long vowel of "grieve"; because of the metrical pattern, the word literally must be given more time than it normally takes to say it, just as the syllable "you" acquires a stronger stress than it would have in conversation. If there were an unstressed syllable between "grieve" and "you," for example, "Let nothing grieve for you," the glide of the long ē—Emily Dickinson's favorite vowel, like a scream—wouldn't require extension because the sound would be encased in the iambic trimeter. As it is, the held note makes a very affecting music.

And the last line of the poem, working within and against the metrical grid, is even more effective and affecting: "Now and forever." Period. Two stresses and a feminine ending. In the ensuing silence after the last, unstressed syllable, after all those three-beat lines, the final beat never comes. Its absence is palpable, as if the silence itself were stressed, an endless incompletion, a longing for something missing, something lost.

The wealth of mystery in the poem, a good part of which is acquired through its rhythm and music, is not obscured by the slightest mystification. Its depths are discovered and displayed in a language absolutely simple and clear, words, as Wittgenstein said, "like film on deep water." Kunitz himself said in *The Paris Review* interview: "I dream of an art so transparent you can look through and see the world." He surely has already accomplished this, and much more, in **"My Sisters."**

Stanley Kunitz was eighty last July. As much as a young poet could learn about writing poetry from his poems, he or she could learn about the vocation of poetry from his prose. The book to mark his birthday appropriately includes poems and essays. But his life with poetry has not been confined to writing. For Kunitz, poetry is a spiritual discipline, a way of being and knowing oneself and the world, and he has purposefully presented himself as an example in a century when it has probably never been harder to live a poet's vocation and never been easier to cultivate a poet's "career," pathetic as such a "career" is next to those valued by corporate society.

In this regard, though his style was initially suffused with Hopkins and the Metaphysical Poets, the figure of John Keats in his "vale of Soul-making" has been Kunitz's main spiritual guide. In **"The Modernity of Keats,"** first published in 1964, he wrote that Keats's "technique was not an aggregate of mechanical skills, but a form of spiritual testimony." And this observation is recast as Kunitz's central assumption a decade later in the foreword to *A Kind of Order, a Kind of Folly*: "One of my unshakeable convictions has been that poetry is more than a craft, important as the craft may be: it is a vocation, a passionate enterprise, rooted in human sympathies and aspirations."

Theoretically, it may appear that this vocation could be a private affair between the poet and his or her own soul, as it surely was for Emily Dickinson and for Hopkins, though even in the latter case this was not necessarily by choice. Hopkins wrote to his friend Dixon in 1878: "What I do regret is the loss of recognition belonging to the work itself. For as to every moral act, being right or wrong, there belongs, of the nature of things, reward or punishment, so to every form perceived by the mind belongs, of the nature of things, admiration or the reverse." And, later in the same letter, more from the gut than from the Jesuit: "Disappointment and humiliation embitter the heart and make an aching in the very bones."

How many poets have sooner or later been poisoned by this bitterness? It's clearly from the desire and need for an audience that disappointment and humiliation and worse have inevitably come. Yet even if this desire and need were eliminated in the poet's heart, "Art is social in origin" (as Jane Ellen Harrison says bluntly in *Ancient Art and Ritual*), and poetry still retains its fundamental social character, even when the difference between the sale of five thousand copies of a volume of poems, which is unusual, and fifty thousand copies, which is almost unheard of, is the difference between minute fractions of one percent of the population. In response, poetry can and sometimes has become hermetic, opaque, precious, and prosaic; it can become difficult—as Eliot said it *must* be in this century—like a child suffering from lack of attention and love. It can refuse to give pleasure, even to the poet who writes it. And the figure of the poet may become the *poète maudit,* Gérard de Nerval walking his lobster on a leash and hanging himself with a shoelace, dandified, flippant—or doomed, as in the sad incarnation of Delmore Schwartz in an essay entitled "The Vocation of the Poet in the Modern World":

> In the unpredictable and fearful future that awaits civilization, the poet must be prepared to be alienated and indestructible. He must dedicate himself to poetry, although no one else seems likely to read what he writes; he must be indestructible as a poet until he is destroyed as a human being.

In the absence of an audience, are the available choices either killing the poetry or killing the poet? It's interesting and moving to watch how poets have tried to negotiate this Scylla and Charybdis in their lives and ideas and work. In his "Preface to *Lyrical Ballads* (1800)," Wordsworth internalizes the conflict between the poet and a culture which has abandoned him because his original social function is served by more efficient institutions and technology. Wordsworth tries to rescue the poet's social role by asserting that "the Poet binds together by passion and knowledge the vast empire of human society, as it is spread over the whole earth, and over all time." Yet, in the same essay, having imagined this grand audience out of the thinnest air, he admits that, in fact, the Poet's "own feelings are his stay and support."

For poets since the Industrial Revolution, Wordsworth articulates the predicament, but his solution is a formula for solipsism or, as Keats charitably called it, the "Wordsworthian or egotistical sublime." Grandiosity ("the vast empire," etc.) and isolation ("his own feelings are his stay and support") can only feed and increase each other, and, if their marriage is insular, can only breed bombast. They can kill the poet's soul and consequently his art, and can even become—as in the case of Delmore Schwartz and the dominant figures of Kunitz's generation—a risk to his life.

This danger is exactly what Whitman is addressing in this great passage from his "Preface" to the 1855 edition of *Leaves of Grass*:

> The soul has that measureless pride which consists in never acknowledging any lessons but its own. But it

has sympathy as measureless as its pride and the one balances the other and neither can stretch too far while it stretches in company with the other. The inmost secrets of art sleep with the twain.

The poet's "own feelings are his stay and support" for Whitman, too, but his "measureless pride," essential to enduring the lack of an audience and its economic and psychological implications, is offset by a "sympathy as measureless" for other people and even for other things outside of the self. This is the crucial counterweight to the solipsism that is Whitman's explicit currency, and from the tension between them he makes his poetry: "The inmost secrets of art sleep with the twain." Tested by poverty and loneliness to the degree that, as Kunitz quotes him in **"At the Tomb of Walt Whitman,"** he sometimes felt his poems "in a pecuniary and worldly sense, have certainly wrecked the life of their author," the balance of "measureless" pride and sympathy is nonetheless the key to Whitman's spiritual discipline and probably to his survival.

It is also a remarkably accurate description of Stanley Kunitz. His poetry, his character, and his ideas are born of these polarities. From his new book, *Next-to-Last Things*:

> If it were not for [the poet's] dream of perfection, which is the emblem of his life-enhancing art, and which he longs to share with others, generations of men and women would gradually sink into passivity, accepting as their lot second-rate or third-rate destinies, or worse. If one is to be taught submission, in the name of progress or national security, it is redemptive to recall the pride of one [Keats] who averred that his only humility was toward "the eternal Being, the Principle of Beauty, and the Memory of great Men."

The paradox, of course, is that a "life-enhancing art" which the poet "longs to share with others" isn't subject to the modification, opinion, or response of any other human being—"the eternal Being, the Principle of Beauty, and the Memory of great Men" being ideas—much less of any audience at large. And if the idea of the poet's preventing "generations" from sinking "into passivity" sounds like Wordsworth, in an earlier essay and somewhat different mood, Kunitz shows himself to be fully aware of the hazards of such "measureless pride":

> One of the dangers of poetry, certainly, is grandiosity. Let us not deceive ourselves: a poet isn't going to change the world with even the most powerful of his poems. The best he can hope for is to conquer a piece of himself.

In Kunitz's view, the spiritual discipline of poetry implies and incorporates the poet's social function. The poet is "an embodiment of resistance":

resistance against universal apathy, mediocrity, conformity, against institutional pressures to make everything look and become alike. This is why he is so involved with contraries.

He is "the representative free man of our time":

> The poet, in the experience of his art, is a whole person, or he is nothing. . . . He is uniquely equipped to defend the worth and power and responsibility of individuals in a world of institutions.

Consequently, and most pointedly:

> The poet speaks to others not only through what he says but through what he is, his symbolic presence, as though he carried a set of flags reading Have a Heart, Let Nothing Get By, Live at the Center of Your Being. His life instructs us that it is not necessary, or even desirable, for everyone to join the crowds streaming onto the professional or business highway, pursuing the bitch goddess.

In other words (though a paraphrase is hardly needed), the poet's vocation has an important social function even if his poetry is drowned out by the noise of TV, movies, commercials, and factories spuming forth new products. It's a vocation inherently subversive to corporate ideology, spoken symbolically and by example:

> Poets are subversive, but they are not really revolutionaries, for revolutionaries are concerned with changing others, while poets want first of all to change themselves.

If those dedicated to social change through civil disobedience spend a lot of time in jail, the poet's dedication to changing himself implies a life of internal exile in a society built for profit, in—as Ronald Reagan calls it—"the age of the entrepreneur." Kunitz's most recent statement, in *The Paris Review* interview, is also his most urgent:

> Evil has become a product of manufacture, it is built into our whole industrial and political system, it is being manufactured every day, it is rolling off the assembly line, it is being sold in the stores, it pollutes the air. . . .
>
> Perhaps the way to cope with the adversary is to confront him in ourselves. We have to fight for our little bit of health. We have to make our living and dying important again. And the living and dying of others. Isn't this what poetry is about?

In this light, a poem as apparently apolitical as **"My Sisters"** takes on political content and becomes a political gesture, ineffective as it may be against the million movies and TV programs in which life is sentimentalized and death is trivialized. The political nature of poetry has no more to do with subject than with its rendering, in making us feel living and dying

are more important than property and "the national interest," in using language clearly and accountably, unlike the way politicians and commercials use it. Insofar as the poet's vocation is a public act, it can be an act of conscience with a social function, though the border between public and publicity in this media culture needs constant checking. If the vocation of poetry Kunitz describes were arranged in a line, it would look like his characterization of "the power of the mind": "to transform, to connect, to communicate"—the first ("to transform") being the poet's relation to himself in his spiritual discipline, the second ("to connect") his relation to the world and to others, and the third ("to communicate") his social function, both through his poetry and his "symbolic presence." Of course, it isn't a line. It's all these at once.

This outline of Kunitz's ideas really is "a kind of translation" from "the Arabian tongue" of his prose. He certainly never presents them this systematically. They have more vitality and nuance combined with his many other convictions, concerns, and affections. Reading his essays, I get a transfusion of his indomitable spirit, his "fierce hold on life," which is much more important to me than my agreement. There are excellent reasons, for the sake of the poetry itself, to try to rescue its social function, even when from all appearances it has none. Poets from Horace to Sidney to Eliot have tried to do so, finding themselves at the edge of exile within the versions of civilization in which they lived. For Kunitz, poetry is a manifestation of hope and life, for the culture as well as for the individual—this is the source of its power and poignance. He argues for the essential seriousness of poetry, and for clarity and depth and music at a time when intelligent critics, perhaps unconsciously reflecting the political atmosphere, indulge triviality and obscurity and praise superficial linguistic invention.

> In the best poetry of our time—but only the best—one is aware of a moral pressure being exerted on the medium in the very act of creation. By "moral" I mean a testing of existence at its highest pitch—what does it feel like to be totally oneself?; an awareness of others beyond the self; a concern with values and meaning rather than with effects; an effort to tap the spontaneity that hides in the depths rather than what forms on the surface; a conviction about the possibility of making right and wrong choices. Lacking this pressure, we are left with nothing but a vacuum occupied by technique.

In exactly this sense, Kunitz's example to poets of my generation is a moral example, put forward consciously with an awareness of the hazards of doing so. He has said, "The poet's first obligation is survival," by which he means spiritual as well as literal, knowing from experience the conflicts between the two for a poet in this culture: "No bolder challenge confronts the modern artist than to stay healthy in a sick world."

Visiting Stanley Kunitz a few years ago, during a difficult period, I made the standard complaints about the poet's life that anyone who has been around poets has heard a thousand times. That means he had heard them a hundred thousand times, and maybe even voiced them once or twice when he was living in absolute obscurity on almost nothing, as he did for over twenty years. But he listened until I was finished, and then replied, "But, Michael, poetry is something you give to the world." If I'm ever able, as Chekhov said, "to squeeze the slave's blood out of my veins," this is the type of blood I would replace it with.

Stanley Kunitz: Selective Bibliography

POETRY AND PROSE:

Intellectual Things. New York: Doubleday, Doran, 1930.

Passport to the War: A Selection of Poems. New York: Holt, Rinehart, and Winston, 1944.

Selected Poems 1928-1958. Boston: Atlantic-Little, Brown, 1958.

The Poems of John Keats (ed.). New York: Crowell, 1965.

The Testing-Tree. Poems. Boston: Atlantic-Little, Brown, 1971.

The Terrible Threshold: Selected Poems 1940-1970. London: Secker & Warburg, 1974.

The Coat without a Seam: Sixty Poems 1930-1972. Northampton, MA: Gehenna Press, 1974.

Robert Lowell: Poet of Terribilità. New York: Pierpont Morgan Library, 1974.

A Kind of Order, a Kind of Folly: Essays and Conversations. Boston: Atlantic-Little, Brown, 1975.

From Feathers to Iron. Washington: Library of Congress, 1976.

The Lincoln Relics: A Poem. Port Townsend, Washington: Greywolf Press, 1978.

The Poems of Stanley Kunitz, 1928-1978. Boston: Atlantic-Little, Brown, 1979.

The Wellfleet Whale and Companion Poems. New York: Sheep Meadow Press, 1983.

Next-to-Last Things: New Poems and Essays. Boston: Atlantic-Little, Brown, 1985.

The Essential Blake (ed.). New York: Ecco Press, 1987.

TRANSLATIONS:

Voznesensky, Andrei. *Anti-Worlds and the Fifth Ace.* Trans. W. H. Auden, Stanley Kunitz et al. Ed. Patricia Blake and Max Hayward. New York: Schocken Books, 1967.

Yevtushenko, Yevgeny. *Stolen Apples.* Ed. Albert Todd. Trans. Stanley Kunitz et al. New York: Doubleday & Co., 1972.

Akhmatova, Anna. *Poems of Akhmatova.* Selected, Translated, and Introduced by Stanley Kunitz with Max Hayward. Boston: Atlantic-Little, Brown, 1973.

Drach, Ivan. *Orchard Lamps.* Ed. Stanley Kunitz and translated with others. New York: Sheep Meadow Press, 1978.

YALE SERIES OF YOUNGER POETS:

Kunitz, Stanley. Foreword. *Collecting Evidence.* By Hugh Seidman. Ed. Stanley Kunitz. New Haven: Yale University Press, 1970.

————. Foreword. *Lugging Vegetables to Nantucket.* By Peter Klappert. Ed. Stanley Kunitz. New Haven: Yale University Press, 1971.

————. Foreword. *Obscenities.* By Michael Casey. Ed. Stanley Kunitz. New Haven: Yale University Press, 1972.

Kunitz, Stanley. Foreword. *Field Guide.* By Robert Hass. Ed. Stanley Kunitz. New Haven: Yale University Press, 1973.

————. Foreword. *Threats instead of Trees.* By Michael Ryan. Ed. Stanley Kunitz. New Haven: Yale University Press, 1974.

————. Foreword. *Snow on Snow.* By Maura Stanton. Ed. Stanley Kunitz. New Haven: Yale University Press, 1975.

————. Foreword. *Gathering the Tribes.* By Carolyn Forché. Ed. Stanley Kunitz. New Haven: Yale University Press, 1976.

————. Foreword. *Beginning with O.* By Olga Broumas. Ed. Stanley Kunitz. New Haven: Yale University Press, 1977.

REFERENCE WORKS EDITED:

Tante, Dilly [Pseud.], ed. *Living Authors: A Book of Biographies.* New York: H. W. Wilson, 1931.

————. *Authors Today and Yesterday: A Companion Volume to Living Authors.* With Howard Haycraft. New York: H. W. Wilson, 1933.

Kunitz, Stanley J., ed. *The Junior Book of Authors: An Introduction to the Lives of Writers and Illustrators for Younger Readers.* With Howard Haycraft. New York: H. W. Wilson, 1934. 2nd ed. 1951.

————. *British Authors of the Nineteenth Century.* With Howard Haycraft. New York: H. W. Wilson, 1936.

————. *American Authors, 1600-1900: A Biographical Dictionary of American Literature.* With Howard Haycraft. New York: H. W. Wilson, 1938.

———. *Twentieth Century Authors: A Biographical Dictionary of Modern Literature.* With Howard Haycraft. New York: H. W. Wilson, 1942.

———. *British Authors before 1800: A Biographical Dictionary.* With Howard Haycraft. New York: H. W. Wilson, 1952.

———. *Twentieth Century Authors: First Supplement.* With Vineta Colby. New York: H. W. Wilson, 1955.

———. *European Authors: 1000-1900, A Biographical Introduction to European Literature.* With Vineta Colby. New York: H. W. Wilson, 1967.

BOOKS CONTRIBUTED TO:

Kunitz, Stanley. "Poetry's Silver Age: An Improbable Dialogue." *Writing in America.* Ed. John Fischer and Robert B. Silvers. New Brunswick, New Jersey: Rutgers University Press, 1960.

———. "The Taste of Self" (on Theodore Roethke's "In a Dark Time"). *The Contemporary Poet as Artist and Critic.* Ed. Anthony Ostroff. Boston: Little, Brown, 1964.

———. "On 'Father and Son.'" Ibid.

———. "Out of the Edge." *Randall Jarrell 1914-1965.* Ed. Robert Lowell, Peter Taylor, and Robert Penn Warren. New York: Farrar, Straus, and Giroux, 1967.

———. Foreword. *Worcester Poets: With Notes toward a Literary History.* By Michael True. Worcester, Massachusetts: Worcester County Poetry Association, 1972.

———. "Where Joy Is" (prefatory note). *To Hold in My Hand: Selected Poems.* By Hilda Morley. New York: Sheep Meadow Press, 1983.

———. "Poet and State." *Poetry and Politics: An Anthology of Essays.* Ed. Richard Jones. New York: Quill, 1985.

———. "Jeremiah: The Fountain Overflows." *Congregation: Contemporary Writers Read the Jewish Bible.* Ed. David Rosenberg. New York: Harcourt Brace Jovanovich, 1987.

———. "James Brooks: Reflections." *James Brooks: The Early 1950s.* New York: Berry-Hill, 1989.

———. "Chariot" (poem). *Varujan Boghosian.* Dartmouth, New Hampshire: Hood Museum of Art, 1989.

ARTICLES AND ESSAYS:

"Dilly Tante Observes." *Wilson Bulletin for Librarians* (title changed to *Wilson Library Bulletin,* 1939). Continued as "The Roving Eye" with initials "S. J. K." January 1928-March 1943.

Kunitz, Stanley. "From Queen Anne to the Jungle." Rev. of Edith Sitwell. *Poetry* 37 Mar. 1931: 339-345.

———. "Horace Gregory's First Book." *Poetry* 38 Apr. 1931: 41-45.

———. "Middle Way." Rev. of "AE" (George William Russell). *Poetry* 38 Aug. 1931: 276-80.

———. "Poetry of Conrad Aiken." *Nation* 14 Oct. 1931: 393-94.

———. "Poet of the War." Rev. of Wilfred Owen. *Poetry* 40 June 1932: 159-62.

———. "Six English Poets." *Poetry* 42 July 1933: 228-33.

———. "Honor of Doubt." Rev. of Harold Monroe. *Poetry* 44 June 1934: 162-64.

———. "Enchanted Pilgrim." Rev. of Elder Olson. *Poetry* 45 Feb. 1935: 279-82.

———. "Lesson from Rilke." Rev. of Rilke trans. *Poetry* 45 Mar. 1935: 328-32.

———. "Between Two Worlds." Rev. of C. Day Lewis. *Poetry* 47 Dec. 1935: 158-62.

———. "Simplicity in Wonder." Rev. of W. H. Davies. *Poetry* 48 July 1936: 232-34.

———. "Poet's Duty." Rev. of C. A. Millspaugh. *Poetry* 50 Apr. 1937: 43-45.

———. "Learned in Violence." Rev. of Conrad Aiken. *Poetry* 50 May 1937: 103-6.

———. "The Single Conscience." Rev. of Mary Colum. *Poetry* 52 May 1938: 86-94.

———. "Profile of a Mask." Rev. of Horace Gregory. *Poetry* 58 June 1941: 152-56.

———. "Pangolin of Poets." Rev. of Marianne Moore. *Poetry* 59 Nov. 1941: 96-98.

———. "The Day Is a Poem." Rev. of Robinson Jeffers. *Poetry* 59 Dec. 1941: 148-54.

———. "Pentagons and Pomegranates." Rev. of Louise Bogan. *Poetry* 60 Apr. 1942: 40-43.

Kunitz, Stanley. "In the Beginning." Rev. of *Five American Poets. Poetry* 60 July 1942: 215-19.

———. "A Tale of a Jar." Rev. of H. D. *Poetry* 70 Apr. 1947: 36-42.

———. "News of the Root." Rev. of Theodore Roethke. *Poetry* 73 Jan. 1949: 222-25.

———. "Bronze by Gold." Rev. of Gwendolyn Brooks and Annie Allen. *Poetry* 76 Apr. 1950: 52-56.

———. "Creative Writing Workshop." *Education* 73 Nov. 1952: 152-56.

———. "Seminar in the Arts." *Education* 73 Nov. 1952: 172-76.

———. "Five Points of the Compass." Rev. of Logan, Hall, Hutchinson, Woods, and Wales. *Poetry* 88 June 1956: 183-91.

———. "Careful Young Men." *Nation* 9 Mar. 1957: 200-201.

———. "Private Eye." Rev. of Kenneth Fearing. *Saturday Review* 29 June 1957: 25.

———. "Identity Is the Problem." Rev. of Lenore G. Marshall. *Saturday Review* 40 July 1957: 28.

———. "No Middle Flight." Rev. of John Berryman. *Poetry* 90 July 1957: 244-49.

———. "Poems Recorded by Richard Wilbur." *Evergreen Review* 8 Spring 1959: 201-2.

———. "American Poetry's Silver Age." *Harper's* 219 Oct. 1959: 173-79.

———. "Process and Thing: A Year of Poetry." *Harper's* 221 Sep. 1960: 96.

———. "New Books." *Harper's* 223 Aug. 1961: 86-91.

———. "The Taste of Self." *New World Writing* 19 1961: 106-14.

———. "The Cold War and the West." *Partisan Review* 29 Winter 1962: 40-42.

———. "Father and Son: A Rejoinder." *New World Writing* 20 1962: 211-15.

———. "Frost, Williams, and Company." *Harper's* 225 Oct. 1962: 100-103.

———. "Graves, Nemerov, Smith." *New York Times Book Review* 21 July 1963: 4.

———. "Robert Lowell: The Sense of a Life." *New York Times Book Review* 14 Oct. 1964: 34.

———. "Roethke: Poet of Transformations." *New Republic* 23 Jan. 1965: 23-29.

———. "Sea Son of the Wave." Rev. of *The Life of Dylan Thomas,* by Constantine Fitzgibbon. *New York Times Book Review* 31 Oct. 1965: 1.

———. "The Hartford Walker." *New Republic* 12 Nov. 1966: 23-26.

———. "A Sum of Approximations." *Translation* Winter 1973: 56-61.

———. "The Life of Poetry." *Antaeus* 37 Spring 1980: 149.

———. "Jean Garrigue: A Symposium." *Twentieth Century Literature* 29 Spring 1983: 13-18.

———. "The Layers." *Ironwood* Fall 1984: 71-74.

———. "Communication and Communion: A Dialogue." *Southern Review* Spring 1985: 404-14.

———. "Jack Tworkov." *Provincetown Arts* Aug. 1985: 5.

———. "At the Tomb of Walt Whitman." *American Poetry Review* Sep./Oct. 1985: 24-27.

———. "The Poet's Quest for the Father." *New York Times Book Review* 22 Feb. 1987: 1. Repr. in *Provincetown Arts* Annual Issue 1992.

———. "Gardening for Love." *New York Times Book Review* 11 Oct. 1987: 53.

———. "An Island Garden." *New York Times Book Review* 11 Dec. 1988: 28.

INTERVIEWS AND CONVERSATIONS:

Kunitz, Stanley. "A Conversation with Robert Lowell." *New York Times Book Review* 4 Oct. 1964. Repr. in Stanley Kunitz, *A Kind of Order, a Kind of Folly: Essays and Conversation,* 1975.

———. "Auden on Poetry: A Conversation with Stanley Kunitz." *Atlantic* 218 Aug. 1966: 94-102.

———. "A Conversation with Andrei Voznesensky." *New York Times Book Review* 16 April 1972. Repr. (fuller text) in *Antaeus* Summer 1972 and *A Kind of Order, a Kind of Folly.*

Russell, Robert. "The Poet in the Classroom." *College English* 28 May 1967: 580-86.

Lupher, David. "A Yale Lit Interview." *Yale Literary Magazine* 136 May 1968: 6-13.

Packard, William. "Craft Interview with Stanley Kunitz." *New York Quarterly* 1 Fall 1970: 9-22. Repr. in *The Poet's Craft: Interviews from The New York Quarterly.* Ed. William Packard. New York: Paragon, 1987. Previously in *The Craft of Poetry: Interviews from the New York Quarterly,* Ed. William Packard. New York: Doubleday, 1974.

Rodman, Selden. *Tongues of Fallen Angels.* New York: New Directions, 1972.

Boyers, Robert. "'Imagine Wrestling with an Angel': An Interview with Stanley Kunitz." *Salmagundi* 22-23 Spring 1973: 71-83. Repr. as "An Interview with Stanley Kunitz." *Contemporary Poetry in America.* Ed. Robert Boyers. New York: Schocken Books, 1974.

Davis, Cynthia, "Interview with Stanley Kunitz." *Contemporary Literature* 15 Winter 1974: 1-14.

Ryan, Michael. "An Interview with Stanley Kunitz." *Iowa Review* 5 1974: 76-85.

Allen, Henry. "The Poet's Poet: Stanley Kunitz at the Library of Congress." *Potomac (Washington Post* supplement) 9 Jan. 1975: 10.

Slaughter, Adele. "Stanley Kunitz on 'The Science of the Night'." *Calvert* Spring 1975: 6-9.

Brantley, Robin. "A Touch of the Poet." *New York Times Magazine* 7 Sept. 1975: 80-83.

Loxterman, Alan, moderator. "Poetry in the Classroom: A Symposium with Marvin Bell, Donald Hall, and Stanley Kunitz." *American Poetry Review* 6 1977: 9-13.

Gross, Harvey. "Stanley Kunitz: Action and Incantation." *Antaeus* 30/31 Spring 1978: 283-95.

Busa, Christopher. "The Art of Poetry XXIX: Stanley Kunitz." *Paris Review* Vol. 24, no. 83 Spring 1982: 205-46. Repr. (revised) in Stanley Kunitz, *Next-to-Last Things: New Poems and Essays.*

Jackson, Richard. "Living the Layers of Time." *Acts of Mind: Conversations with Contemporary Poets.* Ed. Richard Jackson. Alabama: University of Alabama Press, 1983.

"Stanley Kunitz Addresses New York Poets at Gracie Mansion." *Envoy* No. 44 and 45 23 Sept. 1983: 3.

Busa, Christopher. "Stanley Kunitz: A Poet in His Garden." *Garden Design* Winter 1984-85: 46-47, 92.

Sutton, Caroline. "PW Interviews: Stanley Kunitz." *Publishers Weekly* 228 20 Dec. 1985: 67-68.

"A Poet's Garden." *House Beautiful* Apr. 1986: 106.

Weissbort, Daniel. "Translating Anna Akhmatova." *Translating Poetry.* Ed. by Daniel Weissbort. Iowa City: University of Iowa Press, 1989.

Ringold, Francine. "Lighting the Lamp." *Nimrod* April 1991 Vol. 34, no. 2 Spring/Summer 1991: 71-3

Dore Ashton (essay date 1986)

SOURCE: Ashton, Dore. "Kunitz and the Painters." In *A Celebration for Stanley Kunitz on His Eightieth Birthday,* pp. 18-22. Riverdale-on-Hudson, N.Y.: Sheep Meadow Press, 1986.

[*In the following essay, Ashton reflects on Kunitz's establishment of friendships with a number of painters who found the poet's perspective inspiring.*]

"Mark Rothko was such a restless and impatient soul," Kunitz wrote in a brief memoir. "He never could sit through any kind of meeting. The way he squirmed!" Rothko not only squirmed. He paced. In the midst of a dinner he would light a cigarette, thrust back his chair and, on his gumsoles, pad around the kitchen trailing a stream of smoke. Yet, when Kunitz was there, Rothko paused, listened, and often plunged into discussions from which we all profited. There were a half-dozen other painters in those gregarious old days who relished the opportunity to engage Kunitz in talk, talk, talk. He understood them. As he wrote in **A Kind of Order, a Kind of Folly,** he preferred their company to that of poets "who tend to be surly and withdrawn."

If Kunitz was something of a connoisseur, it was because he paid attention. I have an ineffable memory of our first encounter. I was living with my husband, a painter, in a small and rather shabby loft up a narrow flight of stairs. It was sometime in the mid-1950s. Kunitz had just settled down in New York and had somehow broken a leg doing so. Up he clumped in his plaster-cast gait. Then, instead of collapsing into the chair I hastened to offer, he clumped around the studio, face thrust close to the canvases, looking hard. We talked that afternoon for hours. I remember being immensely impressed when he proudly told me that he had planted a thousand trees (or was it five thousand?). I have always associated the determined will that great plantation required with Kunitz's poetic presence in my life, and the lives of my friends among the artists.

Within a matter of months Kunitz had become well acquainted with the most gifted artists around, many of whom were destined to fame as innovative artists of The New York School. (Among those whose company Kunitz sought, and who could be found at long evenings at his home, were Franz Kline, James Rosati, Mark Rothko, Giorgio Cavallon, Adja Yunkers, Philip Guston, Jack Tworkov and Robert Motherwell.) I think what the painters liked—at least those I knew best, Rothko, Kline, Guston and Motherwell—was that Kunitz was a man who spoke unabashedly about a "moral universe." They too were committed to a point of view of existence—an esthetic—that assumed that their place was in a universe created by art and, of necessity, moral.

Their universe was one of constant transformations. Kunitz, who liked to talk about "shapeshifters," was uniquely equipped to understand them. When, shortly after Theodore Roethke's death in 1963, Kunitz wrote about his poetry, he characterized a poetics that could be easily transposed to the works of several of his friends among the painters: "If the transformations of his experience resist division into mineral, vegetable and animal categories, it is because the levels are continually overlapped, intervolved, in the manifold of tissue." During frequent studio visits, at parties, around the dinner table, in his own baroque garden, or strolling through the streets of the Village, Kunitz exchanged views with the painters and sometimes even engaged in Socratic gadflyism. I have known him to provoke for the sake of discussion and I have often noticed his love of paradox when talking with artists. Although I know that the influence of poets is incalculable, I also know that Kunitz's presence among the artists was "intervolved" and in the manifold of their most precious tissue. There were certainly moments in the lives of painters such as Guston, Rothko and Motherwell when Kunitz's prescient remarks sustained their hand.

Some of those remarks during the 1950s I jotted down. In my own case he once startled me, in 1958, by telling me that art critics exaggerated their roles and that they must "give back the man to the work." With a touch of irony that was not lost on me, he reminded me of the value of the quotidian criticism of Sainte-Beuve. During the same year he and I talked a great deal about Mark Rothko, whom Kunitz then saw as "a primitive, a shaman who finds the magic formula and leads people to it." Although Kunitz was the poet who, as he recently said, understood that "the way backward and the way forward are the same," and whose own work so wondrously restores the mythic voice, he never permitted himself to escape the contingent. In 1960 standing in the corner of my kitchen with Guston and Rothko he piqued them, saying: "The artist must come back from his escape into myth and permit himself to be polluted. He must read newspapers." In those days he pondered the distinctions between image and icon, and warned against the production of false icons. He also had a healthy disdain for the *tummlers* of the art world beating away at their crude drums. "The artist goes from *his* own center out to a periphery—as far as he can, but always from his own center, not the center of some school or pack," he told us in 1959. Yet, as he said in a public lecture a couple of years ago, "Every work of art of any interest must be considered as an event." When he peered close, Kunitz made his friends among the artists feel as if they had created an event—a rare and fortifying feeling. I think that the particular artists with whom he was most in communion were exceptionally thoughtful, constantly questioning the larger issues implicit in their own work. When he made grand generalizations they were stimulated. I remember one in particular that struck me: Art does not attack its age with its opposite, but applies homeopathic doses of what the age seems to be demanding until in the end the age dies of nausea. For Philip Guston, whose restlessness Kunitz well understood, such a pronunciamento resounded. Guston was about to inaugurate a new age after administering his own powerful homeopathic dose.

Guston's caricatures of Kunitz—he made several—fearlessly stress the thrust of his large and curious nose and the humor of his intense but skeptical gaze. Caricature was something Kunitz and he understood together. So many others were so bloody earnest that they could never see its virtue. But probably it was Kunitz's willingness to talk about the poets Guston devoured, such as Gerard Manley Hopkins ("the taste of myself in all things") and William Butler Yeats, that attached Guston to Kunitz. During those hard years of

the 1960s Guston understood and needed the voice of ancient and tragic wisdom, a voice he found in Kunitz in such lines as:

> Within the city of the burning cloud,
> Dragging my life behind me in a sack,
> Naked I prowl, scourged by the black
> Temptation of the blood grown proud . . .
>
> **("Open the Gates")**

Kunitz felt artistic affinities with certain painters. A couple of years after Rothko's death he told me that he had been moved by the grandeur of Rothko's work, by its rhetoric of color. "I felt definite affinities between his work and a kind of secrecy that lurks in every poem—an emanation that comes only from language." Kunitz was one of the few men of letters in America who could respect the secret language of the painter; the painter's incarnation of meaning in the language of paint—a language that resists translation but is nonetheless a language.

Probably, though, it is simply Kunitz's capacity for faith that inspires artists. To this day he believes in art. Just a few months ago I had a letter from a young painter telling me that a visit from Kunitz had kept her going for months. If I ask what it was about that visit, and all the other studio visits, I think I can say that it was Kunitz's confirmation of the value of what painters do. His is a mind that, as Coleridge said, "feels the riddle of the world, and may help unravel it." For painters of a contemplative, let's even say romantic, temperament, Kunitz fulfills a great hunger. He proffers a Borges-like view of existence as "a giant web of interconnected filaments that if touched, the whole web trembles"—an ideal vision that many, many painters strive to realize in their works.

Yes, I think, finally, that it is Kunitz's faith that inspirits other artists, and most of all painters. And, perhaps, his wisdom. I was on a plane with him last spring and told him I'd just read an essay by Norbert Weiner in which he predicted that eventually computers could be made so accurate that even a man, rendered into the quantified computer language, could be completely communicated. Kunitz smiled his small smile and answered, "Yes, perhaps, but not a man who could write Dante's *Inferno*."

Tess Gallagher (essay date 1986)

SOURCE: Gallagher, Tess. "To Work and Keep Kind." In *A Celebration for Stanley Kunitz on His Eightieth Birthday*, pp. 60-5. Riverdale-on-Hudson, N.Y.: Sheep Meadow Press, 1986.

[*In the following essay, Gallagher describes her friendship with Kunitz, noting their shared, unrequited longing for their fathers.*]

Of the multitude of spoken and unspoken injunctions handed on from parents, teachers, and friends, there are a simple few the heart selects and pursues with an instinctive recognition. My title comes from Stanley Kunitz's plea to the ghost of his father at the end of the poem **"Father and Son"**:

> "O teach me how to work and keep me kind."

It is just these necessities that Stanley Kunitz has held out to me over the past twelve years of our friendship.

The character of Kunitz's own work and his dedication to the work of young writers over the years continue to inspire and amaze me. The impression is of an energy not unlike that of the salmon he writes so movingly about in **"King of the River"**:

> You would dare to be changed,
> as you are changing now,
> into the shape you dread
> beyond the merely human.

His energy is indeed full of changes, of transformations informed by that final knowledge of our human fatedness, which commands us, as he says in the poem, to "increase and die." His faith in my own endeavors to write poetry and to teach has been a guiding force at the very heart of my writing and living. The luck of this association calls to mind his translation of Anna Akhmatova's lines: "But if I could step outside myself / and contemplate the person that I am / I should know at last what envy is."

The first time I heard Kunitz's name was when Theodore Roethke read aloud to us a Kunitz poem entitled **"The Science of the Night"** in the spring of 1963. After Roethke's sudden death that summer Stanley Kunitz made his first appearance in my life. He came to the University of Washington to read his poems in a special program to commemorate Theodore Roethke. It was the fall of 1963. I had just been swept away as only the young can be by the vision of a life dedicated to the writing of poetry. All summer I'd been washing dishes at night in a restaurant. Days I worked in the newsroom of my hometown paper as a reporter and girl Friday, hoping to be able to afford to return to college. On the occasion of Mr. Kunitz's reading, I was dispirited. Sick at heart. Roethke was gone.

When Kunitz was ushered into the packed lecture hall and seated in the chair directly in front of mine, it was as if an emissary from Roethke had suddenly arrived. I was so shaken by the sense of this that I remember thinking I should ask Mr. Kunitz to sign his book of poems for me—a daring act indeed, since I had denied myself such a request of Roethke out of an assumption that this was probably beneath his dignity. But I was too far gone in need to honor such a scruple now. Nonetheless, my hand refused to make the short reach over the back of the chair to proffer the book. I'm laughable to myself in that moment, but caught too by the earnestness of such attachments to those who shepherd anyone's first tottering gestures in the attempt to write. Not until thirteen years had passed would hands extend the same book of poems into those of Mr. Kunitz.

But the voice that gave his poems that day, full of unsentimental consequence and self-mended yearning, seems to have imprinted itself onto my psyche. I know now, as I didn't then, that the deep recognitions I felt had to do most probably with our common search for our fathers. Kunitz's own father had died as a suicide in a public park the spring before he was born. My father was alive, but distanced from me by drinking and spiritual torments that divided him from everyone. While Kunitz attempted to resurrect his father in order to gain the time they'd never had, I seemed pitted against the clock of my father's life in an effort to construct a language of the heart that would, I hoped, reach him and consequently my own life, before it was too late.

By comparison, I had a bounty of time with my father; and because I seized my task so early, I think my poems had time to grow in clarity and finally did give solace to my father. Yet since his death, I've felt closer to the mysterious ramifications of the loss Kunitz must have lived from the start. There is the cold withdrawal at the end of **"Father and Son"** as the father's ghost turns toward his son "the white ignorant hollow of his face." And, in a similarly eerie moment, the ghost of Abraham Lincoln coexists with a contemporary likeness that bears his "rawboned, warty look, / a gangling fellow in jeans" and then gives way to "that other one / who's tall and lonely." Kunitz has been haunted a lifetime by the sense of one who has been banished forever from the kingdom of the living. Perhaps this is what gives his poems such a strong reserve of mystery—this feeling of presences which have the power to outlast their corporeal forms.

Recently I used the word "mystery" in speaking to a group of writing students in Urbana, Illinois, and they looked at me incredulously, as if I'd just suggested they all dig wells and drink only well water from that day forward. Mystery in poems seemed an anachronism. "I need my grottos," I said. There was a blank look on their faces. At this point I reached for Kunitz's book of essays, *A Kind of Order, a Kind of Folly,* turned to the chapter entitled **"Seedcorn and Windfall,"** and read to them:

> Poets today tend to be clearer—sometimes all too clear. A poem is charged with a secret life. Some of its information ought to circulate continuously within its

perimeter as verbal energy. That, indeed, is the function of form: to contain the energy of a poem, to prevent it from leaking out.

It is this sense of a secret inner life which nourishes the poems, signals its taboos and rituals as they limit or instruct access, that I value in Kunitz's poetry and person. Yet this containment never intends to obfuscate meaning arbitrarily. His mysteries arrive without exertion as a natural extension of his spirit finding voice.

In 1973 I was attending classes at the Iowa Writers' Workshop when I purchased Kunitz's translations of Anna Akhmatova. I had so far not found a female poet in English who wholly captured my imagination. Akhmatova, through Kunitz, came powerfully alive for me. I sat at the kitchen table in the small upstairs apartment and began writing the poem **"Stepping Outside."** It was directed to Akhmatova, telling her how she had allowed me to face some of the hardships of my life through her own example of strength. In a rush of gratitude I typed the poem and sent it off to Stanley Kunitz, whom I had never met.

Having since received many such gifts myself from those who've read my poems or essays, I now understand what a rare thing it was when I took from my mailbox a reply from Kunitz. So often the best intentions to thank or to inquire further toward such volunteer correspondents have been delayed or have escaped me altogether in the rush of travel or teaching. All the more to wonder at the magnanimous reply he made. "Are all your poems this good?" he questioned. "Send me a group. I'm introducing several poets in the *American Poetry Review*." It was to be my poetic debut, the first time a group of my poems would appear in a poetry magazine with a large national circulation. I felt "discovered" and the loneliness of my strivings seemed, at last, to have won an advocate.

Three years later I was able to arrange a meeting when Kunitz accepted an invitation to read his poems at Kirkland College in Upstate New York. I had just joined the teaching staff there. My personal life was a shambles. I was recently divorced from my poet husband and was unsure of what to do next. Kunitz arrived *sans* luggage, *sans* poems. I remember our first task together was to search in the library for periodicals that carried his most recent poems. We talked all the while of Roethke, and I remember a feeling of childlike jubilation on my part—not that of meeting, but of reunion. This visit, crucial as it was, renewed my resolve toward my own writing and confirmed me in the steps I had just taken to leave my unhappy marriage. I cannot do other than think that the fresh reserve of energy that allowed me to leave

America for Ireland shortly afterwards had something to do with the encouragement Kunitz had given me. There I was to write most of the poems that formed the heart of my second book, *Under Stars.*

Since then an intimacy so akin to that of father and daughter has developed that I fear mentioning it as such. Maybe I'm afraid it is spell that allows such an inheritance. Also, I know I'm not the only beneficiary. I have good sisters in his affection—Louise Glück, Carolyn Forché, Cleopatra Mathis, Mary Oliver, Olga Broumas—my friends and some of the leading poets of my generation. And there are others—Michael Ryan, Daniel Halpern, Robert Hass, Gregory Orr—writers who have likewise benefited from his wisdom and support.

I remember his journey to the Northwest in 1978 for a writers' conference in Port Townsend, Washington, and how he drove with me to my birthplace an hour away to go fishing with my father and me for salmon. He caught a beautiful fifteen-pound salmon that day, and we photographed it near my mother's rhododendrons before taking it back to Port Townsend for our supper. My mother led Stanley around her flower garden and they developed an instant rapport—she reciting the names of plants and he often recognizing something aloud before she could tell him, thereby presenting, as unobtrusively as possible, his own credentials as an accomplished gardener.

At some point they got into a lively, but friendly, argument about which was the oldest known tree in the world. My mother insisted it was the Bristlecone Pine. Stanley argued that it was the *Metasequoia glyptostroboides,* commonly known as the Dawn Redwood. "*Pinus aristata,*" my mother declared, and stood firm. Over the next several years I passed clippings from various newspapers and gardening journals back and forth between them proving one or the other case. Clearly neither was going to lose this debate. My mother had proudly displayed her own Bristlecone Pine to Stanley before he left, and this caused Stanley to say to me at the end of one of our visits in the East, "I'd like to give your mother a Dawn Redwood. Sometime I will."

After my father's death in 1982, the time seemed appropriate. The idea of the tree had accumulated sufficient significance. I followed instructions and went to the nursery to make the purchase for Stanley. The next day, to my mother's delight and surprise, a truck arrived with the Dawn Redwood. It was planted a little distance from its adversary, the Bristlecone Pine. This seems to have settled the contest between them, and in its place are my mother's ministrations toward the tree itself, referred to now simply as "Stanley's tree."

I tell this story to commemorate the longevity of the man himself as we celebrate his poetry, criticism, and many personal gifts to the entire literary community in his eightieth year, and to bring us back to kindness, without which the work we do would be bereft of its deepest rewards. Stanley Kunitz's gifts to me as I've sketched them briefly here amount to a debt that can only be answered with love, and that isn't an answer—it is more like two trees, each reputed to be the oldest living tree in the world, growing silently upward, side by side.

Stanley Kunitz and Esther Harriott (interview date May 1990)

SOURCE: Kunitz, Stanley, and Esther Harriott. "'I'm Not Sleepy.'" In *Interviews and Encounters with Stanley Kunitz,* edited by Stanley Moss, pp. 185-92. Riverdale-on-Hudson, N.Y.: Sheep Meadow Press, 1993.

[*In the following interview, conducted in May 1990, Kunitz describes the unexpected "feeling of relief" he experienced when he reached his eighties with enough accomplishments to "justify the life."*]

[*Harriott*]: *About sixty years ago, in the poem "I Dreamed That I Was Old," you wrote, "My wisdom, ripe with body's ruin, found / Itself tart recompense for what was lost / In false exchange." Your view of age is more cheerful now, isn't it?*

[Kunitz]: When I wrote that poem in my early twenties, age and, of course, its companion, death, were terrifying prospects. They haunted me. I'm still not wholly reconciled to the fate of the body, but I can truthfully say that I've found more rewards and compensations in my mid-eighties than I ever expected. Above all, I never imagined that the blessings of love and friendship would endure so long.

What are some of the other rewards and compensations?

Just to be rid of the hangups and anxieties of your youth—that's a kind of blessing too. And then, there's an assurance that comes out of having learned so much about yourself, why you are here, what you have done, how much is left for you to do. There is a—I wouldn't call it serenity—but a feeling of relief that you haven't completely wasted your life. Maybe you can take a little pride in having triumphed over the many difficulties and disasters that beset you. As D. H. Lawrence said, "Look! We have come through!" There remains the nagging question as to how well you have used your resources, and there's a bit of comfort in

being able to reply, "Not so well as I might have hoped, but maybe well enough to feel that there is time still to justify the life." The persons around me who have aged badly are the ones who don't feel justified. They can't forgive themselves for having abused or squandered their talent. When people lose their self-esteem, their moral center collapses.

You speak of being able to say "Look! We've come through!" It's surprising how many of the artists and writers I've interviewed were critically neglected until relatively late in life.

Including me.

Including you. Would you say that perhaps the critical neglect was a factor in your continuing productivity? That it taught you to persevere?

Neglect can kill. But from this vantage point I can see that the years of my deepest discontent, when I was working in the dark, were the most seminal period of my creative life, a time of testing, self-questioning, self-renewal. I learned, as I think every artist must, to recognize my own flaws and limitations, to build on whatever strengths I had, and to affirm and reaffirm the worth of my endeavor. I came to understand that the challenge for poets in our society is to make something virtuous, even heroic, out of the marginality of our existence. It's a risky enterprise.

Isn't this one of the advantages as you grow older— that you can afford to work on your own terms, to feel a freedom from critical opinion?

In the end, there's really only a handful of persons whose opinions you care about.

I'd like to go back to your earlier remark that in your youth you were haunted by the idea of death. Was that because of your father's suicide before you were born?

I wondered how and why he did it. The terror of oblivion haunted my childhood. I dreaded falling asleep at night because of the fear of losing consciousness. I'm sure that affected my biological rhythm because, to this day, I hate going to sleep and fight it off as long as I can. I practically never go to bed before three or four in the morning.

I've been trying to figure out when you do *sleep, because you work at night and, in the summer, presumably you garden during the day, and you're active at the Fine Arts Work Center in Provincetown, and . . .*

Yes, but I have a long day. My writing day usually begins around nine or ten at night and then continues for as long as I can hang on.

When do you sleep then? Off and on?

No, I have a Puritan conscience about sleep, and napping would make me feel guilty. I can't even picture myself taking an afternoon snooze. So what do I do? Last night, say, I went to bed exactly at four forty-five. It then took me an hour before I could fall asleep, and I was up at eight-thirty. That's enough for me to get by on, though I usually want four or five hours. But that's enough. If I have five, I feel that I have slept out completely.

So one of your great assets is that you have an extraordinary amount of energy, compared to people of any age.

That's what my young friends say! [Laughs.]

It's not only that you don't get that much sleep, but that . . .

I'm not sleepy.

Right. Do you attribute that energy to good genes or discipline or to being so engaged with your work and with the world?

I don't think of it as a matter of discipline. My mother lived to age eighty-six and was wonderfully alert till her death. I keep going because of unfinished business. There's still work for me to do. For anyone who has a poem to write or a garden to cultivate, the days are never long enough. How could I ever be bored with existence?

You have many friends in the arts, I know, both poets and painters.

One of the sorrows of longevity is the loss of old friends. I've outlived most of my contemporaries. These days my companions tend to be younger than I, some of them much younger, including a number of former students. In many ways I feel closer to their generation than to my own.

In terms of outlook?

In terms of awareness and concerns. In any case, I'm more conversable with them. With the old, it seems to me that I have little to say. The normal subject of conversation with another octogenarian is pretty obvious. I have other things on my mind!

But that wouldn't be the case, would it, if you were talking to an artist of your generation?

Of course there are exceptions, but it's not uncommon for old artists—I mean in particular the celebrated ones—to retreat into themselves, to wrap themselves in their own mythology, to become, in short, iconic figures. You cannot establish contact with their secret life: it's buried too deep inside them.

That's the penalty not only of age, but of fame, isn't it? Couldn't that also happen with a young superstar—not knowing where the myth leaves off and the true identity begins?

It could, though that's not anything, I guess, for young poets to worry about nowadays. Superstars are creatures of the marketplace.

I was thinking of someone like Andy Warhol.

The success of his career, I've always felt, had some of the elements of a parody. It's undeniable that he created, as celebrities tend to do, a legend about himself, but in his case the legend was an artifact, assembled out of spare parts in what he ironically called his Factory. This isn't what Keats meant when he said that the poet's life is a continual allegory.

What is it an allegory of?

Of human destiny, I suppose. The artist isn't somebody special or exotic, but a representative human being. Coleridge said that the poet is one who puts the whole soul of man into activity. I think of it in a somewhat different way. I have this image of a house. We occupy this house, which is our bodily frame, and for most persons maybe three or four lights in the house are burning and the rest is in darkness. But the creative imagination calls for turning all the lights on, for the house to be ablaze with light. That's what one lives for, really—those moments when you feel that blazing luminosity within.

Is there any way that those of us who are not creative artists can turn on all those lights? Is it a matter of being passionately engaged or curious?

A lot of it has to do with the extent of one's curiosity and caring. What bothers me about so many people is how little curiosity they have about what's happening to others, what's happening in the world, what's happening right now, for example, in Eastern Europe, Israel, the Soviet Union. To me the day's news is terribly important. The first thing I do in the morning is read *The New York Times*. The imagination renews itself by intermeshing with the dynamics of history. If you feel you're irrelevant to history, you fester.

But what is your feeling when you learn that in Eastern Europe or Israel or the Soviet Union there has been a regression to things like hypernationalism and old ethnic hatreds? Don't you despair about progress?

It isn't a question of progress, it's a question of concern. I don't delude myself that people are getting any better. Perhaps the state of the individual has improved at the subsistence level, but the relative quotient of good to evil in the world in this century—a century that includes the Holocaust—has probably deteriorated. To stay human we need to understand that what happens to others is happening to us. That's what the moral imagination is all about.

Did you know that Rollo May used you as an example in his book on creativity, The Courage to Create*? He said that you wrote your poems out of rage. But I think he was quoting from your poem* "The Thief"*—"I write this poem for money, rage, and love"—which was rage directed at having your pocket picked, whereas he interpreted the rage as rage against death.*

Rollo was basing his conclusions on conversations we had more than twenty years ago. There certainly was a period when I raged against all sorts of things. I may have told him it was the idea of being mortal that offended me most. Perhaps it's still at the root of my persistence in staying alive. I want to outwit the enemy.

Could it be that the feeling that there is still work to do contributes to longevity? That you must stay alive in order to finish it?

I can't picture myself ever saying, "I have done everything I could. Now I'm going to sit in the sun and vegetate for the rest of my life."

You have said that your work is to tell what it means to be living and dying at the same time. Your poems express an ambivalent attitude to death. On the one hand, there is the dread of it in "What of the Night?" *when you tell the messenger—that is, death—"in a childish voice" that your father is not home. But in some of your other poems about death, there's an acceptance, almost an attraction. In* "The Long Boat," *for example, the phrase "conscience, ambition, and all that caring" suggests that death would be a relief from those burdens.*

That's a momentary surrender to fatigue on the part of the man in the death-boat, as it puts out to sea. It's not the crux of the poem. Do you recall the conclusion?— "As if it didn't matter / which way was home; / as if he didn't know / he loved the earth so much / he wanted to stay forever."

You've said, "Anybody who remains a poet throughout a lifetime has a terrible will to survive." A terrible will*?*

Yes, exactly. Fierce and terrible. How else would one hang on?

In much of your writing you seem to hold a tragic view of life. And yet you also seem to be blessed with a sanguine temperament.

I'll refer you to Aristotle's *Poetics* for an explanation of why the tragic imagination is more compatible with a sanguine temperament, as you put it, than with a melancholy or depressed one. The tragic view leads to exaltation, not to depression.

You've written that you envy your painter friends because they're not working out of their insides all the time.

My point there is that poetry is spun out of one's breath and tissue. It's an extraordinarily internal affair, more so than any other art, with the possible exception of music.

Is writing essays a different kind of process?

They're hard for me to write. I spend as much care on them as I do on a poem. Sometimes it's excruciating just to get the wording right. I'm not a fluent writer.

Are you more fluent in writing poetry?

To a degree. Expository prose bothers me more because I get so impatient with the bridges, the connections, in the course of plodding from sentence to sentence, paragraph to paragraph. I love the fact that in a poem you are free to leap from pole to pole with a flick of the tongue.

But your prose is extraordinarily fluid. I think that the essays in A Kind of Order, a Kind of Folly *are wonderful.*

That encourages me to proceed with my plan to put out a new and expanded collection. The old one has been out of print for some time. As it happens, I'm in the process now of negotiating contracts for three books—which shows you [laughing] how sanguine I am about the future.

Do you think there has been a change in your style as you've grown older?

Everybody says so. But I also think there is a continuity, an abiding principle.

There has been a continuity in your themes and concerns, but what about the style itself? Do you think there is such a thing as a "late style"? You've said, "In my later years I have wanted to write poems that are simple on the surface, even transparent in their diction." The course of your poetic style reminds me of

Yeats's development. In both cases the early poems are more decorative, the later ones simpler in form and more powerful.

Yeats was one of my early heroes and I learned a lot from him.

Doesn't he have some lines about this kind of thing? "I made my song a coat / Covered with embroideries / Out of old mythologies / . . . there's more enterprise / In walking naked"?

Yes. His early poems were quite soft and misty. He didn't become great until he stepped out of the Celtic twilight and began to speak directly of his feelings about Ireland, about Maude Gonne, and the two themes he eventually spotted as imperative concerns for an old poet: namely, sex and death.

Do you agree with Yeats on that?

It depends on the interpretation of his terms. If you stretch his pair of themes to their referential limits they cover practically everything, the sacred as well as the profane.

In your poem "Raccoon Journal" you speak of "the separate wilderness of age, / where the old, libidinous beasts / assume familiar shapes, / pretending to be tamed." I find that last phrase, "pretending to be tamed," particularly provocative. Would you care to comment?

It's a moment of reversal in the action of the poem. Perhaps I'm saying, "Don't be deceived by this old man's mask of civility and resignation. There's a wilderness inside him. Those obstreperous intruders, the Snopes-like raccoons, may simply be coming home."

The art historian Kenneth Clark said, "If the late style in art can teach us to develop a late style in life, it will have rendered us an incomparable service." Do you think there can be a relationship between art and life in that sense?

I'm not sure of the sense. When Michelangelo was doing his sculpture or when Leonardo was painting, that was "late style" then. Renaissance art is no longer a late style, but it was a late style when it was being practiced. Do you follow me?

Yes, I think I do, but aren't you talking about a school of art? I think Clark was talking about individual artists—the way Michelangelo's style changed in his later years.

It isn't always true. It doesn't always change for the better. It's true of Yeats, at least the late Yeats that I care about. I have no great love for the early Yeats—

the late Yeats is the one who speaks to me. But the late Wordsworth, for example, is probably a more representative example. We don't really expect poets to flourish into their seventies and beyond. We prefer them to comply with the romantic legend and die young. At least that's been true up to now. It may not be true tomorrow, given the spectacular advances in modern medical science. The famous poets of the next century may well be wiser and better Methuselahs. Theoretically, one's late style ought to be more universal than the style of one's egotistical youth.

Egotistical youth? Do you think those two words go together?

Almost inevitably.

I've heard it said, and I don't agree with it, that poets are at their best in their twenties.

That's when poetry is a glandular phenomenon. Your skin secretes it. Everything you touch glistens. At a later stage you have to go down into the depths for your poems, back to your origins, to the first stirrings of the self. You have to plunge as deep into your life as you possibly can, and then you have to fight your way back. The difference is substantial, and I do think it explains the distinction between early and late work. A poet of my age is a many-layered creature. Past, present, and future are all seething together in my mind. My poetry these days may look easy on the surface—transparent, as I like to say—but perhaps it has gained a certain elemental gravity as it keeps cutting through those time-layers, from childhood and youth through the eventful middle years to whatever remains for me to face, including, of course, the last brutal reality. That recognition saturates the text. It both taints and sweetens every word I write.

Selected Bibliography

[Editor's Note: See essay by Michael Ryan earlier in this entry for Selected Bibliography.]

Stanley Kunitz and Genine Lentine (interview date November 2002)

SOURCE: Kunitz, Stanley, and Genine Lentine. "A Curious Gladness: A Garden Conversation with Stanley Kunitz and Genine Lentine." *American Poetry Review* 35, no. 3 (May-June 2006): 11-13.

[In the following interview, conducted in November 2002, Kunitz and his assistant, Genine Lentine, discuss Kunitz's poem "Touch Me" as part of a larger conversation about the influence his lifelong love of gardening had on his writing.]

INTRODUCTION

In the fall of 2002, as a central part of the process of working on *The Wild Braid: A Poet Reflects on a Century in the Garden* (W. W. Norton, 2005), photographs by Marnie Crawford Samuelson, Stanley Kunitz and I began to have a series of conversations exploring gardening and poetry. Our intention was to let the discussions range freely, drawing on the exploratory, interactive fluidity of conversation as a way to generate raw material for what would become the essays in the book. Such a process of course generated more material than we could possibly include, though we needed all of it in order to get to what ultimately became the book. Presented here is one of the first of these talks, from November 2002, centering on the poem **"Touch Me."**

—Genine Lentine

[*Lentine*]: *You often talk about the "essential loneliness" of the artist. Do you think your encounters with animals, such as the snakes in your garden that you speak of in **"The Snakes of September"** help you to bridge that loneliness?*

[Kunitz]: One of the great satisfactions of the human spirit is to feel that one's family extends across the borders of the species and belongs to everything that lives. And one has the same feeling about flowers and plants in general, and shrubs and trees, that they all belongs to your family. That makes one feel more kindred than if you're isolated in your species.

What are some of the ways that sense of kindred spirit presents itself? When you're connecting on a level that's not just about "I'm a human being looking at this animal from a distance" but you're actually connecting, what does that feel like?

You feel you're not only sharing the planet with it, but you're sharing your life, as you do with a domestic animal that has become part of your family.

You refer to the snakes as "co-signers of a covenant." What do you think there is for a writer in having a kind of relationship with plants and animals that is transacted wholly without language? Do you think there's something special about that kind of connection that has to be carried out without language?

I don't think language is the only means of communication. The warmth of one's body is a form of communication. The stroke of one's hand is a means of communication.

So, are those heightened for you in the garden?

Oh, yes. Even with the plants, I know I have a tendency when I'm walking in the garden to brush the flowers as I go by them, and I get a sense of reciprocity that is very comforting, consoling.

I know exactly what you're talking about. Do you ever get a sense of something being communicated to you beyond that core feeling of connection and reciprocity? Do you ever have a sense of anything that feels like information, where somehow, you're actually learning—I don't mean learning by observing, but that something actually is being communicated to you?

I think there are forms of communication beyond language, that have to do not only with the body, but with the spirit itself, and they're so internal, there's no way you can define them. It's a permeation of one's being.

"A curious gladness shook me." The temptation is to try to fit language around it.

Well, the hope is that it will become language and sometimes that happens.

I'm just thinking of when I was with those rugosa roses at Herring Cove and I had just left my garden in Virginia. I was missing a particular rugosa and I had the five leaves—you know how the leaves are in fives—

Yes.

I had the leaves spread against my palm, that crinkly rugosa foliage, and I had this really strong sense that felt like information that I got from that plant, that somehow it was the same *plant. What was communicated to me was, this is the* same *rose as the one in my garden. And you could say that was a way of coping with longing or something, but it somehow felt like a* proposition *that was offered, a sense of continuity of being.*

There's a certain conversation that keeps going on beyond the human level in many ways; as I said before, it's beyond language.

Do you think that's one of the main pleasures of the garden, that it exists beyond language?

Yes.

I know for me that's a huge part of what I love about it. And yet it's also such an occasion for language. All these names for everything, the way they encode a history. There is so much to learn, so much lore, and you can interact with it that way, but you can interact with it in total silence as well.

Yes. And that extends into the atmosphere itself. Weather is a form of communication, I often feel. There is an exchange between the self and the atmosphere, the whole atmosphere.

The way you can tell a storm is coming. You really feel that conversation between yourself and the weather in **"Touch Me."**

Mm hmm.

You can feel that storm coming in all the way through that poem.

It's in the very rhythms. It's a disruptive rhythm.

And in the poem **"End of Summer,"** *when you talk about an agitation of the air. Could you talk a little more about that, that sense of exchange between the self and—*

—This has to do with the sounds of poetry and I agree completely with Wallace Stevens when he says that poetry is mostly sounds. There are sounds even before they coalesce into syllables and words.

I always think of that wavy bed along the path at the bottom tier as being representative of that. There's that undercurrent, and then the tiers become stanzas with this current running beneath them.

The poets I love all are responsive to the sounds of words even beyond the meaning of words.

Hopkins certainly was.

I was thinking of Hopkins in particular.

In **"Touch Me"** *can you talk a little more about what you mean by a disruptive rhythm? By the way, that was the first poem of yours that I heard and—*

—Where was this?

In a class with Richard McCann and someone brought **"Touch Me"** *to class, and the line that really struck me, aside from the, uh, crescendo, was* Outdoors all day under a gunmetal sky—

—*staking my garden down,* those hard consonantal metallic sounds.

Is that line an example of what you're talking about?

Yes, and for example *Words plucked out of the air*— all those vowels—*out of the air,* as opposed to *words plucked.* One is so tactile and the other is so vocal. *Torn almost in two, scatter like leaves,* and then suddenly *this night of whistling wind and rain.* The alternation of the sounds has so much to do with the modifications of the sense. There's no separating the two.

I can feel the wind pick up.

And then we get the crickets, *I kneeled to the crickets trilling underfoot as if about to burst from their crusty shells.* I've always felt that the shells of the crickets were almost metallic, thin metal.

When you say crusty shells, *I don't think metallic. I think husks, papery, granular.*

Well, they have so much tactility. That's the point.

So much resonance. They transmit sound.

Actually if you've ever stroked a cricket—

—*which I have*—

—that's the sensation you get from the shells.

Not only have I stroked a cricket, I watched grasshoppers mating for about 45 minutes one day. I was lying on the grass as they went through this very long process. Quite stirring!

What is their actual bodily connection there?

Well—

—How were they facing?

They're sort of on top of each other.

Only one can be on top of the other.

[laughter]

That's a good point. I was mainly amazed that it kept going on and on. I was just reading about snails. They stay connected for hours.

Well you'd expect snails to take hours.

[A discussion of snail mating practices ensues.]

The crickets are so present in that poem. And there's the repetition of the sound in kneel *and* trill. *Could you go on about that?*

The repetition of the sound for example, you have the crickets trilling underfoot as if to burst from their shells . . . *and like a child again marveled to hear so clear*—hear *and* clear / —hear so clear and brave a music. Brave. I love that word.

What do you love about it?

I love the sound. *Brave. It echoes love.*

And marvel *even continues that repetition of the liquid sounds in* trill *and* kneel. *"So clear and brave a music." What about semantically?* Brave. *Could you say something about the meaning of* brave *in relation to the crickets?*

I'm thinking of *brave* in the sense of expressiveness. That there's no getting away from the crickets' trilling in midsummer there. They take possession of the air. They take possession of the territory, of the garden itself.

What about bravery in the sense of how in the poem, they're an emblem of the brevity of life, and yet they're singing. Could you talk about that sense of bravery?

Well, there they are. They're about to die, and here they are bursting with song. It *is* bravery.

Mm hmm. Do you see the crickets as emblematic there, singing as they are about to die?

Well of course there is a conclusion that can be drawn from that, in terms of doing likewise.

Yes. Then, suddenly we get that word machine.

That's, I think, the surprise word in that observation. And then of course, out of *machine* comes the word *engine,* and then *engine* becomes *desire.* "What makes the engine go? Desire, desire, desire."

Do you remember when you wrote that line, what the process was when you decided to repeat the word. Was it always in that form? Seems to me that's always the way it was in the drafts.

Yes it was. That's the way it appeared instantaneously.

What is it about that word that needs to be repeated?

I love the sound of it. *Desire.* You know. Ahh. It's a cry.

That rising vowel sound. I only ask the question just to hear the answer, of course.

And it rhymes with "Fire. Fire."

It also seems so completely mimetic. This physicality, like the rising of desire. That vowel, and the liquid [consonant]—

—All that gasoline.

The longing for the dance stirs—

—*in the buried life.*

You don't often make this break. What—

—Well I wanted to pause. *One season only.* And then you think, well what about it? Then you say, *and it's done.* The terrible realization. And it speaks not only for the crickets but for the human too.

Yes, the season. *And then there's this turn.*

Yes. And this is the response then, "all right, Storm! Break those windows. Thrash. Mm hmm. Break those branches."

I think of Roethke there also, when he's talking about the greenhouse in the storm. She hove into the teeth of it . . .

Yes.

And in his case, the storm being suggestive of mania or yielding to something beyond reason. It's interesting from a writing standpoint, that the willow is not up against your windows.

Oh yes, I was very aware of that when I was writing, but as far as I was concerned, that brought me back to how, in my childhood, there was a willow that was against the window and it did brush it. It appears in the poem **"Three Floors,"** when I say in that poem, *The wind was walking on my neck. The window panes were crying.* That's exactly the same emotion I had when I was writing this.

The other thing it makes me think about is the story at Yaddo.

Oh yes.

Could you say again what happened there?

There I heard the scratching on the window panes and then the breaking of the glass and then it was as though whatever spirit was out trying to get in had burst into the room. That was so alive that when I tell you this, I shudder.

Really? As you're telling me that, I'm thinking about how in the poem, phenomenologically, we're inside the cricket bursting out, and then the outside is pushing—

—in—

—*into the house, and we're inside. There's so much of a sense of everything being right at the membrane, everything being about to break.*

Yes, mm hmm. The point of breaking is like the point of revelation. The two are inseparable.

When you release your hold on—

—on phenomenal reality to a greater reality.

And do you think desire takes you to that breaking point?

Yes. It's beyond reason, as I titled an early poem.

So, could you talk about that line. Touch me, remind me who I am.

Well, that all came to me. I didn't really know what I was writing. Why of all things, *remind me who I am,* because I think in the great storms of feeling especially of desire, one loses identity, one actually has one's identity merging with another's and that's why. *Do you remember the man . . .* In other words, "who am I, so changed that I have become a different creature completely, and not only to myself but to others?"

So this part at the beginning, my song has flown—which you once said was the saddest line in the poem—*there's this sense of feeling distance and then finding your way back through someone's touch.*

Yes.

Again there's that sense of the membrane.

It's sort of interesting that otherness that I was feeling, *words plucked out of the air some forty years ago when I was wild with love, torn almost in two* and what happens? They *scatter like leaves this night of whistling wind and rain.* It's the loss of one's self in time that is so terrible an experience.

Being subject to that force of the wind. The way there's this distance from the self and trying to reorient toward a different self, it also makes me think of "The Long Boat," when his boat snapped loose.

Mm hmm.

There's this movement out, as if he didn't know which way was home. As if he didn't know he loved the earth so much . . .—*that movement out, and then finding a way back through the connection with the world. It's almost the same gesture*—he loved the earth so much he wanted to stay forever. *So that poem comes back through expressing desire for the physical—*

—reality of existence.

Just in the same way that this does. The path back is through touch or through desire.

Mm hmm. Yes. I haven't thought of the convergence of those two poems, but that's pretty much the way my poems tend to develop in general, out of knowledge, out of losses and out of, in the end, revelation, to a kind of knowing that is beyond sensory experience, the transcendence of the self.

Yes, so there's that point in the poem where that knowing is gained or experienced—moving beyond the body and then in both cases, there's a sense of coming back into the body. There's been a movement out and then the self is reasserted through the body.

Yes. In this poem, there is a refinding of the bodily self at the very end of the poem. "Touch me" is an affirmation of the physicality of existence.

And it's such a vulnerable thing to say.

Yeah.

So open and naked. Would you say that is the most direct gesture toward another human being that exists in your poems?

I think so. It's very different, for example, from one of my very early love poems, **"Among the Gods."**

"Among the Dogs."

"Gods."

I know, but I was thinking of that typo in that Italian magazine.

[laughing] "Among the Dogs."

> Within the grated dungeon of the eye
> The old gods, shaggy with gray lichen, sit
> Like fragments of the antique masonry
> Of heaven, a patient thunder in their stare.

This was written in Rome by the way.

> Huge blocks of language, all my quarried love.
> They justify, and not in random poems,
> But shapes of thing interior to Time
> Hewn out of chaos when the Pure was plain.
>
> Sister, my bride, who were both cloud and bird
> When Zeus came down in a shower of sexual
>   gold,
> Listen! we make a world! I hear the sound
> Of Matter pouring through eternal forms

Now remember, I was twenty-five when I wrote that.

That's so interesting though, that "Listen!"

And the expression is not returning to the body, although there is the sexual impetus there, but *we make a world, I hear the sound of matter pouring through eternal forms.* What's that got to do with loving?

It's creation.

I know.

How much more do you want?

I know.

Creation of the universe. I don't think you can get any more erotic than that.

But, instead of ending in the expression of the body of the impulse of the flesh, I end with the sound of matter pouring.

That's like Sakharov. That's the love poem Sakharov would write about background radiation.

Yes. mm hmm.

But there's something about that Listen! *there, the way that suddenly it's either an address to the reader or to this other person. When you say* We make a world.

Because we have both matter and immaterial flesh. And soul.

It's so interesting though. It makes me think about the crickets though, that idea, in both cases, somehow the erotic is—

—I see a connection. I see a connection between those two poems. I see it now. I didn't see it before.

It's as if you can hear—you've talked about how you feel that you can hear the music of the spheres.

Yes. I have heard it.

In both of those poems, it's almost as if you're getting a little channel into that, and that that is what is somehow spurring this erotic response, somehow there's connection there. It's not hard to see.

Even now, in the middle of the night, if I wake, as I often do, I hear the night. I hear the sound of the night, which is not street noises, or any other, but there's a sound that seems to emanate from the movement of the spheres and I actually can hear it and I keep wondering "where is it coming from?" and then I realize it's not coming from anywhere. It's coming from me.

It's particularly interesting since you say you don't sleep with your hearing aids.

That's true.

It also suggests that it's not your standard auditory connection at work there. Do you hear it the same in Provincetown as you do in New York?

I hear it very strongly in Provincetown. The night air seems to produce all sorts of secret sounds that simply flow through it and you know, often I'll get up and walk through the house and say "Where is the sound coming from?" and it's not coming from anywhere, but I think something is going like a motor. Deep pulsing in the universe.

And you can hear it in the cricket.

And I think there is a connection.

Now this is great, because I was looking at "Touch Me" and I was realizing—it seems very sonnet-like to me, and now we're looking at "Among the Gods" and here it is, twelve lines, not fourteen, but—

—Yes, it's not a sonnet. I've never cared for writing sonnets.

I know that, but I think that you could almost make an argument that you might have written one in "Touch Me."

I doubt it.

I know, but it's sort of an interesting theory. The thing that makes me think about that is that turn. When it takes that turn. It's not even that interesting of a thing to pursue, but—

—No—

—but something about its proportion.

Mm hmm, well, yes, but [pause] no, I don't think this has—the sonnet really has a different kind of motion.

More argumentative.

Yes, and it has a preordained plot. Each quatrain is a summing up and then when you come to the final quatrain there is, how shall I describe it—

[Lorraine enters: "Dinner is ready."]

In the final quatrain, the speaker announces that dinner is ready.

In a way, yes, the poem is ready to end. And the poem is ready to end by turning away from the building up of an argument in the early part and launching into a new discovery. So, in any case, the architecture, I've always thought, was too mechanical. That's what bothers me about it.

Hopkins certainly had his way with the mechanical structure of the sonnet. He didn't let it get the best of him.

I think those, what he called "Terrible Sonnets" are among the great ones of the language.

Yes. That was very—

—That was fun

fun.

FURTHER READING

Biographies

"Stanley Kunitz." *Economist* 379, no. 8479 (27 May 2006): 83.
    Obituary describing Kunitz's impact on the world of literature.

Goodyear, Dana. "The Gardener." *New Yorker* 79, no. 24 (1 September 2003): 104.
    Extended profile of Kunitz.

Criticism

Braham, Jeanne. "Stanley Kunitz: The Layers." In *The Light within the Light: Portraits of Donald Hall, Richard Wilbur, Maxine Kumin, and Stanley Kunitz,* pp. 63-82. Boston: David R. Godine, 2007.
    Critical overview of Kunitz's career.

Additional coverage of Kunitz's life and career is contained in the following sources published by Gale: *American Writers Supplement,* **Vol. 3;** *Concise Major 21st-Century Writers,* **Ed. 1;** *Contemporary Authors,* **Vols. 41-44R, 250;** *Contemporary Authors New Revision Series,* **Vols. 26, 57, 98;** *Contemporary Literary Criticism,* **Vols. 6, 11, 14, 148;** *Contemporary Poets,* **Eds. 1, 2, 3, 4, 5, 6, 7;** *Dictionary of Literary Biography,* **Vol. 48;** *DISCovering Authors 3.0; Literature Resource Center; Major 20th-Century Writers,* **Eds. 1, 2;** *Major 21st-Century Writers,* **(eBook) 2005;** *Modern American Literature,* **Ed. 5;** *Poetry Criticism,* **Vol. 19;** *Poetry for Students,* **Vol. 11; and** *Reference Guide to American Literature,* **Ed. 4.**

David Lodge
1935-

(Full name David John Lodge) English novelist, playwright, critic, and nonfiction writer.

The following entry presents an overview of Lodge's career through 2009. For further information on his life and works, see *CLC*, Volumes 36 and 141.

INTRODUCTION

Lodge is known as a Catholic writer with a talent for carefully constructed novels who helped usher in the new realism of the 1960s and 1970s. Lodge has resisted the label of post-structuralist and has embraced Mikhail Bakhtin's ideas of the dialogic nature of the novel: that every text is informed by every other one, and this continuous interaction results in a dynamic relationship among works and an ongoing reimagining of a complete world view. Lodge's novels often feature an inherent duality and characters whose lives illuminate views on religion, academia, and literary theory.

BIOGRAPHICAL INFORMATION

Lodge was born in South London on January 28, 1935, to William Frederick Lodge, a dance-band saxophonist and clarinetist, and Rosalie Murphy Lodge. Evacuated to the English countryside during World War II, as a boy he attended the St. Joseph's Academy Catholic grammar school and earned his bachelor's and master's degrees at University College, London, in 1955 and 1959, respectively. Also in 1959, Lodge married Mary Frances Jacob, with whom he has two sons and a daughter. In 1960 he earned a Ph.D. at the University of Birmingham and joined its English faculty. In 1969 he worked at the University of California, Berkeley, then took a position as assistant to the British Council in London, becoming Senior Lecturer in 1971 and an instructor from 1973 to 1976. He later accepted an appointment as professor of modern English literature at Birmingham and fellow of the Royal Society of Literature. In 1987 he took early retirement to devote himself to writing full time.

MAJOR WORKS

Lodge's early work draws largely on his own experiences, using settings and themes from the South London suburbs, academia, and Catholicism. His first novel, the unpublished *Devil, the World, and the Flesh*, featured Catholic characters living in London. Lodge wrote his first published work, *The Picturegoers* (1960), when he was twenty-two years old. The novel features the Mallorys, a Catholic family whose members have differing degrees of devotion to the church. Clare, the oldest daughter, had wanted to become a nun but returns home from the convent around the time that the family takes in a lodger, Mark, a lapsed Catholic. Mark's intention is to seduce Clare, but after attending Mass with her, his faith begins to return. By the time Clare falls in love with him, Mark has begun to consider the celibate life of the priesthood. The Mallory family is joined by a large cast of local characters in and outside of the Palladium, a local movie house well past its prime. Lodge has been praised for undertaking such a challenging structural convention in his freshman effort.

Ginger, You're Barmy (1962), Lodge's second novel, is also informed by his personal experience. Jonathan Browne, the protagonist of the story, has chosen to defer his mandatory military service until he has completed his studies, as did the author. In an afterword for the 1982 reissue of the novel, Lodge wrote, "*Ginger, You're Barmy* cleaves very close to the contours of my own military service. . . . [T]here is scarcely a minor character or illustrative incident or detail of setting that is not drawn from the life." The story is not as complex as *The Picturegoers,* but thematically it too concerns Catholicism and faith. Lodge has identified Norman Mailer's *The Naked and the Dead* as a major literary influence while writing *Ginger, You're Barmy* and, retrospectively, has noted the influence of Graham Greene's *The Quiet American,* from which he appropriated the novel's flashback structural elements, as well as the "e" at the end of the protagonist's surname. Lodge later came to view his novel disparagingly, calling it a work of "missed possibilities," at the heart of which was his anger at the military.

Lodge followed *Ginger, You're Barmy* with the comical farce *The British Museum Is Falling Down* (1965), which represents a departure from the realism of his earlier work. This novel, greatly influenced by James Joyce's *Ulysses,* chronicles a single day in the life of its main character, Adam Appleby, and satirizes the Roman Catholic ban on artificial birth control as Adam, a student, fears that following the Church's

"Rhythm Method" policy may have resulted in he and his wife's fourth child. Through *The British Museum Is Falling Down,* Lodge again expresses his concern with the Catholic faith, suggesting that the church's metaphysical functions have been displaced by pedantic diplomacy and administration.

Five years later, Lodge returned to traditional realism, publishing *Out of the Shelter* (1970), a coming-of-age story that begins with a child traumatized by the Blitz. Timothy Young, the main character, a shy, bookish Catholic grammar school student, presents his observations of current events. Autobiographical elements of Lodge's life are told through him as he visits his sister, Kate, in Old Heidelberg, the American headquarters in Europe, and in the epilogue, which finds thirty-year-old Timothy a successful academic in America on a fellowship. Again looking to Joyce for literary inspiration, Lodge is indebted to *A Portrait of the Artist as a Young Man* and *Dubliners* for the structural and tonal elements of *Out of the Shelter.*

Changing Places (1975), the first of a college-campus trilogy, was influenced by Lodge's experiences in America. The novel is a comedy of manners, featuring English academic Phillip Swallow and his American counterpart, Morris Zapp, who swap politics, lifestyles, cars, homes, and even wives. *Changing Places* marked a shift for Lodge to the academic comedy for which he is best known and allowed him to weigh in on the American academic world of the 1960s while, conversely, confronting the typical British academic's life of polite, timid English manners. *Changing Places* was awarded the Hawthornden Prize; the next novel in the trilogy, *How Far Can You Go?* (1980; published in America as *Souls and Bodies*) won the Whitbread Book of the Year; and the final book, *Small World* (1984), was shortlisted for the Booker Prize.

Throughout Lodge's writings, the institution of marriage has been assigned a role that is precarious at best. Characters are often involved in unhappy marriages and have affairs, only to conclude that an unhappy marriage is more satisfying than infidelity. With *Therapy* (1995), Lodge presented a new twist on the position. Protagonist Tubby Passmore has reveled in his happy marriage for thirty years, content and even smug in his successful relationship in an era when so many marriages fail. When his wife leaves him, Tubby is shocked, but, adding insult to injury, he learns that she is not divorcing him for another man—she simply doesn't like him. The middle-aged Tubby is left to desperately, and comically, lunge at every opportunity to catch up on all of the sexual encounters he has missed over the duration of his marriage. He rediscovers his first love, Maureen, and implores her to divorce her husband and marry him; as a devout Catholic, Maureen refuses to consider divorce, but she does settle into an affair with Tubby, who also becomes friends with her husband.

Lodge's most recent novel, *Deaf Sentence* (2008), makes light of the author's own failing hearing. Another comedic examination of human foibles, *Deaf Sentence* follows linguistics professor Desmond Bates, recently retired due to severe hearing loss, as he becomes enmeshed in a relationship with a nubile graduate student completing a dissertation on suicide notes, while also attending to his father's final decline. Despite serious subject matter, *Deaf Sentence* extracts humorous moments from what are usually considered somber situations.

In addition to his fiction, Lodge has written critical works including *After Bakhtin* (1990), *The Art of Fiction* (1992), and *The Practice of Writing* (1996), which includes scholarly papers, book reviews, speeches, and diary entries written since his retirement from academia. He has also written screenplays for television and dramatic works for the stage, including *The Writing Game* (1990) and *Home Truths* (1998).

CRITICAL RECEPTION

Lodge is recognized primarily as a Catholic novelist who became an accomplished humorist. While most of the characters in his later work identify themselves as Catholic, Lodge's shift toward humor and farce allowed him to explore a new subject, academic life, and he earned popular success with his campus trilogy. Critics have praised Lodge for his wit and intelligence and his ability to construct complicated novels with difficult subject matter while remaining accessible. His humor is seen as inclusive and refreshing, never cruel. As Marian E. Crowe observed, "*Therapy,* along with *How Far Can You Go?* and *Paradise News* (1991), is distinguished by Lodge's remarkable ability to imbue his comic novel with a seriousness that gives it added richness. What keeps Tubby's story from being simply another amusing satire is—not only the poignancy of his divorce, a pain familiar to so many contemporary people—but the fact that the story of this likeable scriptwriter draws in and reflects the pain of the wider world." Lodge's writing has been criticized at times for being uneven or unbalanced, but critics tend to forgive him his more heavy-handed work, finding redemptive qualities in the style or structure if not always a compelling narrative.

PRINCIPAL WORKS

The Picturegoers (novel) 1960
Ginger, You're Barmy (novel) 1962

Between These Four Walls [with Malcolm Bradbury and James Duckett] (play) 1963

The British Museum Is Falling Down (novel) 1965

Slap in the Middle [with Duckett and David Turner] (play) 1965

Out of the Shelter (novel) 1970

Changing Places: A Tale of Two Campuses (novel) 1975

How Far Can You Go? [published in the U.S. as *Souls and Bodies*] (novel) 1980

Small World: An Academic Romance (novel) 1984

Write On: Occasional Essays (criticism) 1986

Nice Work (novel) 1988

After Bakhtin: Essays on Fiction and Criticism (criticism) 1990

The Writing Game: A Comedy (play) 1990

Paradise News (novel) 1991

The Art of Fiction (nonfiction) 1992

Therapy (novel) 1995

The Practice of Writing (nonfiction) 1996

Home Truths (play) 1998

Home Truths (novella) 2000

Thinks . . . (novel) 2001

Consciousness and the Novel: Connected Essays (essays) 2002

Author, Author (novel) 2004

Deaf Sentence (novel) 2008

CRITICISM

Robert A. Morace (essay date 1989)

SOURCE: Morace, Robert A. *"The Picturegoers, Ginger, You're Barmy,* and the Art of Narrative Doubling." In *The Dialogic Novels of Malcolm Bradbury and David Lodge,* pp. 109-31. Carbondale and Edwardsville: Southern Illinois University Press, 1989.

[*In the following essay, Morace provides a close examination of Lodge's narrative techniques employed in his first two novels.*]

Taken together, David Lodge's first two published novels provide a useful introduction to his increasingly dialogic—and increasingly self-conscious—practice. Many of the same dialogic concerns and techniques that inform his later works appear here in embryo, as it were, in stumbling, exaggerated form, writ large not so much for the near-blind reader (or critic) as for the tentative would-be novelist. Clearly, *The Picturegoers* is a far less successful and subtle work than the similarly titled *The Moviegoer,* another first novel by another Catholic writer, published one year later. Walker Percy's novel is an existential fic-

tion of a special, even unusual, kind. This comic successor to Dostoevsky's fiction distills the Russian's dialogic breadth in the person, or rather the voice, of Percy's narrator-protagonist, the genial underground man, Binx Boling. Within the moviegoer's seemingly flat discourse one hears echoes of Kierkegaard on the one hand and American popular culture on the other. *The Picturegoers,* as the plural of its title suggests, takes a sociological rather than an existential approach. For Percy's version of Gabriel Marcel's homo viator (sovereign wayfarer), Lodge substitutes a "mass" of Joycean narrative focalizations. He permits each of his picturegoers to speak in his or her own turn and in his or her own voice within the novel's fictive space and limited carnival freedom (Interview with Haffenden 146-147). In his subsequent reading of Bakhtin and Gerard Genette, Lodge found the theoretical rationale behind his inchoate use of essentially dialogic narrative techniques. As he discovered, "the more the characters are allowed to speak for themselves in the narrative text, and the less they are explained by an authoritative narrator, the stronger will be our sense of their individual freedom of choice—and our own interpretive freedom." In overall structure, if not in complexity and execution, *The Picturegoers* anticipates *Changing Places* and especially *Small World* (despite differences in tone), *How Far Can You Go?* (with which it shares a similar religious doubt or reservation), and *The British Museum Is Falling Down* (in which the concatenation of parodies is but a variation on Lodge's dialogic aesthetic, the carnival freedom of styles in this later work parallelling the convergence of characters at the cinema in *The Picturegoers*).

The Palladium Moviehouse, formerly the grander Palladium Theatre, serves the same purpose on the thematic level that the novel itself does in the larger structural sense. It acts as a meeting place, not only for people but for styles, forms, and languages as well. Just as the characters go to the Palladium for a variety of reasons—to be entertained, to be titillated, to fantasize, to rest, to kill time, to earn a living—the reader experiences a similar diversity in the novel as a whole—a variety of characters and overlapping, or intersecting, but nonetheless largely discrete plots. There is Mark Underwood, a lapsed Catholic and aspiring writer, who seems much like Blatcham, the hometown he has left; located midway between city and country, it has elements of both but "belong[s] to neither" (39). Then there is the Mallory family in whose traditionally Catholic home Mark becomes "a willing prisoner," as attracted by the "warmth and humanity" that his own family lacks and to the older daughter Clare, as he is repelled by their simple religious faith. There is the parish priest, Father Kipling, who launches an unsuccessful counteroffensive against the Palladium and its manager, Mr. Berkeley, whose loveless marriage leads him to have an affair with Doreen, one of his young employees. Then there are Bridget and Len whose love leads to marriage but whose marriage seems likely to be dogged both by poverty and their film-induced romantic illusions. And there is the young thug, Harry, who goes to the movies to fuel his sadistic sexual fantasies and in this way to find some release from his desperate loneliness. And finally there are two characters that we do not actually see at the Palladium: Clare's former student, Hilda, who has turned from religion to a nearly lesbian love for Clare and now finally to movie idols in order to satisfy her own need for love, and Damien, a priggish Catholic whose desire for Clare is as abhorrent as it is chaste.

The separate narratives not only focus on different characters, they are narrated in variously stylized ways in the manner of Joyce's "scrupulous meanness" or what Park Honan has called Lodge's "cinematic style." "Lodge's manner with narrative viewpoints is innovative," Honan contends. "In *The Picturegoers,* the novelist's own camera—in that familiar maneuver of impressionism—is set behind the characters' eyes. 'Reality' is perceived and felt by representative South Londoners. But the viewpoints are not developed in the showily imitative fashion of dialogue. Instead, there is a subtle shift between kinds of vocabularies as viewpoints change" (171). Honan's description is accurate, especially insofar as it correctly links Lodge's novel with his theory of the language of fiction. It is nonetheless open to two objections, one because Honan goes too far and the other because he does not go far enough, which is to say not nearly as far as Lodge the novelist does, even in this, his flawed first novel. To begin with, Honan claims that Lodge achieves "the linguistic variety he wants within the limits of cinematic unobtrusiveness" (169). That is, he does not call attention to the stylistic variations themselves, for his goal here is to achieve a heightened realism, not a postmodern self-consciousness. Whatever he may have intended, what Lodge achieves is anything but unobtrusive in a novel marked, or marred, at every turn by the same melodramatic excess that also characterizes (though less noticeably) *Ginger, You're Barmy* and *Out of the Shelter.* Lodge learned to overcome this tendency towards melodrama by gradually adopting, or adapting, a number of distancing poses borrowed from the English comic novel and from postmodern fiction. In *The Picturegoers,* the language is indeed stylized, but the stylizations too often only reflect what the characters all too allegorically "mean": Mark the skeptic and writer-to-be, Clare the whilom nun moving towards sexual love, etc. To a

large extent, the novel Lodge wrote reflects all too well the limitations that Mark discerns in himself: "Were other people like this, he wondered—always observing themselves in a spontaneous emotion? It was the penalty of being (or trying to be) a writer. To create characters you took a rib from your own personality, and shaped a character around it with the dust of experience. But it was a painful debilitating process. Usually the characters were still born, and the old Adam got weaker and weaker, less and less sure of his identity" (93). After reading such lines, Lodge's reader may very well agree with the author's own assessment of *The Picturegoers* as "an immature work . . . which I cannot now read without embarrassment" (*Write On* 61).

Although Lodge's execution is considerably less successful—his prose less cinematically unobtrusive—than Honan claims, his reach is far greater than Honan allows. This narrative cinematism is, I believe, one aspect not only of the modern novel in general as an essentially dialogical genre but of Lodge's novels in particular. They have become so increasingly self-conscious in their dialogism that Lodge the dialogical novelist has in fact come to merge with Lodge the critic who has gone from propounding the language of fiction to working with structuralism and, more recently, to finding in Bakhtin's theoretical writings the articulation of his own aesthetic practice. Thus, *The Picturegoers* includes not only various stylized languages but numerous interpolated and carnivalized forms as well; the sheer number and extent of these carnivalizations suggest that Lodge's first novel may have as much in common with *Ulysses* as it does with either *Dubliners* or *Portrait of the Artist as a Young Man.* The reader finds not only summaries of films, as one would naturally expect in such a novel, but Mark's notebooks, Doreen's fantasies, Damien's imagined conversations with Clare, one of Father Kipling's sermons, hymns, psalms, parts of the Catholic mass, excerpts from Christopher Marlowe's writings, and even a scene from a cheap novel which Harry has apparently memorized: "A blade glinted, and as if by magic a crescent appeared on the man's cheek, with little beads of blood seeping out like juice from an orange" (140). It is not only the content and style of, for example, films and cheap novels that manifest themselves in a given character's language—both his external speech and, more especially in this novel of and about private longings, internal discourse. It is the form as well, as in the case of Mark's thinking, which begins to resemble the trailers he and the other picturegoers watch before the feature film commences. Thus, even as the novel itself is made up of alternating stylizations, these stylizations often recapitulate the novel's larger structure insofar as they are themselves not uniform and whole but dialogized still further. The passage in which Harry "quotes" from a cheap novel illustrates in the simplest possible way the kind of further internal dialogization which pervades the entire novel and which manifests itself in still more striking fashion in a number of passages that deal with Mark and Clare. Thinking back to the sexual passion he has released in Clare, for example, Mark writes in his notebook:

> But not tenderness she wanted now. Passion now.
>
> If dishonoured her, must then make an honest woman of her? Marriage with Clare. Nothing said, but it was expected. Suppose could do worse. Logical really, after what he had said to Pat. Merge with the Mallorys; marry a Mallory. Name the day, bride in white, radiant, nuptial Mass. Our Lady of Perpetual Sucker, till death do us, special graces, Mendelssohn, the happy couple, pause for photo, confetti, into the car, what to say, what the hell does one say—roll on bed? The reception, a buffet, so glad you could come, yes didn't she, yes I am, O ha ha Uncle Tom's sozzled ha ha good Old Uncle Tom, unaccustomed as I am to public speaking, a glass of champagne cider each. I give you the Bride's parents! My own parents looking a bit sick of all the tipsy Irish. Thank God we're going, kippers in the car, confetti, small hotel, double bed, a baby started, could do worse.
>
> (172)

Or Clare, later in the novel, feeling oppressed by the heat and "incapable of sustaining any longer the intolerable labour of love." "How long was this fencing going to continue. She was impatient for the heavy swing of blunt, simple statements: 'I'm sorry'—'I was a bitch'—'It was my fault'—'I love you'" (198). And again, towards the end of this same scene, Clare wonders, "Was that all then? Well good-bye, it's been nice knowing you, I've enjoyed running my hands up and down your spine, it was so nice of you to give me my faith back, we must keep in touch, I do hope you have a nice life, cheerio" (202). Her language captures all too well both her own dismay and Mark's posturing, the hollowness of his spiritual rebirth. In the words that Mark "cries out"—"'I can't be true to the old evil in me, and be false to—whatever may be potentially good in me now!'" (200)—the reader hears echoes not only of Clare's former innocence but of Damien's self-righteousness as well. We witness in their language the fact that Mark and Clare have in effect traded characters. She has become more skeptical and self-consciously dialogical, and he more strident and mono-logically certain. In the thoughts and words of each we hear the echoes of what the other formerly was, though in a form modified by some essential feature of their characters: in Clare's case, her authenticity, in Mark's his posturing.

Earlier in the novel, Mark says of the abrupt, unexpected ending of *Bicycle Thieves,* the picture he and Clare have just seen, "'that's just the brilliance of it. No American or English director would have dared to end it there. . . . The point of the film is the plural of its title'" (141-142). The same cannot be said of *The Picturegoers.* Although its plural title suggests its dialogical point and method, as well as its sociological perspective, Lodge chooses not to end his novel abruptly or brilliantly but, instead, "cautiously." He resembles, in this regard, his own character, Mr. Berkeley, whose showing of a rock and roll film in order to save his ailing theater brings about an unexpected result. "It awaken[s] many dead souls to life." However, when the dead not only awaken but begin dancing in the aisles, Mr. Berkeley decides that things have gone too far. Lodge would undoubtedly understand and sympathize. In *The Picturegoers,* and indeed throughout his career as novelist and as critic, he has always tempered his willingness to explore new narrative and theoretical modes with a healthy sense of caution, or skepticism. The dialogic play of these two tendencies, or voices, is particularly evident in Lodge's second novel, *Ginger, You're Barmy.*

In comments on his second novel, David Lodge has identified three major literary influences ("Introduction" 4). One, the most localized, was Norman Mailer's war novel, *The Naked and the Dead,* which provided Lodge with a simple means for dealing with a then troubling aspect of the book's realism, the obscenities in his characters' speech. Another and far more important influence was John Osborne's play, *Look Back in Anger,* a performance of which Lodge attended while on leave from the same National Service that forms the ostensible subject matter of his own contribution to the literature of Britain's angry young men. As for the third influence, it was only long after the novel had been written that Lodge became aware of how completely he had cast it in the structural mold of Graham Greene's *The Quiet American,* from which he borrowed, "subliminally," that novel's "systematic flashback technique" as well as the final "e" of his protagonist's surname. Looking back on *Ginger, You're Barmy* and on the roles Mailer, Osborne, and Greene played in its conception and composition, Lodge seems to have been afflicted with a belated case of the anxiety of influence, pointing to what he feels are weaknesses in the novel that are clearly the result of a young author's failure to go it on his own. He has come to judge his second novel as a work of "missed possibilities" and has located the chief source of these missed possibilities in the genesis and composition of the novel as "an act of revenge," an angry look backwards at his two-year stint in the National Service ("David Lodge Interviewed" 112). Despite its shortcomings, *Ginger, You're Barmy* is, if not a major novel, then certainly an interesting, even impressive, one. Its strength derives much less from its overt subject matter and Lodge's "angry" response to it than it does from the ways in which he solved "the technical problem" that the writing of the novel posed and from the relation between Lodge's solution to this problem and the ideas about narrative theory and practice that he was then formulating—ideas that he would later bring together under the title *Language of Fiction* ("David Lodge Interviewed" 113).

In an interview with Bernard Bergonzi, published shortly after a second, revised (deMailerized) edition was published in paperback in 1970, Lodge explained the nature of this technical problem. The task he set himself was to create for the reader a sense of the tedium of peacetime military life without actually making the novel itself tedious to read. Lodge hoped to overcome the problem in two ways: one was to concentrate on the first weeks (of basic training) and on the last few days before the protagonist-narrator, Jonathan Browne, is mustered out, and the second was to add to this story a prologue-and-epilogue frame that would allow him to justify the narrative method he had adopted and "to convey some kind of moral comment on my ['somewhat unsympathetic'] narrator. . . . So the prologue-and-epilogue was partly an answer to a formal problem, partly an answer to a moral problem" (113). It was also an answer that seemed to insist upon the protagonist-narrator's development, morally and, as we shall see, aesthetically as well. Later, however, in the introduction he wrote in 1981 for a third (reMailerized) edition (in which "fugg" and "c——t" are restored and the novel transformed into a period piece), Lodge questioned whether his handling of this "technical problem" did not in fact constitute "a failure of nerve" on his part (3). Insofar as the frame insists upon a development of the protagonist's character that the rest of the novel does not adequately prepare for, then, the intentional fallacy notwithstanding, Lodge is undoubtedly correct in his assessment. This "failure of nerve" can, perhaps even should, be understood in a quite different way, however. Rather than constituting either a *deus ex machina* imposed by the author or an unconscious borrowing by a young Catholic novelist from another and more experienced one, Lodge's frame-and-tale structure forms part of a much larger pattern of doublings that in effect makes up the novel's underlying structure, that provides a structural metaphor for the novel's moral substance, and that anticipates as well his later interest in Gerard Genette's structuralist theory of narrative grammars.

To begin simply, the addition of the prologue-and-epilogue frame entails a chronological doubling: "now," in the narrative present, Jonathan looks back on events that occurred "then," during his two years

of National Service, and becomes in the process "a *voyeur* spying on my own experience" (12). And there is as well a similar doubling within the framed tale, a constant shuttling back and forth of the narrative between the last days of Jonathan's tour of duty at Badmore and his first weeks at Catterick (the flashback technique mentioned earlier). The military experience is thus itself doubled—beginning and end, Catterick and Badmore—and within this doubling contrasted with civilian life: "For us soldier-commuters 'home' and 'camp' were two disparate, self-contained worlds, with their own laws and customs; every week we passed from one to the other and back again, changing like chameleons to melt into the new environment" (127). The changes are never quite so complete, however, either for the narrator-protagonist or for the reader. The soldier-commuter is never either wholly soldier or wholly civilian. Each carries the residue, or trace, of the other into their respective environments. The reader, whose reading of the framed tale doubles Jonathan's reading of his manuscript, faces a similar dilemma, for the story he reads not only concerns different temporal and geographical settings but has been composed by Jonathan at different, but not always distinguishable, times. That is to say, we do not read the "confessional outpouring" Jonathan wrote (although we may forget and think we do). What we read is that text as it was subsequently revised—lengthened and "polished." The result may be a Wordsworthian emotion recollected in tranquility or something quite different and far more self-serving. The reader cannot be sure because, while the idea of revision is a textual fact to which Jonathan admits in his prologue and epilogue, the textual evidence of these revisions is missing. To complicate matters a bit more, our reading of the framed story's two textual levels cannot be separated from the fictive author's (Jonathan's) commentary on them in the appended frame and, for readers of the third edition, from Lodge's commentary on them in his introduction. This is not to say that Lodge consciously and meticulously labored to create chronologically discrete compositional stages of Jonathan's narration. He may have, of course, but he did not need to. He needed only to create a Borgesian sense of their presence to lead the reader to intuit that "Jonathan" is not single, or even, as he himself claims, double, but more accurately, multiple, a series of images in a funhouse mirror. In this respect, the character development of which Lodge writes in his introduction to the third edition may be said to constitute a failure of nerve insofar as it attempts to reduce the dialogic complexity of Jonathan's character to the level of simple monologue. As narrator, Jonathan comments on the self he was then, but this is another, different Jonathan who is (was?) already at least double (geographically and narratively split, Catterick and Badmore). And as narrator Jonathan is further multiplied. He is the writer, the reviser, and finally the commentator who addresses the reader directly in the prologue and epilogue. Instead of remaining entirely discrete, these separate selves, each having its own distinct though not always or even often distinguishable voice, merge dialogically to create a surprisingly rich and troublingly complex characterization in a novel that, in the surface texture of its seemingly artless, conventionally realistic prose, suggests a similarly deceptive easy-to-understand narrative depthlessness. As in the case of those realistic novels which Lodge discusses in *Language of Fiction, Ginger, You're Barmy* demands the kind of close critical reading it seems least to invite.[1]

At times, the narrative voice speaks not only as "author" (which Jonathan of course is, fictively) but for its author, Lodge, who in writing *Ginger, You're Barmy* appears, narratively speaking, to have split himself in two. "My response to the Army," Lodge has written, "shifted from an indignant moral resistance to its values . . . to a pragmatic determination to make myself as comfortable as possible and to use my time as profitably as possible" (2-3). That Lodge managed to use his time wisely is evidenced by the fact that he wrote much of his first novel, *The Picturegoers,* while in the National Service. More interesting is the way in which Lodge assigns the halves of his own divided response to army life to two different characters, Jonathan Browne and Mike Brady. Although (to put the matter in a crudely biographical way) Browne and Brady do, almost allegorically, represent sides of Lodge's own mind during his tour of duty, the significant fact is that whereas in his monological introduction the two are conveniently and easily separated, in the novel they exist and intersect dialogically. On the surface of Lodge's narrative, they are in simple opposition to one another. Mike is impulsive, gregarious, idealistic, and naively credulous. Jonathan is calculating, self-centered, pragmatic, and agnostic. The one is virtually a caricature of Irish Catholicism and "grotesque individuality" (50), the other a study in secularism and self-promoting anonymity. Mike suffers from claustrophobia and requires considerable physical as well as psychological space (paradoxically so, given the narrowness of his religious beliefs). Jonathan, on the other hand, though ostensibly a free thinker, actually seems to prefer various forms of confinement, metaphorical "boxes" in which he can prosper in his own preferred narrow fashion. As he explains at one point, "success consisted in determining which box would be most pleasant for you, and getting into it. If you were forced to inhabit an unpleasant box for a time, then you could make it as comfortable as possible until you could get out. . . .

[I]t was better to be in the most uncomfortable box than outside, in the confusion of the elements" (196-197). Better to be inside reading William Empson's *Seven Types of Ambiguity* (as Jonathan does) than to be outside and therefore paradoxically *in* the uncertain ambiguous world.

Keeping the spatial metaphor in mind, we can say that Jonathan is correct in his summary analysis of his and Mike Brady's differences: "My temperament was prudence and my destiny success, as surely as Mike's were foolhardiness and failure" (217). However, Jonathan's syntactically balanced assessment is not without its own ironic double: "'I may not have the virtue of Christian prudence,'" Mike tells him, "'but God help me from the unchristian sort'" (160). The point is not that either Jonathan or Mike is right, but that they somehow share the truth between them. Each qualifies the other, though never to the point that Lodge is able—or at least willing—to posit a monologic synthesis that will resolve the characters' and the reader's moral dilemma. It is, however, difficult to like Jonathan and so to accept that his views have any moral validity whatsoever. If Mike's conscience works overtime, then Jon's appears to work not at all, replaced by selfishness, self-consciousness, and voyeuristic detachment. "I have always tried to avoid occasion for regret, the most lingering of all the unpleasant emotions, by prudent foresight" (46), Jon explains as he ponders whether or not to deflower his girlfriend, Pauline. It is hard to like such a "reasonable" character, especially one as prone as Jonathan is to self-pity, to making himself (Henry Fleming fashion) the object of the world's injustice. On the other hand, it is impossible not to agree that his judgments about himself and others are often correct and that his self-pity is at times warranted. The comment recorded in his army file, for example, "educated up to the university level: thinks too much of himself" (52), is at once accurate and yet (given the context of the army's distrust of and distaste for "education") patently unfair. The syntactical parallelism in this comment reflects the balance of objectivity and subjectivity, of fairness and injustice, as well as the larger dialogical character of the entire novel. Similarly, Jon's voyeurism and reasonableness, although objectionable, cannot be entirely separated from that awareness—especially self-awareness—which so clearly contrasts with Mike's narrowness and which identifies him as a distinctly "modern" character, one who is willing to expose himself, "warts and all," to the reader's own voyeuristic gaze.

> The prospect of parting with Mike . . . aroused ambiguous feelings in me. I could not deceive myself that our friendship had been deep and instinctive: it had been almost artificially forced by our mutual

distaste for the Army. On the other hand I viewed with little enthusiasm life in the Army without Mike's moral support. I mean "moral" literally. Mike's hostility to the Army seemed to have an essentially moral basis, which somehow sanctioned my more self-centred grievances. But it was becoming increasingly clear to me that Mike's "morality" was an unreliable guide to conduct, and I did not wish to become involved in some wild, quixotic crusade against the Army.

(152)

Mike's rigid moral code is as archaic as the army's feudal infrastructure and the "who goes there, friend or foe?" (159) challenge that Jonathan cannot bring himself to take seriously. For Mike, the army is "'evil'"; it deprives him of his "'free will'" and thus makes it impossible for him to fulfill his purpose on earth, which is, he says in a "pedantic," catechetical way, "'to exercise my free will, and to save my soul'" (158). For Jonathan, the army means something quite different: the interruption of his academic studies, the limiting of his personal freedom, and the loss of certain creaturely comforts. It is difficult not to credit to some degree his realistic if self-centered point of view, even as the reader questions the value of a life in which amorality and selfishness are so rigorously pursued.

Instead of promoting a moral position, the novel creates a morally and textually ambiguous world. This ambiguity is most pronounced in Lodge's handling of one of the novel's central narrative events, the death of Percy Higgins. Whether Percy's death is accidental or a suicide is a crucial question that Lodge deliberately leaves unanswered. The novel focuses on the survivors', especially Jonathan's and Mike's, efforts to deal with this ambiguity. (Lodge blurs further all simple distinctions by developing parallels between Percy and Mike on the one hand and Percy and Jonathan on the other. Percy is, for example, like Mike a Catholic fundamentalist and like Jonathan a sheltered loner in need of Mike's help.) The novel in fact opens with an invitation, or rather a challenge, to the reader to read Jonathan's story according to a literary equivalent of the physicist's laws of uncertainty and complementarity. "It is strange to read what I wrote three years ago," the novel begins. "It is like reading another man's writing. Things have certainly not worked out as I expected. Or did I deliberately prevent them from so working out?" (11). If Lodge is concerned with the question of ambiguous meaning, then we would have to say that his narrator is obsessed by it. The book Jonathan reads just before he gains his release from the service, Empson's *Seven Types of Ambiguity,* not only symbolizes this obsession but seems to have influenced his writing as well.

It is true that much of the narrative parallelism in the novel serves a *too clearly* ironic, and therefore nearly monologic, purpose. The soldier who scoffs at Mike's

grief over Percy's death, claiming that what actually troubles Mike is the loss not of Percy but of part of his leave, ironically echoes Jonathan's own selfishness and insensitivity a page or two earlier. But in a later scene, one which in turn echoes the first, we find ambiguity rather than irony. Mike has just been taken into custody after clubbing Sgt. Baker, whom he holds responsible for Percy's death. As he waits to discover Mike's fate, Jonathan lashes out at a small group of soldiers who have (in this case unjustly) claimed he was "'not being very worried about his mate.'" Jonathan calls them "'stupid, selfish bastards'" and especially (and rightly) condemns their "Fugg you Jack, I'm all right" attitude (174-175). Immediately after making this Brady-like outburst, Jonathan discovers that he has been assigned to guard duty. His response—"'Fugg the Army'" (176)—puts him in the same moral as well as linguistic realm as those whom he has just criticized. However, the irony here, while it clearly underscores what appears to be Jonathan's dominant and certainly least appealing trait, does not cancel out what the novel's parallel structure implies: that Jonathan is poised somewhere between self-pity and moral concern. Both the critical irony and the moral ambiguity deepen in a later, and again parallel, scene in which Jonathan visits Mike at the military stockade where, following his escape from his first imprisonment (for striking Sgt. Baker), he has been confined for taking part in an IRA raid on the Badmore camp. Lodge handles the raid much as he handled Percy's death earlier in the novel. He compounds the irony to the point that individual ironies dissolve (though not without leaving a trace) in the larger ambiguous whole that results. For example, Mike is one of the attackers, but his part in the raid is the condition upon which his release from the IRA (whose violence he abhors) is predicated. That Mike should find it necessary to gain his release from the very group, the IRA, that helped free him from his first captivity contributes to the novel's pervasive irony and general blurring of clear-cut distinctions. Similarly, in foiling the IRA attack, Jonathan becomes—at least in the minds of his military supervisors—what for two years he has managed to avoid being: a good soldier. Doing his duty, he saves the camp's officers, whom he loathes, from the same kind of embarrassment he himself suffered moments before when one of those same officers launched his own surprise attack in order to test camp security—and to win a bet. As the ironies multiply, the stable point of view upon which the successful use of moral irony is said to depend dissolves. As a result, the reader finds himself adrift in a morally ambiguous textual world that offers him certain simple facts and connections (Jonathan, for example, foils the IRA raid and so is indirectly responsible for his friend's capture), but that teases the reader with moral conundrums (Jonathan was unaware that Mike was among the attackers, but what would he have done had he known?). As their visit draws to an end, Mike says, "'It's all right, Jon. You were only doing your duty'" (215). His words echo Jonathan's own remark, "It's all right, Jack," just a few pages before. Whatever Mike intends his words to mean, for his auditor and for Lodge's reader they serve both to console and to condemn, as does the sign Mike makes as Jonathan departs, lifting his hand "in a gesture of . . . / . . . of what? Reassurance? Dismissal? Benediction? Would I ever know?" (216). Admittedly, the ironies and uncertainties here and elsewhere in the novel are laid on in a heavy-handed, even melodramatic, fashion, but it is a heavy hand that tells the reader more about the workings of Jonathan's mind, I believe, than about the shortcomings of Lodge's writing.

Just as the structure of the novel betrays doubling and parallelism at all narrative levels, from the meanings of individual words to the construction of syntactically balanced sentences, compounded ironies, parallel scenes, and complementary subchapters, so in similar fashion does Jonathan's style evidence a dual tendency towards the melodramatic on the one hand and the religious on the other. While the former suggests the stilted "literariness" and self-pitying sentimentality of Jonathan's character and point of view, the latter points to one of the ways in which Mike has impressed himself on Jonathan's imagination and on his writing. Together they create an interesting tension between Jonathan's largely selfish views on the one hand and his tentative moral gropings on the other. Certain words evidence this moral, or more accurately, this religious subtext directly: "confession," "contrition," "indoctrinate," "covet," "expiation," "benediction," "mission," "conscience," "transubstantiation," "eremitical"(!), among others. Other instances are less direct—Jonathan's Peter-like denials, first of Percy and later of Mike as "friends," for example, and, more effectively, the echoes of Catholic doctrine in certain of Jonathan's phrasings, "occasion of sin" in his "occasion for regret" and "firm purpose of amendment" from the Catholic sacrament of penance in his "possibilities of amendment."

In the novel's religious subtext the reader detects the residue of Jonathan's studied and all too serious literariness (the parallels he draws between military life and Dante's *Inferno,* another of the books he reads during his National Service) as well as Mike's continuing presence in Jonathan's life and writing. The precise extent of Mike's influence and the uses to which Jonathan puts it are less certain. In his epilogue, Jonathan claims that "my relationship with Mike had been a fuse laid in the bed-rock of my self-complacency" (221), but though he offers this view

Jonathan also tends to reject or at least modify it, noting elsewhere (in the prologue), for example, that Mike's influence has been far less explosive. "I don't think I am a better person, or even a happier one; but perhaps there has been a small advance" (11). Outwardly the change appears considerable. During the three years since he completed his National Service as well as the writing and revision of his manuscript, Jonathan has, like his Biblical namesake, devoted himself to his friend. He has abandoned his academic studies and taken a teaching position in a small rural school in order to be close to the prison where he can visit Mike as often as possible and minister to his needs. Equally startling, now that his friend is to be released and his own "mission" over, Jonathan hopes to "build a life of modest usefulness" (223) as a teacher, husband, and father. "I hope Mike will agree to stay with us for a while," Jonathan writes. "He has been the focal point of my life for so long that I am curiously jealous of the rest of the world with whom he will shortly resume contact. Also, I feel a certain panic when I reflect that he will no longer need my support. It is not a question of what he will do without me, but of what I will do without him" (222). All that Jonathan writes here is understandable, even—in its high degree of honest self-criticism—commendable. But then, in a verbal gesture that is entirely characteristic of the Jonathan of the framed tale, Jonathan as narrator immediately adds, "now he is free, and I am shackled,—by a wife and family I do not greatly love, and by a career that I find no more than tolerable" (222). Jonathan's honesty disarms and appalls the reader, but does it do so because Jonathan's selfishness makes him such a morally appalling figure in the reader's eyes or because the narrative mode in which his tale is told (or, alternately, in which he has chosen to tell his tale)—the religious confession—requires this kind of self-portraiture?

Beginning his work as a "confessional outpouring" (11), the writer monastically ("eremitically") sets himself apart from the hedonish world, specifically Majorca where Jonathan and Pauline's dream vacation turns nightmare. Their island paradise transmogrifies into an inferno of sickness (Pauline's food poisoning), and frustrated longings (psychological, sexual, and linguistic: Jonathan's ignorance of Spanish makes it difficult for him to communicate with anyone on the island). As a result, Jonathan turns to writing, or more particularly to confession, but even the penitent can be seduced. "The demon Form" leads him to turn his "confessional outpouring" into something more aesthetically crafted, but whether this transformation signals transfiguration or falsification—or both—is not made clear; perhaps it cannot be made clear. For all its seeming transparency, *Ginger, You're Barmy* is very much about the ambiguous relationship between art and life. At one point, Jonathan readily admits that his "mission" has been both an unselfish act and an excuse to be nothing more than a nominal husband and father. Much the same can be said of Jonathan's mission as a writer. The self-flagellation of his self-begetting novel at once chronicles life and competes with it, as Pauline quickly comes to realize when she finds she has to compete with the manuscript for Jonathan's attention. Significantly, what first attracted Jonathan to her was her "femininity" (141), by which word Jonathan seems to mean her feminine receptiveness, less as a sexual partner than as an audience for his repressed monologues. Soon after they meet, she asks him to tell her about army life, a topic on which the usually garrulous Mike Brady has been noticeably reticent. "The invitation could not have been more welcome. This was the audience I had been seeking all the week-end" (137). Jonathan is thus not only a character in search of an author (himself), but an author in search of an audience (in this case Pauline). Later, when he goes to Pauline to tell her what Mike has done (struck Sgt. Baker), Jonathan "considered very carefully what version I should give her of what I knew about the incident, and had decided to tell her what I should say when Mike was charged. My motives were, firstly, to rehearse the story properly, and secondly, to position myself as favourably as possible in relation to Pauline. This latter problem was by no means simple" (162). Read in the light of this passage, the ending of the novel puts Jonathan in a particularly ambiguous position. The reader cannot be sure whether Jonathan has indeed grown morally or whether any claim, or even any narrative hint, of such growth on his part may be nothing more than a calculated attempt to once again position himself "as favourably as possible" in relation to his audience. What complicates the reader's dilemma still further is the fact that Jonathan's willingness to put himself before the reader, warts and all, is disarming.

The form of his narration and of Lodge's novel is therefore especially noteworthy in that the story Jonathan tells appears to be an act of self-incrimination, and by exposing himself in this way the teller earns not only the reader's censure but his sympathy as well. Unfortunately, Jonathan's narrative strategy may not be quite as disingenuous as the credulous reader would like to believe. Given that Jonathan's position as narrator parallels Lodge's as author, the former's remarks quoted above curiously anticipate the latter's, quoted earlier in this chapter, on the "technical problem" that the writing of the novel posed. Such a reading would certainly be in keeping with the pragmatic side of Jonathan's personality, evident throughout both his tale and the frame he appends to it: "even now, it seems, I am not immune from the insinuations of Form. It occurs to me that these notes, which I am jotting down on this momentous morning, might usefully form a prologue and epilogue to the main story . . ." (12). On the other hand, the fact that Jonathan has unearthed—or resurrected—his manuscript and revised it for a second time (by adding the frame) suggests the ongoingness of his search to discover the meaning of his military experience and more particularly, through Mike, of himself. In doing so, Jonathan embodies one of the key points upon which Lodge's *Language of Fiction* theory rests: "in literary discourse, the writer discovers what he has to say in the process of saying it, and the reader discovers what is said in responding to the way it is said" (64-65). What Jonathan could not bring himself to tell Pauline, he confides in his manuscript, and it is the writing process itself that enables Jonathan to begin to understand himself. What the reader experiences is not the act of self-discovery, some Joycean epiphany, but the process through which that discovery may occur. The uncertainty is crucial, for synthetic, univocal readings (including the author's in his introduction) are precisely what the novel manages to avoid. Its author David Lodge and its narrator-protagonist Jonathan Browne are poised, as I believe its reader must be, between belief and clerkly skepticism. What the novel ultimately points to is not any "failure of nerve" on Lodge's part but, instead, the open-endedness and necessary incompleteness of the dialogical process—a process for which the unfinished state of Jonathan's manuscript stands as a metaphor.

Ginger, You're Barmy succeeds to the degree that it embodies and not merely espouses such an interplay of conflicting voices, one in which the relation between the formal and moral aspects of art are given a new post-liberal twist. In the *Language of Fiction*, Lodge quotes "a very characteristic statement of Dr. Leavis's": "when we examine the formal perfection of *Emma,* we find that it can be appreciated only in terms of the moral preoccupations that characterize the novelist's peculiar interest in life." Lodge then "emends" the quotation in the following manner: "when we examine the moral preoccupations that characterize Jane Austen's peculiar interest in life as manifested in *Emma,* we find that they can be appreciated only in terms of the formal perfection of the novel" (68). Whether it is or is not useful to speak of the "formal perfection" of *Ginger, You're Barmy* is a moot point. What we can speak of with assurance, however, is its formal consistency as well as the ways in which the novel anticipates, and in some cases recapitulates, many of the same concerns that Lodge has voiced in his critical writings. Bradbury and others have complained that as a critic Lodge favors linguistic analysis over humanistic values, "the demon Form" over "the confessional outpouring." The charge is at once merited and yet—in light of the numerous disclaimers of any such preference that punctuate the *Language of Fiction*—mistaken:

> a true "science" of stylistics is a chimera. . . . [Linguistics can never replace literary criticism because linguistics claims to be science and literature] concerns values. And values are not amenable to scientific method. . . . [W]hile a literary structure has an objective existence which can be objectively (or "scientifically") described, such a description has little value in literary criticism until it is related to a process of human communication which is not amenable to objective description.
>
> (55, 57, 65)

In such disclaimers, as in his contention that the rigorous brand of verbal analysis he advocates and practices must be "applied intuitively," we detect much the same play of contending voices as in **Ginger, You're Barmy.** Certainly, the writing of his story of National Service is Jonathan's most ambiguous and most transformative act. In it biography metamorphoses into fictive autobiography, contingent life into formal art, the narrator's examination of conscience into his examination of narrative. Lodge's second novel evidences a profound concern for "formal perfection" that, on the one hand, necessitates a retreat from the values associated with much humanistic (especially realistic, premodernist) art but that may, at the same time, suggest the most viable means for achieving moral clarification, if not moral certainty, in the modern age.

Note

1. "But in so far as the study of the novelist's language is limited to those who most obviously invite it, because their use of language answers immediately to our view of how literary language works, we risk implying that the language of other, earlier novelists [i.e., the realists/premodernists] is less integrally integrated to their achievements . . ." (Lodge, *Language of Fiction* 30).

Works Cited

Amis, Martin. Rev. of *Rates of Exchange. Observer* 3 Apr. 1983: 29.

Bakhtin, Mikhail. *The Dialogic Imagination: Four Essays.* Trans. Caryl Emerson and Michael Holquist. Ed. Michael Holquist. Austin: U of Texas P, 1981.

———. "Extracts from 'Notes' (1970-1971)." *Bakhtin: Essays and Dialogues on His Work.* Ed. Saul Morson. Chicago: U of Chicago P, 1986. 179-82.

———. *Problems of Dostoevsky's Poetics.* Ed. and trans. Caryl Emerson. Minneapolis: U of Minnesota P, 1984.

———. *Rabelais and His World.* Trans. Helene Iswolsky. Bloomington: Indiana UP, 1984.

Banks, J. R. "Back to Bradbury Lodge." *Critical Quarterly* 27.1 (1985): 79-81.

Barth, John. "The Literature of Exhaustion" (1967). Bradbury, *The Novel Today* 70-83.

———. "The Literature of Replenishment." *Atlantic* Jan. 1980: 65-71.

Barthes, Roland. *A Barthes Reader.* Ed. Susan Sontag. New York: Hill & Wang, 1983.

Booth, Wayne. "Introduction." Bakhtin, *Problems of Dostoevsky's Poetics* xiii-xxvii.

Borges, Jorge Luis. *Labyrinths: Selected Stories & Other Writings.* Ed. Donald A. Yates and James E. Kirby. New York: New Directions, 1964.

Bradbury, Malcolm. *The After Dinner Game.* 1982. London: Arena, 1984.

———. "An Age of Parody: Style in the Modern Arts." *Encounter* July 1980: 36-53.

———. *All Dressed Up and Nowhere to Go.* 1982. London: Arena, 1986. Comprises *Phogey! How to Have Class in a Classless Society* (1960) and *All Dressed Up and Nowhere to Go* (1962).

———. "Coming Out of the Fifties." *Twentieth Century Literature* 29 (1983): 178-189.

———. *Cuts: A Very Short Novel.* London: Hutchinson, 1987.

———. "Dangerous Pilgrimages: Transatlantic Images in Fiction." *Encounter* Dec. 1976: 56-67; Feb. 1977: 50-65; May 1977: 56-71.

———. "A Dog Engulfed by Sand: Abstraction and Irony." *Encounter* Nov. 1978: 51-59; Jan. 1979: 36-42. See Bradbury, "Putting in the Person," below.

———. "Donswapping." Rev. of *Changing Places. New Review* Feb. 1975: 65-66.

———. *Eating People Is Wrong.* 1959. London: Secker & Warburg, 1976. With an "Introduction" by the author.

———. "Foreword." Halio, *British Novelists* xi-xviii.

———. ed. Forster: A Collection of Critical Essays. Englewood Cliffs: Prentice-Hall, 1966.

———. *The History Man.* 1975. New York: Penguin, 1985.

———. Interview with John Haffenden. Haffenden, John. *Novelists in Interview.* London: Methuen, 1985. 25-56.

———. Interview with Christopher Bigsby. *The Radical Imagination and the Liberal Tradition: Interviews with English and American Novelists.* Ed. Heide Ziegler and Christopher Bigsby. London: Junction Books, 1982. 60-78.

————. "An Interview with Malcolm Bradbury." With Richard Todd. *Dutch Quarterly Review of Anglo-American Letters* 11 (1982): 183-196.

————. "The Language Novelists Use." Rev. of *Language of Fiction. Kenyon Review* 29 (1967): 122-136.

————. "Lionel Trilling: End of the Journey." *New Statesman* 14 Nov. 1975: 619.

————. *The Modern American Novel.* New York: Oxford UP, 1983.

————. "Modernism/Postmodernism." *Innovation/ Renovation: New Perspectives on the Humanities.* Ed. Ihab Hassan and Sally Hassan. Madison: U of Wisconsin P, 1983. 311-327.

————. *No, Not Bloomsbury.* London: Deutsch, 1987.

————. "One Man's America." *Author! Author! A Selection from "The Author," the Journal of the Society of Authors since 1890.* Ed. Richard Findlater. London: Faber and Faber, 1984.

————. *Possibilities: Essays on the State of the Novel.* New York: Oxford UP, 1973.

————. "Putting in the Person: Character and Abstraction in Current Writing and Painting." Bradbury and Palmer 181-208. Rpt. in *No, Not Bloomsbury* in revised form, under its original title, "A Dog Engulfed by Sand."

————. *Rates of Exchange.* New York: Knopf, 1983.

————. Rev. of *Mulligan Stew,* by Gilbert Sorrentino. *New York Times Book Review* 26 Aug. 1979: 9, 18.

————. Rev. of *The Stories of John Cheever,* by John Cheever. *New Statesman* 29 June 1979: 956-957.

————. Rev. of *Slow Homecoming,* by Peter Handke. *New York Times Book Review* 4 Aug. 1985: 11.

————. *Saul Bellow.* London: Methuen, 1982.

————. "Second Countries: The Expatriate Tradition in American Writing." *Yearbook of English Studies* 8 (1978): 15-39.

————. *The Social Context of Modern English Literature.* New York: Schocken, 1971.

————. "The State of Criticism Today." *Contemporary Criticism.* Ed. Malcolm Bradbury and David Palmer. London: Arnold, 1970. 11-38.

————. *Stepping Westward.* 1965. London: Secker & Warburg, 1983. With an "Introduction" by the author.

————. *What Is a Novel?* London: Arnold, 1969.

————. *Who Do You Think You Are?: Stories and Parodies.* Rev. ed. London: Arena, 1984. A 2nd revised edition was published in 1987.

Bradbury, Malcolm, ed. *Forster: A Collection of Critical Essays.* Englewood Cliffs: Prentice-Hall, 1966.

————. ed. *The Novel Today: Contemporary Writers on Modern Fiction.* London: Fontana, 1977.

Bradbury, Malcolm, and James McFarlane, eds. *Modernism: 1890-1930.* Hammondsworth: Penguin, 1976.

Bradbury, Malcolm, and David Palmer, eds. *The Contemporary English Novel.* New York: Holmes & Meier, 1979.

Bradbury, Malcolm, and Allan Rodway. *Two Poets.* Nottingham: Byron P, 1966.

Bradbury, Malcolm, and Howard Temperley, eds. *Introduction to American Studies.* London: Longman, 1981.

Burden, Robert. "The Novel Interrogates Itself." *Bradbury and Palmer* 133-155.

Burton, Robert S. "A Plurality of Voices: Malcolm Bradbury's *Rates of Exchange.*" *Critique* 28 (1987): 101-106.

Byatt, A. S. "People in Paper Houses: Attitudes to 'Realism' and 'Experiment' in English Postwar Fiction." Bradbury and Palmer 19-42.

Church, Michael. Rev. of *The History Man. Times Education Supplement* 25 Dec. 1977: 21.

Clark, Katerina, and Michael Holquist. *Mikhail Bakhtin.* Cambridge: Belknap-Harvard UP, 1984.

Culler, Jonathan. *The Pursuit of Signs: Semiotics, Literature, and Deconstruction.* Ithaca: Cornell UP, 1981.

Cunningham, Valentine. Rev. of *The History Man. New Statesman* 7 Nov. 1974: 528.

D'haen, Theo. "Fowles, Lodge and the 'Problematical Novel.'" *Dutch Quarterly Review of Anglo-American Letters* 10 (1980): 160-175.

Dickens, Charles. *Martin Chuzzlewit.* The Works of Charles Dickens. New York: Books, n.d.

Eco, Umberto. *The Role of the Reader: Explorations in the Semiotics of Texts.* Bloomington: Indiana UP, 1979.

————. *Semiotics and the Philosophy of Language.* Bloomington: Indiana UP, 1984.

Evans, Walter. "The English Short Story in the Seventies." *The English Short Story 1945-1980: A Critical History.* Ed. Dennis Vannatta. Boston: Twayne, 1985. 143-45.

Fletcher, John. "Iris Murdoch." Halio, *British Novelists* 546-561.

Friedman, Melvin J. "Malcolm Bradbury." Halio, *British Novelists* 108-116.

Gass, William. *Fiction & the Figures of Life*. Boston: Nonpareil Books, 1971.

Genette, Gerard. *Narrative Discourse: An Essay in Method*. Trans. Jane E. Lewin. Ithaca: Cornell Up, 1980.

Gindin, James. "Bradbury, Malcolm (Stanley)." Vinson, James, ed. *Contemporary Novelists*. 3rd ed. New York: St. Martin's P, 1982. 90-92.

————. "Taking Risks." *Granta* 3 (1980): 155-60.

Green, Martin. "Transatlantic Communications: Malcolm Bradbury's *Stepping Westward* (1966)." *Old Lines, New Forces: Essays on the Contemporary British Novel, 1960-1970*. Ed. Robert K. Morris. Rutherford: Farleigh Dickinson UP, 1976. 53-66.

Haffenden, John. *Novelists in Interview*. London: Methuen, 1985.

Halio, Jay L. Rev. of *The History Man*. *Southern Review* 15 (1979): 706-707.

Halio, Jay L., ed. *British Novelists Since 1960*. Dictionary of Literary Biography 14. Detroit: Gale, 1983.

Hayman, Ronald. *The Novel Today 1967-1975*. Burnt Mill: Longman Group [1976].

Holquist, Michael. "Introduction." Bakhtin, *The Dialogic Imagination* xv-xxxiv.

Honan, Park. "David Lodge and the Cinematic Novel in England." *Novel* 5 (1972): 167-173.

Honan, Park, ed. "Realism, Reality and the Novel: A Symposium." *Novel* 2 (1969): 197-211.

Jackson, Dennis. "David Lodge." Halio, *British Novelists* 469-481.

Joyce, James. *Finnegans Wake*. 1939. New York: Penguin, 1978.

————. *A Portrait of the Artist as a Young Man*. 1916. New York: Viking, 1969.

Kakutani, Michiko. "Letter from London: Novelists Are News Again." *New York Times Book Review* 14 Aug. 1983: 3, 22-23.

Kermode, Frank. *The Sense of an Ending: Studies in the Theory of Fiction*. New York: Oxford UP, 1966.

Kristeva, Julia. *Desire in Language: A Semiotic Approach to Literature and Art*. Trans. Thomas Gora, et al. New York: Columbia UP, 1980.

Leitch, Vincent B. *Deconstructive Criticism: An Advanced Introduction*. New York: Columbia UP, 1983.

Lodge, David. *The British Museum Is Falling Down*. 1965. London: Secker & Warburg, 1981. With an "Introduction" by the author.

————. *Changing Places*. 1975. New York: Penguin, 1979.

————. "David Lodge Interviewed." With Bernard Bergonzi. *Month* Feb. 1970: 108-116.

————. *Evelyn Waugh*. New York: Columbia UP, 1971.

————. *Ginger, You're Barmy*. 3rd ed. London: Secker & Warburg, 1982. With an "Introduction" by the author. Originally published in 1962.

————. *How Far Can You Go?* London: Secker & Warburg, 1980.

————. *Language of Fiction*. 2nd ed. London: Routledge & Kegan Paul, 1984. Originally published in 1966.

————. "Leading Three Lives." Interview with Michael Billington. *New York Times Book Review* 17 Mar. 1985: 7.

————. "Literary Theory in the University: A Survey." *New Literary History* 14 (1983): 435.

————. "Mimesis and Diegesis in Modern Fiction." *Contemporary Approaches to Narrative*. Ed. Anthony Mortimer. Tubingen: Narr, 1984. 85-108.

————. *The Modes of Modern Writing: Metaphor, Metonymy, and the Typology of Modern Literature*. London: Arnold, 1977.

————. *The Novelist at the Crossroads and Other Essays on Fiction and Criticism*. London: Routledge & Kegan Paul, 1971.

————. *Out of the Shelter*. 2nd ed. London: Secker & Warburg, 1985. With an "Introduction" by the author. Originally published in 1970.

————. *The Picturegoers*. London: Macgibbon & Gee, 1960.

————. Rev. of *Roger's Version*, by John Updike. *New York Times Book Review* 31 Aug. 1986: 1, 19.

————. *Small World: An Academic Romance*. London: Secker & Warburg, 1984.

————. *Working with Structuralism: Essays and Reviews on Nineteenth- and Twentieth-Century Literature*. London: Routledge & Kegan Paul, 1981.

————. *Write On: Occasional Essays '65-'85*. London: Secker & Warburg, 1986.

Lodge, David, ed. *20th Century Literary Criticism: A Reader*. London: Longman, 1971.

McCaffery, Larry, ed. *Postmodern Fiction: A Bio-Bibliographical Guide*. New York: Greenwood, 1986.

McEwan, Neil. *The Survival of the Novel: British Fiction in the Later Twentieth Century*. Totowa: Barnes & Noble, 1981.

Malamud, Bernard. *A New Life.* 1961. New York: Pocket Books, 1973.

Martin, Jay. *Harvests of Change: American Literature 1865-1914.* Englewood Cliffs: Prentice-Hall, 1967.

Morgan, Edwin. Rev. of *Stepping Westward. New Statesman* 6 Aug. 1965: 191-92.

Morrison, Blake. Rev. of *Rates of Exchange. Times Literary Supplement* 8 Apr. 1983: 345.

New Yorker 28 Apr. 1986: 4.

Percy, Walker. *Conversations with Walker Percy.* Ed. Lewis A. Lawson and Victor A. Kramer. Jackson: UP of Mississippi, 1986.

Rabate, Jean-Michel. "La 'Fin du Roman' et Les Fins des Romans." *Etudes Anglaises* 36 (1983): 197-212.

Rev. of *Souls and Bodies* [American title of *How Far Can You Go?*]. *Publishers Weekly* 20 Nov. 1981: 44.

Scholes, Robert. *Structuralism in Literature: An Introduction.* New Haven: Yale UP, 1974.

Steiner, George. "Party Lines." Rev. of *The History Man. New Yorker* 3 May 1976: 130-132.

Stevenson, Randall. *The British Novel Since the Thirties: An Introduction.* London: Batsford, 1976.

Sullivan, Jack, Rev. of *Souls and Bodies* [American title of *How Far Can You Go?*]. *Washington Post Book World* 7 Feb. 1982: 4.

Theroux, Paul. Rev. of *Souls and Bodies* [American title of *How Far Can You Go?*]. *New York Times Book Review* 31 Jan. 1982: 3, 23.

Thiher, Allen. *Words in Reflection: Modern Language Theory and Postmodern Fiction.* Chicago: U of Chicago P, 1984.

Todd, Richard. "Malcolm Bradbury's *The History Man*: The Novelist as Reluctant Impresario." *Dutch Quarterly Review of Anglo-American Letters* 11 (1981): 162-182.

Todorov, Tzvetan. *Mikhail Bakhtin: The Dialogical Principle.* Trans. Wlad Godzick. Minneapolis: U of Minnesota P, 1984.

Tucker, Martin. Rev. of *Eating People Is Wrong. New Republic* 2 May 1960: 19-20.

Vinson, James, ed. *Contemporary Novelists.* 3rd ed. New York: St. Martin's P, 1982.

Waugh, Patricia. *Metafiction: The Theory and Practice of Self-Conscious Fiction.* London: Methuen, 1984.

Widdowson, Peter. "The Anti-History Men: Malcolm Bradbury and David Lodge." *Critical Quarterly* 26.4 (1984): 5-32.

Wilson, A. N. Rev. of *Ginger, You're Barmy. Spectator* 31 July 1982: 23-24.

Robert A. Morace (essay date 1989)

SOURCE: Morace, Robert A. "*Out of the Shelter* and the Problem of Literary Recidivism." In *The Dialogic Novels of Malcolm Bradbury and David Lodge,* pp. 142-55. Carbondale and Edwardsville: Southern Illinois University Press, 1989.

[*In the following essay, Morace analyzes Lodge's* Out of the Shelter, *considering its literary form and impact in comparison to the author's earlier novels.*]

The doubleness of Lodge's fourth novel, **Out of the Shelter,** first published in 1970 and recently reissued in 1985 in a substantively revised—or actually restored—edition,[1] is evident even in the history of its composition and publication. Although largely based on a trip that the author made to Germany when, like his protagonist, he was sixteen years old, the novel bears as well the clear impress of Lodge's first trip to the United States, thirteen years later, and it anticipates his second, to assume a visiting professorship at the University of California at Berkeley, which he undertook shortly after completing the manuscript in 1968. The novel is, therefore, as Lodge has pointed out, "autobiographical in origins, but not confessional in intent" (ix). It is confessional in form, however, even if that form is not quite so apparent as it is in **Ginger, You're Barmy.** That **Out of the Shelter** should have more in common with Lodge's second novel (and with his first, **The Picturegoers**) than with his third, the archly parodic **British Museum,** [**The British Museum Is Falling Down**] should not be surprising. It was, after all, conceived before **The British Museum** was written (xii). Moreover, Lodge's career as a novelist has had a curious dialogical rhythm of its own involving the alternating publication of serious and comic works. That Lodge should, with Bradbury's help, have discovered the possibilities of comic narration in the writing of his third novel, and then have composed a work that is "in tone and technique" (xii) closer to **The Picturegoers** and **Ginger, You're Barmy** than to **The British Museum,** does not, therefore, necessarily signal an aesthetic retreat on Lodge's part. However, **Out of the Shelter** does look back to and "double" the past—itself double, biographical and literary—in an aesthetically unsatisfying way, and it does so despite the author's large claims for the book's formidable lineage and at times equally large claims for its aesthetic merits. Ironically, it may be because the book is, as Lodge has said, "the most inclusive and most fully achieved" of his first three "serious" novels that it satisfies so little (quoted in Vinson 401).

As Lodge has noted, **Out of the Shelter** merges two literary forms, the *Bildungsroman* and the Jamesian international novel "of conflicting ethical and cultural values,"² and has as "its most obvious literary models" Joyce's *A Portrait of the Artist as a Young Man* and James's *The Ambassadors* (with touches of *The Dubliners* and *What Maisie Knew* thrown in for good measure and added effect) ("Introduction" ix). Of the two, it is clearly Joyce's influence that is by far the more pervasive and that accounts for the novel's being so "fully achieved." What one finds is not the parodic play of *Ulysses* that Lodge adapted so effectively in *The British Museum*; instead, it is the "realistic truth-telling and poetic intensity" of Joyce's earlier style, the aims of which (Lodge then claimed) were "still worth pursuing" insofar as "the heightened realism" of Joyce and the other "classic modernists" had not yet been "exhausted" (quoted in Vinson 401; "David Lodge Interviewed" 116). Lodge may have been correct, but *Out of the Shelter* does not support his claim of continued viability. Moreover, there is even a certain irony in the fact that Lodge should have written this novel of "personal liberation" in so shackled and disabling a style. The fact that "everything is presented from [the protagonist] Timothy's point of view, but narrated by a 'covert' authorial voice that articulates his adolescent sensibility with a slightly more eloquent and mature style than Timothy would have commanded" ("Introduction" xvi), describes rather well *how* the story is narrated, but sidesteps completely the issue of whether the narrative language is aesthetically effective or not. Much of the prose Lodge wrote ostensibly in imitation and extension of Joyce's early style only seems either to fall flat—"are lights fixed in the palm trees illuminated the pool, but did not penetrate its depths" (269)—or, despite the book's serious subject matter, to parody it in unintentionally comic fashion:

> A squadron of jets suddenly screamed overhead, making the windows rattle. Feeling a commotion beside him, he opened his eyes and he saw Gloria arch her back, kick, and the blue jeans flew off her brown legs. He shut his eyes again. His hand now moved freely under the light tension of her flimsy briefs. He ran his hand over the fine, springy nest of hair, and reached a moist crevice. There was a distant rumble, as of bombs or guns. The sound barrier. He heard her breathing quickly beside him. He scarcely dared to breathe himself. She spread her legs and his index finger slipped in like a seal into a rock pool, slithering against the slippery walls, and touching something that quivered and contracted, fluttering like a shrimp under bare toes at low tide, and he thought he must be losing his senses, for there was a strange smell of shrimps in the room.

(240)

Whether this is "heightened realism" or merely heightened rhetoric hardly seems in doubt, least of all when, his climax over, the sixteen-year-old hero of Lodge's portrait of the specialist in "planning blight"

as a young man has his obligatory epiphany and, deciding not to rush immediately from adolescent sex to Catholic confession, chooses to lay "his unshriven soul as a gift at Gloria's feet" (248). If in *The British Museum* Lodge's parodic technique tends both to undermine the authority of his sources and yet paradoxically to validate them as well, then the language of Lodge's fourth novel works in a similar fashion, though in the reverse direction. It undermines even as the author seeks to validate and extend, so that in large measure the novel becomes not the work of "heightened realism" that Lodge intended but (to borrow a line from Barth's *Lost in the Funhouse*) yet another, and not especially effective, story about a sensitive adolescent.

If the novel succeeds at all, then, it does so not in its imitation of Joyce's verbal mannerisms but in the way it reflects quite another feature of Joyce's (and Lodge's) writing. This is his preoccupation with verges and transitions of all kinds, with a character's (or, in the later works, even a word's) being poised between two worlds, two sets of values, two meanings. "Ever since he [Timothy] had come out from England it seemed to him that he had been looking down from heights, being shown the kingdoms of the world, like Jesus in the Bible" (150). What saves such a passage—and such a book—is that Timothy (as well as the reader) is given more than one world from which to choose, and the choices are dialogically presented rather than monologically distinct. This is not to say that the novel does not seem to posit certain simple oppositions. It is, after all, a work which is set in a period of (as Lodge saw it) "crucial transition" from "austerity" to "affluence," and which grew out of the author's conviction that there indeed was, as the Sixties' Youth Culture insisted, a generation gap, but one that separated those who had experienced the war from those who had not ("Introduction" x). Leaving the shelter of his family and country for the first time, Timothy is struck by what he assumes is the completeness of the separation. Shaking his father's hand becomes not a sign of emotional attachment but instead is "like casting off a rope that had held him for a long time in safe anchorage" (67). And his final glimpse of his mother, from the departing train, provides a perfect if pathetic image of just what he is leaving behind. "That was the last view he had of his mother: standing on the platform, gasping for breath, disappointment lining her face, still holding outstretched, like a rejected gift, the Lyons' Individual Fruit Pie" (72). Coming out of his various literal and figurative shelters, Timothy enters a world that is not only new and different, but geographically, socially, culturally, religiously, and sexually ambiguous. The novel necessarily involves, then, an epistemological doubling: Timothy comes out of the shelter, presumably into the clarifying light, but his vision is invariably obscured in various ways. The bomb smoke that prevents his seeing the deaths of his playmate Jill and her mother near the beginning of the novel is the first of several physical, psychological, and cultural barriers to Timothy's actually achieving that clarity of vision that the novel's title seems to imply. The ambiguity is further complicated by the fact that Timothy is himself double: on the one hand he wants to experience the world and on the other he is another of Lodge's voyeurs who prefer to live their lives vicariously. As Timothy himself realizes (in sentences that reflect in their very syntax the workings of his dialogical mind and Lodge's equally dialogical novel), "there was something deeply ambiguous about his situation—he could see it alternately, and almost simultaneously, as absurd and exciting—enviable and ridiculous. . . . He could convert it into something positively exciting only by grasping its opportunities, and he was not equal to that. . . . He had added to his experiences lately, but the additions were abysses concealing more than they revealed."[3]

Out of the Shelter is a novel of seeming contrasts—childhood and adolescence, adolescence and adulthood, war and peace, secular and spiritual, male and female, the poetic and the prosaic, etc. The starkest of these are geographical and cultural. England means shortages, drabness, privation, confinement, work, sameness, and the narrowness of lower-middle-class Anglo-Catholicism, whereas Heidelberg, as the center of the American occupation forces, represents abundance, variety, color, freedom, play, and a certain secular expansiveness. That England should continue to suffer economically even though it won the war, while German Heidelberg prospers, is one of the signs in this novel that things are not necessarily as one might expect them to be "out of the shelter." But as Don Kowalski, one of Timothy's unofficial mentors, explains, Heidelberg too is a kind of shelter, "full of people who don't want to go home" (87). Timothy's sister, Kate, makes a similar point, though from a quite different point of view. (She is one of those who won't, or, as she would prefer, can't go home again.) What she and the other non-Germans in Heidelberg have in common, she says, is that "we want to forget. . . . We want to live in the present. We want fun and companionship without emotional involvement, without the risk of getting hurt again. And we do have a lot of fun. . . . But it can't go on for ever" (167). Kate and Don provide Timothy not only with alternative explanations as to why people like Kate stay in Heidelberg but with alternative courses to follow in his own life. However, just as the voices of Don, Kate, Timothy's parents, and Kate's friends intersect yet

remain distinct in the reader's mind, so in a similar fashion does Lodge suggest that there is no one voice and no one course of action for Timothy (or the reader or the writer for that matter) to follow—not Don's, or Kate's, or Joyce's.

Individual characters are presented in a similarly ambiguous manner. To her family, for example, Kate—or Kath, as they refer to her—is at once a fairy godmother and a fallen woman. The ambiguity of her character and the ambivalence of her family's response to her evidences itself throughout the novel and is distilled in lines such as, "it was as if Kate were accumulating invisible credits, like indulgences, on which the rest of the family could draw,"[4] a description which neatly combines the financial and religious preoccupations of Timothy's lower-middle-class Catholic family. In addition, the Kate that Timothy visits in Heidelberg is quite unlike the Kath he knew in England, for this "Kate" is poised, self-confident, even attractive. But when they go swimming, Timothy makes a second discovery; he sees in her heavy thighs evidence of "the old fat Kath that she [Kate] normally concealed under her skirts" (129). This is the residue of the past that neither Kate nor any of the other characters can ever escape entirely. For better or worse, their pasts continue to haunt them: individual family backgrounds, the world war, original sin, the modernist literary tradition—Barthelme's Dead Father—in whose shadow the contemporary writer self-consciously seeks to find his own distinctive voice. Lodge thus insists upon the presence of the past, on the ways in which it both hinders and helps his characters. And he insists too on their doubleness and upon the similarity or interpenetration of seeming opposites. Creating contrasts and parallels at every turn of the narrative, he causes the novel's characters and their beliefs to alternately merge and separate, to come in and out of focus.

I noted earlier that the novel is, in a sense, confessional in form. It is also a variation on the theme and structure of that traditional religious subgenre, the dialogue between the flesh and the spirit, but one in which the voices merge and the spirit is hardly allowed an unequivocal triumph. The mingling of the sacred and the profane is evident in the phrase, "credits, like indulgences," quoted above and more especially in the fact that Timothy is simultaneously attracted to and appalled by Kate's friends' "insatiable appetite for diversion," an appetite which "affronted his deepest [Anglo-Catholic] instincts and principles" (151). Don articulates in characteristically dogmatic fashion what Timothy, also characteristically, can only contemplate and even then only in the most general terms, being, as he is, entirely devoid of a necessary grounding in historical fact. As Don sees it, Kate's friends are nothing more than well-heeled "camp-followers": "Just when the Germans—and not just the Germans—began to crawl out of their cellars, clear away the rubble, rebuild their cities, open up the hotels and restaurants and the sights and the casinos—they happened to be the only people around with enough money to take advantage of it. The only people with no currency problems, no passport problems, no visa problems. . . . when you think of what happened in Europe only a few years ago, sackcloth and ashes seem more appropriate than Waikiki shirts" (152-153). Don's critical and irreverent attitude towards the war in general and the Allied victory in particular is merited and, for Timothy, a useful corrective to his uninformed chauvinism. Nonetheless, Don's language here and elsewhere in the novel is excessive; he is no less improvident with his moral pronouncements than Kate's friends are with their money. Moreover, although it is true that Don greatly extends Timothy's critical awareness of society and history, he also draws Timothy back in time and place. His preference for "sackcloth and ashes" and the old-fashioned amateur approach still followed at the London School of Economics, where he hopes to do graduate work, echoes Timothy's own English provincialism and Anglo-Catholic morality. It is, therefore, difficult for the reader to know exactly how to respond to Don, who seems to invite both approval and dismissal. As Timothy comes to realize, "that was the trouble with Don's company—it was something of a strain, like taking an examination all the time" (155). Timothy is right, but since Timothy also confuses Auschwitz with Austerlitz, an examination may be exactly what he needs. Moreover, even though he can spot this flaw in Don's character, he cannot make himself immune to it. After going to bed with Gloria Rose, for example, who is "sort of Jewish," Timothy, sounding like Don's echo, asks her what it is like to be a Jew living in postwar, post-Auschwitz Europe. (Gloria is, however, interested in sex, not questions of religious identity and national guilt.) Like so much in this novel, Don's moral concern is at once persuasive and excessive.

His "sackcloth and ashes" frame of mind leads him, as a descendent of Polish Jews, to want to visit Auschwitz, and something similar causes this typically rootless American to want to study at the London School of Economics. Kate on the other hand, intuiting what she feels is the used-upness of both the past (England) and the present (Heidelberg), chooses to step westward into the future (the United States). Their restlessness contributes to Timothy's uncertainty (he is "sort of half-way") and to the reader's as well in a novel which not only blurs distinctions but follows a course that both invites (insofar as it moves through time in a straightforward manner) and disrupts the

reader's passive consumption. Structurally the novel is divided into three numbered and titled parts, plus a nine-page epilogue. The three parts progressively increase in length, from fifty-one to sixty-one and finally to 139 pages. Each of these parts is further divided into three numbered (but untitled) sections that are, with one exception, again further divided into anywhere from four to twenty-one unnumbered and untitled subsections of varying lengths (from one page to twenty-eight). Within each of the three major parts, the narration tends to be more or less uniform in style (less so in the first), but between them it is subtly different, the Joycean differences reflecting changes in Timothy's (like Stephen Dedalus's) maturing mode of perceiving his changing world. Part One, "The Shelter," deals with the period from 1940 (the year of the London Blitz, when Timothy is five) to 1949. Though chronologically arranged, the narrative is not actually continuous. It leaps from event to event, following (especially in its first half) what a child might remember of the war and written in a style that reflects a child's (and later an adolescent's) efforts to make sense of what he doesn't understand based upon what little knowledge he has acquired up to that point. It begins, "almost the first thing he could remember was his mother standing on a stool in the kitchen, piling tins of food into the top cupboard," followed by the child's query, "what are all those tins for?" (3). And it ends, appropriately enough, with what might most profitably be thought of as a narrative palimpsest. Sitting on the beach, Timothy recalls Arnold's poem, "Dover Beach," and more especially the essay he wrote about it for his mock O-level exams. As Timothy begins mentally to revise his essay, the reader becomes aware in this single narrative moment of the existence of two Timothy's, one past and the other present, psychologically distinct yet narratively co-eval. Though longer by some ten pages, the novel's Part Two, "Coming Out," deals with a much shorter chronological period, covering just the time it takes Timothy to travel by train from London to Heidelberg and his first day and night in this Americanized German city. (There is also, near the beginning, a flashback to the events leading to Kate's invitation and Timothy's acceptance.)

At the beginning of the novel, Lodge moves abruptly from scene to scene but nonetheless manages to achieve a certain degree of narrative continuity based upon the recounting of significant events in a child's life: his perception of these events and his efforts to understand them in the light of his very limited knowledge. The temporal and spatial restrictions of Part Two, on the other hand, are reflected in this section's high degree of narrative continuity. The average length of the ten subsections is 6.1 pages, twice that of either Part One (2.68 pages) or Part Three (3.3 pages). The narrative situation and strategy changes radically in Part Three, **"Out of the Shelter,"** which is set in Heidelberg but which involves numerous geographical, political, theological, psychological, and narrative side trips—as well as side narratives—taken during Timothy's four-week stay. More importantly, the narrative here includes numerous abrupt crosscuts that do more than merely disrupt the narrative flow, for they involve parallel scenes, each serving as an alternative to the other, dialogically qualifying but never monologically cancelling out the other. The result is another kind of narrative palimpsest in which different views and judgments come into conflict in Timothy's and the reader's minds without ever being resolved. Although the subject matter of some of these scenes is undoubtedly overdrawn, the "heightened realism" taking a bathetic pratfall, the technique itself is less obtrusive and far more effective. It enables Lodge not simply to recount but actually to recreate for the reader Timothy's own sense of epistemological uncertainty. Such uncertainty is decidedly at odds with what the novel's title and epilogue seem to imply: development ending in closure.

Like the conclusions of so many nineteenth century novels, Lodge's epilogue serves to round off the story for the reader (and perhaps the author as well) who craves the traditional narrative comfort of knowing how it all turned out. Timothy, now thirty years old, has received a fellowship to study in the United States where he, along with his wife Sheila and their children, pays a brief visit to Kate, now a resident of California. Timothy has done rather well—not as well as he would like, but better certainly than Don (divorced) or Kate's Heidelberg friends Vince and Greg (disgraced) or his parents ("growing dully old") or Jill (dead) or Kate who, though she has returned to the Church, remains vaguely dissatisfied. The novel does not end, however, with the hero's relative triumph, freedom, and happiness. Instead, as Timothy joins his wife in the motel pool, "it came on him again—the familiar fear that he could never entirely eradicate, that this happiness was only a ripening target for fate; that somewhere, around the corner, some disaster awaited him, as he blithely approached" (270). It is of more than passing interest that Lodge makes precisely the same point in *The British Museum,* where, of course, it is rendered in the style of deadpan humor: "Catholics are brought up to expect sudden extinction round every corner and to keep their souls highly polished at all times" (65). Whether the reader of Lodge's novels is to understand the feeling shared by Adam Appleby and Timothy Young as the comic residue of their Catholic upbringing or as a tragic fact of human existence is necessarily and dialogically left uncertain. What is certain is

that unlike Stephen Dedalus, Timothy cannot proudly and defiantly—and pompously—proclaim, "I go to encounter for the millionth time the reality of experience and to forge in the smithy of my soul the uncreated conscience of my race" (253). He can only, and desperately, cry out his wife's name, seeking in her what he had earlier hoped to escape, the need for shelter. His need takes on added urgency given the fact that Kate's dissatisfaction is due, at least in part, to her not having married (the sexual and emotional counterpart of her self-imposed geographical exile from Britain and her parents).

Timothy's "Sheila!" concludes the novel but does not quite complete it. His crying out in the California desert exists not as a merely climactic narrative act but in contrast with the point Timothy makes just a few pages/moments before to Kate: "you can be so grateful for being where you are that you don't want to move on, in case things get worse. I recognize that tendency in myself" (265). The contrast here in the epilogue between Timothy's desire for motion and change and his need for stasis and stability reenacts—or re-voices—the similarly dialogical endings of the novel's first two parts. In the first-and the more effective of the two, discussed briefly above—Timothy recalls Arnold's "Dover Beach" and, almost immediately, his own essay about it, and this in turn leads him to reconsider the poem and to revise his essay mentally. Even as he moves ahead, refining his reading with his more mature insights, he moves back as well, not only to his original understanding—or misunderstanding—of Arnold's lines but even further back to the war, until finally, "alone in the shelter, under cover of night, safe from observation, Timothy lapsed into a heroic dream of his childhood" (52). The play of contending forces—past and present, childhood and adolescence—is rendered so that each has its own distinctive voice. (And the same is true in the epilogue where Timothy speaks reasonably of his need to forge ahead and later cries out emotionally when beset by "the familiar fear he could never entirely eradicate.") Though twenty-five years older than at the beginning of the novel, Timothy still faces essentially the same dilemma. He remains discontented not because he has failed to mature but because the process of "coming out of the shelter" and coming "out of [one's] shell" (265) is, as Lodge defines it, continual. His desire for shelter and his counter desire for freedom cannot be reconciled, only dialogized.[5] Timothy's situation is thus analogous to that of the novelist, again as Lodge has defined it. The writer's freedom to invent is limited by the closed universe of the narrative continuum having realism and metonymy at one end and fabulism and metaphor at the other. The essentially spatial form of Lodge's seemingly, or deceptively, linear novel implies a similar limitation, leading the reader back and forth rather than (simply) ahead. And Lodge has managed to "cautiously" advance his career as a novelist in a similar manner, for the writing of *Out of the Shelter* resulted in a moving forward that was itself the result of a looking back to James/Joyce and the high seriousness of his first two novels.

Notes

1. In revising the badly mangled text printed by Macmillan in 1970 for the new edition to be published by Secker & Warburg (1985), Lodge restored a number of passages, deleted several others, and "made many small stylistic alterations" but otherwise left the text pretty much as it was in an effort "to discover the effective version of the novel I wrote in 1967-8" (Lodge, "Introduction," *Out of the Shelter* xvi). Around the time he was making those changes, he explained to John Haffenden that "if I were writing it now I would not use that restrained monotone, the conventionally realistic mode; I think I would have more stylistic variety, more differences of perspective" (Interview 151).

2. "I tried to write a really ambitious socio-cultural novel, in the form of a *Bildungsroman*: it didn't quite come off . . ." (Interview with Haffenden 151).

3. Lodge, *Out of the Shelter* (London: Macmillan, 1970) 145. The revised version reads: "He had added to his experience lately, but as regards sex the additions were abysses concealing more than they revealed" (139).

4. *Out of the Shelter* (1970) 41.

5. According to Lodge, the epilogue was not intended to show any disillusionment, only that Timothy has been lucky and that he possesses "a temperamental cautiousness which holds him back" (Interview with Haffenden 151).

Works Cited

[Editor's Note: See previous essay for complete list of Works Cited.]

Bernard Bergonzi (essay date 1995)

SOURCE: Bergonzi, Bernard. "Early Novels." In *David Lodge,* pp. 1-12. Plymouth, U.K.: Northcote House, 1995.

[*In the following essay, Bergonzi provides a critical overview of Lodge's novels through* Out of the Shelter *and traces the author's development over the decade during which they were published.*]

David Lodge's first four novels, *The Picturegoers, Ginger, You're Barmy, The British Museum Is Falling Down* and *Out of the Shelter* were published between 1960 and 1970. They contain settings and topics drawn from his own experience which were to recur in different guises in his subsequent work. These include South London suburbia; the academic world, particularly university English departments; Catholicism; and the attractions of the American way of life. The first two novels and the fourth are works of sober realism, but the third, *The British Museum Is Falling Down,* brings together realism and farce and formal invention in a way that looks forward to Lodge's later novels.

The Picturegoers (1960) was published when Lodge was twenty-five, but had been completed two years earlier, and is a strikingly precocious achievement for so young a writer. The setting is the suburban milieu in which he grew up, here called 'Brickley', as opposed to the real-life Brockley, and the formal and thematic focus of the novel is a large local cinema, the Palladium, where the characters go for their Saturday night outings. *The Picturegoers* is precisely located in social history: in the mid-1950s cinema-going was still popular, as it had been in the thirties and forties, though it was under threat from television. The Palladium has come down in the world; once it had been a well-known variety theatre, and now, seedy and dilapidated, it is only just holding on as a cinema.

For the central characters, Saturday evening at the cinema is followed by Sunday morning at Mass. (Lodge has remarked that Alan Sillitoe's title *Saturday Night and Sunday Morning* would have suited his novel very well.) The Mallory family are Catholics, some fervent, some merely dutiful. Mr Mallory is an Englishman and a convert, but his wife is an Irishwoman, and they have had eight children. The eldest son is a priest, and another, still at school, is expected to follow the same path. Their eldest daughter, Clare, is back at home after unsuccessfully trying to be a nun. Other people are brought into the story, because they know the Mallorys or spend Saturday nights at the Palladium. Lodge's presentation of this range of characters is ambitious and assured, taking us in and out of their consciousness, each in an appropriate idiom. In an essay on his debt to Joyce (*WO [Write On: Occasional Essays '65-'85]* 57-69), he has acknowledged the influence on *The Picturegoers* of the 'Wandering Rocks' section of *Ulysses,* where a variety of representative Dubliners pass and repass each other on the streets of the city.

Mark Underwood, a London University undergraduate, takes a room in the Mallory household. He, as it happens, is a lapsed Catholic of raffish and cynical temperament, who is soon captivated by the essential goodness and decency of the Mallory family. He takes out the former aspiring nun, Clare, a virginal but well-built girl, and to please her goes to Mass with her. There he finds his faith dramatically returning, as expressed in a simile echoing another of Lodge's early literary mentors, Graham Greene: 'The priest stretched up, lifting the Host on high. Mark stared at it, and belief leapt in his mind like a child in the womb' (*TP* [*The Picturegoers*] 111). Mark's original intentions towards Clare were not particularly honourable, but before long she falls in love with him. Mark, though, is now thinking of a higher end, in the force of his returning faith: not Christian marriage but the celibate priesthood. Clare has to sacrifice him gracefully. The novel's Catholic aspects now look schematic and exaggerated, and in his introduction to the 1993 reissue of the book Lodge has commented on how remote much of its religious dimension now seems to him. There is, though, an element of comic relief in the discomfiture of Father Kipling, who mistakenly finds himself sitting through a gangster movie with sexy interludes instead of, as he had been expecting, *Song of Bernadette*. I shall defer further discussion of Lodge's treatment of Catholic topics to a later section of this study.

The Picturegoers combines sharp observation, clever guesswork and literary indebtedness. It shows the realistic novelist's capacity to catch the telling and placing details of the appearance of things, and an acute ear for speech and dialogue. The guesswork comes in when the young author has to write about matters he has had no direct experience of, such as the happy and sexually fulfilled marriage of the middle-aged Mallorys (Lodge was still unmarried when he wrote the book). And there are many literary echoes, from Joyce and Greene and more contemporary novelists. The author is out of his depth in his characterization of the Teddy Boy, Harry, a psychopath and potential rapist who seems to be derived from Pinkie in Greene's *Brighton Rock* rather than from observation of life. Harry is unconvincingly redeemed by meeting a nice girl who encourages him to dance in the aisles of the Palladium at a showing of the film *Rock Around the Clock*, a historical detail from the year 1956. What remains notable about *The Picturegoers* is not its inevitable unevenness but its extraordinary assurance in handling a complex narrative. This would have indicated at the time that its author would go on to greater things, even if it offered few clues about the direction he would take.

Lodge's second novel, *Ginger, You're Barmy* (1962), is a simpler story, much narrower in range. From the Second World War until the late 1950s, all able-bodied young men had to put in two years of military service. The system was generally unpopular, regarded by many of those who underwent it as a waste of time which did not usefully add to the military strength of the nation. The British have never had a tradition of peacetime conscription, unlike Continental countries where military service is an integral part of citizenship. Students had to decide whether to get their service in before going to university, thereby interrupting their studies, or to defer it, and have it hanging over them. Jonathan Browne, the central figure of the novel, follows the latter course, as did its author. In the Afterword to the 1982 reissue, Lodge wrote, '*Ginger, You're Barmy* cleaves very closely to the contours of my own military service. Although the story of the three main characters is fictional, there is scarcely a minor character or illustrative incident or detail of setting that is not drawn from the life' (*GYB* [*Ginger, You're Barmy*] 213).

Jonathan Browne is cautious, ambitious, self-regarding and an agnostic; he detests the army but tries to make himself as comfortable as possible within the system (as, Lodge admits, he did himself). He is contrasted with his friend Mike 'Ginger' Brady, an impulsive young man from an Irish Catholic background who is a natural rebel, and falls badly foul of the military machine. The polarity between Jonathan and Mike is an early instance of Lodge's liking for opposed pairs of types or places. Jonathan behaves shabbily towards Mike, who ends up in prison, having lost his girl, Pauline, to his friend.

Lodge admits that *Ginger, You're Barmy* was an act of deliberate revenge against the army. The blend of scrupulous realism, resentment at class distinctions and general bloody-mindedness gives the novel something in common with the work of the new English writers who emerged in the 1950s and were labelled as the 'Angry Young Men'. Its author, though, regards Graham Greene as the dominant influence, realizing after the book was written how much the structure owed to *The Quiet American,* and how the tone was often reminiscent of Greene; 'there is a sentence in the first paragraph of *Ginger* [*Ginger, You're Barmy*] which strikes me now as quintessentially Greenian in its relishing of the paradoxes of the moral life, its cadenced syntax and resonant abstractions: "I could never again write so unflattering an account of myself as the following, because it would open up so many awful possibilities of amendment."' (*GYB* 215). There is, too, the occasional elaborate simile in the manner of Greene: 'It must have been a time when Mike was still very much the link between us, when we anxiously talked and corresponded about him, like two watchers conferring at the bedside of someone gravely ill, our fingers straying imperceptibly towards each other in the darkness of the sick-room' (*GYB* 123). In general, though, the narrative is plain and unsurprising. It does, however, have some memorable touches, like the young soldier called Norman, a minor character but an impressive comic creation, who moves noisily but uselessly through his army career, finally injuring his hand in a typewriter while training to be a clerk.

The main narrative of *Ginger, You're Barmy* is framed by a brief Prologue and Epilogue, in which Jonathan discusses the story a few years later and brings us up to date about subsequent events, when he tries to make amends to Ginger. Lodge has said that he used this framing device to distance Jonathan's unamiable qualities of envy, selfishness and deceit (*GYB* 214). I do not think it works very well, but the failure may be one of technique rather than of nerve. Jonathan's story might have been artistically richer if he were deliberately presented as an 'unreliable narrator', whose assessments of himself and others are not to be trusted. The device is interesting, though, as an early sign of Lodge's inclination to step outside the narrative, to signal an awareness that it is a story and not a simple slice of life, anticipating the more sophisticated self-consciousness of his later novels.

The Picturegoers and *Ginger, You're Barmy* offer the pleasures of skilled story-telling and remain worth reading. They are also fascinating for describing a world that in some ways is remarkably different from our own; when, as Lodge has remarked, the concepts of racism and sexism did not exist; and when well-brought up young men, as well as young women, were expected to remain virgins until marriage, and often did so, whether from principle or lack of opportunity. The Dionysiac release provided by the rock'n'roll movie at the end of *The Picturegoers* was an unrecognized herald of changes to come. In 1962, after Lodge had published his second novel, it could have seemed that there was now nowhere for him to go. Writing in a vein of scrupulous and observant realism, he had used up a lot of experience: a Catholic childhood and family life in *The Picturegoers* and student days and military service in *Ginger, You're Barmy*. He became a lecturer in English at Birmingham University in 1960, and the routines and predictability of academic life might not have offered the stuff of interesting fiction. If Lodge had stopped then, he would not have been the first talented young writer to begin with a couple of promising novels and then give up, whether to become a critic or scholar, or to follow some non-literary career.

In the event, though, he showed himself to possess not only the staying power but the inventiveness to go on writing, and to write a different kind of fiction. Despite occasional humorous passages and a gently ironic tone, there is not much in the first two novels to suggest that Lodge could become a wholeheartedly comic

novelist, as he did in *The British Museum Is Falling Down* (1965). He has described how he did so. At Birmingham he collaborated with his then colleague Malcolm Bradbury and another friend in writing a satirical revue which was put on at the Birmingham Rep in 1963: 'I discovered in myself a zest for satirical, farcical and parodic writing that I had not known I possessed; and this liberated me, I found, from the restrictive decorums of the well-made realistic novel' (*BMFD* [*The British Museum Is Falling Down*] 6).

The British Museum Is Falling Down is a very funny book about a potentially grave subject. In *The Picturegoers* Lodge had painted an idealized picture of Catholic family life, but here the realities are bleaker. Adam Appleby, a penurious Catholic graduate student, already has three small children and is afraid that a fourth may be on the way. As loyal Catholics he and his wife are restricted in their family planning to the elaborate and unpredictable system known as the 'rhythm method' or 'safe period', which involves complex operations with calendar and temperature chart. On the single day in which the novel is set, his wife's period is already ominously late. *The British Museum Is Falling Down* appeared at a time when many Catholics entertained hopes—subsequently disappointed—that the ban on contraception would be lifted, and it reflects their state of mind. Those outside the Catholic Church meanwhile regarded the topic with amused or puzzled interest, and Lodge's novel ministered to their curiosity. He remarked that the problem 'seemed to me a part of experience which could only be treated comically if it were not to be tedious, and rather absurd' (Bergonzi 1, 112).

Adam spends his days in the great domed Reading Room of the British Museum (now known as the British Library, and due to move to a new building), where he is working on a thesis about style in the modern English novel. The treatment of sex in the literature he reads contrasts with his own anxious experiences, and he says of the difference between literature and life: 'Literature is mostly about having sex and not much about having children. Life is the other way round' (*BMFD* 65). (This aphorism has since found its way into dictionaries of modern quotations.) Like *Ulysses*, *The British Museum Is Falling Down* is confined to the events of a single day, and is centred on the Reading Room, though in fact Adam spends very little time reading. He takes a pub lunch with friends, attends a meeting of a Catholic society, visits his academic supervisor, and is caught up in a wild-goose chase in pursuit of the papers of a long-dead Catholic writer, which might provide a scholarly coup and gain him an academic job. Events follow each other with farcical rapidity: there is a false fire alarm in the museum, for which Adam is unwittingly responsible; for a time he is lost in the library stacks; and a precocious schoolgirl, daughter of the custodian of the papers he is after, tries to seduce him in exchange for handing them over, a proposition which tempts him, more out of ambition than out of lust, but which he finally resists. Throughout the day he is worried by his wife's possible pregnancy, which leads him to make many futile phone calls to her. Late that night, when Adam is asleep, her belated period starts; their immediate anxiety is lifted but the larger problem remains.

For many readers it is enough that *The British Museum Is Falling Down* is a dazzling comedy with lively characters and sharp, witty language. Some will also have an interest in its Catholic aspects. And others, especially those professionally concerned with literature, will respond to its exploration of intertextuality, the sense that literature inevitably draws on other literature. Adam reflects that so much experience has already been used up by the great writers of the past, and his aphorism about the difference between life and literature is prompted by the accusation from one of his friends that he no longer knows what the difference is. In his 1981 introduction Lodge refers to what the critic Harold Bloom calls the Anxiety of Influence: 'the sense every young writer must have of the daunting weight of the literary tradition he has inherited, the necessity and yet seeming impossibility of doing something in writing that has not been done before' (*BMFD* 5). Adam, the research student, feels this anxiety, but it really belongs to his creator, the novelist; Lodge deals with it by weaving the problem into the narrative itself. At intervals Adam finds himself responding to the successive events and traumas of the day in the manner of a twentieth-century novelist. When he arrives at the museum in the morning he encounters bureaucratic obstruction on having to get his out-of-date reader's ticket renewed. It is the sort of situation that we readily describe as 'Kafkaesque', but Lodge actually writes it in the manner of Kafka. The talent for parody which he had discovered when contributing material to a stage revue is now directed to the ends of literary self-reflectiveness; Joyce had shown what could be done with the expressive use of parody in the 'Oxen of the Sun' section of *Ulysses*.

The authors parodied include such modern masters as Kafka, Conrad, James, Lawrence, Woolf, Hemingway, and some lesser figures, like C. P. Snow and Baron Corvo; the latter provokes a superb excursion into fantasy, when Adam imagines he has become pope and issues an encyclical permitting the faithful freedom of choice in the matter of contraception. Another Catholic writer, Greene, is invoked when Adam is lost in the stacks; 'He had crossed a frontier—there was no doubt of that; and already he felt himself entering into the invisible community of outcasts and malefactors—all those who were hunted through dark ways shunned by the innocent and respectable . . .

Show me the happy scholar, he thought, and I will show you the bliss of ignorance' (*BMFD* 99). Lodge had closely studied Corvo and Greene in the course of writing a monumentally long MA dissertation on Catholic writers; he also invents a convincing autobiographical fragment by Egbert Merrymarsh, the minor figure from the Chesterbelloc era whose papers Adam is after. His pursuit of Merrymarsh prompts one of the finest parodies, when his genteel tea with the author's middle-aged niece is rendered in the style of Henry James:

> It was with a, for him, unwonted alacrity that our friend, hearing the tinkle of china in the hall, sprang gallantly to the door.
>
> 'I've been admiring your "things",' he said, as he assisted her with the tea-trolley.
>
> 'They're mostly my uncle's,' she said. 'But one does one's best.' She gestured vaguely to a cabinet where reliquaries statuettes and vials of Lourdes water were ranged on shelves, dim dusty devotional.
>
> She made tea in the old leisured way, pouring the water into the pot from a hissing brass urn.
>
> 'One lump or . . . ?' she questioned.
>
> (*BMFD* 115)

In conclusion Lodge turns to Joyce, to Molly Bloom's long unpunctuated soliloquy at the end of *Ulysses,* to provide a climactic parody, and to enable Barbara, Adam's wife, to move into the picture and have her say, and indeed the final word. We share her inner monologue as Adam, unaware that her period has started, lies asleep beside her. Molly Bloom's final word had been 'yes'; Barbara's is a tentative 'perhaps', which Lodge regards as 'more appropriate to Barbara's character and the mingled notes of optimism and resignation on which I wanted to end the novel' (*BMFD* 7).

Out of the Shelter (1970), published five years later, is a very different kind of book. It does not continue the wit, ingenuity and high spirits of *The British Museum Is Falling Down,* but makes a determined return to traditional realism. The first edition was beset by all kinds of problems, both before and after publication, wryly described by Lodge in his introduction to the revised edition of 1985, where he put back cuts demanded by the original publisher and tried to restore the text to something like his original intentions. The book remains something of an oddity, not widely read, and is unlike the common conception of a David Lodge novel. Nevertheless, it contains some of his best writing. It is Lodge's most directly autobiographical novel, and for this extended recreation of personal experience it seems that he needed to return to the straightforwardly realistic mode with which he began. We are back in the milieu of *The Picturegoers,* Catholic family life in the South London suburbs, but the treatment is more detached.

Timothy Young, the central figure, is 5 years old when the novel opens in 1940. The presentation of his consciousness is openly indebted to Joyce's *A Portrait of the Artist as a Young Man*: 'Soon he found out that war was a Mickey Mouse gasmask that steamed up when you breathed and his father getting a tin hat and a whistle and Jill crying because her father was going away to join the Air Force and the wireless on all the time and black paper stuck over the front-door windows and sirens going and getting up in the middle of the night because of the raids. It was fun getting up in the middle of the night' (*OS* [*Out of the Shelter*] 3). Timothy enjoys the snug warmth of the air-raid shelter in the garden. A bomb falls nearby, killing his little playmate and her mother and half burying the shelter with rubble; but Timothy does not want to leave it: 'In the end, one of the men carried him, kicking and screaming, out of the shelter, into the open air.' The implications of this sentence echo throughout the novel.

Lodge is systematically indebted to *A Portrait* in this book, even following Joyce's Continental convention of beginning dialogue with a dash instead of enclosing it in quotation marks. In '**My Joyce**', he acknowledges ***Out of the Shelter***'s debt to *A Portrait,* and also to the rigorous naturalism of *Dubliners,* but admits that he falls far short of the model: '***Out of the Shelter,*** however, plays much safer than *A Portrait* in both surface and deep structure. It quite lacks the bold variation of styles, the poetic rhythms and leitmotifs, the disconcerting temporal gaps, and the uncompromising allusiveness of Joyce's masterpiece' (***WO*** 68).

Timothy, as he grows up, cannot claim the poetic sensibility of Stephen Dedalus, but he has some affinities with him; he is a timid but brainy lad who attends the local Catholic grammar school, where he is hardworking and somewhat priggish, but is kept in touch with the rest of humanity by his interest in sex and football. Lodge skilfully sketches in the various influences on the growing boy: a narrow maternal possessiveness, anxious suburban respectability, and a rigid, rather superstitious form of Catholicism. Meanwhile the war drags on, until 1945 finally brings peace and what Timothy sees as the sudden mysterious replacement of the great war leader Churchill by the colourless Attlee. Shortages and hardships seem unending, and the ministers in the Labour government, Strachey, Shinwell and Cripps, are demonized, replacing the grosser bogeymen, Hitler, Goebbels and Goering. Lodge filters public events through the consciousness of the boy, and effectively catches the climate of feeling of the immediate postwar period.

The greater part of the narrative occurs when Timothy is 16, in 1951. His much older sister, Kate, has already moved out of the shelter of the family, and works as a secretary for the American army in Germany. She has not been home for several years, though she regularly sends back American luxuries and consumer goods, and she invites Timothy to join her for a holiday; with timid eagerness on his part, and many misgivings on his parents', he accepts. What happens to him during his stay in Heidelberg provides a significant rite of passage. Germany itself is not much more than a background: impressions of Old Heidelberg, a sense of Wagnerian menace, crippled ex-soldiers, and wartime nightmares about Hitler (though the city itself escaped war damage, which is why the Americans made it their headquarters). The real impact on Timothy comes from the way of life of the American occupying forces: huge steaks, huge cars, and a bewildering and seductive variety of ice-cream sodas in a drug-store. In every sense, this is rich fare for the naïve and sheltered schoolboy who has just come from the physical shortages and imaginative poverty of postwar England. Even in his dealings with his sister, who is genuinely pleased to see him, culture shock is mixed up with adolescent uncertainties. Timothy upsets her by declining her offer of a shower after his long and tiring train journey, saying that he had had a bath two nights before; he is accustomed to a weekly bath whereas Kate now takes daily showers.

He learns a lot as he emerges from the shelter, and the reader shares the boy's sense of himself as absurd as well as vulnerable. An older woman offers to have sex with him, but he nervously declines; in the end he achieves a kind of sexual initiation when he is masturbated by a worldly but good-hearted American high school girl, as the climax of a bout of heavy petting (another characteristic American custom, at least at that time). One of Lodge's critics, Merritt Moseley, has shrewdly remarked, 'It is a mark of Lodge's control, I believe, that he does not give Timothy the complete sexual success which is a feature, and a very unconvincing one, of so many adolescent-coming-of-age stories' (Moseley, 48).

In the character of Timothy, Lodge shows an acute and sensitive understanding of adolescence. He drew on some of his own youthful experiences; but at the same time Timothy has an archetypal quality, recalling Candide, and the aspiring young men in French and English novels of the nineteenth century who learn to pick their way over social and cultural obstacles as they rise in the world. Lodge has said, 'I tried to write a really ambitious socio-cultural novel, in the form of a *Bildungsroman*: it didn't quite come off, but that was the motivation' (Haffenden, 151). In fact, ***Out of the Shelter*** is only a *Bildungsroman* in a very truncated sense. That mode usually shows the hero moving from youth to early manhood—as in Joyce's *Portrait* or Lawrence's *Sons and Lovers*—but in this novel Lodge skips over that phase. We leave Timothy at the age of 16, and encounter him again in the Epilogue; when he is 30, a successful academic who is touring the United States on a fellowship, with his wife and two children. He is visiting Kate, who now lives in America, and he is gratifying to the full the taste for things American that he first acquired in Heidelberg.

In some respects, Kate is a more interesting character than Timothy, if only because she is older and has got out of the shelter sooner, notwithstanding the pain it causes her parents. Lodge uses her as the focus for a sharp critique of the material and mental smallness of the lower-middle-class suburban world in which she grew up, in the tradition of earlier writers like George Gissing, H. G. Wells and George Orwell. In Heidelberg Kate leads an artificially comfortable life, away from the privations of postwar England and cocooned from the devastation of postwar Germany. But she comes to realize that the expatriate American world is a dangerously unreal community, and that some of her friends are caught up in sexual and financial corruption. She escapes the unreality by emigrating to America itself. As Lodge has indicated, *Out of the Shelter* offers an updated version of the 'international theme' of Henry James's fiction, though here the representatively innocent figure is English rather than American (*OS* ix). In a larger historical context, it dramatizes the impact, physical and imaginative, of American mass culture on English (indeed, European) life and values. Lodge's own early fascination with America comes across in the Epilogue to the novel, which I find a somewhat contrived bringing together of its scattered themes. This fascination is described in his autobiographical essay, **'The Bowling Alley and the Sun'** (*WO* 3-16), and was to be brilliantly embodied in his next novel, *Changing Places*. The major achievement of *Out of the Shelter* is its sharp but moving presentation of a restricted childhood, and an adolescent consciousness trying to overcome the limitations of family and environment. Lodge has not attempted anything quite like this in his other novels; these may be experiences which could be written about only once.

Select Bibliography

Works by David Lodge

Books and Pamphlets

About Catholic Authors (London, 1958).

Introducing Jazz (by D. J. L.) (London, 1959).

The Picturegoers (London, 1960; 2nd edn. with introduction, Harmondsworth, 1993).

Ginger, You're Barmy (London, 1962; New York, 1965; 2nd edn. with afterword, London, 1982).

The British Museum Is Falling Down (London, 1965; New York, 1967; 2nd edn. with introduction, London, 1981).

Graham Greene (New York, 1966).

Language of Fiction: Essays in Criticism and Verbal Analysis of the English Novel (London and New York, 1966; 2nd edn. with afterword, London, 1984).

Out of the Shelter (London, 1970; 2nd edn. revised with introduction, London, 1985; New York, 1989).

The Novelist at the Crossroads and Other Essays on Fiction and Criticism (London and Ithaca, 1971).

Evelyn Waugh (New York, 1971).

Changing Places: A Tale of Two Campuses (London, 1975; New York, 1978).

The Modes of Modern Writing: Metaphor, Metonymy, and the Typology of Modern Literature (London and Ithaca, 1977).

Modernism, Antimodernism and Postmodernism (Birmingham, 1977).

How Far Can You Go? (London, 1980; as *Souls and Bodies,* New York, 1982).

Working with Structuralism: Essays and Reviews on Nineteenth and Twentieth Century Literature (London, 1981).

Small World: An Academic Romance (London, 1984; New York, 1985).

Write On: Occasional Essays '65-'85 (London, 1986).

Nice Work (London, 1988; New York, 1989).

After Bakhtin: Essays on Fiction and Criticism (London and New York, 1990).

Paradise News (London and New York, 1991).

The Writing Game: A Comedy (London, 1991).

The Art of Fiction (London and New York, 1992).

A David Lodge Trilogy (Harmondsworth, 1993). Contains *Changing Places, Small World* and *Nice Work.*

Three Novels (London, 1994). Contains *Ginger, You're Barmy, The British Museum Is Falling Down* and *How Far Can You Go?*

Therapy: A Novel (London and New York, 1995).

Short Stories

'The Man Who Couldn't Get Up', *Weekend Telegraph,* 6 May 1966.

'My First Job', *London Review of Books,* 4 September 1980.

'Where the Climate's Sultry', *Cosmopolitan,* August 1987.

'Hotel des Boobs', in *The Penguin Book of Modern British Short Stories,* ed. M. Bradbury (London, 1988; New York, 1989).

'Pastoral', in *Telling Stories,* ed. D. Minshull (London, 1992).

UNCOLLECTED ESSAYS

'Pay As You Learn', *Listener,* 5 October 1989.

'Fact and Fiction in the Novel: An Author's Note', in *Tensions and Transitions (1869-1990): The Mediating Imagination,* ed. M. Irwin, M. Kinkead-Weekes and A. R. Lee (London, 1990).

'The Novelist Today: Still at the Crossroads?', in *New Writing,* ed. M. Bradbury and J. Cooke (London, 1992).

'Adapting *Nice Work* for Television', in *Novel Images: Literature in Performance,* ed. P. Reynolds (London and New York, 1993).

'Three Weddings and a Big Row' (on Lodge's television adaptation of *Martin Chuzzlewit*), *Independent,* 13 December 1994.

EDITED WORKS AND INTRODUCTIONS

Jane Austen: 'Emma', A Macmillan Casebook (London, 1968).

Jane Austen, *Emma,* with James Kinsley (London, 1971).

Twentieth Century Literary Criticism: A Reader (London, 1972).

George Eliot, *Scenes of Clerical Life* (Harmondsworth, 1973).

Thomas, Hardy, *The Woodlanders* (London, 1974).

The Best of Ring Lardner (London, 1984).

François Mauriac, *Knot of Vipers* (Harmondsworth, 1985).

Henry James, *The Spoils of Poynton* (Harmondsworth, 1987).

Modern Criticism and Theory: A Reader (London, 1988).

Kingsley Amis, *Lucky Jim* (Harmondsworth, 1992).

INTERVIEWS WITH DAVID LODGE

Bergonzi, B., 'David Lodge Interviewed', *The Month* (February, 1970), 108-16.

———. 'A Religious Romance: David Lodge in Conversation', *The Critic* (Fall, 1992), 68-73.

Haffenden, J., 'David Lodge', in *Novelists in Interview* (London, 1985).

Kostrzewa, R., 'The Novel and Its Enemies: A Conversation with David Lodge', *Harkness Report* (December, 1993), 8-11.

Walsh, C., 'David Lodge Interviewed', *Strawberry Fare* (Autumn, 1984), 3-12.

CRITICAL AND BIOGRAPHICAL STUDIES

Bergonzi, B., *The Myth of Modernism and Twentieth Century Literature* (Brighton, 1986). Contains 'The Decline and Fall of the Catholic Novel', an essay relating Lodge to earlier Catholic novelists.

———. *Exploding English: Criticism, Theory, Culture* (Oxford, 1990). Discusses Lodge's criticism and fiction in a critique of academic English study.

Bradbury, M., and D. Palmer (eds), *The Contemporary English Novel* (London, 1979). Contains Robert Burden's 'The Novel Interrogates Itself', which discusses *The British Museum Is Falling Down.*

Halio, J. L. (ed.), *British Novelists Since* 1960 (Detroit, 1983).

Honan, P., 'David Lodge and the Cinematic Novel in England', *Novel* (Winter, 1972), 167-73. On Lodge's early novels.

Morace, R. A., *The Dialogic Novels of Malcolm Bradbury and David Lodge* (Carbondale, 1989).

Moseley, M., *David Lodge: How Far Can You Go?* (San Bernardino, 1991). A lucid survey of Lodge's work up to 1988.

Parnell, M., 'The Novels of David Lodge', *Madog* (Summer, 1979), 8-15.

Smallwood, P., *Modern Critics in Practice: Critical Portraits of British Literary Critics* (London, 1990).

Sutherland, J. A., *Fiction and the Fiction Industry* (London, 1978). Discusses Lodge as a novelist of academic life.

Taylor, D. J., *After the War: The Novel and English Society Since 1945* (London, 1993). Includes scattered idiosyncratic comments on Lodge; praises *The Picturegoers.*

Widdowson, P., 'The Anti-History Men: Malcolm Bradbury and David Lodge', *Critical Quarterly* (Winter, 1984), 5-32.

Woodman, T., *Faithful Fictions: The Catholic Novel in British Literature* (Milton Keynes, 1991). A useful study, which considers Lodge's Catholic aspects in their larger literary context.

Bernard Bergonzi (essay date 1995)

SOURCE: Bergonzi, Bernard. "Catholic Questions." In *David Lodge*, pp. 29-47. Plymouth, U.K.: Northcote House, 1995.

[In the following essay, Bergonzi distills the religious elements of Lodge's fiction.]

There is a distinguished roll-call of English writers who have been Roman Catholics: Newman, Hopkins, Chesterton, Waugh, Greene, David Jones, Muriel Spark. But nearly all of them were converts to Catholicism. This fact separates them from the majority of their co-religionists, the 'cradle-Catholics' whose religion was passed on from their families, and, who, apart from a small number of upper-class 'Old Catholics', were working class or lower middle class, with a strong admixture of Irish immigrants. Their educational attainments and ambitions tended to be limited, and did not often turn them towards literature. Young people from such a background who took advantage of new educational opportunities and became socially mobile often abandoned Catholicism in the process. This has long been the case with Irish writers, most famously Joyce, though his work remained profoundly marked by the religion which he had abandoned. A number of recent English writers have been lapsed Catholics, who look back on Catholicism with affection or hostility, or elements of both. Examples include John Braine and Anthony Burgess, both of Northern English Catholic origin, and a succession of women authors seeking revenge for their convent education.

David Lodge is unusual in being a cradle-Catholic from a lower-middle-class family in South London who is a successful writer and who continues to regard himself as a Catholic, though his ideas about religion have changed greatly over the years. In **'Memories of a Catholic Childhood'** (*WO* [*Write On*] 28-32) he described his origins, which were not altogether typical of cradle-Catholic culture, since he was an only child and his father was not a Catholic:

> My mother was a dutiful but undemonstrative daughter of the Church. I was given a Catholic schooling, but the atmosphere of the home was not distinctively Catholic. There was no great profusion of holy pictures and statues in the house, religion was a topic rarely touched on in conversation, and there was little of the regular and complex social interaction with parish clergy and laity that is a feature of the typical large devout Catholic family. I had no brothers or sisters to reinforce the Catholic cultural code, and my friends in the same street happened not to be Catholic. The result was that as a child I always felt something of an outsider in the Church, anxious to belong, to be accepted, yet hanging back on the periphery through shyness, absence of familial pressure and inadequate grasp of the relevant codes.

The sense of being in the Church and at the same time something of an outsider can be traced in Lodge's novels, which combine detailed knowledge of the institution with cool observation. At school he acquired an idea of the theological foundations of Catholic belief and developed 'a respect for and fascination with its subtleties and complexities'. Reading Joyce and other modern authors extended his intellectual horizons: 'I became more critical of the Catholic "ghetto" culture that I encountered in the parish and at school, especially its suspicious hostility towards the arts. When I discovered *A Portrait of the Artist as a Young Man* I identified immediately with Stephen Daedalus, though I had neither the courage nor the urge to rebel on so spectacular a scale'. Graham Greene and François Mauriac and other authors offered new possibilities within a Catholic world-view, 'presenting authentic religious belief as something equally opposed to the materialism of the secular world and to the superficial pieties of parochial Catholicism'. They drew the sinner as a representative Christian in a way that was exciting to an adolescent with literary ambitions: 'being a Catholic need not entail a life of dull, petty-bourgeois respectability. The extreme situations and exotic settings on which these writers thrived were, however, very remote from my experience; and when I came to try and write fiction for myself I domesticated their themes to the humdrum suburban-parochial milieu that I knew best'.

Lodge's first four novels all contain Catholic characters, but he does not put them through high spiritual dramas. His interest is much more in the subculture of English (or Hiberno-English) Catholics and their dealings with the rest of society. The problems that arise from following their beliefs are more likely to be treated comically than melodramatically. In *The Picturegoers* he presented 'the typical large devout Catholic family', with an Irish mother and an English convert father, basing it on his wife's family rather than his own. Kingsley Amis in a favourable review of *The Picturegoers* described it as 'a Catholic novel, but written without the nose-to-the-grindstone glumness, all sin and significance, that the phrase often implies'. Amis rightly praised Lodge's 'social eye': here and in his other early novels the frame of reference is sociological rather than theological, with much close observation of the minutiae of lower-middle-class Catholic life. When Mark Underwood first enters the Mallory household, he soon encounters the signs of Catholic devotion: 'the plastic holy water stoup askew on the wall, the withered holy Palm, stuck behind a picture of the Sacred Heart which resembled an illustration in a medical text-book, and the statue of St Patrick enthroned upon the dresser' (*TP* [*The Picturegoers*] 44). This milieu has rarely been caught in

English fiction, for the convert Catholic writers had little knowledge of it, and the closest parallels are in Joyce's domestic interiors.

Though the implied attitudes in **The Picturegoers** are entirely orthodox, in ways that seemed remote to Lodge when he wrote his preface to the 1993 reissue, there are elements of distancing irony directed at some of the more extreme manifestations of Catholic fervour. There is the odious Damien O'Brien, an Irish ex-seminarian who lives next door to the Mallorys and lusts after Clare. He is permeated with pharisaical piety, and Lodge gives him the malign vitality of a Dickensian caricature; he is described, in a Greene-ish simile as 'carrying his failure before him like a monstrance'. And there is Father Kipling, the parish priest of Brickley, who starts a campaign against the sinfulness of the cinema. He is an amiably ridiculous figure, whose portrayal suggests the mild anti-clericalism sometimes found in cradle-Catholics (more precisely, cradle-Catholic men).

In **Ginger, You're Barmy** the principal Catholic character is the Irish rebel, Mike Brady, to whom we never become very close, as we know him only through the narrative of his agnostic and ultimately disloyal friend, Jonathan Browne, who is dismissive of Mike's religion. He does, though, recall a poem Mike has written attacking contraception; an ironical touch, in the light of Lodge's next novel, **The British Museum Is Falling Down.** That book broke entirely new ground for a Catholic novel, and despite its comic elements dealt with a serious subject: the ban on contraception and the restiveness that was beginning to be felt about it by married Catholics in the 1960s. Adam Appleby embodies the hopes that were in the air as the Second Vatican Council opened in 1962. Early in the story he gives a lift on his motor-scooter to Father Finbar, an *echt* Irish curate from his parish church, and tries to raise the possibility of a change in the teaching on birth control. Father Finbar will consider no such possibility; as far as he is concerned, the Church's teaching never changes on any subject whatsoever, and the true purpose of marriage is to procreate children and bring them up in the fear and love of God. Adam is hardly surprised, for he and his wife already regard him as the Priest Most Likely to Prevent the Conversion of England. Later in the day, he meets a priest of a very different kind, the radical Dominican, Father Bill Wildfire, who wears workmen's clothes and occupies dangerously advanced theological territory: 'I was preaching at a men's retreat the other day, and I told them, better sleep with a prostitute with some kind of love than with your wife out of habit. Seems some of them took me at my word, and the bishop is rather cross'. Father Wildfire is sympathetic to Adam's difficulties, but the priest's real concern is in larger spiritual dramas: 'In contrast, Adam's moral problem seemed trivial and suburban, and to seek Father Wildfire's advice would be like engaging the services of a big-game hunter to catch a mouse' (**BMFD** [**The British Museum Is Falling Down**] 72).

Father Finbar and Father Wildfire, contrasting caricatures as they are, reflect the divisions that were appearing in English Catholicism and which would deepen over the years. Finding no satisfaction, Adam retreats into his Corvine fantasy of becoming pope and decreeing all methods of birth control acceptable, with the result that 'so many lapsed Catholics are returning to the practice of their Faith that the Churches cannot accommodate them'. But in practice only the rhythm method, or safe period, was permitted to practising Catholics. Adam has already engaged in a fantasy about that, an imaginary article on 'Roman Catholicism' for a Martian encyclopaedia compiled after life on earth had been extinguished by nuclear war:

> Intercourse between married partners was restricted to certain limited periods determined by the calendar and the body-temperature of the female. Martian archaeologists have learned to identify the domiciles of Roman Catholics by the presence of large numbers of complicated graphs, calendars, small booklets full of figures, and quantities of broken thermometers, evidence of the great importance attached to this code. Some scholars have argued that it was merely a method of limiting the number of offspring; but as it has been conclusively proved that the Roman Catholics produced more children on average than any other section of the community, this seems untenable. Other doctrines of the Roman Catholics included a belief in a Divine Redeemer and in life after death.

> (**BMFD** 16)

At the end of the novel, Adam's wife proves not to be pregnant after all, which brings immediate short-term relief, but the large issues remain unresolved. Lodge himself wrote in his Introduction to the new edition of 1981: 'Like most traditional comedy, **The British Museum Is Falling Down** is essentially conservative in its final import, the conflicts and misunderstandings it deals with being resolved without fundamentally disturbing the system which provoked them. (That more fundamental disturbance is the subject of **How Far Can You Go?**') (**BMFD** 3).

The British Museum Is Falling Down was published in 1965, the year in which the Second Vatican Council completed its sessions. That great assembly of bishops from all over the world, called by Pope John XXIII to, in effect, update the Catholic Church, brought about many changes. Latin was replaced by the vernacular in much of the liturgy, theologians and scriptural scholars found a new freedom, and morality was seen less as adherence to rules laid down by an authoritarian system and more a matter of informed and responsible decision-making. The traditional modes of belief and practice described in **The Picturegoers** remained in place, but suffered noticeable and sometimes disturbing modification. Many conservative believers, of whom Evelyn Waugh was one of the most prominent, were distressed or angered by the changes. The Vatican Council did not, however, pronounce on contraception. That subject was removed from its deliberations by the pope and entrusted to a special commission made up of theologians, scientists and other experts. In time it voted by a large majority for a change in the traditional teaching, and such a change was widely expected. Nevertheless, in 1968 John's successor as pope, Paul VI, confuted expectations and reaffirmed the ban in his encyclical, *Humanae Vitae*. Instead of the resigned obedience which such a pronouncement might have prompted before the liberal climate initiated by Vatican II, there was a storm of protest. Married Catholics, at least in the western world, decided that if there was not to be a change in the law about contraception then they would ignore it. *Humanae Vitae* provoked a crisis not only about sexuality but about authority in the Church that is still unresolved.

How Far Can You Go? (1980) is a much more serious novel than **The British Museum Is Falling Down,** in the senses of being both more intellectually and artistically ambitious and less funny, though it has its comic moments; Moseley says of it, 'This is the first novel . . . in which he has actually made being a Catholic a serious, world-historical kind of situation' (Moseley, 77). Lodge describes the enormous changes in the Church brought first by Vatican II and then by *Humanae Vitae* and the reaction to it, as they affect a group of middle-class English Catholics from the early 1950s, when they are students, to the late seventies, when some of them are no longer Catholics. Lodge said of the book in 1984:

> It was a subject nobody else seemed to have dealt with, what had happened to the Catholic Church over the last twenty-five years. Even the people in the Church haven't realized how it's changed out of all recognition, because it was a gradual change, and I needed a large number of characters in order to illustrate all the varieties of change—priests dropping out, for example, and nuns having to throw off their habits and adjust to the modern world; sexual problems in marriage, mixed marriages, changes in the liturgy—I would immediately think of a whole set of incidents and situations that I wanted to incorporate. It would have been a huge saga novel if I had treated it in a realistic mode. I also knew I had to find some way of communicating to a non-Catholic audience a lot of theological and ecclesiastical information. So thinking in terms of a short novel with

a rather rapid pace, with a lot of characters and a lot of information to communicate, I was led inexorably to use a dominant, intrusive authorial voice which would communicate that information in a way I hoped was itself amusing. It meant cutting down the characterization to a fairly summary form, and having many characters of more or less equal importance.

(Haffenden, 154-5)

In **How Far Can You Go?** Lodge departs from the realistic mode only in the limited sense that the novel rejects the Jamesian prescription that the author should always dramatize the story and go in for 'showing' rather than 'telling'. But the knowing story-teller, the dominant, intrusive, omniscient narrator, has been central in a line that runs from Cervantes to Fielding to the major Victorians; Thackeray, for instance, writes at the end of *Vanity Fair,* 'let us shut up the box and the puppets, for our play is played out'. This is every bit as deliberately alienated and distancing as the tone adopted by Lodge's narrator.

The opening of the novel is precisely located in history and geography. The year is 1952, it is 8 o'clock in the morning of a dismal February day—St Valentine's Day—in a sooty Catholic church in central London, where a group of London University students are attending Mass. These are the young Catholics whose fortunes we are to follow through the novel. There is Angela, pretty, blonde, and very devout, reading French. Dennis is a burly youth, reading chemistry, and not very devout; indeed, he is only at the Mass because he is in love with Angela. (They will marry, after a protracted, notionally chaste engagement lasting several years.) Polly is a dark, pretty girl, something of a rebel and destined to lose her virginity and her faith before long. She is reading English, and so is Michael, who is clever, sex-obsessed, and still a virgin, as are all of them at this point. He has a white face and dark greasy hair, and wears what the author piquantly describes as a 'wanker's overcoat'. After graduating Michael writes a thesis on Graham Greene, and references to Greene's new novels as they come out provide a subtext relating Lodge's work to an admired master of the English Catholic novel. Michael will marry Miriam, a convert to Catholicism, and have a happy marriage, though preserving a lively erotic imagination. Although Lodge has said that the characters are intended to be of roughly equal importance, in fact it is the married couples who are at the moral and imaginative centre of the novel: Angela and Dennis; Michael and Miriam; and, to a lesser extent, Edward, a somewhat lugubrious medical student who is acting as Mass server when we first see him, and Tessa, a nurse whom he marries after he qualifies as a doctor, and who willingly becomes a Catholic.

The other characters are more marginal. There is Adrian, a student of economics, who never really comes alive; theologically, he is a dogmatic conservative at the beginning of the book and a dogmatic liberal at the end of it. Ruth is a plain girl with a strong personality, reading botany; she is to become a nun and have an unexpectedly interesting life in the wake of the changes brought by Vatican II. Miles, a recent convert, is the only member of the group to have been at a public school; he becomes an academic historian and struggles with his homosexuality. Violet, reading classics, is a pretty but neurotic girl, who is to be seduced by a young lecturer and then marry him; her spiritual path takes her away from Catholicism, first to Jehovah's Witnesses, and then to Sufism. The person who travels the furthest is the young priest saying Mass. Initially, Father Austin Brierley is narrow-minded and priggish, but he will change enormously during the sixties and seventies. He is one of the priestly rebels against *Humanae Vitae,* but is handled gently by his bishop, who treats him as a managerial rather than a spiritual problem. Father Brierley is removed from parish work and sent on courses of study to keep him out of the way. He becomes more and more radical, discovering new modes of theology and biblical exegesis and moving into the secular discipline of sociology. By the end of the novel he has left the priesthood and married, though still considering himself 'a kind of Catholic'.

Throughout the novel Lodge keeps the focus on the group as a whole, cutting rapidly from one individual or couple to another, and freely using authorial omniscience to look ahead as well as back. Since there are a lot of characters, and *How Far Can You Go?* is not a long novel, their psychological and moral development over the years cannot be shown in any depth and one has to rely on the narrator to inform us about it (a matter of 'telling' rather than 'showing'). Indeed, they are not always sharply differentiated, a point which Lodge has accepted: 'One of the possible weaknesses of the book, which is an almost inevitable result of dealing with a homogeneous social group, is that the characters are likely to be confused with each other in the reader's mind' (Haffenden, 154). He has also acknowledged that the women characters tend to be more complex and interesting than the men; this is 'partly a reflection of the fact that in the period dealt with women have changed a lot more than men' (letter to the present writer, 6 June 1979).

One of the most important characters is the narrator, whose voice is frequently heard. In time it becomes evident that he is a version of David Lodge himself; he cross-refers to his other novels, and at the end of the book, when there is a round-up of what all the characters are doing, he says: 'I teach English literature at a redbrick university and write novels in my spare time, slowly, and hustled by history' (*HFCYG* [*How Far Can You Go?*] 243). Such a device seems to undermine the distinction between 'fiction' and 'reality', but in fact the author-as-character is still an invented figure, and not identical with the historical individual whose name appears on the title-page. Wayne C. Booth provides a classic account of this question in *The Rhetoric of Fiction*; more recently, Lodge himself has written, 'the more nakedly the author appears to reveal himself in such texts, the more inescapable it becomes, paradoxically, that the author as a *voice* is only a function of his own fiction, a rhetorical construct, not a privileged authority but an object of interpretation' (*AB* [**After Bakhtin: Essays on Fiction and Criticism**] 43). Although *How Far Can You Go?* is to a degree a formally innovative novel, its intervening, commenting narrator, who is ready to break off the story to insert little essays on religion or the nature of narrative, is reminiscent of Fielding's narrator in *Tom Jones*; he, too, has a pseudo-identification with the historical author.

The active role of the narrator in *How Far Can You Go?* means that the book contains a good deal of direct discussion of the transformations in Catholicism as well as showing them in the attitudes and behaviour of the characters. The title is first presented in a reminiscence of Michael's schooldays: 'a favourite device of the bolder spirits in the sixth form to enliven Religious Instruction was to tease the old priest who took them for this lesson with casuistical questions of sexual morality, especially the question of How Far You Could Go with the opposite sex. *"Please, Father, how far can you go with a girl, Father?"'* (*HFCYG* 4). By the end of the novel the question has a wider and less literal application; it asks how far can Catholics, or the Church, change and still retain anything identifiable as Catholic identity. Early on the narrator describes the world-picture that his young Catholics would have grown up with. It took the form of a great snakes-and-ladders board with Salvation as the name of the game; at the top was Heaven and at the bottom was Hell; prayers and sacraments and good deeds sent you scuttling up a ladder; sins sent you slithering down a snake. The rules were complicated, but anything you very much liked doing was almost certainly bad, or at least a moral danger. This account would have been regarded by thoughtful Catholics, well before Vatican II, as a caricature, since it excludes any idea of a loving Creator or an autonomous spiritual life. Nevertheless, there is no denying that something like this caricature was what cradle-Catholics often grew up with. In the novel, Lodge's characters gradually come to abandon it, not by a conscious rethinking of doctrine but by a steady change in their sense of what seemed credible. 'At some point in the 1960s', remarks the narrator, 'Hell disappeared. No one could say for certain when this happened. First it was there, then it wasn't'. By the end of the decade the married couples had all taken to using contraception, in defiance of *Humanae Vitae.* The narrator subjects the Catholic position on contraception to a chilly analysis; it was more logical, he suggests, when the Church believed, like Father Finbar in *The British Museum Is Falling Down,* that the purpose of marriage was simply the procreation and education of children. But then the emphasis changed; marital sexual pleasure was regarded as acceptable, even proper (in defiance of ancient traditions), and the use of the safe period, which had been reluctantly tolerated as a means of birth control, was actively encouraged. All of which meant that the ban on contraceptive methods, based on abstruse metaphysical arguments, came to seem less and less cogent. Furthermore, the starry-eyed praise of sexual happiness—in marriage, naturally—by the new theologians meant that young Catholics were disinclined to wait patiently for marriage before enjoying it, as the characters in *How Far Can You Go?* had done. In this novel Lodge opens up an entirely new subject, and describes, with sombre wit and painfully sharp observation, a subculture on the point of meltdown.

The last chapter of the novel contains the script of a television programme, presenting a Paschal Festival put on at Easter 1975 by Catholics for an Open Church, a reformist group which includes the characters of the novel who are still practising believers. At intervals in the programme, a 'voice over' comments on the symbolic and liturgical action and its implications, and Lodge has associated this narratorial voice with his own view of the issues raised. It announces 'the fading away of the traditional Catholic metaphysic—that marvellously complex and ingenious synthesis of theology and cosmology and casuistry, which situated individual souls on a kind of spiritual Snakes and Ladders board, motivated them with equal doses of hope and fear, and promised them, if they persevered in the game, an eternal reward' (*HFCYG* 239). Within another generation or two, the speaker believes, 'it will have disappeared, superseded by something less vivid but more tolerant. Christian unity is now a feasible objective for the first time since the Reformation'. He goes on to propose a future for religion in terms which Lodge has developed elsewhere: belief involves necessary but provisional narratives with which we try to make sense of existence, and which have analogies with literary narratives:

> Just as when reading a novel, or writing one for that matter, we maintain a double consciousness of the characters as both, as it were, real and fictitious, free

and determined, and know that however absorbing and convincing we may find it, it is not the only story we shall want to read (or, as the case may be, write) but part of an endless sequence of stories by which man has sought and will always seek to make sense of life. And death.

> (*HFCYG* 240)

But this speculation is not quite the end of the story. The author moves on a few more pages, and years, and in the final paragraph announces the election in 1978 of a new pope, a Pole and the first non-Italian for 400 years, adding 'all bets are void, the future is uncertain'. It was a prudent intervention, for John Paul II proved to be a pontiff of charismatic, conservative and authoritarian temperament, with little sympathy for modernizing liberal Catholics; he made great efforts to deflect if not reverse the thrust of Vatican II, and to undo many of the changes that stemmed from it. Right-wing and traditionalist groups in the Church revived, and the 'traditional Catholic metaphysic' did not fade away in the manner predicted in *How Far Can You Go?* The divisions between liberals and conservatives remained in place, and argument continued. The ban on contraception was reaffirmed, but was widely disregarded.

In 1991 Lodge returned to the Catholic questions in *Paradise News.* It had a more mixed reception than his last few novels, and it is true that it is milder and gentler, without the inventiveness and displays of wit readers had come to expect. It has a retrospective quality, as he takes the opportunity, after more than thirty years of writing, to revisit the places and themes of his earlier work. The novel is partly set in Rummidge, not in its university but in a rather run-down theological college; one chapter takes us to Brickley, the South London suburb which provided the setting for *The Picturegoers*; and most of the action occurs in Hawaii, where Persse McGarrigle had briefly touched down in *Small World.* Lodge's last 'Catholic' novel raised and tried to answer the question, 'How far can you go?' In *Paradise News* the response is, 'Further still'. In the earlier novel, Father Austin Brierley has passed through many vicissitudes after his conventional beginning, has left the priesthood and married, but remains 'a kind of Catholic'. Bernard Walsh, the central figure of *Paradise News,* has gone further, for he has abandoned not only the priesthood but Catholic belief itself. He is the son of a London Irish family in Brickley, which is reminiscent of the Mallorys, but is shown in a harsher light. At the end of *The Picturegoers* Mark Underwood goes off to become a priest, to the general approbation of the Catholic characters, and, one imagines, the author. One of the Mallory sons, James, is already a priest, and another, Patrick, is expected to become one, though it is not clear how far he shares this expectation. Bernard, like the Mallorys a parishioner of Our Lady of Perpetual Succour, Brickley, enters the priesthood, not out of deep dedication and spiritual zeal, but because his family hope he will become a priest, and he is drawn to the privileges and status of the priestly life and scared of the demands of the larger world. The Mallory family had been depicted as admirable people, but the Walsh family is permeated by self-deception and bad faith. Bernard suggests what might have happened to James or Patrick in the uncertain future that followed Vatican II.

He serves as a priest to the best of his abilities, and becomes a lecturer in theology at a seminary. But his faith, never robust, is steadily dwindling, and Lodge effectively traces the intellectual and psychological process of the decline. The final break is prompted by sex, when Bernard, a 40-year-old celibate and virgin, falls, or is led, into an affair with a woman whom he is supposedly instructing in Catholicism. It ends disastrously for both of them. After he has left the priesthood, Bernard scrapes a modest living as an unbelieving part-time lecturer in theology at a college in Rummidge. Now in his mid-40s, he is a lonely and depressed figure, with few friends, and more or less alienated from his family, who have found it difficult to forgive his abandonment of the priesthood.

The plot transports Bernard from Rummidge to Hawaii. His Aunt Ursula had long ago moved to the United States, like Kate in *Out of the Shelter,* and has retired to Hawaii. She telephones Bernard, whom she has not seen for many years, to tell him that she is suffering from inoperable cancer and may not live much longer. Before she dies she wants to meet again and make her peace with her brother Jack, Bernard's father, from whom she has long been estranged. She urges Bernard to bring Jack to Hawaii, and will pay their fares. Bernard is more than ready to make the trip, but his father, a cantankerous Irish widower who lives alone in Brickley, needs a great deal of persuasion. Eventually he agrees, spurred by the hope of getting something in his sister's will. Bernard finds that a package holiday in Hawaii is much cheaper than two ordinary return air tickets, so they make the long flight as tourists. Lodge moves easily into a comic mode in his description of their fellow travellers—who include Brian Everthorpe, previously encountered in *Nice Work*—and in satirical reflections on the phenomenon of global tourism; he carefully registers the exotic appearances and *mores* of Hawaii, an American state which is in every sense halfway to the Far East. But the comic dimension of the novel is a little perfunctory. The real interest is in the story of Bernard and what happens to him in Hawaii, a gentle, painful and moving story.

Bernard does what he can to make his aunt more comfortable, and her situation makes him think steadily about death. The prayers and liturgy which he used to conduct as a priest are full of references to the world to come, where those who have lived a good life on earth can expect an eternity of happiness with God. According to the Catechism, the Christian is to love and serve God in his life, and be happy with him for ever in the next (Bernard notes sardonically that there is nothing about happiness in *this* life). Hope in heaven is still an essential part of the faith of most Christians, especially those who have found little reward in their earthly existence. But the advanced theologians whom Bernard studies and teaches are silent about an afterlife. Hell quietly disappeared for the liberal Catholics in *How Far Can You Go?,* and it seems that heaven may have gone the same way. If so, a traditional hope for humanity has been snatched away. Ordinary believers, though, may be unaware and unaffected by this shift, since theologians write not for them but for each other; there is an analogy, which Lodge has pursued elsewhere, with the way in which academic literary criticism and theory are now incomprehensible to unprofessional readers of literature.

Bernard dwells on these questions in the intervals of looking after his aunt, and his father, who is injured in a traffic accident on their first day in Hawaii. The woman driving the car which runs into Jack is very concerned about him, though entirely blameless (Jack, not used to traffic coming from the right, was looking the wrong way). She is Yolande, an attractive woman of 40, who came to Hawaii from the continental USA some years before because of her husband's academic job; now they have split up and she is seeking a divorce. After some hesitation on his part, Bernard and Yolande embark on an affair, which is both passionate and tender. He finds unfamiliar happiness and a tentative hope for the future, since their love is shared and the relationship may continue. Yolande is keen to leave Hawaii, having had more than enough of the island paradise and its supposedly perfect climate, and is intrigued by the idea of the English Midlands, despite the weather. It is a thoroughly romantic episode, but Lodge presents it very persuasively.

When he arrives at the airport in Hawaii Bernard picks up a tourist brochure called *Paradise News,* and he soon discovers that practically everything in the islands connects itself to Paradise: 'Paradise Finance Inc., Paradise Sportswear, Paradise Supply Inc., Paradise Beauty and Barber Suppliers, Paradise Beverages, Paradise Puppets, Paradise Snorkel Adventures, Paradise Tinting, Paradise Cleaning and Maintenance Service, Paradise Parking'. The insistent and ultimately meaningless repetition of the word is counterpointed with Bernard's mingled doubts and hopes about the spiritual paradise of Christian tradition. He finds romance in Hawaii, but he is also in a Romance, of the kind that Lodge is very interested in. The image of Hawaii as an earthly paradise is a commercialized vulgarity, but he attempts to redeem the term and revive its ancient associations; in the novel, Hawaii has affinities with the magic island of *The Tempest*, which is quoted more than once, and with the Fortunate Isles of European mythology.

Back in Rummidge, Bernard receives a letter from Yolande, saying that she may marry him in time, and meanwhile wants to come to England to spend Christmas with him. A colleague asks Bernard if he has had good news, and he replies, in the final words of the novel, 'Very good news'. It is indeed, for Bernard at that point in his life; but the phrase 'good news' also referred to the Gospel and the Christian hope for the future. Bernard's experiences in Hawaii may not have restored his faith, but they have given him hope, which is a theological virtue as well as a human quality. The tentatively happy ending of *Paradise News* emphasises its affinities with the Romance mode rather than with the despairing realism of much modern fiction. Lodge's use of the semi-magic plot devices of the Victorian novel is continued from *Nice Work*; there an unexpected legacy arrives from Australia, and in *Paradise News* an overlooked share certificate among Ursula's modest assets proves to have become immensely valuable, enabling her to spend her final weeks in dignity and comfort; and, after her death, to benefit Bernard's sister, who is coping with a brain-damaged child. (He refuses any share in the money.)

In *How Far Can You Go?* and *Paradise News* Lodge considers Catholicism in England during the long aftermath of the Vatican Council. Both novels show his keen if sceptical interest in religious questions, and his reading in modern theology. His personal attitude is not altogether apparent, though it is evident that he has come a long way from the kind of traditional Catholicism which underlay *The Picturegoers*; he has said of *How Far Can You Go?*: 'it brought me in a way to the edges of belief, I would say, writing that novel. I would like to think that as a result I have in some ways a more honest and profound but also a more provisional and metaphorical religious belief now than I had before . . .' (*Walsh,* 5). In 1992, Lodge attempted to define his position further. Graham Greene, one of his early models, described himself, after he had moved on from the tormented orthodoxy of his Catholic novels, as a 'Catholic agnostic'; Lodge prefers to reverse the term and call himself an 'agnostic Catholic'. He remains a practising member of the Church, though he is agnostic about the ultimate reality behind the symbolic and metaphorical languages of liturgy and scripture. Although he has abandoned much of what he has called the 'Catholic metaphysic', he insists that religious language is meaningful, as the perennial symbolic and speculative mode in which we articulate the contradictions and anxieties and hopes which are central to the human condition. Lodge acknowledges that by traditional standards, including those that he professed as a young man, he is probably a heretic; but he believes that many theologians, including Catholic ones, would now hold similar views. His position has affinities with that of the Catholic Modernists of the early twentieth century; and, less certainly, with recent radical Protestant theology. That approach, though, regards divinity as entirely immanent, whereas Lodge finds the idea of transcendence necessary to make sense of existence. Responding to the theme explored in *Paradise News,* he thinks that without some idea of life beyond death there is no point in religion, though the problem is to find an adequate language for that idea (Bergonzi 2, 71-2).

It is for theological experts to decide how far Lodge has in fact gone in moving away from the Catholic mind-set. There is, however, one important respect in which his fiction continues to reflect it, though perhaps for temperamental as much as doctrinal reasons. This has been described by Peter Widdowson:

> Lodge's Catholicism—explored historically in *How Far Can You Go?*—underpins his acceptance of bourgeois marriage as the domain in which people, whatever their frustrations and aspirations need finally to secure themselves: the family is the still point in a world turning ever faster, and the wife (usually) the one woman who has to stand in for . . . all the other women theoretically available in the world of sexual permissiveness. In Lodge's novels, there is always a crucial return (or *nostos*) for the main characters from the wide-open spaces, the fleshpots, the global campus, to a marriage which has to be remade.
>
> (Widdowson, 22)

Widdowson's phrase 'bourgeois marriage' indicates his own ideological agenda, but his point is valid. The marriage of Philip and Hilary Swallow has dwindled into a rather empty relationship; but they come together after the infidelities in *Changing Places,* and again in *Small World* after Philip's affair with Joy, an attractive widow with whom he had spent a night some years before, and, unknown to him, conceived a child. The revived relationship between Philip and Joy has a lot going for it, and is described in very lyrical language. Indeed, Philip wishes to marry Joy, and is on the point of asking Hilary for a divorce when she disconcerts him by telling him that she has got a job as a marriage counsellor, and he cannot bring himself to say anything. The affair comes to an end when Philip is attending a conference in Israel, with Joy in tow. He falls ill with what is at first wrongly diagnosed as Legionnaires' Disease. Panic-stricken, he asks Joy to phone Hilary, who flies out to take him home, like a mother rescuing a naughty boy in trouble. Later, Philip says of himself, 'Basically I failed in the role of romantic hero. I thought I wasn't too old for it, but I was' (*SW* [*Small World*] 336). Meanwhile, Joy is to marry someone else. There is a hint of authorial intervention about this episode, a suggestion of a moral story in favour of the indissolubility of marriage. The Swallow marriage, according to hints in *Nice Work,* does not get any happier, but it endures after a fashion. Hilary, in her new professional role, restores the broken marriage of Swallow's former colleague, Dempsey. Admittedly, the end of *Small World* is, as I have remarked, something of a Shakespearean tableau, where broken marriages are restored and new ones made.

Already, though, in the generally graver and more realistic *How Far Can You Go?* we have seen a similar pattern. Dennis has a brief headlong affair with a much younger woman, Lynn, who thinks she is in love with him; he leaves his family and moves in with her, but after a few weeks of discomfort and sexual exhaustion he goes back to them. Eventually, she marries the ex-priest, Austin Brierley. Again, in *Nice Work,* Vic Wilcox, after his infatuation with Robyn, settles back into what has been established as a pretty unsatisfactory marriage. It is true that he would never have got anywhere with Robyn, but he need not have gone back to the dim and lymphatic Marjorie, though it is suggested that her character might improve once she has a part-time job as a secretary. The underlying assumption seems to be, adapting a remark by Samuel Johnson, that though marriage has many pains, infidelity brings no pleasure.

In his latest novel, *Therapy,* Lodge gives a significant twist to this belief. The main character, Tubby Passmore, a successful television scriptwriter, has been married, happily as he thinks, for thirty years, and he and his wife have been faithful to each other all that time (though he has a girlfriend with whom his relations are quasi-platonic and strictly non-penetrative). He takes great satisfaction at the success of his marriage, when others all around are coming apart, so he is shattered when his wife tells him that she is leaving him; not for someone else, but because she cannot stand him any more. The apparent success of his marriage was based, he discovers (as do the readers), on solipsistic complacency. In his late 50s he starts making desperate and comically unsuccessful efforts to catch up on the sexual opportunities he has long denied

himself. In time he rediscovers Maureen, his first love from forty years before; she is the same age as Tubby, long married, has suffered from cancer and lost a son, and no longer has sex with her husband. Tubby falls in love with her again and begs her to marry him after they have divorced their spouses, but she is a Catholic, as she was when Tubby first knew her—when they meet up again she is making a pilgrimage to the shrine of St James at Santiago in Spain—and so is her husband. Their marriage may be sexless, she tells Tubby, but it is not loveless, and as a Catholic she will not consider divorce. Nevertheless, her conscience is accommodating enough to let her sleep with Tubby from time to time. He and Maureen and her husband, we are told on the last page, are all very great friends; it reads like another version of the fairy-tale ending.

Lodge's treatment of traditional Catholic practices is more sympathetic than in *How Far Can You Go?* or *Paradise News,* particularly in the presentation of Maureen's devotion to St James of Compostella; she knows that there is far more myth than history in his cult, but she still finds spiritual value in it. Notwithstanding his generally sceptical state of mind, Lodge responds warmly to ritual and ceremony, as ways of bringing people together for a higher end, transcending their individuality for a time. This is evident in his account of the devotions in the great Cathedral of Santiago at the end of the pilgrimage; earlier instances include the Paschal Festival in *How Far Can You Go?,* and the Hawaiian Folk Mass in *Paradise News,* which is celebrated on the beach for Ursula after her death, and which impresses the unbelieving Yolande.

Widdowson claims that Lodge's emphasis on marriage and stability, even a dull stability, 'runs counter to the openness and freedom of the novels' "Romance" rhetoric'. This is a fair comment, and the tension between romance and realism does give Lodge's more recent fiction its particular flavour. Widdowson suggests that he unfairly favours 'realism', such as carrying on with a humdrum marriage, against 'romance', which is getting a divorce and making a fresh start. But the more common mode of Romance in the novels is not the Ariostan, which is open-ended, indeed, never-ending, and involves constant fresh adventures. There is also the Shakespearean, which ends firmly, with marriages and ceremony. It first prompted Lodge's interest in Romance when, as an undergraduate, he made a special study of the late plays, with their patterns of reconciliation and transcendence. It is worth noting, too, that he wanted to end his television adaptation of Dickens's *Martin Chuzzlewit* with multiple marriages but was overruled by the director. (See Lodge's article, 'Three Weddings and a Big Row', *Independent,* 13 December 1994, which prints his intended version of the conclusion of the script.)

Unlike many modern novelists who like to humiliate and torment their characters, Lodge treats his creations with respect and affection, even at the risk of being sentimental. He is much concerned with what he calls 'providential plotting', and the happy endings of his recent novels, so against the grain of the age, emphasize the centrality of hope as a virtue, which was made explicit in **Paradise News.** Traditionally, religious literature implied a work with a happy ending, a *commedia*. Despite his agnosticism about doctrinal definitions, it makes sense to regard Lodge as a kind of religious writer.

Select Bibliography

[Editor's Note: See previous essay for Select Bibliography.]

Julian Evans (essay date 16 December 2002)

SOURCE: Evans, Julian. "Notes towards a Supreme Fiction." *New Statesman* 131, no. 4618 (16 December 2002): 112-14.

[*In the following essay, Evans compares the assertions about human consciousness that Lodge makes in* Consciousness and the Novel—*a book of essays—with observations Lodge makes on the subject within his novels.*]

If Karl Marx and Adam Smith were right to believe that science is not a pure enterprise but the reflection of a society's values and outlook, what does its current popularity tell us about society? Not much we didn't know already: that we live in a materialistic culture, that we place our trust in facts and objects rather than ideas and people, that we fear rather than include the irrational in our lives, that we think there must be an explanation for everything. But what if we were to discover that our faith in science was based on an illusion, of the kind that Sigmund Freud describes, that "commend themselves to us because they save us pain and allow us to enjoy pleasure instead"?

What might the illusion be? One answer comes from an unexpected quarter, in the form of two recently published collections of literary essays. In David Lodge's **Consciousness and the Novel,** writing in the intelligent and intelligible, civilised vein that is his hallmark, Lodge discusses the contrasting attempts of novelists and, more recently, scientists to explain human consciousness. Among cognitive and neuroscientists, consciousness was the hot subject—at least in publishing terms—for most of the Nineties. The scientific drift is summed up by Francis Crick in his book *The Astonishing Hypothesis* (1994): "'You', your joys and your sorrows, your memories and your ambitions, your sense of personal identity and free will, are in fact no more than the behaviour of a vast assembly of nerve cells and their associated molecules."

Lodge's interest in the subject was roused when it struck him that this hypothesis had thrown down a "strong challenge to the humanist or Enlightenment idea of man on which the presentation of character in the novel is based". As he says, to cognitive materialists such as Steven Pinker and V S Ramachandran, the human mind is no more than a machine, its sense of itself a mere epiphenomenon caused by an excess of brainpower over and above our evolutionary needs. No self, no soul. Some more recent work has stressed the fundamentally narrative nature of the brain's activity, but even those scientists who agree that we project and protect ourselves by telling stories about who we are regard those stories, and those selves, as ultimate illusions. Lodge's counter-case is strong. Novelists, he says, along with lyric poets, provide a bridge between first-person (subjective) and third-person (scientific) views or narrations of the world. In conveying individual, open-ended experience in all its inconclusiveness, creative writers model the world more fully and helpfully for the consciousness that apprehends it. Drawing on the achievements of Marvell, Henry James, Virginia Woolf, Evelyn Waugh and various others, he edges the hard materialist fringe out of the picture. "If the self is a fiction," he writes, "it may perhaps be the supreme fiction, the greatest achievement of human consciousness, the one that makes us human." (Or as the French poet Paul Valery put it, more wryly, "'*L'Homme pense; donc je suis,' dit l'Univers.*")

Yet, for all Lodge's championing of the novelists' corner, one senses a sympathy with the scientists. Informative and well-argued as his essay is, it has the tone of detached exposition with which we are very familiar from his fiction. Indeed, Lodge did fictionalise what he had learned about the consciousness debate in his most recent novel, **Thinks . . . ,** which I enjoyed as I usually enjoy his novels: with a devil on my shoulder, a devil of impatience hurling silent taunts, urging him or his characters to lose control. Lodge is not known for including a deep emotional heart in his fiction. Cleverness, civilised satire, intelligent gags, yes; passion, no. Likewise his essays: in his preface to **Consciousness and the Novel,** he quotes some words of Gertrude Stein's, to stand as an epigraph for all his literary criticism: "What does literature do and how does it do it. And what does English literature do and how does it do it. And what ways does it use to do what it does." Well, the old *in-accrochable* certainly knew how to repeat herself, but it did not disguise her bafflingly mechanistic view of writing—a view that, however distantly, one feels Lodge shares when he writes of his desire to construct "a poetics of fiction" which is a "systematic and comprehensive description of the [ways] through which novels communicate their meanings".

Perhaps Lodge's objectivity, his substitution of explanation for appreciation, system for passion, are a case of "we grow up among theories and illusions common to our class, our race, our time", as Cyril Connolly wrote in 1938, halfway through *Enemies of Promise*. "We absorb them unawares and their effect is incalculable." It was Connolly who also wrote that "Anxiety is my true condition", who was afraid of suicide and prone to morning tears. A "lazy, irresolute person, overvain and overmodest", he would have been no match for Lodge in the professorial stakes. If Lodge is, like us, a materialist, Connolly, to complicate matters, was one, too. He was excessively material in his longings for manor house in France and helicopter and book-lined belvedere. It was the ultimate reason he failed as a novelist: the world that a writer creates was not available to him, because he was happy with the one that already existed, if only he were rich enough to have it.

But there's a crucial contrast to be drawn between his writing and Lodge's. The absence of emotion that runs through Lodge's essays is interrupted only once, when he agrees in the piece entitled **"Lives in Letters: Kingsley and Martin Amis"** that he felt the same about seeing his father on his deathbed as the younger Amis did; whereas Connolly's two volumes (*Selected Works*) are crammed with his moaning and yearning, with a restless staring into the world and a gloomy relish at nearly all he sees. Connolly's work, in fact, is absolutely defined by that conjunction with his life, the two spinning out in a confessional honesty that is severe and often painful, as whenever he attacks the journalism from which he failed to escape ("The reviewing of novels is the white man's grave of journalism; it corresponds to building bridges in some impossible tropical climate"). The same quality is often simply very funny (in his parodies), and equally often funny and painful (see the devastating analysis of literary corruption in the "Blue Bugloss" section of *Enemies of Promise*).

This contrast between two writers working in the same sub-field of letters—the literary essay—can be read as simply a restatement of the old polarity between head and heart, gown and town, but I believe it goes deeper. Part of Connolly's achievement, for me, is to make me nostalgic for the 20th century, for its aspirations and its geniuses, its very particular messes and its localness. (His diary of 1929 made me remember perfectly Paris in the late Seventies after I graduated, a city of cosy darkness and filth in the outer arrondissements. One cannot find this city now in Chirac's Paris.)

Connolly's brilliant analysis of styles, Mandarin *v* Vernacular, his long and generous pamphlet *The Modern Movement,* his analysis of English poetry from "Paradise Lost" to "The Waste Land", and practically every one of his reviews, communicate a literary partisanship whose contagiousness is rarely forgotten by anyone who reads him. Though Lodge covers much of the same 20th-century ground, I feel little of the same excitement.

No, the contrast is between the rich, roiling, polyglot, flawed (idealist, elitist) current of mid-century, pro-European heterodoxy and the literal, materialist culture in which we at present thrive. The same closed attitudes abounded in Connolly's time. The epicentre of literary materialism was Bloomsbury, its high priestess Virginia Woolf; Connolly despised Bloomsbury's "fastness of private virtue and personal relations", preferring the leafy, open sanctuary of Chelsea in which "leisure, however ill-earned, has seldom been more agreeably and intelligently made use of". Lodge, on this point, is Woolf's defender, mentioning twice her "wonderful diaries" (which is a singular judgement, given that I've never found a single joke in the five volumes and that they make plain her talent for disdain and exclusion).

Let us play Fantasy Culture for a moment. What is the role of the literary essayist today? To believe, perhaps, that the world is most intelligible when seen through the metaphor of literature; to resist cultural orthodoxy; to excite the reader (in particular, his or her talent for resistance). And why is any of this currently important? Because materialism abhors a metaphor. It shrinks everything. Its cultural atmosphere is one of ever more global and commercial yardsticks, and therefore restrictions, which inhibit the free play of the spirit and our vision of the future.

Interestingly, in an essay entitled "Writers and Society", Connolly viewed the Second World War in exactly the same light. "War . . . means less time, less tolerance, less imagination, less curiosity, less play." His answer was to write a 30-page nostrum for the future in *Horizon,* consigning Joyce and Proust temporarily to the scrap heap for their leisurely wastefulness, giving dictatorial powers to a Word Controller to protect a wartime vocabulary exhausted by journalism, and calling for a renaissance, a new place for art "in our conception of the meaning of life". Because, for all his moaning and longing, Connolly was a passionate believer. By comparison, despite all his explanatory virtues, Lodge is a sort of rhetorical shopkeeper, trading his words. For readers, there is a world of difference between the two. John Banville wrote recently how he used to read Connolly's weekly reviews in the *Sunday Times* and could "still vividly recall particular pieces, and the excitement with which I read them". I remember the same feeling on reading the first page of *The Unquiet Grave*, with its austere declaration that "the true function of a writer is to produce a masterpiece" and that "no other task is of any consequence". Excitement is Connolly's legacy. A literal world surrounds us, and science overtakes us (of whose excitement, as with other modern entertainments, we partake only as consumers). But passion is not quite dead—if only to judge by the achievement of Picador's former publisher Peter Straus, in getting these sumptuous volumes of Connolly back into print. Now we could use a few more essays on writers and society, even in a world alternately preoccupied by the enjoyment of its pleasure and tantalised by the threat of another war.

George Walden (essay date 6 September 2004)

SOURCE: Walden, George. "The Truth about Henry." *New Statesman* 133, no. 4704 (6 September 2004): 48-50.

[*In the following essay, Walden assesses Lodge's unconventional biography of Henry James,* Author, Author.]

Genre-bending seems back in fashion, in the shape of biography more or less artfully bent into novel form—John Updike on Jackson Pollock in *Seek My Face,* William Boyd conjuring up every big name from the first half of the 20th century in his *Any Human Heart,* and now David Lodge fictionalising Henry James. Fictionalising James: the very words illustrate the awesomeness of the endeavour, not least since Colm Toíbín has also recently attempted the same, in *The Master.* What chance has Lodge, a lightish novelist albeit a serious scholar and critic, of successfully evoking an author of legendary avoirdupois whose speciality it was to create an atmosphere of misty indeterminacy by slicing living sentiments ever finer and stringing them, still quivering, into endless sentences? Compared to James's, Lodge's fictional style, at its most utilitarian, can seem like boiled cabbage cut up into strips. The simple solution, naturally, would be to take this overblown literary antique apart, aerating his opaque persona with "irreverent" bubbles of jokiness, and have fun with poor Henry's sexual problems.

Which is exactly what Lodge, who probably reveres James the literary critic too much to give him the conventional treatment, declines to do. Any temptation

to guy an old master few people read but whom everyone knows about—long-winded closet queen, right?—has been manfully resisted, in favour of a valiant stab at the truth about James. There is little levity, even when James takes up bicycle-riding, and mercifully few attempts to caricature his hero's literary manner, or force the staid old body, by anachronistic language or psychology, to lighten up. Boldly—controversially, almost—Lodge has refused to populate James's sensual wilderness with a Wildean telegraph boy or two, or retrospectively insert lubricious dreams of ephebes into his over-cerebral, balding head. Sexually, he is presented as irredeemably low-voltage—Lodge claims he never did anything with or to anyone—though with a weakness for young male friendships, and as suffering from occasional mildly concupiscent impulses which, swiftly sublimated, did not drive him to distraction in the way we sexually superior moderns insist they must.

His hero's blunted emotional life is depicted convincingly, by reference to the record, but his real crisis is one of creativity. Yet was a novel the best vehicle to convey these not especially dramatic facts? Here one senses Lodge the academic colliding with Lodge the novelist, an ambivalence that shows itself in textual tergiversation as the book alternates, sometimes violently, between fictional and conventional biographical mode.

So why not a straightforward biography in the first place? Clearly, Lodge has done his research. Equally clearly, Leon Edel (*Henry James: A Life*) got there first, though that was 30 years ago and Lodge has an interesting personal take on James. Perhaps the reasons he has disguised biography as fiction are similar to those that drove James to do his own genre-bending when, after people gave up trying to get to the end of his novels, he tried writing them more succinctly, as rather literary plays. A biography of James, unless it was unconscionably sexed up, would have stood as much chance of competing with the cornucopia of revelations about Oscar Wilde as James's doomed drama *Guy Domville* had of outselling *The Importance of Being Earnest.*

Lodge's dilemma about form is important, given that he has placed the conflict between the tragic and more marketable muses at the heart of his novel. "Something had happened in the culture of the English-speaking world," he has James reflect. "The spread and thinning of literacy, the levelling effects of democracy . . . the distortion of values by journalism and advertising, which made it impossible for a practitioner in the art of fiction to achieve both excellence and popularity

. . ." Either Lodge is lightly mocking James, implying "it was ever thus", or—more likely, given the tone of the book—he sympathises.

If you read **Author, Author** this way, the space devoted to James's close friendship with the *Punch* illustrator (and devoted family man) George du Maurier makes better sense. For it was the rightly unassuming du Maurier who, at the very moment James's reputation was faltering, published *Trilby,* a melodramatic novel that became a colossal success, complete with stage adaptation and, in America, associated merchandise. *Trilby* was a winning confection of devilishness (antihero: Svengali, pronounced with a long "a"), sentimentalism and sauciness (girl poses for Parisian artist in the altogether, in *vie de Bohème* mode, but we forgive her).

Meanwhile, the opening night of *Guy Domville* is taking place, simultaneously with Wilde's *An Ideal Husband.* This, the book's centrepiece, is nicely done. Unable to bear the tension of attending his own, James goes to Wilde's play, where the sight of the audience gurgling with pleasure at the mechanical inversions of Wilde's sometimes facile wit makes him feel worse.

The admiration/envy/sexual apprehension James feels towards Wilde is well evoked, and again it is bold of Lodge, in our worshipful times, to allow it to be suggested that there might be something a trifle tinselly about Oscar. Lodge could have pointed up the astuteness of James's critique of the source of Wilde's appeal to English audiences. Among the direct quotations he uses, Lodge might have included the following from a letter James wrote in 1892 after seeing *Lady Windermere's Fan*:

> There is so much drollery—that is, "cheeky" paradoxical wit of dialogue, and the pit and gallery are so pleased at finding themselves clever enough to "catch on" to four or five of the ingenious—too ingenious—*mots* in the dozen, that it makes them feel quite *décadent* and *raffiné,* and they enjoy the sensation as a change from the stodgy.

(Add "stalls" to pit and gallery, apply it to "cheeky" art as well as to Wilde, and think how little has changed.) Alas, poor Henry, with his 200,000-word *Princess Casamassima* flopping, was coming to be classed among the stodgy. Lodge is informative about just how little he was beginning to sell, and how low were his advances: £70, at one point, for a new book.

The tale is well enough told, but faction is rarely satisfying, on or off screen, and the seams are visible, as straightforward biographical passages are stapled to fictional sections, made more perilous to the novelist by the resonance of the names. At James's opening night Arnold Bennett, G B Shaw, Ellen Terry and H G Wells are in the audience, which wouldn't matter, except when they are given lines such as:

> "What's this you said your name was?"
>
> "Herbert Wells. I write as 'H G' Wells."
>
> "Ah yes . . . Interested in science, aren't you?"

Elsewhere we have Guy de Maupassant shocking James by trying to pick up a woman in a restaurant. "I want a woman. Not an emancipated one, just an ordinary one, as long as she has a pretty face and a nice arse." Cut to James's appalled expression. Maybe the Frenchman said it, maybe this is Lodge in clunky, cinema mode. The demotic imperative obliges him to compensate for all this literary toffery with painfully stylised below-stairs chat between ever so warm-hearted servants. Even as a joke, it is impermissible to write dialogue such as the following, when one of them has a stab at reading James's books:

> "Couldn't make head nor tail of it."
>
> "Well, they weren't written for the likes of us."

Such passages do not confer life and dignity on humble folk; they reduce them to social marionettes. Even in the generally sensitive lines attributed to James there are occasional lapses. On the subject of smoking, Lodge has him saying: "I resort to the occasional gasper myself." On the other hand, the flatly factual descriptions of late-Victorian London and of Rye, where James bought a house, bear the dampening imprint of sedulous research. Does Lodge manage overall to "harmonise fact with fact by the plastic solvent of an idea", as the master once wrote? Writing a work of fiction about a genius of human consciousness was always going to be a tall order. What emerges is a goodish, lightly dramatised biography, worth reading for instruction and understanding, and for Lodge's empathy with James. As a novel, however, it doesn't work, and had it not been a novel at all it might have been a better biography.

Anita Brookner (review date 11 September 2004)

SOURCE: Brookner, Anita. "Rising Far above Failure." *Spectator* 296, no. 9188 (11 September 2004): 45.

[*Below, Brookner presents a positive review of* Author, Author, *Lodge's fictionalized biography of Henry James.*]

Henry James might be gratified by the attention he is currently receiving [including David Lodge's **Author, Author**], but the irony would not be lost on him. It was the absence of success rather than the condemnation of failure that preoccupied him, for this most hermetic of men hankered after vociferous acclaim, comparing himself unfavourably with more astute and marketable novelists like his friends Edith Wharton and Constance Fenimore Woolson, and most notably with George Du Maurier, whose *Trilby,* based on an idea which James and Du Maurier had discussed between them, was a smash hit in 1894.

James, whose every novel and story hovers over some kind of immanence, as if life were reserving surprises which are sensed though rarely directly addressed, felt betrayed by some cosmic intelligence whose business it was to regulate matters of fame and obscurity, and, more importantly, of fame and mere popularity. Rarely rewarded, even in financial terms, he sustained his moral vision, together with his scruples, his fastidiousness and the courtesy which defines him as a writer, throughout his life. The famous advice he offers in *The Ambassadors* was perhaps for others, not for himself. 'Live all you can, it's a mistake not to,' says the older man to the younger. Yet this is perhaps balanced by the tragic summary contained in the story entitled 'The Middle Years': 'We work in the dark—we do what we can—we give what we have. Our doubt is our passion and our passion is our task. The rest is the madness of art.'

There are moral chasms in his novels of which his characters can never remain unaware. Those who do so tend to end up like poor Daisy Miller, struck down by malaria after a midnight stroll with an unsuitable companion. His readers admired him but deemed him less accessible than writers for whom fiction was less a painful pursuit than a lucrative hobby, leaving him alone to draw comparisons between himself and rather too many others. The stoicism which this position entailed conferred a moral excellence of its own, yet as David Lodge shows in this remarkable novel [*Author, Author*], there was a price to pay. It was in James's last days that the beast in the jungle revealed itself. His mind wandering and thus freed from censorship, he believed himself to be Napoleon, and issued instructions for the refurbishment of the Louvre and the Tuileries. There is no need to emphasise the contrast between this illusion and the habitual sweetness and modesty he had displayed throughout his life. It is a device that he himself would have scorned to employ.

It was a life he had designed for himself, and indeed he had obeyed his own advice to live all he could. Blessed with good friends and adequate income from family money (for he earned next to nothing from his books), comfortably housed and waited on, and ac-

customed to agreeable and rewarding foreign travel, he maintained the outward appearance of success. A prodigious walker—almost as prodigious as Dickens—he would, on Sundays, walk from Kensington to Hampstead to visit Du Maurier, walk with him round Hampstead Heath, repair to the Du Mauriers for a meal, and then walk back to Kensington. One hundred and seven dinners are recorded in a single season. That he remained celibate is an obvious difficulty for the modern reader, though this may have been no more than personal choice, or, alternatively, a consequence of the madness of art. If he could hardly imagine the physical act, he appreciated, within limits, the companionship of women and the presence of young men. We draw our own conclusions from these matters. What we cannot do—and what David Lodge makes clear—is internalise the dreadful moment of self-exposure when his play, *Guy Domville,* was a resounding failure and he himself, appearing to take a bow, was loudly booed. And he had anticipated a moment of glory, as he had enjoyed when an earlier play, *The American,* staged in Southport, was deemed a success, and he himself had taken not one but three curtain calls, the reward for a lifetime of good behaviour.

This was not a question of vanity. It was more than that: the validation he had sought and had not received, or had not received in full measure. It may be argued that the late great novels are the consequence of this humiliation, but in fact his dealings with the theatre, which were substantial, had been entirely frustrating. Henceforth he would engage with subjects of such moral refinement that no theatre audience would be able to pierce their mystery, and would therefore be confined to their rightful place, within the covers of a novel.

Prior to the *Guy Domville* episode, his feelings had already been disturbed by the suicide of a friend and occasional companion, Constance Fenimore Woolson, and the letter she had left, or rather the outline of a story, in which she described the principal male character as well set up but with no heart. It was Flaubert and Louise Colet all over again, although Colet was a coarser character whose activities continued more or less undiminished. But the implication was damning. He had enjoyed Fenimore's devotion to him, but had been careful to sidestep her suggestions that they collaborate on a play. His own plays were enough for him. *Guy Domville,* to which David Lodge devotes a brilliant chapter, opened when Oscar Wilde's *An Ideal Husband* was playing to a delighted audience in another theatre. The contrast could not have been more conclusive. And there was no doubt of James's public disgrace. He had been lured to the front of the stage by a friend's cries of 'Author! Author!' Standing there, bewildered by the storm of catcalls, he could be in no doubt that this was the worst moment of his life.

Yet he recovered, almost surprisingly, helped by those ever devoted friends, by excursions to coastal resorts and, most of all, by the acquisition of Lamb House, where, between 1902 and 1904 he wrote his undoubted masterpieces, *The Ambassadors, The Wings of the Dove* and *The Golden Bowl.* David Lodge does not expend his considerable literary judgment on these late novels. This is both tactful and disappointing, for an elucidation of *The Golden Bowl,* in which it is possible to detect a whisper of the madness of art, would be welcome. Instead he fashions his novel, which is not only a novel but also a well-researched chronicle, around the twin episodes of the *Guy Domville* fiasco and the runaway success of *Trilby,* stepping out of the shadows at the end to declare his fealty to the Master, assuring him of his fame, his excellence, his sheer superiority over other writers. This was to some extent assured—in real life—by the award of the Order of Merit when Henry James was dying in his last home, 21 Carlyle Mansions. There is no blue plaque on the facade of this dignified red-brick building. This omission, together with the failure of the New York Edition of his works, is the humbling epitaph to a life for which the terms success and failure are wholly inadequate.

This is a compelling book, which reads seamlessly, organically, as a novel. Never has a character—Henry James himself—been so well served by an author, paying his dues to a writer who scarcely believed in immortality but who was granted it none the less.

Brenda Wineapple (review date 1 November 2004)

SOURCE: Wineapple, Brenda. "About Henry." *Nation* 279, no. 14 (1 November 2004): 34.

[*In the following review, Wineapple compares Lodge's* Author, Author *with Colm Toíbín's historical biography of Henry James,* The Master.]

Henry James is not a name that springs to mind when we think of adventure stories prose epics or historical fiction. His forte was sensibility, not spectacle, in both art and life, and he specialized in capturing the intricacies of consciousness in rich, unmistakable prose. And by all external measures, he lived an uneventful life. Born in New York City in 1843, he moved to Britain as a young adult, and he wrote. He jotted ideas in his notebooks; he penned thousands of witty letters; he contributed essays and tales to magazines; he composed novels, biographies criticism, plays and a

memoir; and at the end of his life set himself the herculean task of revising an entire fictional oeuvre. He never married or entered into any romantic liaison, so far as we know, though he did accept dinner invitations (107 in one year), travel occasionally and entertain guests. In 1897 he purchased a Remington typewriter so he could dictate his novels to a typist instead of writing them longhand. This is not the stuff of high drama.

Still, James has been fortunate in biographers (besides Leon Edel, there's R. W. B. Lewis, Fred Kaplan and Lyndall Gordon, to name just a few), even though he deliberately intended to elude the "publishing scoundrels," as he called the scavenging narrator of "The Aspern Papers," by chucking much of his correspondence into a fire. Yet if "biography first convinces us of the fleeing of the Biographied," as Emily Dickinson (no stranger to the elusive) once observed, it seems that James, oddly, has now landed in the province of novelists. This year alone, two very different writers, first Colm Toíbín and then David Lodge, have tackled the life—and by extension, the art—of Henry James in two very different historical novels.

Both Toíbín's *The Master* and Lodge's **Author, Author** adduce the same anecdotal chestnuts and, taking James's genius for granted, pursue the sources of his art in his various failures either as literary entrepreneur or human being. When a young man, James failed to participate in the American Civil War, unlike two of his brothers, because of an "obscure hurt" received while helping extinguish a fire. In early 1895, as an established author of middle age, he was treated to an interminable fifteen minutes of hisses and boos when he took an ill-advised curtain call after the first performance of his play *Guy Domville* on the London stage. He enjoyed friendships with a number of men and women, in particular the novelist Constance Fenimore Woolson (grand-niece of James Fenimore Cooper), but she hurled herself from an upper-story balcony in Venice and died groaning on the ground below. After sorting through Woolson's correspondence (and torching some of it), James "buried" her dresses in a Venetian lagoon by pitching them overboard, a weird decision by anyone's standards. The unweighted garments bubbled to the surface, yards of velvet and silk ballooning grotesquely on the water. Then there was the move from London to Lamb House, in Rye, and in 1909, seven years before his death, a nervous collapse.

Even more important to both novelists is James's ambition. Lodge's Henry James aspires "to be the Anglo-American Balzac," as he tells his good friend George Du Maurier, the half-blind *Punch* illustrator who eventually writes an enormously popular (and now forgotten) novel, *Trilby*. **Author, Author** subsequently presents Du Maurier's almost inadvertent success in poignant counterpoint to James's career at midlife. Having renounced the pleasures of a conventional domestic life—"literary greatness was incompatible with the obligations of marriage"—as well as sexual intimacy of any kind, Lodge's James is a bachelor novelist committed to an aesthetic of making "life as experienced on the pulses and in the consciousnesses of individual human beings." In other words, he wishes to be considered the successor of Dickens, George Eliot, Hawthorne—and rich besides. Why not? Rider Haggard's potboiler *She* sold 40,000 copies, and Mrs. Humphrey Ward, another lesser light, was raking in cash with her lumbering cliches. By contrast, sales of James's books were plummeting, especially after that long-winded *Princess Casamassima,* to say nothing of its successor, *The Tragic Muse.*

Lodge's James decides to try his luck in theater, crude as it was with theatergoers applauding the likes of Oscar Wilde, whom the celibate James, squeamish about homosexuality and "bohemian sordidness," considers an exhibitionist dandy. ("Something fastidious in him [James] recoiled from any thought of intimate sexual contact involving nakedness," Lodge explains, "the groping and interlocking of private parts, and the spending of seed." If Lodge's repressed hero were to picture himself so compromised, he'd prefer it be with a beautiful young man, but this fantasy merely fuels his nascent and none-too-pleasant homophobia.)

Skilled in all forms of denial—for a connoisseur of the inner life, this James seems oddly impervious to his own—James rationalizes that a theatrical success will buy him time to write "real" literature. But after the humiliating premiere of *Guy Domville,* when his friends call "Author, author" (hence the title of the book) and James unwisely appears onstage, he reconsecrates himself to his art, adapting the conceptual lessons of the theater to narrative prose. To Lodge's James, then, writing is a conscious act of intellectual discernment, formal craft, deliberate decision-making. And so with *Guy Domville* inaugurating James's late phase, James will now write such nuanced masterpieces as *The Ambassadors, The Wings of the Dove* and *The Golden Bowl.* Of course, James can't know his future and dies believing that an "unsympathetic literary world" had perversely neglected his work.

And so Lodge, himself a brilliant critic and author of such gems as **The Novelist at the Crossroads,** will step into the breach at his novel's end, addressing himself directly to *The Master.* "You only contributed one word to the English language," Lodge consoles his dying Henry, "but it's one to be proud of: 'Jamesian.'"

Having confined himself more or less to a limited point of view with James its center, Lodge nonetheless packs James's world with characters like Edmund Gosse, Morton Fullerton and a 5-year-old Agatha Christie, much as if Trollope were rewriting James, or, more precisely, as if Lodge were placing James in one of his hectic novels of academic foible—without however, the foible. He does, however, grant himself omniscience to recount *Guy Domville*'s opening night, when theatergoers like George Bernard Shaw discuss it with the neophyte drama critic H. G. Wells, who'd just sold a serial called *The Time Machine.*

Lodge's novel is spirited historical fiction—the kind that Colm Toíbín's Henry James dismisses. "I view the historical novel as tainted by a fatal cheapness," Toíbín's James roundly declares. Covering roughly the same period (January 1895 to May 1899), Toíbín's evocative novel *The Master,* published this past spring, represents James as a man of regret, reminiscence and not a little self-reflection. "Once I wrote about youth and America," he muses, "and now I am left with exile and middle age and stories of disappointment." This is a James of gesture, not bustle; of susceptibilities rather than speeches. And where Lodge's James briskly advances, stoutly dislodging the slings and arrows of midlife, Toíbín's James fends off his recurrent dreams of the dead with the urge—the compulsion—to write, "anything to numb himself, distract himself."

Yet with the exception of Du Maurier, who does not appear in Toíbín's book, Toíbín invokes most of the same characters and circumstances as Lodge, with a difference: the relationship with Constance Woolson, with whom James shared a house in Bellosguardo, a suburb north of Florence, for a short and clandestine time; the premature death of his beloved cousin Minny Temple, who enters his fiction as Isabel Archer and Milly Theale; the truncated life of his gifted, if waspish, sister Alice; his relationship, never easy, with brother William—all this is rendered as rumination in translucent prose. Keeping vigil one rainy night in Paris, looking upward at the window of a male friend in one of the "truest" hours he ever lived, he ponders over and over "the mystery of having a single consciousness," the knowing that everyone stores away "an entirely private world to which they could return at the sound of a name, or for no reason at all." Such, as Toíbín tenderly traces them, are the deep springs of James's art.

Toíbín's book is organized around images of watching and waiting, of orphans and exiles and crucial moments, largely unspoken; the glance exchanged between James and an Irish manservant, each of them discreetly aware of what passes between them, or so we think, or so James does; his awareness of the bland rapaciousness of the beautiful young sculptor Hendrik Andersen, to whom he is nevertheless attracted. (Toíbín's James is a celibate homosexual but not a squeamish one, and one of his best scenes takes place during an idyllic summer when Minny Temple was vibrantly alive and Oliver Wendell Holmes, ex-soldier, brushed against James as the two young men shared a bed in a New England farmhouse.) His sighting of a young girl on a lawn, unlatching memories of his sister Alice, and the story of his father's nervous breakdown, elegantly recalled, slowly expand into *What Maisie Knew* and *The Turn of the Screw*. Or James remembers with poignant clarity his brother Wilky's bloody homecoming from the war James himself did not experience firsthand. Such luminous incidents, "flashes and moments," bloom into the lustrous tales and novels we recognize, indeed, as Jamesian.

Unlike Lodge's proud and conscience-ridden Anglophile who in 1915 takes up British citizenship as an act of solidarity with his adopted country (and a protest against his native one), Toíbín's James is a perpetual expatriate haunted by the past, unfulfilled desire and even the guilt that seems to presage art (themes in Toíbín's previous fiction). He's the beast in the jungle, ready to spring into action—that is to say, to lose himself in his work. It's this work, fed by solitude, that James protects, not just his fastidious self. What's more, it's worth protecting. "Art makes life, makes interest, makes importance," James famously tells H. G. Wells.

Setting the tone for Lodge's categorical James and Toíbín's more shaded one is James's story, "The Beast in the Jungle," in which John Marcher realizes too late he has neither fully loved nor lived. Is this the lot, then, that these novelists assign James, depicted either as Lodge's prig (who rejects Woolson) or Toíbín's depressive loner committed to his vigils? Are these the only choices available to a post-Freudian world? Isn't it possible that something like friendship—an underrated phenomenon—might have offered James pleasures unavailable to the egotistical Marcher? Still, both Lodge and Toíbín staunchly suggest that art is a pursuit worthy of the energy—the very life—that James lavished on it. *Author, Author* comes out and says so, and *The Master* makes us feel that, despite the cost, this must be true.

In the acknowledgments at the end of *Author, Author,* David Lodge claims he didn't learn of Toíbín's novel until after he delivered his book to his publisher. "I leave it to students of the Zeitgeist," he concludes, "to ponder the significance." So we might. Both Colm Toíbín, the gifted Irish novelist, and Lodge, the British one, take the position that there's something noble about the calling of art (especially if you're Henry

James), and that art involves sacrifice and passion as well as subtlety and diplomacy, qualities not readily associated with America today. Their James is a thoroughgoing American of the best international sort, and one of America's finest exports, for he represents the very subject that James himself eloquently molded, the American innocent whose purity of intent does not protect him from the cruelties, and responsibilities, of experience. Nor does it exonerate him. Lodge's book begins and ends with James's last days and a brutal evocation of war; Toíbín's ends more discreetly, with James tossing aside his brother William's suggestion that he give up a subject matter that dramatizes the insipid and write about something rock-hard, like the Puritans.

But William is now ill, and Henry will prevail to sound, once again, the intricate depths of the human heart. "The moral?" concludes Toíbín's James, half amused. "The moral is the most pragmatic we can imagine, that life is a mystery and that only sentences are beautiful, and that we must be ready for change."

Marian E. Crowe (essay date 2007)

SOURCE: Crowe, Marian E. "Intimations of Immortality: *Paradise News*." In *Aiming at Heaven, Getting the Earth: The English Catholic Novel Today*, pp. 169-85. Lanham, Md.: Lexington, 2007.

[*In the following essay, Crowe presents an in-depth assessment of Lodge's* Paradise News, *noting the presence of the author's trademark theme of religion and concluding that the novel's "tension and paradox . . . are simply a realistic account of the nature of faith in today's world."*]

> *Even for those who believe in the Christian possibility of eternal life, death is still a reality and still stings.*
>
> —Daniel Callahan, "Visions of Eternity"

> *I suspect that our conception of Heaven as merely a state of mind is not unconnected with the fact that the specifically Christian virtue of Hope has in our time grown so languid.*
>
> —C. S. Lewis, *Miracles*

"'The question facing the theologian today is, therefore, what can be salvaged from the eschatological wreckage?'"[1] This question, which begins the last chapter of David Lodge's *Paradise News* (1991), is taken from a lecture given by Bernard Walshe, the novel's protagonist. Bernard, a former priest, has lost his religious faith, but being untrained for any other kind of work, he is teaching part time at an ecumenical theological college. The segment of his lecture that begins the last chapter is a candid and poignant analysis of the dilemma facing Christianity at the end of the twentieth century. Bernard argues that although belief in an afterlife remains a central tenet of Christianity, being the culmination of its "linear plot" of salvation history and a staple of Christian teaching, it has little credibility for many educated people. Furthermore, many of the major theologians of the twentieth century have regarded the idea of an afterlife for individual human beings "with scepticism and embarrassment" or "silently ignored" it (280). Noting that fundamentalism, which *does* continue to promote belief in an anthropomorphic afterlife, is flourishing "'precisely on the eschatological scepticism of responsible theology'" (281), Bernard is reminded of W. B. Yeats's lines:

> The best lack all conviction, while the worst
> Are full of passionate intensity.[2]

But can Christianity afford to marginalize what has been one of its most motivating and inspirational beliefs? As Bernard puts it to his students, "'if you purge Christianity of the promise of eternal life (and, let us be honest, the threat of eternal punishment) which traditionally underpinned it, are you left with anything that is distinguishable from secular humanism?'" (282).

Bernard's question and his keen analysis of the dilemma facing Christianity in our time—the inability of sophisticated and intellectual Christians to emphasize and propound belief in an afterlife at the same time that human longing persists for what has always been a foundational dogma—marks *Paradise News* as a new stage in David Lodge's use of Catholicism in his fiction. Although the novel remains ambivalent on the question of an afterlife, the serious exploration of the possibilities for faith in a postmodern age and a sense of sacramentality in everyday life make *Paradise News* a more nuanced, complex, and theologically interesting novel than any of Lodge's earlier work. Just as the title *How Far Can You Go?* refers to both an adolescent approach to sexual morality and profound theological questions, the *Paradise* in *Paradise News,* refers both to Hawaii and to heaven.

In *Paradise News* Lodge is less concerned with Catholicism as sociological data and the day to day life of ordinary Catholics and is more focused on philosophical questions, especially that of an afterlife, that central Christian belief, which is being de-emphasized by theologians and intellectuals but remains of vital importance for ordinary Christians. In this sense, then, Lodge's theme in this novel is more Christian than specifically Catholic. Nevertheless, with the protagonist a former priest and his father and aunt practicing Catholics, a substantial amount of Catholic material is used. But *Paradise News* is different from Lodge's earlier Catholic novels, not only in its theme and subject matter, but also in its tone. Although critic Bernard Bergonzi found *How Far Can You Go?* bitter in places and marked by a "cold Voltairean irony," I suspect that he, like most readers, finds *Paradise News* more genial, tender, and affirmative.[3]

Lodge describes himself as "by temperament tentative, sceptical, ironic," so it is not surprising that the novel refrains from speaking strongly or authoritatively on the question of religious belief in general and an afterlife in particular.[4] Certain aspects of the novel—some postmodernist narrative techniques, and cynicism associated with the central metaphor of Hawaii as paradise—tend to erode the possibility of any grand philosophical ideal, any absolute. Expectations, preconceptions, and hopes are subverted. Other forces in the novel, however, pull it toward affirmation. The central metaphor, which at first seems to destabilize the possibility of belief, ultimately allows for transformation and life out of death. Although initially described with cynicism and irony, Hawaii at times not only lives up to its promise of paradisaical, unearthly beauty, but also offers transformative possibilities to the characters. Furthermore, the sense of sacramentality that suffuses the novel suggests that God's transforming presence is active, not only in the institutional sacraments of the Church, but in unexpected ways as well.

The "paradise" of the novel's title is both the eschatological goal—heaven—referred to in Bernard's lecture, and Honolulu, Hawaii, where Bernard goes to visit his dying Aunt Ursula, and which is the setting for most of the novel. Bernard articulates the central metaphor when he reflects on his life as a priest: "The Good News is news of eternal life, Paradise news. For my parishioners, I was a kind of travel agent, issuing tickets, insurance, brochures, guaranteeing them ultimate happiness" (153).

The primary meanings of *paradise* are the Garden of Eden and heaven, but the word is also so commonly used to refer to desirable vacation destinations like Hawaii or Tahiti that it is a dead metaphor. In this novel, however, the metaphor is *not* dead. Lodge repeatedly reminds the reader of Hawaii's association with paradise, as one of the tourists, anthropologist Roger Sheldrake, makes a point of noting down every instance of the word's use in Honolulu business:

> *Paradise Bakery*
> *Paradise Dental*
> *Paradise Jet Ski*

(191)

Paradise Finance Inc.
Paradise Sportswear
Paradise Beauty Supply Inc.

(195)

This continual reminder of Hawaii's metaphorical link to paradise foregrounds the word, conflates the three meanings together, and seems to diminish the significance of any of them. Tourists are like pilgrims looking for an Eden-like terrestrial paradise. Christians are spiritual tourists hoping for a heavenly paradise. Both are beset by frustration, disappointment, thwarted expectations, and misleading promises.

For the most part, cynicism, artificiality, and disappointment characterize the presentation of Hawaii. This paradise is tacky. Although the airport is a pleasant surprise—walkways open to the "warm and velvety" air and a "kind of tropical garden . . . next to the terminal building, with artificial ponds and streams, and naked torches burning amid the foliage" (67)—Bernard is disappointed by the drive into the city:

> A melange of amplified music, traffic noise and human voices penetrated the car windows. It reminded Bernard of the crush around Victoria Station, except that everything looked much cleaner. There were even familiar names on the shopfronts—MacDonalds *[sic]*, Kentucky Fried Chicken, Woolworths. . . .
>
> "It's not quite what I imagined," said Bernard. "It's very built-up, isn't it? I had a mental picture of sand, and sea and palm trees."

(73)

Nor does the reality of this tropical "paradise" live up to its reputation:

> Two bosomy blondes in brassières and skirts made of what looked like shiny blue plastic ribbon were gyrating to a kind of Hawaiian rock music. Their fixed, enamelled smiles raked the audience like searchlights. . . .
>
> "It doesn't look very authentic," said Bernard.
>
> "It's rubbish," said Dee. "I've seen more authentic hula dancing at the London Palladium."

(106)

The reason that Bernard's traveling companion, anthropologist Roger Sheldrake, is compiling a list of Hawaiian businesses with the word *paradise* in them is that he sees a parallel between tourism and religion: "'You see, I don't think people really want to go on holiday, any more than they really want to go to church. They've been brainwashed into thinking it will do them good, or make them happy. In fact surveys show the holidays cause incredible amounts of stress'" (62). Tour companies sell "paradise" just as

churches sell heaven. But the product is phony. Pulling out a Travelwise brochure with a picture of an idyllic, near-empty beach, Sheldrake points out that it "'bears no resemblance to reality,'" that almost no tourists find "'a beach as deserted as this one'" (63). He later refines his schema into two types of tourism, both based on religious metaphors. One is the tour as pilgrimage, where the traveller visits famous places—museums, monuments, cities. The other is the tour as paradise, "in which the subject strives to get back to a state of nature, or prelapsarian innocence" (192). Whether paradise is seen as the goal of a religious pilgrimage, which medieval people devoutly believed could help them earn heaven, or the Garden of Eden, which was heaven on earth, Sheldrake's travelers have taken the energy formerly channeled into religious activities and redirected it into vacation travel—the modern path to paradise. According to Sheldrake, however, both religion and tourism proffer empty promises.

The narrative technique also undermines the possibility of an affirmative or comforting answer to eschatological anxiety. Lodge, who is a prolific literary critic, as well as a novelist, has written extensively about postmodern literary techniques, sometimes illustrating his theory with examples from his own fiction.[5] In *Paradise News* he employs several techniques that disrupt the mostly straightforward, realistic narrative, to push it into the self-conscious narrativity of metafiction, thus destabilizing the reader and refusing to allow him or her to stay in the comfortable space of a traditional story. Lodge is fond of switching into the mode of a script, usually near the end of his novels, as he does with the televised Easter celebration at the end of *How Far Can You Go?* The final chapter of *Changing Places* is also in the form of a film script. In *The Art of Fiction* Lodge explains that part of his purpose in *Changing Places* was a formal one: since he had employed so many other kinds of stylistic shifts in earlier chapters—shifts in tense, interpolations of newspaper accounts, letters, and other documents—he needed to provide something even more striking so that the conclusion would not be anticlimactic. He also states that he wished to end the novel on a note of "radical indeterminacy."[6]

Lodge follows a similar course in *Paradise News*. Part of the narrative is in the form of Bernard's journal. Part is a series of postcards sent by various members of Bernard's tour group. Part is a long letter to Bernard from Yolande, a woman he becomes romantically involved with during his stay in Hawaii. In the penultimate chapter, in which Bernard attends a cocktail party to mark the end of the Travelwise tour, narrative techniques include a newspaper article, an advertising video, and a videotape made by one of the Travelwise tourists, titled *Everthorpes in Paradise.* Much of this chapter consists of conversations of the various tour members overlaid with descriptions of what is going on in the videotape. Two sequences are taking place simultaneously: the past-tense events of the trip and the present tense conversation. The tourists intermittently ignore, or are surprised, amused, or embarrassed by what they see on the television screen. Lodge's narration of the video sequence includes details that mark this narrative as an artificial construct.

> The film began with a picture of two teenage boys and an elderly lady waving goodbye from the porch of a mock-Jacobean house with leaded windows and integral garage. "Our boys and my mother," Beryl explained. There followed a long static close-up of a notice board saying *"East Midlands Airport,"* and then a jerky sequence with a painfully high-pitched whine on the soundtrack showing Beryl, in her red and yellow dress and gold bangles, climbing a steep flight of mobile steps into the cabin of a propeller plane. She stopped suddenly at the top and swept round to wave at the camera, causing the passengers behind and beneath her to cannon into each other and bury their faces in each other's bottoms.
>
> (267)

A random sequence of events, it is arranged and "posed" by its creator in such a way as to render it a story of "paradise"; but that *meaning* is clearly at odds with the actual facts. Its artificiality is emphasized. Apologizing that he has not had time to "edit this properly, or dub any music on," Everthorpe asks for patience with his "rough cut" (266). The bored viewers begin to show interest as they recognize themselves and others, saluting themselves "with hoots of laughter, cheers and jeers" (268). The delight of seeing oneself in another story, living two dimensions at once, begins to pale, however, as the artificiality of the film obtrudes:

> The voice of Brian Everthorpe was heard crying, "Cut!" Beryl stopped sauntering and turned to frown at the camera. Then she appeared to get back into bed and to wake up all over again.
>
> "Had to do two takes of this, because of the ambulance," said Brian Everthorpe. "I'll cut the first one out of the finished film, of course."
>
> (268)

As the film becomes more tedious, Everthorpe speeds it up to provide humor. The viewers are denied the pleasure of satisfying closure, however, as Everthorpe suddenly switches off the video machine when he is paged with the news that he must meet an unwelcome guest. If this novel is about the way that the life of faith enjoins living on two parallel tracks at once, drawn toward, tantalized by, in some senses even

misled by, the hope of reaching some kind of "paradise," then metafiction makes an appropriate analogue for that life.

Another destabilizing factor is the narrator's ambivalence about tensions within contemporary Roman Catholicism. Although the novel is saturated with Catholicism, one is hard-pressed to align the narrative voice with one particular perspective. Indeed, the novel reflects attitudes that characterize both liberal and conservative Catholics.

One area of tension in contemporary Catholicism is liturgy: traditionalists favoring ceremony, restraint, formality, and in some cases, Latin; reformists favoring flexibility, spontaneity, exuberance, and the vernacular. There are two celebrations of the Eucharist in the novel: Bernard's father receives Holy Communion in the hospital, and Yolande attends a Mass on Waikiki beach. Both events disclose a tension with regard to modes of celebration: formal versus informal, pre-Vatican II versus post-Vatican II, traditional or charismatic. The novel refuses, however, to speak univocally on this issue. Yolande finds the beach Mass refreshingly natural and authentic, especially in contrast to the ostentatious formality of the only other Mass she has ever attended "in an Italian church . . . stuffed with hideous statuary. . . . like a TV spectacular, with the altar-boys in their red robes, and the priest in his brocade get-up, parading in and out" (287). But this Mass on the beach impresses Yolande with its simplicity and naturalness, the altar "just a simple table set up on the beach, and the congregation sitting or standing around in a loose circle on the sand" (287).

Bernard's father, however, is uncomfortable with a casual approach to the sacraments. When he receives Holy Communion in the hospital, he insists on receiving the host on the tongue in the pre-Vatican II manner and is discomfited and shakes his head "like a startled horse" when the charismatic priest puts his hand on his head to pray for his recovery (134). Aunt Ursula is also discomfited by changes in the Church. Telling Bernard about her return to the Church after years away from it, she says that she "hardly recognized the service" (135). "There was a bunch of kids up at the altar, with tambourines and guitars, and they were singing jolly camp-fire type songs, not the good old hymns I remember. . . . And the mass was in English, not Latin, and there was a *woman* on the altar reading the epistle, and the priest said the mass facing the people—I was quite embarrassed watching him chewing the host" (135). Although Bernard appears patronizing and dismissive of the old people's views, the narrative voice behind Bernard seems to have some sympathy with their distress. There is a disjunction between the fashionable contemporary and the cherished familiar.

As with *How Far Can You Go?*, the aspect of Lodge's portrayal of Catholicism that probably engenders the most sympathy is its critique of Catholic attitudes toward sex. Bernard's Catholic childhood has badly distorted his sexuality. "I was troubled by the things that were happening to my body, and the thoughts that were straying into my mind. I was very worried about sin, about how easily you could commit it, and what the consequences would be if you died in a state of it. That's what Catholic education does for you—did for you in my day, anyway. Basically I was paralysed with fear of hell and ignorance of sex" (145). Bernard's priestly life is described as artificial, self-indulgent, and disconnected from the pulse of real life. For part of his priestly career he was an academic theologian, where he spent most of his time "insulated from the realities and concerns of modern secular society. It was rather like the life of a mid-Victorian Oxford don: celibate, male-centered, high-minded, not exactly ascetic" (146). When he gets into parish work, a woman he has been counseling impulsively kisses him, and Bernard realizes how deprived he has been "of human physical contact, of the animal comfort of touch, during all the long years of [his] training and work as a priest" (166). He also realizes that after the kiss and his decision to leave the priesthood, he feels more alive than he has felt for years and believes that he "was never a more effective confessor than [he] was that evening—compassionate, caring, encouraging" (167). The implicit causal link between the affection and Bernard's more effective ministry prepares the reader for Bernard's transformation into a more generous, warm, and sensitive human being after he becomes sexually involved with Yolande in the second part of the novel.

The harmful effects of the Church's methods of promoting sexual morality, its engendering of fear and shame in order to enforce its strict standards, and the dehumanizing effects of mandatory celibacy for the clergy all tend to erode confidence in the Church as a reliable spiritual guide, a mediator between God and humanity in this life, and a guarantor of eternal salvation in the next. It would be natural and tempting, therefore, to categorize the novel as polemical, a pointed, satiric argument as to why the Church has to modernize and adapt itself to the mores of contemporary, secular society. Such a stance, however, not only would be simplistic, but would fail to acknowledge other parts of the novel. Lodge denies us such easy closure.

Other features of the novel critique aspects of liberal theology. The theological college where Bernard has been teaching is one of those that have adapted to "the more ecumenical spirit of modern times by opening their doors to all denominations, indeed all faiths, and

to laypeople as well as to clerics" (28). Bernard compares the wide variety of courses and beliefs to the variety of products available in a modern supermarket. "On its shelves you could find everything you needed, conveniently stored and attractively packaged. But the very ease of the shopping process brought with it the risk of a certain satiety, a certain boredom. If there was so much choice, perhaps nothing mattered very much" (29).

The promise of the ecumenical movement—a deepening and enhancement of one's own religious tradition through a greater understanding of other faiths—has, in fact, eroded clarity, diminished meaning, and reduced the urgency involved in the life of faith. Bernard notes how the language of contemporary religious discourse has become vacuous and elusive. In a book on process theology, which he is reviewing, he reads a description of God as a cosmic lover: *"His transcendence is in His sheer faithfulness to Himself in love, in His inexhaustibility as lover, and in His capacity for endless adaptation to circumstances in which His love may be active"* (29). Bernard wonders who, apart from theologians, possibly cares about such formulations. "It often seemed to Bernard that the discourse of much modern radical theology was just as implausible and unfounded as the orthodoxy it had displaced" (29). Thus the contemporary Christian is in a kind of no-man's land, straddling two territories: the old orthodoxy—crippled by shame, repression, fear, superstition—but colorful, dramatic, and compelling; and the new ecumenism—enlightened, humane, benevolent—but abstract, boring, and vacuous.

This critique of "advanced" religion strains against the critique of traditional religion, opening up a kind of aporia in religious life. Although the old ways crippled the spirit and distorted one's sensual and emotional maturity, the new way starves the hunger for religious experience and the desire for meaningful answers to ultimate questions. Thus Lodge opens up a kind of postmodernist religious space, in which the old certainties have fallen away to leave the would-be Christian religiously destabilized.

The cynicism and instability, however, are countered by a reconsideration of faith in terms suitable for a postmodern age and by a sense of sacramentality. Although Bernard no longer believes in Christianity, his loss of faith recounted in his diary may be the prelude to a more genuine adult faith, for his early religious "faith" is shown to be largely derivative, immature, and fear-driven.[7] If Bernard is moving toward some new kind of faith, one suspects that it may be similar to the present theological perspective of the author, which, it will be recalled, Lodge himself described as "demythologized, provisional, and in many ways agnostic."[8] It is also a faith that resonates with St. Paul's description of faith as "confident assurance concerning what we hope for, and conviction about things we do not see" (Hebrews 11:1). Although "assurance" *(hupostasis)* and "conviction" *(elegchos)* sound positive, they are yoked with "hope" and "things we do not see," thus linking presence with absence and giving the term a destabilizing, oxymoronic ambience: an appropriate faith for our postmodern age. Furthermore, an element of doubt is seen by some contemporary theologians as essential for a healthy faith. Kenneth Leech in *Experiencing God: Theology as Spirituality* asserts that without "creative doubt, religion becomes hard and cruel, degenerating into the spurious security which breeds intolerance and persecution. . . . But to the eyes of conventional religion, this mingling of faith and doubt appears as atheism."[9]

This idea of creative doubt is further emphasized at the very end of the novel when Yolande includes in her letter to Bernard the following quotation from Miguel de Unamuno's *The Tragic Sense of Life,* which she has photocopied from the *Reader's Digest*:

> In the most secret recess of the spirit of the man who believes that death will put an end to his personal consciousness and even to his memory forever, in that inner recess, even without his knowing it perhaps, a shadow hovers, a vague shadow lurks, a shadow of a shadow of uncertainty, and while he tells himself: "There is nothing for it but to live this passing life, for there is no other!" at the same time he hears, in this most secret recess, his own doubt murmur: "Who knows? . . ." He is not sure he hears aright, but he hears. Likewise, in some recess of the soul of the true believer who has faith in the future life, a muffled voice the voice of uncertainty, murmurs in his spirit's ear: "Who knows?. . . ." Perhaps these voices are no louder than the buzzing of mosquitoes when the wind roars through the trees in the woods; we scarcely make out the humming, and yet, mingled with the roar of the storm, it can be heard. How, without this uncertainty, could we ever live?
>
> (293)[10]

Not only is "creative doubt" healthy; according to Unamuno, it is essential to life itself. The novel suggests that it is also essential to a healthy and realistic religious faith at the end of the twentieth century. Furthermore, although contemporary theologians may de-emphasize it, belief in an afterlife is an important part of such a faith, yet it is as much hope as faith.

In addition to its articulation of a contemporary faith which incorporates doubt in a potentially fruitful way, the novel also offers an approach to God through sacramentality. Sacramentality is prominent in *Paradise News* as incident, image, and theme, imparting to the story a sense of completeness, efficacy, and direction. According to the Catechism, sacraments are "efficacious signs of grace, instituted by Christ and entrusted to the Church, by which divine life is dispensed to us."[11] The principle of sacramentality insists that matter can be a vehicle for spirit, that God's grace comes through material things, that God is still present in the world. Thus the images and reminders of sacramentality, while not providing any definitive answer to the question of an afterlife, provide a sense of connection with the divine and a context for hope that that connection survives bodily death.

Bernard Walshe's contemporary "pilgrimage" includes all seven sacraments in some form. The sacraments of Holy Eucharist and Anointing of the Sick are explicitly celebrated according to the rite of the Catholic Church. Some are present in memory or expectation, others allusively or symbolically. The Holy Eucharist appears in the novel when Bernard's father receives Communion in the hospital, where he is recovering from a minor auto accident, and later at a Hawaiian folk Mass on Waikiki Beach. The hospital chaplain explains to Bernard that he likes bringing the Eucharist to the hospitalized because they seem "to appreciate the Eucharist so much more than parishioners at an ordinary Sunday mass" (134). When Ursula, who is in a different hospital, is told about her brother's receiving Communion, she is envious, wishing that her health plan allowed her to be in a Catholic hospital. This incident leads to Bernard's giving Ursula a quasi-academic lecture on contemporary Eucharistic theology. Annoyed by some of Ursula's remarks, he feels frustrated and impatient with what he perceives as her reductionistic, childish, and naive theology; yet it is clear that for both Ursula and her brother, participating in the ancient rite of the Eucharist provides some kind of spiritual anchor.

After Bernard returns to England, Yolande describes in a letter to him the Mass she has attended on Waikiki Beach. After Aunt Ursula's death, Father McPhee, in accordance with her wishes, takes her ashes to the beach to scatter them in the ocean. He times it to coincide with a Hawaiian folk Mass regularly held on the beach on summer Saturdays. Yolande, who has always considered herself an atheist, has attended only one other Mass, the wedding Mass referred to above that seemed to her like a TV spectacular. This folk Mass on the beach incorporates Hawaiian singing and hula dancing, which amazingly, in the hothouse artificiality of Honolulu, seems genuine and human:

> Even the authentic demonstrations they put on at the Bishop Museum are essentially theatrical, while the hula you see in Waikiki is halfway between belly-dancing and burlesque. So it was quite a shock to see

hula dancing at a Mass. But it worked. I think it worked because the girls weren't particularly good at it, and not particularly good-looking. I mean, they were OK, on both counts, but they were nothing special. . . . And of course they didn't have that fixed, gooey smile that you associate with pro hula girls. They looked serious and reverent.

(288)

This sacrament is transformative. Honolulu now looks different. "I was looking back at the shore, and I must say Oahu was doing its stuff that evening. Even Waikiki was a thing of beauty. The tall buildings were catching the light of the setting sun as if floodlit, thrown into relief against the hills in the background, which were dark with raincloud" (289). Although the phrase "Oahu was doing its stuff" suggests that this beauty is routine in Honolulu, in fact, throughout the novel, Honolulu has been described as vulgar and artificial. The emphasis on sun, sky, and light suggest a connection with the transcendent; and the image of the rainbow not only recalls God's covenant with Noah to preserve the human race but reinforces the yoking together of contrasting realms: the illuminated buildings against the dark, stormy hills, and the human, artificial world set against the God-given natural world. "There was a rainbow over one of the hills, behind the tower block in the Hilton Hawaiian Village with the rainbow mural. . . . I suppose that just about sums up Hawaii: the real rainbow cosying up to the artificial one" (289). This is an image of a sacramental world, the intersection of two realms, the heavenly and the earthly, the natural and the supernatural. Paradise now looks like paradise.

The Anointing of the Sick (formerly known as Extreme Unction) is the sacrament given to those in danger of death from sickness or old age. It consists of anointing with sacred oil, scripture readings, laying on of hands, and prayers. According to the *Catechism,* "The first grace of this sacrament is one of strengthening, peace and courage to overcome the difficulties that go with the condition of serious illness or the frailty of old age."[12] Ursula asks for this sacrament on the day before her meeting with her brother, Bernard's father. This is a decisive moment because it is for this meeting that Bernard and his father have come to Hawaii.

> "One more thing," Ursula said, as they were preparing to leave. "I think maybe I should receive the Last Sacrament."
>
> "That's a good idea," said Tess [Bernard's sister]. "Only we don't call it that any more. Or Extreme Unction. It's called the Sacrament of the Sick."
>
> "Well, whatever it's called, I think I could use it," said Ursula drily.
>
> (243)

It is agreed that she will receive the sacrament at the hospital when they go there for the meeting between Ursula and her brother. Father McPhee, the friendly, charismatic chaplain will be able to celebrate the sacrament when, as Tess says, they are all together as a family.

The sacrament of Holy Orders is present both through Bernard's failed priestly vocation and Father McPhee's apparently successful one. During his stay in Hawaii, Bernard writes a journal/autobiography, in which he writes about his vocation to the priesthood:

> I couldn't talk to my parents: they never mentioned the subject of sex. I was too shy to ask my elder brother. . . . I was astonishingly ignorant, and afraid. I suppose I thought that by committing myself to the priesthood, I would solve all my problems at a stroke: sex, education, career, and eternal salvation. As long as I fixed my aim on becoming a priest I couldn't, as they say, "go wrong."
>
> (145-46)

Not surprisingly, a vocation based on such motives (and never, apparently, strengthened by any nobler ones) ultimately fails. In contrast, Father McPhee, the priest who attends Bernard's father in the hospital and who conducts Aunt Ursula's funeral, is human and approachable, "a youngish, plumpish man, with a short haircut, wearing the stole over a grey clerical shirt and black trousers" (133). He places his hand on the patient's head and prays spontaneously for his recovery (an action one can never imagine the old Bernard doing). Although Father McPhee's ministerial competence is stressed, the language also stresses that he is *priest,* not simply minister. He stands in the line of the ordained that Catholics believe stretches back to the apostles and that validates their special connection to Christ. The language of the passage—"wearing a stole," "acolyte," "host," "ciborium"—connects Father McPhee's ministry to the ordained priesthood in a church where the priest offers the *sacrifice* of the mass and stands *in persona Christi.*

Matrimony is present in a dark ironic way, as the novel is replete with failed and troubled marriages: Ursula's, Yolande's, Bernard's sister's and even a young honeymoon couple on the tour who aren't speaking. Yet the prospect of Bernard and Yolande's eventual marriage, which is a distinct possibility at the end of the novel, suggests that past failures can still be redeemed. Refusing her husband's offer of a reconciliation, Yolande explains to Bernard that, although "Nothing is fixed, nothing is definite," marriage is a possibility. Referring to her husband, she says, "Lewis is all right, but he's not an honest man. Now that I've met one, I can't be content with anything less" (292). Yolande also tells Bernard that although she is not yet sure whether she wants to marry him, she intends "to find out, by getting to know [him] better" (292), thus raising the possibility that a relationship based on carefully acquired knowledge of the other and a love founded on honesty, respect, and integrity might actually stand a chance of being a sacramental marriage.

Confession and Confirmation function more as overarching themes than as discrete entities. Ursula's need to be reconciled with her brother is seminal for the plot. Although Bernard at first appears to be simply the mediator and facilitator for this meeting, it becomes apparent that he also has to "confess" to himself and to another human being the sins of his past life: his inauthentic vocation, his ineffective ministry, his masquerade as an "atheist" priest (154), his failed relationship with a woman at the time he left the priesthood, the falsehood involved in his role as a non-believing "theologian," his desiccated emotional life, and his failure to relate to people.[13] Bernard makes his "confession" in the form of the journal that he writes and lets Yolande read.

Since the sacrament of Confirmation is the celebration of a mature, adult commitment to the faith, it is unwarranted to see the unbelieving Bernard's Hawaiian experience as a sacramental Confirmation. Certainly there is no explicit indication that he has renounced atheism and is moving back toward theism, nor does he give even a hint or suggestion that he will return to Catholic belief and practice. However, the primary meaning of the verb *to confirm,* coming from its Latin roots (*cum,* with + *firmare,* to make firm), is to strengthen, and in this sense accurately describes Bernard's experience. According to Thomistic theology, grace builds on nature; until Bernard is mature on the natural human level, he cannot be a mature Christian. There is no question that in Hawaii he becomes a more mature person and thus is laying the groundwork for the possibility of a mature relationship to God.

Perhaps the most powerful sacramental image in the novel is Bernard's symbolic baptism. About halfway through the novel Bernard has been trying to find an affordable nursing home for his Aunt Ursula when, hot and tired, he decides to go for a swim. The experience is idyllic, almost a kind of bracketed space lifted out of terrestrial, mundane time:

> It was a perfect hour for a swim. The sun was low in the sky and had lost its fierce daytime heat, but the sea was warm and the air balmy. I swam vigorously for about a hundred yards in the general direction of Australia, then floated on my back and gazed up at the overarching sky. Long shreds of mauve-tinted cloud, edged with gold, streamed like banners from the west. . . . Occasionally a bigger wave surged past, swamping me or lifting me into the air like a matchstick, leaving me spluttering in its wake, laughing like a boy. I decided I would do this more often.
>
> (162)

Several elements lift this experience into a supernatural, liturgical realm: the "perfect" hour, the establishment of direction in terms of another continent (the fact that swimming to another continent is a preposterous notion establishes bigger than life parameters for this experience), the "overarching sky," a mauve and gold natural world (instead of the more "natural" colors of blue and green), elevation into the air, the intense joy. Most importantly, the experience is transformative. When Bernard comes out of the water and sees the silhouettes of boats against "a backdrop of shimmering gold," he understands for "perhaps the first time . . . how Hawaii could cast a spell upon the visitor" (163).

He discovers to his horror, however, that his keys are lost, most probably buried somewhere in the sand. His momentary panic and despair is dissipated, however, when he notices that the beams of the sun, which is almost touching the horizon, are "level with the surface of the ocean." He walks "in a perfectly straight line" to the water's edge. "I stopped, turned, and squatted on my heels. I looked back up the gently sloping beach to the spot where I had changed for my swim, and there, a yard or two to the right of my towel, something gleamed and glinted, something reflected back the light of the setting sun, like a tiny star in the immensity of space" (165). Again, the language—"perfectly straight line," "gleamed and glinted," "sun," "star," "immensity of space"—suggests transcendence, and is reminiscent of Dante's imagery in the *Paradiso,* the continual references to the sun recalling Dante's primary symbol for God. From his new angle of vision, keeping his "eyes fixed on the spot where the spark of light had gleamed," Bernard is able to locate the all-essential keys. Thrilled with his newly found competence, he feels "light-hearted and gleeful." Just as Catholicism has traditionally taught that Baptism leaves an indelible mark on the soul, Bernard notes that he clutched the newfound keys so tightly that "the indentations in [his] palms have not yet faded" (165). The found keys, like any car keys, not only open a door but also give Bernard the ability to harness energy from a powerful force and to use it to move in the direction of his choice. From this point on in the novel, Bernard displays new competence, self-confidence, and vitality.

The theology of sacramentality affirms presence, efficacy, and transformation; and the sacramentality in the novel counters the negativist tendencies of the cynicism, fragmentation, and destabilizing narrative techniques, creating a context for affirmation and possibility in the face of the "eschatological wreckage."

When Ursula asks him if he believes in an afterlife, Bernard answers, "'I don't know,'" (205) thereby articulating, not only his personal agnosticism, but the novel's reluctance to speak definitively on the point. However, Ursula's rejoinder, "I don't see the point of religion if there's no heaven" (205), articulates what the average Christian (as opposed to theologians) knows to be a fact: that Christianity cannot afford to marginalize or trivialize this essential doctrine. Part of the problem in trying to answer questions about the afterlife is the lack of any adequate language, either to frame the question or articulate an answer. As Bernard tells Ursula about the ideas of modern theologians, such as the appropriation of the Buddhist idea of "'the extinction of the individual ego, its assimilation into the eternal spirit of the universe,'" Ursula probably speaks for many people when she responds, "'I don't think I like the sound of that'" (206). Bernard sees a difficulty in speaking of heaven as a place. "'A garden. A city. Happy Hunting Grounds. Such solid things'" (206). Yet he himself had written in his journal that when he read a liberal theologian who argued that there is "no god but the religious requirement, the choice of it, the acceptance of its demands, and the liberating self-transcendence it brings about in us," he had to admit that he felt no "liberating self-transcendence" and that this language left him feeling "lonely, hollow, unfulfilled" (154). Against this kind of language, Lodge sets Aunt Ursula's unsophisticated but sensible question, "'Why not be bad, if you're not going to be punished in the long run?'" To Bernard's suggestion that "'virtue is its own reward,'" Ursula's rejoinder is, "'The hell with that'" (205). Thus language presses upon language, leaving us with the alternatives of formulations that are childish, naive, and overly-literal; and others that are vague, lifeless, unconnected to lived experience. Any formulation of that belief/hope is bound to be, in some sense, oxymoronic: "confident assurance concerning what we hope for, and conviction about things we do not see," presence and absence.

Significantly, the term used in the title and throughout the book is primarily *paradise,* not *heaven.* Colleen McDannell and Bernhard Lang point out in their book *Heaven: A History* that the term *paradise* has more earthly, human connotations than *heaven.* Not only is its primary meaning the Garden of Eden, but when used to refer to heaven, it usually indicates a kind of heaven where the joys are more human and terrestrial.[14] Since the paradise that Bernard discovers is, in effect, a completely terrestrial one—one that any good secular humanist could affirm—does the novel imply that that is the only paradise there is? Does Yolande speak with the authority of the narrative voice when she says, "'I think we have to make our own heaven on this earth'" (220)?

Such an interpretation is inadequate. The tension and paradox running through all the discourse about faith—Bernard's account of his loss of faith, Ursula's explanation of her return to it, the eloquent musings of Unamuno—are simply a realistic account of the nature of faith in today's world. Mostly what allows for affirmation, transformation, and possibility are those qualities that make *Paradise News* different from Lodge's earlier Catholic novels: a more sustained and serious engagement with the basic issues of faith, rather than its externals, a more nuanced view of Catholicism, and a sense of both the Church and the world as sacramental, offering a possibility of a connection with the transcendent.

Although Bernard's first impression of Hawaii's pseudoparadise is that it is tacky, tawdry, and downright uncomfortable, gradually it rises to its promise. Bernard has glimpses of transcendence in its natural beauty—especially the ocean. In it he reconnects with his family and acts as peacemaker, intercessor, comforter, and aide, thus confirming that even during his dry, academic, ecclesiastical life, he was growing in virtue. His surprising discovery that he is, in fact, a very good man may be his most precious gift in Hawaii, one indispensable to his ability to re-find his faith and connect to God. He also discovers erotic love, which orients him toward a richer, more fully human life. The Hawaiian "paradise," which originally seemed to betray its promise, ends by living up to it in an unexpected and unforeseen way. Human love, growth in virtue, forgiveness, intimations of transcendence through the natural world all suggest that, though we are denied certainty, we have grounds for believing/hoping that God touches us sacramentally and is drawing us toward a paradise beyond all imagining. The first sentence in the novel is a question: "'What do they see in it, eh?'" (3). The last sentence in the novel is an answer to a question: "'Very good news'" (294).

Notes

1. David Lodge, *Paradise News* (New York: Penguin, 1991), 280. Hereafter cited in the text by page number.

2. The lines, which are quoted on p. 281, are from Yeats's "The Second Coming."

3. Bergonzi, "Decline and Fall," 183.

4. Haffenden, "David Lodge," 152.

5. See, for example, his *The Art of Fiction,* chapters 8 and 50.

6. David Lodge, *Art of Fiction,* 227-28.

7. French theologian François Varone makes the point that a conversion to mature Christianity means leaving behind "the false God pleased-by-duty and by fear, the facile and useful God of efficacious rites" and discovering the God "who exists so that I may exist, who gives an overall meaning to my life so that I can fill out that meaning for myself and for others, the One who gives meaning to my responsi-

bility, searching, doubts and plans. One has to exist in order to be a believer." François Varone, *Ce Dieu absent qui fait problème* (Paris: Cerf, 1981), 62, quoted in Michael Paul Gallagher, S. J., *What Are They Saying About Unbelief?* (New York: Paulist Press, 1995), 64.

8. Lodge, introduction to *The Picturegoers*, ix. One might question whether a theological perspective described in these terms is really deserving of the name *faith*, or whether it is rather a form of hope. What kind of faith can be described as "agnostic"? Yet in the face of the serious challenges posed by contemporary science and Biblical criticism, one might also argue that as much as a robust, unquestioning faith might be desirable, that described by Lodge is probably an accurate and honest description of the faith of many serious, thoughtful contemporary Christians.

9. Kenneth Leech, *Experiencing God: Theology as Spirituality* (San Francisco: Harper and Row, 1985), 25. It will be recalled that I previously made the point that the best Catholic novels leave room for doubt.

10. The passage is found in Miguel de Unamuno, *The Tragic Sense of Life*, vol. 7 of *Selected Works of Miguel de Unamuno*, trans. Anthony Kerrigan (Princeton: Princeton Univ. Press, 1972), 131.

11. *Catechism*, 1131.

12. *Catechism*, 1520.

13. The importance of confession *to another human being* is key in the Catholic understanding of this sacrament. Protestants often wonder why they cannot simply confess their sins to God in private. As explained in the *HarperCollins Encyclopedia of Catholicism*, confession is necessary because of the social nature of sin, which is "an offense against both God and the community. Consequently, Reconciliation is reconciliation with both God and the community. Since every sin has a social dimension, every confession of sin or act of Reconciliation must also have a social dimension" (344).

14. Colleen McDannell and Bernhard Lang. *Heaven: A History* (New York: Random House, Vintage Books, 1990). For example, the happiness of the blessed would consist primarily in the company of loved ones and in aesthetic, intellectual, and in some accounts, even physical pleasures—rather than in the Beatific Vision.

Bibliography

Ableman, Paul. "Booted About." Review of *A Married Man*, by Piers Paul Read. *The Spectator*, November 24, 1979, 21.

Ackroyd, Peter. "Out of Sight." Review of *The Sin Eater*, by Alice Thomas Ellis. *The Spectator*, December 24, 1977, 29-30.

Amis, Kingsley, "How I Lived in a Very Big House and Found God." *Times Literary Supplement*, November 20, 1952, 1352.

Appleby, R. Scott. "Surviving the Shaking of the Foundations: United States Catholicism in the Twenty-First Century." Contextual Introduction. Pp. 1-23 in *Seminaries, Theologates, and the Future of Ministry: An Analysis of Trends and Transitions*, by Katarina Schuth. Collegeville, Minn.: Liturgical Press, 1999.

Augustine, Saint. *The City of God. The City of God*, Book XIV, chapter 1, translated by Marcus Dods, D.D. New York: Modern Library, 1950.

———. The Works of Saint Augustine, edited by John E. Rotelle, O.S.A. Sermons III, translated by Edmund Hill, O.P. Brooklyn: New City Press, 1991.

Bakhtin, Mikhail. *The Dialogic Imagination: Four Essays*. Austin: University of Texas Press, 1981.

Barbey d'Aurevilly, Jules Amédée. *Oeuvres de J. Barbey d'Aurevilly*. Preface to *Une Vielle Maitresse*. Nouvelle Edition. Tome Premier. Paris: Librairie Alphonse Lemerre, n.d.

Bellah, Robert. *The Good Society*. New York: Random House, Vintage Books, 1991.

Belloc, Hilaire. *Europe and the Faith*. New York: Paulist Press, 1920.

———. "A Letter to Dean Inge." In *Essays of a Catholic*. New York: Macmillan, 1931.

———. Survivals and New Arrivals. New York: Macmillan, 1929.

Benson, Robert Hugh. *The Dawn of All*. London: Hutchinson, 1911.

———. Lord of the World. London: Sir Isaac Pitman & Sons, 1907.

Berger, Peter. *A Rumor of Angels: Modern Society and the Rediscovery of the Supernatural*. Garden City, N.Y.: Doubleday Anchor, 1970.

Bergonzi, Bernard. "The Decline and Fall of the Catholic Novel." In *The Myth of Modernism and Twentieth Century Literature*. New York: St. Martin's Press, 1986.

———. "A Conversation with David Lodge." In *War Poets and Other Subjects*. Aldershot, U.K.: Ashgate, 1999.

Bernanos, Georges. *The Diary of a Country Priest*. Trans. Pamela Norris. New York: Carroll & Graf, 1983.

———. Under the Sun of Satan. Trans. Harry L. Binsse. New York: Pantheon, 1949.

Boffetti, Jason. "Tolkien's Catholic Imagination," *Crisis*, November 2001, 34-40.

Bradbury, Malcolm. "A Case of Ilychitis." Review of *A Married* Man, by Piers Paul Read. New *York Times Book Review,* December 30, 1979, 3.

Bretall, Robert, ed. *A Kierkegaard Anthology.* Princeton University Press, 1946.

Brockway, James. "Going Down Bravely." Review of *Polonaise,* by Piers Paul Read. *Books and Bookmen,* Feb. 1977, 22-23.

Buckley, F. J. "The Satirist of the Fall." *Crisis,* January 2003, 27-31.

Caldecott, Stratford. "The Lord & Lady of the Rings: The Hidden Presence of Tolkien's Catholicism in *The Lord of the Rings." Touchstone,* January 2002, 51-57.

Canavan, Francis, "The Dilemma of Liberal Pluralism," *The Human Life Review* 5, no. 3 (summer 1979), 7. Quoted in Stanley Hauerwas, *A Community of Character: Toward a Constructive Christian Social Ethic* (Notre Dame, Ind.: University of Notre Dame Press, 1981), 217.

Carlin, David. *The Decline and Fall of the Catholic Church in America.* Manchester, N.H.: Sophia Institute Press, 2003.

Carroll, Colleen. *The New Faithful: Why Young Adults are Embracing Christian Orthodoxy.* Chicago: Loyola Press, 2002.

Catechism of the Catholic Church. New York: Doubleday, Image Books, 1995.

Chesterton, G. K. "On the Novel with a Purpose." Pp. 225-29 in *The Thing: Why I Am a Catholic.* Pp. 133-335 in *The Collected Works of G. K. Chesterton.* Vol. 3. San Francisco: Ignatius Press, 1990.

———. *Orthodoxy.* San Francisco: Ignatius Press, 1908, 1995.

———. *St. Thomas Aquinas.* Pp. 419-551 in *The Collected Works of G. K. Chesterton.* Vol. 2. San Francisco: Ignatius Press, 1986.

———. *The Well and the Shallows.* In Vol. 3 of *The Collected Works of G. K. Chesterton.* San Francisco: Ignatius Press, 1990.

Christ, Carol P. *Diving Deep and Surfacing: Women Writers on Spiritual Quest.* Boston: Beacon Press, 1980.

Collins, James. *Pilgrim in Love: An Introduction to Dante and His Spirituality.* Chicago: Loyola University Press, 1984.

Collins, James Daniel. *The Mind of Kierkegaard.* Chicago: Henry Regnery, 1953.

Conrad, Joseph. *The Secret Agent: A Simple Tale.* Cambridge and New York: Cambridge University Press, 1990.

Copleston, Frederick, S. J. *Modern Philosophy: Schopenhauer to Nietzsche.* Vol. 7, Part 2 of *A History of Philosophy.* Garden City, N.Y.: Doubleday, Image Books, 1965.

Couto, Maria. *Graham Greene: On the Frontier.* New York: St. Martin's Press, 1988.

Cunneen, Sally. "Big Enough for God: The Fiction of Sara Maitland." *Logos* 6, no. 4 (fall 2003): 122-35.

Cunningham, Lawrence S. *The Catholic Experience.* New York: Crossroad, 1987.

Daiches, David, ed. *The Avenel Companion to English & American Literature.* Vol. 1. New York: Avenel Books, 1981.

Delbanco, Andrew. *The Death of Satan: How Americans Have Lost the Sense of Evil.* New York: Farrar, Straus & Giroux, 1995.

Demers, James. *The Last Roman Catholic.* Carp, Ontario: Creative Bound Inc., 1991.

Desmond, John. "The Heart of the Matter: The Mystery of the Real in *Monsignor Quixote." Religion and Literature* 22, no. 1 (Spring 1990): 59-78.

Duffy, Eamon. *Faith of Our Fathers: Reflections on Catholic Tradition.* London: Continuum, 2004.

Duran, Leopoldo. *Graham Greene.* Trans. Euan Cameron. San Francisco: HarperCollins, 1994.

Eliot, T. S. "Religion and Literature." Pp. 343-54 in *Selected Essays.* New ed. New York: Harcourt, Brace & Co., 1950.

Ellis, Alice Thomas. *The Birds of the Air.* Harmondsworth, Eng.: Penguin, 1983.

———. Interview by author. London. February 7, 2001.

———. *Serpent on the Rock.* London: Hodder and Stoughton, 1994.

———. *The Sin Eater.* Harmondsworth, Eng.: Penguin, 1986.

———. *The 27th Kingdom.* Pleasantville, N.Y.: Akadine Press, 1999.

———. *Unexplained Laughter,* Pleasantville, N.Y.: Akadine Press, 1998.

Ethics and Culture: The Newsletter of the Notre Dame Center for Ethics & Culture, Spring 2005.

Foucauld, Michel. *An Introduction.* Vol. 1 of *The History of Sexuality,* 19-23. Trans. Robert Hirley. London: Allen Lane, 1979. Quoted in Woodman, *Faithful Fictions,* 147.

Fraser, Theodore P. *The Modern Catholic Novel in Europe.* New York: Twayne, 1994.

Friedman, Melvin J., ed. *The Vision Obscured: Perceptions of Some Twentieth-Century Catholic Novelists.* New York: Fordham University Press, 1970.

Frye, Northrop. *Anatomy of Criticism: Four Essays.* Princeton: Princeton University Press, 1957.

Gandolfo, Anita. *Testing the Faith: The New Catholic Fiction in America.* New York: Greenwood Press, 1992.

Gide, André. *Dostoyevsky,* 15. New York: New Directions, 1923, 1961. Quoted in Fraser, *Modern Catholic Novel,* 5.

Gilley, Sheridan. "A Tradition and Culture Lost, To Be Regained?" Pp. 29-45 in *Catholics in England,* edited by Michael P. Hornsby-Smith.

Gilman, Richard. "Salvation, Damnation, and the Religious Novel." *New York Times Book Review,* December 2, 1984, 7, 58-60. Quoted in Fraser, prologue to *Modern Catholic Novel,* xi.

Glendon, Mary Ann. "The Hour of the Laity." *First Things,* November 2002, 23-25.

Godawa, Brian. "Redemption in the Movies." Pp. 433-51 in Ryken, *The Christian Imagination.*

Greeley, Andrew. *The Catholic Imagination.* Berkeley: University of California Press. 2000.

———. *The Catholic Revolution: New Wine, Old Wineskins, and the Second Vatican Council.* Berkeley: University of California Press, 2004.

Green, Julian. *Diary 1928-1957,* 159. Sel. by Kurt Wolff. Trans. Anne Green. New York: Harcourt, Brace & World, 1964, 159.

Green, Martin. *Essays on Literature and Religion: Yeats's Blessings on von Hügel,* 116, 74. London, Longman, 1967. Quoted in Woodman, *Faithful Fictions,* 140.

Greene, Graham. *The End of the Affair.* New York: Viking, 1961.

———. "François Mauriac." Pp. 69-73 in *The Lost Childhood and Other Essays.* New York: Viking Press, 1951.

———. *Monsignor Quixote.* London: Vintage, 2000.

———. *The Power and the Glory.* New York: Penguin, 1977.

———. *Ways of Escape.* New York: Simon and Schuster, 1980.

Haffenden, John. "David Lodge." Pp. 145-67 in *Novelists in Interview.* London: Methuen, 1985.

Haight, Roger, S.J. *Jesus: Symbol of God.* Maryknoll, N.Y.: Orbis, 1999. Quoted in Edward T. Oakes, S.J., "Reconciling Judas: Evangelizing the Theologians," *Crisis,* Oct. 2004, 31-35.

Hansen, Ron. Preface to *A Stay Against Confusion: Essays on Faith and Fiction.* New York: HarperCollins, 2001.

The HarperCollins Encyclopedia of Catholicism. Ed. Richard P. McBrien et al. San Francisco: HarperSanFrancisco, 1995.

The Harper Handbook to Literature. 2d ed. Ed. Northrop Frye et al. New York: Longman, 1997.

Hart, David B. "The Laughter of the Philosophers." *First Things,* Jan. 2005, 31-37.

Hebblethwaite, Peter. "How Catholic Is the Catholic Novel?" *Times Literary Supplement,* 27 July 1967, 678-79.

Heppenstall, Rayner. *Léon Bloy.* Studies in Modern European Literature and Thought. Cambridge: Bowes & Bowes, 1953.

Hoge, Dean et al. *Young Adult Catholics: Religion in the Culture of Choice.* Notre Dame, Ind.: University of Notre Dame Press, 2001.

Hornsby-Smith, Michael P., ed. *Catholics in England 1950-2000: Historical and Sociological Perspectives.* London: Cassell, 1999.

———. "English Catholics at the New Millennium." Pp. 291-306 in HornsbySmith, *Catholics in England.*

———. *Roman Catholic Beliefs in England: Customary Catholicism and Transformations of Religious Authority.* Cambridge: Cambridge University Press, 1991.

———. "A Transformed Church." Pp. 3-25 in Hornsby-Smith, *Catholics in England.*

Hornsby-Smith, Michael P. and R. M. Lee. *Roman Catholic Opinion: A Study of Roman Catholics in England and Wales in the 1970's* (Guildford: University of Surrey, 1979), 117. Quoted in Hornsby-Smith, *Roman Catholic Beliefs in England,* 183.

Howard, Thomas. "*Brideshead Revisited* Revisited." *Touchstone,* summer 1996, 27-32.

Huizinga, Johan. *Homo Ludens: A Study of the Play-Element in Culture,* 18. New York: Roy Publishers, 1950. Quoted in Weinberger, "Religion and Fly Fishing," 282.

Huysmans, Joris-Karl. *En route.* 3rd. ed. Trans. C. Kegan Paul. London: Kegan Paul, Trench, Trubner & Co., 1908.

Jaspers, Karl. *Way to Wisdom.* Trans. Ralph Manheim. New Haven: Yale University Press, 1954.

Jenkins, Philip. *Hidden Gospels: How the Search for Jesus Lost Its Way.* Oxford: Oxford University Press, 2001.

Johnson, Anne Janette. "Read, Piers Paul." Pp. 353-55 in Vol. 36 of *Contemporary Authors*. New Revision Series. Detroit: Gale Research Inc., 1993.

Karl, Frederick R. *A Reader's Guide to the Contemporary English Novel*. Rev. ed. New York: Octagon Books, 1986.

Kellogg, Gene. *The Vital Tradition: The Catholic Novel in a Period of Convergence*. Chicago: Loyola University Press, 1970.

Kennedy, Eugene. *Re-imagining American Catholicism*. New York: Vintage Books, 1985.

Ker, Ian. *The Achievement of John Henry Newman*. Notre Dame, Ind.: University of Notre Dame Press, 1990.

———. *The Catholic Revival in English Literature, 1845-1961*. Notre Dame, Ind.: University of Notre Dame Press, 2003.

Kermode, Frank. *The Sense of an Ending*. New York: Oxford University Press, 1967.

Kierkegaard, Søren. *The Concept of Dread*. Trans. Walter Lowrie. Princeton: Princeton University Press, 1957.

———. *Fear and Trembling & Repetition*. Eds. and Trans. Howard V. Hong and Edna H. Hong. Princeton: Princeton University Press, 1983.

Kilpatrick, William. *The Emperor's New Clothes*. Westchester, Ill.: Crossway, 1985.

Knox, Ronald and Arthur Lunn. *Difficulties*. London: Eyre & Spottiswoode, 1932.

Kort, Wesley. *Narrative Elements and Religious Meanings*. Philadelphia: Fortress Press, 1975.

Kroll, Jack. "Map of Greeneland," *Newsweek,* April 15, 1991, 75.

Lacey, Paul A. "'To Meditate a Saving Strategy': Denise Levertov's Religious Poetry." *Renascence* 50, Nos. 1-2 (fall 1997/winter 1998): 17-32.

"The Languages of Love." Review of *Daughter of Jerusalem,* by Sara Maitland. *Publishers Weekly,* January 30, 1981, 62.

Last, Jonathan V. "God on the Internet." *First Things,* December 2005, 34-40.

Lawson, Mark. "How Far Did He Go?" *The Tablet,* September 4, 2004, 12-14.

Lee, Hermione. "Marriage à la Mode." Review of *Daughter of Jerusalem,* by Sara Maitland. *The Observer,* October 22, 1978, 35.

Leech, Kenneth. *Experiencing God: Theology as Spirituality*. San Francisco: Harper & Row, 1985.

Levertov, Denise. "On Belief in the Physical Resurrection of Jesus." Pp. 115-16 in *The Sands of the Well*. New York: New Directions, 1996.

Lewis, C. S. *Letters to Malcolm: Chiefly on Prayer*. New York: Harcourt, Brace & World, 1964.

———. *Mere Christianity*. Rev. ed. New York: Macmillan, 1960.

———. *Miracles*. New York: Macmillan, 1960

———. *The Problem of Pain*. New York: Macmillan, 1962.

———. *Reflections on the Psalms*. New York: Harcourt Brace Jovanovich, 1958.

———. "Religion Without Dogma?" Pp. 129-46 in *God in the Dock,* edited by Walter Hooper. Grand Rapids: Eerdmans, 1970.

———. *The Screwtape Letters*. New York: Macmillan, 1953.

Lodge, David. *The Art of Fiction*. New York: Penguin, 1992.

———. "The Catholic Church and Cultural Life." Pp. 32-37 in Lodge, *Write On*.

———. "Graham Greene." Pp. 87-118 in Lodge, *Novelist at the Crossroads*.

———. Interview. *Contemporary Authors*. Detroit: Gale Research Inc., 1995.

———. Interview by author. London. March 13, 2001.

———. "Memories of a Catholic Childhood." Pp. 28-31 in Lodge, *Write On*.

———. "My Joyce." Pp. 57-69 in Lodge, *Write On*.

———. "The Novelist at the Crossroads." Pp. 3-34 in Lodge, *Novelist at the Crossroads*.

———. *The Novelist at the Crossroads and Other Essays on Fiction and Criticism*. Ithaca: Cornell University Press, 1971.

———. *Paradise News*. New York: Penguin, 1991.

———. *The Picturegoers*. 1960. New York: Penguin, 1993.

———. *Souls and Bodies*. [American edition of *How Far Can You Go?*] New York: Penguin, 1980.

———. *Therapy*. New York: Penguin, 1995.

———. "The Uses and Abuses of Omniscience: Method and Meaning in Muriel Spark's *The Prime of Miss Jean Brodie*." Pp. 119-44 in *Novelist at the Crossroads*.

———. *Write On: Occasional Essays '65-'85*. London: Secker & Warburg, 1986.

Longenecker, Dwight. "Indifference to Religion on the Rise in Great Britain." *Our Sunday Visitor,* January 30, 2005, 4.

Low, Anthony. "Jon Hassler: Catholic Realist." *Renascence* 47, no. 1 (fall 1994): 59-70.

Lundin, Roger. *The Culture of Interpretation: Christian Faith and the Postmodern World.* Grand Rapids: Eerdmans, 1993.

Lynch, William F., S.J. *Christ and Apollo: The Dimensions of the Literary Imagination.* 1960. Notre Dame, Ind.: University of Notre Dame Press, 1975.

———. *Christ and Prometheus: A New Image of the Secular.* Notre Dame, Ind.: University of Notre Dame Press, 1970.

Maison, Margaret M. *The Victorian Vision: Studies in the Religious Novel.* New York. Sheed & Ward, 1961.

Maitland, Sara. *A Big-Enough God: A Feminist's Search for a Joyful Theology.* New York: Riverhead Books, 1995.

———. *Brittle Joys.* London: Virago Press, 1999.

———. *Daughter of Jerusalem.* New York: Henry Holt & Co., 1978.

———. "Fag Hags: A Field Guide." Pp. 111-118 in *Angel Maker: The Short Stories of Sara Maitland.* New York: Henry Holt & Co., 1996.

———. "The Future of Faith" *Cross Currents,* (spring/summer 2000): 154-56.

———. Interview by author. Austin, Tex. June 18, 1999.

———. *A Map of the New Country: Women and Christianity.* London: Routledge & Kegan Paul, 1983.

———. *Novel Thoughts.* Notre Dame, Ind.: Erasmus Institute, 1999.

———. *Virgin Territory.* New York: Beaufort Books, 1984.

Malin, Irving. "The Deceptions of Muriel Spark." Pp. 95-107 in Friedman, *Vision Obscured.*

Maritain, Jacques. "Christian Art." Pp. 53-57 in *Art and Scholasticism: With Other Essays,* translated by J. F. Scanlan. New York: Charles Scribner's Sons, 1924.

Marshall, John. "Catholic Family Life." Pp. 67-77 in *Catholics in England,* edited by Michael P. Hornsby-Smith.

Mauriac, François. *The Desert of Love.* Trans. Gerard Hopkins. London: Eyre & Spottiswoode, 1949.

———. "On Writing Today." In *Second Thoughts: Reflections on Literature and Life,* 16. New York: World, 1961. Quoted in Fraser, *Modern Catholic Novel,* 37.

———. *The Viper's Tangle.* Trans. Gerard Hopkins. New York: Carroll & Graf, 1987.

McDannell, Colleen and Bernhard Lang. *Heaven: A History.* New York: Random House, Vintage Books, 1990.

McFague, Sallie. *Speaking in Parables: A Study in Metaphor and Theology.* Philadelphia: Fortress Press, 1975.

Miller, J. Hillis. "Literature and Religion." Pp. 31-45 in *Religion and Modern Literature: Essays in Theory and Criticism,* edited by G. B. Tennyson and Edward E. Ericson, Jr. Grand Rapids: Eerdmans, 1975.

Milton, Edith. Review of *The Birds of the Air,* by Alice Thomas Ellis. *New York Magazine,* 7 Sept. 1981, 64-65.

Moeller, Charles. *Man and Salvation in Literature.* Trans. Charles Underhill Quinn. Notre Dame, Ind.: University of Notre Dame Press, 1970.

Mooneyham, Laura. "The Triple Conversions of *Brideshead Revisited.*" *Renascence* 45, no. 4 (summer 1993): 225-35.

Mustich, James, Jr. Afterward to *Unexplained Laughter,* by Alice Thomas Ellis. New York: Akadine Press, 1998.

Myers, John J. "The Church vs. the Culture: The Score Thus Far." *Crisis,* May 2004, 18-22.

Naughton, John. "Leavisites in Yorkshire." Review of *Daughter of Jerusalem,* by Sara Maitland. *The Listener* 100, no. 2586, (16 November 1978): 658-59.

Neary, John. *Like and Unlike God: Religious Imaginations in Modern and Contemporary Fiction.* Atlanta: Scholars Press, 1999.

Neuhaus, Richard John. "Kierkegaard for Grownups." *First Things,* October 2004, 27-33.

———. "The Public Square." *First Things,* August/September 2004, 86-104.

Newman, John Henry Cardinal. *An Essay in Aid of a Grammar of Assent.* Garden City, NY: Doubleday, Image Books, 1955.

———. *The Idea of a University.* Ed. Martin J. Svaglic. New York: Holt, Rinehart & Winston, 1960.

Nichols, Aidan. *The Art of God Incarnate.* New York: Paulist, 1980.

Nicholson, John. Review of *The Other Side of the Fire,* by Alice Thomas Ellis. *Times* (London) 1 December 1983, 13.

Norris, Kathleen. *The Cloister Walk.* New York: Riverhead, 1996.

Novak, Michael. "Abandoned in a Toxic Culture." *Crisis,* December 1992, 15-19.

———. *The Experience of Nothingness,* 15. New York: Harper & Row, 1970. Quoted in Christ, *Diving Deep,* 14-15.

O'Connor, Flannery. "Catholic Novelists and their Readers." Pp. 169-90 in *Mystery and Manners.*

———. *The Complete Stories.* New York: Farrar, Straus & Giroux, 1971.

———. "The Fiction Writer and His Country." Pp. 25-35 in *Mystery and Manners.*

———. *Mystery and Manners.* Ed. Sally and Robert Fitzgerald. New York: Farrar, Straus & Giroux, 1969.

———. "The Nature and Aim of Fiction." Pp. 63-86 in *Mystery and Manners.*

———. "Novelist and Believer." Pp. 154-168 in *Mystery and Manners.*

O'Donnell, Donat [Conor Cruise O'Brien]. *Maria Cross: Imaginative Patterns in a Group of Modern Catholic Writers.* New York: Oxford University Press, 1952.

O'Faolain, Julia. Review of *Unexplained Laughter,* by Alice Thomas Ellis. *Times Literary Supplement,* September 6, 1985, 972.

Oakes, Edward T. "Reconciling Judas: Evangelizing the Theologians." *Crisis,* October 2004, 31-35.

———. "Stanley Fish's Milton." *First Things,* November 2001, 23-34.

Oertling, Margaret. "A Response to Critics of *Brideshead Revisited.*" The Epositor (Trinity University) 2 (1990): 65-75. Quoted in Mooneyham, "Triple Conversions," 232.

Orwell, George. "Inside the Whale." Pp. 215-56 in *A Collection of Essays.* New York: Doubleday, 1954.

Otto, Rudolf. *The Idea of the Holy.* Trans. John W. Harvey. New York: Oxford University Press, 1958.

Péguy, Charles. *The Portal of the Mystery of Hope.* Trans. David Louis Schindler, Jr. Grand Rapids: Eerdmans, 1996.

———. "Un Nouveau théologien: M. Fernand Laudet." *"Oeuvres de prose, 1909-1914.* (Paris: Gallimard/ Bibliothèque de la Pléiade, 1961), 1074-76. Quoted in Fraser, *Modern Catholic Novel,* 21.

Percy, Walker. "On Being a Catholic Novelist." Excerpted from *Conversations with Walker Percy.* Eds. Lewis A. Lawson and Victor A. Kramer. Jackson: University Press of Mississippi, 1985. Pp. 193-94 in Ryken, *The Christian Imagination.*

Pieper, Josef. *In Tune With the World: A Theory of Festivity.* Chicago: Franciscan Herald Press, 1973.

Podhoretz, John. Review of *How Far Can You Go?,* by David Lodge. *The New Republic,* 7 April 1982, 37-38.

Radcliffe, Liat. "Log On for Salvation." *Newsweek,* May 31, 2004, 10.

Randisi, Jennifer Lynn. *On Her Way Rejoicing: The Fiction of Muriel Spark.* Washington, D.C.: The Catholic University of America Press, 1991.

Ranke-Heinemann, Uta. *Eunuchs for the Kingdom of Heaven: Women, Sexuality and the Catholic Church.* New York: Doubleday, 1990.

Ratzinger, Joseph Cardinal. *Salt of the Earth: Christianity and the Catholic Church at the End of the Millennium.* San Francisco: Ignatius Press, 1997.

Read, Piers Paul. "The Catholic Novelist in a Secular Society." Pp. 199-212 in *Hell and Other Destinations.*

———. "A Confession." *Crisis,* September 1995, 14-15.

———. *Hell and Other Destinations: A Novelist's Reflections on This World and the Next.* San Francisco: Ignatius Press, 2006.

———. Interview by author. London. April 11, 2001.

———. *A Married Man.* London: Secker & Warburg, 1979.

———. *Monk Dawson.* Philadelphia: Lippincott, 1970.

———. *On the Third Day.* London: Secker & Warburg, 1990.

———. "Piers Paul Read on the Future of the Church." AD2000 November 1999. <http://www.ad2000.com.au/articles/1999/nov1999p8_286.html> (April 6, 2006).

———. *Polonaise.* London: Orion Books, Phoenix, 1997.

———. "Screwtape Returns." Pp. 76-79 in *Hell and Other Destinations.*

———. "Upon This Rock." Pp. 49-61 in *Hell and Other Destinations*

Reinhardt, Kurt F. *The Theological Novel of Modern Europe: An Analysis of Masterpieces by Eight Authors.* New York: Frederick Ungar, 1969.

Rice, Edward. *The Man in the Sycamore Tree: The Good Times and Hard Life of Thomas Merton.* New York: Doubleday, Image Books, 1972.

Ryken, Leland, ed. *The Christian Imagination.* Rev. ed. Colorado Springs: Waterbrook Press, 2002.

———. "Thinking Christianly About Literature." Pp. 23-34. in Ryken, *The Christian Imagination.*

Sayers, Valerie. "Being a Writer, Being Catholic." *Commonweal,* May 4, 2001, 12-16.

Scott, Nathan, *The Wild Prayer of Longing: Poetry and the Sacred,* 49. New Haven: Yale University Press, 1971. Quoted in Neary, *Like and Unlike God,* 114.

Shannon, William H. "A Note to the Reader." Pp. xix-xxiii in *The Seven Storey Mountain,* by Thomas Merton. 50th Anniversary Edition. San Diego: Harcourt Brace & Co., 1998.

Sidney, Sir Philip. *An Apology for Poetry.* Ed. Forrest G. Robinson. Indianapolis: Bobbs-Merrill, 1970.

Sonnenfeld, Albert. *Crossroads: Essays on the Catholic Novelists.* York, S.C.: French Literature Publications Co., 1982.

Spark, Muriel. *The Comforters.* London: Macmillan, 1957.

———. "My Conversion." *Twentieth Century* 170 (autumn 1961): 58-63.

Speaight, Robert. *The Life of Hilaire Belloc.* London, Hollis & Carter, 1957.

Steinfels, Peter. *A People Adrift: The Crisis of the Roman Catholic Church in America.* New York: Simon & Schuster, 2003.

Stumpf, Samuel Enoch. *Socrates to Sartre: A History of Philosophy.* 3rd ed. New York: McGraw-Hill, 1982.

Tarsitano, Louis. "Passing On True Religion." *Touchstone,* December 2001, 15-17.

Thompson, Peggy. "Comedy and Christianity: Surveying the Ground." *Christianity and Literature* 44, no. 1 (autumn 1994): 59-72.

Tracy, David. *The Analogical Imagination: Christian Theology and the Culture of Pluralism.* New York: Crossroad, 1981.

Ulanov, Barry. "The Ordeal of Evelyn Waugh." Pp. 79-93 in Friedman, *The Vision Obscured.*

Unamuno, Miguel de. *The Tragic Sense of Life,* 131. Vol. 7 of *Selected Works of Miguel de Unamuno.* Trans. Anthony Kerrigan. Princeton: Princeton University Press, 1972. Quoted in Lodge, *Paradise News,* 293.

Varone, François. *Ce Dieu absent qui fait problème.* Paris: Cerf, 1981. Quoted in Michael Paul Gallagher, S.J., *What Are They Saying About Unbelief?* New York: Paulist Press, 1995.

Vitz, Paul C. *Faith of the Fatherless.* Dallas: Spence, 1999.

The Wakefield Second Shepherds' Play. Pp. 44-72 in *An Anthology of English Drama Before Shakespeare,* edited by Robert B. Heilman. New York: Rinehart & Co., 1959.

Walsh, Chad. "A Hope for Literature." Pp. 206-33 in *The Climate of Faith in Modern Literature,* edited by Nathan A. Scott, Jr. New York: Seabury Press, 1964.

Watts, Greg. "Gandalf in London." *Our Sunday Visitor,* March 7, 2004, 18-19.

Waugh, Evelyn, *Brideshead Revisited: The Sacred and Profane Memories of Captain Charles Ryder.* Boston: Little, Brown & Co., 1945.

———. "Come Inside." Pp. 3-9 in *The Road to Damascus: The Spiritual Pilgrimage of Fifteen Converts to Catholicism,* edited by John A. O'Brien. Garden City: N.Y.: Doubleday, Image Books, 1955.

———. *The Essays, Articles and Reviews of Evelyn Waugh,* edited by Donat Gallagher. Boston: Little, Brown & Company, 1983.

———. "Fan-Fare." Pp. 300-4 in Evelyn Waugh, *Essays, Articles and Reviews.*

———. *The Letters of Evelyn Waugh,* edited by Mark Amory. London: Weidenfield & Nicholson, 1980.

Waugh, Harriet, "A Modern Emma Woodhouse." Review of *Unexplained Laughter,* by Alice Thomas Ellis. *The Spectator,* August 31, 1985, 24-25.

Weaver, Richard M. *Ideas Have Consequences.* Chicago: University of Chicago Press, 1948.

Weinberger, Theodore. "Religion and Fly Fishing: Taking Norman Maclean Seriously." *Renascence* 49, no. 4 (summer 1997): 281-89.

West, Christopher. *A Crash Course in the Theology of the Body.* Carpentersville, Il.: The Gift Foundation, 2002. Sound cassette, tape 3.

Whitehouse, J. C. *Vertical Man: The Human Being in the Catholic Novels of Graham Greene, Sigrid Undset, and Georges Bernanos.* London: Saint Austin Press, 1999.

Whittaker, Ruth. *The Faith and Fiction of Muriel Spark.* New York: St. Martin's Press, 1982.

"Why the RCIA Needs Improvement." *Our Sunday Visitor,* March 2, 2003, 2.

Wilson, A. N. Review of *The Other Side of the Fire,* by Alice Thomas Ellis. *The Spectator,* December 31, 1983, 22.

Wojtyla, Karol (Pope John Paul II). "Letter to Artists." 1999. <http://www.ewtn.com/library/papaldoc/jp2artis.htm> (10 April 2006).

Wood, Ralph C. *The Comedy of Redemption: Christian Faith and Comic Vision in Four American Novelists.* Notre Dame, Ind.: University of Notre Dame Press, 1988.

Woodman, Thomas. *Faithful Fictions: The Catholic Novel in British Literature.* Milton Keynes: Open University Press, 1991.

Woodward, Kenneth L. *Making Saints: How the Catholic Church Determines Who Becomes a Saint, Who Doesn't, and Why.* New York: Simon and Schuster, 1990.

Wright, Walter F. "Tone in Fiction." Pp. 297-304 in *The Theory of the Novel: New Essays,* edited by John Halperin. New York: Oxford University Press, 1974. Quoted in Kort, *Narrative Elements,* 100.

Marian E. Crowe (essay date 2007)

SOURCE: Crowe, Marian E. "*Angst* Meets Comedy: *Therapy.*" In *Aiming at Heaven, Getting the Earth: The English Catholic Novel Today,* pp. 187-213. Lanham, Md.: Lexington, 2007.

[*In the following essay, Crowe presents a detailed consideration of the elements of humor, within the frame of Catholicism, in Lodge's fiction.*]

> *Kierkegaard is for the young, but he is also for grownups who have attained the wisdom of knowing how fragile and partial is our knowing in the face of the absolute.*
>
> —Richard John Neuhaus, "Kierkegaard for Grownups"

> *There was never a pilgrim, "who did not come back to his village with one less prejudice and one more idea."*
>
> —Chateaubriand

That a television comedy writer would become captivated by the austere philosophy of Søren Kierkegaard may seem unlikely, but that is exactly what happens in David Lodge's *Therapy* (1995). Laurence Passmore, known as "Tubby" to his friends and relatives, is the very successful scriptwriter of a popular television situation comedy, *The People Next Door.* He is married to an attractive, talented university professor, has a grown son and daughter, a lovely home, and a flat in London, and enjoys the benefits of a large income. Yet, in spite of a life which most people would envy, Tubby is plagued by an inexplicable malaise. One day a friend kiddingly asks him how his *angst* is. Not knowing what the word means, he looks it up in his dictionary, which leads him to reference books to look up Existentialism, which leads him to look up Kierkegaard—and he is off on an experience that transforms his life.

As he begins reading Kierkegaard, Tubby discovers that the philosopher's concepts of dread and despair, his theory about repetition, the role of choice in creating an authentic self, and especially his analysis of the three stages of life—the aesthetic, the ethical, and the religious—begin to play themselves out in his own life. Kierkegaard provides more questions than

answers, but when Tubby's comfortable life is suddenly turned upside down, he faces his own existential crisis, which leads him all the way to the shrine of Santiago de Compostela in Spain.

The relevance of the title is evident early in the novel, for the first section is largely taken up with Tubby's descriptions of the various therapies he utilizes to alleviate his pain. He goes to Roland for physiotherapy, to Alexandra, a psychiatrist, for cognitive behaviour therapy, to Dudley for aromatherapy, and to Miss Wu for acupuncture. Tubby also considers his meetings with Amy, his platonic mistress in London, as "a sort of therapy."[1] Apart from his general despondency, the only reason given for these therapies is a knee operation to correct some sudden mysterious attacks of pain. The operation is not successful, nor is there any really satisfying explanation for the pain. Roland tells him that it is "Internal Derangement of the Knee," or as doctors sometimes refer to it I.D.K. Roland wryly suggests that the letters really stand for "I don't know" (13).

Tubby is not really miserable but just continually feels an inexplicable discontent. His emotional state is given farcical concreteness in the form of a solicitation from an organization called MIND, which comes in the form of an envelope with a balloon and a letter inside. When he blows up the balloon, it shows a profile of a man's head (which Tubby thinks resembles him) and the words: "BEREAVED, UNEMPLOYED, MONEY, SEPARATED, MORTGAGE, DIVORCED, HEALTH." The letter says, "'to you . . . the words on the balloon may seem just that—words. But the events they describe are at the heart of someone's nervous breakdown'" (61). This experience makes Tubby feel guilty because he cannot claim any of these factors as the cause for his unhappiness. He has no good reason to be unhappy, but he is.

Looking up the name *Kierkegaard* in a biographical dictionary, Tubby is transfixed by the titles of his books:

> I can't describe how I felt as I read the titles. If the hairs on the back of my neck were shorter, they would have lifted. *Fear and Trembling, The Sickness Unto Death, The Concept of Dread*—they didn't sound like titles of philosophy books, they seemed to name my condition like arrows thudding into a target. Even the ones I couldn't understand, or guess at the contents of, like *Either/Or* and *Repetition,* seemed pregnant with hidden meaning designed especially for me.

> (64-65)

Tubby starts reading *The Concept of Dread.* Kierkegaard defines *dread* as a "*sympathetic antipathy and an antipathetic sympathy.*"[2] Historian of philosophy Frederick Copleston explains the term this way: "Attraction and repulsion, sympathy and antipathy are interwoven." Dread is different from fear, which has as its object something "quite definite, real or imagined, a snake under the bed, a wasp threatening to sting, whereas dread is concerned with the as yet unknown and indefinite."[3] For Kierkegaard dread also refers to the state of a person who is both attracted to the good and repelled by it. It can also, however, refer to the anxiety one feels at the prospect of freedom. Kierkegaard uses Adam as an example: God's command not to eat the fruit awakens in him "the possibility of freedom." Adam experiences "the alarming possibility of *being able*. What it is he is able to do, of that he has no conception."[4] Adam is both attracted to the possibility of freedom yet also repelled because it involves sin.

Kierkegaard thinks that this state of dread often precedes a transition to another mode of living. His notion of the three stages of life is developed in *Either/Or*, one of the other books Tubby borrows from the library, along with *The Concept of Dread*.[5] The first stage is the aesthetic. Although the name suggests that a person at this stage is primarily concerned with beauty, what Kierkegaard means is actually closer to what is commonly understood by the word *hedonism*, a devotion to pleasure. The pleasures may be those of gross sensuality, but they can also be the refined pleasures of the intellect or of the fine arts, the emotional pleasure of human relationships (such as the Bloomsbury Group advocated), or the romantic idealization of nature (as with Wordsworth). The aesthetic person's highest goal is to enjoy the fullest range of experience, unencumbered by any objective moral norms, ethical principles, or religious faith.

Tubby at the beginning of the novel is a Kierkegaardian aesthete, who certainly enjoys the pleasures of the senses. He relishes good food, particularly at Gabrielli's, the Italian restaurant he frequents with his platonic mistress, Amy; as well as the homemade dishes she sometimes brings to the flat, "*moussaka*, or beef with olives or *coq au vin*" (42). He is fond of the pleasures of sport. "I don't know anything like that glowing, aching tiredness you feel after a keen game of squash or eighteen holes of gold or five sets of tennis" (24). He also enjoys a satisfying sex life with his "sexy wife at home" (31). Furthermore, he enjoys it with comfort and security. "One thing I've never worried about, though, is Sally's fidelity. We've had our ups and downs, of course, in nearly thirty years of marriage, but we've always been faithful to each other. . . . To enjoy sex you need comfort—clean sheets, firm mattresses, warm bedrooms—and continuity" (28).

Tubby is not a bad man. He is not a lecher or a gross sensualist. He is a faithful husband and responsible father. He feels sorry for the squatter who has bedded down in the entryway to his London flat and invites him up rather than have him taken away by the police. He makes people laugh. He is endearing at times, as in his self-description, which he is directed to write by his psychotherapist:

> My stomach was all muscle in those days, . . . but as I got older, in spite of regular exercise, the muscle turned to flab and then spread to my hips and bum, so now I'm more pear-shaped than barrel-shaped. They say that inside every fat man there's a thin man struggling to get out, and I hear his stifled groans every time I look into the bathroom mirror. It's not just the shape of my torso that bothers me, either, and it's not just the torso, come to that. My chest is covered with what looks like a doormat-sized Brillo pad that grows right up to my Adam's apple.

(19)

Although he is a rich, successful television writer, Tubby suffers from the same nagging self doubts and self criticism as most people. His psychotherapist is quick to diagnose his problem as guilt and lack of self-esteem, those ubiquitous whipping boys of the therapeutic culture. Tubby admits that he lacks self-esteem and craves the respect of others. Yet that doesn't seem an adequate explanation of his unhappiness, given all the positives in his life. Tubby's preoccupation with his unhappiness is causing him to be distracted. He sometimes simply fails to hear what people are saying to him.

It may seem hyperbolic to suggest that Tubby is suffering from Kierkegaardian dread or despair—what Amy calls *angst*—but Tubby finds the titles *Fear and Trembling, The Sickness Unto Death,* and *The Concept of Dread* compelling. He does seem to be experiencing the emotion that usually precedes the transition from one stage to another. As one historian of philosophy puts it, "an individual on the aesthetic level is aware, notwithstanding his variety of sense experiences, that his life consists, or *ought* to consist, of more than his emotive and sense experiences."[6] Such a person inevitably suffers from boredom, and his life comes to seem empty and meaningless.

Tubby is puzzled because he cannot identify any reason for his unhappiness. He does mention some annoyances: occasional sleeplessness, his inability to have a climax when he had sex with his wife recently, a predicament about how to write the female star out of the television show when her contract expires. None of these problems, however, seems an adequate explanation.

Reflecting and amplifying his personal unhappiness is Tubby's growing awareness of the pain and violence of the world at large, imaging, as it were, his own sadness writ large. A two-year-old boy is lured away from a butcher shop by two older boys and is later found murdered. Two ten-year-old boys are charged with the crime. Vulgar and sterile new buildings and shopping plazas proliferate, homeless people bed down on London sidewalks, (including one who sleeps in the doorway to Tubby's London flat), bomb alerts are frequent. He learns that the wife of one of his tennis partners has had a sexual fling with the son of the Club's golf pro; and his friend Jake, married less than two years, asks to borrow Tubby's flat to have a rendezvous with a woman. Tubby is further disillusioned when he spots his physician, Dr. Nizar, with a young woman he knows is not his wife. Even the royal family is misbehaving sexually—"Internal Derangement of the Monarchy" (92). The evening news reports the death from cancer of Bobby Moore, hero of Britain's victory in the 1966 World Cup Final. The poor response of a studio audience for the filming of *The People Next Door* is explained by the fact that they have just received notice that the plant where they work is going to shut down and they will all lose their jobs (79). Kierkegaard gives Tubby the vocabulary to describe his emotional state. "Dread is what I feel when I wake in the small hours in a cold sweat. Acute but unspecific Dread" (64).

Tubby resists the idea that what he feels is Kierkegaardian despair, writing in his journal that what he feels is "nothing as dramatic as that" (111), yet he comes to understand that Kierkegaard does not mean despair over some particular thing or event, but a more generalized, diffuse despair. In *The Sickness Unto Death* Kierkegaard writes, "So to despair over something is not yet properly despair. It is the beginning, or it is as when the physician says of a sickness that it has not yet declared itself."[7]

Tubby's vague, unfocused despair suddenly becomes very focused when his wife Sally tells him that she wants a separation. The disease has declared itself.

For the reader, who has been drawn into Tubby's account of his problems with the television show, his various therapy sessions, his discussions with his platonic mistress, and his lavish lifestyle, this development is almost as much of a shock as it is to Tubby. Like him, the reader may have failed to notice some clues that all was not well with the marriage: his remark that these days sex is almost always at Sally's instigation, his admission that he sometimes fails to listen to what Sally is saying to him, his impulsively running off to the filming session of *The People Next Door* when he expressly told Sally that he was not going to go, in consequence of which she had invited the neighbors in for a drink.

This shock propels Tubby into a spate of wild, erratic behavior, including spying on his wife's tennis coach, taking his platonic mistress to Tenerife, and flying to California to try to have a second chance with a woman whose advances he had declined several years before. Sally's announcement is followed by a series of first-person narratives by other characters, giving their version of what has happened. The first one is testimony by Brett Sutton, Sally's handsome tennis coach, relating how someone had tried to break into his house, how he found his ladder outside leaned up against his bedroom window, and how finally he was awakened one night to find Tubby in his bedroom with a torch (flashlight), staring at him. Tubby's first reaction to Sally's request for a separation had been to assume she had a lover and to suspect her virile tennis coach.

Brett's account is followed by Amy's, a description of Tubby's pathetic attempt to turn his platonic relationship with Amy into a sexual one. Amy's story, however, also sheds light on Tubby's marriage and separation: that Sally had told Laurence (as Amy calls him) that "he was like a zombie" (137), that he had spent the whole weekend trying to talk her out of it, that he had asked her if there was someone else and she said there wasn't, and that Sally had once walked out and stayed away for a weekend, and when she returned insisted on marriage counseling, thus explaining how Tubby happened to be going to psychotherapy in the first place. Amy's account is followed by similar narratives by Louise, an executive with a television production company in Hollywood who had once tried to seduce Tubby when he was in California to advise on the American version of *The People Next Door*; Ollie, the producer of *The People Next Door*; Samantha, a beautiful young script director whom Tubby takes along on a weekend in Copenhagen; and finally, Sally herself, who gives an extended account of their courtship, marriage, and the reason why she wants to end the marriage.

Telling the same story from different points of view naturally provides a much fuller and more richly textured view of Tubby, his marital situation, and his fascination with Kierkegaard. Multiple viewpoints are not uncommon in contemporary fiction, but *Therapy* provides a tour de force when Tubby again becomes the narrator and reveals that he has written all of the previous accounts by imagining himself into the psyche of those people. This experiment was done at the direction of his psychotherapist. Tubby recognizes that Alexandra thinks the exercise will help to raise his self-esteem because it should help him to realize that people really do not hate him, but actually like and respect him. The project does not, however, have the intended effect. "Being the sort of writer I am, I couldn't just summarize other people's views of me, I had to let them speak their thoughts in their own voices. And what they said wasn't very flattering" (212). When Alexandra accuses him of having been very hard on himself, he says he had tried to see himself "truthfully from other people's points of view" (212).

The writing of these accounts is a pivotal event in Tubby's moral growth. Kierkegaard's stress on the *individual*—as opposed to generic or abstract *humanity*—is what is distinctive about his philosophy. It is the individual in his or her particularity that is all important, not generic *humanity* or *mankind,* which is the subject of so much philosophy.⁸ Tubby's writing of these various accounts, each of which so perfectly captures the personality, outlook, and even style of speech of each "author," indicates an extraordinary capacity to enter into the particularity of those persons. Although the ability to capture the idiosyncratic flavor of each of the character's speech could be attributed simply to the talent of a practiced scriptwriter, Tubby's ability to enter into other people's mindset and vicariously live their experience goes beyond a good ear for dialogue to an ability to appreciate the uniqueness of those individuals and suggests the beginning of real moral growth. Recall that in the classic conversion story, *A Christmas Carol,* Scrooge's reformation is accomplished through his opportunity to see life through other people's eyes—in particular their views of him.

Tubby's keen awareness of these people as individuals suggests that he is poised to make a transition to Kierkegaard's second stage, the ethical. In *Concluding Unscientific Postscript,* Kierkegaard says, "The ethical is concerned with particular human beings, and with each and everyone of them by himself. If God knows how many hairs there are on a man's head, the ethical knows how many human beings there are; and its enumeration is not in the interest of a total sum, but for the sake of each individual."⁹ Historian of philosophy Samuel Stumpf summarizes Kierkegaard's notion of the ethical man:

> Unlike the aesthetic man, who has no universal standards but only his own taste, the ethical man does recognize and accept rules of conduct that reason formulates. Moral rules give the ethical man's life the elements of form and consistency. Moreover, the ethical man accepts the limitations upon his life that moral responsibility imposes. Kierkegaard illustrates the contrast between the aesthetic man and the ethical man in their attitude toward sexual behavior, saying that whereas the former yields to his impulses wherever there is an attraction, the ethical man accepts the obligations of marriage as an expression of reason, the universal reason of man.¹⁰

It may seem ironic to suggest that Tubby is moving into the ethical stage, considering that previously (when he was apparently an aesthete) he was faithful to his wife during a long marriage, whereas now his greatest desire is to go to bed with other women as soon as possible. Yet his fidelity to Sally was not, in fact, based on strong ethical principles as much as on his penchant for comfort and convenience. It is in the context of explaining why he and Sally have been faithful to each other that he makes the remark about needing "clean sheets, firm mattresses, warm bedrooms—and continuity" to have enjoyable sex (28). Furthermore, in explaining why he and Amy do not have sex, he says, "Amy doesn't really want it and I don't really need it. I get plenty of sex at home" (31). He again appeals to comfort as the reason that he values monogamy over the philandering indulged in by so many of his friends: "What's so wonderful about married sex (and especially middle-aged, post-menopausal sex, when the birth-control business is over and done with) is that you don't have to be thinking about it all the time." Furthermore, Tubby finds that this sense of routine spills over into all aspects of married life so that you "need to speak to each other less and less" (128). So Tubby's "fidelity" does not really qualify him as "ethical" in Kierkegaard's terms.

There are some indications that Tubby has been moving toward the ethical sphere even before the shock of his wife's asking for a separation. Early in the novel, he has written some dialogue for *The People Next Door* that refers to abortion. One of the couples on the show suspects that their unmarried daughter may be pregnant and mentions the possibility of her having a "termination" (57). His producer feels the reference is "too controversial, and too upsetting" (58). Tubby, however, feels that it is unrealistic to expect that an "educated, middle class" couple would not even mention the possibility of abortion in such a situation. To the objection that the lines are not "'absolutely essential'" to the story, Tubby replies, "'Not absolutely essential. . . . Just a little moment of truth'" (58). Although seeing abortion as an option in a problem pregnancy may seem anything but ethical to some readers, it is important to remember that for Kierkegaard the word *ethical* does not mean adherence to any *particular* set of moral proscriptions or religious teachings, but simply the fact that one *does* order one's life by duty and principle, rather than simply by a devotion to pleasure. Tubby here is risking offending segments of his audience in order to depict honestly current thinking on a controversial subject.

Other indications that Tubby is developing some kind of an ethical sensibility are his refusal to let Jake use his London flat for one of his sexual trysts and his reluctance to turn over to the police the young squatter who has taken up residence in his entryway. It is conceivable that in each case Tubby bases his action more on an emotion than on any clearly and consciously held moral principle. He tells Jake that if he allowed him to use his flat for a sexual assignation, he would "'never be able to look Rhoda [Jake's wife] straight in the eye again.'" (48). As for the squatter, Tubby says, "I surprised in myself a strange reluctance to hand the youth over to the power of the law" (115). He invites him upstairs for a cup of tea and gives him fifteen pounds to rent a room for the night. Admittedly, in taking these actions Tubby does not demonstrate the clear adherence to duty and principle that is characteristic of Kierkegaard's ethical man. Yet, he seems to be moving toward a stronger sense of the rights and dignity of other people than he had as the callow youth and television writer presented in the flashbacks. In a stumbling and half-hearted way, Tubby is moving *toward* the ethical.

Kierkegaard's influence in nudging him toward the ethical is most dramatically shown when Tubby takes Samantha, a voluptuous script editor, along with him on a trip to Copenhagen ostensibly to do some research, but, in fact, to see the hallowed places associated with the Danish philosopher. He also has every intention of seducing Samantha, which is why he invites her. Yet when the delectable young woman, who is perfectly aware of his intentions, offers herself to him, he declines. When Samantha says she thought he brought her to Copenhagen to sleep with her, he replies, "'You're quite right, that was why I asked you to come, but when I got here I found I couldn't do it. . . . Because of Kierkegaard'" (190). Furthermore, he confides that Kierkegaard has become a kind of "'spirit or a good angel, saying, "Don't exploit this young girl."'" (190). In fact, what started out to be a sexual escapade ends up being a kind of pilgrimage as Tubby stands in reverence before Kierkegaard's possessions in the Kierkegaard room of the City Museum "as if they were sacred relics" (184). Kierkegaard has metamorphosed into a kind of guardian angel "hovering at [his] shoulder" (209).

If Tubby's Copenhagen trip can be considered a pseudopilgrimage, his next strategy for coping with the pain of the end of his marriage involves him in a very real—if not exactly traditional—pilgrimage. It begins when he starts looking for his first girlfriend, Maureen Kavanagh. Memories of Maureen start popping into his mind even before Sally asks for a separation. Thinking of his expensive car, which he is so proud of, Tubby wonders what Maureen would think of it, given that she considered it such a treat to ride in even an old car when they were dating in the 1950s. When he encounters Kierkegaard's religious ideas, he again thinks of Maureen, whose parents were strict

Catholics, who would only allow him to see Maureen at the Catholic Youth Club at her parish. Although a nominal Anglican, Tubby had feigned interest in Catholicism in order to be allowed to attend the meetings and social events. When the lavender that Tubby's aromatherapist uses on him reminds him of the lavender scented stationery Maureen used to send him letters, it brings back "Maureen in all her specificity. Maureen. My first love. My first breast" (221). He mentions that memories of Maureen have been flitting through his mind ever since he have been writing a journal, as his psychotherapist had directed him to do. He then decides to write a full-fledged memoir of Maureen.

Tubby recounts their meeting at the corner where they each caught different trams going to their different schools. His account of their long, drawn-out, strictly chaperoned courtship, is not only nostalgic but amazingly erotic. He sees and admires her for months without ever speaking a word to her. They finally become acquainted when he helps her pick up her books after she falls when running for her tram. He summons up his nerve to ask her to go to the movies with him, only to be called a "'young blackguard'" by her stern father and gruffly told, "'My daughter's a respectable girl. I won't have her talkin' to strange fellas on street corners, understand?'" (230). Tubby attends every Catholic Youth Club function in order to have some time with her, and at the dances, he actually gets to touch her. The older, memoir-writing Tubby makes an amusing contrast between the dancing of today and the dancing of the 1950s:

> When, nowadays, I put my head inside a discothèque or nightclub patronized by young people, I'm struck by the contrast between the eroticism of the ambience— the dim, lurid lighting, the orgasmic throb of the music, the tight-fitting, provocative clothes—and the tactile impoverishment of the actual dancing. I suppose they have so much physical contact afterwards that they don't miss it on the dance floor, but for us it was the other way round. Dancing meant that, even in a church youth club, you were actually allowed to hold a girl in your arms in public, perhaps a girl you'd never even met before you asked her to dance, feel her thighs brush against yours under her rustling petticoats, sense the warmth of her bosom against your chest, inhale the scent behind her ears or the smell of shampoo from her freshly washed hair as it tickled your cheek.
>
> (235)

Tubby says that they "advanced in physical intimacy slowly, and by infinitesimal degrees" (238). The contrast to the blatantly open and free sexuality of the first part of the novel is striking: the casual philandering of Jake and Tubby's other friends, the eagerness of two young women in Hollywood to go to bed with a man they hardly know, the way that Samantha, aroused by a pornographic film, almost begs Tubby to have sex with her. Looking back, the older Tubby recognizes that Maureen's upbringing and restricted social environment allowed her to have a combination of traits almost unheard of today.

> She had a naturally pure mind, pure without being prudish. Dirty jokes left her looking genuinely blank. She talked about wanting to get married and have children when she grew up, but she didn't seem to connect this with sexuality. Yet she loved to be kissed and cuddled. She purred in my arms like a kitten. Such sensuality and innocence could hardly co-exist nowadays, I believe, when teenagers are exposed to so much sexual information and imagery.
>
> (241)

Yet the scene where Tubby first holds Maureen's breast is more erotic than many explicit descriptions of sexual intercourse that are such a staple of contemporary fiction.[11]

> Holding my breath I gently released a breast, the left one, from its cup. It rolled into my palm like a ripe fruit. God! I've never felt a sensation like it, before or since, like the first feel of Maureen's young breast—so soft, so smooth, so tender, so firm, so elastic, so mysteriously gravity-defying. I lifted the breast a centimetre, and weighed it in my cupped palm, then gently lowered my hand again until it just fitted the shape without supporting it. That her breast should still hang there, proud and firm, seemed as miraculous a phenomenon as the Earth itself floating in space. I took the weight again and gently squeezed the breast as it lolled in my palm like a naked cherub.
>
> (246)

Tubby goes on to recount how Maureen's growing sense of guilt about the liberties she is allowing him led him to end their relationship in a way that he now sees was hurtful and cruel. "I realized *for the first time* what an appalling thing I had done all those years ago. I broke a young girl's heart, callously, selfishly, wantonly" (261). In fact, the writing of this memoir has dramatically changed the way he thinks of Maureen. Whereas in the past, if he thought of her at all, it was just as a nice, naive kid, he now seems overwhelmed, as he was in his youth, by her extraordinary beauty and her warm, affectionate nature.

This development in Tubby's life is important in three ways. First, it connects him more strongly with Kierkegaard, initiating an experience that resonates with the philosopher's ideas in *Repetition*. Second, it signifies a growth in character that is moving him closer to be the ethical sphere. Third, it sets him on the road of pilgrimage.

Ever since Tubby has discovered Kierkegaard, he is as fascinated with the story of the philosopher's relationship with a woman named Regine, as he is with his philosophy. Kierkegaard became engaged to Regine but soon afterward, broke it off quite suddenly. He still loved her, but was convinced that the difference in their temperaments—her lighthearted gaiety and his melancholy, introspection and seriousness—did not bode well for a happy marriage. Furthermore, he was convinced that Regine was "unreflective and unspiritual" and "could never accompany him along the ways of critical reflection."[12] Regine begged him to reconsider, but he would not.

Tubby is impressed with the parallels between Kierkegaard's break with Regine and his own with Maureen so many years ago. He even notes that their names almost rhyme—Regine-Maureen. Also, just as Regine, begging Kierkegaard to change his mind, asked him to kiss her, similarly, Maureen, after telling Tubby that they would have to refrain from kissing as long as she was playing the Virgin Mary in the Nativity play, told him that he could kiss her once before the moratorium and lifted her face. Tubby's response was, "'Oh, grow up, Maureen,'" and he walked away (253). His extended reflection on this era of his life makes him determined to find his old photographs of her and then to find Maureen herself. He feels an urgent need to make up to her for his cruelty.

Kierkegaard's book *Repetition* was written right after his parting from Regine and is to some extent based on it. The narrator is an older gentleman who has become the confidante of a young man who, like Kierkegaard, had become engaged to a young woman he loves, but who decides to break it off for rather complicated reasons. Two views about repetition are expressed in this work. The first is that of the narrator, an aesthete, who believes that it might be possible to retrieve past events by calling them forth from the eternal present where they all reside. In a humorous account of his visit to Berlin in order to test this thesis by staying in the same lodgings and attending the same theater as he had done previously, he learns that this is not possible, partly because he has tried so hard to bring it about. The young man, on the other hand, is obsessed with the story of Job, particularly the way in which Job received back from God everything he had lost and more. The young man considers this a *"repetition."*[13] He admires Job—not for his patience—but because "the disputes at the boundaries of faith are fought out in him, [and] the colossal revolt of the wild and aggressive powers of passion are presented here."[14] God effected a repetition that the young man compares to a thunderstorm. "When everything has stalled, when thought is immobilized, when language is silent, when explanation returns home in despair—then there has to be a thunderstorm. . . . When did it occur for Job? When every *thinkable* human certainty and probability were impossible."[15] Job's ordeal "places him in a purely personal relationship of opposition to God, in a relationship such that he cannot allow himself to be satisfied with any explanation at second hand."[16]

When the young man finds out that his former fiancée has married someone else, he considers that such a thunderstorm heralds a repetition in his own life. He has been "given back" his freedom but without resorting to the strategy suggested by his confidante: that he pretend that he has a mistress. He compares himself with Job. "Is there not, then, a repetition? Did I not get everything double? Did I not get myself again and precisely in such a way that I might have a double sense of its meaning?"[17] The young man is convinced that there is repetition after all although it does not mean literal replication. Even though Job got new children, his original beloved children are still lost to him. True repetition is "repetition of the spirit," not material duplication.[18] Furthermore, this repetition contrasts the attempt of the aesthete to recreate his earlier Berlin experience. According to one Kierkegaard scholar, "his attempt suffers the fate of all repetition pursued on an aesthetic basis: it fails just because it is an *attempt* and because it is *pursued*."[19] "Repetition of the spirit," on the other hand, is a gift from God and comes with the violence and surprise of a thunderstorm. "How beneficent a thunderstorm is! How blessed it is to be rebuked by God!"[20]

Given that Kierkegaard's young man believes that Job's repetition occurs only after "everything has stalled, when thought is immobilized, when language is silent, when explanation returns home in despair," one could argue that the end of Tubby's marriage constitutes a "thunderstorm" in his life.[21] When his comfortable and routinized life is shattered, Tubby starts thinking of different kinds of repetition.

Aside from his ridiculous antics trying to discover Sally's lover—the only explanation Tubby can think of as to why she would want to leave him—his first response is to think of all the opportunities he has had for extramarital sex, opportunities that he has declined. He now wants to make up for lost time by recreating the opportunity but this time going ahead and enjoying the delights of unmarried sex. First he decides to turn his relationship with his platonic mistress into a nonplatonic one. Although he and Amy do, in fact, have sexual intercourse, the whole experience is far from the romantic idyll Tubby envisions, partly because of the vulgarity, commercialism, and downright ugliness of Tenerife, the island where they go for their tryst, ("essentially an enormous lump of coke, and the beaches are made of powdered coke"), and partly because the sex itself is so unsatisfying (152). In trying to go back and remake his relationship with Amy into something else, he ends up spoiling what had been a mutually satisfying friendship.

Tubby's next attempt at remaking the past more closely approximates the attempt of Kierkegaard's narrator when he tries to repeat his theater experience in Berlin. Tubby wants to re-create an experience exactly—only he wants it to end differently. He remembers that when he was in Los Angeles as a consultant for the American version of *The People Next Door,* Louise, an attractive, young television executive, had been very forthright about her willingness to sleep with him. Now that his wife has left him, he wants to go back and accept the offer. He sees it as a possible Kierkegaardian repetition. "It was the lure of Repetition, the idea of having Louise offer herself to me again, making possession doubly sweet, that impelled me to travel all those thousands of miles" (207). Tubby is obsessed with the idea of replicating every detail about the experience he remembers but is continually frustrated. At first Louise doesn't even remember him, although she finally does when Tubby refreshes her memory. When she agrees to have dinner with him, Tubby insists that they eat at the same fish restaurant in Venice that he remembers. It turns out, however, that the fish restaurant is now a Thai eatery. He wants to eat outside and watch a glorious sunset like they did before, but now it is chilly and overcast. He remembers that she had liked whiskey sours and is disappointed when she wants only mineral water. He even orders the same kind of wine, Napa Valley Chardonnay. As Louise says in her memoir (actually written by Tubby), "He was trying to recreate the exact circumstances of that evening four years ago as far as possible in every detail. . . . I guess in his head I was forever sitting at that table beside the ocean, gazing wistfully out to sea and waiting for him to reappear, released from his matrimonial vows, to sweep me into his arms" (167-68). The ultimate disappointment, though, is that Louise will not go to bed with him because she now has a steady boyfriend (by whom she is trying to get pregnant) and only agreed to the dinner date because her boyfriend was out of town.

As Tubby's plans to recapture his lost sexual opportunities are all foiled, he begins thinking more and more of Maureen. He decides to try and find her and returns to Hatchford, the neighborhood where they had lived. He finds it an "eerie" experience, "a dreamlike mixture of the familiar and the unfamiliar" (264) Although the streets and main buildings are familiar, the area is now inhabited mostly by Caribbean and Asian families. Tubby finds the house he lived in has been improved: sealed aluminum units replacing the old sash windows and the wall dividing the two small parlors into one "bright and pleasantly proportioned living-room" (265). Tubby immediately wonders why his family hadn't done that. Maureen's house, however, has not simply been changed, it has been demolished.

Through inquiries at the parish church, he finds a record of Maureen's marriage—to Bede Harrington, who had been an officious, pompous, and unattractive member of the Catholic Youth Club. Finding Bede's number in the London phone book, Tubby calls and then goes to see him. From him he learns that Maureen is in Spain on a pilgrimage.

Impulsively, Tubby decides to go and find her in Spain. His enthusiasm for this daft project is heightened when, after he tells Bede that his wife has left him, Bede responds, "'Then that makes two of us'" (277). Is Tubby's decision to seek Maureen in Spain a Kierkegaardian "leap" or just another impulsive attempt of a newly separated man to ease his pain? Perhaps a little of both. Kierkegaard is clear about his conviction that significant moral growth—from the aesthetic sphere to the ethical and from the ethical to the religious—occurs, not as a slow and gradual process, but as a leap. Tubby's decision to seek Maureen in Spain is such a bold and radical decision that it can be considered a "leap." Having made this decision, his whole focus and attitude change. He stops fighting the divorce, telling Sally's lawyer that he "wouldn't obstruct divorce proceedings any longer, and would agree to appropriate maintenance and a reasonable financial settlement" (278). The terms he offers are deemed by Sally's lawyer to be not only fair but generous.

Whereas his earlier forays to Tenerife and Los Angeles were undertaken with a clear goal in mind (sex!), Tubby does not really know what he wants or expects from Maureen. "I don't really know what I want from Maureen. Not her love back, obviously—it's too late for a Repetition" (278). He is opening himself to the unknown, and in that sense too this action is a leap. In the introduction to the last section of the book, which is a revised memoir of his experience in Spain, Tubby says, "I do feel I've reached the end of something. And, hopefully, a new beginning" (286).

The tone and ambiance of this section are in sharp contrast with the rest of the novel. Nature comes more to the fore, and the accoutrements of living are much more austere and simple than those of Tubby's tennis club, London flat, fine restaurants, and various therapeutic venues. His expensive car, which he has ferried over to the continent, ("the Richmobile," as his daughter calls it) is his only link with his former life. After he crosses the Pyrenees, the weather is fine, and Tubby notes in his journal that "the scenery was spectacular: mountains green to their peaks, valleys smiling in the sunshine, caramel-coloured cows with clinking bells, flocks of mountain sheep, vultures hang-gliding at eye level" (288). The contrast with the earlier descriptions of the ugliness of Tenerife or the congestion of London are obvious. Just as in *Paradise News* the early descriptions of a tawdry, commercialized Hawaii give way to a sensitive rendition of its natural beauty as the protagonist grows into greater spiritual maturity, so here Tubby seems to become sensitive to the natural world for the first time.[22]

Even before Tubby actually finds Maureen, he is drawing close to her world by his encounter with Catholic Spain. When he attends a Catholic Mass at the monastery of Roncesvalles, he likes "the idea of doing something Maureen would certainly have done a few weeks earlier" (290). As in *How Far Can You Go?* and *Paradise News,* Lodge depicts the surprise of someone who hasn't attended Mass in many years and encounters the post-Vatican II liturgy. Tubby notes that "the pilgrim mass didn't bear much resemblance to anything I remembered from the repertory of the Immaculate Conception in the old days. There were several priests saying the mass at the same time and they stood in a semi-circle behind a plain table-style altar . . . facing the congregation" (290-91). Yet there is a sense of connection with the past as well, "the liturgy echoing round the pillars and vaults of the ancient church, as it had for centuries" (291).

Therapy is the only one of Lodge's Catholic novels whose protagonist is not a cradle Catholic, lapsed Catholic, or convert. Approaching Catholicism from the outside, Tubby describes the appearance of this religion to one who, though acquainted with it through Maureen and the Catholic Youth Club, is not conditioned by early indoctrination, fear of hell, or moral guilt. His description of Benediction from his adolescent point of view is classic example of an outsider's view:

> Suddenly there was a clamour of high-pitched bells, and I peeped through the doorway, looking down the aisle to the altar. It was quite a sight, ablaze with dozens of tall, thin lighted candles. The priest, dressed in a heavy embroidered robe of white and gold, was holding up something that flashed and glinted with reflected light, a white disc in a glass case, with golden rays sticking out all round it like a sunburst.
>
> (232)

The exotic strangeness of Catholicism, which was such a strong characteristic of the pre-Vatican II Church, is much attenuated in the Catholicism that Tubby encounters in the 1990s; yet it is there, especially in Spain, for Catholicism drags its long and picturesque, if sometimes tortured, history behind it. In the village of Cebrero, the church "contains relics of some gruesome mediaeval miracle, when the communion bread and wine turned into real flesh and blood, and the place is also said to be associated with the legend of the Holy Grail" (293).

Through patient questioning and searching, Tubby finally does find Maureen. As in Hatchford, he is struck by the changes wrought by the intervening years. The beautiful young girl has become "a plump, solitary woman in baggy cotton trousers and a broad-brimmed straw hat" (293-94). "In truth she looked a wreck . . . her neck was creased like an old garment; and her figure had gone soft and shapeless, with no perceptible waistline between the cushiony mounds of her bosom and the broad beam of her hips" (296). Not only does she look different, but the site of their meeting is far from the idyllic spot he had imagined. "As it was, we met on the edge of an ugly main road in one of the least attractive bits of Castile, deafened by the noise of tyres and engines, choked by exhaust fumes, and buffeted by gusts of gritty air displaced by passing juggernauts" (294).

The biggest shock of all, however, comes one night when Tubby hears Maureen crying in her room in the inn where they have stopped. He goes to her room to comfort her, gets in bed with her, and discovers that where one of her breasts should be, there is a "plateau of skin and bone" and "the erratic line of a scar" (307). Although startled, he is not repulsed. In fact, he kisses the puckered flesh. Maureen says "'that's the nicest thing anybody ever did to me'" (307), a remark that takes on added poignancy when it is later revealed that her husband has had no sexual relations with her since her mastectomy.

Once he and Maureen actually get to Santiago, the cathedral itself is a kind of icon of Catholicism, a montage of its colorful, grotesque, troubled, and romantic past. Tubby describes it as follows:

> The Cathedral is a bit of a dog's breakfast architecturally but, as we say in television, it works. The elaborately decorated façade is eighteenth-century baroque, with a grand staircase between the two towers and spires. Behind it is the portico of the earlier romanesque building, the Portico de la Gloria, carved by a mediaeval genius called Maestro Matteo. It depicts in amazing, often humorous, detail, some two hundred figures, including Jesus, Adam and Eve, Matthew, Mark, Luke and John, twenty-four old codgers with musical instruments from the Book of Revelations, and a selection of the saved and the damned at the Last Judgement. St. James has pride of place, sitting on top of a pillar just under the feet of Jesus.
>
> (309)

The sense of exuberance, bordering on burlesque, and the tumultuous variety of this building capture an aspect of Catholicism that can be as off-putting as it is attractive. The juxtaposition of Tubby's earthy colloquialisms ("dog's breakfast," "old codgers") with the language of high art ("façade," "portico," "ba-

roque," "romanesque") is a linguistic icon of the rich texture of Catholicism that is both awe-inspiring and comic.

Catholicism's insistence on the material as a valid conduit for the spirit is evident in the pillar supporting the statue of St. James, where the custom is for pilgrims to place their fingers into the hollow spaces that have been worn into the marble by previous pilgrims. Maureen does so and closes her eyes in prayer. Behind the main altar pilgrims climb up on a platform behind the statue of St. James and embrace it, the traditional "'hug for St. James'" (310). Even Tubby is swept up in the enthusiasm and, like the other pilgrims, knocks his head against the forehead of the bust of the sculptor, Maestro Matteo, the tradition being that doing so will enable one to acquire something of his wisdom. Tubby is still a comedy writer at heart. "Every now and again somebody would bang their head against the pillar under the statue of St. James as they put their fingers in the holes, and then everybody in the line behind them would follow suit. I was tempted to try slapping my buttocks like a Bavarian folkdancer as I paid homage, just to see if it caught on" (310).

Tubby's droll comments about this spectacle come close to rendering it satire—if not farce. Yet that doesn't quite happen because it is overlaid with a genuine respect for Maureen's faith. When he had stopped at the abbey of Roncesvalles, where all the pilgrims are asked to complete a questionnaire, he had found Maureen's. Under *Motives for journey* the pilgrims could check one or more of the following: *"1. Religious 2. Spiritual 3. Recreational 4. Cultural 5. Sporting"* (290). Maureen has checked only *"Spiritual."* When they arrive in Santiago, Tubby wants to find accommodations, but Maureen wants to go immediately to the Cathedral. Kneeling at the foot of the pillar, she closes her eyes in prayer. When to Tubby's surprise, she reveals that she had booked a room at the most elegant hotel in the city before she had left home, he asks how she could be sure she would arrive on that very day. Her reply: "'I had faith'" (312).

Yet it is not only piety that has inspired Maureen to make this pilgrimage. She is trying to get over the death of her son Damien, who was killed while doing volunteer work in Africa. As she tells Tubby:

> I read an article about the pilgrimage in a magazine, and it seemed just what I needed. Something quite challenging and clearly defined, something that would occupy your whole self, body and soul, for two or three months. I read a book about the history of it, and was completely fascinated. Literally millions of pilgrims went along this road, when the only way of doing it was on foot or on horseback. They must have got

something tremendous out of it, I thought to myself, or people wouldn't have kept on going.

(302-3)

Anyone who has ever read Chaucer's *Canterbury Tales* knows that motives for making pilgrimages have always been mixed. The worldly friar, the wife of Bath, and the crude miller have their counterparts in present day Spain.

> The most numerous were young Spaniards for whom the pilgrimage was obviously an impeccable excuse to get out of the parental home and meet other young Spaniards of the opposite sex. The *refugios* [inns built to accommodate pilgrims] are unsegregated. . . . Then there were the more sophisticated young backpackers from other countries, bronzed and muscular, attracted by the buzz on the international grapevine that Santiago was a really cool trip, with great scenery, cheap wine and free space to spread your bedroll.
>
> (292)

Others have more serious motivations, although they might not be specifically religious. Some are walking for charity, some to celebrate a turning point in their lives, others to step back from their lives and think about their future. Yet rather than dividing into neat categories of religious and nonreligious, the categories merge and blend. Like Maureen, many of the pilgrims would define their motives as "spiritual."

In his determination to find Maureen, Tubby actually becomes a pilgrim himself. When his agent objects to Tubby's taking a holiday in Spain at a critical time, Tubby retorts, "'It's not a holiday . . . it's a pilgrimage'" (280). At one point he and Maureen come upon a television crew filming a documentary about the pilgrimage. They ask to interview Tubby, but he insists, "'I'm not a true pilgrim.'" "'Ah! Who is a true pilgrim?'" asks the director. "'Someone for whom it's an existential act of self-definition,'" proclaims Tubby. "'A leap into the absurd, in Kierkegaard's sense'" (304). Tubby goes on to deliver his existentialist interpretation of pilgrimage to the television audience.[23]

Tubby may not consider himself a true pilgrim, but his Kierkegaardian overlay certainly renders his journey serious and spiritual, if not religious. In Kierkegaard's schema of the three stages, a person reaches the religious stage when, conscious of his own sins, his alienation from God, and his inability to fulfill the moral law by his own efforts, he makes a leap of faith which brings him into relationship with God. He knows God—not as an object—but intimately as a subject. The religious man is not free of suffering; indeed the truly religious person may suffer greatly, but like Job, is rewarded with an intimacy with God.

Tubby has worked out a schema for pilgrims corresponding to Kierkegaard's three stages of personal development. The aesthetic pilgrim is "mainly interested in having a good time," the ethical sees the pilgrimage "as essentially a test of stamina and self-discipline" (304-5). The true pilgrim, the religious one, makes the pilgrimage as a kind of leap into the absurd:

> To Kierkegaard, Christianity was "absurd": if it were entirely rational, there would be no merit in believing it. The whole point was that you chose to believe without rational compulsion—you made a leap into the void and in the process chose yourself. Walking a thousand miles to the shrine of Santiago without knowing whether there was anybody actually buried there was such a leap.[24]
>
> (305)

In fact, however, Tubby's participation in the pilgrimage goes beyond his moral support of Maureen and his endorsement of pilgrimage in the Kierkegaardian sense. He physically joins in. Because Maureen is suffering from strained ligaments, Tubby arranges to drive with her pack to each day's destination, arrange for accommodations, and then walk back, meet Maureen, and walk the rest of the way with her. Amazingly, Tubby's problem knee gives him no trouble. Maureen attributes this "miracle" to St. James: "'It's a well-known phenomenon. He helps you. I'd never have got this far without him. I remember when I was climbing the pass through the Pyrenees . . . feeling I couldn't go any further and would just roll into a ditch and die, I felt a force like a hand in the small of the back pushing me on, and before I knew where I was, I found myself at the top'" (300). Maureen also attributes to St. James the fact that Tubby turned up just when she was feeling hopeless. "'It was like a miracle. St. James again'" (302). At the end Tubby walks the whole last stage of the pilgrimage with Maureen and says that he is very glad he did. "You notice much more on foot than you do in a car, and the slowness of walking itself creates a kind of dramatic tension, delaying the consummation of your journey" (309).

Although it is the very premise of a television comedy writer named Tubby suffering from *angst* that makes the novel so delightfully comic, it may be straining credulity to see him in the process of "leaping" into another Kierkegaardian sphere. Is he in any meaningful sense a pilgrim? Two factors about Tubby suggest that it is not preposterous to see him as a serious pilgrim: his curiosity, and his determination to take a good honest look at himself.

His curiosity is one of the first traits revealed about Tubby. Only three paragraphs into the novel, Tubby has written in his journal, "Gingerly I got to my feet"

(4). Immediately he wonders if the word should be *gingerlyly,* and he looks it up and finds that "adjective and adverb both have the same form." (4). Tubby often looks up words for their correct spelling or definition, and this penchant not only individualizes his character, but indicates a fundamental curiosity about things and a desire to understand. He is always going to "look it up" (49), and looking up *angst* is what leads him to read Kierkegaard. Joseph Conrad wrote in *The Secret Agent,* "Curiosity being one of the forms of self-revelation, a systematically incurious person remains always partly mysterious."[25] Conrad's link between curiosity and self-revelation is intriguing. The incurious person is mysterious because he himself is not open to mystery. Self-revelation and curiosity both stem from the same source: a desire to know and to understand. The curious person reveals himself because in doing so, he learns more about himself. Tubby's curiosity is linked to his determination to see himself honestly, such as his attempt to see himself "truthfully from other people's points of view" (212) when he writes the accounts as if he were other people and his realization of the callousness with which he had broken off his relationship with Maureen.

Pilgrimage not only provides the central narrative framework for the last part of the novel, but also functions as an image of individual spiritual growth and of the Church itself. The phrase "pilgrim church" is one of the key metaphors from the documents of Vatican II that has become a staple of Catholic discourse about the Church.[26] It is often invoked to support the model of a church that is less rigid and hierarchical, and more flexible and porous; less concerned with immutability and more concerned with spiritual growth and responsiveness to a changing world.

The pilgrim church in this novel is clearly a seasoned traveler, weighed down with baggage, with bruised and sore feet, feeling at times, as Maureen says of herself, "'almost at the end of [her] tether'" (302). The pilgrimage experience—the ancient churches, the cult of martyrs, relics, and miracles, the enormous outpouring of piety that can result from a scribal error[27]—is a visible manifestation of the Church's long history, which is both an inspiration and an encumbrance, indeed, at times, an embarrassment. Yet, as Maureen says, people "'must have got something tremendous out of it'" (303).

Like Maureen, the pilgrim church in this novel shows signs of aging; like her she is scarred and disfigured by struggles and has lost her youthful beauty. Like Maureen, when Tubby catches up with her in Spain, the Church sometimes looks "a wreck" (296). Her efforts to maintain integrity and fidelity have led to strategies (the Inquisition, the Crusades) that, though well-intentioned, now seem inhumane. As in Lodge's other Catholic novels, the Church's traditional sexual morality comes under critical scrutiny, especially in the chapters where the young people's burgeoning sexual feeling is crushed, Maureen is burdened by guilt, and Tubby's frustration leads him to end the relationship. Yet Maureen's puritanical upbringing and overprotective father do not seem to have irretrievably warped her burgeoning sexuality. Tubby imagines that she was devastated after he broke off their relationship. Yet when he apologizes to her for his treatment, she admits she cried herself to sleep for ages, but adds, "'young girls are always doing that. You were the first boy I cried over, but not the last.'" In fact, she went on to fall hopelessly in love with a "'wildly handsome registrar'" and have an affair with a houseman in the hospital where she worked (297). It was when she was on the rebound from this affair—not from Tubby—that she married Bede. Tubby is hurt to find that she hasn't thought about him in years.

Although the dour Bede may seem a disappointing and unworthy beneficiary of the erotic energy of such a lovely young woman, there is something solid, even sustaining, about the home and family they have established.[28] Not stylish or sophisticated—"ordinary large inter-war semi, with a long back garden," curtains that match the loose covers in the sitting room, family photographs on display (272-74)—there is, nevertheless, something welcoming here, in spite of the disturbing fact of twin beds in the master bedroom. Just as Maureen's father was presented as *both* overprotective *and* a benevolent guardian (like the Church), so also Bede's effort to shield his children from the worst aspects of modern popular culture by intermittently banning television from their home when his children were growing up is seen, on the one hand, as an unrealistic attempt to shelter them from the real world and, on the other, as a careful attempt to keep harmful influences at bay. Bede himself admits to Tubby that his daughter became completely addicted to television as soon as she left home and had a set of her own and concludes that "'all effort to control other people's lives is completely futile'" (273). Although Bede is undoubtedly right that an effort to control people (even one's own children) is doomed to failure, his exclusion of television very likely contributed to the serious tone in their home that produced children like their son Damien, who was killed in Angola while working for a Catholic aid organization.[29] Similarly Maureen's growing up in the strict, overprotective environment provided by her church and family did not make her into a cold, repressed woman. In fact, so positive does she feel about sex, that she tells Tubby she hopes Damien had sex with his girlfriend before he was killed (302). Maureen's upbringing is certainly not beyond criticism, but especially when she is compared with some of the products of the overly sexualized secular society like Louise and Samantha, her upbringing does not seem all that bad.

Bede and Maureen have stayed connected to their Catholic roots. When Bede tells Tubby that Maureen does a lot of volunteer work for the Church, Tubby asks, "'You both still go to church, then?'" Bede answers curtly, "'Yes'" and with his next breath asks Tubby if he wants milk or sugar with his coffee (274). It is as if their still going to church is just an ordinary fact of life, to be taken for granted, hardly something to explain or defend. Bede and Maureen represent the resilient and tenacious Catholic faith that survives in some people who lived through the tumultuous upheavals of the post-Vatican II years. Sociologist Andrew Greeley attributes such faith to the Catholic sacramental imagination nurtured in "a pervasive religious culture that had been shaped by it and continued to be supported by it."[30] Maureen's belief in St. James, miracles, and prayer, and the importance she attaches to the traditional rites associated with the pilgrimage are evidence of a connection to "the imaginative tradition and the spirituality of the lay folk," which Greeley sees as such a wellspring for faith.[31]

If pilgrimage has functioned in this novel as a useful metaphor for Catholicism—both the institution and the individual Catholic—and provided visual icons of the "dog's breakfast" of Catholicism, the Kierkegaardian themes have further enriched the depiction of religious experience. As we have seen, Kierkegaard believes that one achieves genuine religious faith only through a "leap." Kierkegaard's concept of the "leap" was partly a reaction against the theories of the philosopher Hegel, who proposed that significant change was accomplished through the gradual process of thesis, antithesis, and synthesis. Although Kierkegaard preferred instead the figure of the sudden leap into a higher sphere, the truth, of course, is that growth involves both kinds of movement: gradual Hegelian development and Kierkegaardian leaps, just as the physical development of species (at least according to some biologists) involved long periods of slow, steady evolutionary growth, spurred on by "leaps" of punctuated equilibrium. Frederick Copleston believes that Kierkegaard gives insufficient credit to the part that reason plays in the movement to faith: "As Kierkegaard's dialectic is one of discontinuity, in the sense that the transition from one stage to another is made by choice, by self-commitment, and not through a continuous process of conceptual mediation, he not unnaturally plays down the role of reason and emphasizes that of will when he is treating of religious faith." Copleston goes on to point out that although he finds the analogy of the leap insufficient to describe coming to faith, the life of faith does partake of Kierkegaard's notion of repetition. "And this act of faith is not something which can be performed once and for all. It has to be constantly repeated."[32] One thinks of how much repetition is at the heart of the Christian life and particularly Catholic life: the repetition of scriptural passages, liturgical rites and forms, devotions like the rosary and litanies, and in all the various traditions which have become part of the pilgrimage to Santiago de Compostela.

The use of the pilgrimage theme, with its rich sacramental sense of the sacred conveyed through matter, and the Kierkegaard theme, with its strong "either-or" mode, enables Lodge to achieve something quite remarkable. Andrew Greeley says of this novel, "Combing the two imaginations, analogical and dialectical, in the same 'therapy' is a deft touch, evidence that the two imaginations need not exclude one another."[33]

On their last day together in Spain, Maureen and Tubby drive to Finisterre, which means "end of the world" in Latin. Once again nature is foregrounded in its elemental and primitive beauty, as in those earlier sections of the book in France, as Tubby began his pilgrimage, and in **Paradise News** where the true beauty of Hawaii was revealed in contrast to the vulgar commercialized version presented earlier. These settings feature the characters either alone in a moment of profound self awareness or with another in a moment of genuine intimacy.

> The rolling wooded hills of the country around Santiago gave way to a more rugged, heath-like terrain of windblown grass broken by great slabs of grey rock and the occasional stubborn, slanting tree. As we approached the tip of the peninsula the land seemed to tilt upwards like a ramp, beyond which we could see nothing but sky. You really felt as if you were coming to the end of the world; the end of something, anyway. We parked the car beside a lighthouse, followed a path round to the other side of the building, and there was the ocean spread out beneath us, calm and blue, shading almost imperceptibly into the sky at the hazy horizon. We sat down on a warm, flat rock, amid coarse grass and wildflowers, and watched the sun, like a huge communion wafer behind a thin veil of cloud, slowly decline towards the wrinkled surface of the sea.
>
> (315)

Although Tubby wants Maureen to divorce Bede and marry him, she says she cannot do that. When he asks how she can stay in a loveless marriage, she responds that her marriage may have been sexless, "'but not loveless. . . . And I did marry him, after all, for better or for worse'" (316). So strong, in fact, is Maureen's faith in the permanence of marriage, that she encourages Tubby to try to reconcile with his wife.

As they drive back to Santiago that evening, Tubby stops the car, and they get out to look at the Milky Way, "a pale, glimmering canopy of light." Tubby remarks that the "'ancient Greeks thought it was the way to heaven'" and Maureen says, "'I'm not surprised.'" This exchange, together with the earlier eucharistic imagery and the fact that their dinner that evening had been fresh fish that "they grilled . . . for us over charcoal" reminiscent of the disciples' post Resurrection supper with Jesus by the sea of Tiberius (John 21:9-14) overlays the scene with a shimmer of transcendence (317). As Tubby and Maureen face each other with tenderness, affection and deep honesty, but with profound awareness of the contingency of their lives and their ongoing responsibility for the choices they have made, and as they situate their lives within the mystery and beauty of the larger universe, they brush up against the sacred.

Tubby has been reborn into a new life. Refurnishing the flat, which was robbed while he was in Spain, is "like starting a new life from scratch" (320). His knee pain, the original reason for all his therapies, has mysteriously disappeared, and he handily beats his old tennis partner "rushing the net after every serve and scampering back to the baseline when he tried to lob me" (320). His marriage is over, but Maureen will not leave Bede. Instead the three of them are the best of friends and are planning to go to Copenhagen in the autumn. Tubby and Maureen occasionally "have a siesta" in his London flat. The ending, of course, is not "neat." How could it be? Tubby is still very much on a pilgrimage—perhaps preparing to make another leap?

Therapy, along with *How Far Can You Go?* and *Paradise News* is distinguished by Lodge's remarkable ability to imbue his comic novel with a seriousness that gives it added richness. What keeps Tubby's story from being simply another amusing satire is—not only the poignancy of his divorce, a pain familiar to so many contemporary people—but the fact that the story of this likeable scriptwriter draws in and reflects the pain of the wider world. The MIND balloon with its reminder of all the reasons for depression, the studio audience of workers who have all just lost their jobs, the description of Tubby's father working as a tram driver standing at the controls in the cold for eight hours, the London homeless shelter shown to Tubby by the homeless man camped out in his entryway all keep the narrative from being focused too exclusively on the troubles of one very privileged member of the middle class. It is more than a reminder of the ubiquitous nature of human suffering. There is also a suggestion that larger structures of government, finance, industry, and the military promote pain and unhappiness. Even something intended to promote well-being, like the Rummidge City Centre ends up being ill suited to provide either comfort or visual pleasure. "Now the new buildings, with their stainless steel escalators and glass lifts and piped music, stand expectant and almost empty, like a theme park before opening day, or like some utopian capital city of a third-world country, built for ideological reasons in the middle of the jungle, an object of wonder to the natives but seldom visited by foreigners" (85). After spending a week doing little other than writing his memoir of Maureen, Tubby buys a paper and reads mostly bad news. "Nothing much has changed in the big wide world. Eleven people were killed when the Bosnian Serbs lobbed mortar shells into a football stadium in Sarajevo. Twenty-five UN soldiers were killed in an ambush by General Aidid's troops in Somalia. John Major has the lowest popularity rating of any British Prime Minister since polling began" (259).

This saga of a comedy writer's postdivorce adventure is definitively situated in a broken world, suffering from what Christianity calls original sin. Many secular novelists depict powerfully the pain of the larger world, yet they often do so at the cost of cynical pessimism, and if they use a comic mode, it tends toward irony and dark satire. Lodge's comic tone, however, remains buoyant and optimistic. His Catholic sensibility, I would argue, is partly responsible for his remarkable ability to integrate such a robust comic vision with an uncompromising account of a world which is, at best, disappointing, and at worst, sordid and corrupt.[34]

Kierkegaard's theory of comedy, as explained by Eastern Orthodox theologian David Hart, provides one of the best accounts of what David Lodge achieves in *Therapy* and his other novels.

> The special logic of this theory, after all, is that the *Christian* philosopher [or novelist]—having surmounted the "aesthetic," "ethical," and even in a sense "religious" stages of human existence—is uniquely able to enact a return, back to the things of earth, back to finitude, back to the aesthetic; having found the highest rationality of being in God's *kenosis*—his self-outpouring—in the Incarnation, the Christian philosopher [novelist] is reconciled to the particularity of flesh and form, recognizes all of creation as a purely gratuitous gift of a God of infinite love, and is able to rejoice in the levity of a world created and redeemed purely out of God's "pleasure."[35]

In affirming heaven, Lodge is gaining the earth.

Notes

1. David Lodge, *Therapy* (New York: Penguin, 1995), 14. Hereafter cited in the text by page number.

2. Søren Kierkegaard, *The Concept of Dread,* trans. Walter Lowrie (Princeton: Princeton University Press, 1957), 38. Italics in the original.

3. Frederick Copleston, S.J., *Modern Philosophy: Schopenhauer to Nietzsche,* vol. 7, part 2 of *A History of Philosophy* (Garden City, N.Y.: Doubleday, Image Books, 1965), 120.

4. Kierkegaard, *Concept of Dread,* 40. Italics in the original.

5. Kierkegaard developed his ideas of the three stages in several of his other books, especially *Stages on Life's Way* and *Concluding Unscientific Postscript. Either/Or,* however, the book Tubby borrows, is devoted primarily to a description of the first two stages, the ones that most pertain to Tubby's life.

6. Stumpf, *Socrates to Sartre,* 448.

7. Quoted in Robert Bretall, ed., *A Kierkegaard Anthology* (Princeton: Princeton University Press, 1946), 343.

8. According to Copleston, "Existence . . . was for Kierkegaard a category relating to the free individual. In his use of the term, to exist means realizing oneself through free choice between alternatives, through self-commitment. To exist, therefore, means becoming more and more an individual and less and less a mere member of a group. It means, one can say, transcending universality in favour of individuality." Copleston, *Modern Philosophy,* 105-6.

9. Bretall, *A Kierkegaard Anthology,* 226.

10. Stumpf, *Socrates to Sartre,* 449.

11. The same point is often made about films: that older films where sex was conveyed by innuendo or suggestion are more erotic—certainly more romantic—than contemporary ones where sexual acts are explicitly portrayed with full nudity.

12. James Daniel Collins, *The Mind Of Kierkegaard* (Chicago: Henry Regnery, 1953), 9.

13. Søren Kierkegaard, *Fear and Trembling & Repetition* eds. and trans., Howard V. Hong and Edna H. Hong (Princeton: Princeton University Press, 1983), 212.

14. Kierkegaard, *Fear and Trembling & Repetition,* 210.

15. Kierkegaard, *Fear and Trembling & Repetition,* 212.

16. Kierkegaard, *Fear and Trembling & Repetition,* 210.

17. Kierkegaard, *Fear and Trembling & Repetition,* 220-21.

18. Kierkegaard, *Fear and Trembling & Repetition,* 221.

19. Bretall, *A Kierkegaard Anthology,* 136.

20. Kierkegaard, *Fear and Trembling & Repetition,* 212.

21. Kierkegaard, *Fear and Trembling & Repetition,* 212.

22. Actually, the very first paragraph of the novel has Tubby describing squirrels playing in the leafless trees in his garden. However, although the scene is natural, its barren wintry setting and the frenetic activity of the squirrels seem descriptive of the London/Rummidge life depicted in the first two thirds of the novel:

> I watched two playing tag in the chestnuts just outside my study window: spiralling up a trunk, dodging and feinting among the branches, then scampering along a bough and leaping to the next tree, then zooming down the side of its trunk headfirst, freezing halfway, claws sticking like Velcro to the corrugated bark, then streaking across the grass, one trying to shake off the other by jinking and swerving and turning on a sixpence till he reached the bole of a Canadian poplar and they both rocketed up its side into the thin elastic branches and balanced there, swaying gently and blinking contentedly at each other. Pure play—no question.
>
> (3)

If this is play, it is play London-style. The natural scenes of the last third of the novel, however, are much more peaceful, pastoral, and verdant.

23. According to the *HarperCollins Encyclopedia of Catholicism,* there are three requisites for an authentic pilgrimage: "(1) the belief that God responds to prayer, (2) the conviction that God is present at holy sites, and (3) the desire to make a sacred journey to a holy site." "Pilgrimage," *HarperCollins Encyclopedia of Catholicism,* 1001.

24. Earlier Tubby had pointed out to Maureen that the tradition that St. James is buried in Santiago is believed by many to be due to the error of a scribe, who wrote "Hispaniam" (Spain) for "Hierusalem" (Jerusalem). Such rational quibbles carry no weight with Maureen. "'I think he's around the place somewhere'" she replies. "'With so many people walking to Santiago to pay him homage, he could hardly stay away, could he?'" (300-1).

25. Joseph Conrad, *The Secret Agent: A Simple Tale* (Cambridge and New York: Cambridge University Press, 1990), 179.

26. The metaphor is used in *Lumen Gentium,* the Constitution on the Church.

27. See endnote 24.

28. This is also true of Maureen's working class home, which Tubby used to visit while her father was at work. "Mrs. Kavanagh gave me a cup of tea and a slice of home-made soda bread in her big, dark, chaotic basement kitchen, and burped a baby over her shoulder as she assessed me" (231).

29. The name Damien is one with a particular Catholic resonance, being the name of a nineteenth-century French priest, recently beatified, who spent his life

serving the lepers on the Hawaiian island of Molokai until he himself contracted the disease and died. The name of Maureen and Bede's son and the fact that he was working for a Catholic aid organization suggest that he has absorbed and retained something of the faith tradition of his parents.

30. Greeley, *Catholic Revolution,* 146.

31. Greeley, *Catholic Revolution,* 118.

32. Copleston, *Modern Philosophy,* 115.

33. Greeley, *Catholic Imagination,* 50.

34. David Hart explains how Kierkegaard saw the profound difference between humor and irony:

> Irony can certainly recognize that the incongruities that throng human experience typically frustrate the quest for truth; but, having seen as much, irony is then impotent to do anything more than unveil failure and vanquish pretense. Humor, on the other hand, is born from an altogether higher recognition: that tragic contradiction is not absolute, that finitude is not only pain and folly, and that the absurdity of our human contradictions can even be a cause for joy. Humor is able to receive finitude as a gift, conscious of the suffering intrinsic to human existence, but capable of transcending despair through jest. And this is why the power of humor is most intense in the "religious" sphere: Christianity, seeing all things from the perspective of the Incarnation (that most unexpected of peripeties), is the "most comic" vision of things: it encompasses the greatest contradictions and tragedies of all, but does so in such a way as to take the suffering of existence into the unanticipated absurdity of our redemption. David Hart, "The Laughter of the Philosophers," *First Things,* Jan. 2005, 32.

35. Hart, "Laughter of the Philosophers," 36.

Bibliography

[Editor's Note: See previous essay for complete bibliography.]

Gary Johnson (essay date March 2008)

SOURCE: Johnson, Gary. "Consciousness as Content: Neuronarratives and the Redemption of Fiction." *Mosaic* 41, no. 1 (March 2008): 169-84.

[*In the following essay, Johnson compares the treatment of consciousness in Lodge's* Thinks . . . *and Richard Powers'* Galatea 2.2.]

The opening chapter of David Lodge's 2001 novel, ***Thinks . . . ,*** presents a self-conscious exercise in stream-of-consciousness narration. Ralph Messenger, Lodge's co-protagonist, is a cognitive scientist endeavouring to understand and describe the workings of

the human mind. As the work begins, we encounter Ralph as he dictates his own thoughts into a tape recorder—a quaintly retrograde piece of equipment given his position as the head of a fictional British university's Centre for Cognitive Science. One of the aims of the exercise, he reveals, is "to try to describe the structure of, or rather to produce a specimen, that is to say raw data, on the basis of which one might infer the structure of . . . thought"[1]. Ralph is acutely aware of the "artificiality" of his experiment, recognizing the fact that his consciousness of the exercise will inevitably change the nature of his thoughts and his thought process. He wants "random" thoughts, but his project necessarily imposes some kind of order on those thoughts; it is nearly impossible, it seems, to be aware of one's thinking without allowing that awareness to alter the process itself. As he admits later in the novel, "The brain does a lot of ordering and revising before the words come out of your mouth" (172).

Ralph's experiment is artificial on a second level as well. Although the reader ostensibly takes the place that would be occupied by a specific narratee, Lodge is obliged to construct and reveal Ralph's thoughts in a way that makes them accessible to us. Thus, Ralph's opening monologue provides more information than would be necessary if no audience—other than Ralph himself—were anticipated. The first line of Lodge's novel, in fact, introduces this somewhat artificial manner of narration: "One, two, three, testing, testing, recorder working, OK . . ." (1). Shortly thereafter, Ralph reveals the aim of his exercise, an aim that will prove crucial to the unfolding of the novel's main plot: "Where was I? But that's the point, I'm not anywhere, I haven't made a decision to think about anything specific, the object of the exercise being simply to record the random thoughts, if anything can be random, the random thoughts passing through a man's head [. . .] at a randomly chosen time and place" (1). Such information appears not "naturally," but rather as the result of a conscious decision on Lodge's part to orient his reader.

The subject matter of this novel—the structure of human thought—necessitates this type of orientation. Traditional stream-of-consciousness narratives, to which parts of Lodge's ***Thinks . . .*** bear some resemblance, endeavour "simply" to represent natural human thought. At their most basic level, these narratives aspire to mimesis, the realistic depiction of an individual's consciousness. Thought, therefore, is crucial to the narrative, and the human psyche is certainly one area of the novelists' interest, but cognitive science was not yet a central concern, since cognitive science itself did not yet exist. Lodge's work, in contrast, approaches consciousness from a scientific angle, one made possible by the scientific advances of the last several decades, and one that obliges him not only to represent thought, but also, as Ralph puts it, to describe its structure. As a result, Lodge must both represent and explain.

The problem of explaining human consciousness, or at least of explaining what scientists know of human consciousness, within the framework of a literary text presents the novelist with some interesting and revealing narrative challenges. Chief among these, I believe, is the issue of how to convey to the lay reader scientific information that he or she likely lacks, but that is essential to the narrative itself. And Lodge is not alone in facing this dilemma; indeed, in 1995, Richard Powers published his own neuronarrative (the term I will use to describe a work of fiction that has cognitive science as a, or the, main theme), entitled *Galatea 2.2,* a work that poses narrative challenges similar to those we find in ***Thinks***. . . . While my focus in this essay will be on the works of Lodge and Powers, a growing list of narrative works, including Powers's recent *The Echo Maker,* Ian McEwan's *Saturday,* Jonathan Franzen's *The Corrections,* and A. S. Byatt's *A Whistling Woman,* follows suit in foregrounding the emerging fields of neuroscience and neurobiology. These works, I propose, constitute an emerging subgenre of literature that can provide us with a glimpse of how authors are responding to scientific advances concerning the nature of human consciousness.

In ***Thinks*** . . . , Lodge has provided Ralph—an intellectually stereotypical scientist—with a foil/love interest from the humanities, a novelist named Helen who has accepted a temporary teaching position at Ralph's university. Early in their relationship, as the writer comes to make sense of what it is that a cognitive scientist does, Helen surmises somewhat incredulously that "consciousness is apparently the sort of thing cognitive scientists study" and that those scientists "have decided that consciousness is a 'problem' which has to be 'solved'" (61). Helen's use of scare quotes here is significant; it reveals the fact that, for this humanist, the scientific approach to consciousness is foreign, suspect, and, in a way, threatening. "I've always assumed, I suppose," Helen muses, "that consciousness was the province of the arts, especially literature, and most especially the novel. Consciousness, after all, is what most novels [. . .] are about. [. . .] Consciousness is simply the medium in which one lives, and has a sense of personal identity. The problem is how to *represent* it, especially in different selves from one's own" (61). Helen's interaction with Ralph is significant because it enlarges her understanding of the problem of consciousness; the challenge involved in working with consciousness now has an epistemological dimension as well as a mimetic one.

Indeed, cognitive science purports to know something about consciousness as an object of study that this particular novelist, who takes consciousness "more simply" as a given component of human life, does not.

The contrasting views of Ralph and Helen regarding the nature of consciousness, and Helen's sense of bewilderment with the scientific approach that Ralph both advocates and embodies, can help us to understand the challenges faced by contemporary novelists. As Helen indicates, the issue for authors (especially authors of realistic fiction) has always been how to *represent* consciousness, how, in other words, to construct characters that seem true to life in the sense that they could be real people with their own individual consciousnesses. Seen from this angle, consciousness always pertains to characters (or narrators) and, thus, as Helen reveals, one of the primary tasks of an author involves figuring out *how* to narrate or represent that mind. This places the problem of consciousness squarely in the realm of "discourse," the term that narratologists use for "the expression plane of narrative as opposed to its content plane or story; the 'how' of a narrative as opposed to its 'what'" (Prince 21). This distinction, and the placement of consciousness in it, works particularly well when we think about much of twentieth-century literature; what were the "high modernists" doing if not, among other things, experimenting with modes of representing consciousness?

Helen's emerging grasp of the nature of cognitive science, however, has profound implications for her understanding of consciousness and how it might be relevant to, and treated by, novelists. If she accepts Ralph's position, then she must accept the possibility that consciousness is no longer the sole province of the arts and, more profoundly, that consciousness might fit equally well in the "content plane" of narrative, as a "thing" or a "problem" that is separable from individual selves or characters. As scientists learn more about the general human phenomenon of consciousness, novelists find themselves forced to rethink how that phenomenon manifests itself in their individual narratives. Neuronarratives, I submit, allow readers to see the early results of this new way of thinking about consciousness.

I have divided this essay into two sections in order to pursue two primary objectives. The first is to illustrate how two novelists struggle to approach consciousness as "content" and how that struggle manifests itself in the structure of their respective narratives. My second aim is to argue that the encroachment of neuroscience on the field of literature results in a kind of revaluation of narrative fiction on the part of the novelists who produce it. Even as neurologists, psychologists, medical doctors, and others in the scientific community embrace narrative as a legitimate area of inquiry, Lodge and Powers seem to need to convince themselves of the potential value of narrative fiction. Perhaps because the broad field of what we might call consciousness studies—and, by extension, consciousness as a part of the story world—remains in its infancy, novelists such as Lodge and Powers seem to be struggling with what to do with it and wrestling with what it portends for literature as a field. In Lodge's *Thinks . . .* and Powers's *Galatea 2.2,* this two-fronted struggle produces a plot that turns on the old, and now questionable, "two cultures" split that C. P. Snow described in 1959. In his well-known lectures at Cambridge, Snow argued that a dangerous gulf had come to separate the humanities (especially literature) and the sciences (especially the physical sciences) in the first half of the twentieth century. Snow describes a climate in which writers and scientists "had almost ceased to communicate at all"[2]. The scientists, apparently, did not read (literature) and the writers, apparently, did not understand science. "There seems to be no place," he lamented, "where the cultures meet" (17).

If this was the case in 1959, the intervening half century has brought significant change. Even a cursory survey of recent popular science writing, for example, indicates that scientists do, in fact, read literature and that they are interested in exploring the ways in which literature and the arts more generally can interact with science. Indeed, some of the most popular science writers incorporate some discussion of the humanities in their recent works. (1) Unfortunately, this group of writers, all of whom work from the perspective of evolutionary psychology, write about the humanities in a way that ultimately trivializes the arts and strikes many—especially those of us in humanities fields—as somewhat one-sided, if not predatory.

Other scientists, however, while perhaps less well-known to the general public, take a more balanced view and have gone even further in bridging the divide between the two cultures. These writers include the likes of Antonio Damasio and Gerald Edelman. (2) And, in a recent development, the neurologist Oliver Sacks—known for his narrative approach to the science of the mind—has accepted a position at Columbia as that school's first "Columbia artist," a platform that will allow him to move among, and teach in, a number of different departments, including creative writing (Rich).

Approaching from the other side of the shrinking divide, literary critics have become especially likely to write about science in their works, and even to adopt a scientific frame of reference; this is particularly true of those critics who have an interest in cognitive science.

Writing of literary critics who "are now producing critical works that apply cognitive research" to literary analysis, F. Elizabeth Hart points out that such an approach is necessarily "dependent on scientific studies of the brain and mind and so accepts axiomatically some degree of epistemological efficacy in scientific empiricism" (314). In addition to Hart, other such critics include Lisa Zunshine, Mary Crane, Alan Richardson, and N. Katherine Hayles.[3]

Additionally, the sub-discipline of narratology—an offshoot of structuralism, which itself has a scientific bent—has become increasingly interdisciplinary. David Herman, Alan Palmer, and Nancy Easterlin, for example, are all concerned with the relationships among consciousness, cognition, and narrative.[4] Interest in the relationship between science and narrative flows in the other direction as well, a fact illustrated by the existence of the Program in Narrative Medicine at Columbia University. The promotional material for this unique program indicates that "narrative theory and knowledge provide fundamental conceptual frameworks for all [. . .] dimensions of medicine while narrative skills and methods provide means of achieving narratively competent care."

There is also, I should add, no dearth of literature devoted to exploring the realm of science. There continues to be, of course, a large market of science fiction and fantasy, but even writers outside of these generic confines pursue scientific themes in their works. As Jay Clayton has pointed out, there has been a "veritable explosion" in the last twenty years of "fictional explorations of scientific issues" (808). If we sort through the individual pieces left over from this explosion, we will note some distinctive aspects of those works of literature that focus on neuroscience rather than on one or another of the myriad scientific issues that would make for interesting topics for a work of literature (genetic engineering, global warming, etc.).

One of the most fascinating characteristics of neuronarratives, as I indicated above, is the novelist's perceived need to inform his or her audience about the current state of neuroscience. To put this in narratological terms, the authors seem compelled to facilitate the readers' entry into the "authorial audience." In *Before Reading: Narrative Conventions and the Politics of Interpretation,* Peter Rabinowitz proposes that we recognize three categories for the reader of fictional narratives: the actual audience, which is composed of the individual flesh-and-blood readers; the narrative audience, which Rabinowitz describes as a "role" in which the reader is willing to enter the world of the narrative on its own terms (95-96); and the authorial audience, or the hypothetical audience for whom authors have designed their works (21). In many cases, that authorial audience will be more sophisticated and more educated than the narrative audience, as this former group is expected to be capable of joining "a particular social/interpretive community," one whose membership includes the author him- or herself (22). This audience is a construct that is capable of "getting" the author's intended meaning, even as members of the actual and/or narrative audience might not. Because consciousness is so new as "content"—rather than form—we witness some interesting moves on the part of novelists, moves that are intended, I believe, to allow readers entry into the authorial audience.

In the case of neuronarratives, one way of doing this is to revisit and, in a sense, to reopen the two-culture divide within the fictional world of the narrative, and then to rehearse the closing of that divide. Toward this end, the fortuitous choice of a setting can facilitate the novelist's task, allowing him or her to convey the requisite scientific information in a way that does not compromise the aesthetic integrity of the novel. In short, by setting their novels in a university, both Lodge and Powers can plausibly depict both the separation and the potential for the convergence of the two cultures and also explore the ramifications of that convergence. Indeed, the university has long been recognized as a logical place for this type of convergence. This setting, therefore, allows for—indeed, almost necessitates—the presence of characters from different disciplines and with different ideas about the human condition.

As anyone familiar with a university and its culture of clearly defined and demarcated programs can attest, however, simple proximity does not guarantee convergence. Lodge, who is intimately familiar with the culture of universities, plays with this fact when he has the Dean of Humanities of his fictional university explain to Helen, who is also the narrator at this point in the novel, the layout of the campus:

> They started building at each end of the site, Arts at one end and Sciences at the other, confident that they would soon fill up the intervening acres. But costs rose, the money supply dwindled, and in the nineteen-eighties the Government realized that it would be much cheaper to convert all the polytechnics into universities with a stroke of the pen than to enlarge the existing ones. [. . .] "We're an architectural allegory of the Two Cultures, I'm afraid," Jasper Richmond said, with a wry smile, as we looked out over the campus from his tenth-floor office in the Humanities Tower towards the distant Science buildings.
>
> (11)

In order to overcome this fact of academic life, Lodge and Powers have employed distinct methods of bringing together characters who represent the "two cultures." In *Thinks . . .*, the catalyst for actual convergence is a trusted staple of narrative fiction—physical/romantic attraction. Ralph first encounters Helen at a dinner party hosted by a university dean. Ralph is, of course, something of a rascal, and when he spies Helen walking around campus the following day he begins to plan for ways to "bump into her," apparently serendipitously. Such a meeting does occur several weeks into the semester at the cafeteria of the University's "Staff House." Over lunch, Ralph and Helen engage in a conversation that is weighted heavily toward Ralph's work and interests, which happen to be the intellectual areas in which the reader of Lodge's novel is most likely deficient. As readers, therefore, we tend to share Helen's perspective as well as her need for some remedial work in cognitive science.

Like Helen, the reader is simultaneously intrigued by Ralph and repelled by his stereotypically cold, analytical, scientific way of looking at things. In just a brief conversation, Ralph is able to dismiss the religiously inclined as irrational and unintelligent (33), dismiss the notion of a permanent self, spirit, or soul (35), and even call into question the reality of "our subjective experiences of the world" (36). All of this fits in with Ralph's guiding simile that the "mind is like a computer" (37), and that it is theoretically possible to construct artificially intelligent robots "embodied in some kind of organic material" (38). As a novelist and a committed humanist, Helen represents the alternative to Ralph's radical scientism, and, not surprisingly, she finds much of his talk interesting but disconcerting.

The plot device that keeps this encounter between Helen and Ralph from being the full extent of their relationship is Ralph's desire for Helen. The reader is aware almost from the beginning of the novel of an attraction between these two figures, one that is initially resisted by Helen because Ralph is married and because her own husband has recently and unexpectedly died. Ralph, on the other hand, does not allow his marital status to impede his pursuit of Helen, and he uses the prospect of a tour of the Centre for Cognitive Science as a way of enticing her to spend some time with him. His plan works, and in the novel's third chapter—the first one to be narrated by a third-person narrator (the first consists of Ralph's dictated thoughts, and the second consists of Helen's personal journal entries)—Helen and Ralph find themselves together in the Centre.

The Centre is a modern, technologically advanced building whose distinguishing feature is a large mural that encircles an atrium on the second-floor gallery. As Lodge's third-person narrator describes it, the mural comprises "a series of overlapping scenes, figures, vignettes, painted in a bold, expressionistic style," which, together, give the effect of "a kind of cyclorama" whose colours and figures stand in stark contrast to the "hi-tech austerity of the rest of the building" (49). The "Karinthy Mural" (named for the fictional amateur painter who conceived and executed the project while on a sabbatical year at the Centre) pictorially represents "various well-known theories and thought experiments in cognitive science, evolutionary psychology and the philosophy of mind" (49). The episode of ekphrasis that follows the description of the mural allows Lodge to provide both Helen and the reader with a brief, but essential, history of cognitive science. Indeed, as Lodge is surely aware, the likely reader of his novel is probably more like the scientifically benighted Helen than like Ralph, the scientist. Ralph's interpretation of the mural for Helen doubles as Lodge's way of "showing"—or perhaps it is an interesting combination of showing and telling—this information to the reader. Rather than breaking into his plot to provide the reader with this background information, Lodge has found a more "artful" means of conveying the same material.

A similar centre plays a similar narrative role in Powers's *Galatea 2.2*. In this case, the first person narrator, who shares the author's name, arrives, at the outset of the novel, at an unnamed Midwestern university's "enormous new Center for the Study of Advanced Sciences" (4). "My official title was Visitor," Powers informs us. "Unofficially, I was the token humanist" (4). While the Centre in Lodge's narrative serves as a means of facilitating "convergence" between Ralph and Helen, the Center in Powers's work functions more immediately as the actual manifestation of convergence. In his role as Visitor, Richard is given an office in the expansive Center, a facility so large that one could hardly expect the "embarrassment of talking to the same colleague twice" (6). Our narrator initially welcomes such isolation, as he has recently emerged from a painful romantic separation. As he settles into his new high-tech environment, Richard is drawn into the World Wide Web, as a lurker, and he finds his presence there to be even more acutely isolating and dispiriting: "But the longer I lurked, the sadder the holiday became. [. . .] The web was a neighborhood more efficiently lonely than the one it replaced. Its solitude was bigger and faster" (9).

Just as a work of art (the mural) serves as the lure to get Helen into the Centre for Cognitive Science and into a relationship with Ralph in *Thinks . . . ,* so too does a quintessentially humanist artifact draw Richard out of his dispiriting solitude and into a relationship (albeit not a romantic one) with a scientist in *Galatea 2.2.* For Richard, the artistic seduction takes the form of the middle movement of Mozart's *Clarinet Con-*

certo, a piece that seeps into his consciousness one night as he works in what he assumes is an otherwise empty Center. Richard declares that, in other circumstances, "any sound would have driven me to an emergency exit" (12), but he is drawn to the music and ultimately traces it to a hallway and an office of which he was previously unaware. Inside the office, he finds Philip Lentz, a somewhat surly scientist studying neural networks and connectionism, who is using the Mozart piece as a part of one of his experiments. This human convergence leads to Richard's association with a group of scientists, most of whom are working in related fields of cognitive science and neuroscience. And it is from this connection that the main plot takes shape: a kind of ruse perpetrated by the scientists on the naïve novelist.

Ostensibly, there is a bet among the group of scientists concerning whether or not they could program a computer to pass a masters-level exam in English Literature. Using theories of connectionism and neural nets, Lentz and Richard endeavour to train the machine by reading it works of literature and "teaching" it the power of paraphrase. The novelist believes the bet to be legitimate, and so he earnestly engages himself in the task. At the end of the novel, however, Powers's protagonist and the reader learn that the bet was not about "teaching a machine to read," but rather about "teaching a human to tell" (317-18). The scientists' real interest, in other words, was to see if they could dupe the naive writer into believing that a bogus experiment was legitimate; the bet was a joke and Richard was its butt. Still, though, the project—even if it was never completely serious—provides Powers with an excuse to meditate on cognitive science, neural nets, and connectionism, and to convey a surprising amount of material to his reader in what I consider to be an aesthetically satisfying manner.

One of the many interesting similarities between *Thinks . . .* and *Galatea 2.2* lies in the trajectory of their plots. Both begin with an unexpected, and in many ways exciting, convergence between representatives of the two cultures, both use this convergence as an opportunity for intellectual and emotional growth, and both end with the two "cultures" once again diverging. In Lodge's novel, Helen and Ralph end their relationship, and Helen leaves the university to return full-time to her writing; in *Galatea 2.2,* Richard, put off by the duplicity of his supposed colleagues, leaves the Center and, like Helen, resumes his writing.

Although there are clearly multiple reasons for the eventual dissolution of the relationships between the novelists and the scientists, I believe that the conclusions represent the novelists' attempts to work through the value of the kinds of narratives they want to create, and perhaps ultimately to come to terms with the kinds of narratives they feel have value. In the case of both Lodge and Powers, I sense that their personal experience with the developments in neuroscience have compelled them to re-evaluate and revalue the phenomenon of the fictional narrative.

Although Lodge represents the convergence and the eventual (re)divergence of the two cultures in the plot of *Thinks . . . ,* the novel as a whole is a product of the author's own attempt at an alliance with scientists studying cognition. While we can only hypothesize about whether and how two fictional characters might have benefited intellectually from their temporary fictional relationship, we know definitively that the text itself owes its very existence to convergence of the novel as a genre and the knowledge emerging from the discipline of cognitive science. Lodge's "Acknowledgments" section, which concludes but is not part of the narrative, allows us to see the novel as, at least partly, a product of a relationship the author had cultivated with a scientist. "My biggest single debt," Lodge attests,

> is to Aaron Sloman, Professor of Artificial Intelligence and Cognitive Science in the School of Computer Science at the University of Birmingham. Aaron patiently answered my elementary questions, gave me copies of his publications, introduced me to his colleagues, welcomed me to his departmental seminars, escorted me to an eye-opening international conference on consciousness . . . and generally acted as an indispensable guide to consciousness studies in general and artificial intelligence in particular.
>
> (342)

Even though the story Lodge tells does not offer or represent a good model for a successful alliance between the two cultures, the novel is, perhaps ironically, the fruit of just such an alliance.

We can make the same observation regarding *Galatea 2.2,* a novel that often seems, even more so than *Thinks . . . ,* an excuse for the author to show us all that he has learned about cognitive science, artificial intelligence, and connectionism. In this case, the protagonist is an only slightly fictionalized version of the author who shares his name. Unlike Helen, Richard embraces cognitive science and makes a concerted effort to learn about the field. When he is first teamed with the scientist Philip Lentz as part of the wager on artificial intelligence, Richard, like Lodge, begins reading scientific articles in an effort to understand the task he has undertaken. The fictionalized novelist's convergence with science, he realizes, is literally a mind-altering experience:

> I read the homework Lentz assigned me. An article on hippocampal association that Diana Hartrick co-authored grabbed my imagination. Every sentence, every word I'd ever stored had changed the physical structure of my brain. Even reading this article deformed the cell map of the mind the piece described, the map that took the piece in.
>
> At bottom, at synapse level, I was far more fluid than I'd ever suspected. As fluid as the sum of things that had happened to me, all things retained and apparently lost. Every input to my associative sieve changed the way I sieved the next input.
>
> (56)

The reader senses Richard's excitement about the transformative power of the information he is processing as he familiarizes himself with the current state of cognitive science. Having been introduced to "connectionism," and finding in it a potential means for explaining cognition, Richard is entranced with his new discoveries. "I now couldn't escape the word," he confesses. "I read about it throughout the worldwide electronic note files and in the stack of diversionary texts that replaced my nightly dose of forgotten fiction. Neural simulation's scent of the unprecedented diffused everywhere. I followed along, moving my lips like a child, while Lentz declared in print that we had shot the first rapids of inanimate thought" (29). Clearly infatuated with this new field, Richard abandons his literary projects and seems to be a cultural convert, jumping from the humanities to the sciences.

Yet, even if Richard has replaced the novels on his night table with scientific monographs, the novel we are reading testifies to the interdisciplinary nature of his foray into cognitive science. With every new bit of information, the brain, as our protagonist has learned, is altered, but it is not completely altered, and this is made clear as the novel progresses. Indeed, Richard consistently, and perhaps inevitably, processes the scientific input through his own neural network, one that has been shaped by his humanistic background. When, for example, Richard finds himself out of his depths with the hard science and complex mathematics that underpin connectionism, he reassures himself by redescribing the problem in literary terms: "I could at least follow the pictures, if not the argument's text. I visualized the spin glasses, complex similes for mental topology. I walked through the landscape of imagination, where every valley formed an associative memory. I could follow the *story* of the math, if not the substance" (74). Given his "real" vocation, it should not be surprising that Richard resorts to a narrative metaphor (understanding the "story of the math"), but it is no less instructive for its predictability. Much of Richard's scientific education, in fact, is processed and related in a similarly interdisciplinary way. He is aided in trying to understand how the computer he is helping to program makes certain associations, for example, by again reformulating the neurobiological questions at play in language and in concepts that are more familiar to him, and probably to the reader versed in post-structuralist literary theory as well: "Meaning was not a pitch but an interval. It sprang from the depth of disjunction, the distance between one circuit's center and the edge of another. Representation caught the sign napping, with its semantic pants down. Sense lay in metaphor's embarrassment at having two takes on the same thing. For the first time, I understood Emerson's saying about the use of life being to learn metonymy. . . . Life *was* metonymy, or at least stood for it" (154-55). One senses that this quotation and the previous one come close to expressing Powers's own feelings regarding his encounter with cognitive science; even if he cannot quite pin down the "substance" of the discipline, he can allude to its meaning and tell the story of its broader significance using the tools (language and figures of speech) with which he is both familiar and comfortable.

Lodge's and Powers's neuronarratives serve two important epistemological functions: they implicitly validate the notion that science produces a certain kind of useful and true knowledge and they artfully disseminate that knowledge to the lay public through the narrative devices I have noted above. On the literal level, both of the novelist-characters leave their stories a little wiser than they began them, and they both have material for new works of fiction. In this sense, these characters apparently reflect the experiences that their authors have had in their respective encounters with cognitive studies. We should not, however, underestimate the importance of the dissolution of the relationships between humanists and scientists that occurs in both *Thinks . . .* and *Galatea 2.2.* This aspect of the plots reveals the paradoxical nature of the problem of epistemology for the humanists.

The interdisciplinary exchange of intellectual property, for lack of a better term, is central to both of these neuronarratives. On an epistemological level, the humanist characters—and through them, many of the readers—receive a sort of remedial crash course in cognitive science that informs the novels. These characters must be brought up-to-date concerning the knowledge that is emerging from this field so that they can understand it and determine how it might or might not affect their own disciplines and ways of thinking.

In *Thinks . . .* the remediation is pared down to a bare minimum, as Lodge provides us only with the basic issues at play in "the current scientific and philosophical debate about consciousness" (341), and with a rudimentary working vocabulary, one that includes increasingly common words such as "neu-

rons" and "synapses." Most of Helen's "instruction" comes directly from Ralph and his colleagues as she speaks with them, or indirectly, as she inhabits, albeit from the margins, their intellectual space. Like the reader, however, Helen learns enough to be conversant with the scientists, but not enough to be completely at ease in this new discipline. Both Helen and the reader realize how basic their understanding of cognitive science is when Helen relates the titles ("A phase-state approach to quantum neurodynamics and its relation to the space-time domain of neural coding mechanisms" [313], for example) of some of the papers presented at a conference organized by Ralph. Still, the fact that Helen is forced by the convergence of the two cultures to see the issue of consciousness from a different disciplinary perspective is a salutary intellectual development.

In the two neuronarratives under discussion here, however, the interdisciplinary epistemology tends to flow in one direction: the humanists must learn what the scientists already know, or are in the process of learning. The scientists, on the other hand, are generally skeptical that the humanities have any real knowledge that can benefit them. The dismissive and ironic tone of Lentz's challenge to Richard at the beginning of *Galatea 2.2* captures the general attitude of the scientists: "Tell us," he demands. "What passes for knowledge in your so-called discipline? What does a student of English have to do to demonstrate acceptable reading comprehension?" (43). Lentz's questions strike a sensitive nerve with Richard and with anyone committed to the humanities; indeed, articulating the "knowledge" that one gains through the study of literature, for example, always poses difficulties for the humanist, particularly when the epistemological standard is set by the hard sciences. Ralph Messenger shares Lentz's attitude toward literature. In one of their first discussions, Helen tries to persuade Ralph that one's reason for reading novels—"to find out what goes on in other people's heads" (42)—might mirror the enterprise of cognitive science. Ralph replies, however, that, "all they really find out is what has gone on in the writer's head. It's not real knowledge" (42).

We see in both of the novels the establishment, or at least the representation, of a classic binary opposition between scientific knowledge on the one hand and that ineffable something that the humanities purports to offer on the other. For lack of a better term, we might call that something "understanding," in a hermeneutic rather than an epistemological sense. And at the end of each neuronarrative, the fictionalized novelists seem to recognize the apparent marginality and relative impotence of such understanding vis-a-vis the concrete knowledge produced through scientific investigation.

Helen, for her part, delivers the keynote address at a conference organized by Ralph, and she ends by pointing out that there is "a tragic dimension to consciousness" that has not been discussed at the conference and which literature can help us to understand (319-20). This claim, however, seems susceptible to Ralph's previous retort that this is not "real knowledge," and Ralph admits to Helen that he does not "agree with a word" of what she has said. And even Helen concedes that it is unlikely that she has "converted any scientists" with a speech that is essentially a close reading Andrew Marvell's "The Garden" (321).

In *Galatea 2.2,* Richard is forced to acknowledge that his claim on Helen—the computer they have co-developed—is somehow less tenable than is Lentz's. This acknowledgment occurs as Richard faces the prospect of Lentz dismantling the computer in order to analyze how she has been able to do what she has done. Richard is devastated by this prospect, but realizes that in the context of their convergence, Lentz has the power: "I had no leg to stand on. Lentz owned Helen, her shaped evolution, the lay of her synapses. He owned all the reasoning about her as well. I had some connection to her, by virtue of our long association. But that connection was, at most, emotional. And if Helen lived far enough to be able to feel, it just went to prove that emotions were no more than the sum of their weight vectors. And cuttable, in the name of knowing" (302). The humanist concedes that, in this case, knowledge trumps emotion, but the reader is made to feel that the scientist has failed to understand how significant Helen has become for Richard. Helen has clearly come to mean—and even to be—more than the sum of her parts, but Lentz is incapable or unwilling to see that, a failing that makes him seem somehow less than human, but also quintessentially (or stereotypically) scientific.

The problem of epistemology is the remainder at the end of these two novels and it is, I believe, what prevents the convergence of the two cultures that we see represented in the narratives from enduring. The novelists can tell the story of scientific advances in the field of cognition, but they are unable to abide by the implications of that narrative. If understanding inner reality as a hermeneutic enterprise gives way to understanding the reality of the inner (the mind) through purely scientific means, then the humanities would seem to have lost something, at least if we read the relatively somber endings of these two novels symbolically.

The re-divergence of the two cultures at the end of each of our neuronarratives possibly reveals the extent to which the humanities are still threatened by the potential resolution of the problem of epistemology on

scientific terms and the extent to which the scientific community is still skeptical about the knowledge value of literature and the humanities more generally. As I claimed at the outset of this essay, however, the distance between the two cultures does not seem to be as great in the contemporary real world as it appears to be in these novels. Columbia University alone, in fact, now has Oliver Sacks teaching creative writing students and literary scholars instructing future medical doctors. So why have Lodge and Powers revived a tension between science and literature that has apparently relaxed considerably in the real world?

The obvious answer would be that the conflict between scientists and novelists in these narratives meets some very practical needs for the authors. Explaining the source of this conflict—even if it is somewhat artificial—allows the authors to bring the readers into the authorial audience because it allows them (the authors) to treat consciousness as content. Moreover, and even more practically, a good plot tends to need some kind of conflict, and the divide between the two cultures stands as a ready-made plot element. Yet, the endings of these two novels seem to reveal something significant about their authors' feelings regarding fictional narrative, a genre that both writers have subjected to ridicule through their scientist-characters. One senses in both Lodge and Powers a recognition of the possibility that Messenger and Lentz are not completely wrong in questioning the value of narrative fiction. This feeling, at least for this reader, has its origins in the relatively pathetic author-characters described early on in each novel. Both Helen and Richard appear stilted emotionally and exhausted creatively, neither likely to produce anything truly worth reading. As Richard puts it in *Galatea 2.2,* "Mornings passed when a sick knot in my stomach informed me that I would never write anything again. I had nothing left in me but the autobiography I'd refused from the start even to think about. My life threatened to grow as useless as a three-month old computer magazine" (36). For her part, Lodge's Helen is no more sanguine about her own potential productivity or the state of narrative fiction generally. "Of course one can argue that there's a basic human need for narrative," she recognizes,

> it's one of our fundamental tools for making sense of experience—has been, back as far as you can go in history. But does this, I ask myself, necessarily entail the endless multiplication of new stories? [. . .] It's frightening to think of how many novels I must have read in my lifetime, and how little I retain of the substance of most of them. Should I really be encouraging these bright young people to add their quotient to the dust-heap of forgotten pseudo-lives? Would they perhaps be more profitably occupied designing computer models of the mind in Ralph Messenger's Centre for Cognitive Science?
>
> (83-84)

Despite these misgivings about their own profession, however, by the end of the narratives they inhabit, both fictional authors are reinvigorated and apparently armed with the raw material—the substance or content—for narratives that they must believe will both matter and last. Thus, even as the convergence of the two cultures as symbolized through the interpersonal relationships in the novels does not last, the convergence itself has had a salutary effect. In a sense, the narrative literature that has been demeaned in both works is given fresh import because it has new content. Tellingly, both novels end with a Proustian twist, their author-characters set to emerge from their respective states of writer's block and self-doubt and ready to write something close to the novels we have just finished reading. Richard leaves the Center with the refreshing sense that "I might have another fiction in me after all" (328), and Helen, following her tumultuous experiences with Ralph Messenger, ends up writing a novel, set in a university, with a title that comes directly from her discussions with Ralph and that attests to the fact that neuroscientists still cannot rationally explain all of what humans do or feel: *Crying is a Puzzler.* In both of these neuronarratives, it seems as if the real authors—Lodge and Powers—have endeavoured to introduce their author-characters and their readers to a new area of fictional *content,* human consciousness, that has the potential to refresh and redeem the field of literature.

Notes

1. See, for example, Daniel C. Dennett, *Consciousness Explained* (New York: Penguin, 1993); Steven Pinker, *The Blank Slate: The Modern Denial of Human Nature* (New York: Viking, 2002); and E. O. Wilson, *Consilience: The Unity of Knowledge* (New York: Vintage, 1999).

2. See, for example, Antonio Damasio, *Descartes' Error: Emotion, Reason, and the Human Brain* (New York: Penguin, 2005) and Gerald Edelman, *Second Nature: Brain Science and Human Knowledge* (New Haven, CT: Yale UP, 2006).

3. See, for example, Lisa Zunshine, *Why We Read Fiction: Theory of Mind and the Novel* (Columbus: Ohio State UP, 2006); Mary Crane and Alan Richardson, "Literary Studies and Cognitive Science: Toward a New Interdisciplinarity," *Mosaic* 32.2 (1999): 123-40; and N. Kathryn Hayles, *My Mother Was a Computer: Digital Subjects and Literary Texts* (Chicago: U of Chicago P, 2005).

4. See, for example, David Herman, *Story Logic: Problems and Possibilities of Narrative* (Lincoln: U of Nebraska P, 2004); Alan Palmer, *Fictional Minds* (Lincoln: U of Nebraska P, 2004); Nancy Easterlin, "Making Knowledge: Bioepistemology and the Foundations of Literary Theory," *Mosaic* 32.1 (1999): 131-47.

Works Cited

Clayton, Jay. "Convergence of the Two Cultures: A Geek's Guide to Contemporary Literature." *American Literature* 74 (2002): 807-31.

Hart, F. Elizabeth. "The Epistemology of Cognitive Literary Studies." *Philosophy and Literature* 25.2 (2001): 314-44.

Lodge, David. *Thinks . . . : A Novel.* New York: Viking, 2001.

Program in Narrative Medicine. College of Physicians and Surgeons, Columbia University, <http://narrativemedicine.org/about/about.html> (7 Sept. 2007).

Powers, Richard. *The Echo Maker.* New York: Farrar, Straus, and Giroux, 2006.

———. *Galatea 2.2.* New York: Farrar, Straus, and Giroux, 1995.

Prince, Gerald. *A Dictionary of Narratology.* Lincoln: U of Nebraska P, 1987.

Rabinowitz, Peter. *Before Reading: Narrative Conventions and the Politics of Interpretation.* Ithaca, NY: Cornell UP, 1987.

Rich, Motoko. "Oliver Sacks Joins Columbia Faculty as 'Artist.'" *New York Times Online* 1 September 2007 <http://nytimes.com/2007/09/01/books/01sack.html> (5 Sept. 2007).

Snow, C. P. *The Two Cultures and The Scientific Revolution.* New York: Cambridge UP, 1959.

J. Russell Perkin (essay date spring 2008)

SOURCE: Perkin, J. Russell. "The Pilgrimages of David Lodge." *Christianity and Literature* 57, no. 3 (spring 2008): 419-42.

[*In the following essay, Perkin examines the phenomenon of pilgrimage, both literal and symbolic, in Lodge's fiction.*]

. . . a tourist is half a pilgrim, if a pilgrim is half a tourist.

—Turner and Turner 20

. . . most of the greater pilgrimages have become seedbeds of the literature of "high culture"

—Turner and Turner 23

What are they hoping for? I don't think most of them could tell you if you asked them. Some adventure, some encounter, some miraculous transformation of their ordinary lives.

—Lodge, *Therapy* 214

In spite of the decline of organized religion in much of the western world, the concept of pilgrimage is alive and well, if by pilgrimage one means a purposeful journey, undertaken with some sense of homage or veneration, to a place that is set apart as special by the consensus of a specific community. Some traditional religious pilgrimages still flourish, such as that to Compostela in Spain, while people travel to many other sites with some of the attitudes and expectations of pilgrims: places associated with a writer or popular culture icon (Wordsworth's Lake District, the Oxford of J. R. R. Tolkien and C. S. Lewis, Jim Morrison's grave in Paris) or places that feature in a literary work, or film, or, frequently, in a film made from a literary work. Oxford, a multilayered cultural site, has among its many associations the fact that it is the location of the Inspector Morse series of TV movies, based on detective novels by the Oxford resident Colin Dexter.[1] The phenomenal success of Dan Brown's 2003 novel *The Da Vinci Code* created at least briefly a new pilgrim's way, retracing the journey of the novel's characters. And of course Castle Howard in Yorkshire owes much of its fame to the fact that it was used to represent the fictitious Brideshead in the celebrated miniseries made from Evelyn Waugh's *Brideshead Revisited*. I will return later in this essay to the question of how far such postmodern tourism can be seen to have anything in common with the religious pilgrimage of early or medieval Christianity.

The many versions of pilgrimage in contemporary society have been a recurrent focus in the novels of David Lodge, who is both a Roman Catholic and a keen observer of postmodern culture.[2] In this essay, I will trace his use of the motif of pilgrimage, from his presentation of traditional Catholic religious journeys in several of his novels to much more metaphorical extensions of the concept. I have allowed the term to be used flexibly because a significant theme in Lodge's fiction is the liberating effect of travel, and like many writers—notably Henry James, with whom he has an important intertextual relationship[3]—he often uses a journey to represent a metaphorical journey within the self. One of the places where Lodge signals the significance of this cluster of associations in his imaginative world is at the beginning of *Small World,* the celebration and satire of academic life, and especially of conference going, that was instrumental in establishing Lodge's North American popularity in the 1980s. He begins the Prologue to *Small World* with a modern English paraphrase of one of the most famous openings in English literature:

> When April with its sweet showers has pierced the drought of March to the root, and bathed every vein of earth with that liquid by whose power the flowers are engendered; when the zephyr, too, with its dulcet breath, has breathed life into the tender new shoots in every copse and on every heath, and the young sun has run half his course in the sign of the Rare, and the little birds that sleep all night with their eyes open give song (so Nature prompts them in their hearts), then, as the poet Geoffrey Chaucer observed many years ago, folk long to go on pilgrimages. Only, these days, professional people call them conferences.

(1)

However, the motif of pilgrimage is not especially important in the text of this novel as a whole, except insofar as the idea of pilgrimage can be assimilated to that of the romance quest; motifs from Arthurian literature are much more significant. *Small World* also features some humorous incidents involving tourism, including memorable moments in the Middle East, Japan, and the Lake Isle of Innisfree, and its ceaseless energy does celebrate, in a carnivalesque manner, both the farcical and the transformative possibilities of global travel;[4] but we must look elsewhere in Lodge for an exploration of the analogy between modern tourism and cultural travel and the Catholic concept of the pilgrimage.

Pilgrimage in the west is especially associated with Catholicism, though it has roots in Judaism and is round in most religions. The earliest concept of pilgrimage in Christianity sees human life as the journey of an exile toward the true home, which is in heaven. In *Pilgrimage and Literary Tradition,* Philip Edwards notes that the key biblical passage underlying this understanding of pilgrimage is Heb. 11:13-14, which reads

> These all died in faith, not having received the promises, but having seen them afar off, and were persuaded of them, and embraced them, and confessed that they were strangers and pilgrims on the earth [Vulgate: "peregrini et hospites sunt supra terram"]. For they that say such things declare plainly that they seek a country.

(KJV)

In Christian experience, this metaphorical view of human life chronologically precedes the actual physical journey to places made holy by their associations with Jesus Christ, the apostles, and later saints. In the *Confessions,* St. Augustine views individual human life and the collective experience of the church as a journey toward God, but he was not an advocate of "terrestial pilgrimage" (Edwards 11).[5] Commentators on the concept of pilgrimage often refer to the recurrent tension between the spiritual meaning of the pilgrim journey and the fact that it takes place in a physical world and can incorporate a variety of other motives, such as sightseeing, socializing with others, or getting away from home. In Langland, in Erasmus, and in the Protestant reformers, we see an attack on an overly literalized understanding of pilgrimage. In the post-Reformation English tradition, the idea of the pilgrimage as a metaphor for human life, or at least for the individual Christian's spiritual life, was given a very wide currency through the influence of John Bunyan's *Pilgrim's Progress*.[6]

The destruction of the English shrines and the reform of the Church of England interrupted the tradition of pilgrimage in England from the sixteenth to the nineteenth centuries, although it has been argued that, just as pilgrimage always had an aspect of tourism, so the Grand Tour was not devoid of an aspect of pilgrimage (Champ 9, 104-9).[7] Pilgrimage proper began again in the nineteenth century as a result of the Catholic revival, and by the twentieth century was practiced by Anglicans as well as Roman Catholics. At the same time, the meaning of the word "pilgrimage" had been broadened in secular use to refer to any meaningful journey, such as revisiting one's birthplace in another country.[8] (It is interesting to note that the earliest example of this extended use in the *Oxford English Dictionary* is tentatively dated 1515). Some of the traditional medieval pilgrimages have recently enjoyed a kind of renaissance, notably the Camino de Santiago or Way of St. James, to Santiago de Compostela in Spain. The website of the Canadian Company of Pilgrims, for example, lists and briefly reviews thirteen books in English, most of them very recent, about the Compostela pilgrimage ("Books"). The Compostela pilgrimage figures prominently in David Lodge's novel *Therapy*. Similarly, the Marian shrine in Walsingham, Norfolk, was restored in the twentieth century as a place of pilgrimage for both Roman Catholics and Anglicans.

The East Anglian village of Little Walsingham first became a place of pilgrimage after a vision experienced by the Saxon noblewoman Richeldis de Faverches in 1061 led to the construction of a replica of the house in which the Annunciation took place, according to directions given in the vision. Walsingham became known as "England's Nazareth." Along with other holy places, the shrine was destroyed by Henry VIII; Roman Catholic devotion at the site was revived in 1897, and in the 1920s, as a result of the initiative of the Anglican vicar of Walsingham, Fr. Alfred Hope Patten, Anglican pilgrimages began. Walsingham is now the principal Anglican shrine in the world, and interest in it has grown steadily in spite of the general decline in the Church of England.[9]

Pilgrimages to Walsingham are described in two of Lodge's novels. In his first published novel, *The Picturegoers*, the protagonist Mark Underwood is a student of literature who reverses the pattern of Joyce's *Portrait of the Artist*—a text alluded to several times in *The Picturegoers*—by experiencing a conversion from his secular and cynical devotion to modernist literature to the Roman Catholic church, in which he had been baptized but not brought up. Mark accompanies a group of other University of London students on a pilgrimage called "Student Cross." They are supposed to spend five days walking from London to Walsingham carrying a twelve-foot wooden cross "to perform an act of reparation for the sins of students everywhere" (174). Lodge emphasizes, through Mark's own self-aware analysis, his character's mixed motives for joining the pilgrimage. He is attracted by the idea of an unusual experience and is aware that his efforts will impress the Catholic family with whom he boards, yet he is embarrassed by the public demonstration of piety and the "Augean" purpose of the undertaking: "So what was it that had made him go, but a furtive, half-acknowledged sense that not to have done so would have been like turning one's back on the Crucifixion, that here perhaps at last was the litmus which might determine the validity of his readopted faith?" (175). To narrate the events of the pilgrimage itself, Lodge shifts from the novel's variously focalized third-person narration to excerpts from Mark's diary (as Joyce does with Stephen's at the end of *Portrait*). On Palm Sunday, the second day of the pilgrimage, Mark is suffering excruciating pain from blistered feet, and he is moved by the kindness of those who tend to him. He feels a deepening understanding of the meaning of the cross and of Christian love, but on the third day he gives up the pilgrimage, although he is aware that others are in at least as much pain as he is. He writes "I knew that the Cross would drag me to Cambridge if I allowed myself to be dragged, but I refused" (180). he narration shifts back to third person, and Mark's failure is analyzed: "the task of rebuilding was a daunting one. The foundations might have been securely laid if he had got to Walsingham. But he brought back with him from the pilgrimage no feeling of achievement or merit, only a sense of failure with which he was already too familiar" (180).

In his author's introduction to the 1993 Penguin reprint of *Picturegoers*, Lodge dissociates himself from the Catholic religiosity of his first novel, suggesting that the source was more in the Catholic fiction of "Greene, Waugh, Mauriac, Bernanos and that ilk" (viii) than in any spiritual experience of his own, though he does add

> I did occasionally undertake supererogatory religious exercises like the Student Cross pilgrimage described herein (with similarly ignominious results) in the somewhat superstitious belief that they would do me good. Looking back at that aspect of *The Picturegoers* from my present demythologized, provisional, and in

many ways agnostic theological perspective, it seems like the work of another person.

(viii-ix)

Mark Underwood's experience is repeated by Adrian, one of the large cast of characters in *How Far Can You Go?* (1980), Lodge's most sustained fictional exploration of Roman Catholicism. Adrian interprets his failure to complete the pilgrimage as a bad omen for his forthcoming final examinations, in which he earns a lower second. By this time in his career, Lodge is much more detached in his treatment of Catholicism, and he emphasizes the bathetic dimension of the experience far more than in his first novel. Adrian is "sent home in a wheelchair, sitting in the guard's van amid bales of returned newspapers and crates of disgruntled chickens" (32). It is also noteworthy that the pilgrim experience is given to Adrian, an unimaginative and vehement young man who begins as an apologist for Tridentine Catholicism, and then becomes an equally fervent crusader for a more open church in the aftermath of Vatican II, but who is throughout the novel the object of the narrator's irony.

The journey as a means of self-discovery is a central motif in Lodge's fiction.[10] He has commented in an interview on the importance in his own life of visits in his youth to Germany and Belgium "at a time when it was very difficult for British people to travel to the continent—certainly for people of my class" (Haffenden 148), and in the essay **"The Bowling Alley and the Sun"** he describes the liberating effect of a visit to the United States, an experience that formed the basis of his novel *Changing Places.* Travel plays a prominent role in most of Lodge's novels. In *Ginger, You're Barmy,* Jonathan Browne spends much of a holiday writing the memoir that comprises the bulk of the novel while his girlfriend is sick with food poisoning. His personal transformation is still pending at the end of the novel. *Out of the Shelter,* on the other hand, presents a trip abroad as a coming of age narrative, while *Changing Places* represents a sojourn in the United States as an experience of self-transformation. *Small World,* as I have already noted, describes global travel of a truly epic scale. Travel is especially prominent in *Paradise News* (1991) and *Therapy* (1995), which are the primary focus of this essay, while in *Author, Author* (2004) Lodge imagines travel from the perspective of Henry James. One can see Lodge's most recent novel as the acknowledgment of his immense debt to his American precursor, for—again as the allusion to Chaucer in *Small World* suggests—Lodge's presentation of travel owes as much to his literary preceptors as to his personal experience. The international theme of Henry James receives

comic treatment in Lodge's academic romances, and another key influence was Graham Greene, that most travelled of authors.

In both of his novels of the 1990s, Lodge uses multiple narrative points of view, incorporating texts written by the protagonist either on or immediately after a journey. It is also interesting to note that each of these two novels returns to the world of lower middle-class and working-class Catholic communities in the suburbs of London that Lodge explored in *The Picturegoers,* but the mature works are very different in their perspective. They are self-evidently midlife novels (Lodge was fifty-five in 1990 and sixty-five in 2000) in which the main character has by his educational or career success detached himself from his childhood world but finds himself forced to return in order to deal with unresolved issues from the past. In each case, a journey that has elements of a pilgrimage helps the protagonist to overcome his present problems by coming to terms with this "unfinished business" from earlier in his life. These two works, *Paradise News* and *Therapy,* constitute Lodge's most sustained explorations of the connection between travel and spiritual quest.

Paradise News is one of Lodge's most theological novels (and of course even the title echoes *Paradise Lost*[11]). It is the story of a former priest, Bernard Walsh, who is no longer a religious believer but nevertheless a teacher of theology at a college in Rummidge, Lodge's fictional counterpart to the city of Birmingham. He grew up in Brickley, the fictional suburb of London that is the setting of *The Picturegoers.*[12] Bernard lives a hand-to-mouth existence as an adjunct teacher, owning neither a car nor his own phone and even living in student accommodation on campus. As a result of his loss of faith, he is alienated from his father and sister, who are still practicing Catholics. Bernard's life is turned upside down when he is summoned to Hawaii at the request of a dying aunt. Lodge uses the fact that Paradise is an important concept in both theology and holiday advertising as the basis for a series of analogies between spiritual quest and tourism. Bernard Walsh himself is neither pilgrim nor tourist, as an unbeliever who has abandoned spiritual aspiration to live a life that is "lonely, hollow, unfulfilled" (192), and as someone who is visiting Hawaii on urgent family business rather than in quest of the vacation of a lifetime. But he finds that the experience of a different culture, into which he is forced when he has to care for the needs of his father and aunt, and the experience of falling in love with a woman whom chance throws in his path, have a liberating effect akin to Lodge's own encounter with the United States in the 1960s. Lodge signals his theme in a number of ways. A series of allusions to Shakespeare's *Tempest* underscores the fact that some of the characters in the novel came to Hawaii fleeing personal difficulties elsewhere, while others need forgiveness, whether they realize it or not.[13] Some of the tourists are on their first or second honeymoon, just as Shakespeare's royal party in the *Tempest* are returning from a wedding. But unlike Prospero's enchanted island, Hawaii is not in the Mediterranean; rather, as one of Lodge's characters explains, "We're out on the rim of Western civilization here, hanging on by our fingertips . . ." (175; ellipsis in original text). His trip makes Bernard Walsh realize the limitations of his insular English and Roman Catholic upbringing, while the conclusion to the novel very tentatively points to an alternative form of Catholic spirituality that remains possible for the implied author, and perhaps eventually even for Bernard. Lodge also brings out the archetypal significance of his story through other allusions, which come naturally given that his main character is theologically educated and highly literate. Bernard quotes from Yeats ("News for the Delphic Oracle" and "The Second Coming") and Larkin ("This Be the Verse") as well as *The Tempest,* and Part One of the novel has an epigraph from William Meredith's "An Account of a Visit to Hawaii": "Nightly descending through the baroque cloud / That decorates these hills, riding on air, / Thousands arrive by dream at their desire." Bernard himself sees the journey in a similarly mythopoeic vein, and on the personal level he regards it as an opportunity for remaking himself. In the terms of Victor and Edith Turner's influential anthropological analysis of pilgrimage, Bernard's trip to Hawaii to see his aunt Ursula is a liminal experience,[14] taking him out of his ordinary sphere, on a journey to a place where he suffers a "sea change" before returning to his point of origin a different man, even looking years younger as a result of shaving off his beard and acquiring a new wardrobe. As he reflects, "the journey to which he had impulsively committed himself" is an exhilarating possibility, in spite of its sad occasion: "To fly halfway round the world at a few days' notice was an adventure, whatever the occasion; it would be 'a change', as people said—indeed it would be hard to think of a more dramatic alteration of the dull rhythm of his present existence" (30). Lodge's description of the arrival in Hawaii, narrated here from Bernard's perspective, emphasizes this aspect of the trip:

> And how miraculous, really, that their aircraft had felt its way unerringly across the thousands of miles of dark water to this haven of light. There was something mythical about it—the night sea journey—though the other passengers stretching and yawning around him seemed to take it all for granted.
>
> (83)

The place that awaits them is a version of the Fortunate Isles or earthly paradise, although it is characteristic of Lodge's realism that in describing the tropical air and flowers that greet the travellers in Hawaii he also notes the "hint of petrol" that blends with the smell of frangipani (83).

Lodge also explores the connection between tourism and pilgrimage through the musings of another character, Roger Sheldrake, who intensely dislikes holidays and who is travelling to Hawaii as part of his anthropological research into the phenomenon of tourism. Lodge gently mocks academic behavior in his portrayal of Sheldrake, while using him as the mouthpiece for some serious analysis of the human quest for Paradise and transcendence of the ordinary self. Sheldrake echoes the views of influential anthropologists when he sees tourism as a new global religion, in which sightseeing functions "as secular pilgrimage" (75). The insight of his research in Hawaii is that "*The holiday paradise is inevitably transposed into a site of pilgrimage by the innate momentum of the tourist industry*" (251; italics in the original). Victor and Edith Turner write that "a tourist is half a pilgrim, if a pilgrim is half a tourist. Even when people bury themselves in anonymous crowds on beaches, they are seeking an almost sacred, often symbolic, mode of communitas, generally unavailable to them in the structured life of the office, the shop floor, or the mine" (20).[15] Similarly, Hartmut Berghoff asserts that "Modern tourism may partly be described as a secularized form of pilgrimage because the underlying assumption is that 'recreation'—the term itself has strong religious connotations—requires absence from home" (161). Lodge manages in *Paradise News* to convey a great deal about modern tourism and to reflect on it with characteristic intelligence, in part through the reflections of Bernard Walsh and Roger Sheldrake, and in part through his acute eye for revealing details which makes him a master of realism, crystallizing social trends and movements with striking economy. By seeking Paradise, secularized into a series of holiday images, the tourists in *Paradise News* are really all seeking self-transformation. But the novel is also concerned with the question of Paradise in the sense of an afterlife.[16] A hasty reading of *Paradise News* might suggest that it is about the need to make heaven on earth and might further suggest that Lodge's heaven consists of physical pleasure, and especially sexual gratification. Bernard overcomes his anxieties about sexuality and finds love and a potential life partner on the trip to Hawaii. But the novel cannot be reduced to the cliche of equating religious practice and sexual repression. Bernard's Aunt Ursula is dying, and it is too late for her to experience the fulfillment that was missing in her failed marriage as a result of sexual abuse she suffered as a child. Instead, she seeks to be reconciled with her family, especially her brother, and that action leads to a reconciliation between Bernard and his sister. Lodge shows that for Ursula, unlike Bernard, Catholicism is a source of strength and comfort. As Marian Crowe shows in her analysis of the sacramental imagery in *Paradise News,* Bernard's inadequacy as a priest was personal, the result of not only his repressed upbringing but also his intellectual dishonesty. The novel presents in the charismatic Father McPhee a priest who is comfortable with his vocation, and who as a result is able to minister the comfort of the sacraments to Bernard's aunt and his father. Bernard refuses to receive communion with his father, his aunt, and his sister, but his transformation in Hawaii is accompanied by sacramental imagery. Crowe notes his symbolic baptism in the ocean, which leads to the minor "miracle" of his losing and then finding the key to Ursula's safe-deposit box, where he locates the funds that enable her to die in comfort (Crowe 157-58). Although Lodge does not insist upon the symbolism of the keys of the kingdom, it is a plausible implication.

By relaxing into the new experiences offered by the Hawaiian trip, Bernard gains the self-confidence and self-knowledge that enable him to live a more truly Christian life than he ever did as an ostensibly believing priest. Crowe does not point out another key sacramental image that occurs at the end of the novel. In the last pages, we first see him lecturing at the college, and telling his students:

> To the question, "Why did God make you?" the Catechism answered, "God made me to know him, love him and serve him in this world, and to be happy with him *for ever in the next.*" But the concepts and images of this next world which have come down to us in Christian teaching no longer have any credibility for thoughtful, educated men and women. The very idea of an afterlife for individual human beings has been regarded with scepticism and embarrassment—or silently ignored—by nearly every major twentieth-century theologian.
>
> (352; italics in the original)

However, these are not the last words of the text. After the lecture, with its presentation of skeptical theology, Bernard finds a letter in his mailbox from Yolande, the woman in Hawaii whom he hopes to marry, describing the requiem mass for his aunt Ursula. The language here, mixing traditional Catholicism with yet another reference to the *Tempest,* suggests that the implied author cannot be quite as categorical about the afterlife as can Bernard Walsh, and Yolande's letter is accompanied by a quotation from Unamuno's *The Tragic Sense of Life* that describes the possibility of life after death as "a shadow of a shadow of uncertainty" lurking in the consciousness of the skeptic, just as "the voice of uncertainty" lurks "in some recess of the soul

of the true believer who has faith in the future life" (368). The requiem mass on the beach incorporates hula dancing, and it is followed by a moving passage describing the scattering of Ursula's ashes in the ocean. Bernard's receiving of the letter is accompanied by the sacramental image of the descent of the holy spirit. He reads the letter under the leaves of a copper beech tree whose leaves "blazed, like a tree on fire yet unconsumed" (358). After he has finished reading, "The leaves rustled in the breeze, and one or two fluttered down like tiny tongues of fire" (369). Bernard tells a colleague—in the last words of the novel—that the letter contains "Very good news." Earlier, in his journal, Bernard recorded the fact that the Good News of the gospel is "Paradise news" (190), while on the level of the secular holiday, *Paradise News* was the name of a local newspaper in Hawaii. As a returned pilgrim, Bernard continues to be a rather uninspiring teacher of theology, but in some crucial way his life has been altered, and further transforming possibilities await him.[17] Yolande's letter may be seen as the confirmation of his earlier symbolic baptism in the Pacific Ocean. In spite of Bernard's own radically skeptical world view, Lodge ends his novel with a typological image. The fact that Yolande, his earthly lover, is describing a requiem mass in sympathetic terms leaves the concluding implication that she may ultimately help him to regain some sort of faith.[18]

In *Therapy* (1995), the pilgrimage metaphor becomes actualized as a key part of the plot of the novel. *Therapy* is narrated by Laurence Passmore, known to his friends as Tubby, a TV scriptwriter in his late fifties who is engaged in a variety of forms of therapy for a malady that the reader soon realizes is more spiritual than anything else. He is prompted by Alexandra, his "cognitive behaviour therapist" to make lists of the good and bad things in his life. Judging by the list of good things, he has an enviable life: professional and financial success, a stable marriage and family, a nice house, and expensive car. Under the column of bad things, he writes "Feel unhappy most of the time" adding a few weeks later "Pain in knee" (23), and the knee pain becomes symbolic of his deeper spiritual malaise. Lodge may be drawing here, however unconsciously, on the traditional religious idea, more Catholic than Protestant, that there is an opposition between worldly success and salvation; he is also commenting, again with his typical sharp eye for the minutiae of social history, on the rise of alternative forms of therapy, mental, physical, and spiritual, through the 1990s, including the introduction of Prozac.

Therapy is richly comic, especially in the first two parts. In Part One, Tubby Passmore, dissatisfied with the failure of his various therapists to help him with either his unhappiness or the pain in his knee, begins to read Kierkegaard, prompted by what he finds when he happens to look up the word *Angst.* (Tubby is not a well-educated person, and he compensates for this by frequently looking things up in reference books). He gradually learns about Kierkegaard's life and begins to use existentialist categories to analyze his marriage, all the while unaware that in the view of his wife, Sally, the marriage has irretrievably broken down. When Sally asks him for a separation, he doesn't take in her request, not because he is so shocked by it, but because he has developed the habit of not listening to anything that she says. Tubby has not been unfaithful to his wife sexually, although he has not told her about a close Platonic friendship with Amy, a woman who works with him in television. He becomes fascinated by Kierkegaard's analysis of the dynamics of human sexual attraction. When his marriage breaks down, he undertakes a series of journeys that in varying degrees can be seen as pilgrimages. The first of these is an attempt to compensate for lost opportunities for philandering. He decides to attempt a sexual relationship with his friend Amy on a trip to the Canary Islands. This turns out to be a holiday where everything goes wrong, and Lodge's description of it is a miniature masterpiece of satiric comedy. After things don't go well with Amy, Tubby sets off once again on what turns into a parodic pilgrimage, Tubby's attempt to get laid, a comic epic of sexual dysfunction as he seeks the erotic fulfillment promised by holiday advertising. His second destination is Los Angeles, where he tries to reconnect with an American production executive who once propositioned him. The third journey of the erotic quest is a trip to Copenhagen with an attractive young assistant, ostensibly for the purpose of researching a film about Kierkegaard. Tubby and Samantha walk the streets of Copenhagen, visit Kierkegaard's grave (giving Lodge the opportunity to point out that the name Kierkegaard means churchyard or cemetery, so they visit "Kierkegaard in the *kierkegaard*" [186], which Samantha says is the only joke of the visit), attend a lugubrious Lutheran church service, and visit the City Museum. Tubby pores over the humble artifacts such as Kierkegaard's pipes and magnifying glass "as if they were sacred relics" (184), and as a result he feels that he cannot consummate his lust for Samantha, because the presence of Kierkegaard in the museum exhibit, "like a spirit or a good angel," has prevented him (190). As he puts it, "Call it conscience. Call it Kierkegaard. They have become one and the same thing" (209).

Tubby's epiphany in Copenhagen results from a type of tourism that is growing in popularity, and whose history is analyzed by Nicola Watson in her recent book *The Literary Tourist.* Watson's study traces the

way that since the Romantic movement, the practice of visiting places associated with writers and their works has developed into "a commercially significant phenomenon" (1). The places visited may include the writer's grave, the writer's home as the place where the works were composed, and places associated with the writer's works. Ian Ousby explicitly connects such travelling to pilgrimage, noting the frequency with which accounts of literary tourism use words like "shrine" and "pilgrim" (22). Because a popular writer endures after death in the form of his or her work, Ousby suggests that the writer "proved the ideal hero for a secular culture, the most satisfying object of national pride" (23).[19]

The epigraph to *Therapy* is a quotation from Graham Greene: "Writing is a form of therapy,"[20] and much of the novel is comprised of Tubby Passmore's journal, as he details the various forms of therapy he is involved in and their inability to help him in his predicament. The third part of the novel contains a separate short memoir titled "Maureen," also by Tubby, telling in vivid detail the story of his first girlfriend and the heartless way that he broke up with her. Maureen's family were Roman Catholic, and in narrating the story of Tubby's first love, Lodge again revisits the world of pre-Vatican II suburban London Catholicism that he explored in his early fiction. Maureen is chosen to play the Virgin Mary in a play put on by the church youth group, and after being told by the parish priest what a responsibility this role entails she tells Tubby that they will have to stop kissing and petting while she is playing Mary. He responds by ending their relationship. Lodge creates an obvious parallel between Kierkegaard's rejection of Regine and Tubby's of Maureen. The memoir is thus a literary equivalent of the pilgrimage home; having written it, Tubby actually goes back to Hatchford, the suburb where he grew up, and visits his childhood home and the church that Maureen's family attended (her childhood home is no longer there), and then he decides to find Maureen herself.

This journey home, as I have already noted, is one of the most common types of secularized and individual pilgrimages of the postmodern age. Tubby Passmore's journey is an attempt to understand himself and to come to terms with the past. He largely does this through his writing, which is why I see that writing as an extension of the concept of pilgrimage. Both writing and pilgrimage, in postmodernity, are seen as forms of therapy—better in Lodge's view than many of the alternatives—and given the number of books about the Camino de Santiago, they seem to be very closely connected. As though to spell out this point for the reader, when Tubby sets out to find Maureen again, he discovers from her husband that she has gone off, alone, on the pilgrimage to Santiago de Compostela. So if he is going to find Maureen, he too must become a pilgrim of sorts. As he tells his agent, who is furious that Tubby is leaving at a crucial moment for the television series he writes, "It's not a holiday . . . it's a pilgrimage" (280).

The Compostela pilgrimage experienced a great resurgence in the 1990s, and David Lodge himself was involved in making a television program about it.[21] It has evolved into a rather postmodern phenomenon, with pilgrims often following their own personal quest to visit a place that is holy due to a rather implausible legend. Tubby comments, "I found it hard to understand why millions of people had walked halfway across Europe in times past, often under conditions of appalling discomfort and danger, to visit the dubious shrine of this dubious saint" (289), but as he pursues Maureen—even though he is driving rather than walking—the pilgrimage starts to put a spell on him. The pilgrims are people he can readily identify with: "People at turning-points in their lives—looking for peace, or enlightenment, or just an escape from the daily rat-race" (292). Accounts of the contemporary Compostela pilgrimage make it seem like a mixture of an extreme sports challenge, a Buddhist meditative walk, and an exercise in medievalist cultural tourism, promoted by a strange conjunction of New Age personal spirituality, the Spanish tourist industry, and the Roman Catholic church.[22] Tubby finds a form of therapy in abandoning the incessant demands and conflicts of the television industry, while Maureen uses the pilgrimage as an opportunity to escape temporarily from a difficult impasse in her marriage, so that she can come to terms with the death of a child and the aftermath of breast cancer.[23]

Mary Victoria Wallis's *Among the Pilgrims* is an eclectic account of the camino written by a health-care worker who is both a trained medievalist and a follower of Buddhist spirituality. She describes reading an account of the pilgrimage by a Benedictine monk, Fray Juan Antonio Torres Prieto, titled *Tu Solus Peregrinus.* For Prieto, there is only one true purpose for pilgrimage: "the search for God in one's heart as one follows the sacred path to the Shrine of St. James"[24]. Wallis says ironically that she went on the pilgrimage more for what Prieto identifies as "three bad reasons": cultural tourism, a desire to escape the stress of everyday life, and a desire to meet interesting people (24).

Lodge makes a metafictional joke when Tubby meets up with a British television crew who are recording a programme about the *camino.* "David" the writer and presenter, is not present, because he is annoyed at having had to walk earlier in the day, but the director

excitedly starts filming when Tubby ventures to define the "true pilgrim" in Kierkegaardian terms as one for whom pilgrimage is "an existential act of self-definition" (304). Like the monk Fray Juan, Tubby classifies pilgrims. For him, the cultural tourists are the aesthetic type of pilgrim; those who view the pilgrimage as a personal challenge are the ethical type; the true pilgrim is "the religious pilgrim, religious in the Kierkegaardian sense. . . . The whole point was that you chose to believe without rational compulsion—you made a leap into the void and in the process chose yourself" (305). This is not so different from the monk's idea of searching for God in one's heart. (To prevent his tone from becoming too earnest here, Lodge concludes the incident with another joke. When the English pilgrim is recognized as Tubby Passmore, writer of the hit comedy *The People Next Door,* the director decides that his analysis was just "taking the piss" [305]).

Thus Tubby's romantic quest for his lost childhood love becomes a pilgrimage on which he comes to understand for the first time what "an appalling thing" he did when he broke Maureen's heart (261). His journey is also, therefore, a quest for lost innocence, and for forgiveness of what he comes to think of as the original sin of his life, the source of many of the problems that afflict him in middle age. He realizes that his own memoir of Maureen has resemblances to Kierkegaard's "Seducer's Diary." At the close of the novel, Tubby has accepted the end of his marriage and is spending a lot of time with both Maureen and her husband, while he and Maureen are occasionally lovers. The novel concludes, "The three of us are best of friends. We're going off together for a little autumn break, actually. To Copenhagen. It was my idea. You could call it a pilgrimage" (321). Once again there is a connection with Graham Greene, as Lodge is here rewriting the triangle that structures *The End of the Affair.* Maureen's husband Bede is even, like Henry Miles in Greene's novel, a civil servant. I'm not sure if the echo was conscious on Lodge's part.

In other ways, the conclusion to **Therapy** is very different from the world of Graham Greene. Tubby continues to be successful professionally and materially—at the end of the novel he is contemplating buying a house in Wimbledon, where Maureen and Bede live—and he finds his way out of his mid-life crisis as a result of his pilgrimages to Copenhagen and Compostela. The reader can presume that, like Bernard Walsh in **Paradise News,** he has had the kind of spiritual reawakening that in the postmodern world is the closest most people can get to religious faith. (24) The fact that the novel concludes with the plan for another trip to Copenhagen, explicitly referred to as a "pilgrimage," indicates the importance of Kierkegaard in Tubby's new world-view. It also suggests that for Lodge cultural tourism can take on the dimension of a genuine spirituality. Tubby Passmore was never a Roman Catholic, but his existentialism replicates much of the essence of Catholic spirituality. Lodge explicitly compares the two forms of religiosity when Tubby visits the shrine of St. James in Compostela. He reflects:

> I couldn't help contrasting the pomp and circumstance of the shrine with the small, austerely furnished room in the Copenhagen Bymuseum, its half-dozen cabinets containing a few homely objects, books and pictures, and the modest monument in the Assistens Kirkegard. I wondered whether, if Kierkegaard had been a Catholic, they would have made him a saint by now, and built a basilica over his grave. He would make a good patron saint of neurotics.

(311)

The conclusion of **Paradise News** can be read as affirming a liberal, demythologized form of Catholicism that nevertheless is open to the possibility that there is more than symbolic truth in Christian, and more specifically Catholic, religious language. In **Therapy,** it seems to me that Lodge is more interested in the common elements among the various forms of therapy that are explored in the novel. However, the forms that are truly efficacious are writing, Kierkegaardian existentialism, and Catholic pilgrimage. Lodge does not find it necessary to show Tubby Passmore moving toward Rome at the end of **Therapy**; on the other hand, it is clear that through his personal quest for meaning, culminating in his study of Kierkegaard, he has found a form of genuinely religious experience.

The idea of literary tourism as spiritual pilgrimage seems to me to underlie Lodge's most recent novel, **Author, Author,** a biographical novel about Henry James.[25] If visiting Lamb House is akin to a pilgrimage, as would be the case for many writers and students of literature, Lodge's novel may be seen as an extended imagined visit to Lamb House, an ecphrastic narrative whereby Lodge projects himself into the consciousness of one of the writers he admires most. James's purchase of the house is in fact a major episode in **Author, Author.** Lodge has written about Henry James throughout his career, and his own transatlantic fiction reprises James's international theme.[26] He can be seen preparing to write **Author, Author** in his previous novel, **Thinks . . . ,** which contains a number of references to Henry James. The narrator of part of that novel, Helen Reed, is herself a novelist, and is teaching a course in creative writing where she makes use of passages from James. On a visit to Gloucester, Helen recalls it as the scene of the adulterous tryst of Charlotte and the Prince in *The Golden Bowl* (88), and later she visits the town of

Ledbury to see a church mentioned in one of James's letters: "a noble old church (with detached *campanile*) & a churchyard so full of ancient sweetness, so happy in situation and characteristic detail, that it seemed for me (for the time)—as so many things do—one of the memorable sights of my European experience" (230). Seeking to recapture James's own experience— "Fingers crossed that it is still as James saw it" (231)—Helen goes to visit the church, but her visit, which "began as a kind of Jamesian pilgrimage" (231) ends with her discovering one of her friends having a clandestine lunch with a man who is obviously her adulterous lover, a scene, as she notes, that might have come from one of James's own novels. Beginning as a literary tourist, Helen finds herself re-enacting the discovery scene in *The Ambassadors,* slightly overdetermined by the earlier reference to *The Golden Bowl.*[27]

Author, Author is an extended act of homage, a virtual pilgrimage to the site of Henry James. It is very much a writer's novel, movingly focused on James's friendships with George du Maurier and Constance Fenimore Woolson and his failed attempt to establish himself as a playwright. Lodge's interest in the writerly life, manifested in many of his essays of the last two decades and in the novella **Home Truths,** comes to fruition in **Author, Author.** He incorporates elements of James's own stories of literary life, notably "The Middle Years" and "The Next Time." The Catholic themes of his earlier work are largely occluded.[28]

On the evidence of **Author, Author,** then, religious pilgrimage has been absorbed into a more general spirituality of aesthetic experience. Henry James was himself fascinated by Roman Catholicism,[29] and in **Author, Author,** Lodge's fictional character Henry tells George du Maurier that he feels an attraction to the Roman church, but that his religion is "Consciousness, . . . human consciousness. Refining it, intensifying it—and preserving it" (91). This suggests that the true spiritual life is that of artistic creation. In the concluding pages of **Author, Author,** the postmodern narrator interjects himself, linking the story of James's deathbed to an account of his remarkable literary afterlife in recent decades, of which Lodge's novel is of course a part. Lodge also draws on James's own essay "Is There a Life After Death?" to illustrate the perennial human desire, in the face of all evidence to the contrary, for belief in personal immortality. But the only believing Christian represented in **Author, Author** is a genial broad church Anglican clergyman who is a friend of du Maurier and James, and he has a small part in the novel. It is James's *literary* afterlife that leaves the strongest impression.

David Lodge began his MA thesis with a discussion of George Orwell's claim that the novel is a Protestant form, inherently incompatible with Roman Catholicism (8-9; he returns to the question in the conclusion to the thesis, 721-23). In the first half of the twentieth century, the European Catholic novel sought to disprove Orwell's claim, and Lodge has continued to wrestle with the issue throughout his career. In his novels of the 1990s he explores the relationship between travel and spirituality and connects the modern tourist with the medieval pilgrim. On the evidence of **Thinks . . .** and **Author, Author,** Lodge's fiction has moved toward a much more secularized form of spirituality in which pilgrimage is absorbed into literary tourism, and the eschatology of the original biblical pilgrimage metaphor is radically realized in the here and now, absorbed into the everyday human world of the realist novel. Nevertheless, just as Yolande's letter in **Paradise News** asserts the possibility of a personal immortality, even if only as "a shadow of a shadow of uncertainty" (368), so **Author, Author** ends by imagining, even if only as a rhetorical gesture, the possibility of the consciousness of Henry lames as somewhere still present. Even when he is not writing explicitly about Catholicism, Lodge remains, as Bernard Bergonzi has suggested, "a fundamentally religious writer" ("Conversation" 205).[30]

Notes

1. A sense of the wealth of representations of Oxford can be gleaned from John Dougill's fascinating book.

2. In the early part of his career, Lodge can be identified as a Roman Catholic novelist and intellectual. One of his first publications was in fact a religious tract titled *About Catholic Authors*. It has a fictional frame, that of a series of letters from a priest to a young man doing his National Service, and contains some acute critical observations, though it participates in the insular piety characteristic of the genre. Lodge's extremely long (760 pages!) University of London MA thesis was a study of "Catholic Fiction Since the Oxford Movement" (1959), and his early novels focus on Catholic characters, often from backgrounds resembling his own in suburban London. The novel *How Far Can You Go?* (1980) traces the decline of the Church's authority and the liberalization of attitudes in a group of middle-class Catholics from the late 1950s to the late 1970s; more recently Lodge described himself as an "Agnostic Catholic" (Bergonzi, "Conversation" 203). In an interview with Lidia Vianu published in 2001, Lodge said, "I think if you read my novels in sequence you will see a gradual waning of orthodox religious belief in the 'implied author' I don't propose to comment here on the 'real author's' religious position."

3. The highly intertextual nature of Lodge's fiction is a subject all of its own, and I will take it for granted in this essay. It is a focus in Robert A. Morace's study of the fiction of Lodge and Malcolm Bradbury and is discussed in books by Bruce K. Martin and Barbara Arizti. Intertextuality has also been a preoccupation of Lodge throughout his career as a critic. A particularly interesting recent essay is "Graham Greene and the Anxiety of Influence."

4. For an interesting analysis of the role of rapid means of transportation in the construction of the modern subject see Chapter 9 of John Urry's *Consuming Places,* "Tourism, Travel and the Modern Subject" (141-51). Urry suggests that "The modern subject is a subject on the move. Central to the idea of modernity is that of movement . . ." (141).

5. For the use of metaphors of exodus and pilgrimage in Augustine, see Crouse, Chapter IV, "St. Augustine."

6. This paragraph draws on the excellent overview of the development of the concept of pilgrimage within the Christian tradition in Edwards, Chapter 1 (523).

7. See also Peat for a discussion of the persistence of pilgrim sites as destinations in the literature of the modern period, specifically Forster and Woolf.

8. The essays in Katherine Govier's anthology *Solo: Writers on Pilgrimage* cover topics such as Nuruddin Farah's return to Somalia, Roddy Doyle watching the World Cup on television, and Joy Kogawa's return to the house of her childhood, where she lived before the internment of the Japanese-Canadians.

9. See "The Story So Far" on the Anglican Walsingham website (The Shrine) for a history of the shrine from the vision of Richeldis to the present. Other interesting material is located under the heading "Why Pilgrimage?" A useful chronology may be found on the Roman Catholic Walsingham site ("R. C. National Shrine"). In an exceptional display of equal-opportunity ecumenism, the two churches' sites are entered through a common home page, <http://www.walsingham.org.uk/>. There is an informative discussion of Walsingham and Loreto in Turner and Turner (17587). Edwards devotes a chapter to the literary traces of the Walsingham pilgrimage, which considering its status as one of the principal European Marian shrines are surprisingly few (see Chapter 2, 24-44).

10. Govier's *Solo* is an anthology of accounts of such journeys. In her introduction, Govier defines a pilgrimage as the "one particular, long-imagined journey we have to take" (vii). She comments that her biggest surprise in collecting the narratives that comprise her book was that "by far the most popular destination was home" (ix), a remark that is relevant to David Lodge's *Therapy.*

11. Lodge draws attention to this allusion in the following exchange between Yolande and Bernard: "The history of Hawaii is the history of loss" / "Paradise lost?" I said. / "Paradise stolen. Paradise raped. Paradise infected. Paradise owned, developed, packaged. Paradise sold" (177).

12. The London suburb where Lodge himself was brought up is called Brockley; Lodge described it to John Haffenden as "a somewhat seedy, neglected bit of London" (Haffenden 147).

13. Lodge commented to Bernard Bergonzi that American reviewers were better at picking up the *Tempest* references than British reviewers ("Conversation" 205).

14. Victor and Edith Turner analyze pilgrimage in terms of the concept of "liminality;' which they define as "The state and process of mid-transition in a rite of passage" (249). They note that "For the majority, pilgrimage was the great liminal experience of the religious life. If mysticism is an interior pilgrimage, pilgrimage is exteriorized mysticism" (7).

15. For a summary of the views of several anthropologists on the analogy between tourism and pilgrimage see Urry, *Tourist Gaze* 8-10.

16. Crowe points out that Lodge throughout uses the term paradise rather than heaven, and has a useful analysis of the implications of this choice (159).

17. Lodge is true to his unpretentious roots in the literature of the 1950s when he allows a package tour to Hawaii, rather than some more esoteric kind of experience, to become a means of spiritual grace. It is interesting to note that Sue Wright's "Sun, Sea, Sand and Self-Expression: Mass Tourism as an Individual Experience" argues that one should not dismiss package tours as homogenizing mass experiences, as negative analysis often does, because to their participants they represent a "multiplicity of experiences and meanings" (199).

18. Bruce K. Martin contrasts *Paradise News* with Lodge's earlier Catholic novels and sees it as "post-Catholic" like its protagonist (149). I agree with Martin that there is a much greater degree of provisionality in the novel's treatment of religious issues, but I think the sacramental symbolism is more significant than his discussion implies. Similarly, Martin notes the references to pilgrimage in *Paradise News* (151) but does not spend much time discussing them, although he does acknowledge that the use of such references is more serious than the allusion that commences *Small World*. Bergonzi takes the Catholicism of *Paradise News* more seriously in a brief but suggestive discussion (*David Lodge* 39-44).

19. John Urry notes in *Consuming Places* that "Many of the objects of the tourist gaze are functionally equivalent to the objects of religious pilgrimage in traditional society" (144-45). With specific reference to sites of literary tourism and the parallel phenomenon of visiting places of popular cultural significance, Tobias Döring writes "Even in a contemporary postmodern geography where the experience of space has generally become secularized such spots are marked as remnants of a spatial hierarchy: they remain places inscribed with special meaning. It

seems as if, in a world of the profane, the celebrity shrine might offer a last substitute for the sacred" (256).

20. The quotation is from Greene's *Ways of Escape* "Writing is a form of therapy; sometimes I wonder how all those who do not write, compose or paint can manage to escape the madness, the melancholia, the panic fear which is inherent in the human situation" (237). Greene quotes this statement from his own text in the Preface to the book (xiii). It is probably not an accident that the homeless man who sleeps in the entryway to Tubby's London flat is called "Grahame" (I owe this point to an Internet database note on *Therapy* by Jacalyn Duffin). Lodge is probably imitating the name games beloved by his precursor in the Catholic novel; it was Greene who called the villain of *The Third Man* Harry Lime.

21. In a strange twist of fate, Lodge met the Irish writer Colm Tóibín while on the *camino* or pilgrim way, and Tóibín describes this meeting in his own book on Catholic Europe. For some reason, Tóibín greeted Lodge by asking "'What did Chad's family make their fortune from in Henry James' *The Ambassadors*?'" (Tóibín 150), as if to foreshadow the fact that in 2004 they would both publish books about Henry James. Lodge gives his own version of this meeting in *The Year of Henry James* (40-43). A useful brief account of Lodge's documentary research on the Compostela pilgrimage may be round in Martin (153-54). Martin notes that Lodge published an article about the pilgrimage, much of which is incorporated into *Therapy,* in the *Independent on Sunday* (16 Dec. 1993).

22. The *camino* illustrates the continuing validity of Roland Barthes's famous pronouncement that "Christianity is the chief purveyor of tourism, and one travels only to visit churches" (75). Barthes made this comment in the course of an analysis of the *Blue Guide to Spain*.

23. Wallis suggests that even in the Middle Ages "for many people, the trip to Santiago must also have been a welcome release from the round of everyday life. It was a claustrophobic age. . . . Pilgrimage was a chance to see the world beyond the parish" (22).

24. Philip Edwards concludes *Pilgrimage and the Literary Tradition* with a brief commentary on *Therapy,* and writes that "Laurence Passmore believes that Maureen's pilgrimage is justified to herself as a leap of faith, 'absurd' but necessary in Kierkegaard's view. He does not himself, so far as we hear in the remaining few pages of the novel, accept the leap, but he accepts its possibility, and he shares to some extent in what Maureen has achieved or has been granted" (210).

25. The term "biographical novel" is Lodge's own (*Year* 8).

26. In an interview with Jonathan Derbyshire, Lodge comments that he admires James a great deal,

although not as much as James Joyce, and notes that James is the novelist whom Graham Greene most often refers to in his essays, "which is not something you'd immediately predict or suppose" Lodge's engagement with James can be seen early on, with an essay on *The Ambassadors* in his first major work of criticism ("Strether") and continues with analyses of James in *The Art of Fiction,* editions of *The Spoils of Poynton* and *Daisy Miller,* and extensive discussion in *Consciousness and the Novel.* In the fiction, there are the wickedly funny parody of James in *The British Museum Is Falling Down* (105-08) and numerous references in *Thinks* . . . before the full-scale treatment of James in *Author, Author.*

27. Near the end of *Thinks . . . ,* Helen alludes to Lodge's essay on this discovery scene, "Strether by the River" (314).

28. In *Thinks . . . ,* the novelist Helen Reed has had a Catholic upbringing, and this plays a minor role in the novel, but she herself is more a liberal humanist novelist, a category as rare as the Catholic novelist in the new millennium, as Lodge recognizes when he makes a reviewer describe Helen's latest novel as "so old-fashioned in form as to be almost experimental" (340).

29. See Fussell for a discussion of James and Catholicism.

30. Research for this article was assisted by a Saint Mary's University Research Grant.

Works Cited

Arizti, Barbara. *Textuality as Striptease: The Discourses of Intimacy in David Lodge's* Changing Places *and* Small World. New York and Frankfurt: Peter Lang, 2002.

Barthes, Roland. *Mythologies.* Trans. Annette Lavers. London: Paladin, 1973.

Berghoff, Hartmut. "From Privilege to Commodity? Modern Tourism and the Rise of Consumer Society." Berghoff et al. 159-80.

Berghoff, Hartmut, et al., eds. *The Making of Modern Tourism: The Cultural History of the British Experience, 1600-2000.* Basingstoke: Palgrave, 2002.

Bergonzi, Bernard. "A Conversation with David Lodge" *War Poets and Other Subjects.* Aldershot: Ashgate, 1999. 201-05.

———. *David Lodge.* Plymouth: Northcote House, 1995.

"Books of Interest" Canadian Company of Pilgrims. 5 June 2007. <http://www.santiago.ca/books.html>.

Champ, Judith. *The English Pilgrimage to Rome: A Dwelling for the Soul.* Leominster: Gracewing, 2000.

Crouse, Robert D. *Images of Pilgrimage: Paradise and Wilderness in Christian Spirituality.* Charlottetown, PEI: St. Peter Publications, 1985. 13 December 2007. <http://www.prayerbook.ca/crouse/writings/images_of_pilgrimage.htm>.

Crowe, Marian E. "Intimations of Immortality: Catholicism in David Lodge's *Paradise News." Renascence: Essays on Values in Literature* 52.2 (Winter 2000): 143-61.

Derbyshire, Jonathan. "A Conversation with David Lodge." Jonathan Derbyshire: Literature, Philosophy, Politics. 15 June 2007. <http://jonathanderbyshire.typepad.com/blog/2004/08/index.html>.

Doring, Tobias. "Travelling in Transience: The Semiotics of Necro-Tourism." Berghoff et al. 249-66.

Dougill, John. *Oxford in English Literature: The Making, and Undoing, of 'The English Athens'.* Ann Arbor: U of Michigan P, 1998.

Duffin, Jacalyn. "Literature Annotations: Lodge, David. *Therapy.*" Literature, Arts, and Medicine Database. 14 June 2007. <http://litmed.med.nyu.edu/Annotation?action=view&annid=1275>.

Edwards, Philip. *Pilgrimage and Literary Tradition.* Cambridge: Cambridge UP, 2005.

Fussell, Edwin S. *The Catholic Side of Henry James.* Cambridge: Cambridge UP, 1993.

Govier, Katherine, ed. *Solo: Writers on Pilgrimage.* Toronto: McClelland & Stewart, 2004.

Greene, Graham. *Ways of Escape.* Toronto: Lester & Orpen Dennys, 1980.

Haffenden, John. "David Lodge." *Novelists in Interview.* London: Methuen, 1985. 145-67.

James, Henry. *Daisy Miller.* Ed. David Lodge. London: Penguin, 2007.

———. *The Spoils of Poynton.* Ed. David Lodge. Harmondsworth: Penguin, 1987.

Lodge, David. *About Catholic Authors.* London: St. Paul Publications, 1957.

———. *The Art of Fiction Illustrated from Classic and Modern Texts.* London: Penguin, 1992.

———. *Author, Author.* 2004. London: Penguin, 2005.

———. "The Bowling Alley and the Sun or How I Learned to Stop Worrying and Love America." 1968. *Write On: Occasional Essays '65-'85.* London: Secker & Warburg, 1986. 3-16.

———. *The British Museum Is Falling Down.* 1965. London: Penguin, 1983.

———. "Catholic Fiction Since the Oxford Movement: Its Literary Form and Religious Content." MA Thesis, University of London, 1959.

————. *Changing Places: A Tale of Two Campuses.* 1975. Harmondsworth: Penguin, 1978.

————. *Consciousness & the Novel: Connected Essays.* Cambridge, MA: Harvard UP, 2002.

————. *Ginger, You're Barmy.* 1962. London: Penguin, 1984.

————. "Graham Greene and the Anxiety of Influence." Year 202-23.

————. *Home Truths: A Novella.* 1999. London: Penguin, 2000.

————. *How Far Can You Go?* 1980. London: Penguin, 1981.

————. *Out of the Shelter.* 1970. London: Penguin, 1986.

————. *Paradise News: A Novel.* 1991. London: Penguin, 1992.

————. *The Picturegoers.* 1960. London: Penguin, 1993.

————. *Small World: An Academic Romance.* 1984. Harmondsworth: Penguin, 1985.

————. "Strether by the River" *Language of Fiction: Essays in Criticism and Verbal Analysis of the English Novel.* 1966. London: Routledge, 2002. 200-26.

————. *Therapy: A Novel.* 1995. London: Penguin, 1996.

————. *Thinks. . . .* 2001. New York: Penguin, 2002.

————. *The Year of Henry James or, Timing Is All: The Story of a Novel.* London: Harvill Secker, 2006.

Martin, Bruce K. *David Lodge.* New York: Twayne, 1999.

Morace, Robert A. *The Dialogic Novels of Malcolm Bradbury and David Lodge.* Carbondale and Edwardsville: Southern Illinois UP, 1989.

Ousby, Ian. *The Englishman's England: Taste, Travel and the Rise of Tourism.* Cambridge: Cambridge UP, 1990.

Peat, Alexandra. "Modern Pilgrimage and the Authority of Space in Forster's *A Room with a View* and Woolf's *The Voyage Out.*" *Mosaic* 36.4 (Dec. 2003): 139-53.

"R. C. National Shrine." 14 May 2007. <http://www.walsingham.org.uk/romancatholic/>.

The Shrine of Our Lady of Walsingham. 14 May 2007. <http://www.walsingham.org.uk/>.

Toíbín, Colm. *The Sign of the Cross: Travels in Catholic Europe.* London: Jonathan Cape, 1994.

Turner, Victor, and Edith Turner. *Image and Pilgrimage in Christian Culture: Anthropological Perspectives.* New York: Columbia UP, 1978.

Urry, John. *Consuming Places.* London and New York: Routledge, 1995.

————. *The Tourist Gaze: Leisure and Travel in Contemporary Societies.* London: Sage, 1990.

Vianu, Lidia. "Interview with David Lodge." Desperado Literature. 5 June 2007. <http://lidiavianu.script mania.com/david_lodge.htm>.

Wallis, Mary Victoria. *Among the Pilgrims: Journeys to Santiago de Compostela.* Victoria, B.C.: Trafford, 2003.

Watson, Nicola. *The Literary Tourist: Readers and Places in Romantic & Victorian Britain.* Basingstoke: Palgrave Macmillan, 2006.

Wright, Sue. "Sun, Sea, Sand and Self-Expression: Mass Tourism as an Individual Experience." Berghoff et al. 181-202.

Caroline Moore (review date 3 May 2008)

SOURCE: Moore, Caroline. "The Last Laugh." *Spectator* 307, no. 9375 (3 May 2008): 38-9.

[*In the following review, Moore praises Lodge's "pitch-perfect writing" in* Deaf Sentence.]

David Lodge's writing career spans nearly 50 years. Coincidentally, my son was reading (and hugely enjoying) *How Far Can You Go?* when *Deaf Sentence* arrived for review. It seemed generationally fitting that the teenager should be reading about sex and religion, and his mother a novel about deafness, death, erectile dysfunction and the search for a care home that does not smell of 'urine nauseatingly mixed with air-freshener'.

In the opening sentence, the hero of *Deaf Sentence* is described at a party:

> The tall, bespectacled, grey-haired man standing at the edge of the throng on the main room of the gallery, stooping very close to the young woman in the red silk blouse, his head lowered and angled away from her face, nodding sagely and emitting a phatic murmur from time to time, is not as you might think an off-duty priest whom she has persuaded to hear her confession . . . nor has he adopted this posture the better to look down the front of her blouse, though this is an accidental bonus of his situation, the only one in fact.

In fact, Desmond Bates is deaf—

> not profoundly deaf, but deaf enough to make communication imperfect in most social situations and impossible in some, such as this one.

Deafness has prompted Desmond to take early retirement from his university job as Professor of Linguistics, and his life is now dismayingly empty. He has lost his appetite for research, and 'the question: what shall I do with myself today?' confronts him every morning.

He feels increasingly marginalised in his marriage. His second wife, Winifred (or Fred), is eight years younger than him—'not quite January and May—more like March and April'. But the gap is yawning wider in his apprehensions, as Fred has recently acquired a 'rejuvenating career', and a rejuvenated figure. Desmond now finds himself trailing along behind her at social occasions with 'a vague unfocussed smile on his face', like the gaffe-prone consort of a female monarch.

'Sex had become an object of anxious rather than pleasurable anticipation' and, Desmond asks, 'What will I have to live for, when social and sexual intercourse are effectively at an end?'

The only structure in Desmond's life is provided by his 'duty visits' every four weeks to check on his 89-year-old father—an ex-dance musician living alone in the London suburbs in conditions of ever-increasing squalor. The old man is stripped of all his old life-enhancing interests. 'He has only one hobby these days: saving money, observing prices, economising on food, clothing and household bills'.

Such a synopsis makes this novel sound unrelentingly glum, though it is actually extremely readable. It is deeply embedded in the mundane, without becoming dull; and, at the end, when death strikes (as every reader knows it will, from the title alone), it becomes deeply moving. The descriptions of bereavement read like only thinly-veiled autobiography; and their fine, understated, unsentimental honesty is quite extraordinarily good at evoking the painful ordinariness of grief.

The sections which seem most obviously fictional, and which give the novel its nearest approach to a plot are altogether flimsier though entertaining enough. The main scenario (though emotionally this is a mere subplot) involves Desmond with the young woman, Alex Loom, whose cleavage he is involuntarily inspecting in the opening paragraph. She is a graduate writing a thesis on the language of suicide notes, which is thematically convenient; and rapidly reveals herself to be manipulative and unstable, and to have designs, of a sort, on Desmond. But the levels of suspense are mild, since one never believes that Desmond is threatened with anything more than humiliation—and a drip of small indignities is already his daily lot.

In its primary plot, the novel suffers from low narrative drive, for which there is no pill available on the internet. One feels the author has his own version of Desmond's query, 'what shall I do with my characters today?'

But this rather slight framework is only there to provide a peg for Lodge's real interests. Much of the novel is taken up with Desmond's musings upon deafness. 'Deafness is a kind of pre-death, a drawn-out introduction to the long silence into which we will all eventually lapse'; and the many stages of auricular decay are envisaged as 'a long staircase leading down into the grave'. Yet, as Desmond observes, 'Deafness is comic, as blindness is tragic' (actually though, Mr Magoo-style near-blindness is usually comic too). Lodge's novel brilliantly blends observational comedy with felt pain. Indignities evoke laughter, though the man that slips on a banana-skin may be crippled for life, and old age is experienced as a monstrous practical joke nature's version of happy-slapping.

Desmond, glimpsing *Death Menu* on a computer-screen at the local registry office, muses on what death one might choose if offered the carte by the Angel of Death—'something painless, dignified (no bed-pans and catheters)'. Certainly, one would not pick a comic Special. (Jo Grimond once confessed to my father-in-law that he had been unable to attend the funeral of a relation for fear of laughing; the dead man had been run over while Morris dancing.)

All these reflections on the cruelties of comedy and the compensations of tragedy, however interesting, might have come across as a mere extended essay if Lodge had not also explored these themes through his characters—particularly through the relationship between Desmond and his wife, Fred which is well-drawn, and through the relationship between Desmond and his father, which is one of the most moving things I have read in a long while. *Deaf Sentence* kick-starts into imaginative and emotional life whenever Desmond's stubborn, exasperating, pitiful and admirable father comes on the scene, and Lodge's pitch-perfect writing superbly dodges both mawkishness and mere cleverness.

Chris Bray (review date 2 June 2008)

SOURCE: Bray, Chris. "Seriously Funny." *New Statesman* 137, no. 4899 (2 June 2008): 58-9.

[*Below, Bray gives a mixed review of Lodge's* Deaf Sentence.]

"I'm not bored because I'm deaf," Evelyn Waugh told an interviewer he found more than usually tiresome: "I'm deaf because I'm bored." Desmond Bates, the retired linguistics professor at the centre of David Lodge's characteristically dense new novel [*Deaf Sentence*] is deaf, too—yet although he thinks his post-working life a bore, relieved only by "the troubled introspection for which retirement gives so much scope", the reader can't help but find it fascinating.

For one thing, it gives us the chance to bone up on our phonetics When for instance, the Cheshire Cat asks Alice whether she said "pig or fig" he is in effect asking her whether the noun he misheard began with a bilabial plosive or a labiodental fricative. Lodge the writer still being Lodge the teacher, of course, such lessons come with a mnemonic joke attached. "'F' is called a labiodental fricative because you produce it by bringing your top teeth into contact with your bottom lip and allowing some air to escape between them. It's also called a continuant because you can continue making the sound as long as you have breath: *fffffffffffff* . . . though I can't imagine why you'd want to, unless perhaps you started to say 'Fuck' and thought better of it."

Talking of thinking better of things, Professor Bates has just discovered that a leggy blonde postgraduate student he met at a party has contrived to stuff a pair of knickers in his coat pocket. As Bates half suspects his wife of playing around (the reader is convinced on the matter), you might assume he would be cheered by the find. But Alex Loom, the blonde in question, is as alarming as she is alluring, and her research into the stylistic tropes of notes bodes ill in the happy-go-lucky-fling stakes. Anyway, the good prof is too worried by his elderly and cantankerous father's habit of starting chip-pan fires to have his head turned. Or is he?

I couldn't possibly say, though I will remark that, for all its incidental pleasures and felicities, the big surprise about *Deaf Sentence* is that it's short on big surprises. Lodge aficionados fond of the switchback plotting and the cunning, cross-braided didacticism of his masterpieces (*Nice Work, Small World, Thinks* . . .) may find themselves feeling short-changed as they finish this latest novel.

Yet finish it they will, because while *Deaf Sentence* is short on ideas, it is full to bursting with comic riffs, apercus and insights. Anyone who has ever even for a moment wondered whether a lot of contemporary art might not be up to much will be comforted by Bates's description of his visit to a (fictional) exhibition called "Mis-takes". Looking at this collection of badly exposed photographs, jerky faxes and smeary stats while reading the text-heavy accompanying catalogue, Bates suggests to his wife that "much contemporary art is supported by an immense scaffolding of discourse without which it would simply collapse and be indistinguishable from rubbish".

Elsewhere, Lodge—via Bates—treats us to a fascinating piece of practical criticism on why the famous line from Coward's *Private Lives,* "Very flat, Norfolk," is

quite so funny. The passage ought to be on every freshman literature student's basic reading list. Lodge himself is at his most ridiculously funny—for which read most serious—in his repeated punning on the word deaf: "Deaf, where is thy sting?", "the Deaf Instinct", deafsentence. Reminding us that even though it was not until they lost their own hearing that Beethoven and Goya began to out really great work, Lodge gently coaxes us into the realisation that we tend to regard deafness as a bit of a joke: "What would be the equivalent of a guide dog for the deaf? A parrot on your shoulder squawking into your ear?"

For all the laughs, however, this is a markedly doleful book. At several points, Lodge shows off his knowledge of the canon by quoting from practically any poet who refers to the loss of hearing—finding room to wonder whether that most downcast of poets, Philip Larkin chose not to write about his own deafness because, as a jazz lover, he found it too much of a facer. Certainly Lodge, whose own hearing is on the way out, plumbs new depths of misery here. If he had ditched its metonymic but misguided subplot and concentrated his energies on its entropic, elegiac, still centre, *Deaf Sentence* might have heralded his own late great period. As it is, deaf doesn't quite become him.

Joseph Cunneen (review date 19 January 2009)

SOURCE: Cunneen, Joseph. "Sound of Silence." *America* 200, no. 2 (19 January 2009): 33-4.

[*In the following review, Cunneen concludes that while* Deaf Sentence *is not Lodge's funniest novel, it is worthwhile for its "mellow wit, close observation of language and compassionate understanding of aging and suicide."*]

David Lodge's earlier books won him a reputation as one of the leading comic novelists of the past century. *Small World* and *Nice Work,* both send-ups of the academic world, were finalists for the Booker Prize. What makes several of his novels especially hilarious to America readers is his use of Catholic central characters whose ridiculous actions parody the life situation of a younger Lodge. *The British Museum Is Falling Down,* for example, presents a day in the life of a married Catholic graduate student working on his dissertation. When Adam gets to the library, he is so worried that his wife may again be pregnant that he gets nothing done. (They already have three small children, and have not mastered the rhythm method.) Unfortunately, this wonderful Catholic farce—perhaps somewhat dated today—failed to reach the audience it deserved when published in the United States in 1967, perhaps since most churchgoers were too upset by the church's condemnation of birth control, renewed in Humanae Vitae (1968). Two later novels, ***How Far Can You Go?*** (1980) and ***Paradise News*** (1991), successfully draw on the confusion of Catholics in the aftermath of the Second Vatican Council.

Lodge's new book, ***Deaf Sentence,*** is set in Rummidge, a stand-in for Birmingham; and its hero Desmond Bates, a linguistics professor like the author himself, has taken early retirement because of a severe hearing loss. The humor is mostly restrained, starting with Bates's difficulty in following simple exchanges with his wife, Fred (short for Winifred). Desmond is presented as an agnostic who had a nominal Anglican upbringing; Fred has returned to Catholic practice and launched a successful interior-design business. At an evening party Bates meets Alex Loom, a shapely graduate student from America, who flirts with him in the hope that he will mentor her doctoral thesis. Unable to make out what she is saying in the crowd noise but finding her quite attractive, he is maneuvered into seeing her again at her apartment—but fails to tell his wife about it.

Reminding himself that deafness is comic, while blindness is tragic, Bates starts a journal to keep his life somewhat in order. Alex has revived the sexual desire of late middle age; besides, he enjoys the prospect of helping this young woman make a close study of suicide letters, while drawing on his own specialization in linguistics and discourse. But Lodge is less successful in drawing humor from the Bates-Alex relationship than from sexual intrigues in earlier novels, primarily because readers remain uncertain as to whether they should see the young woman as an opportunist or a victim of her American past.

Bates spends much of his time going to London to see his father, a man who had worked for years as a jazz musician, now nearly 90 and degenerating but stubbornly refusing help. The frustrating relationship between father and son, though treated with sympathy, constantly reveals comic aspects. Messages from Alex bring further confusion, arriving at the same time as e-mail ads for Viagra; he is even driven to write a suicide note he has no intention of acting on.

Events pile up, with varying degrees of emotional impact on Bates. A daughter produces a grandchild; he recalls the grim reality of his first wife's death; there is a threatening note from Alex; he helps his father through the old man's final moments. Lodge somehow manages to bring these disparate threads of his story together with credibility and humanity. ***Deaf Sentence*** is not the author's funniest book, but readers should appreciate its mellow wit, close observation of language and compassionate understanding of aging and suicide.

FURTHER READING

Criticism

Davis, Robert Murray. Review of *Deaf Sentence,* by David Lodge. *World Literature Today* 83, no. 2 (2009): 69.
   Negative review of *Deaf Sentence.*

O'Reilly, Mollie Wilson. Review of *Deaf Sentence,* by David Lodge. *Commonweal* 135, no. 21 (2008): 21.
   Takes issue with some elements of *Deaf Sentence* but describes the novel as "delightful company, enlightening and funny."

Quin, John. "Pardon?" *British Medical Journal* 338, no. 7701 (2009): 1016.
   Review of Lodge's *Deaf Sentence* from a medical perspective.

Additional coverage of Lodge's life and career is contained in the following sources published by Gale: *Bestsellers,* Vol. 90:1; *British Writers Supplement,* Vol. 4; *Concise Major 21st-Century Writers,* Ed. 1; *Contemporary Authors,* Vols. 17-20R; *Contemporary Authors New Revision Series,* Vols. 19, 53, 92, 139, 197; *Contemporary Literary Criticism,* Vols. 36, 141; *Contemporary Novelists,* Eds. 1, 2, 3, 4, 5, 6, 7; *Contemporary Popular Writers*; *Dictionary of Literary Biography,* Vols. 14, 194; *DISCovering Authors Modules: Popular Fiction and Genre Authors*; *Encyclopedia of World Literature in the 20th Century,* Ed. 3; *Literature Resource Center*; *Major 20th-Century Writers,* Eds. 1, 2; *Major 21st-Century Writers,* (eBook) 2005; and *Modern British Literature,* Ed. 2.

Yambo Ouologuem
1940-

(Has also written under pseudonym Utto Rodolph) Malian novelist, essayist, and short story writer.

The following entry presents an overview of Ouologuem's career through 2009. For further information on his life and works, see *CLC,* Volume 146.

INTRODUCTION

Ouologuem is best known for his first novel, *Le devoir de violence* (1968; *Bound to Violence*). After receiving France's Prix Renaudot for the novel, Ouologuem faced accusations of plagiarism, still strongly debated three decades later. In 1969 he published two other works—a pamphlet of essays and a collection of short stories—but neither received widespread critical attention, and Ouologuem withdrew from literary life. A single-volume collection of his writings, *The Yambo Ouologuem Reader,* was published in 2008.

BIOGRAPHICAL INFORMATION

Ouologuem was born in Bandiagara, Sudan (now Mali). His father was a landowner, school inspector, and member of the ruling class. Ouologuem's background allowed him the opportunity to learn several African languages, as well as English, French, and Spanish. He attended a lycée in Mali before going to France in 1960 to continue his education. He taught at the Lycée de Charenton in Paris from 1964 to 1966 before earning his doctorate in sociology. After the controversy that surrounded *Bound to Violence* in the early 1970s, Ouologuem returned to Mali where he worked as a youth center director until 1984. Since then, Ouologuem has led a secluded life in the Sahel region of Africa, reportedly devoting himself to the study and teaching of Islam.

MAJOR WORKS

Bound to Violence, Ouologuem's first publication, tells the story of the family of Raymond Spartacus Kassoumi while simultaneously chronicling the history of a fictitious West African kingdom from the thirteenth century to the end of European colonialism. The novel documents African emperors, Muslims, and then Europeans responsible for the "slave mentality" of black Africans. The structure of the novel employs extensive historical flashbacks and postmodernist conventions. The story, structure, and style of *Bound to Violence,* however, are not what have brought notoriety to the book. At first seen as remarkable for its departure from traditional francophone African themes, it has since been vilified amid allegations of plagiarism. Although much has been written about allegations of plagiarism leveled against Ouologuem, he has maintained that the book's French publishers created the appearance of plagiarism when they altered his manuscript without his permission, removing quotation marks and attributions to other authors.

In the months following *Bound to Violence,* Ouologuem published the collection of essays *Lettre à la France nègre* (1969), a condemnation of French colonialists that was widely viewed as retaliation against what he perceived as his persecution at the hands of the French. One essay frequently pointed to as a commentary on his alleged plagiarism, "Lettre aux pisse-copie, Nègres d'écrivains célèbres," suggests to young black Africans that they employ traditional literary conventions and include eroticism, violence, and suspense in their writing in order to be successful in the West. In the essay, he also instructs young writers to appropriate freely from already published works.

Les milles et une bibles du sexe (1969) was published under the pseudonym Utto Rodolph. Considered by many to be pornographic, the collection of stories is cited as being in the tradition of the Marquis de Sade's *100 Days of Sodom* and Comte de Lautrémont's *Maldoror.* Ouologuem seemed to be following his own advice as laid out in "Lettre aux pisse-copie, Nègres d'écrivains célèbres," although he claimed that the stories were given to him to edit by a man named Utto Rodolph. Discussions of the collection tend to gravitate toward questions of social commentary inherent in pornography that have been put to the genre time and time again. Ouologuem himself asserts political motivation behind *Les milles et une bibles du sexe,* saying that the book was intended to draw attention to the dehumanization of black Africans in France and of African subjects on the continent.

CRITICAL RECEPTION

Bound by Violence was met with a great deal of critical acclaim. It was at first seen as a watershed in sub-Saharan African literature, the first novel to criticize African complicity in European colonialism. Early reviews identify Ouologuem as a new, unique, and authentic voice in the canon. The novel's use of violence and eroticism helped make it a popular success as well, and it earned the prestigious Prix Théophraste-Renaudot the year it was published. The African community at large, however, was less enthusiastic about the work, claiming the very authenticity that Westerners championed was suspect. Many claimed that Ouologuem said things that a real African simply would not say. Idiosyncrasies in the tone and style of the writing were generally put down to Ouologuem's intentional critique of Western literature, but suspicions arose after the publication of *Lettre à la France nègre,* a work that was seen as vastly inferior to *Bound to Violence.* The year or so following the publication of *Bound to Violence* saw the first grumblings that Ouologuem may have appropriated parts of other published works and claimed them as his own. This led to the admission of the publisher that it was aware that parts of the novel strongly resembled passages in André Schwarz-Bart's novel *Le dernier des Justes.* Schwarz-Bart was contacted and reassured Ouologuem's publisher that he was flattered by Ouologuem's borrowing of his work, insisting that it was he, in fact, who was indebted to Ouologuem. The scandal was largely dismissed, the similarities between the books put down to the practice of any young writer emulating others in order to find his or her own voice. Shortly thereafter, however, London's *Times Literary Supplement* published side-by-side passages of *Bound to Violence* and Graham Greene's *It's a Battlefield,* showing almost verbatim similarities. This not only renewed allegations of plagiarism, but altered critical opinions of Ouologuem's work, as shifts in the tone of his book no longer seemed stylistically interesting but rather unintentional and the result of cribbing from another author's composition. Ouologuem defended his work by saying that he had incorporated the work of others in his novel in order to give it a multiplicity of voices but had properly attributed those portions, for example using quotation marks around direct quotes. Ouologuem insisted that the publisher had edited out his attributions; the publisher denied the allegations, and the controversy has gone unresolved for over three decades.

The question of what to do with *Bound to Violence* and whether it was still a valuable work with respect to African authenticity is still disputed among critics. One argument is that it reflects the nature of African art and its authorship is irrelevant because, unlike Western art, African art is skewed toward craftsmanship and has historically functioned as representational of the world view of a collective rather than an individual. A counterargument, however, is that Ouologuem, having been educated at French institutions, must have known he was committing a Western faux pas and, having first tried to hide it and then later embracing it, has discounted the importance of his own novel in the context of any European art or artifact. Ouologuem has ceased to weigh in on the controversy and has given up writing altogether.

PRINCIPAL WORKS

Le devoir de violence (novel) 1968; translated by Ralph Manheim as *Bound to Violence,* 1971
Lettre à la France nègre (essays) 1969
Les milles et un bibles du sexe [as Utto Rodolph] (short stories) 1969
The Yambo Ouologuem Reader [edited by Christopher Wise] (novels and essays) 2008

CRITICISM

Roland-François Lack (essay date November 1995)

SOURCE: Lack, Roland-François. "'La littérature de martial': Plagiarism as Figure in Sade, Lautréamont, Ouologuem, and Sony Labou Tansi." *Romanic Review* 86, no. 4 (November 1995): 681-96.

[*In the following essay, Lack discusses well-known incidents of plagiarism including Ouologuem's* Le devoir de violence *and explores the historical precedent for framing plagiarism as a form of kidnapping.*]

Le mal rongeur s'étend sur toute la figure . . .[1]

Plagiarism is an intertextual literary practice with an abundance of intertexts to its name, not all of them literary. It has a history in legal discourse and its etymologies reveal a violent origin in the real: "PLAGIAT, Delit du plagiaire. Chez les Romains, on appelait *plagiaire* celui qui etait condamne au fouet (*ad plagas*) pour avoir vendu comme esclaves des hommes libres.—Dans notre langue, cette qualification s'applique à l'auteur qui s'approprie les pensées d'autrui."[2]

Within literary discourse, scenes of real, Oedipal violence have been figured by plagiarism: "Plagiarism is kidnapping. A false fatherhood. The OED points to the Latin *plagiarus,* 'one who abducts the child or slave of another'"; "Ainsi, pour l'homme, le plagiat est perversion: il équivaut à une relation incestueuse avec la mère."[3]

The figural power of plagiarism is a power to name something other than itself. In this article that other thing is writing, restrictively figured as violent, gendered, and historicized by my taking "Sadian" writers as exemplars. My first suggestion is that plagiarism is an appropriate figure of intertextual relations that are characterized by violence.

The figurality of plagiarism originates in an elaborate *mise-en-scène* of the legal question by the Latin poet Martial:[4]

> "Ie te recommande nos Livres, Quinctianus, si toutesfois ie puis dire nostres ceux que ton Poëte recite. Si une servitude trop pesante leur donne sujet de se plaindre, vien procurer leur liberté,[5] & ne leur dénie point le secours suffisant: Et quand il voudra s'en rendre le maistre, répons qu'ils m'appartiennent, & et que ie les ay affranchis. Que si tu maintiens cela fortement trois & quatre fois, tu feras recevoir au Plagiaire[6] une grande confusion."

Martial is representing the court of law where his books, as manumitted slaves illicitly re-enslaved, would have to claim their freedom by the agency of a third party (here, the friend to whom the poem is addressed) since they would not, if shown to be slaves, have had the right to speak for themselves. Though the book-as-slave figure had a certain currency in first-century poetry, Martial's book-stealer as slave-stealer is unique in classical Latin.[7] The originating scene complicates plagiarism as literary figure since the plagiarist's crime is not simply to have alienated the property of another, but specifically to have alienated the freedom of the text. Furthermore, as an abducted ex-slave, victim of an original abduction by the first master (Martial), the text is implicated in a founding (or confounding[8]) history of appropriation and reappropriation. Thus the story of the first text to be figured by plagiarism is already a story of recurring violence.

If the association of literary plagiarism with literal abduction seems remote, Suzanne Guerlac, writing of Victor Hugo's *L'Homme qui rit* (where "a child is kidnapped and disfigured by a band of gypsies who have cut his mouth from ear to ear"), has shown how the child-stealer's crime can derive mythic power from the speaking of its proper and resonantly literary name: the mutilation of the child Gwynplaine by Harquenonne is called a work of art, and Harquenonne is hanged for it "as a plagiarist".[9]

The OED's alternative specifications of the plagiarist's crime—child or slave stealer—are actualized in these scenes from Martial and Hugo, though Martial's slave is not actually but only figuratively stolen, and shame is the only punishment imposed. With the archplagiarist Isidore Ducasse, Comte de Lautréamont, we are still speaking in figures: the "mutilation" of Hugo's poem "Tristesse d'Olympio", abducted by Ducasse and put to work in his *Poésies,* if it rivals Harquenonne for "artistry", is not actually violent, and if it is deemed that the crime nonetheless deserves punishment, this too need only be figurative.[10]

Actually punitive measures are, on occasion, imposed for literary crimes, for instance when Yambo Ouologuem's **Le devoir de violence** was withdrawn from circulation on the discovery of his plagiarisms. Such a crime and such a punishment make this text exemplary for my case here. Its very first sentence clearly illuminates a discussion of intertextuality and violence:

> Nos yeux boivent l'éclat du soleil, et, vaincus, s'étonnent de pleurer.

These words have a pretext in André Schwarz-Bart's holocaust-fiction, *Le Dernier des Justes*:

> Nos yeux reçoivent la lumière d'étoiles mortes.[11]

Though Ouologuem is a notorious plagiarist, and Schwarz-Bart is, notoriously, his willing victim,[12] the violence done here by one text to another is not the "délit du plagiaire" defined in Bouillet's dictionary, so deserving of violence in its turn. Ouologuem is using the proximity of his text to the other in order to construct a difference between the situations of the communities represented in each. The exclusively communal first-person subject—we who receive this light, not you the reader—in Schwarz-Bart's opening sentence figures a temporal community, formed through succession. The uninterrupted passage of light through time is influence idealized as tradition. It is a tradition of suffering and death, but influence is, as Harold Bloom insists, "*Influenza*—an astral disease".[13] In his own chronicle of holocaust, on the other hand, Ouologuem's appropriative opening sentence can figure neither time-honoured tradition nor a community able to receive its influence. The sun's splendour is immediate and atemporal; Ouologuem's Africans cannot be as "receptive" as Schwarz-Bart's Jews, they have to metaphorize light into water and transfigure it (astonishedly) into tears. The vanquished communality of the first-person plural here gives way immediately to a babel of intertexts, the poly-vocality[14] of a "community" constructed out of writing (from Schwarz-Bart, the Quran, C. H. Kane, and Césaire, among others).[15]

There is the familiar prospect here of opposing influence and intertextuality, and if I begin to repeat that exercise, it is to situate the violence of plagiarism within that opposition, even if plagiarism turns out to be no more than a more or less appropriate figure of one or the other notion. Bloom theorizes influence as a relation between texts, but enough of his own figurations derive from "agonistic" relations between subjects for a figure of inter-subjective violence such as plagiarism to serve. Intertextuality, in Julia Kristeva's construction of it, displaces such intersubjectivity: "Tout texte se construit comme un mosaïque de citations, tout texte est absorption et transformation d'un autre texte. A la place de la notion d'intersubjectivité s'installe celle d'*intertextualité . . .*"[16] There are violent and non-violent figurations here. The "absorption" and "transformation" of texts is a violence done to them, and there is metatextual violence in "installing" intertextuality in the place of intersubjectivity; plagiarism belongs among such ratios. On the other hand, mosaic-making and interweaving (tesselation and intertexting) are non-linear and benign constructions promising a future of peaceful relations between texts;[17] in such a future, it would seem, there is no place for plagiarism.

These future things are not yet fulfilled, however, and realizing a non-violent intertextual utopia may mean foregoing more than the pleasure of figurations through plagiarism. For example, Kristeva's common recourse to a language of appropriation would have to go.[18] Furthermore, quite acceptable ways of abandoning the literary past—revising the history and reforming the canons—can demand of their practitioners a figuratively violent disposition, especially when the history to be rewritten is a history of violence. On the understanding that the pleasures of the texts to be represented are relative and momentary, this attempt to situate plagiarism as figure uses one such history to present a particularly violent intertext.

Literary history need not be as punctual as, for instance, Denis Hollier's representation of it suggests,[19] but I shall take three points from the literary history of France to stand here for the whole. They represent, at the very least, the continuity of a certain tradition within French letters. These points are marked by texts, the first from 1768:

> [Il] luy a dit de se deshabiller qu'elle luy demanda pourquoy, il luy repondit que c'etoit pour s'amuser, que luy aiant representé que ce n'etoit pas pour cela qu'il l'avoit fait venir, il lui dit que si elle ne se deshabilloit pas, il la tueroit et l'enterreroit luy meme, qu'etant ressorti et l'aiant laissée seule, elle s'est deshabillée, elle ne l'etoit pas encore entierement lors qu'il est revenu et luy aiant encor trouvé sa chemise, il luy dit qu'il falloit aussy l'oter, a quoy aiant repondu

> qu'elle mourreroit plutôt, il a luy meme arraché ladite chemise en la faisant sortir pardessus la tete de la deposante, apres quoy il ra conduit dans une autre chambre auprès de celle la dans le milieu de la quelle il y avoit un lit de repos d'Indienne rouge a tache blanche, l'a jettée sur ledit lit sur le ventre, l'a lié par les quatre members et par le milieu du corps avec des cordes de chanvre, luy a mis un traversin sur le col, . . . Qu'etant attaché sur le lit il a pris une poignée de verges avec la quelle il l'a fouettée luy a fait differentes incisions avec un petit couteau ou canif, a coullé de la cire rouge et de la cire blanche en plus grande quantité sur ces playes apres quoy il a recommencé a la fouetter, faire des incisions et couller de la cire, tous lesquels mauvais traitements il a réiteré jusqu'a sept à huit fois. Que la deposante aiant crié lors de ces mauvais traitements il luy a montre un couteau, et l'a menace, si elle crioit de la tuer et de l'enterrer luy meme comme elle nous l'a deja dit, qu'alors elle a cessé de crier. Ajoutte qu'a chaque reprise qu'il lui donnoit des coups de verges, il luy donnoit aussi des coups de baton. Qu'au milieu de ses tourments la deposante luy avoit fait differentes representations, et l'avoit prié de ne pas la faire mourir parcequ'elle n'avoit pas fait ses paques, a quoy il avoit repondu qu'il la confesseroit luy meme . . . ; que luy aiant fait en cor d'autres representations, il s'est mis a jetter des cris tres hauts et tres effraiants . . .[20]

The second is from 1868:

> Maldoror passait avec son bouledogue; il voit une jeune fille qui dort à l'ombre d'un platane, et il la prit d'abord pour une rose. On ne peut dire qui s'éleva le plus tôt dans son esprit, ou la vue de cette enfant, ou la résolution qui en fut la suite. Il se déshabille rapidement, comme un homme qui sait ce qu'il va faire. Nu comme une pierre, il s'est jeté sur le corps de la jeune fille, et lui a levé la robe pour lui commettre un attentat à la pudeur . . . à la clarté du soleil! Il ne se gênera pas, allez! . . . N'insistons pas sur cette action impure. L'esprit mécontent, il se rhabille avec précipitation, jette un regard de prudence sur la route poudreuse, où personne ne chemine, et ordonne au bouledogue d'étrangler avec le mouvement de ses mâchoires, la jeune fille ensanglantée. Il indique au chien de la montagne la place où respire et hurle la victime souffrante, et se retire à l'écart, pour ne pas être témoin de la rentrée des dents pointues dans les veines roses. L'accomplissement de cet ordre put paraître sévère au bouledogue. Il crut qu'on lui demanda ce qui avait été déjà fait, et se contenta, ce loup, au muffle monstrueux, de violer à son tour la virginité de cette enfant délicate. De son ventre déchiré, le sang coule de nouveau le long de ses jambes, à travers la prairie. Ses gémissements se joignent aux pleurs de l'animal. La jeune fille lui présente la croix d'or qui ornait son cou, afin qu'il l'épargne; elle n'avait pas osé la présenter aux yeux farouches de celui qui, d'abord, avait eu la pensée de profiter de la faiblesse de son âge. Mais le chien n'ignorait pas que, s'il désobéissait à son maître, un couteau lancé de dessous une manche, ouvrirait brusquement ses entrailles, sans crier gare. Maldoror (comme ce nom répugne à prononcer!) entendait les agonies de la douleur, et s'étonnait que la victime eût la vie si dure, pour ne pas être encore morte. Il s'approche de l'autel sacrificatoire, et voit la conduite

de son bouledogue, livré à de bas penchants, et qui élevait sa tête audessus de la jeune fille, comme un naufragé élève la sienne, audessus des vagues en courroux. Il lui donne un coup de pied et lui rend un oeil. Le bouledogue, en colère, s'enfuit dans la campagne, entraînant après lui, pendant un espace de route qui est toujours trop long, pour si court qu'il fût, le corps de la jeune fille suspendue, qui n'a été dégagé que grâce aux mouvements saccadés de la fuite; mais, il craint d'attaquer son maître, qui ne le reverra plus. Celui-ci tire de sa poche un canif américain, composé de dix à douze lames qui servent à divers usages. Il ouvre les pattes anguleuses de cet hydre d'acier; et, muni d'un pareil scalpel, voyant que le gazon n'avait pas encore disparu sous la couleur de tant de sang versé, s'apprête; sans pâlir, à fouiller courageusement le vagin de la malheureuse enfant.[21]

The third is from 1968:

"C'est pas mal chez vous, susurra effrontement Awa. Ce que vous en avez, des livres!"

"Ce sont ceux que j'ai écrits", mentit l'administrateur.

"Ce doit être merveilleux d'écrire." . . .

"Ma chambre á coucher", dit-il, s'éclipsant devant une porte rose, et promenant une lampe.

Awa eut le souffle coupé par le plaisir que provoquèrent en elle les tentures roses, le lit en demi-cercle, la courtepointe en soie, que l'on eût juré jonchée de pétales de roses. . . .

Caressant la croupe creuse du ventre de la femme, il baisa les longues ailes noires de sa nuque et sortit— revint avec deux setters, chiens beaux et robustes, et une camisole.

Les bêtes dardaient sur eux leurs prunelles avides. Leur maître; siffla et Médor s'élança sur Awa, gueule humide et frémissante.

"Médor! jappa-t-il, vas-y! Quartier libre!"

Avant que la femme pût réaliser quoi que ce fût, elle sentit le muffle du setter et ses crocs mettre en pièces ses vêtements, déchirant son pagne et sa camisole, la dénudant à coups de griffes et de pattes, sans érafler la peau. Il devait avoir une habitude peu commune de ce genre de travail, Médor.

Paralysée par une émotion à la fois terrifiée et consentante, Awa se vit dépouillée de ses habits en moins d'une seconde. Lorsqu'elle fut nue, Chevalier se courba vers elle, l'installant au milieu de fourrures recouvertes d'un châle de soie rose.

Il la coucha dessus, promenant sa langue légère sur ses lèvres rouges comme le cuivre, ses cheveux, bleu or comme le fer, ses yeux noirs comme l'argent, ses seins, tièdes et doux comme deux beaux corps de colombes de laine vivante—et soudain ce fut un gémissement, qui s'enfla, quitta les lèvres de la femme, monta, brusquement étouffé par la main de Chevalier.

Les doigts sous ses aisselles, redressée sur ses reins, elle criait, percevant contre ses lèvres la râpeuse âcreté de la gueule de Dick, tandis que Chevalier ralentissait

en grimaçant les caresses sur son bas ventre, et qu'elle sentait toujours, la langue dure et tendue tel un gourdin gluant, Médor fouiller sa vulve.

Elle s'affola sous la fièvre étirante de ces morsures, et finit par lécher la langue parfumée de Chevalier, poussant des cris et se débattant. Ordonnant au chiens de se retirer, l'homme laboura la femme comme une terre en friche, comme un océan frappé par la proue d'une nef . . .[22]

Beyond the spurious punctuality of dates, several things establish this intertext. There is, for one, a Sadian tradition, a succession of names,[23] in which the two later authors can be inscribed. However difficult it is to demonstrate that Sade was read by Ducasse, the link between their names has been insisted upon, not least by Blanchot in his *Lautréamont et Sade* (1949). With Ouologuem, the title of his "pornographic" novel, *Les milles et une bibles du sexe* (1969) joins that of the *120 journées de Sodome* (1785) and the *Chants de Maldoror* within a larger tradition of episodic narratives that includes the *Decameron* and *Les Mille et une nuits,* and his proud assumption of the title "the Black Sade" marks a more specific affiliation to "Sadology".[24]

Even without this extrinsic literary history, there are sufficient features within each text to make of the ensemble a viable intertext. Although the descriptions of sexual violence in the three texts would not alone set them apart, intrinsic correspondences suggest an almost poetic cohesion between them. Sade's "petit couteau ou canif" and Maldoror's "canif américain", or the rape of the child by Maldoror's dog and the two dogs set on Awa by Chevalier make appropriate connections; "connectives", in a Riffaterrean sense,[25] may be read into echoes of the name of the "Rose", Rose Keller, who was Sade's victim in the first scene: Maldoror "voit une jeune fille qui dort à l'ombre d'un platane, et il la prit d'abord pour une rose"; and Chevalier's victim is seduced by the pervasive atmosphere of the association: "Awa eut le souffle coupé par le plaisir que provoquèrent en elle les tentures roses, le lit en demi-cercle, la courtepointe en soie, que l'on eût juré jonchée de pétales de roses."

To return to the premise of this article, plagiarism is a useful figure in covering both intrinsic and extrinsic constants of the intertext. Going beyond the bounds of one literary history into another, all three authors are linked intertextually as plagiarists, not of each other (necessarily), but as eminent practitioners of a literary genre that conceals its borrowings from others.[26] Furthermore, each text is associated with narratives of abduction that make them in the most literal sense plagiaristic. The Sadian text is a straightforward account of a kidnapping, if not of a slave, of a servant at least; in the *Chants de Maldoror,* the plagiarism of young boys or adolescents is Maldoror's most characteristic act; and **Le devoir de violence** tells the history of black Africa as a history of successive appropriations and re-appropriations of "la negraille". Men and women, children, entire peoples, are abducted, sold and re-sold. Plagiarism is a powerful figure of such violence in texts.

Owen Heathcote has analysed the "remarkable complicity between the representation of sexuality, violence and literature", arguing from a diversity of examples that violence in literature is radically *engendered*: "violence is shown to be engendered both in the sense that it is inseparable from particular representations of sexuality, and in the sense that it is only parodically or strategically other than male".[27] The literary elaborations of the violence perpetrated on women within my own, less diversified intertext would bear out this contention. Moreover, the occasions for violence within it have not been exhaustively itemized. The particular power each instance has to disturb, shock, or offend is a violence done to the reader, a violence that is *engendered* by the opportunities offered for readerly identifications. Eileen Julien, reading Ouologuem against another male author, Sony Labou Tansi, has argued that the violence in Ouologuem is radically offensive because it replicates gendered power relations in its attempts to critique political structures, identifying the subject-position of women with victimhood.[28]

Sony Labou Tansi represents rapes no less violently than Sade, Ducasse, or Ouologuem. Having earlier been forced to witness the murder of her father and then eat his remains, the heroine of *La Vie et demie* is raped, in a room daubed with inscriptions, by that same father, who has stubbornly refused to die:

> Martial entra dans une telle colère qu'il battit sa fille comme une bête et coucha avec elle, sans doute pour lui donner une gifle intérieure. A la fin de l'acte, Martial battit de nouveau sa fille qu'il laissa pour morte. Il cracha sur elle avant de partir et tous les écrits disparurent de la chambre, restaient ceux que Chaïdana avait sur les paumes. Elle revint à elle deux jours et deux nuits après la gifle intérieure, elle avait le sexe et le ventre amers, le coeur lourd, sa chair avait franchi une autre étape sur les vides humains.[29]

Despite this, according to Julien, Sony Labou Tansi's heroine resists victimization. The difference is Sony Labou Tansi's attribution to her of an agency that does not have its source in an essentialized femininity. Julien locates two other sources, the first in the power of a woman's writing:

> . . . Elle composa des chansons, des cris, des histoires, des dates, des nombres, un veritable univers ou le centre de gravite etait la solitude de l'etre. Le vieux Lay-

isho les lisait a l'insu de Chaidana qui ne le permettait qu'a Amedandio. Il avait tellement Aime l'espece de poeme intitule "Bouts de viande, troncs de sang" qu'il l'avait recopie et propose a l'editeur nord-americain Jim Panama qui s'etait empresse de lui en demander au moins une dizaine ve cette dimension-la pour en faire un recueil. . . .

Amedandio s'employait a distribuer les ecrits de Chaidana parmi les Gens de Martial. Ainsi naquit la "litterature de Martial" qu'on appelait aussi litterature de passe ou evangile de Martial. Les manuscrits circulaient clandestinement de main en main.

. . . Les plus grands ecrivains katamalanasiens essayaient d'appliquer la methode et la vision chaidaniennes de l'ecriture; Les Mots font pitie, le dernier livre de Chaiadana etait publie par Victorio Lampourta qui se vit incarcerer et interdire toutes ses oeuvres; Sabratana Mouanke fut arrete pour avoir essaye de diffuser Mon pere s'appelait Martial.[30]

"Few of her works, of course, will survive censorship", comments Julien. "They will be burned. Thus language and writing in this context are the site of a constant struggle for power. When Chaidana writes, writing becomes especially subversive because writing is male."[31]

The second source located by Julien is women's power to intervene in political struggle from the critical position of the marginalized: "If Chaidana's rage is in part the rage of a female object of exchange between two rival men . . . , then her acts of vengeance are not only a bid to wrest power from the villainous dictators, but are also an attempt to inveigh against the system of domination that also reduces women to signs between men. . . . It is that from their position of marginality they perceive the nakedness of power. And it is that perception that enables them to envision, to challenge."[32]

Necessarily, the second saving grace is as far removed from the Ducasse and Sade texts as it is from Ouologuem. In all three, however, language and writing are engendered as the site of a struggle for power. Awa is first seduced by the book-lined room and the power it evinces: "Ce doit etre merveilleux d'ecrire". As the agent of the local ruler (Saif) in his struggle with the colonial administrator Chevalier, Awa herself is unlikely to accede to writing; her role is confined to being a conduit of information between men, having made her male aggressor speak despite himself: "Une semaine plus tard, Awa lui deliait la langue, et faisait communiquer a Saif la confirmation d'un attentat." The girl's rape and murder in the *Chants de Maldoror* is presented via a feminine "ecriture", narrated by "la folle qui passe en dansant", the girl's mother: "Elle laisse echapper des lambeaux de phrases dans lesquels, en les recousant, tres-peu trouveraient une signification claire. . . . Elle a laisse tomber de son sein un rouleau de papier. Un inconnu le ramasse, s'enferme chez lui toute la nuit, et lit le manuscrit. . . ." There follows the narrative of the rape, mediated by the "inconnu", Maldoror, in the role of the reader. "A la fin de cette lecture, l'inconnu ne peut plus garder ses forces, et s'evanouit. Il reprend ses sens, et brule le manuscrit."[33]

The Sadian text is, at first sight, the revenge of feminine discourse, a woman speaking out against male aggression—all the more impressively in that Rose Keller, like Awa, did not have writing at her disposal. Her legal deposition concludes: ". . . qui est tout ce qu'elle a dit scavoir, lecture faitte de sa deposition la temoin de ce interpellee a dit iceUe contenir verite y a persite a requis taxe et a declare ne scavoir ecrire ny signer de ce interpellee suivant l'ordonnance. Approuve six mots rayes. Chavane. Lebreton." Unsurprisingly, perhaps, given the several masculine mediations of her text, Rose Keller's speaking out does net triumph, since the conclusion of the case is that she is persuaded to withdraw her accusation, for a price, and Sade is not prosecuted. A defence of plagiarism as figure is not favoured by association with an intertext premised on the silencing of women or on the suppression of their texts, whether or not Sony Labou Tansi's *La Vie et demie* provides, as Julien suggests, a genuine critique of gendered violence. It may even be that plagiarism, as the stealing of words, is a proper name for the act of a speaking in a woman's place. Sony Labou Tansi notes that Chaidana's poem "Bouts de viande, troncs de sang" was plagiarized by Layisho and offered to the American publisher Jim Panama. In *Le devoir de violence,* Awa's admiration for writing provokes Chevalier into plagiarism as he appropriates the books of others: "'Ce ce sont ceux que j'ai ecrits', mentit l'administrateur."[34] The madwoman's manuscript in the *Chants* is appropriated by Maldoror and incorporated wholesale in Ducasse's text. In the rape of Rose Keller, Sade first imposes silence on her—"l'a menace, si elle crioit de la tuer . . . alors elle a cesse de crier"—then answers her "representations" with his own terrible utterance: "il s'est mis a jetter des cris tres hauts et tres effraiants". If they were not, in the overriding first instance, horrific tortures, Sade's "mauvais traitements" might be read as if he were writing on her flesh, inscribing with his penknife and sealing his letter with wax, leaving wounds as traces to be read, later, in evidence against him.[35] Rose Keller suffers the further textual indignity of having her deposition signed for her by two men, Chavane and Lebreton. Finally, being noted in the records variously as Rose Keller, Rose Kailair, Roze Kailair, Roze Kelair, Roze Kelair, etc., she is refused even the security of a stable proper name.

I do not despair entirely of plagiarism as figure, despite its deep association with violence towards women. There remain other bodies of evidence to call on, with the promise of quite other constructions. Many women writers have embraced plagiarism. Marilyn Randall elaborates a case for feminist writing as "une poetique du plagiat" through reference to works by Denise Boucher, Madeleine Gagnon, and Louky Bersianik, to conclude with a discussion of Irigaray's plagiaristic practice as critique of phallogocentrism. I do not want to represent Randall's case here without reading more closely the intertexts she cites,[36] but it can at least be suggested that even a violent plagiarism is not absolutely inimical to an ecriture feminine. Duras seems to renounce the practice, but her appeal to violence may yet accommodate it in reconstructed form:

> . . . we have to turn away from plagiarism. There are many women who write as they think they should write—to imitate men and make a place for themselves in literature. Colette wrote like a little girl, a turbulent and terrible and delightful little girl. So she wrote "feminine literature" as men wanted it. That's not feminine literature in reality. It's feminine literature seen by men and recognized as such. It's the men who enjoy themselves when they read it. I think feminine literature is a violent, direct literature.[37]

In my conclusion, with no guarantee of deflecting the phallogocentric violence of the figure, I want to return to the intertexts first cited in this article, returning thereby to plagiarism's primal, etymological scene.

"Celui qui etait condamne au fouet (ad plagas)". The etymology given by Bouillet of the Latin plagiarius places plagiarism firmly at the scene of Sade whipping Rose Keller with his "poignee de verges", but it must also be present when the gender-roles are reversed. It is present, for example, when Ducasse figures—parodically and proleptically—the direct violence of a feminine "ecriture": a man refuses to have sex with his mother, so mother and wife together punish him by covering him with tar and whipping him with "deux fouets au cordes de plomb": "J'admirais . . . avec quelle exactitude energique les lames de metal, au lieu de glisser a la surface, . . . s'appliquaient, grace au goudron, jusqu'a l'interieur des chairs, marquees par des sillons aussi creux que l'empechement des os pouvait raisonnablement le permettre."[38]

This is a line that leads from the originating primal scene, via a detour through Sade and Ducasse, to Duras and Irigaray. But there is more than one line to be traced, not least because such origins are plural. Different dictionaries evoke different etymological scenes. Chambers's *Twentieth Century,* for example, derives plagiarius from plaga, the "net" with which the kidnapper snares the child or slave. The *Oxford Latin Dictionary* gives the variant reading "a spider's web", such as might be woven by the "araignee de la grande espece" in the scene of Maldoror's torment.[39] Following this thread we arrive at the "benign" figure of intertextuality or weaving latent in Kristeva.

Other etymologies leave still more and different traces. Lewis and Short's Latin dictionary shows Bouillet's "fouets" to be a deceptive metonymy, since plagas are not the instruments but the wounds they inflict. This plaga is connected, then, to the French for wound, returning us to the scene of Rose Keller's suffering and the wax poured onto her "playes", and evoking the "vaste plaie immonde" from Maldoror's struggle with the angel.

> . . . Il se penche, et porte la langue, imbibee de salive, sur cette joue angelique, qui jette des regards suppliants. Il promene quelque temps sa langue sur cette joue. Oh! . . . voyez! . . . voyez done! . . . la joue rose et blanche est devenue noire, comme un charbon! Elle exhale des miasmes putrides. C'est la gangrene; il n'est plus permis d'en douter. Le mal rongeur s'etend sur toute la figure, et de la, exerce ses furies sur les parties basses; bientot, tout le corps n'est qu'une vaste plaie immonde.[40]

The all-embracing, all-accommodating figure of these etymological intertexts must be the "open expanse (of land, sea, or sky)" that, in the Oxford dictionary, is another sense of plaga, a sense that expands, metonymically, into the plage that marks the limits of such an expanse of sea. This sea may as well be "la mer maldororienne", that age-old intertextual figure, or Sollers's Ocean, "ce milieu de resistance a toute science lineaire". The lines can be extended further, of course,[41] but the proliferation of intertexts is less of a help than a hindrance to plagiarism's claims as figure. Plagiarism has lost the necessary economy of the figure; by trailing its intertexts in its wake it has, in effect, transformed itself from a possible aid to interpreting texts into a (one-word) text, itself in need of interpretation. This article concludes by reading plagiarism only as text. As figure, the "future things" plagiarism promises remain to be fulfilled.[42]

Notes

1. Isidore Ducasse, Comte de Lautréamont, *Les Chants de Maldoror, Poésies, Lettres,* ed. Patrick Besnier (Paris: Le Livre de Poche, 1992), II. 11, 93.

2. M.-N. Bouillet, *Dictionnaire universel des sciences, des lettres et des arts* (Paris: Hachette, 1862).

3. Christopher Miller in his book *Blank Darkness: Africanist Discourse in French* (Chicago: University of Chicago Press, 1985), writing of Yambo Ouologuem's *Le Devoir de violence;* and Marilyn Ran-

dall, "L'Ecriture Féministe: Une Poétique du Plagiat?", *Queen's Quarterly,* 96.2 (1989), 275. Randall is summarizing, without necessarily subscribing to, the lesson of Michel Schneider's *Voleurs de Mots, Essai sur le plagiat, la psychanalyse et la pensée* (Paris: Gallimard, 1985).

4. "Commendo tibi, Quinctiane, nostros, (Nostros dicere si tamen libellos Possim, quos recitat tuus Poëta.) Si de servitio gravi queruntur, Assertor venias, satisque præstes; Et, cum se dominum vocabit ille, Dicas esse meos, manuque missos. Hoc si terque quaterque clamitaris; Impones plagiario pudorem." Epigram I.52, from *Toutes les Epigrammes de Martial en latin et en francois, Avec de petittes nottes, En deux parties,* translated by "M. de M." [l'abbé Michel de Marolles] (Paris: "chez Guillaume de Luyne", 1655), vol. I, 76 and 77. I have used this version of Martial to represent this founding text's currency in French literature beyond learned circles. Though substantial, this edition was intended to make Martial available to a wider readership, hence the foregrounding of the vernacular version and the use of the vernacular for the critical materials. At the same time, however, it sought to narrow its readership at strategic points by leaving untranslated the epigrams on sexual topics, "indigne d'estre expliquée". Enjoyment of these was confined to those (presumably male) readers with extra-vernacular competence.

5. "Cecy est une metaphore des Esclaves qu'on affranchissoit." Editor's note in *Toutes les Epigrammes de Martial,* 76.

6. "A celuy qui prend le labeur d'autruy pour s'en glorifier." Editor's note, ibid., 76.

7. In simplified form, it found its way into contemporary usage through Lorenzo Valla in the fifteenth century (Preface to Book II of his *Elegantiarum Latinae Linguae Libri VI,* cited in Peter Howell, *A Commentary on Book One of the Epigrams of Martial* (London: The Athlone Press, 1980), 230). Howell cites Horace's *Epistle* I.20 as the source for the idea of book as slave.

8. To (mis)appropriate George Lang's distinction between "*founding* texts (examples of which are the Bible and the Koran, as well as the myriad traditional cosmologies recorded and unrecorded throughout Africa) and those which are *confounding,* which resist the assimilation of text to history, secular or sacred, and tend toward the disruption of textual identity itself". See "Text, Identity, and Difference: Yambo Ouologuem's *Le Devoir de violence* and Ayi Kwei Armah's *Two Thousand Seasons*", *Comparative Literature Studies,* 24.4 (1987), 387-402 (388, 401).

9. See Suzanne Guerlac, *The Impersonal Sublime: Hugo, Baudelaire, Lautréamont* (Stanford: Stanford University Press, 1990), 35 & 58.

10. Poésies II.69, in *Chants de Maldoror* (1992), 260-61. See my "Intertextuality or influence: Kristeva, Bloom

and the *Poésies* of Isidore Ducasse", in Worton and Still (eds), *Intertextuality: theories and practices* (Manchester: Manchester University Press, 1990), 132-38. The possibility that Ducasse specifically plagiarized *L'Homme qui rit* in the *Chants de Maldoror* is commonly discounted, despite the strong coincidences of theme and expression in the accounts of mutilated mouths, since the first *Chant de Maldoror* appeared in August 1868 and *L'Homme qui rit* did not begin to appear, in serialized form, until January 1869. However, there is the suggestion that *L'Homme qui rit* was available in some form several months before the first *Chant* was published, since Des Essarts, in a letter to Mallarmé, claims to have read some of it in May 1868. See Mallarmé, *Correspondance 1862-1871* (Paris: Gallimard, 1959), 274. Alternatively, it is conceivable that Hugo plagiarized the *Chants de Maldoror,* since we know he received from Ducasse a copy of the first *Chant* around September 1868, and that he read parts of it.

11. See *Le Devoir de violence* (Paris: Seuil, 1968), 9, and *Le Dernier des Justes* (Paris: Seuil, 1959), 11. The difference between these two openings is discussed at length by Kwame Anthony Appiah in *In My Father's House* (Chicago: University of Chicago Press, 1992).

12. "I am especially touched, even overwhelmed, to think that a Black writer should have relied on *Le Dernier des Justes* in creating a book like *Le Devoir de violence.* Thus Mr Ouologuem is not indebted to me, but rather I to him." Letter from Schwarz-Bart, cited in E. Sellin, "The Unknown Voice of Yambo Ouologuem", *Yale French Studies,* 53 (1976), 144.

13. Harold Bloom, *The Anxiety of Influence* (New York: Oxford University Press, 1981 [1973]), 95. In *Le Devoir de violence* influence is better called contagion, contracted through the too-close proximity of texts that some call plagiarism.

14. In "Colonialism, Polyvocality, and Islam in *L'aventure ambiguë* and *Le devoir de violence*" (*MLN,* 107 (1992), 1000-27), Donald R. Wehrs has analysed the noncommunality figured in the opening: "The interplay of multiple perspectives . . . leads to a dispossession of voice that is, in part, a radicalization of Romantic irony" (1012).

15. Traced intertexts or sources to *Le Devoir de violence* as a whole include Graham Greene, Guy de Maupassant, and Camara Laye. Untraced intertexts suggested by Ouologuem himself include Kipling, Portuguese explorer Lope di Pigafeta, detective novelist John MacDonald, and archival documents of the French colonial administration. Those suggested by (generally hostile) critics include Saint-Exupéry, Kateb Yacine, Sartre, Gatti, Godard, Pascal, and Suret-Canale. For a thorough if patronizing account of the "Ouologuem affair", see Sellin, "The Unknown Voice of Yambo Ouologuem", 137-62. In his 'Lettre

aux pisse-copie Nègres d'écrivains célèbres', Ouologuem explicitly illustrates his plagiaristic methods. See *Lettre à la France nègre* (Paris: Edmond Nalis, 1968), 163-72.

16. "Bakhtine, le mot, le dialogue et le roman", *Critique,* 23.239 (1967), 438-65 (440-41).

17. A somewhat less benign, but still non-linear, figure of intertextuality was proposed by Philippe Sollers in a subsequent issue of *Critique,* writing of Ducasse's "strophe de l'océan": "Ce milieu de résistance à toute science linéaire a un 'nom' (parmi d'autres): l'océan. Mais entendons tout de suite *texte* . . ." (*Critique,* 24.245 (1967), 802). A gendered opposition is latent in the distinction between figures of benign weaving or waving and malign linearity, if only because of Freud's memorable association of weaving with femme sexuality and the invention of writing, remembered by Sollers thus (in a footnote): "Suggestion de Freud: l'écriture inventée par des femmes à travers le tissage et le tressage des poils du pubis. Et, par conséquent: investissement maximum à la place du pénis manquant, masturbation déléguée traçant la pensée, seuil 'magique'. L'homme, lui, s'écrirait d'autant plus qu'en pouvant ce manque" (*Tel Quel,* 64 (1976), 30). Then again, this suggests a malignity in weaving that leaves the original opposition wanting.

18. See, for example, her reading of Ducasse's *Poésies,* from *La Révolution du langage poétique* (Paris: Seuil, 1974), 347: "L'appropriation du présupposé se fait en entrant d'abord dans ses contraintes, puis en les quittant, pour ne donner, par la suite, comme opposition, que son propre lieu d'énonciation." Appropriation is, of course, according to Bouillet's dictionary, the act of a plagiarist, "qui *s'approprie* les pensées d'autrui".

19. Denis Hollier (ed.), *New History of French Literature* (Cambridge MA: Harvard University Press, 1989).

20. "Deposition de Rose Keller", in Gilbert Lely, *Vie du Marquis de Sade* (Paris: Gallimard, 1952), 222-23.

21. Isidore Ducasse, Comte de Lautreamont, *Les Chants de Maldoror, Poesies, Lettres* (1992), 120-22.

22. Ouologuem, *Le Devoir de violence,* 68-70. It is in this passage, precisely, that Ouologuem plagiarizes Graham Greene. See *It's a Battlefield* (London: Heinemann, 1970 [1934]), 55-57. As in his use of Schwarz-Bart, the difference Ouologuem makes between the two texts points self-referentially to his plagiaristic practice; for example, the character into whose place the administrator Chevalier comes is called in Greene's text "Mr Surrogate".

23. Which, in one acceptation, can be called a theory: "THEORIE: . . . une longue suite de personnes qui s'avancent en rangs", *Petit Larousse* (Paris: Larousse, 1959). The word is employed in this sense by Ouologuem in *Le Devoir de violence* and taken from

there by Christopher Miller in *Theories of Africans: Francophone Literature and Anthropology in Africa* (Chicago: University of Chicago Press, 1990).

24. See Carolyn J. Dean's article "Sadology" in Hollier (ed.), *A New History of French Literature*, 892-94.

25. See "Compulsory Reader Response: the Intertextual Drive", in Worton and Still (eds), *Intertextuality: theories and practices*, 56-78 (58): ". . . indices [that] direct readers towards the specific and relevant intertexts, and indeed compel them to look for these intertexts even when cultural changes have made their recovery less likely".

26. "La repetition plus ou moins integrale d'un discours anterieur sans indication de sa provenance" is Marilyn Randall's definition of plagiarism ("L'Ecriture Feministe: Une Poetique du Plagiat?", 274). For Ouologuem's plagiarisms, see Sellin, "The Unknown Voice of Yambo Ouologuem", passim; for Ducasse see Peter Nesselroth, "Lautreamont's plagiarisms, or the poetization of prose texts," in Robert L. Mitchell (ed.), *Pre-Text, Text, Context* (Columbus: Ohio State University Press, 1980); for Sade, see Michel Delon, "La copie sadienne", *Litterature*, 69 (1988), 87-99.

27. Owen Heathcote, "The Representation of Violence and the Violence of Representation," *New Comparison*, 14 (1992), 202-09 (208, 209).

28. "Rape, Repression, and Narrative Form in *Le Devoir de violence* and *La Vie et demie*", in *Rape and Representation*, ed. Lynn A. Higgins and Brenda R. Silver (New York: Columbia University Press, 1991), 160-81.

29. Sony Labou Tansi, *La Vie et demie* (Paris: Seuil, 1979), 69.

30. *La Vie et demie*, 76-77. It is tempting to make more of the coincidence of Chaidana's father's name with that of the founding father in my own scenario of textual violence, especially as, in Sony Labou Tansi's text, textuality is a power that passes from men to women. I suggest that plagiarism has effected a similar passage.

31. "Rape, Repression, and Narrative Form in *Le Devoir de violence* and *La Vie et demie*", 177.

32. ibid., 178, 179.

33. *Chants de Maldoror*, III.2 (1992), 118-19, 122. In fainting, Maldoror enacts parodically the response of the sensitive reader aggressed by the violence of the text. In burning the manuscript, he deals with it as Chaidana's enemies dealt with her manuscripts.

34. Ouologuem, *Le Devoir de violence*, 68. This appropriated phrase self-referentially marks its difference from the source in Graham Greene by translating "said" as "mentit", inviting us to see the lie in Ouologuem's own claim to ownership: "'What a lot of books you have.' 'Those are my own,' Mr Surrogate said" (*It's a Battlefield*, 56).

35. See the "Rapport du chirurgien Le Comte sur l'etat de Rose Keller": ". . . une femme qui venoit d'estre maltraite que j'ai appris se nommer Rose Kailair, que j'ai trouve soufrante de plusieurs partie de son corps, que j'ai examine et reconnus toute l'estendu des fesses et une parti des lombes vergete et excorie avec coupure et contusion forte et longue sur l'epine du dos, et en outre une contusion echimose et dechirure sur le dessus de la main gauche, que le tout ma paru estre fait par quelque instrument contundant et tranchant, ay aussi remarque de la cire fondu sur quelqu'une des playes." In Lely, *Vie du Marquis de Sade*, 205.

36. For instance: Denise Boucher, *Cyprine: Essai collage pour etre une femme* (Montréal: L'Aurore, 1978); Madeleine Gagnon, *Autographie. I. Fictions* (Montréal: VLB, 1982); Louky Bersianik, *L'Euguélionne* (Montréal: La Presse, 1976) and *Le Pique-nique sur l'Acropole: Cahiers d'Ancyl* (Montréal: VLB, 1979). I shall cite Randall's conclusion (277): "Qu'elle soit sous forme de citation, de parodie ou, finalement, de plagiat avoué, l'imitation remplit d'abord une fonction de contestation par rapport a la notion meme d'originalité dont la valeur dépend du phallogocentrisme patriarcal qui constitue la cible de l'écriture féministe. Or, pratiquer le tabou va encore plus loin que le désir de transgression: il revient à annoncer un refus absolu de s'inscrire dans l'économie qui légitimise la loi."

37. "Marguerite Duras", in *New French Feminisms*, eds Elaine Marks and L de Courtivron (New York: Schocken Books, 1980), 174 (no French source is given). Cited by Marilyn Randall, "L'Ecriture Feministe: Une Poetique du Plagiat?", 266. Duras's separation of plagiarism and violence rests, as Randall suggests, on a confusion between plagiarism and imitation. See also Duras's remark in Duras and Michelle Porte, *Les Lieux de Marguerite Duras* (Paris: Minuit, 1977), 102: "On n'ecrit pas du tout au meme endroit que les hommes. Et quand les femmes n'ecrivent pas dans le lieu du desir, elles n'ecrivent pas, elles sont dans le plagiat."

38. *Chants de Maldoror* IV.3 (1992), 147.

39. ibid., 192-99.

40. *Chants de Maldoror* II.11 (1992), 92-93. This account of malefic proximity is a mise-en-scene of the all-effacing embrace described by Ducasse in his famous maxim on plagiarism (*Poésies* II.59): "Le plagiat est necessaire. Le progres l'implique. Il serre de pres la phrase d'un auteur, se sert de ses expressions, efface une idee fausse, la remplace par l'idee juste" (*Les Chants de Maldoror, Poesies, Lettres* (1992), 259). This Latin plaga is also at the root of the plague that is so recurrent a topic in the *Chants de Maldoror*. A fuller discussion of plagiarism and intertexuality in Ducasse can be found in my forthcoming *Poetics of the Pretext: Reading Lautreamont* (Exeter: University of Exeter Press, 1996).

41. Eg., into Greek: λάγιζ (oblique) allows Suzanne Guerlac, for instance, to speak convincingly of plagiarism as "the 'oblique' evasion of representation" (*The Impersonal Sublime,* 155 & 215, n.15). The verb connected with this root can mean, appropriately, to turn sideways, to lead astray, to pervert, or to use tortuous methods.

42. See Augustine, *Contra Faustinum,* 4.2: "in illis temporalibus figuras fuisse futurorum quae implerentur in nobis" (in these temporal figures there was the promise of future things, which were to be fulfilled in us). Cited by Erich Auerbach, "Figura", in *Scenes from the Drama of European Literature* (New York: Meridian Books, 1959), p. 41. I am currently researching an anthology of plagiarisms, ancient and modern.

Christopher Wise (essay date summer 1998)

SOURCE: Wise, Christopher. "In Search of Yambo Ouologuem." In *Yambo Ouologuem: Postcolonial Writer, Islamic Militant,* edited by Christopher Wise, pp. 199-218. Boulder and London: Lynne Rienner, 1999.

[*In the following essay, originally published in the summer 1998 issue of* Research in African Literatures, *Wise conveys the state of scholarly understanding of Ouologuem over thirty years after the publication of* Le devoir de violence.]

Yambo Ouologuem, the Malian author of *Le Devoir de violence* and other literary works, has not been interviewed in nearly three decades. In fact, his doings have been shrouded in mystery ever since he "disappeared" from the West, in effect turning his back on literature. Like Arthur Rimbaud, J. D. Salinger, and others, Ouologuem has become an enigma for many, a mysterious figure as well as a highly respected author. The reasons for Ouologuem's silence are complex and will perhaps never be fully known. It is certain, however, that Ouologuem has blamed the publishers of *Le Devoir de violence* for plagiarism controversies that followed the novel's appearance in 1968.[1] In the early 1970s, Ouologuem claimed that numerous unauthorized deletions had been made in his manuscript, specifically references to Graham Greene's *It's a Battlefield,* André Schwartz-Bart's *Le Dernier des justes,* and other sources. Rather than acknowledging these revisions, the novel's publishers simply disavowed all responsibility and placed the onus entirely upon Ouologuem.[2] Nevertheless, Ouologuem's refusal to write cannot be easily attributed to any ancient grudges he might bear toward the French literary establishment. What complicates matters is Ouologuem's wholehearted return to Islam, the faith of his childhood. In the mid-1970s, Ouologuem returned to Mali, where he is now widely known as a devout marabout, or Muslim holy man.[3] However, as I have argued elsewhere,[4] even the writings of Ouologuem's "apostate" period cannot be fully understood without reference to Islam, specifically Tidjaniya Sufism as it has historically been practiced throughout West Africa.

During a year's residency at the Université de Ouagadougou in Burkina Faso, I sought to find Ouologuem and conduct an interview with him, for I hoped to better understand the reasons for his "conversion" to Islam and his rejection of literature. It seemed for a time that my wishes would not be fulfilled. Repeatedly, I was warned that Ouologuem would refuse to see me, or anyone else from the West. Gaoussou Mariko, the U.S. Cultural Affairs Assistant in Bamako, informed me that "Yambo's current state of mind may cause him to be reluctant to meeting [sic] and talking with people." Among my colleagues at the Université de Ouagadougou, I'd also heard many strange rumors and tales. Some claimed that Ouologuem was a great genius—even the "African Joyce"—while others insisted that he was a shameful plagiarist and dangerous lunatic.

My break came during a conference at the Université de Ouagadougou on the literatures of the Sahel, when I delivered a paper on Islam and *Bound to Violence.* In the audience that day happened to be a French professor named Nicole Vinciléoni, who had lived in West Africa for some twenty-five years. After my presentation, Professor Vinciléoni invited me to dinner at her home in Ouagadougou, along with another colleague and friend of mine, Ute Fendler. Professor Vinciléoni told me that she liked my paper in one very important regard: I had suggested that the conflicting demands of secular and religious life among West African Muslims created a kind of "schizophrenia" that could be traced at least as far back as al-Hajj Umar Tall, a thesis that I had first come across in Brad G. Martin's now-classic study, *Muslim Brotherhoods in Nineteenth-Century Africa* (1976). What I had suggested in my presentation was that this non-Western form of "schizophrenia" could be observed in Ouologuem's *Bound to Violence,* although most occidental critics tended to misread Ouologuem's disassociative (or "esoteric") critique of Islam as a blanket dismissal. Professor Vinciléoni had observed such "schizophrenia" often, which for her was not a pejorative term but rather an inadequate, Greek word for an experience little known or understood in the Western world. Since Ouologuem lived in the Sévaré-Mopti area, which was a highly venerated seat for West African Islam, and since Ouologuem had reputedly become a devout Muslim, possibly even a marabout, she recommended that I get in touch with the main religious leaders of the Mosquée Riméibé at Sévaré. If these men felt that Ouologuem should meet with me, it would be difficult for him to refuse an interview.

Professor Vinciléoni also told me that there lived in Ouagadougou a certain al-Hajj Sékou Tall, a well-known local figure and an immediate descendant of al-Hajj Umar Tall, the Peul conqueror and great Sufi *sheikh* who had brought Tidjaniya Islam to the Dogon country—with many prayers and great bloodshed. Through al-Hajj Sékou Tall, it was possible that I could secure an introduction to Ouologuem, or at least to the religious leaders of Sévaré. As it turned out, the husband of Ute Fendler, my German friend who had accompanied me to Professor Vinciléoni's house, was well acquainted with the son of Tall Sékou (or "Sékou Tall," as the name would appear in the West). Jean-Claude Naba, Ute's husband and fellow professor at the Université de Ouagadougou, had once attended school with Tall's son and could probably introduce me to Tall.

In January 1997, Jean-Claude and I drove to Tall's house in one of the older sections of Ouagadougou. After introducing me to Tall's family, including two of Tall's wives, Jean-Claude quietly explained that I was editing a book on Yambo Ouologuem, and that I'd like to include a recent interview and other updated, biographical information. We were concerned, however, because of stories we'd heard about Ouologuem's strange behavior. While Jean-Claude spoke, Tall sat back in his chair, patiently stroking his closely cropped head. He was eighty years old, as I'd found out from Jean-Claude, though he seemed as healthy as a man in his early sixties. In a country where the life expectancy is less than forty years, I was amazed by his vigor and obvious good health. When I got to know him better, I found out that he had some twenty children between four wives. "I saw Yambo four years ago," Tall told us. "At the funeral of his father, Boukary. Yambo's father and I were schoolmates in Bandiagara."

"How did he seem?" Jean-Claude asked. "At the time of the funeral?"

"He's fine. He's not crazy like these people say. It's true that Yambo's a quiet man, but he's not mad. In fact, he teaches French at a lycée in Sévaré."

"So he's not mad?" I said.

"No," Tall said. "He's a religious man, a devout man."

"Is it true he's become a marabout?"

"No, he's a militant, like myself. A marabout teaches the Quran to children. Yambo is serious about his religion, but he's not a marabout. A marabout has a

particular job." In his free hand, Tall clutched a white, intricately woven prayer cap along with a handsome, silver-handled cane. He was a big man with thin, gangly limbs from under his black robe. It was clear that he wanted to say something further but wasn't sure how to begin. "If you like," he said, "I can send my son Mountaga with you. He can introduce you to Yambo on my behalf." When he saw my response, Tall became even more thoughtful. Then he began to tell us that there had been a recent death in his family. One of his brothers, who had been chief at Bandiagara in the Dogon country, had recently died. For a long time, it was believed that Sékou Tall himself, as direct heir of al-Hajj Umar Tall, would be appointed as new chief. However, an older brother had been found, which meant that Tall was now officially second-in-line to become chief at Bandiagara.

Much of this history, Tall told us with a deliberate end, for he had decided to accompany me to Mali himself, along with his son Mountaga, so that he could formally greet his older brother, the recently appointed chief of Bandiagara. First, we would attend to the business of meeting Yambo Ouologuem, Tall said, and then we'd drive on to Bandiagara. What remained now was to work out the details of our journey.

* * *

Because of the excruciating heat that would come to the Sahel after February, our trip to Mali could not be delayed for long. One practical problem was transportation. My own Toyota station wagon worked well within the city of Ouagadougou, but it was not made for trips to the bush (as I had found out the hard way). What we needed was a four-wheel-drive, or *"quatre-quatre,"* which would no doubt quadruple my costs. However, there was a friend of mine, an American named Robert Hans, who worked for the World Bank, and who was willing to take us in his Jeep Cherokee. Besides Tall and his son Mountaga, we had arranged for Robert's driver to accompany us, a Liberian political refugee named James Wade. Due to our late start, we planned to spend the first night in Ouahigouya, Tall's "hometown" of sorts, and then we would drive into Sévaré the next morning.

As the African bush blurred outside the car window, Tall's son Mountaga explained to me the many complicated alliances wherein his father had come to be heir-apparent to the chiefdom of Bandiagara, as well as the "first Muslim" in Ouahigouya. According to Mountaga, Sékou Tall was the great-grandson of al-Hajj Umar Tall; grandson of Aguibou Tall, builder of the palace at Bandiagara; and son of Alpha Maki Tall. Mountaga also informed me that the chief at Bandiagara was in reality chief of the entire Dogon people. At first, this seemed confusing to me given the rather obvious fact that Sékou Tall was himself Peul (or Fulani) and not Dogon. In other words, I couldn't figure out why a Peul was to be appointed chief of the Dogon people. The more Mountaga spoke, however, I gradually began to realize what I should have known from the start: Tall was himself descendant of the very Saifs criticized in Ouologuem's novel, the so-called "black Jews" who, according to Ouologuem, shamefully exploited the teachings of Islam to oppress the masses of Nakem, or the more "primitive" Dogon.

Later, when I asked Tall if it was true that the Peul were Jews, I saw that my use of the word "Jew" had been indiscreet, acceptable only because I was a foreigner. What Tall preferred to say was that the Peul originally came from Palestine, which avoided the more distasteful allusion to Jews. "It is said that the Peul are a white stream in a land of black water," Tall said, "a black stream in a land of white water." The Dogon people that I spoke with in Mali did not take such a lyrical view of things, but the mysterious origins of the Peul turned out to be a favorite topic of Tall's, who was obviously proud of his ancestry.

Still, what I had not fully understood before speaking with Mountaga was that Yambo Ouologuem's grandfather, Umar Karambé Ouologuem—who was of course Dogon—had conspired with the family of al-Hajj Umar Tall to subdue the Dogon country on behalf of the Peul. In fact, this is how Sékou Tall and Boukary Ouologuem, Yambo's father, had come to be childhood friends. For, unlike the vast majority of Malians, Yambo Ouologuem was no *lumpenproletariat,* or poor subaltern, but rather one of the wealthiest and most highly educated men in Mali. However, if Ouologuem came from an elite, aristocratic caste, I saw now that it was because his family had sided with the Peul in ruling over the Dogon people.

From Sékou Tall, I also learned that Ouologuem came from a long line of Tidjaniya Muslims, the very form of Sufism imported by al-Hajj Umar Tall. Sékou Tall himself was a practicing Tidjaniya Muslim, though he preferred not to talk about it, except to say that it was dangerous to discuss such things. Although Yambo Ouologuem would not have been directly exposed to Sufi teachings as a child—since, as Tall pointed out, Sufi teachings are certainly *not* matters for children—Yambo's ancestors on both sides of his family were among the most prominent Tidjaniya Muslims in the region. In other words, for Tall, Yambo Ouologuem was in some sense "born" a Tidjaniya Muslim.

The more I learned about Ouologuem's prominent family, the better I understood Tall's earlier insistence that Yambo Ouologuem was no marabout. For Tall, a

marabout taught the Quran to young children and was supported by his pupils who begged for alms on his behalf. In many Dogon villages today, Mountaga explained, Muslim children as young as four years old commonly leave their parents to follow a marabout for several years, until they have sufficiently mastered the Quran. A child's time with a marabout is determined by his ability to orally recite the Quran from memory. In this way, the marabout can devote his life to religion and to the study of the Quran. Because Yambo Ouologuem came from a wealthy family and because he was freed from the necessity of taking on pupils, this disqualified him in Tall's eyes from being a marabout. In Sévaré, however, others told me that there were marabouts who did not take on pupils, whose wealth made it possible for them to be freed from this obligation. Despite Tall's reservations, the consensus in Sévaré was that Ouologuem was most definitely a marabout. However, as I was soon to learn, Tall was mistaken about Ouologuem in other ways as well.

For, when we finally arrived in Sévaré the next afternoon and began to search for Ouologuem in earnest, Tall was clearly astounded at the reports we heard: at the Mosquée Riméibé, an ancient imam named Pâte-Touré, who was nearly blind and almost toothless, told us that Ouologuem was indeed a marabout but a very dangerous one, a man who walked the hardest of paths. He had become an expert in the Quran, in the Arab language, and in Muslim literature. As the old imam fingered his rosary, Sékou Tall leaned forward in his chair, his mouth agape at the accounts of Ouologuem's doings. As it turned out, Ouologuem not only did *not* teach at the French school, but his hatred of the French was such that he sent his own children to the Arab-language school in Sévaré. At present, he occupied a government post at a *maison de jeunesse,* which required very little of him. This was necessary, the old imam told us, because Yambo did not have many lucid days; in fact, in the eyes of most, Ouologuem was quite mad. Though reluctant to use such terms himself, Pâte-Touré insisted that Yambo's was a special case, a man who had been "touched" by Allah.

The old man told us about the incident, recorded by Thomas Hale in *Scribe, Griot, and Novelist,* when Ouologuem threw rocks at two French tourists who had attempted to photograph the inside of the Mosquée Riméibé. This incident had a quasi-legendary status in Sévaré, and we were to hear several different versions of it during our stay. But there were other incidents as well. Not long ago, Ouologuem had provoked a quarrel at the public courthouse, exhibiting such rage that many fled in terror. On the streets, he might approach a Muslim brother and began expounding upon the most esoteric of questions regarding quranic law, the hadith, dress codes, and other arcane religious matters. While his discourses were often brilliant, he tolerated absolutely no interruptions or contradictions. If his monologues were ever interrupted, he would break off, as if deeply affronted, and then go abruptly about his business.

One incident in particular seemed to bother the old imam. Before prayers one Friday, he had met Ouologuem on his way to the mosque. Under one arm, Yambo had carried a worn edition of the Quran. When the old imam extended his right hand in greeting, Ouologuem declined to shake hands, claiming that he had not yet performed his ablutions. In refusing to shake hands, Ouologuem implied that he was unclean, yet his right hand rested upon his Quran. For Pâte-Touré, no other conclusion was possible: it was not Yambo Ouologuem who was unclean but he himself. Given the saintly demeanor of the old man, such an inference seemed not only highly insulting but comical. It upset Sékou Tall so much he got up from his chair and began pacing the room.

"I can only warn you to be cautious," Pâte-Touré said. "There is a precedent. Two other Americans came before you, and Yambo hid himself in the mosque for two days. I wish you the best of luck in your venture but you must use extreme care. May God's blessing and peace be with you."

We dropped off Sékou Tall and Mountaga at the home of their relatives, and Robert and I took a room at the Hotel Oasis in Sévaré, as it turned out, across from a large piece of property that was owned and managed by Ouologuem. Tall planned on meeting with Ouologuem's uncle that evening, the former mayor of Sévaré, al-Hajj Timbely Umar, to arrange the introduction. From the hotel patron and his son, I heard more stories about Ouologuem, his religious fervor, his wealthy father, and his eccentric behavior. The patron, however, insisted that the best way to meet Ouologuem was not through his uncle, whom Ouologuem distrusted, but through his mother. "Yambo will do anything his mother says," the patron told us. "He listens absolutely to his mother." I declined his offer to take me "vite-vite" to meet Ouologuem's mother, but walked over to Ouologuem's property, where I saw many small gardens and little straw shacks. From the people I had spoken with so far, including Tall's acquaintances in Sévaré, the blind imam, and now the patron and his son, I could only conclude that the majority of people here believed Ouologuem to be a religious fanatic and near lunatic. The word that I heard repeatedly in connection with Ouologuem was "le fou," or madman, yet all agreed that he was the most highly educated person in Mali and a truly great man. "They really treated him very badly over there," the patron said. "You see, the French did this to him."

That night, al-Hajj Timbely Umar came to pay his respects to Sékou Tall as we all sat in the courtyard of Tall's relatives in Sévaré. Timbely was accompanied by nearly a dozen elegantly dressed men, who encircled him as if part of a royal entourage. Timbely himself wore a white *bou-bou* with gold trimming and a white prayer cap. His face was truly remarkable, one of the wisest-looking men I'd ever seen. After Tall and Timbely exchanged greetings, Robert and I were introduced. I explained to Timbely that I was editing a collection of essays on his nephew, Yambo Ouologuem, and I'd like to speak with him. I did not want to disturb him if he truly wished to be left alone, but I wanted to be sure that he was aware of this opportunity to air his views. Timbely listened patiently to my explanation, his hands resting on a scepterlike cane. At last, he told me that he was happy I'd come and that in actuality he'd been anticipating my visit.

"I will do what I can to help you," he said, "but you must know that Yambo has not been himself lately, especially since the death of his father," Timbely paused, carefully searching for the right words. "Life has lost its flavor for Yambo. You might say that he has become disgusted with the business of living. He has rejected all things worldly and spends his time reciting the Quran and praying. He has even built a small mosque in the courtyard of his house. For a long time, all of us have waited for a change to come to him."

One of Timbely's nephews described Yambo's current state of being. As before, we heard of Ouologuem's dislike of the French and apparently for whites in general. We also heard once again that he had difficulty conversing in any meaningful sense: he often lectured on Islam—sometimes brilliantly, sometimes incoherently—but he rarely engaged others in true dialogue. On the streets, Ouologuem at times greeted his friends, but he might just as likely ignore them altogether. One evening, when a group of lycée students, both boys and girls, happened to study together under a streetlight, Ouologuem grew so enraged at the impropriety of this gathering that he grabbed a stick and smashed the streetlight into pieces. He also regularly lectured the Muslim mothers of Sévaré who allowed their daughters to expose their hair outside their veils or who wore any kind of decorative mesh. For the second time, I heard a story about Ouologuem's refusal to accept his government pension, much to the chagrin of his family. Because Ouologuem believed the present Malian government and president to be corrupt, he refused to accept any money from them whatsoever.

"After the death of Yambo's father," Timbely added, "we all gathered at the mosque to read the Quran. It is customary for the son to make a sacrifice on such occasions, and so Yambo came to the mosque carrying several large books, all written in the Arab language. He wanted us to spend the next few weeks reading these books and studying them with him. We agreed to recite the Quran with him, but we refused to even look at the other books. There were so many of them, we would have been reading books for the next two years."

That evening, as friends and relatives described Yambo's behavior, many laughed at his eccentricity, but their laughter seemed indulgent, not ridiculing. If Ouologuem was "fou," he was apparently functioning well enough, living on the inheritance from his father, taking care of his immediate family, and practicing his highly idiosyncratic Islam. When I tried to thank Timbely for helping me, he only shrugged and said that he considered it his duty. Above all, he wanted to help Yambo get over his bitterness. "He speaks often of a certain French publisher and his years in France," Timbely said. "We are not sure here what happened there, but it was obviously something terrible." I explained the best I could the controversies surrounding **Bound to Violence,** how many had accused Ouologuem of plagiarism. I could see, however, that the details of this controversy did not really interest those present: for most, it was simply another example of French irresponsibility toward Africans, but in this case Yambo was the victim. "The important thing is that you have come," Timbely said. "We will attend to Yambo tomorrow."

* * *

During breakfast the next morning, Robert and I reviewed Timbely's plan for meeting Ouologuem. First, Timbely and Sékou Tall would go alone to greet him on the pretext that Tall wanted to express condolences over the death of Yambo's father. (This confused me somewhat since, in Ouagadougou, Tall had originally told me that he'd personally attended the funeral of Boukary Ouologuem.) After sufficient time passed, Robert and I would then casually join them and, in the company of Timbely, Tall, and others, Ouologuem would most likely be on his best behavior. Timbely also warned us to hide Robert's Jeep Cherokee, which still bore the decals of Coopération Française, the French organization from which Robert had purchased the vehicle. If Yambo saw the decals and believed we were French, it was certain he would have nothing to do with us.

When we arrived at our predetermined meeting place, a complication arose when it turned out that Ouologuem was not at home but making a tour of Sévaré. Tall and I were content to await his return, but Robert

grew frustrated and insisted that we drive to the mosque to find him. "Listen, Tall will sit around here chewing kola-nuts all morning," he told me. "Then we'll never get anywhere. Believe me, it's like this at my office. You've got to push these guys at times, or you'll never get anything done." We argued the question for awhile, but Tall himself had no objections to Robert's plan, so we all climbed into the Jeep and began searching for Ouologuem. At last, we found him at the public courthouse, where he'd gone to photocopy some old documents. These documents, we learned later, were letters written by some Frenchmen during Mali's colonial period. Ouologuem wanted them preserved in the public archives as a testament to France's crimes in Sévaré. For now, we carefully hid the Jeep behind a tree, while Tall and Timbely approached Ouologuem on the front steps of the courthouse. A few minutes later, Umar Sow, one of Tall's nephews, motioned for us to come.

Ouologuem never saw our approach because his back faced us, and he was deeply engrossed in conversation with Tall and Timbely. He wore a sky-blue *bou-bou* with a white scarf, white slippers, and a white prayer cap. His arms dramatically flailed about as he spoke, the packet of letters clutched in one hand. He immediately noted our presence but did not break off his speech. When Timbely introduced us, he irritably shook our hands but did not allow the flow of his lecture to be interrupted, an energetic clarification of the different orders of Muslim religious leaders. However, his speech became faster and angrier, his eyes glaringly fastened upon his uncle. As he spoke, I became transfixed by his face, which seemed to me profoundly ugly, not unlike a bust I'd once seen of Socrates, the dog-faced philosopher, or perhaps Danton. His cheeks were round and enormous, and they were set in an intense if not bellicose grimace. I lost his train of thought and only caught up again when he made a heated reference to Judas Ischariot, all the while glowering at his uncle.

Timbely only smiled serenely, and soon we all sat upon metal chairs, brought out by the judge and his secretaries, as Ouologuem continued his discussion of the Muslim laity. I asked him if I could record his voice, but he refused and said, "No, this is not an interview. I came to the courthouse to visit my friends, that is all. Besides, these things can be used against me. I have been exploited before." Nevertheless, his friends repeatedly encouraged him to speak with me or at least to look at the list of questions I'd prepared. In the large circle of his elders and friends, I began to feel sorry for Ouologuem, who had clearly been ambushed by all of us. After awhile, however, he warmed to the idea of being interviewed and even seemed to enjoy the attention he was receiving. He spoke freely on a wide range of subjects, though he never directly answered any of my questions. In fact, he spoke for about three hours altogether. During this time, I listened attentively, wondering how I could possibly remember everything he'd said. Later, after going over my notes with Robert, Sékou Tall, and Mountaga, we all agreed upon the basics of what we'd heard.

However, it was difficult to follow Ouologuem's reasoning since his speech was filled with references to his private dreams, prayers, and religious experiences. He also spoke in parables, analogies, and riddles, insisting that the Greek syllogism was vastly inferior to the paradox in its communicative power. His reading in Muslim literature clearly exceeded that of everyone present, who deferred entirely to him in these matters. Often, he built upon a subtle network of allusions from the Quran and the hadith, which he seemed to assume—erroneously—was shared knowledge by all those present. Repeatedly, he insisted that God speaks through dreams, that the future can be known if we are attentive to our dreams. At times, whenever the subject of French colonialism drifted into his speech, he grew angry all over again, leaning forward in his chair, his voice nearly shouting in rage. His energy was intense, perhaps manic, and when he broke off into a sudden joke, dispelling his previous acrimony, our relief was immense. After one of his jokes, Ouologuem would often slap hands with the judge, with whom he was on very good terms.

Perhaps Ouologuem's most important revelation was that former president Moctar Oul Dada had once offered him a position as minister of education in Mauritania, clearly no job for a "fou." Three times Ouologuem had been asked to journey from Mali to Mauritania to completely reform its educational system. The first two times, Ouologuem had refused the offer, leery of the intent of Mauritania's Arab-led government, whose policies toward blacks have historically verged on the genocidal. Given the fact that Mauritania banned slavery as recently as 1980, Ouologuem was rightly cautious about Dada's offer. However, the third time, Ouologuem had been visited at his house by the ambassador of Mauritania in Mali and by Mali's ambassador in Nouakchott. This time, Ouologuem accepted the offer, contingent upon an interim period of several months, so that he might have time for prayer and reflection. However, for reasons that were never clear to me, Ouologuem had not yet assumed this position, apparently as a result of certain political complications that had later developed. The challenges he would confront there would arise chiefly from his desire to synthesize the requirements of a thoroughly modern and yet thoroughly Quranic education. He was inclined to accept the position, he

told us, because of his desire to end the suffering of his brothers in Mauritania, that is, black Muslims who have historically been oppressed and enslaved by Arab Muslims.

At no point was Ouologuem willing to discuss his writings, and even questions related to literature seemed to irritate him. "I will leave that for you smart ones, the professors," he told me. "I am not a 'smart' man, thanks be to Allah, and 'smart' subjects do not interest me." When I mentioned the name of Wole Soyinka, Ouologuem would not let me finish my sentence. "Another 'smart' one," he said. "An intellectual."

Many of his most hostile remarks were directed at the publishing industry and its many prizes, like the Nobel Prize given to Soyinka. He saw such prizes as a way of controlling African writers and the kind of literature they produced. Ouologuem's criticism, however, was not so much directed against Soyinka as against the publishing industry at large and the way in which Africa's best minds were routinely exploited by faraway presses and the demands of a foreign readership. In his own case, ***Bound to Violence*** had been published before he'd even signed a contract and after numerous unauthorized changes had been made on his manuscript. The most famous editorial change was, of course, his editor's deletion of quotation marks in passages later labeled as "plagiarized," a fact never denied by his publisher. Ouologuem also claimed that his novel had been translated into English without his consent. If neo-colonization was to be fought, Ouologuem said, the book industry itself would have to be entirely restructured. One place to start was the prize system with its seductive but pernicious cash awards. On an even more critical note, Ouologuem spoke harshly of Léopold Sédar Senghor, "the most French" of African writers and "a black man who wished that his skin was white."

In fact, one of Ouologuem's greatest fears seemed to be that he would be turned into a "petit Senghor," a Malian curiosity like the mosque at Djenné or any other tourist attraction. The scorn that Ouologuem heaped upon Senghor echoed a common attitude about the Senegalese throughout the Dogon country. Whereas the Senegalese abused the Dogon as "primitives," the local Dogon (as well as Peul, Malinké, and others) ridiculed the Senegalese as French "bootlickers" and self-hating blacks. In any event, almost everyone present seemed to share Ouologuem's sentiments about Senghor, or they were at least amused by his rapid-fire monologue. When I asked him his views on the Salman Rushdie affair, Ouologuem refused to comment (as he did with any of my direct questions), but it was clear he'd given the matter a great deal of thought.

His friend, the judge, seemed particularly upset that Ouologuem would not respond to my question, and he informed us that they had been discussing Rushdie only a day ago. However, Ouologuem steadfastly refused to comment, except to say that his remarks would probably be misunderstood and used against him. In fact, Ouologuem returned to his invective against Senghor, and to the amusement of all, he began to ridicule négritude, especially its reception in the United States. At this point, it dawned on me that Ouologuem believed I was myself an African American in some remote way, a suspicion that was later confirmed when he confided that he'd foreseen this visit in a dream.

It was evident that the situation of the African American, especially in the United States, incessantly occupied his attention and even formed a private obsession with him. He spoke at length of his time in the United States, his appreciation of Malcolm X, his meetings with Cassius Clay, and his participation in the formation of black studies programs at several American universities. When Robert asked him which states he visited, Ouologuem again refused to answer directly, but he finally laughed and said, "In any case, I was not in any pious state." Unexpectedly, he blurted out, "You know, we Africans cannot be held accountable for the actions of our brothers over there. This is a fallacy. Many would disagree with me, of course, and I have heard it said that if your goat destroys your neighbor's garden, you are responsible for the damage. Still, these Africans who are causing so much trouble are not Muslims." Like Senghor and all advocates of négritude, he said, blacks in the United States are too obsessed with skin color. "They have been infected by too many poisonous ideas. In Islam, however, there is no color." Here, Ouologuem cited two or three hadith wherein it is said that people of all colors are equal in God's eyes.

"Blacks in America must repent," he insisted. "Until they do so, they will continue to live in their own private hell, and this has nothing to do with us in Africa." Here, Ouologuem claimed that his own problem, as well as that of his fellow Malians, was hardly a question of skin color but rather imperialism. With the arrival of the French in Mali, the plight of his fellow Dogon was more closely akin to that of the American Indian, "a new spaghetti Western" in Africa. Above all, he feared that an extraordinarily rich culture and its many ancient customs could be destroyed in favor of the most vulgar technological innovations— all in the name of modernization and "progress." Later, I was to learn how serious he was about this when I discovered that, much to the frustration of his wife and mother, Ouologuem refused to allow electricity to be installed at his house in Sévaré. Ouologuem also

refused to have his photograph taken by me, citing the biblical injunction against graven images. Timbely, Tall, and everyone present expressed their outrage at Ouologuem's refusal and even pleaded with him to change his mind. I also reminded him that I'd seen a movie theater across from the Mosquée Riméibé, but he would not budge. The Quran tolerated no equivocation on this issue, he said. In fact, this was one of the most defining features of Islam, as opposed to more infidel variants of Ibrahimic religion. As for the movie theater, this was a fault of the local Muslim community, much to be regretted.

By now, Robert and some of the others had wandered off, and only a few of us remained. As our discussion wound down, Umar Timbely spoke at length, though he had previously said little. Whatever rancor Ouologuem harbored for his uncle for "betraying" him, he evidently held him in great esteem and was sufficiently respectful to him, not unlike a young man in the presence of his father. Indeed, it was difficult not to be slightly in awe of Timbely, who had all the trappings of a great king. "We are all happy that you have come this far to see Yambo," Timbely said, "and I believe that you will be fair to him, for I can see by your face that you are an honest and just man. That is all we ask really, that you be fair. Yambo has been treated poorly in the past. He has been exploited and misrepresented. It is only right that he receive justice at last."

At the words of his uncle, Yambo's defiant attitude seemed to dissipate, and he relaxed for the first time that morning. He thanked his uncle for his words, and I promised to do my best to be fair to Yambo. In the meantime, Robert had returned, and he was obviously anxious to be on the road. In fact, throughout the interview, Robert had buried himself in a recent issue of *The Economist,* especially during moments in which Ouologuem discussed his private dreams. It was evident that Ouologuem did not know what to make of this American, with his short trousers, CD walkman, and two-day beard stubble. Tall also seemed disturbed, attempting to cajole Robert by informing everyone that he was "le frère de Clinton." Robert disavowed Tall's remark with a shrug and said, "I can't be Clinton's brother. Clinton's a Christian, and I'm a Jew."

If he'd intended to shock everyone, he enjoyed one of his greatest successes. However, there were more surprises in store for us, for in the interim he had instructed his driver to bring the Jeep Cherokee around. When we left together from the courthouse, James stood directly in front of the Coopération Française decal until the moment Yambo turned the corner. At that point, James had been told to step aside and reveal the decal. Later, Robert told me that he'd merely wanted to "get a rise" out of Ouologuem to see if he couldn't "turn Yambo into Rambo." Not surprisingly, Ouologuem was distressed when he saw the French decal, until we were able to assure him that Robert had only purchased his vehicle from the French and that he was indeed a real American.

Afterwards, we were all exhilarated at our great success. Those who knew Yambo were amazed that he'd spoken at such length. Umar Timbely told me that we'd caught Yambo on a good day, when he'd been at his absolute best. Our luck had been extraordinary: He had been lucid, funny, sharp-witted, and entirely coherent. It was true that there had been moments of great intensity, when we all sensed his tremendous anger, but the presence of Timbely, Tall, and the others seemed to have a calming effect upon him. In retrospect, I questioned the local consensus that Ouologuem was mad, which seemed to me entirely too severe a judgment upon him. Sékou Tall also assured me that, in his own estimation, Ouologuem was no madman. "He's a disappointed man," Tall said. "But he's not any madder than the rest of us." In parting, I left a copy of my interview questions with Umar Sow, one of Tall's nephews. Mountaga informed me that Yambo would pray about this matter during our journey to Bandiagara. On our return trip through Sévaré, he would decide whether or not to speak with me any further.

* * *

In Bandiagara, we lost Sékou Tall, who had insisted upon returning to Ouagadougou a day early and taking Mountaga with him. Our parting had not been on the best of terms, so when we returned to Sévaré, there were a few awkward moments when I tried to explain to Tall's relatives what had happened: either Tall had confused our original return dates, or I had somehow misunderstood him. At the moment, Robert was back at the hotel in Mopti, down with a serious upset stomach, so I'd only brought James with me to the house of Tall's relatives. Umar Sow, Tall's oldest nephew, heard me out, and then he walked me over to the house of al-Hajj Umar Timbely, Ouologuem's uncle. There, I explained all over again what had happened with Sékou Tall.

In his own house, which seemed like a palace with its complex of buildings, courtyards, and labyrinthine corridors, Timbely's stature was even further enhanced, and I realized now that he was a man of incredible, even extravagant, wealth. When a friend stopped by, Timbely introduced me as "the one who had come to bring about the change in Yambo." In fact, Timbely was quite excited about what had transpired in my absence. "Yambo came to see me twice," he said. Timbely repeated the word "twice" as if this was a fact of remarkable significance. "The first time, he was furious that I'd dared to bring a Jew into his presence. He told me that this was unforgivable. But he returned the next day, and he was very happy this time. He wanted to know when you were coming back. It is certain he will see you again."

Immediately, we sent out James and a nephew of Timbely's to see if Ouologuem wouldn't come by. They'd been instructed to tell Yambo that I was leaving in the morning and that I wanted to say farewell. In the interim, we discussed the student strike in Ouagadougou, and President Blaise Campaoré's recent amendment to the Burkinabé constitution.[5] Our conversation was interrupted, however, when James and Timbely's nephew returned with news of Yambo. "You must come quick," James said. "He wants you to come to his house." I saw that James was flustered, even radiant, after speaking with Ouologuem. I quickly bid farewell to Timbely and followed James to Ouologuem's house. James smiled broadly and could not contain his excitement. "I didn't know what your mission was," he said. "Robert told me to stay out of it. It was only tonight that I finally understood. But now I've spoken with Yambo, and I can see that he's a great man, a blessed man." James stopped walking for a moment, and then he exploded in laughter. "But, of course, this guy's completely mad."

"What do you mean?" I said.

"His English is good. This guy speaks better English than people in Liberia. He told me that he wouldn't come to his uncle's house because his uncle is a member of a certain political party in this country that's been exploiting him for the past thirty-three years. He said, 'The reason I don't pay any attention to them is because I consider them to be very insignificant. They think that what they are doing is great, but what they are doing is very simple and worthless, and that's why I don't even question them. They think that I'm a fool, but they are the fools. He's sitting over there calling me. Go and tell Christopher that I'm not going to that house.'"

"Tell me exactly what happened," I said. "What did he say when you approached him?"

"He was coming back from a funeral and had been praying all afternoon. When he saw me, he said in English, 'Where is Christopher's friend? The one with the short trousers?'"

"'He's not feeling well,' James told him. 'He has an upset stomach.'"

"'His sins will see him through. He's very insolent.'"

"'No, he's only joking around,'" I told him. "'He likes to joke. He's not really insolent.'"

"'He's a Jew,' he said. 'And you were trying to play smart. I saw you at the car. You went to the car to cover up that sign. What are you trying to hide? Coopération Française? You see, they have bought you. And they reduce you. You have sold your dignity. Just as they have killed Thomas Sankara and taken his body to Wall Street.'"[6]

"He spoke of Sankara?" I asked.

"Yes, he said the body of Thomas Sankara has been taken to Wall Street. So, I asked him, 'Why Wall Street? Why not Paris?'"

"'Blaise Campaoré will account for that,' he said. 'He will explain why they didn't take his body to Paris and instead to Wall Street. Blaise Campaoré will explain that when the time comes. It's just a matter of time. But you Liberians,' he said, 'from the day of your independence, you have been killing one another. And you will continue to kill one another because you have abused your identity. When the Americans realized they were very wicked in dealing with blacks, they decided to export them, to get rid of the rejects. That is what 'Liberia' means. It comes from a Latin word meaning 'the condemned ones,' the ones who were condemned by the whites. They had to find a place for these rejects, and they chose Liberia.'" At this James began to laugh all over again and assured me what a brilliant man Yambo was. "'But the whites made one mistake,' he said. 'They should've left everything with the blacks, but they decided to run things themselves. If they'd done this, today there would be no blacks in America. Instead of giving black Americans the chance to administer their own affairs, they interfered, and today they regret it.'"

"'They got a lot of blacks over in the United States who don't know the direction of their lives, and they are condemned to hell. These blacks say they admire me, they admire my books, but I care nothing for them because they have forgotten their brothers, the suffering masses in Africa. They have sold their dignity. If they really admired me, they would come to Africa and join me for what I have fasted the past ten years, and for what I'm still fasting. I am fasting because I want to see black people everywhere freed from their oppression.'"

By now, we'd arrived at Ouologuem's house, where I was to hear much of what James told me repeated. For the moment, I was too astonished to know how to respond. We knocked on Ouologuem's gate and were greeted by his mother, an ancient, veiled woman who had some trouble with the heavy chains upon the metal posts. The old woman informed us that, unfortunately, Yambo could not speak with us that evening because he was in mourning and occupied with his nightly prayers. We persisted, however, insisting that it was Yambo who had sent for us. "I'm leaving early tomorrow morning," I told her. "I have an important message for him." Finally, she relented and went to get her son. Ouologuem greeted us but refused to shake hands, as he had already performed his ablutions. Our presence did not seem to make him happy, but his mother offered us chairs while he himself sat upon a huge, felled tree limb. It was completely dark now, except for the light of the moon and stars. Ouologuem's courtyard had a wild, unkempt look with scraggly bushes and vegetation everywhere. We were also introduced to Ouologuem's grandmother, who sat in complete darkness further under the house's awnings.

"I will speak with you tonight at your insistence," he said, "but it would be better if I said nothing." He spoke in English now, and James had been right about his mastery of the language, which was total. "You must know that you are in grave danger," he said. "You and the Liberian are in grave danger here. There are people who would like to kill you. I refused to speak with you because I wanted to protect you. For now, I shall pray for you." From where I sat on a short-legged, metal chair, Ouologuem seemed larger than he actually was, his face, scarf, and prayer cap illuminated by moonlight. "It has been four years now since I saw you in a dream," he said, rubbing his eyes. "I dreamed that a Jew would bring me a Liberian and an African-American." Here, he stopped and looked me over: the fact that I did not seem to be black disturbed him, but only slightly. "These things that I know are hard for you to understand, I realize this. I have the authority to speak the way I want to speak, but if I decide to talk to people like you, I must put things in simpler terms. Still, it would be better if I said nothing at all."

"Silence is always better, you see. This is why I refuse to answer your questions. We speak too much, myself included. Jesus was a silent man. Muhammad was a silent man too. We forget this with all our books and radios. We drown ourselves in meaningless noise. But, if you are able to be silent, you will see that it is much better than speaking." He paused for a moment and placed both hands on his knees. He seemed tired now, as if indeed the effort to speak exhausted him. "I have seen Jesus more than fifty times," he said. "I have spoken with him and with the Prophet. The angels too, including Gabriel, and they're mostly silent. You must be very careful with people who speak a lot. They think that they know a lot, but they really know nothing." Ouologuem himself fell into silence at this point, as if listening for the sound of the wind blowing through the trees.

It was James who finally spoke. "You are truly a blessed man," he said softly. "God has truly blessed you."

"I am not a blessed man," Yambo insisted. "Far from it. I am simply a man who is seeking God's blessing."

"But you have knowledge," James said, "and knowledge is power."

"No, knowledge is not power. When you are blessed by God, then you acquire wisdom. And when you acquire wisdom, then you have power. Knowledge in itself is not power. You see, God has allowed me to journey to the very frontiers of the human mind. I have seen them unfold before my eyes." With this Ouologuem swept his hand over his head, urging us to look up at the stars. "The world we live in is truly magnificent," he said. "In Allah, all things are possible if we are only open to them."

There was another long moment of silence, until Ouologuem's mother cleared her throat, signaling for him to dismiss us. "If there's just one message you have," I said quickly, "if there was just one thing you'd like to say to black people in America, what is it?" I'm not sure why I asked such a question, but I said the first thing that came to mind.

"Go back to America and tell my black brothers that I've been fasting for the last ten years on their behalf. I've been fasting so that they'll come back to Africa. Tell them to come back to help ease our suffering, and Allah will be merciful. That is the first thing you must say. Then you may tell them that I am now preparing to take over the leadership of the educational system in Mauritania, where blacks suffer more than anywhere on earth. I hope to help establish there a truly Islamic government that will administer to the total affairs of Mauritanians, including Arabs. The worst enemies for blacks right now are racist Arabs, Arabs who have been satanically blessed with oil and who are now funding the Jews and apartheid-type governments everywhere. It is the Arabs who are sponsoring all these organizations that are against blacks, and who invest their money in Switzerland, America, and South Africa. Many have tried to stop me in this, but I am not so easily defeated. The French have tried to stop me. Even the CIA has offered me a few million dollars. The CIA has already done what it could to me, and they think they have defeated me, but they are mistaken. That is all I have to say."

Ouologuem arose from where he sat, preparing to dismiss us. He again apologized for not shaking our hands and told us that it was time for his evening prayers, that we had detained him long enough. He disappeared into the darkness of his courtyard, and we were led to the gate by his mother.

* * *

That night I had many questions for James about his long walk with Ouologuem while I waited at Timbely's house. Though it had not been possible to record Ouologuem's words, James's short-range memory was excellent—in fact, far better than mine—so I recorded our conversation back at the hotel, as we told Robert about our adventure. Robert was feeling slightly better though his face was quite pale. When James and I had finished speaking, Robert sat up in his bed and laughed. "Yambo's a nutcase," he said. "A paranoid schizophrenic, and what's worse, an anti-Semite. Seriously, the guy could benefit from medication. He might not be able to talk to Jesus all that often, but he could function better." When James repeated that Ouologuem was fine, Robert said, "You don't think he's all that mad because you talk to Jesus all the time. That's the way it is with you religious types."

"Yes," James said simply. "This man is blessed. He said a lot of good things. He's right about blacks in America too. Africa is the place they come from, but blacks over there don't come and help us. Our brothers in America do not care for us. When we are together, they treat us worse than white men do, as if we are inferior to them. If you look around at all these programs in Africa, the majority of Americans who come are white. Why? With the Peace Corps, even the white ladies are willing to go to the villages and teach our people, but blacks are not willing to come. The problem is that we do not love one another."

"Look, it's hard for *all* Americans here," Robert said. "Things are so different in Africa you don't know what the hell's going on half the time. It's even harder for blacks who have to adjust to this place and then deal with all this bullshit about being 'African American.' Most blacks in the United States don't have a clue what goes on in Africa. They've got enough problems of their own."

James listened carefully, but he was far from convinced. I remembered then that he'd lost a child and his wife had lost an arm before they'd fled Liberia as political refugees. Sometime later, James had converted to an anti-Catholic, charismatic form of Christianity, some import from the United States. "Okay," James said, "there is truth in what you say, but Yambo is still right. When I was at a refugee camp in Côte d'Ivoire, a brother of Michael Jackson came to sing for us. He came there, and he stood on a bench. Everyone wanted to see this Jackson hero. We were all suffering, and we were glad this guy came to help us. So we listened, and he said, 'You know, I gotta tell you, America is a useless country. America got itself involved in the Middle East thing, in the Gulf War, wasting billions of dollars when they got you here suffering.' So we all looked at one another and said, 'This guy is mad.' There were many highly educated people among the group, some professors, and they too said, 'This guy is mad.' 'You know, when I get back to America,' he said, 'I'm gonna get to Congress and do something for you.' I tell you," James said. "We wanted to stone him. This useless guy came, and he made a lot of promises. Then he left, doing nothing."

"What was he supposed to do?" Robert said. "Save Africa all by himself? Believe me, it can't be done. It's not possible. You know, I'm not a religious person, but I believe very strongly that God helps those who help themselves. There are many Jews in the United States like myself who have been very successful. But no one helped me. No one gave me a job or cut me a break. My belief is that countries are successful and that people prosper or suffer as a result of their capability to help themselves or not help themselves."

"Yes," said James. "You are right about that. Now you are speaking from the Bible." Both James and Robert were somewhat surprised when I told them that the saying "God helps those who help themselves" did not come from the Bible but was coined by Benjamin Franklin. Robert, in particular, was amused by this, which made him feel all the better about being an American. He was currently in the process of securing an entry visa to the United States for James, and he was certain that once James arrived in America, he'd feel exactly the same way he did.

* * *

My search for Yambo Ouologuem had ended. Back in Ouagadougou, I met several more times with Sékou Tall and Mountaga, both of whom insisted that Ouologuem was no madman. Tall promised to write me a piece for my book, offering his own perspective on Ouologuem's current doings. Mountaga only nodded serenely and said that Yambo was "dur" (or "hard in his faith"), and that was all. He was one of the "hard ones," not unlike his own father. As for the books Yambo had written some years ago, Mountaga said, these were all literary questions, and so they had of course ceased to interest him.

Notes

1. See K. W.'s (Kaye Whiteman) "In Defence of Yambo Ouologuem," *West Africa,* July 21, 1972. In an interview with Ouologuem, Whiteman reports the following:

> To demonstrate the injustice of the charges against him, he spent some time taking me through his original hand-written manuscript (in an old exercise book) of *Le Devoir de violence* showing me all the places where there had been quotation marks, if not actual mentions of his literary allusions and quotations . . . I saw, for instance, where he had written "here ends *The Last of the Just*," a reference omitted like so many others, for whatever reason, from the published version.

(941)

2. The altogether strident response of Ouologuem's publisher is documented in B. P., "Le Devoir de vérité," *Figaro littéraire,* June 10, 1972.

3. See Thomas Hale, *Scribe, Griot, and Novelist: Narrative Interpreters of the Songhay Empire* (Gainesville: University of Florida Press), 1990: 169.

4. Christopher Wise, "Qur'anic Hermeneutics, Sufism, and *Le Devoir de violence*: Yambo Ouologuem as Marabout Novelist," *Religion and Literature,* Vol. 28, No. 1 (Spring 1996): 85-112.

5. In January 1997, Blaise Campaoré altered Burkina Faso's constitution in regard to limitations on the terms of the president. As things stood now, Campaoré could be president for the rest of his life.

6. Thomas Sankara, the former president of Burkina Faso, was assassinated by a gang of thugs during a coup d'état in Burkina Faso in 1987. Afterwards, Blaise Campaoré, who claimed to be ill with malaria at the time, took over the country's leadership.

Bibliography

Abastado, Claude. "Introduction à l'analyse des manifestes." *Littérature,* vol. 39 (October 1980).

Abu-Lughod, Janet. "Cities Blend the Past to Face the Future." *African Report,* vol. 16, no. 6 (June 1971): 12.

Abun-Nasr, Jamil M. *The Tidjaniyya: A Sufi Order in the Modern World.* London: Oxford University Press, 1965.

Achebe, Chinua. *Things Fall Apart.* Portsmouth, N.H.: Heinemann Educational Books, 1958.

Achiriga, Jingiri J. *La Révolte des romanciers noirs de langue française.* Sherbrooke, Quebec: Editions Nadman, 1978.

Adotevi, Stanislas Spero K. *Négritude et négrologues.* Paris: Union Generale d'Éditions, 1972.

Ahmed, Akbar S. *Postmodernism and Islam: Predicament and Promise.* New York: Routledge, 1992.

Aidoo, Ama Ata. "For Whom Things Did Not Change." *No Sweetness Here.* 1970. New York: Feminist Press at the City University of New York, 1995. Pp. 8-29.

Aire, Victor O. "*Le Devoir de violence.*" In *Dictionnaire des oeuvres littéraires négro-africaines de langue française des origines a 1978.* Sous la direction de Ambroise Kom. Sherbrooke, Quebec: Editions Naaman. Paris: Agence de Co-operation Culturelle et Technique, 1983.

Aizenberg, Edna. "Historical Subversion and Violence of Representation in García Marquez and Ouologuem." *PMLA,* Vol. 107, No. 5 (October 1992): 1235-1252.

Andrade, Susan. "The Nigger of the Narcissist: History, Sexuality and Intertextuality in Maryse Condé's *Heremakhonon.*" *Callaloo,* vol. 16, no. 1 (1993): 213-226.

Ansari, Khwaja 'Abdullah. *Intimate Conversations (Munajat).* Trans. by W. M. Thackston, Jr. New York: Paulist Press, 1978.

Appiah, Kwame Anthony. *In My Father's House: Africa in the Philosophy of Culture.* New York and Oxford: Oxford University Press, 1992.

Arnaud, Robert. *L'Islam et la politique musulmane française en Afrique occidentale française.* Paris: Comité de l'Afrique Française, 1912.

Asante, S. K. B. "International Assistance and International Capitalism: Supportive or Counterproductive?" In *African Independence: The First Twenty-Five Years,* Gwendolyn M. Carter and Patrick O'Meara (eds.). Bloomington: Indiana University Press, 1985. Pp. 249-274.

Ashcroft, Bill, Gareth Griffiths, and Helen Tiffin. *The Empire Writes Back: Theory and Practice in Postcolonial Literatures.* New York and London: Routledge, 1989.

Ba, Adam Konaré. *Sonni Ali Ber.* Études Nigériennes no. 40. Niamey: Institut de Recherches en Science Humanines, 1977.

Bâ, Amadou Hampaté. *Vie et enseignement de Tierno Bokar: Le sage de Bandiagara.* Paris: Seuil, 1980.

Bakhtin, Mikhail. "Épopée et Roman." *Recherches Internationales,* No. 76 (1973).

Barkan, Sandra. "*Le Devoir de violence*: A Non-History." In *Interdisciplinary Dimensions of African Literature,* Kofi Anyidoho, Abioseh M. Porter, Daniel Racine, and Janice Spleth (eds.). Washington, D.C.: Three Continents Press, 1985. Pp. 101-112.

Baudelaire, Charles. *Curiosités esthétiques et l'art romantique.* Paris: Garnier, 1962.

Benot, Yves. "*Le Devoir de violence* de Yambo Ouologuem est-il un chef d'oeuvre ou une mystification?" *La Pensée,* No. 149 (January-February 1970): 127-131.

Bernstein, Serge. "De Gaulle and Gaullism in the Fifth Republic." In *De Gaulle and Twentieth Century France,* John Horne and Hugh Gough (eds.). London: Edward Arnold, 1994. Pp. 109-124.

Beverley, John. *Against Literature.* Minneapolis: University of Minnesota Press, 1993.

Boulnois, Jean, and Boubou Hama. *L'Empire de Gao: Histoire, coutumes et magie.* Paris: Adrien-Maisonneuve, 1954.

Bouygues, Claude. "Yambo Ouologuem, ou le silence des canons." *Canadian Journal of African Studies/Revue Canadienne des Études Africaines* Vol. 25, No. 1 (1991): 1-11.

B. P. "Le Devoir de vérité," *Figaro littéraire,* June 10, 1972.

Breitman, George. *The Last Year of Malcolm X: The Evolution of a Revolutionary.* New York: Pathfinder Press, 1988.

Brennan, Timothy. *Salman Rushdie and the Third World.* New York: St. Martin Press, 1989.

Brenner, Louis. *West African Sufi: The Religious Heritage and Spiritual Search of Cerno Bokar Salif Tal.* London: Hurst, 1984.

Bu-Buakei, Jabbi. "Influence and Originality in African Writing." *African Literature Today,* Vol. 10 (1979): 106-123.

Butor, Michel. "La critique et l'invention." In *Répertoire III.* Paris: Éditions de Minuit, 1968.

Césaire, Aimé. *Cahier d'un retour au pays natal.* In *Aimé Césaire: The Collected Poetry,* trans. by Clayton Eshleman and Annette Smith. Berkeley: University of California Press, 1983.

Cham, Mybe B. "Islam in Senegalese Literature and Film." In *Faces of Islam in African Literature,* Kenneth W. Harrow (ed.). Portsmouth, N.H.: Heinemann Educational Books, 1991. Pp. 163-186.

Chaulet-Achour, Christiane. *Abécédaires en devenir.* Algers: Éditions de l'ENAP, 1985.

———. "Langue française et colonialisme en Algérie: De l'abécédaire à la production littéraire." Diss., University of Paris III, 1982, vol. 2: 419-443.

———. "Textes, prétextes, contextes: Quelques interrogations à propos de l'intertextualité." *Langues et Littératures,* Revue de l'Institut des Langues Étrangères de l'Université d'Alger, No. 5 (1993): 115-125.

Chipman, John. *French Power in Africa.* Cambridge: Basil Blackwell, 1989.

Chraibi, Driss. *Le passé simple.* Paris: Denoel, 1954.

Clifford, James. *The Predicament of Culture: Twentieth-Century Ethnography, Literature, and Art.* Cambridge, Mass.: Harvard University Press, 1988.

Coulon, Christian. *Le Marabout et le Prince: Islam et pourvoir au Sénégal.* Paris: Pedone, 1981.

Dabla, Séwanou. *Nouvelles écritures africaines: Romanciers de la seconde génération.* Paris: Éditions L'Harmattan, 1986.

Danner, Victor, and Martin Lings. "Preface." In Ibn 'Ata'illah's *Sufi Aphorisms* (*Kitab al-Hikam*). Leiden: E. J. Brill, 1973. Pp. xi-xiii.

Dathorne, O. R. *African Literature in the Twentieth Century,* Minneapolis: University of Minnesota, 1974.

Decraene, Philippe. "Un Nègre à part entière." *Le Monde,* Supplément au numéro 7386, October 12, 1968: 1.

Delafosse, Maurice. *Les nègres.* Paris: Editions Rieder, 1927.

———. *Les civilisations negro-africaines.* Paris: Librairie Stock, 1925.

———. *L'ame negre.* Paris: Payot, 1922.

———. *Les noirs de l'Afrique.* Paris: Payot, 1922.

de Man, Paul. *Rhetoric of Romanticism.* New York: Columbia University Press, 1984.

de Maupassant, Guy. "Allouma," *Short Stories of the Tragedy and Comedy of Life,* Vol. 4. New York and London: M. Walter Dunne, 1903.

Derrida, Jacques. *Dissemination.* Trans. by Barbara Johnson. Chicago: University of Chicago Press, 1981.

———. *Of Grammatology.* Trans. by Gayatri Chakravorty Spivak. Baltimore: Johns Hopkins University Press, 1974.

Devlin, Tim. "Echoes of Graham Greene Halt Prizewinning Book." *The Times* (London), May 5, 1972: 1.

Dieterlen, Germaine. *Le Titre d'honneur des Arou: Dogon, Mali.* Paris: Société des Africanistes, 1982.

Dunton, Chris. "'Wheyting Be Dat?' The Treatment of Homosexuality in African Literature." *Research in African Literature* Vol. 20, No. 3 (Fall 1989): 422-448.

Eagleton, Terry. *Literary Theory.* Oxford: Blackwell, 1983.

Egejuru, Phanuel Akubueze. *Towards African Literary Independence: A Dialogue with Contemporary African Writers.* Westport, Conn.: Greenwood Press, 1980.

Elaho, Raymond O. "Le Devoir d'amour dans *le devoir de violence* de Yambo Ouologuem." *L'Afrique littéraire at artistique,* Vol. 56 (1979): 65-69.

Erickson, John. "Africa Reborn: Emergence from Myth, Yambo Ouologuem: *Le Devoir de violence.*" In *Nommo: African Fiction in French South of the Sahara.* York, S.C.: French Literature Publications, 1979.

Es-Sa'di, Abderrahman ben Abdallah ben 'Imran ben 'Amir. *Tarîkh es-Soudan.* Trans. by O. Houdas. Paris: École des Languages Orientales Vivants, 1898-1900; 2nd ed., Paris: Adrien-Maisonneuve, 1964.

Esin, Emel. *Mecca the Blessed/Madinah the Radiant.* New York: Crown Publishers, 1963.

Faik, Sully. "Yambo Ouologuem: *Le Devoir de violence,* Prix Renaudot 1968." *Congo-Afrique,* Vol. 9, No. 32 (1969): 91-101.

Fanon, Frantz. *Black Skin, White Masks.* Trans. by Charles Lam Markmann. New York: Grove Weidenfeld, 1968.

———. *Les Damnés de la terre,* Paris: Maspero, 1973.

———. *Peau Noir, Masques Blancs.* Paris: Seuil, 1952.

———. *The Wretched of the Earth.* Trans. by Constance Farrington. New York: Grove Press, 1963.

Fatunde, Tunde. "Images of Working People in Two African Novels: Ouologuem and Iyayi," *Marxism and African Literature,* Georg M. Gugelberger (ed.). Trenton, N.J.: African World Press, 1985. Pp. 110-117.

Fischer, Michael M. J., and Mehdi Abedi. *Debating Muslims: Cultural Dialogues in Postmodernity and Tradition.* Madison: University of Wisconsin Press, 1990.

Flamand, Paul. "Letter to the Editor." *Research in African Literatures,* Vol. 2, No. 2 (1971): 116.

Fleischmann, Ulrich. "Violence dans l'histoire et dans l'utopie: Evolution d'un theme dans le roman africain." *Franzosisch-Heute* (Frankfurt am Main, Germany) No. 2 (June 1982): 93-103.

Foucault, Michel. "La Bibliothèque fantastique." In *Travail de Flaubert.* Paris: Le Seuil, Points, 1983.

Françon, André *La Propriété littéraire et artistique.* Paris: PUF, 1970.

Frazer, Robert. "*Two Thousand Seasons*: Literary Ancestry and Text." In *Critical Perspectives on Ayi Kwei Armah,* Derek Weight (ed.). Washington, D.C.: Three Continents Press, 1992. Pp. 298-314.

Frobenius, Leo. *Histoire de la civilisation africaine.* Traduit par H. Back et D. Ermont. Paris: Gallimard, 1936.

Fuglestad, Finn. *A History of Niger: 1850-1960.* Cambridge: Cambridge University Press, 1983.

Galey, Matthieu. "Un grand roman africain." *Le Monde,* Supplement au numéro 7386, 12 Octobre: i.

Gardet, Louis. *La Cité musulmane, vie sociale et politique.* Paris: Librairie J. Vrin, 1954.

Geertz, Clifford. *Islam Observed.* Chicago: University of Chicago Press, 1968.

Gérard, Albert. "Littérature francophone d'Afrique: Le temps de la releve." *Revue Nouvelle,* Vol. 49 (1969): 198-204.

———. "Historical Origins and Literary Destiny of Negritude," *Diogenes,* No. 48 (1964): 14-38.

Graham, William A. "Qur'an as Spoken Word: An Islamic Contribution to the Understanding of Scripture." In *Approaches to Islam in Religious Studies,* Richard C. Martin (ed.). Tucson: University of Arizona Press, 1985. Pp. 23-40.

Greene, Graham. *It's a Battlefield.* London: Heinemann, 1934.

Habermas, Jürgen. *The Philosophical Discourse of Modernity.* Cambridge, Mass.: MIT Press, 1991.

Hale, Thomas. *Scribe, Griot, and Novelist: Narrative Interpreters of the Songhay Empire.* Gainesville: University of Florida Press, 1990.

Handelman, Susan A. *The Slayers of Moses: The Emergence of Rabbinic Interpretation in Modern Literary Theory.* Albany, N.Y.: SUNY Press, 1982.

Harrison, Christopher. *France and Islam in West Africa: 1860-1960.* Cambridge: Cambridge University Press, 1988.

Harrow, Kenneth. "Camara Laye, Cheikh Hamidou Kane, and Tayeb Salib: Three Sufi Authors." In *Faces of Islam in African Literature,* Kenneth W. Harrow (ed.). Portsmouth, N.H.: Heinemann Educational Books, 1991. Pp. 261-297.

———. "Introduction: Islam(s) in African Literature." In *Faces of Islam in African Literature,* Kenneth W. Harrow (ed.). Portsmouth, N.H.: Heinemann Educational Books, 1991. Pp. 3-20.

Highet, Gilbert. *The Anatomy of Satire.* Princeton: Princeton University Press, 1962.

Huggan, Graham. "Anthropology and Other Frauds." *Comparative Literature,* Vol. 46, No. 2 (Spring 1994): 113-128.

Hunwick, John O. *Shari'a in Songhay: The Replies of al-Maghili to the Questions of Askia al-Hajj Muhammad.* New York: Oxford University Press, 1985.

Ibn 'Abbad of Ronda. *Ibn 'Abbad of Ronda: Letters on the Sufi Path,* trans. by John Renard. New York: Paulist Press, 1986.

Ibn 'Ata'illah. *Sufi Aphorisms* (*Kitab al-Hikam*). Leiden: E. J. Brill, 1973.

"An Interview With Yambo Ouologuem." *Journal of New African Literature and the Arts,* Vols. 9-10 (Winter/ Spring 1971): 134-138.

"Interview: Yambo Ouologuem." *Cultural Events in Africa,* No. 61 (1969): 2.

Irele, Abiola. *The African Experience in Literature and Ideology.* Bloomington: Indiana University Press, 1990.

———. "Negritude and Black Cultural Nationalism." *Journal of Modern African Studies,* Vol. 4 (1965): 321-348.

———. "Negritude Literature and Ideology," *Journal of Modern African Studies,* Vol. 4 (1965): 499-526.

Iyayi, Festus. *Violence.* London: Longman, Drumbeat, 1979.

Jackson, Julian. "De Gaulle and May 1968." In *De Gaulle and Twentieth Century France.* John Horne and Hugh Gough (eds.). London: Edward Arnold, 1994. Pp. 125-146.

Jahn, Janheinz. *Muntu: An Outline of the New African Culture.* New York: Grove Press, 1961.

Johnson, Lemuel. *The Devil, the Gargoyle, and the Buffoon: The Negro as Metaphor in Western Literature.* Port Washington, N.Y.: Kennikat Press, 1969.

Jolles, A. *Formes Simples.* Paris: Le Seuil, 1972.

Julien, Eileen. "Rape, Repression, and Narrative Form in *Le Devoir de violence* and *La Vie et demie.*" In *Rape and Representation,* Lynn A. Higgins and Brenda R. Silver (ed.). New York: Columbia University Press, 1991. Pp. 160-181.

Kaba, Lansine. "The Pen, the Sword, and the Crown: Islam and Revolution in Songhay Reconsidered: 1464-1493." *Journal of African History,* Vol. 25 (1984): 241-256.

Kamal, Ahmad. *The Sacred Journey: Being Pilgrimage to Makkah.* New York: Duell, Sloan, and Pearce, 1961.

Kane, Mohamadou. "Roman africain et traditions," Diss., University of Lille, 1978.

———. "Sur les 'formes traditionnelles' du roman africain." *Revue de littérature comparée,* Nos. 3-4 (July-December 1974): 536-568.

Kâti, Mahmoud. *Tarîkh el-Fettâch ou chronique du chercheur pour servir à l'histoire des villes, des armées et des principaux personnages du Tekrour.* Trans. by O. Houdas and M. Delafosse. Paris: Ernest Leroux, 1913.

Kaufmann, Francine. "Compte-rendu de la soutenance," *Le Monde,* May 14, 1976.

Kerbrat-Orecchioni, C. *L'énonciation de la subjectivité dans le langage.* Paris: Colin, 1980.

Kersteloot, Lylian. *Les Ecrivains noirs de langue française: Naissance d'une littérature.* Brussels: Editions de l'Université de Bruxelles, 1963.

Khatibi, Abdelkebir. *Maghreb pluriel.* Paris: Éditions Denoël, 1983.

Kohn, Ingeborg M. "Satire in African Letters: Black Appraisals of White Ethnologists in the Works of Ferdinand Oyono, Tchicaya U'Tam'si and Yambo Ouologuem." *Studies in Twentieth Century Literature,* Vol. 4, No. 2 (Spring 1980): 213-227.

Kuehl, Linda. "Yambo Ouologuem on Violence, Truth, and Black History." *Commonweal,* June 11, 1971: 311-314.

K. W. (Kaye Whiteman) "In Defence of Yambo Ouologuem." *West Africa,* No. 2875, July 21, 1972: 939-941.

Lack, Roland-François. "'La littérature de Martial': Plagiarism as Figure in Sade, Lautréamont, Ouologuem, and Sony Labou Tansi." *Romantic Review,* Vol. 86, No. 4 (1995): 681-696.

Lang, George. "Text, Identity, and Difference: Yambo Ouologuem's *Le Devoir de violence* and Ayi Kwei Armah's *Two Thousand Seasons.*" *Comparative Literature Studies,* Vol. 24, No. 4 (1987): 387-402.

————. "Through a Prism Darkly: 'Orientalism' in European-Language African Writing." In *Faces of Islam in African Literature,* Kenneth W. Harrow (ed.). Portsmouth, N.H.: Heinemann Educational Books, 1991. Pp. 299-311.

Lanotte, Jacques. "Un Renaudot africain: *Le Devoir de violence.*" *Culture et Développement,* Vol. 1 (1969): 670-676.

Le Carvennec, Ernest. "La Prise du récit dans *Le Devoir de violence* de Yambo Ouologuem." In *Récit et historie,* Jean Bessière (ed.). Paris: Presses Universitaires de France, 1984: 159-175.

Leclech, G. "Ouologuem n'emprunte qu'aux riches." *Le Figaro Littéraire,* Vol. 1356, 13 mai 1972: 15.

Lentriccia, Frank. *After the New Criticism.* Chicago: University of Chicago Press, 1980.

Leusse, Hubert de. *Afrique Occidentale: Heurs et malheurs d'une rencontre: Les romanciers du pay noir.* Paris: Ed. de l'Orante, 1971.

Lings, Martin. *What Is Sufism?* Berkeley and Los Angeles: University of California Press, 1975.

Lukács, Georg. *The Theory of the Novel.* Trans. by Anna Bostock. London: Merlin Press, 1971.

Lusebrink, Hans-Jurgen. "De l'incontournabilité de la fiction dans la connaisance historique: Questionnements theoriques à partir de romans historiques contemporains

d'Alejo Carpentier, de 'Yambo Ouologuem et d'Ousmane Sembene.'" *Neohelicon: Acta Comparationis Litterarum Universarum* (Amsterdam: The Netherlands), Vol. 16, No. 2 (1989): 107-128.

Maes-Jelinek, Hena. "Yambo Ouologuem." *African Literature Today,* Vol. 164 (1970): 54-55.

Maiangwa, Yusufu. "The Duty of Violence in Yambo Ouologuem's *Bound to Violence.*" In *New West African Literature,* Kolawole Obunbesan (ed.). London: Heinemann, 1979. Pp. 70-79.

Maingueneau, D. *Initiation aux méthods de l'analyse du discours.* Paris: Hachette Université, 1976.

Makward, Edris. "Women, Tradition, and Religion in Sembène Ousmane's Work." In *Faces of Islam in African Literature,* ed. Kenneth W. Harrow (ed.). Portsmouth, N.H.: Heinemann Educational Books, 1991: Pp. 187-200.

Martin, Brad G. *Muslim Brotherhoods in Nineteenth-Century Africa.* Cambridge: Cambridge University Press, 1976.

Maupassant, Guy de. *Boule de Suif.* Paris: Societe d'Editions Litteraires et Artistiques, 1902.

Mbelolo, J. Mpiku ya. "From One Mystification to Another: 'Négritude' and 'Négraille' in *Le Devoir de violence.*" *Review of National Literatures* Vol. 2, no. 2 (Fall 1971): 124-147.

McDonald, Robert. "*Bound to Violence*: A case of plagiarism." *Transition,* Vol. 41 (1972): 67-68.

Memmi, Albert. *Dependence: A Sketch for a Portrait of the Dependent.* Trans. by Philip A. Facey. Boston: Beacon Press, 1984.

Miller, Christopher L. *Blank Darkness: Africanist Discourse in French.* Chicago: University of Chicago Press, 1985. Pp. 216-245.

————. *Theories of Africans: Francophone Literature and Anthropology in Africa.* Chicago: University of Chicago Press, 1990.

————. "Trait d'union: Injunction and Dismemberment in Yambo Ouologuem's *Le Devoir de violence.*" *L'Ésprit Createur,* Vol. 23, No. 4 (Winter 1983): 62-73.

Moore, Gerald. "The Debate on Existence in African Literature," *Présence Africaine,* Vol. 81 (1972).

————. "Towards Realism in French African Writing," *Journal of Modern African Studies,* Vol. 1 (1963): 61-73.

Mouralis, Bernard. "Une Carrefour d'écritures: *Le Devoir de violence* by Yambo Ouologuem," *Recherches et Travaux,* "Littératures africaines d'écriture française," University of Grenoble, UER de Lettres, Bulletin No. 27 (1984): 75-92.

———. "Littératures africaines d'écriture française." Université de Grenoble, UER de Lettres, Bulletin No. 27, 1984. Pp. 75-92.

———. "La réception du roman sahélien par la critique de langue française." Paris III, La Sorbonne Nouvelle, 1981.

Mudimbe, Valentin. *Invention of Africa.* Chicago: University of Chicago Press, 1988.

Nelson, Kristina. *The Art of Reciting the Qur'an.* Austin: University of Texas Press, 1985.

Ngaté, Jonathan. *Francophone African Fiction: Reading a Literary Tradition.* Trenton, N.J.: Africa World Press, 1988.

Nicholls, J. A. "Towards a Camusian Reading of *Le Devoir de violence.*" *Australian Journal of French Studies,* Vol. 28, No. 2 (May-August 1991): 211-219.

Nietzsche, Friedrich. *Basic Writings of Nietzsche.* New York: Random House, 1968.

Nwoga, Donatus I. "Plagiarism and Authentic Creativity in West Africa." *Research in African Literature,* Vol. 6, No. 1 (1975): 32-39.

Obiechina, E. N. *"Bound to Violence"* (review). *Okike: An African Journal of New Writing,* Vol. 1, No. 3, 1972: 53.

Ohaegbu, A. E. "An Approach to Ouologuem's *Le Devoir de violence.*" *African Literature Today,* Vol. 10 (1979): 124-133.

Olivier de Sardan, Jean-Pierre. *Concepts et Conceptions songhay-zarma.* Paris: Nubia, 1982.

Olney, James. *Tell Me Africa: An Approach to African Literature.* Princeton: Princeton University Press, 1973.

Oloruntimehin, B. O. *The Segu Tukulor Empire.* London: Longman Group Limited, 1972.

Ouologuem, Yambo. *Bound to Violence.* Trans. by Ralph Mannheim London: Heinemann Educational Books, 1971. New York: Harcourt, Brace, Jovanovich, 1971.

———. "La conscience malheureuse." *Nouvelle poésie négro-africaine, Poésie I,* Nos. 43-45 (January-June 1976): 124.

———. *Le Devoir de violence.* Paris: Éditions du Seuil, 1968.

———. *Lettre à la France nègre.* Paris: Éditions Edmond Nalis, 1968.

——— (under the pseudonym Utto Rodolph). *Les Milles et une bibles du sexe.* Paris: Editions du Dauphin, 1969.

———. "A Mon Mari" *Presence Africaine,* Vol. 57 (1966): 95.

———. *"Le Devoir de violence."* *Figaro litléraire,* 10 June 1972.

Parrinder, Geoffrey. *Jesus in the Qur'an.* New York: Oxford University Press, 1977.

Philipson, Robert. "Chess and Sex in *Le Devoir de violence,*" *Callaloo: A Journal of African-American and African Arts and Letters,* Vol. 12, No. 1 (Winter 1989): 216-232.

Piégay-Gros, Nathalie. *Introduction à l'intertextualité.* Paris: Dunod, 1996.

Prescott, Peter S. "Wanderers in Disaster." *Newsweek,* March 29, 1971: 100.

Qazi, M. A. *A Concise Dictionary of Islamic Terms.* Chicago: Qazi Publications, 1979.

Randall, Marilyn. "Appropriate(d) Discourse: Plagiarism and Decolonization." *New Literary History: A Journal of Theory and Interpretation,* Vol. 22, No. 3 (Summer 1991): 525-541.

———. "Le Presuppose d'originalité et l'art du plagiat: Lecture pragmatique." *Voix et Images: Littérature Quebecoise,* Vol. 15, No. 2 (Winter 1990): 196-208.

Riedel, Alfredo. *Cultura negro africana moderna.* Trieste: Edizioni Umana, 1973.

Rimbaud, Arthur. *Une Saison en enfer.* Paris: Coll. Poésie/Gallimard, 1984.

Robinson, David. "An Approach to Islam in West African History." In *Faces of Islam in African Literature,* Kenneth W. Harrow (ed.). Portsmouth, N.H.: Heinemann Educational Books, 1991: Pp. 107-130.

———. *The Holy War of Umar Tall.* New York: Oxford University Press, 1985.

Rushdie, Salman. *The Satanic Verses.* New York: Viking, 1988.

Rutimirwa, Alec. "A Case of Plagiarism." *Transition,* Vol. 42 (1973): 8-9.

al-'Sadi, 'Abd al-Rahman ibn 'Abd Allah. *Tarîkh es-Soudan,* edit, par O. Houdas, avec la collaboration de Edm. Benoist. Paris: E. Leroux, 1898-1900.

Said, Edward. *The World, the Text and the Critic.* Cambridge: Harvard University Press, 1983.

Saint-Martin, Yves. "Un fils d'El Hadj Omar: Agibou, roi du Dinguiray et du Macina (1843?-1907?)." *Cahier d'Études Africaines,* Vol. 8 (1968).

Schikora, Rosemary G. "Outfoxing the Fox: Game Strategy in *Le Devoir de violence.*" *Perspectives on Contemporary Literature,* No. 6 (1980): 72-79.

Schwarz-Bart, André. *Le Dernier des justes.* Paris: Editions du Seuil, 1959.

Sellin, Eric. "Book Review: *Bound to Violence*," *French Review* 43, no. 1 (October 1969): 64-68.

———. "African Art: Compositional vs. Modal Esthetics." *Yale Review,* Vol. 59, No. 2 (Winter 1970): 215-227.

———. "Ouologuem's Blueprint for *Le Devoir de violence.*" *Research in African Literature,* Vol. 2, No. 2 (1971): 117-120.

———. "Ouologuem, Kourouma, et le nouveau roman africain." In *Littératures ultramarines de langue française: Genèse et jeunesse,* Thomas H. Geno and Roy Julow (eds.). Sherbrooke, Quebec: Naaman, 1974. Pp. 35-50.

———. "The Unknown Voice of Yambo Ouologuem." *Yale French Studies,* Vol. 53 (1976): 137-162.

Semujanga, Josias. "Le Genre comme procès axiologigue et esthetique: Élements pour l'enseignment du roman africain." *Tangence,* Vol. 49 (December 1995): 94-111.

———. "De l'histoire à sa metaphore dans *Le Devoir de violence* de Yambo Ouologuem." *Études Françaises* (Montreal, Canada), Vol. 31, No. 1 (Summer 1995): 71-83.

Scott, Walter Sir. *Minstrelsy of the Scottish Border, with his introductions, additions, and notes.* Edinburgh: A. & C. Black, 1873.

Shah, Indries. *The Elephant in the Dark: Christianity, Islam, and the Sufis.* London: Octagon Press, 1974.

Sharif, M. M. *A History of Muslim Philosophy, Volume II.* Wiesbaden: Otto Harrassowitz, 1966.

Skurnik, Walter A. E. "Léopold Sédar Senghor and African Socialism." *Journal of Modern African Studies,* Vol. 3 (1965), 349-450.

Sklar, Richard L. "The Colonial Imprint on African Political Thought." *African Independence: The First Twenty-Five Years,* Gwendolyn M. Carter and Patrick O'Meara (eds.). Bloomington: Indiana University Press, 1985. 1-30.

Slemon, Stephen. "Post-Colonial Allegory and the Transformation of History." *Journal of Commonwealth Literature.* Vol. 23, No. 1 (1988): 157-181.

"Something *New* Out of Africa?" *Times Literary Supplement,* May 5, 1972: 525.

Songolo, Aliko. "Fiction et Subversion: *Le Devoir de violence.*" *Présence Africaine,* Vol. 120 (1981): 17-34.

———. "The Writer, The Audience and the Critic's Responsibility: The Case of *Bound to Violence.*" In *Artist and Audience: African Literature as a Shared Experience,* Richard Priebe and Thomas A. Hale (eds.). Washington, D.C.: Three Continents Press, 1979. Pp. 126-140.

Soyinka, Wole. *Myth, Literature, and the African World.* Cambridge: Cambridge University Press, 1976. Pp. 104-106.

Spivak, Gayatri Chakravorty. *In Other Worlds: Essays in Cultural Politics.* New York: Routledge, 1988.

Strobbe, Nicolas. "Instituting the Imaginary Subject Colonial: *Men in the Sun* and *Bound to Violence.*" *Southern Review: Literary and Interdisciplinary Essays* (Churchhill, Victoria, Australia [SoRA]), Vol. 27, No. 4 (December 1994): 459-474.

Suret-Canale, J. *Afrique Noire,* Vol. 1, Paris: Éditions Sociales, 1958.

Tassou, Kazaro. "*Le Devoir de violence* face au public." Chapter 3, "La réception du roman sahélien par la critique de langue française," thèse de III cycle, Paris III, La Sorbonne Nouvelle, 1991. Pp. 222-278.

Thibaudeau, J. "Le roman actuel: Flaubert et Lautrémont," In *Interventions: Socialisme, avant-garde, littérature.* Paris: Éditions Sociales, 1972. Pp. 16-19.

Torrey, Charles Cutler. *The Jewish Foundation of Islam.* New York: Ktav Publishing House, 1967.

Trimingham, J. Spencer. *A History of Islam in West Africa.* London, Glasgow, and New York: Oxford University Press, 1962.

Trotsky, Leon. *Literature and Revolution.* New York: Monthly Review Press, 1974.

United States Congress, House Committee on Foreign Affairs, Subcommittee on Human Rights and International Organizations. *Human Rights in the Maghreb and Mauritania,* June 19, 1991. Washington, D.C.: U.S. Government Printing Office, 1991.

"Vient de paraître." *Le Monde* (Supplément au numéro 7344), 24 août 1968: ii.

Vignal, Daniel. "L'homophilie dans le roman négro-africain d'expression anglaise et française." *Peuples Noirs, Peuples Africains,* Vol. 33 (May-June 1983): 63-81.

Watkins, Mel. "Talk with Yambo Ouologuem," *New York Times Book Review,* March 7, 1971, p. 7.

Welch, Claude E., Jr. "Yambo Ouologuem and His Times: Aspects of Literature of Violence." In *Commentaries on a Creative Encounter: Proceedings of a Conference on the Culture and Literature of Francophone Africa.* Albany: African-American Institute, 1988. Pp. 47-51.

Wise, Christopher. "In Search of Yambo Ouologuem." *Research in African Literature,* Vol. 29, No. 2 (Summer 1998): 159-182.

———. "Qur'anic Hermeneutics, Sufism, and *Le Devoir de violence*: Yambo Ouologuem as Marabout Novelist." *Religion and Literature,* Vol. 28, No. 1 (Spring 1996): 85-112.

————. "Yambo Ouologuem dans le postmoderne: Les débats littéraires sur *Le Devoir de violence* depuis 1985." *Littératures du Sahel,* Joseph Paré, Sanou Salaka, and Christopher Wise (eds.). Bellingham, Wash.: CamNexus/Kola Tree Press, 1998. Pp. 117-122.

Woddis, Jack. *New Theories of Revolution.* New York: International Publishers, 1972.

Wolitz, Seth I. "L'Art du plagiat, ou une brève défense de Ouologuem." *Research in African Literature,* Vol. 4, No. 1 (Spring 1973): 130-134.

Wright, Derek. "Orality in the African Historical Novel: Yambo Ouologuem's *Bound to Violence* and Ayi Kwei Armah's *Two Thousand Seasons.*" *Journal of Commonwealth Literature,* Vol. 23, No. 1 (1988): 90-101.

Zhang, Longxi. *The Tao and the Logos: Literary Hermeneutics, East and West.* Durham, N.C.: Duke University Press, 1992.

Zoghby, Samir M. "Blacks and Arabs: Past and Present." *Current Bibliography on African Affairs,* Vol. 3, No. 5 (May 1970): 5-22.

Zupancic, Metka. "Problem plagiata pri Yambu Ouologuem." In *Bajt Drago,* Frane Jerman and Janko Moder (eds.). Iz zgodovine prevajanja na Slovenskem. Ljubljana: Drustvo slovenskih knjizevnih prevajalcev, 1982. Pp. 385-391.

Ann Elizabeth Willey (essay date 1999)

SOURCE: Willey, Ann Elizabeth. "Pornography, or the Politics of Misbehaving? A Feminist Reading of the Voices of Yambo Ouologuem." In *Yambo Ouologuem: Postcolonial Writer, Islamic Militant,* edited by Christopher Wise, pp. 139-51. Boulder and London: Lynne Rienner, 1999.

[In the following essay, Willey asserts that a feminist reading of Ouologuem's three published works contradicts the standard view of his writings as subversive.]

Most readers of Yambo Ouologuem are concerned with the novel *Le Devoir de violence.* Indeed, reams of discourse have been dedicated to this novel; as early as 1972, shortly after it was awarded the Prix Renaudot, *Le Devoir de violence* was at the center of hotly contested debates that have not subsided to this day. And yet in the voluminous and quite thorough scholarship on Yambo Ouologuem, whether celebratory or castigating, very little has been said about Ouologuem's two other major pieces of prose, *Lettre à la France nègre* and *Les Milles et une bibles du sexe.*[1] This chapter will ask of these two lesser-known works the kinds of questions usually posed in reference to *Le Devoir de violence.* In particular, I wonder if these two works can shed some new light on the question of how we can or should receive Ouologuem's troubling corpus.[2] Ouologuem is usually read as engaging in a "politics of misbehavior," but this has been challenged by some readers, particularly those who are concerned with questions raised from feminist standpoints.[3] I suggest that although *Le Devoir de violence* can indeed be read convincingly as a subversive text, when it is looked at in conjunction with *Lettre à la France nègre* and *Les Milles et une bibles du sexe,* this recuperation of Ouologuem is much harder to effect. An extension of the feminist critique to these other two texts seriously weakens any representation of Ouologuem's work as subversive.

Short of Chinua Achebe's *Things Fall Apart,* Yambo Ouologuem's novel *Le Devoir de violence* may be one of the most written-about novels in African literature, but for very different reasons. Whereas Achebe's novel is celebrated as a foundational text in African literature, Ouologuem's novel is infamous for committing a host of sins. Rather than establishing a canon, Ouologuem's novel departs radically from the norms that had shaped the francophone African canon prior to its publication. It is very definitely not a book that had truck with négritude, unless you read it as a scathing critique of the same. It is not lyrically nostalgic like Cheikh Hamidou Kane's *L'Aventure ambiguë,* nor is it a mildly ironic, subtly critical realistic novel bent on exposing the contradictions of the civilizing mission like *Une vie de Boy* or almost any of Mongo Beti's novels. Ouologuem's vitriolic, pugnacious, and scatological version of African history as one of corruption, sadism, and hypocrisy outraged many African readers. Its flagrant plagiarism added fuel to the critical fire. Since its early scandal-ridden appearance on the scene, however, *Le Devoir de violence* has come to mean many different things.

Indeed, the scholarship surrounding *Le Devoir de violence* largely seeks to recoup this objectionable, disruptive text from the early attacks made against it on several fronts. Many have argued that, in fact, this novel was exactly what francophone African literature needed in the late 1960s to counterbalance what were increasingly obvious as the shortfalls of a novelistic tradition shaped by orthodoxies of négritude. In this vein, Wole Soyinka claims *Le Devoir de violence* as a corrective to the types of history posited by Kane's *L'Aventure ambiguë,* calling *Le Devoir de violence* "a studied repudiation of historical blinkers" (100). Kwame Anthony Appiah similarly claims that *Le Devoir de violence* is primarily a work of political critique aimed at contemporary Africa. Appiah describes it as a novel that "seeks to delegitimate the forms of the realist African novel, in part, surely, because what it sought to naturalize was a nationalism that, by 1968, had plainly failed" (150).[4]

Not only is *Le Devoir de violence* read as a critique of foregoing political and literary traditions, its plagiaristic mode is often read as a profoundly subtle and disruptive commentary on the dynamics of colonial discourse and postcolonial relations. Critics such as Aliko Songolo, Jonathan Ngaté, and Christopher Miller respond more directly to the charges of plagiarism and always in such a way as to recoup the plagiarism as a critical statement on discursive relations of power. They argue that Ouologuem's plagiarism is an attempt to disrupt the unidirectional flow of discourse posited by the colonialist enterprise. Miller refers to the novel as "a brazen act of trifling with the idols of literary creation, respecting the taboos of neither the African nor the European literary establishment" (1985: 218), which Ouologuem does in order to look the Africanist tradition in its eye and "disfigure it in his own fashion" (238).[5] Aliko Songolo goes even further in claiming for this novel subversive techniques and goals:

> Cette technique, que je nommerai la technique de la subversion, fait violence non seulement à tout ce que le roman africain représentait avant 1968, mais encore à la notion acquise du rôle social et politique de la tradition d'une part, et d'autre part à la notion de propriété littéraire.[6]

(1981: 25)

Ngaté combines these readings and calls the text "a radical invitation to conspiratorial misbehavior" and again later places the novel firmly in a context of "a politics of misbehavior which [is] shaping the African novel" (44, 58). The readings of Ngaté Miller, and Songolo that emphasize Ouologuem's use and misuse of European literary conventions, his flouting of the laws of patriarchy, all agree: Ouologuem's misbehaving is a politically subversive act that works to undermine the hegemony of colonial discourse about Africa. And these are convincing ways to read Ouologuem's novel. From a feminist standpoint, though, the prospect of men misbehaving is not always a heartening thought.

In an essay that examines the representation of rape in Ouologuem's *Le Devoir de violence,* Eileen Julien, in fact, points out that though Ouologuem's text is radically critical of the hierarchy inherent in European colonialism, it does not challenge hierarchical gender relations; in fact, on a textual level, it reinscribes female passivity.[7] If we extend Julien's argument to the reception of Ouologuem's novel, what we see is, I think, that the defenses of *Le Devoir* depend on reading literary discourse and political discourse as analogous, or metaphors for each other. We see Ouo-

loguem's rejection of European literary norms as a type of rebellion against European political hegemony. Plagiarism becomes guerrilla warfare. And yet, this tropological slide covers over the other norms that Ouologuem leaves in place, most notably unequal gender relations. What happens to "the politics of misbehavior" if we unlink the concepts of the violence of colonial discourse, the violence of Ouologuem's textual practice against that discourse, and the violence against women in Ouologuem's discourse? An awareness of how this third term underpins the first two throughout Ouologuem's work, I argue, seriously challenges the easy metaphorical substitution of plagiarism for radical politics. The transgressions against the European-derived, patriarchically inflected laws of authority and authorship are only subversive in a masculine context. What many claim for Ouologuem— that he is making a call for a new humanism (*pace* Appiah), that he is representing the disenfranchised of Africa (*pace* Fatunde),[8] or even that he posits brutality as part of the human condition (*pace* Julien and Thomas Hale)—begs the question of who is acknowledged as human, disenfranchised, or even brutalized, in Ouologuem's work.

Ouologuem's *Lettre à la France nègre* and *Les Milles et une bibles du sexe* are less well known and certainly less often discussed, though both were published within a year of *Le Devoir de violence.* In 1968, the same year *Le Devoir de violence* appeared, Ouologuem published a collection of satiric essays called *Lettre à la France nègre.* This series of "letters" comprise highly sarcastic attacks on the French and French culture, wherein Ouologuem takes a great deal of pleasure in turning both French and African pieties on their heads. One letter, for example, examines the well-known lament of the négritude poets concerning the negative associations of blackness in the French language. Ouologuem starts off by quoting the famous examples of whiteness as purity, truth, light, and so on, but then goes on to show how whiteness has also been used in the French language to imply things that are not nearly so savory, such as the idea of insubstantial and insincere speech known as blandishments; the treatment of treating symptoms that mask a much more serious underlying disease, known as "un traitement qui ne fait que blanchir" (40); or similarly, the craftiness used in exculpating criminals, referred to as "un bon avocat peut blanchir un criminel" (40). Although this essay is in part a chastisement aimed at the négritude poets for their too simplistic critique of the French language, the letter ends with the observation that France is not nearly as "white" as it would like to think itself either. Ouologuem concludes with the question, "la France est-elle nègre ou pas?" to which he poses the answer, "consulter le Bottin alphabétique, pour voir si y figure l'Afrique des banlieues . . ." (46). This is the type of playful and yet pointed reversal that Ouologuem's critics celebrate in reading *Le Devoir de violence.*

Lettre à la France nègre contains one letter in particular that critics of Ouologuem's work, most notably Christopher Miller and James Olney, have identified as central to a reading of Ouologuem's literary politics. Ouologuem's **"Lettre aux pisse-copie Nègres d'écrivains célèbres"** is a long exegesis on how the black writer in French is in some ways always a "ghostwriter." Miller points out that one meaning of the word *nègre* in French is "ghostwriter"; thus, for the black writer to write in French is always to write as a *nègre*—that is, necessarily as someone writing in a language of which she or he cannot claim ownership. Ouologuem tells the black writer not to despair but instead to relish his anonymity, to leave the task of thinking to others, and instead to get rich by producing mass quantities of hackneyed but lucrative detective fiction quickly and simply by combining elements of already published fiction. In the middle of this essay, he provides a pull-out chart with several passages from popular detective novels conveniently excerpted and classified, complete with plot schematics and possible combinations for effective fiction.

Certainly, his *Lettre à la France nègre* seems to be a nonfiction version of the defense that others have posed in his stead. In his evenhanded attacks on the discourse that promotes both a sense of African victimhood and thus a loss of subjectivity and conversely a sense of French superiority that is both hypocritical and dependent on the presence of African wealth, Ouologuem plays into a reading of his work as subversive or an invitation to misbehavior. The how-to fold-out chart outlining the mechanics of plagiarism is the pinnacle of his exploding of these myths. The excoriating letters to those who would forget their investment in perpetuating the racist tropes of colonialism frame a call to wholesale plunder of French literature that will lead to handsome remuneration for the black writer, even if he cannot take credit for "the white work of thinking" (166). How better to live up to the "radical politics of misbehavior" than to publish a "how-to" book for plagiarists? Ouologuem's *Lettre à la France nègre* fits well into the pattern that would have us read his narratives as an invitation to misbehavior for the purposes of dramatizing the violence-fraught relationship that Africans have to writing in French.

However, even in this work, women are invoked and silenced simultaneously, much as they are *Le Devoir de violence.* In the sometimes very personal essays in which Ouologuem invokes his own childhood or tries to explain the motives for African men in marrying Frenchwomen, women, either European or African, are invoked only as symbols, not subjects. In the first letter, Ouologuem invokes the common image of Africa as a women who has prostituted herself to Europe to explain the neo-colonial context. He uses this image again in the fourth letter through an extended parable about "Binta," a woman who disfigures herself in a vain attempt to become more desirable to the white lovers who eventually abandon her—this is his metaphor for cultural colonialism and the arrival of independence. The seventh letter, titled "Lettre aux femmes nègrement seules" (Letter to blackly alone women") begins with the claim "Femmes seules, vous êtes comme les Nègres, dès lors même que votre état vous tient à l'écart de la vie, reléguées dans la société marginale des groupes minoritaires" (97).[9] From here, Ouologuem goes on to explain how women who remain alone become too interiorized and thus make orphans of themselves, and then he asserts that this is why African women in Europe will not marry African men. Whereas African men who marry European women are seeking a promise of acceptance, African women are shown simply as rejecting African men because of mental maladjustment. The status of woman is explicitly one of silence; she is unable to voice or act on her desires.[10]

Ouologuem's other major piece of writing is *Les Milles et une bibles du sexe* (1969), a collection of erotic, or more accurately, pornographic,[11] short-stories that Ouologuem claims are culled from a thousand such stories handed to him by a Parisian aristocrat named "Utto Rodolph" for his editing. What follows is a series of "poker confessions" of four sexual adventurers whose exploits range from the relatively mild scene of mutual masturbation on a subway train to the outrageous orgies of hundreds of couples each trying to outdo the other in the preposterousness of their sexual appetites. The structure of this collection would seem to follow the program laid out in his **"Lettre aux pisse-copies nègres d'écrivains célèbres"**: Ouologuem hides behind a pen name, the position of the ghostwriter, and engages in producing a series of stories that fall under one of the more formulaic genres of writing, the pornographic short story. Can this pornography also be recouped as part of a politics of misbehavior? Can we claim it as a commentary on the social, political, and discursive relations between France and the ex-colonies that invites subversion?

In his introduction, Ouologuem claims this position for himself and this work. He claims that Utto Rudolph came to him because certain aspects of *Le Devoir de violence* suggested that Ouologuem would be an appropriate editor for a collection of "erotic confessions." Ouologuem writes:

But I do not intend to specialize in this area. This is my first and last effort. I have taken it upon myself to present this thousand and one bibles of sex partly because it was the erotic aspects of my first novel that caused several African countries to close their borders to **Bound to Violence**. In the eyes of the irresponsible and uncultivated heads of state, I was, for having dared to say that the black man makes love, a sell-out to a racist France, which amuses itself by watching a black man strip other black people of their identities and customs as black people. So be it.[12]

Echoing the defenses made on his behalf by critics like Appiah and Soyinka, Ouologuem poses this collection as a political statement aimed at the heads of state in Africa who would keep him from treating African subjects as wholly human.

Critics have been willing in part to accept Ouologuem's own positioning of this text as a political response to the objections launched at **Le Devoir de violence.** James Olney, for example, reads **Les Milles et une bibles du sexe** as a somewhat raunchy retort to the claims that Ouologuem's goal is the perpetuation of the colonialist stereotypes of the barbaric African. The Europeans of **Les Milles et une bibles du sexe** are more savage in their customs than the worst of the Saifs, and indeed some of the most objectionable scenes in **Le Devoir de violence** are repeated here, translated into a European context.[13] Olney points out:

> The erotic adventures in **Les Milles et une bibles du sexe**—and this fact of setting reflects, I think, significantly on actions in **Le Devoir de Violence,** which is located almost entirely in Africa—take place, for the most part, in France and the participants, again for the most part (when they are not dogs or other dumb beasts), are French."
>
> (225)

Olney ascribes a political motive to Ouologuem's translation of the more egregious scenes in **Le Devoir de violence** to a French setting. As Olney says at another point in his reading, Ouologuem is generous in his distributions of vices, neglecting neither the Africans nor the Europeans that he writes about (211). Although Miller (1985) gives Ouologuem much less credit for this collection, (he argues that **Les Milles et une bibles du sexe** is a much less original work [245], which ironically would suggest its appropriateness as an example in Ouologuem's exercises in mass-production of formulaic literature), he follows some of the same lines of argument as Olney, suggesting that Ouologuem's appropriation of sexual discourse about Europe presents itself as a political act.[14]

Although this positioning of **Les Milles et une bibles du sexe** works into the common reading of his corpus as subversive, critics feel compelled to recoup the one

story in the collection that takes place in Africa. The narrator himself displays the same desire: this is the only story which the narrator prefaces with an apology for its content. During the interminable Parisian adventures of the main characters, they arrive one night at an orgy, accompanied by three Liberians. The proprietor of the club they wish to enter will not admit the Liberians. The main character threatens the owner, and eventually they all enter, but the mood has been sullied and they quickly retire. The Liberians, rich businessmen, offer the four Parisians round-trip tickets to Africa as a thank you for their efforts on behalf of the Africans. Ouologuem interrupts the collection of stories to report in his own editorial voice:

> I must somewhat naively declare that I was sorry to see Africa mixed up in this business. I had wished, for form's sake, that Utto Rudolph would have chosen another type of story—a less collective exoticism, perhaps, so problematic did it seem. The leisurely activity of the safari; does it give the traveler anything more than a little local color? One of the confessees wrote on page 732 'Safaris are another thing altogether. They have the refined sex appeal of a hunt with hounds." I had to rewrite the opening of this confession. To reread it. And still I was not satisfied: it lacked the psychological dimension of eroticism.
>
> (275)

What follows is a conversation between Ouologuem and the couple who had submitted this particular story in which he pushes them to explain the connection between safaris and eroticism. The wife compares a safari to a bullfight—an elaborately staged dance that, by implication, always ends in blood. She says later though, that she finds the unequal contest between man and beast unnerving. Her husband identifies this aspect as precisely the root of eroticism. The wife explains:

W:

> It's about the male being seen. A reflection of his masculine power. Of his superiority over the female.

H (TO HIS WIFE):

> Exactly.

W:

> What do you mean "Exactly"?

H:

> Sexual love is very violent.

YO:

> And so the Safari . . .

H:

> It is beautiful . . . the woman on safari is very sweet/ soft.

YO:

She gives the feeling of being a victim?

H:

She is seductive, fascinating.

(276-277)

The characters clearly lay out for us the erotic appeal of unequal relations of power that are doubly displayed in the erotic/exotic safari. As is so often the case in colonialist discourse, the white man claims his power over a feminized landscape. This is not substantially different from the position that the pornographer takes in relation to the female body. In this passage, for example, the wife's objections to the coupling of power and sexuality as a particularly male phenomenon are ignored as the two men agree on the seductiveness of creating victims.

The adventures of our Parisian foursome begin in Liberia with very little "action" whatsoever. The first four pages of this episode are given over instead to a description of the African landscape, the evils of neocolonialism, the interethnic conflicts that bedevil the West Coast, and the abundance of natural resources available. The foursome then decide to travel to Kenya, where they amuse themselves by going on a safari with an African guide who agrees to chaperone them only with great reservations and insists that they do not carry weapons. After driving quite a bit, they decide to stop and make love in the bush while the guard does his best not to look on, but instead looks after the car. When the two couples are surprised making love in the bush by a lion, they soothe him, as Miller points out, by continuing their natural way of being by continuing to have sex. The African guide then masturbates the lion to distraction, tosses a gourd down the lion's throat, and causes it to choke to death. Everyone flees the scene in terror, but the guide calmly returns and rifles through the Europeans' goods, appropriating for himself a cigarette that he proceeds to smoke in an attitude of (postcoital) satisfaction.

This story is indeed fraught with the usual tropes of colonial discourse, from the worried, nagging, effeminate African guide to the naturalness of sex in the African landscape. But to read this scene as Miller and Olney do as one where the African is on a par with the bestial lion (they are, after all, sex partners in a sense here) begs the question of who is fooled by the colonialist trope. Although one could read the African guide as equal to the lion, all one part of the African landscape, one could also read this story as suggesting how the Europeans, in their own misguided projections of what is "natural" on to this landscape, are lulled into unreason, at which point they can be

taken advantage of. The sly little ending of this story indeed suggests that the African will have the last laugh while Europeans breathlessly watch what they think is an African moving in his own natural state. This echoes the dynamics of the first reviewers calling *Le Devoir de violence* "the first truly African novel," suggesting that what they were seeing was the perversions of their own projections. Meanwhile, Ouologuem, having tamed the lion of colonialist discourse, will take his prize money and laugh all the way to the bank.

All three of these texts then, can be read as participating in the "invitation to a politics of misbehavior," an attempt to subvert colonialist discourse. But what I think is at stake in reading Ouologuem as inviting his reader to participate in a politics of misbehavior is a certain construction of the relationship of the discourses of politics and sexuality. If we read these two as being metaphorically related, we can read his stories of rape, torture, and maimed female bodies as a metaphorical representation of Africa under colonialism or in Ouologuem's terms, of man's propensity to mistreat man. Certainly, this is a common trope in Africanist discourse, both in the works of apologists for colonialism who wish to tame Africa and also in the works of those who fight against colonialism in the name of Mother Africa. What happens though, if we read the relationship between discourses of politics and sexuality as being metonymically related in Ouologuem? What if politics and sexuality are not mutually substitutable but instead have been naturalized as such? What happens to Ouologuem's politics of misbehavior if we question this apparent similarity between politics and sex?

The long-standing connection between rhetorics of gender and rhetorics of colonialism do indeed underlie all three of these texts. When discussing *Les Milles et une bibles du sexe,* Ouologuem's critics all point out the disingenuous, at the least, if not frankly tongue in cheek, remark that this collection of pornography was in part the result of a sense of pique on Ouologuem's behalf at *Le Devoir de violence* having been banned in several African countries because, he claims, of its lascivious nature. What few have mentioned is that earlier in the same introduction, Ouologuem sarcastically remarks that he sought the prior approval of the Renaudot Prize jury for this collection. If indeed Ouologuem's African critics are sliding from political objections to sexual objections, his comments suggest a reversal with regard to the jury of the Prix Renaudot where he implies a political intent in his sexual writing. Where Ouologuem posits that African leaders use sex to hide their anxieties about his politics, Ouologuem suggests that the European literary establishment is so wrapped up in his sexual discourse that they fail to perceive the politics of an African describing European sex. As this reversal shows, Ouologuem, along the same lines as his critics, posits another type of misbehavior (in this case sexual rather than literary) as a substitution for political misbehavior.

On one level, Ouologuem's pornography is the perfect fictional working out of his claims in the **"Lettre aux pisse-copies nègres d'écrivains célèbres."** The reams of formulaic prose stitched together under a pen name in a genre that has historically proven lucrative works as an example of how to succeed as an African writer writing in French. The display of European degradation similarly works as a response to the charges that Ouologuem degrades Africa through his portrayal of African atrocities in *Le Devoir de violence.* He is indeed generous with his libel. The subtly ironic nod toward the literary establishment found in his introduction, when he claims to have gotten the prior approval of the Prix Renaudot jury for his salacious undertaking, begs the reader to see Europeans as too occupied with the abstract concern for the French patriarchy (in the case of plagiarism) to be able to see Ouologuem's manipulations of French discourse as a power move. And yet all these readings ignore the trail of maimed and mutilated female bodies that literally litter the paths of Ouologuem's work. In using pornography to turn the tables on the European piety of the plagiarism debacle, Ouologuem cannot, as his defenders suggest, come out the good guy. In order to subvert the paradigms of colonial discourse in its claim to white male authority over Africa, Ouologuem simply reverses the claim by reinscribing African male control over white sexuality. Ouologuem does not subvert the trope; he simply claims the right to be on top. This metaphoric substitution depends on our acceptance of a naturalized relationship between sexuality and politics as both exemplifying male power.

In rethinking the connections we draw between discourses of sexuality and politics, it is useful, I think, to fall back on Paul de Man's distinctions between metaphor and metonym. Although the political discourse of and about Africa has often used a gendered metaphor for the position of Africa (a landscape raped, the Mother Africa that has been abused/ abandoned, and the resulting metaphor of the process of colonization as an emasculation of African people), it is possible, even necessary, to reread the connections between gender and politics in Africa as being metonymically connected. In defining metaphor and metonymy, de Man refers to a choice of rhetorical figures as being motivated by "necessary links" or "perchance":

> a distinction that corresponds to the difference between metaphor and metonymy, necessity and chance being a legitimate way to distinguish between analogy and

contiguity. The inference of identity and totality that is constitutive of metaphor is lacking in the purely relational metonymic contact: an element of truth is involved in taking Achilles for a lion but none in taking Mr. Ford for a motor car.

(14)

To substitute sexuality for politics assumes that there is an element of truth in describing sex as a form of colonization instead of seeing the brutalization of women as an effect of the colonial discourse that Ouologuem would subvert. His texts taken together, then, reinscribe an essential part of the discursive system he would challenge.

Ouologuem does seem to recognize this paradox in *Le Devoir de violence,* but only in limited ways, as Eileen Julien points out. Julien argues that Ouologuem establishes a metonymic relationship between rape and "sickness of political relations": "Rape is represented then not as an isolated, gratuitous instance of violence that can be read metaphorically. . . . It is portrayed rather metonymically, as a quintessential act of violence in a context of rampant abuse" (161). However, in his textual silencing of the women who are subjected to rape, Ouologuem replicates the objectification of women that he thematically depends on as indicating an abusive and intolerable climate.

Though rarer than the metaphoric use cited above, a metonymic understanding of the association of gender power and political power is present in some Africanist discourse but is rarely highlighted. For example, in Ama Ata Aidoo's "For Whom Things Did Not Change," the narrator quite consciously questions the metaphoric relations of political hierarchies as gendered when he questions the metaphorical import of what it means to be a black man who cooks for a white man and then poses the question of what it means to be black man cooking for another black man. To read this metaphorically brings up issues of neocolonialism that reinscribe the association of masculine identity and political power. But to read it metonymically would be to identify the axis along which this particular trope operates and ask what it means to be a black woman cooking for anybody. The black woman's body is erased and naturalized as part of the landscape in the metaphorical tropological system that equates cooking with the loss of political power. Similarly, in Ouologuem's African pornographic story, the African guide who exploits the perverted European notions of nature and sexuality as a trope for Africa does so in a truly male display of the matador: he masturbates as he watches the lion die. As the European recounters of this story argue to the narrator, sexuality is defined as the display of male power over a victim, either a woman or an animal.

To read Yambo Ouologuem's objectification of European women as politically subversive (the role that he himself claims for this collection of stories in the preface, wherein he situates this text as a response in kind to the political reaction to *Le Devoir de violence*) begs the question of what is being subverted. Without the discursive gloss provided by *Lettre à la France nègre,* the pornography of Yambo Ouologuem feels less like a subversion of European hegemony than a restatement of the ultimately nihilistic view presented by *Le Devoir de violence*: that brutality is the human condition. The coupling of exoticism and eroticism, both dependent on an objectification of the "other," is nowhere challenged. Objectifying women to make the point that Europe objectifies Africa writes women out of the picture.

To read Yambo Ouologuem's texts as engaging in a conspiratorial invitation to misbehavior raises the question of to whom this invitation is extended. The metaphorical relationship between plagiarism and political independence, between displaying the depravity of French pornography and staking a claim for social and cultural freedom of/in Africa, depends on reading the relationship between political and sexual discourses along the metaphorical axis of substitution. If we instead ask how these two are related syntagmatically, we are instead confronted with Ouologuem's displacement of political and cultural frustrations onto the bodies of women, white and black, who like the bull in a bullfight find their ultimate fulfillment through their eventual annihilation in a bloody display of male superiority. We can resist this metaphorical reading, though, by recasting the relationship between politics and gender as metonymy. If we understand metonymy as a chance relationship, we can uncouple political and sexual oppressions as naturally or necessarily linked. To read the oppression of women as not linked to political oppression opens up new possibilities for thinking through the position of women vis-à-vis both personal and political violence against their persons. In particular, we can take a look at the tendency of postcolonial discourse to silence women either in the heavily masculine discourse typical of nationalist movements or in the falsely universalized appeals to a "a new humanism," both of which subsume the particular experiences of women to "larger" concerns. To read political and sexual oppression in a metaphoric relation, that is, as analogous, in Ouologuem's body of work serves to naturalize the oppression of women. The subversion of the laws of patriarchy in writing via plagiarism may be enough to kill the father. You may displace him, you may be able to sleep with the mother through pornography, but you will never hear what she has to say about it.

Notes

1. An earlier version of this chapter was presented at the 23rd Annual African Literature Association Conference, Michigan State University, April 16-20, 1997.

2. The two exceptions to this are Christopher Miller, *Blank Darkness,* and James Olney, *Tell Me Africa.*

3. I am thinking here of Eileen Julien's essay, "Rape, Repression, and Narrative Form in *Le Devoir de violence* and *Le Vie et demie*," which will be discussed at length later in the chapter.

4. Appiah goes on to assert that Ouologuem's text ends up promoting a "new humanism" in the name of the downtrodden and oppressed "niggertrash," representative of both the slaves of former times and those who currently suffer under a vast array of African dictators. Although I agree with Appiah's argument that the novel delegitimates the naturalizing tendencies of nationalism, I do not find the extension of this argument to the promotion of a "new humanism" to be convincing. Nihilism does not erect new positive values to replace those that it discredits.

5. Thomas Hale has shown very thoroughly the great extent to which Ouologuem uses African traditions of many types, especially oral epics and Arabic language historians of West and Sahelian Africa. See *Scribe, Griot, and Novelist,* 135-159.

6. "This technique, which I will call the technique of subversion, does violence not only to everything that the African novel represented before 1968, but also, on one hand, to the acquired notions of the political and social roles of tradition, and on the other hand, to the notions of literary propriety." Translation mine.

7. This is a summary of Julien's essay cited in note 3.

8. Later in his essay, Fatunde goes on to question the ideological ramification of Ouologuem's portrayal because the narrative displays the misery of the working class without ever suggesting that the working class responds to the violence wrought against them. In Ouologuem's *Bound to Violence,* they are, Fatunde argues, merely passive victims suffering from an ahistorical and eternal violence against them, and thus Ouologuem's narrative ultimately ends up supporting the exploitative status quo and those who benefit from it. In a response to this type of reading of *Bound to Violence,* Christopher Wise argues that a more careful reading of the novel based in the traditions of Sufism show Ouologuem to be a strident critic of a practice of Islam that has worked to support exploitative governments and tyrants at the expense of both the poor and the true nature of Islam. Thus, Wise argues, we can read Ouologuem as truly speaking up for the liberation of the oppressed—their liberation from secular authorities and secularized Islam used to support those illegitimate authorities. See Wise, "Qur'anic Hermeneutics, Sufism, and *Le Devoir de Violence*: Yambo Ouologuem as Marabout Novelist."

9. "Women alone, you are like Negros in that your status holds you on the outside of life, relegated to the marginal society of minority groups." Translation mine.

10. This echoes a similar distinction made by Fanon in *Black Skins, White Masks.* In her essay, "The Nigger of the Narcissist: History, Sexuality and Intertextuality in Maryse Condé's *Heremakhonon,*" Susan Andrade has shown how Fanon attributes to black men an understandable, if lamentable, motivation in seeking partners of a different race, whereas his discussion of black women who seek partners of a different race claims that they are motivated purely and simply by self-hatred.

11. The difference between pornography and eroticism is indeed a difficult one to draw with any convincing certainty. Here, I refer back to Ouologuem's own definition of pornography as something that lacks the "psychological dimension" of eroticism. The story of the African safari that I discuss in more length below is singled out by Ouologuem as lacking this depth.

12. This text has not been translated in its entirety: short sections of it are translated by both Olney and Miller. This passage and all that follow are my translations, with reference to the parts that Olney and Miller have translated elsewhere. P. 18.

13. Particularly significant in this regard is the use of a scene where a woman is subjected to cunnilingus performed by a dog. It is a scene of this type that raised the most vociferous objections to *Le Devoir de violence.*

14. Miller goes on to argue that Ouologuem is ultimately less successful at disrupting European discourse in this story because he gets caught up in the "trap of libertinism" (245), whereby the act of promoting Africans as equally sexual and free subjects as Europeans recreates the act of reducing them to purely sexual objects.

Bibliography

[Editor's Note: See previous essay for complete bibliography.]

Pius Ngandu Nkashama (essay date summer 2009)

SOURCE: Nkashama, Pius Ngandu. "Lettres maliennes: Figures et configurations de l'activite litteraire au Mali." *Research in African Literatures* 40, no. 2 (summer 2009): 240-41.

[*In the following essay, Nkashama discusses a recently published anthology of Malian authors including content from Ouologuem.*]

Classical anthologies have only retained the "cult" literary figures of Mali—Hampate Ba, Seydou Badian, Yambo Ouologuem, Ibrahima Ly, mythic works, historical place-names (Segou, Djenne, Timbuktu), and symbolic landmarks (Moussa Kankan). Rarely are literary references associated with periods of production, and even less with the political circumstances of their appearances. It is true that those writers made a mark in their time on the literature of Negritude, and their works took up, with particular mastery, the themes of revolt against the colonizer, respect for traditions, or even the coming of a new African history.

Far from the stereotypes made popular in textbooks, the history of Mali disappeared behind fascinating images, even as the specialists of the genre seemed to conceal within literary configurations the social and especially the political tragedies that shook the same country over and over again. The hypothesis of Sebastien Le Potvin's books goes beyond the preliminaries of "Black African" texts. The author capably shows that the writers who seemed to be "visionaries" for the rest of the continent had been persecuted, imprisoned, and often exiled far from their families by the successive dictatorships that held a grip with as much, if not more, cruelty than anywhere else. Their productions are thus borne along by a common destiny that should assume primary place in any analysis of related texts and contexts.

The three parts of the work clearly illustrate these dramatic trajectories and implicate, throughout the critical study, both history and literature, beginning with "l'emprise ideologique sur le discours litteraire" (1960-1968) 'ideological influence on literary discourse (1960-1968),' part 1; "expressions de l'entre-cultures (1969-1991)" 'expressions of the between-cultures period (1969-1991,)' part 2, and finally, "la parole litteraire en quete de reconnaissance de l'autonomie (1992-2004)" 'literary work in search of the recognition of autonomy (1992-2004), part 3.' The "volonte d'historiciser le fait litteraire" 'will to historicize the literary' (14) drives the author to circumscribe acts of writing within the frontiers of a given national territory, and that is often determined by the exigencies of cultures that remain fixed and thus inadequate. Without lapsing into postulates of a "national literature," often decried in criticism, such a position has the advantage of linking the work to its immediate time, "puis aux temps prolonges de l'Histoire" 'then to the prolonged time periods of History.' Nevertheless, in considering "l'histoire politique de chaque pays [qui] s'est deroulee selon des evolutions interieures propres" 'the political history of each country as it has unfurled according to its own internal evolutions,' the author succeeds in explaining the permanent correspondences between the institutions of legitimation and the resulting literary expressions:

> Des textes crees comme des instruments de transformation sociale a la reception des memes textes vecus comme des outrages, les relations des ecrivains avec le pouvoir et avec leur lecteur commun se caracterisent par une histoire houleuse.

> From texts created as instruments of social transformation to the reception of those same texts experienced as outrages, the writers relationships with authority and with their common reader are characterized by a stormy history.

(2310)

To follow the historical dynamic of productions, the research is based upon the receptivity of the texts especially in scholarly and cultural milieux (notably in journals and textbooks), but it also calls upon the numerous experiences of editorial productivity that was sustained or fought by the powers in place.

This book is the result of a harvesting of first-hand facts, but also one of frank collaboration with many of Mali's authors who confided in all lucidity, sometimes at risk of facing the repressive forces of political torturers: prison for Seydou Badian, a mysterious death for Fily Dabo Sissoko, exile in the salt desert for Yambo Ouologuem, too oppressive solitude for Ibrahima Ly or Ismaila Samba Traore. It thus constitutes a sincere homage to the bravery of those who defied the tyrannies of the coups d'etat, and who patiently, at peril to their lives or the security of their respective families, contributed in one way or another to the advent of a new Mali, unshackled from its interior monsters, and turned toward another historical future.

The work is accompanied by many appendices, especially on the "historical chronology of the Republic of Mali," on "published literary production" in French, by genre, period, and place of publication, and finally an important "bio-bibliography" of the authors who figure in the summary.

FURTHER READING

Criticism

Sellin, Eric. "The Unknown Voice of Yambo Ouologuem." In *Yambo Ouologuem: Postcolonial Writer, Islamic Militant,* edited by Christopher Wise, pp. 67-87. Boulder and London: Lynne Rienner, 1999.
　　Traces the history of *Le devoir do violence.*

Willey, Ann Elizabeth. Review of *The Yambo Ouologuem Reader. Research in African Literatures* 40, no. 4 (2009): 190.
　　Notes differences in the latest translations of Ouologuem's writings.

Wise, Christopher, ed. *Yambo Ouologuem: Postcolonial Writer, Islamic Militant.* Boulder, Colo.: Lynne Rienner, 1999, 258 p.
　　Provides critical essays about Ouologuem and interviews with the author.

Additional coverage of Ouologuem's life and career is contained in the following sources published by Gale: *Contemporary Authors,* **Vols. 111, 176;** *Contemporary Literary Criticism,* **Vol. 146; and** *Literature Resource Center.*

How to Use This Index

The main references

Calvino, Italo
1923-1985 .... CLC 5, 8, 11, 22, 33, 39,
73; SSC 3, 48

list all author entries in the following Gale Literary Criticism series:

AAL = *Asian American Literature*
BG = *The Beat Generation: A Gale Critical Companion*
BLC = *Black Literature Criticism*
BLCS = *Black Literature Criticism Supplement*
CLC = *Contemporary Literary Criticism*
CLR = *Children's Literature Review*
CMLC = *Classical and Medieval Literature Criticism*
DC = *Drama Criticism*
FL = *Feminism in Literature: A Gale Critical Companion*
GL = *Gothic Literature: A Gale Critical Companion*
HLC = *Hispanic Literature Criticism*
HLCS = *Hispanic Literature Criticism Supplement*
HR = *Harlem Renaissance: A Gale Critical Companion*
LC = *Literature Criticism from 1400 to 1800*
NCLC = *Nineteenth-Century Literature Criticism*
NNAL = *Native North American Literature*
PC = *Poetry Criticism*
SSC = *Short Story Criticism*
TCLC = *Twentieth-Century Literary Criticism*
WLC = *World Literature Criticism, 1500 to the Present*
WLCS = *World Literature Criticism Supplement*

The cross-references

See also CA 85-88, 116; CANR 23, 61;
DAM NOV; DLB 196; EW 13; MTCW 1, 2;
RGSF 2; RGWL 2; SFW 4; SSFS 12

list all author entries in the following Gale biographical and literary sources:

AAYA = *Authors & Artists for Young Adults*
AFAW = *African American Writers*
AFW = *African Writers*
AITN = *Authors in the News*
AMW = *American Writers*
AMWR = *American Writers Retrospective Supplement*
AMWS = *American Writers Supplement*
ANW = *American Nature Writers*
AW = *Ancient Writers*
BEST = *Bestsellers*
BPFB = *Beacham's Encyclopedia of Popular Fiction: Biography and Resources*
BRW = *British Writers*
BRWS = *British Writers Supplement*
BW = *Black Writers*
BYA = *Beacham's Guide to Literature for Young Adults*
CA = *Contemporary Authors*
CAAS = *Contemporary Authors Autobiography Series*
CABS = *Contemporary Authors Bibliographical Series*
CAD = *Contemporary American Dramatists*
CANR = *Contemporary Authors New Revision Series*
CAP = *Contemporary Authors Permanent Series*
CBD = *Contemporary British Dramatists*
CCA = *Contemporary Canadian Authors*
CD = *Contemporary Dramatists*
CDALB = *Concise Dictionary of American Literary Biography*

CDALBS = Concise Dictionary of American Literary Biography Supplement
CDBLB = Concise Dictionary of British Literary Biography
CMW = St. James Guide to Crime & Mystery Writers
CN = Contemporary Novelists
CP = Contemporary Poets
CPW = Contemporary Popular Writers
CSW = Contemporary Southern Writers
CWD = Contemporary Women Dramatists
CWP = Contemporary Women Poets
CWRI = St. James Guide to Children's Writers
CWW = Contemporary World Writers
DA = DISCovering Authors
DA3 = DISCovering Authors 3.0
DAB = DISCovering Authors: British Edition
DAC = DISCovering Authors: Canadian Edition
DAM = DISCovering Authors: Modules
   DRAM: Dramatists Module; **MST:** Most-studied Authors Module;
   MULT: Multicultural Authors Module; **NOV:** Novelists Module;
   POET: Poets Module; **POP:** Popular Fiction and Genre Authors Module
DFS = Drama for Students
DLB = Dictionary of Literary Biography
DLBD = Dictionary of Literary Biography Documentary Series
DLBY = Dictionary of Literary Biography Yearbook
DNFS = Literature of Developing Nations for Students
EFS = Epics for Students
EW = European Writers
EWL = Encyclopedia of World Literature in the 20th Century
EXPN = Exploring Novels
EXPP = Exploring Poetry
EXPS = Exploring Short Stories
FANT = St. James Guide to Fantasy Writers
FW = Feminist Writers
GFL = Guide to French Literature, Beginnings to 1789, 1798 to the Present
GLL = Gay and Lesbian Literature
HGG = St. James Guide to Horror, Ghost & Gothic Writers
HW = Hispanic Writers
IDFW = International Dictionary of Films and Filmmakers: Writers and Production Artists
IDTP = International Dictionary of Theatre: Playwrights
LAIT = Literature and Its Times
LAW = Latin American Writers
JRDA = Junior DISCovering Authors
MAICYA = Major Authors and Illustrators for Children and Young Adults
MAICYAS = Major Authors and Illustrators for Children and Young Adults Supplement
MAWW = Modern American Women Writers
MJW = Modern Japanese Writers
MTCW = Major 20th-Century Writers
NCFS = Nonfiction Classics for Students
NFS = Novels for Students
PAB = Poets: American and British
PFS = Poetry for Students
RGAL = Reference Guide to American Literature
RGEL = Reference Guide to English Literature
RGSF = Reference Guide to Short Fiction
RGWL = Reference Guide to World Literature
RHW = Twentieth-Century Romance and Historical Writers
SAAS = Something about the Author Autobiography Series
SATA = Something about the Author
SFW = St. James Guide to Science Fiction Writers
SSFS = Short Stories for Students
TCWW = Twentieth-Century Western Writers
WLIT = World Literature and Its Times
WP = World Poets
YABC = Yesterday's Authors of Books for Children
YAW = St. James Guide to Young Adult Writers

Literary Criticism Series
Cumulative Author Index

Adorno, Theodor W(iesengrund)
1903-1969 .... **TCLC 111**
See also CA 89-92; 25-28R; CANR 89;
DLB 242; EWL 3

Ady, Endre 1877-1919 .... **TCLC 11**
See also CA 107; CDWLB 4; DLB 215;
EW 9; EWL 3

A.E.
See Russell, George William

Aelfric c. 955-c. 1010 .... **CMLC 46**
See also DLB 146

Aelred of Rievaulx 1110-1167 ..... **CMLC 123**

Aeschines c. 390B.C.-c. 320B.C. .... **CMLC 47**
See also DLB 176

Aeschylus 525(?)B.C.-456(?)B.C. .. **CMLC 11,
51, 94; DC 8; WLCS**
See also AW 1; CDWLB 1; DA; DAB;
DAC; DAM DRAM, MST; DFS 5, 10,
26; DLB 176; LMFS 1; RGWL 2, 3;
TWA; WLIT 8

Aesop 620(?)B.C.-560(?)B.C. .... **CMLC 24**
See also CLR 14; MAICYA 1, 2; SATA 64

Affable Hawk
See MacCarthy, Sir (Charles Otto) Desmond

Africa, Ben
See Bosman, Herman Charles

Afrika, Jan
See Breytenbach, Breyten

Afton, Effie
See Harper, Frances Ellen Watkins

Agapida, Fray Antonio
See Irving, Washington

Agar, Emile
See Kacew, Romain

Agee, James 1909-1955 ...... **TCLC 1, 19, 180**
See also AAYA 44; AITN 1; AMW; CA 108;
148; CANR 131; CDALB 1941-1968;
DAM NOV; DLB 2, 26, 152; DLBY
1989; EWL 3; LAIT 3; LATS 1:2; MAL
5; MTCW 2; MTFW 2005; NFS 22;
RGAL 4; TUS

Agee, James Rufus
See Agee, James

A Gentlewoman in New England
See Bradstreet, Anne

A Gentlewoman in Those Parts
See Bradstreet, Anne

Aghill, Gordon
See Silverberg, Robert

Agnon, Shmuel Yosef Halevi
See Agnon, S.Y.

Agnon, S.Y. 1888-1970 .... **CLC 4, 8, 14; SSC
30, 120; TCLC 151**
See also CA 17-18; 25-28R; CANR 60, 102;
CAP 2; DLB 329; EWL 3; MTCW 1, 2;
RGHL; RGSF 2; RGWL 2, 3; WLIT 6

Agrippa von Nettesheim, Henry Cornelius
1486-1535 .... **LC 27**

Aguilera Malta, Demetrio
1909-1981 .... **HLCS 1**
See also CA 111; 124; CANR 87; DAM
MULT, NOV; DLB 145; EWL 3; HW 1;
RGWL 3

Agustini, Delmira 1886-1914 .... **HLCS 1**
See also CA 166; DLB 290; HW 1, 2; LAW

Aherne, Owen
See Cassill, R(onald) V(erlin)

Ai 1947-2010 .... **CLC 4, 14, 69; PC 72**
See also CA 85-88; CAAS 13; CANR 70;
CP 6, 7; DLB 120; PFS 16

Aickman, Robert (Fordyce)
1914-1981 .... **CLC 57**
See also CA 5-8R; CANR 3, 72, 100; DLB
261; HGG; SUFW 1, 2

Aidoo, (Christina) Ama Ata
1942- .... **BLCS; CLC 177**
See also AFW; BRWS 15; BW 1; CA 101;
CANR 62, 144; CD 5, 6; CDWLB 3; CN

6, 7; CWD; CWP; DLB 117; DNFS 1, 2;
EWL 3; FW; WLIT 2

Aiken, Conrad 1889-1973 ... **CLC 1, 3, 5, 10,
52; PC 26; SSC 9**
See also AMW; CA 5-8R; 45-48; CANR 4,
60; CDALB 1929-1941; CN 1; CP 1;
DAM NOV, POET; DLB 9, 45, 102; EWL
3; EXPS; HGG; MAL 5; MTCW 1, 2;
MTFW 2005; PFS 24; RGAL 4; RGSF 2;
SATA 3, 30; SSFS 8; TUS

Aiken, Conrad Potter
See Aiken, Conrad

Aiken, Joan (Delano) 1924-2004 ...... **CLC 35**
See also AAYA 1, 25; CA 9-12R, 182; 223;
CAAE 182; CANR 4, 23, 34, 64, 121;
CLR 1, 19, 90; DLB 161; FANT; HGG;
JRDA; MAICYA 1, 2; MTCW 1; RHW;
SAAS 1; SATA 2, 30, 73; SATA-Essay
109; SATA-Obit 152; SUFW 2; WYA;
YAW

Ainsworth, William Harrison
1805-1882 .... **NCLC 13**
See also DLB 21; HGG; RGEL 2; SATA
24; SUFW 1

Aitmatov, Chingiz 1928-2008 .. **CLC 71; SSC
131**
See also CA 103; CANR 38; CWW 2; DLB
302; EWL 3; MTCW 1; RGSF 2; SATA
56

Aitmatov, Chingiz Torekulovich
See Aitmatov, Chingiz

Ajar, Emile
See Kacew, Romain

Akers, Floyd
See Baum, L. Frank

Akhmadulina, Bella 1937- ... **CLC 53; PC 43**
See also CA 65-68; CWP; CWW 2; DAM
POET; EWL 3

Akhmadulina, Bella Akhatovna
See Akhmadulina, Bella

Akhmatova, Anna 1888-1966 ..... **CLC 11, 25,
64, 126; PC 2, 55**
See also CA 19-20; 25-28R; CANR 35;
CAP 1; DA3; DAM POET; DLB 295; EW
10; EWL 3; FL 1:5; MTCW 1, 2; PFS 18,
27, 32; RGWL 2, 3

Aksakov, Sergei Timofeevich
1791-1859 .... **NCLC 2, 181**
See also DLB 198

Aksenov, Vasilii
See Aksyonov, Vassily

Aksenov, Vasilii Pavlovich
See Aksyonov, Vassily

Aksenov, Vassily
See Aksyonov, Vassily

Akst, Daniel 1956- .... **CLC 109**
See also CA 161; CANR 110

Aksyonov, Vassily 1932-2009 ..... **CLC 22, 37,
101**
See also CA 53-56; CANR 12, 48, 77;
CWW 2; DLB 302; EWL 3

Aksyonov, Vassily Pavlovich
See Aksyonov, Vassily

Akutagawa Ryunosuke 1892-1927 ... **SSC 44;
TCLC 16**
See also CA 117; 154; DLB 180; EWL 3;
MJW; RGSF 2; RGWL 2, 3

Alabaster, William 1568-1640 .... **LC 90**
See also DLB 132; RGEL 2

Alain 1868-1951 .... **TCLC 41**
See also CA 163; EWL 3; GFL 1789 to the
Present

Alain de Lille c. 1116-c. 1203 .... **CMLC 53**
See also DLB 208

Alain-Fournier
See Fournier, Henri-Alban

Al-Amin, Jamil Abdullah 1943- ...... **BLC 1:1**
See also BW 1, 3; CA 112; 125; CANR 82;
DAM MULT

Alanus de Insluis
See Alain de Lille

Alarcon, Pedro Antonio de
1833-1891 .... **NCLC 1, 219; SSC 64**

Alas (y Urena), Leopoldo (Enrique Garcia)
1852-1901 .... **TCLC 29**
See also CA 113; 131; HW 1; RGSF 2

Albee, Edward (III) 1928- ..... **CLC 1, 2, 3, 5,
9, 11, 13, 25, 53, 86, 113; DC 11; WLC
1**
See also AAYA 51; AITN 1; AMW; CA
5-8R; CABS 3; CAD; CANR 8, 54, 74,
124; CD 5, 6; CDALB 1941-1968; DA;
DA3; DAB; DAC; DAM DRAM, MST;
DFS 25; DLB 7, 266; EWL 3; INT
CANR-8; LAIT 4; LMFS 2; MAL 5;
MTCW 1, 2; MTFW 2005; RGAL 4; TUS

Albee, Edward Franklin
See Albee, Edward (III)

Alberti, Leon Battista 1404-1472 ...... **LC 173**

Alberti, Rafael 1902-1999 .... **CLC 7**
See also CA 85-88; 185; CANR 81; CWW
2; DLB 108; EWL 3; HW 2; RGWL 2, 3

Alberti Merello, Rafael
See Alberti, Rafael

Albert of Saxony c. 1316-1390 .... **CMLC 110**

Albert the Great 1193(?)-1280 ...... **CMLC 16**
See also DLB 115

Alcaeus c. 620B.C.- .... **CMLC 65**
See also DLB 176

Alcala-Galiano, Juan Valera y
See Valera y Alcala-Galiano, Juan

Alcayaga, Lucila Godoy
See Mistral, Gabriela

Alciato, Andrea 1492-1550 .... **LC 116**

Alcott, Amos Bronson 1799-1888 ... **NCLC 1,
167**
See also DLB 1, 223

Alcott, Louisa May 1832-1888 . **NCLC 6, 58,
83, 218; SSC 27, 98; WLC 1**
See also AAYA 20; AMWS 1; BPFB 1;
BYA 2; CDALB 1865-1917; CLR 1, 38,
109; DA; DA3; DAB; DAC; DAM MST,
NOV; DLB 1, 42, 79, 223, 239, 242;
DLBD 14; FL 1:2; FW; JRDA; LAIT 2;
MAICYA 1, 2; NFS 12; RGAL 4; SATA
100; TUS; WCH; WYA; YABC 1; YAW

Alcuin c. 730-804 .... **CMLC 69**
See also DLB 148

Aldanov, M. A.
See Aldanov, Mark (Alexandrovich)

Aldanov, Mark (Alexandrovich)
1886-1957 .... **TCLC 23**
See also CA 118; 181; DLB 317

Aldhelm c. 639-709 .... **CMLC 90**

Aldington, Richard 1892-1962 .... **CLC 49**
See also CA 85-88; CANR 45; DLB 20, 36,
100, 149; LMFS 2; RGEL 2

Aldiss, Brian W. 1925- .. **CLC 5, 14, 40, 290;
SSC 36**
See also AAYA 42; CA 5-8R, 190; CAAE
190; CAAS 2; CANR 5, 28, 64, 121, 168;
CN 1, 2, 3, 4, 5, 6, 7; DAM NOV; DLB
14, 261, 271; MTCW 1, 2; MTFW 2005;
SATA 34; SCFW 1, 2; SFW 4

Aldiss, Brian Wilson
See Aldiss, Brian W.

Aldrich, Ann
See Meaker, Marijane

Aldrich, Bess Streeter
1881-1954 .... **TCLC 125**
See also CLR 70; TCWW 2

Alegria, Claribel
See Alegria, Claribel

Alegria, Claribel 1924- .... **CLC 75; HLCS 1; PC 26**
See also CA 131; CAAS 15; CANR 66, 94, 134; CWW 2; DAM MULT; DLB 145, 283; EWL 3; HW 1; MTCW 2; MTFW 2005; PFS 21

Alegria, Claribel Joy
See Alegria, Claribel

Alegria, Fernando 1918-2005 .... **CLC 57**
See also CA 9-12R; CANR 5, 32, 72; EWL 3; HW 1, 2

Aleixandre, Vicente 1898-1984 .... **HLCS 1; TCLC 113**
See also CANR 81; DLB 108, 329; EWL 3; HW 2; MTCW 1, 2; RGWL 2, 3

Alekseev, Konstantin Sergeivich
See Stanislavsky, Constantin

Alekseyer, Konstantin Sergeyevich
See Stanislavsky, Constantin

Aleman, Mateo 1547-1615(?) .... **LC 81**

Alencar, Jose de 1829-1877 .... **NCLC 157**
See also DLB 307; LAW; WLIT 1

Alencon, Marguerite d'
See de Navarre, Marguerite

Alepoudelis, Odysseus
See Elytis, Odysseus

Aleshkovsky, Joseph 1929- .... **CLC 44**
See also CA 121; 128; DLB 317

Aleshkovsky, Yuz
See Aleshkovsky, Joseph

Alexander, Barbara
See Ehrenreich, Barbara

Alexander, Lloyd 1924-2007 .... **CLC 35**
See also AAYA 1, 27; BPFB 1; BYA 5, 6, 7, 9, 10, 11; CA 1-4R; 260; CANR 1, 24, 38, 55, 113; CLR 1, 5, 48; CWRI 5; DLB 52; FANT; JRDA; MAICYA 1, 2; MAIC-YAS 1; MTCW 1; SAAS 19; SATA 3, 49, 81, 129, 135; SATA-Obit 182; SUFW; TUS; WYA; YAW

Alexander, Lloyd Chudley
See Alexander, Lloyd

Alexander, Meena 1951- .... **CLC 121**
See also CA 115; CANR 38, 70, 146; CP 5, 6, 7; CWP; DLB 323; FW

Alexander, Rae Pace
See Alexander, Raymond Pace

Alexander, Raymond Pace
1898-1974 .... **SSC 62**
See also CA 97-100; SATA 22; SSFS 4

Alexander, Samuel 1859-1938 .... **TCLC 77**

Alexeiev, Konstantin
See Stanislavsky, Constantin

Alexeyev, Constantin Sergeivich
See Stanislavsky, Constantin

Alexeyev, Konstantin Sergeyevich
See Stanislavsky, Constantin

Alexie, Sherman 1966- .... **CLC 96, 154; NNAL; PC 53; SSC 107**
See also AAYA 28; BYA 15; CA 138; CANR 65, 95, 133, 174; CN 7; DA3; DAM MULT; DLB 175, 206, 278; LATS 1:2; MTCW 2; MTFW 2005; NFS 17, 31; SSFS 18

Alexie, Sherman Joseph, Jr.
See Alexie, Sherman

al-Farabi 870(?)-950 .... **CMLC 58**
See also DLB 115

Alfau, Felipe 1902-1999 .... **CLC 66**
See also CA 137

Alfieri, Vittorio 1749-1803 .... **NCLC 101**
See also EW 4; RGWL 2, 3; WLIT 7

Alfonso X 1221-1284 .... **CMLC 78**

Alfred, Jean Gaston
See Ponge, Francis

Alger, Horatio, Jr. 1832-1899 .... **NCLC 8, 83**
See also CLR 87; DLB 42; LAIT 2; RGAL 4; SATA 16; TUS

Al-Ghazali, Muhammad ibn Muhammad
1058-1111 .... **CMLC 50**
See also DLB 115

Algren, Nelson 1909-1981 ..... **CLC 4, 10, 33; SSC 33**
See also AMWS 9; BPFB 1; CA 13-16R; 103; CANR 20, 61; CDALB 1941-1968; CN 1, 2; DLB 9; DLBY 1981, 1982, 2000; EWL 3; MAL 5; MTCW 1, 2; MTFW 2005; RGAL 4; RGSF 2

al-Hamadhani 967-1007 .... **CMLC 93**
See also WLIT 6

al-Hariri, al-Qasim ibn 'Ali Abu Muhammad al-Basri
1054-1122 .... **CMLC 63**
See also RGWL 3

Ali, Ahmed 1908-1998 .... **CLC 69**
See also CA 25-28R; CANR 15, 34; CN 1, 2, 3, 4, 5; DLB 323; EWL 3

Ali, Tariq 1943- .... **CLC 173**
See also CA 25-28R; CANR 10, 99, 161, 196

Alighieri, Dante
See Dante

al-Kindi, Abu Yusuf Ya'qub ibn Ishaq c.
801-c. 873 .... **CMLC 80**

Allan, John B.
See Westlake, Donald E.

Allan, Sidney
See Hartmann, Sadakichi

Allan, Sydney
See Hartmann, Sadakichi

Allard, Janet .... **CLC 59**

Allen, Betsy
See Harrison, Elizabeth (Allen) Cavanna

Allen, Edward 1948- .... **CLC 59**

Allen, Fred 1894-1956 .... **TCLC 87**

Allen, Paula Gunn 1939-2008 . **CLC 84, 202, 280; NNAL**
See also AMWS 4; CA 112; 143; 272; CANR 63, 130; CWP; DA3; DAM MULT; DLB 175; FW; MTCW 2; MTFW 2005; RGAL 4; TCWW 2

Allen, Roland
See Ayckbourn, Alan

Allen, Sarah A.
See Hopkins, Pauline Elizabeth

Allen, Sidney H.
See Hartmann, Sadakichi

Allen, Woody 1935- ..... **CLC 16, 52, 195, 288**
See also AAYA 10, 51; AMWS 15; CA 33-36R; CANR 27, 38, 63, 128, 172; DAM POP; DLB 44; MTCW 1; SSFS 21

Allende, Isabel 1942- ... **CLC 39, 57, 97, 170, 264; HLC 1; SSC 65; WLCS**
See also AAYA 18, 70; CA 125; 130; CANR 51, 74, 129, 165; CDWLB 3; CLR 99; CWW 2; DA3; DAM MULT; NOV; DLB 145; DNFS 1; EWL 3; FL 1:5; FW; HW 1, 2; INT CA-130; LAIT 5; LAWS 1; LMFS 2; MTCW 1, 2; MTFW 2005; NCFS 1; NFS 6, 18, 29; RGSF 2; RGWL 3; SATA 163; SSFS 11, 16; WLIT 1

Alleyn, Ellen
See Rossetti, Christina

Alleyne, Carla D. .... **CLC 65**

Allingham, Margery (Louise)
1904-1966 .... **CLC 19**
See also CA 5-8R; 25-28R; CANR 4, 58; CMW 4; DLB 77; MSW; MTCW 1, 2

Allingham, William 1824-1889 ...... **NCLC 25**
See also DLB 35; RGEL 2

Allison, Dorothy E. 1949- . **CLC 78, 153, 290**
See also AAYA 53; CA 140; CANR 66, 107; CN 7; CSW; DA3; DLB 350; FW; MTCW 2; MTFW 2005; NFS 11; RGAL 4

Alloula, Malek .... **CLC 65**

Allston, Washington 1779-1843 .... **NCLC 2**
See also DLB 1, 235

Almedingen, E. M.
See Almedingen, Martha Edith von

Almedingen, Martha Edith von
1898-1971 .... **CLC 12**
See also CA 1-4R; CANR 1; SATA 3

Almodovar, Pedro 1949(?)- .... **CLC 114, 229; HLCS 1**
See also CA 133; CANR 72, 151; HW 2

Almqvist, Carl Jonas Love
1793-1866 .... **NCLC 42**

al-Mutanabbi, Ahmad ibn al-Husayn Abu al-Tayyib al-Jufi al-Kindi
915-965 .... **CMLC 66**
See also RGWL 3; WLIT 6

Alonso, Damaso 1898-1990 .... **CLC 14**
See also CA 110; 131; 130; CANR 72; DLB 108; EWL 3; HW 1, 2

Alov
See Gogol, Nikolai

al'Sadaawi, Nawal
See El Saadawi, Nawal

al-Shaykh, Hanan 1945- .... **CLC 218**
See also CA 135; CANR 111; CWW 2; DLB 346; EWL 3; WLIT 6

Al Siddik
See Rolfe, Frederick (William Serafino Austin Lewis Mary)

Alta 1942- .... **CLC 19**
See also CA 57-60

Alter, Robert B. 1935- .... **CLC 34**
See also CA 49-52; CANR 1, 47, 100, 160, 201

Alter, Robert Bernard
See Alter, Robert B.

Alther, Lisa 1944- .... **CLC 7, 41**
See also BPFB 1; CA 65-68; CAAS 30; CANR 12, 30, 51, 180; CN 4, 5, 6, 7; CSW; GLL 2; MTCW 1

Althusser, L.
See Althusser, Louis

Althusser, Louis 1918-1990 .... **CLC 106**
See also CA 131; 132; CANR 102; DLB 242

Altman, Robert 1925-2006 .... **CLC 16, 116, 242**
See also CA 73-76; 254; CANR 43

Alurista
See Urista, Alberto

Alvarez, A. 1929- .... **CLC 5, 13**
See also CA 1-4R; CANR 3, 33, 63, 101, 134; CN 3, 4, 5, 6; CP 1, 2, 3, 4, 5, 6, 7; DLB 14, 40; MTFW 2005

Alvarez, Alejandro Rodriguez
1903-1965 . **CLC 49; DC 32; TCLC 199**
See also CA 131; 93-96; EWL 3; HW 1

Alvarez, Julia 1950- .. **CLC 93, 274; HLCS 1**
See also AAYA 25; AMWS 7; CA 147; CANR 69, 101, 133, 166; DA3; DLB 282; LATS 1:2; LLW; MTCW 2; MTFW 2005; NFS 5, 9; SATA 129; SSFS 27, 31; WLIT 1

Alvaro, Corrado 1896-1956 .... **TCLC 60**
See also CA 163; DLB 264; EWL 3

Amado, Jorge 1912-2001 ... **CLC 13, 40, 106, 232; HLC 1**
See also CA 77-80; 201; CANR 35, 74, 135; CWW 2; DAM MULT; NOV; DLB 113, 307; EWL 3; HW 2; LAW; LAWS 1; MTCW 1, 2; MTFW 2005; RGWL 2, 3; TWA; WLIT 1

Ambler, Eric 1909-1998 .... **CLC 4, 6, 9**
See also BRWS 4; CA 9-12R; 171; CANR 7, 38, 74; CMW 4; CN 1, 2, 3, 4, 5, 6; DLB 77; MSW; MTCW 1, 2; TEA

Ambrose c. 339-c. 397 .... **CMLC 103**

Ambrose, Stephen E. 1936-2002 .... **CLC 145**
See also AAYA 44; CA 1-4R; 209; CANR 3, 43, 57, 83, 105; MTFW 2005; NCFS 2; SATA 40, 138

4, 5, 6, 7; CPW; DA; DA3; DAC; DAM
MST, MULT, POET, POP; DFS 3, 11, 16;
DLB 5, 7, 16, 38; DLBD 8; EWL 3; MAL
5; MTCW 1, 2; MTFW 2005; PFS 9;
RGAL 4; TCLE 1:1; TUS; WP

Baratynsky, Evgenii Abramovich
1800-1844 .... **NCLC 103**
See also DLB 205

Barbauld, Anna Laetitia
1743-1825 .... **NCLC 50, 185**
See also DLB 107, 109, 142, 158, 336;
RGEL 2

Barbellion, W. N. P.
See Cummings, Bruce F.

Barber, Benjamin R. 1939- .... **CLC 141**
See also CA 29-32R; CANR 12, 32, 64, 119

Barbera, Jack 1945- .... **CLC 44**
See also CA 110; CANR 45

Barbera, Jack Vincent
See Barbera, Jack

Barbey d'Aurevilly, Jules-Amedee
1808-1889 .... **NCLC 1, 213; SSC 17**
See also DLB 119; GFL 1789 to the Present

Barbour, John c. 1316-1395 .... **CMLC 33**
See also DLB 146

Barbusse, Henri 1873-1935 .... **TCLC 5**
See also CA 105; 154; DLB 65; EWL 3;
RGWL 2, 3

Barclay, Alexander c. 1475-1552 .... **LC 109**
See also DLB 132

Barclay, Bill
See Moorcock, Michael

Barclay, William Ewert
See Moorcock, Michael

Barclay, William Ewert
See Moorcock, Michael

Barea, Arturo 1897-1957 .... **TCLC 14**
See also CA 111; 201

Barfoot, Joan 1946- .... **CLC 18**
See also CA 105; CANR 141, 179

Barham, Richard Harris
1788-1845 .... **NCLC 77**
See also DLB 159

Baring, Maurice 1874-1945 .... **TCLC 8**
See also CA 105; 168; DLB 34; HGG

Baring-Gould, Sabine 1834-1924 ... **TCLC 88**
See also DLB 156, 190

Barker, Clive 1952- .... **CLC 52, 205; SSC 53**
See also AAYA 10, 54; BEST 90:3; BPFB
1; CA 121; 129; CANR 71, 111, 133, 187;
CPW; DA3; DAM POP; DLB 261; HGG;
INT CA-129; MTCW 1, 2; MTFW 2005;
SUFW 2

Barker, George Granville
1913-1991 .... **CLC 8, 48; PC 77**
See also CA 9-12R; 135; CANR 7, 38; CP
1, 2, 3, 4, 5; DAM POET; DLB 20; EWL
3; MTCW 1

Barker, Harley Granville
See Granville-Barker, Harley

Barker, Howard 1946- .... **CLC 37**
See also CA 102; CBD; CD 5, 6; DLB 13,
233

Barker, Jane 1652-1732 .... **LC 42, 82; PC 91**
See also DLB 39, 131

Barker, Pat 1943- .... **CLC 32, 94, 146**
See also BRWS 4; CA 117; 122; CANR 50,
101, 148, 195; CN 6, 7; DLB 271, 326;
INT CA-122

Barker, Patricia
See Barker, Pat

Barlach, Ernst (Heinrich)
1870-1938 .... **TCLC 84**
See also CA 178; DLB 56, 118; EWL 3

Barlow, Joel 1754-1812 .... **NCLC 23, 223**
See also AMWS 2; DLB 37; RGAL 4

Barnard, Mary (Ethel) 1909- .... **CLC 48**
See also CA 21-22; CAP 2; CP 1

Barnes, Djuna 1892-1982 .... **CLC 3, 4, 8, 11,
29, 127; SSC 3; TCLC 212**
See also AMWS 3; CA 9-12R; 107; CAD;
CANR 16, 55; CN 1, 2, 3; CWD; DLB 4,
9, 45; EWL 3; GLL 1; MAL 5; MTCW 1,
2; MTFW 2005; RGAL 4; TCLE 1:1;
TUS

Barnes, Jim 1933- .... **NNAL**
See also CA 108, 175, 272; CAAE 175,
272; CAAS 28; DLB 175

Barnes, Julian 1946- .... **CLC 42, 141**
See also BRWS 4; CA 102; CANR 19, 54,
115, 137, 195; CN 4, 5, 6, 7; DAB; DLB
194; DLBY 1993; EWL 3; MTCW 2;
MTFW 2005; SSFS 24

Barnes, Julian Patrick
See Barnes, Julian

Barnes, Peter 1931-2004 .... **CLC 5, 56**
See also CA 65-68; 230; CAAS 12; CANR
33, 34, 64, 113; CBD; CD 5, 6; DFS 6;
DLB 13, 233; MTCW 1

Barnes, William 1801-1886 .... **NCLC 75**
See also DLB 32

Baroja, Pio 1872-1956 .... **HLC 1; SSC 112;
TCLC 8**
See also CA 104; 247; EW 9

Baroja y Nessi, Pio
See Baroja, Pio

Baron, David
See Pinter, Harold

Baron Corvo
See Rolfe, Frederick (William Serafino
Austin Lewis Mary)

Barondess, Sue K. 1926-1977 .... **CLC 3, 8**
See also CA 1-4R; 69-72; CANR 1

Barondess, Sue Kaufman
See Barondess, Sue K.

Baron de Teive
See Pessoa, Fernando

Baroness Von S.
See Zangwill, Israel

Barres, (Auguste-)Maurice
1862-1923 .... **TCLC 47**
See also CA 164; DLB 123; GFL 1789 to
the Present

Barreto, Afonso Henrique de Lima
See Lima Barreto, Afonso Henrique de

Barrett, Andrea 1954- .... **CLC 150**
See also CA 156; CANR 92, 186; CN 7;
DLB 335; SSFS 24

Barrett, Michele
See Barrett, Michele

Barrett, Michele 1949- .... **CLC 65**
See also CA 280

Barrett, Roger Syd
See Barrett, Syd

Barrett, Syd 1946-2006 .... **CLC 35**

Barrett, William (Christopher)
1913-1992 .... **CLC 27**
See also CA 13-16R; 139; CANR 11, 67;
INT CANR-11

Barrett Browning, Elizabeth
1806-1861 ...... **NCLC 1, 16, 61, 66, 170;
PC 6, 62; WLC 1**
See also AAYA 63; BRW 4; CDBLB 1832-
1890; DA; DA3; DAB; DAC; DAM MST,
POET; DLB 32, 199; EXPP; FL 1:2; PAB;
PFS 2, 16, 23; TEA; WLIT 4; WP

Barrie, Baronet
See Barrie, J. M.

Barrie, J. M. 1860-1937 .... **TCLC 2, 164**
See also BRWS 3; BYA 4, 5; CA 104; 136;
CANR 77; CDBLB 1890-1914; CLR 16,
124; CWRI 5; DA3; DAB; DAM DRAM;
DFS 7; DLB 10, 141, 156, 352; EWL 3;
FANT; MAICYA 1, 2; MTCW 2; MTFW
2005; SATA 100; SUFW; WCH; WLIT 4;
YABC 1

Barrie, James Matthew
See Barrie, J. M.

Barrington, Michael
See Moorcock, Michael

Barrol, Grady
See Bograd, Larry

Barry, Mike
See Malzberg, Barry N(athaniel)

Barry, Philip 1896-1949 .... **TCLC 11**
See also CA 109; 199; DFS 9; DLB 7, 228;
MAL 5; RGAL 4

Barry, Sebastian 1955- .... **CLC 282**
See also CA 117; CANR 122, 193; CD 5,
6; DLB 245

Bart, Andre Schwarz
See Schwarz-Bart, Andre

Barth, John 1930- ... **CLC 1, 2, 3, 5, 7, 9, 10,
14, 27, 51, 89; SSC 10, 89**
See also AITN 1, 2; AMW; BPFB 1; CA
1-4R; CABS 1; CANR 5, 23, 49, 64, 113,
204; CN 1, 2, 3, 4, 5, 6, 7; DAM NOV;
DLB 2, 227; EWL 3; FANT; MAL 5;
MTCW 1; RGAL 4; RGSF 2; RHW;
SSFS 6; TUS

Barth, John Simmons
See Barth, John

Barthelme, Donald 1931-1989 ... **CLC 1, 2, 3,
5, 6, 8, 13, 23, 46, 59, 115; SSC 2, 55**
See also AMWS 4; BPFB 1; CA 21-24R;
129; CANR 20, 58, 188; CN 1, 2, 3, 4;
DA3; DAM NOV; DLB 2, 234; DLBY
1980, 1989; EWL 3; FANT; LMFS 2;
MAL 5; MTCW 1, 2; MTFW 2005;
RGAL 4; RGSF 2; SATA 7; SATA-Obit
62; SSFS 17

Barthelme, Frederick 1943- ...... **CLC 36, 117**
See also AMWS 11; CA 114; 122; CANR
77; CN 4, 5, 6, 7; CSW; DLB 244; DLBY
1985; EWL 3; INT CA-122

Barthes, Roland (Gerard)
1915-1980 .... **CLC 24, 83; TCLC 135**
See also CA 130; 97-100; CANR 66; DLB
296; EW 13; EWL 3; GFL 1789 to the
Present; MTCW 1, 2; TWA

Bartram, William 1739-1823 .... **NCLC 145**
See also ANW; DLB 37

Barzun, Jacques (Martin) 1907- ..... **CLC 51,
145**
See also CA 61-64; CANR 22, 95

Bashevis, Isaac
See Singer, Isaac Bashevis

Bashevis, Yitskhok
See Singer, Isaac Bashevis

Bashkirtseff, Marie 1859-1884 .... **NCLC 27**

Basho, Matsuo
See Matsuo Basho

Basil of Caesaria c. 330-379 .... **CMLC 35**

Basket, Raney
See Edgerton, Clyde

Bass, Kingsley B., Jr.
See Bullins, Ed

Bass, Rick 1958- . **CLC 79, 143, 286; SSC 60**
See also AMWS 16; ANW; CA 126; CANR
53, 93, 145, 183; CSW; DLB 212, 275

Bassani, Giorgio 1916-2000 .... **CLC 9**
See also CA 65-68; 190; CANR 33; CWW
2; DLB 128, 177, 299; EWL 3; MTCW 1;
RGHL; RGWL 2, 3

Bassine, Helen
See Yglesias, Helen

Bastian, Ann .... **CLC 70**

Bastos, Augusto Roa
See Roa Bastos, Augusto

Bataille, Georges 1897-1962 .... **CLC 29;
TCLC 155**
See also CA 101; 89-92; EWL 3

Bates, H(erbert) E(rnest)
1905-1974 .... **CLC 46; SSC 10**
See also CA 93-96; 45-48; CANR 34; CN 1; DA3; DAB; DAM POP; DLB 162, 191; EWL 3; EXPS; MTCW 1, 2; RGSF 2; SSFS 7

Bauchart
See Camus, Albert

Baudelaire, Charles 1821-1867 . **NCLC 6, 29, 55, 155; PC 1, 106; SSC 18; WLC 1**
See also DA; DA3; DAB; DAC; DAM MST, POET; DLB 217; EW 7; GFL 1789 to the Present; LMFS 2; PFS 21; RGWL 2, 3; TWA

Baudouin, Marcel
See Peguy, Charles (Pierre)

Baudouin, Pierre
See Peguy, Charles (Pierre)

Baudrillard, Jean 1929-2007 .... **CLC 60**
See also CA 252; 258; DLB 296

Baum, L. Frank 1856-1919 ...... **TCLC 7, 132**
See also AAYA 46; BYA 16; CA 108; 133; CLR 15, 107; CWRI 5; DLB 22; FANT; JRDA; MAICYA 1, 2; MTCW 1, 2; NFS 13; RGAL 4; SATA 18, 100; WCH

Baum, Louis F.
See Baum, L. Frank

Baum, Lyman Frank
See Baum, L. Frank

Baumbach, Jonathan 1933- .... **CLC 6, 23**
See also CA 13-16R, 284; CAAE 284; CAAS 5; CANR 12, 66, 140; CN 3, 4, 5, 6, 7; DLBY 1980; INT CANR-12; MTCW 1

Bausch, Richard 1945- .... **CLC 51**
See also AMWS 7; CA 101; CAAS 14; CANR 43, 61, 87, 164, 200; CN 7; CSW; DLB 130; MAL 5

Bausch, Richard Carl
See Bausch, Richard

Baxter, Charles 1947- .... **CLC 45, 78**
See also AMWS 17; CA 57-60; CANR 40, 64, 104, 133, 188; CPW; DAM POP; DLB 130; MAL 5; MTCW 2; MTFW 2005; TCLE 1:1

Baxter, Charles Morley
See Baxter, Charles

Baxter, George Owen
See Faust, Frederick

Baxter, James K(eir) 1926-1972 .... **CLC 14**
See also CA 77-80; CP 1; EWL 3

Baxter, John
See Hunt, E. Howard

Bayer, Sylvia
See Glassco, John

Bayle, Pierre 1647-1706 .... **LC 126**
See also DLB 268, 313; GFL Beginnings to 1789

Baynton, Barbara 1857-1929 . **TCLC 57, 211**
See also DLB 230; RGSF 2

Beagle, Peter S. 1939- .... **CLC 7, 104**
See also AAYA 47; BPFB 1; BYA 9, 10, 16; CA 9-12R; CANR 4, 51, 73, 110; DA3; DLBY 1980; FANT; INT CANR-4; MTCW 2; MTFW 2005; SATA 60, 130; SUFW 1, 2; YAW

Beagle, Peter Soyer
See Beagle, Peter S.

Bean, Normal
See Burroughs, Edgar Rice

Beard, Charles A(ustin)
1874-1948 .... **TCLC 15**
See also CA 115; 189; DLB 17; SATA 18

Beardsley, Aubrey 1872-1898 .... **NCLC 6**

Beatrice of Nazareth 1200-1268 .. **CMLC 114**

Beattie, Ann 1947- ..... **CLC 8, 13, 18, 40, 63, 146, 293; SSC 11, 130**
See also AMWS 5; BEST 90:2; BPFB 1; CA 81-84; CANR 53, 73, 128; CN 4, 5, 6, 7; CPW; DA3; DAM NOV, POP; DLB 218, 278; DLBY 1982; EWL 3; MAL 5; MTCW 1, 2; MTFW 2005; RGAL 4; RGSF 2; SSFS 9; TUS

Beattie, James 1735-1803 .... **NCLC 25**
See also DLB 109

Beauchamp, Katherine Mansfield
See Mansfield, Katherine

Beaumarchais, Pierre-Augustin Caron de
1732-1799 .... **DC 4; LC 61**
See also DAM DRAM; DFS 14, 16; DLB 313; EW 4; GFL Beginnings to 1789; RGWL 2, 3

Beaumont, Francis 1584(?)-1616 .. **DC 6; LC 33**
See also BRW 2; CDBLB Before 1660; DLB 58; TEA

Beauvoir, Simone de 1908-1986 .... **CLC 1, 2, 4, 8, 14, 31, 44, 50, 71, 124; SSC 35; TCLC 221; WLC 1**
See also BPFB 1; CA 9-12R; 118; CANR 28, 61; DA; DA3; DAB; DAC; DAM MST, NOV; DLB 72; DLBY 1986; EW 12; EWL 3; FL 1:5; FW; GFL 1789 to the Present; LMFS 2; MTCW 1, 2; MTFW 2005; RGSF 2; RGWL 2, 3; TWA

Beauvoir, Simone Lucie Ernestine Marie Bertrand de
See Beauvoir, Simone de

Becker, Carl (Lotus) 1873-1945 ..... **TCLC 63**
See also CA 157; DLB 17

Becker, Jurek 1937-1997 .... **CLC 7, 19**
See also CA 85-88; 157; CANR 60, 117; CWW 2; DLB 75, 299; EWL 3; RGHL

Becker, Walter 1950- .... **CLC 26**

Becket, Thomas a 1118(?)-1170 .... **CMLC 83**

Beckett, Samuel 1906-1989 .. **CLC 1, 2, 3, 4, 6, 9, 10, 11, 14, 18, 29, 57, 59, 83; DC 22; SSC 16, 74; TCLC 145; WLC 1**
See also BRWC 2; BRWR 1; BRWS 1; CA 5-8R; 130; CANR 33, 61; CBD; CDBLB 1945-1960; CN 1, 2, 3, 4; CP 1, 2, 3, 4; DA; DA3; DAB; DAC; DAM DRAM, MST, NOV; DFS 2, 7, 18; DLB 13, 15, 233, 319, 321, 329; DLBY 1990; EWL 3; GFL 1789 to the Present; LATS 1:2; LMFS 2; MTCW 1, 2; MTFW 2005; RGSF 2; RGWL 2, 3; SSFS 15; TEA; WLIT 4

Beckett, Samuel Barclay
See Beckett, Samuel

Beckford, William 1760-1844 .... **NCLC 16, 214**
See also BRW 3; DLB 39, 213; GL 2; HGG; LMFS 1; SUFW

Beckham, Barry (Earl) 1944- .... **BLC 1:1**
See also BW 1; CA 29-32R; CANR 26, 62; CN 1, 2, 3, 4, 5, 6; DAM MULT; DLB 33

Beckman, Gunnel 1910- .... **CLC 26**
See also CA 33-36R; CANR 15, 114; CLR 25; MAICYA 1, 2; SAAS 9; SATA 6

Becque, Henri 1837-1899 .... **DC 21; NCLC 3**
See also DLB 192; GFL 1789 to the Present

Becquer, Gustavo Adolfo
1836-1870 .... **HLCS 1; NCLC 106**
See also DAM MULT

Beddoes, Thomas Lovell 1803-1849 .. **DC 15; NCLC 3, 154**
See also BRWS 11; DLB 96

Bede c. 673-735 .... **CMLC 20**
See also DLB 146; TEA

Bedford, Denton R. 1907-(?) .... **NNAL**

Bedford, Donald F.
See Fearing, Kenneth

Beecher, Catharine Esther
1800-1878 .... **NCLC 30**
See also DLB 1, 243

Beecher, John 1904-1980 .... **CLC 6**
See also AITN 1; CA 5-8R; 105; CANR 8; CP 1, 2, 3

Beer, Johann 1655-1700 .... **LC 5**
See also DLB 168

Beer, Patricia 1924- .... **CLC 58**
See also BRWS 14; CA 61-64; 183; CANR 13, 46; CP 1, 2, 3, 4, 5, 6; CWP; DLB 40; FW

Beerbohm, Max
See Beerbohm, (Henry) Max(imilian)

Beerbohm, (Henry) Max(imilian)
1872-1956 .... **TCLC 1, 24**
See also BRWS 2; CA 104; 154; CANR 79; DLB 34, 100; FANT; MTCW 2

Beer-Hofmann, Richard
1866-1945 .... **TCLC 60**
See also CA 160; DLB 81

Beethoven, Ludwig van
1770(?)-1827 .... **NCLC 227**

Beg, Shemus
See Stephens, James

Begiebing, Robert J(ohn) 1946- .... **CLC 70**
See also CA 122; CANR 40, 88

Begley, Louis 1933- .... **CLC 197**
See also CA 140; CANR 98, 176; DLB 299; RGHL; TCLE 1:1

Behan, Brendan 1923-1964 ...... **CLC 1, 8, 11, 15, 79**
See also BRWS 2; CA 73-76; CANR 33, 121; CBD; CDBLB 1945-1960; DAM DRAM; DFS 7; DLB 13, 233; EWL 3; MTCW 1, 2

Behan, Brendan Francis
See Behan, Brendan

Behn, Aphra 1640(?)-1689 .. **DC 4; LC 1, 30, 42, 135; PC 13, 88; WLC 1**
See also BRWR 3; BRWS 3; DA; DA3; DAB; DAC; DAM DRAM, MST, NOV, POET; DFS 16, 24; DLB 39, 80, 131; FW; TEA; WLIT 3

Behrman, S(amuel) N(athaniel)
1893-1973 .... **CLC 40**
See also CA 13-16; 45-48; CAD; CAP 1; DLB 7, 44; IDFW 3; MAL 5; RGAL 4

Bekederemo, J. P. Clark
See Clark-Bekederemo, J. P.

Belasco, David 1853-1931 .... **TCLC 3**
See also CA 104; 168; DLB 7; MAL 5; RGAL 4

Belben, Rosalind 1941- .... **CLC 280**
See also CA 291

Belben, Rosalind Loveday
See Belben, Rosalind

Belcheva, Elisaveta Lyubomirova
1893-1991 .... **CLC 10**
See also CA 178; CDWLB 4; DLB 147; EWL 3

Beldone, Phil ''Cheech''
See Ellison, Harlan

Beleno
See Azuela, Mariano

Belinski, Vissarion Grigoryevich
1811-1848 .... **NCLC 5**
See also DLB 198

Belitt, Ben 1911- .... **CLC 22**
See also CA 13-16R; CAAS 4; CANR 7, 77; CP 1, 2, 3, 4, 5, 6; DLB 5

Belknap, Jeremy 1744-1798 .... **LC 115**
See also DLB 30, 37

Bell, Gertrude (Margaret Lowthian)
1868-1926 .... **TCLC 67**
See also CA 167; CANR 110; DLB 174

Bell, J. Freeman
See Zangwill, Israel

Bell, James Madison 1826-1902 ..... **BLC 1:1; TCLC 43**
See also BW 1; CA 122; 124; DAM MULT; DLB 50

Breton, Nicholas c. 1554-c. 1626 .... **LC 133**
See also DLB 136

Breytenbach, Breyten 1939(?)- .. **CLC 23, 37, 126**
See also CA 113; 129; CANR 61, 122, 202; CWW 2; DAM POET; DLB 225; EWL 3

Bridgers, Sue Ellen 1942- .... **CLC 26**
See also AAYA 8, 49; BYA 7, 8; CA 65-68; CANR 11, 36; CLR 18; DLB 52; JRDA; MAICYA 1, 2; SAAS 1; SATA 22, 90; SATA-Essay 109; WYA; YAW

Bridges, Robert (Seymour)
1844-1930 .... **PC 28; TCLC 1**
See also BRW 6; CA 104; 152; CDBLB 1890-1914; DAM POET; DLB 19, 98

Bridie, James
See Mavor, Osborne Henry

Brin, David 1950- .... **CLC 34**
See also AAYA 21; CA 102; CANR 24, 70, 125, 127; INT CANR-24; SATA 65; SCFW 2; SFW 4

Brink, Andre 1935- .... **CLC 18, 36, 106**
See also AFW; BRWS 6; CA 104; CANR 39, 62, 109, 133, 182; CN 4, 5, 6, 7; DLB 225; EWL 3; INT CA-103; LATS 1:2; MTCW 1, 2; MTFW 2005; WLIT 2

Brink, Andre Philippus
See Brink, Andre

Brinsmead, H. F(ay)
See Brinsmead, H(esba) F(ay)

Brinsmead, H. F.
See Brinsmead, H(esba) F(ay)

Brinsmead, H(esba) F(ay) 1922- ...... **CLC 21**
See also CA 21-24R; CANR 10; CLR 47; CWRI 5; MAICYA 1, 2; SAAS 5; SATA 18, 78

Brittain, Vera (Mary)
1893(?)-1970 .... **CLC 23; TCLC 228**
See also BRWS 10; CA 13-16; 25-28R; CANR 58; CAP 1; DLB 191; FW; MTCW 1, 2

Broch, Hermann 1886-1951 ... **TCLC 20, 204**
See also CA 117; 211; CDWLB 2; DLB 85, 124; EW 10; EWL 3; RGWL 2, 3

Brock, Rose
See Hansen, Joseph

Brod, Max 1884-1968 .... **TCLC 115**
See also CA 5-8R; 25-28R; CANR 7; DLB 81; EWL 3

Brodkey, Harold (Roy) 1930-1996 .. **CLC 56; TCLC 123**
See also CA 111; 151; CANR 71; CN 4, 5, 6; DLB 130

Brodskii, Iosif
See Brodsky, Joseph

Brodskii, Iosif Alexandrovich
See Brodsky, Joseph

Brodsky, Iosif Alexandrovich
See Brodsky, Joseph

Brodsky, Joseph 1940-1996 ..... **CLC 4, 6, 13, 36, 100; PC 9; TCLC 219**
See also AAYA 71; AITN 1; AMWS 8; CA 41-44R; 151; CANR 37, 106; CWW 2; DA3; DAM POET; DLB 285, 329; EWL 3; MTCW 1, 2; MTFW 2005; PFS 35; RGWL 2, 3

Brodsky, Michael 1948- .... **CLC 19**
See also CA 102; CANR 18, 41, 58, 147; DLB 244

Brodsky, Michael Mark
See Brodsky, Michael

Brodzki, Bella .... **CLC 65**

Brome, Richard 1590(?)-1652 .... **LC 61**
See also BRWS 10; DLB 58

Bromell, Henry 1947- .... **CLC 5**
See also CA 53-56; CANR 9, 115, 116

Bromfield, Louis (Brucker)
1896-1956 .... **TCLC 11**
See also CA 107; 155; DLB 4, 9, 86; RGAL 4; RHW

Broner, E(sther) M(asserman)
1930- .... **CLC 19**
See also CA 17-20R; CANR 8, 25, 72; CN 4, 5, 6; DLB 28

Bronk, William (M.) 1918-1999 .... **CLC 10**
See also CA 89-92; 177; CANR 23; CP 3, 4, 5, 6, 7; DLB 165

Bronstein, Lev Davidovich
See Trotsky, Leon

Bronte, Anne
See Bronte, Anne

Bronte, Anne 1820-1849 ..... **NCLC 4, 71, 102**
See also BRW 5; BRWR 1; DA3; DLB 21, 199, 340; NFS 26; TEA

Bronte, (Patrick) Branwell
1817-1848 .... **NCLC 109**
See also DLB 340

Bronte, Charlotte
See Bronte, Charlotte

Bronte, Charlotte 1816-1855 ...... **NCLC 3, 8, 33, 58, 105, 155, 217; WLC 1**
See also AAYA 17; BRW 5; BRWC 2; BRWR 1; BYA 2; CDBLB 1832-1890; DA; DA3; DAB; DAC; DAM MST, NOV; DLB 21, 159, 199, 340; EXPN; FL 1:2; GL 2; LAIT 2; NFS 4; TEA; WLIT 4

Bronte, Emily
See Bronte, Emily

Bronte, Emily 1818-1848 .... **NCLC 16, 35, 165; PC 8; WLC 1**
See also AAYA 17; BPFB 1; BRW 5; BRWC 1; BRWR 1; BYA 3; CDBLB 1832-1890; DA; DA3; DAB; DAC; DAM MST, NOV, POET; DLB 21, 32, 199, 340; EXPN; FL 1:2; GL 2; LAIT 1; NFS 2; PFS 33; TEA; WLIT 3

Bronte, Emily Jane
See Bronte, Emily

Brontes
See Bronte, Anne; Bronte, (Patrick) Branwell; Bronte, Charlotte; Bronte, Emily

Brooke, Frances 1724-1789 .... **LC 6, 48**
See also DLB 39, 99

Brooke, Henry 1703(?)-1783 .... **LC 1**
See also DLB 39

Brooke, Rupert 1887-1915 . **PC 24; TCLC 2, 7; WLC 1**
See also BRWS 3; CA 104; 132; CANR 61; CDBLB 1914-1945; DA; DAB; DAC; DAM MST, POET; DLB 19, 216; EXPP; GLL 2; MTCW 1, 2; MTFW 2005; PFS 7; TEA

Brooke, Rupert Chawner
See Brooke, Rupert

Brooke-Haven, P.
See Wodehouse, P. G.

Brooke-Rose, Christine 1923(?)- ..... **CLC 40, 184**
See also BRWS 4; CA 13-16R; CANR 58, 118, 183; CN 1, 2, 3, 4, 5, 6, 7; DLB 14, 231; EWL 3; SFW 4

Brookner, Anita 1928- . **CLC 32, 34, 51, 136, 237**
See also BRWS 4; CA 114; 120; CANR 37, 56, 87, 130; CN 4, 5, 6, 7; CPW; DA3; DAB; DAM POP; DLB 194, 326; DLBY 1987; EWL 3; MTCW 1, 2; MTFW 2005; NFS 23; TEA

Brooks, Cleanth 1906-1994 . **CLC 24, 86, 110**
See also AMWS 14; CA 17-20R; 145; CANR 33, 35; CSW; DLB 63; DLBY 1994; EWL 3; INT CANR-35; MAL 5; MTCW 1, 2; MTFW 2005

Brooks, George
See Baum, L. Frank

Brooks, Gwendolyn 1917-2000 .... **BLC 1:1, 2:1; CLC 1, 2, 4, 5, 15, 49, 125; PC 7; WLC 1**
See also AAYA 20; AFAW 1, 2; AITN 1; AMWS 3; BW 2, 3; CA 1-4R; 190; CANR 1, 27, 52, 75, 132; CDALB 1941-1968; CLR 27; CP 1, 2, 3, 4, 5, 6, 7; CWP; DA; DA3; DAC; DAM MST, MULT, POET; DLB 5, 76, 165; EWL 3; EXPP; FL 1:5; MAL 5; MBL; MTCW 1, 2; MTFW 2005; PFS 1, 2, 4, 6, 32; RGAL 4; SATA 6; SATA-Obit 123; TUS; WP

Brooks, Gwendolyn Elizabeth
See Brooks, Gwendolyn

Brooks, Mel 1926-
See Kaminsky, Melvin
See also CA 65-68; CANR 16; DFS 21

Brooks, Peter 1938- .... **CLC 34**
See also CA 45-48; CANR 1, 107, 182

Brooks, Peter Preston
See Brooks, Peter

Brooks, Van Wyck 1886-1963 .... **CLC 29**
See also AMW; CA 1-4R; CANR 6; DLB 45, 63, 103; MAL 5; TUS

Brophy, Brigid 1929-1995 ...... **CLC 6, 11, 29, 105**
See also CA 5-8R; 149; CAAS 4; CANR 25, 53; CBD; CN 1, 2, 3, 4, 5, 6; CWD; DA3; DLB 14, 271; EWL 3; MTCW 1, 2

Brophy, Brigid Antonia
See Brophy, Brigid

Brosman, Catharine Savage 1934- ..... **CLC 9**
See also CA 61-64; CANR 21, 46, 149

Brossard, Nicole 1943- .... **CLC 115, 169; PC 80**
See also CA 122; CAAS 16; CANR 140; CCA 1; CWP; CWW 2; DLB 53; EWL 3; FW; GLL 2; RGWL 3

Brother Antoninus
See Everson, William

Brothers Grimm
See Grimm, Jacob Ludwig Karl; Grimm, Wilhelm Karl

The Brothers Quay
See Quay, Stephen; Quay, Timothy

Broughton, T(homas) Alan 1936- ..... **CLC 19**
See also CA 45-48; CANR 2, 23, 48, 111

Broumas, Olga 1949- .... **CLC 10, 73**
See also CA 85-88; CANR 20, 69, 110; CP 5, 6, 7; CWP; GLL 2

Broun, Heywood 1888-1939 .... **TCLC 104**
See also DLB 29, 171

Brown, Alan 1950- .... **CLC 99**
See also CA 156

Brown, Charles Brockden
1771-1810 .... **NCLC 22, 74, 122**
See also AMWS 1; CDALB 1640-1865; DLB 37, 59, 73; FW; GL 2; HGG; LMFS 1; RGAL 4; TUS

Brown, Christy 1932-1981 .... **CLC 63**
See also BYA 13; CA 105; 104; CANR 72; DLB 14

Brown, Claude 1937-2002 ..... **BLC 1:1; CLC 30**
See also AAYA 7; BW 1, 3; CA 73-76; 205; CANR 81; DAM MULT

Brown, Dan 1964- .... **CLC 209**
See also AAYA 55; CA 217; LNFS 1; MTFW 2005

Brown, Dee 1908-2002 .... **CLC 18, 47**
See also AAYA 30; CA 13-16R; 212; CAAS 6; CANR 11, 45, 60, 150; CPW; CSW; DA3; DAM POP; DLBY 1980; LAIT 2; MTCW 1, 2; MTFW 2005; NCFS 5; SATA 5, 110; SATA-Obit 141; TCWW 1, 2

Brown, Dee Alexander
See Brown, Dee

Chapman, Graham 1941-1989 .... **CLC 21**
See also AAYA 7; CA 116; 129; CANR 35, 95

Chapman, John Jay 1862-1933 .... **TCLC 7**
See also AMWS 14; CA 104; 191

Chapman, Lee
See Bradley, Marion Zimmer

Chapman, Walker
See Silverberg, Robert

Chappell, Fred (Davis) 1936- .... **CLC 40, 78, 162, 293; PC 105**
See also CA 5-8R, 198; CAAE 198; CAAS 4; CANR 8, 33, 67, 110; CN 6; CP 6, 7; CSW; DLB 6, 105; HGG

Char, Rene 1907-1988 ..... **CLC 9, 11, 14, 55; PC 56**
See also CA 13-16R; 124; CANR 32; DAM POET; DLB 258; EWL 3; GFL 1789 to the Present; MTCW 1, 2; RGWL 2, 3

Char, Rene-Emile
See Char, Rene

Charby, Jay
See Ellison, Harlan

Chardin, Pierre Teilhard de
See Teilhard de Chardin, (Marie Joseph) Pierre

Chariton fl. 1st cent. (?)- .... **CMLC 49**

Charlemagne 742-814 .... **CMLC 37**

Charles I 1600-1649 .... **LC 13**

Charriere, Isabelle de 1740-1805 .. **NCLC 66**
See also DLB 313

Charron, Pierre 1541-1603 .... **LC 174**
See also GFL Beginnings to 1789

Chartier, Alain c. 1392-1430 .... **LC 94**
See also DLB 208

Chartier, Emile-Auguste
See Alain

Charyn, Jerome 1937- .... **CLC 5, 8, 18**
See also CA 5-8R; CAAS 1; CANR 7, 61, 101, 158, 199; CMW 4; CN 1, 2, 3, 4, 5, 6, 7; DLBY 1983; MTCW 1

Chase, Adam
See Marlowe, Stephen

Chase, Mary (Coyle) 1907-1981 .... **DC 1**
See also CA 77-80; 105; CAD; CWD; DFS 11; DLB 228; SATA 17; SATA-Obit 29

Chase, Mary Ellen 1887-1973 .... **CLC 2; TCLC 124**
See also CA 13-16; 41-44R; CAP 1; SATA 10

Chase, Nicholas
See Hyde, Anthony

Chase-Riboud, Barbara (Dewayne Tosi)
1939- .... **BLC 2:1**
See also BW 2; CA 113; CANR 76; DAM MULT; DLB 33; MTCW 2

Chateaubriand, Francois Rene de
1768-1848 .... **NCLC 3, 134**
See also DLB 119; EW 5; GFL 1789 to the Present; RGWL 2, 3; TWA

Chatelet, Gabrielle-Emilie Du
See du Chatelet, Emilie

Chatterje, Saratchandra -(?)
See Chatterji, Sarat Chandra

Chatterji, Bankim Chandra
1838-1894 .... **NCLC 19**

Chatterji, Sarat Chandra
1876-1936 .... **TCLC 13**
See also CA 109; 186; EWL 3

Chatterton, Thomas 1752-1770 ..... **LC 3, 54; PC 104**
See also DAM POET; DLB 109; RGEL 2

Chatwin, (Charles) Bruce
1940-1989 .... **CLC 28, 57, 59**
See also AAYA 4; BEST 90:1; BRWS 4; CA 85-88; 127; CPW; DAM POP; DLB 194, 204; EWL 3; MTFW 2005

Chaucer, Daniel
See Ford, Ford Madox

Chaucer, Geoffrey 1340(?)-1400 ... **LC 17, 56, 173; PC 19, 58; WLCS**
See also BRW 1; BRWC 1; BRWR 2; CD-BLB Before 1660; DA; DA3; DAB; DAC; DAM MST, POET; DLB 146; LAIT 1; PAB; PFS 14; RGEL 2; TEA; WLIT 3; WP

Chaudhuri, Nirad C(handra)
1897-1999 .... **TCLC 224**
See also CA 128; 183; DLB 323

Chavez, Denise 1948- .... **HLC 1**
See also CA 131; CANR 56, 81, 137; DAM MULT; DLB 122; FW; HW 1; LLW; MAL 5; MTCW 2; MTFW 2005

Chaviaras, Strates 1935- .... **CLC 33**
See also CA 105

Chayefsky, Paddy 1923-1981 .... **CLC 23**
See also CA 9-12R; 104; CAD; CANR 18; DAM DRAM; DFS 26; DLB 23; DLBY 7, 44; RGAL 4

Chayefsky, Sidney
See Chayefsky, Paddy

Chedid, Andree 1920- .... **CLC 47**
See also CA 145; CANR 95; EWL 3

Cheever, John 1912-1982 ..... **CLC 3, 7, 8, 11, 15, 25, 64; SSC 1, 38, 57, 120; WLC 2**
See also AAYA 65; AMWS 1; BPFB 1; CA 5-8R; 106; CABS 1; CANR 5, 27, 76; CDALB 1941-1968; CN 1, 2, 3; CPW; DA; DA3; DAB; DAC; DAM MST, NOV, POP; DLB 2, 102, 227; DLBY 1980, 1982; EWL 3; EXPS; INT CANR-5; MAL 5; MTCW 1, 2; MTFW 2005; RGAL 4; RGSF 2; SSFS 2, 14; TUS

Cheever, Susan 1943- .... **CLC 18, 48**
See also CA 103; CANR 27, 51, 92, 157, 198; DLBY 1982; INT CANR-27

Chekhonte, Antosha
See Chekhov, Anton

Chekhov, Anton 1860-1904 ...... **DC 9; SSC 2, 28, 41, 51, 85, 102; TCLC 3, 10, 31, 55, 96, 163; WLC 2**
See also AAYA 68; BYA 14; CA 104; 124; DA; DA3; DAB; DAC; DAM DRAM, MST; DFS 1, 5, 10, 12, 26; DLB 277; EW 7; EWL 3; EXPS; LAIT 3; LATS 1:1; RGSF 2; RGWL 2, 3; SATA 90; SSFS 5, 13, 14, 26, 29; TWA

Chekhov, Anton Pavlovich
See Chekhov, Anton

Cheney, Lynne V. 1941- .... **CLC 70**
See also CA 89-92; CANR 58, 117, 193; SATA 152

Cheney, Lynne Vincent
See Cheney, Lynne V.

Chenier, Andre-Marie de 1762-1794 . **LC 174**
See also EW 4; GFL Beginnings to 1789; TWA

Chernyshevsky, Nikolai Gavrilovich
See Chernyshevsky, Nikolay Gavrilovich

Chernyshevsky, Nikolay Gavrilovich
1828-1889 .... **NCLC 1**
See also DLB 238

Cherry, Carolyn Janice
See Cherryh, C.J.

Cherryh, C.J. 1942- .... **CLC 35**
See also AAYA 24; BPFB 1; CA 65-68; CANR 10, 147, 179; DLBY 1980; FANT; SATA 93, 172; SCFW 2; YAW

Chesler, Phyllis 1940- .... **CLC 247**
See also CA 49-52; CANR 4, 59, 140, 189; FW

Chesnutt, Charles W(addell)
1858-1932 .... **BLC 1; SSC 7, 54, 139; TCLC 5, 39**
See also AFAW 1, 2; AMWS 14; BW 1, 3; CA 106; 125; CANR 76; DAM MULT;

DLB 12, 50, 78; EWL 3; MAL 5; MTCW 1, 2; MTFW 2005; RGAL 4; RGSF 2; SSFS 11, 26

Chester, Alfred 1929(?)-1971 .... **CLC 49**
See also CA 196; 33-36R; DLB 130; MAL 5

Chesterton, G. K. 1874-1936 . **PC 28; SSC 1, 46; TCLC 1, 6, 64**
See also AAYA 57; BRW 6; CA 104; 132; CANR 73, 131; CDBLB 1914-1945; CMW 4; DAM NOV, POET; DLB 10, 19, 34, 70, 98, 149, 178; EWL 3; FANT; MSW; MTCW 1, 2; MTFW 2005; RGEL 2; RGSF 2; SATA 27; SUFW 1

Chesterton, Gilbert Keith
See Chesterton, G. K.

Chettle, Henry 1560-1607(?) .... **LC 112**
See also DLB 136; RGEL 2

Chiang, Pin-chin 1904-1986 .... **CLC 68**
See also CA 118; DLB 328; EWL 3; RGWL 3

Chiang Ping-chih
See Chiang, Pin-chin

Chief Joseph 1840-1904 .... **NNAL**
See also CA 152; DA3; DAM MULT

Chief Seattle 1786(?)-1866 .... **NNAL**
See also DA3; DAM MULT

Ch'ien, Chung-shu 1910-1998 .... **CLC 22**
See also CA 130; CANR 73; CWW 2; DLB 328; MTCW 1, 2

Chikamatsu Monzaemon 1653-1724 ... **LC 66**
See also RGWL 2, 3

Child, Francis James 1825-1896 . **NCLC 173**
See also DLB 1, 64, 235

Child, L. Maria
See Child, Lydia Maria

Child, Lydia Maria 1802-1880 .. **NCLC 6, 73**
See also DLB 1, 74, 243; RGAL 4; SATA 67

Child, Mrs.
See Child, Lydia Maria

Child, Philip 1898-1978 .... **CLC 19, 68**
See also CA 13-14; CAP 1; CP 1; DLB 68; RHW; SATA 47

Childers, (Robert) Erskine
1870-1922 .... **TCLC 65**
See also CA 113; 153; DLB 70

Childress, Alice 1920-1994 .... **BLC 1:1; CLC 12, 15, 86, 96; DC 4; TCLC 116**
See also AAYA 8; BW 2, 3; BYA 2; CA 45-48; 146; CAD; CANR 3, 27, 50, 74; CLR 14; CWD; DA3; DAM DRAM, MULT, NOV; DFS 2, 8, 14, 26; DLB 7, 38, 249; JRDA; LAIT 5; MAICYA 1, 2; MAICYAS 1; MAL 5; MTCW 1, 2; MTFW 2005; RGAL 4; SATA 7, 48, 81; TUS; WYA; YAW

Chin, Frank 1940- ..... **AAL; CLC 135; DC 7**
See also CA 33-36R; CAD; CANR 71; CD 5, 6; DAM MULT; DLB 206, 312; LAIT 5; RGAL 4

Chin, Frank Chew, Jr.
See Chin, Frank

Chin, Marilyn 1955- .... **PC 40**
See also CA 129; CANR 70, 113; CWP; DLB 312; PFS 28

Chin, Marilyn Mei Ling
See Chin, Marilyn

Chislett, (Margaret) Anne 1943- ...... **CLC 34**
See also CA 151

Chitty, Thomas Willes 1926- .... **CLC 6, 11**
See also CA 5-8R; CN 1, 2, 3, 4, 5, 6; EWL 3

Chivers, Thomas Holley
1809-1858 .... **NCLC 49**
See also DLB 3, 248; RGAL 4

Chlamyda, Jehudil
See Gorky, Maxim

DA3; DAB; DAC; DAM MST, NOV; DLB 39, 95, 101, 336; JRDA; LAIT 1; LMFS 1; MAICYA 1, 2; NFS 9, 13, 30; RGEL 2; SATA 22; TEA; WCH; WLIT 3

de Gouges, Olympe
See de Gouges, Olympe

de Gouges, Olympe 1748-1793 .... **LC 127**
See also DLB 313

de Gourmont, Remy(-Marie-Charles)
See Gourmont, Remy(-Marie-Charles) de

de Gournay, Marie le Jars
1566-1645 .... **LC 98**
See also DLB 327; FW

de Hartog, Jan 1914-2002 .... **CLC 19**
See also CA 1-4R; 210; CANR 1, 192; DFS 12

de Hostos, E. M.
See Hostos (y Bonilla), Eugenio Maria de

de Hostos, Eugenio M.
See Hostos (y Bonilla), Eugenio Maria de

Deighton, Len
See Deighton, Leonard Cyril

Deighton, Leonard Cyril 1929- ..... **CLC 4, 7, 22, 46**
See also AAYA 57, 6; BEST 89:2; BPFB 1; CA 9-12R; CANR 19, 33, 68; CDBLB 1960- Present; CMW 4; CN 1, 2, 3, 4, 5, 6, 7; CPW; DA3; DAM NOV, POP; DLB 87; MTCW 1, 2; MTFW 2005

Dekker, Thomas 1572(?)-1632 ..... **DC 12; LC 22, 159**
See also CDBLB Before 1660; DAM DRAM; DLB 62, 172; LMFS 1; RGEL 2

de Laclos, Pierre Ambroise Franois
See Laclos, Pierre-Ambroise Francois

Delacroix, (Ferdinand-Victor-)Eugene
1798-1863 .... **NCLC 133**
See also EW 5

Delafield, E. M.
See Dashwood, Edmee Elizabeth Monica de la Pasture

de la Mare, Walter (John)
1873-1956 ..... **PC 77; SSC 14; TCLC 4, 53; WLC 2**
See also AAYA 81; CA 163; CDBLB 1914-1945; CLR 23, 148; CWRI 5; DA3; DAB; DAC; DAM MST, POET; DLB 19, 153, 162, 255, 284; EWL 3; EXPP; HGG; MAICYA 1, 2; MTCW 2; MTFW 2005; RGEL 2; RGSF 2; SATA 16; SUFW 1; TEA; WCH

de Lamartine, Alphonse
See Lamartine, Alphonse de

Delaney, Franey
See O'Hara, John

Delaney, Shelagh 1939- .... **CLC 29**
See also CA 17-20R; CANR 30, 67; CBD; CD 5, 6; CDBLB 1960 to Present; CWD; DAM DRAM; DFS 7; DLB 13; MTCW 1

Delany, Martin Robison
1812-1885 .... **NCLC 93**
See also DLB 50; RGAL 4

Delany, Mary (Granville Pendarves)
1700-1788 .... **LC 12**

Delany, Samuel R., Jr. 1942- .... **BLC 1:1; CLC 8, 14, 38, 141**
See also AAYA 24; AFAW 2; BPFB 1; BW 2, 3; CA 81-84; CANR 27, 43, 116, 172; CN 2, 3, 4, 5, 6, 7; DAM MULT; DLB 8, 33; FANT; MAL 5; MTCW 1, 2; RGAL 4; SATA 92; SCFW 1, 2; SFW 4; SUFW 2

Delany, Samuel Ray
See Delany, Samuel R., Jr.

de la Parra, Ana Teresa Sonojo
See de la Parra, Teresa

de la Parra, Teresa 1890(?)-1936 .... **HLCS 2; TCLC 185**
See also CA 178; HW 2; LAW

Delaporte, Theophile
See Green, Julien

De La Ramee, Marie Louise
1839-1908 .... **TCLC 43**
See also CA 204; DLB 18, 156; RGEL 2; SATA 20

de la Roche, Mazo 1879-1961 .... **CLC 14**
See also CA 85-88; CANR 30; DLB 68; RGEL 2; RHW; SATA 64

De La Salle, Innocent
See Hartmann, Sadakichi

de Laureamont, Comte
See Lautreamont

Delbanco, Nicholas 1942- ..... **CLC 6, 13, 167**
See also CA 17-20R, 189; CAAE 189; CAAS 2; CANR 29, 55, 116, 150, 204; CN 7; DLB 6, 234

Delbanco, Nicholas Franklin
See Delbanco, Nicholas

del Castillo, Michel 1933- .... **CLC 38**
See also CA 109; CANR 77

Deledda, Grazia (Cosima)
1875(?)-1936 .... **TCLC 23**
See also CA 123; 205; DLB 264, 329; EWL 3; RGWL 2, 3; WLIT 7

Deleuze, Gilles 1925-1995 .... **TCLC 116**
See also DLB 296

Delgado, Abelardo (Lalo) B(arrientos)
1930-2004 .... **HLC 1**
See also CA 131; 230; CAAS 15; CANR 90; DAM MST, MULT; DLB 82; HW 1, 2

Delibes, Miguel
See Delibes Setien, Miguel

Delibes Setien, Miguel 1920-2010 ...... **CLC 8, 18**
See also CA 45-48; CANR 1, 32; CWW 2; DLB 322; EWL 3; HW 1; MTCW 1

DeLillo, Don 1936- ..... **CLC 8, 10, 13, 27, 39, 54, 76, 143, 210, 213**
See also AMWC 2; AMWS 6; BEST 89:1; BPFB 1; CA 81-84; CANR 21, 76, 92, 133, 173; CN 3, 4, 5, 6, 7; CPW; DA3; DAM NOV, POP; DLB 6, 173; EWL 3; MAL 5; MTCW 1, 2; MTFW 2005; NFS 28; RGAL 4; TUS

de Lisser, H. G.
See De Lisser, H(erbert) G(eorge)

De Lisser, H(erbert) G(eorge)
1878-1944 .... **TCLC 12**
See also BW 2; CA 109; 152; DLB 117

Deloire, Pierre
See Peguy, Charles (Pierre)

Deloney, Thomas 1543(?)-1600 .... **LC 41; PC 79**
See also DLB 167; RGEL 2

Deloria, Ella (Cara) 1889-1971(?) ..... **NNAL**
See also CA 152; DAM MULT; DLB 175

Deloria, Vine, Jr. 1933-2005 .... **CLC 21, 122; NNAL**
See also CA 53-56; 245; CANR 5, 20, 48, 98; DAM MULT; DLB 175; MTCW 1; SATA 21; SATA-Obit 171

Deloria, Vine Victor, Jr.
See Deloria, Vine, Jr.

del Valle-Inclan, Ramon
See Valle-Inclan, Ramon del

Del Vecchio, John M(ichael) 1947- .. **CLC 29**
See also CA 110; DLBD 9

de Man, Paul (Adolph Michel)
1919-1983 .... **CLC 55**
See also CA 128; 111; CANR 61; DLB 67; MTCW 1, 2

de Mandiargues, Andre Pieyre
See Pieyre de Mandiargues, Andre

DeMarinis, Rick 1934- .... **CLC 54**
See also CA 57-60, 184; CAAE 184; CAAS 24; CANR 9, 25, 50, 160; DLB 218; TCWW 2

de Maupassant, Guy
See Maupassant, Guy de

Dembry, R. Emmet
See Murfree, Mary Noailles

Demby, William 1922- ...... **BLC 1:1; CLC 53**
See also BW 1, 3; CA 81-84; CANR 81; DAM MULT; DLB 33

de Menton, Francisco
See Chin, Frank

Demetrius of Phalerum c.
307B.C.- .... **CMLC 34**

Demijohn, Thom
See Disch, Thomas M.

De Mille, James 1833-1880 .... **NCLC 123**
See also DLB 99, 251

Democritus c. 460B.C.-c. 370B.C. . **CMLC 47**

de Montaigne, Michel
See Montaigne, Michel de

de Montherlant, Henry
See Montherlant, Henry de

Demosthenes 384B.C.-322B.C. ...... **CMLC 13**
See also AW 1; DLB 176; RGWL 2, 3; WLIT 8

de Musset, (Louis Charles) Alfred
See Musset, Alfred de

de Natale, Francine
See Malzberg, Barry N(athaniel)

de Navarre, Marguerite 1492-1549 .... **LC 61, 167; SSC 85**
See also DLB 327; GFL Beginnings to 1789; RGWL 2, 3

Denby, Edwin (Orr) 1903-1983 .... **CLC 48**
See also CA 138; 110; CP 1

de Nerval, Gerard
See Nerval, Gerard de

Denham, John 1615-1669 .... **LC 73**
See also DLB 58, 126; RGEL 2

Denis, Claire 1948- .... **CLC 286**
See also CA 249

Denis, Julio
See Cortazar, Julio

Denmark, Harrison
See Zelazny, Roger

Dennis, John 1658-1734 .... **LC 11, 154**
See also DLB 101; RGEL 2

Dennis, Nigel (Forbes) 1912-1989 ...... **CLC 8**
See also CA 25-28R; 129; CN 1, 2, 3, 4; DLB 13, 15, 233; EWL 3; MTCW 1

Dent, Lester 1904-1959 .... **TCLC 72**
See also CA 112; 161; CMW 4; DLB 306; SFW 4

Dentinger, Stephen
See Hoch, Edward D.

De Palma, Brian 1940- .... **CLC 20, 247**
See also CA 109

De Palma, Brian Russell
See De Palma, Brian

de Pizan, Christine
See Christine de Pizan

De Quincey, Thomas 1785-1859 ..... **NCLC 4, 87, 198**
See also BRW 4; CDBLB 1789-1832; DLB 110, 144; RGEL 2

De Ray, Jill
See Moore, Alan

Deren, Eleanora 1908(?)-1961 .. **CLC 16, 102**
See also CA 192; 111

Deren, Maya
See Deren, Eleanora

Derleth, August (William)
1909-1971 .... **CLC 31**
See also BPFB 1; BYA 9, 10; CA 1-4R; 29-32R; CANR 4; CMW 4; CN 1; DLB 9; DLBD 17; HGG; SATA 5; SUFW 1

Der Nister 1884-1950 .... **TCLC 56**
See also DLB 333; EWL 3

de Routisie, Albert
See Aragon, Louis

Derrida, Jacques 1930-2004 ...... **CLC 24, 87, 225**
See also CA 124; 127; 232; CANR 76, 98, 133; DLB 242; EWL 3; LMFS 2; MTCW 2; TWA

Derry Down Derry
See Lear, Edward

Dersonnes, Jacques
See Simenon, Georges

Der Stricker c. 1190-c. 1250 .... **CMLC 75**
See also DLB 138

Derzhavin, Gavriil Romanovich
1743-1816 .... **NCLC 215**
See also DLB 150

Desai, Anita 1937- . **CLC 19, 37, 97, 175, 271**
See also BRWS 5; CA 81-84; CANR 33, 53, 95, 133; CN 1, 2, 3, 4, 5, 6, 7; CWRI 5; DA3; DAB; DAM NOV; DLB 271, 323; DNFS 2; EWL 3; FW; MTCW 1, 2; MTFW 2005; SATA 63, 126; SSFS 28, 31

Desai, Kiran 1971- .... **CLC 119**
See also BRWS 15; BYA 16; CA 171; CANR 127; NFS 28

de Saint-Luc, Jean
See Glassco, John

de Saint Roman, Arnaud
See Aragon, Louis

Desbordes-Valmore, Marceline
1786-1859 .... **NCLC 97**
See also DLB 217

Descartes, Rene 1596-1650 .... **LC 20, 35, 150**
See also DLB 268; EW 3; GFL Beginnings to 1789

Deschamps, Eustache 1340(?)-1404 .. **LC 103**
See also DLB 208

De Sica, Vittorio 1901(?)-1974 .... **CLC 20**
See also CA 117

Desnos, Robert 1900-1945 .... **TCLC 22**
See also CA 121; 151; CANR 107; DLB 258; EWL 3; LMFS 2

Destouches, Louis-Ferdinand
See Celine, Louis-Ferdinand

de Teran, Lisa St. Aubin
See St. Aubin de Teran, Lisa

de Tolignac, Gaston
See Griffith, D.W.

Deutsch, Babette 1895-1982 .... **CLC 18**
See also BYA 3; CA 1-4R; 108; CANR 4, 79; CP 1, 2, 3; DLB 45; SATA 1; SATA-Obit 33

Devenant, William 1606-1649 .... **LC 13**

Devi, Mahasweta 1926- .... **CLC 290**

Deville, Rene
See Kacew, Romain

Devkota, Laxmiprasad 1909-1959 . **TCLC 23**
See also CA 123

De Voto, Bernard (Augustine)
1897-1955 .... **TCLC 29**
See also CA 113; 160; DLB 9, 256; MAL 5; TCWW 1, 2

De Vries, Peter 1910-1993 ..... **CLC 1, 2, 3, 7, 10, 28, 46**
See also CA 17-20R; 142; CANR 41; CN 1, 2, 3, 4, 5; DAM NOV; DLB 6; DLBY 1982; MAL 5; MTCW 1, 2; MTFW 2005

Dewey, John 1859-1952 .... **TCLC 95**
See also CA 114; 170; CANR 144; DLB 246, 270; RGAL 4

Dexter, John
See Bradley, Marion Zimmer

Dexter, Martin
See Faust, Frederick

Dexter, Pete 1943- .... **CLC 34, 55**
See also BEST 89:2; CA 127; 131; CANR 129; CPW; DAM POP; INT CA-131; MAL 5; MTCW 1; MTFW 2005

Diamano, Silmang
See Senghor, Leopold Sedar

Diamant, Anita 1951- .... **CLC 239**
See also CA 145; CANR 126

Diamond, Neil 1941- .... **CLC 30**
See also CA 108

Diaz, Junot 1968- .... **CLC 258**
See also BYA 12; CA 161; CANR 119, 183; LLW; SSFS 20

Diaz del Castillo, Bernal c.
1496-1584 .... **HLCS 1; LC 31**
See also DLB 318; LAW

di Bassetto, Corno
See Shaw, George Bernard

Dick, Philip K. 1928-1982 ... **CLC 10, 30, 72; SSC 57**
See also AAYA 24; BPFB 1; BYA 11; CA 49-52; 106; CANR 2, 16, 132; CN 2, 3; CPW; DA3; DAM NOV, POP; DLB 8; MTCW 1, 2; MTFW 2005; NFS 5, 26; SCFW 1, 2; SFW 4

Dick, Philip Kindred
See Dick, Philip K.

Dickens, Charles 1812-1870 . **NCLC 3, 8, 18, 26, 37, 50, 86, 105, 113, 161, 187, 203, 206, 211, 217, 219; SSC 17, 49, 88; WLC 2**
See also AAYA 23; BRW 5; BRWC 1, 2; BYA 1, 2, 3, 13, 14; CDBLB 1832-1890; CLR 95; CMW 4; DA; DA3; DAB; DAC; DAM MST, NOV; DLB 21, 55, 70, 159, 166; EXPN; GL 2; HGG; JRDA; LAIT 1, 2; LATS 1:1; LMFS 1; MAICYA 1, 2; NFS 4, 5, 10, 14, 20, 25, 30, 33; RGEL 2; RGSF 2; SATA 15; SUFW 1; TEA; WCH; WLIT 4; WYA

Dickens, Charles John Huffam
See Dickens, Charles

Dickey, James 1923-1997 .... **CLC 1, 2, 4, 7, 10, 15, 47, 109; PC 40; TCLC 151**
See also AAYA 50; AITN 1, 2; AMWS 4; BPFB 1; CA 9-12R; 156; CABS 2; CANR 10, 48, 61, 105; CDALB 1968-1988; CP 1, 2, 3, 4, 5, 6; CPW; CSW; DA3; DAM NOV, POET, POP; DLB 5, 193, 342; DLBD 7; DLBY 1982, 1993, 1996, 1997, 1998; EWL 3; INT CANR-10; MAL 5; MTCW 1, 2; NFS 9; PFS 6, 11; RGAL 4; TUS

Dickey, James Lafayette
See Dickey, James

Dickey, William 1928-1994 .... **CLC 3, 28**
See also CA 9-12R; 145; CANR 24, 79; CP 1, 2, 3, 4; DLB 5

Dickinson, Charles 1951- .... **CLC 49**
See also CA 128; CANR 141

Dickinson, Emily 1830-1886 ... **NCLC 21, 77, 171; PC 1; WLC 2**
See also AAYA 22; AMW; AMWR 1; CDALB 1865-1917; DA; DA3; DAB; DAC; DAM MST, POET; DLB 1, 243; EXPP; FL 1:3; MBL; PAB; PFS 1, 2, 3, 4, 5, 6, 8, 10, 11, 13, 16, 28, 32, 35; RGAL 4; SATA 29; TUS; WP; WYA

Dickinson, Emily Elizabeth
See Dickinson, Emily

Dickinson, Mrs. Herbert Ward
See Phelps, Elizabeth Stuart

Dickinson, Peter 1927- .... **CLC 12, 35**
See also AAYA 9, 49; BYA 5; CA 41-44R; CANR 31, 58, 88, 134, 195; CLR 29, 125; CMW 4; DLB 87, 161, 276; JRDA; MAICYA 1, 2; SATA 5, 62, 95, 150; SFW 4; WYA; YAW

Dickinson, Peter Malcolm de Brissac
See Dickinson, Peter

Dickson, Carr
See Carr, John Dickson

Dickson, Carter
See Carr, John Dickson

Diderot, Denis 1713-1784 .... **LC 26, 126**
See also DLB 313; EW 4; GFL Beginnings to 1789; LMFS 1; RGWL 2, 3

Didion, Joan 1934- . **CLC 1, 3, 8, 14, 32, 129**
See also AITN 1; AMWS 4; CA 5-8R; CANR 14, 52, 76, 125, 174; CDALB 1968-1988; CN 2, 3, 4, 5, 6, 7; DA3; DAM NOV; DLB 2, 173, 185; DLBY 1981, 1986; EWL 3; MAL 5; MBL; MTCW 1, 2; MTFW 2005; NFS 3; RGAL 4; TCLE 1:1; TCWW 2; TUS

di Donato, Pietro 1911-1992 .... **TCLC 159**
See also AMWS 20; CA 101; 136; DLB 9

Dietrich, Robert
See Hunt, E. Howard

Difusa, Pati
See Almodovar, Pedro

di Lampedusa, Giuseppe Tomasi
See Lampedusa, Giuseppe di

Dillard, Annie 1945- ...... **CLC 9, 60, 115, 216**
See also AAYA 6, 43; AMWS 6; ANW; CA 49-52; CANR 3, 43, 62, 90, 125; DA3; DAM NOV; DLB 275, 278; DLBY 1980; LAIT 4, 5; MAL 5; MTCW 1, 2; MTFW 2005; NCFS 1; RGAL 4; SATA 10, 140; TCLE 1:1; TUS

Dillard, R(ichard) H(enry) W(ilde)
1937- .... **CLC 5**
See also CA 21-24R; CAAS 7; CANR 10; CP 2, 3, 4, 5, 6, 7; CSW; DLB 5, 244

Dillon, Eilis 1920-1994 .... **CLC 17**
See also CA 9-12R, 182; 147; CAAE 182; CAAS 3; CANR 4, 38, 78; CLR 26; MAICYA 1, 2; MAICYAS 1; SATA 2, 74; SATA-Essay 105; SATA-Obit 83; YAW

Dimont, Penelope
See Mortimer, Penelope (Ruth)

Dinesen, Isak
See Blixen, Karen

Ding Ling
See Chiang, Pin-chin

Diodorus Siculus c. 90B.C.-c.
31B.C. .... **CMLC 88**

Diphusa, Patty
See Almodovar, Pedro

Disch, Thomas M. 1940-2008 .... **CLC 7, 36**
See also AAYA 17; BPFB 1; CA 21-24R; 274; CAAS 4; CANR 17, 36, 54, 89; CLR 18; CP 5, 6, 7; DA3; DLB 8, 282; HGG; MAICYA 1, 2; MTCW 1, 2; MTFW 2005; SAAS 15; SATA 92; SATA-Obit 195; SCFW 1, 2; SFW 4; SUFW 2

Disch, Thomas Michael
See Disch, Thomas M.

Disch, Tom
See Disch, Thomas M.

d'Isly, Georges
See Simenon, Georges

Disraeli, Benjamin 1804-1881 ... **NCLC 2, 39, 79**
See also BRW 4; DLB 21, 55; RGEL 2

D'Israeli, Isaac 1766-1848 .... **NCLC 217**
See also DLB 107

Ditcum, Steve
See Crumb, R.

Dixon, Paige
See Corcoran, Barbara (Asenath)

Dixon, Stephen 1936- .... **CLC 52; SSC 16**
See also AMWS 12; CA 89-92; CANR 17, 40, 54, 91, 175; CN 4, 5, 6, 7; DLB 130; MAL 5

Dixon, Thomas, Jr. 1864-1946 ..... **TCLC 163**
See also RHW

Djebar, Assia 1936- .... **BLC 2:1; CLC 182; SSC 114**
See also CA 188; CANR 169; DLB 346; EWL 3; RGWL 3; WLIT 2

Doak, Annie
See Dillard, Annie

Dobell, Sydney Thompson
1824-1874 .... **NCLC 43; PC 100**
See also DLB 32; RGEL 2

Doblin, Alfred
See Doeblin, Alfred

Dobroliubov, Nikolai Aleksandrovich
See Dobrolyubov, Nikolai Alexandrovich

Dobrolyubov, Nikolai Alexandrovich
1836-1861 .... **NCLC 5**
See also DLB 277

Dobson, Austin 1840-1921 .... **TCLC 79**
See also DLB 35, 144

Dobyns, Stephen 1941- .... **CLC 37, 233**
See also AMWS 13; CA 45-48; CANR 2,
18, 99; CMW 4; CP 4, 5, 6, 7; PFS 23

Doctorow, Cory 1971- .... **CLC 273**
See also CA 221; CANR 203

Doctorow, E. L. 1931- ...... **CLC 6, 11, 15, 18,
37, 44, 65, 113, 214**
See also AAYA 22; AITN 2; AMWS 4;
BEST 89:3; BPFB 1; CA 45-48; CANR
2, 33, 51, 76, 97, 133, 170; CDALB 1968-
1988; CN 3, 4, 5, 6, 7; CPW; DA3; DAM
NOV, POP; DLB 2, 28, 173; DLBY 1980;
EWL 3; LAIT 3; MAL 5; MTCW 1, 2;
MTFW 2005; NFS 6; RGAL 4; RGHL;
RHW; SSFS 27; TCLE 1:1; TCWW 1, 2;
TUS

Doctorow, Edgar Laurence
See Doctorow, E. L.

Dodgson, Charles Lutwidge
See Carroll, Lewis

Dodsley, Robert 1703-1764 .... **LC 97**
See also DLB 95; RGEL 2

Dodson, Owen (Vincent)
1914-1983 .... **BLC 1:1; CLC 79**
See also BW 1; CA 65-68; 110; CANR 24;
DAM MULT; DLB 76

Doeblin, Alfred 1878-1957 .... **TCLC 13**
See also CA 110; 141; CDWLB 2; DLB 66;
EWL 3; RGWL 2, 3

Doerr, Harriet 1910-2002 .... **CLC 34**
See also CA 117; 122; 213; CANR 47; INT
CA-122; LATS 1:2

Domecq, Honorio Bustos
See Bioy Casares, Adolfo; Borges, Jorge
Luis

Domini, Rey
See Lorde, Audre

Dominic, R. B.
See Hennissart, Martha

Dominique
See Proust, Marcel

Don, A
See Stephen, Sir Leslie

Donaldson, Stephen R. 1947- ... **CLC 46, 138**
See also AAYA 36; BPFB 1; CA 89-92;
CANR 13, 55, 99; CPW; DAM POP;
FANT; INT CANR-13; SATA 121; SFW
4; SUFW 1, 2

Donleavy, J(ames) P(atrick) 1926- .... **CLC 1,
4, 6, 10, 45**
See also AITN 2; BPFB 1; CA 9-12R;
CANR 24, 49, 62, 80, 136; CBD; CD 5,
6; CN 1, 2, 3, 4, 5, 6, 7; DLB 6, 173; INT
CANR-24; MAL 5; MTCW 1, 2; MTFW
2005; RGAL 4

Donnadieu, Marguerite
See Duras, Marguerite

Donne, John 1572-1631 ... **LC 10, 24, 91; PC
1, 43; WLC 2**
See also AAYA 67; BRW 1; BRWC 1;
BRWR 2; CDBLB Before 1660; DA;
DAB; DAC; DAM MST, POET; DLB
121, 151; EXPP; PAB; PFS 2, 11, 35;
RGEL 3; TEA; WLIT 3; WP

Donnell, David 1939(?)- .... **CLC 34**
See also CA 197

Donoghue, Denis 1928- .... **CLC 209**
See also CA 17-20R; CANR 16, 102

Donoghue, Emma 1969- .... **CLC 239**
See also CA 155; CANR 103, 152, 196;
DLB 267; GLL 2; SATA 101

Donoghue, P.S.
See Hunt, E. Howard

Donoso, Jose 1924-1996 ..... **CLC 4, 8, 11, 32,
99; HLC 1; SSC 34; TCLC 133**
See also CA 81-84; 155; CANR 32, 73; CD-
WLB 3; CWW 2; DAM MULT; DLB 113;
EWL 3; HW 1, 2; LAW; LAWS 1; MTCW
1, 2; MTFW 2005; RGSF 2; WLIT 1

Donoso Yanez, Jose
See Donoso, Jose

Donovan, John 1928-1992 .... **CLC 35**
See also AAYA 20; CA 97-100; 137; CLR
3; MAICYA 1, 2; SATA 72; SATA-Brief
29; YAW

Don Roberto
See Cunninghame Graham, Robert Bontine

Doolittle, Hilda 1886-1961 . **CLC 3, 8, 14, 31,
34, 73; PC 5; WLC 3**
See also AAYA 66; AMWS 1; CA 97-100;
CANR 35, 131; DA; DAC; DAM MST,
POET; DLB 4, 45; EWL 3; FL 1:5; FW;
GLL 1; LMFS 2; MAL 5; MBL; MTCW
1, 2; MTFW 2005; PFS 6, 28; RGAL 4

Doppo
See Kunikida Doppo

Doppo, Kunikida
See Kunikida Doppo

Dorfman, Ariel 1942- .... **CLC 48, 77, 189;
HLC 1**
See also CA 124; 130; CANR 67, 70, 135;
CWW 2; DAM MULT; DFS 4; EWL 3;
HW 1, 2; INT CA-130; WLIT 1

Dorn, Edward (Merton)
1929-1999 .... **CLC 10, 18**
See also CA 93-96; 187; CANR 42, 79; CP
1, 2, 3, 4, 5, 6, 7; DLB 5; INT CA-93-96;
WP

Dor-Ner, Zvi .... **CLC 70**

Dorris, Michael 1945-1997 .... **CLC 109;
NNAL**
See also AAYA 20; BEST 90:1; BYA 12;
CA 102; CANR 19, 46, 75; CLR 58;
DA3; DAM MULT, NOV; DLB 175;
LAIT 5; MTCW 2; MTFW 2005; NFS 3;
RGAL 4; SATA 75; SATA-Obit 94;
TCWW 2; YAW

Dorris, Michael A.
See Dorris, Michael

Dorris, Michael Anthony
See Dorris, Michael

Dorsan, Luc
See Simenon, Georges

Dorsange, Jean
See Simenon, Georges

Dorset
See Sackville, Thomas

Dos Passos, John 1896-1970 ...... **CLC 1, 4, 8,
11, 15, 25, 34, 82; WLC 2**
See also AMW; BPFB 1; CA 1-4R; 29-32R;
CANR 3; CDALB 1929-1941; DA; DA3;
DAB; DAC; DAM MST, NOV; DLB 4,
9, 274, 316; DLBD 1, 15; DLBY 1996;
EWL 3; MAL 5; MTCW 1, 2; MTFW
2005; NFS 14; RGAL 4; TUS

Dos Passos, John Roderigo
See Dos Passos, John

Dossage, Jean
See Simenon, Georges

Dostoevsky, Fedor
See Dostoevsky, Fyodor

Dostoevsky, Fedor Mikhailovich
See Dostoevsky, Fyodor

Dostoevsky, Fyodor 1821-1881 ... **NCLC 2, 7,
21, 33, 43, 119, 167, 202; SSC 2, 33, 44,
134; WLC 2**
See also AAYA 40; DA; DA3; DAB; DAC;
DAM MST, NOV; DLB 238; EW 7;
EXPN; LATS 1:1; LMFS 1, 2; NFS 28;
RGSF 2; RGWL 2, 3; SSFS 8, 30; TWA

Doty, Mark 1953(?)- .... **CLC 176; PC 53**
See also AMWS 11; CA 161, 183; CAAE
183; CANR 110, 173; CP 7; PFS 28

Doty, Mark A.
See Doty, Mark

Doty, Mark Alan
See Doty, Mark

Doty, M.R.
See Doty, Mark

Doughty, Charles M(ontagu)
1843-1926 .... **TCLC 27**
See also CA 115; 178; DLB 19, 57, 174

Douglas, Ellen 1921- .... **CLC 73**
See also CA 115; CANR 41, 83; CN 5, 6,
7; CSW; DLB 292

Douglas, Gavin 1475(?)-1522 .... **LC 20**
See also DLB 132; RGEL 2

Douglas, George
See Brown, George Douglas

Douglas, Keith (Castellain)
1920-1944 .... **PC 106; TCLC 40**
See also BRW 7; CA 160; DLB 27; EWL
3; PAB; RGEL 2

Douglas, Leonard
See Bradbury, Ray

Douglas, Michael
See Crichton, Michael

Douglas, (George) Norman
1868-1952 .... **TCLC 68**
See also BRW 6; CA 119; 157; DLB 34,
195; RGEL 2

Douglas, William
See Brown, George Douglas

Douglass, Frederick 1817(?)-1895 .. **BLC 1:1;
NCLC 7, 55, 141; WLC 2**
See also AAYA 48; AFAW 1, 2; AMWC 1;
AMWS 3; CDALB 1640-1865; DA; DA3;
DAC; DAM MST, MULT; DLB 1, 43, 50,
79, 243; FW; LAIT 2; NCFS 2; RGAL 4;
SATA 29

Dourado, (Waldomiro Freitas) Autran
1926- .... **CLC 23, 60**
See also CA 25-28R; 179; CANR 34, 81;
DLB 145, 307; HW 2

Dourado, Waldomiro Freitas Autran
See Dourado, (Waldomiro Freitas) Autran

Dove, Rita 1952- . **BLC 2:1; BLCS; CLC 50,
81; PC 6**
See also AAYA 46; AMWS 4; BW 2; CA
109; CAAS 19; CANR 27, 42, 68, 76, 97,
132; CDALBS; CP 5, 6, 7; CSW; CWP;
DA3; DAM MULT, POET; DLB 120;
EWL 3; EXPP; MAL 5; MTCW 2; MTFW
2005; PFS 1, 15; RGAL 4

Dove, Rita Frances
See Dove, Rita

Doveglion
See Villa, Jose Garcia

Dowell, Coleman 1925-1985 .... **CLC 60**
See also CA 25-28R; 117; CANR 10; DLB
130; GLL 2

Downing, Major Jack
See Smith, Seba

Dowson, Ernest (Christopher)
1867-1900 .... **TCLC 4**
See also CA 105; 150; DLB 19, 135; RGEL
2

Doyle, A. Conan
See Doyle, Sir Arthur Conan

Doyle, Sir Arthur Conan
    1859-1930 ..... **SSC 12, 83, 95; TCLC 7; WLC 2**
        See also AAYA 14; BPFB 1; BRWS 2; BYA 4, 5, 11; CA 104; 122; CANR 131; CD-BLB 1890-1914; CLR 106; CMW 4; DA; DA3; DAB; DAC; DAM MST, NOV; DLB 18, 70, 156, 178; EXPS; HGG; LAIT 1; MSW; MTCW 1, 2; MTFW 2005; NFS 28; RGEL 2; RGSF 2; RHW; SATA 24; SCFW 1, 2; SFW 4; SSFS 2; TEA; WCH; WLIT 4; WYA; YAW

Doyle, Conan
        See Doyle, Sir Arthur Conan

Doyle, John
        See Graves, Robert

Doyle, Roddy 1958- .... **CLC 81, 178**
        See also AAYA 14; BRWS 5; CA 143; CANR 73, 128, 168, 200; CN 6, 7; DA3; DLB 194, 326; MTCW 2; MTFW 2005

Doyle, Sir A. Conan
        See Doyle, Sir Arthur Conan

Dr. A
        See Asimov, Isaac; Silverstein, Alvin; Silverstein, Virginia B.

Drabble, Margaret 1939- ...... **CLC 2, 3, 5, 8, 10, 22, 53, 129**
        See also BRWS 4; CA 13-16R; CANR 18, 35, 63, 112, 131, 174; CDBLB 1960 to Present; CN 1, 2, 3, 4, 5, 6, 7; CPW; DA3; DAB; DAC; DAM MST, NOV, POP; DLB 14, 155, 231; EWL 3; FW; MTCW 1, 2; MTFW 2005; RGEL 2; SATA 48; TEA

Drakulic, Slavenka
        See Drakulic, Slavenka

Drakulic, Slavenka 1949- .... **CLC 173**
        See also CA 144; CANR 92, 198; DLB 353

Drakulic-Ilic, Slavenka
        See Drakulic, Slavenka

Drakulic-Ilic, Slavenka
        See Drakulic, Slavenka

Drapier, M. B.
        See Swift, Jonathan

Drayham, James
        See Mencken, H. L.

Drayton, Michael 1563-1631 . **LC 8, 161; PC 98**
        See also DAM POET; DLB 121; RGEL 2

Dreadstone, Carl
        See Campbell, Ramsey

Dreiser, Theodore 1871-1945 .... **SSC 30, 114; TCLC 10, 18, 35, 83; WLC 2**
        See also AMW; AMWC 2; AMWR 2; BYA 15, 16; CA 106; 132; CDALB 1865-1917; DA; DA3; DAC; DAM MST, NOV; DLB 9, 12, 102, 137; DLBD 1; EWL 3; LAIT 2; LMFS 2; MAL 5; MTCW 1, 2; MTFW 2005; NFS 8, 17; RGAL 4; TUS

Dreiser, Theodore Herman Albert
        See Dreiser, Theodore

Drexler, Rosalyn 1926- .... **CLC 2, 6**
        See also CA 81-84; CAD; CANR 68, 124; CD 5, 6; CWD; MAL 5

Dreyer, Carl Theodor 1889-1968 ...... **CLC 16**
        See also CA 116

Drieu la Rochelle, Pierre
    1893-1945 .... **TCLC 21**
        See also CA 117; 250; DLB 72; EWL 3; GFL 1789 to the Present

Drieu la Rochelle, Pierre-Eugene 1893-1945
        See Drieu la Rochelle, Pierre

Drinkwater, John 1882-1937 .... **TCLC 57**
        See also CA 109; 149; DLB 10, 19, 149; RGEL 2

Drop Shot
        See Cable, George Washington

Droste-Hulshoff, Annette Freiin von
    1797-1848 .... **NCLC 3, 133**
        See also CDWLB 2; DLB 133; RGSF 2; RGWL 2, 3

Drummond, Walter
        See Silverberg, Robert

Drummond, William Henry
    1854-1907 .... **TCLC 25**
        See also CA 160; DLB 92

Drummond de Andrade, Carlos
    1902-1987 .... **CLC 18; TCLC 139**
        See also CA 132; 123; DLB 307; EWL 3; LAW; RGWL 2, 3

Drummond of Hawthornden, William
    1585-1649 .... **LC 83**
        See also DLB 121, 213; RGEL 2

Drury, Allen (Stuart) 1918-1998 .... **CLC 37**
        See also CA 57-60; 170; CANR 18, 52; CN 1, 2, 3, 4, 5, 6; INT CANR-18

Druse, Eleanor
        See King, Stephen

Dryden, John 1631-1700 ..... **DC 3; LC 3, 21, 115; PC 25; WLC 2**
        See also BRW 2; BRWR 3; CDBLB 1660-1789; DA; DAB; DAC; DAM DRAM, MST, POET; DLB 80, 101, 131; EXPP; IDTP; LMFS 1; RGEL 2; TEA; WLIT 3

du Aime, Albert
        See Wharton, William

du Aime, Albert William
        See Wharton, William

du Bellay, Joachim 1524-1560 .... **LC 92**
        See also DLB 327; GFL Beginnings to 1789; RGWL 2, 3

Duberman, Martin 1930- .... **CLC 8**
        See also CA 1-4R; CAD; CANR 2, 63, 137, 174; CD 5, 6

Dubie, Norman (Evans) 1945- .... **CLC 36**
        See also CA 69-72; CANR 12, 115; CP 3, 4, 5, 6, 7; DLB 120; PFS 12

Du Bois, W. E. B. 1868-1963 .... **BLC 1:1; CLC 1, 2, 13, 64, 96; HR 1:2; TCLC 169; WLC 2**
        See also AAYA 40; AFAW 1, 2; AMWC 1; AMWS 2; BW 1, 3; CA 85-88; CANR 34, 82, 132; CDALB 1865-1917; DA; DA3; DAC; DAM MST, MULT, NOV; DLB 47, 50, 91, 246, 284; EWL 3; EXPP; LAIT 2; LMFS 2; MAL 5; MTCW 1, 2; MTFW 2005; NCFS 1; PFS 13; RGAL 4; SATA 42

Du Bois, William Edward Burghardt
        See Du Bois, W. E. B.

Dubus, Andre 1936-1999 ..... **CLC 13, 36, 97; SSC 15, 118**
        See also AMWS 7; CA 21-24R; 177; CANR 17; CN 5, 6; CSW; DLB 130; INT CANR-17; RGAL 4; SSFS 10; TCLE 1:1

Duca Minimo
        See D'Annunzio, Gabriele

Ducharme, Rejean 1941- .... **CLC 74**
        See also CA 165; DLB 60

du Chatelet, Emilie 1706-1749 .... **LC 96**
        See also DLB 313

Duchen, Claire .... **CLC 65**

Duck, Stephen 1705(?)-1756 .... **PC 89**
        See also DLB 95; RGEL 2

Duclos, Charles Pinot- 1704-1772 .... **LC 1**
        See also GFL Beginnings to 1789

Ducornet, Erica 1943- .... **CLC 232**
        See also CA 37-40R; CANR 14, 34, 54, 82; SATA 7

Ducornet, Rikki
        See Ducornet, Erica

Dudek, Louis 1918-2001 .... **CLC 11, 19**
        See also CA 45-48; 215; CAAS 14; CANR 1; CP 1, 2, 3, 4, 5, 6, 7; DLB 88

Duerrematt, Friedrich
        See Durrenmatt, Friedrich

Duffy, Bruce 1953(?)- .... **CLC 50**
        See also CA 172

Duffy, Maureen 1933- .... **CLC 37**
        See also CA 25-28R; CANR 33, 68; CBD; CN 1, 2, 3, 4, 5, 6, 7; CP 5, 6, 7; CWD; CWP; DFS 15; DLB 14, 310; FW; MTCW 1

Duffy, Maureen Patricia
        See Duffy, Maureen

Du Fu
        See Tu Fu

Dugan, Alan 1923-2003 .... **CLC 2, 6**
        See also CA 81-84; 220; CANR 119; CP 1, 2, 3, 4, 5, 6, 7; DLB 5; MAL 5; PFS 10

du Gard, Roger Martin
        See Martin du Gard, Roger

Duhamel, Georges 1884-1966 .... **CLC 8**
        See also CA 81-84; 25-28R; CANR 35; DLB 65; EWL 3; GFL 1789 to the Present; MTCW 1

du Hault, Jean
        See Grindel, Eugene

Dujardin, Edouard (Emile Louis)
    1861-1949 .... **TCLC 13**
        See also CA 109; DLB 123

Duke, Raoul
        See Thompson, Hunter S.

Dulles, John Foster 1888-1959 .... **TCLC 72**
        See also CA 115; 149

Dumas, Alexandre (pere)
    1802-1870 .... **NCLC 11, 71; WLC 2**
        See also AAYA 22; BYA 3; CLR 134; DA; DA3; DAB; DAC; DAM MST, NOV; DLB 119, 192; EW 6; GFL 1789 to the Present; LAIT 1, 2; NFS 14, 19; RGWL 2, 3; SATA 18; TWA; WCH

Dumas, Alexandre (fils) 1824-1895 ...... **DC 1; NCLC 9**
        See also DLB 192; GFL 1789 to the Present; RGWL 2, 3

Dumas, Claudine
        See Malzberg, Barry N(athaniel)

Dumas, Henry L. 1934-1968 . **BLC 2:1; CLC 6, 62; SSC 107**
        See also BW 1; CA 85-88; DLB 41; RGAL 4

du Maurier, Daphne 1907-1989 .. **CLC 6, 11, 59; SSC 18, 129; TCLC 209**
        See also AAYA 37; BPFB 1; BRWS 3; CA 5-8R; 128; CANR 6, 55; CMW 4; CN 1, 2, 3, 4; CPW; DA3; DAB; DAC; DAM MST, POP; DLB 191; GL 2; HGG; LAIT 3; MSW; MTCW 1, 2; NFS 12; RGEL 2; RGSF 2; RHW; SATA 27; SATA-Obit 60; SSFS 14, 16; TEA

Du Maurier, George 1834-1896 ..... **NCLC 86**
        See also DLB 153, 178; RGEL 2

Dunbar, Alice
        See Nelson, Alice Ruth Moore Dunbar

Dunbar, Alice Moore
        See Nelson, Alice Ruth Moore Dunbar

Dunbar, Paul Laurence
    1872-1906 .... **BLC 1:1; PC 5; SSC 8; TCLC 2, 12; WLC 2**
        See also AAYA 75; AFAW 1, 2; AMWS 2; BW 1, 3; CA 104; 124; CANR 79; CDALB 1865-1917; DA; DA3; DAC; DAM MST, MULT, POET; DLB 50, 54, 78; EXPP; MAL 5; PFS 33; RGAL 4; SATA 34

Dunbar, William 1460(?)-1520(?) .... **LC 20; PC 67**
        See also BRWS 8; DLB 132, 146; RGEL 2

Dunbar-Nelson, Alice
        See Nelson, Alice Ruth Moore Dunbar

Dunbar-Nelson, Alice Moore
        See Nelson, Alice Ruth Moore Dunbar

Duncan, Dora Angela
        See Duncan, Isadora

Duncan, Isadora 1877(?)-1927 .... **TCLC 68**
See also CA 118; 149

Duncan, Lois 1934- .... **CLC 26**
See also AAYA 4, 34; BYA 6, 8; CA 1-4R;
CANR 2, 23, 36, 111; CLR 29, 129;
JRDA; MAICYA 1, 2; MAICYAS 1;
MTFW 2005; SAAS 2; SATA 1, 36, 75,
133, 141; SATA-Essay 141; WYA; YAW

Duncan, Robert 1919-1988 ... **CLC 1, 2, 4, 7,
15, 41, 55; PC 2, 75**
See also BG 1:2; CA 9-12R; 124; CANR
28, 62; CP 1, 2, 3, 4; DAM POET; DLB
5, 16, 193; EWL 3; MAL 5; MTCW 1, 2;
MTFW 2005; PFS 13; RGAL 4; WP

Duncan, Sara Jeannette
1861-1922 .... **TCLC 60**
See also CA 157; DLB 92

Dunlap, William 1766-1839 .... **NCLC 2**
See also DLB 30, 37, 59; RGAL 4

Dunn, Douglas (Eaglesham) 1942- .... **CLC 6,
40**
See also BRWS 10; CA 45-48; CANR 2,
33, 126; CP 1, 2, 3, 4, 5, 6, 7; DLB 40;
MTCW 1

Dunn, Katherine 1945- .... **CLC 71**
See also CA 33-36R; CANR 72; HGG;
MTCW 2; MTFW 2005

Dunn, Stephen 1939- .... **CLC 36, 206**
See also AMWS 11; CA 33-36R; CANR
12, 48, 53, 105; CP 3, 4, 5, 6, 7; DLB
105; PFS 21

Dunn, Stephen Elliott
See Dunn, Stephen

Dunne, Finley Peter 1867-1936 ...... **TCLC 28**
See also CA 108; 178; DLB 11, 23; RGAL
4

Dunne, John Gregory 1932-2003 ..... **CLC 28**
See also CA 25-28R; 222; CANR 14, 50;
CN 5, 6, 7; DLBY 1980

Dunsany, Lord
See Dunsany, Edward John Moreton Drax
Plunkett

**Dunsany, Edward John Moreton Drax
Plunkett** 1878-1957 .... **TCLC 2, 59**
See also CA 104; 148; DLB 10, 77, 153,
156, 255; FANT; MTCW 2; RGEL 2;
SFW 4; SUFW 1

Duns Scotus, John 1266(?)-1308 ... **CMLC 59**
See also DLB 115

Duong, Thu Huong 1947- .... **CLC 273**
See also CA 152; CANR 106, 166; DLB
348; NFS 23

Duong Thu Huong
See Duong, Thu Huong

du Perry, Jean
See Simenon, Georges

Durang, Christopher 1949- .... **CLC 27, 38**
See also CA 105; CAD; CANR 50, 76, 130;
CD 5, 6; MTCW 2; MTFW 2005

Durang, Christopher Ferdinand
See Durang, Christopher

Duras, Claire de 1777-1832 .... **NCLC 154**

Duras, Marguerite 1914-1996 . **CLC 3, 6, 11,
20, 34, 40, 68, 100; SSC 40**
See also BPFB 1; CA 25-28R; 151; CANR
50; CWW 2; DFS 21; DLB 83, 321; EWL
3; FL 1:5; GFL 1789 to the Present; IDFW
4; MTCW 1, 2; RGWL 2, 3; TWA

Durban, (Rosa) Pam 1947- .... **CLC 39**
See also CA 123; CANR 98; CSW

Durcan, Paul 1944- .... **CLC 43, 70**
See also CA 134; CANR 123; CP 1, 5, 6, 7;
DAM POET; EWL 3

d'Urfe, Honore
See Urfe, Honore d'

Durfey, Thomas 1653-1723 .... **LC 94**
See also DLB 80; RGEL 2

Durkheim, Emile 1858-1917 .... **TCLC 55**
See also CA 249

Durrell, Lawrence 1912-1990 .... **CLC 1, 4, 6,
8, 13, 27, 41**
See also BPFB 1; BRWR 3; BRWS 1; CA
9-12R; 132; CANR 40, 77; CDBLB 1945-
1960; CN 1, 2, 3, 4; CP 1, 2, 3, 4, 5; DAM
NOV; DLB 15, 27, 204; DLBY 1990;
EWL 3; MTCW 1, 2; RGEL 2; SFW 4;
TEA

Durrell, Lawrence George
See Durrell, Lawrence

Durrenmatt, Friedrich
See Durrenmatt, Friedrich

Durrenmatt, Friedrich 1921-1990 . **CLC 1, 4,
8, 11, 15, 43, 102**
See also CA 17-20R; CANR 33; CDWLB
2; CMW 4; DAM DRAM; DLB 69, 124;
EW 13; EWL 3; MTCW 1, 2; RGHL;
RGWL 2, 3

Dutt, Michael Madhusudan
1824-1873 .... **NCLC 118**

Dutt, Toru 1856-1877 .... **NCLC 29**
See also DLB 240

Dwight, Timothy 1752-1817 .... **NCLC 13**
See also DLB 37; RGAL 4

Dworkin, Andrea 1946-2005 ..... **CLC 43, 123**
See also CA 77-80; 238; CAAS 21; CANR
16, 39, 76, 96; FL 1:5; FW; GLL 1; INT
CANR-16; MTCW 1, 2; MTFW 2005

Dwyer, Deanna
See Koontz, Dean

Dwyer, K.R.
See Koontz, Dean

Dybek, Stuart 1942- .... **CLC 114; SSC 55**
See also CA 97-100; CANR 39; DLB 130;
SSFS 23

Dye, Richard
See De Voto, Bernard (Augustine)

Dyer, Geoff 1958- .... **CLC 149**
See also CA 125; CANR 88

Dyer, George 1755-1841 .... **NCLC 129**
See also DLB 93

Dylan, Bob 1941- .... **CLC 3, 4, 6, 12, 77; PC
37**
See also AMWS 18; CA 41-44R; CANR
108; CP 1, 2, 3, 4, 5, 6, 7; DLB 16

Dyson, John 1943- .... **CLC 70**
See also CA 144

Dzyubin, Eduard Georgievich
1895-1934 .... **TCLC 60**
See also CA 170; EWL 3

E. V. L.
See Lucas, E(dward) V(errall)

Eagleton, Terence
See Eagleton, Terry

Eagleton, Terence Francis
See Eagleton, Terry

Eagleton, Terry 1943- .... **CLC 63, 132**
See also CA 57-60; CANR 7, 23, 68, 115,
198; DLB 242; LMFS 2; MTCW 1, 2;
MTFW 2005

Early, Jack
See Scoppettone, Sandra

East, Michael
See West, Morris L(anglo)

Eastaway, Edward
See Thomas, (Philip) Edward

Eastlake, William (Derry)
1917-1997 .... **CLC 8**
See also CA 5-8R; 158; CAAS 1; CANR 5,
63; CN 1, 2, 3, 4, 5, 6; DLB 6, 206; INT
CANR-5; MAL 5; TCWW 1, 2

Eastman, Charles A(lexander)
1858-1939 .... **NNAL; TCLC 55**
See also CA 179; CANR 91; DAM MULT;
DLB 175; YABC 1

Eaton, Edith Maude
1865-1914 .... **AAL; TCLC 232**
See also CA 154; DLB 221, 312; FW

Eaton, (Lillie) Winnifred 1875-1954 .... **AAL**
See also CA 217; DLB 221, 312; RGAL 4

Eberhart, Richard 1904-2005 ...... **CLC 3, 11,
19, 56; PC 76**
See also AMW; CA 1-4R; 240; CANR 2,
125; CDALB 1941-1968; CP 1, 2, 3, 4, 5,
6, 7; DAM POET; DLB 48; MAL 5;
MTCW 1; RGAL 4

Eberhart, Richard Ghormley
See Eberhart, Richard

Eberstadt, Fernanda 1960- .... **CLC 39**
See also CA 136; CANR 69, 128

Ebner, Margaret c. 1291-1351 ...... **CMLC 98**

**Echegaray (y Eizaguirre), Jose (Maria
Waldo)** 1832-1916 .... **HLCS 1; TCLC 4**
See also CA 104; CANR 32; DLB 329;
EWL 3; HW 1; MTCW 1

Echeverria, (Jose) Esteban (Antonino)
1805-1851 .... **NCLC 18**
See also LAW

Echo
See Proust, Marcel

Eckert, Allan W. 1931- .... **CLC 17**
See also AAYA 18; BYA 2; CA 13-16R;
CANR 14, 45; INT CANR-14; MAICYA
2; MAICYAS 1; SAAS 21; SATA 29, 91;
SATA-Brief 27

Eckhart, Meister 1260(?)-1327(?) .. **CMLC 9,
80**
See also DLB 115; LMFS 1

Eckmar, F. R.
See de Hartog, Jan

Eco, Umberto 1932- .... **CLC 28, 60, 142, 248**
See also BEST 90:1; BPFB 1; CA 77-80;
CANR 12, 33, 55, 110, 131, 195; CPW;
CWW 2; DA3; DAM NOV, POP; DLB
196, 242; EWL 3; MSW; MTCW 1, 2;
MTFW 2005; NFS 22; RGWL 3; WLIT 7

Eddison, E(ric) R(ucker)
1882-1945 .... **TCLC 15**
See also CA 109; 156; DLB 255; FANT;
SFW 4; SUFW 1

Eddy, Mary (Ann Morse) Baker
1821-1910 .... **TCLC 71**
See also CA 113; 174

Edel, (Joseph) Leon 1907-1997 .. **CLC 29, 34**
See also CA 1-4R; 161; CANR 1, 22, 112;
DLB 103; INT CANR-22

Eden, Emily 1797-1869 .... **NCLC 10**

Edgar, David 1948- .... **CLC 42**
See also CA 57-60; CANR 12, 61, 112;
CBD; CD 5, 6; DAM DRAM; DFS 15;
DLB 13, 233; MTCW 1

Edgerton, Clyde 1944- .... **CLC 39**
See also AAYA 17; CA 118; 134; CANR
64, 125, 195; CN 7; CSW; DLB 278; INT
CA-134; TCLE 1:1; YAW

Edgerton, Clyde Carlyle
See Edgerton, Clyde

Edgeworth, Maria 1768-1849 ... **NCLC 1, 51,
158; SSC 86**
See also BRWS 3; CLR 153; DLB 116, 159,
163; FL 1:3; FW; RGEL 2; SATA 21;
TEA; WLIT 3

Edmonds, Paul
See Kuttner, Henry

Edmonds, Walter D(umaux)
1903-1998 .... **CLC 35**
See also BYA 2; CA 5-8R; CANR 2; CWRI
5; DLB 9; LAIT 1; MAICYA 1, 2; MAL
5; RHW; SAAS 4; SATA 1, 27; SATA-
Obit 99

Edmondson, Wallace
See Ellison, Harlan

Edson, Margaret 1961- .... **CLC 199; DC 24**
See also AMWS 18; CA 190; DFS 13; DLB
266

Edson, Russell 1935- .... **CLC 13**
See also CA 33-36R; CANR 115; CP 2, 3, 4, 5, 6, 7; DLB 244; WP

Edwards, Bronwen Elizabeth
See Rose, Wendy

Edwards, Eli
See McKay, Claude

Edwards, G(erald) B(asil)
1899-1976 .... **CLC 25**
See also CA 201; 110

Edwards, Gus 1939- .... **CLC 43**
See also CA 108; INT CA-108

Edwards, Jonathan 1703-1758 .... **LC 7, 54**
See also AMW; DA; DAC; DAM MST; DLB 24, 270; RGAL 4; TUS

Edwards, Marilyn
See French, Marilyn

Edwards, Sarah Pierpont 1710-1758 .. **LC 87**
See also DLB 200

Efron, Marina Ivanovna Tsvetaeva
See Tsvetaeva, Marina

Egeria fl. 4th cent. - .... **CMLC 70**

Eggers, Dave 1970- .... **CLC 241**
See also AAYA 56; CA 198; CANR 138; MTFW 2005

Egoyan, Atom 1960- .... **CLC 151, 291**
See also AAYA 63; CA 157; CANR 151

Ehle, John (Marsden, Jr.) 1925- ...... **CLC 27**
See also CA 9-12R; CSW

Ehrenbourg, Ilya (Grigoryevich)
See Ehrenburg, Ilya (Grigoryevich)

Ehrenburg, Ilya (Grigoryevich)
1891-1967 .... **CLC 18, 34, 62**
See Erenburg, Ilya (Grigoryevich)
See also CA 102; 25-28R; EWL 3

Ehrenburg, Ilyo (Grigoryevich)
See Ehrenburg, Ilya (Grigoryevich)

Ehrenreich, Barbara 1941- ..... **CLC 110, 267**
See also BEST 90:4; CA 73-76; CANR 16, 37, 62, 117, 167; DLB 246; FW; LNFS 1; MTCW 1, 2; MTFW 2005

Ehrlich, Gretel 1946- .... **CLC 249**
See also ANW; CA 140; CANR 74, 146; DLB 212, 275; TCWW 2

Eich, Gunter
See Eich, Gunter

Eich, Gunter 1907-1972 .... **CLC 15**
See also CA 111; 93-96; DLB 69, 124; EWL 3; RGWL 2, 3

Eichendorff, Joseph 1788-1857 .... **NCLC 8, 225**
See also DLB 90; RGWL 2, 3

Eigner, Larry
See Eigner, Laurence (Joel)

Eigner, Laurence (Joel) 1927-1996 ..... **CLC 9**
See also CA 9-12R; 151; CAAS 23; CANR 6, 84; CP 1, 2, 3, 4, 5, 6, 7; DLB 5; WP

Eilhart von Oberge c. 1140-c. 1195 .... **CMLC 67**
See also DLB 148

Einhard c. 770-840 .... **CMLC 50**
See also DLB 148

Einstein, Albert 1879-1955 .... **TCLC 65**
See also CA 121; 133; MTCW 1, 2

Eiseley, Loren
See Eiseley, Loren Corey

Eiseley, Loren Corey 1907-1977 .... **CLC 7**
See also AAYA 5; ANW; CA 1-4R; 73-76; CANR 6; DLB 275; DLBD 17

Eisenstadt, Jill 1963- .... **CLC 50**
See also CA 140

Eisenstein, Sergei (Mikhailovich)
1898-1948 .... **TCLC 57**
See also CA 114; 149

Eisner, Simon
See Kornbluth, C(yril) M.

Eisner, Will 1917-2005 .... **CLC 237**
See also AAYA 52; CA 108; 235; CANR 114, 140, 179; MTFW 2005; SATA 31, 165

Eisner, William Erwin
See Eisner, Will

Ekeloef, Bengt Gunnar
See Ekelof, Gunnar

Ekeloef, Gunnar
See Ekelof, Gunnar

Ekelof, Gunnar 1907-1968 ... **CLC 27; PC 23**
See also CA 123; 25-28R; DAM POET; DLB 259; EW 12; EWL 3

Ekelund, Vilhelm 1880-1949 .... **TCLC 75**
See also CA 189; EWL 3

Ekman, Kerstin (Lillemor) 1933- ... **CLC 279**
See also CA 154; CANR 124; DLB 257; EWL 3

Ekwensi, C. O. D.
See Ekwensi, Cyprian

Ekwensi, Cyprian 1921-2007 .... **BLC 1:1; CLC 4**
See also AFW; BW 2, 3; CA 29-32R; CANR 18, 42, 74, 125; CDWLB 3; CN 1, 2, 3, 4, 5, 6; CWRI 5; DAM MULT; DLB 117; EWL 3; MTCW 1, 2; RGEL 2; SATA 66; WLIT 2

Ekwensi, Cyprian Odiatu Duaka
See Ekwensi, Cyprian

Elaine
See Leverson, Ada Esther

El Conde de Pepe
See Mihura, Miguel

El Crummo
See Crumb, R.

Elder, Lonne III 1931-1996 .. **BLC 1:1; DC 8**
See also BW 1, 3; CA 81-84; 152; CAD; CANR 25; DAM MULT; DLB 7, 38, 44; MAL 5

Eleanor of Aquitaine 1122-1204 ... **CMLC 39**

Elia
See Lamb, Charles

Eliade, Mircea 1907-1986 .... **CLC 19**
See also CA 65-68; 119; CANR 30, 62; CD-WLB 4; DLB 220; EWL 3; MTCW 1; RGWL 3; SFW 4

Eliot, A. D.
See Jewett, Sarah Orne

Eliot, Alice
See Jewett, Sarah Orne

Eliot, Dan
See Silverberg, Robert

Eliot, George 1819-1880 ...... **NCLC 4, 13, 23, 41, 49, 89, 118, 183, 199, 209; PC 20; SSC 72, 139; WLC 2**
See also BRW 5; BRWC 1, 2; BRWR 2; CDBLB 1832-1890; CN 7; CPW; DA; DA3; DAB; DAC; DAM MST, NOV; DLB 21, 35, 55; FL 1:3; LATS 1:1; LMFS 1; NFS 17, 20, 34; RGEL 2; RGSF 2; SSFS 8; TEA; WLIT 3

Eliot, John 1604-1690 .... **LC 5**
See also DLB 24

Eliot, T. S. 1888-1965 .. **CLC 1, 2, 3, 6, 9, 10, 13, 15, 24, 34, 41, 55, 57, 113; DC 28; PC 5, 31, 90; TCLC 236; WLC 2**
See also AAYA 28; AMW; AMWC 1; AMWR 1; BRW 7; BRWR 2; CA 5-8R; 25-28R; CANR 41; CBD; CDALB 1929-1941; DA; DA3; DAB; DAC; DAM DRAM, MST, POET; DFS 4, 13; DLB 7, 10, 45, 63, 245, 329; DLBY 1988; EWL 3; EXPP; LAIT 3; LATS 1:1; LMFS 2; MAL 5; MTCW 1, 2; MTFW 2005; NCFS 5; PAB; PFS 1, 7, 20, 33; RGAL 4; RGEL 2; TUS; WLIT 4; WP

Eliot, Thomas Stearns
See Eliot, T. S.

Elisabeth of Schonau c. 1129-1165 .... **CMLC 82**

Elizabeth 1866-1941 .... **TCLC 41**

Elizabeth I, Queen of England
1533-1603 .... **LC 118**
See also BRWS 16; DLB 136

Elkin, Stanley L. 1930-1995 ..... **CLC 4, 6, 9, 14, 27, 51, 91; SSC 12**
See also AMWS 6; BPFB 1; CA 9-12R; 148; CANR 8, 46; CN 1, 2, 3, 4, 5, 6; CPW; DAM NOV, POP; DLB 2, 28, 218, 278; DLBY 1980; EWL 3; INT CANR-8; MAL 5; MTCW 1, 2; MTFW 2005; RGAL 4; TCLE 1:1

Elledge, Scott .... **CLC 34**

Eller, Scott
See Shepard, Jim

Elliott, Don
See Silverberg, Robert

Elliott, Ebenezer 1781-1849 .... **PC 96**
See also DLB 96, 190; RGEL 2

Elliott, George P(aul) 1918-1980 .... **CLC 2**
See also CA 1-4R; 97-100; CANR 2; CN 1, 2; CP 3; DLB 244; MAL 5

Elliott, Janice 1931-1995 .... **CLC 47**
See also CA 13-16R; CANR 8, 29, 84; CN 5, 6, 7; DLB 14; SATA 119

Elliott, Sumner Locke 1917-1991 ..... **CLC 38**
See also CA 5-8R; 134; CANR 2, 21; DLB 289

Elliott, William
See Bradbury, Ray

Ellis, A. E. .... **CLC 7**

Ellis, Alice Thomas
See Haycraft, Anna

Ellis, Bret Easton 1964- ..... **CLC 39, 71, 117, 229**
See also AAYA 2, 43; CA 118; 123; CANR 51, 74, 126; CN 6, 7; CPW; DA3; DAM POP; DLB 292; HGG; INT CA-123; MTCW 2; MTFW 2005; NFS 11

Ellis, (Henry) Havelock
1859-1939 .... **TCLC 14**
See also CA 109; 169; DLB 190

Ellis, Landon
See Ellison, Harlan

Ellis, Trey 1962- .... **CLC 55**
See also CA 146; CANR 92; CN 7

Ellison, Harlan 1934- .... **CLC 1, 13, 42, 139; SSC 14**
See also AAYA 29; BPFB 1; BYA 14; CA 5-8R; CANR 5, 46, 115; CPW; DAM POP; DLB 8, 335; HGG; INT CANR-5; MTCW 1, 2; MTFW 2005; SCFW 2; SFW 4; SSFS 13, 14, 15, 21; SUFW 1, 2

Ellison, Ralph 1914-1994 .... **BLC 1:1, 2:2; CLC 1, 3, 11, 54, 86, 114; SSC 26, 79; WLC 2**
See also AAYA 19; AFAW 1, 2; AMWC 2; AMWR 2; AMWS 2; BPFB 1; BW 1, 3; BYA 2; CA 9-12R; 145; CANR 24, 53; CDALB 1941-1968; CN 1, 2, 3, 4, 5; CSW; DA; DA3; DAB; DAC; DAM MST, MULT, NOV; DLB 2, 76, 227; DLBY 1994; EWL 3; EXPN; EXPS; LAIT 4; MAL 5; MTCW 1, 2; MTFW 2005; NCFS 3; NFS 2, 21; RGAL 4; RGSF 2; SSFS 1, 11; YAW

Ellison, Ralph Waldo
See Ellison, Ralph

Ellmann, Lucy 1956- .... **CLC 61**
See also CA 128; CANR 154

Ellmann, Lucy Elizabeth
See Ellmann, Lucy

Ellmann, Richard (David)
1918-1987 .... **CLC 50**
See also BEST 89:2; CA 1-4R; 122; CANR 2, 28, 61; DLB 103; DLBY 1987; MTCW 1, 2; MTFW 2005

FitzGerald, Edward 1809-1883 ...... **NCLC 9, 153; PC 79**
See also BRW 4; DLB 32; RGEL 2

Fitzgerald, F. Scott 1896-1940 ...... **SSC 6, 31, 75; TCLC 1, 6, 14, 28, 55, 157; WLC 2**
See also AAYA 24; AITN 1; AMW; AMWC 2; AMWR 1; BPFB 1; CA 110; 123; CDALB 1917-1929; DA; DA3; DAB; DAC; DAM MST, NOV; DLB 4, 9, 86, 219, 273; DLBD 1, 15, 16; DLBY 1981, 1996; EWL 3; EXPN; EXPS; LAIT 3; MAL 5; MTCW 1, 2; MTFW 2005; NFS 2, 19, 20; RGAL 4; RGSF 2; SSFS 4, 15, 21, 25; TUS

Fitzgerald, Francis Scott Key
See Fitzgerald, F. Scott

Fitzgerald, Penelope 1916-2000 . **CLC 19, 51, 61, 143**
See also BRWS 5; CA 85-88; 190; CAAS 10; CANR 56, 86, 131; CN 3, 4, 5, 6, 7; DLB 14, 194, 326; EWL 3; MTCW 2; MTFW 2005

Fitzgerald, Robert (Stuart) 1910-1985 .... **CLC 39**
See also CA 1-4R; 114; CANR 1; CP 1, 2, 3, 4; DLBY 1980; MAL 5

FitzGerald, Robert D(avid) 1902-1987 .... **CLC 19**
See also CA 17-20R; CP 1, 2, 3, 4; DLB 260; RGEL 2

Fitzgerald, Zelda (Sayre) 1900-1948 .... **TCLC 52**
See also AMWS 9; CA 117; 126; DLBY 1984

Flanagan, Thomas (James Bonner) 1923-2002 .... **CLC 25, 52**
See also CA 108; 206; CANR 55; CN 3, 4, 5, 6, 7; DLBY 1980; INT CA-108; MTCW 1; RHW; TCLE 1:1

Flashman, Harry Paget
See Fraser, George MacDonald

Flaubert, Gustave 1821-1880 .... **NCLC 2, 10, 19, 62, 66, 135, 179, 185; SSC 11, 60; WLC 2**
See also DA; DA3; DAB; DAC; DAM MST, NOV; DLB 119, 301; EW 7; EXPS; GFL 1789 to the Present; LAIT 2; LMFS 1; NFS 14; RGSF 2; RGWL 2, 3; SSFS 6; TWA

Flavius Josephus
See Josephus, Flavius

Flecker, Herman Elroy
See Flecker, (Herman) James Elroy

Flecker, (Herman) James Elroy 1884-1915 .... **TCLC 43**
See also CA 109; 150; DLB 10, 19; RGEL 2

Fleming, Ian 1908-1964 ... **CLC 3, 30; TCLC 193**
See also AAYA 26; BPFB 1; BRWS 14; CA 5-8R; CANR 59; CDBLB 1945-1960; CMW 4; CPW; DA3; DAM POP; DLB 87, 201; MSW; MTCW 1, 2; MTFW 2005; RGEL 2; SATA 9; TEA; YAW

Fleming, Ian Lancaster
See Fleming, Ian

Fleming, Thomas 1927- .... **CLC 37**
See also CA 5-8R; CANR 10, 102, 155, 197; INT CANR-10; SATA 8

Fleming, Thomas James
See Fleming, Thomas

Fletcher, John 1579-1625 . **DC 6; LC 33, 151**
See also BRW 2; CDBLB Before 1660; DLB 58; RGEL 2; TEA

Fletcher, John Gould 1886-1950 .... **TCLC 35**
See also CA 107; 167; DLB 4, 45; LMFS 2; MAL 5; RGAL 4

Fleur, Paul
See Pohl, Frederik

Flieg, Helmut
See Heym, Stefan

Flooglebuckle, Al
See Spiegelman, Art

Flying Officer X
See Bates, H(erbert) E(rnest)

Fo, Dario 1926- .... **CLC 32, 109, 227; DC 10**
See also CA 116; 128; CANR 68, 114, 134, 164; CWW 2; DA3; DAM DRAM; DFS 23; DLB 330; DLBY 1997; EWL 3; MTCW 1, 2; MTFW 2005; WLIT 7

Foden, Giles 1967- .... **CLC 231**
See also CA 240; DLB 267; NFS 15

Fogarty, Jonathan Titulescu Esq.
See Farrell, James T(homas)

Follett, Ken 1949- .... **CLC 18**
See also AAYA 6, 50; BEST 89:4; BPFB 1; CA 81-84; CANR 13, 33, 54, 102, 156, 197; CMW 4; CPW; DA3; DAM NOV, POP; DLB 87; DLBY 1981; INT CANR-33; LNFS 3; MTCW 1

Follett, Kenneth Martin
See Follett, Ken

Fondane, Benjamin 1898-1944 ..... **TCLC 159**

Fontane, Theodor 1819-1898 . **NCLC 26, 163**
See also CDWLB 2; DLB 129; EW 6; RGWL 2, 3; TWA

Fonte, Moderata 1555-1592 .... **LC 118**

Fontenelle, Bernard Le Bovier de 1657-1757 .... **LC 140**
See also DLB 268, 313; GFL Beginnings to 1789

Fontenot, Chester .... **CLC 65**

Fonvizin, Denis Ivanovich 1744(?)-1792 .... **LC 81**
See also DLB 150; RGWL 2, 3

Foote, Albert Horton
See Foote, Horton

Foote, Horton 1916-2009 .... **CLC 51, 91**
See also AAYA 82; CA 73-76; 284; CAD; CANR 34, 51, 110; CD 5, 6; CSW; DA3; DAM DRAM; DFS 20; DLB 26, 266; EWL 3; INT CANR-34; MTFW 2005

Foote, Mary Hallock 1847-1938 .. **TCLC 108**
See also DLB 186, 188, 202, 221; TCWW 2

Foote, Samuel 1721-1777 .... **LC 106**
See also DLB 89; RGEL 2

Foote, Shelby 1916-2005 .... **CLC 75, 224**
See also AAYA 40; CA 5-8R; 240; CANR 3, 45, 74, 131; CN 1, 2, 3, 4, 5, 6, 7; CPW; CSW; DA3; DAM NOV, POP; DLB 2, 17; MAL 5; MTCW 2; MTFW 2005; RHW

Forbes, Cosmo
See Lewton, Val

Forbes, Esther 1891-1967 .... **CLC 12**
See also AAYA 17; BYA 2; CA 13-14; 25-28R; CAP 1; CLR 27, 147; DLB 22; JRDA; MAICYA 1, 2; RHW; SATA 2, 100; YAW

Forche, Carolyn 1950- .. **CLC 25, 83, 86; PC 10**
See also CA 109; 117; CANR 50, 74, 138; CP 4, 5, 6, 7; CWP; DA3; DAM POET; DLB 5, 193; INT CANR-47; MAL 5; MTCW 2; MTFW 2005; PFS 18; RGAL 4

Forche, Carolyn Louise
See Forche, Carolyn

Ford, Elbur
See Hibbert, Eleanor Alice Burford

Ford, Ford Madox 1873-1939 ... **TCLC 1, 15, 39, 57, 172**
See also BRW 6; CA 104; 132; CANR 74; CDBLB 1914-1945; DA3; DAM NOV; DLB 34, 98, 162; EWL 3; MTCW 1, 2; NFS 28; RGEL 2; RHW; TEA

Ford, Henry 1863-1947 .... **TCLC 73**
See also CA 115; 148

Ford, Jack
See Ford, John

Ford, John 1586-1639 .... **DC 8; LC 68, 153**
See also BRW 2; CDBLB Before 1660; DA3; DAM DRAM; DFS 7; DLB 58; IDTP; RGEL 2

Ford, John 1895-1973 .... **CLC 16**
See also AAYA 75; CA 187; 45-48

Ford, Richard 1944- ... **CLC 46, 99, 205, 277**
See also AMWS 5; CA 69-72; CANR 11, 47, 86, 128, 164; CN 5, 6, 7; CSW; DLB 227; EWL 3; MAL 5; MTCW 2; MTFW 2005; NFS 25; RGAL 4; RGSF 2

Ford, Webster
See Masters, Edgar Lee

Foreman, Richard 1937- .... **CLC 50**
See also CA 65-68; CAD; CANR 32, 63, 143; CD 5, 6

Forester, C. S. 1899-1966 ..... **CLC 35; TCLC 152**
See also CA 73-76; 25-28R; CANR 83; DLB 191; RGEL 2; RHW; SATA 13

Forester, Cecil Scott
See Forester, C. S.

Forez
See Mauriac, Francois (Charles)

Forman, James
See Forman, James D.

Forman, James D. 1932- .... **CLC 21**
See also AAYA 17; CA 9-12R; CANR 4, 19, 42; JRDA; MAICYA 1, 2; SATA 8, 70; YAW

Forman, James Douglas
See Forman, James D.

Forman, Milos 1932- .... **CLC 164**
See also AAYA 63; CA 109

Fornes, Maria Irene 1930- .... **CLC 39, 61, 187; DC 10; HLCS 1**
See also CA 25-28R; CAD; CANR 28, 81; CD 5, 6; CWD; DFS 25; DLB 7, 341; HW 1, 2; INT CANR-28; LLW; MAL 5; MTCW 1; RGAL 4

Forrest, Leon (Richard) 1937-1997 .... **BLCS; CLC 4**
See also AFAW 2; BW 2; CA 89-92; 162; CAAS 7; CANR 25, 52, 87; CN 4, 5, 6; DLB 33

Forster, E. M. 1879-1970 .. **CLC 1, 2, 3, 4, 9, 10, 13, 15, 22, 45, 77; SSC 27, 96; TCLC 125; WLC 2**
See also AAYA 2, 37; BRW 6; BRWR 2; BYA 12; CA 13-14; 25-28R; CANR 45; CAP 1; CDBLB 1914-1945; DA; DA3; DAB; DAC; DAM MST, NOV; DLB 34, 98, 162, 178, 195; DLBD 10; EWL 3; EXPN; LAIT 3; LMFS 1; MTCW 1, 2; MTFW 2005; NCFS 1; NFS 3, 10, 11; RGEL 2; RGSF 2; SATA 57; SUFW 1; TEA; WLIT 4

Forster, Edward Morgan
See Forster, E. M.

Forster, John 1812-1876 .... **NCLC 11**
See also DLB 144, 184

Forster, Margaret 1938- .... **CLC 149**
See also CA 133; CANR 62, 115, 175; CN 4, 5, 6, 7; DLB 155, 271

Forsyth, Frederick 1938- .... **CLC 2, 5, 36**
See also BEST 89:4; CA 85-88; CANR 38, 62, 115, 137, 183; CMW 4; CN 3, 4, 5, 6, 7; CPW; DAM NOV, POP; DLB 87; MTCW 1, 2; MTFW 2005

Fort, Paul
See Stockton, Francis Richard

Forten, Charlotte
See Grimke, Charlotte L. Forten

Forten, Charlotte L. 1837-1914
See Grimke, Charlotte L. Forten

Friis-Baastad, Babbis Ellinor
1921-1970 .... **CLC 12**
See also CA 17-20R; 134; SATA 7
Frisch, Max 1911-1991 ...... **CLC 3, 9, 14, 18, 32, 44; TCLC 121**
See also CA 85-88; 134; CANR 32, 74; CD-WLB 2; DAM DRAM, NOV; DFS 25; DLB 69, 124; EW 13; EWL 3; MTCW 1, 2; MTFW 2005; RGHL; RGWL 2, 3
Froehlich, Peter
See Gay, Peter
Fromentin, Eugene (Samuel Auguste)
1820-1876 .... **NCLC 10, 125**
See also DLB 123; GFL 1789 to the Present
Frost, Frederick
See Faust, Frederick
Frost, Robert 1874-1963 . **CLC 1, 3, 4, 9, 10, 13, 15, 26, 34, 44; PC 1, 39, 71; TCLC 236; WLC 2**
See also AAYA 21; AMW; AMWR 1; CA 89-92; CANR 33; CDALB 1917-1929; CLR 67; DA; DA3; DAB; DAC; DAM MST, POET; DLB 54, 284, 342; DLBD 7; EWL 3; EXPP; MAL 5; MTCW 1, 2; MTFW 2005; PAB; PFS 1, 2, 3, 4, 5, 6, 7, 10, 13, 32, 35; RGAL 4; SATA 14; TUS; WP; WYA
Frost, Robert Lee
See Frost, Robert
Froude, James Anthony
1818-1894 .... **NCLC 43**
See also DLB 18, 57, 144
Froy, Herald
See Waterhouse, Keith
Fry, Christopher 1907-2005 .. **CLC 2, 10, 14; DC 36**
See also BRWS 3; CA 17-20R; 240; CAAS 23; CANR 9, 30, 74, 132; CBD; CD 5, 6; CP 1, 2, 3, 4, 5, 6, 7; DAM DRAM; DLB 13; EWL 3; MTCW 1, 2; MTFW 2005; RGEL 2; SATA 66; TEA
Frye, (Herman) Northrop
1912-1991 .... **CLC 24, 70; TCLC 165**
See also CA 5-8R; 133; CANR 8, 37; DLB 67, 68, 246; EWL 3; MTCW 1, 2; MTFW 2005; RGAL 4; TWA
Fuchs, Daniel 1909-1993 .... **CLC 8, 22**
See also CA 81-84; 142; CAAS 5; CANR 40; CN 1, 2, 3, 4, 5; DLB 9, 26, 28; DLBY 1993; MAL 5
Fuchs, Daniel 1934- .... **CLC 34**
See also CA 37-40R; CANR 14, 48
Fuentes, Carlos 1928- .. **CLC 3, 8, 10, 13, 22, 41, 60, 113, 288; HLC 1; SSC 24, 125; WLC 2**
See also AAYA 4, 45; AITN 2; BPFB 1; CA 69-72; CANR 10, 32, 68, 104, 138, 197; CDWLB 3; CWW 2; DA; DA3; DAB; DAC; DAM MST, MULT, NOV; DLB 113; DNFS 2; EWL 3; HW 1, 2; LAIT 3; LATS 1:2; LAW; LAWS 1; LMFS 2; MTCW 1, 2; MTFW 2005; NFS 8; RGSF 2; RGWL 2, 3; TWA; WLIT 1
Fuentes, Gregorio Lopez y
See Lopez y Fuentes, Gregorio
Fuentes Macias, Carlos Manuel
See Fuentes, Carlos
Fuertes, Gloria 1918-1998 .... **PC 27**
See also CA 178, 180; DLB 108; HW 2; SATA 115
Fugard, Athol 1932- .... **CLC 5, 9, 14, 25, 40, 80, 211; DC 3**
See also AAYA 17; AFW; BRWS 15; CA 85-88; CANR 32, 54, 118; CD 5, 6; DAM DRAM; DFS 3, 6, 10, 24; DLB 225; DNFS 1, 2; EWL 3; LATS 1:2; MTCW 1; MTFW 2005; RGEL 2; WLIT 2
Fugard, Harold Athol
See Fugard, Athol

Fugard, Sheila 1932- .... **CLC 48**
See also CA 125
Fujiwara no Teika 1162-1241 .... **CMLC 73**
See also DLB 203
Fukuyama, Francis 1952- .... **CLC 131**
See also CA 140; CANR 72, 125, 170
Fuller, Charles (H.), (Jr.) 1939- ..... **BLC 1:2; CLC 25; DC 1**
See also BW 2; CA 108; 112; CAD; CANR 87; CD 5, 6; DAM DRAM, MULT; DFS 8; DLB 38, 266; EWL 3; INT CA-112; MAL 5; MTCW 1
Fuller, Henry Blake 1857-1929 .... **TCLC 103**
See also CA 108; 177; DLB 12; RGAL 4
Fuller, John (Leopold) 1937- .... **CLC 62**
See also CA 21-24R; CANR 9, 44; CP 1, 2, 3, 4, 5, 6, 7; DLB 40
Fuller, Margaret 1810-1850 ...... **NCLC 5, 50, 211**
See also AMWS 2; CDALB 1640-1865; DLB 1, 59, 73, 183, 223, 239; FW; LMFS 1; SATA 25
Fuller, Roy (Broadbent) 1912-1991 ... **CLC 4, 28**
See also BRWS 7; CA 5-8R; 135; CAAS 10; CANR 53, 83; CN 1, 2, 3, 4, 5; CP 1, 2, 3, 4, 5; CWRI 5; DLB 15, 20; EWL 3; RGEL 2; SATA 87
Fuller, Sarah Margaret
See Fuller, Margaret
Fuller, Thomas 1608-1661 .... **LC 111**
See also DLB 151
Fulton, Alice 1952- .... **CLC 52**
See also CA 116; CANR 57, 88, 200; CP 5, 6, 7; CWP; DLB 193; PFS 25
Fundi
See Baraka, Amiri
Furey, Michael
See Ward, Arthur Henry Sarsfield
Furphy, Joseph 1843-1912 .... **TCLC 25**
See also CA 163; DLB 230; EWL 3; RGEL 2
Furst, Alan 1941- .... **CLC 255**
See also CA 69-72; CANR 12, 34, 59, 102, 159, 193; DLB 350; DLBY 01
Fuson, Robert H(enderson) 1927- .... **CLC 70**
See also CA 89-92; CANR 103
Fussell, Paul 1924- .... **CLC 74**
See also BEST 90:1; CA 17-20R; CANR 8, 21, 35, 69, 135; INT CANR-21; MTCW 1, 2; MTFW 2005
Futabatei, Shimei 1864-1909 .... **TCLC 44**
See also CA 162; DLB 180; EWL 3; MJW
Futabatei Shimei
See Futabatei, Shimei
Futrelle, Jacques 1875-1912 .... **TCLC 19**
See also CA 113; 155; CMW 4
GAB
See Russell, George William
Gaberman, Judie Angell
See Angell, Judie
Gaboriau, Emile 1835-1873 .... **NCLC 14**
See also CMW 4; MSW
Gadda, Carlo Emilio 1893-1973 ...... **CLC 11; TCLC 144**
See also CA 89-92; DLB 177; EWL 3; WLIT 7
Gaddis, William 1922-1998 ... **CLC 1, 3, 6, 8, 10, 19, 43, 86**
See also AMWS 4; BPFB 1; CA 17-20R; 172; CANR 21, 48, 148; CN 1, 2, 3, 4, 5, 6; DLB 2, 278; EWL 3; MAL 5; MTCW 1, 2; MTFW 2005; RGAL 4
Gage, Walter
See Inge, William (Motter)

Gaiman, Neil 1960- .... **CLC 195**
See also AAYA 19, 42, 82; CA 133; CANR 81, 129, 188; CLR 109; DLB 261; HGG; MTFW 2005; SATA 85, 146, 197; SFW 4; SUFW 2
Gaiman, Neil Richard
See Gaiman, Neil
Gaines, Ernest J. 1933- ..... **BLC 1:2; CLC 3, 11, 18, 86, 181; SSC 68, 137**
See also AAYA 18; AFAW 1, 2; AITN 1; BPFB 2; BW 2, 3; BYA 6; CA 9-12R; CANR 6, 24, 42, 75, 126; CDALB 1968-1988; CLR 62; CN 1, 2, 3, 4, 5, 6, 7; CSW; DA3; DAM MULT; DLB 2, 33, 152; DLBY 1980; EWL 3; EXPN; LAIT 5; LATS 1:2; MAL 5; MTCW 1, 2; MTFW 2005; NFS 5, 7, 16; RGAL 4; RGSF 2; RHW; SATA 86; SSFS 5; YAW
Gaines, Ernest James
See Gaines, Ernest J.
Gaitskill, Mary 1954- .... **CLC 69**
See also CA 128; CANR 61, 152; DLB 244; TCLE 1:1
Gaitskill, Mary Lawrence
See Gaitskill, Mary
Gaius Suetonius Tranquillus
See Suetonius
Galdos, Benito Perez
See Perez Galdos, Benito
Gale, Zona 1874-1938 .... **DC 30; TCLC 7**
See also CA 105; 153; CANR 84; DAM DRAM; DFS 17; DLB 9, 78, 228; RGAL 4
Galeano, Eduardo 1940- ... **CLC 72; HLCS 1**
See also CA 29-32R; CANR 13, 32, 100, 163; HW 1
Galeano, Eduardo Hughes
See Galeano, Eduardo
Galiano, Juan Valera y Alcala
See Valera y Alcala-Galiano, Juan
Galilei, Galileo 1564-1642 .... **LC 45**
Gallagher, Tess 1943- .... **CLC 18, 63; PC 9**
See also CA 106; CP 3, 4, 5, 6, 7; CWP; DAM POET; DLB 120, 212, 244; PFS 16
Gallant, Mavis 1922- ..... **CLC 7, 18, 38, 172, 288; SSC 5, 78**
See also CA 69-72; CANR 29, 69, 117; CCA 1; CN 1, 2, 3, 4, 5, 6, 7; DAC; DAM MST; DLB 53; EWL 3; MTCW 1, 2; MTFW 2005; RGEL 2; RGSF 2
Gallant, Roy A(rthur) 1924- .... **CLC 17**
See also CA 5-8R; CANR 4, 29, 54, 117; CLR 30; MAICYA 1, 2; SATA 4, 68, 110
Gallico, Paul (William) 1897-1976 ..... **CLC 2**
See also AITN 1; CA 5-8R; 69-72; CANR 23; CN 1, 2; DLB 9, 171; FANT; MAICYA 1, 2; SATA 13
Gallo, Max Louis 1932- .... **CLC 95**
See also CA 85-88
Gallois, Lucien
See Desnos, Robert
Gallup, Ralph
See Whitemore, Hugh (John)
Galsworthy, John 1867-1933 .... **SSC 22; TCLC 1, 45; WLC 2**
See also BRW 6; CA 104; 141; CANR 75; CDBLB 1890-1914; DA; DA3; DAB; DAC; DAM DRAM, MST, NOV; DLB 10, 34, 98, 162, 330; DLBD 16; EWL 3; MTCW 2; RGEL 2; SSFS 3; TEA
Galt, John 1779-1839 .... **NCLC 1, 110**
See also DLB 99, 116, 159; RGEL 2; RGSF 2
Galvin, James 1951- .... **CLC 38**
See also CA 108; CANR 26
Gamboa, Federico 1864-1939 .... **TCLC 36**
See also CA 167; HW 2; LAW
Gandhi, M. K.
See Gandhi, Mohandas Karamchand

130, 175; CDALBS; CLR 6, 73; CP 2, 3, 4, 5, 6, 7; CSW; CWP; CWRI 5; DA; DA3; DAB; DAC; DAM MST, MULT, POET; DLB 5, 41; EWL 3; EXPP; INT CANR-18; MAICYA 1, 2; MAL 5; MTCW 1, 2; MTFW 2005; PFS 17, 28, 35; RGAL 4; SATA 24, 107, 208; TUS; YAW

Giovanni, Yolanda Cornelia
See Giovanni, Nikki

Giovanni, Yolande Cornelia
See Giovanni, Nikki

Giovanni, Yolande Cornelia, Jr.
See Giovanni, Nikki

Giovene, Andrea 1904-1998 .... **CLC 7**
See also CA 85-88

Gippius, Zinaida 1869-1945 .... **TCLC 9**
See also CA 106; 212; DLB 295; EWL 3

Gippius, Zinaida Nikolaevna
See Gippius, Zinaida

Giraudoux, Jean 1882-1944 ... **DC 36; TCLC 2, 7**
See also CA 104; 196; DAM DRAM; DLB 65, 321; EW 9; EWL 3; GFL 1789 to the Present; RGWL 2, 3; TWA

Giraudoux, Jean-Hippolyte
See Giraudoux, Jean

Gironella, Jose Maria (Pous) 1917-2003 .... **CLC 11**
See also CA 101; 212; EWL 3; RGWL 2, 3

Gissing, George (Robert) 1857-1903 .... **SSC 37, 113; TCLC 3, 24, 47**
See also BRW 5; CA 105; 167; DLB 18, 135, 184; RGEL 2; TEA

Gitlin, Todd 1943- .... **CLC 201**
See also CA 29-32R; CANR 25, 50, 88, 179

Giurlani, Aldo
See Palazzeschi, Aldo

Gladkov, Fedor Vasil'evich
See Gladkov, Fyodor (Vasilyevich)

Gladkov, Fyodor (Vasilyevich) 1883-1958 .... **TCLC 27**
See also CA 170; DLB 272; EWL 3

Gladstone, William Ewart 1809-1898 .... **NCLC 213**
See also DLB 57, 184

Glancy, Diane 1941- .... **CLC 210; NNAL**
See also CA 136, 225; CAAE 225; CAAS 24; CANR 87, 162; DLB 175

Glanville, Brian (Lester) 1931- .... **CLC 6**
See also CA 5-8R; CAAS 9; CANR 3, 70; CN 1, 2, 3, 4, 5, 6, 7; DLB 15, 139; SATA 42

Glasgow, Ellen 1873-1945 .... **SSC 34, 130; TCLC 2, 7, 239**
See also AMW; CA 104; 164; DLB 9, 12; MAL 5; MBL; MTCW 2; MTFW 2005; RGAL 4; RHW; SSFS 9; TUS

Glasgow, Ellen Anderson Gholson
See Glasgow, Ellen

Glaspell, Susan 1882(?)-1948 ..... **DC 10; SSC 41, 132; TCLC 55, 175**
See also AMWS 3; CA 110; 154; DFS 8, 18, 24; DLB 7, 9, 78, 228; MBL; RGAL 4; SSFS 3; TCWW 2; TUS; YABC 2

Glassco, John 1909-1981 .... **CLC 9**
See also CA 13-16R; 102; CANR 15; CN 1, 2; CP 1, 2, 3; DLB 68

Glasscock, Amnesia
See Steinbeck, John

Glasser, Ronald J. 1940(?)- .... **CLC 37**
See also CA 209

Glassman, Joyce
See Johnson, Joyce

Gleick, James (W.) 1954- .... **CLC 147**
See also CA 131; 137; CANR 97; INT CA-137

Glendinning, Victoria 1937- .... **CLC 50**
See also CA 120; 127; CANR 59, 89, 166; DLB 155

Glissant, Edouard (Mathieu) 1928- .... **CLC 10, 68**
See also CA 153; CANR 111; CWW 2; DAM MULT; EWL 3; RGWL 3

Gloag, Julian 1930- .... **CLC 40**
See also AITN 1; CA 65-68; CANR 10, 70; CN 1, 2, 3, 4, 5, 6

Glowacki, Aleksander
See Prus, Boleslaw

Gluck, Louise 1943- . **CLC 7, 22, 44, 81, 160, 280; PC 16**
See also AMWS 5; CA 33-36R; CANR 40, 69, 108, 133, 182; CP 1, 2, 3, 4, 5, 6, 7; CWP; DA3; DAM POET; DLB 5; MAL 5; MTCW 2; MTFW 2005; PFS 5, 15; RGAL 4; TCLE 1:1

Gluck, Louise Elisabeth
See Gluck, Louise

Glyn, Elinor 1864-1943 .... **TCLC 72**
See also DLB 153; RHW

Gobineau, Joseph-Arthur 1816-1882 .... **NCLC 17**
See also DLB 123; GFL 1789 to the Present

Godard, Jean-Luc 1930- .... **CLC 20**
See also CA 93-96

Godden, (Margaret) Rumer 1907-1998 .... **CLC 53**
See also AAYA 6; BPFB 2; BYA 2, 5; CA 5-8R; 172; CANR 4, 27, 36, 55, 80; CLR 20; CN 1, 2, 3, 4, 5, 6; CWRI 5; DLB 161; MAICYA 1, 2; RHW; SAAS 12; SATA 3, 36; SATA-Obit 109; TEA

Godoy Alcayaga, Lucila
See Mistral, Gabriela

Godwin, Gail 1937- ...... **CLC 5, 8, 22, 31, 69, 125**
See also BPFB 2; CA 29-32R; CANR 15, 43, 69, 132; CN 3, 4, 5, 6, 7; CPW; CSW; DA3; DAM POP; DLB 6, 234, 350; INT CANR-15; MAL 5; MTCW 1, 2; MTFW 2005

Godwin, Gail Kathleen
See Godwin, Gail

Godwin, William 1756-1836 .. **NCLC 14, 130**
See also BRWS 15; CDBLB 1789-1832; CMW 4; DLB 39, 104, 142, 158, 163, 262, 336; GL 2; HGG; RGEL 2

Goebbels, Josef
See Goebbels, (Paul) Joseph

Goebbels, (Paul) Joseph 1897-1945 .... **TCLC 68**
See also CA 115; 148

Goebbels, Joseph Paul
See Goebbels, (Paul) Joseph

Goethe, Johann Wolfgang von 1749-1832 . **DC 20; NCLC 4, 22, 34, 90, 154; PC 5; SSC 38; WLC 3**
See also CDWLB 2; DA; DA3; DAB; DAC; DAM DRAM, MST, POET; DLB 94; EW 5; GL 2; LATS 1; LMFS 1:1; RGWL 2, 3; TWA

Gogarty, Oliver St. John 1878-1957 .... **TCLC 15**
See also CA 109; 150; DLB 15, 19; RGEL 2

Gogol, Nikolai 1809-1852 .... **DC 1; NCLC 5, 15, 31, 162; SSC 4, 29, 52; WLC 3**
See also DA; DAB; DAC; DAM DRAM, MST; DFS 12; DLB 198; EW 6; EXPS; RGSF 2; RGWL 2, 3; SSFS 7; TWA

Gogol, Nikolai Vasilyevich
See Gogol, Nikolai

Goines, Donald 1937(?)-1974 .... **BLC 1:2; CLC 80**
See also AITN 1; BW 1, 3; CA 124; 114; CANR 82; CMW 4; DA3; DAM MULT, POP; DLB 33

Gold, Herbert 1924- ... **CLC 4, 7, 14, 42, 152**
See also CA 9-12R; CANR 17, 45, 125, 194; CN 1, 2, 3, 4, 5, 6, 7; DLB 2; DLBY 1981; MAL 5

Goldbarth, Albert 1948- .... **CLC 5, 38**
See also AMWS 12; CA 53-56; CANR 6, 40; CP 3, 4, 5, 6, 7; DLB 120

Goldberg, Anatol 1910-1982 .... **CLC 34**
See also CA 131; 117

Goldemberg, Isaac 1945- .... **CLC 52**
See also CA 69-72; CAAS 12; CANR 11, 32; EWL 3; HW 1; WLIT 1

Golding, Arthur 1536-1606 .... **LC 101**
See also DLB 136

Golding, William 1911-1993 . **CLC 1, 2, 3, 8, 10, 17, 27, 58, 81; WLC 3**
See also AAYA 5, 44; BPFB 2; BRWR 1; BRWS 1; BYA 2; CA 5-8R; 141; CANR 13, 33, 54; CD 5; CDBLB 1945-1960; CLR 94, 130; CN 1, 2, 3, 4; DA; DA3; DAB; DAC; DAM MST, NOV; DLB 15, 100, 255, 326, 330; EWL 3; EXPN; HGG; LAIT 4; MTCW 1, 2; MTFW 2005; NFS 2; RGEL 2; RHW; SFW 4; TEA; WLIT 4; YAW

Golding, William Gerald
See Golding, William

Goldman, Emma 1869-1940 .... **TCLC 13**
See also CA 110; 150; DLB 221; FW; RGAL 4; TUS

Goldman, Francisco 1954- .... **CLC 76**
See also CA 162; CANR 185

Goldman, William 1931- .... **CLC 1, 48**
See also BPFB 2; CA 9-12R; CANR 29, 69, 106; CN 1, 2, 3, 4, 5, 6, 7; DLB 44; FANT; IDFW 3, 4; NFS 31

Goldman, William W.
See Goldman, William

Goldmann, Lucien 1913-1970 .... **CLC 24**
See also CA 25-28; CAP 2

Goldoni, Carlo 1707-1793 .... **LC 4, 152**
See also DAM DRAM; DFS 27; EW 4; RGWL 2, 3; WLIT 7

Goldsberry, Steven 1949- .... **CLC 34**
See also CA 131

Goldsmith, Oliver 1730(?)-1774 .... **DC 8; LC 2, 48, 122; PC 77; WLC 3**
See also BRW 3; CDBLB 1660-1789; DA; DAB; DAC; DAM DRAM, MST, NOV, POET; DFS 1; DLB 39, 89, 104, 109, 142, 336; IDTP; RGEL 2; SATA 26; TEA; WLIT 3

Goldsmith, Peter
See Priestley, J(ohn) B(oynton)

Goldstein, Rebecca 1950- .... **CLC 239**
See also CA 144; CANR 99, 165; TCLE 1:1

Goldstein, Rebecca Newberger
See Goldstein, Rebecca

Gombrowicz, Witold 1904-1969 .... **CLC 4, 7, 11, 49**
See also CA 19-20; 25-28R; CANR 105; CAP 2; CDWLB 4; DAM DRAM; DLB 215; EW 12; EWL 3; RGWL 2, 3; TWA

Gomez de Avellaneda, Gertrudis 1814-1873 .... **NCLC 111**
See also LAW

Gomez de la Serna, Ramon 1888-1963 .... **CLC 9**
See also CA 153; 116; CANR 79; EWL 3; HW 1, 2

Goncharov, Ivan Alexandrovich 1812-1891 .... **NCLC 1, 63**
See also DLB 238; EW 6; RGWL 2, 3

Goncourt, Edmond de 1822-1896 ... **NCLC 7**
See also DLB 123; EW 7; GFL 1789 to the Present; RGWL 2, 3

Goncourt, Edmond Louis Antoine Huot de
See Goncourt, Edmond de

Goncourt, Jules Alfred Huot de
See Goncourt, Jules de

Goncourt, Jules de 1830-1870 .... **NCLC 7**
See Goncourt, Jules de
See also DLB 123; EW 7; GFL 1789 to the Present; RGWL 2, 3

Gongora (y Argote), Luis de
1561-1627 .... **LC 72**
See also RGWL 2, 3

Gontier, Fernande 19(?)- .... **CLC 50**

Gonzalez Martinez, Enrique
See Gonzalez Martinez, Enrique

Gonzalez Martinez, Enrique
1871-1952 .... **TCLC 72**
See also CA 166; CANR 81; DLB 290; EWL 3; HW 1, 2

Goodison, Lorna 1947- .... **BLC 2:2; PC 36**
See also CA 142; CANR 88, 189; CP 5, 6, 7; CWP; DLB 157; EWL 3; PFS 25

Goodman, Allegra 1967- .... **CLC 241**
See also CA 204; CANR 162, 204; DLB 244, 350

Goodman, Paul 1911-1972 ..... **CLC 1, 2, 4, 7**
See also CA 19-20; 37-40R; CAD; CANR 34; CAP 2; CN 1; DLB 130, 246; MAL 5; MTCW 1; RGAL 4

GoodWeather, Hartley
See King, Thomas

Goodweather, Hartley
See King, Thomas

Googe, Barnabe 1540-1594 .... **LC 94**
See also DLB 132; RGEL 2

Gordimer, Nadine 1923- ...... **CLC 3, 5, 7, 10, 18, 33, 51, 70, 123, 160, 161, 263; SSC 17, 80; WLCS**
See also AAYA 39; AFW; BRWS 2; CA 5-8R; CANR 3, 28, 56, 88, 131, 195; CN 1, 2, 3, 4, 5, 6, 7; DA; DA3; DAB; DAC; DAM MST, NOV; DLB 225, 326, 330; EWL 3; EXPS; INT CANR-28; LATS 1:2; MTCW 1, 2; MTFW 2005; NFS 4; RGEL 2; RGSF 2; SSFS 2, 14, 19, 28, 31; TWA; WLIT 2; YAW

Gordon, Adam Lindsay
1833-1870 .... **NCLC 21**
See also DLB 230

Gordon, Caroline 1895-1981 . **CLC 6, 13, 29, 83; SSC 15**
See also AMW; CA 11-12; 103; CANR 36; CAP 1; CN 1, 2; DLB 4, 9, 102; DLBD 17; DLBY 1981; EWL 3; MAL 5; MTCW 1, 2; MTFW 2005; RGAL 4; RGSF 2

Gordon, Charles William
1860-1937 .... **TCLC 31**
See also CA 109; DLB 92; TCWW 1, 2

Gordon, Mary 1949- .. **CLC 13, 22, 128, 216; SSC 59**
See also AMWS 4; BPFB 2; CA 102; CANR 44, 92, 154, 179; CN 4, 5, 6, 7; DLB 6; DLBY 1981; FW; INT CA-102; MAL 5; MTCW 1

Gordon, Mary Catherine
See Gordon, Mary

Gordon, N. J.
See Bosman, Herman Charles

Gordon, Sol 1923- .... **CLC 26**
See also CA 53-56; CANR 4; SATA 11

Gordone, Charles 1925-1995 .... **BLC 2:2; CLC 1, 4; DC 8**
See also BW 1, 3; CA 93-96, 180; 150; CAAE 180; CAD; CANR 55; DAM DRAM; DLB 7; INT CA-93-96; MTCW 1

Gore, Catherine 1800-1861 .... **NCLC 65**
See also DLB 116, 344; RGEL 2

Gorenko, Anna Andreevna
See Akhmatova, Anna

Gor'kii, Maksim
See Gorky, Maxim

Gorky, Maxim 1868-1936 ..... **SSC 28; TCLC 8; WLC 3**
See also CA 105; 141; CANR 83; DA; DAB; DAC; DAM DRAM, MST, NOV; DFS 9; DLB 295; EW 8; EWL 3; MTCW 2; MTFW 2005; RGSF 2; RGWL 2, 3; TWA

Goryan, Sirak
See Saroyan, William

Gosse, Edmund (William)
1849-1928 .... **TCLC 28**
See also CA 117; DLB 57, 144, 184; RGEL 2

Gotlieb, Phyllis 1926-2009 .... **CLC 18**
See also CA 13-16R; CANR 7, 135; CN 7; CP 1, 2, 3, 4; DLB 88, 251; SFW 4

Gotlieb, Phyllis Fay Bloom
See Gotlieb, Phyllis

Gottesman, S. D.
See Kornbluth, C(yril) M.; Pohl, Frederik

Gottfried von Strassburg fl. c.
1170-1215 .... **CMLC 10, 96**
See also CDWLB 2; DLB 138; EW 1; RGWL 2, 3

Gotthelf, Jeremias 1797-1854 .... **NCLC 117**
See also DLB 133; RGWL 2, 3

Gottschalk, Laura Riding
See Jackson, Laura

Gould, Lois 1932(?)-2002 .... **CLC 4, 10**
See also CA 77-80; 208; CANR 29; MTCW 1

Gould, Stephen Jay 1941-2002 .... **CLC 163**
See also AAYA 26; BEST 90:2; CA 77-80; 205; CANR 10, 27, 56, 75, 125; CPW; INT CANR-27; MTCW 1, 2; MTFW 2005

Gourmont, Remy(-Marie-Charles) de
1858-1915 .... **TCLC 17**
See also CA 109; 150; GFL 1789 to the Present; MTCW 2

Gournay, Marie le Jars de
See de Gournay, Marie le Jars

Govier, Katherine 1948- .... **CLC 51**
See also CA 101; CANR 18, 40, 128; CCA 1

Gower, John c. 1330-1408 .... **LC 76; PC 59**
See also BRW 1; DLB 146; RGEL 2

Goyen, (Charles) William
1915-1983 .... **CLC 5, 8, 14, 40**
See also AITN 2; CA 5-8R; 110; CANR 6, 71; CN 1, 2, 3; DLB 2, 218; DLBY 1983; EWL 3; INT CANR-6; MAL 5

Goytisolo, Juan 1931- .... **CLC 5, 10, 23, 133; HLC 1**
See also CA 85-88; CANR 32, 61, 131, 182; CWW 2; DAM MULT; DLB 322; EWL 3; GLL 2; HW 1, 2; MTCW 1, 2; MTFW 2005

Gozzano, Guido 1883-1916 .... **PC 10**
See also CA 154; DLB 114; EWL 3

Gozzi, (Conte) Carlo 1720-1806 .... **NCLC 23**

Grabbe, Christian Dietrich
1801-1836 .... **NCLC 2**
See also DLB 133; RGWL 2, 3

Grace, Patricia 1937- .... **CLC 56**
See also CA 176; CANR 118; CN 4, 5, 6, 7; EWL 3; RGSF 2

Grace, Patricia Frances
See Grace, Patricia

Gracian, Baltasar 1601-1658 .... **LC 15, 160**

Gracian y Morales, Baltasar
See Gracian, Baltasar

Gracq, Julien 1910-2007 ..... **CLC 11, 48, 259**
See also CA 122; 126; 267; CANR 141; CWW 2; DLB 83; GFL 1789 to the present

Grade, Chaim 1910-1982 .... **CLC 10**
See also CA 93-96; 107; DLB 333; EWL 3; RGHL

Grade, Khayim
See Grade, Chaim

Graduate of Oxford, A
See Ruskin, John

Grafton, Garth
See Duncan, Sara Jeannette

Grafton, Sue 1940- .... **CLC 163**
See also AAYA 11, 49; BEST 90:3; CA 108; CANR 31, 55, 111, 134, 195; CMW 4; CPW; CSW; DA3; DAM POP; DLB 226; FW; MSW; MTFW 2005

Graham, John
See Phillips, David Graham

Graham, Jorie 1950- .... **CLC 48, 118; PC 59**
See also AAYA 67; CA 111; CANR 63, 118, 205; CP 4, 5, 6, 7; CWP; DLB 120; EWL 3; MTFW 2005; PFS 10, 17; TCLE 1:1

Graham, R. B. Cunninghame
See Cunninghame Graham, Robert Bontine

Graham, Robert
See Haldeman, Joe

Graham, Robert Bontine Cunninghame
See Cunninghame Graham, Robert Bontine

Graham, Tom
See Lewis, Sinclair

Graham, W(illiam) S(ydney)
1918-1986 .... **CLC 29**
See also BRWS 7; CA 73-76; 118; CP 1, 2, 3, 4; DLB 20; RGEL 2

Graham, Winston (Mawdsley)
1910-2003 .... **CLC 23**
See also CA 49-52; 218; CANR 2, 22, 45, 66; CMW 4; CN 1, 2, 3, 4, 5, 6, 7; DLB 77; RHW

Grahame, Kenneth 1859-1932 ...... **TCLC 64, 136**
See also BYA 5; CA 108; 136; CANR 80; CLR 5, 135; CWRI 5; DA3; DAB; DLB 34, 141, 178; FANT; MAICYA 1, 2; MTCW 2; NFS 20; RGEL 2; SATA 100; TEA; WCH; YABC 1

Granger, Darius John
See Marlowe, Stephen

Granin, Daniil 1918- .... **CLC 59**
See also DLB 302

Granovsky, Timofei Nikolaevich
1813-1855 .... **NCLC 75**
See also DLB 198

Grant, Skeeter
See Spiegelman, Art

Granville-Barker, Harley
1877-1946 .... **TCLC 2**
See also CA 104; 204; DAM DRAM; DLB 10; RGEL 2

Granzotto, Gianni
See Granzotto, Giovanni Battista

Granzotto, Giovanni Battista
1914-1985 .... **CLC 70**
See also CA 166

Grasemann, Ruth Barbara
See Rendell, Ruth

Grass, Guenter
See Grass, Gunter

Grass, Gunter 1927- .. **CLC 1, 2, 4, 6, 11, 15, 22, 32, 49, 88, 207; WLC 3**
See also BPFB 2; CA 13-16R; CANR 20, 75, 93, 133, 174; CDWLB 2; CWW 2; DA; DA3; DAB; DAC; DAM MST, NOV; DLB 330; EW 13; EWL 3; MTCW 1, 2; MTFW 2005; RGHL; RGWL 2, 3; TWA

Grass, Gunter Wilhelm
See Grass, Gunter

Gratton, Thomas
  See Hulme, T(homas) E(rnest)
Grau, Shirley Ann 1929- .... CLC 4, 9, 146;
    SSC 15
  See also CA 89-92; CANR 22, 69; CN 1, 2,
    3, 4, 5, 6, 7; CSW; DLB 2, 218; INT CA-
    89-92; CANR-22; MTCW 1
Gravel, Fern
  See Hall, James Norman
Graver, Elizabeth 1964- .... CLC 70
  See also CA 135; CANR 71, 129
Graves, Richard Perceval
    1895-1985 .... CLC 44
  See also CA 65-68; CANR 9, 26, 51
Graves, Robert 1895-1985 ... CLC 1, 2, 6, 11,
    39, 44, 45; PC 6
  See also BPFB 2; BRW 7; BYA 4; CA 5-8R;
    117; CANR 5, 36; CDBLB 1914-1945;
    CN 1, 2, 3; CP 1, 2, 3, 4; DA3; DAB;
    DAC; DAM MST, POET; DLB 20, 100,
    191; DLBD 18; DLBY 1985; EWL 3;
    LATS 1:1; MTCW 1, 2; MTFW 2005;
    NCFS 2; NFS 21; RGEL 2; RHW; SATA
    45; TEA
Graves, Robert von Ranke
  See Graves, Robert
Graves, Valerie
  See Bradley, Marion Zimmer
Gray, Alasdair 1934- .... CLC 41, 275
  See also BRWS 9; CA 126; CANR 47, 69,
    106, 140; CN 4, 5, 6, 7; DLB 194, 261,
    319; HGG; INT CA-126; MTCW 1, 2;
    MTFW 2005; RGSF 2; SUFW 2
Gray, Amlin 1946- .... CLC 29
  See also CA 138
Gray, Francine du Plessix 1930- ..... CLC 22,
    153
  See also BEST 90:3; CA 61-64; CAAS 2;
    CANR 11, 33, 75, 81, 197; DAM NOV;
    INT CANR-11; MTCW 1, 2; MTFW 2005
Gray, John (Henry) 1866-1934 ...... TCLC 19
  See also CA 119; 162; RGEL 2
Gray, John Lee
  See Jakes, John
Gray, Simon 1936-2008 .... CLC 9, 14, 36
  See also AITN 1; CA 21-24R; 275; CAAS
    3; CANR 32, 69; CBD; CD 5, 6; CN 1, 2,
    3; DLB 13; EWL 3; MTCW 1; RGEL 2
Gray, Simon James Holliday
  See Gray, Simon
Gray, Spalding 1941-2004 .... CLC 49, 112;
    DC 7
  See also AAYA 62; CA 128; 225; CAD;
    CANR 74, 138; CD 5, 6; CPW; DAM
    POP; MTCW 2; MTFW 2005
Gray, Thomas 1716-1771 . LC 4, 40, 178; PC
    2, 80; WLC 3
  See also BRW 3; CDBLB 1660-1789; DA;
    DA3; DAB; DAC; DAM MST; DLB 109;
    EXPP; PAB; PFS 9; RGEL 2; TEA; WP
Grayson, David
  See Baker, Ray Stannard
Grayson, Richard (A.) 1951- .... CLC 38
  See also CA 85-88, 210; CAAE 210; CANR
    14, 31, 57; DLB 234
Greeley, Andrew M. 1928- .... CLC 28
  See also BPFB 2; CA 5-8R; CAAS 7;
    CANR 7, 43, 69, 104, 136, 184; CMW 4;
    CPW; DA3; DAM POP; MTCW 1, 2;
    MTFW 2005
Green, Anna Katharine
    1846-1935 .... TCLC 63
  See also CA 112; 159; CMW 4; DLB 202,
    221; MSW
Green, Brian
  See Card, Orson Scott
Green, Hannah
  See Greenberg, Joanne (Goldenberg)

Green, Hannah 1927(?)-1996 .... CLC 3
  See also CA 73-76; CANR 59, 93; NFS 10
Green, Henry
  See Yorke, Henry Vincent
Green, Julian
  See Green, Julien
Green, Julien 1900-1998 .... CLC 3, 11, 77
  See also CA 21-24R; 169; CANR 33, 87;
    CWW 2; DLB 4, 72; EWL 3; GFL 1789
    to the Present; MTCW 2; MTFW 2005
Green, Julien Hartridge
  See Green, Julien
Green, Paul (Eliot) 1894-1981 .. CLC 25; DC
    37
  See also AITN 1; CA 5-8R; 103; CAD;
    CANR 3; DAM DRAM; DLB 7, 9, 249;
    DLBY 1981; MAL 5; RGAL 4
Greenaway, Peter 1942- .... CLC 159
  See also CA 127
Greenberg, Ivan 1908-1973 .... CLC 24
  See also CA 85-88; DLB 137; MAL 5
Greenberg, Joanne (Goldenberg)
    1932- .... CLC 7, 30
  See also AAYA 12, 67; CA 5-8R; CANR
    14, 32, 69; CN 6, 7; DLB 335; NFS 23;
    SATA 25; YAW
Greenberg, Richard 1959(?)- .... CLC 57
  See also CA 138; CAD; CD 5, 6; DFS 24
Greenblatt, Stephen J(ay) 1943- ...... CLC 70
  See also CA 49-52; CANR 115; LNFS 1
Greene, Bette 1934- .... CLC 30
  See also AAYA 7, 69; BYA 3; CA 53-56;
    CANR 4, 146; CLR 2, 140; CWRI 5;
    JRDA; LAIT 4; MAICYA 1, 2; NFS 10;
    SAAS 16; SATA 8, 102, 161; WYA; YAW
Greene, Gael .... CLC 8
  See also CA 13-16R; CANR 10, 166
Greene, Graham 1904-1991 .. CLC 1, 3, 6, 9,
    14, 18, 27, 37, 70, 72, 125; SSC 29, 121;
    WLC 3
  See also AAYA 61; AITN 2; BPFB 2;
    BRWR 2; BRWS 1; BYA 3; CA 13-16R;
    133; CANR 35, 61, 131; CBD; CDBLB
    1945-1960; CMW 4; CN 1, 2, 3, 4; DA;
    DA3; DAB; DAC; DAM MST, NOV;
    DLB 13, 15, 77, 100, 162, 201, 204;
    DLBY 1991; EWL 3; MSW; MTCW 1, 2;
    MTFW 2005; NFS 16, 31; RGEL 2;
    SATA 20; SSFS 14; TEA; WLIT 4
Greene, Graham Henry
  See Greene, Graham
Greene, Robert 1558-1592 .... LC 41
  See also BRWS 8; DLB 62, 167; IDTP;
    RGEL 2; TEA
Greer, Germaine 1939- .... CLC 131
  See also AITN 1; CA 81-84; CANR 33, 70,
    115, 133, 190; FW; MTCW 1, 2; MTFW
    2005
Greer, Richard
  See Silverberg, Robert
Gregor, Arthur 1923- .... CLC 9
  See also CA 25-28R; CAAS 10; CANR 11;
    CP 1, 2, 3, 4, 5, 6, 7; SATA 36
Gregor, Lee
  See Pohl, Frederik
Gregory, Lady Isabella Augusta (Persse)
    1852-1932 .... TCLC 1, 176
  See also BRW 6; CA 104; 184; DLB 10;
    IDTP; RGEL 2
Gregory, J. Dennis
  See Williams, John A(lfred)
Gregory of Nazianzus, St.
    329-389 .... CMLC 82
Gregory of Nyssa c. 335-c. 394 ... CMLC 118
Gregory of Rimini 1300(?)-1358 . CMLC 109
  See also DLB 115
Grekova, I.
  See Ventsel, Elena Sergeevna

Grekova, Irina
  See Ventsel, Elena Sergeevna
Grendon, Stephen
  See Derleth, August (William)
Grenville, Kate 1950- .... CLC 61
  See also CA 118; CANR 53, 93, 156; CN
    7; DLB 325
Grenville, Pelham
  See Wodehouse, P. G.
Greve, Felix Paul (Berthold Friedrich)
    1879-1948 .... TCLC 4
  See also CA 104; 141, 175; CANR 79;
    DAC; DAM MST; DLB 92; RGEL 2;
    TCWW 1, 2
Greville, Fulke 1554-1628 .... LC 79
  See also BRWS 11; DLB 62, 172; RGEL 2
Grey, Lady Jane 1537-1554 .... LC 93
  See also DLB 132
Grey, Zane 1872-1939 .... TCLC 6
  See also BPFB 2; CA 104; 132; DA3; DAM
    POP; DLB 9, 212; MTCW 1, 2; MTFW
    2005; RGAL 4; TCWW 1, 2; TUS
Griboedov, Aleksandr Sergeevich
    1795(?)-1829 .... NCLC 129
  See also DLB 205; RGWL 2, 3
Grieg, (Johan) Nordahl (Brun)
    1902-1943 .... TCLC 10
  See also CA 107; 189; EWL 3
Grieve, C. M. 1892-1978 ... CLC 2, 4, 11, 19,
    63; PC 9
  See also BRWS 12; CA 5-8R; 85-88; CANR
    33, 107; CDBLB 1945-1960; CP 1, 2;
    DAM POET; DLB 20; EWL 3; MTCW 1;
    RGEL 2
Grieve, Christopher Murray
  See Grieve, C. M.
Griffin, Gerald 1803-1840 .... NCLC 7
  See also DLB 159; RGEL 2
Griffin, John Howard 1920-1980 ..... CLC 68
  See also AITN 1; CA 1-4R; 101; CANR 2
Griffin, Peter 1942- .... CLC 39
  See also CA 136
Griffith, David Lewelyn Wark
  See Griffith, D.W.
Griffith, D.W. 1875(?)-1948 .... TCLC 68
  See also AAYA 78; CA 119; 150; CANR 80
Griffith, Lawrence
  See Griffith, D.W.
Griffiths, Trevor 1935- .... CLC 13, 52
  See also CA 97-100; CANR 45; CBD; CD
    5, 6; DLB 13, 245
Griggs, Sutton (Elbert)
    1872-1930 .... TCLC 77
  See also CA 123; 186; DLB 50
Grigson, Geoffrey (Edward Harvey)
    1905-1985 .... CLC 7, 39
  See also CA 25-28R; 118; CANR 20, 33;
    CP 1, 2, 3, 4; DLB 27; MTCW 1, 2
Grile, Dod
  See Bierce, Ambrose
Grillparzer, Franz 1791-1872 .... DC 14;
    NCLC 1, 102; SSC 37
  See also CDWLB 2; DLB 133; EW 5;
    RGWL 2, 3; TWA
Grimble, Reverend Charles James
  See Eliot, T. S.
Grimke, Angelina Emily Weld
  See Grimke, Angelina Weld
Grimke, Angelina Weld 1880-1958 ... DC 38;
    HR 1:2
  See also BW 1; CA 124; DAM POET; DLB
    50, 54; FW
Grimke, Charlotte L. Forten
    1837(?)-1914 .... BLC 1:2; TCLC 16
  See also BW 1; CA 117; 124; DAM MULT,
    POET; DLB 50, 239
Grimke, Charlotte Lottie Forten
  See Grimke, Charlotte L. Forten

Grimm, Jacob Ludwig Karl
1785-1863 .... **NCLC 3, 77; SSC 36, 88**
See also CLR 112; DLB 90; MAICYA 1, 2;
RGSF 2; RGWL 2, 3; SATA 22; WCH

Grimm, Wilhelm Karl 1786-1859 .. **NCLC 3,
77; SSC 36**
See also CDWLB 2; CLR 112; DLB 90;
MAICYA 1, 2; RGSF 2; RGWL 2, 3;
SATA 22; WCH

Grimm and Grim
See Grimm, Jacob Ludwig Karl; Grimm,
Wilhelm Karl

Grimm Brothers
See Grimm, Jacob Ludwig Karl; Grimm,
Wilhelm Karl

**Grimmelshausen, Hans Jakob Christoffel
von**
See Grimmelshausen, Johann Jakob Christoffel von

**Grimmelshausen, Johann Jakob Christoffel
von** 1621-1676 .... **LC 6**
See also CDWLB 2; DLB 168; RGWL 2, 3

Grindel, Eugene 1895-1952 .... **PC 38; TCLC
7, 41**
See also CA 104; 193; EWL 3; GFL 1789
to the Present; LMFS 2; RGWL 2, 3

Grisham, John 1955- .... **CLC 84, 273**
See also AAYA 14, 47; BPFB 2; CA 138;
CANR 47, 69, 114, 133; CMW 4; CN 6,
7; CPW; CSW; DA3; DAM POP; LNFS
1; MSW; MTCW 2; MTFW 2005

Grosseteste, Robert 1175(?)-1253 . **CMLC 62**
See also DLB 115

Grossman, David 1954- .... **CLC 67, 231**
See also CA 138; CANR 114, 175; CWW
2; DLB 299; EWL 3; RGHL; WLIT 6

Grossman, Vasilii Semenovich
See Grossman, Vasily (Semenovich)

Grossman, Vasily (Semenovich)
1905-1964 .... **CLC 41**
See also CA 124; 130; DLB 272; MTCW 1;
RGHL

Grove, Frederick Philip
See Greve, Felix Paul (Berthold Friedrich)

Grubb
See Crumb, R.

Grumbach, Doris 1918- .... **CLC 13, 22, 64**
See also CA 5-8R; CAAS 2; CANR 9, 42,
70, 127; CN 6, 7; INT CANR-9; MTCW
2; MTFW 2005

Grundtvig, Nikolai Frederik Severin
1783-1872 .... **NCLC 1, 158**
See also DLB 300

Grunge
See Crumb, R.

Grunwald, Lisa 1959- .... **CLC 44**
See also CA 120; CANR 148

Gryphius, Andreas 1616-1664 .... **LC 89**
See also CDWLB 2; DLB 164; RGWL 2, 3

Guare, John 1938- .... **CLC 8, 14, 29, 67; DC
20**
See also CA 73-76; CAD; CANR 21, 69,
118; CD 5, 6; DAM DRAM; DFS 8, 13;
DLB 7, 249; EWL 3; MAL 5; MTCW 1,
2; RGAL 4

Guarini, Battista 1538-1612 .... **LC 102**
See also DLB 339

Gubar, Susan 1944- .... **CLC 145**
See also CA 108; CANR 45, 70, 139, 179;
FW; MTCW 1; RGAL 4

Gubar, Susan David
See Gubar, Susan

Gudjonsson, Halldor Kiljan
1902-1998 .... **CLC 25**
See also CA 103; 164; CWW 2; DLB 293,
331; EW 12; EWL 3; RGWL 2, 3

Guedes, Vicente
See Pessoa, Fernando

Guenter, Erich
See Eich, Gunter

Guest, Barbara 1920-2006 ... **CLC 34; PC 55**
See also BG 1:2; CA 25-28R; 248; CANR
11, 44, 84; CP 1, 2, 3, 4, 5, 6, 7; CWP;
DLB 5, 193

Guest, Edgar A(lbert) 1881-1959 ... **TCLC 95**
See also CA 112; 168

Guest, Judith 1936- .... **CLC 8, 30**
See also AAYA 7, 66; CA 77-80; CANR
15, 75, 138; DA3; DAM NOV, POP;
EXPN; INT CANR-15; LAIT 5; MTCW
1, 2; MTFW 2005; NFS 1, 33

Guest, Judith Ann
See Guest, Judith

Guevara, Che
See Guevara (Serna), Ernesto

Guevara (Serna), Ernesto
1928-1967 .... **CLC 87; HLC 1**
See also CA 127; 111; CANR 56; DAM
MULT; HW 1

Guicciardini, Francesco 1483-1540 ..... **LC 49**

Guido delle Colonne c. 1215-c.
1290 .... **CMLC 90**

Guild, Nicholas M. 1944- .... **CLC 33**
See also CA 93-96

Guillemin, Jacques
See Sartre, Jean-Paul

Guillen, Jorge 1893-1984 . **CLC 11; HLCS 1;
PC 35; TCLC 233**
See also CA 89-92; 112; DAM MULT,
POET; DLB 108; EWL 3; HW 1; RGWL
2, 3

Guillen, Nicolas 1902-1989 ... **BLC 1:2; CLC
48, 79; HLC 1; PC 23**
See also BW 2; CA 116; 125; 129; CANR
84; DAM MST, MULT, POET; DLB 283;
EWL 3; HW 1; LAW; RGWL 2, 3; WP

Guillen, Nicolas Cristobal
See Guillen, Nicolas

Guillen y Alvarez, Jorge
See Guillen, Jorge

Guillevic, (Eugene) 1907-1997 .... **CLC 33**
See also CA 93-96; CWW 2

Guillois
See Desnos, Robert

Guillois, Valentin
See Desnos, Robert

Guimaraes Rosa, Joao 1908-1967 ... **CLC 23;
HLCS 1**
See also CA 175; 89-92; DLB 113, 307;
EWL 3; LAW; RGSF 2; RGWL 2, 3;
WLIT 1

Guiney, Louise Imogen
1861-1920 .... **TCLC 41**
See also CA 160; DLB 54; RGAL 4

Guinizelli, Guido c. 1230-1276 ...... **CMLC 49**
See also WLIT 7

Guinizzelli, Guido
See Guinizelli, Guido

Guiraldes, Ricardo (Guillermo)
1886-1927 .... **TCLC 39**
See also CA 131; EWL 3; HW 1; LAW;
MTCW 1

Guma, Alex La
See La Guma, Alex

Gumilev, Nikolai (Stepanovich)
1886-1921 .... **TCLC 60**
See also CA 165; DLB 295; EWL 3

Gumilyov, Nikolay Stepanovich
See Gumilev, Nikolai (Stepanovich)

Gump, P. Q.
See Card, Orson Scott

Gunesekera, Romesh 1954- .... **CLC 91**
See also BRWS 10; CA 159; CANR 140,
172; CN 6, 7; DLB 267, 323

Gunn, Bill
See Gunn, William Harrison

Gunn, Thom 1929-2004 ..... **CLC 3, 6, 18, 32,
81; PC 26**
See also BRWR 3; BRWS 4; CA 17-20R;
227; CANR 9, 33, 116; CDBLB 1960 to
Present; CP 1, 2, 3, 4, 5, 6, 7; DAM
POET; DLB 27; INT CANR-33; MTCW
1; PFS 9; RGEL 2

Gunn, William Harrison
1934(?)-1989 .... **CLC 5**
See also AITN 1; BW 1, 3; CA 13-16R;
128; CANR 12, 25, 76; DLB 38

Gunn Allen, Paula
See Allen, Paula Gunn

Gunnars, Kristjana 1948- .... **CLC 69**
See also CA 113; CCA 1; CP 6, 7; CWP;
DLB 60

Gunter, Erich
See Eich, Gunter

Gurdjieff, G(eorgei) I(vanovich)
1877(?)-1949 .... **TCLC 71**
See also CA 157

Gurganus, Allan 1947- .... **CLC 70**
See also BEST 90:1; CA 135; CANR 114;
CN 6, 7; CPW; CSW; DAM POP; DLB
350; GLL 1

Gurney, A. R.
See Gurney, A(lbert) R(amsdell), Jr.

Gurney, A(lbert) R(amsdell), Jr.
1930- .... **CLC 32, 50, 54**
See also AMWS 5; CA 77-80; CAD; CANR
32, 64, 121; CD 5, 6; DAM DRAM; DLB
266; EWL 3

Gurney, Ivor (Bertie) 1890-1937 ... **TCLC 33**
See also BRW 6; CA 167; DLBY 2002;
PAB; RGEL 2

Gurney, Peter
See Gurney, A(lbert) R(amsdell), Jr.

Guro, Elena (Genrikhovna)
1877-1913 .... **TCLC 56**
See also DLB 295

Gustafson, James M(oody) 1925- ... **CLC 100**
See also CA 25-28R; CANR 37

Gustafson, Ralph (Barker)
1909-1995 .... **CLC 36**
See also CA 21-24R; CANR 8, 45, 84; CP
1, 2, 3, 4, 5, 6; DLB 88; RGEL 2

Gut, Gom
See Simenon, Georges

Guterson, David 1956- .... **CLC 91**
See also CA 132; CANR 73, 126, 194; CN
7; DLB 292; MTCW 2; MTFW 2005;
NFS 13

Guthrie, A(lfred) B(ertram), Jr.
1901-1991 .... **CLC 23**
See also CA 57-60; 134; CANR 24; CN 1,
2, 3; DLB 6, 212; MAL 5; SATA 62;
SATA-Obit 67; TCWW 1, 2

Guthrie, Isobel
See Grieve, C. M.

Gutierrez Najera, Manuel
1859-1895 .... **HLCS 2; NCLC 133**
See also DLB 290; LAW

Guy, Rosa 1925- .... **CLC 26**
See also AAYA 4, 37; BW 2; CA 17-20R;
CANR 14, 34, 83; CLR 13, 137; DLB 33;
DNFS 1; JRDA; MAICYA 1, 2; SATA 14,
62, 122; YAW

Guy, Rosa Cuthbert
See Guy, Rosa

Gwendolyn
See Bennett, (Enoch) Arnold

H. D.
See Doolittle, Hilda

H. de V.
See Buchan, John

Haavikko, Paavo Juhani 1931- .. **CLC 18, 34**
See also CA 106; CWW 2; EWL 3

Habbema, Koos
See Heijermans, Herman

DRAM, MST, MULT; DFS 2; DLB 7, 38;
EWL 3; FL 1:6; FW; LAIT 4; MAL 5;
MTCW 1, 2; MTFW 2005; RGAL 4; TUS

Hansberry, Lorraine Vivian
See Hansberry, Lorraine

Hansen, Joseph 1923-2004 .... **CLC 38**
See also BPFB 2; CA 29-32R; 233; CAAS
17; CANR 16, 44, 66, 125; CMW 4; DLB
226; GLL 1; INT CANR-16

Hansen, Karen V. 1955- .... **CLC 65**
See also CA 149; CANR 102

Hansen, Martin A(lfred)
1909-1955 .... **TCLC 32**
See also CA 167; DLB 214; EWL 3

Hanson, Kenneth O(stlin) 1922- .... **CLC 13**
See also CA 53-56; CANR 7; CP 1, 2, 3, 4,
5

Han Yu 768-824 .... **CMLC 122**

Hardwick, Elizabeth 1916-2007 .... **CLC 13**
See also AMWS 3; CA 5-8R; 267; CANR
3, 32, 70, 100, 139; CN 4, 5, 6; CSW;
DA3; DAM NOV; DLB 6; MBL; MTCW
1, 2; MTFW 2005; TCLE 1:1

Hardwick, Elizabeth Bruce
See Hardwick, Elizabeth

Hardy, Thomas 1840-1928 . **PC 8, 92; SSC 2,
60, 113; TCLC 4, 10, 18, 32, 48, 53, 72,
143, 153, 229; WLC 3**
See also AAYA 69; BRW 6; BRWC 1, 2;
BRWR 1; CA 104; 123; CDBLB 1890-
1914; DA; DA3; DAB; DAC; DAM MST,
NOV, POET; DLB 18, 19, 135, 284; EWL
3; EXPN; EXPP; LAIT 2; MTCW 1, 2;
MTFW 2005; NFS 3, 11, 15, 19, 30; PFS
3, 4, 18; RGEL 2; RGSF 2; TEA; WLIT
4

Hare, David 1947- . **CLC 29, 58, 136; DC 26**
See also BRWS 4; CA 97-100; CANR 39,
91; CBD; CD 5, 6; DFS 4, 7, 16; DLB
13, 310; MTCW 1; TEA

Harewood, John
See Van Druten, John (William)

Harford, Henry
See Hudson, W(illiam) H(enry)

Hargrave, Leonie
See Disch, Thomas M.

**Hariri, Al- al-Qasim ibn 'Ali Abu
Muhammad al-Basri**
See al-Hariri, al-Qasim ibn 'Ali Abu Mu-
hammad al-Basri

Harjo, Joy 1951- ..... **CLC 83; NNAL; PC 27**
See also AMWS 12; CA 114; CANR 35,
67, 91, 129; CP 6, 7; CWP; DAM MULT;
DLB 120, 175, 342; EWL 3; MTCW 2;
MTFW 2005; PFS 15, 32; RGAL 4

Harlan, Louis R. 1922-2010 .... **CLC 34**
See also CA 21-24R; CANR 25, 55, 80

Harlan, Louis Rudolph
See Harlan, Louis R.

Harling, Robert 1951(?)- .... **CLC 53**
See also CA 147

Harmon, William (Ruth) 1938- .... **CLC 38**
See also CA 33-36R; CANR 14, 32, 35;
SATA 65

Harper, Edith Alice Mary
See Wickham, Anna

Harper, F. E. W.
See Harper, Frances Ellen Watkins

Harper, Frances E. W.
See Harper, Frances Ellen Watkins

Harper, Frances E. Watkins
See Harper, Frances Ellen Watkins

Harper, Frances Ellen
See Harper, Frances Ellen Watkins

Harper, Frances Ellen Watkins
1825-1911 . **BLC 1:2; PC 21; TCLC 14,
217**
See also AFAW 1, 2; BW 1, 3; CA 111; 125;
CANR 79; DAM MULT, POET; DLB 50,
221; MBL; RGAL 4

Harper, Michael S(teven) 1938- ..... **BLC 2:2;
CLC 7, 22**
See also AFAW 2; BW 1; CA 33-36R, 224;
CAAE 224; CANR 24, 108; CP 2, 3, 4, 5,
6, 7; DLB 41; RGAL 4; TCLE 1:1

Harper, Mrs. F. E. W.
See Harper, Frances Ellen Watkins

Harpur, Charles 1813-1868 .... **NCLC 114**
See also DLB 230; RGEL 2

Harris, Christie
See Harris, Christie (Lucy) Irwin

Harris, Christie (Lucy) Irwin
1907-2002 .... **CLC 12**
See also CA 5-8R; CANR 6, 83; CLR 47;
DLB 88; JRDA; MAICYA 1, 2; SAAS 10;
SATA 6, 74; SATA-Essay 116

Harris, Frank 1856-1931 .... **TCLC 24**
See also CA 109; 150; CANR 80; DLB 156,
197; RGEL 2

Harris, George Washington
1814-1869 .... **NCLC 23, 165**
See also DLB 3, 11, 248; RGAL 4

Harris, Joel Chandler 1848-1908 ..... **SSC 19,
103; TCLC 2**
See also CA 104; 137; CANR 80; CLR 49,
128; DLB 11, 23, 42, 78, 91; LAIT 2;
MAICYA 1, 2; RGSF 2; SATA 100; WCH;
YABC 1

**Harris, John (Wyndham Parkes Lucas)
Beynon** 1903-1969 .... **CLC 19**
See also BRWS 13; CA 102; 89-92; CANR
84; DLB 255; SATA 118; SCFW 1, 2;
SFW 4

Harris, MacDonald
See Heiney, Donald (William)

Harris, Mark 1922-2007 .... **CLC 19**
See also CA 5-8R; 260; CAAS 3; CANR 2,
55, 83; CN 1, 2, 3, 4, 5, 6, 7; DLB 2;
DLBY 1980

Harris, Norman .... **CLC 65**

Harris, (Theodore) Wilson 1921- ... **BLC 2:2;
CLC 25, 159**
See also BRWS 5; BW 2, 3; CA 65-68;
CAAS 16; CANR 11, 27, 69, 114; CD-
WLB 3; CN 1, 2, 3, 4, 5, 6, 7; CP 1, 2, 3,
4, 5, 6, 7; DLB 117; EWL 3; MTCW 1;
RGEL 2

Harrison, Barbara Grizzuti
1934-2002 .... **CLC 144**
See also CA 77-80; 205; CANR 15, 48; INT
CANR-15

Harrison, Elizabeth (Allen) Cavanna
1909-2001 .... **CLC 12**
See also CA 9-12R; 200; CANR 6, 27, 85,
104, 121; JRDA; MAICYA 1; SAAS 4;
SATA 1, 30; YAW

Harrison, Harry 1925- .... **CLC 42**
See also CA 1-4R; CANR 5, 21, 84; DLB
8; SATA 4; SCFW 2; SFW 4

Harrison, Harry Max
See Harrison, Harry

Harrison, James
See Harrison, Jim

Harrison, James Thomas
See Harrison, Jim

Harrison, Jim 1937- .... **CLC 6, 14, 33, 66,
143; SSC 19**
See also AMWS 8; CA 13-16R; CANR 8,
51, 79, 142, 198; CN 5, 6; CP 1, 2, 3, 4,
5, 6; DLBY 1982; INT CANR-8; RGAL
4; TCWW 2; TUS

Harrison, Kathryn 1961- .... **CLC 70, 151**
See also CA 144; CANR 68, 122, 194

Harrison, Tony 1937- .... **CLC 43, 129**
See also BRWS 5; CA 65-68; CANR 44,
98; CBD; CD 5, 6; CP 2, 3, 4, 5, 6, 7;
DLB 40, 245; MTCW 1; RGEL 2

Harriss, Will(ard Irvin) 1922- .... **CLC 34**
See also CA 111

Hart, Ellis
See Ellison, Harlan

Hart, Josephine 1942(?)- .... **CLC 70**
See also CA 138; CANR 70, 149; CPW;
DAM POP

Hart, Moss 1904-1961 .... **CLC 66**
See also CA 109; 89-92; CANR 84; DAM
DRAM; DFS 1; DLB 7, 266; RGAL 4

Harte, Bret 1836(?)-1902 .. **SSC 8, 59; TCLC
1, 25; WLC 3**
See also AMWS 2; CA 104; 140; CANR
80; CDALB 1865-1917; DA; DA3; DAC;
DAM MST; DLB 12, 64, 74, 79, 186;
EXPS; LAIT 2; RGAL 4; RGSF 2; SATA
26; SSFS 3; TUS

Harte, Francis Brett
See Harte, Bret

Hartley, L(eslie) P(oles) 1895-1972 ... **CLC 2,
22; SSC 125**
See also BRWS 7; CA 45-48; 37-40R;
CANR 33; CN 1; DLB 15, 139; EWL 3;
HGG; MTCW 1, 2; MTFW 2005; RGEL
2; RGSF 2; SUFW 1

Hartman, Geoffrey H. 1929- .... **CLC 27**
See also CA 117; 125; CANR 79; DLB 67

Hartmann, Sadakichi 1869-1944 ... **TCLC 73**
See also CA 157; DLB 54

Hartmann von Aue c. 1170-c.
1210 .... **CMLC 15**
See also CDWLB 2; DLB 138; RGWL 2, 3

Hartog, Jan de
See de Hartog, Jan

Haruf, Kent 1943- .... **CLC 34**
See also AAYA 44; CA 149; CANR 91, 131

Harvey, Caroline
See Trollope, Joanna

Harvey, Gabriel 1550(?)-1631 .... **LC 88**
See also DLB 167, 213, 281

Harvey, Jack
See Rankin, Ian

Harwood, Ronald 1934- .... **CLC 32**
See also CA 1-4R; CANR 4, 55, 150; CBD;
CD 5, 6; DAM DRAM, MST; DLB 13

Hasegawa Tatsunosuke
See Futabatei, Shimei

Hasek, Jaroslav 1883-1923 ... **SSC 69; TCLC
4**
See also CA 104; 129; CDWLB 4; DLB
215; EW 9; EWL 3; MTCW 1, 2; RGSF
2; RGWL 2, 3

Hasek, Jaroslav Matej Frantisek
See Hasek, Jaroslav

Hass, Robert 1941- ...... **CLC 18, 39, 99, 287;
PC 16**
See also AMWS 6; CA 111; CANR 30, 50,
71, 187; CP 3, 4, 5, 6, 7; DLB 105, 206;
EWL 3; MAL 5; MTFW 2005; RGAL 4;
SATA 94; TCLE 1:1

Hassler, Jon 1933-2008 .... **CLC 263**
See also CA 73-76; 270; CANR 21, 80, 161;
CN 6, 7; INT CANR-21; SATA 19; SATA-
Obit 191

Hassler, Jon Francis
See Hassler, Jon

Hastings, Hudson
See Kuttner, Henry

Hastings, Selina .... **CLC 44**
See also CA 257

Hastings, Selina Shirley
See Hastings, Selina

Hastings, Victor
See Disch, Thomas M.

Hellman, Lillian 1905-1984 . **CLC 2, 4, 8, 14, 18, 34, 44, 52; DC 1; TCLC 119**
See also AAYA 47; AITN 1, 2; AMWS 1; CA 13-16R; 112; CAD; CANR 33; CWD; DA3; DAM DRAM; DFS 1, 3, 14; DLB 7, 228; DLBY 1984; EWL 3; FL 1:6; FW; LAIT 3; MAL 5; MBL; MTCW 1, 2; MTFW 2005; RGAL 4; TUS

Hellman, Lillian Florence
See Hellman, Lillian

Heloise c. 1095-c. 1164 .... **CMLC 122**

Helprin, Mark 1947- .... **CLC 7, 10, 22, 32**
See also CA 81-84; CANR 47, 64, 124; CDALBS; CN 7; CPW; DA3; DAM NOV, POP; DLB 335; DLBY 1985; FANT; MAL 5; MTCW 1, 2; MTFW 2005; SSFS 25; SUFW 2

Helvetius, Claude-Adrien 1715-1771 .. **LC 26**
See also DLB 313

Helyar, Jane Penelope Josephine
1933- .... **CLC 17**
See also CA 21-24R; CANR 10, 26; CWRI 5; SAAS 2; SATA 5; SATA-Essay 138

Hemans, Felicia 1793-1835 ...... **NCLC 29, 71**
See also DLB 96; RGEL 2

Hemingway, Ernest 1899-1961 .. **CLC 1, 3, 6, 8, 10, 13, 19, 30, 34, 39, 41, 44, 50, 61, 80; SSC 1, 25, 36, 40, 63, 117, 137; TCLC 115, 203; WLC 3**
See also AAYA 19; AMW; AMWC 1; AMWR 1; BPFB 2; BYA 2, 3, 13, 15; CA 77-80; CANR 34; CDALB 1917-1929; DA; DA3; DAB; DAC; DAM MST, NOV; DLB 4, 9, 102, 210, 308, 316, 330; DLBD 1, 15, 16; DLBY 1981, 1987, 1996, 1998; EWL 3; EXPN; EXPS; LAIT 3, 4; LATS 1:1; MAL 5; MTCW 1, 2; MTFW 2005; NFS 1, 5, 6, 14; RGAL 4; RGSF 2; SSFS 17; TUS; WYA

Hemingway, Ernest Miller
See Hemingway, Ernest

Hempel, Amy 1951- .... **CLC 39**
See also CA 118; 137; CANR 70, 166; DA3; DLB 218; EXPS; MTCW 2; MTFW 2005; SSFS 2

Henderson, F. C.
See Mencken, H. L.

Henderson, Mary
See Mavor, Osborne Henry

Henderson, Sylvia
See Ashton-Warner, Sylvia (Constance)

Henderson, Zenna (Chlarson)
1917-1983 .... **SSC 29**
See also CA 1-4R; 133; CANR 1, 84; DLB 8; SATA 5; SFW 4

Henkin, Joshua 1964- .... **CLC 119**
See also CA 161; CANR 186; DLB 350

Henley, Beth 1952- ... **CLC 23, 255; DC 6, 14**
See also AAYA 70; CA 107; CABS 3; CAD; CANR 32, 73, 140; CD 5, 6; CSW; CWD; DA3; DAM DRAM, MST; DFS 2, 21, 26; DLBY 1986; FW; MTCW 1, 2; MTFW 2005

Henley, Elizabeth Becker
See Henley, Beth

Henley, William Ernest 1849-1903 .. **TCLC 8**
See also CA 105; 234; DLB 19; RGEL 2

Hennissart, Martha 1929- .... **CLC 2**
See also BPFB 2; CA 85-88; CANR 64; CMW 4; DLB 306

Henry VIII 1491-1547 .... **LC 10**
See also DLB 132

Henry, O. 1862-1910 . **SSC 5, 49, 117; TCLC 1, 19; WLC 3**
See also AAYA 41; AMWS 2; CA 104; 131; CDALB 1865-1917; DA; DA3; DAB; DAC; DAM MST; DLB 12, 78, 79; EXPS; MAL 5; MTCW 1, 2; MTFW 2005; RGAL 4; RGSF 2; SSFS 2, 18, 27, 31; TCWW 1, 2; TUS; YABC 2

Henry, Oliver
See Henry, O.

Henry, Patrick 1736-1799 .... **LC 25**
See also LAIT 1

Henryson, Robert 1430(?)-1506(?) ..... **LC 20, 110; PC 65**
See also BRWS 7; DLB 146; RGEL 2

Henschke, Alfred
See Klabund

Henson, Lance 1944- .... **NNAL**
See also CA 146; DLB 175

Hentoff, Nat(han Irving) 1925- .... **CLC 26**
See also AAYA 4, 42; BYA 6; CA 1-4R; CAAS 2; CANR 5, 25, 77, 114; CLR 1, 52; DLB 345; INT CANR-25; JRDA; MAICYA 1, 2; SATA 42, 69, 133; SATA-Brief 27; WYA; YAW

Heppenstall, (John) Rayner
1911-1981 .... **CLC 10**
See also CA 1-4R; 103; CANR 29; CN 1, 2; CP 1, 2, 3; EWL 3

Heraclitus c. 540B.C.-c. 450B.C. ... **CMLC 22**
See also DLB 176

Herbert, Edward 1583-1648 .... **LC 177**
See also DLB 121, 151, 252; RGEL 2

Herbert, Frank 1920-1986 ... **CLC 12, 23, 35, 44, 85**
See also AAYA 21; BPFB 2; BYA 4, 14; CA 53-56; 118; CANR 5, 43; CDALBS; CPW; DAM POP; DLB 8; INT CANR-5; LAIT 5; MTCW 1, 2; MTFW 2005; NFS 17, 31; SATA 9, 37; SATA-Obit 47; SCFW 1, 2; SFW 4; YAW

Herbert, George 1593-1633 . **LC 24, 121; PC 4**
See also BRW 2; BRWR 2; CDBLB Before 1660; DAB; DAM POET; DLB 126; EXPP; PFS 25; RGEL 2; TEA; WP

Herbert, Zbigniew 1924-1998 ..... **CLC 9, 43; PC 50; TCLC 168**
See also CA 89-92; 169; CANR 36, 74, 177; CDWLB 4; CWW 2; DAM POET; DLB 232; EWL 3; MTCW 1; PFS 22

Herbert of Cherbury, Lord
See Herbert, Edward

Herbst, Josephine (Frey)
1897-1969 .... **CLC 34**
See also CA 5-8R; 25-28R; DLB 9

Herder, Johann Gottfried von
1744-1803 .... **NCLC 8, 186**
See also DLB 97; EW 4; TWA

Heredia, Jose Maria 1803-1839 ...... **HLCS 2; NCLC 209**
See also LAW

Hergesheimer, Joseph 1880-1954 ... **TCLC 11**
See also CA 109; 194; DLB 102, 9; RGAL 4

Herlihy, James Leo 1927-1993 .... **CLC 6**
See also CA 1-4R; 143; CAD; CANR 2; CN 1, 2, 3, 4, 5

Herman, William
See Bierce, Ambrose

Hermogenes fl. c. 175- .... **CMLC 6**

Hernandez, Jose 1834-1886 .... **NCLC 17**
See also LAW; RGWL 2, 3; WLIT 1

Herodotus c. 484B.C.-c. 420B.C. .. **CMLC 17**
See also AW 1; CDWLB 1; DLB 176; RGWL 2, 3; TWA; WLIT 8

Herr, Michael 1940(?)- .... **CLC 231**
See also CA 89-92; CANR 68, 142; DLB 185; MTCW 1

Herrick, Robert 1591-1674 .. **LC 13, 145; PC 9**
See also BRW 2; BRWC 2; DA; DAB; DAC; DAM MST, POP; DLB 126; EXPP; PFS 13, 29; RGAL 4; RGEL 2; TEA; WP

Herring, Guilles
See Somerville, Edith Oenone

Herriot, James 1916-1995 .... **CLC 12**
See also AAYA 1, 54; BPFB 2; CA 77-80; 148; CANR 40; CLR 80; CPW; DAM POP; LAIT 3; MAICYA 2; MAICYAS 1; MTCW 2; SATA 86, 135; SATA-Brief 44; TEA; YAW

Herris, Violet
See Hunt, Violet

Herrmann, Dorothy 1941- .... **CLC 44**
See also CA 107

Herrmann, Taffy
See Herrmann, Dorothy

Hersey, John 1914-1993 .. **CLC 1, 2, 7, 9, 40, 81, 97**
See also AAYA 29; BPFB 2; CA 17-20R; 140; CANR 33; CDALBS; CN 1, 2, 3, 4, 5; CPW; DAM POP; DLB 6, 185, 278, 299; MAL 5; MTCW 1, 2; MTFW 2005; RGHL; SATA 25; SATA-Obit 76; TUS

Hersey, John Richard
See Hersey, John

Hervent, Maurice
See Grindel, Eugene

Herzen, Aleksandr Ivanovich
1812-1870 .... **NCLC 10, 61**
See also DLB 277

Herzen, Alexander
See Herzen, Aleksandr Ivanovich

Herzl, Theodor 1860-1904 .... **TCLC 36**
See also CA 168

Herzog, Werner 1942- .... **CLC 16, 236**
See also CA 89-92

Hesiod fl. 8th cent. B.C.- .... **CMLC 5, 102**
See also AW 1; DLB 176; RGWL 2, 3; WLIT 8

Hesse, Hermann 1877-1962 ... **CLC 1, 2, 3, 6, 11, 17, 25, 69; SSC 9, 49; TCLC 148, 196; WLC 3**
See also AAYA 43; BPFB 2; CA 17-18; CAP 2; CDWLB 2; DA; DA3; DAB; DAC; DAM MST, NOV; DLB 66, 330; EW 9; EWL 3; EXPN; LAIT 1; MTCW 1, 2; MTFW 2005; NFS 6, 15, 24; RGWL 2, 3; SATA 50; TWA

Hewes, Cady
See De Voto, Bernard (Augustine)

Heyen, William 1940- .... **CLC 13, 18**
See also CA 33-36R, 220; CAAE 220; CAAS 9; CANR 98, 188; CP 3, 4, 5, 6, 7; DLB 5; RGHL

Heyerdahl, Thor 1914-2002 .... **CLC 26**
See also CA 5-8R; 207; CANR 5, 22, 66, 73; LAIT 4; MTCW 1, 2; MTFW 2005; SATA 2, 52

Heym, Georg (Theodor Franz Arthur)
1887-1912 .... **TCLC 9**
See also CA 106; 181

Heym, Stefan 1913-2001 .... **CLC 41**
See also CA 9-12R; 203; CANR 4; CWW 2; DLB 69; EWL 3

Heyse, Paul (Johann Ludwig von)
1830-1914 .... **TCLC 8**
See also CA 104; 209; DLB 129, 330

Heyward, (Edwin) DuBose
1885-1940 .... **HR 1:2; TCLC 59**
See also CA 108; 157; DLB 7, 9, 45, 249; MAL 5; SATA 21

Heywood, John 1497(?)-1580(?) .... **LC 65**
See also DLB 136; RGEL 2

Heywood, Thomas 1573(?)-1641 . **DC 29; LC 111**
See also DAM DRAM; DLB 62; LMFS 1; RGEL 2; TEA

Hiaasen, Carl 1953- .... **CLC 238**
See also CA 105; CANR 22, 45, 65, 113, 133, 168; CMW 4; CPW; CSW; DA3; DLB 292; LNFS 2, 3; MTCW 2; MTFW 2005; SATA 208

Johnson, Samuel 1709-1784 . **LC 15, 52, 128; PC 81; WLC 3**
See also BRW 3; BRWR 1; CDBLB 1660-1789; DA; DAB; DAC; DAM MST; DLB 39, 95, 104, 142, 213; LMFS 1; RGEL 2; TEA

Johnson, Stacie
See Myers, Walter Dean

Johnson, Uwe 1934-1984 .. **CLC 5, 10, 15, 40**
See also CA 1-4R; 112; CANR 1, 39; CD-WLB 2; DLB 75; EWL 3; MTCW 1; RGWL 2, 3

Johnston, Basil H. 1929- .... **NNAL**
See also CA 69-72; CANR 11, 28, 66; DAC; DAM MULT; DLB 60

Johnston, George (Benson) 1913- ... **CLC 51**
See also CA 1-4R; CANR 5, 20; CP 1, 2, 3, 4, 5, 6, 7; DLB 88

Johnston, Jennifer (Prudence)
1930- .... **CLC 7, 150, 228**
See also CA 85-88; CANR 92; CN 4, 5, 6, 7; DLB 14

Joinville, Jean de 1224(?)-1317 ..... **CMLC 38**

Jolley, Elizabeth 1923-2007 ..... **CLC 46, 256, 260; SSC 19**
See also CA 127; 257; CAAS 13; CANR 59; CN 4, 5, 6, 7; DLB 325; EWL 3; RGSF 2

Jolley, Monica Elizabeth
See Jolley, Elizabeth

Jones, Arthur Llewellyn 1863-1947 . **SSC 20; TCLC 4**
See Machen, Arthur
See also CA 104; 179; DLB 36; HGG; RGEL 2; SUFW 1

Jones, D(ouglas) G(ordon) 1929- ..... **CLC 10**
See also CA 29-32R; CANR 13, 90; CP 1, 2, 3, 4, 5, 6, 7; DLB 53

Jones, David (Michael) 1895-1974 .... **CLC 2, 4, 7, 13, 42**
See also BRW 6; BRWS 7; CA 9-12R; 53-56; CANR 28; CDBLB 1945-1960; CP 1, 2; DLB 20, 100; EWL 3; MTCW 1; PAB; RGEL 2

Jones, David Robert 1947- .... **CLC 17**
See also CA 103; CANR 104

Jones, Diana Wynne 1934- .... **CLC 26**
See also AAYA 12; BYA 6, 7, 9, 11, 13, 16; CA 49-52; CANR 4, 26, 56, 120, 167; CLR 23, 120; DLB 161; FANT; JRDA; MAICYA 1, 2; MTFW 2005; SAAS 7; SATA 9, 70, 108, 160; SFW 4; SUFW 2; YAW

Jones, Edward P. 1950- .. **BLC 2:2; CLC 76, 223**
See also AAYA 71; BW 2, 3; CA 142; CANR 79, 134, 190; CSW; LNFS 2; MTFW 2005; NFS 26

Jones, Edward Paul
See Jones, Edward P.

Jones, Ernest Charles
1819-1869 .... **NCLC 222**
See also DLB 32

Jones, Everett LeRoi
See Baraka, Amiri

Jones, Gayl 1949- .. **BLC 1:2; CLC 6, 9, 131, 270**
See also AFAW 1, 2; BW 2, 3; CA 77-80; CANR 27, 66, 122; CN 4, 5, 6, 7; CSW; DA3; DAM MULT; DLB 33, 278; MAL 5; MTCW 1, 2; MTFW 2005; RGAL 4

Jones, James 1921-1977 ...... **CLC 1, 3, 10, 39**
See also AITN 1, 2; AMWS 11; BPFB 2; CA 1-4R; 69-72; CANR 6; CN 1, 2; DLB 2, 143; DLBD 17; DLBY 1998; EWL 3; MAL 5; MTCW 1; RGAL 4

Jones, John J.
See Lovecraft, H. P.

Jones, LeRoi
See Baraka, Amiri

Jones, Louis B. 1953- .... **CLC 65**
See also CA 141; CANR 73

Jones, Madison 1925- .... **CLC 4**
See also CA 13-16R; CAAS 11; CANR 7, 54, 83, 158; CN 1, 2, 3, 4, 5, 6, 7; CSW; DLB 152

Jones, Madison Percy, Jr.
See Jones, Madison

Jones, Mervyn 1922-2010 .... **CLC 10, 52**
See also CA 45-48; CAAS 5; CANR 1, 91; CN 1, 2, 3, 4, 5, 6, 7; MTCW 1

Jones, Mick 1956(?)- .... **CLC 30**

Jones, Nettie (Pearl) 1941- .... **CLC 34**
See also BW 2; CA 137; CAAS 20; CANR 88

Jones, Peter 1802-1856 .... **NNAL**

Jones, Preston 1936-1979 .... **CLC 10**
See also CA 73-76; 89-92; DLB 7

Jones, Robert F(rancis) 1934-2003 .... **CLC 7**
See also CA 49-52; CANR 2, 61, 118

Jones, Rod 1953- .... **CLC 50**
See also CA 128

Jones, Terence Graham Parry
1942- .... **CLC 21**
See also CA 112; 116; CANR 35, 93, 173; INT CA-116; SATA 67, 127; SATA-Brief 51

Jones, Terry
See Jones, Terence Graham Parry

Jones, Thom (Douglas) 1945(?)- ..... **CLC 81; SSC 56**
See also CA 157; CANR 88; DLB 244; SSFS 23

Jong, Erica 1942- .... **CLC 4, 6, 8, 18, 83**
See also AITN 1; AMWS 5; BEST 90:2; BPFB 2; CA 73-76; CANR 26, 52, 75, 132, 166; CN 3, 4, 5, 6, 7; CP 2, 3, 4, 5, 6, 7; CPW; DA3; DAM NOV, POP; DLB 2, 5, 28, 152; FW; INT CANR-26; MAL 5; MTCW 1, 2; MTFW 2005

Jonson, Ben 1572(?)-1637 ... **DC 4; LC 6, 33, 110, 158; PC 17; WLC 3**
See also BRW 1; BRWC 1; BRWR 1; CD-BLB Before 1660; DA; DAB; DAC; DAM DRAM, MST, POET; DFS 4, 10; DLB 62, 121; LMFS 1; PFS 23, 33; RGEL 2; TEA; WLIT 3

Jonson, Benjamin
See Jonson, Ben

Jordan, June 1936-2002 .. **BLCS; CLC 5, 11, 23, 114, 230; PC 38**
See also AAYA 2, 66; AFAW 1, 2; BW 2, 3; CA 33-36R; 206; CANR 25, 70, 114, 154; CLR 10; CP 3, 4, 5, 6, 7; CWP; DAM MULT, POET; DLB 38; GLL 2; LAIT 5; MAICYA 1, 2; MTCW 1; SATA 4, 136; YAW

Jordan, June Meyer
See Jordan, June

Jordan, Neil 1950- .... **CLC 110**
See also CA 124; 130; CANR 54, 154; CN 4, 5, 6, 7; GLL 2; INT CA-130

Jordan, Neil Patrick
See Jordan, Neil

Jordan, Pat(rick M.) 1941- .... **CLC 37**
See also CA 33-36R; CANR 121

Jorgensen, Ivar
See Ellison, Harlan

Jorgenson, Ivar
See Silverberg, Robert

Joseph, George Ghevarughese .... **CLC 70**

Josephson, Mary
See O'Doherty, Brian

Josephus, Flavius c. 37-100 ..... **CMLC 13, 93**
See also AW 2; DLB 176; WLIT 8

Josh
See Twain, Mark

Josiah Allen's Wife
See Holley, Marietta

Josipovici, Gabriel 1940- ...... **CLC 6, 43, 153**
See also CA 37-40R; 224; CAAE 224; CAAS 8; CANR 47, 84; CN 3, 4, 5, 6, 7; DLB 14, 319

Josipovici, Gabriel David
See Josipovici, Gabriel

Joubert, Joseph 1754-1824 .... **NCLC 9**

Jouve, Pierre Jean 1887-1976 .... **CLC 47**
See also CA 252; 65-68; DLB 258; EWL 3

Jovine, Francesco 1902-1950 .... **TCLC 79**
See also DLB 264; EWL 3

Joyaux, Julia
See Kristeva, Julia

Joyce, James 1882-1941 .... **DC 16; PC 22; SSC 3, 26, 44, 64, 118, 122; TCLC 3, 8, 16, 35, 52, 159; WLC 3**
See also AAYA 42; BRW 7; BRWC 1; BRWR 3; BYA 11, 13; CA 104; 126; CD-BLB 1914-1945; DA; DA3; DAB; DAC; DAM MST, NOV, POET; DLB 10, 19, 36, 162, 247; EWL 3; EXPN; EXPS; LAIT 3; LMFS 1, 2; MTCW 1, 2; MTFW 2005; NFS 7, 26; RGSF 2; SSFS 1, 19; TEA; WLIT 4

Joyce, James Augustine Aloysius
See Joyce, James

Jozsef, Attila 1905-1937 .... **TCLC 22**
See also CA 116; 230; CDWLB 4; DLB 215; EWL 3

Juana Ines de la Cruz, Sor
1651(?)-1695 ... **HLCS 1; LC 5, 136; PC 24**
See also DLB 305; FW; LAW; RGWL 2, 3; WLIT 1

Juana Inez de La Cruz, Sor
See Juana Ines de la Cruz, Sor

Juan Manuel, Don 1282-1348 .... **CMLC 88**

Judd, Cyril
See Kornbluth, C(yril) M.; Pohl, Frederik

Juenger, Ernst 1895-1998 .... **CLC 125**
See also CA 101; 167; CANR 21, 47, 106; CDWLB 2; DLB 56; EWL 3; RGWL 2, 3

Julian of Norwich 1342(?)-1416(?) . **LC 6, 52**
See also BRWS 12; DLB 146; LMFS 1

Julius Caesar 100B.C.-44B.C. .... **CMLC 47**
See also AW 1; CDWLB 1; DLB 211; RGWL 2, 3; WLIT 8

Jung, Patricia B.
See Hope, Christopher

Junger, Ernst
See Juenger, Ernst

Junger, Sebastian 1962- .... **CLC 109**
See also AAYA 28; CA 165; CANR 130, 171; MTFW 2005

Juniper, Alex
See Hospital, Janette Turner

Junius
See Luxemburg, Rosa

Junzaburo, Nishiwaki
See Nishiwaki, Junzaburo

Just, Ward 1935- .... **CLC 4, 27**
See also CA 25-28R; CANR 32, 87; CN 6, 7; DLB 335; INT CANR-32

Just, Ward Swift
See Just, Ward

Justice, Donald 1925-2004 ... **CLC 6, 19, 102; PC 64**
See also AMWS 7; CA 5-8R; 230; CANR 26, 54, 74, 121, 122, 169; CP 1, 2, 3, 4, 5, 6, 7; CSW; DAM POET; DLBY 1983; EWL 3; INT CANR-26; MAL 5; MTCW 2; PFS 14; TCLE 1:1

Justice, Donald Rodney
See Justice, Donald

Juvenal c. 55-c. 127 .... **CMLC 8, 115**
See also AW 2; CDWLB 1; DLB 211; RGWL 2, 3; WLIT 8

Juvenis
See Bourne, Randolph S(illiman)

K., Alice
See Knapp, Caroline

Kabakov, Sasha .... **CLC 59**

Kabir 1398(?)-1448(?) .... **LC 109; PC 56**
See also RGWL 2, 3

Kacew, Romain 1914-1980 .... **CLC 25**
See also CA 108; 102; DLB 83, 299; RGHL

Kacew, Roman
See Kacew, Romain

Kadare, Ismail 1936- .... **CLC 52, 190**
See also CA 161; CANR 165; DLB 353;
EWL 3; RGWL 3

Kadohata, Cynthia 1956(?)- ..... **CLC 59, 122**
See also AAYA 71; CA 140; CANR 124,
205; CLR 121; LNFS 1; SATA 155, 180

Kadohata, Cynthia L.
See Kadohata, Cynthia

Kafka, Franz 1883-1924 ... **SSC 5, 29, 35, 60,
128; TCLC 2, 6, 13, 29, 47, 53, 112,
179; WLC 3**
See also AAYA 31; BPFB 2; CA 105; 126;
CDWLB 2; DA; DA3; DAB; DAC; DAM
MST, NOV; DLB 81; EW 9; EWL 3;
EXPS; LATS 1:1; LMFS 2; MTCW 1, 2;
MTFW 2005; NFS 7, 34; RGSF 2; RGWL
2, 3; SFW 4; SSFS 3, 7, 12; TWA

Kafu
See Nagai, Kafu

Kahanovitch, Pinchas
See Der Nister

Kahanovitsch, Pinkhes
See Der Nister

Kahanovitsh, Pinkhes
See Der Nister

Kahn, Roger 1927- .... **CLC 30**
See also CA 25-28R; CANR 44, 69, 152;
DLB 171; SATA 37

Kain, Saul
See Sassoon, Siegfried

Kaiser, Georg 1878-1945 .... **TCLC 9, 220**
See also CA 106; 190; CDWLB 2; DLB
124; EWL 3; LMFS 2; RGWL 2, 3

Kaledin, Sergei .... **CLC 59**

Kaletski, Alexander 1946- .... **CLC 39**
See also CA 118; 143

Kalidasa fl. c. 400-455 .... **CMLC 9; PC 22**
See also RGWL 2, 3

Kallman, Chester (Simon)
1921-1975 .... **CLC 2**
See also CA 45-48; 53-56; CANR 3; CP 1,
2

Kaminsky, Melvin .... **CLC 12, 217**
See Brooks, Mel
See also AAYA 13, 48; DLB 26

Kaminsky, Stuart
See Kaminsky, Stuart M.

Kaminsky, Stuart M. 1934-2009 ...... **CLC 59**
See also CA 73-76; 292; CANR 29, 53, 89,
161, 190; CMW 4

Kaminsky, Stuart Melvin
See Kaminsky, Stuart M.

Kamo no Chomei 1153(?)-1216 .... **CMLC 66**
See also DLB 203

Kamo no Nagaakira
See Kamo no Chomei

Kandinsky, Wassily 1866-1944 .... **TCLC 92**
See also AAYA 64; CA 118; 155

Kane, Francis
See Robbins, Harold

Kane, Paul
See Simon, Paul

Kane, Sarah 1971-1999 .... **DC 31**
See also BRWS 8; CA 190; CD 5, 6; DLB
310

Kanin, Garson 1912-1999 .... **CLC 22**
See also AITN 1; CA 5-8R; 177; CAD;
CANR 7, 78; DLB 7; IDFW 3, 4

Kaniuk, Yoram 1930- .... **CLC 19**
See also CA 134; DLB 299; RGHL

Kant, Immanuel 1724-1804 ..... **NCLC 27, 67**
See also DLB 94

Kantor, MacKinlay 1904-1977 .... **CLC 7**
See also CA 61-64; 73-76; CANR 60, 63;
CN 1, 2; DLB 9, 102; MAL 5; MTCW 2;
RHW; TCWW 1, 2

Kanze Motokiyo
See Zeami

Kaplan, David Michael 1946- .... **CLC 50**
See also CA 187

Kaplan, James 1951- .... **CLC 59**
See also CA 135; CANR 121

Karadzic, Vuk Stefanovic
1787-1864 .... **NCLC 115**
See also CDWLB 4; DLB 147

Karageorge, Michael
See Anderson, Poul

Karamzin, Nikolai Mikhailovich
1766-1826 .... **NCLC 3, 173**
See also DLB 150; RGSF 2

Karapanou, Margarita 1946- .... **CLC 13**
See also CA 101

Karinthy, Frigyes 1887-1938 .... **TCLC 47**
See also CA 170; DLB 215; EWL 3

Karl, Frederick R(obert)
1927-2004 .... **CLC 34**
See also CA 5-8R; 226; CANR 3, 44, 143

Karr, Mary 1955- .... **CLC 188**
See also AMWS 11; CA 151; CANR 100,
191; MTFW 2005; NCFS 5

Kastel, Warren
See Silverberg, Robert

Kataev, Evgeny Petrovich
1903-1942 .... **TCLC 21**
See also CA 120; DLB 272

Kataphusin
See Ruskin, John

Katz, Steve 1935- .... **CLC 47**
See also CA 25-28R; CAAS 14, 64; CANR
12; CN 4, 5, 6, 7; DLBY 1983

Kauffman, Janet 1945- .... **CLC 42**
See also CA 117; CANR 43, 84; DLB 218;
DLBY 1986

Kaufman, Bob (Garnell)
1925-1986 .... **CLC 49; PC 74**
See also BG 1:3; BW 1; CA 41-44R; 118;
CANR 22; CP 1; DLB 16, 41

Kaufman, George S. 1889-1961 ...... **CLC 38;
DC 17**
See also CA 108; 93-96; DAM DRAM;
DFS 1, 10; DLB 7; INT CA-108; MTCW
2; MTFW 2005; RGAL 4; TUS

Kaufman, Moises 1963- .... **DC 26**
See also CA 211; DFS 22; MTFW 2005

Kaufman, Sue
See Barondess, Sue K.

Kavafis, Konstantinos Petrov
See Cavafy, Constantine

Kavan, Anna 1901-1968 .... **CLC 5, 13, 82**
See also BRWS 7; CA 5-8R; CANR 6, 57;
DLB 255; MTCW 1; RGEL 2; SFW 4

Kavanagh, Dan
See Barnes, Julian

Kavanagh, Julie 1952- .... **CLC 119**
See also CA 163; CANR 186

Kavanagh, Patrick (Joseph)
1904-1967 .... **CLC 22; PC 33, 105**
See also BRWS 7; CA 123; 25-28R; DLB
15, 20; EWL 3; MTCW 1; RGEL 2

Kawabata, Yasunari 1899-1972 ..... **CLC 2, 5,
9, 18, 107; SSC 17**
See also CA 93-96; 33-36R; CANR 88;
DAM MULT; DLB 180, 330; EWL 3;
MJW; MTCW 2; MTFW 2005; RGSF 2;
RGWL 2, 3; SSFS 29

Kawabata Yasunari
See Kawabata, Yasunari

Kaye, Mary Margaret
See Kaye, M.M.

Kaye, M.M. 1908-2004 .... **CLC 28**
See also CA 89-92; 223; CANR 24, 60, 102,
142; MTCW 1, 2; MTFW 2005; RHW;
SATA 62; SATA-Obit 152

Kaye, Mollie
See Kaye, M.M.

Kaye-Smith, Sheila 1887-1956 .... **TCLC 20**
See also CA 118; 203; DLB 36

Kaymor, Patrice Maguilene
See Senghor, Leopold Sedar

Kazakov, Iurii Pavlovich
See Kazakov, Yuri Pavlovich

Kazakov, Yuri Pavlovich 1927-1982 . **SSC 43**
See also CA 5-8R; CANR 36; DLB 302;
EWL 3; MTCW 1; RGSF 2

Kazakov, Yury
See Kazakov, Yuri Pavlovich

Kazan, Elia 1909-2003 .... **CLC 6, 16, 63**
See also CA 21-24R; 220; CANR 32, 78

Kazantzakis, Nikos 1883(?)-1957 .... **TCLC 2,
5, 33, 181**
See also BPFB 2; CA 105; 132; DA3; EW
9; EWL 3; MTCW 1, 2; MTFW 2005;
RGWL 2, 3

Kazin, Alfred 1915-1998 ..... **CLC 34, 38, 119**
See also AMWS 8; CA 1-4R; CAAS 7;
CANR 1, 45, 79; DLB 67; EWL 3

Keane, Mary Nesta 1904-1996 .... **CLC 31**
See also CA 108; 114; 151; CN 5, 6; INT
CA-114; RHW; TCLE 1:1

Keane, Mary Nesta Skrine
See Keane, Mary Nesta

Keane, Molly
See Keane, Mary Nesta

Keates, Jonathan 1946(?)- .... **CLC 34**
See also CA 163; CANR 126

Keaton, Buster 1895-1966 .... **CLC 20**
See also AAYA 79; CA 194

Keats, John 1795-1821 ...... **NCLC 8, 73, 121,
225; PC 1, 96; WLC 3**
See also AAYA 58; BRW 4; BRWR 1; CD-
BLB 1789-1832; DA; DA3; DAB; DAC;
DAM MST, POET; DLB 96, 110; EXPP;
LMFS 1; PAB; PFS 1, 2, 3, 9, 17, 32;
RGEL 2; TEA; WLIT 3; WP

Keble, John 1792-1866 .... **NCLC 87**
See also DLB 32, 55; RGEL 2

Keene, Donald 1922- .... **CLC 34**
See also CA 1-4R; CANR 5, 119, 190

Keillor, Garrison 1942- ..... **CLC 40, 115, 222**
See also AAYA 2, 62; AMWS 16; BEST
89:3; BPFB 2; CA 111; 117; CANR 36,
59, 124, 180; CPW; DA3; DAM POP;
DLBY 1987; EWL 3; MTCW 1, 2; MTFW
2005; SATA 58; TUS

Keillor, Gary Edward
See Keillor, Garrison

Keith, Carlos
See Lewton, Val

Keith, Michael
See Hubbard, L. Ron

Kell, Joseph
See Burgess, Anthony

Keller, Gottfried 1819-1890 .... **NCLC 2; SSC
26, 107**
See also CDWLB 2; DLB 129; EW; RGSF
2; RGWL 2, 3

Keller, Nora Okja 1965- .... **CLC 109, 281**
See also CA 187

Kellerman, Jonathan 1949- .... **CLC 44**
See also AAYA 35; BEST 90:1; CA 106;
CANR 29, 51, 150, 183; CMW 4; CPW;
DA3; DAM POP; INT CANR-29

NOV; DLB 157, 227; DNFS 1; EWL 3;
EXPS; FW; LATS 1:2; LMFS 2; MAL 5;
MTCW 2; MTFW 2005; NCFS 1; NFS 3;
SSFS 5, 7; TUS; WWE 1; YAW

King, Francis (Henry) 1923- .... **CLC 8, 53,
145**
See also CA 1-4R; CANR 1, 33, 86; CN 1,
2, 3, 4, 5, 6, 7; DAM NOV; DLB 15, 139;
MTCW 1

King, Kennedy
See Brown, George Douglas

King, Martin Luther, Jr.
1929-1968 ... **BLC 1:2; CLC 83; WLCS**
See also BW 2, 3; CA 25-28; CANR 27,
44; CAP 2; DA; DA3; DAB; DAC; DAM
MST, MULT; LAIT 5; LATS 1:2; MTCW
1, 2; MTFW 2005; SATA 14

King, Stephen 1947- .... **CLC 12, 26, 37, 61,
113, 228, 244; SSC 17, 55**
See also AAYA 1, 17, 82; AMWS 5; BEST
90:1; BPFB 2; CA 61-64; CANR 1, 30,
52, 76, 119, 134, 168; CLR 124; CN 7;
CPW; DA3; DAM NOV, POP; DLB 143,
350; DLBY 1980; HGG; JRDA; LAIT 5;
LNFS 1; MTCW 1, 2; MTFW 2005;
RGAL 4; SATA 9, 55, 161; SSFS 30;
SUFW 1, 2; WYAS 1; YAW

King, Stephen Edwin
See King, Stephen

King, Steve
See King, Stephen

King, Thomas 1943- .... **CLC 89, 171, 276;
NNAL**
See also CA 144; CANR 95, 175; CCA 1;
CN 6, 7; DAC; DAM MULT; DLB 175,
334; SATA 96

King, Thomas Hunt
See King, Thomas

Kingman, Lee
See Natti, Lee

Kingsley, Charles 1819-1875 .... **NCLC 35**
See also BRWS 16; CLR 77; DLB 21, 32,
163, 178, 190; FANT; MAICYA 2; MAI-
CYAS 1; RGEL 2; WCH; YABC 2

Kingsley, Henry 1830-1876 .... **NCLC 107**
See also DLB 21, 230; RGEL 2

Kingsley, Sidney 1906-1995 .... **CLC 44**
See also CA 85-88; 147; CAD; DFS 14, 19;
DLB 7; MAL 5; RGAL 4

Kingsolver, Barbara 1955- .... **CLC 55, 81,
130, 216, 269**
See also AAYA 15; AMWS 7; CA 129; 134;
CANR 60, 96, 133, 179; CDALBS; CN
7; CPW; CSW; DA3; DAM POP; DLB
206; INT CA-134; LAIT 5; MTCW 2;
MTFW 2005; NFS 5, 10, 12, 24; RGAL
4; TCLE 1:1

Kingston, Maxine Hong 1940- .... **AAL; CLC
12, 19, 58, 121, 271; SSC 136; WLCS**
See also AAYA 8, 55; AMWS 5; BPFB 2;
CA 69-72; CANR 13, 38, 74, 87, 128;
CDALBS; CN 6, 7; DA3; DAM MULT,
NOV; DLB 173, 212, 312; DLBY 1980;
EWL 3; FL 1:6; FW; INT CANR-13;
LAIT 5; MAL 5; MBL; MTCW 1, 2;
MTFW 2005; NFS 6; RGAL 4; SATA 53;
SSFS 3; TCWW 2

Kingston, Maxine Ting Ting Hong
See Kingston, Maxine Hong

Kinnell, Galway 1927- ..... **CLC 1, 2, 3, 5, 13,
29, 129; PC 26**
See also AMWS 3; CA 9-12R; CANR 10,
34, 66, 116, 138, 175; CP 1, 2, 3, 4, 5, 6,
7; DLB 5, 342; DLBY 1987; EWL 3; INT
CANR-34; MAL 5; MTCW 1, 2; MTFW
2005; PAB; PFS 9, 26, 35; RGAL 4;
TCLE 1:1; WP

Kinsella, Thomas 1928- .... **CLC 4, 19, 138,
274; PC 69**
See also BRWS 5; CA 17-20R; CANR 15,
122; CP 1, 2, 3, 4, 5, 6, 7; DLB 27; EWL
3; MTCW 1, 2; MTFW 2005; RGEL 2;
TEA

Kinsella, W.P. 1935- .... **CLC 27, 43, 166**
See also AAYA 7, 60; BPFB 2; CA 97-100,
222; CAAE 222; CAAS 7; CANR 21, 35,
66, 75, 129; CN 4, 5, 6, 7; CPW; DAC;
DAM NOV, POP; FANT; INT CANR-21;
LAIT 5; MTCW 1, 2; MTFW 2005; NFS
15; RGSF 2; SSFS 30

Kinsey, Alfred C(harles)
1894-1956 .... **TCLC 91**
See also CA 115; 170; MTCW 2

Kipling, Joseph Rudyard
See Kipling, Rudyard

Kipling, Rudyard 1865-1936 . **PC 3, 91; SSC
5, 54, 110; TCLC 8, 17, 167; WLC 3**
See also AAYA 32; BRW 6; BRWC 1, 2;
BRWR 3; BYA 4; CA 105; 120; CANR
33; CDBLB 1890-1914; CLR 39, 65;
CWRI 5; DA; DA3; DAB; DAC; DAM
MST, POET; DLB 19, 34, 141, 156, 330;
EWL 3; EXPS; FANT; LAIT 3; LMFS 1;
MAICYA 1, 2; MTCW 1, 2; MTFW 2005;
NFS 21; PFS 22; RGEL 2; RGSF 2; SATA
100; SFW 4; SSFS 8, 21, 22; SUFW 1;
TEA; WCH; WLIT 4; YABC 2

Kircher, Athanasius 1602-1680 .... **LC 121**
See also DLB 164

Kirk, Russell (Amos) 1918-1994 .. **TCLC 119**
See also AITN 1; CA 1-4R; 145; CAAS 9;
CANR 1, 20, 60; HGG; INT CANR-20;
MTCW 1, 2

Kirkham, Dinah
See Card, Orson Scott

Kirkland, Caroline M. 1801-1864 . **NCLC 85**
See also DLB 3, 73, 74, 250, 254; DLBD
13

Kirkup, James 1918-2009 .... **CLC 1**
See also CA 1-4R; CAAS 4; CANR 2; CP
1, 2, 3, 4, 5, 6, 7; DLB 27; SATA 12

Kirkwood, James 1930(?)-1989 .... **CLC 9**
See also AITN 2; CA 1-4R; 128; CANR 6,
40; GLL 1

Kirsch, Sarah 1935- .... **CLC 176**
See also CA 178; CWW 2; DLB 75; EWL
3

Kirshner, Sidney
See Kingsley, Sidney

Kis, Danilo 1935-1989 .... **CLC 57**
See also CA 109; 118; 129; CANR 61; CD-
WLB 4; DLB 181; EWL 3; MTCW 1;
RGSF 2; RGWL 2, 3

Kissinger, Henry A(lfred) 1923- ..... **CLC 137**
See also CA 1-4R; CANR 2, 33, 66, 109;
MTCW 1

Kittel, Frederick August
See Wilson, August

Kivi, Aleksis 1834-1872 .... **NCLC 30**

Kizer, Carolyn 1925- ..... **CLC 15, 39, 80; PC
66**
See also CA 65-68; CAAS 5; CANR 24,
70, 134; CP 1, 2, 3, 4, 5, 6, 7; CWP; DAM
POET; DLB 5, 169; EWL 3; MAL 5;
MTCW 2; MTFW 2005; PFS 18; TCLE
1:1

Klabund 1890-1928 .... **TCLC 44**
See also CA 162; DLB 66

Klappert, Peter 1942- .... **CLC 57**
See also CA 33-36R; CSW; DLB 5

Klausner, Amos
See Oz, Amos

Klein, A. M. 1909-1972 .... **CLC 19**
See also CA 101; 37-40R; CP 1; DAB;
DAC; DAM MST; DLB 68; EWL 3;
RGEL 2; RGHL

Klein, Abraham Moses
See Klein, A. M.

Klein, Joe
See Klein, Joseph

Klein, Joseph 1946- .... **CLC 154**
See also CA 85-88; CANR 55, 164

Klein, Norma 1938-1989 .... **CLC 30**
See also AAYA 2, 35; BPFB 2; BYA 6, 7,
8; CA 41-44R; 128; CANR 15, 37; CLR
2, 19; INT CANR-15; JRDA; MAICYA
1, 2; SAAS 1; SATA 7, 57; WYA; YAW

Klein, T.E.D. 1947- .... **CLC 34**
See also CA 119; CANR 44, 75, 167; HGG

Klein, Theodore Eibon Donald
See Klein, T.E.D.

Kleist, Heinrich von 1777-1811 .... **DC 29;
NCLC 2, 37, 222; SSC 22**
See also CDWLB 2; DAM DRAM; DLB
90; EW 5; RGSF 2; RGWL 2, 3

Klima, Ivan 1931- .... **CLC 56, 172**
See also CA 25-28R; CANR 17, 50, 91;
CDWLB 4; CWW 2; DAM NOV; DLB
232; EWL 3; RGWL 3

Klimentev, Andrei Platonovich
See Klimentov, Andrei Platonovich

Klimentov, Andrei Platonovich
1899-1951 .... **SSC 42; TCLC 14**
See also CA 108; 232; DLB 272; EWL 3

Klinger, Friedrich Maximilian von
1752-1831 .... **NCLC 1**
See also DLB 94

Klingsor the Magician
See Hartmann, Sadakichi

Klopstock, Friedrich Gottlieb
1724-1803 .... **NCLC 11, 225**
See also DLB 97; EW 4; RGWL 2, 3

Kluge, Alexander 1932- .... **SSC 61**
See also CA 81-84; CANR 163; DLB 75

Knapp, Caroline 1959-2002 .... **CLC 99**
See also CA 154; 207

Knebel, Fletcher 1911-1993 .... **CLC 14**
See also AITN 1; CA 1-4R; 140; CAAS 3;
CANR 1, 36; CN 1, 2, 3, 4, 5; SATA 36;
SATA-Obit 75

Knickerbocker, Diedrich
See Irving, Washington

Knight, Etheridge 1931-1991 .... **BLC 1:2;
CLC 40; PC 14**
See also BW 1, 3; CA 21-24R; 133; CANR
23, 82; CP 1, 2, 3, 4, 5; DAM POET; DLB
41; MTCW 2; MTFW 2005; RGAL 4;
TCLE 1:1

Knight, Sarah Kemble 1666-1727 .... **LC 7**
See also DLB 24, 200

Knister, Raymond 1899-1932 .... **TCLC 56**
See also CA 186; DLB 68; RGEL 2

Knowles, John 1926-2001 ... **CLC 1, 4, 10, 26**
See also AAYA 10, 72; AMWS 12; BPFB
2; BYA 3; CA 17-20R; 203; CANR 40,
74, 76, 132; CDALB 1968-1988; CLR 98;
CN 1, 2, 3, 4, 5, 6, 7; DA; DAC; DAM
MST, NOV; DLB 6; EXPN; MTCW 1, 2;
MTFW 2005; NFS 2; RGAL 4; SATA 8,
89; SATA-Obit 134; YAW

Knox, Calvin M.
See Silverberg, Robert

Knox, John c. 1505-1572 .... **LC 37**
See also DLB 132

Knye, Cassandra
See Disch, Thomas M.

Koch, C(hristopher) J(ohn) 1932- .... **CLC 42**
See also CA 127; CANR 84; CN 3, 4, 5, 6,
7; DLB 289

Koch, Christopher
See Koch, C(hristopher) J(ohn)

Koch, Kenneth 1925-2002 .... **CLC 5, 8, 44;
PC 80**
See also AMWS 15; CA 1-4R; 207; CAD;
CANR 6, 36, 57, 97, 131; CD 5, 6; CP 1,

2, 3, 4, 5, 6, 7; DAM POET; DLB 5; INT
CANR-36; MAL 5; MTCW 2; MTFW
2005; PFS 20; SATA 65; WP

Kochanowski, Jan 1530-1584 .... **LC 10**
See also RGWL 2, 3

Kock, Charles Paul de 1794-1871 . **NCLC 16**

Koda Rohan
See Koda Shigeyuki

Koda Rohan
See Koda Shigeyuki

Koda Shigeyuki 1867-1947 .... **TCLC 22**
See also CA 121; 183; DLB 180

Koestler, Arthur 1905-1983 ... **CLC 1, 3, 6, 8,
15, 33**
See also BRWS 1; CA 1-4R; 109; CANR 1,
33; CDBLB 1945-1960; CN 1, 2, 3;
DLBY 1983; EWL 3; MTCW 1, 2; MTFW
2005; NFS 19; RGEL 2

Kogawa, Joy 1935- .... **CLC 78, 129, 262, 268**
See also AAYA 47; CA 101; CANR 19, 62,
126; CN 6, 7; CP 1; CWP; DAC; DAM
MST, MULT; DLB 334; FW; MTCW 2;
MTFW 2005; NFS 3; SATA 99

Kogawa, Joy Nozomi
See Kogawa, Joy

Kohout, Pavel 1928- .... **CLC 13**
See also CA 45-48; CANR 3

Koizumi, Yakumo
See Hearn, Lafcadio

Kolmar, Gertrud 1894-1943 .... **TCLC 40**
See also CA 167; EWL 3; RGHL

Komunyakaa, Yusef 1947- . **BLC 2:2; BLCS;
CLC 86, 94, 207; PC 51**
See also AFAW 2; AMWS 13; CA 147;
CANR 83, 164; CP 6, 7; CSW; DLB 120;
EWL 3; PFS 5, 20, 30; RGAL 4

Konigsberg, Alan Stewart
See Allen, Woody

Konrad, George
See Konrad, Gyorgy

Konrad, George
See Konrad, Gyorgy

Konrad, Gyorgy 1933- .... **CLC 4, 10, 73**
See also CA 85-88; CANR 97, 171; CD-
WLB 4; CWW 2; DLB 232; EWL 3

Konwicki, Tadeusz 1926- .... **CLC 8, 28, 54,
117**
See also CA 101; CAAS 9; CANR 39, 59;
CWW 2; DLB 232; EWL 3; IDFW 3;
MTCW 1

Koontz, Dean 1945- .... **CLC 78, 206**
See also AAYA 9, 31; BEST 89:3, 90:2; CA
108; CANR 19, 36, 52, 95, 138, 176;
CMW 4; CPW; DA3; DAM NOV, POP;
DLB 292; HGG; MTCW 1; MTFW 2005;
SATA 92, 165; SFW 4; SUFW 2; YAW

Koontz, Dean R.
See Koontz, Dean

Koontz, Dean Ray
See Koontz, Dean

Kopernik, Mikolaj
See Copernicus, Nicolaus

Kopit, Arthur (Lee) 1937- ..... **CLC 1, 18, 33;
DC 37**
See also AITN 1; CA 81-84; CABS 3;
CAD; CD 5, 6; DAM DRAM; DFS 7, 14,
24; DLB 7; MAL 5; MTCW 1; RGAL 4

Kopitar, Jernej (Bartholomaus)
1780-1844 .... **NCLC 117**

Kops, Bernard 1926- .... **CLC 4**
See also CA 5-8R; CANR 84, 159; CBD;
CN 1, 2, 3, 4, 5, 6, 7; CP 1, 2, 3, 4, 5, 6,
7; DLB 13; RGHL

Kornbluth, C(yril) M. 1923-1958 .... **TCLC 8**
See also CA 105; 160; DLB 8; SCFW 1, 2;
SFW 4

Korolenko, V.G.
See Korolenko, Vladimir G.

Korolenko, Vladimir
See Korolenko, Vladimir G.

Korolenko, Vladimir G.
1853-1921 .... **TCLC 22**
See also CA 121; DLB 277

Korolenko, Vladimir Galaktionovich
See Korolenko, Vladimir G.

Korzybski, Alfred (Habdank Skarbek)
1879-1950 .... **TCLC 61**
See also CA 123; 160

Kosinski, Jerzy 1933-1991 ..... **CLC 1, 2, 3, 6,
10, 15, 53, 70**
See also AMWS 7; BPFB 2; CA 17-20R;
134; CANR 9, 46; CN 1, 2, 3, 4; DA3;
DAM NOV; DLB 2, 299; DLBY 1982;
EWL 3; HGG; MAL 5; MTCW 1, 2;
MTFW 2005; NFS 12; RGAL 4; RGHL;
TUS

Kostelanetz, Richard (Cory) 1940- .. **CLC 28**
See also CA 13-16R; CAAS 8; CANR 38,
77; CN 4, 5, 6; CP 2, 3, 4, 5, 6, 7

Kostrowitzki, Wilhelm Apollinaris de
1880-1918
See Apollinaire, Guillaume

Kotlowitz, Robert 1924- .... **CLC 4**
See also CA 33-36R; CANR 36

Kotzebue, August (Friedrich Ferdinand) von
1761-1819 .... **NCLC 25**
See also DLB 94

Kotzwinkle, William 1938- ..... **CLC 5, 14, 35**
See also BPFB 2; CA 45-48; CANR 3, 44,
84, 129; CLR 6; CN 7; DLB 173; FANT;
MAICYA 1, 2; SATA 24, 70, 146; SFW
4; SUFW 2; YAW

Kowna, Stancy
See Szymborska, Wislawa

Kozol, Jonathan 1936- .... **CLC 17**
See also AAYA 46; CA 61-64; CANR 16,
45, 96, 178; MTFW 2005

Kozoll, Michael 1940(?)- .... **CLC 35**

Krakauer, Jon 1954- .... **CLC 248**
See also AAYA 24; AMWS 18; BYA 9; CA
153; CANR 131; MTFW 2005; SATA 108

Kramer, Kathryn 19(?)- .... **CLC 34**

Kramer, Larry 1935- .... **CLC 42; DC 8**
See also CA 124; 126; CANR 60, 132;
DAM POP; DLB 249; GLL 1

Krasicki, Ignacy 1735-1801 .... **NCLC 8**

Krasinski, Zygmunt 1812-1859 .... **NCLC 4**
See also RGWL 2, 3

Kraus, Karl 1874-1936 .... **TCLC 5**
See also CA 104; 216; DLB 118; EWL 3

Kraynay, Anton
See Gippius, Zinaida

Kreve (Mickevicius), Vincas
1882-1954 .... **TCLC 27**
See also CA 170; DLB 220; EWL 3

Kristeva, Julia 1941- .... **CLC 77, 140**
See also CA 154; CANR 99, 173; DLB 242;
EWL 3; FW; LMFS 2

Kristofferson, Kris 1936- .... **CLC 26**
See also CA 104

Krizanc, John 1956- .... **CLC 57**
See also CA 187

Krleza, Miroslav 1893-1981 .... **CLC 8, 114**
See also CA 97-100; 105; CANR 50; CD-
WLB 4; DLB 147; EW 11; RGWL 2, 3

Kroetsch, Robert (Paul) 1927- .... **CLC 5, 23,
57, 132, 286**
See also CA 17-20R; CANR 8, 38; CCA 1;
CN 2, 3, 4, 5, 6, 7; CP 6, 7; DAC; DAM
POET; DLB 53; MTCW 1

Kroetz, Franz
See Kroetz, Franz Xaver

Kroetz, Franz Xaver 1946- .... **CLC 41**
See also CA 130; CANR 142; CWW 2;
EWL 3

Kroker, Arthur (W.) 1945- .... **CLC 77**
See also CA 161

Kroniuk, Lisa
See Berton, Pierre (Francis de Marigny)

Kropotkin, Peter 1842-1921 .... **TCLC 36**
See also CA 119; 219; DLB 277

Kropotkin, Peter Alekseievich
See Kropotkin, Peter

Kropotkin, Petr Alekseevich
See Kropotkin, Peter

Krotkov, Yuri 1917-1981 .... **CLC 19**
See also CA 102

Krumb
See Crumb, R.

Krumgold, Joseph (Quincy)
1908-1980 .... **CLC 12**
See also BYA 1, 2; CA 9-12R; 101; CANR
7; MAICYA 1, 2; SATA 1, 48; SATA-Obit
23; YAW

Krumwitz
See Crumb, R.

Krutch, Joseph Wood 1893-1970 ..... **CLC 24**
See also ANW; CA 1-4R; 25-28R; CANR
4; DLB 63, 206, 275

Krutzch, Gus
See Eliot, T. S.

Krylov, Ivan Andreevich
1768(?)-1844 .... **NCLC 1**
See also DLB 150

Kubin, Alfred (Leopold Isidor)
1877-1959 .... **TCLC 23**
See also CA 112; 149; CANR 104; DLB 81

Kubrick, Stanley 1928-1999 .... **CLC 16;
TCLC 112**
See also AAYA 30; CA 81-84; 177; CANR
33; DLB 26

Kueng, Hans
See Kung, Hans

Kumin, Maxine 1925- .... **CLC 5, 13, 28, 164;
PC 15**
See also AITN 2; AMWS 4; ANW; CA
1-4R; 271; CAAE 271; CAAS 8; CANR
1, 21, 69, 115, 140; CP 2, 3, 4, 5, 6, 7;
CWP; DA3; DAM POET; DLB 5; EWL
3; EXPP; MTCW 1, 2; MTFW 2005;
PAB; PFS 18; SATA 12

Kumin, Maxine Winokur
See Kumin, Maxine

Kundera, Milan 1929- . **CLC 4, 9, 19, 32, 68,
115, 135, 234; SSC 24**
See also AAYA 2, 62; BPFB 2; CA 85-88;
CANR 19, 52, 74, 144; CDWLB 4; CWW
2; DA3; DAM NOV; DLB 232; EW 13;
EWL 3; MTCW 1, 2; MTFW 2005; NFS
18, 27; RGSF 2; RGWL 3; SSFS 10

Kunene, Mazisi 1930-2006 .... **CLC 85**
See also BW 1, 3; CA 125; 252; CANR 81;
CP 1, 6, 7; DLB 117

Kunene, Mazisi Raymond
See Kunene, Mazisi

Kunene, Mazisi Raymond Fakazi Mngoni
See Kunene, Mazisi

Kung, Hans
See Kung, Hans

Kung, Hans 1928- .... **CLC 130**
See also CA 53-56; CANR 66, 134; MTCW
1, 2; MTFW 2005

Kunikida, Tetsuo
See Kunikida Doppo

Kunikida Doppo 1869(?)-1908 .... **TCLC 99**
See also DLB 180; EWL 3

Kunikida Tetsuo
See Kunikida Doppo

Kunitz, Stanley 1905-2006 ..... **CLC 6, 11, 14,
148, 293; PC 19**
See also AMWS 3; CA 41-44R; 250; CANR
26, 57, 98; CP 1, 2, 3, 4, 5, 6, 7; DA3;
DLB 48; INT CANR-26; MAL 5; MTCW
1, 2; MTFW 2005; PFS 11; RGAL 4

Kunitz, Stanley Jasspon
See Kunitz, Stanley

Kunze, Reiner 1933- .... **CLC 10**
See also CA 93-96; CWW 2; DLB 75; EWL 3

Kuprin, Aleksander Ivanovich 1870-1938 .... **TCLC 5**
See also CA 104; 182; DLB 295; EWL 3

Kuprin, Aleksandr Ivanovich
See Kuprin, Aleksander Ivanovich

Kuprin, Alexandr Ivanovich
See Kuprin, Aleksander Ivanovich

Kureishi, Hanif 1954- ...... **CLC 64, 135, 284; DC 26**
See also BRWS 11; CA 139; CANR 113, 197; CBD; CD 5, 6; CN 6, 7; DLB 194, 245, 352; GLL 2; IDFW 4; WLIT 4; WWE 1

Kurosawa, Akira 1910-1998 ..... **CLC 16, 119**
See also AAYA 11, 64; CA 101; 170; CANR 46; DAM MULT

Kushner, Tony 1956- .... **CLC 81, 203; DC 10**
See also AAYA 61; AMWS 9; CA 144; CAD; CANR 74, 130; CD 5, 6; DA3; DAM DRAM; DFS 5; DLB 228; EWL 3; GLL 1; LAIT 5; MAL 5; MTCW 2; MTFW 2005; RGAL 4; RGHL; SATA 160

Kuttner, Henry 1915-1958 .... **TCLC 10**
See also CA 107; 157; DLB 8; FANT; SCFW 1, 2; SFW 4

Kutty, Madhavi
See Das, Kamala

Kuzma, Greg 1944- .... **CLC 7**
See also CA 33-36R; CANR 70

Kuzmin, Mikhail (Alekseevich) 1872(?)-1936 .... **TCLC 40**
See also CA 170; DLB 295; EWL 3

Kyd, Thomas 1558-1594 .. **DC 3; LC 22, 125**
See also BRW 1; DAM DRAM; DFS 21; DLB 62; IDTP; LMFS 1; RGEL 2; TEA; WLIT 3

Kyprianos, Iossif
See Samarakis, Antonis

L. S.
See Stephen, Sir Leslie

Labe, Louise 1521-1566 .... **LC 120**
See also DLB 327

Labrunie, Gerard
See Nerval, Gerard de

La Bruyere, Jean de 1645-1696 .. **LC 17, 168**
See also DLB 268; EW 3; GFL Beginnings to 1789

LaBute, Neil 1963- .... **CLC 225**
See also CA 240

Lacan, Jacques (Marie Emile) 1901-1981 .... **CLC 75**
See also CA 121; 104; DLB 296; EWL 3; TWA

Laclos, Pierre-Ambroise Francois 1741-1803 .... **NCLC 4, 87**
See also DLB 313; EW 4; GFL Beginnings to 1789; RGWL 2, 3

La Colere, Francois
See Aragon, Louis

Lacolere, Francois
See Aragon, Louis

Lactantius c. 250-c. 325 .... **CMLC 118**

La Deshabilleuse
See Simenon, Georges

Lady Gregory
See Gregory, Lady Isabella Augusta (Persse)

Lady of Quality, A
See Bagnold, Enid

La Fayette, Marie-(Madelaine Pioche de la Vergne) 1634-1693 .... **LC 2, 144**
See also DLB 268; GFL Beginnings to 1789; RGWL 2, 3

Lafayette, Marie-Madeleine
See La Fayette, Marie-(Madelaine Pioche de la Vergne)

Lafayette, Rene
See Hubbard, L. Ron

La Flesche, Francis 1857(?)-1932 ...... **NNAL**
See also CA 144; CANR 83; DLB 175

La Fontaine, Jean de 1621-1695 .... **LC 50**
See also DLB 268; EW 3; GFL Beginnings to 1789; MAICYA 1, 2; RGWL 2, 3; SATA 18

LaForet, Carmen 1921-2004 .... **CLC 219**
See also CA 246; CWW 2; DLB 322; EWL 3

LaForet Diaz, Carmen
See LaForet, Carmen

Laforgue, Jules 1860-1887 .... **NCLC 5, 53, 221; PC 14; SSC 20**
See also DLB 217; EW 7; GFL 1789 to the Present; RGWL 2, 3

Lagerkvist, Paer 1891-1974 ... **CLC 7, 10, 13, 54; SSC 12; TCLC 144**
See also CA 85-88; 49-52; DA3; DAM DRAM, NOV; DLB 259, 331; EW 10; EWL 3; MTCW 1, 2; MTFW 2005; RGSF 2; RGWL 2, 3; TWA

Lagerkvist, Paer Fabian
See Lagerkvist, Paer

Lagerkvist, Par
See Lagerkvist, Paer

Lagerloef, Selma
See Lagerlof, Selma

Lagerloef, Selma Ottiliana Lovisa
See Lagerlof, Selma

Lagerlof, Selma 1858-1940 .... **TCLC 4, 36**
See also CA 108; 188; CLR 7; DLB 259, 331; MTCW 2; RGWL 2, 3; SATA 15; SSFS 18

Lagerlof, Selma Ottiliana Lovisa
See Lagerlof, Selma

La Guma, Alex 1925-1985 .. **BLCS; CLC 19; TCLC 140**
See also AFW; BW 1, 3; CA 49-52; 118; CANR 25, 81; CDWLB 3; CN 1, 2, 3; CP 1; DAM NOV; DLB 117, 225; EWL 3; MTCW 1, 2; MTFW 2005; WLIT 2; WWE 1

La Guma, Justin Alexander
See La Guma, Alex

Lahiri, Jhumpa 1967- .... **CLC 282; SSC 96**
See also AAYA 56; CA 193; CANR 134, 184; DLB 323; MTFW 2005; NFS 31; SSFS 19, 27

Laidlaw, A. K.
See Grieve, C. M.

Lainez, Manuel Mujica
See Mujica Lainez, Manuel

Laing, R(onald) D(avid) 1927-1989 . **CLC 95**
See also CA 107; 129; CANR 34; MTCW 1

Laishley, Alex
See Booth, Martin

Lamartine, Alphonse de 1790-1869 .... **NCLC 11, 190; PC 16**
See also DAM POET; DLB 217; GFL 1789 to the Present; RGWL 2, 3

Lamartine, Alphonse Marie Louis Prat de
See Lamartine, Alphonse de

Lamb, Charles 1775-1834 ..... **NCLC 10, 113; SSC 112; WLC 3**
See also BRW 4; CDBLB 1789-1832; DA; DAB; DAC; DAM MST; DLB 93, 107, 163; RGEL 2; SATA 17; TEA

Lamb, Lady Caroline 1785-1828 ... **NCLC 38**
See also DLB 116

Lamb, Mary Ann 1764-1847 ...... **NCLC 125; SSC 112**
See also DLB 163; SATA 17

Lame Deer 1903(?)-1976 .... **NNAL**
See also CA 69-72

Lamming, George (William) 1927- . **BLC 1:2, 2:2; CLC 2, 4, 66, 144**
See also BW 2, 3; CA 85-88; CANR 26, 76; CDWLB 3; CN 1, 2, 3, 4, 5, 6, 7; CP 1; DAM MULT; DLB 125; EWL 3; MTCW 1, 2; MTFW 2005; NFS 15; RGEL 2

L'Amour, Louis 1908-1988 .... **CLC 25, 55**
See also AAYA 16; AITN 2; BEST 89:2; BPFB 2; CA 1-4R; 125; CANR 3, 25, 40; CPW; DA3; DAM NOV, POP; DLB 206; DLBY 1980; MTCW 1, 2; MTFW 2005; RGAL 4; TCWW 1, 2

Lampedusa, Giuseppe di 1896-1957 .... **TCLC 13**
See also CA 111; 164; DLB 177; EW 11; EWL 3; MTCW 2; MTFW 2005; RGWL 2, 3; WLIT 7

Lampman, Archibald 1861-1899 .. **NCLC 25, 194**
See also DLB 92; RGEL 2; TWA

Lancaster, Bruce 1896-1963 .... **CLC 36**
See also CA 9-10; CANR 70; CAP 1; SATA 9

Lanchester, John 1962- .... **CLC 99, 280**
See also CA 194; DLB 267

Landau, Mark Alexandrovich
See Aldanov, Mark (Alexandrovich)

Landau-Aldanov, Mark Alexandrovich
See Aldanov, Mark (Alexandrovich)

Landis, Jerry
See Simon, Paul

Landis, John 1950- .... **CLC 26**
See also CA 112; 122; CANR 128

Landolfi, Tommaso 1908-1979 .... **CLC 11, 49**
See also CA 127; 117; DLB 177; EWL 3

Landon, Letitia Elizabeth 1802-1838 .... **NCLC 15**
See also DLB 96

Landor, Walter Savage 1775-1864 .... **NCLC 14**
See also BRW 4; DLB 93, 107; RGEL 2

Landwirth, Heinz
See Lind, Jakov

Lane, Patrick 1939- .... **CLC 25**
See also CA 97-100; CANR 54; CP 3, 4, 5, 6, 7; DAM POET; DLB 53; INT CA-97-100

Lane, Rose Wilder 1887-1968 ...... **TCLC 177**
See also CA 102; CANR 63; SATA 29; SATA-Brief 28; TCWW 2

Lang, Andrew 1844-1912 .... **TCLC 16**
See also CA 114; 137; CANR 85; CLR 101; DLB 98, 141, 184; FANT; MAICYA 1, 2; RGEL 2; SATA 16; WCH

Lang, Fritz 1890-1976 .... **CLC 20, 103**
See also AAYA 65; CA 77-80; 69-72; CANR 30

Lange, John
See Crichton, Michael

Langer, Elinor 1939- .... **CLC 34**
See also CA 121

Langland, William 1332(?)-1400(?) .... **LC 19, 120**
See also BRW 1; DA; DAB; DAC; DAM MST, POET; DLB 146; RGEL 2; TEA; WLIT 3

Langstaff, Launcelot
See Irving, Washington

Lanier, Sidney 1842-1881 . **NCLC 6, 118; PC 50**
See also AMWS 1; DAM POET; DLB 64; DLBD 13; EXPP; MAICYA 1; PFS 14; RGAL 4; SATA 18

Lanyer, Aemilia 1569-1645 .... **LC 10, 30, 83; PC 60**
See also DLB 121

Lightfoot, Gordon 1938- .... **CLC 26**
See also CA 109; 242
Lightfoot, Gordon Meredith
See Lightfoot, Gordon
Lightman, Alan P. 1948- .... **CLC 81**
See also CA 141; CANR 63, 105, 138, 178;
MTFW 2005; NFS 29
Lightman, Alan Paige
See Lightman, Alan P.
Ligotti, Thomas 1953- .... **CLC 44; SSC 16**
See also CA 123; CANR 49, 135; HGG;
SUFW 2
Ligotti, Thomas Robert
See Ligotti, Thomas
Li Ho 791-817 .... **PC 13**
Li Ju-chen c. 1763-c. 1830 .... **NCLC 137**
Liking, Werewere 1950- .... **BLC 2:2**
See also CA 293; EWL 3
Lilar, Francoise
See Mallet-Joris, Francoise
Liliencron, Detlev
See Liliencron, Detlev von
Liliencron, Detlev von 1844-1909 .. **TCLC 18**
See also CA 117
Liliencron, Friedrich Adolf Axel Detlev von
See Liliencron, Detlev von
Liliencron, Friedrich Detlev von
See Liliencron, Detlev von
Lille, Alain de
See Alain de Lille
Lillo, George 1691-1739 .... **LC 131**
See also DLB 84; RGEL 2
Lilly, William 1602-1681 .... **LC 27**
Lima, Jose Lezama
See Lezama Lima, Jose
Lima Barreto, Afonso Henrique de
1881-1922 .... **TCLC 23**
See also CA 117; 181; DLB 307; LAW
Lima Barreto, Afonso Henriques de
See Lima Barreto, Afonso Henrique de
Limonov, Eduard
See Limonov, Edward
Limonov, Edward 1944- .... **CLC 67**
See also CA 137; DLB 317
Lin, Frank
See Atherton, Gertrude (Franklin Horn)
Lin, Yutang 1895-1976 .... **TCLC 149**
See also CA 45-48; 65-68; CANR 2; RGAL
4
Lincoln, Abraham 1809-1865 .... **NCLC 18,
201**
See also LAIT 2
Lincoln, Geoffrey
See Mortimer, John
Lind, Jakov 1927-2007 ... **CLC 1, 2, 4, 27, 82**
See also CA 9-12R; 257; CAAS 4; CANR
7; DLB 299; EWL 3; RGHL
Lindbergh, Anne Morrow
1906-2001 .... **CLC 82**
See also BPFB 2; CA 17-20R; 193; CANR
16, 73; DAM NOV; MTCW 1, 2; MTFW
2005; SATA 33; SATA-Obit 125; TUS
Lindbergh, Anne Spencer Morrow
See Lindbergh, Anne Morrow
Lindholm, Anna Margaret
See Haycraft, Anna
Lindsay, David 1878(?)-1945 .... **TCLC 15**
See also CA 113; 187; DLB 255; FANT;
SFW 4; SUFW 1
Lindsay, Nicholas Vachel
See Lindsay, Vachel
Lindsay, Vachel 1879-1931 ..... **PC 23; TCLC
17; WLC 4**
See also AMWS 1; CA 114; 135; CANR
79; CDALB 1865-1917; DA; DA3; DAC;
DAM MST, POET; DLB 54; EWL 3;
EXPP; MAL 5; RGAL 4; SATA 40; WP

Linke-Poot
See Doeblin, Alfred
Linney, Romulus 1930- .... **CLC 51**
See also CA 1-4R; CAD; CANR 40, 44,
79; CD 5, 6; CSW; RGAL 4
Linton, Eliza Lynn 1822-1898 .... **NCLC 41**
See also DLB 18
Li Po 701-763 .... **CMLC 2, 86; PC 29**
See also PFS 20; WP
Lippard, George 1822-1854 .... **NCLC 198**
See also DLB 202
Lipsius, Justus 1547-1606 .... **LC 16**
Lipsyte, Robert 1938- .... **CLC 21**
See also AAYA 7, 45; CA 17-20R; CANR
8, 57, 146, 189; CLR 23, 76; DA; DAC;
DAM MST, NOV; JRDA; LAIT 5; MAI-
CYA 1, 2; SATA 5, 68, 113, 161, 198;
WYA; YAW
Lipsyte, Robert Michael
See Lipsyte, Robert
Lish, Gordon 1934- .... **CLC 45; SSC 18**
See also CA 113; 117; CANR 79, 151; DLB
130; INT CA-117
Lish, Gordon Jay
See Lish, Gordon
Lispector, Clarice 1925(?)-1977 .... **CLC 43;
HLCS 2; SSC 34, 96**
See also CA 139; 116; CANR 71; CDWLB
3; DLB 113, 307; DNFS 1; EWL 3; FW;
HW 2; LAW; RGSF 2; RGWL 2, 3; WLIT
1
Liszt, Franz 1811-1886 .... **NCLC 199**
Littell, Robert 1935(?)- .... **CLC 42**
See also CA 109; 112; CANR 64, 115, 162;
CMW 4
Little, Malcolm
See Malcolm X
Littlewit, Humphrey Gent.
See Lovecraft, H. P.
Litwos
See Sienkiewicz, Henryk (Adam Alexander
Pius)
Liu, E. 1857-1909 .... **TCLC 15**
See also CA 115; 190; DLB 328
Lively, Penelope 1933- .... **CLC 32, 50**
See also BPFB 2; CA 41-44R; CANR 29,
67, 79, 131, 172; CLR 7; CN 5, 6, 7;
CWRI 5; DAM NOV; DLB 14, 161, 207,
326; FANT; JRDA; MAICYA 1, 2;
MTCW 1, 2; MTFW 2005; SATA 7, 60,
101, 164; TEA
Lively, Penelope Margaret
See Lively, Penelope
Livesay, Dorothy (Kathleen)
1909-1996 .... **CLC 4, 15, 79**
See also AITN 2; CA 25-28R; CAAS 8;
CANR 36, 67; CP 1, 2, 3, 4, 5; DAC;
DAM MST, POET; DLB 68; FW; MTCW
1; RGEL 2; TWA
Livius Andronicus c. 284B.C.-c.
204B.C. .... **CMLC 102**
Livy c. 59B.C.-c. 12 .... **CMLC 11**
See also AW 2; CDWLB 1; DLB 211;
RGWL 2, 3; WLIT 8
Li Yaotang
See Jin, Ba
Lizardi, Jose Joaquin Fernandez de
1776-1827 .... **NCLC 30**
See also LAW
Llewellyn, Richard
See Llewellyn Lloyd, Richard Dafydd Viv-
ian
Llewellyn Lloyd, Richard Dafydd Vivian
1906-1983 .... **CLC 7, 80**
See also CA 53-56; 111; CANR 7, 71; DLB
15; NFS 30; SATA 11; SATA-Obit 37
Llosa, Jorge Mario Pedro Vargas
See Vargas Llosa, Mario

Llosa, Mario Vargas
See Vargas Llosa, Mario
Lloyd, Manda
See Mander, (Mary) Jane
Lloyd Webber, Andrew 1948- .... **CLC 21**
See also AAYA 1, 38; CA 116; 149; DAM
DRAM; DFS 7; SATA 56
Llull, Ramon c. 1235-c. 1316 .... **CMLC 12,
114**
Lobb, Ebenezer
See Upward, Allen
Lochhead, Liz 1947- .... **CLC 286**
See also CA 81-84; CANR 79; CBD; CD 5,
6; CP 2, 3, 4, 5, 6, 7; CWD; CWP; DLB
310
Locke, Alain Leroy 1885-1954 .... **BLCS; HR
1:3; TCLC 43**
See also AMWS 14; BW 1, 3; CA 106; 124;
CANR 79; DLB 51; LMFS 2; MAL 5;
RGAL 4
Locke, John 1632-1704 .... **LC 7, 35, 135**
See also DLB 31, 101, 213, 252; RGEL 2;
WLIT 3
Locke-Elliott, Sumner
See Elliott, Sumner Locke
Lockhart, John Gibson 1794-1854 .. **NCLC 6**
See also DLB 110, 116, 144
Lockridge, Ross (Franklin), Jr.
1914-1948 .... **TCLC 111**
See also CA 108; 145; CANR 79; DLB 143;
DLBY 1980; MAL 5; RGAL 4; RHW
Lockwood, Robert
See Johnson, Robert
Lodge, David 1935- .... **CLC 36, 141, 293**
See also BEST 90:1; BRWS 4; CA 17-20R;
CANR 19, 53, 92, 139, 197; CN 1, 2, 3,
4, 5, 6, 7; CPW; DAM POP; DLB 14,
194; EWL 3; INT CANR-19; MTCW 1,
2; MTFW 2005
Lodge, David John
See Lodge, David
Lodge, Thomas 1558-1625 .... **LC 41**
See also DLB 172; RGEL 2
Loewinsohn, Ron(ald William)
1937- .... **CLC 52**
See also CA 25-28R; CANR 71; CP 1, 2, 3,
4
Logan, Jake
See Smith, Martin Cruz
Logan, John (Burton) 1923-1987 .... **CLC 5**
See also CA 77-80; 124; CANR 45; CP 1,
2, 3, 4; DLB 5
Lo-Johansson, (Karl) Ivar
1901-1990 .... **TCLC 216**
See also CA 102; 131; CANR 20, 79, 137;
DLB 259; EWL 3; RGWL 2, 3
Lo Kuan-chung 1330(?)-1400(?) .... **LC 12**
Lomax, Pearl
See Cleage, Pearl
Lomax, Pearl Cleage
See Cleage, Pearl
Lombard, Nap
See Johnson, Pamela Hansford
Lombard, Peter 1100(?)-1160(?) ... **CMLC 72**
Lombino, Salvatore
See Hunter, Evan
London, Jack 1876-1916 .... **SSC 4, 49, 133;
TCLC 9, 15, 39; WLC 4**
See also AAYA 13, 75; AITN 2; AMW;
BPFB 2; BYA 4, 13; CA 110; 119; CANR
73; CDALB 1865-1917; CLR 108; DA;
DA3; DAB; DAC; DAM MST, NOV;
DLB 8, 12, 78, 212; EWL 3; EXPS;
JRDA; LAIT 3; MAICYA 1, 2,; MAL 5;
MTCW 1, 2; MTFW 2005; NFS 8, 19;
RGAL 4; RGSF 2; SATA 18; SFW 4; YAW
SSFS 7; TCWW 1, 2; TUS; WYA; YAW
London, John Griffith
See London, Jack

Macumber, Mari
  See Sandoz, Mari(e Susette)
Madach, Imre 1823-1864 .... **NCLC 19**
Madden, (Jerry) David 1933- .... **CLC 5, 15**
  See also CA 1-4R; CAAS 3; CANR 4, 45;
  CN 3, 4, 5, 6, 7; CSW; DLB 6; MTCW 1
Maddern, Al(an)
  See Ellison, Harlan
Madhubuti, Haki R. 1942- .... **BLC 1:2; CLC 2; PC 5**
  See also BW 2, 3; CA 73-76; CANR 24,
  51, 73, 139; CP 2, 3, 4, 5, 6, 7; CSW;
  DAM MULT, POET; DLB 5, 41; DLBD
  8; EWL 3; MAL 5; MTCW 2; MTFW
  2005; RGAL 4
Madison, James 1751-1836 .... **NCLC 126**
  See also DLB 37
Maepenn, Hugh
  See Kuttner, Henry
Maepenn, K. H.
  See Kuttner, Henry
Maeterlinck, Maurice 1862-1949 .... **DC 32; TCLC 3**
  See also CA 104; 136; CANR 80; DAM
  DRAM; DLB 192, 331; EW 8; EWL 3;
  GFL 1789 to the Present; LMFS 2; RGWL
  2, 3; SATA 66; TWA
Maginn, William 1794-1842 .... **NCLC 8**
  See also DLB 110, 159
Mahapatra, Jayanta 1928- .... **CLC 33**
  See also CA 73-76; CAAS 9; CANR 15,
  33, 66, 87; CP 4, 5, 6, 7; DAM MULT;
  DLB 323
Mahfouz, Nagib
  See Mahfouz, Naguib
Mahfouz, Naguib 1911(?)-2006 . **CLC 52, 55, 153; SSC 66**
  See also AAYA 49; AFW; BEST 89:2; CA
  128; 253; CANR 55, 101; DA3; DAM
  NOV; DLB 346; DLBY 1988; MTCW 1,
  2; MTFW 2005; RGSF 2; RGWL 2, 3;
  SSFS 9; WLIT 2
Mahfouz, Naguib Abdel Aziz Al-Sabilgi
  See Mahfouz, Naguib
Mahfouz, Najib
  See Mahfouz, Naguib
Mahfuz, Najib
  See Mahfouz, Naguib
Mahon, Derek 1941- .... **CLC 27; PC 60**
  See also BRWS 6; CA 113; 128; CANR 88;
  CP 1, 2, 3, 4, 5, 6, 7; DLB 40; EWL 3
Maiakovskii, Vladimir
  See Mayakovski, Vladimir
Mailer, Norman 1923-2007 ... **CLC 1, 2, 3, 4, 5, 8, 11, 14, 28, 39, 74, 111, 234**
  See also AAYA 31; AITN 2; AMW; AMWC
  2; AMWR 2; BPFB 2; CA 9-12R; 266;
  CABS 1; CANR 28, 74, 77, 130, 196;
  CDALB 1968-1988; CN 1, 2, 3, 4, 5, 6,
  7; CPW; DA; DA3; DAB; DAC; DAM
  MST, NOV, POP; DLB 2, 16, 28, 185,
  278; DLBD 3; DLBY 1980, 1983; EWL
  3; MAL 5; MTCW 1, 2; MTFW 2005;
  NFS 10; RGAL 4; TUS
Mailer, Norman Kingsley
  See Mailer, Norman
Maillet, Antonine 1929- .... **CLC 54, 118**
  See also CA 115; 120; CANR 46, 74, 77,
  134; CCA 1; CWW 2; DAC; DLB 60;
  INT CA-120; MTCW 2; MTFW 2005
Maimonides, Moses 1135-1204 ..... **CMLC 76**
  See also DLB 115
Mais, Roger 1905-1955 .... **TCLC 8**
  See also BW 1, 3; CA 105; 124; CANR 82;
  CDWLB 3; DLB 125; EWL 3; MTCW 1;
  RGEL 2
Maistre, Joseph 1753-1821 .... **NCLC 37**
  See also GFL 1789 to the Present

Maitland, Frederic William
  1850-1906 .... **TCLC 65**
Maitland, Sara (Louise) 1950- .... **CLC 49**
  See also BRWS 11; CA 69-72; CANR 13,
  59; DLB 271; FW
Major, Clarence 1936- ...... **BLC 1:2; CLC 3, 19, 48**
  See also AFAW 2; BW 2, 3; CA 21-24R;
  CAAS 6; CANR 13, 25, 53, 82; CN 3, 4,
  5, 6, 7; CP 2, 3, 4, 5, 6, 7; CSW; DAM
  MULT; DLB 33; EWL 3; MAL 5; MSW
Major, Kevin (Gerald) 1949- .... **CLC 26**
  See also AAYA 16; CA 97-100; CANR 21,
  38, 112; CLR 11; DAC; DLB 60; INT
  CANR-21; JRDA; MAICYA 1, 2; MAIC-
  YAS 1; SATA 32, 82, 134; WYA; YAW
Maki, James
  See Ozu, Yasujiro
Makin, Bathsua 1600-1675(?) .... **LC 137**
Makine, Andrei
  See Makine, Andrei
Makine, Andrei 1957- .... **CLC 198**
  See also CA 176; CANR 103, 162; MTFW
  2005
Malabaila, Damiano
  See Levi, Primo
Malamud, Bernard 1914-1986 .. **CLC 1, 2, 3, 5, 8, 9, 11, 18, 27, 44, 78, 85; SSC 15; TCLC 129, 184; WLC 4**
  See also AAYA 16; AMWS 1; BPFB 2;
  BYA 15; CA 5-8R; 118; CABS 1; CANR
  28, 62, 114; CDALB 1941-1968; CN 1, 2,
  3, 4; CPW; DA; DA3; DAB; DAC; DAM
  MST, NOV, POP; DLB 2, 28, 152; DLBY
  1980, 1986; EWL 3; EXPS; LAIT 4;
  LATS 1:1; MAL 5; MTCW 1, 2; MTFW
  2005; NFS 27; RGAL 4; RGHL; RGSF 2;
  SSFS 8, 13, 16; TUS
Malan, Herman
  See Bosman, Herman Charles; Bosman,
  Herman Charles
Malaparte, Curzio 1898-1957 .... **TCLC 52**
  See also DLB 264
Malcolm, Dan
  See Silverberg, Robert
Malcolm, Janet 1934- .... **CLC 201**
  See also CA 123; CANR 89, 199; NCFS 1
Malcolm X 1925-1965 ..... **BLC 1:2; CLC 82, 117; WLCS**
  See also BW 1, 3; CA 125; 111; CANR 82;
  DA; DA3; DAB; DAC; DAM MST,
  MULT; LAIT 5; MTCW 1, 2; MTFW
  2005; NCFS 3
Malebranche, Nicolas 1638-1715 .... **LC 133**
  See also GFL Beginnings to 1789
Malherbe, Francois de 1555-1628 .... **LC 5**
  See also DLB 327; GFL Beginnings to 1789
Mallarme, Stephane 1842-1898 ...... **NCLC 4, 41, 210; PC 4, 102**
  See also DAM POET; DLB 217; EW 7;
  GFL 1789 to the Present; LMFS 2; RGWL
  2, 3; TWA
Mallet-Joris, Francoise 1930- .... **CLC 11**
  See also CA 65-68; CANR 17; CWW 2;
  DLB 83; EWL 3; GFL 1789 to the Present
Malley, Ern
  See McAuley, James Phillip
Mallon, Thomas 1951- .... **CLC 172**
  See also CA 110; CANR 29, 57, 92, 196;
  DLB 350
Mallowan, Agatha Christie
  See Christie, Agatha
Maloff, Saul 1922- .... **CLC 5**
  See also CA 33-36R
Malone, Louis
  See MacNeice, (Frederick) Louis
Malone, Michael (Christopher)
  1942- .... **CLC 43**
  See also CA 77-80; CANR 14, 32, 57, 114

Malory, Sir Thomas 1410(?)-1471(?) . **LC 11, 88; WLCS**
  See also BRW 1; BRWR 2; CDBLB Before
  1660; DA; DAB; DAC; DAM MST; DLB
  146; EFS 2; RGEL 2; SATA 59; SATA-
  Brief 33; TEA; WLIT 3
Malouf, David 1934- .... **CLC 28, 86, 245**
  See also BRWS 12; CA 124; CANR 50, 76,
  180; CN 3, 4, 5, 6, 7; CP 1, 3, 4, 5, 6, 7;
  DLB 289; EWL 3; MTCW 2; MTFW
  2005; SSFS 24
Malouf, George Joseph David
  See Malouf, David
Malraux, Andre 1901-1976 . **CLC 1, 4, 9, 13, 15, 57; TCLC 209**
  See also BPFB 2; CA 21-22; 69-72; CANR
  34, 58; CAP 2; DA3; DAM NOV; DLB
  72; EW 12; EWL 3; GFL 1789 to the
  Present; MTCW 1, 2; MTFW 2005;
  RGWL 2, 3; TWA
Malraux, Georges-Andre
  See Malraux, Andre
Malthus, Thomas Robert
  1766-1834 .... **NCLC 145**
  See also DLB 107, 158; RGEL 2
Malzberg, Barry N(athaniel) 1939- ... **CLC 7**
  See also CA 61-64; CAAS 4; CANR 16;
  CMW 4; DLB 8; SFW 4
Mamet, David 1947- .. **CLC 9, 15, 34, 46, 91, 166; DC 4, 24**
  See also AAYA 3, 60; AMWS 14; CA 81-
  84; CABS 3; CAD; CANR 15, 41, 67, 72,
  129, 172; CD 5, 6; DA3; DAM DRAM;
  DFS 2, 3, 6, 12, 15; DLB 7; EWL 3;
  IDFW 4; MAL 5; MTCW 1, 2; MTFW
  2005; RGAL 4
Mamet, David Alan
  See Mamet, David
Mamoulian, Rouben (Zachary)
  1897-1987 .... **CLC 16**
  See also CA 25-28R; 124; CANR 85
Mandelshtam, Osip
  See Mandelstam, Osip
  See also DLB 295
Mandelstam, Osip 1891(?)-1943(?) .... **PC 14; TCLC 2, 6, 225**
  See Mandelshtam, Osip
  See also CA 104; 150; EW 10; EWL 3;
  MTCW 2; RGWL 2, 3; TWA
Mandelstam, Osip Emilievich
  See Mandelstam, Osip
Mander, (Mary) Jane 1877-1949 ... **TCLC 31**
  See also CA 162; RGEL 2
Mandeville, Bernard 1670-1733 .... **LC 82**
  See also DLB 101
Mandeville, Sir John fl. 1350- ...... **CMLC 19**
  See also DLB 146
Mandiargues, Andre Pieyre de
  See Pieyre de Mandiargues, Andre
Mandrake, Ethel Belle
  See Thurman, Wallace (Henry)
Mangan, James Clarence
  1803-1849 .... **NCLC 27**
  See also BRWS 13; RGEL 2
Maniere, J. E.
  See Giraudoux, Jean
Mankell, Henning 1948- .... **CLC 292**
  See also CA 187; CANR 163, 200
Mankiewicz, Herman (Jacob)
  1897-1953 .... **TCLC 85**
  See also CA 120; 169; DLB 26; IDFW 3, 4
Manley, (Mary) Delariviere
  1672(?)-1724 .... **LC 1, 42**
  See also DLB 39, 80; RGEL 2
Mann, Abel
  See Creasey, John
Mann, Emily 1952- .... **DC 7**
  See also CA 130; CAD; CANR 55; CD 5,
  6; CWD; DLB 266

Maxwell, William (Keepers, Jr.)
1908-2000 .... **CLC 19**
See also AMWS 8; CA 93-96; 189; CANR
54, 95; CN 1, 2, 3, 4, 5, 6, 7; DLB 218,
278; DLBY 1980; INT CA-93-96; MAL
5; SATA-Obit 128

May, Elaine 1932- .... **CLC 16**
See also CA 124; 142; CAD; CWD; DLB
44

Mayakovski, Vladimir 1893-1930 ... **TCLC 4,
18**
See also CA 104; 158; EW 11; EWL 3;
IDTP; MTCW 2; MTFW 2005; RGWL 2,
3; SFW 4; TWA; WP

Mayakovski, Vladimir Vladimirovich
See Mayakovski, Vladimir

Mayakovsky, Vladimir
See Mayakovski, Vladimir

Mayhew, Henry 1812-1887 .... **NCLC 31**
See also BRWS 16; DLB 18, 55, 190

Mayle, Peter 1939(?)- .... **CLC 89**
See also CA 139; CANR 64, 109, 168

Maynard, Joyce 1953- .... **CLC 23**
See also CA 111; 129; CANR 64, 169

Mayne, William (James Carter)
1928- .... **CLC 12**
See also AAYA 20; CA 9-12R; CANR 37,
80, 100; CLR 25, 123; FANT; JRDA;
MAICYA 1, 2; MAICYAS 1; SAAS 11;
SATA 6, 68, 122; SUFW 2; YAW

Mayo, Jim
See L'Amour, Louis

Maysles, Albert 1926- .... **CLC 16**
See also CA 29-32R

Maysles, David 1932-1987 .... **CLC 16**
See also CA 191

Mazer, Norma Fox 1931-2009 .... **CLC 26**
See also AAYA 5, 36; BYA 1, 8; CA 69-72;
292; CANR 12, 32, 66, 129, 189; CLR
23; JRDA; MAICYA 1, 2; SAAS 1; SATA
24, 67, 105, 168, 198; WYA; YAW

Mazzini, Guiseppe 1805-1872 .... **NCLC 34**

McAlmon, Robert (Menzies)
1895-1956 .... **TCLC 97**
See also CA 107; 168; DLB 4, 45; DLBD
15; GLL 1

McAuley, James Phillip 1917-1976 .. **CLC 45**
See also CA 97-100; CP 1, 2; DLB 260;
RGEL 2

McBain, Ed
See Hunter, Evan

McBrien, William 1930- .... **CLC 44**
See also CA 107; CANR 90

McBrien, William Augustine
See McBrien, William

McCabe, Pat
See McCabe, Patrick

McCabe, Patrick 1955- .... **CLC 133**
See also BRWS 9; CA 130; CANR 50, 90,
168, 202; CN 6, 7; DLB 194

McCaffrey, Anne 1926- .... **CLC 17**
See also AAYA 6, 34; AITN 2; BEST 89:2;
BPFB 2; BYA 5; CA 25-28R, 227; CAAE
227; CANR 15, 35, 55, 96, 169; CLR 49,
130; CPW; DA3; DAM NOV, POP; DLB
8; JRDA; MAICYA 1, 2; MTCW 1, 2;
MTFW 2005; SAAS 11; SATA 8, 70, 116,
152; SATA-Essay 152; SFW 4; SUFW 2;
WYA; YAW

McCaffrey, Anne Inez
See McCaffrey, Anne

McCall, Nathan 1955(?)- .... **CLC 86**
See also AAYA 59; BW 3; CA 146; CANR
88, 186

McCall Smith, Alexander
See Smith, Alexander McCall

McCann, Arthur
See Campbell, John W(ood, Jr.)

McCann, Edson
See Pohl, Frederik

McCarthy, Charles
See McCarthy, Cormac

McCarthy, Charles, Jr.
See McCarthy, Cormac

McCarthy, Cormac 1933- .... **CLC 4, 57, 101,
204**
See also AAYA 41; AMWS 8; BPFB 2; CA
13-16R; CANR 10, 42, 69, 101, 161, 171;
CN 6, 7; CPW; CSW; DA3; DAM POP;
DLB 6, 143, 256; EWL 3; LATS 1:2;
LNFS 3; MAL 5; MTCW 2; MTFW 2005;
TCLE 1:2; TCWW 2

McCarthy, Mary 1912-1989 ...... **CLC 1, 3, 5,
14, 24, 39, 59; SSC 24**
See also AMW; BPFB 2; CA 5-8R; 129;
CANR 16, 50, 64; CN 1, 2, 3, 4; DA3;
DLB 2; DLBY 1981; EWL 3; FW; INT
CANR-16; MAL 5; MBL; MTCW 1, 2;
MTFW 2005; RGAL 4; TUS

McCarthy, Mary Therese
See McCarthy, Mary

McCartney, James Paul
See McCartney, Paul

McCartney, Paul 1942- .... **CLC 12, 35**
See also CA 146; CANR 111

McCauley, Stephen (D.) 1955- .... **CLC 50**
See also CA 141

McClaren, Peter .... **CLC 70**

McClure, Michael (Thomas) 1932- ... **CLC 6,
10**
See also BG 1:3; CA 21-24R; CAD; CANR
17, 46, 77, 131; CD 5, 6; CP 1, 2, 3, 4, 5,
6, 7; DLB 16; WP

McCorkle, Jill (Collins) 1958- .... **CLC 51**
See also CA 121; CANR 113; CSW; DLB
234; DLBY 1987; SSFS 24

McCourt, Francis
See McCourt, Frank

McCourt, Frank 1930-2009 .... **CLC 109**
See also AAYA 61; AMWS 12; CA 157;
288; CANR 97, 138; MTFW 2005; NCFS
1

McCourt, James 1941- .... **CLC 5**
See also CA 57-60; CANR 98, 152, 186

McCourt, Malachy 1931- .... **CLC 119**
See also SATA 126

McCoy, Edmund
See Gardner, John

McCoy, Horace (Stanley)
1897-1955 .... **TCLC 28**
See also AMWS 13; CA 108; 155; CMW 4;
DLB 9

McCrae, John 1872-1918 .... **TCLC 12**
See also CA 109; DLB 92; PFS 5

McCreigh, James
See Pohl, Frederik

McCullers, Carson 1917-1967 . **CLC 1, 4, 10,
12, 48, 100; DC 35; SSC 9, 24, 99;
TCLC 155; WLC 4**
See also AAYA 21; AMW; AMWC 2; BPFB
2; CA 5-8R; 25-28R; CABS 1, 3; CANR
18, 132; CDALB 1941-1968; DA; DA3;
DAB; DAC; DAM MST, NOV; DFS 5,
18; DLB 2, 7, 173, 228; EWL 3; EXPS;
FW; GLL 1; LAIT 3, 4; MAL 5; MBL;
MTCW 1, 2; MTFW 2005; NFS 6, 13;
RGAL 4; RGSF 2; SATA 27; SSFS 5;
TUS; YAW

McCullers, Lula Carson Smith
See McCullers, Carson

McCulloch, John Tyler
See Burroughs, Edgar Rice

McCullough, Colleen 1937- ...... **CLC 27, 107**
See also AAYA 36; BPFB 2; CA 81-84;
CANR 17, 46, 67, 98, 139, 203; CPW;
DA3; DAM NOV, POP; MTCW 1, 2;
MTFW 2005; RHW

McCunn, Ruthanne Lum 1946- .... **AAL**
See also CA 119; CANR 43, 96; DLB 312;
LAIT 2; SATA 63

McDermott, Alice 1953- .... **CLC 90**
See also AMWS 18; CA 109; CANR 40,
90, 126, 181; CN 7; DLB 292; MTFW
2005; NFS 23

McElroy, Joseph 1930- .... **CLC 5, 47**
See also CA 17-20R; CANR 149; CN 3, 4,
5, 6, 7

McElroy, Joseph Prince
See McElroy, Joseph

McEwan, Ian 1948- ... **CLC 13, 66, 169, 269;
SSC 106**
See also BEST 90:4; BRWS 4; CA 61-64;
CANR 14, 41, 69, 87, 132, 179; CN 3, 4,
5, 6, 7; DAM NOV; DLB 14, 194, 319,
326; HGG; MTCW 1, 2; MTFW 2005;
NFS 32; RGSF 2; SUFW 2; TEA

McEwan, Ian Russell
See McEwan, Ian

McFadden, David 1940- .... **CLC 48**
See also CA 104; CP 1, 2, 3, 4, 5, 6, 7; DLB
60; INT CA-104

McFarland, Dennis 1950- .... **CLC 65**
See also CA 165; CANR 110, 179

McGahern, John 1934-2006 .... **CLC 5, 9, 48,
156; SSC 17**
See also CA 17-20R; 249; CANR 29, 68,
113, 204; CN 1, 2, 3, 4, 5, 6, 7; DLB 14,
231, 319; MTCW 1

McGinley, Patrick (Anthony) 1937- . **CLC 41**
See also CA 120; 127; CANR 56; INT CA-
127

McGinley, Phyllis 1905-1978 .... **CLC 14**
See also CA 9-12R; 77-80; CANR 19; CP
1, 2; CWRI 5; DLB 11, 48; MAL 5; PFS
9, 13; SATA 2, 44; SATA-Obit 24

McGinniss, Joe 1942- .... **CLC 32**
See also AITN 2; BEST 89:2; CA 25-28R;
CANR 26, 70, 152; CPW; DLB 185; INT
CANR-26

McGivern, Maureen Daly
See Daly, Maureen

McGivern, Maureen Patricia Daly
See Daly, Maureen

McGrath, Patrick 1950- .... **CLC 55**
See also CA 136; CANR 65, 148, 190; CN
5, 6, 7; DLB 231; HGG; SUFW 2

McGrath, Thomas (Matthew)
1916-1990 .... **CLC 28, 59**
See also AMWS 10; CA 9-12R; 132; CANR
6, 33, 95; CP 1, 2, 3, 4, 5; DAM POET;
MAL 5; MTCW 1; SATA 41; SATA-Obit
66

McGuane, Thomas 1939- .. **CLC 3, 7, 18, 45,
127**
See also AITN 2; BPFB 2; CA 49-52;
CANR 5, 24, 49, 94, 164; CN 2, 3, 4, 5,
6, 7; DLB 2, 212; DLBY 1980; EWL 3;
INT CANR-24; MAL 5; MTCW 1;
MTFW 2005; TCWW 1, 2

McGuane, Thomas Francis III
See McGuane, Thomas

McGuckian, Medbh 1950- .... **CLC 48, 174;
PC 27**
See also BRWS 5; CA 143; CP 4, 5, 6, 7;
CWP; DAM POET; DLB 40

McHale, Tom 1942(?)-1982 .... **CLC 3, 5**
See also AITN 1; CA 77-80; 106; CN 1, 2,
3

McHugh, Heather 1948- .... **PC 61**
See also CA 69-72; CANR 11, 28, 55, 92;
CP 4, 5, 6, 7; CWP; PFS 24

McIlvanney, William 1936- .... **CLC 42**
See also CA 25-28R; CANR 61; CMW 4;
DLB 14, 207

McIlwraith, Maureen Mollie Hunter
See Hunter, Mollie

Merimee, Prosper 1803-1870 . **DC 33; NCLC 6, 65; SSC 7, 77**
See also DLB 119, 192; EW 6; EXPS; GFL 1789 to the Present; RGSF 2; RGWL 2, 3; SSFS 8; SUFW

Merkin, Daphne 1954- .... **CLC 44**
See also CA 123

Merleau-Ponty, Maurice
1908-1961 .... **TCLC 156**
See also CA 114; 89-92; DLB 296; GFL 1789 to the Present

Merlin, Arthur
See Blish, James

Mernissi, Fatima 1940- .... **CLC 171**
See also CA 152; DLB 346; FW

Merrill, James 1926-1995 ...... **CLC 2, 3, 6, 8, 13, 18, 34, 91; PC 28; TCLC 173**
See also AMWS 3; CA 13-16R; 147; CANR 10, 49, 63, 108; CP 1, 2, 3, 4; DA3; DAM POET; DLB 5, 165; DLBY 1985; EWL 3; INT CANR-10; MAL 5; MTCW 1, 2; MTFW 2005; PAB; PFS 23; RGAL 4

Merrill, James Ingram
See Merrill, James

Merriman, Alex
See Silverberg, Robert

Merriman, Brian 1747-1805 .... **NCLC 70**

Merritt, E. B.
See Waddington, Miriam

Merton, Thomas 1915-1968 ..... **CLC 1, 3, 11, 34, 83; PC 10**
See also AAYA 61; AMWS 8; CA 5-8R; 25-28R; CANR 22, 53, 111, 131; DA3; DLB 48; DLBY 1981; MAL 5; MTCW 1, 2; MTFW 2005

Merton, Thomas James
See Merton, Thomas

Merwin, William Stanley
See Merwin, W.S.

Merwin, W.S. 1927- ..... **CLC 1, 2, 3, 5, 8, 13, 18, 45, 88; PC 45**
See also AMWS 3; CA 13-16R; CANR 15, 51, 112, 140; CP 1, 2, 3, 4, 5, 6, 7; DA3; DAM POET; DLB 5, 169, 342; EWL 3; INT CANR-15; MAL 5; MTCW 1, 2; MTFW 2005; PAB; PFS 5, 15; RGAL 4

Metastasio, Pietro 1698-1782 .... **LC 115**
See also RGWL 2, 3

Metcalf, John 1938- .... **CLC 37; SSC 43**
See also CA 113; CN 4, 5, 6, 7; DLB 60; RGSF 2; TWA

Metcalf, Suzanne
See Baum, L. Frank

Mew, Charlotte (Mary) 1870-1928 .. **PC 107; TCLC 8**
See also CA 105; 189; DLB 19, 135; RGEL 2

Mewshaw, Michael 1943- .... **CLC 9**
See also CA 53-56; CANR 7, 47, 147; DLBY 1980

Meyer, Conrad Ferdinand
1825-1898 .... **NCLC 81; SSC 30**
See also DLB 129; EW; RGWL 2, 3

Meyer, Gustav 1868-1932 .... **TCLC 21**
See also CA 117; 190; DLB 81; EWL 3

Meyer, June
See Jordan, June

Meyer, Lynn
See Slavitt, David R.

Meyer, Stephenie 1973- .... **CLC 280**
See also AAYA 77; CA 253; CANR 192; CLR 142; SATA 193

Meyer-Meyrink, Gustav
See Meyer, Gustav

Meyers, Jeffrey 1939- .... **CLC 39**
See also CA 73-76, 186; CAAE 186; CANR 54, 102, 159; DLB 111

Meynell, Alice (Christina Gertrude Thompson) 1847-1922 .... **TCLC 6**
See also CA 104; 177; DLB 19, 98; RGEL 2

Meyrink, Gustav
See Meyer, Gustav

Mhlophe, Gcina 1960- .... **BLC 2:3**

Michaels, Leonard 1933-2003 ..... **CLC 6, 25; SSC 16**
See also AMWS 16; CA 61-64; 216; CANR 21, 62, 119, 179; CN 3, 45, 6, 7; DLB 130; MTCW 1; TCLE 1:2

Michaux, Henri 1899-1984 .... **CLC 8, 19**
See also CA 85-88; 114; DLB 258; EWL 3; GFL 1789 to the Present; RGWL 2, 3

Micheaux, Oscar (Devereaux)
1884-1951 .... **TCLC 76**
See also BW 3; CA 174; DLB 50; TCWW 2

Michelangelo 1475-1564 .... **LC 12**
See also AAYA 43

Michelet, Jules 1798-1874 ...... **NCLC 31, 218**
See also EW 5; GFL 1789 to the Present

Michels, Robert 1876-1936 .... **TCLC 88**
See also CA 212

Michener, James A. 1907(?)-1997 . **CLC 1, 5, 11, 29, 60, 109**
See also AAYA 27; AITN 1; BEST 90:1; BPFB 2; CA 5-8R; 161; CANR 21, 45, 68; CN 1, 2, 3, 4, 5, 6; CPW; DA3; DAM NOV, POP; DLB 6; MAL 5; MTCW 1, 2; MTFW 2005; RHW; TCWW 1, 2

Michener, James Albert
See Michener, James A.

Mickiewicz, Adam 1798-1855 . **NCLC 3, 101; PC 38**
See also EW 5; RGWL 2, 3

Middleton, (John) Christopher
1926- .... **CLC 13**
See also CA 13-16R; CANR 29, 54, 117; CP 1, 2, 3, 4, 5, 6, 7; DLB 40

Middleton, Richard (Barham)
1882-1911 .... **TCLC 56**
See also CA 187; DLB 156; HGG

Middleton, Stanley 1919-2009 ...... **CLC 7, 38**
See also CA 25-28R; 288; CAAS 23; CANR 21, 46, 81, 157; CN 1, 2, 3, 4, 5, 6, 7; DLB 14, 326

Middleton, Thomas 1580-1627 ...... **DC 5; LC 33, 123**
See also BRW 2; DAM DRAM, MST; DFS 18, 22; DLB 58; RGEL 2

Mieville, China 1972(?)- .... **CLC 235**
See also AAYA 52; CA 196; CANR 138; MTFW 2005

Migueis, Jose Rodrigues 1901-1980 . **CLC 10**
See also DLB 287

Mihura, Miguel 1905-1977 .... **DC 34**
See also CA 214

Mikszath, Kalman 1847-1910 .... **TCLC 31**
See also CA 170

Miles, Jack .... **CLC 100**
See also CA 200

Miles, John Russiano
See Miles, Jack

Miles, Josephine (Louise)
1911-1985 .... **CLC 1, 2, 14, 34, 39**
See also CA 1-4R; 116; CANR 2, 55; CP 1, 2, 3, 4; DAM POET; DLB 48; MAL 5; TCLE 1:2

Militant
See Sandburg, Carl

Mill, Harriet (Hardy) Taylor
1807-1858 .... **NCLC 102**
See also FW

Mill, John Stuart 1806-1873 ... **NCLC 11, 58, 179, 223**
See also CDBLB 1832-1890; DLB 55, 190, 262; FW 1; RGEL 2; TEA

Millar, Kenneth 1915-1983 .. **CLC 1, 2, 3, 14, 34, 41**
See also AAYA 81; AMWS 4; BPFB 2; CA 9-12R; 110; CANR 16, 63, 107; CMW 4; CN 1, 2, 3; CPW; DA3; DAM POP; DLB 2, 226; DLBD 6; DLBY 1983; MAL 5; MSW; MTCW 1, 2; MTFW 2005; RGAL 4

Millar, E. Vincent
See Millay, Edna St. Vincent

Millay, Edna St. Vincent 1892-1950 ..... **PC 6, 61; TCLC 4, 49, 169; WLCS**
See also AMW; CA 104; 130; CDALB 1917-1929; DA; DA3; DAB; DAC; DAM MST, POET; DFS 27; DLB 45, 249; EWL 3; EXPP; FL 1:6; GLL 1; MAL 5; MBL; MTCW 1, 2; MTFW 2005; PAB; PFS 3, 17, 31, 34; RGAL 4; TUS; WP

Miller, Arthur 1915-2005 ..... **CLC 1, 2, 6, 10, 15, 26, 47, 78, 179; DC 1, 31; WLC 4**
See also AAYA 15; AITN 1; AMW; AMWC 1; CA 1-4R; 236; CABS 3; CAD; CANR 2, 30, 54, 76, 132; CD 5, 6; CDALB 1941-1968; DA; DA3; DAB; DAC; DAM DRAM, MST; DFS 1, 3, 8, 27; DLB 7, 266; EWL 3; LAIT 1, 4; LATS 1:2; MAL 5; MTCW 1, 2; MTFW 2005; RGAL 4; RGHL; TUS; WYAS 1

Miller, Frank 1957- .... **CLC 278**
See also AAYA 45; CA 224

Miller, Henry (Valentine)
1891-1980 .... **CLC 1, 2, 4, 9, 14, 43, 84; TCLC 213; WLC 4**
See also AMW; BPFB 2; CA 9-12R; 97-100; CANR 33, 64; CDALB 1929-1941; CN 1, 2; DA; DA3; DAB; DAC; DAM MST, NOV; DLB 4, 9; DLBY 1980; EWL 3; MAL 5; MTCW 1, 2; MTFW 2005; RGAL 4; TUS

Miller, Hugh 1802-1856 .... **NCLC 143**
See also DLB 190

Miller, Jason 1939(?)-2001 .... **CLC 2**
See also AITN 1; CA 73-76; 197; CAD; CANR 130; DFS 12; DLB 7

Miller, Sue 1943- .... **CLC 44**
See also AMWS 12; BEST 90:3; CA 139; CANR 59, 91, 128, 194; DA3; DAM POP; DLB 143

Miller, Walter M(ichael, Jr.)
1923-1996 .... **CLC 4, 30**
See also BPFB 2; CA 85-88; CANR 108; DLB 8; SCFW 1, 2; SFW 4

Millett, Kate 1934- .... **CLC 67**
See also AITN 1; CA 73-76; CANR 32, 53, 76, 110; DA3; DLB 246; FW; GLL 1; MTCW 1, 2; MTFW 2005

Millhauser, Steven 1943- ... **CLC 21, 54, 109; SSC 57**
See also AAYA 76; CA 110; 111; CANR 63, 114, 133, 189; CN 6, 7; DA3; DLB 2, 350; FANT; INT CA-111; MAL 5; MTCW 2; MTFW 2005

Millhauser, Steven Lewis
See Millhauser, Steven

Millin, Sarah Gertrude 1889-1968 ... **CLC 49**
See also CA 102; 93-96; DLB 225; EWL 3

Milne, A. A. 1882-1956 .... **TCLC 6, 88**
See also BRWS 5; CA 104; 133; CLR 1, 26, 108; CMW 4; CWRI 5; DA3; DAB; DAC; DAM MST; DLB 10, 77, 100, 160, 352; FANT; MAICYA 1, 2; MTCW 1, 2; MTFW 2005; RGEL 2; SATA 100; WCH; YABC 1

Milne, Alan Alexander
See Milne, A. A.

Milner, Ron(ald) 1938-2004 .. **BLC 1:3; CLC 56**
See also AITN 1; BW 1; CA 73-76; 230; CAD; CANR 24, 81; CD 5, 6; DAM MULT; DLB 38; MAL 5; MTCW 1

Milnes, Richard Monckton
1809-1885 .... **NCLC 61**
See also DLB 32, 184
Milosz, Czeslaw 1911-2004 .... **CLC 5, 11, 22, 31, 56, 82, 253; PC 8; WLCS**
See also AAYA 62; CA 81-84; 230; CANR 23, 51, 91, 126; CDWLB 4; CWW 2; DA3; DAM MST, POET; DLB 215, 331; EW 13; EWL 3; MTCW 1, 2; MTFW 2005; PFS 16, 29, 35; RGHL; RGWL 2, 3
Milton, John 1608-1674 ..... **LC 9, 43, 92; PC 19, 29; WLC 4**
See also AAYA 65; BRW 2; BRWR 2; CD-BLB 1660-1789; DA; DA3; DAB; DAC; DAM MST, POET; DLB 131, 151, 281; EFS 1; EXPP; LAIT 1; PAB; PFS 3, 17; RGEL 2; TEA; WLIT 3; WP
Min, Anchee 1957- .... **CLC 86, 291**
See also CA 146; CANR 94, 137; MTFW 2005
Minehaha, Cornelius
See Wedekind, Frank
Miner, Valerie 1947- .... **CLC 40**
See also CA 97-100; CANR 59, 177; FW; GLL 2
Minimo, Duca
See D'Annunzio, Gabriele
Minot, Susan (Anderson) 1956- ...... **CLC 44, 159**
See also AMWS 6; CA 134; CANR 118; CN 6, 7
Minus, Ed 1938- .... **CLC 39**
See also CA 185
Mirabai 1498(?)-1550(?) .... **LC 143; PC 48**
See also PFS 24
Miranda, Javier
See Bioy Casares, Adolfo
Mirbeau, Octave 1848-1917 .... **TCLC 55**
See also CA 216; DLB 123, 192; GFL 1789 to the Present
Mirikitani, Janice 1942- .... **AAL**
See also CA 211; DLB 312; RGAL 4
Mirk, John (?)-c. 1414 .... **LC 105**
See also DLB 146
Miro (Ferrer), Gabriel (Francisco Victor)
1879-1930 .... **TCLC 5**
See also CA 104; 185; DLB 322; EWL 3
Misharin, Alexandr .... **CLC 59**
Mishima, Yukio
See Hiraoka, Kimitake
Mishima Yukio
See Hiraoka, Kimitake
Miss C. L. F.
See Grimke, Charlotte L. Forten
Mister X
See Hoch, Edward D.
Mistral, Frederic 1830-1914 .... **TCLC 51**
See also CA 122; 213; DLB 331; GFL 1789 to the Present
Mistral, Gabriela 1899-1957 .... **HLC 2; PC 32; TCLC 2**
See also BW 2; CA 104; 131; CANR 81; DAM MULT; DLB 283, 331; DNFS; EWL 3; HW 1, 2; LAW; MTCW 1, 2; MTFW 2005; RGWL 2, 3; WP
Mistry, Rohinton 1952- ... **CLC 71, 196, 281; SSC 73**
See also BRWS 10; CA 141; CANR 86, 114; CCA 1; CN 6, 7; DAC; DLB 334; SSFS 6
Mitchell, Clyde
See Ellison, Harlan; Silverberg, Robert
Mitchell, Emerson Blackhorse Barney
1945- .... **NNAL**
See also CA 45-48
Mitchell, James Leslie 1901-1935 .... **TCLC 4**
See also BRWS 14; CA 104; 188; DLB 15; RGEL 2

Mitchell, Joni 1943- .... **CLC 12**
See also CA 112; CCA 1
Mitchell, Joseph (Quincy)
1908-1996 .... **CLC 98**
See also CA 77-80; 152; CANR 69; CN 1, 2, 3, 4, 5, 6; CSW; DLB 185; DLBY 1996
Mitchell, Margaret 1900-1949 .... **TCLC 11, 170**
See also AAYA 23; BPFB 2; BYA 1; CA 109; 125; CANR 55, 94; CDALBS; DA3; DAM NOV, POP; DLB 9; LAIT 2; MAL 5; MTCW 1, 2; MTFW 2005; NFS 9; RGAL 4; RHW; TUS; WYAS 1; YAW
Mitchell, Margaret Munnerlyn
See Mitchell, Margaret
Mitchell, Peggy
See Mitchell, Margaret
Mitchell, S(ilas) Weir 1829-1914 .... **TCLC 36**
See also CA 165; DLB 202; RGAL 4
Mitchell, W(illiam) O(rmond)
1914-1998 .... **CLC 25**
See also CA 77-80; 165; CANR 15, 43; CN 1, 2, 3, 4, 5, 6; DAC; DAM MST; DLB 88; TCLE 1:2
Mitchell, William (Lendrum)
1879-1936 .... **TCLC 81**
See also CA 213
Mitford, Mary Russell 1787-1855 ... **NCLC 4**
See also DLB 110, 116; RGEL 2
Mitford, Nancy 1904-1973 .... **CLC 44**
See also BRWS 10; CA 9-12R; CN 1; DLB 191; RGEL 2
Miyamoto, (Chujo) Yuriko
1899-1951 .... **TCLC 37**
See also CA 170, 174; DLB 180
Miyamoto Yuriko
See Miyamoto, (Chujo) Yuriko
Miyazawa, Kenji 1896-1933 .... **TCLC 76**
See also CA 157; EWL 3; RGWL 3
Miyazawa Kenji
See Miyazawa, Kenji
Mizoguchi, Kenji 1898-1956 .... **TCLC 72**
See also CA 167
Mo, Timothy (Peter) 1950- .... **CLC 46, 134**
See also CA 117; CANR 128; CN 5, 6, 7; DLB 194; MTCW 1; WLIT 4; WWE 1
Mo, Yan
See Yan, Mo
Moberg, Carl Arthur
See Moberg, Vilhelm
Moberg, Vilhelm 1898-1973 .... **TCLC 224**
See also CA 97-100; 45-48; CANR 135; DLB 259; EW 11; EWL 3
Modarressi, Taghi (M.) 1931-1997 ... **CLC 44**
See also CA 121; 134; INT CA-134
Modiano, Patrick (Jean) 1945- .... **CLC 18, 218**
See also CA 85-88; CANR 17, 40, 115; CWW 2; DLB 83, 299; EWL 3; RGHL
Mofolo, Thomas 1875(?)-1948 .... **BLC 1:3; TCLC 22**
See also AFW; CA 121; 153; CANR 83; DAM MULT; DLB 225; EWL 3; MTCW 2; MTFW 2005; WLIT 2
Mofolo, Thomas Mokopu
See Mofolo, Thomas
Mohr, Nicholasa 1938- .... **CLC 12; HLC 2**
See also AAYA 8, 46; CA 49-52; CANR 1, 32, 64; CLR 22; DAM MULT; DLB 145; HW 1, 2; JRDA; LAIT 5; LLW; MAICYA 2; MAICYAS 1; RGAL 4; SAAS 8; SATA 8, 97; SATA-Essay 113; WYA; YAW
Moi, Toril 1953- .... **CLC 172**
See also CA 154; CANR 102; FW
Mojtabai, A(nn) G(race) 1938- ..... **CLC 5, 9, 15, 29**
See also CA 85-88; CANR 88

Moliere 1622-1673 ..... **DC 13; LC 10, 28, 64, 125, 127; WLC 4**
See also DA; DA3; DAB; DAC; DAM DRAM, MST; DFS 13, 18, 20; DLB 268; EW 3; GFL Beginnings to 1789; LATS 1:1; RGWL 2, 3; TWA
Molin, Charles
See Mayne, William (James Carter)
Molina, Antonio Munoz 1956- .... **CLC 289**
See also DLB 322
Molnar, Ferenc 1878-1952 .... **TCLC 20**
See also CA 109; 153; CANR 83; CDWLB 4; DAM DRAM; DLB 215; EWL 3; RGWL 2, 3
Momaday, N. Scott 1934- ...... **CLC 2, 19, 85, 95, 160; NNAL; PC 25; WLCS**
See also AAYA 11, 64; AMWS 4; ANW; BPFB 2; BYA 12; CA 25-28R; CANR 14, 34, 68, 134; CDALBS; CN 2, 3, 4, 5, 6, 7; CPW; DA; DA3; DAB; DAC; DAM MST, MULT, NOV, POP; DLB 143, 175, 256; EWL 3; EXPP; INT CANR-14; LAIT 4; LATS 1:2; MAL 5; MTCW 1, 2; MTFW 2005; NFS 10; PFS 2, 11; RGAL 4; SATA 48; SATA-Brief 30; TCWW 1, 2; WP; YAW
Momaday, Navarre Scott
See Momaday, N. Scott
Momala, Ville i
See Moberg, Vilhelm
Monette, Paul 1945-1995 .... **CLC 82**
See also AMWS 10; CA 139; 147; CN 6; DLB 350; GLL 1
Monroe, Harriet 1860-1936 .... **TCLC 12**
See also CA 109; 204; DLB 54, 91
Monroe, Lyle
See Heinlein, Robert A.
Montagu, Elizabeth 1720-1800 .... **NCLC 7, 117**
See also DLB 356; FW
Montagu, Mary (Pierrepont) Wortley
1689-1762 .... **LC 9, 57; PC 16**
See also DLB 95, 101; FL 1:1; RGEL 2
Montagu, W. H.
See Coleridge, Samuel Taylor
Montague, John (Patrick) 1929- ..... **CLC 13, 46; PC 106**
See also BRWS 15; CA 9-12R; CANR 9, 69, 121; CP 1, 2, 3, 4, 5, 6, 7; DLB 40; EWL 3; MTCW 1; PFS 12; RGEL 2; TCLE 1:2
Montaigne, Michel de 1533-1592 .... **LC 8, 105; WLC 4**
See also DA; DAB; DAC; DAM MST; DLB 327; EW 2; GFL Beginnings to 1789; LMFS 1; RGWL 2, 3; TWA
Montaigne, Michel Eyquem de
See Montaigne, Michel de
Montale, Eugenio 1896-1981 ... **CLC 7, 9, 18; PC 13**
See also CA 17-20R; 104; CANR 30; DLB 114, 331; EW 11; EWL 3; MTCW 1; PFS 22; RGWL 2, 3; TWA; WLIT 7
Montesquieu, Charles-Louis de Secondat
1689-1755 .... **LC 7, 69**
See also DLB 314; EW 3; GFL Beginnings to 1789; TWA
Montessori, Maria 1870-1952 ...... **TCLC 103**
See also CA 115; 147
Montgomery, Bruce 1921(?)-1978 .... **CLC 22**
See also CA 179; 104; CMW 4; DLB 87; MSW
Montgomery, L. M. 1874-1942 ..... **TCLC 51, 140**
See also AAYA 12; BYA 1; CA 108; 137; CLR 8, 91, 145; DA3; DAC; DAM MST; DLB 92; DLBD 14; JRDA; MAICYA 1, 2; MTCW 2; MTFW 2005; RGEL 2; SATA 100; TWA; WCH; WYA; YABC 1

Montgomery, Lucy Maud
See Montgomery, L. M.

Montgomery, Marion, Jr. 1925- .... **CLC 7**
See also AITN 1; CA 1-4R; CANR 3, 48, 162; CSW; DLB 6

Montgomery, Marion H. 1925-
See Montgomery, Marion, Jr.

Montgomery, Max
See Davenport, Guy (Mattison, Jr.)

Montgomery, Robert Bruce
See Montgomery, Bruce

Montherlant, Henry de 1896-1972 .... **CLC 8, 19**
See also CA 85-88; 37-40R; DAM DRAM; DLB 72, 321; EW 11; EWL 3; GFL 1789 to the Present; MTCW 1

Montherlant, Henry Milon de
See Montherlant, Henry de

Monty Python
See Chapman, Graham; Cleese, John (Marwood); Gilliam, Terry; Idle, Eric; Jones, Terence Graham Parry; Palin, Michael

Moodie, Susanna (Strickland) 1803-1885 .... **NCLC 14, 113**
See also DLB 99

Moody, Hiram
See Moody, Rick

Moody, Hiram F. III
See Moody, Rick

Moody, Minerva
See Alcott, Louisa May

Moody, Rick 1961- .... **CLC 147**
See also CA 138; CANR 64, 112, 179; MTFW 2005

Moody, William Vaughan 1869-1910 .... **TCLC 105**
See also CA 110; 178; DLB 7, 54; MAL 5; RGAL 4

Mooney, Edward 1951- .... **CLC 25**
See also CA 130

Mooney, Ted
See Mooney, Edward

Moorcock, Michael 1939- ...... **CLC 5, 27, 58, 236**
See also AAYA 26; CA 45-48; CAAS 5; CANR 2, 17, 38, 64, 122, 203; CN 5, 6, 7; DLB 14, 231, 261, 319; FANT; MTCW 1, 2; MTFW 2005; SATA 93, 166; SCFW 1, 2; SFW 4; SUFW 1, 2

Moorcock, Michael John
See Moorcock, Michael

Moorcock, Michael John
See Moorcock, Michael

Moore, Al
See Moore, Alan

Moore, Alan 1953- .... **CLC 230**
See also AAYA 51; CA 204; CANR 138, 184; DLB 261; MTFW 2005; SFW 4

Moore, Alice Ruth
See Nelson, Alice Ruth Moore Dunbar

Moore, Brian 1921-1999 ... **CLC 1, 3, 5, 7, 8, 19, 32, 90**
See also BRWS 9; CA 1-4R; 174; CANR 1, 25, 42, 63; CCA 1; CN 1, 2, 3, 4, 5, 6; DAB; DAC; DAM MST; DLB 251; EWL 3; FANT; MTCW 1, 2; MTFW 2005; RGEL 2

Moore, Edward
See Muir, Edwin

Moore, G. E. 1873-1958 .... **TCLC 89**
See also DLB 262

Moore, George Augustus 1852-1933 .... **SSC 19, 134; TCLC 7**
See also BRW 6; CA 104; 177; DLB 10, 18, 57, 135; EWL 3; RGEL 2; RGSF 2

Moore, Lorrie 1957- ..... **CLC 39, 45, 68, 165**
See also AMWS 10; CA 116; CANR 39, 83, 139; CN 5, 6, 7; DLB 234; MTFW 2005; SSFS 19

Moore, Marianne 1887-1972 . **CLC 1, 2, 4, 8, 10, 13, 19, 47; PC 4, 49; WLCS**
See also AMW; CA 1-4R; 33-36R; CANR 3, 61; CDALB 1929-1941; CP 1; DA; DA3; DAB; DAC; DAM MST, POET; DLB 45; DLBD 7; EWL 3; EXPP; FL 1:6; MAL 5; MBL; MTCW 1, 2; MTFW 2005; PAB; PFS 14, 17; RGAL 4; SATA 20; TUS; WP

Moore, Marianne Craig
See Moore, Marianne

Moore, Marie Lorena
See Moore, Lorrie

Moore, Michael 1954- .... **CLC 218**
See also AAYA 53; CA 166; CANR 150

Moore, Thomas 1779-1852 .... **NCLC 6, 110**
See also DLB 96, 144; RGEL 2

Moorhouse, Frank 1938- .... **SSC 40**
See also CA 118; CANR 92; CN 3, 4, 5, 6, 7; DLB 289; RGSF 2

Mora, Pat 1942- .... **HLC 2**
See also AMWS 13; CA 129; CANR 57, 81, 112, 171; CLR 58; DAM MULT; DLB 209; HW 1, 2; LLW; MAICYA 2; MTFW 2005; PFS 33, 35; SATA 92, 134, 186

Moraga, Cherrie 1952- ... **CLC 126, 250; DC 22**
See also CA 131; CANR 66, 154; DAM MULT; DLB 82, 249; FW; GLL 1; HW 1, 2; LLW

Moran, J.L.
See Whitaker, Rod

Morand, Paul 1888-1976 .... **CLC 41; SSC 22**
See also CA 184; 69-72; DLB 65; EWL 3

Morante, Elsa 1918-1985 .... **CLC 8, 47**
See also CA 85-88; 117; CANR 35; DLB 177; EWL 3; MTCW 1, 2; MTFW 2005; RGHL; RGWL 2, 3; WLIT 7

Moravia, Alberto
See Pincherle, Alberto

Morck, Paul
See Rolvaag, O.E.

More, Hannah 1745-1833 .... **NCLC 27, 141**
See also DLB 107, 109, 116, 158; RGEL 2

More, Henry 1614-1687 .... **LC 9**
See also DLB 126, 252

More, Sir Thomas 1478(?)-1535 ... **LC 10, 32, 140**
See also BRWC 1; BRWS 7; DLB 136, 281; LMFS 1; NFS 29; RGEL 2; TEA

Moreas, Jean
See Papadiamantopoulos, Johannes

Moreton, Andrew Esq.
See Defoe, Daniel

Moreton, Lee
See Boucicault, Dion

Morgan, Berry 1919-2002 .... **CLC 6**
See also CA 49-52; 208; DLB 6

Morgan, Claire
See Highsmith, Patricia

Morgan, Edwin 1920- .... **CLC 31**
See also BRWS 9; CA 5-8R; CANR 3, 43, 90; CP 1, 2, 3, 4, 5, 6, 7; DLB 27

Morgan, Edwin George
See Morgan, Edwin

Morgan, (George) Frederick 1922-2004 .... **CLC 23**
See also CA 17-20R; 224; CANR 21, 144; CP 2, 3, 4, 5, 6, 7

Morgan, Harriet
See Mencken, H. L.

Morgan, Jane
See Cooper, James Fenimore

Morgan, Janet 1945- .... **CLC 39**
See also CA 65-68

Morgan, Lady 1776(?)-1859 .... **NCLC 29**
See also DLB 116, 158; RGEL 2

Morgan, Robin (Evonne) 1941- .... **CLC 2**
See also CA 69-72; CANR 29, 68; FW; GLL 2; MTCW 1; SATA 80

Morgan, Scott
See Kuttner, Henry

Morgan, Seth 1949(?)-1990 .... **CLC 65**
See also CA 185; 132

Morgenstern, Christian (Otto Josef Wolfgang) 1871-1914 .... **TCLC 8**
See also CA 105; 191; EWL 3

Morgenstern, S.
See Goldman, William

Mori, Rintaro
See Mori Ogai

Mori, Toshio 1910-1980 ... **AAL; SSC 83, 123**
See also CA 116; 244; DLB 312; RGSF 2

Moricz, Zsigmond 1879-1942 .... **TCLC 33**
See also CA 165; DLB 215; EWL 3

Morike, Eduard (Friedrich) 1804-1875 .... **NCLC 10, 201**
See also DLB 133; RGWL 2, 3

Morin, Jean-Paul
See Whitaker, Rod

Mori Ogai 1862-1922 .... **TCLC 14**
See also CA 110; 164; DLB 180; EWL 3; MJW; RGWL 3; TWA

Moritz, Karl Philipp 1756-1793 .... **LC 2, 162**
See also DLB 94

Morland, Peter Henry
See Faust, Frederick

Morley, Christopher (Darlington) 1890-1957 .... **TCLC 87**
See also CA 112; 213; DLB 9; MAL 5; RGAL 4

Morren, Theophil
See Hofmannsthal, Hugo von

Morris, Bill 1952- .... **CLC 76**
See also CA 225

Morris, Julian
See West, Morris L(anglo)

Morris, Steveland Judkins (?)-
See Wonder, Stevie

Morris, William 1834-1896 . **NCLC 4; PC 55**
See also BRW 5; CDBLB 1832-1890; DLB 18, 35, 57, 156, 178, 184; FANT; RGEL 2; SFW 4; SUFW

Morris, Wright (Marion) 1910-1998 . **CLC 1, 3, 7, 18, 37; TCLC 107**
See also AMW; CA 9-12R; 167; CANR 21, 81; CN 1, 2, 3, 4, 5, 6; DLB 2, 206, 218; DLBY 1981; EWL 3; MAL 5; MTCW 1, 2; MTFW 2005; RGAL 4; TCWW 1, 2

Morrison, Arthur 1863-1945 .... **SSC 40; TCLC 72**
See also CA 120; 157; CMW 4; DLB 70, 135, 197; RGEL 2

Morrison, Chloe Anthony Wofford
See Morrison, Toni

Morrison, James Douglas 1943-1971 .... **CLC 17**
See also CA 73-76; CANR 40

Morrison, Jim
See Morrison, James Douglas

Morrison, John Gordon 1904-1998 ... **SSC 93**
See also CA 103; CANR 92; DLB 260

Morrison, Toni 1931- . **BLC 1:3, 2:3; CLC 4, 10, 22, 55, 81, 87, 173, 194; SSC 126; WLC 4**
See also AAYA 1, 22, 61; AFAW 1, 2; AMWC 1; AMWS 3; BPFB 2; BW 2, 3; CA 29-32R; CANR 27, 42, 67, 113, 124, 204; CDALB 1968-1988; CLR 99; CN 3, 4, 5, 6, 7; CPW; DA; DA3; DAB; DAC; DAM MST, MULT, NOV, POP; DLB 6, 33, 143, 331; DLBY 1981; EWL 3; EXPN; FL 1:6; FW; GL 3; LAIT 2, 4; LATS 1:2; LMFS 2; MAL 5; MBL;

Murray, James Augustus Henry
1837-1915 .... **TCLC 117**

Murray, Judith Sargent
1751-1820 .... **NCLC 63**
See also DLB 37, 200

Murray, Les 1938- .... **CLC 40**
See also BRWS 7; CA 21-24R; CANR 11,
27, 56, 103, 199; CP 1, 2, 3, 4, 5, 6, 7;
DAM POET; DLB 289; DLBY 2001;
EWL 3; RGEL 2

Murray, Leslie Allan
See Murray, Les

Murry, J. Middleton
See Murry, John Middleton

Murry, John Middleton
1889-1957 .... **TCLC 16**
See also CA 118; 217; DLB 149

Musgrave, Susan 1951- .... **CLC 13, 54**
See also CA 69-72; CANR 45, 84, 181;
CCA 1; CP 2, 3, 4, 5, 6, 7; CWP

Musil, Robert (Edler von)
1880-1942 ... **SSC 18; TCLC 12, 68, 213**
See also CA 109; CANR 55, 84; CDWLB
2; DLB 81, 124; EW 9; EWL 3; MTCW
2; RGSF 2; RGWL 2, 3

Muske, Carol
See Muske-Dukes, Carol

Muske, Carol Anne
See Muske-Dukes, Carol

Muske-Dukes, Carol 1945- .... **CLC 90**
See also CA 65-68, 203; CAAE 203; CANR
32, 70, 181; CWP; PFS 24

Muske-Dukes, Carol Ann
See Muske-Dukes, Carol

Muske-Dukes, Carol Anne
See Muske-Dukes, Carol

Musset, Alfred de 1810-1857 . **DC 27; NCLC
7, 150**
See also DLB 192, 217; EW 6; GFL 1789
to the Present; RGWL 2, 3; TWA

Musset, Louis Charles Alfred de
See Musset, Alfred de

Mussolini, Benito (Amilcare Andrea)
1883-1945 .... **TCLC 96**
See also CA 116

Mutanabbi, Al-
See al-Mutanabbi, Ahmad ibn al-Husayn
Abu al-Tayyib al-Jufi al-Kindi

Mutis, Alvaro 1923- .... **CLC 283**
See also CA 149; CANR 118; DLB 283;
EWL 3; HW 1; LAWS 1

My Brother's Brother
See Chekhov, Anton

Myers, L(eopold) H(amilton)
1881-1944 .... **TCLC 59**
See also CA 157; DLB 15; EWL 3; RGEL
2

Myers, Walter Dean 1937- ...... **BLC 1:3, 2:3;
CLC 35**
See also AAYA 4, 23; BW 2; BYA 6, 8, 11;
CA 33-36R; CANR 20, 42, 67, 108, 184;
CLR 4, 16, 35, 110; DAM MULT, NOV;
DLB 33; INT CANR-20; JRDA; LAIT 5;
LNFS 1; MAICYA 1, 2; MAICYAS 1;
MTCW 2; MTFW 2005; NFS 30, 33;
SAAS 2; SATA 41, 71, 109, 157, 193;
SATA-Brief 27; SSFS 31; WYA; YAW

Myers, Walter M.
See Myers, Walter Dean

Myles, Symon
See Follett, Ken

Nabokov, Vladimir 1899-1977 ... **CLC 1, 2, 3,
6, 8, 11, 15, 23, 44, 46, 64; SSC 11, 86;
TCLC 108, 189; WLC 4**
See also AAYA 45; AMW; AMWC 1;
AMWR 1; BPFB 2; CA 5-8R; 69-72;
CANR 20, 102; CDALB 1941-1968; CN
1, 2; CP 2; DA; DA3; DAB; DAC; DAM
MST, NOV; DLB 2, 244, 278, 317; DLBD
3; DLBY 1980, 1991; EWL 3; EXPS;
LATS 1:2; MAL 5; MTCW 1, 2; MTFW
2005; NCFS 4; NFS 9; RGAL 4; RGSF
2; SSFS 6, 15; TUS

Nabokov, Vladimir Vladimirovich
See Nabokov, Vladimir

Naevius c. 265B.C.-201B.C. .... **CMLC 37**
See also DLB 211

Nagai, Kafu 1879-1959 .... **TCLC 51**
See also CA 117; 276; DLB 180; EWL 3;
MJW

Nagai, Sokichi
See Nagai, Kafu

Nagai Kafu
See Nagai, Kafu

na gCopaleen, Myles
See O Nuallain, Brian

na Gopaleen, Myles
See O Nuallain, Brian

Nagy, Laszlo 1925-1978 .... **CLC 7**
See also CA 129; 112

Naidu, Sarojini 1879-1949 .... **TCLC 80**
See also EWL 3; RGEL 2

Naipaul, Shiva 1945-1985 .... **CLC 32, 39;
TCLC 153**
See also CA 110; 112; 116; CANR 33; CN
2, 3; DA3; DAM NOV; DLB 157; DLBY
1985; EWL 3; MTCW 1, 2; MTFW 2005

Naipaul, Shivadhar Srinivasa
See Naipaul, Shiva

Naipaul, V. S. 1932- . **CLC 4, 7, 9, 13, 18, 37,
105, 199; SSC 38, 121**
See also BPFB 2; BRWS 1; CA 1-4R;
CANR 1, 33, 51, 91, 126, 191; CDBLB
1960 to Present; CDWLB 3; CN 1, 2, 3,
4, 5, 6, 7; DA3; DAB; DAC; DAM MST,
NOV; DLB 125, 204, 207, 326, 331;
DLBY 1985, 2001; EWL 3; LATS 1:2;
MTCW 1, 2; MTFW 2005; RGEL 2;
RGSF 2; SSFS 29; TWA; WLIT 4; WWE
1

Naipaul, Vidiahar Surajprasad
See Naipaul, V. S.

Nair, Kamala
See Das, Kamala

Nakos, Lilika 1903-1989 .... **CLC 29**
See also CA 217

Nalapat, Kamala
See Das, Kamala

Napoleon
See Yamamoto, Hisaye

Narayan, R. K. 1906-2001 ..... **CLC 7, 28, 47,
121, 211; SSC 25**
See also BPFB 2; CA 81-84; 196; CANR
33, 61, 112; CN 1, 2, 3, 4, 5, 6, 7; DA3;
DAM NOV; DLB 323; DNFS 1; EWL 3;
MTCW 1, 2; MTFW 2005; RGEL 2;
RGSF 2; SATA 62; SSFS 5, 29; WWE 1

Narayan, Rasipuram Krishnaswami
See Narayan, R. K.

Nash, Frediric Ogden
See Nash, Ogden

Nash, Ogden 1902-1971 ...... **CLC 23; PC 21;
TCLC 109**
See also CA 13-14; 29-32R; CANR 34, 61,
185; CAP 1; CP 1; DAM POET; DLB 11;
MAICYA 1, 2; MAL 5; MTCW 1, 2; PFS
31; RGAL 4; SATA 2, 46; WP

Nashe, Thomas 1567-1601(?) . **LC 41, 89; PC
82**
See also DLB 167; RGEL 2

Nathan, Daniel
See Dannay, Frederic

Nathan, George Jean 1882-1958 .... **TCLC 18**
See also CA 114; 169; DLB 137; MAL 5

Natsume, Kinnosuke
See Natsume, Soseki

Natsume, Soseki 1867-1916 .... **TCLC 2, 10**
See also CA 104; 195; DLB 180; EWL 3;
MJW; RGWL 2, 3; TWA

Natsume Soseki
See Natsume, Soseki

Natti, Lee 1919- .... **CLC 17**
See also CA 5-8R; CANR 2; CWRI 5;
SAAS 3; SATA 1, 67

Natti, Mary Lee
See Natti, Lee

Navarre, Marguerite de
See de Navarre, Marguerite

Naylor, Gloria 1950- . **BLC 1:3; CLC 28, 52,
156, 261; WLCS**
See also AAYA 6, 39; AFAW 1, 2; AMWS
8; BW 2, 3; CA 107; CANR 27, 51, 74,
130; CN 4, 5, 6, 7; CPW; DA; DA3;
DAC; DAM MST, MULT, NOV, POP;
DLB 173; EWL 3; FW; MAL 5; MTCW
1, 2; MTFW 2005; NFS 4, 7; RGAL 4;
TCLE 1:2; TUS

Ndebele, Njabulo (Simakahle)
1948- .... **SSC 135**
See also CA 184; DLB 157, 225; EWL 3

Neal, John 1793-1876 .... **NCLC 161**
See also DLB 1, 59, 243; FW; RGAL 4

Neff, Debra .... **CLC 59**

Neihardt, John Gneisenau
1881-1973 .... **CLC 32**
See also CA 13-14; CANR 65; CAP 1; DLB
9, 54, 256; LAIT 2; TCWW 1, 2

Nekrasov, Nikolai Alekseevich
1821-1878 .... **NCLC 11**
See also DLB 277

Nelligan, Emile 1879-1941 .... **TCLC 14**
See also CA 114; 204; DLB 92; EWL 3

Nelson, Alice Ruth Moore Dunbar
1875-1935 .... **HR 1:2; SSC 132**
See also BW 1, 3; CA 122; 124; CANR 82;
DLB 50; FW; MTCW 1

Nelson, Willie 1933- .... **CLC 17**
See also CA 107; CANR 114, 178

Nemerov, Howard 1920-1991 .... **CLC 2, 6, 9,
36; PC 24; TCLC 124**
See also AMW; CA 1-4R; 134; CABS 2;
CANR 1, 27, 53; CN 1, 2, 3; CP 1, 2, 3,
4, 5; DAM POET; DLB 5, 6; DLBY 1983;
EWL 3; INT CANR-27; MAL 5; MTCW
1, 2; MTFW 2005; PFS 10, 14; RGAL 4

Nemerov, Howard Stanley
See Nemerov, Howard

Nepos, Cornelius c. 99B.C.-c.
24B.C. .... **CMLC 89**
See also DLB 211

Neruda, Pablo 1904-1973 .. **CLC 1, 2, 5, 7, 9,
28, 62; HLC 2; PC 4, 64; WLC 4**
See also CA 19-20; 45-48; CANR 131; CAP
2; DA; DA3; DAB; DAC; DAM MST,
MULT, POET; DLB 283, 331; DNFS 2;
EWL 3; HW 1; LAW; MTCW 1, 2;
MTFW 2005; PFS 11, 28, 33, 35; RGWL
2, 3; TWA; WLIT 1; WP

Nerval, Gerard de 1808-1855 ... **NCLC 1, 67;
PC 13; SSC 18**
See also DLB 217; EW 6; GFL 1789 to the
Present; RGSF 2; RGWL 2, 3

Nervo, (Jose) Amado (Ruiz de)
1870-1919 .... **HLCS 2; TCLC 11**
See also CA 109; 131; DLB 290; EWL 3;
HW 1; LAW

Nesbit, Malcolm
See Chester, Alfred

Nessi, Pio Baroja y
See Baroja, Pio

Nestroy, Johann 1801-1862 .... **NCLC 42**
See also DLB 133; RGWL 2, 3

Netterville, Luke
See O'Grady, Standish (James)

Nossack, Hans Erich 1901-1977 .... **CLC 6**
See also CA 93-96; 85-88; CANR 156;
DLB 69; EWL 3

Nostradamus 1503-1566 .... **LC 27**

Nosu, Chuji
See Ozu, Yasujiro

Notenburg, Eleanora (Genrikhovna) von
See Guro, Elena (Genrikhovna)

Nova, Craig 1945- .... **CLC 7, 31**
See also CA 45-48; CANR 2, 53, 127

Novak, Joseph
See Kosinski, Jerzy

Novalis 1772-1801 .... **NCLC 13, 178**
See also CDWLB 2; DLB 90; EW 5; RGWL
2, 3

Novick, Peter 1934- .... **CLC 164**
See also CA 188

Novis, Emile
See Weil, Simone

Nowlan, Alden (Albert) 1933-1983 ... **CLC 15**
See also CA 9-12R; CANR 5; CP 1, 2, 3;
DAC; DAM MST; DLB 53; PFS 12

Noyes, Alfred 1880-1958 ...... **PC 27; TCLC 7**
See also CA 104; 188; DLB 20; EXPP;
FANT; PFS 4; RGEL 2

Nugent, Richard Bruce
1906(?)-1987 .... **HR 1:3**
See also BW 1; CA 125; CANR 198; DLB
51; GLL 2

Nunez, Elizabeth 1944- .... **BLC 2:3**
See also CA 223

Nunn, Kem .... **CLC 34**
See also CA 159; CANR 204

Nussbaum, Martha Craven 1947- .. **CLC 203**
See also CA 134; CANR 102, 176

Nwapa, Flora (Nwanzuruaha)
1931-1993 .... **BLCS; CLC 133**
See also BW 2; CA 143; CANR 83; CD-
WLB 3; CWRI 5; DLB 125; EWL 3;
WLIT 2

Nye, Robert 1939- .... **CLC 13, 42**
See also BRWS 10; CA 33-36R; CANR 29,
67, 107; CN 1, 2, 3, 4, 5, 6, 7; CP 1, 2, 3,
4, 5, 6, 7; CWRI 5; DAM NOV; DLB 14,
271; FANT; HGG; MTCW 1; RHW;
SATA 6

Nyro, Laura 1947-1997 .... **CLC 17**
See also CA 194

O. Henry
See Henry, O.

Oates, Joyce Carol 1938- .. **CLC 1, 2, 3, 6, 9,
11, 15, 19, 33, 52, 108, 134, 228; SSC 6,
70, 121; WLC 4**
See also AAYA 15, 52; AITN 1; AMWS 2;
BEST 89:2; BPFB 2; BYA 11; CA 5-8R;
CANR 25, 45, 74, 113, 129, 165; CDALB
1968-1988; CN 1, 2, 3, 4, 5, 6, 7; CP 5,
6, 7; CPW; CWP; DA; DA3; DAB; DAC;
DAM MST, NOV, POP; DLB 2, 5, 130;
DLBY 1981; EWL 3; EXPS; FL 1:6; FW;
GL 3; HGG; INT CANR-25; LAIT 4;
MAL 5; MBL; MTCW 1, 2; MTFW 2005;
NFS 8, 24; RGAL 4; RGSF 2; SATA 159;
SSFS 1, 8, 17; SUFW 2; TUS

O'Brian, E.G.
See Clarke, Arthur C.

O'Brian, Patrick 1914-2000 .... **CLC 152**
See also AAYA 55; BRWS 12; CA 144; 187;
CANR 74, 201; CPW; MTCW 2; MTFW
2005; RHW

O'Brien, Darcy 1939-1998 .... **CLC 11**
See also CA 21-24R; 167; CANR 8, 59

O'Brien, Edna 1932- ..... **CLC 3, 5, 8, 13, 36,
65, 116, 237; SSC 10, 77**
See also BRWS 5; CA 1-4R; CANR 6, 41,
65, 102, 169; CDBLB 1960 to Present;
CN 1, 2, 3, 4, 5, 6, 7; DA3; DAM NOV;
DLB 14, 231, 319; EWL 3; FW; MTCW
1, 2; MTFW 2005; RGSF 2; WLIT 4

O'Brien, E.G.
See Clarke, Arthur C.

O'Brien, Fitz-James 1828-1862 ..... **NCLC 21**
See also DLB 74; RGAL 4; SUFW

O'Brien, Flann
See O Nuallain, Brian

O'Brien, Richard 1942- .... **CLC 17**
See also CA 124

O'Brien, Tim 1946- .... **CLC 7, 19, 40, 103,
211; SSC 74, 123**
See also AAYA 16; AMWS 5; CA 85-88;
CANR 40, 58, 133; CDALBS; CN 5, 6,
7; CPW; DA3; DAM POP; DLB 152;
DLBD 9; DLBY 1980; LATS 1:2; MAL
5; MTCW 2; MTFW 2005; RGAL 4;
SSFS 5, 15, 29; TCLE 1:2

O'Brien, William Timothy
See O'Brien, Tim

Obstfelder, Sigbjorn 1866-1900 ..... **TCLC 23**
See also CA 123; DLB 354

O'Casey, Brenda
See Haycraft, Anna

O'Casey, Sean 1880-1964 .... **CLC 1, 5, 9, 11,
15, 88; DC 12; WLCS**
See also BRW 7; CA 89-92; CANR 62;
CBD; CDBLB 1914-1945; DA3; DAB;
DAC; DAM DRAM, MST; DFS 19; DLB
10; EWL 3; MTCW 1, 2; MTFW 2005;
RGEL 2; TEA; WLIT 4

O'Cathasaigh, Sean
See O'Casey, Sean

Occom, Samson 1723-1792 .... **LC 60; NNAL**
See also DLB 175

Occomy, Marita (Odette) Bonner
1899(?)-1971 ..... **HR 1:2; PC 72; TCLC
179**
See also BW 2; CA 142; DFS 13; DLB 51,
228

Ochs, Phil(ip David) 1940-1976 .... **CLC 17**
See also CA 185; 65-68

O'Connor, Edwin (Greene)
1918-1968 .... **CLC 14**
See also CA 93-96; 25-28R; MAL 5

O'Connor, Flannery 1925-1964 ..... **CLC 1, 2,
3, 6, 10, 13, 15, 21, 66, 104; SSC 1, 23,
61, 82, 111; TCLC 132; WLC 4**
See also AAYA 7; AMW; AMWR 2; BPFB
3; BYA 16; CA 1-4R; CANR 3, 41;
CDALB 1941-1968; DA; DA3; DAB;
DAC; DAM MST, NOV; DLB 2, 152;
DLBD 12; DLBY 1980; EWL 3; EXPS;
LAIT 5; MAL 5; MBL; MTCW 1, 2;
MTFW 2005; NFS 3, 21; RGAL 4; RGSF
2; SSFS 2, 7, 10, 19; TUS

O'Connor, Frank 1903-1966
See O'Donovan, Michael Francis

O'Connor, Mary Flannery
See O'Connor, Flannery

O'Dell, Scott 1898-1989 .... **CLC 30**
See also AAYA 3, 44; BPFB 3; BYA 1, 2,
3, 5; CA 61-64; 129; CANR 12, 30, 112;
CLR 1, 16, 126; DLB 52; JRDA; MAI-
CYA 1, 2; SATA 12, 60, 134; WYA; YAW

Odets, Clifford 1906-1963 ..... **CLC 2, 28, 98;
DC 6**
See also AMWS 2; CA 85-88; CAD; CANR
62; DAM DRAM; DFS 3, 17, 20; DLB 7,
26, 341; EWL 3; MAL 5; MTCW 1, 2;
MTFW 2005; RGAL 4; TUS

O'Doherty, Brian 1928- .... **CLC 76**
See also CA 105; CANR 108

O'Donnell, K. M.
See Malzberg, Barry N(athaniel)

O'Donnell, Lawrence
See Kuttner, Henry

O'Donovan, Michael Francis
1903-1966 .... **CLC 14, 23; SSC 5, 109**
See also BRWS 14; CA 93-96; CANR 84;
DLB 162; EWL 3; RGSF 2; SSFS 5

Oe, Kenzaburo 1935- .. **CLC 10, 36, 86, 187;
SSC 20**
See also CA 97-100; CANR 36, 50, 74, 126;
CWW 2; DA3; DAM NOV; DLB 182,
331; DLBY 1994; EWL 3; LATS 1:2;
MJW; MTCW 1, 2; MTFW 2005; RGSF
2; RGWL 2, 3

Oe Kenzaburo
See Oe, Kenzaburo

O'Faolain, Julia 1932- .... **CLC 6, 19, 47, 108**
See also CA 81-84; CAAS 2; CANR 12,
61; CN 2, 3, 4, 5, 6, 7; DLB 14, 231, 319;
FW; MTCW 1; RHW

O'Faolain, Sean 1900-1991 ...... **CLC 1, 7, 14,
32, 70; SSC 13; TCLC 143**
See also CA 61-64; 134; CANR 12, 66; CN
1, 2, 3, 4; DLB 15, 162; MTCW 1, 2;
MTFW 2005; RGEL 2; RGSF 2

O'Flaherty, Liam 1896-1984 .... **CLC 5, 34;
SSC 6, 116**
See also CA 101; 113; CANR 35; CN 1, 2,
3; DLB 36, 162; DLBY 1984; MTCW 1,
2; MTFW 2005; RGEL 2; RGSF 2; SSFS
5, 20

Ogai
See Mori Ogai

Ogilvy, Gavin
See Barrie, J. M.

O'Grady, Standish (James)
1846-1928 .... **TCLC 5**
See also CA 104; 157

O'Grady, Timothy 1951- .... **CLC 59**
See also CA 138

O'Hara, Frank 1926-1966 .... **CLC 2, 5, 13,
78; PC 45**
See also CA 9-12R; 25-28R; CANR 33;
DA3; DAM POET; DLB 5, 16, 193; EWL
3; MAL 5; MTCW 1, 2; MTFW 2005;
PFS 8, 12, 34; RGAL 4; WP

O'Hara, John 1905-1970 . **CLC 1, 2, 3, 6, 11,
42; SSC 15**
See also AMW; BPFB 3; CA 5-8R; 25-28R;
CANR 31, 60; CDALB 1929-1941; DAM
NOV; DLB 9, 86, 324; DLBD 2; EWL 3;
MAL 5; MTCW 1, 2; MTFW 2005; NFS
11; RGAL 4; RGSF 2

O'Hara, John Henry
See O'Hara, John

O'Hehir, Diana 1929- .... **CLC 41**
See also CA 245; CANR 177

O'Hehir, Diana F.
See O'Hehir, Diana

Ohiyesa
See Eastman, Charles A(lexander)

Okada, John 1923-1971 .... **AAL**
See also BYA 14; CA 212; DLB 312; NFS
25

O'Kelly, Seamus 1881(?)-1918 .... **SSC 136**

Okigbo, Christopher 1930-1967 ..... **BLC 1:3;
CLC 25, 84; PC 7; TCLC 171**
See also AFW; BW 1, 3; CA 77-80; CANR
74; CDWLB 3; DAM MULT, POET; DLB
125; EWL 3; MTCW 1, 2; MTFW 2005;
RGEL 2

Okigbo, Christopher Ifenayichukwu
See Okigbo, Christopher

Okri, Ben 1959- .... **BLC 2:3; CLC 87, 223;
SSC 127**
See also AFW; BRWS 5; BW 2, 3; CA 130;
138; CANR 65, 128; CN 5, 6, 7; DLB
157, 231, 319, 326; EWL 3; INT CA-138;
MTCW 2; MTFW 2005; RGSF 2; SSFS
20; WLIT 2; WWE 1

Old Boy
See Hughes, Thomas

Olds, Sharon 1942- .. **CLC 32, 39, 85; PC 22**
See also AMWS 10; CA 101; CANR 18,
41, 66, 98, 135; CP 5, 6, 7; CPW; CWP;

Peirce, Charles Sanders
1839-1914 .... **TCLC 81**
See also CA 194; DLB 270
Pelagius c. 350-c. 418 .... **CMLC 118**
Pelecanos, George P. 1957- .... **CLC 236**
See also CA 138; CANR 122, 165, 194;
DLB 306
Pelevin, Victor 1962- .... **CLC 238**
See also CA 154; CANR 88, 159, 197; DLB
285
Pelevin, Viktor Olegovich
See Pelevin, Victor
Pellicer, Carlos 1897(?)-1977 .... **HLCS 2**
See also CA 153; 69-72; DLB 290; EWL 3;
HW 1
Pena, Ramon del Valle y
See Valle-Inclan, Ramon del
Pendennis, Arthur Esquir
See Thackeray, William Makepeace
Penn, Arthur
See Matthews, (James) Brander
Penn, William 1644-1718 .... **LC 25**
See also DLB 24
PEPECE
See Prado (Calvo), Pedro
Pepys, Samuel 1633-1703 ... **LC 11, 58; WLC 4**
See also BRW 2; CDBLB 1660-1789; DA;
DA3; DAB; DAC; DAM MST; DLB 101,
213; NCFS 4; RGEL 2; TEA; WLIT 3
Percy, Thomas 1729-1811 .... **NCLC 95**
See also DLB 104
Percy, Walker 1916-1990 .... **CLC 2, 3, 6, 8, 14, 18, 47, 65**
See also AMWS 3; BPFB 3; CA 1-4R; 131;
CANR 1, 23, 64; CN 1, 2, 3, 4; CPW;
CSW; DA3; DAM NOV, POP; DLB 2;
DLBY 1980, 1990; EWL 3; MAL 5;
MTCW 1, 2; MTFW 2005; RGAL 4; TUS
Percy, William Alexander
1885-1942 .... **TCLC 84**
See also CA 163; MTCW 2
Perdurabo, Frater
See Crowley, Edward Alexander
Perec, Georges 1936-1982 .... **CLC 56, 116**
See also CA 141; DLB 83, 299; EWL 3;
GFL 1789 to the Present; RGHL; RGWL
3
Pereda (y Sanchez de Porrua), Jose Maria de 1833-1906 .... **TCLC 16**
See also CA 117
Pereda y Porrua, Jose Maria de
See Pereda (y Sanchez de Porrua), Jose
Maria de
Peregoy, George Weems
See Mencken, H. L.
Perelman, S(idney) J(oseph)
1904-1979 .. **CLC 3, 5, 9, 15, 23, 44, 49; SSC 32**
See also AAYA 79; AITN 1, 2; BPFB 3;
CA 73-76; 89-92; CANR 18; DAM
DRAM; DLB 11, 44; MTCW 1, 2; MTFW
2005; RGAL 4
Peret, Benjamin 1899-1959 .... **PC 33; TCLC 20**
See also CA 117; 186; GFL 1789 to the
Present
Perets, Yitskhok Leybush
See Peretz, Isaac Loeb
Peretz, Isaac Leib (?)-
See Peretz, Isaac Loeb
Peretz, Isaac Loeb 1851-1915 .... **SSC 26; TCLC 16**
See Peretz, Isaac Leib
See also CA 109; 201; DLB 333
Peretz, Yitzkhok Leibush
See Peretz, Isaac Loeb

Perez Galdos, Benito 1843-1920 ..... **HLCS 2; TCLC 27**
See also CA 125; 153; EW 7; EWL 3; HW
1; RGWL 2, 3
Peri Rossi, Cristina 1941- .. **CLC 156; HLCS 2**
See also CA 131; CANR 59, 81; CWW 2;
DLB 145, 290; EWL 3; HW 1, 2
Perlata
See Peret, Benjamin
Perloff, Marjorie G(abrielle)
1931- .... **CLC 137**
See also CA 57-60; CANR 7, 22, 49, 104
Perrault, Charles 1628-1703 .... **LC 2, 56**
See also BYA 4; CLR 79, 134; DLB 268;
GFL Beginnings to 1789; MAICYA 1, 2;
RGWL 2, 3; SATA 25; WCH
Perrotta, Tom 1961- .... **CLC 266**
See also CA 162; CANR 99, 155, 197
Perry, Anne 1938- .... **CLC 126**
See also CA 101; CANR 22, 50, 84, 150,
177; CMW 4; CN 6, 7; CPW; DLB 276
Perry, Brighton
See Sherwood, Robert E(mmet)
Perse, St.-John
See Leger, Alexis Saint-Leger
Perse, Saint-John
See Leger, Alexis Saint-Leger
Persius 34-62 .... **CMLC 74**
See also AW 2; DLB 211; RGWL 2, 3
Perutz, Leo(pold) 1882-1957 .... **TCLC 60**
See also CA 147; DLB 81
Peseenz, Tulio F.
See Lopez y Fuentes, Gregorio
Pesetsky, Bette 1932- .... **CLC 28**
See also CA 133; DLB 130
Peshkov, Alexei Maximovich
See Gorky, Maxim
Pessoa, Fernando 1888-1935 .... **HLC 2; PC 20; TCLC 27**
See also CA 125; 183; CANR 182; DAM
MULT; DLB 287; EW 10; EWL 3; RGWL
2, 3; WP
Pessoa, Fernando Antonio Nogueira
See Pessoa, Fernando
Peterkin, Julia Mood 1880-1961 ...... **CLC 31**
See also CA 102; DLB 9
Peters, Joan K(aren) 1945- .... **CLC 39**
See also CA 158; CANR 109
Peters, Robert L(ouis) 1924- .... **CLC 7**
See also CA 13-16R; CAAS 8; CP 1, 5, 6,
7; DLB 105
Peters, S. H.
See Henry, O.
Petofi, Sandor 1823-1849 .... **NCLC 21**
See also RGWL 2, 3
Petrakis, Harry Mark 1923- .... **CLC 3**
See also CA 9-12R; CANR 4, 30, 85, 155;
CN 1, 2, 3, 4, 5, 6, 7
Petrarch 1304-1374 .... **CMLC 20; PC 8**
See also DA3; DAM POET; EW 2; LMFS
1; RGWL 2, 3; WLIT 7
Petrarch, Francesco
See Petrarch
Petronius c. 20-66 .... **CMLC 34**
See also AW 2; CDWLB 1; DLB 211;
RGWL 2, 3; WLIT 8
Petrov, Eugene
See Kataev, Evgeny Petrovich
Petrov, Evgenii
See Kataev, Evgeny Petrovich
Petrov, Evgeny
See Kataev, Evgeny Petrovich
Petrovsky, Boris
See Mansfield, Katherine

Petry, Ann 1908-1997 .. **CLC 1, 7, 18; TCLC 112**
See also AFAW 1, 2; BPFB 3; BW 1, 3;
BYA 2; CA 5-8R; 157; CAAS 6; CANR
4, 46; CLR 12; CN 1, 2, 3, 4, 5, 6; DLB
76; EWL 3; JRDA; LAIT 1; MAICYA 1,
2; MAICYAS 1; MTCW 1; NFS 33;
RGAL 4; SATA 5; SATA-Obit 94; TUS
Petry, Ann Lane
See Petry, Ann
Petursson, Halligrimur 1614-1674 .... **LC 8**
Peychinovich
See Vazov, Ivan (Minchov)
Phaedrus c. 15B.C.-c. 50 .... **CMLC 25**
See also DLB 211
Phelge, Nanker
See Richards, Keith
Phelps (Ward), Elizabeth Stuart
See Phelps, Elizabeth Stuart
Phelps, Elizabeth Stuart
1844-1911 .... **TCLC 113**
See also CA 242; DLB 74; FW
Pheradausi
See Ferdowsi, Abu'l Qasem
Philippe de Remi c. 1247-1296 ... **CMLC 102**
Philips, Katherine 1632-1664 ..... **LC 30, 145; PC 40**
See also DLB 131; RGEL 2
Philipson, Ilene J. 1950- .... **CLC 65**
See also CA 219
Philipson, Morris H. 1926- .... **CLC 53**
See also CA 1-4R; CANR 4
Phillips, Caryl 1958- ..... **BLCS; CLC 96, 224**
See also BRWS 5; BW 2; CA 141; CANR
63, 104, 140, 195; CBD; CD 5, 6; CN 5,
6, 7; DA3; DAM MULT; DLB 157; EWL
3; MTCW 2; MTFW 2005; WLIT 4;
WWE 1
Phillips, David Graham
1867-1911 .... **TCLC 44**
See also CA 108; 176; DLB 9, 12, 303;
RGAL 4
Phillips, Jack
See Sandburg, Carl
Phillips, Jayne Anne 1952- .... **CLC 15, 33, 139; SSC 16**
See also AAYA 57; BPFB 3; CA 101;
CANR 24, 50, 96, 200; CN 4, 5, 6, 7;
CSW; DLBY 1980; INT CANR-24;
MTCW 1, 2; MTFW 2005; RGAL 4;
RGSF 2; SSFS 4
Phillips, Richard
See Dick, Philip K.
Phillips, Robert (Schaeffer) 1938- .... **CLC 28**
See also CA 17-20R; CAAS 13; CANR 8;
DLB 105
Phillips, Ward
See Lovecraft, H. P.
Philo c. 20B.C.-c. 50 .... **CMLC 100**
See also DLB 176
Philostratus, Flavius c. 179-c.
244 .... **CMLC 62**
Phiradausi
See Ferdowsi, Abu'l Qasem
Piccolo, Lucio 1901-1969 .... **CLC 13**
See also CA 97-100; DLB 114; EWL 3
Pickthall, Marjorie L(owry) C(hristie)
1883-1922 .... **TCLC 21**
See also CA 107; DLB 92
Pico della Mirandola, Giovanni
1463-1494 .... **LC 15**
See also LMFS 1
Piercy, Marge 1936- .... **CLC 3, 6, 14, 18, 27, 62, 128; PC 29**
See also BPFB 3; CA 21-24R; 187; CAAE
187; CAAS 1; CANR 13, 43, 66, 111; CN
3, 4, 5, 6, 7; CP 1, 2, 3, 4, 5, 6, 7; CWP;

Queen, Ellery
See Dannay, Frederic; Hoch, Edward D.; Lee, Manfred B.; Marlowe, Stephen; Sturgeon, Theodore (Hamilton); Vance, Jack

Queneau, Raymond 1903-1976 ..... **CLC 2, 5, 10, 42; TCLC 233**
See also CA 77-80; 69-72; CANR 32; DLB 72, 258; EW 12; EWL 3; GFL 1789 to the Present; MTCW 1, 2; RGWL 2, 3

Quevedo, Francisco de 1580-1645 ...... **LC 23, 160**

Quiller-Couch, Sir Arthur (Thomas) 1863-1944 .... **TCLC 53**
See also CA 118; 166; DLB 135, 153, 190; HGG; RGEL 2; SUFW 1

Quin, Ann 1936-1973 .... **CLC 6**
See also CA 9-12R; 45-48; CANR 148; CN 1; DLB 14, 231

Quin, Ann Marie
See Quin, Ann

Quincey, Thomas de
See De Quincey, Thomas

Quindlen, Anna 1953- .... **CLC 191**
See also AAYA 35; AMWS 17; CA 138; CANR 73, 126; DA3; DLB 292; MTCW 2; MTFW 2005

Quinn, Martin
See Smith, Martin Cruz

Quinn, Peter 1947- .... **CLC 91**
See also CA 197; CANR 147

Quinn, Peter A.
See Quinn, Peter

Quinn, Simon
See Smith, Martin Cruz

Quintana, Leroy V. 1944- ...... **HLC 2; PC 36**
See also CA 131; CANR 65, 139; DAM MULT; DLB 82; HW 1, 2

Quintilian c. 40-c. 100 .... **CMLC 77**
See also AW; DLB 211; RGWL 2, 3

Quiroga, Horacio (Sylvestre) 1878-1937 ... **HLC 2; SSC 89; TCLC 20**
See also CA 117; 131; DAM MULT; EWL 3; HW 1; LAW; MTCW 1; RGSF 2; WLIT 1

Quoirez, Francoise 1935-2004 ... **CLC 3, 6, 9, 17, 36**
See also CA 49-52; 231; CANR 6, 39, 73; CWW 2; DLB 83; EWL 3; GFL 1789 to the Present; MTCW 1, 2; MTFW 2005; TWA

Raabe, Wilhelm (Karl) 1831-1910 . **TCLC 45**
See also CA 167; DLB 129

Rabe, David (William) 1940- .. **CLC 4, 8, 33, 200; DC 16**
See also CA 85-88; CABS 3; CAD; CANR 59, 129; CD 5, 6; DAM DRAM; DFS 3, 8, 13; DLB 7, 228; EWL 3; MAL 5

Rabelais, Francois 1494-1553 .... **LC 5, 60; WLC 5**
See also DA; DAB; DAC; DAM MST; DLB 327; EW 2; GFL Beginnings to 1789; LMFS 1; RGWL 2, 3; TWA

Rabi'a al-'Adawiyya c. 717-c. 801 .... **CMLC 83**
See also DLB 311

Rabinovitch, Sholem 1859-1916 .... **SSC 33, 125; TCLC 1, 35**
See also CA 104; DLB 333; TWA

Rabinovitsh, Sholem Yankev
See Rabinovitch, Sholem

Rabinowitz, Sholem Yakov
See Rabinovitch, Sholem

Rabinowitz, Solomon
See Rabinovitch, Sholem

Rabinyan, Dorit 1972- .... **CLC 119**
See also CA 170; CANR 147

Rachilde
See Vallette, Marguerite Eymery; Vallette, Marguerite Eymery

Racine, Jean 1639-1699 .. **DC 32; LC 28, 113**
See also DA3; DAB; DAM MST; DLB 268; EW 3; GFL Beginnings to 1789; LMFS 1; RGWL 2, 3; TWA

Radcliffe, Ann 1764-1823 .. **NCLC 6, 55, 106, 223**
See also BRWR 3; DLB 39, 178; GL 3; HGG; LMFS 1; RGEL 2; SUFW; WLIT 3

Radclyffe-Hall, Marguerite
See Hall, Radclyffe

Radiguet, Raymond 1903-1923 ...... **TCLC 29**
See also CA 162; DLB 65; EWL 3; GFL 1789 to the Present; RGWL 2, 3

Radishchev, Aleksandr Nikolaevich 1749-1802 .... **NCLC 190**
See also DLB 150

Radishchev, Alexander
See Radishchev, Aleksandr Nikolaevich

Radnoti, Miklos 1909-1944 .... **TCLC 16**
See also CA 118; 212; CDWLB 4; DLB 215; EWL 3; RGHL; RGWL 2, 3

Rado, James 1939- .... **CLC 17**
See also CA 105

Radvanyi, Netty 1900-1983 .... **CLC 7**
See also CA 85-88; 110; CANR 82; CD-WLB 2; DLB 69; EWL 3

Rae, Ben
See Griffiths, Trevor

Raeburn, John (Hay) 1941- .... **CLC 34**
See also CA 57-60

Ragni, Gerome 1942-1991 .... **CLC 17**
See also CA 105; 134

Rahv, Philip
See Greenberg, Ivan

Rai, Navab
See Srivastava, Dhanpat Rai

Raimund, Ferdinand Jakob 1790-1836 .... **NCLC 69**
See also DLB 90

Raine, Craig 1944- .... **CLC 32, 103**
See also BRWS 13; CA 108; CANR 29, 51, 103, 171; CP 3, 4, 5, 6, 7; DLB 40; PFS 7

Raine, Craig Anthony
See Raine, Craig

Raine, Kathleen (Jessie) 1908-2003 .. **CLC 7, 45**
See also CA 85-88; 218; CANR 46, 109; CP 1, 2, 3, 4, 5, 6, 7; DLB 20; EWL 3; MTCW 1; RGEL 2

Rainis, Janis 1865-1929 .... **TCLC 29**
See also CA 170; CDWLB 4; DLB 220; EWL 3

Rakosi, Carl
See Rawley, Callman

Ralegh, Sir Walter
See Raleigh, Sir Walter

Raleigh, Richard
See Lovecraft, H. P.

Raleigh, Sir Walter 1554(?)-1618 .... **LC 31, 39; PC 31**
See also BRW 1; CDBLB Before 1660; DLB 172; EXPP; PFS 14; RGEL 2; TEA; WP

Rallentando, H. P.
See Sayers, Dorothy L(eigh)

Ramal, Walter
See de la Mare, Walter (John)

Ramana Maharshi 1879-1950 .... **TCLC 84**

Ramoacn y Cajal, Santiago 1852-1934 .... **TCLC 93**

Ramon, Juan
See Jimenez, Juan Ramon

Ramos, Graciliano 1892-1953 .... **TCLC 32**
See also CA 167; DLB 307; EWL 3; HW 2; LAW; WLIT 1

Rampersad, Arnold 1941- .... **CLC 44**
See also BW 2, 3; CA 127; 133; CANR 81; DLB 111; INT CA-133

Rampling, Anne
See Rice, Anne

Ramsay, Allan 1686(?)-1758 .... **LC 29**
See also DLB 95; RGEL 2

Ramsay, Jay
See Campbell, Ramsey

Ramus, Peter
See La Ramee, Pierre de

Ramus, Petrus
See La Ramee, Pierre de

Ramuz, Charles-Ferdinand 1878-1947 .... **TCLC 33**
See also CA 165; EWL 3

Rand, Ayn 1905-1982 ...... **CLC 3, 30, 44, 79; SSC 116; WLC 5**
See also AAYA 10; AMWS 4; BPFB 3; BYA 12; CA 13-16R; 105; CANR 27, 73; CDALBS; CN 1, 2, 3; CPW; DA; DA3; DAC; DAM MST, NOV, POP; DLB 227, 279; MTCW 1, 2; MTFW 2005; NFS 10, 16, 29; RGAL 4; SFW 4; TUS; YAW

Randall, Dudley 1914-2000 ... **BLC 1:3; CLC 1, 135; PC 86**
See also BW 1, 3; CA 25-28R; 189; CANR 23, 82; CP 1, 2, 3, 4, 5; DAM MULT; DLB 41; PFS 5

Randall, Dudley Felker
See Randall, Dudley

Randall, Robert
See Silverberg, Robert

Ranger, Ken
See Creasey, John

Rank, Otto 1884-1939 .... **TCLC 115**

Rankin, Ian 1960- .... **CLC 257**
See also BRWS 10; CA 148; CANR 81, 137, 171; DLB 267; MTFW 2005

Rankin, Ian James
See Rankin, Ian

Ransom, John Crowe 1888-1974 .. **CLC 2, 4, 5, 11, 24; PC 61**
See also AMW; CA 5-8R; 49-52; CANR 6, 34; CDALBS; CP 1, 2; DA3; DAM POET; DLB 45, 63; EWL 3; EXPP; MAL 5; MTCW 1, 2; MTFW 2005; RGAL 4; TUS

Rao, Raja 1908-2006 . **CLC 25, 56, 255; SSC 99**
See also CA 73-76; 252; CANR 51; CN 1, 2, 3, 4, 5, 6; DAM NOV; DLB 323; EWL 3; MTCW 1, 2; MTFW 2005; RGEL 2; RGSF 2

Raphael, Frederic (Michael) 1931- ... **CLC 2, 14**
See also CA 1-4R; CANR 1, 86; CN 1, 2, 3, 4, 5, 6, 7; DLB 14, 319; TCLE 1:2

Raphael, Lev 1954- .... **CLC 232**
See also CA 134; CANR 72, 145; GLL 1

Ratcliffe, James P.
See Mencken, H. L.

Rathbone, Julian 1935-2008 .... **CLC 41**
See also CA 101; 269; CANR 34, 73, 152

Rathbone, Julian Christopher
See Rathbone, Julian

Rattigan, Terence 1911-1977 . **CLC 7; DC 18**
See also BRWS 7; CA 85-88; 73-76; CBD; CDBLB 1945-1960; DAM DRAM; DFS 8; DLB 13; IDFW 3, 4; MTCW 1, 2; MTFW 2005; RGEL 2

Rattigan, Terence Mervyn
See Rattigan, Terence

Ratushinskaya, Irina 1954- .... **CLC 54**
See also CA 129; CANR 68; CWW 2

CSW; DA3; DAM POP; DLB 292; GL 3; GLL 2; HGG; MTCW 2; MTFW 2005; SUFW 2; YAW

Rice, Elmer (Leopold) 1892-1967 ...... **CLC 7, 49; TCLC 221**
See also CA 21-22; 25-28R; CAP 2; DAM DRAM; DFS 12; DLB 4, 7; EWL 3; IDTP; MAL 5; MTCW 1, 2; RGAL 4

Rice, Tim 1944- .... **CLC 21**
See also CA 103; CANR 46; DFS 7

Rice, Timothy Miles Bindon
See Rice, Tim

Rich, Adrienne 1929- ..... **CLC 3, 6, 7, 11, 18, 36, 73, 76, 125; PC 5**
See also AAYA 69; AMWR 2; AMWS 1; CA 9-12R; CANR 20, 53, 74, 128, 199; CDALBS; CP 1, 2, 3, 4, 5, 6, 7; CSW; CWP; DA3; DAM POET; DLB 5, 67; EWL 3; EXPP; FL 1:6; FW; MAL 5; MBL; MTCW 1, 2; MTFW 2005; PAB; PFS 15, 29; RGAL 4; RGHL; WP

Rich, Adrienne Cecile
See Rich, Adrienne

Rich, Barbara
See Graves, Robert

Rich, Robert
See Trumbo, Dalton

Richard, Keith
See Richards, Keith

Richards, David Adams 1950- .... **CLC 59**
See also CA 93-96; CANR 60, 110, 156; CN 7; DAC; DLB 53; TCLE 1:2

Richards, I(vor) A(rmstrong)
1893-1979 .... **CLC 14, 24**
See also BRWS 2; CA 41-44R; 89-92; CANR 34, 74; CP 1, 2; DLB 27; EWL 3; MTCW 2; RGEL 2

Richards, Keith 1943- .... **CLC 17**
See also CA 107; CANR 77

Richardson, Anne
See Roiphe, Anne

Richardson, Dorothy Miller
1873-1957 .... **TCLC 3, 203**
See also BRWS 13; CA 104; 192; DLB 36; EWL 3; FW; RGEL 2

Richardson, Ethel Florence Lindesay
1870-1946 .... **TCLC 4**
See also CA 105; 190; DLB 197, 230; EWL 3; RGEL 2; RGSF 2; RHW

Richardson, Henrietta
See Richardson, Ethel Florence Lindesay

Richardson, Henry Handel
See Richardson, Ethel Florence Lindesay

Richardson, John 1796-1852 .... **NCLC 55**
See also CCA 1; DAC; DLB 99

Richardson, Samuel 1689-1761 ...... **LC 1, 44, 138; WLC 5**
See also BRW 3; CDBLB 1660-1789; DA; DAB; DAC; DAM MST, NOV; DLB 39; RGEL 2; TEA; WLIT 3

Richardson, Willis 1889-1977 .... **HR 1:3**
See also BW 1; CA 124; DLB 51; SATA 60

Richardson Robertson, Ethel Florence Lindesay
See Richardson, Ethel Florence Lindesay

Richler, Mordecai 1931-2001 .... **CLC 3, 5, 9, 13, 18, 46, 70, 185, 271**
See also AITN 1; CA 65-68; 201; CANR 31, 62, 111; CCA 1; CLR 17; CN 1, 2, 3, 4, 5, 7; CWRI 5; DAC; DAM MST, NOV; DLB 53; EWL 3; MAICYA 1, 2; MTCW 1, 2; MTFW 2005; RGEL 2; RGHL; SATA 44, 98; SATA-Brief 27; TWA

Richter, Conrad (Michael)
1890-1968 .... **CLC 30**
See also AAYA 21; AMWS 18; BYA 2; CA 5-8R; 25-28R; CANR 23; DLB 9, 212;

LAIT 1; MAL 5; MTCW 1, 2; MTFW 2005; RGAL 4; SATA 3; TCWW 1, 2; TUS; YAW

Ricostranza, Tom
See Ellis, Trey

Riddell, Charlotte 1832-1906 .... **TCLC 40**
See also CA 165; DLB 156; HGG; SUFW

Riddell, Mrs. J. H.
See Riddell, Charlotte

Ridge, John Rollin 1827-1867 ...... **NCLC 82; NNAL**
See also CA 144; DAM MULT; DLB 175

Ridgeway, Jason
See Marlowe, Stephen

Ridgway, Keith 1965- .... **CLC 119**
See also CA 172; CANR 144

Riding, Laura
See Jackson, Laura

Riefenstahl, Berta Helene Amalia
1902-2003 .... **CLC 16, 190**
See also CA 108; 220

Riefenstahl, Leni
See Riefenstahl, Berta Helene Amalia

Riffe, Ernest
See Bergman, Ingmar

Riffe, Ernest Ingmar
See Bergman, Ingmar

Riggs, (Rolla) Lynn
1899-1954 .... **NNAL; TCLC 56**
See also CA 144; DAM MULT; DLB 175

Riis, Jacob A(ugust) 1849-1914 ..... **TCLC 80**
See also CA 113; 168; DLB 23

Rikki
See Ducornet, Erica

Riley, James Whitcomb 1849-1916 .... **PC 48; TCLC 51**
See also CA 118; 137; DAM POET; MAI-CYA 1, 2; RGAL 4; SATA 17

Riley, Tex
See Creasey, John

Rilke, Rainer Maria 1875-1926 .... **PC 2; TCLC 1, 6, 19, 195**
See also CA 104; 132; CANR 62, 99; CD-WLB 2; DA3; DAM POET; DLB 81; EW 9; EWL 3; MTCW 1, 2; MTFW 2005; PFS 19, 27; RGWL 2, 3; TWA; WP

Rimbaud, Arthur 1854-1891 ..... **NCLC 4, 35, 82, 227; PC 3, 57; WLC 5**
See also DA; DA3; DAB; DAC; DAM MST, POET; DLB 217; EW 7; GFL 1789 to the Present; LMFS 2; PFS 28; RGWL 2, 3; TWA; WP

Rimbaud, Jean Nicholas Arthur
See Rimbaud, Arthur

Rinehart, Mary Roberts
1876-1958 .... **TCLC 52**
See also BPFB 3; CA 108; 166; RGAL 4; RHW

Ringmaster, The
See Mencken, H. L.

Ringwood, Gwen(dolyn Margaret) Pharis
1910-1984 .... **CLC 48**
See also CA 148; 112; DLB 88

Rio, Michel 1945(?)- .... **CLC 43**
See also CA 201

Rios, Alberto 1952- .... **PC 57**
See also AAYA 66; AMWS 4; CA 113; CANR 34, 79, 137; CP 6, 7; DLB 122; HW 2; MTFW 2005; PFS 11

Rios, Alberto Alvaro
See Rios, Alberto

Ritsos, Giannes
See Ritsos, Yannis

Ritsos, Yannis 1909-1990 .... **CLC 6, 13, 31**
See also CA 77-80; 133; CANR 39, 61; EW 12; EWL 3; MTCW 1; RGWL 2, 3

Ritter, Erika 1948(?)- .... **CLC 52**
See also CD 5, 6; CWD

Rivera, Jose Eustasio 1889-1928 ... **TCLC 35**
See also CA 162; EWL 3; HW 1, 2; LAW

Rivera, Tomas 1935-1984 .... **HLCS 2**
See also CA 49-52; CANR 32; DLB 82; HW 1; LLW; RGAL 4; SSFS 15; TCWW 2; WLIT 1

Rivers, Conrad Kent 1933-1968 .... **CLC 1**
See also BW 1; CA 85-88; DLB 41

Rivers, Elfrida
See Bradley, Marion Zimmer

Riverside, John
See Heinlein, Robert A.

Rizal, Jose 1861-1896 .... **NCLC 27**
See also DLB 348

Roa Bastos, Augusto 1917-2005 ...... **CLC 45; HLC 2**
See also CA 131; 238; CWW 2; DAM MULT; DLB 113; EWL 3; HW 1; LAW; RGSF 2; WLIT 1

Roa Bastos, Augusto Jose Antonio
See Roa Bastos, Augusto

Robbe-Grillet, Alain 1922-2008 ..... **CLC 1, 2, 4, 6, 8, 10, 14, 43, 128, 287**
See also BPFB 3; CA 9-12R; 269; CANR 33, 65, 115; CWW 2; DLB 83; EW 13; EWL 3; GFL 1789 to the Present; IDFW 3, 4; MTCW 1, 2; MTFW 2005; RGWL 2, 3; SSFS 15

Robbins, Harold 1916-1997 .... **CLC 5**
See also BPFB 3; CA 73-76; 162; CANR 26, 54, 112, 156; DA3; DAM NOV; MTCW 1, 2

Robbins, Thomas Eugene 1936- . **CLC 9, 32, 64**
See also AAYA 32; AMWS 10; BEST 90:3; BPFB 3; CA 81-84; CANR 29, 59, 95, 139; CN 3, 4, 5, 6, 7; CPW; CSW; DA3; DAM NOV, POP; DLBY 1980; MTCW 1, 2; MTFW 2005

Robbins, Tom
See Robbins, Thomas Eugene

Robbins, Trina 1938- .... **CLC 21**
See also AAYA 61; CA 128; CANR 152

Robert de Boron fl. 12th cent. - .... **CMLC 94**

Roberts, Charles G(eorge) D(ouglas)
1860-1943 .... **SSC 91; TCLC 8**
See also CA 105; 188; CLR 33; CWRI 5; DLB 92; RGEL 2; RGSF 2; SATA 88; SATA-Brief 29

Roberts, Elizabeth Madox
1886-1941 .... **TCLC 68**
See also CA 111; 166; CLR 100; CWRI 5; DLB 9, 54, 102; RGAL 4; RHW; SATA 33; SATA-Brief 27; TCWW 2; WCH

Roberts, Kate 1891-1985 .... **CLC 15**
See also CA 107; 116; DLB 319

Roberts, Keith (John Kingston)
1935-2000 .... **CLC 14**
See also BRWS 10; CA 25-28R; CANR 46; DLB 261; SFW 4

Roberts, Kenneth (Lewis)
1885-1957 .... **TCLC 23**
See also CA 109; 199; DLB 9; MAL 5; RGAL 4; RHW

Roberts, Michele 1949- .... **CLC 48, 178**
See also BRWS 15; CA 115; CANR 58, 120, 164, 200; CN 6, 7; DLB 231; FW

Roberts, Michele Brigitte
See Roberts, Michele

Robertson, Ellis
See Ellison, Harlan; Silverberg, Robert

Robertson, Thomas William
1829-1871 .... **NCLC 35**
See also DAM DRAM; DLB 344; RGEL 2

Robertson, Tom
See Robertson, Thomas William

Robeson, Kenneth
See Dent, Lester

Rostand, Edmond 1868-1918 . DC 10; TCLC 6, 37
See also CA 104; 126; DA; DA3; DAB; DAC; DAM DRAM, MST; DFS 1; DLB 192; LAIT 1; MTCW 1; RGWL 2, 3; TWA

Rostand, Edmond Eugene Alexis
See Rostand, Edmond

Roth, Henry 1906-1995 ... CLC 2, 6, 11, 104; SSC 134
See also AMWS 9; CA 11-12; 149; CANR 38, 63; CAP 1; CN 1, 2, 3, 4, 5, 6; DA3; DLB 28; EWL 3; MAL 5; MTCW 1, 2; MTFW 2005; RGAL 4

Roth, (Moses) Joseph 1894-1939 ... TCLC 33
See also CA 160; DLB 85; EWL 3; RGWL 2, 3

Roth, Philip 1933- ... CLC 1, 2, 3, 4, 6, 9, 15, 22, 31, 47, 66, 86, 119, 201; SSC 26, 102; WLC 5
See also AAYA 67; AMWR 2; AMWS 3; BEST 90:3; BPFB 3; CA 1-4R; CANR 1, 22, 36, 55, 89, 132, 170; CDALB 1968-1988; CN 3, 4, 5, 6, 7; CPW 1; DA; DA3; DAB; DAC; DAM MST, NOV, POP; DLB 2, 28, 173; DLBY 1982; EWL 3; MAL 5; MTCW 1, 2; MTFW 2005; NFS 25; RGAL 4; RGHL; RGSF 2; SSFS 12, 18; TUS

Roth, Philip Milton
See Roth, Philip

Rothenberg, Jerome 1931- ... CLC 6, 57
See also CA 45-48; CANR 1, 106; CP 1, 2, 3, 4, 5, 6, 7; DLB 5, 193

Rotter, Pat ... CLC 65

Roumain, Jacques 1907-1944 ... BLC 1:3; TCLC 19
See also BW 1; CA 117; 125; DAM MULT; EWL 3

Roumain, Jacques Jean Baptiste
See Roumain, Jacques

Rourke, Constance Mayfield 1885-1941 ... TCLC 12
See also CA 107; 200; MAL 5; YABC 1

Rousseau, Jean-Baptiste 1671-1741 ... LC 9

Rousseau, Jean-Jacques 1712-1778 .... LC 14, 36, 122; WLC 5
See also DA; DA3; DAB; DAC; DAM MST; DLB 314; EW 4; GFL Beginnings to 1789; LMFS 1; RGWL 2, 3; TWA

Roussel, Raymond 1877-1933 ... TCLC 20
See also CA 117; 201; EWL 3; GFL 1789 to the Present

Rovit, Earl (Herbert) 1927- ... CLC 7
See also CA 5-8R; CANR 12

Rowe, Elizabeth Singer 1674-1737 ... LC 44
See also DLB 39, 95

Rowe, Nicholas 1674-1718 ... LC 8
See also DLB 84; RGEL 2

Rowlandson, Mary 1637(?)-1678 ... LC 66
See also DLB 24, 200; RGAL 4

Rowley, Ames Dorrance
See Lovecraft, H. P.

Rowley, William 1585(?)-1626 ... LC 100, 123
See also DFS 22; DLB 58; RGEL 2

Rowling, J.K. 1965- ... CLC 137, 217
See also AAYA 34, 82; BRWS 16; BYA 11, 13, 14; CA 173; CANR 128, 157; CLR 66, 80, 112; LNFS 1, 2, 3; MAICYA 2; MTFW 2005; SATA 109, 174; SUFW 2

Rowling, Joanne Kathleen
See Rowling, J.K.

Rowson, Susanna Haswell 1762(?)-1824 ... NCLC 5, 69, 182
See also AMWS 15; DLB 37, 200; RGAL 4

Roy, Arundhati 1960(?)- ... CLC 109, 210
See also CA 163; CANR 90, 126; CN 7; DLB 323, 326; DLBY 1997; EWL 3; LATS 1:2; MTFW 2005; NFS 22; WWE 1

Roy, Gabrielle 1909-1983 ... CLC 10, 14
See also CA 53-56; 110; CANR 5, 61; CCA 1; DAB; DAC; DAM MST; DLB 68; EWL 3; MTCW 1; RGWL 2, 3; SATA 104; TCLE 1:2

Royko, Mike 1932-1997 ... CLC 109
See also CA 89-92; 157; CANR 26, 111; CPW

Rozanov, Vasilii Vasil'evich
See Rozanov, Vassili

Rozanov, Vasily Vasilyevich
See Rozanov, Vassili

Rozanov, Vassili 1856-1919 ... TCLC 104
See also DLB 295; EWL 3

Rozewicz, Tadeusz 1921- ... CLC 9, 23, 139
See also CA 108; CANR 36, 66; CWW 2; DA3; DAM POET; DLB 232; EWL 3; MTCW 1, 2; MTFW 2005; RGHL; RGWL 3

Ruark, Gibbons 1941- ... CLC 3
See also CA 33-36R; CAAS 23; CANR 14, 31, 57; DLB 120

Rubens, Bernice (Ruth) 1923-2004 . CLC 19, 31
See also CA 25-28R; 232; CANR 33, 65, 128; CN 1, 2, 3, 4, 5, 6, 7; DLB 14, 207, 326; MTCW 1

Rubin, Harold
See Robbins, Harold

Rudkin, (James) David 1936- ... CLC 14
See also CA 89-92; CBD; CD 5, 6; DLB 13

Rudnik, Raphael 1933- ... CLC 7
See also CA 29-32R

Ruffian, M.
See Hasek, Jaroslav

Rufinus c. 345-410 ... CMLC 111

Ruiz, Jose Martinez
See Martinez Ruiz, Jose

Ruiz, Juan c. 1283-c. 1350 ... CMLC 66

Rukeyser, Muriel 1913-1980 . CLC 6, 10, 15, 27; PC 12
See also AMWS 6; CA 5-8R; 93-96; CANR 26, 60; CP 1, 2, 3; DA3; DAM POET; DLB 48; EWL 3; FW; GLL 2; MAL 5; MTCW 1, 2; PFS 10, 29; RGAL 4; SATA-Obit 22

Rule, Jane 1931-2007 ... CLC 27, 265
See also CA 25-28R; 266; CAAS 18; CANR 12, 87; CN 4, 5, 6, 7; DLB 60; FW

Rule, Jane Vance
See Rule, Jane

Rulfo, Juan 1918-1986 .. CLC 8, 80; HLC 2; SSC 25
See also CA 85-88; 118; CANR 26; CD-WLB 3; DAM MULT; DLB 113; EWL 3; HW 1, 2; LAW; MTCW 1, 2; RGSF 2; RGWL 2, 3; WLIT 1

Rumi
See Rumi, Jalal al-Din

Rumi, Jalal al-Din 1207-1273 ... CMLC 20; PC 45
See also AAYA 64; RGWL 2, 3; WLIT 6; WP

Runeberg, Johan 1804-1877 ... NCLC 41

Runyon, (Alfred) Damon 1884(?)-1946 ... TCLC 10
See also CA 107; 165; DLB 11, 86, 171; MAL 5; MTCW 2; RGAL 4

Rush, Norman 1933- ... CLC 44
See also CA 121; 126; CANR 130; INT CA-126

Rushdie, Ahmed Salman
See Rushdie, Salman

Rushdie, Salman 1947- ... CLC 23, 31, 55, 100, 191, 272; SSC 83; WLCS
See also AAYA 65; BEST 89:3; BPFB 3; BRWS 4; CA 108; 111; CANR 33, 56, 108, 133, 192; CLR 125; CN 4, 5, 6, 7; CPW 1; DA3; DAB; DAM MST, NOV, POP; DLB 194, 323, 326; EWL 3; FANT; INT CA-111; LATS 1:2; LMFS 2; MTCW 1, 2; MTFW 2005; NFS 22, 23; RGEL 2; RGSF 2; TEA; WLIT 4

Rushforth, Peter 1945-2005 ... CLC 19
See also CA 101; 243

Rushforth, Peter Scott
See Rushforth, Peter

Ruskin, John 1819-1900 ... TCLC 63
See also BRW 5; BYA 5; CA 114; 129; CD-BLB 1832-1890; DLB 55, 163, 190; RGEL 2; SATA 24; TEA; WCH

Russ, Joanna 1937- ... CLC 15
See also BPFB 3; CA 25-28; CANR 11, 31, 65; CN 4, 5, 6, 7; DLB 8; FW; GLL 1; MTCW 1; SCFW 1, 2; SFW 4

Russ, Richard Patrick
See O'Brian, Patrick

Russell, George William 1867-1935 ... TCLC 3, 10
See also BRWS 8; CA 104; 153; CDBLB 1890-1914; DAM POET; DLB 19; EWL 3; RGEL 2

Russell, Jeffrey Burton 1934- ... CLC 70
See also CA 25-28R; CANR 11, 28, 52, 179

Russell, (Henry) Ken(neth Alfred) 1927- ... CLC 16
See also CA 105

Russell, William Martin 1947- ... CLC 60
See also CA 164; CANR 107; CBD; CD 5, 6; DLB 233

Russell, Willy
See Russell, William Martin

Russo, Richard 1949- ... CLC 181
See also AMWS 12; CA 127; 133; CANR 87, 114, 194; NFS 25

Rutebeuf fl. c. 1249-1277 ... CMLC 104
See also DLB 208

Rutherford, Mark
See White, William Hale

Ruysbroeck, Jan van 1293-1381 ... CMLC 85

Ruyslinck, Ward
See Belser, Reimond Karel Maria de

Ryan, Cornelius (John) 1920-1974 ... CLC 7
See also CA 69-72; 53-56; CANR 38

Ryan, Michael 1946- ... CLC 65
See also CA 49-52; CANR 109, 203; DLBY 1982

Ryan, Tim
See Dent, Lester

Rybakov, Anatoli (Naumovich) 1911-1998 ... CLC 23, 53
See also CA 126; 135; 172; DLB 302; RGHL; SATA 79; SATA-Obit 108

Rybakov, Anatolii (Naumovich)
See Rybakov, Anatoli (Naumovich)

Ryder, Jonathan
See Ludlum, Robert

Ryga, George 1932-1987 ... CLC 14
See also CA 101; 124; CANR 43, 90; CCA 1; DAC; DAM MST; DLB 60

Rymer, Thomas 1643(?)-1713 ... LC 132
See also DLB 101, 336

S. H.
See Hartmann, Sadakichi

S. L. C.
See Twain, Mark

S. S.
See Sassoon, Siegfried

Sa'adawi, al- Nawal
See El Saadawi, Nawal

Saadawi, Nawal El
See El Saadawi, Nawal

Saadiah Gaon 882-942 .... **CMLC 97**

Saba, Umberto 1883-1957 .... **TCLC 33**
See also CA 144; CANR 79; DLB 114;
EWL 3; RGWL 2, 3

Sabatini, Rafael 1875-1950 .... **TCLC 47**
See also BPFB 3; CA 162; RHW

Sabato, Ernesto 1911- ... **CLC 10, 23; HLC 2**
See also CA 97-100; CANR 32, 65; CD-
WLB 3; CWW 2; DAM MULT; DLB 145;
EWL 3; HW 1, 2; LAW; MTCW 1, 2;
MTFW 2005

Sa-Carneiro, Mario de 1890-1916 . **TCLC 83**
See also DLB 287; EWL 3

Sacastru, Martin
See Bioy Casares, Adolfo

Sacher-Masoch, Leopold von
1836(?)-1895 .... **NCLC 31**

Sachs, Hans 1494-1576 .... **LC 95**
See also CDWLB 2; DLB 179; RGWL 2, 3

Sachs, Marilyn 1927- .... **CLC 35**
See also AAYA 2; BYA 6; CA 17-20R;
CANR 13, 47, 150; CLR 2; JRDA; MAI-
CYA 1, 2; SAAS 2; SATA 3, 68, 164;
SATA-Essay 110; WYA; YAW

Sachs, Marilyn Stickle
See Sachs, Marilyn

Sachs, Nelly 1891-1970 .. **CLC 14, 98; PC 78**
See also CA 17-18; 25-28R; CANR 87;
CAP 2; DLB 332; EWL 3; MTCW 2;
MTFW 2005; PFS 20; RGHL; RGWL 2,
3

Sackler, Howard (Oliver)
1929-1982 .... **CLC 14**
See also CA 61-64; 108; CAD; CANR 30;
DFS 15; DLB 7

Sacks, Oliver 1933- .... **CLC 67, 202**
See also CA 53-56; CANR 28, 50, 76, 146,
187; CPW; DA3; INT CANR-28; MTCW
1, 2; MTFW 2005

Sacks, Oliver Wolf
See Sacks, Oliver

Sackville, Thomas 1536-1608 .... **LC 98**
See also DAM DRAM; DLB 62, 132;
RGEL 2

Sadakichi
See Hartmann, Sadakichi

Sa'dawi, Nawal al-
See El Saadawi, Nawal

Sade, Donatien Alphonse Francois
1740-1814 .... **NCLC 3, 47**
See also DLB 314; EW 4; GFL Beginnings
to 1789; RGWL 2, 3

Sade, Marquis de
See Sade, Donatien Alphonse Francois

Sadoff, Ira 1945- .... **CLC 9**
See also CA 53-56; CANR 5, 21, 109; DLB
120

Saetone
See Camus, Albert

Safire, William 1929-2009 .... **CLC 10**
See also CA 17-20R; 290; CANR 31, 54,
91, 148

Safire, William L.
See Safire, William

Safire, William Lewis
See Safire, William

Sagan, Carl 1934-1996 .... **CLC 30, 112**
See also AAYA 2, 62; CA 25-28R; 155;
CANR 11, 36, 74; CPW; DA3; MTCW 1,
2; MTFW 2005; SATA 58; SATA-Obit 94

Sagan, Francoise
See Quoirez, Francoise

Sahgal, Nayantara (Pandit) 1927- .... **CLC 41**
See also CA 9-12R; CANR 11, 88; CN 1,
2, 3, 4, 5, 6, 7; DLB 323

Said, Edward W. 1935-2003 .... **CLC 123**
See also CA 21-24R; 220; CANR 45, 74,
107, 131; DLB 67, 346; MTCW 2; MTFW
2005

Saikaku, Ihara 1642-1693 .... **LC 141**
See also RGWL 3

Saikaku Ihara
See Saikaku, Ihara

Saint, H(arry) F. 1941- .... **CLC 50**
See also CA 127

St. Aubin de Teran, Lisa 1953- .... **CLC 36**
See also CA 118; 126; CN 6, 7; INT CA-
126

Saint Birgitta of Sweden c.
1303-1373 .... **CMLC 24**

St. E. A. of M. and S
See Crowley, Edward Alexander

Sainte-Beuve, Charles Augustin
1804-1869 .... **NCLC 5; PC 110**
See also DLB 217; EW 6; GFL 1789 to the
Present

Saint-Exupery, Antoine de
1900-1944 .... **TCLC 2, 56, 169; WLC**
See also AAYA 63; BPFB 3; BYA 3; CA
108; 132; CLR 10, 142; DA3; DAM
NOV; DLB 72; EW 12; EWL 3; GFL
1789 to the Present; LAIT 3; MAICYA 1,
2; MTCW 1, 2; MTFW 2005; NFS 30;
RGWL 2, 3; SATA 20; TWA

Saint-Exupery, Antoine Jean Baptiste Marie
Roger de
See Saint-Exupery, Antoine de

St. John, David
See Hunt, E. Howard

St. John, Henry 1678-1751 .... **LC 178**
See also DLB 101, 336

St. John, J. Hector
See Crevecoeur, J. Hector St. John de

Saint-John Perse
See Leger, Alexis Saint-Leger

Saintsbury, George (Edward Bateman)
1845-1933 .... **TCLC 31**
See also CA 160; DLB 57, 149

Sait Faik
See Abasiyanik, Sait Faik

Saki 1870-1916 .... **SSC 12, 115; TCLC 3;**
WLC 5
See also AAYA 56; BRWS 6; BYA 11; CA
104; 130; CANR 104; CDBLB 1890-
1914; DA; DA3; DAB; DAC; DAM MST,
NOV; DLB 34, 162; EXPS; LAIT 2;
MTCW 1, 2; MTFW 2005; RGEL 2;
SSFS 1, 15; SUFW

Sala, George Augustus 1828-1895 . **NCLC 46**

Saladin 1138-1193 .... **CMLC 38**

Salama, Hannu 1936- .... **CLC 18**
See also CA 244; EWL 3

Salamanca, J(ack) R(ichard) 1922- .. **CLC 4,**
15
See also CA 25-28R, 193; CAAE 193

Salas, Floyd Francis 1931- .... **HLC 2**
See also CA 119; CAAS 27; CANR 44, 75,
93; DAM MULT; DLB 82; HW 1, 2;
MTCW 2; MTFW 2005

Sale, J. Kirkpatrick
See Sale, Kirkpatrick

Sale, John Kirkpatrick
See Sale, Kirkpatrick

Sale, Kirkpatrick 1937- .... **CLC 68**
See also CA 13-16R; CANR 10, 147

Salinas, Luis Omar 1937- ... **CLC 90; HLC 2**
See also AMWS 13; CA 131; CANR 81,
153; DAM MULT; DLB 82; HW 1, 2

Salinas (y Serrano), Pedro
1891(?)-1951 .... **TCLC 17, 212**
See also CA 117; DLB 134; EWL 3

Salinger, J.D. 1919-2010 ...... **CLC 1, 3, 8, 12,**
55, 56, 138, 243; SSC 2, 28, 65; WLC 5
See also AAYA 2, 36; AMW; AMWC 1;
BPFB 3; CA 5-8R; CANR 39, 129;
CDALB 1941-1968; CLR 18; CN 1, 2, 3,
4, 5, 6, 7; CPW 1; DA; DA3; DAB; DAC;
DAM MST, NOV, POP; DLB 2, 102, 173;
EWL 3; EXPN; LAIT 4; MAICYA 1, 2;
MAL 5; MTCW 1, 2; MTFW 2005; NFS
1, 30; RGAL 4; RGSF 2; SATA 67; SSFS
17; TUS; WYA; YAW

Salinger, Jerome David
See Salinger, J.D.

Salisbury, John
See Caute, (John) David

Sallust c. 86B.C.-35B.C. .... **CMLC 68**
See also AW 2; CDWLB 1; DLB 211;
RGWL 2, 3

Salter, James 1925- .... **CLC 7, 52, 59, 275;**
SSC 58
See also AMWS 9; CA 73-76; CANR 107,
160; DLB 130; SSFS 25

Saltus, Edgar (Everton) 1855-1921 . **TCLC 8**
See also CA 105; DLB 202; RGAL 4

Saltykov, Mikhail Evgrafovich
1826-1889 .... **NCLC 16**
See also DLB 238:

Saltykov-Shchedrin, N.
See Saltykov, Mikhail Evgrafovich

Samarakis, Andonis
See Samarakis, Antonis

Samarakis, Antonis 1919-2003 .... **CLC 5**
See also CA 25-28R; 224; CAAS 16; CANR
36; EWL 3

Samigli, E.
See Schmitz, Aron Hector

Sanchez, Florencio 1875-1910 .... **TCLC 37**
See also CA 153; DLB 305; EWL 3; HW 1;
LAW

Sanchez, Luis Rafael 1936- .... **CLC 23**
See also CA 128; DLB 305; EWL 3; HW 1;
WLIT 1

Sanchez, Sonia 1934- . **BLC 1:3, 2:3; CLC 5,**
116, 215; PC 9
See also BW 2, 3; CA 33-36R; CANR 24,
49, 74, 115; CLR 18; CP 2, 3, 4, 5, 6, 7;
CSW; CWP; DA3; DAM MULT; DLB 41;
DLBD 8; EWL 3; MAICYA 1, 2; MAL 5;
MTCW 1, 2; MTFW 2005; PFS 26; SATA
22, 136; WP

Sancho, Ignatius 1729-1780 .... **LC 84**

Sand, George 1804-1876 .... **DC 29; NCLC 2,**
42, 57, 174; WLC 5
See also DA; DA3; DAB; DAC; DAM
MST, NOV; DLB 119, 192; EW 6; FL 1:3;
FW; GFL 1789 to the Present; RGWL 2,
3; TWA

Sandburg, Carl 1878-1967 ...... **CLC 1, 4, 10,**
15, 35; PC 2, 41; WLC 5
See also AAYA 24; AMW; BYA 1, 3; CA
5-8R; 25-28R; CANR 35; CDALB 1865-
1917; CLR 67; DA; DA3; DAB; DAC;
DAM MST, POET; DLB 17, 54, 284;
EWL 3; EXPP; LAIT 2; MAICYA 1, 2;
MAL 5; MTCW 1, 2; MTFW 2005; PAB;
PFS 3, 6, 12, 33; RGAL 4; SATA 8; TUS;
WCH; WP; WYA

Sandburg, Carl August
See Sandburg, Carl

Sandburg, Charles
See Sandburg, Carl

Sandburg, Charles A.
See Sandburg, Carl

Sanders, Ed 1939- .... **CLC 53**
See also BG 1:3; CA 13-16R; CAAS 21;
CANR 13, 44, 78; CP 1, 2, 3, 4, 5, 6, 7;
DAM POET; DLB 16, 244

Sanders, Edward
See Sanders, Ed

Sanders, James Edward
See Sanders, Ed

Sanders, Lawrence 1920-1998 .... **CLC 41**
See also BEST 89:4; BPFB 3; CA 81-84;
165; CANR 33, 62; CMW 4; CPW; DA3;
DAM POP; MTCW 1

Shaw, George Bernard 1856-1950 ..... DC 23;
TCLC 3, 9, 21, 45, 205; WLC 5
See also AAYA 61; BRW 6; BRWC 1;
BRWR 2; CA 104; 128; CDBLB 1914-
1945; DA; DA3; DAB; DAC; DAM
DRAM, MST; DFS 1, 3, 6, 11, 19, 22;
DLB 10, 57, 190, 332; EWL 3; LAIT 3;
LATS 1:1; MTCW 1, 2; MTFW 2005;
RGEL 2; TEA; WLIT 4
Shaw, Henry Wheeler 1818-1885 .. NCLC 15
See also DLB 11; RGAL 4
Shaw, Irwin 1913-1984 .... CLC 7, 23, 34
See also AITN 1; BPFB 3; CA 13-16R; 112;
CANR 21; CDALB 1941-1968; CN 1, 2,
3; CPW; DAM DRAM, POP; DLB 6,
102; DLBY 1984; MAL 5; MTCW 1, 21;
MTFW 2005
Shaw, Robert (Archibald)
1927-1978 .... CLC 5
See also AITN 1; CA 1-4R; 81-84; CANR
4; CN 1, 2; DLB 13, 14
Shaw, T. E.
See Lawrence, T. E.
Shawn, Wallace 1943- .... CLC 41
See also CA 112; CAD; CD 5, 6; DLB 266
Shaykh, al- Hanan
See al-Shaykh, Hanan
Shchedrin, N.
See Saltykov, Mikhail Evgrafovich
Shea, Lisa 1953- .... CLC 86
See also CA 147
Sheed, Wilfrid 1930- .... CLC 2, 4, 10, 53
See also CA 65-68; CANR 30, 66, 181; CN
1, 2, 3, 4, 5, 6, 7; DLB 6; MAL 5; MTCW
1, 2; MTFW 2005
Sheed, Wilfrid John Joseph
See Sheed, Wilfrid
Sheehy, Gail 1937- .... CLC 171
See also CA 49-52; CANR 1, 33, 55, 92;
CPW; MTCW 1
Sheldon, Alice Hastings Bradley
1915(?)-1987 .... CLC 48, 50
See also CA 108; 122; CANR 34; DLB 8;
INT CA-108; MTCW 1; SCFW 1, 2; SFW
4
Sheldon, John
See Bloch, Robert (Albert)
Sheldon, Raccoona
See Sheldon, Alice Hastings Bradley
Shelley, Mary
See Shelley, Mary Wollstonecraft
Shelley, Mary Wollstonecraft
1797-1851 .... NCLC 14, 59, 103, 170;
SSC 92; WLC 5
See also AAYA 20; BPFB 3; BRW 3;
BRWC 2; BRWR 3; BRWS 3; BYA 5;
CDBLB 1789-1832; CLR 133; DA; DA3;
DAB; DAC; DAM MST, NOV; DLB 110,
116, 159, 178; EXPN; FL 1:3; GL 3;
HGG; LAIT 1; LMFS 1, 2; NFS 1; RGEL
2; SATA 29; SCFW 1, 2; SFW 4; TEA;
WLIT 3
Shelley, Percy Bysshe 1792-1822 .. NCLC 18,
93, 143, 175; PC 14, 67; WLC 5
See also AAYA 61; BRW 4; BRWR 1; CD-
BLB 1789-1832; DA; DA3; DAB; DAC;
DAM MST, POET; DLB 96, 110, 158;
EXPP; LMFS 1; PAB; PFS 2, 27, 32;
RGEL 2; TEA; WLIT 3; WP
Shepard, James R.
See Shepard, Jim
Shepard, Jim 1956- .... CLC 36
See also AAYA 73; CA 137; CANR 59, 104,
160, 199; SATA 90, 164
Shepard, Lucius 1947- .... CLC 34
See also CA 128; 141; CANR 81, 124, 178;
HGG; SCFW 2; SFW 4; SUFW 2

Shepard, Sam 1943- .... CLC 4, 6, 17, 34, 41,
44, 169; DC 5
See also AAYA 1, 58; AMWS 3; CA 69-72;
CABS 3; CAD; CANR 22, 120, 140; CD
5, 6; DA3; DAM DRAM; DFS 3, 6, 7,
14; DLB 7, 212, 341; EWL 3; IDFW 3, 4;
MAL 5; MTCW 1, 2; MTFW 2005;
RGAL 4
Shepherd, Jean (Parker)
1921-1999 .... TCLC 177
See also AAYA 69; AITN 2; CA 77-80; 187
Shepherd, Michael
See Ludlum, Robert
Sherburne, Zoa (Lillian Morin)
1912-1995 .... CLC 30
See also AAYA 13; CA 1-4R; 176; CANR
3, 37; MAICYA 1, 2; SAAS 18; SATA 3;
YAW
Sheridan, Frances 1724-1766 .... LC 7
See also DLB 39, 84
Sheridan, Richard Brinsley
1751-1816 . DC 1; NCLC 5, 91; WLC 5
See also BRW 3; CDBLB 1660-1789; DA;
DAB; DAC; DAM DRAM, MST; DFS
15; DLB 89; WLIT 3
Sherman, Jonathan Marc 1968- .... CLC 55
See also CA 230
Sherman, Martin 1941(?)- .... CLC 19
See also CA 116; 123; CAD; CANR 86;
CD 5, 6; DFS 20; DLB 228; GLL 1;
IDTP; RGHL
Sherwin, Judith Johnson
See Johnson, Judith
Sherwood, Frances 1940- .... CLC 81
See also CA 146, 220; CAAE 220; CANR
158
Sherwood, Robert E(mmet)
1896-1955 .... DC 36; TCLC 3
See also CA 104; 153; CANR 86; DAM
DRAM; DFS 11, 15, 17; DLB 7, 26, 249;
IDFW 3, 4; MAL 5; RGAL 4
Shestov, Lev 1866-1938 .... TCLC 56
Shevchenko, Taras 1814-1861 .... NCLC 54
Shiel, M. P. 1865-1947 .... TCLC 8
See also CA 106; 160; DLB 153; HGG;
MTCW 2; MTFW 2005; SCFW 1, 2;
SFW 4; SUFW
Shiel, Matthew Phipps
See Shiel, M. P.
Shields, Carol 1935-2003 . CLC 91, 113, 193;
SSC 126
See also AMWS 7; CA 81-84; 218; CANR
51, 74, 98, 133; CCA 1; CN 6, 7; CPW;
DA3; DAC; DLB 334, 350; MTCW 2;
MTFW 2005; NFS 23
Shields, David 1956- .... CLC 97
See also CA 124; CANR 48, 99, 112, 157
Shields, David Jonathan
See Shields, David
Shiga, Naoya 1883-1971 .... CLC 33; SSC 23;
TCLC 172
See also CA 101; 33-36R; DLB 180; EWL
3; MJW; RGWL 3
Shiga Naoya
See Shiga, Naoya
Shilts, Randy 1951-1994 .... CLC 85
See also AAYA 19; CA 115; 127; 144;
CANR 45; DA3; GLL 1; INT CA-127;
MTCW 2; MTFW 2005
Shimazaki, Haruki 1872-1943 .... TCLC 5
See also CA 105; 134; CANR 84; DLB 180;
EWL 3; MJW; RGWL 3
Shimazaki Toson
See Shimazaki, Haruki
Shirley, James 1596-1666 .... DC 25; LC 96
See also DLB 58; RGEL 2
Shirley Hastings, Selina
See Hastings, Selina

Sholem Aleykhem
See Rabinovitch, Sholem
Sholokhov, Mikhail 1905-1984 ..... CLC 7, 15
See also CA 101; 112; DLB 272, 332; EWL
3; MTCW 1, 2; MTFW 2005; RGWL 2,
3; SATA-Obit 36
Sholokhov, Mikhail Aleksandrovich
See Sholokhov, Mikhail
Sholom Aleichem 1859-1916
See Rabinovitch, Sholem
Shone, Patric
See Hanley, James
Showalter, Elaine 1941- .... CLC 169
See also CA 57-60; CANR 58, 106; DLB
67; FW; GLL 2
Shreve, Susan
See Shreve, Susan Richards
Shreve, Susan Richards 1939- .... CLC 23
See also CA 49-52; CAAS 5; CANR 5, 38,
69, 100, 159, 199; MAICYA 1, 2; SATA
46, 95, 152; SATA-Brief 41
Shue, Larry 1946-1985 .... CLC 52
See also CA 145; 117; DAM DRAM; DFS
7
Shu-Jen, Chou 1881-1936 . SSC 20; TCLC 3
See also CA 104; EWL 3
Shulman, Alix Kates 1932- .... CLC 2, 10
See also CA 29-32R; CANR 43, 199; FW;
SATA 7
Shuster, Joe 1914-1992 .... CLC 21
See also AAYA 50
Shute, Nevil 1899-1960 .... CLC 30
See also BPFB 3; CA 102; 93-96; CANR
85; DLB 255; MTCW 2; NFS 9; RHW 4;
SFW 4
Shuttle, Penelope (Diane) 1947- .... CLC 7
See also CA 93-96; CANR 39, 84, 92, 108;
CP 3, 4, 5, 6, 7; CWP; DLB 14, 40
Shvarts, Elena 1948- .... PC 50
See also CA 147
Sidhwa, Bapsi 1939-
See Sidhwa, Bapsy (N.)
Sidhwa, Bapsy (N.) 1938- .... CLC 168
See also CA 108; CANR 25, 57; CN 6, 7;
DLB 323; FW
Sidney, Mary 1561-1621 .... LC 19, 39
See also DLB 167
Sidney, Sir Philip 1554-1586 .... LC 19, 39,
131; PC 32
See also BRW 1; BRWR 2; CDBLB Before
1660; DA; DA3; DAB; DAC; DAM MST,
POET; DLB 167; EXPP; PAB; PFS 30;
RGEL 2; TEA; WP
Sidney Herbert, Mary
See Sidney, Mary
Siegel, Jerome 1914-1996 .... CLC 21
See also AAYA 50; CA 116; 169; 151
Siegel, Jerry
See Siegel, Jerome
Sienkiewicz, Henryk (Adam Alexander Pius)
1846-1916 .... TCLC 3
See also CA 104; 134; CANR 84; DLB 332;
EWL 3; RGSF 2; RGWL 2, 3
Sierra, Gregorio Martinez
See Martinez Sierra, Gregorio
Sierra, Maria de la O'LeJarraga Martinez
See Martinez Sierra, Maria
Sigal, Clancy 1926- .... CLC 7
See also CA 1-4R; CANR 85, 184; CN 1,
2, 3, 4, 5, 6, 7
Siger of Brabant 1240(?)-1284(?) . CMLC 69
See also DLB 115
Sigourney, Lydia H.
See Sigourney, Lydia Howard
See also DLB 73, 183
Sigourney, Lydia Howard
1791-1865 .... NCLC 21, 87
See Sigourney, Lydia H.
See also DLB 1, 42, 239, 243

Sigourney, Lydia Howard Huntley
See Sigourney, Lydia Howard
Sigourney, Lydia Huntley
See Sigourney, Lydia Howard
Siguenza y Gongora, Carlos de
1645-1700 .... **HLCS 2; LC 8**
See also LAW
Sigurjonsson, Johann
See Sigurjonsson, Johann
Sigurjonsson, Johann 1880-1919 ... **TCLC 27**
See also CA 170; DLB 293; EWL 3
Sikelianos, Angelos 1884-1951 .... **PC 29; TCLC 39**
See also EWL 3; RGWL 2, 3
Silkin, Jon 1930-1997 .... **CLC 2, 6, 43**
See also CA 5-8R; CAAS 5; CANR 89; CP 1, 2, 3, 4, 5, 6; DLB 27
Silko, Leslie 1948- ...... **CLC 23, 74, 114, 211; NNAL; SSC 37, 66; WLCS**
See also AAYA 14; AMWS 4; ANW; BYA 12; CA 115; 122; CANR 45, 65, 118; CN 4, 5, 6, 7; CP 4, 5, 6, 7; CPW 1; CWP; DA; DA3; DAC; DAM MST, MULT, POP; DLB 143, 175, 256, 275; EWL 3; EXPP; EXPS; LAIT 4; MAL 5; MTCW 2; MTFW 2005; NFS 4; PFS 9, 16; RGAL 4; RGSF 2; SSFS 4, 8, 10, 11; TCWW 1, 2
Silko, Leslie Marmon
See Silko, Leslie
Sillanpaa, Frans Eemil 1888-1964 ... **CLC 19**
See also CA 129; 93-96; DLB 332; EWL 3; MTCW 1
Sillitoe, Alan 1928- .. **CLC 1, 3, 6, 10, 19, 57, 148**
See also AITN 1; BRWS 5; CA 9-12R, 191; CAAE 191; CAAS 2; CANR 8, 26, 55, 139; CDBLB 1960 to Present; CN 1, 2, 3, 4, 5, 6; CP 1, 2, 3, 4, 5; DLB 14, 139; EWL 3; MTCW 1, 2; MTFW 2005; RGEL 2; RGSF 2; SATA 61
Silone, Ignazio 1900-1978 .... **CLC 4**
See also CA 25-28; 81-84; CANR 34; CAP 2; DLB 264; EW 12; EWL 3; MTCW 1; RGSF 2; RGWL 2, 3
Silone, Ignazione
See Silone, Ignazio
Siluriensis, Leolinus
See Jones, Arthur Llewellyn
Silver, Joan Micklin 1935- .... **CLC 20**
See also CA 114; 121; INT CA-121
Silver, Nicholas
See Faust, Frederick
Silverberg, Robert 1935- .... **CLC 7, 140**
See also AAYA 24; BPFB 3; BYA 7, 9; CA 1-4R, 186; CAAE 186; CAAS 3; CANR 1, 20, 36, 85, 140, 175; CLR 59; CN 6, 7; CPW; DAM POP; DLB 8; INT CANR-20; MAICYA 1, 2; MTCW 1, 2; MTFW 2005; SATA 13, 91; SATA-Essay 104; SCFW 1, 2; SFW 4; SUFW 2
Silverstein, Alvin 1933- .... **CLC 17**
See also CA 49-52; CANR 2; CLR 25; JRDA; MAICYA 1, 2; SATA 8, 69, 124
Silverstein, Shel 1932-1999 .... **CLC 49**
See also AAYA 40; BW 3; CA 107; 179; CANR 47, 74, 81; CLR 5, 96; CWRI 5; JRDA; MAICYA 1, 2; MTCW 2; MTFW 2005; SATA 33, 92; SATA-Brief 27; SATA-Obit 116
Silverstein, Sheldon Allan
See Silverstein, Shel
Silverstein, Virginia B. 1937- .... **CLC 17**
See also CA 49-52; CANR 2; CLR 25; JRDA; MAICYA 1, 2; SATA 8, 69, 124
Silverstein, Virginia Barbara Opshelor
See Silverstein, Virginia B.
Sim, Georges
See Simenon, Georges

Simak, Clifford D(onald) 1904-1988 . **CLC 1, 55**
See also CA 1-4R; 125; CANR 1, 35; DLB 8; MTCW 1; SATA-Obit 56; SCFW 1, 2; SFW 4
Simenon, Georges 1903-1989 .... **CLC 1, 2, 3, 8, 18, 47**
See also BPFB 3; CA 85-88; 129; CANR 35; CMW 4; DA3; DAM POP; DLB 72; DLBY 1989; EW 12; EWL 3; GFL 1789 to the Present; MSW; MTCW 1, 2; MTFW 2005; RGWL 2, 3
Simenon, Georges Jacques Christian
See Simenon, Georges
Simic, Charles 1938- .... **CLC 6, 9, 22, 49, 68, 130, 256; PC 69**
See also AAYA 78; AMWS 8; CA 29-32R; CAAS 4; CANR 12, 33, 52, 61, 96, 140; CP 2, 3, 4, 5, 6, 7; DA3; DAM POET; DLB 105; MAL 5; MTCW 2; MTFW 2005; PFS 7, 33; RGAL 4; WP
Simmel, Georg 1858-1918 .... **TCLC 64**
See also CA 157; DLB 296
Simmons, Charles (Paul) 1924- .... **CLC 57**
See also CA 89-92; INT CA-89-92
Simmons, Dan 1948- .... **CLC 44**
See also AAYA 16, 54; CA 138; CANR 53, 81, 126, 174, 204; CPW; DAM POP; HGG; SUFW 2
Simmons, James (Stewart Alexander)
1933- .... **CLC 43**
See also CA 105; CAAS 21; CP 1, 2, 3, 4, 5, 6, 7; DLB 40
Simmons, Richard
See Simmons, Dan
Simms, William Gilmore
1806-1870 .... **NCLC 3**
See also DLB 3, 30, 59, 73, 248, 254; RGAL 4
Simon, Carly 1945- .... **CLC 26**
See also CA 105
Simon, Claude 1913-2005 ... **CLC 4, 9, 15, 39**
See also CA 89-92; 241; CANR 33, 117; CWW 2; DAM NOV; DLB 83, 332; EW 13; EWL 3; GFL 1789 to the Present; MTCW 1
Simon, Claude Eugene Henri
See Simon, Claude
Simon, Claude Henri Eugene
See Simon, Claude
Simon, Marvin Neil
See Simon, Neil
Simon, Myles
See Follett, Ken
Simon, Neil 1927- .... **CLC 6, 11, 31, 39, 70, 233; DC 14**
See also AAYA 32; AITN 1; AMWS 4; CA 21-24R; CAD; CANR 26, 54, 87, 126; CD 5, 6; DA3; DAM DRAM; DFS 2, 6, 12, 18, 24, 27; DLB 7, 266; LAIT 4; MAL 5; MTCW 1, 2; MTFW 2005; RGAL 4; TUS
Simon, Paul 1941(?)- .... **CLC 17**
See also CA 116; 153; CANR 152
Simon, Paul Frederick
See Simon, Paul
Simonon, Paul 1956(?)- .... **CLC 30**
Simonson, Rick .... **CLC 70**
Simpson, Harriette
See Arnow, Harriette (Louisa) Simpson
Simpson, Louis 1923- ... **CLC 4, 7, 9, 32, 149**
See also AMWS 9; CA 1-4R; CAAS 4; CANR 1, 61, 140; CP 1, 2, 3, 4, 5, 6, 7; DAM POET; DLB 5; MAL 5; MTCW 1, 2; MTFW 2005; PFS 7, 11, 14; RGAL 4
Simpson, Mona 1957- .... **CLC 44, 146**
See also CA 122; 135; CANR 68, 103; CN 6, 7; EWL 3

Simpson, Mona Elizabeth
See Simpson, Mona
Simpson, N(orman) F(rederick)
1919- .... **CLC 29**
See also CA 13-16R; CBD; DLB 13; RGEL 2
Sinclair, Andrew (Annandale) 1935- . **CLC 2, 14**
See also CA 9-12R; CAAS 5; CANR 14, 38, 91; CN 1, 2, 3, 4, 5, 6, 7; DLB 14; FANT; MTCW 1
Sinclair, Emil
See Hesse, Hermann
Sinclair, Iain 1943- .... **CLC 76**
See also BRWS 14; CA 132; CANR 81, 157; CP 5, 6, 7; HGG
Sinclair, Iain MacGregor
See Sinclair, Iain
Sinclair, Irene
See Griffith, D.W.
Sinclair, Julian
See Sinclair, May
Sinclair, Mary Amelia St. Clair (?)-
See Sinclair, May
Sinclair, May 1865-1946 .... **TCLC 3, 11**
See also CA 104; 166; DLB 36, 135; EWL 3; HGG; RGEL 2; RHW; SUFW
Sinclair, Roy
See Griffith, D.W.
Sinclair, Upton 1878-1968 ...... **CLC 1, 11, 15, 63; TCLC 160; WLC 5**
See also AAYA 63; AMWS 5; BPFB 3; BYA 2; CA 5-8R; 25-28R; CANR 7; CDALB 1929-1941; DA; DA3; DAB; DAC; DAM MST, NOV; DLB 9; EWL 3; INT CANR-7; LAIT 3; MAL 5; MTCW 1, 2; MTFW 2005; NFS 6; RGAL 4; SATA 9; TUS; YAW
Sinclair, Upton Beall
See Sinclair, Upton
Singe, (Edmund) J(ohn) M(illington)
1871-1909 .... **WLC**
Singer, Isaac
See Singer, Isaac Bashevis
Singer, Isaac Bashevis 1904-1991 .. **CLC 1, 3, 6, 9, 11, 15, 23, 38, 69, 111; SSC 3, 53, 80; WLC 5**
See also AAYA 32; AITN 1, 2; AMW; AMWR 2; BPFB 3; BYA 1, 4; CA 1-4R; 134; CANR 1, 39, 106; CDALB 1941-1968; CLR 1; CN 1, 2, 3, 4; CWRI 5; DA; DA3; DAB; DAC; DAM MST, NOV; DLB 6, 28, 52, 278, 332, 333; DLBY 1991; EWL 3; EXPS; HGG; JRDA; LAIT 3; MAICYA 1, 2; MAL 5; MTCW 1, 2; MTFW 2005; RGAL 4; RGHL; RGSF 2; SATA 3, 27; SATA-Obit 68; SSFS 2, 12, 16, 27, 30; TUS; TWA
Singer, Israel Joshua 1893-1944 .... **TCLC 33**
See also CA 169; DLB 333; EWL 3
Singh, Khushwant 1915- .... **CLC 11**
See also CA 9-12R; CAAS 9; CANR 6, 84; CN 1, 2, 3, 4, 5, 6, 7; DLB 323; EWL 3; RGEL 2
Singleton, Ann
See Benedict, Ruth
Singleton, John 1968(?)- .... **CLC 156**
See also AAYA 50; BW 2, 3; CA 138; CANR 67, 82; DAM MULT
Siniavskii, Andrei
See Sinyavsky, Andrei (Donatevich)
Sinibaldi, Fosco
See Kacew, Romain
Sinjohn, John
See Galsworthy, John
Sinyavsky, Andrei (Donatevich)
1925-1997 .... **CLC 8**
See also CA 85-88; 159; CWW 2; EWL 3; RGSF 2

Sinyavsky, Andrey Donatovich
See Sinyavsky, Andrei (Donatevich)
Sirin, V.
See Nabokov, Vladimir
Sissman, L(ouis) E(dward)
1928-1976 .... CLC 9, 18
See also CA 21-24R; 65-68; CANR 13; CP
2; DLB 5
Sisson, C(harles) H(ubert)
1914-2003 .... CLC 8
See also BRWS 11; CA 1-4R; 220; CAAS
3; CANR 3, 48, 84; CP 1, 2, 3, 4, 5, 6, 7;
DLB 27
Sitting Bull 1831(?)-1890 .... NNAL
See also DA3; DAM MULT
Sitwell, Dame Edith 1887-1964 ..... CLC 2, 9,
67; PC 3
See also BRW 7; CA 9-12R; CANR 35;
CDBLB 1945-1960; DAM POET; DLB
20; EWL 3; MTCW 1, 2; MTFW 2005;
RGEL 2; TEA
Siwaarmill, H. P.
See Sharp, William
Sjoewall, Maj 1935- .... CLC 7
See also BPFB 3; CA 65-68; CANR 73;
CMW 4; MSW
Sjowall, Maj
See Sjoewall, Maj
Skelton, John 1460(?)-1529 ..... LC 71; PC 25
See also BRW 1; DLB 136; RGEL 2
Skelton, Robin 1925-1997 .... CLC 13
See also AITN 2; CA 5-8R; 160; CAAS 5;
CANR 28, 89; CCA 1; CP 1, 2, 3, 4, 5, 6;
DLB 27, 53
Skolimowski, Jerzy 1938- .... CLC 20
See also CA 128
Skram, Amalie (Bertha)
1846-1905 .... TCLC 25
See also CA 165; DLB 354
Skvorecky, Josef 1924- . CLC 15, 39, 69, 152
See also CA 61-64; CAAS 1; CANR 10,
34, 63, 108; CDWLB 4; CWW 2; DA3;
DAC; DAM NOV; DLB 232; EWL 3;
MTCW 1, 2; MTFW 2005
Skvorecky, Josef Vaclav
See Skvorecky, Josef
Slade, Bernard 1930-
See Newbound, Bernard Slade
Slaughter, Carolyn 1946- .... CLC 56
See also CA 85-88; CANR 85, 169; CN 5,
6, 7
Slaughter, Frank G(ill) 1908-2001 ... CLC 29
See also AITN 2; CA 5-8R; 197; CANR 5,
85; INT CANR-5; RHW
Slavitt, David R. 1935- .... CLC 5, 14
See also CA 21-24R; CAAS 3; CANR 41,
83, 166; CN 1, 2; CP 1, 2, 3, 4, 5, 6, 7;
DLB 5, 6
Slavitt, David Rytman
See Slavitt, David R.
Slesinger, Tess 1905-1945 .... TCLC 10
See also CA 107; 199; DLB 102
Slessor, Kenneth 1901-1971 .... CLC 14
See also CA 102; 89-92; DLB 260; RGEL
2
Slowacki, Juliusz 1809-1849 .... NCLC 15
See also RGWL 3
Smart, Christopher 1722-1771 .... LC 3, 134;
PC 13
See also DAM POET; DLB 109; RGEL 2
Smart, Elizabeth 1913-1986 .... CLC 54;
TCLC 231
See also CA 81-84; 118; CN 4; DLB 88
Smiley, Jane 1949- ...... CLC 53, 76, 144, 236
See also AAYA 66; AMWS 6; BPFB 3; CA
104; CANR 30, 50, 74, 96, 158, 196; CN
6, 7; CPW 1; DA3; DAM POP; DLB 227,
234; EWL 3; INT CANR-30; MAL 5;
MTFW 2005; NFS 32; SSFS 19

Smiley, Jane Graves
See Smiley, Jane
Smith, A(rthur) J(ames) M(arshall)
1902-1980 .... CLC 15
See also CA 1-4R; 102; CANR 4; CP 1, 2,
3; DAC; DLB 88; RGEL 2
Smith, Adam 1723(?)-1790 .... LC 36
See also DLB 104, 252, 336; RGEL 2
Smith, Alexander 1829-1867 .... NCLC 59
See also DLB 32, 55
Smith, Alexander McCall 1948- ..... CLC 268
See also CA 215; CANR 154, 196; SATA
73, 179
Smith, Anna Deavere 1950- ...... CLC 86, 241
See also CA 133; CANR 103; CD 5, 6; DFS
2, 22; DLB 341
Smith, Betty (Wehner) 1904-1972 .... CLC 19
See also AAYA 72; BPFB 3; BYA 3; CA
5-8R; 33-36R; DLBY 1982; LAIT 3; NFS
31; RGAL 4; SATA 6
Smith, Charlotte (Turner)
1749-1806 .... NCLC 23, 115; PC 104
See also DLB 39, 109; RGEL 2; TEA
Smith, Clark Ashton 1893-1961 .... CLC 43
See also AAYA 76; CA 143; CANR 81;
FANT; HGG; MTCW 2; SCFW 1, 2; SFW
4; SUFW
Smith, Dave
See Smith, David (Jeddie)
Smith, David (Jeddie) 1942- .... CLC 22, 42
See also CA 49-52; CAAS 7; CANR 1, 59,
120; CP 3, 4, 5, 6, 7; CSW; DAM POET;
DLB 5
Smith, Iain Crichton 1928-1998 .... CLC 64
See also BRWS 9; CA 21-24R; 171; CN 1,
2, 3, 4, 5, 6; CP 1, 2, 3, 4, 5, 6; DLB 40,
139, 319, 352; RGSF 2
Smith, John 1580(?)-1631 .... LC 9
See also DLB 24, 30; TUS
Smith, Johnston
See Crane, Stephen
Smith, Joseph, Jr. 1805-1844 .... NCLC 53
Smith, Kevin 1970- .... CLC 223
See also AAYA 37; CA 166; CANR 131,
201
Smith, Lee 1944- .... CLC 25, 73, 258
See also CA 114; 119; CANR 46, 118, 173;
CN 7; CSW; DLB 143; DLBY 1983;
EWL 3; INT CA-119; RGAL 4
Smith, Martin
See Smith, Martin Cruz
Smith, Martin Cruz 1942- .. CLC 25; NNAL
See Smith, Martin Cruz
See also BEST 89:4; BPFB 3; CA 85-88;
CANR 6, 23, 43, 65, 119, 184; CMW 4;
CPW; DAM MULT, POP; HGG; INT
CANR-23; MTCW 2; MTFW 2005;
RGAL 4
Smith, Patti 1946- .... CLC 12
See also CA 93-96; CANR 63, 168
Smith, Pauline (Urmson)
1882-1959 .... TCLC 25
See also DLB 225; EWL 3
Smith, R. Alexander McCall
See Smith, Alexander McCall
Smith, Rosamond
See Oates, Joyce Carol
Smith, Seba 1792-1868 .... NCLC 187
See also DLB 1, 11, 243
Smith, Sheila Kaye
See Kaye-Smith, Sheila
Smith, Stevie 1902-1971 .... CLC 3, 8, 25, 44;
PC 12
See also BRWR 3; BRWS 2; CA 17-18; 29-
32R; CANR 35; CAP 2; CP 1; DAM
POET; DLB 20; EWL 3; MTCW 1, 2;
PAB; PFS 3; RGEL 2; TEA

Smith, Wilbur 1933- .... CLC 33
See also CA 13-16R; CANR 7, 46, 66, 134,
180; CPW; MTCW 1, 2; MTFW 2005
Smith, Wilbur Addison
See Smith, Wilbur
Smith, William Jay 1918- .... CLC 6
See also AMWS 13; CA 5-8R; CANR 44,
106; CP 1, 2, 3, 4, 5, 6, 7; CSW; CWRI
5; DLB 5; MAICYA 1, 2; SAAS 22;
SATA 2, 68, 154; SATA-Essay 154; TCLE
1:2
Smith, Woodrow Wilson
See Kuttner, Henry
Smith, Zadie 1975- .... CLC 158
See also AAYA 50; CA 193; CANR 204;
DLB 347; MTFW 2005
Smolenskin, Peretz 1842-1885 .... NCLC 30
Smollett, Tobias (George) 1721-1771 ... LC 2,
46
See also BRW 3; CDBLB 1660-1789; DLB
39, 104; RGEL 2; TEA
Snodgrass, Quentin Curtius
See Twain, Mark
Snodgrass, Thomas Jefferson
See Twain, Mark
Snodgrass, W. D. 1926-2009 .... CLC 2, 6, 10,
18, 68; PC 74
See also AMWS 6; CA 1-4R; 282; CANR
6, 36, 65, 85, 185; CP 1, 2, 3, 4, 5, 6, 7;
DAM POET; DLB 5; MAL 5; MTCW 1,
2; MTFW 2005; PFS 29; RGAL 4; TCLE
1:2
Snodgrass, W. de Witt
See Snodgrass, W. D.
Snodgrass, William de Witt
See Snodgrass, W. D.
Snodgrass, William De Witt
See Snodgrass, W. D.
Snorri Sturluson 1179-1241 .... CMLC 56
See also RGWL 2, 3
Snow, C(harles) P(ercy) 1905-1980 ... CLC 1,
4, 6, 9, 13, 19
See also BRW 7; CA 5-8R; 101; CANR 28;
CDBLB 1945-1960; CN 1, 2; DAM NOV;
DLB 15, 77; DLBD 17; EWL 3; MTCW
1, 2; MTFW 2005; RGEL 2; TEA
Snow, Frances Compton
See Adams, Henry
Snyder, Gary 1930- . CLC 1, 2, 5, 9, 32, 120;
PC 21
See also AAYA 72; AMWS 8; ANW; BG
1:3; CA 17-20R; CANR 30, 60, 125; CP
1, 2, 3, 4, 5, 6, 7; DA3; DAM POET; DLB
5, 16, 165, 212, 237, 275, 342; EWL 3;
MAL 5; MTCW 2; MTFW 2005; PFS 9,
19; RGAL 4; WP
Snyder, Gary Sherman
See Snyder, Gary
Snyder, Zilpha Keatley 1927- .... CLC 17
See also AAYA 15; BYA 1; CA 9-12R; 252;
CAAE 252; CANR 38, 202; CLR 31, 121;
JRDA; MAICYA 1, 2; SAAS 2; SATA 1,
28, 75, 110, 163; SATA-Essay 112, 163;
YAW
Soares, Bernardo
See Pessoa, Fernando
Sobh, A.
See Shamlu, Ahmad
Sobh, Alef
See Shamlu, Ahmad
Sobol, Joshua 1939- .... CLC 60
See also CA 200; CWW 2; RGHL
Sobol, Yehoshua 1939-
See Sobol, Joshua
Socrates 470B.C.-399B.C. .... CMLC 27
Soderberg, Hjalmar 1869-1941 ...... TCLC 39
See also DLB 259; EWL 3; RGSF 2
Soderbergh, Steven 1963- .... CLC 154
See also AAYA 43; CA 243

Soderbergh, Steven Andrew
See Soderbergh, Steven
Sodergran, Edith 1892-1923 .... **TCLC 31**
See also CA 202; DLB 259; EW 11; EWL
3; RGWL 2, 3
Soedergran, Edith Irene
See Sodergran, Edith
Softly, Edgar
See Lovecraft, H. P.
Softly, Edward
See Lovecraft, H. P.
Sokolov, Alexander V. 1943- .... **CLC 59**
See also CA 73-76; CWW 2; DLB 285;
EWL 3; RGWL 2, 3
Sokolov, Alexander Vsevolodovich
See Sokolov, Alexander V.
Sokolov, Raymond 1941- .... **CLC 7**
See also CA 85-88
Sokolov, Sasha
See Sokolov, Alexander V.
Solo, Jay
See Ellison, Harlan
Sologub, Fedor
See Teternikov, Fyodor Kuzmich
Sologub, Feodor
See Teternikov, Fyodor Kuzmich
Sologub, Fyodor
See Teternikov, Fyodor Kuzmich
Solomons, Ikey Esquir
See Thackeray, William Makepeace
Solomos, Dionysios 1798-1857 .... **NCLC 15**
Solwoska, Mara
See French, Marilyn
Solzhenitsyn, Aleksandr 1918-2008 ... **CLC 1,
2, 4, 7, 9, 10, 18, 26, 34, 78, 134, 235;
SSC 32, 105; WLC 5**
See also AAYA 49; AITN 1; BPFB 3; CA
69-72; CANR 40, 65, 116; CWW 2; DA;
DA3; DAB; DAC; DAM MST, NOV;
DLB 302, 332; EW 13; EWL 3; EXPS;
LAIT 4; MTCW 1, 2; MTFW 2005; NFS
6; RGSF 2; RGWL 2, 3; SSFS 9; TWA
Solzhenitsyn, Aleksandr I.
See Solzhenitsyn, Aleksandr
Solzhenitsyn, Aleksandr Isayevich
See Solzhenitsyn, Aleksandr
Somers, Jane
See Lessing, Doris
Somerville, Edith Oenone
1858-1949 .... **SSC 56; TCLC 51**
See also CA 196; DLB 135; RGEL 2; RGSF
2
Somerville & Ross
See Martin, Violet Florence; Somerville,
Edith Oenone
Sommer, Scott 1951- .... **CLC 25**
See also CA 106
Sommers, Christina Hoff 1950- ...... **CLC 197**
See also CA 153; CANR 95
Sondheim, Stephen 1930- .. **CLC 30, 39, 147;
DC 22**
See also AAYA 11, 66; CA 103; CANR 47,
67, 125; DAM DRAM; DFS 25, 27; LAIT
4
Sondheim, Stephen Joshua
See Sondheim, Stephen
Sone, Monica 1919- .... **AAL**
See also DLB 312
Song, Cathy 1955- .... **AAL; PC 21**
See also CA 154; CANR 118; CWP; DLB
169, 312; EXPP; FW; PFS 5
Sontag, Susan 1933-2004 ... **CLC 1, 2, 10, 13,
31, 105, 195, 277**
See also AMWS 3; CA 17-20R; 234; CANR
25, 51, 74, 97, 184; CN 1, 2, 3, 4, 5, 6, 7;
CPW; DA3; DAM POP; DLB 2, 67; EWL
3; MAL 5; MBL; MTCW 1, 2; MTFW
2005; RGAL 4; RHW; SSFS 10

Sophocles 496(?)B.C.-406(?)B.C. .... **CMLC 2,
47, 51, 86; DC 1; WLCS**
See also AW 1; CDWLB 1; DA; DA3;
DAB; DAC; DAM DRAM, MST; DFS 1,
4, 8, 24; DLB 176; LAIT 1; LATS 1:1;
LMFS 1; RGWL 2, 3; TWA; WLIT 8
Sordello 1189-1269 .... **CMLC 15**
Sorel, Georges 1847-1922 .... **TCLC 91**
See also CA 118; 188
Sorel, Julia
See Drexler, Rosalyn
Sorokin, Vladimir .... **CLC 59**
See also CA 258; DLB 285
Sorokin, Vladimir Georgievich
See Sorokin, Vladimir
Sorrentino, Gilbert 1929-2006 .... **CLC 3, 7,
14, 22, 40, 247**
See also CA 77-80; 250; CANR 14, 33, 115,
157; CN 3, 4, 5, 6, 7; CP 1, 2, 3, 4, 5, 6,
7; DLB 5, 173; DLBY 1980; INT
CANR-14
Soseki
See Natsume, Soseki
Soto, Gary 1952- ... **CLC 32, 80; HLC 2; PC
28**
See also AAYA 10, 37; BYA 11; CA 119;
125; CANR 50, 74, 107, 157; CLR 38;
CP 4, 5, 6, 7; DAM MULT; DLB
82; EWL 3; EXPP; HW 1, 2; INT CA-
125; JRDA; LLW; MAICYA 2; MAIC-
YAS 1; MAL 5; MTCW 2; MTFW 2005;
PFS 7, 30; RGAL 4; SATA 80, 120, 174;
WYA; YAW
Soupault, Philippe 1897-1990 .... **CLC 68**
See also CA 116; 147; 131; EWL 3; GFL
1789 to the Present; LMFS 2
Souster, (Holmes) Raymond 1921- .... **CLC 5,
14**
See also CA 13-16R; CAAS 14; CANR 13,
29, 53; CP 1, 2, 3, 4, 5, 6, 7; DA3; DAC;
DAM POET; DLB 88; RGEL 2; SATA 63
Southern, Terry 1924(?)-1995 .... **CLC 7**
See also AMWS 11; BPFB 3; CA 1-4R;
150; CANR 1, 55, 107; CN 1, 2, 3, 4, 5,
6; DLB 2; IDFW 3, 4
Southerne, Thomas 1660-1746 .... **LC 99**
See also DLB 80; RGEL 2
Southey, Robert 1774-1843 .... **NCLC 8, 97**
See also BRW 4; DLB 93, 107, 142; RGEL
2; SATA 54
Southwell, Robert 1561(?)-1595 .... **LC 108**
See also DLB 167; RGEL 2; TEA
Southworth, Emma Dorothy Eliza Nevitte
1819-1899 .... **NCLC 26**
See also DLB 239
Souza, Ernest
See Scott, Evelyn
Soyinka, Wole 1934- .. **BLC 1:3, 2:3; CLC 3,
5, 14, 36, 44, 179; DC 2; WLC 5**
See also AFW; BW 2, 3; CA 13-16R;
CANR 27, 39, 82, 136; CD 5, 6; CDWLB
3; CN 6, 7; CP 1, 2, 3, 4, 5, 6 ,7; DA;
DA3; DAB; DAC; DAM DRAM, MST,
MULT; DFS 10, 26; DLB 125, 332; EWL
3; MTCW 1, 2; MTFW 2005; PFS 27;
RGEL 2; TWA; WLIT 2; WWE 1
Spackman, W(illiam) M(ode)
1905-1990 .... **CLC 46**
See also CA 81-84; 132
Spacks, Barry (Bernard) 1931- .... **CLC 14**
See also CA 154; CANR 33, 109; CP 3, 4,
5, 6, 7; DLB 105
Spanidou, Irini 1946- .... **CLC 44**
See also CA 185; CANR 179
Spark, Muriel 1918-2006 .... **CLC 2, 3, 5, 8,
13, 18, 40, 94, 242; PC 72; SSC 10, 115**
See also BRWS 1; CA 5-8R; 251; CANR
12, 36, 76, 89, 131; CDBLB 1945-1960;
CN 1, 2, 3, 4, 5, 6, 7; CP 1, 2, 3, 4, 5, 6,

7; DA3; DAB; DAC; DAM MST, NOV;
DLB 15, 139; EWL 3; FW; INT CANR-
12; LAIT 4; MTCW 1, 2; MTFW 2005;
NFS 22; RGEL 2; SSFS 28; TEA; WLIT
4; YAW
Spark, Muriel Sarah
See Spark, Muriel
Spaulding, Douglas
See Bradbury, Ray
Spaulding, Leonard
See Bradbury, Ray
Speght, Rachel 1597-c. 1630 .... **LC 97**
See also DLB 126
Spence, J. A. D.
See Eliot, T. S.
Spencer, Anne 1882-1975 ...... **HR 1:3; PC 77**
See also BW 2; CA 161; DLB 51, 54
Spencer, Elizabeth 1921- .... **CLC 22; SSC 57**
See also CA 13-16R; CANR 32, 65, 87; CN
1, 2, 3, 4, 5, 6, 7; CSW; DLB 6, 218;
EWL 3; MTCW 1; RGAL 4; SATA 14
Spencer, Leonard G.
See Silverberg, Robert
Spencer, Scott 1945- .... **CLC 30**
See also CA 113; CANR 51, 148, 190;
DLBY 1986
Spender, Stephen 1909-1995 ..... **CLC 1, 2, 5,
10, 41, 91; PC 71**
See also BRWS 2; CA 9-12R; 149; CANR
31, 54; CDBLB 1945-1960; CP 1, 2, 3, 4,
5, 6; DAM POET; DLB 20; EWL
3; MTCW 1, 2; MTFW 2005; PAB; PFS
23; RGEL 2; TEA
Spender, Stephen Harold
See Spender, Stephen
Spengler, Oswald (Arnold Gottfried)
1880-1936 .... **TCLC 25**
See also CA 118; 189
Spenser, Edmund 1552(?)-1599 ...... **LC 5, 39,
117; PC 8, 42; WLC 5**
See also AAYA 60; BRW 1; CDBLB Before
1660; DA; DA3; DAB; DAC; DAM MST,
POET; DLB 167; EFS 2; EXPP; PAB;
PFS 32; RGEL 2; TEA; WLIT 3; WP
Spicer, Jack 1925-1965 .... **CLC 8, 18, 72**
See also BG 1:3; CA 85-88; DAM POET;
DLB 5, 16, 193; GLL 1; WP
Spiegelman, Art 1948- .... **CLC 76, 178**
See also AAYA 10, 46; CA 125; CANR 41,
55, 74, 124; DLB 299; MTCW 2; MTFW
2005; RGHL; SATA 109, 158; YAW
Spielberg, Peter 1929- .... **CLC 6**
See also CA 5-8R; CANR 4, 48; DLBY
1981
Spielberg, Steven 1947- .... **CLC 20, 188**
See also AAYA 8, 24; CA 77-80; CANR
32; SATA 32
Spillane, Frank Morrison
See Spillane, Mickey
Spillane, Mickey 1918-2006 .. **CLC 3, 13, 241**
See also BPFB 3; CA 25-28R; 252; CANR
28, 63, 125; CMW 4; DA3; DLB 226;
MSW; MTCW 1, 2; MTFW 2005; SATA
66; SATA-Obit 176
Spinoza, Benedictus de 1632-1677 . **LC 9, 58,
177**
Spinrad, Norman (Richard) 1940- ... **CLC 46**
See also BPFB 3; CA 37-40R, 233; CAAE
233; CAAS 19; CANR 20, 91; DLB 8;
INT CANR-20; SFW 4
Spitteler, Carl 1845-1924 .... **TCLC 12**
See also CA 109; DLB 129, 332; EWL 3
Spitteler, Karl Friedrich Georg
See Spitteler, Carl
Spivack, Kathleen (Romola Drucker)
1938- .... **CLC 6**
See also CA 49-52

Strugatsky, Boris Natanovich
See Strugatskii, Boris
Strummer, Joe 1952-2002 .... **CLC 30**
Strunk, William, Jr. 1869-1946 ...... **TCLC 92**
See also CA 118; 164; NCFS 5
Stryk, Lucien 1924- .... **PC 27**
See also CA 13-16R; CANR 10, 28, 55, 110; CP 1, 2, 3, 4, 5, 6, 7
Stuart, Don A.
See Campbell, John W(ood, Jr.)
Stuart, Ian
See MacLean, Alistair
Stuart, Jesse (Hilton) 1906-1984 ... **CLC 1, 8, 11, 14, 34; SSC 31**
See also CA 5-8R; 112; CANR 31; CN 1, 2, 3; DLB 9, 48, 102; DLBY 1984; SATA 2; SATA-Obit 36
Stubblefield, Sally
See Trumbo, Dalton
Sturgeon, Theodore (Hamilton) 1918-1985 .... **CLC 22, 39**
See also AAYA 51; BPFB 3; BYA 9, 10; CA 81-84; 116; CANR 32, 103; DLB 8; DLBY 1985; HGG; MTCW 1, 2; MTFW 2005; SCFW; SFW 4; SUFW
Sturges, Preston 1898-1959 .... **TCLC 48**
See also CA 114; 149; DLB 26
Styron, William 1925-2006 .. **CLC 1, 3, 5, 11, 15, 60, 232, 244; SSC 25**
See also AMW; AMWC 2; BEST 90:4; BPFB 3; CA 5-8R; 255; CANR 6, 33, 74, 126, 191; CDALB 1968-1988; CN 1, 2, 3, 4, 5, 6, 7; CPW; CSW; DA3; DAM NOV, POP; DLB 2, 143, 299; DLBY 1980; EWL 3; INT CANR-6; LAIT 2; MAL 5; MTCW 1, 2; MTFW 2005; NCFS 1; NFS 22; RGAL 4; RGHL; RHW; TUS
Styron, William C.
See Styron, William
Styron, William Clark
See Styron, William
Su, Chien 1884-1918 .... **TCLC 24**
See also CA 123; EWL 3
Suarez Lynch, B.
See Bioy Casares, Adolfo; Borges, Jorge Luis
Suassuna, Ariano Vilar 1927- .... **HLCS 1**
See also CA 178; DLB 307; HW 2; LAW
Suckert, Kurt Erich
See Malaparte, Curzio
Suckling, Sir John 1609-1642 . **LC 75; PC 30**
See also BRW 2; DAM POET; DLB 58, 126; EXPP; PAB; RGEL 2
Suckow, Ruth 1892-1960 .... **SSC 18**
See also CA 193; 113; DLB 9, 102; RGAL 4; TCWW 2
Sudermann, Hermann 1857-1928 .. **TCLC 15**
See also CA 107; 201; DLB 118
Sue, Eugene 1804-1857 .... **NCLC 1**
See also DLB 119
Sueskind, Patrick
See Suskind, Patrick
Suetonius c. 70-c. 130 .... **CMLC 60**
See also AW 2; DLB 211; RGWL 2, 3; WLIT 8
Su Hsuan-ying
See Su, Chien
Su Hsuean-ying
See Su, Chien
Sukenick, Ronald 1932-2004 ..... **CLC 3, 4, 6, 48**
See also CA 25-28R; 209; 229; CAAE 209; CAAS 8; CANR 32, 89; CN 3, 4, 5, 6, 7; DLB 173; DLBY 1981
Suknaski, Andrew 1942- .... **CLC 19**
See also CA 101; CP 3, 4, 5, 6, 7; DLB 53
Sullivan, Vernon
See Vian, Boris

Sully Prudhomme, Rene-Francois-Armand 1839-1907 .... **TCLC 31**
See also CA 170; DLB 332; GFL 1789 to the Present
Sulpicius Severus c. 363-c. 425 ... **CMLC 120**
Su Man-shu
See Su, Chien
Sumarokov, Aleksandr Petrovich 1717-1777 .... **LC 104**
See also DLB 150
Summerforest, Ivy B.
See Kirkup, James
Summers, Andrew James
See Summers, Andy
Summers, Andy 1942- .... **CLC 26**
See also CA 255
Summers, Hollis (Spurgeon, Jr.) 1916- .... **CLC 10**
See also CA 5-8R; CANR 3; CN 1, 2, 3; CP 1, 2, 3, 4; DLB 6; TCLE 1:2
Summers, (Alphonsus Joseph-Mary Augustus) Montague 1880-1948 .... **TCLC 16**
See also CA 118; 163
Sumner, Gordon Matthew
See Sting
Sun Tzu c. 400B.C.-c. 320B.C. ...... **CMLC 56**
Surayya, Kamala
See Das, Kamala
Surayya Kamala
See Das, Kamala
Surdas c. 1478-c. 1583 .... **LC 163**
See also RGWL 2, 3
Surrey, Henry Howard 1517-1574 ... **LC 121; PC 59**
See also BRW 1; RGEL 2
Surtees, Robert Smith 1805-1864 .. **NCLC 14**
See also DLB 21; RGEL 2
Susann, Jacqueline 1921-1974 .... **CLC 3**
See also AITN 1; BPFB 3; CA 65-68; 53-56; MTCW 1, 2
Su Shi
See Su Shih
Su Shih 1036-1101 .... **CMLC 15**
See also RGWL 2, 3
Suskind, Patrick 1949- .... **CLC 44, 182**
See also BPFB 3; CA 145; CWW 2
Suso, Heinrich c. 1295-1366 .... **CMLC 87**
Sutcliff, Rosemary 1920-1992 .... **CLC 26**
See also AAYA 10; BRWS 16; BYA 1, 4; CA 5-8R; 139; CANR 37; CLR 1, 37, 138; CPW; DAB; DAC; DAM MST, POP; JRDA; LATS 1:1; MAICYA 1, 2; MAIC-YAS 1; RHW; SATA 6, 44, 78; SATA-Obit 73; WYA; YAW
Sutherland, Efua (Theodora Morgue) 1924-1996 .... **BLC 2:3**
See also AFW; BW 1; CA 105; CWD; DLB 117; EWL 3; IDTP; SATA 25
Sutro, Alfred 1863-1933 .... **TCLC 6**
See also CA 105; 185; DLB 10; RGEL 2
Sutton, Henry
See Slavitt, David R.
Su Yuan-ying
See Su, Chien
Su Yuean-ying
See Su, Chien
Suzuki, D. T.
See Suzuki, Daisetz Teitaro
Suzuki, Daisetz T.
See Suzuki, Daisetz Teitaro
Suzuki, Daisetz Teitaro 1870-1966 .... **TCLC 109**
See also CA 121; 111; MTCW 1, 2; MTFW 2005
Suzuki, Teitaro
See Suzuki, Daisetz Teitaro

Svareff, Count Vladimir
See Crowley, Edward Alexander
Svevo, Italo
See Schmitz, Aron Hector
Swados, Elizabeth 1951- .... **CLC 12**
See also CA 97-100; CANR 49, 163; INT CA-97-100
Swados, Elizabeth A.
See Swados, Elizabeth
Swados, Harvey 1920-1972 .... **CLC 5**
See also CA 5-8R; 37-40R; CANR 6; CN 1; DLB 2, 335; MAL 5
Swados, Liz
See Swados, Elizabeth
Swan, Gladys 1934- .... **CLC 69**
See also CA 101; CANR 17, 39; TCLE 1:2
Swanson, Logan
See Matheson, Richard
Swarthout, Glendon (Fred) 1918-1992 .... **CLC 35**
See also AAYA 55; CA 1-4R; 139; CANR 1, 47; CN 1, 2, 3, 4, 5; LAIT 5; NFS 29; SATA 26; TCWW 1, 2; YAW
Swedenborg, Emanuel 1688-1772 ..... **LC 105**
Sweet, Sarah C.
See Jewett, Sarah Orne
Swenson, May 1919-1989 ...... **CLC 4, 14, 61, 106; PC 14**
See also AMWS 4; CA 5-8R; 130; CANR 36, 61, 131; CP 1, 2, 3, 4; DA; DAB; DAC; DAM MST, POET; DLB 5; EXPP; GLL 2; MAL 5; MTCW 1, 2; MTFW 2005; PFS 16, 30; SATA 15; WP
Swift, Augustus
See Lovecraft, H. P.
Swift, Graham 1949- .... **CLC 41, 88, 233**
See also BRWC 2; BRWS 5; CA 117; 122; CANR 46, 71, 128, 181; CN 4, 5, 6, 7; DLB 194, 326; MTCW 2; MTFW 2005; NFS 18; RGSF 2
Swift, Jonathan 1667-1745 ..... **LC 1, 42, 101; PC 9; WLC 6**
See also AAYA 41; BRW 3; BRWC 1; BRWR 1; BYA 5, 14; CDBLB 1660-1789; CLR 53; DA; DA3; DAB; DAC; DAM MST, NOV, POET; DLB 39, 95, 101; EXPN; LAIT 1; NFS 6; PFS 27; RGEL 2; SATA 19; TEA; WCH; WLIT 3
Swinburne, Algernon Charles 1837-1909 ... **PC 24; TCLC 8, 36; WLC 6**
See also BRW 5; CA 105; 140; CDBLB 1832-1890; DA; DA3; DAB; DAC; DAM MST, POET; DLB 35, 57; PAB; RGEL 2; TEA
Swinfen, Ann .... **CLC 34**
See also CA 202
Swinnerton, Frank (Arthur) 1884-1982 .... **CLC 31**
See also CA 202; 108; CN 1, 2, 3; DLB 34
Swinnerton, Frank Arthur 1884-1982 .... **CLC 31**
See also CA 108; DLB 34
Swithen, John
See King, Stephen
Sylvia
See Ashton-Warner, Sylvia (Constance)
Symmes, Robert Edward
See Duncan, Robert
Symonds, John Addington 1840-1893 .... **NCLC 34**
See also BRWS 14; DLB 57, 144
Symons, Arthur 1865-1945 .... **TCLC 11**
See also BRWS 14; CA 107; 189; DLB 19, 57, 149; RGEL 2

Symons, Julian (Gustave)
1912-1994 .... **CLC 2, 14, 32**
See also CA 49-52; 147; CAAS 3; CANR 3, 33, 59; CMW 4; CN 1, 2, 3, 4, 5; CP 1, 3, 4; DLB 87, 155; DLBY 1992; MSW; MTCW 1

Synge, Edmund John Millington
See Synge, John Millington

Synge, J. M.
See Synge, John Millington

Synge, John Millington 1871-1909 ...... **DC 2;**
TCLC 6, 37
See also BRW 6; BRWR 1; CA 104; 141; CDBLB 1890-1914; DAM DRAM; DFS 18; DLB 10, 19; EWL 3; RGEL 2; TEA; WLIT 4

Syruc, J.
See Milosz, Czeslaw

Szirtes, George 1948- .... **CLC 46; PC 51**
See also CA 109; CANR 27, 61, 117; CP 4, 5, 6, 7

Szymborska, Wislawa 1923- ... **CLC 99, 190;**
PC 44
See also AAYA 76; CA 154; CANR 91, 133, 181; CDWLB 4; CWP; CWW 2; DA3; DLB 232, 332; DLBY 1996; EWL 3; MTCW 2; MTFW 2005; PFS 15, 27, 31, 34; RGHL; RGWL 3

T. O., Nik
See Annensky, Innokenty (Fyodorovich)

Tabori, George 1914-2007 .... **CLC 19**
See also CA 49-52; 262; CANR 4, 69; CBD; CD 5, 6; DLB 245; RGHL

Tacitus c. 55-c. 117 .... **CMLC 56**
See also AW 2; CDWLB 1; DLB 211; RGWL 2, 3; WLIT 8

Tadjo, Veronique 1955- .... **BLC 2:3**
See also EWL 3

Tagore, Rabindranath 1861-1941 .... **PC 8;**
SSC 48; TCLC 3, 53
See also CA 104; 120; DA3; DAM DRAM, POET; DFS 26; DLB 323, 332; EWL 3; MTCW 1, 2; MTFW 2005; PFS 18; RGEL 2; RGSF 2; RGWL 2, 3; TWA

Taine, Hippolyte Adolphe
1828-1893 .... **NCLC 15**
See also EW 7; GFL 1789 to the Present

Talayesva, Don C. 1890-(?) .... **NNAL**

Talese, Gay 1932- .... **CLC 37, 232**
See also AITN 1; AMWS 17; CA 1-4R; CANR 9, 58, 137, 177; DLB 185; INT CANR-9; MTCW 1, 2; MTFW 2005

Tallent, Elizabeth 1954- .... **CLC 45**
See also CA 117; CANR 72; DLB 130

Tallmountain, Mary 1918-1997 .... **NNAL**
See also CA 146; 161; DLB 193

Tally, Ted 1952- .... **CLC 42**
See also CA 120; 124; CAD; CANR 125; CD 5, 6; INT CA-124

Talvik, Heiti 1904-1947 .... **TCLC 87**
See also EWL 3

Tamayo y Baus, Manuel
1829-1898 .... **NCLC 1**

Tammsaare, A(nton) H(ansen)
1878-1940 .... **TCLC 27**
See also CA 164; CDWLB 4; DLB 220; EWL 3

Tam'si, Tchicaya U
See Tchicaya, Gerald Felix

Tan, Amy 1952- ..... **AAL; CLC 59, 120, 151,**
257
See also AAYA 9, 48; AMWS 10; BEST 89:3; BPFB 3; CA 136; CANR 54, 105, 132; CDALBS; CN 6, 7; CPW 1; DA3; DAM MULT, NOV, POP; DLB 173, 312; EXPN; FL 1:6; FW; LAIT 3, 5; MAL 5; MTCW 2; MTFW 2005; NFS 1, 13, 16, 31; RGAL 4; SATA 75; SSFS 9; YAW

Tan, Amy Ruth
See Tan, Amy

Tandem, Carl Felix
See Spitteler, Carl

Tandem, Felix
See Spitteler, Carl

Tania B.
See Blixen, Karen

Tanizaki, Jun'ichiro 1886-1965 ... **CLC 8, 14,**
28; SSC 21
See also CA 93-96; 25-28R; DLB 180; EWL 3; MJW; MTCW 2, MTFW 2005; RGSF 2; RGWL 2

Tanizaki Jun'ichiro
See Tanizaki, Jun'ichiro

Tannen, Deborah 1945- .... **CLC 206**
See also CA 118; CANR 95

Tannen, Deborah Frances
See Tannen, Deborah

Tanner, William
See Amis, Kingsley

Tante, Dilly
See Kunitz, Stanley

Tao Lao
See Storni, Alfonsina

Tapahonso, Luci 1953- .... **NNAL; PC 65**
See also CA 145; CANR 72, 127; DLB 175

Tarantino, Quentin 1963- .... **CLC 125, 230**
See also AAYA 58; CA 171; CANR 125

Tarantino, Quentin Jerome
See Tarantino, Quentin

Tarassoff, Lev
See Troyat, Henri

Tarbell, Ida 1857-1944 .... **TCLC 40**
See also CA 122; 181; DLB 47

Tarbell, Ida Minerva
See Tarbell, Ida

Tarchetti, Ugo 1839(?)-1869 .... **SSC 119**

Tardieu d'Esclavelles,
Louise-Florence-Petronille
See Epinay, Louise d'

Tarkington, (Newton) Booth
1869-1946 .... **TCLC 9**
See also BPFB 3; BYA 3; CA 110; 143; CWRI 5; DLB 9, 102; MAL 5; MTCW 2; NFS 34; RGAL 4; SATA 17

Tarkovskii, Andrei Arsen'evich
See Tarkovsky, Andrei (Arsenyevich)

Tarkovsky, Andrei (Arsenyevich)
1932-1986 .... **CLC 75**
See also CA 127

Tartt, Donna 1964(?)- .... **CLC 76**
See also AAYA 56; CA 142; CANR 135; LNFS 2; MTFW 2005

Tasso, Torquato 1544-1595 .... **LC 5, 94**
See also EFS 2; EW 2; RGWL 2, 3; WLIT 7

Tate, (John Orley) Allen 1899-1979 .. **CLC 2,**
4, 6, 9, 11, 14, 24; PC 50
See also AMW; CA 5-8R; 85-88; CANR 32, 108; CN 1, 2; CP 1, 2; DLB 4, 45, 63; DLBD 17; EWL 3; MAL 5; MTCW 1, 2; MTFW 2005; RGAL 4; RHW

Tate, Ellalice
See Hibbert, Eleanor Alice Burford

Tate, James (Vincent) 1943- ..... **CLC 2, 6, 25**
See also CA 21-24R; CANR 29, 57, 114; CP 1, 2, 3, 4, 5, 6, 7; DLB 5, 169; EWL 3; PFS 10, 15; RGAL 4; WP

Tate, Nahum 1652(?)-1715 .... **LC 109**
See also DLB 80; RGEL 2

Tauler, Johannes c. 1300-1361 ...... **CMLC 37**
See also DLB 179; LMFS 1

Tavel, Ronald 1936-2009 .... **CLC 6**
See also CA 21-24R; 284; CAD; CANR 33; CD 5, 6

Taviani, Paolo 1931- .... **CLC 70**
See also CA 153

Taylor, Bayard 1825-1878 .... **NCLC 89**
See also DLB 3, 189, 250, 254; RGAL 4

Taylor, C(ecil) P(hilip) 1929-1981 .... **CLC 27**
See also CA 25-28R; 105; CANR 47; CBD

Taylor, Edward 1642(?)-1729 ..... **LC 11, 163;**
PC 63
See also AMW; DA; DAB; DAC; DAM MST, POET; DLB 24; EXPP; PFS 31; RGAL 4; TUS

Taylor, Eleanor Ross 1920- .... **CLC 5**
See also CA 81-84; CANR 70

Taylor, Elizabeth 1912-1975 .... **CLC 2, 4, 29;**
SSC 100
See also CA 13-16R; CANR 9, 70; CN 1, 2; DLB 139; MTCW 1; RGEL 2; SATA 13

Taylor, Frederick Winslow
1856-1915 .... **TCLC 76**
See also CA 188

Taylor, Henry 1942- .... **CLC 44**
See also CA 33-36R; CAAS 7; CANR 31, 178; CP 6, 7; DLB 5; PFS 10

Taylor, Henry Splawn
See Taylor, Henry

Taylor, Kamala
See Markandaya, Kamala

Taylor, Mildred D. 1943- .... **CLC 21**
See also AAYA 10, 47; BW 1; BYA 3, 8; CA 85-88; CANR 25, 115, 136; CLR 9, 59, 90, 144; CSW; DLB 52; JRDA; LAIT 3; MAICYA 1, 2; MTFW 2005; SAAS 5; SATA 135; WYA; YAW

Taylor, Peter (Hillsman) 1917-1994 .. **CLC 1,**
4, 18, 37, 44, 50, 71; SSC 10, 84
See also AMWS 5; BPFB 3; CA 13-16R; 147; CANR 9, 50; CN 1, 2, 3, 4, 5; CSW; DLB 218, 278; DLBY 1981, 1994; EWL 3; EXPS; INT CANR-9; MAL 5; MTCW 1, 2; MTFW 2005; RGSF 2; SSFS 9; TUS

Taylor, Robert Lewis 1912-1998 .... **CLC 14**
See also CA 1-4R; 170; CANR 3, 64; CN 1, 2; SATA 10; TCWW 1, 2

Tchekhov, Anton
See Chekhov, Anton

Tchicaya, Gerald Felix 1931-1988 .. **CLC 101**
See also CA 129; 125; CANR 81; EWL 3

Tchicaya U Tam'si
See Tchicaya, Gerald Felix

Teasdale, Sara 1884-1933 .... **PC 31; TCLC 4**
See also CA 104; 163; DLB 45; GLL 1; PFS 14; RGAL 4; SATA 32; TUS

Tecumseh 1768-1813 .... **NNAL**
See also DAM MULT

Tegner, Esaias 1782-1846 .... **NCLC 2**

Teilhard de Chardin, (Marie Joseph) Pierre
1881-1955 .... **TCLC 9**
See also CA 105; 210; GFL 1789 to the Present

Temple, Ann
See Mortimer, Penelope (Ruth)

Tennant, Emma 1937- .... **CLC 13, 52**
See also BRWS 9; CA 65-68; CAAS 9; CANR 10, 38, 59, 88, 177; CN 3, 4, 5, 6, 7; DLB 14; EWL 3; SFW 4

Tenneshaw, S.M.
See Silverberg, Robert

Tenney, Tabitha Gilman
1762-1837 .... **NCLC 122**
See also DLB 37, 200

Tennyson, Alfred 1809-1892 ... **NCLC 30, 65,**
115, 202; PC 6, 101; WLC 6
See also AAYA 50; BRW 4; BRWR 3; CD-BLB 1832-1890; DA; DA3; DAB; DAC; DAM MST, POET; DLB 32; EXPP; PAB; PFS 1, 2, 4, 11, 15, 19; RGEL 2; TEA; WLIT 4; WP

Teran, Lisa St. Aubin de
See St. Aubin de Teran, Lisa

Tibullus c. 54B.C.-c. 18B.C. .... **CMLC 36**
See also AW 2; DLB 211; RGWL 2, 3;
WLIT 8

Ticheburn, Cheviot
See Ainsworth, William Harrison

Tieck, (Johann) Ludwig
1773-1853 ..... **NCLC 5, 46; SSC 31, 100**
See also CDWLB 2; DLB 90; EW 5; IDTP;
RGSF 2; RGWL 2, 3; SUFW

Tiger, Derry
See Ellison, Harlan

Tilghman, Christopher 1946- .... **CLC 65**
See also CA 159; CANR 135, 151; CSW;
DLB 244

Tillich, Paul (Johannes)
1886-1965 .... **CLC 131**
See also CA 5-8R; 25-28R; CANR 33;
MTCW 1, 2

Tillinghast, Richard (Williford)
1940- .... **CLC 29**
See also CA 29-32R; CAAS 23; CANR 26,
51, 96; CP 2, 3, 4, 5, 6, 7; CSW

Tillman, Lynne (?)- .... **CLC 231**
See also CA 173; CANR 144, 172

Timrod, Henry 1828-1867 .... **NCLC 25**
See also DLB 3, 248; RGAL 4

Tindall, Gillian (Elizabeth) 1938- ...... **CLC 7**
See also CA 21-24R; CANR 11, 65, 107;
CN 1, 2, 3, 4, 5, 6, 7

Ting Ling
See Chiang, Pin-chin

Tiptree, James, Jr.
See Sheldon, Alice Hastings Bradley

Tirone Smith, Mary-Ann 1944- .... **CLC 39**
See also CA 118; 136; CANR 113; SATA
143

Tirso de Molina 1580(?)-1648 .... **DC 13;
HLCS 2; LC 73**
See also RGWL 2, 3

Titmarsh, Michael Angelo
See Thackeray, William Makepeace

**Tocqueville, Alexis (Charles Henri Maurice
Clerel Comte) de** 1805-1859 .. **NCLC 7,
63**
See also EW 6; GFL 1789 to the Present;
TWA

Toe, Tucker
See Westlake, Donald E.

Toer, Pramoedya Ananta
1925-2006 .... **CLC 186**
See also CA 197; 251; CANR 170; DLB
348; RGWL 3

Toffler, Alvin 1928- .... **CLC 168**
See also CA 13-16R; CANR 15, 46, 67,
183; CPW; DAM POP; MTCW 1, 2

Toibin, Colm 1955- .... **CLC 162, 285**
See also CA 142; CANR 81, 149; CN 7;
DLB 271

Tolkien, J. R. R. 1892-1973 ... **CLC 1, 2, 3, 8,
12, 38; TCLC 137; WLC 6**
See also AAYA 10; AITN 1; BPFB 3;
BRWC 2; BRWS 2; CA 17-18; 45-48;
CANR 36, 134; CAP 2; CDBLB 1914-
1945; CLR 56, 152; CN 1; CPW 1; CWRI
5; DA; DA3; DAB; DAC; DAM MST,
NOV, POP; DLB 15, 160, 255; EFS 2;
EWL 3; FANT; JRDA; LAIT 1; LATS
1:2; LMFS 2; MAICYA 1, 2; MTCW 1,
2; MTFW 2005; NFS 8, 26; RGEL 2;
SATA 2, 32, 100; SATA-Obit 24; SFW 4;
SUFW; TEA; WCH; WYA; YAW

Tolkien, John Ronald Reuel
See Tolkien, J. R. R.

Toller, Ernst 1893-1939 .... **TCLC 10, 235**
See also CA 107; 186; DLB 124; EWL 3;
RGWL 2, 3

Tolson, M. B.
See Tolson, Melvin B(eaunorus)

Tolson, Melvin B(eaunorus)
1898(?)-1966 .... **BLC 1:3; CLC 36, 105;
PC 88**
See also AFAW 1, 2; BW 1, 3; CA 124; 89-
92; CANR 80; DAM MULT, POET; DLB
48, 76; MAL 5; RGAL 4

Tolstoi, Aleksei Nikolaevich
See Tolstoy, Alexey Nikolaevich

Tolstoi, Lev
See Tolstoy, Leo

Tolstoy, Aleksei Nikolaevich
See Tolstoy, Alexey Nikolaevich

Tolstoy, Alexey Nikolaevich
1882-1945 .... **TCLC 18**
See also CA 107; 158; DLB 272; EWL 3;
SFW 4

Tolstoy, Leo 1828-1910 ..... **SSC 9, 30, 45, 54,
131; TCLC 4, 11, 17, 28, 44, 79, 173;
WLC 6**
See also AAYA 56; CA 104; 123; DA; DA3;
DAB; DAC; DAM MST, NOV; DLB 238;
EFS 2; EW 7; EXPS; IDTP; LAIT 2;
LATS 1:1; LMFS 1; NFS 10, 28; RGSF
2; RGWL 2, 3; SATA 26; SSFS 5, 28;
TWA

Tolstoy, Count Leo
See Tolstoy, Leo

Tolstoy, Leo Nikolaevich
See Tolstoy, Leo

Tomalin, Claire 1933- .... **CLC 166**
See also CA 89-92; CANR 52, 88, 165;
DLB 155

Tomasi di Lampedusa, Giuseppe
See Lampedusa, Giuseppe di

Tomlin, Lily 1939(?)- .... **CLC 17**
See also CA 117

Tomlin, Mary Jane
See Tomlin, Lily

Tomlin, Mary Jean
See Tomlin, Lily

Tomline, F. Latour
See Gilbert, W(illiam) S(chwenck)

Tomlinson, (Alfred) Charles 1927- .... **CLC 2,
4, 6, 13, 45; PC 17**
See also CA 5-8R; CANR 33; CP 1, 2, 3, 4,
5, 6, 7; DAM POET; DLB 40; TCLE 1:2

Tomlinson, H(enry) M(ajor)
1873-1958 .... **TCLC 71**
See also CA 118; 161; DLB 36, 100, 195

Tomlinson, Mary Jane
See Tomlin, Lily

Tonna, Charlotte Elizabeth
1790-1846 .... **NCLC 135**
See also DLB 163

Tonson, Jacob fl. 1655(?)-1736 .... **LC 86**
See also DLB 170

Toole, John Kennedy 1937-1969 ..... **CLC 19,
64**
See also BPFB 3; CA 104; DLBY 1981;
MTCW 2; MTFW 2005

Toomer, Eugene
See Toomer, Jean

Toomer, Eugene Pinchback
See Toomer, Jean

Toomer, Jean 1894-1967 ... **BLC 1:3; CLC 1,
4, 13, 22; HR 1:3; PC 7; SSC 1, 45,
138; TCLC 172; WLCS**
See also AFAW 1, 2; AMWS 3, 9; BW 1;
CA 85-88; CDALB 1917-1929; DA3;
DAM MULT; DLB 45, 51; EWL 3; EXPP;
EXPS; LMFS 2; MAL 5; MTCW 1, 2;
MTFW 2005; NFS 11; PFS 31; RGAL 4;
RGSF 2; SSFS 5

Toomer, Nathan Jean
See Toomer, Jean

Toomer, Nathan Pinchback
See Toomer, Jean

Torley, Luke
See Blish, James

Tornimparte, Alessandra
See Ginzburg, Natalia

Torre, Raoul della
See Mencken, H. L.

Torrence, Ridgely 1874-1950 .... **TCLC 97**
See also DLB 54, 249; MAL 5

Torrey, E. Fuller 1937- .... **CLC 34**
See also CA 119; CANR 71, 158

Torrey, Edwin Fuller
See Torrey, E. Fuller

Torsvan, Ben Traven
See Traven, B.

Torsvan, Benno Traven
See Traven, B.

Torsvan, Berick Traven
See Traven, B.

Torsvan, Berwick Traven
See Traven, B.

Torsvan, Bruno Traven
See Traven, B.

Torsvan, Traven
See Traven, B.

Toson
See Shimazaki, Haruki

Tourneur, Cyril 1575(?)-1626 ...... **LC 66, 181**
See also BRW 2; DAM DRAM; DLB 58;
RGEL 2

Tournier, Michel 1924- .... **CLC 6, 23, 36, 95,
249; SSC 88**
See also CA 49-52; CANR 3, 36, 74, 149;
CWW 2; DLB 83; EWL 3; GFL 1789 to
the Present; MTCW 1, 2; SATA 23

Tournier, Michel Edouard
See Tournier, Michel

Tournimparte, Alessandra
See Ginzburg, Natalia

Towers, Ivar
See Kornbluth, C(yril) M.

Towne, Robert (Burton) 1936(?)- ..... **CLC 87**
See also CA 108; DLB 44; IDFW 3, 4

Townsend, Sue 1946- .... **CLC 61**
See also AAYA 28; CA 119; 127; CANR
65, 107, 202; CBD; CD 5, 6; CPW; CWD;
DAB; DAC; DAM MST; DLB 271, 352;
INT CA-127; SATA 55, 93; SATA-Brief
48; YAW

Townsend, Susan Lilian
See Townsend, Sue

Townshend, Pete
See Townshend, Peter

Townshend, Peter 1945- .... **CLC 17, 42**
See also CA 107

Townshend, Peter Dennis Blandford
See Townshend, Peter

Tozzi, Federigo 1883-1920 .... **TCLC 31**
See also CA 160; CANR 110; DLB 264;
EWL 3; WLIT 7

Trafford, F. G.
See Riddell, Charlotte

Traherne, Thomas 1637(?)-1674 .. **LC 99; PC
70**
See also BRW 2; BRWS 11; DLB 131;
PAB; RGEL 2

Traill, Catharine Parr 1802-1899 .. **NCLC 31**
See also DLB 99

Trakl, Georg 1887-1914 ...... **PC 20; TCLC 5,
239**
See also CA 104; 165; EW 10; EWL 3;
LMFS 2; MTCW 2; RGWL 2, 3

Trambley, Estela Portillo
See Portillo Trambley, Estela

Tranquilli, Secondino
See Silone, Ignazio

Transtroemer, Tomas Gosta
See Transtromer, Tomas

van Itallie, Jean-Claude 1936- .... **CLC 3**
See also CA 45-48; CAAS 2; CAD; CANR
1, 48; CD 5, 6; DLB 7
Van Loot, Cornelius Obenchain
See Roberts, Kenneth (Lewis)
van Ostaijen, Paul 1896-1928 .... **TCLC 33**
See also CA 163
Van Peebles, Melvin 1932- .... **CLC 2, 20**
See also BW 2, 3; CA 85-88; CANR 27,
67, 82; DAM MULT
van Schendel, Arthur(-Francois-Emile)
1874-1946 .... **TCLC 56**
See also EWL 3
Van See, John
See Vance, Jack
Vansittart, Peter 1920-2008 .... **CLC 42**
See also CA 1-4R; 278; CANR 3, 49, 90;
CN 4, 5, 6, 7; RHW
Van Vechten, Carl 1880-1964 ... **CLC 33; HR
1:3**
See also AMWS 2; CA 183; 89-92; DLB 4,
9, 51; RGAL 4
van Vogt, A(lfred) E(lton) 1912-2000 . **CLC 1**
See also BPFB 3; BYA 13, 14; CA 21-24R;
190; CANR 28; DLB 8, 251; SATA 14;
SATA-Obit 124; SCFW 1, 2; SFW 4
Vara, Madeleine
See Jackson, Laura
Varda, Agnes 1928- .... **CLC 16**
See also CA 116; 122
Vargas Llosa, Jorge Mario Pedro
See Vargas Llosa, Mario
Vargas Llosa, Mario 1936- .. **CLC 3, 6, 9, 10,
15, 31, 42, 85, 181; HLC 2**
See also BPFB 3; CA 73-76; CANR 18, 32,
42, 67, 116, 140, 173; CDWLB 3; CWW
2; DA; DA3; DAB; DAC; DAM MST,
MULT, NOV; DLB 145; DNFS 2; EWL
3; HW 1, 2; LAIT 5; LATS 1:2; LAW;
LAWS 1; MTCW 1, 2; MTFW 2005;
RGWL 2, 3; SSFS 14; TWA; WLIT 1
Varnhagen von Ense, Rahel
1771-1833 .... **NCLC 130**
See also DLB 90
Vasari, Giorgio 1511-1574 .... **LC 114**
Vasilikos, Vasiles
See Vassilikos, Vassilis
Vasiliu, Gheorghe
See Bacovia, George
Vassa, Gustavus
See Equiano, Olaudah
Vassilikos, Vassilis 1933- .... **CLC 4, 8**
See also CA 81-84; CANR 75, 149; EWL 3
Vaughan, Henry 1621-1695 .... **LC 27; PC 81**
See also BRW 2; DLB 131; PAB; RGEL 2
Vaughn, Stephanie .... **CLC 62**
Vazov, Ivan (Minchov) 1850-1921 . **TCLC 25**
See also CA 121; 167; CDWLB 4; DLB
147
Veblen, Thorstein B(unde)
1857-1929 .... **TCLC 31**
See also AMWS 1; CA 115; 165; DLB 246;
MAL 5
Vega, Lope de 1562-1635 ... **HLCS 2; LC 23,
119**
See also EW 2; RGWL 2, 3
Veldeke, Heinrich von c. 1145-c.
1190 .... **CMLC 85**
Vendler, Helen 1933- .... **CLC 138**
See also CA 41-44R; CANR 25, 72, 136,
190; MTCW 1, 2; MTFW 2005
Vendler, Helen Hennessy
See Vendler, Helen
Venison, Alfred
See Pound, Ezra
Ventsel, Elena Sergeevna
1907-2002 .... **CLC 59**
See also CA 154; CWW 2; DLB 302

Venttsel', Elena Sergeevna
See Ventsel, Elena Sergeevna
Verdi, Marie de
See Mencken, H. L.
Verdu, Matilde
See Cela, Camilo Jose
Verga, Giovanni (Carmelo)
1840-1922 ..... **SSC 21, 87; TCLC 3, 227**
See also CA 104; 123; CANR 101; EW 7;
EWL 3; RGSF 2; RGWL 2, 3; WLIT 7
Vergil 70B.C.-19B.C. .. **CMLC 9, 40, 101; PC
12; WLCS**
See also AW 2; CDWLB 1; DA; DA3;
DAB; DAC; DAM MST, POET; DLB
211; EFS 1; LAIT 1; LMFS 1; RGWL 2,
3; WLIT 8; WP
Vergil, Polydore c. 1470-1555 .... **LC 108**
See also DLB 132
Verhaeren, Emile (Adolphe Gustave)
1855-1916 .... **TCLC 12**
See also CA 109; EWL 3; GFL 1789 to the
Present
Verlaine, Paul 1844-1896 ... **NCLC 2, 51; PC
2, 32**
See also DAM POET; DLB 217; EW 7;
GFL 1789 to the Present; LMFS 2; RGWL
2, 3; TWA
Verlaine, Paul Marie
See Verlaine, Paul
Verne, Jules 1828-1905 .... **TCLC 6, 52**
See also AAYA 16; BYA 4; CA 110; 131;
CLR 88; DA3; DLB 123; GFL 1789 to
the Present; JRDA; LAIT 2; LMFS 2;
MAICYA 1, 2; MTFW 2005; NFS 30, 34;
RGWL 2, 3; SATA 21; SCFW 1, 2; SFW
4; TWA; WCH
Verne, Jules Gabriel
See Verne, Jules
Verus, Marcus Annius
See Aurelius, Marcus
Very, Jones 1813-1880 .... **NCLC 9; PC 86**
See also DLB 1, 243; RGAL 4
Very, Rev. C.
See Crowley, Edward Alexander
Vesaas, Tarjei 1897-1970 .... **CLC 48**
See also CA 190; 29-32R; DLB 297; EW
11; EWL 3; RGWL 3
Vialis, Gaston
See Simenon, Georges
Vian, Boris 1920-1959(?) .... **TCLC 9**
See also CA 106; 164; CANR 111; DLB
72, 321; EWL 3; GFL 1789 to the Present;
MTCW 2; RGWL 2, 3
Viator, Vacuus
See Hughes, Thomas
Viaud, Julien 1850-1923 .... **TCLC 11, 239**
See also CA 107; DLB 123; GFL 1789 to
the Present
Viaud, Louis Marie Julien
See Viaud, Julien
Vicar, Henry
See Felsen, Henry Gregor
Vicente, Gil 1465-c. 1536 .... **LC 99**
See also DLB 318; IDTP; RGWL 2, 3
Vicker, Angus
See Felsen, Henry Gregor
Vico, Giambattista
See Vico, Giovanni Battista
Vico, Giovanni Battista 1668-1744 .... **LC 138**
See also EW 3; WLIT 7
Vidal, Eugene Luther Gore
See Vidal, Gore
Vidal, Gore 1925- ...... **CLC 2, 4, 6, 8, 10, 22,
33, 72, 142, 289**
See also AAYA 64; AITN 1; AMWS 4;
BEST 90:2; BPFB 3; CA 5-8R; CAD;
CANR 13, 45, 65, 100, 132, 167; CD 5,
6; CDALBS; CN 1, 2, 3, 4, 5, 6, 7; CPW;
DA3; DAM NOV, POP; DFS 2; DLB 6,

152; EWL 3; GLL 1; INT CANR-13;
MAL 5; MTCW 1, 2; MTFW 2005;
RGAL 4; RHW; TUS
Viereck, Peter 1916-2006 .... **CLC 4; PC 27**
See also CA 1-4R; 250; CANR 1, 47; CP 1,
2, 3, 4, 5, 6, 7; DLB 5; MAL 5; PFS 9,
14
Viereck, Peter Robert Edwin
See Viereck, Peter
Vigny, Alfred de 1797-1863 .... **NCLC 7, 102;
PC 26**
See also DAM POET; DLB 119, 192, 217;
EW 5; GFL 1789 to the Present; RGWL
2, 3
Vigny, Alfred Victor de
See Vigny, Alfred de
Vilakazi, Benedict Wallet
1906-1947 .... **TCLC 37**
See also CA 168
Vile, Curt
See Moore, Alan
Villa, Jose Garcia 1914-1997 ... **AAL; PC 22;
TCLC 176**
See also CA 25-28R; CANR 12, 118; CP 1,
2, 3, 4; DLB 312; EWL 3; EXPP
Villard, Oswald Garrison
1872-1949 .... **TCLC 160**
See also CA 113; 162; DLB 25, 91
Villarreal, Jose Antonio 1924- .... **HLC 2**
See also CA 133; CANR 93; DAM MULT;
DLB 82; HW 1; LAIT 4; RGAL 4
Villaurrutia, Xavier 1903-1950 .... **TCLC 80**
See also CA 192; EWL 3; HW 1; LAW
Villaverde, Cirilo 1812-1894 .... **NCLC 121**
See also LAW
Villehardouin, Geoffroi de
1150(?)-1218(?) .... **CMLC 38**
Villiers, George 1628-1687 .... **LC 107**
See also DLB 80; RGEL 2
**Villiers de l'Isle Adam, Jean Marie Mathias
Philippe Auguste** 1838-1889 ... **NCLC 3;
SSC 14**
See also DLB 123, 192; GFL 1789 to the
Present; RGSF 2
Villon, Francois 1431-1463(?) .... **LC 62, 166;
PC 13**
See also DLB 208; EW 2; RGWL 2, 3;
TWA
Vine, Barbara
See Rendell, Ruth
Vinge, Joan (Carol) D(ennison)
1948- .... **CLC 30; SSC 24**
See also AAYA 32; BPFB 3; CA 93-96;
CANR 72; SATA 36, 113; SFW 4; YAW
Viola, Herman J(oseph) 1938- .... **CLC 70**
See also CA 61-64; CANR 8, 23, 48, 91;
SATA 126
Violis, G.
See Simenon, Georges
Viramontes, Helena Maria 1954- .... **HLCS 2**
See also CA 159; CANR 182; CLR 285;
DLB 122, 350; HW 2; LLW
Virgil
See Vergil
Visconti, Luchino 1906-1976 .... **CLC 16**
See also CA 81-84; 65-68; CANR 39
Vitry, Jacques de
See Jacques de Vitry
Vittorini, Elio 1908-1966 .... **CLC 6, 9, 14**
See also CA 133; 25-28R; DLB 264; EW
12; EWL 3; RGWL 2, 3
Vivekananda, Swami 1863-1902 .... **TCLC 88**
Vives, Juan Luis 1493-1540 .... **LC 170**
See also DLB 318

Vizenor, Gerald Robert 1934- .... **CLC 103, 263; NNAL**
See also CA 13-16R, 205; CAAE 205; CAAS 22; CANR 5, 21, 44, 67; DAM MULT; DLB 175, 227; MTCW 2; MTFW 2005; TCWW 2

Vizinczey, Stephen 1933- .... **CLC 40**
See also CA 128; CCA 1; INT CA-128

Vliet, R(ussell) G(ordon) 1929-1984 .... **CLC 22**
See also CA 37-40R; 112; CANR 18; CP 2, 3

Vogau, Boris Andreevich
See Vogau, Boris Andreyevich

Vogau, Boris Andreyevich 1894-1938 .... **SSC 48; TCLC 23**
See also CA 123; 218; DLB 272; EWL 3; RGSF 2; RGWL 2, 3

Vogel, Paula A. 1951- .. **CLC 76, 290; DC 19**
See also CA 108; CAD; CANR 119, 140; CD 5, 6; CWD; DFS 14; DLB 341; MTFW 2005; RGAL 4

Vogel, Paula Anne
See Vogel, Paula A.

Voigt, Cynthia 1942- .... **CLC 30**
See also AAYA 3, 30; BYA 1, 3, 6, 7, 8; CA 106; CANR 18, 37, 40, 94, 145; CLR 13, 48, 141; INT CANR-18; JRDA; LAIT 5; MAICYA 1, 2; MAICYAS 1; MTFW 2005; SATA 48, 79, 116, 160; SATA-Brief 33; WYA; YAW

Voigt, Ellen Bryant 1943- .... **CLC 54**
See also CA 69-72; CANR 11, 29, 55, 115, 171; CP 5, 6, 7; CSW; CWP; DLB 120; PFS 23, 33

Voinovich, Vladimir 1932- .. **CLC 10, 49, 147**
See also CA 81-84; CAAS 12; CANR 33, 67, 150; CWW 2; DLB 302; MTCW 1

Voinovich, Vladimir Nikolaevich
See Voinovich, Vladimir

Vollmann, William T. 1959- ...... **CLC 89, 227**
See also AMWS 17; CA 134; CANR 67, 116, 185; CN 7; CPW; DA3; DAM NOV, POP; DLB 350; MTCW 2; MTFW 2005

Voloshinov, V. N.
See Bakhtin, Mikhail Mikhailovich

Voltaire 1694-1778 .. **LC 14, 79, 110; SSC 12, 112; WLC 6**
See also BYA 13; DA; DA3; DAB; DAC; DAM DRAM, MST; DLB 314; EW 4; GFL Beginnings to 1789; LATS 1:1; LMFS 1; NFS 7; RGWL 2, 3; TWA

von Aschendrof, Baron Ignatz
See Ford, Ford Madox

von Chamisso, Adelbert
See Chamisso, Adelbert von

von Daeniken, Erich 1935- .... **CLC 30**
See also AITN 1; CA 37-40R; CANR 17, 44

von Daniken, Erich
See von Daeniken, Erich

von Eschenbach, Wolfram c. 1170-c. 1220 .... **CMLC 5**
See also CDWLB 2; DLB 138; EW 1; RGWL 2, 3

von Hartmann, Eduard 1842-1906 .... **TCLC 96**

von Hayek, Friedrich August
See Hayek, F(riedrich) A(ugust von)

von Heidenstam, (Carl Gustaf) Verner
See Heidenstam, (Carl Gustaf) Verner von

von Heyse, Paul (Johann Ludwig)
See Heyse, Paul (Johann Ludwig von)

von Hofmannsthal, Hugo
See Hofmannsthal, Hugo von

von Horvath, Odon
See von Horvath, Odon

von Horvath, Odon
See von Horvath, Odon

von Horvath, Odon 1901-1938 .... **TCLC 45**
See also CA 118; 184, 194; DLB 85, 124; RGWL 2, 3

von Horvath, Oedoen
See von Horvath, Odon

von Kleist, Heinrich
See Kleist, Heinrich von

Vonnegut, Kurt, Jr.
See Vonnegut, Kurt

Vonnegut, Kurt 1922-2007 .... **CLC 1, 2, 3, 4, 5, 8, 12, 22, 40, 60, 111, 212, 254; SSC 8; WLC 6**
See also AAYA 6, 44; AITN 1; AMWS 2; BEST 90:4; BPFB 3; BYA 3, 14; CA 1-4R; 259; CANR 1, 25, 49, 75, 92; CDALB 1968-1988; CN 1, 2, 3, 4, 5, 6, 7; CPW 1; DA; DA3; DAB; DAC; DAM MST, NOV, POP; DLB 2, 8, 152; DLBD 3; DLBY 1980; EWL 3; EXPN; EXPS; LAIT 4; LMFS 2; MAL 5; MTCW 1, 2; MTFW 2005; NFS 3, 28; RGAL 4; SCFW; SFW 4; SSFS 5; TUS; YAW

Von Rachen, Kurt
See Hubbard, L. Ron

von Sternberg, Josef
See Sternberg, Josef von

Vorster, Gordon 1924- .... **CLC 34**
See also CA 133

Vosce, Trudie
See Ozick, Cynthia

Voznesensky, Andrei 1933- ..... **CLC 1, 15, 57**
See also CA 89-92; CANR 37; CWW 2; DAM POET; EWL 3; MTCW 1

Voznesensky, Andrei Andreievich
See Voznesensky, Andrei

Voznesensky, Andrey
See Voznesensky, Andrei

Wace, Robert c. 1100-c. 1175 .... **CMLC 55**
See also DLB 146

Waddington, Miriam 1917-2004 .... **CLC 28**
See also CA 21-24R; 225; CANR 12, 30; CCA 1; CP 1, 2, 3, 4, 5, 6, 7; DLB 68

Wade, Alan
See Vance, Jack

Wagman, Fredrica 1937- .... **CLC 7**
See also CA 97-100; CANR 166; INT CA-97-100

Wagner, Linda W.
See Wagner-Martin, Linda (C.)

Wagner, Linda Welshimer
See Wagner-Martin, Linda (C.)

Wagner, Richard 1813-1883 ..... **NCLC 9, 119**
See also DLB 129; EW 6

Wagner-Martin, Linda (C.) 1936- .... **CLC 50**
See also CA 159; CANR 135

Wagoner, David (Russell) 1926- .... **CLC 3, 5, 15; PC 33**
See also AMWS 9; CA 1-4R; CAAS 3; CANR 2, 71; CN 1, 2, 3, 4, 5, 6, 7; CP 1, 2, 3, 4, 5, 6, 7; DLB 5, 256; SATA 14; TCWW 1, 2

Wah, Fred(erick James) 1939- .... **CLC 44**
See also CA 107; 141; CP 1, 6, 7; DLB 60

Wahloo, Per 1926-1975 .... **CLC 7**
See also BPFB 3; CA 61-64; CANR 73; CMW 4; MSW

Wahloo, Peter
See Wahloo, Per

Wain, John 1925-1994 ...... **CLC 2, 11, 15, 46**
See also BRWS 16; CA 5-8R; 145; CAAS 4; CANR 23, 54; CDBLB 1960 to Present; CN 1, 2, 3, 4, 5; CP 1, 2, 3, 4, 5; DLB 15, 27, 139, 155; EWL 3; MTCW 1, 2; MTFW 2005

Wajda, Andrzej 1926- .... **CLC 16, 219**
See also CA 102

Wakefield, Dan 1932- .... **CLC 7**
See also CA 21-24R, 211; CAAE 211; CAAS 7; CN 4, 5, 6, 7

Wakefield, Herbert Russell 1888-1965 .... **TCLC 120**
See also CA 5-8R; CANR 77; HGG; SUFW

Wakoski, Diane 1937- ...... **CLC 2, 4, 7, 9, 11, 40; PC 15**
See also CA 13-16R, 216; CAAE 216; CAAS 1; CANR 9, 60, 106; CP 1, 2, 3, 4, 5, 6, 7; CWP; DAM POET; DLB 5; INT CANR-9; MAL 5; MTCW 2; MTFW 2005

Wakoski-Sherbell, Diane
See Wakoski, Diane

Walcott, Derek 1930- . **BLC 1:3, 2:3; CLC 2, 4, 9, 14, 25, 42, 67, 76, 160, 282; DC 7; PC 46**
See also BW 2; CA 89-92; CANR 26, 47, 75, 80, 130; CBD; CD 5, 6; CDWLB 3; CP 1, 2, 3, 4, 5, 6, 7; DA3; DAB; DAC; DAM MST, MULT, POET; DLB 117, 332; DLBY 1981; DNFS 1; EFS 1; EWL 3; LMFS 2; MTCW 1, 2; MTFW 2005; PFS 6, 34; RGEL 2; TWA; WWE 1

Walcott, Derek Alton
See Walcott, Derek

Waldman, Anne (Lesley) 1945- .... **CLC 7**
See also BG 1:3; CA 37-40R; CAAS 17; CANR 34, 69, 116; CP 1, 2, 3, 4, 5, 6, 7; CWP; DLB 16

Waldo, E. Hunter
See Sturgeon, Theodore (Hamilton)

Waldo, Edward Hamilton
See Sturgeon, Theodore (Hamilton)

Waldrop, Rosmarie 1935- .... **PC 109**
See also CA 101; CAAS 30; CANR 18, 39, 67; CP 6, 7; CWP; DLB 169

Walker, Alice 1944- .... **BLC 1:3, 2:3; CLC 5, 6, 9, 19, 27, 46, 58, 103, 167; PC 30; SSC 5; WLCS**
See also AAYA 3, 33; AFAW 1, 2; AMWS 3; BEST 89:4; BPFB 3; BW 2, 3; CA 37-40R; CANR 9, 27, 49, 66, 82, 131, 191; CDALB 1968-1988; CN 4, 5, 6, 7; CPW; CSW; DA; DA3; DAB; DAC; DAM MST, MULT, NOV, POET, POP; DLB 6, 33, 143; EWL 3; EXPN; EXPS; FL 1:6; FW; INT CANR-27; LAIT 3; MAL 5; MBL; MTCW 1, 2; MTFW 2005; NFS 5; PFS 30, 34; RGAL 4; RGSF 2; SATA 31; SSFS 2, 11; TUS; YAW

Walker, Alice Malsenior
See Walker, Alice

Walker, David Harry 1911-1992 ...... **CLC 14**
See also CA 1-4R; 137; CANR 1; CN 1, 2; CWRI 5; SATA 8; SATA-Obit 71

Walker, Edward Joseph 1934-2004 .. **CLC 13**
See also CA 21-24R; 226; CANR 12, 28, 53; CP 1, 2, 3, 4, 5, 6, 7; DLB 40

Walker, George F(rederick) 1947- .. **CLC 44, 61**
See also CA 103; CANR 21, 43, 59; CD 5, 6; DAB; DAC; DAM MST; DLB 60

Walker, Joseph A. 1935-2003 .... **CLC 19**
See also BW 1, 3; CA 89-92; CAD; CANR 26, 143; CD 5, 6; DAM DRAM, MST; DFS 12; DLB 38

Walker, Margaret 1915-1998 .... **BLC 1:3; CLC 1, 6; PC 20; TCLC 129**
See also AFAW 1, 2; BW 2, 3; CA 73-76; 172; CANR 26, 54, 76, 136; CN 1, 2, 3, 4, 5, 6; CP 1, 2, 3, 4, 5, 6; CSW; DAM MULT; DLB 76, 152; EXPP; FW; MAL 5; MTCW 1, 2; MTFW 2005; PFS 31; RGAL 4; RHW

Walker, Ted
See Walker, Edward Joseph

Wallace, David Foster 1962-2008 .... **CLC 50, 114, 271, 281; SSC 68**
See also AAYA 50; AMWS 10; CA 132; 277; CANR 59, 133, 190; CN 7; DA3; DLB 350; MTCW 2; MTFW 2005

Wallace, Dexter
See Masters, Edgar Lee
Wallace, (Richard Horatio) Edgar
1875-1932 .... **TCLC 57**
See also CA 115; 218; CMW 4; DLB 70;
MSW; RGEL 2
Wallace, Irving 1916-1990 .... **CLC 7, 13**
See also AITN 1; BPFB 3; CA 1-4R; 132;
CAAS 1; CANR 1, 27; CPW; DAM NOV,
POP; INT CANR-27; MTCW 1, 2
Wallant, Edward Lewis 1926-1962 ... **CLC 5, 10**
See also CA 1-4R; CANR 22; DLB 2, 28,
143, 299; EWL 3; MAL 5; MTCW 1, 2;
RGAL 4; RGHL
Wallas, Graham 1858-1932 .... **TCLC 91**
Waller, Edmund 1606-1687 .... **LC 86; PC 72**
See also BRW 2; DAM POET; DLB 126;
PAB; RGEL 2
Walley, Byron
See Card, Orson Scott
Walpole, Horace 1717-1797 ..... **LC 2, 49, 152**
See also BRW 3; DLB 39, 104, 213; GL 3;
HGG; LMFS 1; RGEL 2; SUFW 1; TEA
Walpole, Hugh 1884-1941 .... **TCLC 5**
See also CA 104; 165; DLB 34; HGG;
MTCW 2; RGEL 2; RHW
Walpole, Hugh Seymour
See Walpole, Hugh
Walrond, Eric (Derwent) 1898-1966 . **HR 1:3**
See also BW 1; CA 125; DLB 51
Walser, Martin 1927- .... **CLC 27, 183**
See also CA 57-60; CANR 8, 46, 145;
CWW 2; DLB 75, 124; EWL 3
Walser, Robert 1878-1956 ..... **SSC 20; TCLC 18**
See also CA 118; 165; CANR 100, 194;
DLB 66; EWL 3
Walsh, Gillian Paton
See Paton Walsh, Jill
Walsh, Jill Paton
See Paton Walsh, Jill
Walter, Villiam Christian
See Andersen, Hans Christian
Walter of Chatillon c. 1135-c.
1202 .... **CMLC 111**
Walters, Anna L(ee) 1946- .... **NNAL**
See also CA 73-76
Walther von der Vogelweide c.
1170-1228 .... **CMLC 56**
Walton, Izaak 1593-1683 .... **LC 72**
See also BRW 2; CDBLB Before 1660;
DLB 151, 213; RGEL 2
Walzer, Michael 1935- .... **CLC 238**
See also CA 37-40R; CANR 15, 48, 127,
190
Walzer, Michael Laban
See Walzer, Michael
Wambaugh, Joseph, Jr. 1937- ...... **CLC 3, 18**
See also AITN 1; BEST 89:3; BPFB 3; CA
33-36R; CANR 42, 65, 115, 167; CMW
4; CPW 1; DA3; DAM NOV, POP; DLB
6; DLBY 1983; MSW; MTCW 1, 2
Wambaugh, Joseph Aloysius
See Wambaugh, Joseph, Jr.
Wang Wei 699(?)-761(?) . **CMLC 100; PC 18**
See also TWA
Warburton, William 1698-1779 .... **LC 97**
See also DLB 104
Ward, Arthur Henry Sarsfield
1883-1959 .... **TCLC 28**
See also AAYA 80; CA 108; 173; CMW 4;
DLB 70; HGG; MSW; SUFW
Ward, Douglas Turner 1930- .... **CLC 19**
See also BW 1; CA 81-84; CAD; CANR
27; CD 5, 6; DLB 7, 38
Ward, E. D.
See Lucas, E(dward) V(errall)

Ward, Mrs. Humphry 1851-1920
See Ward, Mary Augusta
See also RGEL 2
Ward, Mary Augusta 1851-1920 ... **TCLC 55**
See Ward, Mrs. Humphry
See also DLB 18
Ward, Nathaniel 1578(?)-1652 .... **LC 114**
See also DLB 24
Ward, Peter
See Faust, Frederick
Warhol, Andy 1928(?)-1987 .... **CLC 20**
See also AAYA 12; BEST 89:4; CA 89-92;
121; CANR 34
Warner, Francis (Robert Le Plastrier)
1937- .... **CLC 14**
See also CA 53-56; CANR 11; CP 1, 2, 3, 4
Warner, Marina 1946- .... **CLC 59, 231**
See also CA 65-68; CANR 21, 55, 118; CN
5, 6, 7; DLB 194; MTFW 2005
Warner, Rex (Ernest) 1905-1986 ...... **CLC 45**
See also CA 89-92; 119; CN 1, 2, 3, 4; CP
1, 2, 3, 4; DLB 15; RGEL 2; RHW
Warner, Susan (Bogert)
1819-1885 .... **NCLC 31, 146**
See also AMWS 18; DLB 3, 42, 239, 250,
254
Warner, Sylvia (Constance) Ashton
See Ashton-Warner, Sylvia (Constance)
Warner, Sylvia Townsend
1893-1978 .. **CLC 7, 19; SSC 23; TCLC 131**
See also BRWS 7; CA 61-64; 77-80; CANR
16, 60, 104; CN 1, 2; DLB 34, 139; EWL
3; FANT; FW; MTCW 1, 2; RGEL 2;
RGSF 2; RHW
Warren, Mercy Otis 1728-1814 .... **NCLC 13, 226**
See also DLB 31, 200; RGAL 4; TUS
Warren, Robert Penn 1905-1989 .. **CLC 1, 4, 6, 8, 10, 13, 18, 39, 53, 59; PC 37; SSC 4, 58, 126; WLC 6**
See also AITN 1; AMW; AMWC 2; BPFB
3; BYA 1; CA 13-16R; 129; CANR 10,
47; CDALB 1968-1988; CN 1, 2, 3, 4;
CP 1, 2, 3, 4; DA; DA3; DAB; DAC;
DAM MST, NOV, POET; DLB 2, 48, 152,
320; DLBY 1980, 1989; EWL 3; INT
CANR-10; MAL 5; MTCW 1, 2; MTFW
2005; NFS 13; RGAL 4; RGSF 2; RHW;
SATA 46; SATA-Obit 63; SSFS 8; TUS
Warrigal, Jack
See Furphy, Joseph
Warshofsky, Isaac
See Singer, Isaac Bashevis
Warton, Joseph 1722-1800 ... **LC 128; NCLC 118**
See also DLB 104, 109; RGEL 2
Warton, Thomas 1728-1790 .... **LC 15, 82**
See also DAM POET; DLB 104, 109, 336;
RGEL 2
Waruk, Kona
See Harris, (Theodore) Wilson
Warung, Price
See Astley, William
Warwick, Jarvis
See Garner, Hugh
Washington, Alex
See Harris, Mark
Washington, Booker T. 1856-1915 . **BLC 1:3; TCLC 10**
See also BW 1; CA 114; 125; DA3; DAM
MULT; DLB 345; LAIT 2; RGAL 4;
SATA 28
Washington, Booker Taliaferro
See Washington, Booker T.
Washington, George 1732-1799 .... **LC 25**
See also DLB 31

Wassermann, (Karl) Jakob
1873-1934 .... **TCLC 6**
See also CA 104; 163; DLB 66; EWL 3
Wasserstein, Wendy 1950-2006 . **CLC 32, 59, 90, 183; DC 4**
See also AAYA 73; AMWS 15; CA 121;
129; 247; CABS 3; CAD; CANR 53, 75,
128; CD 5, 6; CWD; DA3; DAM DRAM;
DFS 5, 17; DLB 228; EWL 3; FW; INT
CA-129; MAL 5; MTCW 2; MTFW 2005;
SATA 94; SATA-Obit 174
Waterhouse, Keith 1929-2009 .... **CLC 47**
See also BRWS 13; CA 5-8R; 290; CANR
38, 67, 109; CBD; CD 6; CN 1, 2, 3, 4, 5,
6, 7; DLB 13, 15; MTCW 1, 2; MTFW
2005
Waterhouse, Keith Spencer
See Waterhouse, Keith
Waters, Frank (Joseph) 1902-1995 .. **CLC 88**
See also CA 5-8R; 149; CAAS 13; CANR
3, 18, 63, 121; DLB 212; DLBY 1986;
RGAL 4; TCWW 1, 2
Waters, Mary C. .... **CLC 70**
Waters, Roger 1944- .... **CLC 35**
Watkins, Frances Ellen
See Harper, Frances Ellen Watkins
Watkins, Gerrold
See Malzberg, Barry N(athaniel)
Watkins, Gloria Jean
See hooks, bell
Watkins, Paul 1964- .... **CLC 55**
See also CA 132; CANR 62, 98
Watkins, Vernon Phillips
1906-1967 .... **CLC 43**
See also CA 9-10; 25-28R; CAP 1; DLB
20; EWL 3; RGEL 2
Watson, Irving S.
See Mencken, H. L.
Watson, John H.
See Farmer, Philip Jose
Watson, Richard F.
See Silverberg, Robert
Watson, Sheila 1909-1998 .... **SSC 128**
See also AITN 2; CA 155; CCA 1; DAC;
DLB 60
Watts, Ephraim
See Horne, Richard Henry Hengist
Watts, Isaac 1674-1748 .... **LC 98**
See also DLB 95; RGEL 2; SATA 52
Waugh, Auberon (Alexander)
1939-2001 .... **CLC 7**
See also CA 45-48; 192; CANR 6, 22, 92;
CN 1, 2, 3; DLB 14, 194
Waugh, Evelyn 1903-1966 ... **CLC 1, 3, 8, 13, 19, 27, 44, 107; SSC 41; TCLC 229; WLC 6**
See also AAYA 78; BPFB 3; BRW 7; CA
85-88; 25-28R; CANR 22; CDBLB 1914-
1945; DA; DA3; DAB; DAC; DAM MST,
NOV, POP; DLB 15, 162, 195, 352; EWL
3; MTCW 1, 2; MTFW 2005; NFS 13,
17, 34; RGEL 2; RGSF 2; TEA; WLIT 4
Waugh, Evelyn Arthur St. John
See Waugh, Evelyn
Waugh, Harriet 1944- .... **CLC 6**
See also CA 85-88; CANR 22
Ways, C.R.
See Blount, Roy, Jr.
Waystaff, Simon
See Swift, Jonathan
Webb, Beatrice 1858-1943 .... **TCLC 22**
See also CA 117; 162; DLB 190; FW
Webb, Beatrice Martha Potter
See Webb, Beatrice
Webb, Charles 1939- .... **CLC 7**
See also CA 25-28R; CANR 114, 188
Webb, Charles Richard
See Webb, Charles

Webb, Frank J. .... **NCLC 143**
  See also DLB 50
Webb, James, Jr.
  See Webb, James
Webb, James 1946- .... **CLC 22**
  See also CA 81-84; CANR 156
Webb, James H.
  See Webb, James
Webb, James Henry
  See Webb, James
Webb, Mary Gladys (Meredith)
  1881-1927 .... **TCLC 24**
  See also CA 182; 123; DLB 34; FW; RGEL 2
Webb, Mrs. Sidney
  See Webb, Beatrice
Webb, Phyllis 1927- .... **CLC 18**
  See also CA 104; CANR 23; CCA 1; CP 1, 2, 3, 4, 5, 6, 7; CWP; DLB 53
Webb, Sidney 1859-1947 .... **TCLC 22**
  See also CA 117; 163; DLB 190
Webb, Sidney James
  See Webb, Sidney
Webber, Andrew Lloyd
  See Lloyd Webber, Andrew
Weber, Lenora Mattingly
  1895-1971 .... **CLC 12**
  See also CA 19-20; 29-32R; CAP 1; SATA 2; SATA-Obit 26
Weber, Max 1864-1920 .... **TCLC 69**
  See also CA 109; 189; DLB 296
Webster, John 1580(?)-1634(?) ...... **DC 2; LC 33, 84, 124; WLC 6**
  See also BRW 2; CDBLB Before 1660; DA; DAB; DAC; DAM DRAM, MST; DFS 17, 19; DLB 58; IDTP; RGEL 2; WLIT 3
Webster, Noah 1758-1843 .... **NCLC 30**
  See also DLB 1, 37, 42, 43, 73, 243
Wedekind, Benjamin Franklin
  See Wedekind, Frank
Wedekind, Frank 1864-1918 .... **TCLC 7**
  See also CA 104; 153; CANR 121, 122; CDWLB 2; DAM DRAM; DLB 118; EW 8; EWL 3; LMFS 2; RGWL 2, 3
Wehr, Demaris .... **CLC 65**
Weidman, Jerome 1913-1998 .... **CLC 7**
  See also AITN 2; CA 1-4R; 171; CAD; CANR 1; CD 1, 2, 3, 4, 5; DLB 28
Weil, Simone 1909-1943 .... **TCLC 23**
  See also CA 117; 159; EW 12; EWL 3; FW; GFL 1789 to the Present; MTCW 2
Weil, Simone Adolphine
  See Weil, Simone
Weininger, Otto 1880-1903 .... **TCLC 84**
Weinstein, Nathan
  See West, Nathanael
Weinstein, Nathan von Wallenstein
  See West, Nathanael
Weir, Peter (Lindsay) 1944- .... **CLC 20**
  See also CA 113; 123
Weiss, Peter (Ulrich) 1916-1982 .. **CLC 3, 15, 51; DC 36; TCLC 152**
  See also CA 45-48; 106; CANR 3; DAM DRAM; DFS 3; DLB 69, 124; EWL 3; RGHL; RGWL 2, 3
Weiss, Theodore (Russell)
  1916-2003 .... **CLC 3, 8, 14**
  See also CA 9-12R; 189; 216; CAAE 189; CAAS 2; CANR 46, 94; CP 1, 2, 3, 4, 5, 6, 7; DLB 5; TCLE 1:2
Welch, (Maurice) Denton
  1915-1948 .... **TCLC 22**
  See also BRWS 8; CA 121; 148; RGEL 2
Welch, James 1940-2003 .... **CLC 6, 14, 52, 249; NNAL; PC 62**
  See also CA 85-88; 219; CANR 42, 66, 107; CN 5, 6, 7; CP 2, 3, 4, 5, 6, 7; CPW; DAM MULT, POP; DLB 175, 256; LATS 1:1; NFS 23; RGAL 4; TCWW 1, 2

Welch, James Phillip
  See Welch, James
Weld, Angelina Grimke
  See Grimke, Angelina Weld
Weldon, Fay 1931- . **CLC 6, 9, 11, 19, 36, 59, 122**
  See also BRWS 4; CA 21-24R; CANR 16, 46, 63, 97, 137; CDBLB 1960 to Present; CN 3, 4, 5, 6, 7; CPW; DAM POP; DLB 14, 194, 319; EWL 3; FW; HGG; INT CANR-16; MTCW 1, 2; MTFW 2005; RGEL 2; RGSF 2
Wellek, Rene 1903-1995 .... **CLC 28**
  See also CA 5-8R; 150; CAAS 7; CANR 8; DLB 63; EWL 3; INT CANR-8
Weller, Michael 1942- .... **CLC 10, 53**
  See also CA 85-88; CAD; CD 5, 6
Weller, Paul 1958- .... **CLC 26**
Wellershoff, Dieter 1925- .... **CLC 46**
  See also CA 89-92; CANR 16, 37
Welles, (George) Orson 1915-1985 .. **CLC 20, 80**
  See also AAYA 40; CA 93-96; 117
Wellman, John McDowell 1945- .... **CLC 65**
  See also CA 166; CAD; CD 5, 6; RGAL 4
Wellman, Mac
  See Wellman, John McDowell; Wellman, John McDowell
Wellman, Manly Wade 1903-1986 ... **CLC 49**
  See also CA 1-4R; 118; CANR 6, 16, 44; FANT; SATA 6; SATA-Obit 47; SFW 4; SUFW
Wells, Carolyn 1869(?)-1942 .... **TCLC 35**
  See also CA 113; 185; CMW 4; DLB 11
Wells, H. G. 1866-1946 . **SSC 6, 70; TCLC 6, 12, 19, 133; WLC 6**
  See also AAYA 18; BPFB 3; BRW 6; CA 110; 121; CDBLB 1914-1945; CLR 64, 133; DA; DA3; DAB; DAC; DAM MST, NOV; DLB 34, 70, 156, 178; EWL 3; EXPS; HGG; LAIT 3; LMFS 2; MTCW 1, 2; MTFW 2005; NFS 17, 20; RGEL 2; RGSF 2; SATA 20; SCFW 1, 2; SFW 4; SSFS 3; SUFW; TEA; WCH; WLIT 4; YAW
Wells, Herbert George
  See Wells, H. G.
Wells, Rosemary 1943- .... **CLC 12**
  See also AAYA 13; BYA 7, 8; CA 85-88; CANR 48, 120, 179; CLR 16, 69; CWRI 5; MAICYA 1, 2; SAAS 1; SATA 18, 69, 114, 156, 207; YAW
Wells-Barnett, Ida B(ell)
  1862-1931 .... **TCLC 125**
  See also CA 182; DLB 23, 221
Welsh, Irvine 1958- .... **CLC 144, 276**
  See also CA 173; CANR 146, 196; CN 7; DLB 271
Welty, Eudora 1909-2001 .... **CLC 1, 2, 5, 14, 22, 33, 105, 220; SSC 1, 27, 51, 111; WLC 6**
  See also AAYA 48; AMW; AMWR 1; BPFB 3; CA 9-12R; 199; CABS 1; CANR 32, 65, 128; CDALB 1941-1968; CN 1, 2, 3, 4, 5, 6, 7; CSW; DA; DA3; DAB; DAC; DAM MST, NOV; DFS 26; DLB 2, 102, 143; DLBD 12; DLBY 1987, 2001; EWL 3; EXPS; HGG; LAIT 3; MAL 5; MBL; MTCW 1, 2; MTFW 2005; NFS 13, 15; RGAL 4; RGSF 2; RHW; SSFS 2, 10, 26; TUS
Welty, Eudora Alice
  See Welty, Eudora
Wen I-to 1899-1946 .... **TCLC 28**
  See also EWL 3
Wentworth, Robert
  See Hamilton, Edmond

Werfel, Franz (Viktor) 1890-1945 .... **PC 101; TCLC 8**
  See also CA 104; 161; DLB 81, 124; EWL 3; RGWL 2, 3
Wergeland, Henrik Arnold
  1808-1845 .... **NCLC 5**
  See also DLB 354
Werner, Friedrich Ludwig Zacharias
  1768-1823 .... **NCLC 189**
  See also DLB 94
Werner, Zacharias
  See Werner, Friedrich Ludwig Zacharias
Wersba, Barbara 1932- .... **CLC 30**
  See also AAYA 2, 30; BYA 6, 12, 13; CA 29-32R, 182; CAAE 182; CANR 16, 38; CLR 3, 78; DLB 52; JRDA; MAICYA 1, 2; SAAS 2; SATA 1, 58; SATA-Essay 103; WYA; YAW
Wertmueller, Lina 1928- .... **CLC 16**
  See also CA 97-100; CANR 39, 78
Wescott, Glenway 1901-1987 .. **CLC 13; SSC 35**
  See also CA 13-16R; 121; CANR 23, 70; CN 1, 2, 3, 4; DLB 4, 9, 102; MAL 5; RGAL 4
Wesker, Arnold 1932- .... **CLC 3, 5, 42**
  See also CA 1-4R; CAAS 7; CANR 1, 33; CBD; CD 5, 6; CDBLB 1960 to Present; DAB; DAM DRAM; DLB 13, 310, 319; EWL 3; MTCW 1; RGEL 2; TEA
Wesley, Charles 1707-1788 .... **LC 128**
  See also DLB 95; RGEL 2
Wesley, John 1703-1791 .... **LC 88**
  See also DLB 104
Wesley, Richard (Errol) 1945- .... **CLC 7**
  See also BW 1; CA 57-60; CAD; CANR 27; CD 5, 6; DLB 38
Wessel, Johan Herman 1742-1785 .... **LC 7**
  See also DLB 300
West, Anthony (Panther)
  1914-1987 .... **CLC 50**
  See also CA 45-48; 124; CANR 3, 19; CN 1, 2, 3, 4; DLB 15
West, C. P.
  See Wodehouse, P. G.
West, Cornel 1953- .... **BLCS; CLC 134**
  See also CA 144; CANR 91, 159; DLB 246
West, Cornel Ronald
  See West, Cornel
West, Delno C(loyde), Jr. 1936- .... **CLC 70**
  See also CA 57-60
West, Dorothy 1907-1998 .... **HR 1:3; TCLC 108**
  See also AMWS 18; BW 2; CA 143; 169; DLB 76
West, Edwin
  See Westlake, Donald E.
West, (Mary) Jessamyn 1902-1984 ... **CLC 7, 17**
  See also CA 9-12R; 112; CANR 27; CN 1, 2, 3; DLB 6; DLBY 1984; MTCW 1, 2; RGAL 4; RHW; SATA-Obit 37; TCWW 2; TUS; YAW
West, Morris L(anglo) 1916-1999 ..... **CLC 6, 33**
  See also BPFB 3; CA 5-8R; 187; CANR 24, 49, 64; CN 1, 2, 3, 4, 5, 6; CPW; DLB 289; MTCW 1, 2; MTFW 2005
West, Nathanael 1903-1940 ...... **SSC 16, 116; TCLC 1, 14, 44, 235**
  See also AAYA 77; AMW; AMWR 2; BPFB 3; CA 104; 125; CDALB 1929-1941; DA3; DLB 4, 9, 28; EWL 3; MAL 5; MTCW 1, 2; MTFW 2005; NFS 16; RGAL 4; TUS
West, Owen
  See Koontz, Dean

Wight, James Alfred
See Herriot, James
Wilbur, Richard 1921- .. **CLC 3, 6, 9, 14, 53, 110; PC 51**
See also AAYA 72; AMWS 3; CA 1-4R; CABS 2; CANR 2, 29, 76, 93, 139; CDALBS; CP 1, 2, 3, 4, 5, 6, 7; DA; DAB; DAC; DAM MST, POET; DLB 5, 169; EWL 3; EXPP; INT CANR-29; MAL 5; MTCW 1, 2; MTFW 2005; PAB; PFS 11, 12, 16, 29; RGAL 4; SATA 9, 108; WP
Wilbur, Richard Purdy
See Wilbur, Richard
Wild, Peter 1940- .... **CLC 14**
See also CA 37-40R; CP 1, 2, 3, 4, 5, 6, 7; DLB 5
Wilde, Oscar 1854(?)-1900 ... **DC 17; SSC 11, 77; TCLC 1, 8, 23, 41, 175; WLC 6**
See also AAYA 49; BRW 5; BRWC 1, 2; BRWR 2; BYA 15; CA 104; 119; CANR 112; CDBLB 1890-1914; CLR 114; DA; DA3; DAB; DAC; DAM DRAM, MST, NOV; DFS 4, 8, 9, 21; DLB 10, 19, 34, 57, 141, 156, 190, 344; EXPS; FANT; GL 3; LATS 1:1; NFS 20; RGEL 2; RGSF 2; SATA 24; SSFS 7; SUFW; TEA; WCH; WLIT 4
Wilde, Oscar Fingal O'Flahertie Willis
See Wilde, Oscar
Wilder, Billy
See Wilder, Samuel
Wilder, Samuel 1906-2002 .... **CLC 20**
See also AAYA 66; CA 89-92; 205; DLB 26
Wilder, Stephen
See Marlowe, Stephen
Wilder, Thornton 1897-1975 ..... **CLC 1, 5, 6, 10, 15, 35, 82; DC 1, 24; WLC 6**
See also AAYA 29; AITN 2; AMW; CA 13-16R; 61-64; CAD; CANR 40, 132; CDALBS; CN 1, 2; DA; DA3; DAB; DAC; DAM DRAM, MST, NOV; DFS 1, 4, 16; DLB 4, 7, 9, 228; DLBY 1997; EWL 3; LAIT 3; MAL 5; MTCW 1, 2; MTFW 2005; NFS 24; RGAL 4; RHW; WYAS 1
Wilder, Thornton Niven
See Wilder, Thornton
Wilding, Michael 1942- ...... **CLC 73; SSC 50**
See also CA 104; CANR 24, 49, 106; CN 4, 5, 6, 7; DLB 325; RGSF 2
Wiley, Richard 1944- .... **CLC 44**
See also CA 121; 129; CANR 71
Wilhelm, Kate
See Wilhelm, Katie
Wilhelm, Katie 1928- .... **CLC 7**
See also AAYA 20; BYA 16; CA 37-40R; CAAS 5; CANR 17, 36, 60, 94; DLB 8; INT CANR-17; MTCW 1; SCFW 2; SFW 4
Wilhelm, Katie Gertrude
See Wilhelm, Katie
Wilkins, Mary
See Freeman, Mary E(leanor) Wilkins
Willard, Nancy 1936- .... **CLC 7, 37**
See also BYA 5; CA 89-92; CANR 10, 39, 68, 107, 152, 186; CLR 5; CP 2, 3, 4, 5; CWP; CWRI 5; DLB 5, 52; FANT; MAICYA 1, 2; MTCW 1; SATA 37, 71, 127, 191; SATA-Brief 30; SUFW 2; TCLE 1:2
William of Malmesbury c. 1090B.C.-c. 1140B.C. .... **CMLC 57**
William of Moerbeke c. 1215-c. 1286 .... **CMLC 91**
William of Ockham 1290-1349 ..... **CMLC 32**
Williams, Ben Ames 1889-1953 ..... **TCLC 89**
See also CA 183; DLB 102

Williams, Charles
See Collier, James Lincoln
Williams, Charles 1886-1945 ..... **TCLC 1, 11**
See also BRWS 9; CA 104; 163; DLB 100, 153, 255; FANT; RGEL 2; SUFW 1
Williams, Charles Walter Stansby
See Williams, Charles
Williams, C.K. 1936- .... **CLC 33, 56, 148**
See also CA 37-40R; CAAS 26; CANR 57, 106; CP 1, 2, 3, 4, 5, 6, 7; DAM POET; DLB 5; MAL 5
Williams, Ella Gwendolen Rees
See Rhys, Jean
Williams, Emlyn 1905-1987 .... **CLC 15**
See also CA 104; 123; CANR 36; DAM DRAM; DLB 10, 77; IDTP; MTCW 1
Williams, George Emlyn
See Williams, Emlyn
Williams, Hank 1923-1953 .... **TCLC 81**
See Williams, Hiram King
See also CA 188
Williams, Helen Maria 1761-1827 .... **NCLC 135**
See also DLB 158
Williams, Hiram King 1923-1953
See Williams, Hank
Williams, Hugo (Mordaunt) 1942- ... **CLC 42**
See also CA 17-20R; CANR 45, 119; CP 1, 2, 3, 4, 5, 6, 7; DLB 40
Williams, J. Walker
See Wodehouse, P. G.
Williams, John A(lfred) 1925- .... **BLC 1:3; CLC 5, 13**
See also AFAW 2; BW 2, 3; CA 53-56, 195; CAAE 195; CAAS 3; CANR 6, 26, 51, 118; CN 1, 2, 3, 4, 5, 6, 7; CSW; DAM MULT; DLB 2, 33; EWL 3; INT CANR-6; MAL 5; RGAL 4; SFW 4
Williams, Jonathan 1929-2008 .... **CLC 13**
See also CA 9-12R; 270; CAAS 12; CANR 8, 108; CP 1, 2, 3, 4, 5, 6, 7; DLB 5
Williams, Jonathan Chamberlain
See Williams, Jonathan
Williams, Joy 1944- .... **CLC 31**
See also CA 41-44R; CANR 22, 48, 97, 168; DLB 335; SSFS 25
Williams, Norman 1952- .... **CLC 39**
See also CA 118
Williams, Roger 1603(?)-1683 .... **LC 129**
See also DLB 24
Williams, Sherley Anne 1944-1999 .... **BLC 1:3; CLC 89**
See also AFAW 2; BW 2, 3; CA 73-76; 185; CANR 25, 82; DAM MULT, POET; DLB 41; INT CANR-25; SATA 78; SATA-Obit 116
Williams, Shirley
See Williams, Sherley Anne
Williams, Tennessee 1911-1983 . **CLC 1, 2, 5, 7, 8, 11, 15, 19, 30, 39, 45, 71, 111; DC 4; SSC 81; WLC 6**
See also AAYA 31; AITN 1, 2; AMW; AMWC 1; CA 5-8R; 108; CABS 3; CAD; CANR 31, 132, 174; CDALB 1941-1968; CN 1, 2, 3; DA; DA3; DAB; DAC; DAM DRAM, MST; DFS 17; DLB 7, 341; DLBD 4; DLBY 1983; EWL 3; GLL 1; LAIT 4; LATS 1:2; MAL 5; MTCW 1, 2; MTFW 2005; RGAL 4; TUS
Williams, Thomas (Alonzo) 1926-1990 .... **CLC 14**
See also CA 1-4R; 132; CANR 2
Williams, Thomas Lanier
See Williams, Tennessee
Williams, William C.
See Williams, William Carlos

Williams, William Carlos 1883-1963 .... **CLC 1, 2, 5, 9, 13, 22, 42, 67; PC 7, 109; SSC 31; WLC 6**
See also AAYA 46; AMW; AMWR 1; CA 89-92; CANR 34; CDALB 1917-1929; DA; DA3; DAB; DAC; DAM MST, POET; DLB 4, 16, 54, 86; EWL 3; EXPP; MAL 5; MTCW 1, 2; MTFW 2005; NCFS 4; PAB; PFS 1, 6, 11, 34; RGAL 4; RGSF 2; SSFS 27; TUS; WP
Williamson, David (Keith) 1942- ..... **CLC 56**
See also CA 103; CANR 41; CD 5, 6; DLB 289
Williamson, Jack
See Williamson, John Stewart
Williamson, John Stewart 1908-2006 .... **CLC 29**
See also AAYA 76; CA 17-20R; 255; CAAS 8; CANR 23, 70, 153; DLB 8; SCFW 1, 2; SFW 4
Willie, Frederick
See Lovecraft, H. P.
Willingham, Calder (Baynard, Jr.) 1922-1995 .... **CLC 5, 51**
See also CA 5-8R; 147; CANR 3; CN 1, 2, 3, 4, 5; CSW; DLB 2, 44; IDFW 3, 4; MTCW 1
Willis, Charles
See Clarke, Arthur C.
Willis, Nathaniel Parker 1806-1867 .... **NCLC 194**
See also DLB 3, 59, 73, 74, 183, 250; DLBD 13; RGAL 4
Willy
See Colette
Willy, Colette
See Colette
Wilmot, John 1647-1680 .... **LC 75; PC 66**
See also BRW 2; DLB 131; PAB; RGEL 2
Wilson, A. N. 1950- .... **CLC 33**
See also BRWS 6; CA 112; 122; CANR 156, 199; CN 4, 5, 6, 7; DLB 14, 155, 194; MTCW 2
Wilson, Andrew Norman
See Wilson, A. N.
Wilson, Angus 1913-1991 .... **CLC 2, 3, 5, 25, 34; SSC 21**
See also BRWS 1; CA 5-8R; 134; CANR 21; CN 1, 2, 3, 4; DLB 15, 139, 155; EWL 3; MTCW 1, 2; MTFW 2005; RGEL 2; RGSF 2
Wilson, Angus Frank Johnstone
See Wilson, Angus
Wilson, August 1945-2005 .... **BLC 1:3, 2:3; CLC 39, 50, 63, 118, 222; DC 2, 31; WLCS**
See also AAYA 16; AFAW 2; AMWS 8; BW 2, 3; CA 115; 122; 244; CAD; CANR 42, 54, 76, 128; CD 5, 6; DA; DA3; DAB; DAC; DAM DRAM, MST, MULT; DFS 3, 7, 15, 17, 24; DLB 228; EWL 3; LAIT 4; LATS 1:2; MAL 5; MTCW 1, 2; MTFW 2005; RGAL 4
Wilson, Brian 1942- .... **CLC 12**
Wilson, Colin 1931- .... **CLC 3, 14**
See also CA 1-4R; CAAS 5; CANR 1, 22, 33, 77; CMW 4; CN 1, 2, 3, 4, 5, 6; DLB 14, 194; HGG; MTCW 1; SFW 4
Wilson, Colin Henry
See Wilson, Colin
Wilson, Dirk
See Pohl, Frederik
Wilson, Edmund 1895-1972 .. **CLC 1, 2, 3, 8, 24**
See also AMW; CA 1-4R; 37-40R; CANR 1, 46, 110; CN 1; DLB 63; EWL 3; MAL 5; MTCW 1, 2; MTFW 2005; RGAL 4; TUS

Wilson, Ethel Davis (Bryant)
1888(?)-1980 .... **CLC 13**
See also CA 102; CN 1, 2; DAC; DAM
POET; DLB 68; MTCW 1; RGEL 2

Wilson, Harriet
See Wilson, Harriet E. Adams

Wilson, Harriet E.
See Wilson, Harriet E. Adams

Wilson, Harriet E. Adams
1827(?)-1863(?) ..... **BLC 1:3; NCLC 78,
219**
See also DAM MULT; DLB 50, 239, 243

Wilson, John 1785-1854 .... **NCLC 5**
See also DLB 110

Wilson, John Anthony Burgess
See Burgess, Anthony

Wilson, John Burgess
See Burgess, Anthony

Wilson, Katharina .... **CLC 65**

Wilson, Lanford 1937- .. **CLC 7, 14, 36, 197;
DC 19**
See also CA 17-20R; CABS 3; CAD; CANR
45, 96; CD 5, 6; DAM DRAM; DFS 4, 9,
12, 16, 20; DLB 7, 341; EWL 3; MAL 5;
TUS

Wilson, Robert M. 1941- .... **CLC 7, 9**
See also CA 49-52; CAD; CANR 2, 41; CD
5, 6; MTCW 1

Wilson, Robert McLiam 1964- .... **CLC 59**
See also CA 132; DLB 267

Wilson, Sloan 1920-2003 .... **CLC 32**
See also CA 1-4R; 216; CANR 1, 44; CN
1, 2, 3, 4, 5, 6

Wilson, Snoo 1948- .... **CLC 33**
See also CA 69-72; CBD; CD 5, 6

Wilson, William S(mith) 1932- .... **CLC 49**
See also CA 81-84

Wilson, (Thomas) Woodrow
1856-1924 .... **TCLC 79**
See also CA 166; DLB 47

Winchester, Simon 1944- .... **CLC 257**
See also AAYA 66; CA 107; CANR 90, 130,
194

Winchilsea, Anne (Kingsmill) Finch
1661-1720
See Finch, Anne
See also RGEL 2

Winckelmann, Johann Joachim
1717-1768 .... **LC 129**
See also DLB 97

Windham, Basil
See Wodehouse, P. G.

Wingrove, David 1954- .... **CLC 68**
See also CA 133; SFW 4

Winnemucca, Sarah 1844-1891 .... **NCLC 79;
NNAL**
See also DAM MULT; DLB 175; RGAL 4

Winstanley, Gerrard 1609-1676 .... **LC 52**

Wintergreen, Jane
See Duncan, Sara Jeannette

Winters, Arthur Yvor
See Winters, Yvor

Winters, Janet Lewis
See Lewis, Janet

Winters, Yvor 1900-1968 .. **CLC 4, 8, 32; PC
82**
See also AMWS 2; CA 11-12; 25-28R; CAP
1; DLB 48; EWL 3; MAL 5; MTCW 1;
RGAL 4

Winterson, Jeanette 1959- .... **CLC 64, 158**
See also BRWS 4; CA 136; CANR 58, 116,
181; CN 5, 6, 7; CPW; DA3; DAM POP;
DLB 207, 261; FANT; FW; GLL 1;
MTCW 2; MTFW 2005; RHW; SATA 190

Winthrop, John 1588-1649 .... **LC 31, 107**
See also DLB 24, 30

Winthrop, Theodore 1828-1861 ... **NCLC 210**
See also DLB 202

Winton, Tim 1960- .... **CLC 251; SSC 119**
See also AAYA 34; CA 152; CANR 118,
194; CN 6, 7; DLB 325; SATA 98

Wirth, Louis 1897-1952 .... **TCLC 92**
See also CA 210

Wiseman, Frederick 1930- .... **CLC 20**
See also CA 159

Wister, Owen 1860-1938 ..... **SSC 100; TCLC
21**
See also BPFB 3; CA 108; 162; DLB 9, 78,
186; RGAL 4; SATA 62; TCWW 1, 2

Wither, George 1588-1667 .... **LC 96**
See also DLB 121; RGEL 2

Witkacy
See Witkiewicz, Stanislaw Ignacy

Witkiewicz, Stanislaw Ignacy
1885-1939 .... **TCLC 8, 237**
See also CA 105; 162; CDWLB 4; DLB
215; EW 10; EWL 3; RGWL 2, 3; SFW 4

Wittgenstein, Ludwig (Josef Johann)
1889-1951 .... **TCLC 59**
See also CA 113; 164; DLB 262; MTCW 2

Wittig, Monique 1935-2003 .... **CLC 22**
See also CA 116; 135; 212; CANR 143;
CWW 2; DLB 83; EWL 3; FW; GLL 1

Wittlin, Jozef 1896-1976 .... **CLC 25**
See also CA 49-52; 65-68; CANR 3; EWL
3

Wodehouse, P. G. 1881-1975 ..... **CLC 1, 2, 5,
10, 22; SSC 2, 115; TCLC 108**
See also AAYA 65; AITN 2; BRWS 3; CA
45-48; 57-60; CANR 3, 33; CDBLB
1914-1945; CN 1, 2; CPW 1; DA3; DAB;
DAC; DAM NOV; DLB 34, 162, 352;
EWL 3; MTCW 1, 2; MTFW 2005; RGEL
2; RGSF 2; SATA 22; SSFS 10

Wodehouse, Pelham Grenville
See Wodehouse, P. G.

Woiwode, L.
See Woiwode, Larry

Woiwode, Larry 1941- .... **CLC 6, 10**
See also CA 73-76; CANR 16, 94, 192; CN
3, 4, 5, 6, 7; DLB 6; INT CANR-16

Woiwode, Larry Alfred
See Woiwode, Larry

Wojciechowska, Maia (Teresa)
1927-2002 .... **CLC 26**
See also AAYA 8, 46; BYA 3; CA 9-12R,
183; 209; CAAE 183; CANR 4, 41; CLR
1; JRDA; MAICYA 1, 2; SAAS 1; SATA
1, 28, 83; SATA-Essay 104; SATA-Obit
134; YAW

Wojtyla, Karol (Jozef)
See John Paul II, Pope

Wojtyla, Karol (Josef)
See John Paul II, Pope

Wolf, Christa 1929- ...... **CLC 14, 29, 58, 150,
261**
See also CA 85-88; CANR 45, 123; CD-
WLB 2; CWW 2; DLB 75; EWL 3; FW;
MTCW 1; RGWL 2, 3; SSFS 14

Wolf, Naomi 1962- .... **CLC 157**
See also CA 141; CANR 110; FW; MTFW
2005

Wolfe, Gene 1931- .... **CLC 25**
See also AAYA 35; CA 57-60; CAAS 9;
CANR 6, 32, 60, 152, 197; CPW; DAM
POP; DLB 8; FANT; MTCW 2; MTFW
2005; SATA 118, 165; SCFW 2; SFW 4;
SUFW 2

Wolfe, Gene Rodman
See Wolfe, Gene

Wolfe, George C. 1954- .... **BLCS; CLC 49**
See also CA 149; CAD; CD 5, 6

Wolfe, Thomas 1900-1938 ..... **SSC 33, 113;
TCLC 4, 13, 29, 61; WLC 6**
See also AMW; BPFB 3; CA 104; 132;
CANR 102; CDALB 1929-1941; DA;
DA3; DAB; DAC; DAM MST, NOV;

DLB 9, 102, 229; DLBD 2, 16; DLBY
1985, 1997; EWL 3; MAL 5; MTCW 1,
2; NFS 18; RGAL 4; SSFS 18; TUS

Wolfe, Thomas Clayton
See Wolfe, Thomas

Wolfe, Thomas Kennerly
See Wolfe, Tom, Jr.

Wolfe, Tom, Jr. 1931- .... **CLC 1, 2, 9, 15, 35,
51, 147**
See also AAYA 8, 67; AITN 2; AMWS 3;
BEST 89:1; BPFB 3; CA 13-16R; CANR
9, 33, 70, 104; CN 5, 6, 7; CPW; CSW;
DA3; DAM POP; DLB 152, 185 185;
EWL 3; INT CANR-9; LAIT 5; MTCW
1, 2; MTFW 2005; RGAL 4; TUS

Wolff, Geoffrey 1937- .... **CLC 41**
See also CA 29-32R; CANR 29, 43, 78, 154

Wolff, Geoffrey Ansell
See Wolff, Geoffrey

Wolff, Sonia
See Levitin, Sonia

Wolff, Tobias 1945- .... **CLC 39, 64, 172; SSC
63, 136**
See also AAYA 16; AMWS 7; BEST 90:2;
BYA 12; CA 114; 117; CAAS 22; CANR
54, 76, 96, 192; CN 5, 6, 7; CSW; DA3;
DLB 130; EWL 3; INT CA-117; MTCW
2; MTFW 2005; RGAL 4; RGSF 2; SSFS
4, 11

Wolff, Tobias Jonathan Ansell
See Wolff, Tobias

Wolitzer, Hilma 1930- .... **CLC 17**
See also CA 65-68; CANR 18, 40, 172; INT
CANR-18; SATA 31; YAW

Wollstonecraft, Mary 1759-1797 .... **LC 5, 50,
90, 147**
See also BRWS 3; CDBLB 1789-1832;
DLB 39, 104, 158, 252; FL 1:1; FW;
LAIT 1; RGEL 2; TEA; WLIT 3

Wonder, Stevie 1950- .... **CLC 12**
See also CA 111

Wong, Jade Snow 1922-2006 .... **CLC 17**
See also CA 109; 249; CANR 91; SATA
112; SATA-Obit 175

Wood, Ellen Price
See Wood, Mrs. Henry

Wood, Mrs. Henry 1814-1887 ...... **NCLC 178**
See also CMW 4; DLB 18; SUFW

Wood, James 1965- .... **CLC 238**
See also CA 235

Woodberry, George Edward
1855-1930 .... **TCLC 73**
See also CA 165; DLB 71, 103

Woodcott, Keith
See Brunner, John (Kilian Houston)

Woodruff, Robert W.
See Mencken, H. L.

Woodward, Bob 1943- .... **CLC 240**
See also CA 69-72; CANR 31, 67, 107, 176;
MTCW 1

Woodward, Robert Upshur
See Woodward, Bob

Woolf, Adeline Virginia
See Woolf, Virginia

Woolf, Virginia 1882-1941 .... **SSC 7, 79;
TCLC 1, 5, 20, 43, 56, 101, 123, 128;
WLC 6**
See also AAYA 44; BPFB 3; BRW 7;
BRWC 2; BRWR 1; CA 104; 130; CANR
64, 132; CDBLB 1914-1945; DA; DA3;
DAB; DAC; DAM MST, NOV; DLB 36,
100, 162; DLBD 10; EWL 3; EXPS; FL
1:6; FW; LAIT 3; LATS 1:1; LMFS 2;
MTCW 1, 2; MTFW 2005; NCFS 2; NFS
8, 12, 28; RGEL 2; RGSF 2; SSFS 4, 12;
TEA; WLIT 4

Woollcott, Alexander (Humphreys)
1887-1943 .... **TCLC 5**
See also CA 105; 161; DLB 29

Literary Criticism Series
Cumulative Topic Index

This index lists all topic entries in Gale's *Children's Literature Review* (CLR), *Classical and Medieval Literature Criticism* (CMLC), *Contemporary Literary Criticism* (CLC), *Drama Criticism* (DC), *Literature Criticism from 1400 to 1800* (LC), *Nineteenth-Century Literature Criticism* (NCLC), *Short Story Criticism* (SSC), and *Twentieth-Century Literary Criticism* (TCLC). The index also lists topic entries in the Gale Critical Companion Collection, which includes the following publications: *The Beat Generation* (BG), *Feminism in Literature* (FL), *Gothic Literature* (GL), and *Harlem Renaissance* (HR).

Topic Index

Topic Index

Topic Index

CLC Cumulative Nationality Index

Nationality Index

Nationality Index

CLC-293 Title Index

ISBN-13: 978-1-4144-4607-3
ISBN-10: 1-4144-4607-1